Fodor's 26th Edition

Canad

The complete guide, thoroughly up-to-date

Packed with details that will make your trip

The must-see sights, off and on the beaten path

What to see, what to skip

Mix-and-match vacation itineraries

City strolls, countryside adventures

Smart lodging and dining options

Essential local do's and taboos

Transportation tips, distances and directions

Key contacts, savvy travel tips

When to go, what to pack

Clear, accurate, easy-to-use maps

Books to read, videos to watch

Fodor's Travel Publications • New York, Toronto, London, Sydney, Auckland
www.fodors.com

Fodor's Canada

EDITORS: Chris Swiac, Shannon Kelly

Editorial Contributors: Rosemary Allerston, Monica Andreef, Bruce Bishop, Milan Chvostek, Lisa Dunford, Liza Finlay, Kim Goodson, Sue Kernaghan, Laura M. Kidder, Ed Kirby, Jack Kohane, Helga Loverseed, Randal McIlroy, Jens Nielsen, Susan Randles, Shawna Richer, Helayne Schiff, Bree Scott, Tina Sebert, Dave Stephens, Don Thacker, Elizabeth Thompson, Katherine Thompson, Isobel Warren, Julie Waters, Paul Waters, Ana Watts, Sara Waxman

Editorial Production: Kristin Milavec

Maps: David Lindroth, *cartographer*; Robert Blake, *map editor*

Design: Fabrizio La Rocca, *creative director*; Guido Caroti, *art director*; Jolie Novak, *senior picture editor*; Melanie Marin, *photo editor*

Cover Design: Pentagram

Production/Manufacturing: Yexenia Markland

Cover Photograph: Philip and Karen Smith/Stone

Copyright

Twenty-Sixth Edition

ISBN 0–676–90210–3

ISSN 0160–3906

Important Tip

Although all prices, opening times, and other details in this book are based on information supplied to us at press time, changes occur all the time in the travel world, and Fodor's cannot accept responsibility for facts that become outdated or for inadvertent errors or omissions. So **always confirm information when it matters,** especially if you're making a detour to visit a specific place.

Special Sales

Fodor's Travel Publications are available at special discounts for bulk purchases for sales promotions or premiums. Special editions, including personalized covers, excerpts of existing guides, and corporate imprints, can be created in large quantities for special needs. For more information, contact your local bookseller or write to Special Markets, Fodor's Travel Publications, 280 Park Avenue, New York, NY 10017. Inquiries from Canada should be directed to your local Canadian bookseller or sent to Random House of Canada, Ltd., Marketing Department, 2775 Matheson Boulevard East, Mississauga, Ontario L4W 4P7. Inquiries from the United Kingdom should be sent to Fodor's Travel Publications, 20 Vauxhall Bridge Road, London SW1V 2SA, England.

PRINTED IN THE UNITED STATES OF AMERICA

10 9 8 7 6 5 4 3 2 1

CONTENTS

Maps and Plans

ON THE ROAD WITH FODOR'S

THE MORE YOU KNOW before you go, the better your trip will be. One of Canada's loveliest museums (or a highly acclaimed restaurant) could be just around the corner from your hotel, but if you don't know it's there, it might as well be on the other side of the globe. That's where this book comes in. It's a great step toward making sure your next trip lives up to your expectations. Here at Fodor's, and at our on-line arm, Fodors.com, our focus is on providing you with information that's not only useful but accurate and on target. Every day Fodor's editors put enormous effort into getting things right, beginning with the search for the right contributors—people who have objective judgment, broad travel experience, and the writing ability to put their insights into words. There's no substitute for advice from a like-minded friend who has just come back from where you're going, but our writers, having seen all corners of Canada, are the next best thing. They're the kind of people you'd poll for tips yourself if you knew them.

Editor of the magazine *Up Here, Life in Canada's North* for 10 years, **Rosemary Allerston,** who updated the Northwest Territories and Nunavut sections of Wilderness Canada and the Ontario chapter, travels frequently in the region; she is based in Ontario. **Monica Andreef,** an Alberta-born freelance journalist, spends a lot of time in the Rocky Mountains. She covers the area, and the rest of her province, for this book. **Bruce Bishop,** who updated the Toronto Exploring section, is president of the Travel Media Association of Canada. Based in Toronto, he is a freelance travel writer and has written for the *Globe and Mail* and the *Toronto Star,* among others. Travel writers and broadcasters **Milan Chvostek and Isobel Warren** contributed to the Nova Scotia and Prince Edward Island chapters. **Liza Finlay,** who freshened the Shopping and Nightlife and the Arts sections of Toronto, is a journalist, communications expert, and self-confessed shopping addict. A former managing editor of *Flare,* she contributes to several Canadian magazines and newspapers. Food columnist **Kim Goodson,** who updated the Halifax sections of the Nova Scotia chapter, indulges her food, wine, and travel passions at every opportunity. Vancouver-born freelance writer **Sue Kernaghan,** now a Salt Spring Island resident, enjoyed getting reacquainted with her hometown for this book. She also covered a lot of dirt roads, open water, and country pubs while researching the Vancouver and British Columbia chapters. **Ed Kirby,** editor of the *Newfoundland and Labrador Travel Guide,* lives in St. John's. He checked out his area's latest places. **Jack Kohane,** a travel and business writer, particularly enjoyed searching out the best in bed-and-breakfasts for the Toronto lodging section. **Helga Loverseed,** a well-traveled freelance journalist and photographer based in Magog in the Eastern Townships, shared her insights on Québec province. She also updated Smart Travel Tips A to Z, to make your travels even easier. **Randal McIlroy,** who revised Winnipeg and Elsewhere in Manitoba in the Prairie Provinces, is assistant editor of *Style Manitoba* and has written on the arts for the *Globe and Mail,* the *Winnipeg Free Press,* and other publications. **Jens Nielsen,** a writer based in Saskatoon, Saskatchewan, updated the Saskatchewan sections of the Prairie Provinces chapter. **Susan Randles,** who contributed to the Prince Edward Island chapter with her late husband, Dave Stephens, has written extensively on the province in newspapers, books, and magazines. **Shawna Richer,** updater of the Outdoor Activities and Sports section of Toronto, is sports editor of globeandmail.com, the national newspaper's Web site. **Tina Sebert,** updater of the Yukon section and also a film scout, lives in Whitehorse. She leads tours of the region and enjoys backpacking and rafting the Yukon River. **Elizabeth Thompson** covers the Canadian government as an Ottawa–based reporter for *The Gazette.* Until 2001she lived in Québec City (her Fodor's beat), which she delights in exploring. **Katherine Thompson** of Montréal travels extensively as part of her job at a Canadian airline. A Cordon Bleu–trained chef, she turns her attentions to her city's shopping scene for this book. **Paul and Julie Waters** are a travel-writing team from Montréal, most of which they cover for the book. Paul, who also wrote the book introduction, is travel editor of *The Gazette*; Julie works for various travel trade magazines. Fredericton columnist **Ana Watts** is passionate about her province, New Brunswick; she freshened that chapter for us. **Sara Waxman,** who wrote the Toronto dining section and the dining reviews for the Niagara Peninsula and Stratford, is the restaurant critic for the *Toronto Sun*.

Don't Forget to Write

Your experiences—positive and negative—matter to us. If we have missed or misstated something, we want to hear about it. We follow up on all suggestions. Contact the Canada editor at editors@ fodors.com or c/o Fodor's, 280 Park Avenue, New York, New York 10017. And have a fabulous trip!

Karen Cure

Karen Cure
Editorial Director

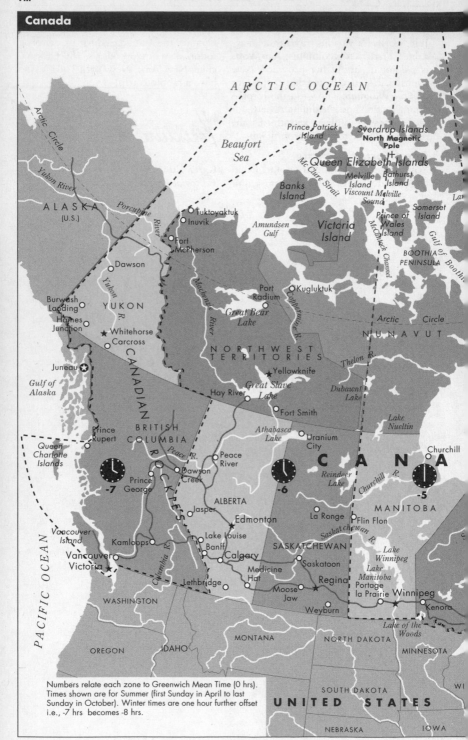

ARCTIC OCEAN

Prince Patrick Island

Sverdrup Islands
North Magnetic Pole

Queen Elizabeth Islands

Beaufort Sea

Mc Clure Strait

Melville Island
Bathurst Island
Viscount Melville Sound

Somerset Island

Banks Island

Prince of Wales Island

Amundsen Gulf

Victoria Island

McClintock Channel

BOOTHIA PENINSULA

Gulf of Booth

Arctic Circle

Yukon River

ALASKA (U.S.)

Porcupine River

Tuktoyaktuk
Inuvik

Fort McPherson

Mackenzie River

Port Radium

Kugluktuk

Dawson

Great Bear Lake

Burwash Landing

YUKON

Yukon R.

Haines Junction

Whitehorse
Carcross

NORTHWEST TERRITORIES

Arctic Circle

NUNAVUT

Thelon R.

Juneau

CANADIAN

Yellowknife

Great Slave Lake

Dubawnt Lake

Lake Nueltin

Gulf of Alaska

Hay River

Fort Smith

Prince Rupert

BRITISH COLUMBIA

Athabasca Lake

Uranium City

C   A   N   A   A

Churchill

Queen Charlotte Islands

Peace R.

Peace River

Reindeer Lake

Churchill R.

-7

Prince George

Dawson Creek

-6

-5

MANITOBA

ROCKIES

ALBERTA

La Ronge

Flin Flon

Jasper

Saskatchewan R.

Vancouver Island

Edmonton

Kamloops

Lake Louise

Lake Winnipeg

Banff

SASKATCHEWAN

Vancouver
Victoria

Columbia R.

Calgary

Saskatoon

Lake Manitoba

Medicine Hat

Portage la Prairie

Winnipeg

Lethbridge

Regina

Moose Jaw

Kenora

PACIFIC OCEAN

WASHINGTON

Weyburn

Lake of the Woods

OREGON

IDAHO

MONTANA

NORTH DAKOTA

MINNESOTA

Numbers relate each zone to Greenwich Mean Time (0 hrs). Times shown are for Summer (first Sunday in April to last Sunday in October). Winter times are one hour further offset i.e., -7 hrs becomes -8 hrs.

SOUTH DAKOTA

WI

UNITED   STATES

NEBRASKA

IOWA

SMART TRAVEL TIPS A TO Z

Basic Information on Traveling in Canada, Savvy Tips to Make Your Trip a Breeze, and Companies and Organizations to Contact

AIR TRAVEL

BOOKING

When you book **look for nonstop flights** and **remember that "direct" flights stop at least once.** Try to avoid connecting flights, which require a change of plane. For more booking tips and to check prices and make on-line flight reservations, log on to www.fodors.com.

CARRIERS

When flying internationally, you must usually choose between a domestic carrier, the national flag carrier of the country you are visiting, and a foreign carrier from a third country. You may, for example, choose to fly Air Canada to Canada. National flag carriers have the greatest number of nonstops. Domestic carriers may have better connections to your hometown and serve a greater number of gateway cities. Third-party carriers may have a price advantage.

Of the U.S. airlines, American flies to Calgary, Montréal, Ottawa, Toronto, and Vancouver; Continental flies to Montréal and Toronto; Delta and United serve Montréal, Toronto, and Vancouver; Northwest serves Calgary, Edmonton, Halifax, Montréal, Ottawa, Toronto, Vancouver, Winnipeg; and US Airways flies to Hamilton, London, Montréal, Ottawa, and Toronto.

Among smaller carriers, Alaska Airlines flies to Vancouver from many western U.S. cities and Horizon Air serves Calgary, Edmonton, Vancouver, and Victoria.

Within Canada, regularly scheduled flights to every major city and to most smaller cities are available on Air Canada and the regional feeder airlines associated with it. Since the end of 1999, when it took over the smaller, financially troubled Canadian Airlines, Air Canada has dominated 90% of Canada's airline industry. The lack of competition has consumers bracing for airfare increases. A few upstart carriers have entered the fray to compete with Air Canada, but at press time one (RootsAir) had already suspended flight operations at least temporarily.

WestJet, which serves destinations in western Canada, added a couple of eastern routes in 2000, to Hamilton and Ottawa. CanJet, a low-cost Canada 3000 subsidiary, serves Moncton, Ottawa, Québec City, Thunder Bay (Ontario), Toronto, and Winnipeg.

Smaller regional airlines airBC, airOntario, and airNova come under the Air Canada umbrella. AirNova flies in the Atlantic region, airOntario in the Ontario region, and airBC serves British Columbia and Alberta, with extended service out of Portland and Seattle. Canadian North and First Air service communities in Alberta, the Yukon, Nunavut, and the Northwest Territories. Air Labrador offers service in the Atlantic region.

From the United Kingdom, Canadian charter lines Canada 3000 Airlines (and its subsidiary Royal Airlines) and Air Transat offer flights to Montréal and Toronto, though not in winter. These carriers also fly between many major Canadian cities, and offer lower rates than Air Canada.

For regulations and for the locations of air bases that allow private flights, check with the regional tourist agencies for charter companies and with the District Controller of Air Services in the territorial (and provincial) capitals. Private pilots should obtain information from the Canada Map Office, which has the "Canada Flight Supplement" (lists of airports with Canada Customs services) as well as aeronautical charts.

➤ MAJOR AIRLINES: **Air Canada** (☎ 800/776–3000). **American** (☎ 800/433–7300). **Continental** (☎ 800/525–0280). **Delta** (☎ 800/241–4141). **Northwest** (☎ 800/225–2525). **TWA** (☎ 800/221–2000). **United** (☎ 800/241–6522). **US Airways** (☎ 800/428–4322).

➤ SMALLER AIRLINES: **Alaska Airlines** (☎ 800/426–0333). **Horizon Air** (☎ 800/547–9308).

➤ FROM THE U.K.: **Air Canada** (☎ 0870/524–7226). **British Airways** (☎ 0845/722–2111). **Canada 3000 Airlines** (☎ 877/973–3000). **Royal Airlines** (☎ 877/769–2524).

➤ WITHIN CANADA: **airBC** (☎ 888/247–2262). **Air Canada** (☎ 800/776–3000). **Air Labrador** (☎ 888/247–2262). **AirNova** (☎ 888/247–2262). **Air Ontario** (☎ 888/247–2262). **Air Transat** (877/872–6728). **Canada 3000 Airlines** (☎ 877/973–3000). **Canadian North** (☎ 867/873–4484). **CanJet** (☎ 800/809–7777). **First Air** (☎ 867/920–2500). **Royal Airlines** (☎ 888/828–9797). **WestJet Airlines** (☎ 800/538–5696).

➤ CONTACTS FOR PRIVATE PILOTS: **Canada Map Office** (✉ 130 Bentley Ave., Nepean, Ontario K1A 0E9, ☎ 800/465–6277).

CHECK-IN & BOARDING

Assuming that not everyone with a ticket will show up, airlines routinely overbook planes. When everyone does, airlines ask for volunteers to give up their seats. In return, these volunteers usually get a certificate for a free flight and are rebooked on the next flight out. If there are not enough volunteers, the airline must choose who will be denied boarding. The first to get bumped are passengers who checked in late and those flying on discounted tickets, so **get to the gate and check in as early as possible**, especially during peak periods.

Always **bring a government-issued photo ID to the airport** even when you don't need one; a passport is best. You will be asked to show it before you are allowed to check in. U.S. Customs and Immigration maintains offices at the airports in Montréal, Toronto, and Vancouver; U.S.-bound passengers should arrive early enough to clear customs before their flight.

Security measures at Canadian airports are similar to those in the United States. Be sure you're not carrying anything that could be construed as a weapon: a letter opener, Swiss Army knife, or a toy weapon, for example. Arriving passengers from overseas flights might find a beagle in a green coat sniffing their luggage; he's looking for forbidden agricultural products.

Departing passengers in Montréal and Vancouver must pay a $10 airport-improvement fee before they can board their plane.

CUTTING COSTS

The least expensive airfares to Canada must usually be purchased in advance and are nonrefundable. It's smart to **call a number of airlines**, and when you are quoted a good price, **book it on the spot**—the same fare may not be available the next day. Always **check different routings** and look into using different airports. Travel agents, especially low-fare specialists (☞ Discounts & Deals), are helpful.

Consolidators are another good source. They buy tickets for scheduled international flights at reduced rates from the airlines, then sell them at prices that beat the best fare available directly from the airlines, usually without restrictions. Sometimes you can even get your money back if you need to return the ticket. Carefully read the fine print detailing penalties for changes and cancellations, and **confirm your consolidator reservation with the airline.**

➤ CONSOLIDATORS: **Cheap Tickets** (☎ 800/377–1000). **Discount Airline Ticket Service** (☎ 800/576–1600). **Unitravel** (☎ 800/325–2222). **Up & Away Travel** (☎ 212/889–2345). **World Travel Network** (☎ 800/409–6753).

ENJOYING THE FLIGHT

For more legroom, **request an emergency-aisle seat.** Don't sit in the row in front of the emergency aisle or in front of a bulkhead, where seats may not recline. If you have dietary concerns, **ask for special meals when booking.** These can be vegetarian, low-cholesterol, or kosher, for example. On long flights, try to maintain a normal routine, to help fight jet lag. At night, **get some sleep.** By day, **eat light meals, drink water** (not alcohol), and **move around the cabin** to stretch your legs. For additional jet-lag tips consult *Fodor's FYI: Travel Fit & Healthy* (available at bookstores everywhere).

None of the major airlines or charter lines permit smoking.

FLYING TIMES

Flying time to Montréal is 1½ hours from New York, 2 hours from Chicago, 6 hours from Los Angeles, and 6½ hours from London. Toronto is 1½ hours from New York and Chicago and 4½ hours from Los Angeles. Vancouver is 6½ hours from Montréal, 4 hours from Chicago, and 2½ hours from Los Angeles.

HOW TO COMPLAIN

If your baggage goes astray or your flight goes awry, complain right away. Most carriers require that you **file a claim immediately.**

➤ AIRLINE COMPLAINTS: U.S. Department of Transportation **Aviation Consumer Protection Division** (✉ C-75, Room 4107, Washington, DC 20590, ☎ 202/366–2220, WEB www.dot.gov/airconsumer). **Federal Aviation Administration Consumer Hotline** (☎ 800/322–7873).

AIRPORTS

The major airports are Montréal's Dorval International Airport (airport code YUL), Toronto's Lester B. Pearson International Airport (YYZ), and Vancouver International Airport (YVR). For airports in other provinces and territories, *see* the A to Z sections in each chapter.

➤ AIRPORT INFORMATION: **Dorval International** (☎ 514/394–7377). **Lester B. Pearson International Airport** (☎ 416/247–7678). **Vancouver International Airport** (☎ 604/276–6101).

BIKE TRAVEL

Despite Canada's harsh climate and demanding landscape, bicycle travel has become very popular since the 1980s. Long-distance bicycle travel is most popular on the Atlantic coast, in Québec and Eastern Ontario, in the Rockies, and along the Pacific coast. Some terrain in these areas is steep and hilly, but it's always varied and interesting. Pedaling across the Prairie Provinces, on the other hand, can be a bit of a chore.

Many provinces have developed bicycle routes composed of both bike-only trails and specially marked lanes on regular highways. Prince Edward Island, for example, has converted an abandoned rail line into a trail that runs from one end of the province to the other. Québec is in the middle of developing the Route Verte, a 3,500-km (2,170-mi) network of trails covering the southern half of the province. One of the most spectacular trails in Western Canada follows the abandoned 600-km-long (370-mi-long) Kettle Valley Railway through the mountains of British Columbia.

Nationally, the Trans-Canada Trail—linking the Atlantic to both the Pacific and Arctic oceans—will allow bicycles along much of its length when the project is finished (parts of it opened in 2000). Though cyclists aren't allowed on most multiple-lane, limited-access highways, much of the Trans-Canada Highway is a two-lane blacktop with broad, paved shoulders that are widely used by cyclists crossing the country. There are also plenty of secondary roads that see little traffic (and almost no truck traffic).

For maps and information on bicycle routes, consult the provincial tourist information offices.

BIKES IN FLIGHT

Most airlines accommodate bikes as luggage, provided they are dismantled and boxed. Bike boxes, often free at bike shops, cost about $5 if you purchase them from airlines; bike bags cost about $100. International travelers can sometimes substitute a bike for a piece of checked luggage at no charge; otherwise, the cost is about $100. Domestic and Canadian airlines charge $25 to $50.

BOAT & FERRY TRAVEL

Car ferries provide essential transportation on both the east and west coasts of Canada. Ferries also operate between the state of Washington and British Columbia's Vancouver Island.

British Columbia (BC) Ferry Corporation has 42 ports of call on the west coast. Marine Atlantic runs ferries between Nova Scotia and Newfoundland. Northumberland and Bay Ferries Ltd. operates a high-speed catamaran car ferry between Bar Harbor, Maine, and Nova Scotia as well as regular car ferries between New Brunswick and Nova Scotia. Prince of Fundy Cruises sails between Portland, Maine, and Nova Scotia.

For additional information about regional ferry service, *see* individual chapters.

➤ BOAT & FERRY INFORMATION: **British Columbia (BC) Ferry Corporation** (✉ 1112 Fort St., Victoria, BC V8V 4V2, ☎ 250/386–3431). **Marine Atlantic** (✉ 355 Purves St., North Sydney, NS B2A 3V2, ☎ 800/341–7981, WEB www.marine-atlantic.ca). **Northumberland and Bay Ferries Ltd.** (✉ 121 Eden St., Bar Harbor, ME 04609, ☎ 888/249–7245). **Prince of Fundy Cruises** (☎ 800/341–7540).

BOOKS

FICTION

The late Mordecai Richler's *St. Urbain's Horseman* and *The Apprenticeship of Duddy Kravitz* (made into a movie starring Richard Dreyfuss) are classics about growing up Jewish in Montréal. Margaret Atwood, a prolific poet and novelist, is regarded as a stateswoman of sorts in her native Canada. Her novel *Cat's Eye* is set in northern Canada and Toronto. Alice Munro writes about small-town life in Ontario in *The Progress of Love*. The mordant wit of the late Robertson Davies lovingly skewers Canadian academic life in works such as *The Deptford Trilogy* and *The Lyre of Orpheus*. *Northern Lights*, by Howard Norman, focuses on a child's experiences growing up in Manitoba and, later, Toronto. Howard Engel's mystery series follows the adventures of Bennie Cooperman, a Toronto-based detective; *The Suicide Murders* is especially compelling. Jack Hodgin's *Spit Delaney's Island* is peopled with loggers, construction workers, and other rural Canadians. Joy Kogawa's

first novel, *Obasan*, tells about the Japanese community of Canada during World War II. *Medicine River* is a collection of short stories by Native American writer Thomas King. For an excellent view of New Brunswick, especially the famed salmon-fishing region called the Miramichi, look for the humorous books *The Americans Are Coming* and *The Last Tasmanian* by local author Herb Curtis. Thomas Raddall's *His Majesty's Yankees* is a vivid account of a local family's deeply divided loyalties during the American Revolution. E. Annie Proulx's Pulitzer Prize–winning *The Shipping News* gives a feeling for life in a Newfoundland outport today.

NONFICTION

Stuart McLean's *Welcome Home: Travels in Small-Town Canada* profiles seven small towns across the country. *Canada North* is a more recent title by Farley Mowat, whose *Never Cry Wolf* is a humorous account of a naturalist who goes to a remote part of Canada to commune with wolves. Andrew Malcolm gives a cultural and historical overview of the country in *The Canadians*. Stephen Brook's *The Maple Leaf Rag* is a collection of idiosyncratic travel essays. *Why We Act Like Canadians: A Personal Exploration of Our National Character* is one of Pierre Berton's many popular nonfiction books focusing on Canada's history and culture; another is *Niagara: A History of the Falls*. *Klondike*, one of Berton's best books, recounts the sensational history of the Klondike gold rush. *Short History of Canada*, by Desmond Morton, is a historical account of the country. *Local Colour—Writers Discovering Canada*, edited by Carol Marin, is a series of articles about Canadian places by leading travel writers. Thomas King, Cheryl Calver, and Helen Hoy collaborated on *The Native in Literature*, about the literary treatment of Native Canadians.

BUS TRAVEL

The bus is an essential form of transportation in Canada, especially if you want to visit out-of-the-way towns that do not have airports or rail lines. Greyhound Lines and Voyageur offer interprovincial service. SMT operates bus service throughout Atlantic Canada.

CUTTING COSTS

Greyhound's Canada Coach Pass provides unlimited bus travel for 7, 15, 30, or 60 days between points from Montréal to the west coast. Canada Coach Pass Plus gives more access to the rest of Québec and the Maritime Provinces. These passes must be purchased in Canada at any Greyhound terminal. They represent an excellent value for travelers who want to wander the highways and byways of the country, packing a lot of miles into a relatively short period of time. However, for occasional, short day trips (from Montréal to Ottawa, for example, or Toronto to Windsor) they're hardly worth it.

FARES & SCHEDULES

Bus terminals in major cities and even in many smaller ones are usually efficient operations with service all week and plenty of agents on hand to handle ticket sales. In villages and some smaller towns, the bus station is simply a counter in a local convenience store, gas station, or snack bar. Getting information on schedules beyond the local ones is sometimes difficult in these places. In rural Québec, it's advisable to **bring along a French–English dictionary,** although most merchants and clerks can handle a simple ticket sale in English.

➤ Bus Information: **Greyhound Lines** (✉ 877 Greyhound Way SW, Calgary, AB T3C 3V8, ☎ 800/661–8747 in Canada; 800/231–2222 in the U.S., WEB www.greyhound.ca). **SMT** (☎ 506/859–5105; 800/567–5151 within Nova Scotia, New Brunswick, and Prince Edward Island, WEB www.smtbus.com). **Voyageur** (✉ 505 E. Boulevard Maisonneuve, Montréal, QC H2L 1Y4, ☎ 514/842–2281). In the U.K.: **Greyhound International** (✉ Sussex House, London Rd., E. Grinstead, East Sussex RHI9 1LD, U.K., ☎ 01342/317317).

PAYING

In major bus terminals, most bus lines accept at least some of the major credit cards. Some smaller lines require cash or take only Visa or Mas-

terCard. All accept travelers' checks in U.S. or Canadian currency with suitable identification, but it's advisable to exchange foreign currency (including U.S. currency) at a bank or exchange office. To buy a ticket in really small centers, it's best to use cash.

RESERVATIONS

Most bus lines do not accept reservations. You should plan on picking up your tickets at least 45 minutes before the bus's scheduled departure time.

BUSINESS HOURS

BANKS & OFFICES

Most banks in Canada are open Monday through Thursday 10–3 and Friday 10–5 or 6. Some banks are open longer hours and also on Saturday morning. All banks are closed on national holidays. Most banks (and some gas stations) have automatic teller machines (ATMs) that are accessible around the clock.

GAS STATIONS

Most highway and city gas stations in Canada are open daily (although there's rarely a mechanic on duty Sunday) and some are open around the clock. In small towns, gas stations are often closed on Sunday, although they may take turns staying open.

MUSEUMS & SIGHTS

Hours at museums vary, but most open at 10 or 11 and close in the evening. Some smaller museums close for lunch. Many museums are closed on Monday; some make up for it by staying open late on Wednesday, often waiving admission.

The days when all churches were always open are gone; vandalism, theft, and the drop in general piety have seen to that. But the major churches in big cities—the Basilique Notre-Dame-de-Montréal, for example—are open daily, usually about 9–6.

SHOPS

Stores, shops, and supermarkets usually are open Monday through Saturday 9–6, although in major cities supermarkets are often open 7:30 AM–9 PM and some food stores are open around the clock. Blue laws are in effect in much of Canada, but in a growing number of provinces, stores—even liquor stores—have limited Sunday hours, usually noon–5; shops in areas highly frequented by tourists are usually open Sunday. Stores often stay open Thursday and Friday evenings, most shopping malls until 9 PM. Drugstores in major cities are often open until 11 PM, and convenience stores tend to be open 24 hours a day, seven days a week.

CAMERAS & PHOTOGRAPHY

Canada is one of the world's most scenic countries. Particularly intriguing for photographers are the misty light of West Coast, the big-sky clarity of the Prairie Provinces, and the dramatic fogs of the Atlantic shore. Photographers who want to catch the country at its most dramatically beautiful should consider a winter trip. City and country take on a whole new glamour when they're buried deep in snow.

The *Kodak Guide to Shooting Great Travel Pictures* (available at bookstores everywhere) is loaded with tips.

➤ PHOTO HELP: **Kodak Information Center** (☎ 800/242–2424).

EQUIPMENT PRECAUTIONS

Don't pack film and equipment in checked luggage, where it is much more susceptible to damage. X-ray machines used to view checked luggage are becoming much more powerful and therefore are more likely to ruin your film. Always **keep film and tape out of the sun.** Carry an extra supply of batteries, and **be prepared to turn on your camera or camcorder** to prove to security personnel that the device is real. Always **ask for hand inspection of film,** which becomes clouded after repeated exposure to airport X-ray machines, and **keep videotapes away from metal detectors.**

CAR RENTAL

Rates in Montréal begin at $45 a day and $290 a week for an economy car with air-conditioning, a manual transmission, and unlimited free kilometers. Rates begin at $49 a day and $290 a week in Toronto and $44

a day and $204 a week in Vancouver. If you prefer a manual-transmission car, check whether the rental agency of your choice offers stick shifts; some companies, such as Avis, don't in Canada.

➤ MAJOR AGENCIES: **Alamo** (☎ 800/522–9696; 020/8759–6200 in the U.K., WEB www.alamo.com). **Avis** (☎ 800/331–1084; 800/879–2847 in Canada; 02/9353–9000 in Australia; 09/525–1982 in New Zealand; 0870/606–0100 in the U.K., WEB www.avis.com). **Budget** (☎ 800/527–0700; 0870/156–5656 in the U.K., WEB www.budget.com). **Dollar** (☎ 800/800–6000; 0124/622–0111 in the U.K., where it's affiliated with Sixt; 02/9223–1444 in Australia, WEB www.dollar.com). **Hertz** (☎ 800/654–3001; 800/263–0600 in Canada; 020/8897–2072 in the U.K.; 02/9669–2444 in Australia; 09/256–8690 in New Zealand, WEB www.hertz.com). **National Car Rental** (☎ 800/227–7368; 020/8680–4800 in the U.K., WEB www.nationalcar.com).

CUTTING COSTS

To get the best deal, **book through a travel agent who shops around.** Also **price local car-rental companies,** although the service and maintenance may not be as good as those of a major player. Remember to ask about required deposits, cancellation penalties, and drop-off charges if you're planning to pick up the car in one city and leave it in another. If you're traveling during a holiday period, also make sure that a confirmed reservation guarantees you a car.

Do **look into wholesalers,** companies that do not own fleets but rent in bulk from those that do and often offer better rates than traditional car-rental operations. Payment must be made before you leave home.

INSURANCE

When driving a rented car you are generally responsible for any damage to or loss of the vehicle as well as for any property damage or personal injury that you may cause. Before you rent, see what coverage your personal auto-insurance policy and credit cards provide.

REQUIREMENTS & RESTRICTIONS

In Canada your own driver's license is acceptable. Some provinces have age restrictions on younger drivers. In Ontario, for example, drivers must be 21; in Québec, drivers under 25 often have to pay a surcharge of $5 a day. Rental-car companies have not set an upper age limit.

SURCHARGES

Before you pick up a car in one city and leave it in another, **ask about drop-off charges or one-way service fees,** which can be substantial. Note, too, that some rental agencies charge extra if you return the car before the time specified in your contract. To avoid a hefty refueling fee, **fill the tank just before you turn in the car,** but be aware that gas stations near the rental outlet may overcharge.

CAR TRAVEL

Canada's highway system is excellent. It includes the Trans-Canada Highway, which uses several numbers and is the longest highway in the world—running about 8,000 km (5,000 mi) from Victoria, British Columbia, to St. John's, Newfoundland, using ferries to bridge coastal waters at each end. The second-longest Canadian highway, the Yellowhead Highway (Highway 16), follows a route from the Pacific Coast and over the Rockies to the prairies. North of the population centers, roads become fewer and less developed.

FROM THE U.S.

Drivers must carry owner registration and proof of insurance coverage, which is compulsory in Canada. The Canadian Non-Resident Inter-Provincial Motor Vehicle Liability Insurance Card, available from any U.S. insurance company, is accepted as evidence of financial responsibility in Canada. The minimum liability coverage in Canada is C$200,000, except in Québec, where the minimum is C$50,000. If you are driving a car that is not registered in your name, carry a letter from the owner that authorizes your use of the vehicle.

The U.S. Interstate Highway System leads directly into Canada: I–95 from Maine to New Brunswick; I–91 and I–89 from Vermont to Québec; I–87 from New York to Québec; I–81 and a spur off I–90 from New York to Ontario; I–94, I–96, and I–75 from Michigan to Ontario; I–29 from North Dakota to Manitoba; I–15 from Montana to Alberta; and I–5 from Washington state to British Columbia. Most of these connections hook up with the Trans-Canada Highway within a few miles. There are many smaller highway crossings between the two countries as well. From Alaska, take the Alaska Highway (from Fairbanks), the Klondike Highway (from Skagway), and the Top of the World Highway (to Dawson City).

➤ INSURANCE INFORMATION: **Insurance Bureau of Canada** (☎ 416/362–9528; 800/387–2880 in Canada, WEB www.ibc.ca).

GASOLINE

Gas prices in Canada have been on the rise. At press time, the per-liter price was up at 85¢. Gasoline tends to be least expensive in Alberta, the heart of Canada's petroleum industry, and most expensive in places such as Newfoundland, where transport costs and high provincial taxes boost the price.

Distances are always shown in kilometers, and gasoline is always sold in liters. (A gallon has 3.8 liters.)

RULES OF THE ROAD

By law, you are required to wear seat belts (and to use infant seats). Some provinces have a statutory requirement to drive with vehicle headlights on for extended periods after dawn and before sunset. In the Yukon, the law requires that you drive with your headlights on when using territory highways. Right turns are permitted on red signals in all provinces except Québec. At press time, the Québec government was toying with idea of changing this law, by permitting right turns in a limited number of rural towns on an experimental basis. Radar-detection devices are illegal in many provinces, and their possession in a car, even if they are not in operation, is illegal in the provinces of Ontario and Québec. Speed limits, given in.

kilometers, vary from province to province, but they are usually within the 90–110 kph (50–68 mph) range outside the cities.

CHILDREN IN CANADA

Travelers crossing the border with children should **carry identification for them** similar to that required by adults (i.e., passport or birth certificate). Children traveling with one parent or other adult should **bring a letter of permission** from the other parent, parents, or legal guardian. Divorced parents with shared custody rights should **carry legal documents establishing their status.**

If you are renting a car, don't forget to **arrange for a car seat** when you reserve.

FLYING

If your children are two or older, **ask about children's airfares.** As a general rule, infants under two not occupying a seat fly at greatly reduced fares or even free. When booking, **confirm carry-on allowances** if you're traveling with infants. In general, for babies charged 10% of the adult fare you are allowed one carry-on bag and a collapsible stroller; if the flight is full, the stroller may have to be checked or you may be limited to less.

Experts agree that it's a good idea to use safety seats aloft for children weighing less than 40 pounds. Airlines set their own policies: U.S. carriers usually require that the child be ticketed, even if he or she is young enough to ride free, since the seats must be strapped into regular seats. Do **check your airline's policy about using safety seats during takeoff and landing.** And since safety seats are not allowed everywhere in the plane, get your seat assignments early.

When reserving, **request children's meals or a freestanding bassinet** if you need them. But note that bulkhead seats, where you must sit to use the bassinet, may lack an overhead bin or storage space on the floor.

LODGING

Most hotels in Canada allow children under a certain age to stay in their parents' room at no extra charge, but others charge for them as extra

adults; be sure to **find out the cutoff age for children's discounts.**

SIGHTS & ATTRACTIONS

Places that are especially appealing to children are indicated by a rubber-duckie icon (🐤) in the margin.

CONSUMER PROTECTION

Whenever shopping or buying travel services in Canada, **pay with a major credit card,** if possible, so you can cancel payment or get reimbursed if there's a problem. If you're buying a package or tour, always **consider travel insurance** that includes default coverage (☞ Insurance).

CUSTOMS & DUTIES

When shopping, **keep receipts** for all purchases. Upon reentering the country, **be ready to show customs officials what you've bought.** If you feel a duty is incorrect or object to the way your clearance was handled, note the inspector's badge number and ask to see a supervisor. If the problem isn't resolved, write to the appropriate authorities, beginning with the port director at your point of entry.

U.S. Customs and Immigration has preclearance services at international airports in Calgary, Edmonton, Montréal, Ottawa, Vancouver, and Winnipeg. This allows U.S.-bound air passengers to depart their airplane directly on arrival at their U.S. destination without further inspection and delays.

➤ INFORMATION: **U.S. Customs Service** (✉ 1300 Pennsylvania Ave. NW, Room 6.3D, Washington, DC 20229, WEB www.customs.gov; inquiries ☎ 202/354–1000; complaints c/o ✉ 1300 Pennsylvania Ave. NW, Room 5.4D, Washington, DC 20229; registration of equipment c/o Office of Passenger Programs, ☎ 202/927–0530).

IN AUSTRALIA

Australian residents who are 18 or older may bring home A$400 worth of souvenirs and gifts (including jewelry), 250 cigarettes or 250 grams of tobacco, and 1,125 ml of alcohol (including wine, beer, and spirits). Residents under 18 may bring back

A$200 worth of goods. Prohibited items include meat products. Seeds, plants, and fruits need to be declared upon arrival.

➤ INFORMATION: **Australian Customs Service** (Regional Director, ✉ Box 8, Sydney, NSW 2001, Australia, ☎ 02/9213–2000, FAX 02/9213–4000, WEB www.customs.gov.au).

IN CANADA

American and British visitors may bring in the following items duty-free: 200 cigarettes, 50 cigars, and 7 ounces of tobacco; 1 bottle (1.1 liters or 40 imperial ounces) of liquor or wine, or 24 355-ml (12-ounce) bottles or cans of beer for personal consumption. Any alcohol and tobacco products in excess of these amounts is subject to duty, provincial fees, and taxes. You can also bring in gifts up to a total value of C$750.

A deposit is sometimes required for trailers (refunded upon return). Cats and dogs must have a certificate issued by a licensed veterinarian that clearly identifies the animal and certifies that it has been vaccinated against rabies during the preceding 36 months. Guide dogs are allowed into Canada without restriction. Plant material must be declared and inspected. There may be restrictions on some live plants, bulbs, and seeds. With certain restrictions or prohibitions on some fruits and vegetables, visitors may bring food with them for their own use, providing the quantity is consistent with the duration of the visit.

Canada's firearms laws are significantly stricter than those in the United States. All handguns and semiautomatic and fully automatic weapons are prohibited and cannot be brought into the country. Sporting rifles and shotguns may be imported provided they are to be used for sporting, hunting, or competition while in Canada. All firearms must be declared to Canada Customs at the first point of entry. Failure to declare firearms will result in their seizure, and criminal charges may be made. Regulations require visitors to have a confirmed "Firearms Declaration" to bring any guns into Canada; a fee of $50 applies, good for one year. For more information, contact the Canadian Firearms Centre.

➤ INFORMATION: **Revenue Canada** (✉ 2265 St. Laurent Blvd. S, Ottawa, ON K1G 4K3, ☎ 613/993–0534; 800/461–9999 in Canada). **Canadian Firearms Centre** (☎ 800/731–4000).

IN NEW ZEALAND

Homeward-bound residents 17 or older may bring back NZ$700 worth of souvenirs and gifts. Your duty-free allowance also includes 4.5 liters of wine or beer; one 1,125-ml bottle of spirits; and either 200 cigarettes, 250 grams of tobacco, 50 cigars, or a combination of the three up to 250 grams. Prohibited items include meat products, seeds, plants, and fruits.

➤ INFORMATION: **New Zealand Customs** (Custom House, ✉ 50 Anzac Ave., Box 29, Auckland, New Zealand, ☎ 09/300–5399, FAX 09/359–6730, WEB www.customs.govt.nz).

IN THE U.K.

From countries outside the European Union, including Canada, you may bring home, duty-free, 200 cigarettes or 50 cigars; 1 liter of spirits or 2 liters of fortified or sparkling wine or liqueurs; 2 liters of still table wine; 60 ml of perfume; 250 ml of toilet water; plus £145 worth of other goods, including gifts and souvenirs. If returning from outside the EU, prohibited items include meat products, seeds, plants, and fruits.

➤ INFORMATION: **HM Customs and Excise** (✉ Dorset House, Stamford St., Bromley, Kent BR1 1XX, U.K., ☎ 020/7202–4227, WEB www.hmce.gov.uk).

DINING

The restaurants we list are the cream of the crop in each price category. Properties indicated by an ✕🏠 are lodging establishments whose restaurant warrants a special trip. For information about regional dining, including a price chart, *see* Dining *in* Pleasures and Pastimes at the beginning of each chapter.

RESERVATIONS & DRESS

Reservations are always a good idea: we mention them only when they're essential or not accepted. Book as far ahead as you can, and reconfirm as soon as you arrive. We mention dress only when men are required to wear a jacket or a jacket and tie.

DISABILITIES & ACCESSIBILITY

Travelers with disabilities do not have the same blanket legal protection in Canada that they have in the United States. Indeed, some facilities aren't easy to use in a wheelchair—the subway systems in Montréal and Toronto, for example, and city buses just about everywhere. However, thanks to increased awareness and government-incentive programs, most major attractions—museums, churches, theaters—are equipped with ramps and lifts to handle wheelchairs. National and provincial institutions—parks, public monuments, and government buildings—almost always are accessible.

The Canadian Paraplegic Association National Office has information about touring in Canada. Kéroul, which was founded by travelers with disabilities to promote tourism in Québec among people in similar circumstances, rates hotels and attractions, organizes trips, and lobbies for improved facilities.

To file a complaint about transportation obstacles at Canadian airports (including flights), railroads, or ferries, contact the Director, Accessible Transportation Directorate, at the Canadian Transportation Agency (WEB www.cta-otc.gc.ca).

▶ COMPLAINTS: In the U.S.: **Aviation Consumer Protection Division** (✉ C-75, Room 4107, Washington, DC 20590, ☎ 202/366–2220, WEB www.dot.gov/airconsumer) for airline-related problems. **Civil Rights Office** (✉ U.S. Department of Transportation, Departmental Office of Civil Rights, S-30, 400 7th St. SW, Room 10215, Washington, DC 20590, ☎ 202/366–4648, FAX 202/366–9371, WEB www.dot.gov/ost/docr/index.htm) for problems with surface transportation. **Disability Rights Section** (✉ U.S. Department of Justice, Civil Rights Division, Box 66738, Washington, DC 20035-6738, ☎ 202/514–0301 or 800/514–0301; 202/514–0383 TTY; 800/514–0383 TTY, FAX 202/307–1198, WEB www.usdoj.gov/crt/ada/

adahom1.htm) for general complaints. In Canada: **Accessible Transportation Directorate** (✉ 15 Eddy St., Hull, QC K1A 0N9, ☎ 819/997–6828 or 800/883–1813). **Council of Canadians with Disabilities** (✉ 294 Portage Ave., Suite 926, Winnipeg, MN R3C 0B9, ☎ 204/947–0303, FAX 204/942–4625).

▶ LOCAL RESOURCES: **Canadian Paraplegic Association National Office** (✉ 1101 Prince of Wales Dr., Ottawa, ON K2C 3W7, ☎ 613/723–1033, WEB www.canparaplegic.org). **Kéroul** (✉ Box 1000, Branch M, Montréal, QC H1V 3R2, ☎ 514/252–3104, WEB www.keroul.qc.ca).

LODGING

When discussing accessibility with an operator or reservations agent, **ask hard questions.** Are there any stairs, inside *or* out? Are there grab bars next to the toilet *and* in the shower/tub? How wide is the doorway to the room? To the bathroom? For the most extensive facilities meeting the latest legal specifications, **opt for newer accommodations.**

TRAVEL AGENCIES

In the United States, the Americans with Disabilities Act requires that travel firms serve the needs of all travelers. Some agencies specialize in working with people with disabilities.

▶ TRAVELERS WITH MOBILITY PROBLEMS: **Access Adventures** (✉ 206 Chestnut Ridge Rd., Scottsville, NY 14624, ☎ 716/889–9096, dltravel@prodigy.net), run by a former physical-rehabilitation counselor. **CareVacations** (✉ No. 5, 5110–50 Ave., Leduc, Alberta T9E 6V4, Canada, ☎ 780/986–6404 or 877/478–7827, FAX 780/986–8332, WEB www.carevacations.com), for group tours and cruise vacations. **Flying Wheels Travel** (✉ 143 W. Bridge St., Box 382, Owatonna, MN 55060, ☎ 507/451–5005 or 800/535–6790, FAX 507/451–1685, WEB www.flyingwheelstravel.com).

DISCOUNTS & DEALS

Be a smart shopper and **compare all your options** before making decisions. A plane ticket bought with a promotional coupon from travel clubs, coupon books, and direct-mail offers or on the Internet may not be cheaper than the least expensive fare from a discount ticket agency. And always keep in mind that what you get is just as important as what you save.

DISCOUNT RESERVATIONS

To save money, **look into discount reservations services** with toll-free numbers, which use their buying power to get a better price on hotels, airline tickets, even car rentals. When booking a room, always **call the hotel's local toll-free number** (if one is available) rather than the central reservations number—you'll often get a better price. Always ask about special packages or corporate rates.

When shopping for the best deal on hotels and car rentals, **look for guaranteed exchange rates,** which protect you against a falling U.S. dollar. With your rate locked in, you won't pay more, even if the price goes up in the local currency.

➤ Airline Tickets: ☎ **800/FLY–ASAP.**

➤ Hotel Rooms: **Hotel Reservations Network** (☎ 800/964–6835, WEB www.hoteldiscount.com). **Players Express Vacations** (☎ 800/458–6161, WEB www.playersexpress.com). **RMC Travel** (☎ 800/245–5738, WEB www.rmcwebtravel.com). **Steigenberger Reservation Service** (☎ 800/223–5652, WEB www.srs-worldhotels.com). **Turbotrip.com** (☎ 800/473–7829, WEB www.turbotrip.com).

PACKAGE DEALS

Don't confuse packages and guided tours. When you buy a package, you travel on your own, just as though you had planned the trip yourself. Fly/drive packages, which combine airfare and car rental, are often a good deal.

ECOTOURISM

Canada's rugged wilderness areas often have very delicate ecosystems. Travelers in northern parts of the country should stick to marked trails and avoid disturbing the local flora. Sand dunes in both western and eastern Canada, important nesting grounds for seabirds, often are protected.

EMBASSIES

All embassies are in Ottawa; there are consulates in some major cities. Emergency information is given in the A to Z section at the end of each chapter.

➤ Australia: **Australian High Commission** (✉ 50 O'Connor St., Suite 710, Ottawa, ☎ 613/236–0841).

➤ New Zealand: **New Zealand High Commission** (✉ 99 Bank St., Suite 727, Ottawa, ☎ 613/238–5991).

➤ United Kingdom: **British High Commission** (✉ 80 Elgin St., Ottawa, ☎ 613/237–1530).

➤ United States: **U.S. Embassy** (✉ 490 Sussex Dr., Ottawa, ☎ 613/238–5335).

GAY & LESBIAN TRAVEL

Canada is generally a fairly tolerant country, and same-sex couples should face few problems in the major metropolitan areas. All the big cities—including the once stodgily puritanical Toronto and the former Roman Catholic bastion of Montréal—actively and avidly compete for gay visitors. Montréal, Toronto, and Vancouver all have large, visible, and very active gay and lesbian communities.

Montréal's gay community is centered in Le Village, a cluster of bars, restaurants, boutiques, and antiques shops in the once run-down area between rues Amherst and Papineau. The annual Parade de la Fierté Gaie et Lesbienne, on the first weekend in August, is one of the city's biggest parades and ends a week of gay cultural activities. The community supports three magazines—*Fugues, RG,* and *Gazelle.*

The annual Pride Toronto Parade (www.pridetoronto.com), held in late June, is the biggest street event of the year in Toronto, attracting well over 500,000 spectators and capping a week of cultural activities. The community's main focus is the area around Church and Wellsely streets. The beach and park at Hanlon's Point on the Toronto Islands are also very popular with gay people. The main gay publications are *Fab* and *Xtra.*

The epicenter of Vancouver's gay scene is the stretch of Davie Street between Burrard and Jervis streets—a cluster of cafés, casual eating places, and shops offering designer T-shirts and sleek housewares. Pride, held the first weekend of August, features parties, tea dances, and cruises, and culminates in a parade on Sunday.

Same-sex couples might not get as warm and open a welcome in rural areas as they do in the big cities. Parts of the Atlantic region, the Ottawa Valley in Ontario, and much of Alberta and the British Columbia interior harbor more conservative views.

For details about the gay and lesbian scenes in Vancouver, Montréal, and Toronto, consult *Fodor's Gay Guide to the USA* (available in bookstores everywhere).

➤ GAY- & LESBIAN-FRIENDLY TRAVEL AGENCIES: **Different Roads Travel** (✉ 8383 Wilshire Blvd., Suite 902, Beverly Hills, CA 90211, ☎ 323/651–5557 or 800/429–8747, FAX 323/651–3678, lgernert@tzell.com). **Kennedy Travel** (✉ 314 Jericho Turnpike, Floral Park, NY 11001, ☎ 516/352–4888 or 800/237–7433, FAX 516/354–8849, WEB www.kennedytravel.com). **Now Voyager** (✉ 4406 18th St., San Francisco, CA 94114, ☎ 415/626–1169 or 800/255–6951, FAX 415/626–8626, WEB www.nowvoyager.com). **Skylink Travel and Tour** (✉ 1006 Mendocino Ave., Santa Rosa, CA 95401, ☎ 707/546–9888 or 800/225–5759, FAX 707/546–9891, WEB www.skylinktravel.com), serving lesbian travelers.

GUIDEBOOKS

Plan well and you won't be sorry. Guidebooks are excellent tools—and you can take them with you. You may want to check out color-photo-illustrated *Fodor's Exploring Canada,* thorough with culture and history, or pocket-size *Citypack Montréal* and *Citypack Toronto,* which include supersize foldout maps. All are available at on-line retailers and bookstores everywhere.

HOLIDAYS

Canadian national holidays for 2002 are as follows: New Year's Day, Good Friday (March 29), Easter Monday (April 14), Victoria Day (May 21), Canada Day (July 1), Labour Day (September 2), Thanksgiving (October 14), Remembrance Day (November 11), Christmas, and Boxing Day (December 26).

Provincial holidays for 2002 are as follows: Heritage Day (August 7), in Alberta; British Columbia Day (August 7); New Brunswick Day (August 7); in Newfoundland, St. Patrick's Day (March 20), St. George's Day (April 24), Discovery Day (June 26), Memorial Day (July 1), and Orangemen's Day (July 10); in Manitoba, the Northwest Territories, Ontario, Saskatchewan, and Nova Scotia, Civic Holiday (August 7); Nunavut Day (April 1); in Québec, St. Jean Baptiste Day (June 24); and in Yukon, Discovery Day (August 21).

INSURANCE

The most useful travel-insurance plan is a comprehensive policy that includes coverage for trip cancellation and interruption, default, trip delay, and medical expenses (with a waiver for preexisting conditions).

Without insurance you will lose all or most of your money if you cancel your trip, regardless of the reason. Default insurance covers you if your tour operator, airline, or cruise line goes out of business. Trip-delay covers expenses that arise because of bad weather or mechanical delays. Study the fine print when comparing policies.

Always **buy travel policies directly from the insurance company**; if you buy them from a cruise line, airline, or tour operator that goes out of business you probably will not be covered for the agency or operator's default, a major risk. Before making any purchase, **review your existing health and home-owner's policies** to find what they cover away from home.

British and Australian citizens need extra medical coverage when traveling overseas.

➤ TRAVEL INSURERS: In the U.S.: **Access America** (✉ 6600 W. Broad St., Richmond, VA 23230, ☎ 800/

SMART TRAVEL TIPS A TO Z

284–8300, FAX 804/673–1491, WEB www.etravelprotection.com). **Travel Guard International** (⊠ 1145 Clark St., Stevens Point, WI 54481, ☎ 715/345–0505 or 800/826–1300, FAX 800/955–8785, WEB www.noelgroup.com). In Canada: **RBC Travel Insurance** (⊠ 6880 Financial Dr., Mississauga, ON L5N 7Y5, ☎ 905/816–2700 or 800/387–4357, WEB www. rbcinsurance.com).

LANGUAGE

Canada's two official languages are English and French. Although English is widely spoken, it is useful to **learn a few French phrases** if you plan to travel to the province of Québec or to the French-Canadian communities in the Maritimes (Nova Scotia, New Brunswick, and Prince Edward Island), northern Manitoba, and Ontario. Canadian French has many distinctive words and expressions, but it's no more different from the language of France than North American English is from the language of Great Britain.

LANGUAGES FOR TRAVELERS

A phrase book and language-tape set can help get you started. *Fodor's French for Travelers* (available at bookstores everywhere) is excellent.

LODGING

In the cities you have a choice of luxury hotels, moderately priced modern properties, and smaller older hotels with perhaps fewer conveniences but more charm. Options in smaller towns and in the country include large, full-service resorts; small, privately owned hotels; roadside motels; and bed-and-breakfasts. Even here you need to make reservations at least on the day on which you plan to pull into town.

Canada doesn't have a national government rating system for hotels, but many provinces do rate their accommodations. For example, in British Columbia and Alberta, a blue Approved Accommodation decal on the window or door of a hotel or motel indicates that it has met provincial hotel-association standards for courtesy, comfort, and cleanliness. Ontario's voluntary rating system includes about 1,000 Ontario proper-

ties. Québec's tourism ministry rates the province's hotels; the stars are more a reflection of the number of facilities than of the hotel's overall atmosphere or welcome.

Expect accommodations to cost more in summer than in the off-season (except for places such as ski resorts, where winter is high season). When making reservations, **ask about special deals and packages.** Big-city hotels that cater to business travelers often offer weekend packages, and many city hotels offer rooms at up to 50% off in winter. If you're planning to visit a major city or resort area in high season, **book well in advance.** Also be aware of any special events or festivals that may coincide with your visit and fill every room for miles around. For resorts and lodges, consider the winter ski-season high as well and plan accordingly.

The lodgings we list are the cream of the crop in each price category. We always list the facilities that are available—but we don't specify whether they cost extra; when pricing accommodations, always ask what's included and what costs extra. Properties indicated by an ✕⌷ are lodging establishments whose restaurant warrants a special trip. For price charts, *see* Lodging *in* Pleasures and Pastimes at the beginning of each chapter.

Assume that hotels operate on the European Plan (EP, with no meals) unless it's otherwise specified that they use the Continental Plan (CP, with a Continental breakfast daily), Breakfast Plan (BP, with a full breakfast), Modified American Plan (MAP, with breakfast and dinner daily), or the American Plan (AP, with all meals).

APARTMENT & VILLA RENTALS

If you want a home base that's roomy enough for a family and comes with cooking facilities, **consider a furnished rental.** These can save you money, especially if you're traveling with a group. Home-exchange directories sometimes list rentals as well as exchanges.

➤ INTERNATIONAL AGENTS: **Hideaways International** (⊠ 767 Islington St., Portsmouth, NH 03801, ☎ 603/

430–4433 or 800/843–4433, FAX 603/
430–4444, WEB www.hideaways.com;
membership $129).

B & B S

Bed-and-breakfasts can be found in
both the country and the cities. For
assistance in booking these, **contact
the appropriate provincial tourist
board,** which either has a listing of
B&Bs or can refer you to an association that can help you secure reservations. Be sure to **check out the B&B's
Web site,** which may have useful
information, although you should
also find out how up-to-date it is.
Room quality varies from house to
house as well, so you can **ask to see
a room before making a choice.**

CAMPING

Campgrounds in Canada range from
rustic woodland settings far from the
nearest paved road to facility-packed
open fields full of sleek motor homes
next to major highways. Some of the
best sites are in national and provincial parks—well cared for, well
equipped, and close to plenty of
nature and activity programs for both
children and adults. The campgrounds
in the coastal regions of the Maritime
Provinces and Québec, on the Great
Lakes in Ontario, and the mountains
of Alberta and British Columbia are
particularly beautiful. Campers tend
to be working- or middle-class families with a fair sprinkling of seniors,
but their tastes and practices are as
varied as the campsites they favor.
Some see camping simply as a way to
get practical, low-cost lodgings on a
road trip, whereas other, more seden-
tary campers move into one campground with as much elaborate
equipment as they can and set up for
a long stay. Wilderness camping for
hikers and canoeists is available in
national and provincial parks across
the country. True adventurers can
even trek into remote campsites in the
Canadian Arctic.

HOSTELS

No matter what your age, you can
**save on lodging costs by staying at
hostels.** In some 4,500 locations in
more than 70 countries around the
world, Hostelling International (HI),
the umbrella group for a number of

national youth-hostel associations,
offers single-sex, dorm-style beds and,
at many hostels, rooms for couples
and family accommodations. Membership in any HI national hostel
association, open to travelers of all
ages, allows you to stay in HI-affili-
ated hostels at member rates; one-
year membership is about $25 for
adults (C$26.75 in Canada, £12.50 in
the U.K., A$52 in Australia, and
NZ$30 in New Zealand); hostels run
about $10–$25 per night. Members
have priority if the hostel is full;
they're also eligible for discounts
around the world, even on rail and
bus travel in some countries.

➤ ORGANIZATIONS: **Hostelling International—American Youth Hostels**
(✉ 733 15th St. NW, Suite 840,
Washington, DC 20005, ☎ 202/783–
6161, FAX 202/783–6171, WEB www.
hiayh.org). **Hostelling International—
Canada** (✉ 400–205 Catherine St.,
Ottawa, Ontario K2P 1C3, Canada,
☎ 613/237–7884, FAX 613/237–7868,
WEB www.hostellingintl.ca). **Youth
Hostel Association of England and
Wales** (✉ Trevelyan House, 8 St.
Stephen's Hill, St. Albans, Hertford-
shire AL1 2DY, U.K., ☎ 0870/
8708808, FAX 01727/844126, WEB
www.yha.org.uk). **Australian Youth
Hostel Association** (✉ 10 Mallett St.,
Camperdown, NSW 2050, Australia,
☎ 02/9565–1699, FAX 02/9565–1325,
WEB www.yha.com.au). **Youth Hostels
Association of New Zealand** (✉
Level 3, 193 Cashel St., Box 436,
Christchurch, New Zealand, ☎
03/379–9970, FAX 03/365–4476,
WEB www.yha.org.nz).

HOTELS

All hotels listed have private bath
unless otherwise noted.

MAIL & SHIPPING

In Canada you can buy stamps at the
post office or from vending machines
in most hotel lobbies, railway stations, airports, bus terminals, many
retail outlets, and some newsstands.
If you're sending mail to or within
Canada, **be sure to include the postal
code** (six digits and letters). Note
that the suite number often appears
before the street number in an address, followed by a hyphen.

SMART TRAVEL TIPS A TO Z

Following are postal abbreviations for provinces and territories: Alberta, AB; British Columbia, BC; Manitoba, MB; New Brunswick, NB; Newfoundland and Labrador, NF; Northwest Territories and Nunavut, NT; Nova Scotia, NS; Ontario, ON; Prince Edward Island, PE; Québec, QC; Saskatchewan, SK; Yukon, YT.

POSTAL RATES

Within Canada, postcards and letters up to 30 grams cost 47¢; between 31 grams and 50 grams, the cost is 75¢; and between 51 grams and 100 grams, the cost is 94¢. Letters and postcards to the United States cost 60¢ for up to 30 grams, 85¢ for between 31 and 50 grams, and $1.30 for up to 100 grams. Prices include GST (Goods and Services Tax).

International mail and postcards run $1.05 for up to 20 grams, $1.60 for 21 to 50 grams, and $2.50 for 51 to 100 grams.

RECEIVING MAIL

Visitors may have mail sent to them c/o General Delivery in the town they are visiting, for pickup in person within 15 days, after which it will be returned to the sender.

MEDIA

NEWSPAPERS & MAGAZINES

Maclean's and *Saturday Night* are Canada's two main general-interest magazines. Both cover arts and culture as well as politics. Canada has two national newspapers, the *National Post* and the *Globe and Mail*—both are published in Toronto and both are available at newsstands in major foreign cities, especially the big weekend editions, which are published on Saturday. The arts-and-entertainment sections of both papers have advance news of major events and exhibitions across the country. Both also have Web sites with limited information on cultural events. For more-detailed information, it is advisable to rely on metropolitan papers. The biggest newspaper in Canada is the *Toronto Star* (www.thestar.com), which has extensive listings for Toronto. Southam, the biggest newspaper chain in Canada, owns the *National Post*, and its Web site,

www.southam.com, has links to daily newspapers in most other Canadian cities.

RADIO & TELEVISION

U.S. television dominates Canada's airwaves. In border areas—where most Canadians live—Fox, PBS, NBC, CBS, and ABC are readily available. Canada's two major networks, the state-owned Canadian Broadcasting Corporation (CBC) and the private CTV, and the smaller Global Network broadcast a steady diet of U.S. sitcoms and dramas in prime time with only a scattering of Canadian-produced dramas and comedies. The selection of Canadian-produced current-affairs programs, however, is much wider. The CBC also has a parallel French-language network, Radio-Canada. Canadian cable subscribers have the usual vast menu of specialty channels to choose from, including the all-news outlets operated by CTV and CBC.

The CBC operates the country's only truly national radio network. In fact, it operates four of them, two in English and two in French. Its Radio 1 network, usually broadcast on the AM band, has a daily schedule rich in news, current-affairs, and discussion programs. One of the most popular shows, "As It Happens," takes a quirky and highly entertaining look at national, world, and weird events every evening at 6. Radio 2, usually broadcast on FM, emphasizes music and often features live classical concerts by some of Canada's best orchestras, opera companies, and choral groups. The two French-language networks more or less follow the same pattern.

MONEY MATTERS

Throughout this book, unless otherwise stated, all prices, including dining and lodging, are given in Canadian dollars.

The following typical prices are for Toronto: a soda (pop), $1.25–$1.75; glass of beer, $3–$6; a sandwich, $3.50–$6; a taxi, as soon as the meter is turned on, $2.50, and $1 for every kilometer (½ mi); movie admission for one, about $8.50. Prices in other cities and regions are often lower.

Prices throughout this guide are given for adults. Substantially reduced fees are almost always available for children, students, and senior citizens.

ATMS

ATMs are available in most bank, trust-company, and credit-union branches across the country, as well as in many convenience stores, malls, and gas stations.

CREDIT CARDS

Throughout this guide, the following abbreviations are used: **AE**, American Express; **D**, Discover; **DC**, Diners Club; **MC**, MasterCard; and **V**, Visa.

➤ REPORTING LOST CARDS: **American Express** (☎ 800/528–4800). **Diners Club** (☎ 800/234–6377). **Discover** (☎ 800/347–2683). **MasterCard** (☎ 800/307–7309). **Visa** (☎ 800/336–8472).

CURRENCY

U.S. dollars are accepted in much of Canada (especially in communities near the border). However, to get the most favorable exchange rate, **exchange at least some of your money into Canadian funds at a bank or other financial institution.** Traveler's checks (some are available in Canadian dollars) and major U.S. credit cards are accepted in most areas.

The units of currency in Canada are the Canadian dollar (C$) and the cent, in almost the same denominations as U.S. currency ($5, $10, $20, 1¢, 5¢, 10¢, 25¢, etc.). The $1 and $2 bill are no longer used; they have been replaced by $1 and $2 coins (known as a "loonie," because of the loon that appears on the coin, and a "toonie," respectively). At press time the exchange rate was US$1 to C$1.56, £1 to C$2.29, C$1 to 81 Australian cents, and C$1 to 68 New Zealand cents.

CURRENCY EXCHANGE

For the most favorable rates, **change money through banks.** Although ATM transaction fees may be higher abroad than at home, ATM rates are excellent because they are based on wholesale rates offered only by major banks. You won't do as well at exchange booths in airports or rail and bus stations, in hotels, in restaurants, or in stores. To avoid lines at airport exchange booths, **get a bit of local currency before you leave home.**

➤ EXCHANGE SERVICES: **International Currency Express** (☎ 888/278–6628 for orders, WEB www.foreignmoney. com). **Thomas Cook Currency Services** (☎ 800/287–7362 for telephone orders and retail locations, WEB www.us.thomascook.com).

NATIONAL PARKS

If you plan to visit several parks in a region, you may be able to **save money on park fees by buying a multipark pass.** Parks Canada offers seven passes: the PEI Combo Pass, the Alberta Federal and Provincial Historic Sites Pass, the Atlantic Regional National Park Pass, the Eastern Newfoundland National Historic Sites Pass, the Saskatchewan National Historic Sites Pass, the Viking Pass, and the Western Canada Annual Pass. Parks Canada is decentralized, so it's best to contact the park you plan to visit for information. You can buy passes at the parks covered by the pass.

➤ PARK PASSES: **Parks Canada** (national office: ✉ 25 Eddy St., Hull, QC K1A 0M5, ☎ 800/213–7275, WEB www.parkscanada.pch.gc.ca).

OUTDOORS & SPORTS

BICYCLING

➤ ASSOCIATION: **Canadian Cycling Association** (✉ 702–2197 Riverside Drive,, Ottawa, ON K1H 7X3, ☎ 613/248–1353, FAX 613/248–9311, WEB www.canadian-cycling.com).

CANOEING AND KAYAKING

Provincial tourist offices can be of assistance, especially in locating an outfitter to suit your needs. You may also contact the Canadian Recreational Canoeing Association.

➤ ASSOCIATION: **Canadian Recreational Canoeing Association** (✉ Box 398, Merrickville, ON K0G 1N0, ☎ 613/269–2910 or 888/252–6292, FAX 613/269–2908, WEB www.crca.ca).

CLIMBING/MOUNTAINEERING

➤ ASSOCIATION: **Alpine Club of Canada** (✉ Box 8040, Canmore, AB

T1W 2T8, ☎ 403/678–3200, FAX 403/678–3224, WEB www.alpineclubof-canada.ca).

GOLF

➤ ASSOCIATION: **Royal Canadian Golf Association** (✉ 1333 Dorval Dr., Oakville, ON L6J 4Z3, ☎ 905/849–9700, FAX 905/845–7040, WEB www.rcga.org).

SCUBA DIVING

➤ ASSOCIATION: **Canadian Amateur Diving Association** (✉ 703–2197 Riverside Dr., Ottawa, ON K1H 7X3, ☎ 613/736–5238, FAX 613/736–0409, WEB www.diving.ca).

TENNIS

➤ ASSOCIATION: **Tennis Canada** (✉ 3111 Steeles Ave. W, Downsview, ON M3J 3H2, ☎ 416/665–9777, FAX 416/665–9017, WEB www.tenniscanada.com).

PACKING

If you plan on camping or hiking in the deep woods in summer, particularly in northern Canada, **always carry insect repellent,** especially in June, which is blackfly season.

In your carry-on luggage, **pack an extra pair of eyeglasses or contact lenses and enough of any medication** you take to last the entire trip. You may also ask your doctor to write a spare prescription using the drug's generic name, since brand names may vary from country to country. In luggage to be checked, **never pack prescription drugs or valuables.** To avoid customs delays, carry medications in their original packaging. And don't forget to carry with you the addresses of offices that handle refunds of lost traveler's checks. Check *Fodor's How to Pack* (available in bookstores everywhere) for more tips.

CHECKING LUGGAGE

How many carry-on bags you can bring with you is up to the airline. Many allow two, but not always, so make sure that everything you carry aboard will fit under your seat or in the overhead bin, and get to the gate early. Note that if you have a seat at the back of the plane, you'll probably board first, while the overhead bins are still empty.

If you are flying internationally, note that baggage allowances may be determined not by piece but by weight—generally 88 pounds (40 kilograms) in first class, 66 pounds (30 kilograms) in business class, and 44 pounds (20 kilograms) in economy.

Airline liability for baggage is limited to $1,250 per person on flights within the United States. On international flights it amounts to $9.07 per pound or $20 per kilogram for checked baggage (roughly $640 per 70-pound bag) and $400 per passenger for unchecked baggage. You can buy additional coverage at check-in for about $10 per $1,000 of coverage, but it excludes a rather extensive list of items, shown on your airline ticket.

Before departure, **itemize your bags' contents** and their worth, and label the bags with your name, address, and phone number. (If you use your home address, cover it so potential thieves can't see it readily.) Inside each bag, **pack a copy of your itinerary.** At check-in, **make sure that each bag is correctly tagged** with the destination airport's three-letter code. If your bags arrive damaged or fail to arrive at all, file a written report with the airline before leaving the airport.

PASSPORTS & VISAS

When traveling internationally, **carry your passport** even if you don't need one (it's always the best form of I.D.) and **make two photocopies of the data page** (one for someone at home and another for you, carried separately from your passport). If you lose your passport, promptly call the nearest embassy or consulate and the local police.

ENTERING CANADA

Citizens and legal residents of the United States do not need a passport or a visa to enter Canada, but proof of citizenship (a birth certificate or valid passport) and some form of photo identification will be requested. Naturalized U.S. residents should carry their naturalization certificate. Permanent residents who are not citizens should carry their "green card." U.S. residents entering Canada from a third country must have a valid passport, naturalization certificate, or "green card."

Citizens of the United Kingdom need only a valid passport to enter Canada for stays of up to six months.

PASSPORT OFFICES

The best time to apply for a passport or to renew is in fall and winter. Before any trip, check your passport's expiration date, and, if necessary, renew it as soon as possible.

SENIOR-CITIZEN TRAVEL

To qualify for age-related discounts, **mention your senior-citizen status up front** when booking hotel reservations (not when checking out) and before you're seated in restaurants (not when paying the bill). When renting a car, ask about promotional car-rental discounts, which can be cheaper than senior-citizen rates.

➤ EDUCATIONAL PROGRAMS: **Elderhostel** (✉ 11 Ave. de Lafayette, Boston, MA 02111–1746, ☎ 877/426–8056, FAX 877/426–2166, WEB www.elderhostel.org). **Interhostel** (✉ University of New Hampshire, 6 Garrison Ave., Durham, NH 03824, ☎ 603/862–1147 or 800/733–9753, FAX 603/862–1113, WEB www.learn.unh.edu).

SHOPPING

Shopping in Canada ranges from the midway-style glitz of the West Edmonton Mall in Alberta (one of the world's biggest) to the exclusive fashion boutiques of Toronto's Yorkville district. The most varied shopping is in the three major cities: Montréal, Toronto, and Vancouver.

Montréal owes its founding to the fur trade and is still the fur capital of Canada; it's also a good place to hunt for antiques and to buy clothes direct from manufacturers. Toronto has some of the most stylish shops in the country, selling everything from fashions to housewares, but it's the city's markets that make it a mecca for shoppers, especially Kensington and the flea markets on the harborfront. Vancouver is the place to find West Coast native art—prints, etchings, and carvings.

Some smaller regions and towns have become known for particular products. Ontario's Kitchener-Waterloo area, for example, produces dozens of different German sausages; farmers in rural Québec produce more than 75% of the world's supply of maple syrup and often have roadside stands where you can buy sugar, taffy, and syrup; Calgary, home of the world's biggest rodeo, has a wide selection of Western-style paraphernalia, from embossed saddles to bolo ties; and craftswomen in the tiny Newfoundland outport of St. Anthony's make parkas, caps, and mittens out of heavy fabric called Grenfell cloth.

SMART SOUVENIRS

The hooked rugs produced by Acadian artisans (usually women) are either kitschy or naively charming, depending on your point of view. The best are available in the Cape Breton village of Chéticamp for prices that range from $15 into the hundreds. Québec pop and folk music is linguistically distinctive, and French-Canadian stars range from rock hunks such as Roch Voisine to passionate chansoniers Félix Leclerc and Gilles Vigneault. From the West Coast, heavy woolen sweaters with unique designs made by Cowichan natives sell for about $200. Cistercian monks in the Lac St-Jean area of northern Québec make chocolate-covered blueberries in summer. They're available all over the province of Québec but vanish almost as quickly as they're made. However, you can purchase other, less-perishable blueberry products from this area.

WATCH OUT

Americans should note that it is illegal for them to buy Cuban cigars and to take them home.

STUDENTS IN CANADA

Persons under 18 years of age who are not accompanied by their parents should **bring a letter from a parent or guardian** giving them permission to travel to Canada.

➤ I.D.S & SERVICES: **Council Travel** (CIEE; ✉ 205 E. 42nd St., 15th floor, New York, NY 10017, ☎ 212/822–2700 or 888/268–6245, FAX 212/822–2699, WEB www.councilexchanges.org) for mail orders only, in the U.S.

Travel Cuts (✉ 187 College St., Toronto, Ontario M5T 1P7, Canada, ☎ 416/979–2406; 800/667–2887 in Canada, FAX 416/979–8167, WEB www.travelcuts.com).

TAXES

A goods and services tax (GST) of 7% applies on virtually every transaction in Canada except for the purchase of basic groceries.

In addition to imposing the GST, all provinces except Alberta, the Northwest Territories, and the Yukon levy a sales tax from 6% to 12% on most items purchased in shops, on restaurant meals, and sometimes on hotel rooms. In Newfoundland, Nova Scotia, and New Brunswick, the single harmonized sales tax (HST) of 15% is used.

GST REFUNDS

You can **get a GST refund** on purchases taken out of the country and on short-term accommodations of less than one month, but not on food, drink, tobacco, car or motorhome rentals, or transportation; rebate forms, which must be submitted within 60 days of leaving Canada, may be obtained from certain retailers, duty-free shops, customs officials, or from the Canada Customs and Revenue Agency. Instant cash rebates up to a maximum of $500 are provided by some duty-free shops when you leave Canada, and most provinces do not tax goods that are shipped directly by the vendor to the purchaser's home. Always **save your original receipts** from stores and hotels (not just credit-card receipts), and **be sure the name and address of the establishment is shown on the receipt.** Original receipts are not returned. To be eligible for a refund, receipts must total at least $200, and each individual receipt must show a minimum purchase of $50.

➤ INFORMATION: **Canada Customs and Revenue Agency** (✉ Visitor Rebate Program, Summerside Tax Centre, 275 Pope Rd., Suite 104, Summerside, PE C1N 6C6, ☎ 902/432–5608; 800/668–4748 in Canada, WEB www.ccra-adrc.gc.ca).

PROVINCIAL TAX REFUNDS

Manitoba and Québec offer a sales-tax rebate system similar to the federal one. For provincial tax refunds, **call the provincial toll-free visitor information lines for details** (☞ Visitor Information). Most provinces do not tax goods shipped directly by the vendor to the visitor's home address.

TIPPING

Tips and service charges are not usually added to a bill in Canada. In general, tip 15% of the total bill. This goes for waiters, waitresses, barbers and hairdressers, and taxi drivers. Porters and doormen should get about $2 a bag. For maid service, leave at least $2 per person a day ($3 in luxury hotels).

TOURS & PACKAGES

Because everything is prearranged on a prepackaged tour or independent vacation, you spend less time planning—and often get it all at a good price.

BOOKING WITH AN AGENT

Travel agents are excellent resources. But it's a good idea to collect brochures from several agencies because some agents' suggestions may be influenced by relationships with tour and package firms that reward them for volume sales. If you have a special interest, **find an agent with expertise in that area.** The American Society of Travel Agents (☞ Travel Agencies) has a database of specialists worldwide.

Make sure your travel agent knows the accommodations and other services of the place being recommended. Ask about the hotel's location, room size, beds, and whether it has a pool, room service, or programs for children, if you care about these. Has your agent been there in person or sent others whom you can contact?

Do some homework on your own, too: local tourism boards can provide information about lesser-known and small-niche operators, some of which may sell only direct.

BUYER BEWARE

Each year consumers are stranded or lose their money when tour operators—even large ones with excellent reputations—go out of business. So **check out the operator.** Ask several travel agents about its reputation, and try to **book with a company that has a consumer-protection program.** (Look for information in the company's brochure.) In the United States, members of the National Tour Association and the United States Tour Operators Association are required to set aside funds to cover your payments and travel arrangements in the event that the company defaults. It's also a good idea to choose a company that participates in the American Society of Travel Agents' Tour Operator Program (TOP); ASTA will act as mediator in any disputes between you and your tour operator.

Remember that the more your package or tour includes the better you can predict the ultimate cost of your vacation. Make sure you know exactly what is covered, and **beware of hidden costs.** Are taxes, tips, and transfers included? Entertainment and excursions? These can add up.

➤ TOUR-OPERATOR RECOMMENDATIONS: **American Society of Travel Agents** (☞ Travel Agencies). **National Tour Association** (NTA; ⊠ 546 E. Main St., Lexington, KY 40508, ☎ 859/226–4444 or 800/682–8886, WEB www.ntaonline.com). **United States Tour Operators Association** (USTOA; ⊠ 342 Madison Ave., Suite 1522, New York, NY 10173, ☎ 212/599–6599 or 800/468–7862, FAX 212/599–6744, WEB www.ustoa.com).

THEME TRIPS

The companies listed below offer multiday tours in Canada. Additional local or regionally based companies that have different-length trips with these themes are listed in each chapter, either with information about the town or in the A to Z section that concludes the chapter.

➤ ADVENTURE: **Ecosummer Expeditions** (⊠ Box 1765, Clearwater, BC V0E 1N0, ☎ 250/674–0102 or 800/465–8884, WEB www.ecosummer.com). **Gorp Travel** (⊠ Box 1486, Boulder, CO 80306, ☎ 303/444–2622 or 800/444–0099, FAX 303/635–0658,

WEB www.gorptravel.com). **Mountain Travel-Sobek** (⊠ 6420 Fairmount Ave., El Cerrito, CA 94530, ☎ 510/527–8100 or 888/687–6235, FAX 510/525–7710, WEB www.mtsobek.com). **Nahanni River Adventures** (⊠ Box 4869, Whitehorse Y1A 4N6, ☎ 867/668–3180 or 800/297–6927, FAX 867/668–3056). **O.A.R.S.** (⊠ Box 67, Angels Camp, CA 95222, ☎ 209/736–4677 or 800/346–6277, FAX 209/736–2902, WEB www.oars.com). **Trek America** (⊠ Box 189, Rockaway, NJ 07866, ☎ 973/983–1144 or 800/221–0596, FAX 973/983–8551, WEB www.trekamerica.com).

➤ BICYCLING: **Backroads** (⊠ 801 Cedar St., Berkeley, CA 94710-1800, ☎ 510/527–1555 or 800/462–2848, FAX 510/527–1444, WEB www.backroads.com). **Bicycle Adventures** (⊠ Box 11219, Olympia, WA 98508, ☎ 360/786–0989 or 800/443–6060, FAX 360/786–9661). **Bike Rider Tours** (⊠ Box 130254, Boston, MA 02113, ☎ 617/723–2354 or 800/473–7040, FAX 617/723–2355, WEB www.bikeridertours.com). **Butterfield & Robinson** (⊠ 70 Bond St., Toronto, ON M5B 1X3, ☎ 416/864–1354 or 800/678–1147, FAX 416/864–0541, WEB www.butterfield.com). **Easy Rider Tours** (⊠ Box 228, Newburyport, MA 01950, ☎ 978/463–6955 or 800/488–8332, FAX 978/463 6988, WEB www.easyridertours.com). **Imagine Tours** (⊠ Box 475, Davis, CA 95617, ☎ 530/758–8782 or 800/924–2453, FAX 530/758–8778, WEB www.imaginetours.com). **Rocky Mountain Worldwide Cycle Tours** (⊠ Box 268, Garibaldi Highlands, Squamish, BC V0N 1T0, ☎ 604/898–8488 or 800/661–2453, FAX 604/898–8489). **Timberline Adventures** (⊠ 7975 E. Harvard, Suite J, Denver, CO 80231, ☎ 303/759–3804 or 800/417–2453, FAX 303/368–1651, WEB www.timberbtours.com). **Vermont Bicycle Touring** (⊠ Box 711, Bristol, VT 05443-0711, ☎ 800/245–3868 or 802/453–4811, FAX 802/453–4806, WEB www.vbt.com). **Les Voyages du Tour de l'Île,** (⊠ 1251 rue Rache Est, Montréal, QC H2J 2J9, ☎ 514/521–8356 or 888/899–1111, FAX 514/512–5711, WEB www.velo.qc.ca).

➤ DUDE RANCHES: **Gorp Travel** (✉ Box 1486, Boulder, CO 80306, ☎ 303/444–2622 or 800/444–0099, FAX 303/635–0658, WEB www.gorptravel.com).

➤ FISHING: **Cutting Loose Expeditions** (✉ Box 447, Winter Park, FL 32790-0447, ☎ 407/629–4700 or 800/533–4746, FAX 407/740–7816, WEB www.gorp.com/cutloose/samer.htm). **Fishing International** (✉ Box 2132, Santa Rosa, CA 95405, ☎ 707/542–4242 or 800/950–4242, FAX 707/526–3474, WEB www.travelsource.com/fishing). **Rod & Reel Adventures** (✉ 566 Thomson La., Copperopolis, CA 95228, ☎ 209/785–0444 or 800/356–6982, FAX 209/785–0447, WEB www.rodreeladventures.com).

➤ PHOTOGRAPHY: **Joseph Van Os Photo Safaris** (✉ Box 655, Vashon, WA 98070, ☎ 206/463–5383, FAX 206/463–5484, WEB www.photosafari.com).

➤ SKIING: **Canadian Mountain Holidays** (✉ 217 Bear St., Banff, AB T0L 0C0, ☎ 403/762–7100 or 800/661–0252, FAX 403/762–5879, WEB www.cmhhike.com). **Selkirk Tangiers Helicopter Skiing** (✉ Box 130, Revelstoke, BC V0E 2S0, ☎ 250/837–5378 or 800/663–7080, FAX 250/837–5766, WEB www.atplay.com). **Skican** (✉ 443 Mt. Pleasant Rd., Toronto, ON M4S 2L8, ☎ 416/488–1169 or 888/475–4226, FAX 416/488–7620, WEB www.skican.com). **Whistler Heli-Skiing** (✉ Box 894, Whistler, BC V0N 1B0, ☎ 604/932–7007 or 888/435–4754, FAX 604/932–9992, WEB www.whistlerheliskiing.com).

➤ SPAS: **Spa-Finders** (✉ 91 5th Ave., Suite 600, New York, NY 10003-3039, ☎ 212/924–6800 or 800/255–7727, WEB www.spafinders.com).

➤ WALKING/HIKING: **Backroads** (✉ 801 Cedar St., Berkeley, CA 94710-1800, ☎ 510/527–1555 or 800/462–2848, FAX 510/527–1444, WEB www.backroads.com). **Butterfield & Robinson** (✉ 70 Bond St., Toronto, ON M5B 1X3, ☎ 416/864–1354 or 800/678–1147, FAX 416/864–0541, WEB www.butterfield.com). **Canadian Mountain Holidays** (✉ 217 Bear St., Banff, AB T0L 0C0, ☎ 403/762–7100 or 800/661–0252, FAX 403/762–

5879, WEB www.cmhhike.com). **Country Walkers** (✉ Box 180, Waterbury, VT 05676-0180, ☎ 802/244–1387 or 800/464–9255, FAX 802/244–5661, WEB www.countrywalkers.com). **New England Hiking Holidays** (✉ Box 1648, North Conway, NH 03860, ☎ 603/356–9696 or 800/869–0949, WEB www.nehikingholidays.com). **Timberline Adventures** (✉ 7975 E. Harvard, Suite J, Denver, CO 80231, ☎ 303/759–3804 or 800/417–2453, FAX 303/368–1651, WEB www.timberbtours.com). **Walking the World** (✉ Box 1186, Fort Collins, CO 80522, ☎ 970/498–0500 or 800/340–9255, FAX 970/498–9100, WEB www.gorp.com/walkingtheworld); specializes in tours for ages 50 and older.

TRAIN TRAVEL

Amtrak has service from New York to Montréal, New York and Buffalo to Toronto, Chicago to Toronto, and Seattle to Vancouver, providing connections between Amtrak's U.S.-wide network and VIA Rail's Canadian routes. VIA Rail Canada provides transcontinental rail service. Rocky Mountaineer Railtours operates a variety of spectacular all-daylight rail trips through the Canadian Rockies from the west coast.

CUTTING COSTS

If you're planning to travel a lot by train, **look into the Canrail pass.** It allows 12 days of coach-class travel within a 30-day period; sleeping cars are available, but they sell out very early and must be reserved at least a month in advance during the high season (June to mid-October), when the pass is $658 (discounts for youths and seniors). Low-season rates (October 16 to May) are $411. The pass is not valid during the Christmas period (December 15 through January 5). For more information and reservations, contact a travel agent in the U.S. In the United Kingdom, Long-Haul Leisurail represents both VIA Rail and Rocky Mountaineer Railtours.

Train travelers can **check out the 30-day North American RailPass** offered by Amtrak and VIA Rail. It allows unlimited coach–economy travel in the U.S. and Canada. You must indicate the itinerary when purchasing the pass. The cost is $1,004 from June to October 15, $702 at other times.

➤ TRAIN INFORMATION: **Amtrak** (☎ 800/872–7245). **Long-Haul Leisurail** (✉ Box 113, Peterborough, PE3 8HY U.K., ☎ 01733/335599). **Rocky Mountaineer Railtours** (☎ 800/665–7245). **VIA Rail Canada** (☎ 800/561–3949).

TRAVEL AGENCIES

A good travel agent puts your needs first. Look for an agency that has been in business at least five years, emphasizes customer service, and has someone on staff who specializes in your destination. In addition, **make sure the agency belongs to a professional trade organization.** The American Society of Travel Agents (ASTA), with more than 26,000 members in some 170 countries, is the largest and most influential in the field. Operating under the motto "Without a travel agent, you're on your own," it maintains and enforces a strict code of ethics and will step in to help mediate any agent-client disputes if necessary. ASTA also maintains a Web site that includes a directory of agents. (If a travel agency is also acting as your tour operator, *see* Buyer Beware *in* Tours & Packages).

➤ LOCAL AGENT REFERRALS: **American Society of Travel Agents** (ASTA; ✉ 1101 King St., Suite 200, Alexandria, VA 22314 ☎ 800/965–2782 24-hr hot line, FAX 703/739–7642, WEB www.astanet.com). **Association of British Travel Agents** (✉ 68–71 Newman St., London W1T 3AH, U.K., ☎ 020/7637–2444, FAX 020/7637–0713, WEB www.abtanet.com). **Association of Canadian Travel Agents** (✉ 130 Albert St., Suite 1705, Ottawa, Ontario K1P 5G4, Canada, ☎ 613/237–3657, FAX 613/237–7052, WEB www.acta.net). **Australian Federation of Travel Agents** (✉ Level 3, 309 Pitt St., Sydney NSW 2000, Australia, ☎ 02/9264–3299, FAX 02/9264–1085, WEB www.afta.com.au). **Travel Agents' Association of New Zealand** (✉ Level 5, Paxus House, 79 Boulcott St., Box 1888, Wellington 10033, New Zealand, ☎ 04/499–0104, FAX 04/499–0827, WEB www.taanz.org.nz).

VISITOR INFORMATION

➤ TOURIST INFORMATION: **Canadian Tourism Commission** (☎ 613/946–1000, WEB www.canadatourism.com). Alberta: **Travel Alberta** (✉ Box 2500, Edmonton, T5J 2Z1, ☎ 800/661–8888 or 780/427–4321, WEB www.travelalberta.com). British Columbia: **Tourism B. C.** (✉ Plaza Level, 200 Burrard St., Vancouver, V6C 3L6, ☎ 800/663–6000, WEB www.hellobc.com). Manitoba: **Travel Manitoba** (✉ 155 Carlton St., 7th floor, Winnipeg, R3C 3H8, ☎ 800/665–0040, WEB www.travelmanitoba.com). New Brunswick: **Tourism New Brunswick** (✉ Box 12345, Campbellton, E3N 3T6, ☎ 800/561–0123, WEB www.tourismnewbrunswick.ca). Newfoundland and Labrador: **Tourism Newfoundland and Labrador** (✉ Box 8730, St. John's, A1B 4K2, ☎ 800/563–6353, WEB www.gov.nf.ca//tourism). Northwest Territories: **NWT Arctic Tourism** (✉ Box 610, Yellowknife, X1A 2N5, ☎ 800/661–0788, WEB www.nwttravel.nt.ca). Nova Scotia: **Nova Scotia Tourism** (✉ Box 519, Halifax, B3J 2R7, ☎ 800/565–0000, WEB www.gov.ns.ca/tourism). Nunavut: **Nunavut Tourism** (✉ Box 1450, Iqaluit, X0A 0H0, ☎ 800/491–7910, WEB www.nunavuttourism.com). Ontario: **Ontario Travel** (✉ 1243 Islington Ave., Suite 200, Toronto, M8X 2Y3, ☎ 800/668–2746, WEB www.ontariotravel.net). Prince Edward Island: **Tourism PEI** (✉ Box 940, Charlottetown, C1A 7M5, ☎ 888/734–7529, WEB www.peiplay.com). Québec: **Tourisme Québec** (✉ C.P. 979, Montréal, H3C 2W3, ☎ 800/363–7777, WEB www.bonjourquebec.com). Saskatchewan: **Tourism Saskatchewan** (✉ 1922 Park St., Regina S4P 3V7, ☎ 800/667–7191, WEB www.sasktourism.com). Yukon: **Tourism Yukon** (✉ Box 2703, Whitehorse, Y1A 2C6, ☎ 867/667–5340, WEB www.touryukon.com).

➤ IN THE U.K.: **Québec Tourism** (✉ 59 Pall Mall, London SW1Y 5JH, ☎ 0990/561–705 or 020/7930–8314). **Visit Canada Center** (✉ 62–65 Trafalgar Sq., London, WC2 5DY, ☎ 0891/715–000, 50p per minute peak rate and 45p per minute cheap rate).

WEB SITES

Do check out the World Wide Web when planning your trip. You'll find everything from weather forecasts to virtual tours of famous cities. Be sure to **visit Fodors.com** (www.fodors.com), a complete travel-planning site. You can research prices and book plane tickets, hotel rooms, rental cars, vacation packages, and more. In addition, you can post your pressing questions in the Travel Talk section and, in the site's Rants & Raves section, read comments about some of the restaurants and hotels in this book—and chime in yourself. Other planning tools include a currency converter and weather reports, and there are loads of links to travel resources.

For Canadian festivals, check out www.festivalseeker.com.

WHEN TO GO

CLIMATE

The following are average daily maximum and minimum temperatures for some major cities.

➤ FORECASTS: **Weather Channel Connection** (☎ 900/932–8437), 95¢ (U.S.) per minute from a Touch-Tone phone.

CALGARY

Jan.	23F	− 5C	May	61F	16C	Sept.	63F	17C
	2	−17		37	3		39	4
Feb.	29F	− 2C	June	67F	19C	Oct.	54F	12C
	8	−13		44	7		30	− 1
Mar.	34F	1C	July	74F	23C	Nov.	38F	3C
	14	−10		49	9		17	− 8
Apr.	49F	9C	Aug.	72F	22C	Dec.	29F	− 2C
	27	− 3		47	8		8	−13

HALIFAX

Jan.	33F	1C	May	58F	14C	Sept.	67F	19C
	20	− 7		41	5		53	12
Feb.	33F	1C	June	67F	19C	Oct.	58F	14C
	19	− 7		50	10		44	7
Mar.	39F	4C	July	73F	23C	Nov.	48F	9C
	26	− 3		57	14		36	2
Apr.	48F	9C	Aug.	73F	24C	Dec.	37F	3C
	33	1		58	13		25	4

MONTRÉAL

Jan.	23F	− 5C	May	65F	18C	Sept.	68F	20C
	9	−13		48	9		53	12
Feb.	25F	− 4C	June	74F	23C	Oct.	57F	14C
	12	−11		58	14		43	6
Mar.	36F	2C	July	79F	26C	Nov.	42F	6C
	23	− 5		63	17		32	0
Apr.	52F	11C	Aug.	76F	24C	Dec.	27F	− 3C
	36	2		61	16		16	− 9

OTTAWA

Jan.	20F	− 7C	May	65F	18C	Sept.	68F	20C
	4	−16		44	7		49	9
Feb.	23F	− 5C	June	75F	24C	Oct.	57F	14C
	6	−14		54	12		39	4
Mar.	34F	1C	July	80F	27C	Nov.	41F	5C
	18	− 8		58	14		29	− 2
Apr.	51F	11C	Aug.	77F	25C	Dec.	25F	− 4C
	33	1		56	13		12	−11

TORONTO

Jan.	30F	– 1C	May	64F	18C	Sept.	71F	22C
	18	– 8		47	8		54	12
Feb.	32F	0C	June	76F	24C	Oct.	60F	16C
	19	– 7		57	14		45	7
Mar.	40F	4C	July	80F	27C	Nov.	46F	8C
	27	– 3		62	17		35	2
Apr.	53F	12C	Aug.	79F	26C	Dec.	34F	1C
	38	3		61	16		23	– 5

VANCOUVER

Jan.	42F	6C	May	60F	16C	Sept.	65F	18C
	33	1		47	8		52	11
Feb.	45F	7C	June	65F	18C	Oct.	56F	13C
	36	2		52	11		45	7
Mar.	48F	9C	July	70F	21C	Nov.	48F	9C
	37	3		55	13		39	4
Apr.	54F	12C	Aug.	70F	21C	Dec.	43F	6C
	41	5		55	13		35	2

SMART TRAVEL TIPS A TO Z

1 DESTINATION: CANADA

A GRAND PLACE

ET'S FACE IT—Canadians have an image problem. To most people we come across as a bit, well, dull. Nice enough and certainly polite. But boring. Good at driving in snow, perhaps, and excellent at helping little old ladies across the street, but not the kind of people you're likely to run into in a soap opera or a gunfight. Not heroic or sexy and certainly not nasty. Canadians can't even curse each other without adding a faintly interrogatory "eh" at the end, as if seeking approval for the harsh words. As in "Go to hell, eh?"

We also get overlooked a lot. The *Boston Globe* runs a regular quiz in its travel section, and one week it asked which country most foreign visitors to the United States come from. The answer given was Japan. Huh? What about us? We're foreign, too, and on any given night there are more Canadians bedding down in Vermont than there are Japanese in all 50 states.

So, given all this, how do you explain hockey—12 guys on ice with steel blades on their feet and big sticks in their hands, slamming each other around in a wood and Plexiglas box? That's not the sort of thing you'd expect from a polite and diffident people. But it's our national passion—almost a religion in some places. "You don't like hockey," Stuart McLean writes in his delightful *Welcome Home*, "you believe in it." And the reputation we have is dreadful. Russians, the conventional wisdom goes, play with skill. Americans play with heart. Canadians just play dirty.

Mary Henderson sees no contradiction. She's a sweet and tiny lady who runs a day-care center in Manitoba and helps raise money for the local hospital. But every Saturday night from September through April, she watches *Hockey Night in Canada* on CBC television with blood in her eye and heat in her heart. "We're so nice, everybody takes us for granted," she says. "In hockey we're allowed to be nasty. We can even break the rules. You can't take us for granted there."

Maybe she's right. It's hard to overlook Brendan Shanahan or Eric Lindros on the ice, no matter whose sweater they're wearing. Or maybe it's just that hockey is one of the few patriotic outlets Canadians allow themselves. The rest of the time we're too busy being diffident to indulge in any kind of showy display. Sometimes this goes to ridiculous extremes. My daughter goes to a French high school for girls in Montréal. One day the school took everyone to Ottawa, the nation's capital. On the way home, some of the girls, mostly English-speaking ones, wanted to sing "O Canada." The teachers said "non." It might offend the Québec nationalists on the bus. Even if they sang it in French.

Canada's kind of an accident, a big, disjointed puzzle spread across the top of a continent. There are only 30 million Canadians—no more than the population of New York and California combined—scattered across a land bigger than China. It's true that most Canadians live within 325 km (202 mi) of the American border, and 75% of them live in cities, but even that doesn't create much density. Cole Harris, an editor of *The Canadian Encyclopedia,* described the inhabited part of Canada as "an island archipelago spread over 4,000 east–west miles."

In a particularly unkind moment, Lucien Bouchard, the leader of the separatist Parti Québécois, angered the nation by saying Canada wasn't a real country at all—this from a man who served as the noncountry's ambassador to France for several years. Still, he had something of a point. Canada's not so much a country as a work in progress, an unfinished symphony. And we can be irritatingly undecided about who we are. Take our spelling, for example. We see plays in "theatres" just like the English, but we live in "neighborhoods" just like the Americans.

Then there's our birthday. We celebrate it on July 1 because on that day in 1867, the British Parliament joined the four provinces of Québec, Ontario, Nova Scotia, and New Brunswick into a new and independent federation. Well, sort of independent. The holiday used to be called Dominion Day, because Canada was once officially a dominion, whatever that is. Then, for some reason, the name was changed to Canada Day, a lamentable choice. There's no such thing as Greece Day or France Day. And it gives the unfortunate impression that Canada popped out of nowhere in 1867, without history or feeling. And that just isn't true.

THE CONSTITUTIONAL conundrum that is Canada was actually conceived, if not born, in a flash of smoke and passion more than 100 years earlier on a warm September night in 1759 when Major-General James Wolfe scrambled up the 300-ft cliffs outside Québec City and mustered his men on the Plains of Abraham. Wolfe had about 4,500 men on the field that day, and so did his French opponent, General the Marquis de Montcalm. A lot of Montcalm's soldiers, however, were militiamen, good at cat-and-mouse tactics, but lacking the stand-and-take-it discipline required to fight a pitched battle in the 18th century. Once Wolfe had lured them out of their fortified position, his hardened regulars took about an hour to drive them from the field. When it was over, the British crown had a new French-speaking colony to govern, the "Canadiens" had new imperial masters to manipulate, and the undertakers had two dead generals to bury.

It all worked fairly well for a while. As conquerors go, the British were pretty benign, and the French kept their faith, their language, and their seigneurs. Then those pesky Americans to the south rebelled against their British masters. Tory refugees—traitors at home, Loyalists to us—fled north. Presto—biculturalism was born. And so was the struggle that consumes our poetry and our politics.

The province of Québec is the true cradle of Canada. Its population is about 85% French, and it totters on the brink of going it alone, of leaving the federation. Its most popular politicians are separatists, and its poets and singers are relentlessly nationalist. Talk of independence is everywhere.

Eric Deschênes is a merry little man who's mayor of Godbout on the North Shore of the Gulf of St. Lawrence. It's a tiny place of austere beauty, but it's Eric's hometown and he loves it dearly. He gave up an academic career to go back there to fish and hunt and to run a little inn. He's cheerfully matter-of-fact about his nationalism. Eric took my family for a boat ride on his favorite lake and then to his fishing camp on the Rivière Godbout. He tried to explain the reluctance of half the province's population to buy the nationalist dream. A lack of self-confidence, he suggested. "People here thought Godbout was finished when the American paper company pulled out," he said. "They were wrong. People have to learn to rely on themselves. And they will."

But there are signs that Canadians in other parts of the country are getting impatient—not so much at Québec's demands for independence as at its indecisiveness. "I wish Québec would decide one way or the other," accountant Kevin MacIntyre of Calgary told me. "Then the rest of us could get on with the job of making this the best country in the world." Others point out that the province has certainly had its fair share of national power—prime ministers from Québec have governed the country for nearly 29 of the past 30 years.

But Québec seems determined to remain indecisive. Support for independence hovers between 30% and 40%—not enough to accomplish it, but certainly enough to remain a force. The odd thing about all this is the civilized way in which this passionate debate is conducted. Rancorous things get said, all right, and spokespeople for both sides can sometimes come off sounding like bigots, but all in all we seldom lose our cool. When floods wiped out thousands of homes in the notoriously nationalist Saguenay–Lac-St-Jean region of Québec in summer 1996, Canadians raised $28 million in aid and sent the area truckloads of clothing, toys, and food. Even on October 30, 1995, when a Québec referendum on independence ended in a virtual dead heat, nothing much happened. Tempers were high and patience thin, but there were no riots or angry demonstrations, just a few scuffles outside the various campaign headquarters. Then everyone went out for a drink.

To many Canadians, of course, the endless debate and the "neverendums" are irrelevant, even plain silly. A lot of people have moved to Canada since 1867—people from Italy, Greece, China, Ukraine, Portugal, Ireland, Iceland, India, Spain, the Caribbean, and, most recently, Latin America. They've brought their faiths and their customs, their food and their music, and sometimes even their own quarrels. And they have irrevocably changed the country: women in veils drive Montréal buses; Edmonton has an Ethiopian restaurant; and at least one Mountie wears a turban. Toronto is now the most multicultural city on earth; French-speaking Montréal counts smoked meat and bagels among its distinctive dishes; and Vancouver is accommodating the thousands of Hong Kong Chinese who have poured into the city. Most of these people have a hard time understanding what the English and the French are fighting about.

"What this country needs is a real problem," a Guatemalan refugee told me. He smiled when he said it, but I could see the pain in his eyes. He was sitting in a church-sponsored legal clinic finding out what he had to do to become a landed immigrant. "There are people who look at Canada from afar. Canada—big, rich, and beautiful—and they just can't understand what's happening." He, too, has a point. Our economy is shaky, the national debt is high, and our social safety net has taken a bit of a beating. But all those troubles must seem pretty trivial to someone from Guatemala or India or Vietnam.

F OR THIS IS STILL a rich and tolerant land. No one has to go hungry, medical care is free for anyone who needs it, and even the poorest of our poor are affluent beyond the imagining of much of the world. The cities where most of us live are safe and clean, with downtowns that are full of life.

And there's always that landscape, that endless and achingly beautiful landscape. We may be an urban people now, but the wilderness is never far away. I live in Montréal, one of the country's great metropolises, but in 2 hours I can be skiing on Mont Tremblant, in 4 I can be hopelessly lost in the tundra of Charlevoix, and in 12 I can be on the shore of James Bay, celebrating the annual goose hunt with Cree whose lifestyle has changed little over the centuries.

Canadians make much ado about winter. They love to whine about the cold and daydream about palm trees. But the truth is, winter is part of what makes us Canadian, and many of us revel in it. "Mon pays, ce n'est pas un pays, c'est l'hiver," chansonnier Gilles Vigneault sang in his most famous song. "My country's not a country; it's winter."

I remember walking along the shores of Lac Turgeon in the middle of northeastern Québec on a cold January night. The drifts were deep enough to bury me standing up and stiff enough to bear my weight. The snow squeaked as I walked, and my sinuses crackled every time I inhaled. But the air smelled sweetly of wood smoke, and the black velvet sky sparkled with a million stars.

And all this landscape and beauty is ours. From the coves of Newfoundland to the mountains of British Columbia, from the Great Lakes to the Arctic desert. It's all ours—the wheat farms of the prairies, the beef ranches of the Rocky Mountain foothills, the Gaelic songs of Cape Breton, the great cathedrals of Québec, the vineyards of the Niagara Peninsula, the clouds of snow geese that fill our sky every spring and fall—ours to hold, ours to pass on to our children and our grandchildren, ours to share with whoever wants to join us.

One July 1, I rode into the Yukon backcountry with a Tutchone grandfather named Fred Brown. He's a lean, wiry whip of a man who owns a modern bungalow with all the conveniences but who prefers to live in the bush. We spent the morning plodding a zigzag course from a hot, dusty valley to the cool uplands of the Ruby Mountains. In the evening we camped by a lake whose water was so clean and cold we could lie on our stomachs and suck it up the way the horses did. I caught a trout and Fred fried it over an open fire. We drank tea and he told me outrageous stories about how his grandmother used to snare moose. At midnight it was still bright enough outside to play cards without a lantern. We hadn't said anything about Dominion Day or Canada Day, but just before we turned in, Fred looked at me with a smile and said, "This is a grand place, white man. Be thankful."

And so I am.

— Paul Waters

Paul Waters, a Canadian journalist, was raised and educated on the Atlantic coast and has lived in all three of Canada's major cities: Montréal, Toronto, and Vancouver. He now lives in Montréal with his family.

NEW AND NOTEWORTHY

Whether you're planning to visit Canada's great outdoors, its beautiful Atlantic and Pacific coasts, or its sophisticated cities, it's good to know that your dollar will stretch further (even with higher Canadian taxes), making the country a great travel value. Following the trend of the past few years, the exchange rate (summer 2001) is about US$1 to C$1.56, and £1 to C$2.29.

➤ ONTARIO: The National Gallery in **Ottawa** is mounting the first major retrospective in 30 years of works by the legendary Canadian painter Tom Thomson, from June to September 2002. Thomson's innovative vision of the wilderness redefined Canadian art. *Expressionist Portrait, 1905–1935*, on display from October 2002 to January 2003, exhibits the tradition-shattering works of such giants as Kokashcka, Schiele, and Nolde.

➤ PRINCE EDWARD ISLAND: Founders' Hall—the Canadian Birthplace Experience, opened in **Charlottetown** as a legacy to the "Birthplace of Canada." Canadian Confederation is explored through interactive multimedia displays, vignettes, and walking tours of Historic Charlottetown.

➤ QUÉBEC: The Québec government has imposed municipal mergers in the **Québec City** and **Montréal** areas that could result in street and city name changes. In Québec City for example, Sillery, Ste. Foy, Cap Rouge, and some other suburbs are becoming part of Québec City. In Montréal, all of the cities and towns on the island are being merged into one megacity. The changes could result in more than one street with the same name in a merged city area, so a number of streets may have to be renamed.

A cool new lodging option has opened just outside Québec City: the Ice Hotel. Made from 4,500 tons of snow and 250 tons of ice, it must be dismantled for warmer months; guests spend the night tucked in sleeping bags on a bed of deer pelts.

At the ever-expanding **Mont Tremblant,** a new 18-hole golf course—built to international standards and designed by Fred Couples—opened in spring 2001.

WHAT'S WHERE

The sections below correspond to regional chapters in this book; major cities that have their own chapters are indicated below in boldface type.

British Columbia

British Columbia's caffeine addicts have a choice between two major coffee shop chains—Seattle's Starbucks and Toronto's Second Cup. Local legend has it that they usually let their Pacific sympathies triumph over their Canadian ones. This clash of the coffees illustrates once again that British Columbia is clearly a world apart, a brash young province with a population that sees its future on the Pacific Rim. Even winter in much of British Columbia is different—soft, gentle, and very un-Canadian. **Victoria,** the provincial capital, has a climate like that of Devon in Great Britain, with springs that are glorious with flowers and sunshine. **Vancouver,** the province's vibrant metropolis, is rainier but just as mild. Visitors to British Columbia can visit a Haida village, catch a chinook salmon, ski and play golf in the mountains (often on the same day), and shop for native art in the boutiques of Vancouver.

Canadian Rockies

Much of what sets British Columbia apart is this broad granite spine that straddles the British Columbia–Alberta line from the U.S. border north through the Yukon. The mountains were once a block to Canada's western expansion—the first prime minister, Sir John A. Macdonald, had to promise to push a railroad through these formidable ranges to entice the British colonies on the west coast to join the fledgling Confederation—but now they are one of the country's favorite playgrounds. National and provincial parks like Banff and Jasper protect much of the land from development and attract skiers, hikers, climbers, horseback riders, and anglers.

New Brunswick

New Brunswick is where the great Canadian forest, sliced by sweeping river valleys and modern highways, meets the Atlantic. To the north and east, the gentle, warm Gulf Stream washes quiet beaches.

Besides the seacoast, there are pure inland streams, pretty towns, and historic cities such as Fredericton and Saint John. The province's dual heritage (35% of its population is Acadian French) provides added cultural interest.

Newfoundland and Labrador

The youngest member of the Canadian family, the island of Newfoundland and Labrador on the mainland joined the Confederation in 1949. But the province has a long history. Norsemen settled briefly in L'Anse-aux-Meadows around 1000, and explorer John Cabot landed on the rocky coast in 1497. The land has a raw beauty, with steep cliffs, roaring salmon rivers, and fishing villages that perch precariously on naked rock. Its people are a rich mix of English, Irish, and Scots who have a colorful grasp of language and a talent for acerbic commentary. St. John's, the capital, is a classic harbor city.

Nova Scotia

Almost an island, Nova Scotia is a little province on the Atlantic coast with a long history and a rich culture. Shaped by its rugged coastline and honed by the sea, it has been a haven for blacks arriving as freemen or escaped slaves, Scots, Germans, and Loyalists from the American Revolution, but its earliest colonial history was enriched by the Acadians and scarred by their brutal deportation. This multicultural mix, dating back 400 years, may account for Nova Scotia's rich musical climate, which includes the Gaelic ceilidh—gatherings wild with fiddles and step dancing—and the folk songs of sailors and the sea. Salty little ports dot the coastline, their extravagant Victorian mansions—many of them now hospitable bed-and-breakfasts—bespeaking the wealth of shipwrights and merchants trading with the world a century and more ago. Today, Nova Scotia maintains its unique outlook: worldly, warm, and sturdily independent.

Ontario

Ontario has both Canada's political capital, Ottawa, and its commercial capital, **Toronto.** It's also big (four times the size of Great Britain), rich, and growing. You can see a first-rate musical in cosmopolitan Toronto, ice-skate on a canal in Ottawa, ski at first-rate resorts, indulge in Shakespeare in rural Stratford, sail on four of the Great Lakes, or go get lost in a wilderness that stretches all the way to the shores of James Bay. And in the past 20 years or so, Ontario has shuffled off its staid, Scottish ways and learned to eat and drink well and even how to party, thanks largely to an influx of settlers from just about every country on earth.

Prairie Provinces

Fewer than 5 million people live in Alberta, Saskatchewan, and Manitoba, which together fill an area twice the size of France. This makes for a lot of wide and lonely landscapes that have produced people who combine a rugged individualism with a sense of community unrivaled anywhere in the country. The climate is harsh—frigid in winter and hot and dry in summer—but the region is Canada's breadbasket and the source of much of its oil and natural gas. The area's major cities—Calgary, Edmonton, Saskatoon, Regina, and Winnipeg—provide a good base for exploring the area's history: dinosaurs, native sites, frontier forts, and a variety of ethnic communities. National and provincial parks preserve grasslands, badlands, waterways, and forests.

Prince Edward Island

In the Gulf of St. Lawrence north of Nova Scotia and New Brunswick, Prince Edward Island seems too good to be true, with its crisply painted farmhouses, manicured green fields rolling down to sandy beaches, warm ocean water, lobster boats in trim little harbors, and a vest-pocket capital city, Charlottetown, packed with architectural heritage. The opening of the Confederation Bridge in 1997 has made the Island more easily accessible to the mainland.

Québec

Québec is probably what all North America would have been like if the French rather than the English had won the Seven Years' War. This eastern province has always been able to find an excuse for a party. Its historic capital, **Québec City,** for example, celebrates one of the world's most brutal winters with a carnival that features parades of majorettes and teams who race boats across an ice-choked river. Throughout the province, the rest of the year is full of festivals celebrating jazz, international folklore, film, classical music, fireworks, beer, and hot-air balloons. What really sets Québec apart, of course, is language. The island city of **Montréal** is the second-largest French-speaking city in the world. French in Québec is more than the language of love—it's the language of law, business, politics, and culture and of more than 80% of the people.

Wilderness Canada

Stretched across the top of Canada above the 60th parallel is the country's last frontier—the Yukon, the Northwest Territories, and Nunavut. Here, tundra plains reach to the Arctic Ocean, remote ice fields engulf the St. Elias Mountains, and white-water rivers snake through mountain ranges and deep canyons. In this thinly populated expanse, native cultures have survived the coming of the white man and are showing signs of new vitality. You can cross the Arctic tundra by dogsled with Inuit hunters or visit native soapstone carvers, painters, printmakers, and clothes-makers.

PLEASURES AND PASTIMES

Flavors

Canadian fine dining really began in Québec, where eating out in a good restaurant with a good bottle of wine has long been a traditional part of life. Eating out was slower to catch on elsewhere, however, and until the early 1970s, Toronto was notorious for its poor food and barbarous drinking laws. But immigrants from places like Italy, Greece, Portugal, Japan, China, and India changed all that. Soon, even the stuffiest Torontonians were learning how to pronounce things like velouté, forestière, tagliolini, manicotti, and tzatziki. In Vancouver there is plenty of West Coast flair and creative use of local specialties from salmon to Pacific halibut and Dungeness crab. The country, of course, is rich in the basic ingredients—native cheeses from Québec and Ontario; lobster, mussels, salmon, and sole from both oceans; fine beef from Alberta; and lots of local delicacies like fiddlehead ferns, wild rice, and game meat.

The Great Outdoors

Most Canadians live in towns and cities within 325 km (202 mi) of the American border, but the country does have a splendid backyard to play in. Even major cities like Montréal and Vancouver are just a few hours' drive from a wilderness full of rivers, lakes, and mountains. A network of more than 30 national parks, from Kluane in Yukon to Cape Breton Highlands in Nova Scotia, is backed by dozens of provincial and regional parks. All this wilderness provides opportunities for bicycling, camping, canoeing, hiking, boating, horseback riding, mountain climbing, skiing, white-water rafting, and fishing. The coasts of British Columbia, the Gulf of St. Lawrence, and the Atlantic provinces are also ideal for whale-watching.

Nightlife and the Arts

Canadians rejoice in their cities, which are clean, safe, and lively. A night on the town still means just that. Dinner, a play or concert, drinks, and maybe even a late show can be squeezed into an evening. And you can walk or take public transport from one event to the next. If you prefer, you can just stroll the brightly lighted, crowded streets and do some people-watching.

Musically, Canada has managed to hold its own against its giant neighbor to the south. Festivals celebrating everything from fiddles to fugues ornament summer schedules across the country and provide showcases for local talent. Names like Teresa Stratas, Anne Murray, k. d. lang, Joni Mitchell, Céline Dion, Alanis Morisette, and Bryan Adams are already familiar south of the border. Less well-known people to look for are the Tragically Hip, perhaps the country's most popular rock band, and Ashley MacIsaac, who has made Scottish fiddle music popular among the urban young. In French there are the heartbreaking lyrics of traditional chansonniers like Gilles Vigneault and Felix Leclerc and the carefully crafted pop rock of Daniel Bélanger. On the classical scene, conductor Charles Dutoît has given the Orchestre Symphonique de Montréal international luster, and Toronto's Canadian Opera Company is highly rated. Norbert Kraft is an outstanding classical guitarist, and Ben Heppner is one of the world's most sought-after operatic tenors.

Toronto has emerged as the third most important center for English-language theater after London and New York. The city has more than four dozen venues staging original plays, musicals, classics, and touring big hits. Montréal is a center of French-language production, with 65 theaters and more than 100 theater and dance companies, including the nationally acclaimed Cirque du Soleil. Shakespeare's classics are honored along with more-modern plays at the Stratford Festival in rural Ontario every summer, and the works of George Bernard Shaw anchor another major festival at Niagara-on-the-Lake, Ontario.

Shopping

Distinctively Canadian items include furs from Montréal, fashions from Montréal and Toronto, wood carvings from rural Québec, woven goods and hooked rugs from the Maritimes, quilts from the Mennonite communities of Ontario, Inuit carvings from the Northwest Territories and Nunavut, native art and prints from the West Coast, native handicrafts from the prairies, and antiques from Montréal, Toronto, and Victoria. Some of the most distinctive Canadian products, of course, come from the maple tree—sugar, syrup, taffy, candy, and even liqueur. Québec, in fact, produces more than three-quarters of the world's supplies of such products.

Sports to Watch

Officially, Canada's national sport is lacrosse, but the nation's dominant passion is hockey. There are only six Canadian teams in the NHL—the Vancouver Canucks, Calgary Flames, Edmonton Oilers, Toronto Maple Leafs, Ottawa Senators, and Montréal Canadiens—but American teams are well stocked with Canadian-born stars. Getting tickets to a Toronto Maple Leafs' game is exceedingly difficult; there is a seven-year waiting list for season tickets, so you may have to settle for haggling with scalpers in front of the Air Canada Centre and paying steep prices. Seats in the NHL's other Canadian cities aren't tough to find and can usually be had just by calling the box office.

Canadians also excel at curling, a game invented in Scotland. It looks a little like bowling, except that it's played on ice with 40-pound lumps of polished granite. Millions of Canadians participate in local leagues, especially in the prairie provinces, and major competitions, called bonspiels, get national television coverage.

Other sports do have their fans. There are two major-league baseball teams—the Montréal Expos and the Toronto Blue Jays—and two National Basketball As-

sociation franchises—the Toronto Raptors and the Vancouver Grizzlies. As for football, Canada has its own version of the game played with three downs on a bigger field than the American version.

Winter

If asked, most Canadians would probably claim they hate winter. But the fact is, the country revels in winter. There are major carnivals celebrating the season in Québec City, Ottawa, Montréal, Winnipeg, and Edmonton. Every town and village has at least a few skating rinks, and everyone has a favorite toboggan hill. In January and February anglers erect whole villages of little huts on frozen rivers and lakes, and dog teams yap through the forest as soon as the snow is deep enough. There are thousands of miles of cross-country ski trails, and first-rate downhill ski resorts in Québec, Alberta, and British Columbia. Several major ski magazines have rated the Whistler and Blackcomb mountains, north of Vancouver, the best ski destinations in the world; in the Laurentian Mountains in Québec, the revitalized Tremblant resort at Mont-Tremblant is winning new fans. One of the fastest-growing sports is snowmobiling. A network of 112,255 km (69,600 mi) of trails with its own restaurants, road signs, and maps crisscrosses much of the country, but purists head for the backcountry to roar through untracked powder.

FODOR'S CHOICE

No two people will agree on what makes a perfect vacation, but it's fun and helpful to know what others think. We hope you'll have a chance to experience some of Fodor's Choices yourself in Canada. For detailed information about each entry, refer to the appropriate chapter.

Historic Sites

★ **Upper Canada Village, Morrisburg, Ontario.** Step into the past as interpreters in period costume re-create typical activities of the 1860s amid a collection of more than 40 historic buildings.

★ **Basilique Notre-Dame-de-Montréal, Montréal.** The enormous (3,800-seat) neo-Gothic church, opened in 1829, has a medieval-style interior with stained-glass windows.

★ **Basilique Ste-Anne-de-Beaupré, outside Québec City.** The monumental church is an important shrine that draws hordes of pilgrims. According to local legend, St. Anne was responsible over the years for saving voyagers from shipwrecks.

★ **Vieux-Québec, Québec City.** The immaculately preserved old town is small and dense, steeped in four centuries of history and French tradition.

★ **Plains of Abraham, Québec City.** The site of the famous 1759 battle between the French and the British that decided the fate of New France is now part of a large park overlooking the St. Lawrence River.

★ **Abbaye St-Benoî-du-Lac, Eastern Townships, Québec.** This Benedictine monastery is a religious retreat and a stunning example of early-20th-century church architecture, set amid rolling hills high above Lac Memphrémagog.

★ **Kings Landing Historical Settlement, outside Fredericton, New Brunswick.** This reconstructed village—including homes, a school, working farms, and a sawmill—illustrates life in the central Saint John River valley between 1790 and 1900.

★ **Fortress of Louisbourg National Historic Site of Canada, Louisbourg, Cape Breton, Nova Scotia.** Costumed actors recreate lives of 18th-century French soldiers, settlers, and tradespeople at this reconstructed fortress.

★ **Dawson City, the Yukon, Wilderness Canada.** The entire town tells the story of the fascination with gold. Century-old Klondike Gold Rush buildings stand next to the log homes of present-day miners.

Parks and Gardens

★ **Butchart Gardens, Victoria, British Columbia.** Stunning display gardens exhibit more than 700 varieties of flowers and have Italian, Japanese, and English rose gardens.

★ **Pacific Rim National Park Reserve, Vancouver Island, British Columbia.** This park on Canada's far west coast comprises a hard-packed white-sand beach, a group of islands, and a demanding coastal hiking trail with panoramic views of the sea and the rain forest.

★ **Banff National Park, Canadian Rockies.** Canada's first national park includes Lake Louise and part of the Icefields Parkway. Its spectacular mountain peaks, forests, and wildlife remain relatively untouched by human development.

★ **Assiniboine Park, Winnipeg, Manitoba.** Rolling alongside the Assiniboine River, this 328-acre park blends an art gallery and concert stage with tree-lined paths for walkers and cyclists. In the summer it is the best place to see Winnipeg at play.

★ **Ouimet Canyon Provincial Park, Ontario.** The canyon, so deep that Arctic plants grow on its floor, is a breathtaking stopover along Lake Superior's scenic North Shore.

★ **Royal Botanical Gardens, Burlington, Ontario.** These rank among the best, with collections of lilacs, acres of roses, and thousands of specimen shrubs and trees along 50 km (30 mi) of walking paths.

★ **Jardin Botanique, Montréal.** This botanical garden, with 181 acres of gardens in summer and 10 greenhouses open all year, has one of the best bonsai collections in the West and the largest Ming-style garden outside Asia.

★ **Prince Edward Island National Park, Prince Edward Island.** Along the north shore of the Island, sky and sea meet red sandstone cliffs, rolling dunes, and long stretches of sand.

★ **Cape Breton Highlands National Park of Canada, Nova Scotia.** A wilderness of wooded valleys, plateau barrens, and steep cliffs, the park stretches across the northern peninsula of Nova Scotia's Cape Breton Island.

★ **Nahanni National Park, Northwest Territories, Wilderness Canada.** Access to this mountainous park in the Northwest Territories is possible only by helicopter or plane; inside the park, canoes and rafts are the principal means of travel.

★ **Kluane National Park, Yukon, Wilderness Canada.** Kluane is home to the largest and most diverse wildlife population north of the 60th parallel, the highest mountains in Canada, and the largest nonpolar ice field in the world.

Views to Remember

★ **Chesterman Beach, Tofino, British Columbia.** The open Pacific Ocean meets old-growth forest at Canada's western edge. The beauty of winter storms has made even harsh weather an attraction.

★ **The view from the Jasper Tramway, Canadian Rockies.** From the steep flank of Whistlers Mountain you can see Mt. Robson (the Canadian Rockies' highest mountain), the Miette Valley to the west, and Athabasca Valley to the east.

★ **View of Niagara Falls by helicopter, Ontario.** Niagara Helicopters Ltd. takes you over the Giant Whirlpool, up Niagara Gorge, and past American Falls and banks around the curve of Horseshoe Falls.

★ **View of St. Lawrence River from Route 362, Québec.** Driving through Charlevoix on Route 362, just before the village of les Eboulements, you can enjoy a sweeping view over the St. Lawrence River, Québec's colonial "highway."

★ **Peggy's Cove, Nova Scotia.** At the mouth of a bay facing the open Atlantic, the cove, with its houses huddled around the narrow slit in the boulders, has the only Canadian post office in a lighthouse.

★ **Signal Hill National Historic Site, St. John's, Newfoundland.** Overlooking the snug, punch-bowl harbor of St. John's and the sea, this hilltop was taken and re-taken by opposing forces in the 17th and 18th centuries.

★ **Arctic Circle from the Dempster Highway, Yukon, Wilderness Canada.** This is an immense tundra vista, inhabited by caribou, wolves, foxes, bears, and eagles, with the gently curving Richardson Mountains catching the midnight sun in the distance.

Dining

★ **Auberge Hatley, North Hatley, Québec.** The sommelier at this inn has been voted one of the best in the world. The dining room overlooks Lac Massawippi, and the wine vault stocks thousands of bottles. $$$$

★ **C, Vancouver.** The name and decor are minimalist, but innovative seafood and the marina-side location make this one of the city's most exciting restaurants. $$$$

★ **Centro, Toronto.** French-Mediterranean style joins fine regional ingredients at a restaurant that sets city standards of excellence. $$$$

★ **L'Eau à la Bouche, Ste-Adèle, Québec.** At this Bavarian-style property you'll find a superb marriage of nouvelle cuisine and traditional Québec cooking in such dishes as roast veal in a cognac and Roquefort sauce. $$$$

★ **Post Hotel, Lake Louise, Canadian Rockies.** Dining on the creative modern and classic European fare in the hotel's restaurant is one of the outstanding culinary experiences in the region; the Alberta rack of lamb is notable. $$$$

★ **Toqué!, Montréal.** This is the city's most fashionable and most zany restaurant. The menu depends on what the two chefs found fresh that day and on which way their ever-creative spirit moves them. $$$$

★ **Laurie Raphaël, Québec City.** International and French flavors mingle on the menu of this stellar eatery. $$$–$$$$

★ **Lion Inn, Lunenburg, Nova Scotia.** Scallops with sweet onions, mussels in wine, rack of lamb, and sinful desserts are prepared by a chef who cooks for the love of it. The homey yet elegant ambience is accented by candlelight and cool jazz. $$

Lodging

★ **Four Seasons Toronto.** The most exclusive property in town has a great location, fine service, and afternoon tea—what could be more civilized? $$$$

★ **Kingsbrae Arms, St. Andrews by-the-Sea, New Brunswick.** The antique furnishings in this restored 1897 estate are eclectic and amusing. Guests are well pampered. $$$$

★ **Sooke Harbour House, Sooke, British Columbia.** This oceanfront inn west of Victoria looks like the home of a discerning art collector; the restaurant is one of Canada's finest. $$$$

★ **Gowerie House, Sydney Mines, Nova Scotia.** Filled with art and antiques and surrounded by trees and flower beds, this Georgian house is a gem of a country inn; dinners are outstanding. $$–$$$$

★ **Auberge du Vieux-Port, Montréal.** In an 1880s building in Vieux-Montréal, the inn overlooks the Vieux-Port and has tall windows and exposed beams. $$–$$$

★ **West Point Lighthouse, West Point, Prince Edward Island.** A functioning lighthouse in a provincial park, this small inn sits next to the beach. $–$$

FESTIVALS AND SEASONAL EVENTS

Contact local or provincial tourist boards for more information about these and other festivals.

WINTER

DEC.➤ British Columbia: The **Carol Ships,** sailboats full of carolers and decorated with colored lights, ply Vancouver harbor.

Newfoundland and Labrador: In St. John's revelers ring in the **New Year** on the waterfront.

JAN.➤ Alberta: The **Jasper Winter Festival** in Jasper and Marmot Basin presents dogsledding, skating, and ice sculpting. The 16-day **Banff/Lake Louise Winter Festival** includes winter sports competitions, displays of artwork, and an ice-sculpting contest. As part of the **Ice Magic** ice-sculpting contest, January 19 through March 2, the work of ice carvers from around the world is shown at numerous venues around Lake Louise in Banff National Park. The **Canmore International Dogsled Race** attracts more than 100 international teams in eight classes of racing.

British Columbia: Skiing competitions take place at most alpine ski resorts (through February).

Ontario: The **Niagara Falls Festival of Lights** is an extravaganza of colored lights in the parks surrounding the falls.

FEB.➤ Alberta: Calgary Winter Festival is a 10-day celebration with winter sports and ice sculpting.

Manitoba: Festival du Voyageur, in St. Boniface, Winnipeg, celebrates the area's early fur traders.

Ontario: Ontario Winter Carnival Bon Soo animates Sault Ste. Marie. Toronto's **Winter Fest** celebrates the season with ice-skating shows, plays, and food. Ottawa's **Winterlude** encourages ice sculpting, snowshoe racing, and ice boating.

Québec: Winter Carnival in Québec City is an 11-day festival of winter-sports competitions, ice-sculpture contests, and parades. *La Fête des Neiges* is Winter Carnival in Montréal.

Yukon: The winter blahs are driven away by the **Frostbite Music Festival.** The **Yukon Sourdough Rendezvous** has leg wrestling, log-sawing, and snowshoe racing. Mushers completing the 1,620-km-long (1,004-mi-long) **Yukon Quest International Dog Sled Race** from Fairbanks, Alaska, to Whitehorse, celebrate in town.

SPRING

MAR.➤ British Columbia: The **Pacific Rim Whale Festival** on Vancouver Island celebrates the spring migration of gray whales with guided tours by whale experts and music and dancing.

Manitoba: The **Royal Manitoba Winter Fair** takes place in Brandon.

Newfoundland and Labrador: From March or April through June, the east coast of Newfoundland from St. Anthony to St. John's is a great place to see **icebergs** floating by.

Northwest Territories: The **Caribou Carnival** fills three days with traditional Inuit and Dene games, ice sculpting, cultural exhibits, and races in Yellowknife. The **Canadian Championship Dog Derby** is a three-day dogsled race on frozen Great Slave Lake that attracts top mushers.

Yukon: The **Celebration of Swans,** held outside Whitehorse, marks the return of thousands of trumpeter and tundra swans.

APR.➤ Alberta: Silver Buckle Rodeo at Red Deer attracts cowboys from all over North America.

British Columbia: TerrifVic Jazz Party, in Victoria, has top international bands. The **Vancouver Playhouse International Wine Festival** is held at this time.

Northwest Territories: Inuvik's **Muskrat Jamboree** is an old-fashioned spring festival with muskrat-skinning contests, dogsled and snowmobile races, log-sawing duels, and more.

Ontario: The Maple Syrup Festival sweetens Elmira. Niagara-on-the-Lake's distinguished **Shaw Festival** (through November) presents plays by George Bernard Shaw and his contemporaries.

Québec: Sugaring-off parties celebrate the maple syrup season.

MAY➤ **Alberta:** The **International Children's Festival** in Calgary and Edmonton draws musicians, mimes, jugglers, clowns, puppeteers, and singers. At the **Red Deer Annual Westerner Spring Quarter Horse Show,** horses from western Canada and the United States compete.

British Columbia: Cloverdale Rodeo in Surrey is rated sixth in the world by the Pro Rodeo Association. **Vancouver Children's Festival** provides free open-air stage performances.

New Brunswick: Celebrations of **Loyalist Day** take place on May 18 in Saint John.

Nova Scotia: In the Annapolis Valley, from Windsor to Digby, the **Apple Blossom Festival** includes dancing, parades, good food, and entertainment. Truro pays tribute to the tulip with its three-day **Tulip Festival.**

Ontario: The internationally known **Stratford Festival,** in Stratford, presents many of Shakespeare's plays (through early November). The **Canadian Tulip Festival** in Ottawa celebrates spring with 3 million tulips.

Saskatchewan: The **International Band and Choral Festival,** in Moose Jaw, attracts 7,000 musicians. **Vesna Festival,** in Saskatoon, is the world's largest Ukrainian cabaret, with traditional Ukrainian food and crafts.

SUMMER

JUNE➤ **Alberta: Jazz City International Festival** in Edmonton has 10 days of jazz concerts, workshops, and free outdoor events. The **Ponoka Annual Stampede** professional rodeo attracts participants from across the continent. **Banff Festival of the Arts** (through August) showcases nearly 1,000 artists in music, dance, drama, comedy, and visual arts.

British Columbia: The **Canadian International Dragon Boat Festival,** in Vancouver, includes entertainment and the ancient "awakening the dragons" ritual with long, slender boats decorated with dragon heads. **Whistler Summer Festivals** (through September) present street entertainment and a variety of music at the resort.

Manitoba: Winnipeg's **Red River Exhibition** features lumberjack contests and performing animals. Winnipeg **International Children's Festival** provides top national and international entertainment.

Northwest Territories: The **Midnight Classic Golf Tournament** in Yellowknife tees off at midnight on the first day of summer. The **Kingalik Jamboree** is a typical Inuit spring celebration, with a week of friendly contests from square dancing to duck plucking.

Nova Scotia: The **International Blues Festival** draws music lovers to Halifax.

Ontario: Toronto's Metro International Caravan is a large ethnic fair. The **Downtown Toronto Jazz Festival** swings through Toronto late in the month. **Changing of the Guard** begins at Ottawa's Parliament Buildings (through August).

Prince Edward Island: Charlottetown Festival Theatre offers concerts and musicals (through October). In Summerside the annual **Summerside Highland Gathering** kicks off a summer of concerts and "Come to the Ceilidh" evenings.

Québec: Some of the world's best drivers compete in the **Air Canada Grand Prix** in Montréal. Québec City hops with the **International Jazz Festival.**

Saskatchewan: Frontier Days Regional Fair and Rodeo, in Swift Current, is a community fair with parades, a horse show, and a rodeo. **Mosaic,** in Regina, celebrates cultures from around the world.

Yukon: The **Yukon International Festival of Storytelling** in Whitehorse draws storytellers from all over the world.

JULY➤ **Alberta: Ukrainian Pysanka Festival** in Vegreville celebrates with costumes and song and dance. **Calgary Exhibition and Stampede** is one of the most popular Canadian events and includes 10 days of western showmanship, hot-air balloon races, chuck-wagon races, agricultural shows, and crafts. **Edmonton's Klondike Days** celebrate the town's early frontier community with pancake breakfasts, gold panning, and raft races.

British Columbia: The **Symphony of Fire,** an international musical fireworks competition, blasts off over four evenings from a barge in English Bay in Vancouver.

Manitoba: At the **Winnipeg Folk Festival,** in Birds Hill Park, 24 km (15 mi) northeast of Winnipeg, country, bluegrass, folk, Acadian music, and jazz can be heard on 10 stages. The **Winnipeg Fringe Festival** presents 10 days of challenging new theater in many downtown locations. **Manitoba Stampede and Exhibition** in Morris is an agricultural fair with rodeos and races.

New Brunswick: The **Shediac Lobster Festival** takes place in the town that calls itself the Lobster Capital of the World. There's an **Irish Festival** in Miramichi. The **New Brunswick Highland Games & Scottish Festival** is in Fredericton. In Edmunston the **Foire Brayonne** has music, cultural events, and sports.

Newfoundland and Labrador: The **Exploits Valley Salmon Festival** is in the Grand Falls area. The **Fish, Fun and Folk Festival** is in Twillingate. The **Conception Bay Folk Festival** in held in Carbonear. **Signal Hill Tattoo** (through August), in St. John's, reenacts the final 1762 battle of the Seven Years' War between the British and the French. The **Burin Peninsula Festival of Folk Song and Dance** features traditional entertainment.

Northwest Territories: The annual **Great Northern Arts Festival** in Inuvik presents displays, workshops, and live performances for the region's premier cultural event. The **Midway Lake Festival,** in Fort McPherson, showcases musicians from across Canada's north and elsewhere, who play alongside Dene drummers and folk and country artists. Participants in the **Great Norman Wells Fossil Hunt** search local Devonian shale and limestone for amazing fossils; prizes go to the best finds.

Nova Scotia: Antigonish Highland Games, staged annually since 1861, has Scottish music, dance, and such ancient sporting events as the caber toss. Halifax hosts the **Nova Scotia International Tattoo.** The **Atlantic Jazz Festival** is a Halifax highlight. The **Stan Rogers Music Festival** presents three days of gospel, bluegrass, and folk music in an outdoor venue in Canso.

Ontario: Ottawa celebrates **Canada Day** (July 1) with entertainment and fireworks. The two-week **International Freedom Festival** celebrates two nations' birthdays in Windsor and neighboring Detroit. The **Molson INDY** race roars through Toronto. The huge **Caribana** festival (late July through August) celebrates Toronto's West Indian community. At the **Beaches Jazz Festival** in Toronto, jazz fans sway and gyrate to the music. The **Glengarry Highland Games** in Maxville is North America's largest Highland gathering.

Prince Edward Island: Summerside's Lobster Carnival is a weeklong feast of lobster.

Québec: Festival International de Jazz de Montréal draws more than 2,000 musicians from all over the world for this 11-day series. **Québec International Summer Festival** offers entertainment in the streets and parks of old Québec City. Montréal's **Juste pour Rire** (Just for Laughs) comedy festival features international comics, in French and English. At **Festival Orford** international artists perform in Orford Park's music center (through August).

Saskatchewan: *The Trial of Louis Riel,* in Regina, one of Canada's longest-running stage shows, reenacts the events surrounding the Northwest Rebellion of 1885 (late July through August). **Shakespeare on the Saskatchewan Festival,** in Saskatoon, has productions near the South Saskatchewan River (early July through late August).

Yukon: The **Dawson City Music Festival** brings musicians from across North America to this small gold rush town.

AUG.➤ **Alberta:** The **Fringe Theatre Festival,** in Edmonton, is one of the major festivals for alternative theater in North America.

British Columbia: Squamish Days Logger Sports Festival draws loggers from around the world to compete in a series of logging feats.

Manitoba: Folklorama, a large multicultural festival, sets up more than 40 pavilions throughout Winnipeg. The **National Ukrainian Festival,** in Dauphin, offers costumes, artifacts, exhibits, fiddling contests, dancing, and workshops. The **Icelandic Festival,** in Gimli, gathers the largest Icelandic community outside of Iceland. **Pioneer Days,** in Steinbach, celebrates the heritage of the Mennonites with a parade, a horse show, and Mennonite foods.

New Brunswick: At the **Summer Chamber Music Festival** in Fredericton, classical musicians perform and lecture. The **Miramichi Folk Song Festival** has songs steeped in Maritime lore. **Acadian Festival,** at Caraquet, celebrates Acadian heritage with folk singing and food. Saint John's **Festival by the Sea** draws hundreds of singers, dancers, and musicians. The **Chocolate Festival,** in St. Stephen, includes suppers, displays, and children's events.

Newfoundland and Labrador: Gander's **Festival of Flight** celebrates this town as the aviation "Crossroads of the World," with dances, parades, and a folk festival. The **Folk Festival** in St. John's is an outstanding traditional music event.

Northwest Territories: The **South Slave Festival,** in Fort Smith, is a weekend of music and dancing.

Nova Scotia: Lunenburg holds the **Nova Scotia Fisheries Exhibition and Fishermen's Reunion.** The **Festival of Cape Breton Fiddling,** in St. Ann's, celebrates Scottish culture on the grounds of the only Gaelic college in North America. The **Halifax International Buskerfest** has daily outdoor shows by street performers and a food festival.

Ontario: Brantford's **Six Nations Native Pageant** celebrates Iroquois culture and history. The huge **Canadian National Exhibition** in Toronto lasts until Labor Day and has rides, displays, performances, and an air show.

Prince Edward Island: Old Home Week fills Charlottetown with nostalgia. Kensington stages an annual **Harvest Festival,** the province's biggest country fair.

Québec: Montréal hosts a **World Film Festival. St-Jean-sur-Richelieu's Hot Air Balloon Festival** is the largest gathering of hot-air balloons in Canada.

Saskatchewan: Buffalo Days Exhibition, in Regina, includes rides, livestock judging, and horse racing.

AUTUMN

SEPT.➤ **Alberta: Spruce Meadows Masters' Tournament,** in Calgary, is an international horse-jumping competition at one of North America's leading equestrian centers.

British Columbia: The **Vancouver International Film Festival** showcases lesser-known international filmmakers.

New Brunswick: World-class musicians and up-and-coming Atlantic Canadian talent flood Fredericton with slick jazz, gritty blues, spicy Cajun, and world-beat music for five days at the **Harvest Jazz & Blues Festival.** The **Atlantic Balloon Fiesta,** in Sussex, attracts about 30 brightly colored hot-air balloons; it also offers helicopter rides, parachute demonstrations, and other festival fun. Six days of French cinema can be enjoyed at the **Festival du Cinéma Francophone en Acadie** in Moncton; directors and actors from around the world attend.

Ontario: The **Canadian Open Golf Championship** takes place in Oakville. Toronto's **International Film Festival** salutes the world of film. St. Catharines toasts the **Niagara Grape and Wine Festival.**

Prince Edward Island: Festival Acadien de la Région Evangeline is an agricultural fair with Acadian music, a parade, and lobster suppers, at Wellington Station.

Québec: Québec International Film Festival screens in Québec City. The **Gatineau Hot Air Balloon Festival** brings together hot-air balloons from across Canada, the United States, and Europe.

OCT.➤ **British Columbia:** The **Okanagan Wine Festival** takes place in the Okanagan Valley area.

Nova Scotia: The 10-day **Celtic Colors International Festival,** one of the premier Celtic events in the world, celebrates traditional music in two dozen locations across Cape Breton.

Ontario: Kitchener–Waterloo's Oktoberfest attracts more than a half-million enthusiasts to its beer halls and tents.

Québec: The **Festival of Colors** celebrates foliage throughout the province.

Nov> **Ontario:** Toronto's **Royal Agricultural Fair** draws exhibitors and contestants to the world's largest indoor agricultural fair and equestrian competition.

Prince Edward Island: The Prince Edward Island Crafts Council **Annual Christmas Craft Fair** brings juried craftspeople to Charlottetown.

2 VANCOUVER

The spectacular setting of cosmopolitan Vancouver has drawn people from around the world to settle here. The ocean and mountains form a dramatic backdrop to downtown's gleaming towers of commerce and make it easy to pursue all kinds of outdoor pleasures. You can trace the city's history in Gastown and Chinatown, savor the wilderness only blocks from the city center in Stanley Park, or dine on superb ethnic or Pacific Northwest cuisine before you sample the city's nightlife.

By Sue
Kernaghan

VANCOUVER IS A YOUNG CITY, even by North American standards. It was not yet a town when British Columbia became part of the Canadian confederation in 1871. The city's history, such as it is, remains visible to the naked eye: eras are stacked east to west along the waterfront, from cobblestone late-Victorian Gastown to shiny postmodern glass cathedrals of commerce.

The Chinese, among the first to recognize the possibilities of Vancouver's setting, came to British Columbia during the 1850s seeking the gold that inspired them to name the province Gum-shan, or Gold Mountain. As laborers they built the Canadian Pacific Railway, giving Vancouver a purpose, one beyond the natural splendor that Royal Navy captain George Vancouver admired during his cruise around its harbor on June 13, 1792. The Canadian transcontinental railway, along with the city's Great White Fleet of clipper ships, gave Vancouver a full week's edge over the California ports in shipping tea and silk to New York at the end of the 19th century.

For its original inhabitants, the Coast Salish peoples, Vancouver was the sacred spot where the mythical Thunderbird and Killer Whale flung wind and rain all about the heavens during their epic battles. How else to explain the coast's fits of meteorological temper? Devotees of a later religious tradition might worship in the groves of Stanley Park or in the fir and cedar interior of Christ Church Cathedral, the city's oldest church.

These days, Vancouver, with a metropolitan-area population of 2 million, is booming. Many Asians have migrated here, mainly from Hong Kong, but other regions are represented as well. The mild climate, exquisite natural scenery, and relaxed, outdoor lifestyle are attracting new residents to British Columbia's business center, and the number of visitors is increasing for the same reasons. People often get their first glimpse of Vancouver when catching an Alaskan cruise, and many return at some point to spend more time here.

Pleasures and Pastimes

Dining

Vancouver has a diverse array of gastronomical offerings, including downtown bistros, waterfront seafood palaces, and upscale pan-Asian restaurants. Several cutting-edge establishments are perfecting and defining Pacific Northwest fare, which incorporates regional seafood, notably salmon, and locally grown produce, often accompanied by British Columbian wines.

The Great Outdoors

Nature has truly blessed this city, surrounding it with verdant forests, towering mountains, coves, inlets, rivers, and the wide sea. Biking, hiking, skiing, snowboarding, and sailing are among the many outdoor activities possible in or near the city. Whether you prefer to relax on a beach by yourself or join a kayaking tour with an outfitter, Vancouver has plenty to offer.

Nightlife and the Arts

Vancouver residents support the arts enthusiastically, especially during the city's film, jazz, folk, and theater festivals, most of which take place between June and October. The opera, ballet, and symphonic companies are thriving. And the city offers a range of live music venues, pubs, and nightclubs, though the province's peculiar liquor laws can be baffling (you can, for example, play darts, but not Scrabble, in a

Greater Vancouver *(Boxes Refer to Detail Maps)*

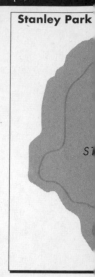

Stanley Park

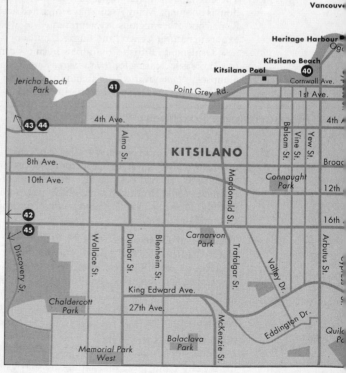

Burrard Inlet

English Bay

Vancouve

Heritage Harbour

Kitsilano Beach

Kitsilano Pool

40

Cornwall Ave.

1st Ave.

Jericho Beach Park

41

Point Grey Rd.

4th Ave.

4th A

43 **44**

Alma St.

Balsam St.

Vine St.

Yew St.

KITSILANO

Broad

8th Ave.

Macdonald St.

Connaught Park

12th

10th Ave.

16th

42

45

Discovery St.

Wallace St.

Dunbar St.

Blenheim St.

Carnarvon Park

Trafalgar St.

Valley Dr.

Arbutus St.

King Edward Ave.

Chaldercott Park

27th Ave.

McKenzie St.

Eddington Dr.

Quilo Pa

Memorial Park West

Balaclava Park

NORTH VANCOUVER

Burrard Inlet

N

0   1 mile
0   1 km

Lions Gate Br.

52
53
54

1A
99A

NLEY PARK

Denman St.

Downtown Vancouver

W. Pender St.
W. Hastings St.
W. Georgia St.
Robson St.
Dunsmuir
Haro St.
Cordova St.
Hornby St.
Davie St.
Burrard St.
Howe St.
Thurlow St.
Granville St.
Seymour St.
Homer St.
Cambie
Richards St.

Centennial
Powell St.
Hastings St.
7A
Powell St.

Dunlevy Ave.

Aquatic Centre

39
38 37
Vanier Park
Burrard Br.
Pacific Blvd
Davie St.

Chestnut St.
Burrard St.

48
50
Plaza of Nations
51
Terminal Ave.

Strathcona Park
Clark

49

Granville Br.
Granville Island

Granville
Granville Island

Granville Island

False Creek

Cambie Br.

Quebec St.

2nd Ave.

Broadway

Granville St.
Hemlock St.
Oak St.
Heather St.
Cambie St.
Manitoba St.
Main St.
Fraser St.

12th Ave.
16th Ave.

Shaughnessy Park

Matthews Ave.
99
28th Ave.
King Edward

hena rk

46
47
33rd Ave.

7
Cedar Cottage Park

Windsor St.
1A

bar). A bylaw bans smoking indoors in all public places in Vancouver, including pubs and bars, though observance is uneven.

EXPLORING VANCOUVER

The heart of Vancouver, which includes downtown, Stanley Park, Yaletown, and the West End, sits on a peninsula bordered by English Bay and the Pacific Ocean to the west; by False Creek, the inlet home to Granville Island, to the south; and by Burrard Inlet, the city's working port, to the north, where the North Shore Mountains loom. The oldest parts of the city, Gastown and Chinatown, lie at the edge of Burrard Inlet, around Main Street, which runs north–south and is roughly the dividing line between the east and west sides. All the avenues, which are numbered, have east and west designations. One note about printed Vancouver street addresses: suite numbers often appear *before* the street number, followed by a hyphen.

There are places of interest elsewhere in the city as well, either on the North Shore across Burrard Inlet, south of downtown in the Kitsilano area across English Bay, or in the Granville Island area across False Creek.

Great Itineraries

IF YOU HAVE 1 OR 2 DAYS

If you have only one day in Vancouver, start with an early morning walk, bike, or shuttle ride through Stanley Park to see the Vancouver Aquarium Marine Science Centre, the views from Prospect Point, and take a stroll along the seawall. Head northeast from the park on Denman Street to Robson Street for lunch, meander on foot through the trendy shops between Denman and Burrard Street, and then walk northeast on Burrard to view the many buildings of architectural interest. Stop along the way at the Vancouver Art Gallery, the Canadian Museum of Craft and Design, and the Pacific Mineral Museum. On Day 2 take a leisurely walking tour of the shops, eateries, and cobblestone streets of Gastown, Chinatown, and Yaletown.

IF YOU HAVE 3 OR 4 DAYS

If you have another day to tour Vancouver and have followed the itinerary above, head to the south side of False Creek and English Bay on Day 3 to delve into the public market and the many boutiques, eateries, and theaters of Granville Island. Buses and ferries provide easy transit, and touring the island is best accomplished on foot. (If you drive, parking is available, but traffic to the island can be congested, especially on weekends.)

On Day 4, tour the sights beyond downtown Vancouver. Make time for the Museum of Anthropology on the campus of the University of British Columbia. Also visit the Vancouver Museum, the H. R. MacMillan Space Centre, and the Vancouver Maritime Museum, all in the Kitsilano area. If you'd rather play outside, head to the North Shore Mountains, where you can swing high above the Capilano River on a suspension bridge or take in the panoramic city views as you ride the Skyride to the top of Grouse Mountain.

Robson to the Waterfront

Numbers in the text correspond to numbers in the margin and on the Downtown Vancouver map.

Museums and buildings of architectural and historical significance are the primary draw in downtown Vancouver, but there's also plenty of fine shopping.

A Good Walk

Begin at the northwest end of **Robson Street** ①, at Bute or Thurlow Street. Follow Robson southeast to Hornby Street to reach landscaped **Robson Square** ②, on your right. The **Vancouver Art Gallery** ③ is on the left. Head northeast on Hornby Street to get to the **Fairmont Hotel Vancouver** ④, a city landmark.

The **HSBC Bank Building** is at Georgia and Hornby streets, catercorner to the Hotel Vancouver. Its five-story-high public lobby atrium has a café, regularly changing art exhibitions, and one of the city's more intriguing public-art installations; *Pendulum,* by B.C. artist Alan Storey, is a 90-ft-long hollow aluminum sculpture that arcs hypnotically overhead. The 1991 **Cathedral Place** office tower, on the other side of Hornby Street, is one of Vancouver's most attractive postmodern buildings. The three large sculptures of nurses at the corners of the building are replicas of the statues that adorned the Georgia Medical–Dental Building, the art deco structure that previously occupied this site; the faux copper roof mimics that of the Fairmont Hotel Vancouver. Step into the lobby to see another interesting sculpture, Robert Studer's *Navigational Device,* suspended from high on the north wall.

The north exit of Cathedral Place (beside the café) leads to a peaceful green courtyard, with the **Canadian Museum of Craft and Design** ⑤. The Gothic-style **Christ Church Cathedral** ⑥ is farther to the west of Cathedral Place. About three blocks north (toward the water), the Art Deco **Marine Building** ⑦ is on the left side of Burrard Street.

Facing the water, make a right onto Hastings Street and follow it east less than a half block for a look at the exterior of the exclusive Vancouver Club. *Working Landscape* by Daniel Laskarin, an art installation that consists of three revolving wooden platforms, is in the tiny public park next door. The Vancouver Club marks the start of the old financial district, which runs southeast along Hastings. The district's older temple-style banks, investment houses, and businesspeople's clubs are the surviving legacy of the city's sophisticated pre–World War I architecture.

The **Pacific Mineral Museum** ⑧ is on the south side of Hastings past Hornby Street. Continue along Hastings to **Sinclair Centre** ⑨, between Howe and Granville streets. The magnificently restored complex of government buildings houses offices and retail shops. At 698 W. Hastings Street, near Granville Street, the jewelry store Birks now occupies the Roman-influenced former headquarters of the **Canadian Imperial Bank of Commerce** (CIBC). The 1907 cast-iron clock that stands outside was, at its previous location at Granville and Georgia streets, a favorite rendezvous point for generations of Vancouverites. The imposing 1931 **Royal Bank** building stands directly across the street. The elevator to the **Lookout at Harbour Centre** ⑩ is at Hastings and Seymour streets, about a block southeast of here.

On Seymour, head toward Burrard Inlet to the **Waterfront Station** ⑪. Take a peek at the murals inside the 19th-century structure, then take the west staircase (to your left, with your back to the entrance) up to Granville Square Plaza where you can see the working harbor to your right. Walk straight across the plaza to the SkyTrain station and turn right to see the soaring canopies of **Canada Place** ⑫, where you can stroll around the cruise-ship–style decks for great ocean and mountain views or catch a film at the IMAX theater. The **Vancouver Tourist Info Centre** is across Canada Place Way (next door to the Waterfront Centre Hotel).

TIMING

This tour takes about an hour to walk, not counting stops along the way. The Canadian Museum of Craft and Design, Pacific Mineral Museum, and the Vancouver Art Gallery each warrant an hour or more, depending on the exhibits.

Sights to See

⑫ **Canada Place.** When Vancouver hosted the Expo '86 world's fair, a former cargo pier was transformed into the off-site Canadian pavilion. The complex, which now encompasses the luxurious **Pan Pacific Hotel**, the **Vancouver Convention and Exhibition Centre**, Vancouver's **World Trade Centre**, and the city's main **cruise-ship terminal**, mimics the style, and size, of a luxury ocean liner. Visitors can stroll its exterior promenade to admire views of Burrard Inlet, Stanley Park, and the North Shore mountains. At the prow (the north end), the **CN IMAX Theatre** (☎ 604/682–4629) shows films on a five-story-tall screen. The Canada Place roof, shaped like five sails, has become a landmark of Vancouver's skyline. ☒ *999 Canada Place Way,* ☎ *604/775–8687,* WEB *www.canadaplace.ca.* ☒ *IMAX $10.50.*

⑤ **Canadian Museum of Craft and Design.** One of Vancouver's most interesting cultural facilities, the craft and design museum displays functional and decorative modern and historical crafts in an attractive, two-tiered postmodern building. Exhibits change year-round, so there's always something new to see. The gift shop has an excellent selection of one-of-a-kind Canadian crafts, and the courtyard is a quiet place to take a break. ☒ *Cathedral Place Courtyard, 639 Hornby St. (also accessible from 925 W. Georgia St.),* ☎ *604/687–8266.* ☒ *$5; donation Thurs. 5–9.* ☉ *Apr. 16–Oct. 14., Mon.–Wed. and Fri.–Sun. 10–5, Thurs. 10–9; Oct. 15–Apr. 15, Mon and Wed. noon–5, Thurs. noon–9, Fri.–Sun. noon–5.*

⑥ **Christ Church Cathedral.** The oldest church in Vancouver was built in 1889–95. Constructed in the Gothic style, it looks like the parish church of an English village from the outside, though underneath its sandstone-clad exterior, it's made of Douglas fir from what is now South Vancouver. The 32 stained-glass windows depict Old and New Testament scenes, often set against Vancouver landmarks (St. Nicholas presiding over the Lions Gate Bridge, for example). The building's excellent acoustics enhance the choral evensong, carols, and Gregorian chants frequently sung here. ☒ *690 Burrard St.,* ☎ *604/682–3848.* ☉ *Weekdays 10–4. Services Sun. 8 AM, 10:30 AM, 9:30 PM; weekdays 12:10 PM.*

④ **Fairmont Hotel Vancouver.** One of the last railway-built hotels in Canada, the Fairmont Hotel Vancouver was designed in the château style, its architectural details reminiscent of a medieval French castle. Construction began in 1928, and wrapped up just in time for King George VI of England's 1939 visit. The exterior of the building, one of the most recognizable in Vancouver's skyline, has carvings of malevolent-looking gargoyles at the corners, native chiefs on the Hornby Street side, and an assortment of figures from classical mythology decorating the building's facade. ☒ *900 W. Georgia St.,* ☎ *604/684–3131,* WEB *www.fairmont.com.*

🖐 ⑩ **Lookout at Harbour Centre.** The lookout looks like a flying saucer stuck atop a high-rise. At 553 ft high, it affords one of the best views of Vancouver. A glass elevator whizzes you up 50 stories to the circular observation deck, where knowledgeable guides point out the sights. On a clear day you can see Vancouver Island. Tickets are good all day, so you can visit in daytime and return for another peek after dark. The

Downtown Vancouver

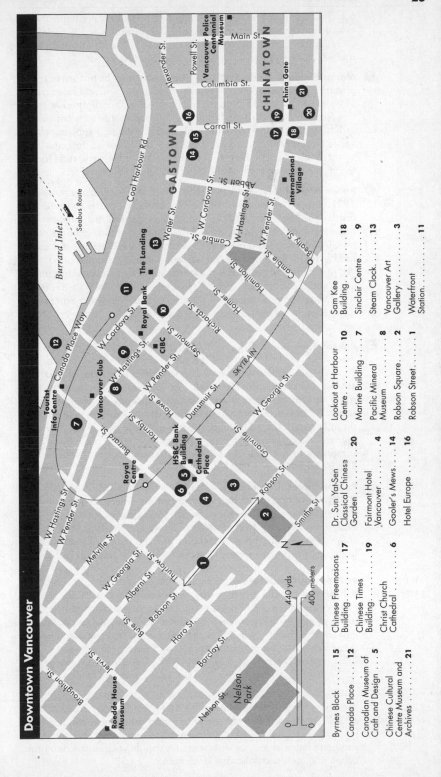

Burrard Inlet

Seabus Route

GASTOWN

CHINATOWN

Vancouver Police
Centennial
Museum

Main St.

Powell St.

Alexander St.

Columbia St.

China Gate

Carrall St.

Coal Harbour Rd.

Water St.

W. Cordova St.

Abbott St.

W. Hastings St.

W. Pender St.

Beatty St.

International
Village

The Landing

Cambie St.

Hamilton St.

Homer St.

Richards St.

SKYTRAIN

Canada Place Way

Tourist
Info Centre

Royal Bank

CIBC

W. Cordova St.

Vancouver Club

W. Hastings St.

Seymour St.

W. Pender St.

Dunsmuir St.

W. Georgia St.

Granville St.

Robson St.

Smithe St.

W. Hastings St.

W. Pender St.

Royal
Centre

HSBC Bank
Building

Cathedral
Place

Melville St.

Hornby St.

Howe St.

Burrard St.

W. Georgia St.

Thurlow St.

Alberni St.

Robson St.

Haro St.

Barclay St.

Bute St.

Nicola St.

Nelson St.

Nelson
Park

Broughton St.

Jervis St.

Roedde House
Museum

N

440 yds
400 meters

Byrnes Block **15**

Canada Place **12**

Canadian Museum of
Craft and Design . . . **5**

Chinese Cultural
Centre Museum and
Archives **21**

Chinese Freemasons
Building **17**

Chinese Times
Building **19**

Christ Church
Cathedral **6**

Dr. Sun Yat-Sen
Classical Chinese
Garden **20**

Fairmont Hotel
Vancouver **4**

Gaoler's Mews . . . **14**

Hotel Europe **16**

Lookout at Harbour
Centre **10**

Marine Building **7**

Pacific Mineral
Museum **8**

Robson Square **2**

Robson Street **1**

Sam Kee
Building **18**

Sinclair Centre **9**

Steam Clock **13**

Vancouver Art
Gallery **3**

Waterfront
Station **11**

top-floor restaurant makes one complete revolution per hour; the elevator ride up is free for diners. ⊠ *555 W. Hastings St.,* ☎ *604/689–0421,* WEB *www.vancouverlookout.com.* ⊡ *$9.* ☉ *Mid-May–late Sept., daily 8:30 AM–10:30 PM; late Sept.–mid-May, daily 9–9.*

❼ Marine Building. Terra-cotta bas-reliefs depicting the history of transportation, such as airships, steamships, locomotives, and submarines, as well as Mayan and Egyptian motifs and images of marine life adorn this Art Deco structure erected in 1930. These motifs were considered radical at the time because most architects were still applying classical or Gothic ornamentation. Step inside for a look at the beautifully restored interior, and then walk to the corner of Hastings and Hornby streets for the best view of the building. ⊠ *355 Burrard St.*

❽ Pacific Mineral Museum. Vancouver's newest museum, in a renovated 1921 building, opened in early 2000. Launched partly to house and display the University of B.C.'s mineral collection, the museum also hosts regularly changing fossil exhibits, such as dinosaur bones or the remains of ice age mammals. The permanent vault gallery, tucked behind a real bank vault door, showcases stunning examples of gold, silver, platinum, and gems. The museum shop sells collectors' specimens, gifts, and souvenirs. ⊠ *848 W. Hastings St.,* ☎ *604/689–8700,* WEB *www.pacificmineralmuseum.org.* ⊡ *$4.* ☉ *Mid-May–early Sept., weekdays 10–5, weekends 10–6; early Sept.–mid-May, Tues.–Fri. 10–5, weekends 10–6.*

❷ Robson Square. Architect Arthur Erickson designed this plaza, which was completed in 1979, to be *the* gathering place of downtown Vancouver. Landscaped walkways connect the Vancouver Art Gallery, government offices, and law courts. An ice-skating rink (used for ballroom dancing in summer) and restaurants occupy the level below the street. Political protests and impromptu demonstrations take place on the gallery stairs, a tradition that dates from the days when the building was a courthouse. At press time, plans were in place for a redevelopment of the site. ⊠ *Bordered by Howe, Hornby, Robson, and Smithe Sts.*

❶ Robson Street. Ultrachic Robson Street is often called Vancouver's Rodeo Drive because of its many see-and-be-seen sidewalk cafés and high-end boutiques. The street, which links downtown and the West End, is particularly lively between Jervis and Burrard streets. The shops may be like those elsewhere, but the people-watching, café-lounging, window-shopping scene draws crowds day and night.

OFF THE BEATEN PATH | **ROEDDE HOUSE MUSEUM –** Two short blocks south of the fast pace of Robson Street, and a century away, is the Roedde (pronounced "roady") House Museum, an 1893 mansion in the Queen Anne revival style, set among Victorian-style gardens. Though the gardens (free) are worth a visit anytime, the only way to see the restored, antiques-furnished interior is to catch one of the guided tours. ⊠ *1415 Barclay St. between Broughton and Nicola,* ☎ *604/684–7040,* WEB *www.roeddehouse.org.* ⊡ *$4; $5 Sun., including tea.* ☉ *Tours year-round, call for times..*

NEED A BREAK? | The pastry chefs at **Senses Bakery** (⊠ 801 West Georgia St., ☎ 604/633–0138) create some of Vancouver's most decadent treats. Stop in for a piece of Champagne truffle cake, some hand-rolled chocolates, a raspberry financier tart, or whatever suits your fancy. You can also grab coffee or a soup and sandwich lunch here.

9 Sinclair Centre. The outstanding Vancouver architect Richard Henriquez knitted four government office buildings into Sinclair Centre, an office–retail complex. The two Hastings Street buildings—the 1910 **Post Office,** which has an elegant clock tower, and the 1911 **Winch Building**—are linked with the 1937 **Post Office Extension** and the 1913 **Customs Examining Warehouse** to the north. As part of a meticulous $37 million restoration in the mid-1980s, the post-office facade was moved to the Granville Street side of the complex. The original clockwork from the old clock tower is on display inside, on the upper level of the arcade. ⊠ *757 W. Hastings St.*

3 Vancouver Art Gallery. Painter Emily Carr's haunting evocations of the British Columbian hinterland are the biggest attraction at the city's main art gallery. Carr (1871–1945), a grocer's daughter from Victoria, fell in love with the wilderness around her and shocked middle-class Victorian society by running off to paint it. Her work accentuates the mysticism and the danger of B.C.'s wilderness—no pretty landscapes here—and records the passing of native cultures. The gallery, which also hosts touring historical and contemporary exhibitions, is housed in a 1911 courthouse that Arthur Erickson redesigned in the early 1980s. Lions guard the majestic front steps, and columns and domes are among the original Classical architectural elements. The Gallery Café has a fine terrace, and the gallery's shop has a noteworthy selection of prints and cards. You can visit the café and shop without an admission ticket. ⊠ *750 Hornby St.,* ☎ *604/662–4719,* WEB *www.vanartgallery.bc.ca.* ⊠ *$10, donation Thurs. 5–9.* ⊙ *Easter–mid-Oct., Mon.–Wed. and Fri.–Sun. 10–5:30, Thurs. 10–9; closed Mon. and Tues. mid-Oct. to Easter.*

Vancouver Tourist Info Centre. Here you can find brochures and personnel to answer questions, book tours, reserve accommodations, and see a nice view to boot. ⊠ *200 Burrard St.,* ☎ *604/683–2000,* WEB *www.tourismvancouver.com.* ⊙ *Sept.–late May, weekdays 8:30–5, Sat. 9–5; late May–Aug., daily 8–6.*

11 Waterfront Station. This former Canadian Pacific Railway passenger terminal was built between 1912 and 1914 as the western terminus for Canada's transcontinental railway. After Canada's railways merged, the station became obsolete, but a 1978 renovation turned it into an office–retail complex and depot for SkyTrain, SeaBus, and West Coast Express passengers. In the main concourse, panels near the ceiling depict the scenery travelers once saw on journeys across Canada. Here you can catch a 13-minute SeaBus trip across the harbor to the waterfront public market at Lonsdale Quay in North Vancouver. ⊠ *601 W. Cordova St.,* ☎ *604/521–0400 for SeaBus and SkyTrain; 604/683–7245 for West Coast Express.*

Gastown and Chinatown

Gastown is where Vancouver originated after "Gassy" Jack Deighton canoed into Burrard Inlet in 1867 with his wife, some whiskey, and a few amenities. The smooth-talking Deighton convinced local mill workers into building him a saloon in exchange for a barrel of whiskey. (It didn't take much convincing. His saloon was on the edge of lumber-company land, where alcohol was forbidden.) In 1885, when the Canadian Pacific Railway announced that Burrard Inlet would be the terminus for the new transcontinental railway, the little town—called Granville Townsite at the time—saw its population grow fivefold over a few months. But on June 13, 1886, two short months after Granville's incorporation as the city of Vancouver, a clearing fire got out of control and burned down the entire town. It was rebuilt by the time the first transcontinental train arrived, in May 1887, and Vancouver became a transfer point for trade with the Far East and soon was crowded with hotels, warehouses, brothels, and saloons. The Klondike gold rush encouraged further development that lasted until 1912, when the so-called Golden Years ended. From the 1930s to the 1950s, hotels were converted into rooming houses, and the warehouse district shifted elsewhere. The neglected area gradually became run down. These days, Gastown, which along with Chinatown was declared a historic district in 1971 and has been revitalized, is home to boutiques, cafés, loft apartments, and souvenir shops.

Chinatown has some of the city's oldest buildings and is one of the largest such areas in North America. A sizable Chinese community was already here at the time of the 1880s immigration boom because of the 1858 Caribou gold rush in central British Columbia. The greatest influx from China came during construction of the Canadian Pacific Railway in the 1880s, when more than 10,000 laborers were recruited. Though they were performing the valuable and hazardous task of blasting the rail bed through the Rocky Mountains, the Chinese were discriminated against. The Anti-Asiatic Riots of 1907 stopped population growth in Chinatown for 50 years, and immigration from China was discouraged by increasingly restrictive policies that climaxed in a $500-per-head tax during the 1920s. In the 1960s the city council planned bulldozer urban renewal for Strathcona, the residential part of Chinatown, as well as freeway connections through the most historic blocks of the district. Fortunately the project was halted. Though much of Vancouver's Chinese community has now shifted to suburban Richmond, Chinatown is still a vital neighborhood, fueled by the investments of immigrants from Hong Kong and elsewhere. The style of architecture in Vancouver's Chinatown is patterned on that of Guangzhou (Canton).

Numbers in the text correspond to numbers in the margin and on the Downtown Vancouver map.

A Good Walk

Start at **The Landing,** a former warehouse at the corner of Water and Richards streets, downtown. Built in 1905 with gold rush money, it was renovated in 1988 to include upscale shops, a brew pub, and a restaurant. The window at the rear of the lobby offers good views of Burrard Inlet and the North Shore Mountains. A block east, at the corner of Water and Cambie streets, you can see and hear the world's first **steam clock** ⑬. **Gaoler's Mews** ⑭ is about two blocks east on the other side of the street, tucked behind 12 Water Street. **Byrnes Block** ⑮, on the corner of Water and Carrall streets, and the **Hotel Europe** ⑯, at Powell and Alexander streets, are two buildings of historical and architectural interest. A statue of Gassy Jack Deighton stands on the west side of Maple Tree Square, at the intersection of Water, Powell, Alexander, and Carrall streets, where he built his first saloon.

From Maple Tree Square it's only three blocks south on Carrall Street to Pender Street, where Chinatown begins. Note: This route passes through a rough part of town, so it's much safer to backtrack two blocks on Water Street through Gastown to Cambie Street, then head south (left) to Pender Street and east (left again) to Carrall Street. If you're interested in law and order, though, consider a detour to the **Vancouver Police Centennial Museum** at Cordova and Gore streets, just east of Main Street.

Walking along Pender Street, you pass International Village, a shopping and cinema development. Old Chinatown starts at the corner of

Carrall and Pender streets. The **Chinese Freemasons Building** ⑰ and the **Sam Kee Building** ⑱ are here, and directly across Carrall Street is the **Chinese Times Building** ⑲. The **Dr. Sun Yat-Sen Classical Chinese Garden** ⑳ is about a half block east and·across Pender, tucked into a courtyard behind the brightly painted China Gate, a four-column entranceway originally built for the Chinese Pavilion at Expo '86. The free, public Dr. Sun Yat-Sen Park is next to the garden. At press time, plans were in place to construct a seven-story pagoda with cultural displays and a tearoom in the southeast corner of Dr. Sun Yat-Sen Park.

A short path through the park takes you out to Columbia Street, where the entrance to the **Chinese Cultural Centre Museum and Archives** ㉑ (not to be confused with the Chinese Cultural Centre that fronts Pender Street) is on your left.

Finish your tour of Chinatown by poking around in the open-front markets, bakeries, herbalist and import shops that line several blocks of Pender and Keefer streets running east. **Ming Wo Cookware,** at 23 E. Pender, has a great selection of Eastern and Western culinary supplies. **Ten Ren Tea and Ginseng Company,** at 550 Main, and **Ten Lee Hong Tea and Ginseng,** at 500 Main, carry every kind of tea imaginable. For art, ceramics, and rosewood furniture, have a look at **Yeu Hua Handicraft Ltd.,** at 173 E. Pender. If you're in the area in summer on a Friday, Saturday, or Sunday, check out the bustling **Night Market,** for which the 200 block of East Pender is closed to traffic 6:30–11.

TIMING
The walk takes about an hour. Allow extra time for a guided tour of the Dr. Sun Yat-Sen Classical Chinese Garden. This tour is best done by day, though shops and restaurants are open into the night in both areas.

Sights to See

⑮ **Byrnes Block.** George Byrnes constructed Vancouver's oldest brick building on the site of Gassy Jack Deighton's second saloon after the 1886 Great Fire, which wiped out most of the fledgling settlement of Vancouver. For a while this building was Vancouver's top luxury hotel, the Alhambra Hotel, charging a dollar a night. The site of Deighton's original saloon, east of the Byrnes Block where his statue now stands, is the zero point from which all Vancouver street addresses start. ✉ 2 *Water St.*

㉑ **Chinese Cultural Centre Museum and Archives.** This Ming Dynasty–style facility is dedicated to promoting an understanding of Chinese-Canadian history and culture. The art gallery on the first floor hosts traveling exhibits by Chinese and Canadian artists. A compelling permanent exhibit on the second floor traces British Columbia's history from a Chinese point of view. ✉ *555 Columbia St.,* ☎ *604/658–8880,* WEB *www.cccvan.com.* ✉ *$4.* ☉ *Tues.–Fri., 1–5; weekends 11–5.*

⑰ **Chinese Freemasons Building.** Two completely different facades distinguish this structure on the northwest corner of Pender and Carrall streets. The side facing Pender represents a fine example of Cantonese recessed balconies. The Carrall Street side displays the standard Victorian style common throughout the British Empire. Dr. Sun Yat-Sen hid for months in this building from agents of the Manchu Dynasty while he raised funds for its overthrow, which he accomplished in 1911. ✉ *3 W. Pender St.*

⑲ **Chinese Times Building.** Police officers during the early 20th century could hear the clicking sounds of clandestine mah-jongg games played after sunset on the hidden mezzanine floor of this 1902 structure. But attempts by vice squads to enforce restrictive policies against the Chinese gamblers proved fruitless because police were unable to find the players. The office building isn't open to the public. ⊠ *1 E. Pender St.*

★ ⑳ **Dr. Sun Yat-Sen Classical Chinese Garden.** The first authentic Ming Dynasty–style garden outside China, this garden was built in 1986 by 52 artisans from Suzhou, the Garden City of the People's Republic. It incorporates design elements and traditional materials from several of that city's centuries-old private gardens. No power tools, screws, or nails were used in the construction. Guided tours (45 minutes long), included in the ticket price, are offered throughout the day; they are valuable in understanding the philosophy and symbolism that are central to the garden's design. (Call ahead for times.) Friday evenings from mid-June through September, musicians perform traditional Chinese music in the garden. The free public park next door is also designed as a traditional Chinese garden. ⊠ *578 Carrall St.,* ☎ *604/689–7133 or 604/662–3207.* ⊡ *$7.50.* ☼ *May–June 14 and Sept., daily 10–6; June 15–Aug., daily 9:30–7; Oct.–Apr., daily 10–4:30.*

⑭ **Gaoler's Mews.** Once the site of the city's first civic buildings—the constable's cabin and customs house, and a two-cell log jail—this atmospheric cobblestone courtyard today is home to cafés and architectural offices. ⊠ *Behind 12 Water St.*

⑯ **Hotel Europe.** Once billed as the best hotel in the city, this 1908 flatiron building is one of the world's best examples of this style of triangular architecture. Now used for government-subsidized housing and not open to the public, the hotel still has its original Italian tile work and lead-glass windows. The glass tiles in the sidewalk on Alexander Street once provided light for an underground saloon. ⊠ *43 Powell St.*

⑱ **Sam Kee Building.** *Ripley's Believe It or Not!* recognizes this 6-ft-wide structure as the narrowest office building in the world. In 1913, after the city confiscated most of the then-owner's land to widen Pender Street, he built a store on what was left in protest. Customers had to be served through the windows. These days the building houses an insurance agency, whose employees make do within the 4-ft-10-inch-wide interior. The glass panes in the sidewalk on Pender Street once provided light for Chinatown's public baths, which, in the early 20th century, were in the basement here. The presence of this and other underground sites has fueled rumors that Chinatown and Gastown were connected by tunnels that enabled residents of the latter to anonymously enjoy the vices of the former. Tunnels haven't been found, however. ⊠ *8 W. Pender St.*

⑬ **Steam clock.** An underground steam system, which also heats many local buildings, supplies the world's first steam clock—possibly Vancouver's most-photographed attraction. The whistle blows every quarter hour, and on the hour a huge cloud of steam spews from the apparatus. The original design, based on an 1875 mechanism, was built in 1977 by Ray Saunders of Landmark Clocks (at 123 Cambie Street) to commemorate the community effort that saved Gastown from demolition. ⊠ *Water and Cambie Sts.*

OFF THE
BEATEN PATH

VANCOUVER POLICE CENTENNIAL MUSEUM – It's not in the best of neighborhoods, and its morgue and autopsy areas may be off-putting to some, but this museum provides an intriguing glimpse into the history of the Vancouver police. Firearms and counterfeit money are on exhibit, as are clues from some of the city's unsolved crimes. ⊠ *240 E. Cordova St.,* ☎ *604/665–3346,* ⓦⓔⓑ *www.city.vancouver.bc.ca/police/museum.* ⊡ *$5.* ☼ *May–Aug., weekdays 9–3, Sat. 10–3; Sept.–Apr., weekdays 9–3.*

Stanley Park

A 1,000-acre wilderness park only blocks from the downtown section of a major city is both a rarity and a treasure. In the 1860s, because of a threat of American invasion, the area that is now Stanley Park was designated a military reserve, though it was never needed. When the city of Vancouver was incorporated in 1886, the council's first act was to request that the land be set aside as a park. In 1888 permission was granted and the grounds were named Stanley Park after Lord Stanley, then governor general of Canada.

If you're driving to Stanley Park, head northwest on Georgia Street from downtown. If you're taking public transit, catch any bus labeled STAN-LEY PARK at the corner of Hastings and Granville streets downtown.

You can also catch North Vancouver Bus 240 or 246 from anywhere on West Georgia Street to the park entrance at Georgia and Chilco streets, or a Robson Bus 5 to Robson and Denman streets, where there are a number of bicycle-rental outlets.

To reach Stanley Park's main attractions, you can bike, walk, drive, or take the free park shuttle. The seawall path, a 9-km (5½-mi) paved shoreline route popular with walkers, cyclists, and rollerbladers, is one of several car-free zones within the park. If you have the time (about a half day) and the energy, strolling the entire seawall is an exhilarating experience. Cyclists must ride in a counterclockwise direction and stay on their side of the path.

The free **Stanley Park Shuttle** (☎ 604/257–8400) operates mid-June to mid-September, providing frequent (15-minute intervals) transportation between 14 major park sights. Pick it up on Pipeline Road, near the Georgia Street park entrance, or at any of the stops in the park.

From mid-September to mid-May, the traffic in Stanley Park is lighter than at other times of the year and there's little competition for parking. Lots are available at or near all the major attractions; one ticket ($5 April through September; $3 the rest of the year) allows you to park all day and to move between lots. Another way to see the park is on one of the Stanley Park Horse Drawn Tours.

Numbers in the text correspond to numbers in the margin and on the Stanley Park map.

A Good Tour

If you're walking or cycling, start at the foot of Alberni Street, beside Lost Lagoon. Go through the underpass and veer right, following the cycle-path markings, to the seawall. If you're driving, enter the park at the foot of Georgia Street. Be sure to stay in the right lane, or you'll have to go over the Lions Gate Bridge. Keep to your right and go beneath an underpass. This puts you on scenic Stanley Park Drive, which circles the park.

Whether you're on the seawall or Stanley Park Drive, the old wooden structure that you pass on your right is the Vancouver Rowing Club, a private athletic club established in 1903. Just ahead and to your left is a parking lot, an information booth (staffed year-round, weather permitting), and the turnoff to the **Vancouver Aquarium Marine Science Centre** ㉒, the **Miniature Railway and Children's Farmyard** ㉓, and **Painters' Corner,** where artists sell their work. There's also a **Salmon Demonstration Stream** near the information booth, with facts about the life cycle of this important fish.

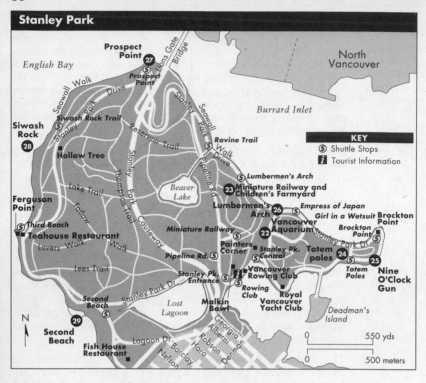

Stanley Park

KEY

ⓢ Shuttle Stops

ℹ Tourist Information

Continue along and pass the Royal Vancouver Yacht Club. The causeway to **Deadman's Island,** a former burial ground for local Salish people and early settlers is about ½ km (⅓ mi) farther. It's now a small naval installation, HMCS *Discovery,* and isn't open to the public. The **totem poles** ㉔, which are a bit farther down Stanley Park Drive and slightly inland on your left, are a popular photo stop. The **Nine O'Clock Gun** ㉕ is ahead at the water's edge, just past the sign for Hallelujah Point. Brockton Point and its small lighthouse and foghorn is to the north.

Brockton Oval, where you can catch a rugby game in winter or cricket in summer, is inland on your left. Next, on the water side, watch for the ***Girl in a Wetsuit,*** a sculpture on a rock offshore that mimics Copenhagen's *Little Mermaid.* A little farther along the seashore, there's a replica of the dragon-shape figurehead from the SS *Empress of Japan,* which plied these waters between 1891 and 1922.

Lumbermen's Arch ㉖, a log archway, is at Km 3 (Mi 2) of the drive. There's a picnic area, a snack bar, and a small beach here. The **Children's Water Park,** across the road, is a big draw throughout the summer. Cyclists and walkers can turn off here for a shortcut back to the aquarium, the Miniature Railway and Children's Farmyard, and the park entrance.

The Lions Gate Bridge is about 2 km (1 mi) farther along the seawall or Stanley Park Drive. Here drivers and cyclists part company. Cyclists ride under the bridge and past the cormorants' nests tucked beneath **Prospect Point** ㉗. Drivers pass over the bridge and reach a viewpoint and café at the top of Prospect Point. Both routes then continue around to the English Bay side of the park and the beginning of sandy beaches. The imposing monolith offshore (though not visible from the road) is **Siwash Rock** ㉘, the focus of a native legend. If you're driving, watch for a sign for the Hollow Tree. This massive burnt cedar stump gives an idea of how large some of the old growth trees were. Continue along to reach the swimming area and snack bar at Third Beach.

The next attraction along the seawall is the large heated pool at **Second Beach** ㉙. If you're walking or cycling, you can take a shortcut from here back to Lost Lagoon by taking the perpendicular pathway behind the pool that cuts into the park. Either of the footbridges ahead leads to a path along the south side of the lagoon that takes you back to your starting point at the foot of Alberni or Georgia streets. If you continue along the seawall from Second Beach, you will emerge from the park into a residential neighborhood of high-rises, the West End. You can walk back to Alberni Street along Denman Street, where there are places to stop for coffee, a drink, or ice cream. **Mum's Gelati,** at 855 Denman Street, serves delicious ice cream.

TIMING
The driving tour takes about an hour. Parking is available near most of the sights in the park. Biking time depends on your speed, but with stops to see the sights, expect the ride to take several hours. It takes at least two hours to see the aquarium thoroughly. If you're going to walk the park and take in most of the sights, plan on spending the day. The seawall can get crowded on summer weekends, but inside the park is a 28-km (17-mi) network of peaceful, usually deserted, walking and cycling paths through old- and second-growth forest. Take a map—they're available at park concession stands—and don't go into the woods alone or after dusk.

Sights to See

㉖ **Lumbermen's Arch.** Made of one massive log, this archway, erected in 1952, is dedicated to the workers in Vancouver's first industry. Beside the arch is an asphalt path that leads back to Lost Lagoon and the Vancouver Aquarium.

㉓ **Miniature Railway and Children's Farmyard.** A child-size steam train takes kids and adults on a ride through the woods. Next door there's a farmyard full of critters, including goats, rabbits, and guinea pigs. At Christmastime, an elaborate light display illuminates the route. ⊠ *Off Pipeline Rd.,* ☎ *604/257–8530.* ☞ *$2.50 for railway, $2.50 for farmyard. Higher fees during Christmas season.* ☉ *June–Sept., daily 11–4; Oct.–Dec. 4 and Jan. 4–Apr. 1, weekends 11–4 (weather permitting); early Dec. to early Jan., daily 3–10.*

㉕ **Nine O'Clock Gun.** This cannonlike apparatus by the water was installed in 1890 to alert fishermen to a curfew ending weekend fishing. Now it signals 9 o'clock every night.

㉗ **Prospect Point.** Cormorants build their seaweed nests along the cliff ledges here. The large black diving birds are distinguished by their long necks and beaks. When not nesting, they often perch atop floating logs or boulders. Another remarkable bird found along the park's shore is the beautiful great blue heron. Herons prey on fish. The oldest heron rookery in British Columbia is in the trees near the aquarium, where the birds like to horn in during feeding time for the whales. Prospect Point at 211 feet, the highest point in the park, offers striking views of the North Shore and Burrard Inlet. There's also a souvenir shop, a snack bar, and a restaurant here.

NEED A
BREAK?

Prospect Point Café (☎ 604/669–2737) is at the top of Prospect Point, with a deck overlooking the Lions Gate Bridge. It specializes in all manner of salmon dishes and makes a good lunch or dinner stop, if you can squeeze in among the tour groups.

🖐 ㉙ **Second Beach.** In summer visitors love the 50-m pool, which has life-guards and water slides. The shallow end fills up on hot days, but the lap-swimming end is usually deserted. The sandy beach also has a play-ground and covered picnic areas. ☎ 604/257–8371, WEB *www.city.van-couver.bc.ca/parks/2.htm.* 🖼 *Beach free, pool $4.* ☉ *Pool late May–mid-June, weekdays noon–8:45, weekends 10–8:45; mid-June–Labor Day 10–8:45.*

㉘ **Siwash Rock.** Legend tells of a young First Nations man who, about to become a father, bathed persistently to wash his sins away so that his son could be born pure. For his devotion he was blessed by the gods and immortalized in the shape of Siwash Rock, just offshore. Two small rocks, said to be his wife and child, are on the cliff above the site. The rock is visible from the seawall; if you're driving, you need to park and take a short path through the woods.

㉔ **Totem poles.** Totem poles were not made in the Vancouver area but were an important art form among B.C.'s native people. These eight poles include replicas of poles originally brought to the park from the north coast in the 1920s, as well as poles carved specifically for the park by First Nations artists. The several styles of poles represent a cross-section of B.C. native groups, including the Kwakiutl, Haida, and Nishga. The combination of carved animals, fish, birds, and mytho-logical creatures represents clan history. An information center near the site has a snack bar and interpretive materials about the poles.

★ 🖐 ㉒ **Vancouver Aquarium Marine Science Centre.** This excellent research and educational facility is a delight for children and natural-history buffs. In the Amazon rain-forest gallery you can walk through a jungle set-ting populated with piranhas, caimans, and tropical birds and vege-tation. Other displays, many with hands-on features for kids, show the underwater life of coastal British Columbia, the Canadian Arctic, and the tropics. Huge tanks have large windows for underwater viewing of beluga whales and playful sea otters. Whale shows are held several times a day. You can even hear whale sounds on radio station ORCA FM, which picks up the wild calls with an underwater microphone off Vancouver Island. A listening post is downstairs by the whale pool. A Pacific Canada Pavilion, built in 1999, looks at the aquatic life in the waters of British Columbia, and a demonstration salmon stream flows through Stanley Park from Burrard Inlet to the aquarium. There's also a café and a gift shop. Be prepared for lines on weekends and school holidays. ☎ 604/659–3474, WEB *www.vanaqua.org.* 🖼 *$12.95.* ☉ *July–Labor Day, daily 9:30–7; Labor Day–June, daily 10–5:30.*

Granville Island

One of North America's most successful urban-redevelopment schemes was just a sandbar until World War I, when the federal government dredged False Creek for access to the sawmills that lined the shore. The sludge from the creek was heaped onto the sandbar to create the is-land. It was used to house much-needed industrial and logging-equip-ment plants, but the businesses had begun to deteriorate by the 1960s. In the early '70s, the federal government came up with a creative plan to redevelop the island with a public market, marine activities, and ar-tisans' studios but to retain the architecture's industrial character. The refurbished Granville Island opened to the public in 1979 and was an immediate hit with locals and visitors alike.

Besides the popular public market, the island is home to a marina, an art college, three theaters, several restaurants and pubs, park space, playgrounds, and dozens of craft shops and artisans studios. It's also

URBAN SAFARI

DURING WORLD WAR II, the Canadian military set up watchtowers along Vancouver's Point Grey so soldiers could detect signs of a Japanese invasion. The lookouts called the alarm once, when they spotted a large, submerged object making its way into Burrard Inlet. Tension mounted, but Japanese subs rarely sport blow holes, so the innocent whale was left alone. You won't see many whales in Vancouver's harbor these days—they're across the way, off Vancouver Island—but in and near this city on the edge of a rain forest you do have a better chance of spotting wildlife than in almost any other urban area.

A good place to start is **Stanley Park** (☎ 604/257–8400), a 1,000-acre forest abutting the downtown core. Here long-necked black cormorants nest in the cliffs under Prospect Point and blue herons stroll the public beaches. There's also a big heron rookery at the edge of the whale pool at Stanley Park's aquarium—over the years the birds have learned about the fish that appear at feeding time. There are outgoing (though hardly tame) raccoons and squirrels posing for photos throughout the park, as well, heed the signs asking visitors not to feed them. Skunks and coyotes are more withdrawn but they also live here and, like the others, they sometimes amble into the West End, a high-rise residential neighborhood bordering the park. An excellent way to learn more about Stanley Park's wildlife is to join a guided walk with the staff from the **Lost Lagoon Nature House** (☎ 604/257–8544). The nature house is at the edge of Lost Lagoon, by the bus loop at the foot of Alberni Street.

The 850-acre **Reifel Migratory Bird Sanctuary** (✉ 5191 Robertson Rd., Delta, ☎ 604/946–6980 for directions), on Westham Island about an hour's drive south of Vancouver, is a stopping-off point for at least 268 species of migratory birds traveling along North America's Pacific Flyway. The sanctuary hosts Canada geese, snow geese, and one of the largest populations of waterfowl to winter anywhere in Canada.

One species is the focus of the **Brackendale Eagles' Park.** About an hour's drive north of Vancouver, the reserve, which was recently made a provincial park, is 7 km (4 mi) north of Squamish in the town of Brackendale (follow signs from Highway 99). Every November to February since time immemorial, eagles from all over North America have gathered here to feed on spawning salmon. Each January eagle-watchers attend the **Brackendale Winter Eagle Festival and Count,** sponsored by the Brackendale Art Gallery (✉ 41950 Government Rd., ☎ 604/898–3333, WEB www.mntn.net/~gallery); it started simply as a bird count and has since blossomed into a month long music, arts, and social event. In 2001, a team of volunteer eagle-counters tallied 2,035 individuals.

Less common, but all the more heart-stopping should you run into one on a trail, are the big mammals—the cougars, black bears, and other animals that once had the run of this territory. Most of the 3,000 or so cougars and 140,000 black bears in British Columbia avoid humans, but sightings have increased in recent years as urban development encroaches on their habitats. Cougars have been spotted in suburban North Vancouver, and in downtown Victoria. Black bears have appeared in North and West Vancouver's suburban backyards. From May through October in Whistler, it's not unusual to see bears near, or even in, the village, so it's important to follow a few rules. Don't leave food or garbage lying about. If you see a bear, don't approach it; back away slowly and speak in a calm voice.

among the venues for Vancouver's comedy, jazz, and fringe-theater festivals, and a great place to catch top-quality street entertainment.

Though the island is now technically a peninsula, connected years ago by landfill to the south shore of False Creek, its distinct atmosphere sets it apart from the rest of the city.

Numbers in the text correspond to numbers in the margin and on the Granville Island map.

A Good Walk

To reach Granville Island on foot, make the 15-minute walk from downtown Vancouver to the south end of Hornby Street. Aquabus Ferries depart from here and deliver passengers across False Creek at the **Granville Island Public Market** ㉚. False Creek Ferries leave every five minutes for Granville Island from a dock behind the Vancouver Aquatic Centre, on Beach Avenue. Still another option is to take a 20-minute ride on a TransLink bus; from Waterfront Station or stops on Granville Street, take False Creek South Bus 50 to the edge of the island. Or, from Granville Street and Broadway, catch Granville Island Bus 51 for direct service to Granville Island. If you drive, parking is free for up to three hours, and paid parking is available in four garages on the island.

Another way to travel is to hop the **Downtown Historic Railway** (☎ 604/665–3903), two early 20th-century electric trams that on summer weekends and holiday afternoons run from Science World to Granville Island.

The Granville Island Public Market, which has a slew of food and other stalls, is a short walk from the bus, ferry, or tram stop.

From the market, to start a clockwise tour of the island, walk south on Johnston Street or take the waterside boardwalk behind the Arts Club Theatre. Either way, past the shops and studios in the Creekhouse building is **Ocean Art Works,** an open space where you can watch First Nations artists at work. Right before you reach **Emily Carr Institute of Art and Design** ㉛, you pass Ocean Cement, one of the last of the island's industries (its lease does not expire until 2004). Past the **Charles H. Scott Gallery,** turn left and follow a walkway along the south side of the art school to Sea Village, one of the only houseboat communities in Vancouver. Then take the boardwalk that starts at the houseboats and continues partway around the island. Beyond the Granville Island Hotel is a small hill called The Mound, a natural amphitheater for outdoor performances.

Turn right onto **Cartwright Street.** This end of the island is home to a mix of crafts galleries, studios, and workshops, and is a great place to watch artisans at work. You can see wooden boats being built at the Alder Bay Boat Company and view printmakers in action at New Leaf Editions, for instance. The Federation of Canadian Artists Gallery, the Crafts Association of B.C. Crafthouse, and the Gallery of B.C. Ceramics all showcase local works. At Studio Glass, around the corner at 1440 Old Bridge Street, you can watch glassblowers at work. Railspur Alley, home to about a dozen artisans' studios, is off Old Bridge Street.

Back on Cartwright Street, you can pick up maps and find out about special events, including the festivals, outdoor concerts, and dance performances often held on the island, at the **Granville Island Information Centre** (open daily 9–6). The **Granville Island Water Park** ㉜, behind the information center, and the **Kids' Market** ㉝, a bit farther down the street, make any child's visit to Granville Island a thrill. Adults can head for the microbrewery tour at **Granville Island Brewing** ㉞, across the street from the Kids' Market.

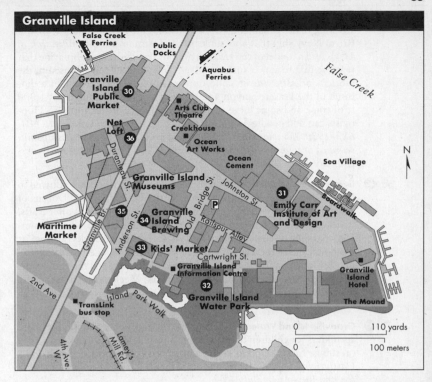

Granville Island

Cross Anderson Street and walk north on Duranleau Street. The **Granville Island Museums** ㉟, with fishing, train, and model-boat displays, are on your left. The sea-oriented shops of the Maritime Market are next. The upscale **Net Loft** ㊱ shopping arcade is the last place to explore. Once you have come full circle, you can either take the ferry back to downtown Vancouver or stay for dinner and catch a play at the Arts Club or the Waterfront Theatre.

TIMING

If your schedule is tight, you can tour Granville Island in three to four hours. If you like to shop, or if there's a festival in progress, you likely need a full day.

Sights to See

㉛ **Emily Carr Institute of Art and Design.** The institute's three main buildings—tin-plated structures formerly used for industrial purposes—were renovated in the 1970s. The **Charles H. Scott Gallery** to the right of the main entrance hosts contemporary exhibitions in various media. ✉ *1399 Johnston St.,* ☎ *604/844–3811.* 🎟 *Free.* ☉ *Weekdays noon–5, weekends 10–5.*

㉞ **Granville Island Brewing.** Tours of Canada's first modern microbrewery last about a half hour and include a souvenir glass and a taste of four brews, including some that aren't on the market yet. Kids are welcome; they get a taste of root beer. ✉ *1441 Cartwright St.,* ☎ *604/687–2739.* 🎟 *$7.* ☉ *Daily, 10–7 (call for tour times).*

㉟ **Granville Island Museums.** Here are three museums under one roof. The **Sport Fishing Museum** houses one of North America's leading collections of angling artifacts, including the world's biggest collection of Hardy reels and fly plates, and a mounted replica of the largest salmon ever caught with a rod and reel. The collection of the **Model Ships Mu-**

seum includes exquisitely detailed early 20th-century military and working vessels, including a 13-ft replica of the HMS *Hood*, the British Royal Navy ship that was sunk by the German warship *Bismarck* in 1941, and a model of the *Hunley*, an 1863 confederate submarine that was the first to sink a surface vessel. The **Model Trains Museum,** the world's largest toy-train collection on public display, includes a diorama of the Fraser Canyon and the Kettle Valley that involves 1,000 ft of track and some large-scale (3 ft high) model steam trains. Hobbyists can find goodies in the gift shop. ⊠ *1502 Duranleau St.,* ☎ *604/683–1939,* WEB *www.sportfishingmuseum.ca or www.modelshipsmuseum.ca or www.modeltrainsmuseum.ca.* ⊠ *$7 for all three museums.* ☉ *Daily 10–5:30.*

★ ③⓪ **Granville Island Public Market.** Because no chain stores are allowed in this 50,000-square-ft building, each outlet here is unique. Dozens of stalls sell locally grown produce direct from the farm; others offer crafts, wine, chocolates, cheeses, fish, meat, flowers, and exotic foods. In summer, market gardeners sell fruit and vegetables from trucks outside. At the north end of the market you can pick up a snack, espresso, or fixings for lunch on the wharf. The Market Courtyard, on the water side, is a good place to catch street entertainers. Weekends can get madly busy here. ⊠ *1689 Johnston St.,* ☎ *604/666–6477,* WEB *www.granvilleisland.com.* ☉ *Daily 9–6.*

☙ ③② **Granville Island Water Park.** This kids' paradise has slides, pipes, and sprinklers for children to shower one another. Parents can keep an eye on things from the patio of the **Cat's Meow** café next door. ⊠ *1318 Cartwright St.,* ☎ *604/257–8195.* ⊠ *Free.* ☉ *Late May–late June, call for hrs; July–Aug., daily 10–6.*

☙ ③③ **Kids' Market.** A slice of kids' heaven on Granville Island, the Kids' Market has an indoor play area and two floors of small shops that sell all kinds of toys, magic gear, books, and other fun stuff. ⊠ *1496 Cartwright St.,* ☎ *604/689–8447.* ☉ *Daily 10–6.*

③⑥ **Net Loft.** This blue-and-red building includes a bookstore, a café, and a collection of high-quality boutiques selling imported and locally made crafts, exotic fabrics, handmade paper, and First Nations art. ⊠ *1666 Johnston St., across from Public Market,* ☎ *no phone.* ☉ *Individual shop hours vary, but most are open daily 10–6.*

Kitsilano

The beachfront district of Kitsilano (popularly known as Kits), south of downtown Vancouver, is among the trendiest of Canadian neighborhoods. Originally inhabited by the Squamish people, whose Chief Khahtsahlanough gave the area its name, Kitsilano began to attract daytrippers from Vancouver in the early part of the 20th century. Some stayed and built lavish waterfront mansions; others built simpler Craftsman-style houses farther up the slope. After a period of decline in the mid-20th century, Kits, which contains many restored wood-frame Craftsman houses, is once again chic.

Kitsilano is home to three museums, some fashionable shops, and popular pubs and cafés. Kits has hidden treasures, too: rare boats moored at Heritage Harbour, stately mansions on forested lots, and, all along the waterfront, quiet coves and shady paths within a stone's throw of Canada's liveliest beach.

Numbers in the text correspond to numbers in the margin and on the Greater Vancouver map.

A Good Walk

Vanier Park, the grassy beachside setting for three museums and the best kite-flying venue in Vancouver, is the logical gateway to Kits. The most enjoyable way to get here is by False Creek Ferries, from Granville Island or from behind the Vancouver Aquatic Centre, on Beach Avenue. The ferries dock at Heritage Harbour behind the Vancouver Maritime Museum. You can also walk or cycle about 1 km (½ mi) along the waterfront pathway from Granville Island (leave the island by Anderson Street and keep to your right along the waterfront). If you prefer to come by road, drive over the Burrard Street Bridge, turn right at Chestnut Street, and park in either of the museum parking lots, or take Bus 2 or 22 traveling south on Burrard Street downtown, get off at Cypress Street and Cornwall Avenue, and walk over to the park.

Vancouver Museum ㊲, which showcases the city's natural and cultural history, shares a building with the **H.R. MacMillan Space Centre** ㊳, a high-tech museum focusing on outer space. The **Vancouver Maritime Museum** ㊴, which traces the maritime history of the West Coast, is to the west and toward the water. Each museum has hands-on exhibits that appeal to kids.

Behind the Maritime Museum, where the ferries dock, is Heritage Harbour, home to a rotating series of boats of historical interest, including *BCP 45,* the picturesque fishing boat that used to appear on Canada's $5 bill. In summer the big tent, set up in Vanier Park, is the venue for the Bard on the Beach Shakespeare series.

There's a quiet, grassy beach west of the Maritime Museum. A staircase leads up from the beach to a paved walkway. Take a moment to look at the 100-ft-tall replica Kwakiutl totem pole in front of the museum, and then follow the walkway west to popular **Kitsilano Beach** ㊵. Across the water you can see Stanley Park, and Vancouver's downtown core is behind you. Continue past the pool, keeping to the water, and enter a shady pathway lined with blackberry bushes that runs behind the Kitsilano Yacht Club. Soon the lane opens up to a viewpoint and gives access to another sandy cove.

About ½ km (¼ mi) from the yacht club, the path ends at a wooden staircase. This leads up to a viewpoint and a park on Point Grey Road. Across the street from the top of the staircase, at 2590 Point Grey Road, is an Edwardian-era mansion that was built by a member of Kitsilano's early elite. Double back the way you came, heading east toward Kits Beach, but this time follow Point Grey Road for a look at the front of the homes you could see from the beach path. The 1909 Logan House, at 2530 Point Grey Road, is an ivory-color Edwardian dream home with a curved balcony.

Follow Point Grey Road as it curves to the right, and cross Cornwall Avenue at Balsam Street. Turn left on either York or 1st Avenue and walk two blocks to Yew Street, where in summer you can find one of the biggest concentrations of sidewalk pubs and cafés in Greater Vancouver. Alternatively, you can hike up the hill to 4th Avenue, once the heart of the hippie district, and explore the shops between Balsam and Burrard streets. You can catch a bus back to downtown Vancouver on Cornwall or 4th Avenue, or cut across Kits Beach Park back to Vanier Park.

TIMING

The walk alone takes about 1½ hours. Add two hours to see the MacMillan Space Centre and an hour for each of the other museums. With time out for shopping or swimming, a visit to Kitsilano could easily fill a whole day.

Sights to See

🐣 ➍⓿ **Kitsilano Beach.** Picnic sites, a playground, Vancouver's biggest out-door pool, and some fine people-watching can all be found at Kits Beach. Inland from the pool, the **Kitsilano Showboat** hosts free performances, mostly of the children's dancing variety, in summer. ⊠ *Off Cornwall Ave.,* ☎ *604/738–8535 for beach information; 604/731–0011 for pool (both summer only),* WEB *www.city.vancouver.bc.ca/parks/2.htm.* ☐ *Beach free, pool $4.* ☉ *Pool: late May–mid-June, weekdays noon–8:45, weekends and holidays 10 AM–8:45 PM; mid-June–mid-Sept., weekdays 7 AM–9 AM (adults only), 9 AM–8:45 PM (general public). Week-ends and holidays 10 AM–8:45 PM.*

🐣 ➌⓼ **H.R. MacMillan Space Centre.** The interactive exhibits and high-tech learning systems at this museum include a Virtual Voyages ride, where visitors can take a simulated space journey (definitely not for those afraid of flying); Ground Station Canada, showcasing Canada's achieve-ments in space; and the Cosmic Courtyard, full of hands-on space-ori-ented exhibits. You can catch daytime astronomy shows or evening music and laser shows at the **H.R. MacMillan Planetarium.** When the sky is clear, the half-meter telescope at the **Gordon MacMillan Southam Ob-servatory** (☎ 604/738–2855) is focused on whatever stars or planets are worth watching that night. Admission to the observatory is free, and it's open year-round on weekend evenings, weather permitting (call for hours). ⊠ *Vanier Park, 1100 Chestnut St.,* ☎ *604/738–7827,* WEB *www.hrmacmillanspacecentre.com.* ☐ *$12.75.* ☉ *July–Aug., daily 10–5; Sept.–June, Tues.–Sun. 10–5.*

🐣 ➌⓽ **Vancouver Maritime Museum.** About a third of the museum has been turned over to kids, with touchable displays that provide a chance to drive a tug, maneuver an underwater robot, or dress up as a seafarer. Toddlers and school-age children appreciate the hands-on displays in Pirates' Cove and the Children's Maritime Discovery Centre. The mu-seum also has an extensive collection of model ships and is the last moor-age for the *St. Roch,* the first ship to sail in both directions through the treacherous Northwest Passage. Historic boats are moored at **Her-itage Harbour,** behind the museum, and a huge replica of a Kwakiutl totem pole stands out front. ⊠ *Vanier Park, 1905 Ogden Ave., north end of Cypress St.,* ☎ *604/257–8300,* WEB *www.vmm.bc.ca.* ☐ *Mu-seum $7, Heritage Harbour free.* ☉ *Mid-May–Labor Day, daily 10–5; Labor Day–mid-May, Tues.–Sat. 10–5, Sun. noon–5.*

🐣 ➌⓻ **Vancouver Museum.** Life-size replicas of a trading post, the sleeping quarters of an immigrant ship, a Victorian parlor, a 1910 kitchen, and a 19th-century Canadian Pacific Railway passenger car are some of the highlights of this museum that focuses on the city's history, from early European exploration to the Edwardian era. The museum is also a major venue for national and international touring exhibitions. ⊠ *Vanier Park, 1100 Chestnut St.,* ☎ *604/736–4431,* WEB *www.vanmu-seum.bc.ca.* ☐ *$8.* ☉ *Fri.–Wed. 10–5; Thurs. 10–9.*

Greater Vancouver

Some of Vancouver's best gardens, natural sights, and museums, in-cluding the renowned Museum of Anthropology, are south of down-town, on the campus of the University of British Columbia and in the city's southern residential districts. Individual attractions are easily reached by TransLink buses, but you need a car to see them all com-fortably in a day.

Numbers in the text correspond to numbers in the margin and on the Greater Vancouver map.

A Good Drive

From downtown Vancouver, cross the **Burrard Street Bridge** and follow the marked scenic route. This takes you along Cornwall Avenue, which becomes Point Grey Road and follows the waterfront to Alma Street. The little wooden structure at the corner of Point Grey Road and Alma Street is the **Old Hastings Mill Store Museum** ㊶, Vancouver's first retail shop. If you're a golf fan, you might take a detour to the **British Columbia Golf Museum** ㊷, on Blanca Street at the edge of the University Golf Course.

The scenic route continues south on Alma Street and then west (to the right) on 4th Avenue. Take the right fork onto **Northwest Marine Drive,** which winds past Jericho, Locarno, and Spanish Banks beaches and up to the University of British Columbia (UBC). The **Museum of Anthropology** ㊸ is here (opposite Gate 4), which houses one of the world's best collections of Pacific Northwest First Nations artifacts. **Nitobe Memorial Garden** ㊹, a Japanese-style strolling garden, is across Marine Drive. There's limited and expensive metered parking at the Museum of Anthropology. Pay parking is also available in two parkades within walking distance of the museum and the garden. To find them, turn left off Northwest Marine Drive at University Gate 4 or 6, then follow the signs.

The **University of British Columbia Botanical Garden** ㊺, which has plenty of parking, is three kilometers (2 miles) farther along Marine Drive. For more gardens, follow Marine Drive through the university grounds and take the left fork onto 41st Avenue. Turn left again onto Oak Street to reach the entrance of the **VanDusen Botanical Garden** ㊻, on your left. The complex is planted with an English-style maze, water and herb gardens, and more. Return to 41st Avenue, continue farther east (turn left), and then turn left again on Cambie Street to reach **Queen Elizabeth Park** ㊼, which overlooks the city. To get back downtown, continue north on Cambie Street and over the Cambie Street Bridge.

TIMING
Except during rush hour, it takes about 30 minutes to drive from downtown to the University of British Columbia. You should add another 30 to 45 minutes of driving time for the rest of the tour, and about two hours to visit each of the main attractions.

Sights to See

㊷ **British Columbia Golf Museum.** This offbeat museum at the edge of the University Golf Club is a treat for those who can't get enough of the game. Housed in a 1930 colonial bungalow that once served as the course clubhouse, the museum has a fine collection of historic photos, trophies, antique clubs, and other golfing memorabilia. The exhibits are arranged like a golf course in 18 sections, or holes, with a theme for each. ⊠ *2545 Blanca St.,* ☎ *604/222–4653,* WEB *www.bcgolfmuseum.org.* ⊠ *Free.* ☉ *Tues.–Sun. noon–4.*

★ ㊸ **Museum of Anthropology.** Part of the University of British Columbia's Department of Anthropology, the MOA has one of the world's leading collections of Pacific Northwest First Nations Art. The Great Hall displays dramatic cedar poles, bentwood boxes, and dugout canoes adorned with images from First Nations mythology. On clear days, the gallery's 50-ft-tall windows provide a striking backdrop of mountains and sea. Another highlight is the work of the late Bill Reid, one of Canada's most respected Haida carvers. His *The Raven and the First Men* (1980), carved in yellow cedar, tells the Haida story of creation. Reid's gold and silver jewelry work is also on display, as are exquisite carvings of gold, silver, and argillite (a black shale found in the Queen

Charlotte Islands) by other First Nations artists. The museum's visible storage section displays, in drawers and cases, thousands of examples of tools, textiles, masks, and other artifacts from around the world. The experience is like poking around the attic of a Victorian explorer. The Koerner Ceramics Gallery contains several hundred pieces from 15th- to 19th-century Europe. Behind the museum are two Haida houses, set on the cliff over the water. This otherwise excellent museum lacks detailed labeling, but the free guided tours—given twice daily in summer, usually at 11 and 2 (call to confirm times)—are very informative. Another option is to visit the museum as part of a First Nations culture tour. Arthur Erickson designed the cliff-top structure that houses the MOA, which also has a good book and souvenir shop and a summertime café. To reach the museum by transit, take a UBC Bus 4 or 10 from Granville Street downtown to the university loop, a 10-minute walk from the museum. ⊠ *University of British Columbia, 6393 N.W. Marine Dr.,* ☎ *604/822–3825,* WEB *www.moa.ubc.ca.* 🎫 *$7, free Tues. 5–9.* ☉ *Memorial Day–Labor Day, Tues. 10–9, Mon. and Wed.–Sun. 10–5; Labor Day–Memorial Day, Tues. 11–9, Wed.– Sun. 11–5.*

44 **Nitobe Memorial Garden.** Opened in 1960 in memory of Japanese scholar and diplomat Dr. Inazo Nitobe (1862–1933), this 2½-acre walled garden, which includes a pond and a ceremonial tea house, is considered one of the most authentic Japanese tea and strolling gardens outside Japan. Designed by Professor Kannosuke Mori of Japan's Chiba University, the garden incorporates many native British Columbia trees and shrubs, pruned and trained in the Japanese fashion and interplanted with Japanese maples and flowering shrubs. The circular path around the park symbolizes the cycle of life and provides a tranquil view from every direction. Cherry blossoms are the highlight in April and May, and in June the irises are magnificent. ⊠ *University of British Columbia, 1903 West Mall,* ☎ *604/822–9666,* WEB *www.ubcbotanicalgarden.org.* 🎫 *Mid-Mar.–mid-Oct. $2.75, mid-Oct.–mid-Mar. by donation.* ☉ *Mid-Mar.–mid-Oct., daily 10–6; mid-Oct.–mid-Mar., weekdays 10–2:30.*

41 **Old Hastings Mill Store Museum.** Vancouver's first store was built in 1865 at the foot of Dunlevy Street in Gastown and moved to this seaside spot in 1930. The only building to predate the 1886 Great Fire, the site is a museum with displays of First Nations artifacts and pioneer household goods. ⊠ *1575 Alma St.,* ☎ *604/734–1212.* 🎫 *Donation.* ☉ *mid-June–mid-Sept., Tues.–Sun. 11–4; mid-Sept.–Nov. and Feb.–mid-June, weekends 1–4. Closed Dec.–Jan.*

47 **Queen Elizabeth Park.** Besides views of downtown, the park has lavish sunken gardens, a rose garden, and an abundance of grassy picnicking spots. Other park facilities include 20 tennis courts, pitch and putt, and a restaurant. In the **Bloedel Conservatory** you can see tropical and desert plants and 60 species of free-flying tropical birds in a glass geodesic dome. To reach the park by public transportation, take a Cambie Bus 15 from the corner of Robson and Burrard streets downtown to 33rd Avenue. ⊠ *Cambie St. and 33rd Ave.,* ☎ *604/257–8570,* WEB *www.city.vancouver.bc.ca/parks/2.htm.* 🎫 *Conservatory $3.75.* ☉ *Apr.–Sept., weekdays 9–8, weekends 10–9; Oct.–Mar., daily 10–5:30.*

45 **University of British Columbia Botanical Garden.** Ten thousand trees, shrubs, and rare plants from around the world thrive on this 70-acre research site on the university campus. The complex includes an Asian garden, a garden of medicinal plants, and an Alpine garden with some of the world's rarest plants. Guided tours, included in the price of admission, are given Wednesday and Saturday at 1 in summer (call to confirm). The extensive shop is a paradise for gardeners. ✉ *6804 S.W. Marine Dr.,* ☎ *604/822–9666,* WEB *www.ubcbotanicalgarden.org.* ✉ *Summer $4.75, winter free.* ◷ *Mid-Mar.–mid-Oct., daily 10–6; mid-Oct.–mid-Mar., daily 10–dusk.*

㊻ VanDusen Botanical Garden. On what was a 55-acre golf course grows one of Canada's largest botanical gardens. Displays from every continent include an Elizabethan maze, five lakes, an Asian medicinal garden, a North American native medicinal garden with a medicine wheel of standing stones, and a Sino-Himalayan garden. There's also a shop, a library, and a restaurant. The first weekend in June the garden produces North America's largest (in attendance and area) outdoor flower and garden show. During the last three weeks of December, a big draw is the festival of lights (5–9 PM daily). The gardens are wheelchair accessible. An Oak Bus 17 gets you here from downtown. Queen Elizabeth Park is a ½-mi walk away, on W. 37th Avenue. ✉ *5251 Oak St., at W. 37th Ave.,* ☎ *604/878–9274 for garden; 604/261–0011 for restaurant,* WEB *www.vandusengarden.org.* ✉ *$6.50 Apr.–Sept., $3.25 Oct.–Mar.* ◷ *June–mid-Aug., daily 10–9; call for off-season hrs.*

Yaletown and False Creek

In 1985–86, the provincial government cleared up a derelict industrial site on the north shore of False Creek, built a world's fair, and invited the world. Twenty million people showed up at Expo '86. Now the site of the fair has become one of the largest urban-redevelopment projects in North America, creating—and, in some cases, reclaiming—a whole new downtown district.

Tucked in among the forest of green-glass, high-rise condo towers is the old warehouse district of Yaletown. First settled by railroad workers who had followed the newly laid tracks from the town of Yale in the Fraser Canyon, Yaletown in the 1880s and '90s was probably the most lawless place in Canada; the Royal Canadian Mounted Police complained it was too far through the forest for them to police it. It's now one of the city's most fashionable neighborhoods, and the Victorian brick loading docks have become terraces for cappuccino bars. The area—which also has restaurants, brew pubs, retail and wholesale fashion outlets, and shops selling upscale home decor—makes the most of its waterfront location, with a seaside walk and cycle path that runs completely around the shore of False Creek. Parking is tight in Yaletown, though there's a lot at Library Square. It's easier to walk, come by False Creek Ferry, or catch a Yaletown Bus 2 on Burrard or Pender Street.

Numbers in the text correspond to numbers in the margin and on the Greater Vancouver map.

A Good Walk

Start at **Library Square** ㊽ at Homer and Georgia streets. Leave by the Robson Street (east) exit, cross Robson, and continue south on Hamilton Street. On your right there's a row of Victorian frame houses built between 1895 and 1900, which look out of place among the surrounding high-rises. In 1995 these historic homes were plucked from the West End and moved here to protect them from the onslaught of development.

Cross Smithe Street, and continue down Mainland Street to Nelson Street and you're now in the heart of Yaletown. Stop for a coffee at one of Yaletown's loading-dock cafés or poke around the shops on Hamilton and Mainland streets.

From the foot of Mainland Street, turn left on Davie Street and cross Pacific Boulevard. This takes you to the **Roundhouse** ㊾, a former turnaround point for trains that is now a showcase for local arts groups. **David Lam Park,** Yaletown's waterfront green space, is behind the Roundhouse. Continue to the waterfront at the foot of Davie Street. Here there's an intriguing iron and concrete sculpture with panels that display archival images of events around False Creek. Also at the foot of Davie Street is the Yaletown dock for Aquabus Ferries (☎ 604/689–5858), where you can catch a boat to Granville Island, Science World, Hornby Street, or Stamp's Landing.

From here you can access Vancouver's seaside path, a car-free, bike, in-line skating, and pedestrian pathway that, with a few detours around construction sites, continues all the way around False Creek. You can rent a bike or Rollerblades at the foot of Davie. A right turn takes you, in about 3 km (2 mi), to the West End and Stanley Park.

To continue this tour, turn left. After about 1 km (½ mi) is the **Plaza of Nations,** the heart of the old Expo site. Cross the plaza toward Pacific Boulevard and take the pedestrian overpass to B.C. Place Stadium. Walk around to Gate A and the **B.C. Sports Hall of Fame and Museum** ㊿. As you leave the museum, the Terry Fox Memorial is on your left. This archway at the foot of Robson Street was built in honor of Terry Fox (1958–81), a local student whose cross-Canada run raised millions of dollars for cancer research. From here, you can continue a block west to return to Library Square. To continue the tour, walk two blocks north on Beatty Street and take the SkyTrain one stop east, or retrace your steps to the waterfront and walk another 1 km (½ mi) east to **Science World** (51), a hands-on museum. From Science World, the SkyTrain takes you back downtown, or you can catch a ferry back to Yaletown or to other stops on False Creek. If you're here on a summer weekend, you can catch the Downtown Historic Railway to Granville Island.

TIMING

It takes about 1½ hours to walk around all the sights. Allow about an hour for the B.C. Sports Hall of Fame and museum and two hours for Science World.

Sights to See

㊿ **B.C. Sports Hall of Fame and Museum.** Inside the B.C. Place Stadium complex, this museum celebrates the province's sports achievers in a series of historical displays. You can test your sprinting, rowing, climbing, and throwing prowess in the high-tech participation gallery. An hour-long audio tour is included with admission. ✉ *B.C. Place, 777 Pacific Blvd. S, Gate A,* ☎ *604/687–5520.* *$6.* ⏲ *Daily 10–5.*

㊽ **Library Square.** The spiraling library building, open plazas, and shaded atriums of Library Square, completed in the mid-1990s, were built to evoke images of the Colosseum in Rome. A high-tech library is the core of the structure; the outer edge of the spiral houses cafés and boutiques. ✉ *350 W. Georgia St.,* ☎ *604/331–3600,* WEB *www.vpl.vancouver.bc.ca.* ⏲ *Mon.–Thurs. 10–8, Fri.–Sat. 10–5, Sun. 1–5.*

Plaza of Nations. The centerpiece of Expo '86 is one of the World's Fair's least used legacies. Now home to a casino and a comedy club, it's at its liveliest in the evening, though a café and a pub with outdoor seating are open during the day. ✉ *700 block of Pacific Blvd.*

㊾ **Roundhouse.** This round brick structure was built in 1888 as the turnaround point for transcontinental trains reaching the end of the line at Vancouver. A spirited local campaign helped to create a home here (in a glass pavilion on the Davie Street side) for **Engine 374**, which pulled the first passenger train into Vancouver on May 23, 1887. Now a community center, the Roundhouse hosts festivals and exhibitions. ⊠ *181 Roundhouse Mews*, ☎ *604/713–1800.* ⌦ *Free; admission may be charged to some events.* ☉ *Weekdays 9 AM–10 PM, weekends 9–5.*

⸽⸽⸽

NEED A BREAK?   Across from the Roundhouse, **Urban Fare** (⊠ 177 Davie St., ☎ 604/975–7550) supplies, among other things, truffles, foie gras, and bread air-freighted from France to Yaletown's Francophiles and foodies. It's open daily 6 AM–midnight. You can sample the wares at the café.

⸽⸽⸽

   ⟳ ⑤ **Science World.** In a gigantic, shiny dome built over an Omnimax Theater, this hands-on science center encourages children to participate in interactive exhibits and demonstrations. Exhibits change throughout the year, so there's always something new to see. ⊠ *1455 Quebec St.*, ☎ *604/443–7443,* ⓌⒺⒷ *www.scienceworld.bc.ca.* ⌦ *Science World $11.75, Science World and Omnimax theater $14.75.* ☉ *July–Aug., daily 10–6; Sept.–June, weekdays 10–5, weekends and holidays 10–6.*

North Vancouver

The mountains that form a stunning backdrop to Vancouver lie in the district of North Vancouver, a bridge or SeaBus ride away on the North Shore of Burrard Inlet. Although the area is part suburb, the mountainous terrain has kept large parts of North Vancouver forested. This is where Vancouverites and visitors go for easily accessible hiking, skiing, and views of the city lights.

Numbers in the text correspond to numbers in the margin and on the Greater Vancouver map.

A Good Drive

From downtown, drive west down Georgia Street to Stanley Park and across the Lions Gate Bridge to North Vancouver. Stay in the right lane, take the North Vancouver exit, then turn left onto Capilano Road. In about 2 km (1 mi), you come to the **Capilano Suspension Bridge and Park** ㉒. A few hundred yards up Capilano Road, on the left, is the entrance to the Capilano Salmon Hatchery, which is part of **Capilano River Regional Park** ㉓. North of the Salmon Hatchery and also part of the park is Cleveland Dam, where you can stop for great views of the mountains. As you continue north, Capilano Road becomes Nancy Greene Way, which ends at the base of **Grouse Mountain** ㉔. From here, a cable car to the summit gives you great city views.

Alternatively, you can take the SeaBus from Waterfront Station to Lonsdale Quay and then catch a Grouse Mountain Bus 236. This stops at the Capilano Suspension Bridge and near the Salmon Hatchery on its way to the base of Grouse Mountain.

TIMING

You need a half day to see the sights, a full day if you want to hike at Grouse Mountain or Capilano River Regional Park. To save a lot of time, avoid crossing the Lions Gate Bridge during weekday rush hours (about 7–9 AM and 3–6 PM).

Sights to See

   ⟳ ㉓ **Capilano River Regional Park.** The park contains hiking trails and footbridges over the Capilano River where it cuts through a dramatic gorge. At the park's **Capilano Salmon Hatchery** (4500 Capilano Park Rd., ☎ 604/666–1790), viewing areas and exhibits illustrate the life cycle of the salmon. The best time of year to see the salmon run is between July and November. The **Cleveland Dam** (⊠ Capilano Rd., about 2 km [1 mi] past main park entrance) is at the north end of the park. Built in 1954 and named for Dr. E. A. Cleveland, a former chief commissioner of the Greater Vancouver Water District, it dams the Capilano River to create the 5½-km-long (3½-mi-long) Capilano Reservoir. A hundred yards from the parking lot, you can walk across the top of the dam to enjoy striking views of the reservoir and mountains behind it. The two sharp peaks to the west are the Lions, for which the Lions Gate Bridge is named. ⊠ *Capilano Rd., North Vancouver,* ☎ *604/224–5739.* ☒ *Free.* ☉ *Park daily 8 AM–dusk; hatchery June–Aug., daily 8–8 (call for off-season hrs).*

🐣 �52 **Capilano Suspension Bridge and Park.** At Vancouver's oldest tourist attraction (the original bridge was built in 1889), you can get a taste of the mountains and test your mettle on the swaying, 450-ft cedar-plank suspension bridge that hangs 230 ft above the rushing Capilano River. The park also has viewing decks, nature trails, a totem park and carving center (where you can watch First Nations carvers at work), history and forestry exhibits, a massive gift shop in the original 1911 tea house, and a restaurant. Most of the attractions are on the near side of the bridge, so you don't have to cross it to enjoy the site. May through October, guides in 19th-century costumes offer free tours throughout the day and First Nations dancers perform three times daily. ⊠ *3735 Capilano Rd., North Vancouver,* ☎ *604/985-7474,* WEB *www.capbridge.com.* ☒ *May–Oct. $11.95; Nov.–Apr. $9.35 (plus $2 for parking).* ☉ *Apr.–Oct., daily 8:30–dusk; Nov.–Mar., daily 9–5.*

★ 🐣 �54 **Grouse Mountain.** North America's largest aerial tramway, the **Skyride** is a great way to take in the city, sea, and mountain vistas (be sure to pick a clear day or evening), and there's plenty to do when you arrive at the top of Grouse Mountain. The Skyride makes the 1-mi climb up to the peak every 15 minutes. A Skyride ticket includes a half-hour video presentation at the Theatre in the Sky. Other mountaintop activities include lumberjack shows, chairlift rides, walking and mountain-bike tours, hiking, tandem paragliding, helicopter tours, and, in winter, snowshoeing, snowboarding, downhill and cross-country skiing, ice-skating, and Sno-Cat-drawn sleigh rides. The mountaintop also has a café, a bistro, and a fine dining restaurant. The **híwus Feast House** (☎ 604/980–9311) presents a traditional First Nations feast and entertainment in a mountaintop longhouse. It's open May through October, and reservations are essential. ⊠ *6400 Nancy Greene Way, North Vancouver,* ☎ *604/980–9311,* WEB *www.grousemountain.com.* ☒ *Skyride and most activities $17.95.* ☉ *Daily 9 AM–10 PM.*

OFF THE
BEATEN PATH

LYNN CANYON PARK – With a steep canyon landscape, a temperate rain forest complete with waterfalls, and a suspension bridge 165 ft above raging Lynn Creek, this park provides thrills to go with its scenic views. The on-site Ecology Centre distributes maps of area hiking trails and has information about the flora and fauna. To get to the park, take the Lions Gate Bridge and Capilano Road, go east on Highway 1, take the Lynn Valley Road exit, and turn right on Peters Road. You can also take the SeaBus to Lonsdale Quay or Bus 228 or 229 from downtown Vancouver; both stop near the park. A snack bar is open in summer. ⊠ *3663 Park Rd. (at the end of Peters Rd.), North Vancouver,* ☎ *604/981-3103,* WEB *www.dnv.org/ecology.* ☒ *Ecology Centre by donation; suspension bridge free.* ☉ *Apr.–Sept., daily 10–5; Oct.–Mar., weekdays 10–5, weekends noon–4.*

DINING

Vancouver dining is fairly informal. Casual but neat dress is appropriate everywhere. Smoking is prohibited by law in all Vancouver restaurants (indoors). A 15% tip is expected. A 10% liquor tax is charged on wine, beer, and spirits. Some restaurants build this into the price of the beverage, but others add it to the bill. *See* the Downtown Vancouver Dining map to locate downtown restaurants and the Greater Vancouver Dining map to locate restaurants in Kitsilano, Granville Island, and other neighborhoods.

CATEGORY	COST*
$$$$	over $32
$$$	$22–$32
$$	$13–$21
$	under $13

*per person, in Canadian dollars, for a main course at dinner

Downtown Vancouver

Cafés

$ ✕ **Bread Garden Bakery Café.** Salads, quiches, elaborate cakes and pies, giant muffins, and fine cappuccinos draw a steady stream of hungry locals to the many branches of this growing, Vancouver-based chain. (It has a few Greater Vancouver locations, too.) Most of the outlets open at 6 AM and stay open at least until midnight. ✉ *812 Bute St., at Robson St.,* ☎ *604/688–3213;* ✉ *1040 Denman St.,* ☎ *604/685–2996;* ✉ *101–889 West Pender St.,* ☎ *604/638–3982. West Pender St. branch closed weekends. AE, DC, MC, V.*

Casual

$–$$ ✕ **Earl's.** This locally grown chain is a favorite among Vancouverites looking for a lively place to go with a group. Big rooms, cheery decor, cozy booths, upbeat music, chipper service, and consistently good burgers, soups, sandwiches, pastas, steaks, and vegetarian options keep people coming back. Food and drink is served all day until midnight, and the Robson Street location has a big outdoor deck away from traffic. ✉ *1185 Robson St.,* ☎ *604/669–0020. AE, MC, V.*

Chinese

$$–$$$$ ✕ **Imperial Chinese Seafood.** The two-story floor-to-ceiling windows at
★ this Cantonese restaurant in the Art Deco Marine Building have stupendous views of Stanley Park and the North Shore Mountains across Coal Harbour. Any dish with lobster, crab, or shrimp from the live tanks is recommended, as is the dim sum, served daily 11 AM to 2:30 PM. ✉ *355 Burrard St.,* ☎ *604/688–8191. Reservations essential. DC, MC, V.*

$$–$$$ ✕ **Kirin Mandarin Restaurant.** A striking silver mural of a *kirin*, a mythical dragon, presides over this elegant two-tiered restaurant two blocks from most of the major downtown hotels. The specialties here are northern Chinese (Mandarin and Szechuan) dishes, which tend to be richer and spicier than the Cantonese cuisine served at Kirin's other locations. Try the Peking duck, or the kung pao lobster, which features sautéed lobster meat served with a deep fried lobster claw. Dim sum is served daily. ✉ *1166 Alberni St.,* ☎ *604/682–8833. Reservations essential. AE, DC, MC, V.*

$ ✕ **Hon's Wun-Tun House.** Mr. Hon has been keeping Vancouver residents in Chinese comfort food since the 1970s. The best bets on the 300-item menu are the pot stickers (dumplings), the wonton and noodle dishes, and anything with barbecued meat. The Robson Street outlet has a separate kitchen for vegetarians and an army of fast-moving

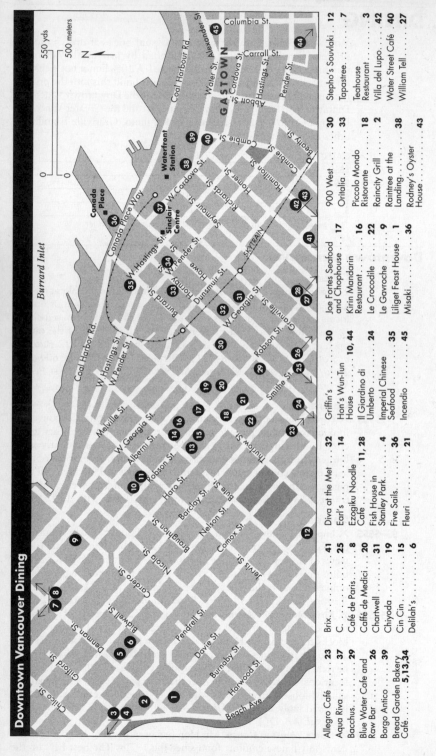

Downtown Vancouver Dining

Allegro Café 23
Aqua Riva 37
Bacchus 29
Blue Water Cafe and Raw Bar 26
Borgo Antico 39
Bread Garden Bakery Café 5,13,34
Brix 41
C. 25
Café de Paris 8
Caffè de Medici 20
Chartwell 31
Chiyoda 19
Cin Cin 15
Delilah's 6
Diva at the Met 32
Earl's 14
Ezogiku Noodle Cafe 11, 28
Fish House in Stanley Park 4
Five Sails 36
Fleuri 21
Griffin's 30
Hon's Wun-Tun House 10, 44
Il Giardino di Umberto 24
Imperial Chinese Seafood 35
Incendio 45
Joe Fortes Seafood and Chophouse . . . 17
Kirin Mandarin Restaurant 16
Le Crocodile 22
Le Gavroche 9
Liliget Feast House . . . 1
Misaki 36
900 West 30
Oritalia 33
Piccolo Mondo Ristorante 18
Raincity Grill 2
Raintree at the Landing 38
Rodney's Oyster House 43
Stepho's Souvlaki . . . 12
Tapastree 7
Teahouse Restaurant 3
Villa del Lupo 42
Water Street Café . . . 40
William Tell 27

waitresses. The original Keefer Street location is in the heart of Chinatown. ✉ *1339 Robson St.,* ☎ *604/685–0871. Reservations not accepted. MC, V.* ✉ *268 Keefer St.,* ☎ *604/688–0871. Reservations not accepted. No credit cards.*

Contemporary

$$$–$$$$ ✗ **Chartwell.** Named after Sir Winston Churchill's country home (a painting of it hangs over one of this elegant restaurant's two fireplaces), the flagship dining room at the Four Seasons hotel has rich wood paneling, plush banquettes, deep leather chairs, and is gaining a reputation for its innovative contemporary cuisine. The seasonally changing menu makes the most of British Columbia's regional bounty. Highlights include braised Salt Spring Island lamb shoulder served with truffled flageolet cassoulet, and poached lobster with grapefruit risotto. ✉ *791 W. Georgia St.,* ☎ *604/844–6715. Reservations essential. AE, D, DC, MC, V. No lunch Sat.*

$$$–$$$$ ✗ **Diva at the Met.** At this multitiered restaurant in the Metropolitan Hotel, the presentation of the innovative contemporary cuisine is as appealing as the art deco decor. The menu changes seasonally, but top creations from the open kitchen have included smoked Alaska black cod, and hazelnut-crusted-venison chop with garlic roasted pumpkin hash. The after-theater crowd heads here for late-evening snacks and desserts. The creative breakfasts and weekend brunches are also popular. ✉ *645 Howe St.,* ☎ *604/602–7788. AE, D, DC, MC, V.*

$$$–$$$$ ✗ **Five Sails.** This special-occasion restaurant at the Pan Pacific Hotel commands a sweeping view of Canada Place, Lions Gate Bridge, and the lights of the North Shore. The broad-reaching, seasonally changing menu takes its inspiration from both Europe and the Pacific Rim. Highlights have included slow-roasted translucent B.C. salmon, and roasted duck with foie gras and pear mille-feuille. ✉ *Pan Pacific Hotel, 300–999 Canada Pl.,* ☎ *604/891–2892. AE, DC, MC, V. No lunch.*

$$$–$$$$ ✗ **900 West.** Half of this lofty room in the Fairmont Hotel Vancouver is the city's most fashionable (and, to be fair, its only) wine bar; the other half is an elegant dining room serving innovative contemporary cuisine. Using European techniques, fresh British Columbia ingredients, and ideas from around the globe, chef and sommelier Dino Renaerts's creations are inventive, sometimes complex, and very West Coast. The evolving menu has included veal medallions with prawns, halibut marinated in miso and sake, and—the signature starter—a rare ahi tuna tower. The extensive wine list includes 75 varieties by the glass. ✉ *Fairmont Hotel Vancouver, 900 W. Georgia St.,* ☎ *604/669–9378. AE, D, DC, MC, V. No lunch weekends.*

$$–$$$ ✗ **Aqua Riva.** The views over the harbor and the North Shore Mountains are stunning from this lofty, lively modern room just yards from the Canada Place cruise-ship terminal. Food from the wood-fired oven, rotisserie, and grill includes thin-crust pizzas with innovative toppings, grilled salmon, and spit-roasted chicken. There's also a good selection of pastas, salads, and sandwiches and a long list of microbrewery beers and martinis. ✉ *200 Granville St.,* ☎ *604/683–5599. Reservations essential. AE, DC, MC, V.*

$$–$$$ ✗ **Brix.** The pretty courtyard tucked in beside a 1912 Yaletown warehouse (it used to be the carriage turnaround) is a romantic summer dining spot, and if you want to dine here, reservations are a must. Inside, the long narrow room is simple and comfortable, with exposed brick and white tablecloths. The Pacific Northwest cuisine, with Asian and French influences, changes seasonally, but has featured entrées like cherry marinated duckling, and ahi tuna served with a parsnip taro root spring roll. An all-day tapas menu, more than 40 wines available by the glass, and live jazz on summer Sunday evenings add up to make this a pop-

ular hangout year-round. ✉ *1138 Homer St.,* ☎ *604/915–9463. AE, MC, V. No lunch weekends. No dinner Sun. Jan.–Feb.*

$$–$$$ ✕ **Delilah's.** Cherubs dance on the ceiling, candles flicker on the tables, and martini glasses clink during toasts at this popular restaurant. The contemporary cuisine is innovative and beautifully presented. The menu, which changes seasonally, is divided into two- or four-course prix-fixe dinners. Try, if you can, the pheasant and pistachio sausage with a mushroom ragout as an appetizer, followed by blackened orange roughy with pear chutney and ginger sautéed spinach. The Szechuan-style rack of lamb is so popular it's always on the menu. Reservations are accepted only for groups of six or larger. ✉ *1789 Comox St.,* ☎ *604/687–3424. AE, DC, MC, V. No lunch.*

$$–$$$ ✕ **Griffin's.** Bright yellow walls, bold black and white tiles, an open kitchen, and splashy artwork keep things lively at this high-energy bistro in the Fairmont Hotel Vancouver. The Pacific Northwest buffets—for breakfast, lunch, evening appetizers, and dessert—are the main attractions here. An à la carte menu features salads, burgers, pizza, pasta, and seafood. ✉ *Fairmont Hotel Vancouver, 900 W. Georgia St.,* ☎ *604/662–1900. AE, D, DC, MC, V.*

$$–$$$ ✕ **Raincity Grill.** The sophisticated candlelit room and views of English Bay at this West End hot spot play second fiddle to a creative menu that owner Harry Kambolis likes to call "stubbornly regional." The best of local and regional products are featured, from salmon and shellfish to game and seasonal produce. Grilled romaine spears give the Caesar salad a delightful smoky flavor. Varying preparations of salmon and duck are usually available, as is at least one vegetarian selection. The exclusively Pacific Northwest and Californian wine list offers 120 choices by the glass. Weekend brunches are a local favorite. ✉ *1193 Denman St.,* ☎ *604/685–7337. AE, DC, MC, V.*

$$–$$$ ✕ **Raintree at the Landing.** In a beautifully renovated historic building in Gastown, Vancouver's original Pacific Northwest restaurant has waterfront views, fireplaces, a Pacific Northwest wine list, and cuisine based on fresh, often organic, regional ingredients. The seasonal menus and daily specials feature innovative treatments of such local bounty as Salt Spring Island lamb and smoked salmon–wrapped halibut, as well as rich soups, breads baked in-house, and a handful of vegetarian options. A summer favorite is the Pacific Northwest salmon bounty, featuring several varieties of smoked salmon. ✉ *375 Water St.,* ☎ *604/ 688–5570. Reservations essential. AE, DC, MC, V.*

$$–$$$ ✕ **Teahouse Restaurant.** The former officers' mess in Stanley Park is perfectly poised for watching sunsets over the water. The seasonally changing Pacific Northwest menu includes such specialties as roasted pear salad, seafood risotto, and rack of lamb. In summer you can dine on the patio, or, year-round, enjoy a traditional English afternoon tea. ✉ *7501 Stanley Park Dr., Ferguson Point,* ☎ *604/669–3281. Reservations essential. AE, MC, V. No afternoon tea Sunday.*

$$–$$$ ✕ **Water Street Café.** The tables at this popular Gastown café spill out onto the sidewalk for front-row views of the steam clock across the street. Inside, the slate-blue-and-white decor with tall windows overlooking bustling Water Street creates a cheerful, casual lunch or dinner atmosphere. It's tempting to pick one of the 12 varieties of pasta, but the crab chowder and the Fanny Bay oysters also are good choices. The breads are baked fresh daily. ✉ *300 Water St.,* ☎ *604/689–2832. AE, MC, V.*

Continental

$$–$$$$ ✕ **Fleuri.** Floral tablecloths, molded ceilings, damask wall coverings, and lush garden scenes depicted in original artwork create an elegant, springlike feel at this spacious restaurant in the Sutton Place Hotel. Classic French Continental cuisine takes on Pacific Northwest influ-

ences in such dishes as lobster and salmon tartare, pheasant with prosciutto and foie gras, and rack of lamb in a lemon-thyme *jus*, served with Stilton pudding. The dessert cart is tempting but, for ultimate decadence, try the Chocoholic Bar, a 20-item buffet with chocolate fondues, cakes, pies, crêpes, and more served Thursday through Sunday evenings. ✉ *The Sutton Place Hotel, 845 Burrard St.,* ☎ *604/642–2900. Reservations essential. AE, D, DC, MC, V.*

$$–$$$ ✕ **William Tell.** Silver service plates, embossed linen napkins, and a silver vase on each table set a tone of Swiss luxury at this establishment in the Georgian Court Hotel. The menu features such Continental classics as filet mignon, steak tartare, and chateaubriand, as well as such Swiss dishes as cheese fondue and thinly sliced veal with mushrooms in a light white-wine sauce. Sunday night there's an all-you-can-eat Swiss buffet. Lunch is served only in the bar-and-bistro area, which caters to a more casual crowd than the main restaurant. ✉ *765 Beatty St.,* ☎ *604/688–3504. Reservations essential. AE, DC, MC, V. Main dining room closed Mon.*

Eclectic

$$–$$$ ✕ **Oritalia.** An offshoot of the San Francisco establishment of the same name, this downtown restaurant features a fusion of Asian and Mediterranean (Italian, specifically) cuisines, hence the euphonic name. Signature dishes on the frequently changing menu include a starter of tuna tartare and such innovative entrées as five-spice–rubbed duck breast and grilled vegetable and buffalo bocconcini terrine. The 119-seat room, attached to the equally fashionable Sheraton Suites Le Soleil hotel, reflects the East-meets-West theme with rich golds, dark woods, and abstract Asia-inspired wall murals. The tables on the mezzanine offer vertiginous views of the open kitchen and a bird's-eye perspective of the striking handmade golden-glass and wrought-iron chandeliers. ✉ *567 Hornby St.,* ☎ *604/689–8862. AE, DC, MC, V.*

$ ✕ **Tapastree.** This bistro-style restaurant near Stanley Park was among the first of Vancouver's tapas-style eateries. It's also where a number of local chefs enjoy after-work snacks. The dishes, all appetizer-size and under $10 each, run the gamut from an Asian seafood salad with papaya, scallops, and prawns, to Japanese eggplant with pesto and goat cheese or lamb chops with sun-dried tomatoes and gorgonzola. The decor is upbeat, with small theatrical touches, including splashy paintings and candelabra sconces shaped like human arms. An extensive wine list rounds out the evening, which can last until 10:30 on weeknights and midnight on weekends. ✉ *1829 Robson St.,* ☎ *604/606–4680. Reservations essential. AE, DC, MC, V. No lunch.*

French

$$$–$$$$ ✕ **Bacchus.** Low lighting, velvet drapes, and Venetian glass lamps, presided over by a large canvas of Bacchus, the Greek god of wine and revelry, create a decadent feel at this luxurious restaurant in the Wedgewood Hotel. The chef shines with such French-influenced delicacies as truffle and thyme–roasted quail, Chilean sea bass with sauce vierge, and duck breast with duck leg confit and rosemary polenta. ✉ *845 Hornby St.,* ☎ *604/608–5319. Reservations essential. AE, D, DC, MC, V.*

$$$–$$$$ ✕ **Le Gavroche.** Classic French cuisine receives contemporary accents at this romantic restaurant, set in a century-old house with mountain views. Seafood entrées range from salmon in sauce vierge, to smoked sablefish with fava beans; meat options include a rich beef tenderloin with goat cheese and pine nuts. The chef also prepares such vegetarian options as sweet potato Napoleon, and caramelized onion tart. The 5,000-label wine cellar stresses Bordeaux and Californian varieties. ✉ *1616 Alberni St.,* ☎ *604/685–3924. Reservations essential. AE, DC, MC, V. No lunch weekends.*

$$–$$$ ✗ **Café de Paris.** Lace café curtains, helpful waiters in aprons and neck-ties, an old-fashioned dessert cart, and some of the best *pommes frites* (french fries) in town make this long-established West End eatery a fa-vorite among lovers of classic French bistro food, at neighborhood-restaurant prices. Bouillabaisse, cassoulet, mussels steamed in white wine, and steak tartare are all here. The prix-fixe menus, offering three courses for under $20 at lunch and under $35 at dinner, are good val-ues. ⊠ *751 Denman St.,* ☎ *604/687–1418. Reservations essential. AE, DC, MC, V. No lunch Sat.*

$$–$$$ ✗ **Le Crocodile.** Chef and owner Michel Jacob specializes in tradi-tional Alsatian food at this elegant restaurant on Smithe Street off Bur-rard. Golden yellow walls, café curtains, and burgundy banquettes keep things cozy. Favorite dishes, many of which also appear at lower prices at lunch, include caramel-sweet onion tart, calf's liver with garlic-spinach butter, and venison with chanterelle sauce. ⊠ *100–909 Bur-rard St.,* ☎ *604/669–4298. Reservations essential. AE, DC, MC, V. Closed Sun. No lunch Sat.*

Greek

$ ✗ **Stepho's Souvlaki.** Regulars swear by, and are quite prepared to wait in line for, Stepho's inexpensive and tasty roast lamb, moussaka, and souvlaki, served in a dark and bustling taverna. Its take-out menu is handy for picnics on the beach just down the street. ⊠ *1124 Davie St.,* ☎ *604/683–2555. Reservations not accepted. AE, MC, V.*

Italian

$$–$$$$ ✗ **Cin Cin.** Warm gold walls, high arched windows, and terra-cotta tiles give this fashionable Italian restaurant a comfortable, Tuscan air. The heated second-floor terrace, surrounded by trees, feels a long way from busy Robson Street below. The food, from the open kitchen and the wood-fired grill, oven, and rotisserie, reflects chef Romy Prasad's experience cooking in New York City, Italy, Spain, and France. The appetizer platter for two includes house-smoked trout, ahi tuna, egg-plant caviar, and wood-grilled baby octopus. Popular main dishes in-clude hot smoked-duck risotto, and roasted black sea bass. The upbeat music and the social scene around the hand-carved marble bar make for a lively atmosphere. ⊠ *1154 Robson St. (upstairs),* ☎ *604/688–7338. Reservations essential. AE, DC, MC, V. No lunch weekends.*

$$–$$$ ✗ **Borgo Antico.** Terra-cotta tiles and graceful archways give this spa-cious Gastown room a classical feel. A sister restaurant to Il Giardino di Umberto, Borgo Antico offers such Tuscan dishes as grilled calamari salad, gnocchi with artichokes and sun-dried tomatoes, veal medallions with lemon and capers, and osso buco with risotto. The wine cellar has more than 300 selections. ⊠ *321 Water St.,* ☎ *604/683–8376. Reser-vations essential. AE, DC, MC, V. Closed Sun. No lunch Sat.*

$$–$$$ ✗ **Caffé de Medici.** This elegant Northern Italian restaurant has ornate
★   molded ceilings, portraits of the Medici family, and a peaceful ambi-ence. Run by the same family (with many of the same customers) since 1980, it is—despite its location on Vancouver's most fashionable street—pleasantly free of attitude. House-made ravioli with lobster and Dungeness crab served in a thyme-infused saffron cream sauce, or spinach salad with goat cheese are recommended starters. Main courses include consistently good rack of lamb with a fresh herb crust, and grilled jumbo prawns and scallops over a mascarpone risotto. The quiet atmo-sphere and gracious service make this a good choice for business lunches or romantic dinners. ⊠ *109–1025 Robson St.,* ☎ *604/669–9322. Reservations essential. AE, MC, V. No lunch weekends.*

$$–$$$ ✗ **Il Giardino di Umberto.** This little yellow house at the end of Hornby
★   Street hides an attractive jumble of four terra-cotta–tile rooms and a vine-draped courtyard with a wood-burning oven. The Tuscan food

features grilled salmon with saffron and fennel vinaigrette, and roast reindeer loin with a wine reduction. Umberto Menghi, a long-established Vancouver restaurateur, also operates Circolo (☒ 1116 Mainland St., ☎ 604/687–1116), a modern Italian restaurant in Yaletown. ☒ *1382 Hornby St.,* ☎ *604/669–2422. Reservations essential. AE, DC, MC, V. Closed Sun. No lunch Sat.*

$$–$$$ ✗ **Piccolo Mondo Ristorante.** Soft candlelight, bountiful flower arrangements, and fine European antiques create an intimate feel at this Northern Italian restaurant on a quiet street a block off Robson. The menu changes seasonally, but favorites have included grilled spot prawns with fennel and anise seed vinaigrette, or beef tenderloin with polenta and walnut and black truffle sauce. A classic osso buco is always on the menu. The wine cellar has more than 4,000 bottles (480 varieties). ☒ *850 Thurlow St.,* ☎ *604/688–1633. Reservations essential. AE, DC, MC, V. Closed Sun. No lunch Sat.*

$$–$$$ ✗ **Villa del Lupo.** Country-house-elegant decor sets a romantic tone at this Victorian house on the edge of trendy Yaletown, home to one of Vancouver's most established Italian restaurants. The contemporary menu takes its inspiration from various regions of Italy. Canadian black cod stuffed with black tiger prawns and wrapped with Parma prosciutto, and osso buco in a sauce of tomatoes, red wine, cinnamon, and lemon are favorites here. The restaurant serves lunch only to groups of 10 or more. ☒ *869 Hamilton St.,* ☎ *604/688–7436. Reservations essential. AE, DC, MC, V. No lunch.*

Japanese

$$–$$$$ ✗ **Misaki.** Local and visiting sushi lovers head for this elegant restaurant in the Pan Pacific Hotel. With its striking black-granite sushi bar and three intimate tatami rooms, Misaki has a relaxing ambience. The chefs here specialize in edomae-style sushi, featuring fresh ingredients from the sea, but the menu also includes traditional Japanese dishes such as miso-broth hot pot, soba noodles, teppan yaki, and lobster and salmon tempura. ☒ *300–999 Canada Pl.,* ☎ *604/891–2893. AE, DC, MC, V. No lunch Sat. Closed Sun.*

$–$$ ✗ **Chiyoda.** A sushi bar and a *robata* (grill) bar curve through Chiyoda's chic modern main room: on one side are the customers and an array of flat baskets full of the day's offerings; the chefs and grills are on the other. There are usually more than 35 choices of items to grill, from black cod marinated in miso paste to squid, snapper, oysters, and shiitake mushrooms—all fresh from the market. The kitchen also turns out tempura and beef katsu (deep-fried beef). ☒ *200–1050 Alberni St.,* ☎ *604/688–5050. Reservations essential. AE, DC, MC, V. Closed Sun. No lunch Sat.*

$ ✗ **Ezogiku Noodle Cafe.** Noodles—or, more precisely, Japanese ramen noodles—are the specialty at these cheap and cheerful hole-in-the-wall cafés. The two Robson Street locations fill quickly with hungry shoppers and homesick Japanese students. Some say the noodles and soups here are just like those in Tokyo. With nothing over $10, Ezogiku offers one of the best values on this chic shopping strip. ☒ *270 Robson St., at Hamilton St.,* ☎ *604/685–9466;* ☒ *1329 Robson St., at Jervis St.,* ☎ *604/685–8606. Reservations not accepted. No credit cards.*

Mediterranean

$–$$ ✗ **Allegro Café.** Cushy curved booths, low lighting, friendly staff, and a long martini menu give this downtown place near Robson Square a romantic—even flirtatious—feel. The menu is playful, too, with such rich and offbeat concoctions as pasta bundles with roasted butternut squash and gorgonzola cream, and roast chicken breast with herbs, goat cheese, and peach-and-fig chutney. The rich daily soups and fair prices make this a good weekday lunch stop. ☒ *888 Nelson St.,* ☎ *604/683–8485. AE, DC, MC, V. No lunch weekends.*

Native American

$$–$$$ ✕ **Liliget Feast House.** This intimate downstairs room looks like the
★   interior of a longhouse, with wooden walkways across pebble floors,
contemporary First Nations art on the walls, and cedar-plank tables
with tatami-style benches. Liliget is one of the few places in the world
serving the original Northwest Coast First Nations cuisine. A feast platter lets you try most of the offerings, which include bannock bread,
baked sweet potato with hazelnuts, alder-grilled salmon, rabbit with
wild berry sauce, venison strips, oysters, mussels, and steamed fern
shoots. ⊠ *1724 Davie St.,* ☎ *604/681–7044. Reservations essential.
AE, DC, MC, V. No lunch. Closed Tues. and Wed. in Feb. and Mar.*

Pizza

$ ✕ **Incendio.** The hand-flipped thin-crust pizzas, with innovative top-
pings including Asiago cheese, prosciutto, roasted garlic, and sun-
dried tomatoes, and the mix-and-match pastas and sauces (try the hot
smoked-duck sausage, artichoke, and tomato combination, or the
mango-basil-butter sauce) draw crowds to this Gastown eatery. The
room, in a circa 1900 heritage building, with exposed brick, local artwork, and big curved windows, has plenty of atmosphere. ⊠ *103
Columbia St.,* ☎ *604/688–8694. AE, MC, V. No lunch weekends.*

Seafood

$$$–$$$$ ✕ **C.** With dishes such as ultrarare grilled ahi tuna served with potato
★   and pea samosa, roasted sablefish with Israeli couscous, and octopus–
bacon-wrapped scallops, C has established itself as Vancouver's most
innovative seafood restaurant. In addition to the lunch and dinner menus,
C has a raw bar offering sashimi, shellfish, and caviar, an elaborate
Sunday brunch, and, at weekday lunch, a West Coast seafood dim sum.
The ultramodern interior is done in cool grays (described by some as
Captain Nemo meets Zen). The patio, overlooking a marina and well
away from traffic, is a pleasant place to spend a summer afternoon.
⊠ *2–1600 Howe St.,* ☎ *604/681–1164. Reservations essential. AE,
DC, MC, V. No lunch Sat.*

$$–$$$$ ✕ **Blue Water Cafe and Raw Bar.** This fashionable Yaletown restaurant shows its architectural bones with exposed timbers, beams, and
brick that arrived here a century ago as ships' ballast. Fresh, local, well-
presented seafood is the theme here, with such catch-dependent features as Queen Charlotte Island halibut, weathervane scallops, and B.C.
sablefish. There are three bars: a main bar backed by a wall of wine,
an ice bar (surfaced in ice) serving chilled vodka, sake, and Champagne,
and the restaurant's proudest feature: a raw bar offering oysters, sushi,
sashimi, caviar, and seafood towers designed for sharing. The menu
also has meat dishes, including Canadian prime beef, as well as vegetarian options. A former loading dock makes an attractive outdoor terrace. ⊠ *1095 Hamilton St.,* ☎ *604/688–8078. AE, DC, MC, V. No
lunch in winter.*

$$–$$$$ ✕ **Joe Fortes Seafood and Chophouse.** This seafood hot spot and chop
house just off Robson Street has a piano bar, a bistro, an oyster bar,
and a delightful rooftop patio with a marquée and an herb garden.
Named for a much-loved English Bay lifeguard, Joe Fortes brings to-
gether a casual ambience, 19th-century dark wood and stained-glass
decor, and generous portions of fresh seafood. Try the cedar-smoked
salmon, Joe's cioppino (a seafood stew), or the lifeguard tower on ice—
a starter of mussels, clams, scallops, prawns, shrimp, lobster and crab
that's meant to be shared. The restaurant is a chop house, too, and it
cuts your steaks to order. ⊠ *777 Thurlow St.,* ☎ *604/669–1940.
Reservations essential. AE, D, DC, MC, V.*

$$–$$$ ✕ **Fish House in Stanley Park.** Tucked between Stanley Park's tennis courts and putting green, this 1930s former sports pavilion with a veranda and fireplace has a relaxed country-house ambience. Chef Karen Barnaby writes cookbooks, and the titles, *Pacific Passions* and *Screamingly Good Food,* say a lot about the food here, which is hearty, flavorful, and unpretentious. Good choices are the ahi tuna steak Diane or the cornhusk-wrapped salmon with a maple glaze. Before dinner head straight for the oyster bar, or arrive between 5 and 6 to take advantage of the early-bird specials. The Fish House also serves a traditional English afternoon tea between 2 and 4 daily. ✉ *8901 Stanley Park Dr., near Stanley Park's Beach Ave. entrance,* ☎ *604/681–7275. Reservations essential. AE, D, DC, MC, V.*

$–$$ ✕ **Rodney's Oyster House.** This Yaletown fishing-shack look-alike has one of the widest selection of oysters in town (up to 18 varieties), from locally harvested bivalves to exotic Japanese kumamotos. You can pick your oysters individually—they're laid out on ice behind the bar and priced at $1.50 to about $3 each—or try the clams, scallops, mussels, periwinkles, and other mollusks from the steamer kettles. Chowders and other hot dishes are on offer as well. ✉ *1228 Hamilton St.,* ☎ *604/609–0080. AE, DC, MC, V. Closed Sun.*

Greater Vancouver

Cafés

$$ ✕ **Boleto at Ecco Il Panne.** During the day, this upmarket Italian bakery serves biscotti, baked sweets, and sandwiches made with its own country breads (which you can buy by the loaf); lunch involves frittatas and other light meals. On Friday and Saturday evenings, the staff puts out tablecloths for a full dinner menu. The decor is very *Roman Holiday,* with potted palms, relief murals, and a scattering of high-backed upholstered chairs. ✉ *2563 W. Broadway,* ☎ *604/739–1314. Reservations essential for dinner. MC, V. No dinner Sun.–Thurs.*

$ ✕ **Bread Garden Bakery Café.** The Granville Street branch of this local chain is open 24 hours. ✉ *1880 W. 1st Ave., Kitsilano,* ☎ *604/738–6681; 2996 Granville St.,* ☎ *604/736–6465;* ✉ *20–601 W. Broadway,* ☎ *604/638–0883. AE, DC, MC, V.*

Casual

$–$$ ✕ **Earl's.** The Greater Vancouver offshoots of this local chain have all the features of a popular casual restaurant: wood-fired pizzas, juicy burgers, homemade desserts, comfy booths, chipper staff, and a relaxed atmosphere. ✉ *901 W. Broadway,* ☎ *604/734–5995;* ✉ *1601 W. Broadway,* ☎ *604/736–5663. AE, MC, V.*

Chinese

$$–$$$$ ✕ **Grand King Seafood.** In a city noted for its Chinese restaurants, the Grand King is widely considered one of the best. Decorated like most of the city's upmarket Cantonese establishments, with chandelier lighting and round white tables set for large groups, the Grand King emphasizes Cantonese seafood, including lobster with black bean sauce and crab claw in shrimp purée. But the large selection of nonseafood items, like ostrich slices in spicy pepper sauce and sautéed chicken with lily bulbs, is equally exciting. The best bets are the set dinner menus for groups of 2–10. The Grand King also has innovative, popular dim sum, served from the menu rather than from trolleys. ✉ *705 W. Broadway,* ☎ *604/876–7855. AE, DC, MC, V.*

$$–$$$$ ✕ **Sun Sui Wah.** Sails in the ceiling, reminiscent of Vancouver's land-
★ mark Convention and Exhibition Centre, add a lofty elegance to this bright and bustling East Side Cantonese restaurant. An offshoot of a popular Hong Kong establishment, Sun Sui Wah is best known for its

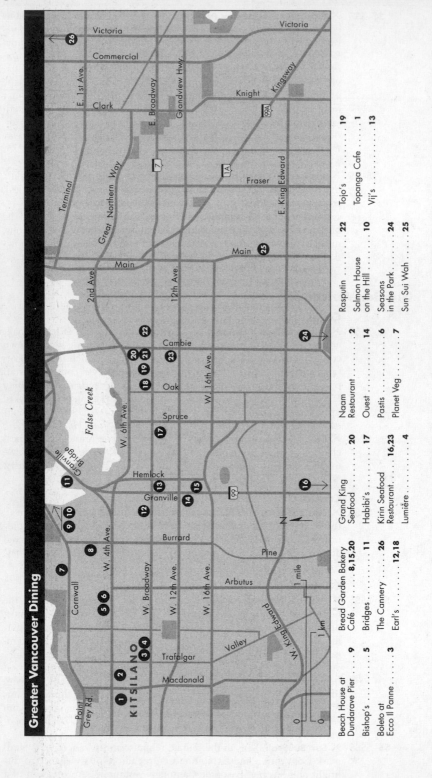

dim sum (served 10:30–3 weekdays, 10–3 on weekends), which ranges from traditional handmade dumplings to some highly adventurous offerings with Japanese touches. It's worth coming back for dinner for house specialties such as roasted squab and enormous king crab from the live tanks. There's another location in Richmond, the suburban heart of Vancouver's Chinese community. ⊠ *3888 Main St.,* ☎ *604/872–8822;* ⊠ *4940 No. 3 Rd., Richmond,* ☎ *604/273–8208. AE, MC, V, DC.*

$$–$$$ ✕ **Kirin Seafood Restaurant.** The Greater Vancouver outposts of this upscale operation focus on seafood and Cantonese creations, which are milder than the northern Chinese cuisine served at Kirin Mandarin Restaurant. Fresh dim sum is served daily at lunchtime. ⊠ *555 W. 12th Ave., 2nd floor,* ☎ *604/879–8038;* ⊠ *2nd floor, 3 West Centre, 7900 Westminster Hwy., Richmond,* ☎ *604/303–8833;* ⊠ *1163 Pinetree Way, Coquitlam,* ☎ *604/944–8833. AE, DC, MC, V.*

Contemporary

$$$–$$$$ ✕ **Bishop's.** One of Vancouver's most highly regarded restaurants, this
★ refined Kitsilano room serves West Coast cuisine with an emphasis on organic, regional produce. The menu changes seasonally, but highlights have included such starters as tea-smoked duck breast with apple and celeriac salad, and intriguing main courses like steamed smoked black cod with scallion potato cake, and Dungeness crab cakes with pear and sun-dried cranberry chutney. All are beautifully presented and impeccably served. The split-level room displays elaborate flower arrangements and selections from owner John Bishop's extensive art collection. ⊠ *2183 W. 4th Ave.,* ☎ *604/738–2025. Reservations essential. AE, DC, MC, V. No lunch. Closed 1st wk in Jan.*

$$$–$$$$ ✕ **Bridges.** On summer afternoons, locals hang out on the massive outdoor deck of this three-in-one restaurant complex on Granville Island, near the public market. Overlooking False Creek, the deck serves casual bistro fare, such as burgers, sandwiches, and quesadillas. Indoors and upstairs, a more formal restaurant serves West Coast cuisine with an emphasis on seafood. The menu features salmon, sea bass, lobster, and lamb dishes. Exposed beams in the high ceiling contrast with the elegant rosewood paneling and white tablecloths. French doors open onto another deck, perched high above the marina, but the tall windows mean views are good from anywhere in the room. Bridges has a cozy pub on the main floor. Reservations are essential for the restaurant; bistro reservations are not accepted May through September. ⊠ *1696 Duranleau St.,* ☎ *604/687–4400. AE, DC, MC, V. Restaurant: no lunch Mon.–Sat.; closed Sun. and Jan.–Feb.*

$$–$$$ ✕ **Beach House at Dundarave Pier.** It's worth the drive over the Lions Gate Bridge to West Vancouver for an evening at this 1912 seaside house. Whether inside the lofty room or outside on the heated beachside patio, virtually every table has expansive views over Burrard Inlet and Stanley Park. The Pacific Rim menu changes frequently, but the chef favors updated versions of the classics, with a variety of innovative game and seafood entrées. After dinner, you can take a stroll along the pier or the seaside walkway. ⊠ *150–25th St., West Vancouver,* ☎ *604/922–1414. Reservations essential. AE, DC, MC, V.*

$$–$$$ ✕ **Seasons in the Park.** Two levels of seating and tall windows allow every table here a commanding view over the gardens in Queen Elizabeth Park, to the city and mountains beyond. Light-wood furnishings and white tablecloths in the comfortable dining room make for an elegant atmosphere that is mirrored in the contemporary Pacific Northwest fare. Menu highlights include such innovative items as seared Chilean sea bass with grapes, pecans, crispy sage, and pinot noir sauce, as well as such standards as confit of Muscovy duck. Weekend brunch is popular, and there's a heated patio for year-round outdoor dining.

⊠ *Queen Elizabeth Park, W. 33rd Ave. and Cambie St.,* ☎ *604/874–8008 or 800/632–9422. Reservations essential. AE, MC, V.*

French

$$$$ ✕ **Lumière.** The contemporary French cuisine at this light and airy Kit-
★   silano restaurant isn't so much served as it's orchestrated, arranged in
one of chef Robert Feenie's frequently changing 8- to 11-course set
menus. The tasting menu features a cross-section of the chef's creations
with such dishes as seared scallops with truffle buerre blanc, leek and
mascarpone ravioli, and roasted duck breast with glazed spices on
Israeli couscous with duck confit. A seafood menu makes the most of
what's at the docks that day, and a vegetarian selection, with courses
such as wild-mushroom torte and passion-fruit sorbet with hibiscus
jus, elevates meatless dining to haute cuisine. The 11-course signature
menu is a memorable dining experience, as is an evening at the chef's
table when it's available. It's also possible to sample individual dishes
at the bar or choose a three-course meal from the à la carte menu. ⊠
2551 W. Broadway, ☎ *604/739–8185. Reservations essential. AE, DC,
MC, V. Closed Mon. No lunch.*

$$$–$$$$ ✕ **Ouest.** Ouest (French for "west") serves contemporary French cui-
sine with New World innovations in a chic modern room on South
Granville. Some highlights on the seasonally changing menu include
roast lingcod with ragout of Manila clams; roast saddle of rabbit with
black trumpets, pearl barley, and truffle velouté; and loin of venison
with celeriac purée and chocolate sauce. The decor is sleek and urban,
with warm, camel-colored leather on the walls and chairs, a cherrywood
bar, marble flooring, high ceilings, and generous table spacing. The
kitchen is visible, but a glass partition keeps the dining room peace-
ful. The wine selection, featuring French and New World varieties and
a good choice of half bottles, is so extensive the waiters need ladders
to reach some of the vintages. ⊠ *2881 Granville St.,* ☎ *604/738–8938.
AE, DC, MC, V. No lunch.*

$$–$$$ ✕ **Pastis.** This intimate, candlelit Kitsilano bistro created a stir as soon
as it opened in early 1999. The simple decor of brown wicker chairs
and white tablecloths belies the elegance of the food. Try the fig and
Belgian endive salad with Roquefort and hazelnut vinaigrette; the
roasted duck breast and Québec foie gras with Belgian endive, plums,
and honey-lime reduction; or the grilled Atlantic salmon fillet with a
jus of saffron and pearl onion, layered with pea shoots and smoked
salmon. The three- and five-course set menus are good values, and the
bistro offers one of the largest selections of wine by the glass in the
city. A cozy eight-seat bar area is ideal for single diners. ⊠ *2153 W.
4th Ave.,* ☎ *604/731–5020. Reservations essential. AE, MC, V. No
lunch.*

Indian

$$ ✕ **Vij's.** Vikram Vij, the genial proprietor of Vancouver's most inno-
★   vative Indian restaurant, uses local ingredients and Western ideas to
create exciting takes on the cuisines of the subcontinent. Highlights on
the brief, seasonally changing menu include garlic and fenugreek ri-
cotta-filled pastries in Bengali sauce, and Portobello mushrooms in fennel curry, as well as main dishes like pork medallions in garam masala
cream curry. The dishes are far from traditional but are spiced beautifully, allowing exotic flavors such as mango, tamarind, and fenugreek
to shine through. The simple room, with bare walls, Indian antiques,
and warm lighting from lanterns, doesn't detract from the art on the
plate. You can enjoy snacks and drinks in the lounge while you wait
for your table. ⊠ *1480 W. 11th Ave.,* ☎ *604/736–6664. Reservations
not accepted. AE, DC, MC, V. No lunch.*

Japanese

$$–$$$ ✕ **Tojo's.** Hidekazu Tojo is a sushi-making legend in Vancouver, with
★ more than 2,000 special preparations stored in his creative mind. His
handsome tatami rooms on the second floor of a modern green-glass
tower on West Broadway provide the proper ambience for intimate dining, but Tojo's 10-seat sushi bar is a convivial ringside seat for watching the creation of edible art. Reserve the spot at the end for the best
view. ✉ *202–777 W. Broadway,* ☎ *604/872–8050. Reservations essential. AE, DC, MC, V. Closed Sun. No lunch.*

Middle Eastern

$ ✕ **Habibi's.** The Lebanese home cooking at this family-run café is one
of the area's best values. All the dishes are vegetarian, all are lovingly
prepared, and all are the same price—just $6.50. Most of the dishes
are meze-size and eaten as dips with warm pita bread. The idea is to
try several, and experiment with such specialties as *lebneh* (a yogurt
cheese with spices), *balila* (warm chickpeas with garlic and olive oil),
and *warak anab* (rice-stuffed grape leaves marinated in lemon juice).
Wooden booths, soft blues music, and family photos from the old country make a welcome change from most eateries in this price range. ✉
1128 W. Broadway, ☎ *604/732–7487. Reservations not accepted. V.
No lunch. Closed Sun.*

Russian

$$–$$$ ✕ **Rasputin.** Don't let the glowering portrait of Rasputin on the wall
put you off—this place is fun, and meals here are long and joyous occasions. The borscht, served with sour cream and a garnish of herbs
and dill, is rich and flavorful. The towering appetizer arrangements,
featuring salmon caviar with crêpes, smoked salmon, and chopped egg,
are meant for sharing, and the main dishes, including kebabs, cabbage
rolls, handmade pierogi, and trout stuffed with couscous pilaf, are consistently top-notch. The bar stocks 40 kinds of vodka, and musicians
playing balalaikas, or Gypsy violins (often backed up by the regulars
in good voice), perform six nights a week. ✉ *457 W. Broadway,* ☎
604/879–6675. AE, DC, MC, V. No lunch.

Seafood

$$–$$$ ✕ **The Cannery.** This long-established East Side favorite has striking
views over the harbor and the mountains beyond. Though the tables
are set with white linen and china, the rustic nautical decor, including
a retired fishing boat out front, gives a pretty clear indication of the
specialty here. Vegetarian and meat options are available, but most diners come for the seafood classics: bouillabaisse, Dungeness crab, Nova
Scotia lobster, treats from the daily fresh sheet, or The Cannery's signature salmon Wellington with a pinot-noir sauce. ✉ *2205 Commissioner St. (north foot of Victoria Dr., then right on Commissioner),* ☎
*604/254–9606 or 877/254–9606. Reservations essential. AE, D, DC,
MC, V. No lunch weekends.*

$$–$$$ ✕ **Salmon House on the Hill.** Perched halfway up a mountain in West
Vancouver, this restaurant has stunning water and city views by day,
and expansive vistas of city lights by night. The Salmon House is best
known for its alder-grilled salmon, though the grilled oysters, British
Columbia prawns, and treats from the daily fresh sheet are also tempting. The Northwest Coast First Nations–theme decor is tastefully done,
though it can hardly compete with what's outside the windows. The
Salmon House is about 15 to 30 minutes from Vancouver by car (depending on traffic). Go over the Lions Gate Bridge and take the Folkestone Way exit off Highway 1 west. ✉ *2229 Folkestone Way, West
Vancouver,* ☎ *604/926–3212. Reservations essential. AE, DC, MC, V.*

Tex-Mex

$–$$ ✕ **Topanga Café.** The California-style Mexican food at this 40-seat Kitsilano classic hasn't changed much since 1978, when the Topanga started dishing up fresh salsa and homemade tortilla chips. Quantities are still huge and prices low. Kids can color blank menu covers while waiting for their food; a hundred of their best efforts are framed on the walls. The summer patio is popular. ⊠ *2904 W. 4th Ave.,* ☎ *604/ 733–3713. Reservations not accepted. MC, V. Closed Sun.*

Vegetarian

$ ✕ **Naam Restaurant.** Vancouver's oldest natural-foods eatery is open 24 hours, so if you need to satisfy a late-night craving for a veggie burger, rest easy. The Naam also serves vegetarian stir-fries, wicked chocolate desserts, and wine, beer, cappuccinos, and fresh juices. Wood tables, an open fireplace, and live blues, folk, and jazz every evening create a homey atmosphere. On warm summer evenings you can sit in the outdoor courtyard. ⊠ *2724 W. 4th Ave.,* ☎ *604/738–7151. AE, MC, V.*

$ ✕ **Planet Veg.** The influences on the fare at this fast-food restaurant range as far afield as India, Mexico, and the Mediterranean. Among the most inspired cheap eats to be found in Kitsilano are the roti rolls, spicy treats in Indian flatbread that are fun, filling, and an excellent value. Eat in, or gather a picnic to take to nearby Kits Beach. ⊠ *1941 Cornwall Ave.,* ☎ *604/734–1001. Reservations not accepted. No credit cards.*

LODGING

Vancouver hotels, especially the more expensive properties downtown, contain fairly comparable facilities. Unless otherwise noted, expect to find the following amenities: minibars, in-room movies, no-smoking rooms and/or floors, room service, massage, baby-sitting, laundry service and dry cleaning, concierge, business services, meeting rooms, and parking (there's usually an additional fee). Lodgings in the inexpensive-to-moderate category generally do not have these amenities. The chart below shows high-season prices, but from mid-October through May, rates throughout the city can drop as much as 50%.

CATEGORY	COST*
$$$$	over $200
$$$	$150–$200
$$	$100–$150
$	under $100

All prices are in Canadian dollars, for a standard double room, excluding 10% room tax and 7% GST.

$$$$ ▣ **Delta Pinnacle.** The soaring 50-ft-high atrium lobby makes a striking entrance to this 38-story hotel a block from the cruise-ship terminal and central business district. Decorated in modern pale woods and neutral tones, each room has almost a full wall of windows. The rooms on the north side of the 17th floor and above have panoramic views of Burrard Inlet and the North Shore Mountains. The hotel's Show Case restaurant and bar serves up West Coast cuisine with global influences. ⊠ *1128 W. Hastings St., V6E 4R5,* ☎ *604/684–1128,* ℻ *604/639– 4027,* ⓦⓔⓑ *www.deltapinnacle.bc.ca. 424 rooms, 10 suites. Restaurant, bar, café, in-room data ports, in-room safes, in-room VCRs, minibars, no-smoking floor, room service, indoor lap pool, hot tub, massage, sauna, steam room, gym, shops, concierge, concierge floor, business services, meeting rooms, parking (fee). AE, DC, MC, V.*

$$$$ ▣ **Delta Vancouver Suites.** Attached to the city's newest conference center (the Morris J. Wosk Centre for Dialogue), this modern luxury hotel is a nice example of early millennial chic. The striking marble and cherry-wood lobby soars four stories. The suites have blond art deco furnishings, floor-to-ceiling windows, movable work tables, high-speed Internet access, and sliding doors or Japanese screens to close off the bedroom. Slightly pricier Signature Club suites offer a private lounge, Continental breakfast, evening refreshments, and turndown service. The hotel's restaurant, Manhattan, is hidden away from the madding crowd. ⊠ *550 W. Hastings St., V6B 1L6,* ☎ *604/689–8188 or 888/663–8811,* FAX *604/605–8881,* WEB *www.deltavancouversuites.ca. 7 rooms, 219 suites. Restaurant, lobby lounge, in-room data ports, indoor pool, hot tub, sauna, gym, shops, convention center, parking (fee). AE, D, DC, MC, V.*

$$$$ 🏨 **Fairmont Hotel Vancouver.** The copper roof of this 1939 château-
★ style hotel dominates Vancouver's skyline. Even the standard guest rooms have an air of prestige, with high ceilings, mahogany furniture, sitting areas, and down duvets. Rooms on the Entrée Gold floor have extra services, including a private lounge and its own concierge. A full-service salon and day spa add to the pampering. ⊠ *900 W. Georgia St., V6C 2W6,* ☎ *604/684–3131 or 800/441–1414,* FAX *604/662–1929,* WEB *www.fairmont.com. 556 rooms, 42 suites. 2 restaurants, lobby lounge, in-room data ports, indoor lap pool, wading pool, hair salon, hot tub, sauna, spa, health club, shops, car rental. AE, D, DC, MC, V.*

$$$$ 🏨 **The Fairmont Waterfront.** An underground walkway leads from this striking 23-story glass hotel to Vancouver's Convention and Exhibition Centre and cruise-ship terminal. Views from the lobby and from 70% of the guest rooms are of Burrard Inlet, Stanley Park, and the North Shore Mountains. Other rooms look onto a terraced herb garden. The spacious rooms have big picture windows and are attractively furnished with blond-wood furniture and contemporary Canadian artwork. Large corner rooms have the best views. Rooms on the Entrée Gold floor have extra amenities, including in-room safes, a private lounge, and a concierge ⊠ *900 Canada Pl. Way, V6C 3L5,* ☎ *604/691–1991 or 800/441–1414,* FAX *604/691–1999,* WEB *www.fairmont.com. 489 rooms, 29 suites. Restaurant, lobby lounge, pool, hot tub, massage, sauna, steam room, gym, car rental. AE, D, DC, MC, V.*

$$$$ 🏨 **Four Seasons.** This 30-story downtown luxury hotel is famous for
★ pampering guests. The lobby is lavish, with seemingly acres of couches and a fountain in the lounge. Standard rooms, with understated black-and-cream or rust-and-cream color schemes and marble bathroom fixtures, are elegantly furnished, as are the roomier corner rooms with sitting areas. The two opulent split-level suites are handy for putting up visiting royalty. Service at the Four Seasons is top-notch, and the attention to detail is outstanding. The many amenities include free evening limousine service. The formal dining room, Chartwell, is one of the best in the city. ⊠ *791 W. Georgia St., V6C 2T4,* ☎ *604/689–9333,* FAX *604/684–4555,* WEB *www.fourseasons.com. 318 rooms, 67 suites. 2 restaurants, lobby lounge, in-room data ports, indoor-outdoor pool, hot tub, sauna, gym, children's programs, business services, meeting rooms, parking (fee). AE, D, DC, MC, V.*

$$$$ 🏨 **Granville Island Hotel.** Granville Island is one of Vancouver's more entertaining neighborhoods, but unless you've moored up in your own houseboat, the only overnight option is the Granville Island Hotel. The exterior of this modern water's-edge hotel looks like it's made of Lego toy blocks; inside, the decor is more refined, with marble floors and Persian rugs in the lobby and guest rooms. Most rooms have water views, and all have big soaking tubs. Rooms on the top floor (the third) have small balconies. The corridor overlooks vats brewing away for the fashionable brew pub and restaurant downstairs. Rooms that don't overlook the pub's summertime patio are the quietest. Thirty rooms

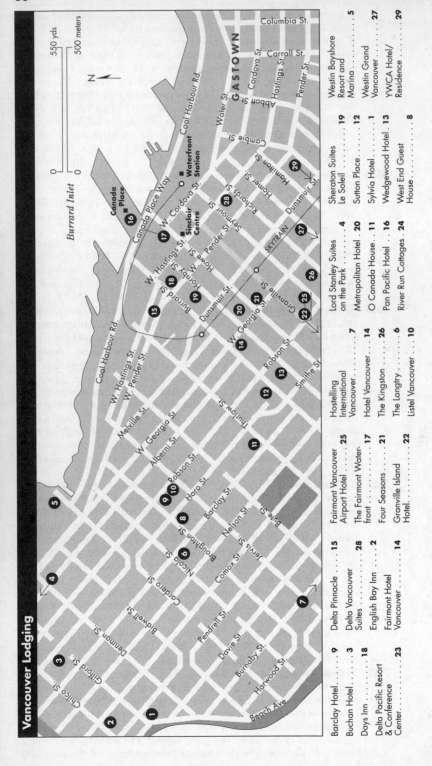

Vancouver Lodging

Barclay Hotel **9**
Buchan Hotel **3**
Days Inn **18**
Delta Pacific Resort & Conference Center **23**

Delta Pinnacle **15**
Delta Vancouver Suites **28**
English Bay Inn **2**
Fairmont Hotel Vancouver **14**

Fairmont Vancouver Airport Hotel . . . **25**
The Fairmont Waterfront **17**
Four Seasons **21**
Granville Island Hotel **22**

Hostelling International Vancouver **7**
Hotel Vancouver . . . **14**
The Kingston **26**
The Langtry **6**
Listel Vancouver . . . **10**

Lord Stanley Suites on the Park **4**
Metropolitan Hotel . . **20**
O Canada House . . . **11**
Pan Pacific Hotel . . **16**
River Run Cottages . . **24**

Sheraton Suites Le Soleil **19**
Sutton Place **12**
Sylvia Hotel **1**
Wedgewood Hotel . . **13**
West End Guest House **8**

Westin Bayshore Resort and Marina **5**
Westin Grand Vancouver **27**
YWCA Hotel/ Residence **29**

in a 2001 addition include two large (1,000 sq. ft) penthouse suites, each with a hot tub, kitchen, jet tub, and fireplace. ✉ *1253 Johnston St., V6H 3R9,* ☎ *604/683–7373 or 800/663–1840,* FAX *604/683–3061,* WEB *www.granvilleislandhotel.com. 83 rooms, 2 suites. Restaurant, pub, in-room data ports, hot tub, sauna, billiards, meeting rooms. AE, DC, MC, V.*

$$$$ ⊞ **Metropolitan Hotel.** The structure was built in 1984 as the Mandarin Oriental Hotel, based on the principles of feng shui, and those precepts have been respected in all renovations since. The spacious rooms are decorated in muted colors, and public areas have Asian art. All rooms have high-speed Internet access and business-class rooms come with printers, fax machines, and cordless phones. Standard rooms have bathrobes, newspapers, down comforters, and other luxury amenities. The popular junior suites are even bigger and only slightly more expensive than standard rooms. You can catch glimpses of the hotel's restaurant, Diva at the Met, through an etched-glass wall in the lobby. ✉ *645 Howe St., V6C 2Y9,* ☎ *604/687–1122 or 800/667–2300,* FAX *604/643–7267,* WEB *www.metropolitan.com. 179 rooms, 18 suites. Restaurant, bar, in-room data ports, indoor lap pool, hot tub, sauna, steam room (men only), gym, racquetball. AE, D, DC, MC, V.*

$$$$ ⊞ **Pan Pacific Hotel.** A centerpiece of the waterfront Canada Place, the
★ luxurious Pan Pacific is convenient to the Vancouver Convention and Exhibition Centre and Vancouver's main cruise-ship terminal. Among the dramatic features of the three-story atrium lobby are a totem pole and waterfall. The lounge, restaurant, and café all have huge windows with views of the harbor and mountains. Eighty percent of the rooms have water views, and all have high-speed Internet access. ✉ *300–999 Canada Pl., V6C 3B5,* ☎ *604/662–8111; 800/663–1515 in Canada; 800/937–1515 in the U.S.;* FAX *604/685–8690,* WEB *www.panpac.com. 504 rooms, 39 suites. 3 restaurants, coffee shop, lobby lounge, in-room data ports, in-room safes, pool, hair salon, hot tub, outdoor hot tub, sauna, spa, steam room, aerobics, health club, indoor track, racquetball, squash, billiards, business services, convention center, travel services. AE, DC, MC, V.*

$$$$ ⊞ **Sheraton Suites Le Soleil.** Cozy and stylish, this boutique hotel, opened in spring 1999 in the central business district, is popular with independent travelers and businesspeople. Neither tour groups nor conventions book here, and the staff prides itself on attentive, personal service. The golden yellow decor and intimate fireplace in the Neoclassical lobby, and the vibrant gold and crimson fabrics in the guest rooms—most are small suites—radiate warmth. With lots of luxurious touches, such as 300-thread-count Egyptian cotton sheets, marble bathrooms, and custom-designed Biedermeier-style furniture, Le Soleil is also the first hotel in Canada with Internet TV, offering unlimited Web use. Two penthouse suites have 24-ft ceilings and wraparound terraces. The hotel doesn't have a pool or fitness facilities, but guests have access to the YWCA next door. The hotel's restaurant, Oritalia, is highly regarded. ✉ *567 Hornby St., V6C 2E8,* ☎ *604/632–3000,* FAX *604/632–3001,* WEB *www.lesoleilhotel.com. 10 rooms, 112 suites. Restaurant, bar, in-room data ports, in-room safes, room service, concierge, business services, meeting rooms. AE, DC, MC, V.*

$$$$ ⊞ **Sutton Place.** The feel here is more of an exclusive European guest
★ house than a large modern hotel. Guest rooms are furnished with rich, dark woods, and the service is gracious and attentive. The hotel's Fleuri restaurant is known for its French Continental cuisine, Sunday brunch, and weekend evening chocoholic bar. A full European health spa (also open to nonguests) offers Le Stone therapy—a massage using river stones—as well as wraps, facials, manicures, reflexology, and massage therapy. La Grande Residence (part of Sutton Place), an apart-

ment hotel suitable for stays of at least a week, is next door, at 855 Burrard. ✉ *845 Burrard St., V6Z 2K6,* ☎ *604/682–5511 or 800/961–7555,* FAX *604/682–5513,* WEB *www.suttonplace.com. 350 rooms, 47 suites, 164 apartments. Restaurant, bar, indoor lap pool, hot tub, sauna (women only), spa, steam room (men only), health club. AE, D, DC, MC, V.*

$$$$ 🏨 **Wedgewood Hotel.** The small, lavish Wedgewood is run by an
★ owner who cares fervently about her guests. The lobby and guest rooms are decorated in a traditional European style with original artwork and antiques selected by the proprietor on her European travels. Guest rooms are capacious and each has a balcony, a bar, and a desk. The four penthouse suites have fireplaces. All the extra touches are here, too: afternoon ice delivery, dark-out drapes, robes, and a morning newspaper. The turndown service incudes homemade cookies and bottled water. The sensuous Bacchus restaurant and lounge is in the lobby. ✉ *845 Hornby St., V6Z 1V1,* ☎ *604/689–7777 or 800/663–0666,* FAX *604/608–5348,* WEB *www.wedgewoodhotel.com. 51 rooms, 38 suites. Restaurant, lobby lounge, in-room data ports, in-room safes, sauna, gym, meeting rooms. AE, D, DC, MC, V.*

$$$$ 🏨 **Westin Bayshore Resort and Marina.** Perched on the best part of the harbor, adjacent to Stanley Park, the Bayshore has truly fabulous views. The rooms in the tower have small balconies and 90° mountain and harbor views; those in the main building feature floor-to-ceiling windows, and many of these rooms also have striking views. The only downtown resort hotel, this is the perfect place to stay in warm weather, especially for families, because of its extensive recreational facilities. A development completed in 2000 added a convention center, marina, and attractive landscaping, including gardens, waterfalls, and ponds. Fishing charters and sightseeing cruises are available from the Bayshore, which is connected to Stanley Park and the Vancouver Convention and Exhibition Centre via seaside walkway. ✉ *1601 Bayshore Dr. (off Cardero St.), V6G 2V4,* ☎ *604/682–3377,* FAX *604/691–6980,* WEB *www.westin.com. 478 rooms, 32 suites. 2 restaurants, 2 bars, coffee shop, 1 indoor and 1 outdoor pool, hot tub, massage, sauna, steam room, aerobics, gym, jogging, boating, fishing, bicycles, shops, piano, children's programs, convention center, travel services. AE, DC, MC, V.*

$$$$ 🏨 **Westin Grand Vancouver.** With its strikingly minimalist decor, cherry-wood and marble lobby, and all-suites layout, the Westin Grand, shaped like a grand piano, is one of the more stylish of the many hotels that have opened here since 1999. Most of the compact studios and one-bedroom suites have floor-to-ceiling windows with skyline views, and all units have fully equipped kitchenettes with microwaves and dishwashers tucked into armoires. Corner suites are larger and have small balconies. Office suites come with a combination fax–photocopier–printer; all rooms have high-speed Internet access. The hotel is close to the main sports and entertainment district and to the fashionable restaurants of Yaletown. ✉ *433 Robson St., V6B 6L9,* ☎ *604/602–1999 or 888/680–9393,* FAX *604/647–2502,* WEB *www.westingrandvancouver.com. 23 rooms, 184 suites. Restaurant, bar, in-room data ports, kitchenettes, outdoor lap pool, outdoor hot tub, sauna, steam room, gym, nightclub, piano, children's programs, travel services. AE, DC, MC, V.*

$$$–$$$$ 🏨 **English Bay Inn.** Antiques furnish these two beautifully decorated 1930s
★ Tudor-style houses a block from the ocean and Stanley Park. One house, the original inn, has an ornate Gothic dining table in the breakfast room, a parlor with wing chairs, a fireplace, a gilt Louis XV clock and candelabra, and a tiny Italianate garden out back. The guest rooms are just as lavish: three have sleigh beds, one has a romantic four-poster, and the suite has a loft bedroom with its own fireplace. The equally beau-

tiful Chilco House across the street is decorated in traditional French style with warm colors and rich fabrics. It opens onto a small park and has its own sitting and breakfast room. The suite here is especially lavish, with brocade drapes and bed curtains and a wood-burning fireplace. Full breakfast is included, and port and sherry are served each afternoon and evening at both houses. ⊠ *1968 Comox St., V6G 1R4,* ☎ *604/683–8002,* FAX *604/683–8089,* WEB *www.englishbayinn.com. 6 rooms, 2 suites. Free parking. No smoking. AE, MC, V.*

$$$–$$$$ 🔢 **Fairmont Vancouver Airport Hotel.** Airport hotels don't get more convenient than this. The Fairmont is in the Vancouver International Airport terminal building; the lobby is reached via an overhead walkway from the U.S. departures level. Rooms and public areas are decorated in a minimalist art deco–style, with pale woods, calming neutrals, extensive use of local cedar and slate, and artworks commissioned from local artists. All rooms have soaker tubs, shower stalls, and free high-speed Internet access; they also have floor-to-ceiling windows, the triple-pane construction that provides near-perfect soundproofing. Rooms on the north side have mountain views. A health club is free for guests and is open to nonguests for $15. There's also a full-service day spa for pre- or post-flight pampering. ⊠ *Vancouver International Airport, Box 23798, Richmond V7B 1X9,* ☎ *604/207–5200,* FAX *604/ 248–3219,* WEB *www.fairmont.com. 390 rooms, 2 suites. Restaurant, bar, in-room data ports, in-room safes, indoor pool, hot tub, wading pool, massage, sauna, spa, health club, piano, concierge, concierge floor, business services, meeting rooms. AE, DC, MC, V.*

$$$–$$$$ 🔢 **O Canada House.** Designated as a Heritage Site by the city of Van-
★   couver, this beautifully restored 1897 Victorian within walking distance of downtown is where the first version of *O Canada,* the national anthem, was written in 1909. Each spacious bedroom is appointed with late-Victorian antiques; modern comforts such as in-room VCRs, phones, and bathrobes make things homey. The top-floor room is enormous, with two double beds and a private sitting area. A separate one-room coach house in the garden is the most romantic option. Full breakfast is included, and guests have the use of a pantry and a parlor with a fireplace. ⊠ *1114 Barclay St., V6E 1H1,* ☎ *604/688–0555 or 877/688–1114,* FAX *604/488–0556,* WEB *www.ocanadahouse.com. 7 rooms. Free parking. No smoking. MC, V.*

$$$ $$$$ 🔢 **River Run Cottages.** A unique bed-and-breakfast, River Run sits in
★   the serene Fraser River delta in the village of Ladner, a 30-minute drive south of downtown, 10 minutes north of the ferry terminal, and near Highway 99 on the way from Seattle. The accommodations include a little gem of a floating house; a loft with a Japanese soaking tub on the deck and a cozy captain's bed; and two river's-edge cottages, each with a fireplace and a deck over the water. A TV and VCR are available on request. Full breakfast and afternoon refreshments are included in the rates at this nonsmoking property. ⊠ *4551 River Rd. W, Ladner V4K 1R9,* ☎ *604/946–7778,* FAX *604/940–1970,* WEB *www.river-runcottages.com. 2 rooms, 2 suites. Refrigerator, boating, bicycles, free parking. MC, V. BP.*

$$–$$$$ 🔢 **West End Guest House.** This Victorian house, built in 1906, is a true
★   "painted lady," from its gracious front parlor, cozy fireplace, and early 1900s furniture to its bright pink exterior. Most of the handsome rooms have high brass beds, antiques, and gorgeous linens, as well as TVs and phones; two larger rooms have gas fireplaces. The inn is in a residential neighborhood, a two-minute walk from Robson Street. Room rates include full breakfast. Book by March for summer. ⊠ *1362 Haro St., V6E 1G2,* ☎ *604/681–2889 or 888/546–3327,* FAX *604/ 688–8812,* WEB *www.westendguesthouse.com. 8 rooms. Bicycles, free parking. No smoking. AE, D, MC, V.*

$$$ ⊡ **Delta Pacific Resort & Conference Center.** The recreational facilities make this 14-acre site a resort: three swimming pools (one indoor, with a 225-ft-long water slide), two squash courts, four tennis courts, aqua-exercise classes, outdoor volleyball nets, a play center and summer camps for children, and a playground. The hotel, 15 minutes from the airport and about a 30-minute drive south of downtown Vancouver, is large but casual and friendly. Guest rooms are modern, with contemporary decor and offer mountain or city views. ⊠ *10251 St. Edwards Dr., Richmond V6X 2M9,* ☎ *604/278–9611 or 800/268–1133,* FAX *604/276–1121,* WEB *www.deltapacific.bc.ca. 434 rooms, 4 suites. 2 restaurants, lobby lounge, 3 pools, hair salon, hot tub, massage, sauna, 4 tennis courts, gym, squash, bicycles, children's programs, convention center, airport shuttle, parking (fee). AE, DC, MC, V.*

$$$ ⊡ **The Langtry.** Inside this 1939 former apartment building near Robson Street and Stanley Park are five apartment-size suites furnished with antiques (including a Jacobean sofa and chair in one suite) and equipped with complete kitchens and dining areas, feather beds, and private phone lines. Host Haike Kingma sets out a beautiful breakfast table (full breakfast is included) in the dining room, or will deliver it to your suite if you prefer. He can also book sightseeing and outdoor adventures around town. The Langtry, named for British stage actress Lily Langtry (1853–1929), is completely no-smoking. ⊠ *968 Nicola St., V6G 2C8,* ☎ *604/687–7798,* FAX *604/687–7892,* WEB *www.thelangtry.com. 5 suites. In-room fax, in-room VCRs, coin laundry, travel services, free parking. MC, V.*

$$$ ⊡ **Lord Stanley Suites on the Park.** Here's a secret: these small, attractive, fully equipped suites built in 1998 on the edge of Stanley Park are privately owned and thus charge less than a comparable hotel for a nightly stay (weekly rates are even better). Each suite has an office nook as well as a sitting room, one or two bedrooms, a galley kitchen, and a washer/dryer. Each suite overlooking busy Georgia Street has an enclosed sunroom; those backing onto quieter Alberni Street have balconies. You can find many good restaurants on Denman Street, a block away. A Continental breakfast is included. ⊠ *1889 Alberni St.,* ☎ *604/688–9299 or 888/767–7829,* FAX *604/688–9297,* WEB *www.lord-stanley.com. 100 suites. In-room data ports, in-room VCRs, no-smoking floor, sauna, gym, meeting rooms, parking (fee). AE, DC, MC, V.*

$$–$$$ ⊡ **Days Inn.** Opened as the Abbotsford in 1920, this six-story hotel is one of the few moderately priced hotels in the business district, and it's conveniently close to the convention center and the U.S. consulate. Rooms are bright, clean, and utilitarian, with phones, TVs, and mini-refrigerators. The two-bedroom–one-bathroom units are a good value for groups and families. There's no room service or air-conditioning, but in-room data ports and voice mail are available. ⊠ *921 W. Pender St., V6C 1M2,* ☎ *604/681–4335 or 877/681–4335,* FAX *604/681–7808,* WEB *www.daysinnvancouver.com. 80 rooms, 5 suites. Restaurant, lounge, fans, in-room data ports, in-room safes, coin laundry. AE, D, DC, MC, V.*

$–$$ ⊡ **Barclay Hotel.** A great location, low rates, and such basic amenities as in-room phones and TVs (though no elevator) make this three-story former apartment building one of the city's best-value pension-style hotels. The guest rooms, with white painted furniture and orange bedspreads, are clean if basic, but the 1930s building, with its wide corridors, skylights, and mahogany staircase, has a certain old-world charm. The Barclay is steps from the shops and restaurants of Robson Street, and a 15-minute walk to either the business district or Stanley Park. Most of the front rooms overlooking Robson Street have mountain views, but the back rooms are quieter. ⊠ *1348 Robson St., V6E 1C5,* ☎ *604/688–8850,* FAX *604/688–2534,* WEB *www.barclayhotel.com. 65 rooms, 20 suites. Breakfast room, no-smoking floor, refrigerators (some), concierge, parking (fee). AE, D, DC, MC, V.*

$–$$ ⊡ **Buchan Hotel.** The three-story Buchan, built in the 1930s, sits on a tree-lined residential street a block from Stanley Park. The hotel's rooms have basic furnishings, ceiling fans, and color TVs, but no phones or air-conditioning. The lounge has a fireplace, and there's storage for bikes and skis. The 35 pension-style rooms with shared baths may be the most affordable accommodations near downtown. The Buchan doesn't have an elevator. Zev's, a fashionable restaurant with an outdoor courtyard, is on the main floor. ⊠ *1906 Haro St., V6G 1H7,* ☎ *604/685–5354 or 800/668–6654,* [FAX] *604/685–5367,* [WEB] *www.buchanhotel.com. 55 rooms, 25 with bath. Restaurant, coin laundry. No smoking. AE, DC, MC, V.*

$–$$ ⊡ **The Kingston.** Convenient to shopping, the Kingston is an old-style four-story building, the type of establishment you'd find in Europe. Small and immaculate, the spartan rooms all have phones; some rooms have TVs and private baths. Continental breakfast is included. ⊠ *757 Richards St., V6B 3A6,* ☎ *604/684–9024 or 888/713–3304,* [FAX] *604/ 684–9917,* [WEB] *www.kingstonhotelvancouver.com. 55 rooms, 9 with bath. Breakfast room, pub, no-smoking floor, room service, sauna, coin laundry. AE, MC, V.*

$–$$ ⊡ **Sylvia Hotel.** To stay at the Sylvia June through August, you need to book six months to a year ahead. This ivy-covered 1912 building is popular because of its low rates and near-perfect location: about 25 ft from the beach on scenic English Bay, 200 ft from Stanley Park, and a 20-minute walk from Robson Street. The unadorned rooms all have private baths, phones, and TVs. Some suites are huge, and all have kitchens. ⊠ *1154 Gilford St., V6G 2P6,* ☎ *604/681–9321,* [FAX] *604/682–3551,* [WEB] *www.sylviahotel.com. 97 rooms, 22 suites. Restaurant, bar, room service, dry cleaning, laundry service, parking (fee). AE, DC, MC, V.*

$–$$
★ ⊡ **YWCA Hotel/Residence.** A secure, 12-story building in the heart of the entertainment district, the YWCA has bright, comfortable rooms— some big enough to sleep five. All have nightstands and desks, minirefrigerators, phones, sinks, and air-conditioning. Some share a bath down the hall, some share a bath between two rooms, and others have private baths. Some rooms have TVs, and shared kitchens are available for all guests. The hotel is open to men and women and offers special rates for seniors, students, and YWCA members; weekly and monthly rates are available in the off-season. Rates include use of the YWCA adults-only pool and fitness facility, a 15-minute walk away at 535 Hornby Street. ⊠ *733 Beatty St., V6B 2M4,* ☎ *604/895–5830 or 800/663–1424,* [FAX] *604/681–2550,* [WEB] *www.ywcahotel.com. 155 rooms. Café, in-room data ports, no-smoking floor, refrigerator, coin laundry, meeting rooms, parking (fee). AE, MC, V.*

$
★ ⊡ **Hostelling International Vancouver.** Vancouver has two Hostelling International locations: a big hostel set in parkland at Jericho Beach in Kitsilano, and a smaller, downtown hostel near English Bay and Stanley Park. Each has private rooms for two to four people; bunks in men's, women's, and coed dorms; a shared kitchen and dining room; and coin laundry, a TV lounge, bicycle rental, luggage and bike storage, lockers, Internet kiosks, and a range of low-cost tours and activities. The downtown hostel also has a rooftop patio, an on-site travel agency, a meeting room, games room, and a library, and is accessible to people who use wheelchairs. The Jericho Beach hostel has a café with a liquor license. A free shuttle bus runs between the hostels and the bus and train station. *Downtown:* ⊠ *1114 Burnaby St., V6E 1P1,* ☎ *604/684– 4565 or 888/203–4302,* [FAX] *604/684–4540,* [WEB] *www.hihostels.bc.ca. 23 rooms, 44 4-bed dorms. Jericho Beach:* ⊠ *1515 Discovery St., V6R 4K5,* ☎ *604/224–3208 or 888/203–4303,* [FAX] *604/224–4852. 286 beds in dorms and private rooms. MC, V.*

NIGHTLIFE AND THE ARTS

For **events information,** pick up a copy of the free *Georgia Straight* (available at cafés and bookstores around town) or look in the entertainment section of the *Vancouver Sun* (Thursday's paper has listings in the "Queue" section). The **Arts Hotline** (☎ 604/684–2787) has the latest entertainment information. Tickets for many venues can be booked through **Ticketmaster** (☎ 604/280–4444).

The Arts

Dance

The **Scotia Bank Dance Centre** (✉ 677 Davie St., ☎ 604/606–6400) is the hub of dance in British Columbia. The striking building, built in 2000, with an art deco facade, has performance and rehearsal space and provides information about dance in the province.

Ballet British Columbia (☎ 604/732–5003), based at the Queen Elizabeth Theatre, mounts productions and hosts out-of-town companies November through May. A few of the many modern-dance companies in town are Karen Jamieson, DanceArts Vancouver, and JumpStart; besides the Scotia Bank Dance Centre, the Firehall Arts Centre and the Vancouver East Cultural Centre are among their performance venues.

Film

Tickets are half price Tuesday at most chain-owned Vancouver movie theaters. The **Vancouver International Film Festival** (☎ 604/685–0260, WEB www.viff.org) is held in late September and early October in several theaters around town.

Several movie theaters in Vancouver show foreign and independent films. The **Blinding Light** (✉ 36 Powell St., ☎ 604/684–8288), on the edge of Gastown, showcases short and experimental films. Occasionally audience members are invited to bring their own films or you may catch a live band improvising scores to silent movies.

The **Fifth Avenue Cinemas** (✉ 2110 Burrard St., ☎ 604/734–7469) is a small multiplex featuring foreign and independent films. The **Pacific Cinémathèque** (✉ 1131 Howe St., ☎ 604/688–8202) shows esoteric and foreign and art films. The **Ridge Theatre** (✉ 3131 Arbutus St., ☎ 604/738–6311 is a long-established art house cinema.

Music

CHAMBER MUSIC AND SMALL ENSEMBLES

Early Music Vancouver (☎ 604/732–1610) performs medieval, Renaissance, and Baroque music year-round and hosts the Vancouver Early Music Programme and Festival from late July to mid-August at the University of British Columbia. Concerts by the **Friends of Chamber Music** (☎ 604/437–5747) are worth watching for in the local-newspaper entertainment listings. The **Vancouver Recital Society** (☎ 604/602–0363) presents both emerging and well-known classical musicians in recital September–May at the Chan Centre for the Performing Arts and the Vancouver Playhouse. In summer the society produces the Vancouver Chamber Music Festival, on the grounds of **Crofton House School** (✉ 3200 W. 41st Ave.).

CHORAL GROUPS

The **Vancouver Bach Choir** (☎ 604/921–8012) performs a five-concert series at the Orpheum Theatre between September and June. The **Vancouver Cantata Singers** (☎ 604/921–8588) present choral performances at various venues around town. The **Vancouver Chamber Choir** (☎ 604/738–6822) performs at several venues, including the Orpheum and the Chan Centre.

Festival Vancouver (✉ 4255 W. 12th Ave., ☎ 604/221–0080, WEB www.festivalvancouver.bc.ca) is Vancouver's biggest music event, with up to 60 performances of orchestral, chamber, choral, world music, early music, opera, and jazz in venues around the city during late July and early August.

ORCHESTRAS
The **Vancouver Symphony Orchestra** (☎ 604/876–3434) is the resident company at the **Orpheum Theatre** (✉ 601 Smithe St.).

Opera
Vancouver Opera (☎ 604/682–2871) stages four productions a year from October through May at the Queen Elizabeth Theatre.

Theater
The **Arts Club Theatre** (✉ 1585 Johnston St., ☎ 604/687–1644) operates two stages on Granville Island (the **Arts Club Theatre** and the **Arts Club Review Stage**) as well as the **Stanley Theatre** at 2750 Granville Street. All three stages present theatrical performances year-round.

Carousel Theatre (☎ 604/669–3410) performs for children and young people at the **Waterfront Theatre** (✉ 1411 Cartwright St.) on Granville Island. The **Chan Centre for the Performing Arts** (✉ 6265 Crescent Rd., on the University of British Columbia campus, ☎ 604/822–2697) contains a 1,200-seat concert hall, a theater, and a cinema.

The **Firehall Arts Centre** (✉ 280 E. Cordova St., ☎ 604/689–0926) showcases Canadian works in an intimate downtown space. The **Queen Elizabeth Theatre** (✉ 600 Hamilton St., ☎ 604/665–3050) is a major venue for ballet, opera, and other events. **Vancouver East Cultural Centre** (✉ 1895 Venables St., ☎ 604/254–9578) is a multipurpose performance space. In the same complex as the Queen Elizabeth Theatre, the **Vancouver Playhouse** (✉ 649 Cambie St., ☎ 604/665–3050) is the leading venue in Vancouver for mainstream theatrical shows. **The Vogue Theatre** (✉ 918 Granville St., ☎ 604/331–7909), a former movie palace, hosts a variety of theatrical events.

Bard on the Beach (☎ 604/739–0559) is a summer series of Shakespeare's plays performed in tents on the beach at Vanier Park. **Theatre Under the Stars** (☎ 604/687–0174) performs musicals at Malkin Bowl, an outdoor amphitheater in Stanley Park, during July and August. The **Vancouver Fringe Festival** (☎ 604/257–0350, WEB www.vancouver-fringe.com), an annual theater festival, is staged in September at various venues in Yaletown and on Granville Island.

Nightlife

Bars, Pubs, and Lounges
Unpretentious is the word at the **Atlantic Trap & Gill** (✉ 612 Davie St., ☎ 604/806–6393), a downtown pub designed to help folks from Atlantic Canada (and everyone else) feel at home, with beer kegs for tables, old couches topped with afghans, Atlantic folk music, and goodies such as clam strips on the menu. The **Bacchus Lounge** (✉ 845 Hornby St., ☎ 604/608–5319), in the Wedgewood Hotel, is a relaxing place with plush couches, a fireplace, and a pianist.

Near Stanley Park and attached to the seaside restaurant of the same name, **Cardero's Pub** (✉ 1583 Coal Harbour Quay, ☎ 604/669–7666) has deep leather couches, marina views, and recycled ship timbers and other nautical touches. The pub grub is top-notch. A fountain, greenery, and soft, comfy chairs make the atriumlike **Garden Terrace** (✉ 791 W. Georgia St., ☎ 604/689–9333) in the Four Seasons a peaceful place to relax over cocktails or a meal. The adjacent Terrace Bar is an elegant space with a copper-topped circular bar and Murano glass light fixtures. The fireplace, wing chairs, dark wood, and leather at the **Gerard Lounge** (✉ Sutton Place Hotel, 845 Burrard St., ☎ 604/682–5511) provide a suitably stylish setting for the film-industry types who hang out here. For a pint of properly poured Guinness and live Irish music, try the **Irish Heather** (✉ 217 Carrall St., ☎ 604/688–9779) in Gastown. Traditional Irish food is served in the pub and in the restaurant upstairs.The **900 West** (✉ 900 W. Georgia St., ☎ 604/669–9378) wine bar at the Fairmont Hotel Vancouver has 75 wines available by the glass.

There are a couple of choices on Granville Island. **Bridges** (✉ 1696 Duranleau St., ☎ 604/687–4400), near the Public Market, has a big outdoor deck and a cozy, nautical-theme pub. You could spend a whole evening at the **Sand Bar** (✉ 1535 Johnson St., ☎ 604/669–9030). It's part seafood restaurant with an oyster bar and crab and lobster from live tanks, and part pub, with an all-day tapas menu, deep leather chairs, and a rooftop patio with striking views of False Creek. On weekend evenings it morphs into a nightclub as patrons hit the dance floor.

Brew Pubs

The Creek (✉ Granville Island Hotel, 1253 Johnston St., ☎ 604/685–7070) is a popular microbrewery lounge with plush velour booths and leather chairs, a fireplace, a pool table, and a seaside patio. The in-house vats brew eight varieties of German-style lagers and ales. **Dix Brew Pub** (✉ 871 Beatty St., ☎ 604/682–2739), near Yaletown and B.C. Place Stadium, is a relaxed and good-looking place, with exposed brick and beams, a fireplace, a long mahogany bar, and vats brewing up a variety of lagers. Dix also serves a fine Southern-style barbecue, slow-smoked in-house in an apple or cherry-wood smoker. The brewmasters at **Steamworks** (✉ 375 Water St., ☎ 604/689–2739), on the edge of Gastown, use an age-old steam process and large copper kettles (visible through glass walls in the dining room downstairs) to fashion several brews, including Lions Gate Lager, Coal Porter, and Cascadia Cream Ale. The pub area upstairs has sweeping views of Burrard Inlet and the North Shore Mountains. There's also a restaurant downstairs. The **Yaletown Brewing Company** (✉ 1111 Mainland St., ☎ 604/681–2739) is based in a huge renovated warehouse with a glassed-in brewery turning out eight tasty beers. It also has a lively singles'-scene pub and a restaurant with an open-grill kitchen.

Casinos

Vancouver has a few casinos; proceeds go to local charities and arts groups. No alcohol is served and guests must be at least 19 years old. The **Great Canadian Casino** (✉ 1133 W. Hastings St., ☎ 604/682–8415) is in the Renaissance Hotel. The **Royal City Star** (✉ Westminster Quay, New Westminster, ☎ 604/878–9999) is a Mississippi riverboat moored on the Fraser River. Its five decks include 30 gaming tables, 300 slot machines, a lounge, and a restaurant. It's open 10 AM–3 AM daily, and takes cruises on the river daily between May and October. Admission is free. The **Royal Diamond Casino** (✉ 750 Pacific Blvd. S, ☎ 604/685–2340) is in the Plaza of Nations Expo site downtown.

Coffeehouses

Coffeehouses play a big role in Vancouver's social life. The Starbucks invasion is nearly complete—there are blocks in town with two branches—but there are other, more colorful places to have a cappuccino, write that novel, or watch the world go by.

Granville Island has many coffee places, but only the **Blue Parrot Café** (✉ Granville Island Public Market, 1689 Johnston St., ☎ 604/688–5127) provides such sweeping views of the boats on False Creek. Like the public market, the Blue Parrot is madly crowded on weekends. Cushy couches and wholesome goodies make **Bojangles Café** (✉ 785 Denman St., ☎ 604/687–3622) a good place to rest after a walk around Stanley Park. The closest thing in Vancouver to a *La Dolce Vita* set is the **Calabria Café** (✉ 1745 Commercial Dr., ☎ 604/253–7017), with its marble tables, plaster statues, and posters of Italian movie stars. Everyone seems to know everyone else at **Delaney's** (✉ 1105 Denman St., ☎ 604/662–3344), a friendly and often crowded coffee bar near English Bay. Cozy wooden booths and stacks of magazines might tempt you to spend a rainy afternoon here. One cannot live by coffee alone, as proven by the vast selection of teas and related paraphernalia at **Tearoom T** (✉ 1568 W. Broadway, ☎ 604/730–8390).

Comedy Clubs

The **Gastown Comedy Store** (✉ 19 Water St., ☎ 604/682–1727) has stand-up and other comedy acts. The **TheatreSports League** (☎ 604/738–7013), a hilarious improv troupe, performs at the New Review Stage on Granville Island. The **Vancouver International Comedy Festival** (☎ 604/683–0883), held in late July and early August, brings an international collection of improv, stand-up, circus, and other acts to Granville Island. **Yuk Yuks Comedy Club** (✉ 750 Pacific Blvd. S, in the Plaza of Nations Expo site, ☎ 604/687–5233) is a popular stand-up venue.

Gay and Lesbian Nightlife

Celebrities (✉ 1022 Davie St., ☎ 604/689–3180), one of Canada's largest gay bars, was closed for renovations at press time, so call first before heading out here. The **Dufferin** (✉ 900 Seymour St., ☎ 604/683–4251), a downtown pub, has male dancers, female impersonators, and drag karaoke. **Odyssey** (✉ 1251 Howe St., ☎ 604/689–5256) is a dance club with drag shows, go-go boys, and theme nights.

Music

DANCE CLUBS

The **Commodore Ballroom** (✉ 868 Granville St., ☎ 604/739–7469), a 1929 dance hall rich with memories for generations of Vancouverites, reopened in late 1999 after years of closure. Restored to its Art Deco glory, complete with its massive dance floor, the Commodore has done a lot to revitalize the city's live-music scene. Live bands, which have included such major Canadian names as Bryan Adams and Blue Rodeo, play here six nights a week; Tuesday is DJ night.

The funky, brick-lined **Bar None** (✉ 1222 Hamilton St., ☎ 604/689–7000) in Yaletown has R&B, hip hop and top-40 dance tunes on weekends; on Monday and Tuesday, the 10-piece house band plays jazz, funk, and soul. DJs at the cozy, subterranean **Chameleon Urban Lounge** (✉ 801 W. Georgia St., ☎ 604/669–0806), in the basement of the Crowne Plaza Hotel Georgia, spin lounge, soul, hip hop, acid jazz, and funk for a laid-back crowd. The **Purple Onion Cabaret** (✉ 15 Water St., ☎ 604/602–9442) in Gastown has both a lounge featuring live jazz, funk, reggae, and hip hop, and a dance club with DJs. **Richard's on Richards** (✉ 1036 Richards St., ☎ 604/687–6794) is one of Vancouver's most established dance clubs, with live bands on weekdays. **Sonar** (✉ 66 Water St., ☎ 604/683–6695) in Gastown has international dance sounds and frequent touring guest DJs.

The fashionable **Voda** (✉ 783 Homer St., ☎ 604/684–3003), in the Westin Grand Hotel, is one of the few places that Vancouverites dress up for. The intimate club is popular with a thirtysomething professional crowd, who come for the live salsa on Tuesdays, and the Motown, underground house, and soul selections the rest of the week.

FOLK

The **Vancouver Folk Music Festival** (☎ 604/602–9798 or 800/883–3655), one of the world's leading folk- and world-music events, takes place at Jericho Beach Park the third weekend of July. For folk and traditional Celtic concerts year-round, call the **Rogue Folk Club** (☎ 604/736–3022).

JAZZ AND SOUL

The hot line of the **Coastal Jazz and Blues Society** (☎ 604/872–5200) has information about concerts and clubs. The society also runs the Vancouver International Jazz Festival, which lights up 40 venues around town every June.

You can hear live jazz six nights a week at the **Cellar Jazz Café** (✉ 3611 W. Broadway, ☎ 604/738–1959). Thursdays through Saturdays you can catch the best of the live local jazz scene at **O'Doul's Restaurant & Bar** (✉ 1300 Robson St., ☎ 604/661–1400) in the Listel Hotel.

ROCK AND BLUES

The **Backstage Bar and Grill** (✉ 1585 Johnston St., ☎ 604/687–1354) behind the main stage at the Arts Club Theatre on Granville Island, features local bands Wednesday through Saturday nights. The **Rage** (✉ 750 Pacific Blvd. S, ☎ 604/685–5585) is a rock disco most nights, but also hosts occasional touring bands. In the early evening, the **Railway Club** (✉ 579 Dunsmuir St., ☎ 604/681–1625) attracts film and media types to its pub-style rooms; after 8 it becomes a venue for local rock bands. Technically it's a private social club, but everyone's welcome. The **Starfish Room** (✉ 1055 Homer St., ☎ 604/682–4171) showcases local and major touring concert bands in a nightclub setting. **The Vogue Theatre** (✉ 918 Granville St., ☎ 604/331–7909), a former movie palace, hosts a variety of concerts by visiting performers. Vancouver's most established rhythm-and-blues bar, **The Yale** (✉ 1300 Granville St., ☎ 604/681–9253), has live bands most nights.

Pool Halls

Most of the city's "hot" pool halls are in Yaletown. The loud, industrial-theme **Automotive Billiards Club** (✉ 1095 Homer St., ☎ 604/682–0040) attracts a twenties crowd. The chic **Soho Café & Billiards** (✉ 1144 Homer St., ☎ 604/688–1180) has a few tables tucked in behind a trendy café.

OUTDOOR ACTIVITIES AND SPORTS

Beaches

An almost continuous string of beaches runs from Stanley Park to the University of British Columbia. The water is cool, but the beaches are sandy, edged by grass. All have lifeguards, washrooms, concession stands, and limited parking, unless otherwise noted. Liquor is prohibited in parks and on beaches. For information, call the **Vancouver Board of Parks and Recreation** (☎ 604/738–8535 summer only).

Kitsilano Beach, over the Burrard Bridge from downtown, has a lifeguard and is the city's busiest beach—in-line skaters, volleyball games, and sleek young people are ever present. The part of the beach nearest the Vancouver Maritime Museum is the quietest. Facilities include a playground, tennis courts, a heated pool, concession stands, and nearby restaurants and cafés.

The **Point Grey beaches**—Jericho, Locarno, and Spanish Banks—begin at the end of Point Grey Road and offer huge expanses of sand, especially at low tide. The shallow water, warmed slightly by sun and sand, is good for swimming. Farther out, toward Spanish Banks, the beach becomes less crowded. Past Point Grey is Wreck Beach, Vancouver's nude beach.

Among the **West End beaches,** Second Beach and Third Beach, along Beach Drive in Stanley Park, draw families. Second Beach has a guarded pool. A water slide, kayak rentals, street performers, and artists keep things interesting all summer at English Bay Beach, at the foot of Denman Street. Farther along Beach Drive, Sunset Beach is a little too close to the downtown core for clean, safe swimming.

Participant Sports

Biking

One of the best ways to see the city is to cycle along at least part of the **Seaside Bicycle Route.** This 39-km (23-mi), flat, car-free route starts at Canada Place downtown, follows the waterfront around Stanley Park, and continues, with a few detours, all the way around False Creek to Spanish Banks Beach.

Rentals are available from **Bayshore Bicycles** (⊠ 745 Denman St., ☎ 604/688–2453), which is open year-round at Robson and Denman near Stanley Park. You can get coffee, bikes, and Rollerblades at **Spokes Bicycle Rentals & Espresso Bar** (⊠ 1798 W. Georgia St., ☎ 604/688–5141), at Denman and Georgia near Stanley Park. Bikes or Rollerblades can be rented on the Yaletown section of the seaside path from **Reckless, the Bike Store** (⊠ 110 Davie St., ☎ 604/648–2600). Cycling helmets, a legal requirement in Vancouver, come with the rentals.

Boating

You can charter motorboats and sailboats from Granville Island through **Blue Pacific Yacht Charters** (⊠ 1519 Foreshore Walk, Granville Island, ☎ 604/682–2161 or 800/237–2392, WEB www.blue-pacific-charters.com). **Cooper Boating Centre** (⊠ 1620 Duranleau St., Granville Island, ☎ 604/687–4110 or 888/999–6419, WEB www.cooperboating.com) has a three-hour introduction to sailing around English Bay, as well as longer cruise-and-learn trips that last from five days to two weeks.

Fishing

You can fish for salmon all year in coastal British Columbia. **Sewell's Marina Horseshoe Bay** (⊠ 6695 Nelson Ave., Horseshoe Bay, ☎ 604/921–3474, WEB www.sewellsmarina.com) offers guided and self-drive salmon-fishing charters on Howe Sound. For trout-fishing day trips, contact **Trout Fishing Adventures** (☎ 604/838–5873, WEB www.trout-fishingguide.com). **Westin Bayshore Yacht Charters** (⊠ 1601 Bayshore Drive, off W. Georgia St., ☎ 604/691–6936) operates fishing and yacht charters.

Golf

For advance tee-time bookings at any of 60 British Columbia courses, or for a spur of the moment game, call **Last Minute Golf** (☎ 604/878–1833 or 800/684–6344, WEB www.lastminutegolf.net). The company matches golfers and courses, sometimes at substantial greens-fee discounts. The half-day packages at **West Coast Golf Shuttle** (☎ 604/351–6833 or 888/599–6800, WEB www.golfshuttle.com) include the greens fee, power cart, and hotel pickup; rental clubs are available.

The challenging 18-hole, par-72 course at **Furry Creek Golf and Country Club** (✉ Hwy. 99, Furry Creek, ☏ 604/922–9576 or 888/922–9462, WEB www.furrycreekgolf.com), a 45-minute drive north of Vancouver, has an $80–$95 greens fee and includes a mandatory cart. The course is closed late October to early March. The facilities of the 18-hole, par-71 public **McCleery Golf Course** (✉ 7188 McDonald St., ☏ 604/257–8191; 604/280–1818 for advance bookings) include a driving range. The greens fee is $36–$39; an optional cart costs $26. **Northview Golf and Country Club** (✉ 6857 168th St., Surrey, ☏ 604/576–4653 or 888/574–2211, WEB www.northviewgolf.com) has two Arnold Palmer–designed 18-hole courses (both par 72) and is home of the Air Canada Championship (a Professional Golfers' Association, or PGA, tour event). The greens fee for the Ridge course (open March through October), where the PGA tour plays, is $85–$95; the fee for the Canal course (open all year) is $60–$70. An optional cart at either course costs $30. At the 18-hole, par-72 course (closed November through March) at the **Westwood Plateau Golf and Country Club** (✉ 3251 Plateau Blvd., Coquitlam, ☏ 604/552–0777 or 800/580–0785, WEB www.westwoodplateaugolf.bc.ca), the greens fee, which includes a cart, is $99–$149. The club also has a 9-hole course that's open year-round and a restaurant.

Health and Fitness Clubs

The **Bentall Centre Athletic Club** (✉ 1055 Dunsmuir St., lower plaza, ☏ 604/689–4424) specializes in squash, and also has racquetball courts, and weight and cardio gyms; aerobics classes are given as well. The **YMCA** (✉ 955 Burrard St., ☏ 604/689–9622), downtown, has daily rates. Facilities include a pool, a men's steam room and women's sauna, two cardio gyms and a weight room, as well as racquetball, squash, and handball courts, basketball, volleyball, and a boxing room. The **YWCA** (✉ 535 Hornby St., ☏ 604/895–5777) has an ozone pool, a cardio room, co-ed and women-only weight rooms, fitness classes, a whirlpool, and steam rooms.

Hiking

The weather can change quickly in the mountains, so go prepared and leave word with someone in the city as to your route and when you expect to be back. For **mountain-weather forecasts,** call ☏ 604/664–9021.

The seaside **Lighthouse Park** (✉ Beacon La., off Marine Dr.) in West Vancouver has fairly flat forested trails leading to the rocky shoreline. The rugged **Pacific Spirit Regional Park** (✉ 4915 W. 16th Ave., ☏ 604/224–5739), near the University of British Columbia, has fairly level forested trails and is popular with mountain bikers and hikers. **Stanley Park** (☏ 604/257–8400) has miles of trails to explore.

In the mountains of North Vancouver, **Capilano River Regional Park** (☏ 604/224–5739) has trails along the edge of a dramatic gorge. **Cypress Provincial Park** (✉ Cypress Bowl Rd., West Vancouver, ☏ 604/924–2200) is a good choice for serious hikers. North Vancouver's **Lower Seymour Conservation Reserve** (✉ end of Lillooet Rd., North Vancouver, ☏ 604/432–6286) has some easy rain-forest walks. **Mount Seymour Provincial Park** (✉ Mount Seymour Rd. off Seymour Pkwy., North Vancouver, ☏ 604/924–2200) offers challenging mountain trails for experienced, well-equipped hikers.

The **Grouse Grind** is a steep (rising 2,800 ft in fewer than 2 mi), grueling trail from the Grouse Mountain parking lot to the top of the mountain; the path is packed with fit Vancouverites most summer afternoons. There are also hiking trails at the top of the mountain, accessed via the Grouse Mountain Skyride.

A number of companies conduct guided walks and hikes in nearby parks and wilderness areas.

Jogging

The **Running Room** (✉ 679 Denman St., ☎ 604/684–9771) is a good source for information about fun runs in the area.

The seawall around **Stanley Park** (☎ 604/257–8400) is 9 km (5½ mi) long; running it provides an excellent minitour of the city. You can take a shorter run of 4 km (2½ mi) in the park around Lost Lagoon.

Skiing

CROSS-COUNTRY

The best cross-country skiing, with 16 km (10 mi) of groomed trails, is at **Cypress Bowl Ski Area** (✉ Cypress Bowl Ski Area Rd., West Vancouver, Exit 8 off Hwy. 1 westbound, ☎ 604/922–0825). **Grouse Mountain** has cross-country trails as well as downhill skiing.

DOWNHILL

Whistler/Blackcomb, a top-ranked ski destination, is a two-hour drive from Vancouver.

The North Shore Mountains hold three ski areas. All have rentals, lessons, and night skiing. **Cypress Bowl** (✉ Cypress Bowl Ski Area Rd., West Vancouver, Exit 8 off Hwy. 1 westbound, ☎ 604/926–5612; 604/419–7669 for snow report) has 25 runs, four chairlifts, and a vertical drop of 1,750 ft. The mountain also has a tobogganing and snow-tubing area. **Grouse Mountain** (✉ 6400 Nancy Greene Way, ☎ 604/980–9311; 604/986–6262 snow report) has four chairlifts, three surface lifts, a vertical drop of 1,210 ft, extensive night skiing, restaurants, bars, ice-skating, a snowshoeing park, and great city views from the runs. **Mount Seymour** (✉ 1700 Mt. Seymour Rd., ☎ 604/986–2261; 604/718–7771 snow report) has three chairlifts and a vertical drop of 1,042 ft. The mountain also has a half-pipe for snowboarding, as well as snowshoeing, tobogganing, and snow-tubing facilities.

Tennis

There are 180 free public courts around town. Contact the **Vancouver Board of Parks and Recreation** (☎ 604/257–8400) for locations. **Stanley Park** (☎ 604/257–8400) has 18 well-surfaced outdoor courts near English Bay Beach. Some courts charge a fee and can be booked in advance.

Water Sports

KAYAKING

Kayaks are a fun way to explore the waters of False Creek and the shoreline of English Bay. **Ecomarine Ocean Kayak Centre** offers lessons and rentals year-round from Granville Island (✉ 1668 Duranleau St., ☎ 604/689–7575, WEB www.ecomarine.com), and from mid-May to early September at Jericho Beach (☎ 604/222–3565). Between early April and the end of October **Ocean West Expeditions** (☎ 800/660–0051, WEB www.ocean-west.com) rents kayaks and offers lessons and tours from English Bay Beach.

RAFTING

The **Canadian Outback Adventure Company** (☎ 604/921–7250 or 800/565–8735, WEB www.canadianoutback.com) runs white-water rafting and scenic (not white-water) floats on day trips from Vancouver.

WINDSURFING

Sailboards and lessons are available in summer at **Windsure Windsurfing School** (✉ Jericho Beach, ☎ 604/224–0615). The winds aren't heavy on English Bay, making it a perfect locale for learning the sport. You

RAINY DAYS

T'S NO SECRET that it rains in Vancouver—the secret is that some people quite like it.

For many it's the atmosphere. Bobbing among the harbor freighters on the SeaBus or taking a stroll on the **Stanley Park Seawall,** you can gain a certain nautical cachet in bad weather. The **Museum of Anthropology** is best seen on a wet day, when dark skies and streaming windows evoke the northern rain forest from which the artifacts came.

The best thing about rain, though, is that it forces many Vancouverites to slow down. This is probably why the city has so embraced the coffeehouse culture. Favorite places to let your umbrella drip include **Delaney's,** quite the social center, and **Bojangles,** a cozy place near Stanley Park. The wraparound windows at Granville Island's **Blue Parrot Café** afford views of people and boats.

Or you could take tea—that's proper tea, with cakes and sandwiches. A logical place, is, of course, **The Teahouse** in Stanley Park. The **Fish House,** also in Stanley Park, serves afternoon tea as well, as do several downtown hotels. Try the **900 West** lounge in the Fairmont Hotel Vancouver, or **La Promenade,** in the Sutton Place Hotel.

have to travel north to Squamish for more-challenging high-wind conditions.

Spectator Sports

Vancouver's professional basketball and hockey teams play at **General Motors Place** (✉ 800 Griffiths Way, ☎ 604/899–7400). **Ticketmaster** (☎ 604/280–4400) sells tickets to many local sports events.

Football
The **B.C. Lions** (☎ 604/930–5466) Canadian Football League team plays home games at **B.C. Place Stadium** (✉ 777 Pacific Blvd. S, ☎ 604/669–2300).

Hockey
The **Vancouver Canucks** (☎ 604/899–7400) of the National Hockey League play at General Motors Place.

SHOPPING

Unlike many cities where suburban malls have taken over, Vancouver is full of individual boutiques and specialty shops. Antiques stores, ethnic markets, art galleries, high-fashion outlets, and fine department stores abound. Store hours are generally 9:30 to 6 Monday, Tuesday, Wednesday, and Saturday; 9:30 to 9 Thursday and Friday; and 10 to 5 Sunday.

Shopping Districts and Malls

About two dozen high-end art galleries, antiques shops, and Oriental-rug emporiums are packed end to end between 5th and 15th avenues on Granville Street, in an area known as **Gallery Row. Oakridge Shopping Centre** (✉ 650 W. 41st Ave., at Cambie St., ☎ 604/261–2511) has chic, expensive stores that are fun to browse. The **Pacific Centre Mall** (✉ 700 W. Georgia St., ☎ 604/688–7236), on two levels and mostly underground, takes up three city blocks in the heart of downtown. **Robson Street** stretching from Burrard to Bute streets is full of boutiques and cafés. A commercial center has developed around **Sinclair Centre** (✉ 757 W. Hastings St.), catering to sophisticated and pricey tastes.

Bustling **Chinatown**—centered on Pender and Main streets—is full of restaurants and markets. **Commercial Drive** north of East 1st Avenue is the center of Vancouver's Italian and Latin American communities. You can sip cappuccino in coffee bars, or buy sun-dried tomatoes or an espresso machine. In **Little India,** on Main Street around 50th Avenue, curry houses, sweets shops, grocery stores, discount jewelers, and silk shops abound. Treasure hunters like the 300 block of **West Cordova Street** near Gastown, where offbeat shops sell curios, vintage clothing, and local designer goods.

Department Stores

The Bay (✉ 674 Granville St., at Georgia St., ☎ 604/681–6211), founded as part of the fur trade in the 17th century, is now a midprice department store downtown. Modeled on Paris's Colette store, **Bruce** (✉ 1038 Alberni St., ☎ 604/688–8802) is Vancouver's first "lifestyle" department store, offering the latest in designer fashion, home decor, and eyewear. **Eaton's** (✉ 701 Granville St., ☎ 604/685–7112) is a midprice, fashion-oriented department store. **Holt Renfrew** (✉ 633 Granville St., ☎ 604/681–3121) focuses on high fashion for men and women.

Specialty Stores

Antiques

Three key antiques hunting grounds are Gallery Row on Granville Street, the stretch of antiques stores along Main Street from 16th to 30th avenues, and along Front Street, between 6th Street and Begbie Street (near New Westminster Quay) in New Westminster. **Love's Auctioneers** (✉ 1635 W. Broadway, ☎ 604/733–1157) auctions antiques on the last Wednesday and Thursday of each month at 6 PM. **Vancouver Antique Centre** (✉ 422 Richards St., ☎ 604/669–7444) has 15 antiques and collectibles dealers under one roof.

Art Galleries

Gallery Row along Granville Street between 5th and 15th avenues is home to about a dozen high-end contemporary-art galleries. The **Diane Farris Gallery** (✉ 1565 W. 7th Ave., ☎ 604/737–2629) often showcases hot new artists. The **Douglas Reynolds Gallery** (✉ 2335 Granville St., ☎ 604/731–9292) has one of the city's finest collections of Northwest Coast First Nations art.

There are also a number of notable galleries on the downtown peninsula. **Buschlen Mowatt** (✉ 1445 W. Georgia St., ☎ 604/682–1234) exhibits the works of contemporary Canadian and international artists. The **Inuit Gallery of Vancouver** (✉ 206 Cambie St. in Gastown, ☎ 888/615–8399, or 604/688–7323) exhibits Northwest Coast and Inuit art. The **Marion Scott Gallery** (✉ 481 Howe St., ☎ 604/685–1934) specializes in Inuit art.

Books

Vancouver's two **Chapters** stores (✉ 788 Robson St., ☎ 604/682–4066; ✉ 2505 Granville St., at Broadway, ☎ 604/731–7822) are enormous, with a café in each and a series of author readings and other performances. At press time, Chapters had been purchased by another chain, Indigo, so it may be getting a new name. **Duthie Books** (⊠ 2239 W. 4th Ave., ☎ 604/732–5344) is a long-established homegrown favorite. **MacLeod's Books** (⊠ 455 W. Pender St., ☎ 604/681–7654) is one of the city's best antiquarian and used bookstores. **Wanderlust** (⊠ 1929 W. 4th Ave., ☎ 604/739–2182) carries thousands of travel books and maps, as well as luggage and travel accessories.

Clothes

For unique men's and women's clothing, try **Dorothy Grant** (⊠ 757 W. Hastings St., ☎ 604/681–0201), in Sinclair Centre, where traditional Haida designs meld with modern fashion. **Dream** (⊠ 311 W. Cordova St., ☎ 604/683–7326) is where up-and-coming local designers sell their wares. Men's and women's fashions by Versace, Dolce Gabbana, Prada, and others are available at **Leone** (⊠ 757 W. Hastings St., ☎ 604/683–1133), in Sinclair Centre. Handmade Italian suits, knitwear and accessories, and other upscale menswear are sold at stylish **Madison Men's Wear** (⊠ 1050 W. Pender St., ☎ 604/683–2122). If your tastes are traditional, don't miss **Straiths** (⊠ 900 W. Georgia St., ☎ 604/685–3301), in the Fairmont Hotel Vancouver. It offers tailored designer fashions for men and women. **Wear Else?** (⊠ 2372 W. 4th Ave., ☎ 604/732–3521; ⊠ 4401 W. 10th Ave., ☎ 604/221–7755; ⊠ Oakridge Shopping Centre, 650 W. 41st Ave., at Cambie St., ☎ 604/266–3613) is a popular womenswear shop with attentive service, offering both business and casual clothes, including shoes and accessories.

Gifts

Museum and gallery gift shops are among the best places to buy high-quality souvenirs—West Coast native art, books, music, jewelry, and other items. The **Clamshell Gift Shop** (⊠ Vancouver Aquarium Marine Science Centre, ☎ 604/659–3413), in Stanley Park, features souvenir clothing and aquatic-theme toys and gifts. The **Gallery Shop** (⊠ 750 Hornby St., ☎ 604/662–4706), in the Vancouver Art Gallery, has a good selection of prints and cards. The **Museum of Anthropology Gift Shop** (⊠ 6393 N.W. Marine Dr., ☎ 604/822–3825), on the University of British Columbia campus, features Northwest Coast jewelry, carvings, and prints, as well as a good collection of books on First Nations history and culture. The **Museum Shop** (⊠ 639 Hornby St., ☎ 604/687–8266), in the Canadian Museum of Craft and Design, has a delightful collection of one-of-a-kind handmade items.

Hill's Native Art (⊠ 165 Water St., ☎ 604/685–4249) in Gastown has Vancouver's largest selection of First Nations art. **Lattimer Gallery** (⊠ 1590 W. 2nd Ave., ☎ 604/732–4556), near Granville Island, is full of native arts and crafts in all price ranges. At the **Salmon Shop** (⊠ 1689 Johnston St., ☎ 604/669–3474), in the Granville Island Public Market, you can pick up fresh or smoked salmon wrapped for travel. One of Vancouver's most extensive, but least known, native-art collections is hidden in the back room at **The Three Vets** (⊠ 2200 Yukon St., ☎ 604/872–5475), a camping-equipment store. Ask any staff member to show you.

Jewelry

Vancouver's leading jewelry shops are clustered along Hastings Street. **Birks** (⊠ 698 W. Hastings St., ☎ 604/669–3333) takes up the grand lower floor of a Neoclassical building that was the former headquarters of the Canadian Imperial Bank of Commerce. **Cartier Jewellers** (⊠ 408 Howe St., ☎ 604/683–6878) is the Vancouver outlet of the famous jewelry chain. **Palladio** (⊠ 855 W. Hastings St., ☎ 604/685–3885) carries modern, high-fashion jewelry in gold and platinum.

Outdoor Equipment

Outdoor-oriented Vancouver is a great place to pick up camping and hiking gear. **Coast Mountain Sports** (⊠ 2201 W. 4th Ave., ☎ 604/731–6181; ⊠ Park Royal Shopping Centre, Marine Dr., West Vancouver, ☎ 604/926–6126; ⊠ Metrotown Shopping Centre, Burnaby, ☎ 604/434–9397) has high-performance (and high-fashion) gear. The massive **Mountain Equipment Co-op** (⊠ 130 W. Broadway, ☎ 604/872–7858) is a local institution with a good selection of high-performance and midprice clothing and equipment. A one-time $5 membership is required. **The Three Vets** (⊠ 2200 Yukon St., ☎ 604/872–5475), near Cambie Street and Broadway, is an army-surplus–style store with budget-price family camping equipment. Ask to see the native art collections.

VANCOUVER A TO Z

To research prices, get advice from other travelers, and book travel arrangements, visit www.fodors.com.

AIR TRAVEL TO AND FROM VANCOUVER

Air B.C., operated by Air Canada, serves destinations around the province, including the Vancouver airport. West Coast Air and Harbour Air Seaplanes operate 35-minute harbor-to-harbor service (downtown Vancouver to downtown Victoria) several times a day. Planes leave from near the Pan Pacific Hotel at 300–999 Canada Place. Helijet International has helicopter service from downtown Vancouver and the Vancouver airport to downtown Seattle and Victoria. The heliport is near Vancouver's Pan Pacific Hotel.

➤ AIRLINES AND CONTACTS: **Air B.C.** (☎ 888/247–2262). **Harbour Air Seaplanes** (☎ 604/688–1277 or 800/665–0212, WEB www.harbour-air.com). **Helijet International** (☎ 800/665–4354 or 604/273–1414, WEB www.helijet.com). **West Coast Air** (☎ 604/606–6888 or 800/347–2222, WEB www.westcoastair.com).

AIRPORTS AND TRANSFERS

Vancouver International Airport is on Sea Island, about 23 km (14 mi) south of downtown off Highway 99. An airport-improvement fee is assessed on all flight departures: $5 for flights within British Columbia or the Yukon; $10 for other flights within North America; $15 for overseas flights. Major credit cards and Canadian and United States currencies are accepted. Alaska, America West, American, British Airways, Continental, Northwest, Qantas, Reno, and United serve the airport. The two major domestic carriers are Air Canada and Canadian Airlines.

➤ AIRPORT INFORMATION: **Vancouver International Airport** (⊠ Grant McConachie Way, Richmond, ☎ 604/276–6101, WEB www.yvr.ca).

AIRPORT TRANSFER

The drive from the airport to downtown takes 20 to 45 minutes, depending on the time of day. Airport hotels provide shuttle service to and from the airport. If you're driving, go over the Arthur Laing Bridge and north on Granville Street (also signposted as Highway 99). Signs direct you to Vancouver City Centre.

The Vancouver Airporter Service bus leaves the international- and domestic-arrivals levels of the terminal building approximately every half hour, stopping at major downtown hotels. It operates from 5:23 AM until midnight. The fare is $12 one way and $18 round-trip.

Taxi stands are in front of the terminal building on domestic- and international-arrivals levels. The taxi fare to downtown is about $23. Area cab companies include Black Top and Yellow.

Limousine service from LimoJet Gold costs about $34, a bit more than the taxi fare to downtown.

➤ Taxis and Shuttles: **Black Top** (☎ 604/681–2181). **LimoJet Gold** (☎ 604/273–1331). **Vancouver Airporter Service** (☎ 604/946–8866 or 800/668–3141). **Yellow** (☎ 604/681–1111).

BOAT AND FERRY TRAVEL

BC Ferries operates two major ferry terminals outside Vancouver. From Tsawwassen to the south (an hour's drive from downtown), ferries sail to Victoria and Nanaimo on Vancouver Island and to the Gulf Islands (the small islands between the mainland and Vancouver Island). From Horseshoe Bay (45 minutes north of downtown), ferries sail to the Sunshine Coast and to Nanaimo on Vancouver Island.

The SeaBus is a 400-passenger commuter ferry that crosses Burrard Inlet from Waterfront Station downtown to the foot of Lonsdale Avenue in North Vancouver. The ride takes 13 minutes and costs the same as the TransLink bus. With a transfer, connection can be made to any TransLink bus or SkyTrain.

Aquabus Ferries connect several stations on False Creek including Science World, Granville Island, Stamp's Landing, Yaletown, and the Hornby Street dock. Some Aquabus ferries take bicycles, and the company also operates two historic wooden boats on some runs.

False Creek Ferries offers foot passenger service between the Aquatic Centre on Beach Avenue, Granville Island, Science World, Stamp's Landing, and Vanier Park.

False Creek and Aquabus Ferries are not part of the TransLink system, so bus transfers aren't accepted.

FARES AND SCHEDULES
Vehicle reservations on Vancouver to Victoria and Nanaimo routes are optional and cost $15 in addition to the fare. There's no extra charge for reservations on Gulf Island routes.

➤ Boat and Ferry Information: **Aquabus Ferries** (☎ 604/689–5858, WEB www.aquabus.bc.ca). **BC Ferries** (☎ 250/386–3431; 888/223–3779 in British Columbia, WEB www.bcferries.com). **False Creek Ferries** (☎ 604/684–7781, WEB www.falsecreekferries.bc.ca). **SeaBus** (☎ 604/521–0400, www.translink.bc.ca).

BUS TRAVEL TO AND FROM VANCOUVER

Greyhound Lines is the largest bus line serving Vancouver. Pacific Central Station is the depot for Greyhound Lines. Quick Shuttle bus service runs between downtown Vancouver, Vancouver Airport, Seattle (Seatac) Airport, and downtown Seattle five times a day in winter and up to eight times a day in summer. The downtown Vancouver depot is at the Holiday Inn though the shuttle picks up at most downtown Vancouver hotels by prior arrangement.

➤ Bus Information: **Greyhound Lines** (☎ 604/482–8747; 800/661–8747 in Canada; 800/231–2222 in the U.S.). **Pacific Central Station** (✉ 1150 Station St., ☎ no phone). **Quick Shuttle** (☎ 604/940–4428 or 800/665–2122). **Vancouver depot** (✉ 1110 Howe St., ☎ no phone).

BUS TRAVEL WITHIN VANCOUVER

A guide called "Discover Vancouver on Transit" is available free at the Tourist Info Centre. Buses to West Vancouver (on the North Shore) are operated by West Vancouver Transit. TransLink buses provide regular service throughout Vancouver and its suburbs (except West Vancouver).

Exact change is needed to ride TransLink buses: $1.75 for normal rides or $2.50 to $3.50 for weekday trips to the suburbs, including the SeaBus to the North Shore. Books of 10 tickets are sold at convenience stores and newsstands; look for a red, white, and blue FARE DEALER sign. Day passes, good for unlimited travel all day, cost $7. They are available from fare dealers and at any SeaBus or SkyTrain station. Transfers (ask for one when you board) are valid for 90 minutes, allow travel in both directions, and are good on buses, SkyTrain, and SeaBus.

➤ BUS INFORMATION: **TransLink** (☎ 604/521–0400, WEB www. translink.bc.ca). **West Vancouver Transit** (☎ 604/985–7777).

CAR RENTAL

➤ MAJOR AGENCIES: **Avis** (☎ 604/606–2847 or 800/331–1212). **Budget** (☎ 604/668–7000 or 800/527–0700). **Thrifty Car Rental** (☎ 604/606–1666 or 800/847–4389).

CAR TRAVEL

Interstate 5 in Washington State becomes Highway 99 at the U.S.–Canada border. Vancouver is a three-hour drive (226 km, or 140 mi) from Seattle.

A car can be handy for touring areas outside the city center, but it isn't essential. On the compact downtown peninsula, however, it's generally easier to get around on foot or by public transport, especially in light of the congestion, limited parking, and many one-way streets.

EMERGENCY SERVICES

The British Columbia Automobile Association provides 24-hour emergency road service for members of the American and the Canadian automobile associations.

➤ CONTACTS: **British Columbia Automobile Association** (☎ 604/293–2222).

PARKING

Parking downtown is expensive and tricky to find. Two large underground pay parking garages that usually have space are the Library Square lot and the Pacific Centre lot. Parking fees run about $6 to $10 a day. Don't leave anything in your car, even in the trunk; break-ins are quite common downtown (hotel parking tends to be more secure than public lots). Parking outside the downtown core is an easier proposition.

➤ PARKING INFORMATION: **Library Square lot** (✉ 775 Hamilton St., off Robson St., ☎ 604/669–4183). **Pacific Centre lot** (✉ 700 block of Howe St., east side, ☎ 604/684–9715).

TRAFFIC

It's best to avoid border crossings during peak times such as holidays and weekends. Highway 1, the Trans-Canada Highway, enters Vancouver from the east. To avoid traffic, arrive after rush hour (9 AM).

Vancouver's rush-hour traffic, about 7–9 weekday mornings and starting at 3 PM weekday afternoons, can be horrendous. The worst bottlenecks outside the city center are the North Shore bridges (especially Lions Gate Bridge), the George Massey Tunnel on Highway 99 south of Vancouver, and Highway 1 through Coquitlam and Surrey.

Right turns are allowed at most red lights after you've come to a full stop.

CONSULATES

➤ AUSTRALIA: (✉ 1225–888 Dunsmuir St., ☎ 604/684–1177).
➤ NEW ZEALAND: (✉ 1200–888 Dunsmuir St., ☎ 604/684–7388).
➤ UNITED KINGDOM: (✉ 800–1111 Melville St., ☎ 604/683–4421).
➤ UNITED STATES: (✉ 1095 W. Pender St., ☎ 604/685–4311).

EMERGENCIES
➤ EMERGENCY SERVICES: **Ambulance, fire, police** (☎ 911).
➤ HOSPITALS: **Medicentre** (✉ 1055 Dunsmuir St., lower level, ☎ 604/
683–8138), a drop-in clinic in Bentall Centre, is open weekdays 8 AM
to 4:30 PM. The emergency ward at **St. Paul's Hospital** (✉ 1081 Burrard St., ☎ 604/682–2344), a downtown facility, is open 24 hours.
➤ 24-HOUR PHARMACIES: **Shopper's Drug Mart** (✉ 1125 Davie St., ☎
604/669–2424).

LODGING
Super, Natural B.C., operated by the provincial Ministry of Tourism,
can book accommodations anywhere in British Columbia. Town &
Country Bed and Breakfast Reservation Service specializes in B&Bs.
➤ RESERVATION SERVICES: **Super, Natural B.C.** (☎ 604/663–6000 or 800/
435–5622, WEB www.hellobc.com). **Town & Country Bed and Break-
fast Reservation Service** (✉ Box 74542, 2803 W. 4th Ave., V6K 1K2,
☎ FAX 604/731–5942, WEB www.townandcountrybedandbreakfast.com).

RAPID-TRANSIT TRAVEL
A one-line, 25-km (16-mi) rapid-transit system called SkyTrain travels underground downtown and is elevated for the rest of its route to
New Westminster and Surrey. A line to Coquitlam was under construction at press time. Trains leave about every five minutes. Tickets,
sold at each station from machines (correct change is not necessary),
must be carried with you as proof of payment. You may use transfers
from SkyTrain to SeaBus and TransLink buses and vice versa. SkyTrain
is convenient for transit between downtown, B.C. Place Stadium, Pacific Central Station, and Science World.
➤ SUBWAY INFORMATION: **SkyTrain** (☎ 604/521–0400, WEB www.
translink.bc.ca).

TAXIS
It's difficult to hail a cab in Vancouver. Unless you're near a hotel, you'll
have better luck calling a taxi service. Try Black Top or Yellow.
➤ TAXI COMPANIES: **Black Top** (☎ 604/681–2181). **Yellow** (☎ 604/
681–1111).

TOURS
Tour prices fluctuate, so inquire about rates when booking.

AIRPLANE TOURS
You can see Vancouver from the air for about $80 for 20 minutes, or
take a one hour flight ($167–$188) over mountains and glaciers with
Harbour Air Seaplanes, which leaves from beside the Pan Pacific Hotel.
➤ FEES AND SCHEDULES: **Harbour Air Seaplanes** (☎ 604/688–1277 or
800/665–0212, WEB www.harbour-air.com).

BIKE TOURS
By Cycle Tours runs bicycle tours around Vancouver's parks and green
spaces. Bikes and helmets are supplied, and the guides pick up and drop
off guests at downtown hotels. Velo-City Cycle Tours offers daily trips
around the Stanley Park seawall, through the North Shore rain forest,
and to Pacific Spirit Park, as well as day trips to Squamish, Whistler,
and the Sunshine Coast. All equipment is supplied.
➤ FEES AND SCHEDULES: **By Cycle Tours** (☎ 604/936–2453). **Velo-City
Cycle Tours** (☎ 604/924–0288, WEB www.velo-city.com).

BOAT TOURS
Aquabus Ferries operates 25-minute minicruises around False Creek
for about $6. From May through October, it also offers 45-minute tours

of False Creek on vintage wooden ferries. The tours cost $8 and leave every 20 minutes from the Aquabus dock on Granville Island.

False Creek Ferries has a 20-minute False Creek tour for $5, and a 40-minute tour for $8; both leave from Granville Island daily, about four times an hour in summer, hourly in winter.

Harbour Cruises, at the north foot of Denman Street on Coal Harbour, operates a 1¼-hour narrated tour of Burrard Inlet aboard the paddle wheeler MPV *Constitution*. Tours are given from April through October and cost less than $20. Harbour Cruises also offers sunset dinner cruises, four-hour lunch cruises up scenic Indian Arm, cruises to golf at Furry Creek Golf Club, and links with the Royal Hudson Steam Train to make a daylong boat–train excursion to Howe Sound.

Paddlewheeler Riverboat Tours, in the New Westminster Public Market can take you out on the Fraser River in an 1800s-style paddle wheeler. Choose from a two-hour gold rush–theme tour with a lunch buffet, a Wild West–theme day trip to historic Fort Langley, or a sunset dinner cruise.

➤ FEES AND SCHEDULES: **Aquabus Ferries** (☎ 604/689–5858, WEB www.aquabus.bc.ca). **False Creek Ferries** (☎ 604/684–7781, WEB www.granvilleislandferries.bc.ca). **Harbour Cruises** (✉ end of Denman St., ☎ 604/688–7246 or 800/663–1500, WEB www.boatcruises.com). **Paddlewheeler Riverboat Tours** (✉ Unit 139, 810 Quayside Dr., New Westminster, ☎ 604/525–4465 or 877/825–1302, WEB www.vancouverpaddlewheeler.com).

BUS TOURS

Gray Line offers a 3½-hour Grand City bus tour year-round. The tour picks up at all major downtown hotels and includes Stanley Park, Chinatown, Gastown, English Bay, and Queen Elizabeth Park. The fee is about $42. From May through October, Gray Line also has a narrated city tour aboard double-decker buses; passengers can get on and off as they choose and can travel free the next day. Adult fare is about $24.
➤ FEES AND SCHEDULES: **Gray Line** (☎ 604/879–3363 or 800/667–0882, WEB www.grayline.ca).

ECOLOGICAL TOURS

In December and January, thousands of bald eagles gather at Brackendale, about an hour north of Vancouver. With Canadian Outback Adventures, you can watch and photograph the eagles from a slow-moving raft on the river. Vancouver All-Terrain Adventures runs four-wheel-drive trips into the mountains near Vancouver, including an eagle-viewing trip.

A number of companies run sea-kayaking trips out of Vancouver. Most trips offer a good chance of spotting orca whales, and some are suitable for first-timers. Ecosummer Expeditions offers weekend and longer sailing trips, in addition to sea kayaking. From May through October, Lotus Land Tours runs a four-hour sea-kayak trip—including a salmon barbecue lunch—to Twin Island (an uninhabited provincial marine park) to explore marine life in the intertidal zone. Experience is not required; the kayaks are easy for beginners to handle. You can choose to take the same trip by motorboat. Ocean West Expeditions, on English Bay beach at the foot of Denman Street, offers guided half-day sea-kayaking trips around English Bay and Stanley Park, as well as kayak rentals and multiday trips out of Vancouver.
➤ FEES AND SCHEDULES: **Canadian Outback Adventures** (☎ 604/921–7250 or 800/565–8735). **Ecosummer Expeditions** (☎ 250/674–0102 or 800/465–8884, WEB www.ecosummer.ca). **Lotus Land Tours** (☎ 604/684–4922 or 800/528–3531, www.lotuslandtours.com). **Ocean West**

Expeditions (☎ 800/660–0051, WEB www.ocean-west.com). **Vancouver All-Terrain Adventures** (☎ 604/984–2374 or 888/754–5601).

HELICOPTER TOURS

Tour Vancouver, the harbor, or the mountains of the North Shore by helicopter. For $110 to $215 per person (minimum of three people), Helijet Charters flies from downtown to the Harbour Heliport. Shorter tours are also available from the top of Grouse Mountain.
➤ FEES AND SCHEDULES: **Helijet Charters** (✉ 455 Waterfront Rd., ☎ 604/270–1484 or 800/987–4354, WEB www.helijet.com).

HIKING TOURS

Hike B.C. conducts guided hikes and snowshoe trips to the North Shore Mountains between May and October. Guided walks through the rain forests and canyons surrounding the city, including a popular day trip to Bowen Island in Howe Sound, are run by Rockwood Adventures.
➤ FEES AND SCHEDULES: **Hike B.C.** (☎ 604/540–2499). **Rockwood Adventures** (☎ 604/926–7705 or 888/236–6606, WEB www.rockwoodadventures.com).

ORIENTATION TOURS

The one-hour Stanley Park Horse Drawn Tours operate March 15 to the end of October and cost $18.65 per person. The tours leave every 20 to 30 minutes from near the information booth on Stanley Park Drive. The Vancouver Trolley Company runs old-style trolleys through Vancouver on a two-hour narrated tour of Stanley Park, Gastown, English Bay, Granville Island, and Chinatown, among other sights. A day pass allows you to complete one full circuit, getting off and on as often as you like. Start the trip at any of the 16 sights and buy a ticket ($24) on board. The four-hour City Highlights tour run by West Coast City and Nature Sightseeing is about $46. Pickup is available from all major hotels downtown.

North Shore tours usually include any or several of the following: a gondola ride up Grouse Mountain, a walk across the Capilano Suspension Bridge, a stop at a salmon hatchery, a visit to the Lonsdale Quay Market, and a ride back to town on the SeaBus. North Shore tours are offered early March through late October by Landsea Tours and all year by West Coast City and Nature Sightseeing. The half-day tours are $45 to $55.
➤ FEES AND SCHEDULES: **Landsea Tours** (☎ 604/255–7272 or 877/669–2277, WEB www.vancouvertours.com). **Stanley Park Horse Drawn Tours** (☎ 604/681–5115, WEB www.stanleyparktours.com). **Vancouver Trolley Company** (☎ 604/801–5515 or 888/451–5581, WEB www.vancouvertrolley.com). **West Coast City and Nature Sightseeing** (☎ 604/451–1600, WEB www.vancouversightseeing.com).

PRIVATE GUIDES

Early Motion Tours picks you up at your hotel for a spin through Vancouver in a 1930 Model-A Ford convertible. Vancouver All-Terrain Adventures offers customized city tours in a luxury four-wheel-drive Suburban at $75 an hour for up to seven passengers. Individual and group tours in six European languages are available from VIP Tourguide Services.
➤ FEES AND SCHEDULES: **Early Motion Tours** (☎ 604/687–5088). **Vancouver All-Terrain Adventures** (☎ 604/984–2374 or 888/754–5601). **VIP Tourguide Services** (☎ 604/214–4677, WEB www3.telus.net/tourguides).

SPECIAL-INTEREST TOURS

West Coast City and Nature Sightseeing gives a daily, four-hour Native Culture tour, with expert guides offering insights into the history and culture of Vancouver-area First Nations peoples. The tours take in the Stanley Park totem poles, the Museum of Anthropology, and two community facilities—the First Nations House of Learning and the Native Education Centre. The $41 fee includes admission to the Museum of Anthropology.

➤ FEES AND SCHEDULES: **West Coast City and Nature Sightseeing** (☎ 604/451–1600, WEB www.vancouversightseeing.com).

TRAIN TOURS

You can sample West Coast cuisine in the vintage rail coaches of the Pacific Starlight Dinner Train, which leaves the North Vancouver B.C. Rail station at 6:15 PM, stops at scenic Porteau Cove on Howe Sound, and returns to the station at 10 PM. The train runs Friday through Sunday, May through October. Fares, including a three-course meal, are $85.95 for salon seating, $109.95 for the dome car. Reservations are essential.

The *Royal Hudson,* a vintage train, leaves the North Vancouver B.C. Rail station for a trip along the mountainous coast up Howe Sound to the town of Squamish. After a break there, you can return by train or sail back to Vancouver on the MV *Britannia.* The trip runs from Wednesday through Sunday late May–late September. The round-trip train fare is $50 or $83 including brunch or high tea. By train and boat the trip costs about $70. Reservations are advised.

➤ FEES AND SCHEDULES: **Pacific Starlight Dinner Train** (☎ 604/631–3500 or 800/663–8238, WEB www.bcrail.com). **Royal Hudson** (☎ 604/631–3500 or 800/663–8238, WEB www.bcrail.com).

WALKING TOURS

Students from the Architectural Institute of British Columbia lead free 90-minute walking tours of the city's top heritage sites July through September. The Gastown Business Improvement Society sponsors free 90-minute historical and architectural walking tours daily June through August. Meet the guide at 2 PM at the statue of "Gassy" Jack in Maple Tree Square. Rockwood Adventures has guided walks around Vancouver neighborhoods, including Gastown, Granville Island, and Chinatown, and a special walk for art lovers. Guides with Walkabout Historic Vancouver dress in 19th-century costume for their two-hour historical walking tours around Downtown and Gastown or Granville Island. Tours run mid-February to mid-November and cost $18.

➤ FEES AND SCHEDULES: **Architectural Institute of British Columbia** (☎ 604/683–8588, WEB www.aibc.bc.ca). **Gastown Business Improvement Society** (☎ 604/683–5650). **Rockwood Adventures** (☎ 604/926–7705 or 888/236–6606, WEB www.rockwoodadventures.com). **Walkabout Historic Vancouver** (☎ 604/720–0006, WEB www.darkroombytes.com/walkabout.html).

TRAIN TRAVEL

The Pacific Central Station, at Main Street and Terminal Avenue, near the Main Street SkyTrain station, is the hub for rail service. Amtrak operates its *Cascades* train service between Vancouver and Eugene, Oregon. VIA Rail provides transcontinental service through Jasper to Toronto three times a week. Passenger trains leave the BC Rail Station for Whistler and the interior of British Columbia.

Rail buffs take note: trains are becoming an increasingly convenient way to get around Vancouver, as well. Part of an effort to revive streetcar service around False Creek, the volunteer-run Downtown Historic Railway operates two restored electric trams (built in 1905 and 1913) along a 5-km (3-mi) track between Science World and Granville Island. The trams, which also stop at First Avenue and Ontario Street and at

Leg-in-Boot Square, near Sixth Avenue and Moberly Street, operate 12:30 to 5 PM weekends and holidays from late May to early October. The adult fare is $2.

➤ TRAIN INFORMATION: **Amtrak** (☎ 800/872–7245, WEB www.am-trak.com). **B.C. Rail Station** (✉ 1311 W. 1st St., North Vancouver, ☎ 604/631–3500 or 800/663–8238, WEB www.bcrail.com). **Downtown Historic Railway** (☎ 604/665–3903 or 604/325–9990, WEB www.city.van-couver.bc.ca/engsvcs/streetcar). **Pacific Central Station** (✉ 1150 Station St., ☎ no phone). **VIA Rail** (☎ 800/561–8630 in Canada; 800/561–3949 in the U.S., WEB www.viarail.ca).

VISITOR INFORMATION

➤ TOURIST INFORMATION: **Granville Island Information Centre** (✉ 1398 Cartwright St., ☎ 604/666–5784, WEB www.granvilleisland.com). **Super, Natural B.C.** (☎ 800/435–5622, WEB www.hellobc.com). **Vancouver Tourist Info Centre** (✉ 200 Burrard St., ☎ 604/683–2000, WEB www.tourismvancouver.com).

3 VICTORIA AND VANCOUVER ISLAND

Islands have long held a fascination for travelers, and Vancouver Island, the largest island off North America's West Coast, is no exception. At 300 mi tip to tip, it offers an immense variety of landscapes—from the rolling farmland and protected beaches of the southeast, to the sparsely inhabited forests of the north and the crashing surf on the west. On the southern tip, Victoria, the capital of British Columbia, has shed its tea-cozy image and reemerged as a Pacific Rim metropolis that celebrates its native, Asian, and European roots.

B EACHES, WILDERNESS PARKS, mountains, deep temperate rain forests, and a wealth of wildlife have long drawn adventurous visitors to the West Coast's largest island. These days, however, a slew of excellent restaurants, country inns, spas, and ecologically sensitive resorts means visitors can enjoy all that beauty in comfort—though roughing it is still an option.

By Sue
Kernaghan

Despite its growing popularity with visitors, the island rarely feels crowded. Fewer than a million people live here, and virtually all of them cluster on the island's sheltered eastern side, between Victoria and Campbell River; half live in Victoria itself. The island's west coast, facing the open ocean, is wild and often inhospitable, with few roads and only a handful of small settlements. Nevertheless, the old-growth forests, magnificent stretch of beach, and challenging trails of the Pacific Rim National Park Reserve, as well as the chance to see whales offshore, are major draws for campers, hikers, kayakers, and even surfers.

As rich as Vancouver Island's natural bounty is the cultural heritage of the Pacific Coast First Nations peoples—the Kwakiutl, Nootka, and others—who had occupied the land for more than 12,000 years before the first Europeans arrived en masse in the late 19th century. Their art and culture are on display throughout the island, in totems and petroglyphs, in city art galleries, and in the striking collections at the Royal British Columbia Museum in Victoria and the Quw'utsun Cultural and Conference Centre in Duncan.

Pleasures and Pastimes

Dining

Restaurants in the region generally are casual. Smoking is banned in all public places, including restaurants and bars, in Greater Victoria and on the Gulf Islands.

CATEGORY	COST*
$$$$	over $32
$$$	$22–$32
$$	$13–$21
$	under $13

*per person, in Canadian dollars, for a main course at dinner

Lodging

Accommodations on Vancouver Island range from bed-and-breakfasts and country inns to rustic cabins to deluxe ecotourism lodges. Victoria in particular has a great selection of English-style B&Bs. Most small inns and B&Bs on the island ban smoking indoors, and virtually all hotels in the area offer no-smoking rooms. Advance reservations are always a good idea, especially in some of the more isolated towns.

CATEGORY	COST*
$$$$	over $250
$$$	$170–$250
$$	$90–$170
$	under $90

*All prices are for a standard double room, excluding 10% provincial accommodation tax, service charge, and 7% GST, in Canadian dollars.

Outdoor Activities and Sports

CANOEING AND KAYAKING

The island-dotted Strait of Georgia, on the east side of Vancouver Island, provides fairly protected seagoing, stunning scenery, and plenty of opportunities to spot orcas, eagles, and other local fauna. The Broken Group Islands, off the island's west coast, draw kayakers from around the world to their protected, wildlife-rich waters. The mountainous Strathcona Provincial Park offers scenic lake and river paddling.

FISHING

Miles of coastline and numerous lakes, rivers, and streams lure anglers to Vancouver Island. Though salmon doesn't run as thickly as it once did, both coasts of the island still provide excellent salmon fishing, and many operators offer fishing charters.

HIKING

The West Coast Trail, one of the world's most famous trails, runs along the western side of Vancouver Island. Other trails also offer plenty of challenge, including the Juan de Fuca Marine Trail and those in Strathcona Provincial Park. But you can find fine hiking-trail networks in almost all of the island's many parks.

WHALE-WATCHING

Three resident and several transient pods of orcas (killer whales) travel the island's eastern coastal waters. These, and the gray whales that migrate along the west coast, are the primary focus of the many whale-watching boat tours leaving Victoria, Telegraph Cove, Ucluelet, Bamfield, and Tofino in spring and summer months. July, August, and September are the best months to see orcas; in March and April, thousands of migrating gray whales pass close to the west coast of Vancouver Island on their way from Baja California to Alaska. Harbor seals, sea lions, porpoises, and marine-bird sightings are a safe bet anytime.

First Nations Culture

Before the arrival of Europeans, the lush landscapes of the Pacific Northwest gave rise to one of the richest and most artistically prolific cultures on the continent. Two of the best places to appreciate it are Victoria's Royal British Columbia Museum and, in Duncan, the Quw'utsun Cultural and Conference Centre, which is run by First Nations people.

Exploring Vancouver Island

Vancouver Island, touched by Pacific currents, has the mildest climate in Canada. Temperatures are usually above 32°F in winter and below 80°F in summer, although winter brings frequent rains (especially on the west coast).

When traveling by car, keep in mind that most of Vancouver Island's west coast has very few roads and is accessible mainly by sea or air.

Numbers in the text correspond to numbers in the margin and on the Vancouver Island map.

Great Itineraries

IF YOU HAVE 1-3 DAYS

For a short trip, ⊞ **Victoria** ①–⑯ is a fine place to begin. There's plenty to explore, from the flower-fringed Inner Harbour and the museums and attractions nearby to Market Square and the red gates of Chinatown. World-famous Butchart Gardens is only half an hour away by car, and you might take a full day to explore the beautiful grounds. On Day 3, head west to ⊞ **Sooke** ⑰ or north, over the scenic Malahat region, to **Duncan** ⑱, **Chemainus** ⑲, or **Nanaimo** ⑳, which has ferry service to the mainland.

IF YOU HAVE 4-6 DAYS

A brief stay in ⊞ **Victoria** ①–⑯ can be followed by a tour of Vancouver Island. Follow the itinerary above, heading to **Sooke** ⑰ on Day 3.

Vancouver Island

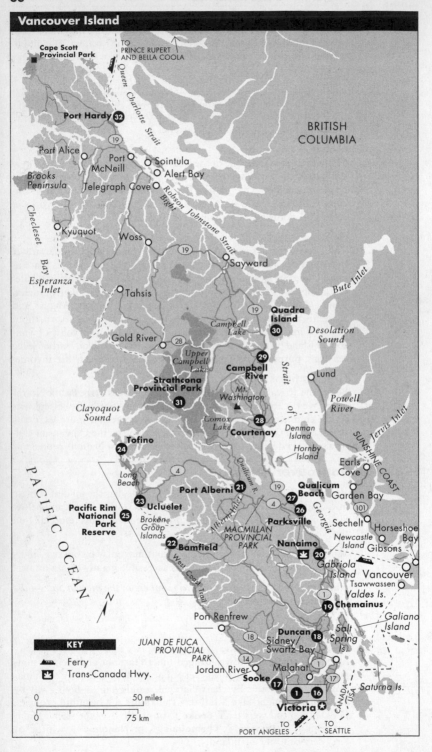

Cape Scott
Provincial Park

TO PRINCE RUPERT
AND BELLA COOLA

Port Hardy 32

BRITISH
COLUMBIA

19

Port Alice

Port
McNeill

Sointula

Alert Bay

*Brooks
Peninsula*

Telegraph Cove

Robson Johnstone Strait

*Checleset
Bay*

Kyuquot

Woss

Sayward

19

*Esperanza
Inlet*

Tahsis

Bute Inlet

Gold River

28

*Campbell
Lake*

19

**Quadra
Island** 30

*Desolation
Sound*

*Upper
Campbell
Lake*

**Campbell
River** 29

Lund

**Strathcona
Provincial Park** 31

Mt.
Washington ▲

28

Strait

*Powell
River*

*Clayoquot
Sound*

*Comox
Lake*

Courtenay 28

*Denman
Island*

*Hornby
Island*

of

SUNSHINE COAST

Jervis Inlet

Tofino 24

*Long
Beach*

4

Earls
Cove

19

**Qualicum
Beach** 27

Garden Bay

101

Port Alberni 21

26

Georgia

Sechelt

Ucluelet 23

4

Parksville 26

Horseshoe
Bay

**Pacific Rim
National
Park
Reserve** 25

*Broken
Group
Islands*

*MACMILLAN
PROVINCIAL
PARK*

*Newcastle
Island*

Gibsons

Bamfield 22

Alberni Inlet

Nanaimo 20

*Gabriola
Island* **Vancouver**

West Coast Trail

Tsawwassen

Valdes Is.

Chemainus 19

*Galiano
Island*

N

Port Renfrew

Duncan 18

*Salt
Spring
Is.*

18

Sidney/
Swartz Bay

*JUAN DE FUCA
PROVINCIAL
PARK*

14

Jordan River

Malahat

1

17

Saturna Is.

Sooke 17

Victoria 1 16 ✛

TO
PORT ANGELES

TO
SEATTLE

CANADA
USA

KEY

⛴ Ferry

🍁 Trans-Canada Hwy.

0 ——— 50 miles

0 ——— 75 km

Day 4 allows time to see the Quw'utsun Cultural and Conference Centre in **Duncan** ⑱ and the murals and restored Victorian buildings of ⛴ **Chemainus** ⑲. On Day 5, one alternative is to trek across the island to the scenic west coast to visit ⛴ **Tofino** ㉔ and ⛴ **Ucluelet** ㉓ (pick one for your overnight) and spend some time whale-watching or hiking around **Pacific Rim National Park Reserve** ㉕. Another choice is to continue up the east coast to visit **Strathcona Provincial Park** ㉛ or to do some salmon fishing from ⛴ **Campbell River** ㉙. Spend Day 6 retracing your steps to Victoria or Nanaimo, for ferry service to the mainland.

IF YOU HAVE 7–10 DAYS

A longer trip allows more time to explore the area in and around the **Pacific Rim National Park Reserve** ㉕, or to visit **Bamfield** ㉒ or the **Broken Group Islands** on the *Lady Rose*, a coastal freighter that sails from **Port Alberni** ㉑. If you're exploring the east coast, you could visit one of the rustic off-shore islands; **Quadra** ㉚, **Denman**, and **Hornby** islands are all easily reached by ferry. Otherwise, head north toward **Port Hardy** ㉜ to see the resident whale pods near Telegraph Cove. From Port Hardy, you can continue a tour of British Columbia on an Inside Passage cruise.

When to Tour Vancouver Island

Though summer is the most popular time to visit, in winter the island has skiing at Mount Washington, near Courtenay, and, off the west coast, dramatic storms that can be fun to watch from a cozy inn. March and April are the best time to see migrating whales off the west coast.

VICTORIA

Originally Fort Victoria, Victoria was the first European settlement on Vancouver Island. It was chosen to be the westernmost trading outpost of the British-owned Hudson's Bay Company in 1843 and became the capital of British Columbia in 1868. Victoria has since evolved into a walkable, livable seaside town of gardens, waterfront pathways, and restored 19th-century architecture. Often described as the country's most British city, these days—except for the odd red phone box, good beer, and well-mannered drivers—Victoria has been working to change that image, preferring to celebrate its combined native, Asian, and European heritage.

The city is 71 km (44 mi), or 1½ hours by ferry plus 1½ hours by car, south of Vancouver, or a 2½-hour ferry ride from Seattle.

Downtown Victoria

Numbers in the text correspond to numbers in the margin and on the Downtown Victoria map.

A Good Walk

Begin on the waterfront at the **Visitors Information Centre,** at 812 Wharf Street. Across the way on Government Street is the **Fairmont Empress** ①, a majestic hotel that opened in 1908. A short walk around the harbor along the Inner Harbour Walk (take any of the staircases from Government Street down to the water level) takes you to the **Royal London Wax Museum** ②. Across Belleville Street is the **Parliament Buildings** ③ complex, seat of the provincial government. Cross Government Street to reach the **Royal British Columbia Museum** ④, one of Canada's most impressive museums. Behind the museum and bordering Douglas Street are the totem poles and ceremonial longhouse of Thunderbird Park; **Helmcken House** ⑤, the oldest house in Victoria; and the tiny 19th-century St. Ann's Schoolhouse. A walk south on Douglas Street leads to the beautiful **Beacon Hill Park** ⑥. A few blocks west of the park on Government Street is the **Emily Carr House** ⑦, the birthplace of one of British Columbia's best-known artists. Walk back to Beacon Hill Park, and then proceed north on Douglas Street until you reach Blanshard Street, on your right. Take Blanshard, where just past Academy Close (on the right) you can see the entrance to **St. Ann's Academy** ⑧, a former convent school with parklike grounds. (There's also a footpath to the academy from Southgate Street.) From St. Ann's, follow Belleville Street west. The next stop, at the corner of Douglas and Belleville streets, is the glass-roofed **Crystal Garden Conservation Centre** ⑨.

From Crystal Garden, take Belleville Street west one block to Government Street, Victoria's liveliest shopping street. Head north about five blocks to Government and View streets, where you can see the entrance to the cobblestoned **Bastion Square** ⑩, the original site of Fort Victoria and the Hudson's Bay Company trading post, which now has restaurants and small shops. Just north of Government and View, on the right-hand side of Government Street, is the entrance to Trounce Alley, a pretty pedestrian-only shopping arcade.

At Bastion Square, you can stop in the **Maritime Museum of British Columbia** ⑪ to learn about an important part of the province's history. Around the corner (to the south) on Wharf Street is the **Victoria Bug Zoo** ⑫, a creepy-crawly attraction popular with kids. North of Bastion Square a few blocks, on Store Street between Johnson Street and Pandora Avenue, is **Market Square** ⑬, one of the city's most picturesque shopping districts. Across Pandora Avenue is the entrance to the narrow, shop-lined Fan Tan Alley, which leads to Fisgard Street, the heart of **Chinatown** ⑭.

You can head back south on Government Street until you hit Fort Street. From here, a 25-minute walk or a short drive east takes you to Joan Crescent and lavish **Craigdarroch Castle** ⑮. Down the hill on Moss Street is the **Art Gallery of Greater Victoria** ⑯.

In summer, a ride on Harbour Ferries from the Inner Harbour takes you to **Point Ellice House,** a historic waterside home and garden.

TIMING

Many of the attractions in downtown Victoria are within easy walking distance of one another. You can walk this tour in a day, but there's so much to see at the Royal British Columbia Museum and the other museums that you could easily fill two days. This would allow time for some shopping and a visit to Craigdarroch Castle.

Sights to See

⑯ Art Gallery of Greater Victoria. Attached to an 1889 mansion, this modern building houses one of the largest collections of Chinese and Japanese artifacts in Western Canada. The Japanese garden between the buildings is home to the only authentic Shinto shrine in North America. The gallery, which is a few blocks west of Craigdarroch Castle, off Fort Street, features regularly changing exhibits of Asian and historical and contemporary Western art. ✉ *1040 Moss St.*, ☎ *250/384–4101,* WEB *www.aggv.bc.ca.* ✄ *$5; Mon. by donation.* ☉ *Mon.–Wed. and Fri.–Sat. 10–5, Thurs. 10–9, Sun. 1–5.*

⑩ Bastion Square. James Douglas, the fur trader and former colonial governor for whom Douglas Street was named, chose this spot for the original Fort Victoria and Hudson's Bay Company trading post. Offices, boutiques, and restaurants occupy the old brick buildings. ✉ *Off Wharf St. at the end of View St.*

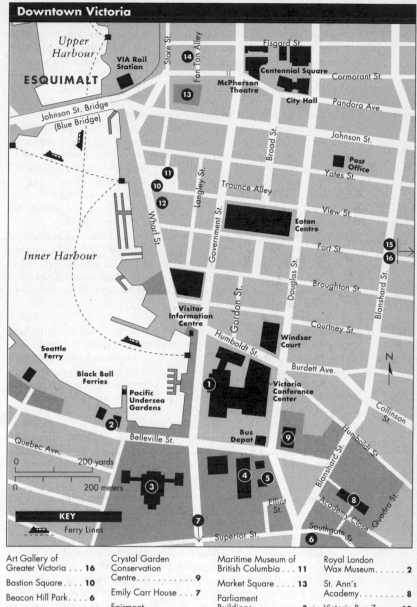

Downtown Victoria

Art Gallery of
Greater Victoria . . . **16**

Bastion Square **10**

Beacon Hill Park **6**

Chinatown **14**

Craigdarroch
Castle **15**

Crystal Garden
Conservation
Centre **9**

Emily Carr House . . . **7**

Fairmont
Empress **1**

Helmcken House **5**

Maritime Museum of
British Columbia . . . **11**

Market Square **13**

Parliament
Buildings **3**

Royal British
Columbia
Museum **4**

Royal London
Wax Museum **2**

St. Ann's
Academy **8**

Victoria Bug Zoo . . . **12**

★ ℃ ❻ **Beacon Hill Park.** The southern lawns of this spacious park have great views of the Olympic Mountains and the Strait of Juan de Fuca. Also here are ponds, jogging and walking paths, abundant flowers and gardens, a petting zoo, and a cricket pitch. The park is also home to Mile Zero of the Trans-Canada Highway. ⊠ *East of Douglas St., south of Southgate St.,* ☎ *250/361–0600 City of Victoria Parks Division; 250/ 381–2532 petting zoo.*

OFF THE
BEATEN PATH
BUTCHART GARDENS – Originally a private estate and still family-run, this stunning 50-acre garden about 21 km (13 mi) north of downtown Victoria has been drawing visitors since it was planted in a limestone quarry in 1904. The site's Japanese, Italian, rose, and sunken gardens grow 700 varieties of flowers in a setting that's beautiful year-round. From mid-June to mid-September, the gardens are illuminated at night, and musicians and other entertainers perform in the afternoons and evenings. In July and August, fireworks light the sky over the gardens on Saturday nights. Also on the premises are a seed and gift shop, two restaurants, and a café. ⊠ *800 Benvenuto Ave., Brentwood Bay,* ☎ *250/652–5256 or 250/652–4422; 250/652–8222 for dining reservations,* WEB *www.butchartgardens.com.* ☜ *$19.25 June 15–Sept. 30; $17.25 May 15–June 14 and Oct. 1–14; call about remainder of the year.* ☉ *June 15–Sept. 1, daily 9 AM–10:30 PM; Sept. 2–15, daily 9–9; Sept. 16–June 14, 9 AM–dusk.*

⓮ **Chinatown.** Chinese immigrants built much of the Canadian Pacific Railway in the 19th century, and their influence still marks the region. Victoria's Chinatown, founded in 1858, is the oldest and most intact such district in Canada. If you enter Chinatown from Government Street, you'll pass under the elaborate **Gate of Harmonious Interest,** made of Taiwanese ceramic tiles and decorative panels. Along Fisgard Street, merchants display paper lanterns, embroidered silks, and produce. Mah-jongg, fan-tan, and dominoes were among the games of chance played on narrow **Fan Tan Alley.** Once the gambling and opium center of Chinatown, it's now lined with offbeat shops. Look for the alley on the south side of Fisgard Street between Nos. 545½ and 549½. ⊠ *Fisgard St. between Government and Store Sts.*

⓯ **Craigdarroch Castle.** This resplendent mansion was built as the home of one of British Columbia's wealthiest men, coal baron Robert Dunsmuir, who died in 1889, just a few months before the castle's completion. Converted into a museum depicting life in the late 1800s, the castle has ornate Victorian furnishings, stained-glass windows, carved woodwork (precut in Chicago for Dunsmuir and sent by rail), and a beautifully restored painted ceiling in the drawing room. A winding staircase climbs four floors to a ballroom and a tower overlooking Victoria. ⊠ *1050 Joan Crescent,* ☎ *250/592–5323,* WEB *www.craigdarrochcastle.com.* ☜ *$8.* ☉ *Mid-June–Sept. 2, daily 9–7; Sept. 3– mid-June, daily 10–4:30.*

℃ ❾ **Crystal Garden Conservation Centre.** Opened in 1925 as the largest saltwater swimming pool in the British Empire, this glass-roof building today houses exotic flora and a variety of endangered tropical mammals, reptiles, and birds, including flamingos, tortoises, macaws, lemurs, bats, and butterflies. ⊠ *713 Douglas St.,* ☎ *250/381–1213,* WEB *www.bcpcc.com/crystal.* ☜ *$7.50.* ☉ *July–Aug., daily 8:30–8; Sept.–Oct. and Apr.–June, daily 9–6; Nov.–Mar., daily 10–4:30.*

❼ **Emily Carr House.** One of Canada's most celebrated artists and a respected writer, Emily Carr (1871–1945) was born and raised in this very proper wooden Victorian house before abandoning her middle-class life to live in, and paint, the wilds of British Columbia. Carr's own descriptions, from her autobiography *Book of Small*, were used to restore the house. Occasional exhibitions of her work are also held here. ⊠ *207 Government St.,* ☎ *250/383–5843,* WEB *www. heritage.gov.bc.ca/emily/emily.htm.* ▦ *$5.35.* ☉ *Mid-May–mid-Oct., daily 10–5; Dec. 1–24 and Dec. 27–31, daily 11–4. By arrangement or during special exhibits the rest of the year.*

❶ **Fairmont Empress.** Opened in 1908 by the Canadian Pacific Railway, the Empress is one of the grand château-style hotels that grace many Canadian cities. Designed by Francis Rattenbury, who also designed the Parliament Buildings across the way, the Empress, with its solid Edwardian grandeur, has become a symbol of the city. The elements that made the hotel an attraction for travelers in the past—old-world architecture, ornate decor, and a commanding view of the Inner Harbour—are still here. You can stop in for afternoon tea, which is served daily. Reservations are recommended, and the dress code calls for smart casual wear. The archives, a historical photo display, are open to the public anytime. **Miniature World** (☎ 250/385–9731, ▦ $8), a display of doll-size dioramas, is on the Humboldt Street side of the complex. ⊠ *721 Government St.,* ☎ *250/384–8111,* WEB *www.fairmont.com.* ▦ *Free; afternoon tea $46 June–Sept. (call about remainder of the year).*

OFF THE BEATEN PATH | **FORT RODD HILL AND FISGARD LIGHTHOUSE** – This 1895 coast artillery fort and the oldest (and still functioning) lighthouse on Canada's west coast are about 15 km (9 mi) west of Victoria, off Highway 1A on the way to Sooke. ⊠ *603 Fort Rodd Hill Rd. off Ocean Blvd.,* ☎ *250/ 478–5849,* WEB *www.parkscanada.gc.ca/rodd.* ▦ *$4.* ☉ *Mar.–Oct., daily 10–5:30; Nov.–Feb., daily 9–4:30.*

Next door to Fort Rodd is **Hatley Castle,** the former estate of coal and railway baron James Dunsmuir. The 1909 castle is on 650 acres of beautifully landscaped grounds (including Italian, Japanese, and English rose gardens) that are open daily until dusk all year. Garden and castle tours are given daily in summer (call for times). ⊠ *2005 Sooke Rd.,* ☎ *250/391–2600 Ext. 4456 or 250/391–2511.* ▦ *Grounds free; castle $3 (by tour only).*

❺ **Helmcken House.** The oldest house in Victoria was erected in 1852 for pioneer doctor and statesman John Sebastian Helmcken. Audio tours of the house, whose holdings include the family's original Victorian furnishings and the doctor's 19th-century medical tools, last 20 minutes. Next door are St. Ann's Schoolhouse, one of the first schools in British Columbia (you can view the interior through the door), and Thunderbird Park, with totem poles and a ceremonial longhouse constructed by Kwakwaka'wakw chief Mungo Martin. ⊠ *10 Elliot St., near Douglas and Belleville Sts.,* ☎ *250/361–0021,* WEB *www.heritage. gov.bc.ca/helm/helm.htm.* ▦ *$5.* ☉ *May–Oct., daily 10–5; Nov.–Apr., Thurs.–Mon. noon–4.*

⑪ **Maritime Museum of British Columbia.** The model ships, hand-built wooden boats, Royal Navy charts, photographs, uniforms, and ship bells at this museum, in Victoria's original courthouse, chronicle the province's seafaring history. An 1899 hand-operated cage elevator, believed to be the oldest continuously operating lift in North America, ascends to the third floor, where the original 1888 vice-admiralty courtroom looks ready for a court-martial. ⊠ *28 Bastion Sq.,* ☎ *250/ 385–4222,* WEB *www.mmbc.bc.ca.* ▦ *$6.* ☉ *Daily 9:30–4:30.*

⑬ **Market Square.** During the late 19th century, this three-level square, built like an old inn courtyard, provided everything a sailor, miner, or lumberjack could want. Restored to its original architectural, if not commercial, character, it's a pedestrian-only, café- and boutique-lined hangout—now, as then, a great spot for people-watching. ⊠ *560 Johnson St.,* ☎ *250/386–2441.*

★ ❸ **Parliament Buildings.** These massive stone structures, designed by Francis Rattenbury and completed in 1898, dominate the Inner Harbour. Two statues flank the main entrance: one of Sir James Douglas, who chose the site where Victoria was built, and the other of Sir Matthew Baille Begbie, the man in charge of law and order during the gold-rush era. Atop the central dome is a gilded statue of Captain George Vancouver, the first European to sail around Vancouver Island. A statue of Queen Victoria reigns over the front of the complex. The Parliament Buildings, which are outlined with more than 3,000 lights at night, typify the rigid symmetry and European elegance of much of the city's architecture. The interior is lavishly done with marble floors, stained-glass windows, and murals depicting scenes from the province's history. When the legislature is in session (usually in spring and early summer), you can sit in the public gallery and watch British Columbia's often polarized democracy at work (custom has the opposing parties sitting 2½ sword lengths apart). Free, informative half-hour tours are obligatory on summer weekends (June 1 until September 2) and optional the rest of the time. ⊠ *501 Belleville St.,* ☎ *250/387–3046,* WEB *www.BC2000.gov.bc.ca.* ⊡ *Free.* ☉ *June–Sept. 2, daily 8:30–5; Sept. 3–May, weekdays 8:30–5.*

OFF THE BEATEN PATH   **POINT ELLICE HOUSE –** The O'Reilly family home, an 1860s Italianate villa overlooking the Upper Harbour, has been restored to its original splendor, with the largest collection of Victorian furnishings in Western Canada. Tea and baked goods are served on the lawn (noon–4). Visitors can also take an audio tour of the house, stroll in the gardens, or try their hand at croquet. Point Ellice House is a few minutes' drive north of downtown, but it's much more fun to come by sea. (Harbour Ferries leave from a dock in front of the Fairmont Empress hotel.) ⊠ *2616 Pleasant St.,* ☎ *250/380–6506,* WEB *www.heritage.gov.bc.ca/point/ point.htm.* ⊡ *$5; $17 including tea.* ☉ *Mother's Day–Labor Day, daily noon–5.*

★ ☝ ❹ **Royal British Columbia Museum.** The museum, easily the best attraction in Victoria, is as much a research and educational center as a draw for the public. The definitive First Peoples exhibit includes a genuine Kwakwaka'wakw longhouse (the builders retain rights to its ceremonial use) and provides insights into the daily life, art, and mythology of both coastal and lesser-known interior peoples, before and after the arrival of Europeans. The Modern History Gallery re-creates most of a frontier town, complete with cobblestone streets, silent movies, and rumbling train sounds. The Natural History Gallery realistically reproduces the sights, sounds, and smells of many of the province's natural habitats, and the Open Ocean mimics, all too realistically, a submarine journey. Century Hall reviews British Columbia's 20th century; an IMAX theater shows National Geographic films on a six-story-tall screen. ⊠ *675 Belleville St.,* ☎ *250/387–3701 or 888/447–7977,* WEB *www.royalbcmuseum.bc.ca.* ⊡ *$10.65; IMAX theater $9.50; combination ticket $18.15.* ☉ *Museum Sat.–Wed. 9–5; Thurs. and Fri. 9–7:45; theater daily 10–8 (call for show times).*

❷ **Royal London Wax Museum.** A collection of life-size wax figures resides in this elegant colonnaded building, once Victoria's steamship terminal. The 300-plus characters include members of the British royal family, famous Canadians, Hollywood stars, and some unfortunate souls in a Chamber of Horrors. ⊠ *470 Belleville St.,* ☎ *250/388–4461,* WEB *www.waxworld.com.* ☜ *$8.50.* ☉ *May–Aug., daily 9–7:30; Sept.–Apr., daily 9:30–5.*

❽ **St. Ann's Academy.** This former convent and school, founded in 1858, played a central role in British Columbia's pioneer life. Closed in 1974, it was carefully restored and reopened as a historic site in 1997. The academy's little chapel—the first Roman Catholic cathedral in Victoria—now looks just as it did in the 1920s. The six acres of grounds, with their fruit trees and herb and flower gardens, are being restored as historic landscapes. ⊠ *835 Humboldt St.,* ☎ *250/953–8828,* WEB *www.bcpcc.com/stanns.* ☜ *Free.* ☉ *June–Sept., daily 10–4; other times by appointment.*

☺ ⑫ **Victoria Bug Zoo.** Kids of all ages are drawn to this offbeat, two-room minizoo. Many of the bugs—mostly large tropical varieties, such as stick insects, scorpions, and centipedes—can be held, and staff members are on hand to dispense scientific information. ⊠ *1107 Wharf St.,* ☎ *250/384–2847,* WEB *www.bugzoo.bc.ca.* ☜ *$6.* ☉ *July–Aug., daily 9–9; Sept.–June, daily 9:30–5:30.*

Visitor Information Centre. You can get the lowdown on Victoria's attractions at this facility near the harbor ferries. The staff here can help you with maps, theater and concert tickets, accommodation reservations, and outdoor-adventure day trips. ⊠ *812 Wharf St.,* ☎ *250/953–2033,* WEB *www.tourismvictoria.com.* ☉ *June 1–Sept. 2, daily 8:30–6:30; Sept. 3–May, daily 9–5.*

Dining

Cafés

$ ✗ **Willie's Bakery.** Four generations of the Wille family ran a bakery in this handsome Victorian building near Market Square before closing shop in the 1970s. The site was reborn as a bakery–café, serving wholesome breakfasts, rich soups, delicious sandwiches made with house baked bread, and tasty muffins, cookies, and bagels. The brick patio with an outdoor fireplace and little fountain is a great place to watch the world go by. ⊠ *537 Johnson St.,* ☎ *250/381–8414. Reservations not accepted. AE, MC, V. No dinner.*

Chinese

$–$$ ✗ **Don Mee's.** A large neon sign invites you inside this traditional Chinese restaurant that's been in business since 1923. The entrées served in the expansive dining room include sweet-and-sour chicken, Peking duck, and ginger fried beef. Dim sum is served at lunchtime. ⊠ *538 Fisgard St.,* ☎ *250/383–1032. AE, DC, MC, V.*

Contemporary

$$$–$$$$ ✗ **Empress Room.** Beautifully presented Pacific Northwest cuisine vies
★ for attention with the elegant setting, where candlelight dances on tapestried walls beneath a carved mahogany ceiling. Fresh local ingredients go into imaginative seasonal dishes such as corn-crusted sea scallops with sugar-beet couscous, guinea fowl with rock-shrimp risotto, and rack of lamb with a macadamia-nut coating. The 500-label wine list is excellent, as are the table d'hôte menus. ⊠ *Fairmont Empress, 721 Government St.,* ☎ *250/389–2727. Reservations essential. AE, D, DC, MC, V. No lunch.*

$$–$$$$ ✗ **The Victorian Restaurant.** This 45-seat, candlelight restaurant in the
★ Delta Victoria Ocean Pointe Resort and Spa has striking views over the Inner Harbour. The chef offers elegantly presented regional dishes such as wild mushroom and truffle soup, roast rack of lamb with a maple and juniper glaze, and pheasant breast with goat cheese and sun-

dried cranberry mousse. The wine list has won a number of awards, including Wine Spectator's Award of Excellence in 1999. ⊠ *Delta Victoria Ocean Pointe Resort and Spa, 45 Songhees Rd. (across the Johnson Street Bridge from downtown Victoria),* ☎ *250/360–5800. Reservations essential. AE, DC, MC, V. Closed Jan. and Mon.–Tues. in Nov.–Apr. No lunch.*

$$$ ✕ **Cassis.** John Hall, the chef-owner of this intimate restaurant in Cook Street Village, a few minutes' drive from the Inner Harbour, seeks out local organic ingredients to create a menu that reads like a map of the surrounding countryside. The menu changes seasonally but has included Cowichan Valley chicken breast with olive tapenade, celeriac purée, and balsamic–rosemary pan *jus,* roast Saanich Peninsula organic rabbit, and medallions of Metchosin pork tenderloin. Most of the main courses also are available in an appetizer size, so you can sample several. ⊠ *253 Cook St.,* ☎ *250/384–1932. Reservations essential. MC, V. Closed Mon. Oct.–Apr. No lunch Tues.–Sat.*

$$–$$$ ✕ **Cafe Brio.** A little north of the Inner Harbour, a building resembling
★ an Italian villa is the setting for one of Victoria's most enjoyable restaurants. Candlelight, hardwood floors, lush Modigliani nudes, and rich gold walls create a warm glow. The daily menu depends on what's fresh that day—very fresh. The café works in partnership with local organic farms and serves the produce the same day it's harvested. Favorites have included confit of duck with potato gnocchi and truffle oil, red wine–braised lamb shank, and seared jumbo Alaskan scallops served with sorrel butter and preserved lemon. The vegetarian options are always good, and the extensive wine list goes easy on the markups. ⊠ *944 Fort St.,* ☎ *250/383–0009. AE, MC, V. No lunch Sat.–Mon. and Nov. and Jan.–Apr.*

$$–$$$ ✕ **Camille's.** The seasonal menu emphasizes fresh local products as well as such exotica as ostrich, quail, and emu. The setting, on the lower floor of a historic brick building in Bastion Square, is candlelight and romantic, with exposed brick and intimate booths. The wine cellar is one of the city's best. ⊠ *45 Bastion Sq.,* ☎ *250/381–3433. AE, MC, V. No lunch. No dinner Mon. Nov.–June.*

$$–$$$ ✕ **Herald Street Caffe.** Intriguing combinations are the hallmarks of
★ this art-filled bistro in Victoria's warehouse district. The menu, which changes seasonally, always lists fresh local cuisine, daily fish grills, great fresh pastas, and good vegetarian selections. Try, if available, calamari in tomato-dill ratatouille with crumbled feta, or free-range beef tenderloin stuffed with a wild mushroom–chestnut paté. The wine list is excellent. The restaurant's lounge is open for dinner as well as for late-night snacks until midnight Friday and Saturday nights. ⊠ *546 Herald St.,* ☎ *250/381–1441. Reservations essential. AE, DC, MC, V. No lunch Mon.–Tues.*

$$ ✕ **Malahat Mountain Inn.** If you're heading up Highway 1, consider a stop at this roadhouse on the top of the Malahat hill about 30 minutes north of Victoria. It doesn't look like much from the highway, but inside the eagle's eye view over Finlayson Arm and the Gulf Islands is magnificent. The scenery is especially striking from the big outdoor deck. The lunch and dinner menus list such casual fare as burgers, quesadillas, and salads, as well as heartier pasta, seafood, and meat dishes. ⊠ *265 Trans-Canada Hwy., Malahat,* ☎ *250/478–1944. AE, MC, V.*

Eclectic

$$–$$$ ✕ **Süze Lounge and Restaurant.** Candlelight, red velveteen drapes, exposed brick, a vintage mahogany bar, and a long martini list give this friendly, downtown lounge and restaurant a stylish air. The frequently changing menu and daily specials sheet include pastas, pizzas, fish, lamb, and some creative Asia-influenced dishes. Popular options are the

Bento Box, a Japanese appetizer sampler, and the pad Thai—a spicy dish of vegetables with peanut sauce and cilantro. Luscious desserts and a wide range of teas also are specialties. The patio is a popular summer hangout. Dinner is served until midnight Sunday to Wednesday and until 1 AM the rest of the week. ⊠ *515 Yates St.,* ☎ *250/383–2829. Reservations essential. AE, DC, MC, V. No lunch.*

Indian

$$ ✕ **Bengal Lounge.** Buffet lunches and dinners in the elegant Empress hotel include vegetarian and meat curries with extensive condiment trays of coconut, nuts, cool *raita* (yogurt with mint or cucumber), and chutney. Popular with cabinet ministers and bureaucrats, the curries are almost as much a Victorian tradition as afternoon tea. Halibut and chips, crab cakes, and rib-eye steak are on the à la carte menu. ⊠ *Fairmont Empress, 721 Government St.,* ☎ *250/384–8111. AE, D, DC, MC, V. No dinner buffet Fri.–Sat.*

Italian

$$–$$$$ ✕ **Il Terrazzo.** A charming redbrick terrace edged with potted green-
★ ery and warmed by fireplaces and overhead heaters makes Il Terrazzo—tucked away off Waddington Alley near Market Square and not visible from the street—the locals' choice for romantic alfresco dining. Starters include mussels steamed with banana peppers, sun-dried tomatoes, cilantro, garlic, Asiago cheese, and cream. Main courses, like the Dijon-encrusted rack of lamb and osso buco with porcini mushrooms, come piping hot from the restaurant's wood oven. ⊠ *555 Johnson St., off Waddington Alley (call for directions),* ☎ *250/361–0028. Reservations essential. AE, MC, V. No lunch Sun. No lunch Sat. Oct.–Apr.*

Seafood

$$–$$$ ✕ **Blue Crab Bar and Grill.** Fresh daily seafood and expansive harbor views make this modern and airy restaurant a popular lunch and dinner spot. Signature dishes include roasted spring salmon with sweet-and-sour fennel, Dungeness crab and shrimp cakes, and a sautée of scallops and jumbo prawns. Still, there's usually something tempting on the long list of daily blackboard specials. Breads and desserts, made in-house, and a wine list that focuses on British Columbia and California round out the menu. The attached lounge area, open until 1 AM nightly, offers less-expensive meals and equally impressive views. ⊠ *Coast Harbourside Hotel and Marina, 146 Kingston St.,* ☎ *250/480–1999. AE, D, DC, MC, V.*

$$–$$$ ✕ **The Marina Restaurant.** A prime spot for Sunday brunch, the Marina has a 180° view over Oak Bay. The extensive menu usually lists a variety of pastas, grills, and seafood entrées, such as grilled rare ahi tuna and slow-roasted B.C. spring salmon. There's also a sushi bar. Downstairs is a more casual café–deli with seating on the patio overlooking the marina. ⊠ *1327 Beach Dr.,* ☎ *250/598–8555. AE, DC, MC, V.*

$ ✕ **Barb's Place.** Funky Barb's, a blue-painted take-out shack, floats on the quay where the fishing boats dock, west of the Inner Harbour off Erie Street. Cod, halibut, oysters, seafood burgers, chowder, and carrot cake are all prepared fresh on the premises. The picnic tables on the wharf offer a front-row view of interesting vessels, including a paddle wheeler, houseboats, and some vintage fishing boats. There's also a grassy park nearby. Ferries sail to Fisherman's Wharf from the Inner Harbour. ⊠ *Fisherman's Wharf, Erie St.,* ☎ *250/384–6515. MC, V. Closed late Oct.–early Mar.*

Vegetarian

$–$$ ✕ **Re-Bar Modern Food.** Bright and casual, this kid-friendly café in Bastion Square is *the* place for vegetarians in Victoria; the almond burgers, enchiladas, decadent home-baked goodies, and big breakfasts keep omnivores happy, too. An extensive tea and fresh-juice selection shares space on the drinks list with espresso, microbrews, and local wines. ⊠ *50 Bastion Sq.,* ☎ *250/361–9223. AE, MC, V. No dinner Sun. No dinner Mon. Oct.–Mar.*

Lodging

$$$$ ⊡ **The Aerie.** The million-dollar view of Finlayson Arm and the Gulf
★ Islands persuaded Maria Schuster to build her luxury resort on this scenic hilltop, 30 km (19 mi) north of Victoria. Most of the plush rooms in the no-smoking Mediterranean-style villa have a patio, a fireplace, and a whirlpool tub. Chocolate truffles and fresh flowers are part of the pampering treatment, which includes a spa with a full selection of aesthetic and wellness treatments. The dining room ($$$–$$$$) has stunning views over the Gulf Islands and is open to the public for lunch and dinner. The top-notch Pacific Northwest cuisine relies almost exclusively on local ingredients and incorporates organic products and heritage produce varieties into its à la carte, vegetarian, and multicourse tasting menus. Full breakfast is included. ⊠ *600 Ebedora La., Box 108, Malahat V0R 2L0,* ☎ *250/743–7115 or 800/518–1933,* 𝖥𝖠𝖷 *250/743–4766,* 𝖶𝖤𝖡 *www.aerie.bc.ca. 10 rooms, 19 suites. Restaurant, bar, fans, indoor pool, indoor and outdoor hot tubs, sauna, spa, tennis court, hiking, library, meeting rooms, helipad, free parking. AE, DC, MC, V. BP.*

$$$$ ⊡ **Coast Harbourside Hotel and Marina.** West of the Inner Harbour and on the water, the Coast Harbourside is handy to downtown but removed from the traffic on Government Street. The ambience is friendly, the decor modern but soothing. The rooms, in pink and blue with rosewood furniture, all have balconies, and some have striking harbor views. Fishing and whale-watching charters and the harbor ferries stop at the hotel's marina, and there's a free downtown shuttle. The Blue Crab Bar and Grill is a popular dining spot. ⊠ *146 Kingston St., V8V 1V4,* ☎ *250/360–1211 or 800/663–1144,* 𝖥𝖠𝖷 *250/360–1418,* 𝖶𝖤𝖡 *www.coasthotels.com. 126 rooms, 6 suites. Restaurant, bar, air-conditioning, in-room data ports, minibars, no-smoking floors, room service, indoor-outdoor pool, hot tub, sauna, gym, dock, laundry service, business services, meeting rooms, free parking. AE, D, DC, MC, V.*

$$$$ ⊡ **The Fairmont Empress.** For empire builders, movie stars, and a great
★ many others, the Empress is the only place to stay in Victoria. Opened in 1908, this harborside château has aged gracefully, with sympathetically restored Edwardian decor, discreet modern amenities, and service standards that recall a more gracious age. Rooms are spacious, with conservative decor, muted colors, and high ceilings; many of those facing Government Street offer front-row views of the Inner Harbour. This Victoria landmark is among the most expensive lodgings in town, but many feel the first-class service and historic ambience are worth it. ⊠ *721 Government St., V8W 1W5,* ☎ *250/384–8111 or 800/441–1414,* 𝖥𝖠𝖷 *250/381–5959,* 𝖶𝖤𝖡 *www.fairmont.com. 457 rooms, 19 suites. 2 restaurants, lounge, fans, in-room data ports, minibars, no-smoking floors, room service, indoor pool, wading pool, hot tub, sauna, spa, gym, shops, laundry service, concierge, concierge floor, business services, convention center, parking (fee). AE, D, DC, MC, V.*

$$$$ ⊡ **Humboldt House.** Sparkling wine and chocolate truffles greet you in your room at this unabashedly romantic hideaway on a quiet side street. The prettily restored Victorian has five rooms, each with elaborate boudoir decor, a wood-burning fireplace, down duvets, a CD player, fresh flowers, candles, and a whirlpool tub (in the bedroom); however, rooms don't have phones or TVs, for the sake of romance, and smoking is not permitted. (A suite with a detached bath and a pretty two-bedroom cottage, about 1 km, or ½ mi, south of the house, also are available.) You can sip sherry in the red velvet parlor, but the real treat arrives in the morning: a picnic basket loaded with breakfast goodies and delivered to your room through a butler's pantry. ⊠ *867 Humboldt St., V8V 2Z6,* ☎ *250/383–0152 or 888/383–0327,* FAX *250/ 383–6402,* WEB *www.humboldthouse.com. 5 rooms, 1 suite, 1 cottage. Refrigerator, free parking. MC, V. BP.*

$$$–$$$$ 🏨 **Abigail's Hotel.** A Tudor-style inn built in 1930, Abigail's is within
★ walking distance of downtown. The guest rooms are attractively furnished in an English Arts and Crafts style. Down comforters, together with whirlpool tubs and fireplaces in many rooms, add to the pampering atmosphere. Six large rooms in the Coach House building are especially lavish, with whirlpool tubs, four-poster king beds, and wood-burning fireplaces. All rooms have telephones but no TVs, and smoking isn't permitted. Full breakfast is included. ⊠ *906 McClure St., V8V 3E7,* ☎ *250/388–5363 or 800/561–6565,* FAX *250/388–7787,* WEB *www.abigailshotel.com. 22 rooms. Breakfast room, library, laundry service, free parking. AE, MC, V. BP.*

$$$–$$$$ 🏨 **Beaconsfield Inn.** This 1905 registered historic building four blocks
★ from the Inner Harbour is one of Victoria's most faithfully restored Edwardian mansions. Though the rooms and suites all have antique furniture, mahogany floors, fireplaces, stained-glass windows, Ralph Lauren fabrics, and period details, each has a unique look; one room even includes an Edwardian wooden canopied tub. Lavish breakfasts, afternoon tea in the conservatory, and evening sherry around the library fire complete the English country-manor ambience. (No smoking in the hotel.) ⊠ *998 Humboldt St., V8V 2Z8,* ☎ *250/384–4044,* FAX *250/384–4052,* WEB *www.beaconsfieldinn.com. 7 rooms, 2 suites. Breakfast room, library, free parking. MC, V. BP.*

$$$–$$$$ 🏨 **Delta Victoria Ocean Pointe Resort and Spa.** Across the "blue
★ bridge" (Johnson Street Bridge) from downtown Victoria, this property has a resort's worth of facilities, including a full spa and an art gallery. The hotel's two-story lobby and half of its guest rooms offer romantic views of the Inner Harbour and the lights of the Parliament Buildings across the water. Standard rooms are spacious and airy, and the apartment-size suites have kitchenettes and separate living and dining areas. The Victorian Restaurant serves fine Pacific Northwest cuisine in a scenic setting. ⊠ *45 Songhees Rd., V9A 6T3,* ☎ *250/360– 2999 or 800/667–4677,* FAX *250/360–5856,* WEB *www.oprhotel.com. 212 rooms, 34 suites. 2 restaurants, bar, wine shop, air-conditioning, in-room data ports, minibars, room service, indoor pool, hot tub, sauna, spa, 2 tennis courts, health club, jogging, racquetball, squash, baby-sitting, laundry service, concierge, business services, meeting rooms, travel services, parking (fee). AE, DC, MC, V.*

$$$–$$$$ 🏨 **A Haterleigh Heritage Inn.** Lead- and stained-glass windows and or-
nate plasterwork on 11-ft ceilings transport you to a more gracious time at this 1901 Queen Anne–style mansion two blocks from the Inner Harbour. Several of the Victorian-theme guest rooms have whirlpool tubs or original claw-foot tubs. The Secret Garden room, with a balcony and oval whirlpool tub, is a romantic choice, as is the Day Dreams room on the main floor, with its double whirlpool tub and private sitting room. Full breakfast and afternoon refreshments are included in the rates; smoking isn't permitted. ⊠ *243 Kingston St., V8V 1V5,* ☎ *250/384–9995 or 866/234–2244,* FAX *250/384–1935,* WEB *www.haterleigh.com. 6 rooms, 2 suites. Breakfast room, free parking. MC, V. BP.*

$$$–$$$$ 🏨 **Oak Bay Beach Hotel & Marine Resort.** This family-run, Tudor-style
★ country inn is beside the ocean in Oak Bay, 10 minutes from downtown. Guest rooms are decorated in an 18th-century European style, with muted tones and sumptuous antiques. Many of the rooms have striking views

over the landscaped gardens and the islands in Haro Strait; several have balconies, gas fireplaces, and big soaking tubs. An on-site tour company can arrange just about anything you might like to do in Victoria, including kayaking, whale-watching, and golf, as well as city tours. The restaurant, Bentley's on the Bay, serves Continental cuisine and, in summer, an elaborate high tea; the pub has a cozy British ambience. ⊠ *1175 Beach Dr., V8S 2N2,* ☎ *250/598–4556 or 800/668–7758,* FAX *250/ 598–6180,* WEB *www.oakbaybeachhotel.com. 50 rooms. Restaurant, pub, in-room data ports, no-smoking floor, room service, massage, dock, boating, mountain bikes, piano, baby-sitting, laundry service, convention center, travel services, free parking. AE, DC, MC, V.*

$$$–$$$$ 🏨 **Victoria Regent.** Originally an apartment building, this nearly all-suites hotel has an excellent waterfront location, a few minutes' walk from the Inner Harbour. The outside is plain, with a glass facade, but the large apartment-size suites are attractively decorated with rosewood furniture and contemporary art (the regular rooms have a similar look). Each suite has a kitchen, living room, dining room, balcony, and one or two bedrooms with bath, making the Victoria Regent a good choice for families. Many suites have water views, and the pricier executive suites each include a fireplace, den, and jet tub. ⊠ *1234 Wharf St., V8W 3H9,* ☎ *250/386–2211 or 800/663–7472,* FAX *250/386– 2622,* WEB *www.victoriaregent.com. 11 rooms, 35 suites. Breakfast room, minibars, free parking. AE, D, DC, MC, V. CP.*

$$–$$$$ 🏨 **Hotel Grand Pacific.** A landscaped courtyard with fountains and statuary creates a striking entrance to this modern full-service hotel overlooking the Inner Harbour. The Parliament Buildings are next door and the Royal British Columbia Museum, along with other central Victoria sights, are a short walk away. The guest rooms are spacious and fairly conservative, with muted colors and rosewood furniture, and many have great harbor views. Several of the suites have fireplaces and whirlpool tubs. The health-club facilities are extensive. ⊠ *463 Belleville St., V8V 1X3* ☎ *250/386–0450 or 800/458–6262,* FAX *250/386–8779,* WEB *www.hotelgrandpacific.com. 268 rooms, 40 suites. Restaurant, bar, air-conditioning, in-room data ports, in-room safes, minibars, no-smoking floor, room service, indoor lap pool, wading pool, hair salon, hot tub, massage, sauna, aerobics, health club, racquetball, shops, dry cleaning, laundry service, concierge, meeting rooms, free parking. AE, D, DC, MC, V.*

$$$ 🏨 **Admiral Motel.** This small, friendly blue and white gabled motel along a quiet part of the Inner Harbour is a good choice for families. About half the rooms have kitchens or kitchenettes, and all have private entrances and a balcony or patio. There's a guest lounge with a fireplace. Small pets are permitted. ⊠ *257 Belleville St., V8V 1X1,* ☎ *888/823– 6472,* ☎ FAX *250/388–6267,* WEB *www.admiral.bc.ca. 22 rooms, 10 suites. Kitchenettes (some), refrigerators, bicycles, piano, coin laundry, free parking. AE, D, MC, V. CP.*

$$$ 🏨 **Laurel Point Inn.** Every room has water views at this modern resort and convention hotel on a 6-acre peninsula in the Inner Harbour. The decor, especially in the newer Arthur Erickson–designed suites, is light and airy, with a strong Asian influence. Chinese art decorates many public areas, and the summer-only Terrace Room restaurant overlooks a Japanese garden. All rooms have balconies. ⊠ *680 Montreal St., V8V 1Z8,* ☎ *250/386–8721 or 800/663–7667,* FAX *250/386–9547,* WEB *www.laurelpoint.com. 135 rooms, 65 suites. 2 restaurants, lounge, no-smoking floor, room service, indoor pool, hot tub, sauna, laundry service, business services, meeting rooms, free parking. AE, DC, MC, V.*

$$$ 🏨 **Prior House Bed & Breakfast Inn.** In a beautifully restored 1912 manor
★   home on a quiet street near Craigdarroch Castle, this B&B has a pretty garden, a guest library, two parlors, antique furniture, lead-glass win-

dows, and oak paneling. All guest rooms (all no-smoking) have TVs and fireplaces; some have whirlpool tubs and private balconies. The Garden Suite, with a private entrance and two bedrooms, is an especially good value. A chef prepares the lavish breakfasts and afternoon teas, which are included in the rates. ⊠ *620 St. Charles St., V8S 3N7,* ☎ *250/592–8847 or 877/924–3300,* FAX *250/592–8223,* WEB *www.priorhouse.com. 3 rooms, 3 suites. Breakfast room, in-room VCRs, library, free parking. MC, V. BP.*

$$–$$$ ☷ **Château Victoria.** Wonderful views from the upper-floor suites and rooftop restaurant are a plus at this friendly, centrally located 19-story hotel. Most of the property was freshly decorated in 2001; the look is airy, with rose and blue fabrics and either rosewood or pine furniture. The apartment-size suites are a good choice for families: all have balconies and sitting areas, and some have kitchenettes. Standard rooms are spacious, too. ⊠ *740 Burdett Ave., V8W 1B2,* ☎ *250/382–4221 or 800/663–5891,* FAX *250/380–1950,* WEB *www.chateauvictoria.com. 59 rooms, 118 suites. 2 restaurants, 2 lounges, kitchenettes (some), in-room data ports, no-smoking floor, room service, indoor pool, hot tub, gym, baby-sitting, laundry service, concierge, business services, meeting rooms, free parking. AE, D, DC, MC, V.*

$$–$$$ ☷ **Holland House Inn.** This stylish art- and antiques-filled Italian Re-
★   naissance–style home is in a quiet residential neighborhood two blocks from the Inner Harbour. Guest rooms all have sitting areas, and many have fireplaces, balconies, and canopied four-poster beds. An Arts and Crafts–style addition, linked to the main building through a conservatory, has seven large rooms with fireplaces and double soaking tubs. Full breakfast is included. This is a smoke-free hotel. ⊠ *595 Michigan St., V8V 1S7,* ☎ *250/384–6644 or 800/335–3466,* FAX *250/384–6117,* WEB *www.hollandhouse.ca. 17 rooms. Breakfast room, free parking. AE, MC, V. BP.*

$$–$$$ ☷ **Mulberry Manor.** The last building designed by Victoria architect Samuel McClure has been restored and decorated to magazine-cover perfection with antiques, luxurious linens, and tile baths. The Jasmine suite includes a wood-burning fireplace and a tub for two. The Tudor-style mansion sits behind a high stone wall on an acre of manicured grounds. The inn is a five-minute drive from the Inner Harbour, among the mansions of the Rockland neighborhood. A full breakfast is included. Smoking is not permitted. ⊠ *611 Foul Bay Rd., V8S 1H2,* ☎ *250/370–1918 or 877/370–1918,* FAX *250/370–1968,* WEB *www.mulberry-manor.com. 3 rooms, 1 suite. Breakfast room, free parking. MC, V. BP.*

$$–$$$ ☷ **Spinnakers Guest House.** Three delightful houses make up the ac-
★   commodations at this B&B—run by the owner of the popular Spinnakers Brew Pub—across the Johnson Street Bridge from downtown. A newer Italian villa–style house has four suites that surround an ivy-draped courtyard. Suites have private entrances and are decorated with Asian antiques, Balinese teak butlers, and other objects gathered during the owner's world travels. Two other houses are beautifully renovated Victorian homes, decorated with original local art and English and Welsh antiques. Most rooms have fireplaces and whirlpool tubs and some suites have kitchens. A full breakfast is included at this non-smoking, adult-oriented B&B (children must be over age 12). ⊠ *308 Catherine St., V9A 3S8,* ☎ *250/384–2739 or 877/838–2739,* WEB *www.spinnakers.com. 5 rooms, 5 suites. Restaurant, pub, free parking. AE, D, DC, MC, V. BP.*

$$–$$$ ☷ **Swans.** Near the waterfront in Victoria's Old Town and within walking distance of most of the major sights, this 1913 former warehouse is one of the city's most attractive boutique hotels. The first floor has a brewery, a restaurant, and a pub, and there's a nightclub in the cellar. Large, apartmentlike suites with kitchens, high ceilings, and Pa-

cific Northwest art fill the upper floors. The two-level penthouse suite has a hot tub on its private rooftop patio. ⊠ *506 Pandora Ave., V8W 1N6,* ☎ *250/361–3310 or 800/668–7926,* FAX *250/361–3491,* WEB *www.swanshotel.com. 30 suites. Restaurant, pub, wine shop, no-smoking room, room service, nightclub, coin laundry, meeting rooms, parking (fee). AE, D, DC, MC, V.*

$ ⊡ **Hostelling International Victoria.** This hostel, in a restored historic building, is in the thick of things near the waterfront and Market Square. The accommodations include private rooms with shared baths as well as beds in men's, women's, and co-ed dorms. Among the amenities: a game room, TV lounge, private lockers, laundry facilities, two shared kitchens, Internet terminals, and loads of travel information for your trip. The reception is staffed 24 hours a day. ⊠ *516 Yates St., V8W 1K8,* ☎ *250/385–4511 or 888/883–0099,* FAX *250/385–3232,* WEB *www.hihostels.bc.ca. 110 beds in 10 single-sex and co-ed dorms; 5 private rooms (2–8 people) without bath; 1 private room with bath. Coin laundry, travel services. MC, V.*

Nightlife and the Arts

For entertainment listings, pick up a free copy of *Monday Magazine* (it comes out every Thursday), or call the **Talking Telus Pages** (☎ 250/ 953–9000).

The Arts
MUSIC
The **TerriVic Jazz Party** (☎ 250/953–2011) showcases internationally acclaimed musicians every April at seven venues around Victoria. The **Victoria Jazz Society** (☎ 250/388–4423) organizes the annual JazzFest International in late June and the Vancouver Island Blues Bash in Victoria every Labor Day weekend.

The **Victoria Symphony** (☎ 250/385–6515) plays in the Royal Theatre (⊠ 805 Broughton St., ☎ 250/386–6121) and at the University Centre Auditorium (⊠ Finnerty Rd., ☎ 250/721–8480).

OPERA
Pacific Opera Victoria (☎ 250/385–0222) performs three productions a year at the Royal Theatre.

THEATER
An old church houses the **Belfry Theatre** (⊠ 1291 Gladstone Ave., ☎ 250/385–6815), where a resident company specializes in contemporary Canadian dramas. **Langham Court Theatre** (⊠ 805 Langham Ct., ☎ 250/384–2142), a small theater in a residential neighborhood, is the home stage of the long-established Victoria Theatre Guild, which stages the works of well-known playwrights. **McPherson Playhouse** (⊠ 3 Centennial Sq., ☎ 250/386–6121) hosts touring theater and dance companies. University of Victoria students stage productions on campus at the **Phoenix Theatre** (⊠ off the Ring Rd., ☎ 250/721–8000 or 250/721–7993).

Nightlife
BARS AND CLUBS
Deep leather sofas and a Bengal tiger skin help to recreate the days of British Raj at the **Bengal Lounge** in the Fairmont Empress Hotel. Martinis and a curry buffet are the draws through the week. On Friday and Saturday nights a jazz band takes the stage. High-energy dance music draws a young crowd to the **Boom Boom Room** (⊠ 1208 Wharf St., ☎ 250/381–2331), on the waterfront. The DJs at **Liquid** (⊠ 15 Bastion Sq., ☎ 250/385–2626) play Top 40, dance, R&B, and hip-hop tunes. With its cozy Tudor ambience and a waterside deck, the **Snug Pub** (1175 Beach

Dr., ☎ 250/598–4556), about 10 minutes from downtown in the Oak Bay Beach Hotel & Marine Resort, is the nearest thing to a traditional English pub in Victoria. **Steamers Public House** (✉ 570 Yates St., ☎ 250/381–4340) has four pool tables and live music every night. The **Strathcona Hotel** (✉ 919 Douglas St., ☎ 250/383–7137) is something of an entertainment complex, with a pub and restaurant, a sports bar, a hillbilly-theme bar, and a nightclub—not to mention beach volleyball played on the roof in summer. The DJs at the dance club **Sweetwater's** (✉ Market Square, 27–560 Johnson St., ☎ 250/383–7844) appeal to a wide age group with Top 40 dance and old-time rock and roll tunes.

BREW PUBS

The deck at the **Harbour Canoe Club** (✉ 450 Swift St., ☎ 250/361–1940), a marine brew pub, looks over the Gorge and is a delightful place to spend a summer afternoon; you can even rent canoes and kayaks here. Inside, the former power station has been stylishly redone, with high ceilings, exposed brick and beams, a wide range of in-house brews (including one made with maple syrup), top-notch bar snacks, and a restaurant. Chic and arty **Hugo's** (✉ 625 Courtney St., ☎ 250/920–4844) serves lunch, dinner, and four of its own brews. This multi-purpose nightspot is a pub by day, a lounge in the early evening, and a dance club at night. Across the Johnson Street Bridge from downtown, **Spinnakers Brew Pub** (✉ 308 Catherine St., ☎ 250/386–2739) pours Victoria's most extensive menu of microbrews in an atmospheric setting, with a waterfront patio, a double-sided fireplace, and a multitude of cozy rooms filled with pub paraphernalia. The excellent pub grub and the in-house restaurant make this a popular eatery, too. **Swan's Pub** (✉ 1601 Store St., ☎ 250/361–3310) serves its own microbrews in a room decorated with Pacific Northwest art; musicians play Sunday through Thursday nights.

Outdoor Activities and Sports

Boating

The quiet upper section of Victoria's harbor, called the Gorge, is a popular boating spot. You can rent a kayak, canoe, motorboat, or rowboat at **Harbour Rentals** (✉ Heritage Quay, 450 Swift St., ☎ 250/386–2277). Guided trips, scooters, and bicycles are also available.

To rent a powerboat or to book almost any kind of guided marine activity, including seaplane tours, fishing, and kayaking expeditions, contact the **Victoria Marine Adventure Centre** (✉ 950 Wharf St., ☎ 250/995–2211 or 800/575–6700), on the Inner Harbour near the Visitor Information Centre. You can also rent scooters and bicycles here.

Golf

Several companies in Victoria offer advance tee-time bookings and golf packages.

The **Cordova Bay Golf Course** (✉ 5333 Cordova Bay Rd., ☎ 250/658–4444) is an 18-hole, par-72 course with views of Cordova Bay and the San Juan Islands. The greens fee is $52. An optional cart costs $30.

Hiking

The **Galloping Goose Regional Trail** (☎ 250/478–3344), an old railroad track that's been reclaimed for walkers, cyclists, and equestrians, runs from downtown Victoria to just north of Sooke. It links with the Peninsula Trail to Sidney to create a continuous 100-km (62-mi) car-free route. **Goldstream Provincial Park** (☎ 250/478–9414), 19 km (12 mi) northwest of Victoria on Highway 1 at Finlayson Arm Road, has an extensive trail system, old-growth forest, waterfalls, a salt marsh, and a river. Park staff lead walks and interpretive programs. Goldstream is a prime site for viewing bald eagles in December and January. **Swan Lake Nature Sanctuary** (⊠ 3873 Swan Lake Rd., ☎ 250/479–0211), a few miles from downtown, has a 23-acre lake set in 143 acres of fields and wetlands. From the 2½-km (1½-mi) trail and floating boardwalk, birders can spot a variety of waterfowl even in winter, as well as nesting birds in the tall grass. The sanctuary's Nature House is open weekdays 8:30–4 and weekends noon–4.

Whale-Watching

To see the pods of orcas and other species that travel in the waters around Vancouver Island, you can take charter boat tours from Victoria.

Great Pacific Adventures (☎ 250/386–2277) operates Zodiac (motor-powered inflatable-boat) tours year-round. A three-hour tour costs $75. **Ocean Explorations** (☎ 250/383–6722 or 888/442–6722) offers two-hour marine tours in winter and three-hour whale-watching trips in summer—all on Zodiacs. Tours cost $69 in summer and $55 in winter. **Seacoast Expeditions** (☎ 250/383–2254) has whale-watching and marine wildlife tours. A three-hour tour (April through October) in either a Zodiac or on a high-speed covered vessel, with two naturalists on board, is $79. Two-hour wildlife-watching trips are $59 and are run during the rest of the year.

The **Oak Bay Beach Hotel & Marine Resort** (☎ 250/592–3474 or 800/668–7758) offers whale-watching trips, with a naturalist and lunch, on a 45-ft catamaran. It also offers other wildlife-spotting and outdoor-adventure trips, including a cycling winery tour in the Cowichan Bay area, guided kayak tours, and sunset dinner cruises.

The **Victoria Marine Adventure Centre** (⊠ 950 Wharf St., ☎ 250/995–2211 or 800/575–6700) can arrange whale-watching trips. Prices start at $79 per person for a three-hour trip in either a covered boat or on a Zodiac (both with naturalists on board).

Shopping

Shopping Districts and Malls

For a wide selection, head to the larger shopping centers downtown. **Victoria Eaton Centre** (⊠ 1 Victoria Eaton Centre, at Government and Fort Sts., ☎ 250/381–4012), a department store and mall, has about 100 boutiques and restaurants.

Antique Row, on Fort Street between Blanshard and Cook streets, is home to more than 60 antiques, curio, and collectibles shops. **Market Square** (⊠ 560 Johnson St., ☎ 250/386–2441) has everything from fudge, music, and comic books to jewelry, local arts, and New Age accoutrements. High-end fashion boutiques, craft shops, and galleries line **Trounce Alley,** a pedestrian-only lane north of View Street between Broad and Government streets.

Specialty Stores

Shopping in Victoria is easy: virtually everything can be found in the downtown area on or near Government Street stretching north from the Fairmont Empress hotel.

At **Artina's** (⊠ 1002 Government St., ☎ 250/386–7000 or 877/386–7700) you can find unusual Canadian art jewelry—mostly handmade, one-of-a-kind pieces. The **Cowichan Trading Co., Ltd.** (⊠ 1328 Government St., ☎ 250/383–0321) sells First Nations jewelry, art, moccasins, and Cowichan Indian sweaters. The **Fran Willis Gallery** (⊠ 1619 Store St., upstairs, ☎ 250/381–3422) shows contemporary Canadian paintings and sculpture. **Hill's Native Art** (⊠ 1008 Government St., ☎ 250/385–3911) has souvenirs and original West Coast First Nations art. As the name would suggest, **Irish Linen Stores** (⊠ 1019 Government St., ☎ 250/383–6812) stocks fine linen, lace, and hand-embroidered items—hankies, napkins, tablecloths, and place mats. **Munro's Books** (⊠ 1108 Government St., ☎ 250/382–2464), in a restored 1909 building, is one of Canada's prettiest bookstores. If the British spirit of Victoria has you searching for fine teas, head to **Murchie's** (⊠ 1110 Government St., ☎ 250/383–3112) for a choice of 40 varieties, plus blended coffees, tarts, and cakes. At **Starfish Glassworks** (⊠ 630 Yates St., ☎ 250/388–7827) you can watch glassblowers create original works.

Victoria A to Z

To research prices, get advice from other travelers, and book travel arrangements, visit www.fodors.com.

AIR TRAVEL TO AND FROM VICTORIA

Victoria International Airport is served by Air B.C., Canadian, Horizon, Pacific Coastal, and WestJet airlines. Air B.C. provides airport-to-airport service from Vancouver to Victoria at least hourly. Flights take about 35 minutes.

West Coast Air and Harbour Air offer 35-minute harbor-to-harbor service (between downtown Vancouver and downtown Victoria) several times a day. Kenmore Air Harbour operates direct daily floatplane service from Seattle to Victoria's Inner Harbour.

Helijet International helicopter service is available from downtown Vancouver, the Vancouver airport, and downtown Seattle to downtown Victoria.

➤ CONTACTS: **Harbour Air** (☎ 604/688–1277 or 800/665–0212, WEB www.harbour-air.com). **Helijet International** (☎ 800/665–4354, 604/273–1414, or 250/382–6222, WEB www.helijet.com). **Kenmore Air Harbour** (☎ 425/486–1257 or 800/543–9595). **West Coast Air** (☎ 604/606–6888 or 800/347–2222, WEB www.westcoastair.com).

AIRPORTS AND TRANSFERS

Victoria International Airport is 25 km (15 mi) north of downtown Victoria, off Highway 17.
➤ AIRPORT INFORMATION: **Victoria International Airport** (⊠ 201–1640 Electra Blvd., off Hwy. 17, Sidney, ☎ 250/953–7500, WEB www.victoriaairport.com).

AIRPORT TRANSFER
To drive from the airport to downtown, take Highway 17 south. A taxi ride costs between $35 and $40, plus tip. The Airporter bus service drops off passengers at most major hotels. The fare is $13 one way, $23 round-trip.
➤ SHUTTLES: **Airporter** (☎ 250/386–2525, WEB www.airporter.travel.bc.ca).

BOAT AND FERRY TRAVEL

BC Ferries operates daily service between Vancouver and Victoria. Ferries arrive at and depart from the Swartz Bay Terminal at the end of Highway 17 (the Patricia Bay Highway), 32 km (20 mi) north of downtown Victoria. Sailing time is about 1½ hours. Peak-season weekend fares are $9.50 per adult passenger and $33.50 per vehicle each way; lower rates apply midweek and in the off-season. Vehicle reservations on Vancouver–Victoria and Nanaimo routes are optional and cost $15 in addition to the fare.

Black Ball Transport operates car ferries daily year-round between Victoria and Port Angeles, Washington. The Oak Bay Beach Hotel & Marine Resort operates a daily, summer-only foot-passenger and bicycle ferry to Roche Harbor on San Juan Island, Washington.

The *Victoria Clipper* offers daily year-round passenger-only service between Victoria and Seattle. The round-trip fare from mid-May to late September is US$109 to US$125, depending on the time of day; the rest of the year the round-trip is US$99. You receive a discount if you order 14-day advance tickets, which have some restrictions.

Washington State Ferries travel daily between Sidney, about 30 km (18 mi) north of Victoria, and Anacortes, Washington.

Within Victoria, Victoria Harbour Ferries serve the Inner Harbour, with stops that include the Fairmont Empress, Chinatown, Point Ellice House, Ocean Pointe Resort Hotel, and Fisherman's Wharf. Fares start at $3. Boats make the rounds every 12 to 20 minutes daily March through October and on sunny weekends the rest of the year. If you're by the Inner Harbour at 9:45 on a Sunday morning in summer, you can catch the little ferries performing a water ballet—they gather together and do maneuvers set to classical music that's blasted over loudspeakers.

➤ BOAT AND FERRY INFORMATION: **BC Ferries** (☎ 250/386–3431; 888/223–3779 in British Columbia; 604/444–2890 or 888/724–5223 for vehicle reservations, WEB www.bcferries.com). **Black Ball Transport** (☎ 250/386–2202 or 360/457–4491, WEB www.northolympic.com/coho). *Victoria Clipper* (☎ 206/448–5000 in Seattle; 800/888–2535 elsewhere, WEB www.victoriaclipper.com). **Oak Bay Beach Hotel & Marine Resort** (✉ ☎ 250/592–3474 or 800/668–7758). **Victoria Harbour Ferries** (☎ 250/708–0201, WEB www.harbourferry.com). **Washington State Ferries** (☎ 250/381–1551 or 206/464–6400; 888/808–7977 in WA, WEB www.wsdot.wa.gov/ferries).

BUS TRAVEL TO AND FROM VICTORIA

Pacific Coach Lines operates daily, connecting service between Victoria and Vancouver using BC Ferries.

➤ BUS INFORMATION: **Pacific Coach Lines** (☎ 250/385–4411 or 800/661–1725, WEB www.pacificcoach.com).

BUS TRAVEL WITHIN VICTORIA

BC Transit serves Victoria and the surrounding areas. An all-day pass costs $5.50.

➤ BUS INFORMATION: **BC Transit** (☎ 250/382–6161, WEB www.bc-transit.com).

CAR RENTAL

➤ MAJOR AGENCIES: **Avis** (☎ 250/386–8468). **Budget** (☎ 250/953–5300). **Enterprise** (☎ 250/475–6900). **National Tilden** (☎ 250/386–1213).

➤ LOCAL AGENCIES: **Island Autos** (☎ 250/384–4881).

EMERGENCIES

➤ EMERGENCY SERVICES: **Ambulance, fire, police** (☎ 911).

➤ HOSPITALS: **Victoria General Hospital** (✉ 1 Hospital Way, off Helmcken Rd., ☎ 250/727–4212).

➤ LATE-NIGHT PHARMACIES: **London Drugs** (✉ 911 Yates St., ☎ 250/381–1113); open Mon.–Sat. until 10 PM.

LODGING

Reservations for lodging can be made through Super, Natural British Columbia.

➤ RESERVATION SERVICES: **Super, Natural British Columbia** (☎ 800/435–5622, WEB www.hellobc.com).

TAXIS
➤ TAXI COMPANIES: **Empress Taxi** (☎ 250/381–2222).

TRAIN TRAVEL
VIA Rail's Esquimalt & Nanaimo Rail Liner serves Duncan, Chemainus, Nanaimo, and Courtenay from Victoria's VIA Rail Station, at the east end of the Johnson Street Bridge.
➤ TRAIN INFORMATION: **Esquimalt & Nanaimo Rail Liner** (☎ 800/561–8630 in Canada; 800/561–3949 in the U.S., WEB www.viarail.ca). **VIA Rail Station** (✉ 450 Pandora Ave., ☎ no phone).

TOURS
BOAT TOURS
The best way to see the sights of the Inner Harbour is by Victoria Harbour Ferries; harbor tours are $12 to $14.
➤ FEES AND SCHEDULES: **Victoria Harbour Ferries** (☎ 250/708–0201, WEB www.harbourferry.com).

BUS TOURS
Gray Line double-decker bus tours visit the city center, Chinatown, Antique Row, Oak Bay, and Beacon Hill Park; a combination tour includes Butchart Gardens.
➤ FEES AND SCHEDULES: **Gray Line** (☎ 250/388–5248 or 800/663–8390, WEB www.victoriatours.com).

CARRIAGE TOURS
Tally-Ho Horsedrawn Tours and Victoria Carriage Tours offer horsedrawn tours of the city.
➤ FEES AND SCHEDULES: **Tally-Ho Horsedrawn Tours** (mailing address: ✉ 8615 Ebor Terrace, V8L 1L7, ☎ 250/383–5067, WEB www.tallyhotours.com). **Victoria Carriage Tours** (✉ 251 Superior St., V8V 1T4, ☎ 877/663–2207 or 250/383–2207, WEB victoriacarriage.com).

THEME TOURS
The Ale Trail runs tours and beer tastings at Victoria's microbreweries and brew pubs.
➤ FEES AND SCHEDULES: **Ale Trail** (✉ 214–733 Johnson St., ☎ 250/658–5367 or 800/667–2291, WEB www.firstislandtours.com).

TRAIN TOURS
The Pacific Wilderness Railway Company runs a 2½-hour round-trip vintage-train excursion from Victoria's Pandora Street station to the top of Malahat mountain, north of Victoria. The trip is made twice a day early June to late September. The regular fare is $32; a first-class ticket, which includes lunch, is $69.
➤ FEES AND SCHEDULES: **Pacific Wilderness Railway Company** (☎ 800/267–0610 or 250/381–8600, WEB www.pacificwildernessrailway.com).

WALKING TOURS
The Architectural Institute of British Columbia offers free walking tours of Victoria's historic neighborhoods during July and August.
➤ FEES AND SCHEDULES: **Architectural Institute of British Columbia** (☎ 800/667–0753; 604/683–8588 Vancouver office).

VISITOR INFORMATION
➤ TOURIST INFORMATION: **Super, Natural British Columbia** (☎ 800/435–5622, WEB www.hellobc.com). **Tourism Victoria** (✉ 812 Wharf St., ☎ 250/953–2033, WEB www.tourismvictoria.com).

VANCOUVER ISLAND

The largest island on Canada's west coast, Vancouver Island stretches 564 km (350 mi) from Victoria in the south to Cape Scott in the north. A ridge of mountains, blanketed in spruce, cedar, and Douglas fir, crowns the island's center, providing opportunities for skiing, climbing, and hiking. Mining, logging, and tourism are the important island industries, although tourism—especially ecotourism—has become increasingly important in recent years.

Outside Victoria and Nanaimo, most towns on the island are so small as to be dwarfed by the surrounding wilderness. However, many have a unique charm, from pretty Victorian Chemainus to such isolated fishing villages as Bamfield and growing ecotourism centers, including Tofino.

Sooke

⑰ *42 km (26 mi) west of Victoria on Hwy. 14.*

The village of Sooke provides a peaceful seaside escape, with rugged beaches, hiking trails through the surrounding rain forest, and views of Washington's Olympic Mountains across the Strait of Juan de Fuca. **East Sooke Regional Park,** on the east side of Sooke Harbour, has more than 3,500 acres of beaches, hiking trails, and wildflower-dotted meadows. A popular hiking and biking route, the **Galloping Goose Regional Trail** (☎ 250/478–3344) is a former railway line that runs all the way to Victoria. The **Sooke Potholes Provincial Park** (⊠ end of Sooke River Rd., off Hwy. 14) has a series of swimming holes carved out of the sandstone by the Sooke River. **Whiffen Spit,** a natural breakwater about a mile long, makes a scenic walk with great bird-watching. It's at the end of Whiffen Spit Road, west of the village.

The **Sooke Region Museum and Visitor Information Centre** (⊠ 2070 Phillips Rd., ☎ 250/642–6351) displays Salish and Nootka crafts and artifacts from 19th-century Sooke. It's open daily 9–6 in July and August, Tuesday through Sunday 9–5 the rest of the year. Donations are accepted.

OFF THE BEATEN PATH
JUAN DE FUCA PROVINCIAL PARK – This park between Jordan River and Port Renfrew has campsites and a long series of beaches, including Botanical Beach, which has amazing tidal pools. The **Juan de Fuca Marine Trail** is a tough 47-km (30-mi) hike set up as an alternative to the overly popular West Coast Trail that begins at China Beach, west of the Jordan River. There are three other trailheads, each with a parking lot: Sombrio Beach, Parkinson Creek, and Botanical Beach (which is 5 km, or 3 mi, southeast of Port Renfrew). ⊠ *Off Hwy. 14, between Jordan River (southeast end) and Port Renfrew (at the northwest end),* ☎ *250/ 391–2300,* ☞ *Free; $5 a night for camping.*

Dining and Lodging

$$ ✕ **Seventeen Mile House.** Originally built as a hotel, this 1894 house is a study in island architecture at the end of the 19th century. It's a good place for pub fare, a beer, or fresh local seafood on the road between Sooke and Victoria. Low-cost rooms, with a do-it-yourself breakfast, are also available here. ⊠ *5126 Sooke Rd.,* ☎ *250/642–5942. MC, V.*

$$$$ ✕🏠 **Sooke Harbour House.** People (including incognito movie stars)
★ who are discerning about their R&R are drawn to this 1929 oceanfront clapboard inn with its elegant yet relaxed ambience and one of Canada's finest dining rooms. Dining here is an adventure: the cuisine

is organic, seasonal, and uniquely Canadian, and makes the most of the local bounty. The menu changes daily, the seafood is just-caught fresh, and much of the produce is grown on the property. The inn is also home to one of Canada's best wine cellars. The guest rooms, each with a sitting area and fireplace, are individually decorated (some with bird or seaside themes) and photo-shoot perfect; all but one have ocean views and private decks or patios. The striking conference room and common area have a First Nations motif, with a river-rock fireplace, totem poles, and murals and statues. ✉ *1528 Whiffen Spit Rd., V0S 1N0,* ☎ *250/642–3421 or 800/889–9688,* FAX *250/642–6988,* WEB *www.sookeharbourhouse.com. 28 rooms. Restaurant, in-room data ports, refrigerator, room service, massage, hiking, piano, laundry service, business services, meeting rooms. MC, V. BP.*

$$–$$$ ⊞ **Markham House Bed & Breakfast.** Owners Sally and Lyall Markham make you feel welcome in this Tudor house set amid extensive grounds that include a trout pond, a putting green, and walking trails. The bedrooms have comfy mattresses with feather beds and are decorated with family pieces, including paintings of and by Lyall's relatives. The Garden Suite, which has a double Jacuzzi, and the Country Room are spacious; the Green Room is cozy but small and its bathroom is down the hall. Tucked away in the woods is the country-style Honeysuckle Cottage, a favorite for romantics. Its private deck has a barbecue and a hot tub, and there's a small kitchenette inside—but breakfast (which is delicious) can be delivered to the door. Despite its Victoria address, the Markham House is closer to Sooke. ✉ *1853 Connie Rd., off Hwy. 14, Victoria V9C 4C2,* ☎ *250/642–7542 or 888/256–6888,* FAX *250/ 642–7538,* WEB *www.markhamhouse.com. 2 rooms, 1 suite, 1 cabin. Breakfast room, in-room VCRs (some). AE, D, DC, MC, V. BP.*

$$–$$$ ⊞ **Point No Point.** Here's a place for your inner Robinson Crusoe. Twenty-two cabins sit on the edge of a cliff, overlooking a mile of sandy private beach and the open Pacific. The one- and two-bedroom cabins, in single, duplex, and quad units, range from rustic to romantic. Seven newer cabins have tall windows, water views, and hot tubs; the older, less expensive cabins are basic, with the original 1960s furniture (pets are allowed in two of these). Every unit has a kitchen, a fireplace or woodstove, and a deck. The lodge restaurant serves lunch, afternoon tea, and dinner (no dinner Monday and Tuesday) from a seafood-oriented menu. Each table has a pair of binoculars for spotting whales and ships on the open sea. ✉ *1505 West Coast Rd., 15 mi west of Sooke, V0S 1N0,* ☎ *250/646–2020,* FAX *250/646–2294,* WEB *www.pointnopointresort.com. 25 cabins. Restaurant, no-smoking room, hiking. AE, MC, V.*

Shopping

At the **Blue Raven Gallery** (✉ 1971 Kaltasin Rd., ☎ 250/881–0528), Victor, Carey, and Edith Newman, a family team of Kwakiutl and Salish artists, display traditional and modern prints, masks, jewelry, and clothing. January through March the shop is open only by appointment.

Duncan

⑱ *60 km (37 mi) north of Victoria on the Trans-Canada Hwy., or Hwy. 1.*

★ ☾ Duncan is nicknamed City of Totems for the many totem poles that dot the small community. The **Quw'utsun Cultural and Conference Centre,** covering 6 acres on the banks of the tree-lined Cowichan River, is one of Canada's leading First Nations cultural and educational facilities. You can see the work (including a stunning whaling-canoe diorama) of some of the Northwest's most renowned artists in a lofty longhouse-style gallery, learn about the history of the Cowichan people from a multimedia show, and sample traditional foods at the Riverwalk Café. You can also watch artisans at work in the world's largest carving house and even try your hand at carving on a visitors' pole. Craft demonstrations and performances take place in summer. ☒ *200 Cowichan Way,* ☏ *250/746–8119 or 877/746–8119,* WEB *www.quwutsun.ca.* ☞ *$10.* ☉ *Daily 9–5; café closed Nov.–Apr.*

The **British Columbia Forest Discovery Centre,** more a park than a museum, spans some 100 acres, combining indoor and outdoor exhibits that focus on the history of forestry in the province. In summer you can ride an original steam locomotive around the property. The *Forest Renewal B.C.* exhibition has a theater, computer games, aquariums, and hands-on displays about the province's ecosystems. There are also nature trails on the property. ☒ *2892 Drinkwater Rd. (Trans-Canada Hwy.),* ☏ *250/715–1113,* WEB *www.bcforestmuseum.com.* ☞ *$8.* ☉ *Easter–Labor Day, daily 10–6; Sept. 3–Oct. 7, daily 10–4.*

Shopping

Duncan is the home of Cowichan wool sweaters, hand-knit by the Cowichan people. They are available at the **Quw'utsun Cultural and Conference Centre.** In addition, **Hill's Native Art** (☏ 250/746–6731), on the main Highway 1, about 1½ km (1 mi) south of Duncan, sells hand-knit Cowichan sweaters along with other crafts.

Chemainus

★ ⑲ *25 km (16 mi) north of Duncan.*

Chemainus is known for the bold epic murals that decorate its townscape, as well as for its beautifully restored Victorian homes. Once dependent on the lumber industry, the small community began to revitalize itself in the early 1980s when its mill closed down. Since then, the town has brought in international artists to paint more than 30 murals depicting local historical events around town. Footprints on the sidewalk lead you on a self-guided tour of the murals. Restaurants, shops, tearooms, coffee bars, art galleries, a minitrain line, horse-and-carriage tours, several B&Bs, and antiques dealers have helped to create one of the prettiest little towns on Vancouver Island. The **Chemainus Dinner Theatre** (☒ 9737 Chemainus Rd., ☏ 250/246–9820 or 800/565–7738) presents family-oriented performances along with dinner.

Dining and Lodging

$$ ✕ **Hummingbird Restaurant.** A husband-and-wife team runs this little two-room café, which offers soup, salad, and sandwich lunches as well as more-elaborate dinners, including a popular warm goat-cheese salad starter and a variety of seafood and pasta entrées. Personal touches, such as the organic flowers decorating each plate, make this a popular stop. ☒ *9893 Maple St.,* ☏ *250/246–2290. AE, V. No dinner Tues. July–Aug. Closed Tues.–Wed. Sept.–June.*

$–$$ ✕ **The Waterford Restaurant.** French-trained chef Dwayne Maslen and his wife, Linda, run this tiny restaurant tucked into a historic house near the center of town. Some highlights on the French-influenced menu are the scallop and prawns Provençal, breast of chicken stuffed with bay scallops and smoked salmon, and roast local venison with a currant demi-glace. ☒ *9875 Maple St.,* ☏ *250/246–1046. AE, MC, V. Closed Mon.*

$$$$ 🏰 **Castlebury Cottage.** This medieval-theme single-suite castle–cottage is a good place to act out your Camelot fantasies. From the royal-purple velveteen duvet and two-sided fireplace to the vaulted ceiling, 18th-century church window, frescoed walls, and suit of armor (sal-

vaged from the *Addams Family* film set), the apartment-size suite is decorated in a delightfully theatrical style. A double soaking tub, TV with VCR, CD player, and a kitchen with a microwave and dishwasher are nods to the modern world, and stairs climb to a little Juliette balcony with views over the town and sea. Breakfast is delivered to the door in a basket. The proprietors can arrange packages including horse-and-carriage rides, theater evenings, and even medieval-theme dinners with a harpist, with advance notice. Note that a two-night minimum is required on weekends. ⊠ *9910 Croft St., V0R 1K0,* ☎ *250/246–9228,* FAX *250/246–2909,* WEB *www.castleburycottage.com. 1 suite. AE, MC, V. BP.*

$$ ⊡ **Bird Song Cottage.** The whimsical white and lavender Victorian cot-
★ tage, an easy walk from the beach and town, has been playfully decorated with antiques and collectibles, including a grand piano, a Celtic harp, and Victorian hats. A full breakfast (often with piano accompaniment) is served in a glassed-in sunporch. The Nightingale room has a private garden and a claw-foot tub, and the other two rooms have baths with showers; every room has a window seat. ⊠ *9909 Maple St., Box 1432, V0R 1K0,* ☎ *250/246–9910,* FAX *250/246–2909,* WEB *www.romanticBB.com. 3 rooms. Piano. AE, MC, V. BP.*

Nanaimo

⑳ *25 km (16 mi) north of Chemainus, 110 km (68 mi) northwest of Victoria.*

Nanaimo is the primary commercial and transport link for the mid-island, with direct ferry service to the mainland. The **Nanaimo District Museum** (⊠ 100 Cameron Rd., ☎ 250/753–1821) has exhibits on the local First Nations' culture and the region's coal-mining history, as well as a variety of interesting temporary exhibits. May through September the museum is open 9–5 daily; the rest of the year it's open Tuesday through Saturday 9–5. Admission is $2.

From Nanaimo, you can take a 10-minute ferry ride (☎ 250/753–5141) in summer to **Newcastle Island** (☎ 250/391–2300), a car-free provincial park where you can camp ($12 per site per night), picnic, bike, walk trails leading past old mines and quarries, and catch glimpses of deer, rabbits, and eagles.

Dining and Lodging

$$–$$$ ✕ **Dar Lebanon.** From the outside, this restaurant near the harbor looks like the top floor of a historic house. Inside, the look is more night-at-the-casbah, with plaster arches, fringed light fixtures, and embroidered tablecloths. The food is Lebanese but takes its inspiration from both sides of the Mediterranean. Try the starter of tiger prawns in mustard, orange, cilantro, and garlic sauce; or, as a main course, kibbeh, a patty of lean beef mixed with cracked wheat and basil, and stuffed with ground walnuts and pomegranate juice. The menu also has such traditional items as stuffed grape leaves, tabbouleh, and moussaka, and plenty of vegetarian options. A few Indian dishes, such as curried chicken, vegetarian samosas, and tandoori chicken, are also available. ⊠ *347 Wesley St.,* ☎ *250/755–9150. MC, V. No lunch Sun. Closed Sun. in Jan. and Feb.*

$$–$$$ ✕ **Mahle House.** Much of the innovative Pacific Northwest cuisine served
★ at this cozy 1904 farmhouse is raised on site, in the restaurant's organic garden, or in the neighborhood. The menu changes weekly, but highlights have included different versions of lamb, rabbit, venison, mussels, and salmon, as well as good vegetarian options. On Wednesday night, you can try the Adventure Dining Experience: for $27 you get five courses chosen by the chef, and your dinner companions (up to a

party of four) each get something different. Mahle House is about 12 km (7 mi) south of Nanaimo. ⊠ *2104 Hemer Rd., at Cedar Rd., call for directions,* ☎ *250/722–3621,* WEB *www.mahlehouse.com. AE, MC, V. Closed Mon.–Tues. and first half of Jan. No lunch.*

$ ✕ **Crow and Gate Neighbourhood Pub.** With its low beams, weathered furniture, and pub paraphernalia, the Crow and Gate is probably the most authentic-looking British-style pub in the province. Set in acres of lawns on a country road about 15 km (9 mi) south of Nanaimo, the pub serves the expected pot pies, ploughman's lunches, and roast beef with Yorkshire pudding, as well as such local items as Fanny Bay oysters. The bar stocks both British and local brews, including hard-to-find Vancouver Island microbrews and estate cider. From Highway 1 between Ladysmith and Nanaimo, follow the signs for Yellow Point Lodge, then the signs for the pub. ⊠ *2313 Yellow Point Rd., Ladysmith,* ☎ *250/722–3731. Reservations not accepted. MC, V.*

$$–$$$ ⌂ **Yellow Point Lodge.** Since the 1930s, this lodge on a spit of land 24 ★ km (15 mi) south of Nanaimo has been a kind of adults-only summer camp. Everything's included, from the use of kayaks, bicycles, and tennis courts to the three full meals and snacks served communally in the dining room (rates are for two people). Accommodations range from comfortable lodge rooms to cozy cottages with minirefrigerators and bed frames made with logs. In addition, some very basic summer-only cabins share a bathhouse and don't have running water. The main lodge, with its great stone fireplace and ocean views, is a wonderful place to unwind; you can also stroll the resort's 165 acres, lounge on its secluded beaches, or, in summer, take a tour on the owner's cutter. Guests must be over age 14. ⊠ *3700 Yellow Point Rd., Ladysmith V9G 1E8,* ☎ *250/245–7422,* FAX *250/245–7411,* WEB *www.yellowpointlodge.com. 9 lodge rooms, 25 rooms without running water, 9 units in shared cabins, 12 private cabins. Dining room, saltwater pool, outdoor hot tub, sauna, 2 tennis courts, badminton, jogging, volleyball, boating, mountain bikes, meeting rooms. AE, MC, V. AP.*

$$ ⌂ **Coast Bastion Inn Nanaimo.** This business hotel downtown overlooks the harbor. The rooms are large and modern, and all have water views. Corner rooms on the 7th floor and higher are larger and have sitting areas and panoramic ocean views. ⊠ *11 Bastion St., V9R 6E4,* ☎ *250/753–6601,* FAX *250/753–4155,* WEB *www.coasthotels.com. 173 rooms, 4 suites. Restaurant, lounge, no-smoking floor, room service, hot tub, sauna, gym, laundry service, business services, meeting rooms. AE, D, DC, MC, V.*

Outdoor Activities and Sports

GOLF

Fairwinds Golf and Country Club (⊠ 3730 Fairwinds Dr., Nanoose Bay, ☎ 250/468–7666 or 888/781–2777) is an 18-hole, par-71 course that's open all year. Greens fees are about $50.

KAYAKING

Kayak rentals and one- to six-day guided sea-kayak expeditions are offered by **Wild Heart Adventure Tours** (⊠ 1560 Brebber Rd., ☎ 250/722–3683, WEB www.kayakbc.com).

Gabriola Island

3½ nautical mi (20-minute ferry ride) east of Nanaimo.

You can stay overnight on rustic, rural Gabriola Island, about a 20-minute ferry ride from Nanaimo. The small island, where about 4,000 people live full time, has beaches, parks, campgrounds, several B&Bs, two marinas, three pubs, and a small shopping area near the ferry terminal. A number of artists' studios are open to the public. The island is also known for its prehistoric petroglyphs, and delightful coastal rock formations. **BC Ferries** (☎ 250/386–3431; 888/223–3779 in British Columbia) runs car and passenger service from Nanaimo.

Port Alberni

㉑ *80 km (50 mi) northwest of Nanaimo, 195 km (121 mi) northwest of Victoria.*

Port Alberni, a pulp- and sawmill town, is a stopover on the way to Ucluelet and Tofino on Vancouver Island's west coast. The salmon-rich waters here attract anglers. The town's old industrial waterfront, at the foot of Argyle Street, has been revitalized into **Alberni Harbour Quay,** an attractive waterfront shopping area. Here you can see the maritime-related exhibits at the **Maritime Discovery Centre,** a building designed like a lighthouse. The center is open daily in July and August; admission is free. The **Alberni Valley Museum** (⊠ 4255 Wallace St., ☎ 250/723–2181, WEB www.alberniheritage.com) features First Nations cultural exhibits as well as local industrial history and a folk-art collection. It's open daily 10–5, with late hours (until 8) on Thursday. It's closed Sundays October through April; admission is by donation.

A 1929 Baldwin Steam Locomotive leaves several times a day Thursday through Monday from the railway station at the foot of Argyle Street for a scenic 35-minute ride to the **McLean Mill National Historic Site** (⊠ 5633 Smith Rd., off Beaver Creek Rd., ☎ 250/723–1376, WEB www.alberniheritage.com). The restored 1925 lumber camp and operating steam sawmill includes bunkhouses, a cookhouse, a blacksmith's forge, and much of the original steam-driven sawmill equipment. A theater troupe performs a daily stage show and leads tours through the forested site. There's also a café and gift shop. The mill is open 10–6 daily from May 20 to September 30. Admission is $6.50, or $20 including the train trip.

From Port Alberni, you can take a breathtaking 4½-hour trip aboard the *Lady Rose*, a Scottish ship built in 1937, to Bamfield. It's run by **Lady Rose Marine Services** (☎ 250/723–8313; 800/663–7192 for reservations Apr.–Sept., WEB www.ladyrosemarine.com). The boat leaves Argyle Pier (⊠ 5425 Argyle St.) at 8 AM Tuesday, Thursday, and Saturday year-round, with additional Friday and Sunday sailings in July and August. The round-trip fare is $45. Or you can take the newer M.V. *Francis Barkley*, which sails to the Broken Group Islands ($40 round-trip) or Ucluelet ($50). It leaves Argyle Pier at 8 AM Monday, Wednesday, and Friday between early June and late September.

About 13 km (8 mi) west of town on Highway 4 is **Sproat Lake Provincial Park,** with a swimming beach and trails leading to ancient petroglyphs. Sproat Lake is also home to the only two Martin Mars water bombers still in existence. Originally World War II troop carriers, they are now used to fight forest fires. The park is open sunrise to sunset and is free.

Lodging

$$ ☷ **Cedar Wood Lodge.** Built in 1998, this clapboard lodge is on 2 acres of gardens. The rooms, most of which can sleep four, are decorated in rich greens and burgundies, with attractive art-deco furniture, gas fireplaces, and whirlpool tubs. The comfortable lounge has a pool table and leather couches set around a fireplace. You also have access to swimming, canoeing, and fishing in the river across the road. Smoking is not permitted. ⊠ *5895 River Rd. (Hwy. 4), V9Y 6Z5,* ☎ *250/724–6800 or 877/314–6800,* FAX *250/724–6887,* WEB *www.cedarwood.bc.ca. 8 rooms. Breakfast room, in-room data ports, fishing, billiards, meeting rooms. AE, MC, V. CP.*

Bamfield

㉒ *100 km (62 mi) southwest of Port Alberni by gravel road.*

In Bamfield, a remote village of about 500, the seaside boardwalk affords an uninterrupted view of ships heading up the inlet to Port Alberni. The town is well equipped to handle overnight visitors. It's also a good base for fishing, boating trips to the Broken Group Islands, and hikes along the West Coast Trail of the Pacific Rim National Park Reserve. You can take a boat here from Port Alberni to protect your car from the gravel road.

Dining and Lodging

$$$$ ✕⊡ **Eagle Nook Ocean Wilderness Resort.** This wilderness country inn,
  ★   accessible only by sea or air, sits on a narrow strip of land in Barkley Sound. For all its blissful isolation, Eagle Nook offers highly civilized comforts. Every spacious room has a minibalcony and a water view. Two self-contained cabins with fireplaces and kitchens are also available. The dining room has a stone fireplace, floor-to-ceiling windows, and fine Pacific Northwest cuisine, which you can enjoy inside or alfresco. Hiking trails lace the woods, and many activities, including fishing, kayaking, and nature cruises, can be prebooked. Getting here—by floatplane from Seattle or Vancouver or on the inn's own water taxi from Port Alberni—is a scenic adventure in its own right. There's a two-night minimum stay; prices are per person and include meals, the water taxi from Port Alberni, a marine nature tour, and all nonguided activities. ⊠ *Box 575, Port Alberni V9Y 7M9,* ☎ *250/723–1000 or 800/760–2777,* FAX *250/723–6609,* WEB *www.wildernessgetaway.com. 23 rooms, 2 cabins. Restaurant, lounge, outdoor hot tub, sauna, hiking, dock, boating, fishing, meeting rooms, helipad. AE, MC, V. Closed mid-Oct.–mid-May. AP.*

Ucluelet

㉓ *100 km (62 mi) west of Port Alberni, 295 km (183 mi) northwest of Victoria.*

Ucluelet, which in the Nuchahnuth First Nations language means "people with a safe landing place," is, along with Bamfield and Tofino, one of the towns serving Pacific Rim National Park Reserve. Whale-watching is another main draw, though visitors increasingly have been coming in the off-season to watch the dramatic winter storms that pound the coast here.

Various charter companies take boats to greet the 26,000 gray whales that pass close to Ucluelet on their migration to the Bering Sea every March and April. However, some gray whales remain in the area year-round. The **Pacific Rim Whale Festival,** a two-week event (here and in Tofino), welcomes the whales each spring. The Ucluelet Chamber of Commerce (⊠ 100 Main St., Box 428, V0R 3A0, ☎ 250/726–4641) has information.

Amphitrite Point Lighthouse, (⊠ end of Coast Guard Rd.), which has a panoramic view of the beach, is an access point for the Wild Pacific Trail, a level path along the coast and through the rain forest. When completed (in about 2003), the trail is to link Ucluelet to Long Beach in Pacific Rim National Park Reserve.

Dining and Lodging

$–$$ ✕ **Matterson House.** In a tiny 1931 cottage with seven tables and an outdoor deck in summer, husband-and-wife team Sandy and Jennifer Clark serve up generous portions of seafood, burgers, pasta, and filling standards such as prime rib and veal cutlets. It's simple food, prepared well with fresh local ingredients; everything, including soups, desserts, and the wonderful bread, is homemade. The wine list has local island wines unavailable elsewhere and worth trying. Matterson House is also a good breakfast stop. ⊠ *1682 Peninsula Rd.*, ☎ *250/726–2200. MC, V.*

$$$–$$$$ 🏨 **Roots Lodge at Reef Point.** The cabins at this resort on the edge of Ucluelet are set along a boardwalk in the woods overlooking the sea. They are beautifully decorated with leather furniture and rich woodsy colors, and have mezzanine bedrooms and fireplaces. Eight suites are also nicely done, though they lack views. Hiking trails through a nearby park start at the resort's edge. Roots Lodge is a good place for self-catering and escapism. ⊠ *131 Seabridge Way, Box 730, V0R 3A0,* ☎ *250/726–2700; 888/594–7333 in British Columbia,* FAX *250/726–2701,* WEB *www.livehotels.net. 8 suites, 14 cabins (for 2–6). Restaurant, kitchenettes, hiking, mountain bikes. AE, DC, MC, V.*

$$$–$$$$ 🏨 **A Snug Harbour Inn.** Set on a cliff above the Pacific, this couples-oriented B&B offers some of the most dramatic views anywhere. The rooms, all with fireplaces, private balconies or decks, whirlpool baths, and ocean views, are decorated in a highly individual style. The Sawadee room, for instance, includes art and fabrics from Thailand, and the Lighthouse room winds up three levels for great views. Eagles nest nearby, and trails through the woods lead to the seaside. ⊠ *460 Marine Dr., Box 367, V0R 3A0,* ☎ *250/726–2686 or 888/936–5222,* FAX *250/726–2685,* WEB *www.awesomeview.com. 4 rooms. Breakfast room, outdoor hot tub, hiking, helipad. MC, V. BP.*

$$$ 🏨 **Tauca Lea by the Sea.** This all-suites complex of blue-stained cedar lodges is on a peninsula on Ucluelet Inlet, but is walking distance to the village (a road connects the island). Hand-crafted furniture and terra-cotta tiles decorate the suites, which also have ocean-view balconies, kitchens, soaking tubs, sofa beds, and gas fireplaces. A boardwalk around the property leads to a sheltered viewpoint for spotting eagles, sea lions, and bears across the inlet. At press time, a marina-view restaurant was set to open, and an espresso bar and a First Nations art gallery were already open. ⊠ *1971 Harbour Crescent, V0R 3A0,* ☎ *250/726–4625 or 800/979–9303,* WEB *www.taucalearesort.com. 27 suites. In-room data ports, boating, fishing, coin laundry, laundry service, business services, meeting rooms. AE, DC, MC, V.*

$–$$$ 🏨 **Canadian Princess Fishing Resort.** If vintage ships are to your liking, you may want to book a cabin on the converted 1932 230-ft, steam-powered survey ship that's part of this complex. Though hardly opulent, the staterooms are comfortable; each has one to four berths, and all but one share bathrooms. The original captain's cabin has a living room, bedroom, and a private bath with a claw-foot tub. Larger than the ship cabins, shoreside rooms in the resort have private entrances, more-contemporary furnishings, and balconies; a few have fireplaces and some are large enough to sleep six. This unique resort appeals to nature enthusiasts and anglers. Fishing charters and whale-watching can be arranged. The Stewart Dining Room and Lounge is open to nonguests; the specialty is (no surprise) seafood. ⊠ *Boat Basin, 1943 Peninsula Rd., Box 939, V0R 3A0,* ☎ *250/726–7771 or 800/663–7090,* FAX *250/726–7121,* WEB *www.obmg.com. 40 shoreside rooms, 35 shipboard cabins without bath and 1 suite. Restaurant, bar, dock, fishing, meeting rooms. AE, DC, MC, V. Closed late Sept.–early Mar.*

Outdoor Activities and Sports

The **Canadian Princess Fishing Resort** (⊠ Boat Basin, 1943 Peninsula Rd., ☎ 250/726–7771 or 800/663–7090) has 10 comfortable fishing and whale-watching boats with heated cabins and bathrooms. **Island West Fishing Resort** (⊠ foot of Bay St., ☎ 250/726–7515) specializes in fishing charters, and also offers accommodations, boat moorage, and floatplane sightseeing tours in the Ucluelet area. **Jamie's Whaling Station** (☎ 250/726–7444) is one of the longest established whale-watching operators in the area, with offices in Ucluelet and Tofino. A great way to learn about the area's ecosystems is on a guided walk or hike with **Long Beach Nature** (☎ 250/726–7099, WEB www.oceansedge.bc.ca). Led by a naturalist and biologist, the day trips range from easy to challenging, and include looks at intertidal life, wildflowers, and the old-growth forest, as well as bird- and whale-watching, photography-oriented walks, and storm-watching walks in winter. **Subtidal Adventures** (☎ 250/726–7336 or 877/444–1134) specializes in whale-watching in spring and nature tours to the Broken Group Islands in summer; there's a choice of a Zodiac (a motorized inflatable boat) or a 36-ft former coast-guard rescue boat.

Tofino

★ ㉔ *42 km (26 mi) northwest of Ucluelet, 337 km (209 mi) northwest of Victoria.*

The end of the road makes a great stage—and Tofino is certainly that. On a narrow peninsula just beyond the north end of the Pacific Rim National Park Reserve, this is as far west as you can go on Vancouver Island by paved road. One look at the pounding Pacific surf and the old-growth forest along the shoreline convinces many people that they've reached not just the end of the road but the end of the Earth.

Tofino's tiny number of year-round residents know what they like and have made what could have been a tourist trap into a funky little town with several art galleries, an excellent bookstore, sociable cafés, and plenty of opportunity to get out to the surrounding wilds—to see the old-growth forests of Meares Island, the natural hot springs at Hot Springs Cove, the long stretches of beach, and, of course, the whales and other wildlife. At the **Tofino Botanical Gardens** (☎ 250/725–1220, WEB www.tofinobotanicalgardens.com), trails wind through displays of indigenous plant life. The 12-acre waterfront site about 2 km (1 mi) south of the village on the Pacific Rim Highway is open 9 to dusk daily, and the $10 admission is good for three days. There's also a restaurant on site (open 10 AM–10 PM daily). Tofino has plenty of accommodations and campsites in and around town, and a full-service spa at the Wickaninnish Inn, but advance reservations are highly recommended if you're visiting Tofino in the summertime.

Dining and Lodging

$$–$$$ ✕ **RainCoast Café.** The draws at this intimate central Tofino restaurant include a good selection of vegetarian dishes as well as local seafood creatively prepared using Asian techniques. For starters, consider the salad of baby greens, smoked wild salmon, and goat cheese, or the Indonesian sweet potato, peanut, and coconut cream soup. Main courses include sake-roasted halibut with Thai red-curry coconut cream, and wild black rice cakes with roasted cashew–ginger sauce. The decor is minimalist and candlelight, with peekaboo sea views. ⊠ *101–120 4th St.,* ☎ *250/725–2215. AE, MC, V. No lunch.*

$$–$$$ ✕ **The Schooner Restaurant.** You can't miss this 1930s-era red clapboard building in central Tofino—it's the one with the schooner sticking out the back; the front half of the boat takes up a chunk of the cozy rooms. The menu changes every two weeks or so. Try, if they're available, the oysters nami nori (blackened Cajun oysters); the halibut Bombay, a halibut fillet stuffed with brie, pine nuts, crab, and shrimp in an apple–brandy cream sauce; the charbroiled seafood platter; or any of the daily oyster or pasta specials. The lunch menu includes sand-

wiches, burgers, and pastas. The Schooner also serves hearty break-fasts. ⊠ *331 Campbell St.,* ☎ *250/725 3111. AE, MC, V.*

$$$$ ✕🖬 **The Wickaninnish Inn.** Set on a rocky promontory above Chester-
★ man Beach, with open ocean on three sides and old-growth forest as
a backdrop, this three-story weathered cedar building is a comfortable
place to enjoy the area's dramatic wilderness scenery, summer or winter. The inn, 5 km (3 mi) south of Tofino, is no-smoking and every room
has a sitting area, an ocean view, and its own balcony, fireplace, and
soaking tub. The staff takes very good care of you, and the full-service Ancient Cedars Spa (also open to nonguests) adds to the pampering.
The glass-enclosed Pointe Restaurant offers 240° views of the crashing surf and is renowned in Canada for its Pacific Northwest cuisine;
the kitchen makes the most of such local delicacies as oysters, goose-
neck barnacles, wild mushrooms, Dungeness crab, and Pacific salmon.
⊠ *Osprey La., at Chesterman Beach, Box 250, V0R 2Z0,* ☎ *250/725–
3100 or 800/333–4604,* 𝔽𝔸𝕏 *250/725–3110,* 𝕎𝔼𝔹 *www.wickinn.com. 46
rooms. Restaurant, lounge, in-room data ports, minibars, room service, massage, spa, steam room, hiking, beach, fishing, laundry service,
meeting rooms. AE, DC, MC, V.*

$$$$ 🖬 **Clayoquot Wilderness Resorts.** This luxury wilderness retreat offers
two options: a floating lodge moored in Clayoquot Sound, a Unesco
Biosphere Reserve 25 minutes by water taxi from Tofino, or high-style
camping on the edge of Strathcona Provincial Park. The lodge is
moored next to its own 127-acre wilderness backyard, with lakes, extensive hiking trails, and acres of old-growth forest. You can enjoy fishing, whale-watching, kayaking, hiking, and nature cruises, as well as
the restaurant's fine Pacific Northwest cuisine. The comfortable rooms
all have water or forest views and private decks. The rates are per person and include all meals and water-taxi pickup from Tofino. The tents
at Wilderness Outpost, a safari-style camp on Bedwell River—a pristine area about 30 minutes by boat from the lodge—sit on wooden platforms and come with queen or twin beds, Persian-style carpets, heaters,
Adirondack furniture, and porches overlooking the water. Campers can
enjoy a hot tub, a sauna, and elegant cuisine served on china and crystal. The activities at the Outpost, including sailing, canoeing, kayaking, horseback riding, mountain biking, hiking, and fishing, are included
in the rates, as are all meals and water-taxi pickup from Tofino. A two-
night minimum stay applies for both. At press time, a spa and longhouse-style conference facility were planned for the lodge. ⊠ *Box
130, V0R 2Z0,* ☎ *250/726–8235 or 888/333–5405,* 𝔽𝔸𝕏 *250/726–
8558,* 𝕎𝔼𝔹 *www.wildretreat.com. 16 rooms, 10 tents. Lodge: restaurant, lounge, outdoor hot tub, sauna, gym, dock, boating, meeting rooms,
helipad. AE, MC, V. Lodge closed Dec.–mid-March; Outpost closed
Oct.–Apr. AP.*

$$–$$$$ 🖬 **Middle Beach Lodge.** A longtime favorite on the beach 3 km (2 mi)
south of Tofino has a choice of three lodges. The Lodge at the Beach,
a wooden, adults-only building on the forest edge, has basic rooms (no
phones or TVs), some with sea views, and a path down to the beach.
The newer (1996) Headlands complex, made with recycled timber and
perched on an oceanfront bluff, offers larger, more-luxurious rooms,
some with fireplaces and ocean-view balconies. The Beach House,
built in 2000, has six luxurious suites, each with a full kitchen. The
suites overlook the bay, so you can watch the waves from your soak-
ing tub. Middle Beach also has several family-size cabins with kitch-
enettes and fireplaces, and some with private outdoor hut tubs. Each
lodge has a common room with a floor-to-ceiling stone fireplace and
ocean views. In July and August dinner is available Wednesday through
Sunday; the rest of the year it's served only on Saturday. Smoking is
not permitted. ⊠ *400 McKenzie Beach Rd., Box 100, V0R 2Z0,* ☎

250/725–2900, FAX 250/725–2901, WEB *www.middlebeach.com. 64 rooms, 10 suites, 19 cabins. Dining room, gym, beach, coin laundry, meeting rooms. AE, MC, V. CP.*

$$$ 🏨 **Chesterman Beach Bed and Breakfast.** The front yard of this small, rustic, West Coast cedar B&B on the beach is the rolling ocean surf. The self-contained two-bedroom suite in the main house and the Lookout room are both romantic and cozy; the former has a sauna, gas fireplace, and a kitchen, and the latter has a gas fireplace and a private ocean-view balcony. The self-sufficient one-bedroom Garden Cottage has a secluded garden, a large deck, a kitchen, and a fireplace and is a good option for families. ✉ *1345 Chesterman Beach Rd., Box 72, V0R 2Z0,* ☎ *250/725–3726,* FAX *250/725–3706,* WEB *www.island.net/~surfsand. 1 room, 2 suites. No-smoking room, beach. MC, V. CP.*

$$–$$$ 🏨 **Inn at Tough City.** The owners of this inn on Tofino Harbour scoured the province for such nifty recyclables as vintage advertising paraphernalia and added First Nations artwork to create a fun and funky ambience in the lobby and common rooms. The name is derived from Tofino's old nickname, from the days before roads, when life was fairly rough here. It certainly isn't anymore: the guest rooms, decorated in rich, bold colors, have stained-glass windows, hardwood floors, antiques, covered decks or balconies, and down duvets. Six of them have striking views over Tofino Harbour and Clayoquot Sound; several have fireplaces and soaking tubs. The main floor has a cozy common room with leather sofas and a woodstove, a wraparound veranda, and a sushi bar. ✉ *350 Main St., V0R 2Z0,* ☎ *250/725–2021 or 877/725–2021,* FAX *250/725–2088,* WEB *www.alberni.net/toughcity. 8 rooms. Sushi bar, no-smoking rooms. AE, MC, V.*

$$ 🏨 **Red Crow Guest House.** On the sheltered side of the Tofino peninsula, about 2 km (1 mi) south of the village, sits this Cape Cod–style house amid 17 acres of cedar and hemlock. Two large rooms underneath the main part of the house open onto a covered veranda and a private pebble beach, offering stunning east-facing views over island-dotted Clayoquot Sound. Decorated with family heirlooms and First Nations art, each of the large, comfortable rooms has a king bed, gas fireplace, coffeemaker, and breakfast table. A lavish breakfast made by the owner, a former Four Seasons chef, is delivered to your door. A rustic cedar cottage in the woods has a full kitchen and sleeps six. Canoes are available for guests, and walking trails lace the property. The bird-watching here is excellent. Smoking is not permitted. ✉ *1084 Pacific Rim Hwy., Box 37, V0R 2Z0,* ☎ FAX *250/725–2275,* WEB *www.tofinoredcrow.com. 2 rooms, 1 cottage. Refrigerators, boating. V, MC. BP.*

$ 🏨 **Paddlers' Inn.** This multiple-business inn on the waterfront in the center of Tofino covers all the bases. Downstairs, an espresso bar and bookstore overlook a kayaking outlet. Upstairs, five clean rooms have Scandinavian furniture and futons but no phones or TVs. The rooms share a bathroom and a kitchen. The inn is completely no-smoking. ✉ *320 Main St., Box 620, V0R 2Z0,* ☎ *250/725–4222 or 800/863–4664,* FAX *250/725–2070,* WEB *www.tofino-kayaking.com. 5 rooms without bath. Café, boating. MC, V. Closed Nov.–Feb. CP.*

$ 🏨 **Whalers on the Point Guesthouse (Hostelling International Tofino).** On Tofino Harbour, this modern seaside hostel has pretty much everything a budget traveler could want: there's a game room and TV lounge; a shared kitchen, living room, dining room, and patio overlooking the bay; and even surfboard storage and Internet access. Accommodation is available in private rooms and dorms. ✉ *81 West St., Box 296, V0R 2Z0,* ☎ *250/725–3443,* FAX *250/725–3463,* WEB *www.tofinohostel.com. 7 rooms, 3 with bath; 15 4-bed dorms. Sauna, bicycles, billiards, coin laundry. MC, V.*

Outdoor Activities and Sports

GOLF

Long Beach Golf Course (✉ Pacific Rim Hwy., ☎ 250/725–3332), a 9-hole, par-36 course, is open all year.

KAYAKING

Remote Passages Sea Kayaking (✉ 71 Wharf St., ☎ 250/725–3330 or 800/666–9833, WEB www.remotepassages.com) has guided day and evening paddles; no experience is necessary. **Tofino Sea-Kayaking Company** (✉ 320 Main St., ☎ 250/725–4222 or 800/863–4664, WEB www.tofino-kayaking.com) rents kayaks and runs a kayaking school and wilderness kayaking trips.

SURFING

Tofino, despite the chilling waters, is a popular place to surf. **Live to Surf** (✉ 1180 Pacific Rim Hwy., ☎ 250/725–4464, WEB www.livetosurf.com) rents boards and wetsuits and offers surfing lessons.

WHALE-WATCHING AND MARINE EXPEDITIONS

In March and April, gray whales migrate along the coast here; resident grays can be seen anytime between May and November. In addition, humpback whales, sea otters, and other wildlife are increasingly seen in the area. Most whale-watching operators also offer boat trips to Meares Island, with its stands of old-growth forest, and Hot Springs Cove, where you can soak in natural rock pools.

Chinook Charters (✉ 450 Campbell St., ☎ 250/725–3431 or 800/665–3646) offers whale-watching, fishing, and Hot Springs Cove trips. **Jamie's Whaling Station** (✉ 606 Campbell St., ☎ 250/725–3919; 800/667–9913 in Canada, WEB www.jamies.com) is one of the most established whale-watching operators on the coast. It has both Zodiacs and more-comfortable 65-ft tour boats. **Remote Passages Marine Excursions** (✉ 71 Wharf St., ☎ 250/725–3330 or 800/666–9833), a well-established operator, runs whale-watching and other wildlife-viewing trips with an ecological focus. It also has trips to Hot Springs Cove and bear-watching outings in sheltered waters. **Sea Trek Tours and Expeditions** (☎ 250/725–4412 or 800/811–9155, WEB www.seatrektour.bc.ca) operates whale- and bear-watching and harbor tours as well as day trips to Hot Spring Cove and Meares Island. **Weigh West Marine Resort** (☎ 250/725–3277 or 800/665–8922, WEB www.weighwest.com) offers fishing charters (including saltwater fly-fishing) and whale-watching and Hot Springs Cove tours. It can arrange complete packages including accommodations, meals, and guides. The **Whale Centre** (✉ 411 Campbell St., ☎ 250/725–2132 or 888/474–2288) has a maritime museum with a 40-ft whale skeleton you can study while waiting for your boat. The center, which has open and closed boats, offers bird-, bear-, and whale-watching trips and goes to Hot Springs Cove.

Shopping

In a traditional longhouse, the magnificent **Eagle Aerie Gallery** (✉ 350 Campbell St., ☎ 250/725–3235) houses a collection of prints, paintings, and carvings by the renowned artist Roy Henry Vickers. **House of Himwitsa** (✉ 300 Main St., ☎ 250/725–2017 or 800/899–1947) sells native crafts, jewelry, and clothing. The complex also has a seafood restaurant and lodge rooms. **Islandfolk Gallery** (✉ 120 4th St., ☎ 250/725–3130) sells the work of Tofino wildlife and landscape artist Mark Hobson and other Vancouver Island artists. Photographs, paintings, carvings, pottery, and jewelry by local artists are available at **Reflecting Spirit Gallery** (✉ 411 Campbell St., ☎ 250/725–2472), which also runs a children's art program in summer. **Wildside Booksellers** (✉ 320

Main St., ☎ 250/725–4222) has an extensive selection of books and an espresso bar.

Pacific Rim National Park Reserve

★ ㉕ *105 km (63 mi) west of Port Alberni, 9 km (5 mi) south of Tofino.*

This national park has some of Canada's most stunning coastal and rain-forest scenery, abundant wildlife, and a unique marine environment. It comprises three separate areas—Long Beach, the Broken Group Islands, and the West Coast Trail—for a combined area of 123,431 acres and stretches 130 km (81 mi) along Vancouver Island's West Coast. The **Park Information Centre** (2 km [1 mi] north of the Tofino–Ucluelet junction on Hwy. 4, ☎ 250/726–4212) is open daily mid-June to mid-September, 9:30–5. Park-use fees apply in all sections of the park.

The **Long Beach** unit gets its name from a 16-km (10-mi) strip of hard-packed sand strewn with driftwood, shells, and the occasional Japanese glass fishing float. Long Beach is the most accessible part of the park, and the roads can get busy in summer. People come in the off-season to watch winter storms and to see migrating whales in early spring. An $8 daily group pass, available from dispensers in the parking lots, is required for each private vehicle and includes admission to the Wickaninnish Interpretive Centre. You can camp at Long Beach at the Green Point Campground; it's off Highway 4 just north of the Tofino–Ucluelet junction. Walk-in sites are issued on a first-come, first-serve basis and fill quickly. Drive-in sites (with no RV hookups) can be reserved by calling ☎ 800/689–9025, or through www.discovercamping.ca.

A first stop for many Pacific Rim National Park visitors, the **Wickaninnish Interpretive Centre** (✉ Hwy. 4, ☎ 250/726–4701 for center; 250/726–7706 for restaurant) is on the ocean edge about 16 km (10 mi) north of Ucluelet. It's a great place to learn about the wilderness; theater programs and exhibits provide information about the park's marine ecology and rain-forest environment. Open daily mid-March to mid-October, 10:30–6, the center is also a good lunch stop—it was originally an inn, and its restaurant still serves up hearty seafood lunches and dinners (until 9 PM). Park information is available here when the Park Information Centre is closed.

The 100-plus islands of the **Broken Group Islands** can be reached only by boat. Many commercial charter tours are available from Ucluelet, at the southern end of Long Beach, and from Tofino, Bamfield, and Port Alberni. The islands and their waters are alive with sea lions, seals, and whales. The inner waters near Gibraltar, Jacques, and Hand islands offer protection and good boating conditions, but go with a guide if it's your first trip.

The third element of the park, the **West Coast Trail**, runs along the coast from Bamfield to Port Renfrew. This extremely rugged 75-km (47-mi) trail is for experienced hikers. It can be traveled only on foot, takes an average of six days to complete, and is open May through September. The park controls the number of people allowed on the trail, so it's best to reserve a spot. A number of fees apply: $25 for a reservation (paid when you book), $70 in park-use fees, and $25 in ferry fares. Reservations can be made up to three months in advance via Super, Natural British Columbia (☎ 800/435–5622) from March through September. ✉ *Mailing address: 2185 Ocean Terrace Rd., Box 280, Ucluelet V0R 3A0, ☎ 250/726–7721, ꜰꜰ 250/726–4720, ᴡᴇʙ www.parkscan.harbour.com/pacrim.*

En Route Heading back to the east coast from Port Alberni, stop at **Cathedral Grove** in MacMillan Provincial Park on Highway 4. Walking trails lead past Douglas fir trees and western red cedars, some as much as 800 years old. Their remarkable height creates a spiritual effect, as though you were gazing at a cathedral ceiling.

Parksville

㉖ *47 km (29 mi) east of Port Alberni, 38 km (24 mi) northwest of Nanaimo, 72 km (45 mi) southeast of Courtenay, 154 km (95 mi) north of Victoria.*

Parksville is one of the primary resort areas on the eastern side of the island; lodges and waterfront motels here cater to families, campers, and boaters. In **Rathtrevor Beach Provincial Park** (✉ off Hwy. 19, ☎ 250/954–4600), 2 km (1 mi) south of Parksville, high tide brings ashore the warmest ocean water in British Columbia. It's a good place for a swim.

OFF THE
BEATEN PATH

COOMBS – If you're traveling from Parksville to Port Alberni, it's worth taking the quieter Highway 4A past this odd little village, best known for the goats grazing on the grass-covered roof of its Old Country Market. Also worth a stop is **Butterfly World** (✉ 1080 Winchester Rd., ☎ 250/248–7026), where you can wander through an atrium filled with hundreds of free-flying butterflies. It's open March and October daily 10–4 and April through September daily 10–5. Admission is $6.50.

Lodging

$$–$$$ 🏨 **Tigh-Na-Mara Resort.** About 2 km (1 mi) south of Parksville on Highway 19A, this resort on 22 forested seaside acres attracts families in summertime and hosts conferences and romantic getaways the rest of the year. The beach, with its warm water and wide tidal flats, is just right for the bucket-and-spade brigade, as are the playgrounds, playhouse, and extensive summertime children's programs. The log-construction accommodations include a three-story lodge high over the water (a winding pathway leads down to the beach), a more basic inland lodge, and several one- and two-bedroom cabins in the woods. All oceanside units have fireplaces and decks with expansive views over Craig Bay; some have whirlpool tubs. ✉ *1095 East Island Hwy., V9P 2E5,* ☎ *250/248–2072 or 800/663–7373,* FAX *250/248–4140,* WEB *www.tigh-na-mara.com. 33 rooms, 116 suites, 37 cabins. Restaurant, lounge, kitchenettes, no-smoking floor, refrigerators, indoor pool, hot tub, massage, steam room, horseshoes, Ping-Pong, volleyball, beach, bicycles, children's programs (ages 4–12), playground, coin laundry, convention center, travel services, car rental. AE, DC, MC, V.*

Outdoor Activities and Sports
Morningstar Golf Course (✉ 525 Lowry's Rd., ☎ 250/248–8161) is an 18-hole, par-72 course that's open all year.

Qualicum Beach

㉗ *10 km (6 mi) north of Parksville.*

Qualicum Beach is known largely for its salmon fishing and opportunities for beachcombing. The **Old School House Arts Centre** (✉ 122 Fern Rd. W, ☎ 250/752–6133) shows and sells the work of British Columbia artists and artisans.

Guided and self-guided spelunking tours for all levels are offered April through October at **Horne Lake Caves Provincial Park** (☎ 250/248–7829, WEB www.hornelake.com). Prices start at $15 for a 1½-hour tour.

The turnoff for the park, from Highway 19, is Exit 75; it's 18 km (11 mi) north of Qualicum Beach. From the exit the park is another 13 km (8 mi).

En Route   Between Qualicum Beach and the twin cities of Courtenay and Comox is tiny Buckley Bay, where BC Ferries leave for **Denman Island,** with connecting service to **Hornby Island.** Both these pretty rural islands have crafts shops, cafés, walking trails, and accommodations. Hornby is best known for its long, sandy beaches.

Courtenay

28   *220 km (136 mi) northwest of Victoria, 17 nautical mi west of Powell River, 57 km (34 mi) northwest of Qualicum Beach.*

This commercial town provides a base for Mt. Washington skiers. You can catch the **Esquimalt & Nanaimo** small-gauge railway (☎ 800/561–8630 in Canada; 800/561–3949 in the U.S., WEB www.viarail.ca) in Courtenay to Nanaimo, Victoria, and other South Island stops.

Dinosaur fans should love the **Courtenay and District Museum and Paleontology Centre** (✉ 207 Fourth St., ☎ 250/334–0686, WEB www.courtenaymuseum.bc.ca), one of British Columbia's leading paleontology centers. It's home to the reconstructed skeleton of a 43-ft elasmosaur—a dinosaur-era sea creature found in the Comox Valley. It also has some interesting First Nations and pioneer artifacts, and arranges fossil-hunting day trips in the area. Admission is $3. The museum is open daily 10–5 June through August and, during the other months, Tuesday through Saturday 10–5 and Sunday noon to 4.

OFF THE BEATEN PATH
COMOX – East of Courtenay about 6 km (4 mi) is the twin town of Comox, which also serves as a base for Mt. Washington skiers. It's best known as the home to Canadian Forces Base Comox, an air force base.

At the **Filberg Heritage Lodge and Park** (✉ 61 Filberg Rd., ☎ 250/339–2715), you can stroll around 9 acres of beautifully landscaped waterfront grounds and tour the rustic 1929 lodge. The lodge is open 11–5 daily June through August, Friday through Monday in May and September. In summer, a separate petting zoo and seaside tea house are also open. Admission to the gardens, which are open dawn to dusk all year, is free; lodge admission is $1.

The **Comox Air Force Museum** (☎ 250/339–8162), at Canadian Forces Base Comox in Lazo, about 1 km (½ mi) north of Comox, has an interesting collection of air force memorabilia and historic aircraft in the nearby airpark. The museum is open daily 10–4 June through August and, during the other months, Thursday and Friday noon to 4 and weekends 10–4. The airpark is open daily 10–4 June through September only. Admission is by donation.

Dining and Lodging

$–$$$
★   ✕ **Old House Restaurant.** This riverside restaurant set among gardens (though also overlooking a pulp mill across the way) provides casual dining in a restored 1938 house with cedar beams, four stone fireplaces, and a patio for dining. People flock here for the West Coast home-style cuisine—sandwiches and salads at lunch; seafood, steaks, and pastas, along with fancier, more-innovative dishes (prawn-and-scallop stir-fry, Fanny Bay oysters), at dinner—and the fresh daily specials. ✉ *1760 Riverside La.,* ☎ *250/338–5406. AE, DC, MC, V.*

$$–$$$$
★   ▥ **Kingfisher Oceanside Resort and Spa.** Soothing is the word to describe this seaside resort about 7 km (4½ mi) south of Courtenay. Thirty-six beachfront suites—all with decks or patios, kitchenettes, gas

fireplaces, in-room data ports and VCRs, and expansive ocean views—are decorated in soft sea blues and greens. All rooms are no-smoking. A full-service spa, also open to nonguests, offers the works, including beauty treatments, aromatherapy, hydrotherapy, and massage. The steam room looks like a mermaid's cave, and the gym has an ocean view. The original, lower-price rooms, set a little farther back from the water, are also modern and spacious, and some have kitchens. ⊠ *4330 S. Island Hwy., R.R. 6, Site 672, C-1, V9N 8H9,* ☎ *250/338–1323 or 800/663–7929,* FAX *250/338–0058,* WEB *www.spa2001.com. 28 rooms, 36 suites. Restaurant, lounge, no-smoking floor, room service, pool, outdoor hot tub, sauna, tennis court, beach, boating, fishing, bicycles, playground, laundry service, business services, meeting rooms. AE, D, DC, MC, V.*

$ ⓘ **Greystone Manor.** About 3 km (2 mi) south of Courtenay, this 1918 house has a lovingly tended 1½-acre English garden and views over Comox Bay, where seals are often visible. Inside, the original hardwood floors, period furnishings, and a woodstove make things cozy. Two of the prettily decorated rooms have baths with showers; the third has a claw-foot tub in a room across the hall. The hosts, Mike and Maureen Shipton, from Bath, England, serve a full hot breakfast, which is included in the rates. ⊠ *4014 Haas Rd., R.R. 6, Site 684, C-2, V9N 8H9,* ☎ *250/338–1422,* WEB *www.bbcanada.com/1334.html. 3 rooms. Breakfast room, piano. MC, V. BP.*

Outdoor Activities and Sports

GOLF

The 18-hole, par-72 course at the **Crown Isle Resort & Golf Community** (⊠ 399 Clubhouse Dr., off Ryan Rd., ☎ 250/703–5050 or 888/338–8439) is, at 7,024 yards, the longest course on Vancouver Island. The resort also has on-site accommodation and a lavish clubhouse. It's one of several courses in the area.

SKIING

Mt. Washington Alpine Resort (☎ 250/338–1386; 888/231–1499 for lodging reservations), 30 km (18 mi) from Courtenay via Strathcona Parkway, has 50 downhill runs, a 1,657-ft vertical drop, five chairlifts, three surface lifts, and an elevation of 5,200 ft; it's the island's largest ski area. The resort also has 40 km (25 mi) of track-set cross-country trails, two snowboard parks, snow-tubing chutes, and, in summer, miles of hiking and mountain-bike trails accessible by chairlift, as well as a disc golf course and horseback riding. The resort has a good selection of restaurants, shops, and hotel and B&B accommodations.

Campbell River

㉙ *50 km (31 mi) north of Courtenay, 155 km (96 mi) northwest of Nanaimo, 270 km (167 mi) northwest of Victoria.*

Campbell River draws people who want to fish; some of the biggest salmon ever caught on a line have been landed just off the coast here. Cutthroat trout are also plentiful in the river.

The primary access to Strathcona Provincial Park is on Highway 28 west of town. Other recreational activities include diving in **Discovery Passage,** where a battleship has been sunk, kayaking, and taking a summer whale-watching tour. For information, contact the **Campbell River Visitor Information Centre** (⊠ 1235 Shoppers Row, Box 400, V9W 5B6, ☎ 250/287–4636 or 800/463–4386).

Haig-Brown House Education Centre (⊠ 2250 Campbell River Rd., ☎ 250/286–6646, WEB www.haig-brown.bc.ca), the preserved home of conservationist and writer Roderick Haig-Brown, is set in 2 acres of formal gardens surrounded by 20 acres of trail-laced woods. The center runs seminars and workshops on topics ranging from conservation to writing, and also offers B&B rooms. Tours of the house are given in July and August, at 1:30 daily, and by special arrangement during the rest of the year. Admission is by donation.

Dining and Lodging

$-$$ ✗ **Royal Coachman Neighbourhood Pub.** Informal, blackboard-menu restaurants like this one dot the landscape of Vancouver Island. The menu, which changes daily, is surprisingly daring for what is essentially a high-end pub, and the inn draws crowds nightly, especially Tuesday and Saturday (prime-rib nights). More-interesting combinations have included Thai ginger beef over Caesar salad and lamb medallions in a martini sauce. Come early for both lunch and dinner to avoid a wait. ⊠ *84 Dogwood St.,* ☎ *250/286–0231. AE, MC, V.*

$$-$$$$ 🏠 **Painter's Lodge.** Bob Hope, John Wayne, and their fishing buddies came to this lodge overlooking Discovery Passage to catch big Tyee (spring salmon) in the 1940s and '50s. The attractive cedar complex (a newer building on the same site) now draws nature-oriented visitors and whale-watchers as well as anglers; the resort's own fleet runs guided fishing and nature cruises. The 15 rooms in the lodge and the rooms, suites, and one- to three-bedroom cabins spread around the property all have balconies or patios, and some have kitchens, fireplaces, and whirlpool baths. The owner, the Oak Bay Marine Group, also runs a water taxi to Painter's sister resort, April Point Lodge, on Quadra Island, where you can kayak or explore biking and hiking trails. Painter's Lodge is 8 km (5 mi) north of Campbell River. ⊠ *1625 McDonald Rd., Box 460, V9W 5C1,* ☎ *250/286–1102 or 800/663–7090,* FAX *250/286–0158,* WEB *www.painterslodge.com. 90 rooms, 4 cabins. Restaurant, lounge, pub, pool, 2 outdoor hot tubs, 2 tennis courts, gym, fishing, bicycles, playground, meeting rooms. AE, D, DC, MC, V. Closed mid-Oct.–mid-Mar.*

Outdoor Activities and Sports

Storey Creek Golf Club (⊠ 300 McGimpsey Rd., ☎ 250/923–3673) is an 18-hole, par-72 course 15 minutes south of Campbell River.

Quadra Island

➌⓪ *10 minutes by ferry from Campbell River.*

Quadra is a thickly forested island, rich with wildlife and laced with hiking trails. The **Kwagiulth Museum and Cultural Centre** (⊠ 34 Weway Rd., Cape Mudge Village, ☎ 250/285–3733) houses a collection of potlatch (ceremonial feast) regalia and historical photos. The museum is open daily in summer, closed Sunday October through May; admission is by donation.

Dining and Lodging

$$ ✗🏠 **Tsa-Kwa-Luten Lodge.** Authentic Pacific Coast native food and cultural activities are highlights of this resort operated by members of the Cape Mudge First Nations band. The main lodge, on a high bluff amid 1,100 acres of forest, has a lofty foyer built in the style of a longhouse. The guest rooms, decorated with modern furniture and Kwagiulth artwork, all have balconies or patios overlooking Discovery Passage; many also have fireplaces or lofts. Three two-bedroom beachfront cottages have gas fireplaces, whirlpool tubs, kitchenettes, and private verandas. A four-bedroom guest house is great for groups. You can visit nearby petroglyphs, kayak, bike, hike, fish, dive, snorkel, take a whale- or bear-watching or sightseeing cruise, and even try archery here. Reflexology and massage are available, too. The restaurant, which serves

traditional Kwagiulth cuisine—such as venison stew, clam fritters, and a breakfast dish of hamatsa hash, a traditional salmon-and-potato hash topped with two eggs—is open to nonguests; reservations are recommended. ⊠ *Lighthouse Rd., Box 460, Quathiaski Cove V0P 1N0,* ☎ *250/285–2042 or 800/665–7745,* FAX *250/285–2532,* WEB *www.cape-mudgeresort.bc.ca. 30 rooms, 4 cottages. Restaurant, lounge, kitchenettes (some), no-smoking room, outdoor hot tub, sauna, archery, boccie, gym, boating, fishing, mountain bikes, laundry service, business services, meeting rooms. AE, DC, MC, V. Closed Oct.–May.*

$$–$$$ 🏨 **April Point Lodge and Fishing Resort.** This former fishing lodge, spread across a point and surrounded by forest, is now a family-oriented eco-tourism getaway, with whale- and bird-watching, kayaking, hiking, and saltwater fishing available. The accommodations include lodge rooms and suites, many with fireplaces, and guest houses with kitchens, fireplaces, and sundecks. Guests have access, via free water taxi, to the pool, hot tubs, tennis courts, and fitness center at Painter's Lodge, near Campbell River. ⊠ *900 Quathiaski Cove, Box 248, Quadra Island V0P 1N0,* ☎ *250/285–2222 or 800/663–7090,* FAX *250/285–2411,* WEB *www.aprilpoint.com. 49 rooms, 8 guest houses. Restaurant, lounge, picnic area, sushi bar, no-smoking room, hiking, dock, boating, bicycles, baby-sitting, meeting rooms, helipad. AE, D, DC, MC, V. Closed Nov.–Mar.*

Strathcona Provincial Park

★ ③ *40 km (25 mi) west of Campbell River.*

The largest provincial park on Vancouver Island, Strathcona Provincial Park (☎ 250/954–4600) encompasses **Mt. Golden Hinde,** at 7,220 ft the island's highest mountain, and **Della Falls,** one of Canada's highest waterfalls, reaching 1,440 ft. This strikingly scenic wilderness park's lakes and 161 campsites attract summer canoeists, hikers, anglers, and campers. The main access is by Highway 28 from Campbell River; Mt. Washington ski area, next to the park, can be reached by roads out of Courtenay. If you're not camping, park entry is free; for walk-in campsites, it's $5 per person.

Lodging

$–$$ 🏨 **Strathcona Park Lodge and Outdoor Education Centre.** A privately owned lakefront resort on the outskirts of Strathcona Provincial Park, the center has reasonably priced lodge rooms, lakefront cabins, and a variety of outdoor-adventure programs—including rock climbing, canoeing, kayaking, and sailing—available to the public in summer. It's about 45 km (28 mi) west of Campbell River on Highway 28. Note that the on-site restaurant is closed November through April, though lodging is available all year. ⊠ *Box 2160, Campbell River V9W 5C5,* ☎ *250/286–3122,* FAX *250/286–6010,* WEB *www.strathcona.bc.ca. 38 rooms, 10 cabins. Restaurant, hiking, boating, children's programs (ages 6–18), meeting rooms. MC, V.*

Johnstone Strait

East side of Vancouver Island, roughly between Campbell River and Telegraph Cove.

In mid- to late June of each year, pods of orca return to the east coast of Vancouver Island, following the salmon runs down from northern British Columbia, and usually stay through the winter.

In Robson Bight (a bight is a bay), orca like rubbing against the soft pebble beaches. Whales are most often seen during the salmon runs of July, August, and September. Because of their presence, Robson Bight has been declared an ecological reserve: whales here must not be dis-turbed by human observers. Some of Vancouver Island's best whale-watching tours, however, are conducted nearby, out of Alert Bay and Telegraph Cove, a village built on pilings over water.

There are other things to do in the area. From Port McNeill, a 40-minute ferry ride takes you to Alert Bay, where you can see the First Nations artifacts at the **U'mista Cultural Centre** (✉ Front St., Box 253, Alert Bay, ☎ 250/974–5403). Or you can go to **Sointula,** a 20-minute ferry ride from Port McNeill, to visit the remains of a Finnish Utopian community.

Outdoor Activities and Sports

KAYAKING

North Island Kayak (☎ 250/949–7707), with outlets at Telegraph Cove, Alder Bay, and Port Hardy, rents kayaks and runs guided paddles.

WHALE-WATCHING

Most trips run from late June through October. **Robson Bight Charters** (✉ 40 Sayward Rd., Box 99, Sayward V0P 1R0, ☎ 250/282–3833; 800/658–0022 in British Columbia) offers full-day whale- and bear-watching expeditions. **Stubbs Island Whale Watching** (☎ 250/928–3185 or 800/665–3066, WEB www.stubbs-island.com) runs half-day whale-watching trips on its two 60-ft vessels. The boats are equipped with hydrophones, for listening to the whales.

Port Hardy

32 *238 km (148 mi) northwest of Campbell River, 499 km (309 mi) northwest of Victoria, 274 nautical mi southeast of Prince Rupert.*

Port Hardy is the departure and arrival point for BC Ferries' year-round trips through the scenic Inside Passage to and from Prince Rupert, the coastal port serving the Queen Charlotte Islands, and, in summer, to Bella Coola and other small communities along the mainland's mid-coast. In summer Port Hardy can be crowded, so book your accommodations early. Ferry reservations for the trip between Port Hardy and Prince Rupert or Bella Coola should also be made well in advance. **North Island Transportation** (☎ 250/949–6300) runs a shuttle bus between most Port Hardy hotels and the ferry terminal. The fare is $5.25.

OFF THE
BEATEN PATH

CAPE SCOTT PROVINCIAL PARK – At the northern tip of Vancouver Island and 67 km (42 mi) north of Port Hardy by gravel road is a wilderness camping region suitable for well-equipped and experienced hikers. To camp, it's $5 per person per night. ☎ *250/954–4600.* ✐ *Free.*

Lodging

$$ ⚑ **Glen Lyon Inn.** Eagles can often be spotted scouting the water for fish to prey on from this modern hotel next to the marina on Hardy Bay. All rooms have full ocean views; most have balconies, microwaves, and refrigerators. Some of the suites have whirlpool tubs and fireplaces and several units have kitchenettes. The inn is one of the closest to the ferry terminal, 7 km (4 mi) away. Fishing and whale-watching charters can be arranged from here. ✉ *6435 Hardy Bay Rd., Box 103, V0N 2P0,* ☎ *250/949–7115 or 877/949–7115,* FAX *250/949–7415,* WEB *www.glenlyoninn.com. 37 rooms, 7 suites. Restaurant, pub, in-room data ports, kitchenettes (some), no-smoking rooms, refrigerators, gym, coin laundry, meeting rooms. AE, MC, V.*

$$ ⚑ **Quarterdeck Inn and Marine Resort.** All rooms have water views at this hotel on Port Hardy's waterfront. The rooms are bright and spacious with modern decor and rich colors; some have kitchenettes. The two suites have fireplaces and whirlpool tubs. Salmon fishing, day hikes,

and whale-watching can be arranged from the hotel, which is a 10-minute drive from the ferry terminal. ⊠ *6555 Hardy Bay Rd., Box 910, VON 2P0,* ☎ *250/902–0455 or 877/902–0459,* FAX *250/902–0454,* WEB *www.quarterdeckresort.net. 38 rooms, 2 suites. Pub, in-room data ports, kitchenettes (some), no-smoking floor, hot tub, gym, marina, meeting rooms. AE, D, DC, MC, V. CP.*

Vancouver Island A to Z

To research prices, get advice from other travelers, and book travel arrangements, visit www.fodors.com.

AIR TRAVEL

Air B.C., operated by Air Canada, is the dominant carrier. Kenmore Air Harbour offers direct daily flights from Seattle to Victoria year-round, and has summer service from Seattle to Nanaimo, Campbell River, Quadra Island, and other North Island and Inside Passage destinations. North Vancouver Air links Tofino with Vancouver and Seattle. Northwest Seaplanes offers summer floatplane service between Seattle and Tofino, Campbell River, and Port Hardy.

➤ AIRLINES AND CONTACTS: **Air B.C.** (☎ 888/247–2262). **Kenmore Air Harbour** (☎ 425/486–1257 or 800/543–9595, WEB www.kenmore-air.com). **North Vancouver Air** (☎ 604/278–1608 or 800/228–6608, WEB www.northvanair.com). **Northwest Seaplanes** (☎ 425/277–1590 or 800/690–0086, WEB www.nwseaplanes.com).

AIRPORTS

Vancouver Island is served by Victoria International Airport. Otherwise, there are domestic airports in or near many towns on the island, including Campbell River, Comox, and Nanaimo. Tofino and Port Hardy have airports that don't have phones.

➤ AIRPORT INFORMATION: **Campbell River Airport** (⊠ 2000 Jubilee Pkwy., Campbell River, ☎ 250/923–5012). **Comox airport** (⊠ Canadian Forces Base, ☎ 250/897–3123). **Nanaimo airport** (⊠ 3350 Spitfire Rd., Cassidy, ☎ 250/245–2157).

BOAT AND FERRY TRAVEL

BC Ferries has frequent, year-round passenger and vehicle service to Vancouver Island: a 1½-hour crossing from Tsawwassen (about an hour's drive south of Vancouver) to Swartz Bay (a 30-minute drive north of Victoria); a two-hour crossing from Tsawwassen to Duke Point, 15 km (9 mi) south of Nanaimo; and a 1½-hour crossing from Horseshoe Bay (a 30-minute drive north of Vancouver) to Departure Bay, 3 km (2 mi) north of Nanaimo. Vehicle reservations can be made for any of these routes; a $15 reservation fee applies.

BC Ferries also has year-round passenger and vehicle service to most of the inhabited islands off Vancouver Island's east coast and links Comox with Powell River on the Sunshine Coast, though reservations cannot be made for this route.

Lady Rose Marine Services takes passengers on packet freighters from Port Alberni to Vancouver Island's west coast. The M.V. *Lady Rose,* a Scottish ship built in 1937, makes the 4½-hour trip to Bamfield at 8 AM Tuesday, Thursday, and Saturday year-round, with additional Friday and Sunday sailings in July and August. The round-trip fare is $45. The newer M.V. *Francis Barkley* sails from Port Alberni to the Broken Group Islands and Ucluelet at 8 AM Monday, Wednesday, and Friday between early June and late September. The round-trip fare is $50 to Ucluelet, $40 to the Broken Group Islands. Both ships leave from Argyle Pier (⊠ 5425 Argyle St.).

The M.V. *Uchuck,* a 100-passenger coastal packet freighter, sails from Gold River, 100 km (62 mi) west of Campbell River at the end of Highway 28, to a number of isolated west-coast settlements. Day trips ($40–$45 per person) and overnight trips ($310 per couple, including one night's bed and breakfast) are available all year. Reservations (and good sea legs) are essential.

➤ BOAT AND FERRY INFORMATION: **BC Ferries** (☎ 250/386–3431; 888/ 223–3779 in B.C.; 604/444–2890 for vehicle reservations; 888/724– 5223 in B.C., WEB www.bcferries.com). **Lady Rose Marine Services** (☎ 250/723–8313; 800/663–7192 for reservations Apr.–Sept., WEB www.la-dyrosemarine.com). **M.V.** *Uchuck* (☎ 250/283–2515 or 250/283– 2325, WEB www.mvuchuck.com).

BUS TRAVEL
Laidlaw Coach Lines serves most towns on Vancouver Island. The Link runs a scheduled shuttle-bus service along the island's west coast, serving Ucluelet, Tofino, Tofino Airport, and the Pacific Rim National Park Reserve. From Vancouver, Greyhound serves Nanaimo.

➤ BUS INFORMATION: **Greyhound** (☎ 604/482–8747 or 800/661–8747). **Laidlaw Coach Lines** (☎ 250/385–4411; 800/318–0818 in British Columbia; 800/663–8390 from the U.S.). **The Link** (☎ 250/726– 7779, WEB www.newshuttle.com).

CAR RENTAL
Most major agencies, including Avis, Budget, Hertz, and National Tilden, serve cities throughout Vancouver Island.

CAR TRAVEL
Major roads on Vancouver Island, and most secondary roads, are paved and well engineered. Many wilderness and park-access roads are unpaved. Inquire locally about logging activity before using logging or forestry service roads. B.C. Highways has 24-hour highway reports; the toll call is 75¢ a minute.

Highway 17 connects the Swartz Bay ferry terminal on the Saanich Peninsula with downtown Victoria. The Trans-Canada Highway (Highway 1) runs from Victoria to Nanaimo. The Island Highway (Highway 19) connects Nanaimo to Port Hardy. (Highway 19A, the old road, runs parallel. It's a slower, seaside option.) Highway 14 connects Victoria to Sooke and Port Renfrew on the west coast. Highway 4 crosses the island from Parksville to Tofino and Pacific Rim National Park Reserve.

➤ CONTACTS: **B.C. Highways** (☎ 900/565–4997, 75¢ a minute).

EMERGENCIES
➤ CONTACTS: **Ambulance, fire, poison control, police** (☎ 911).

LODGING
Reservations for lodging anywhere in the province can be made through Super, Natural British Columbia's reservation service. From March through October, the provincial government also runs a toll-free Campground Reservation Line.

Best Canadian Bed and Breakfast Network and Garden City B&B Reservation Service can book B&B accommodations on Vancouver Island.

➤ RESERVATION SERVICES: **Best Canadian Bed and Breakfast Network** (✉ 1064 Balfour Ave., Vancouver V6H 1X1, ☎ 604/738–7207, FAX 604/732–4998, WEB www.balfourbb.com). **Campground Reservation Line** (☎ 800/689–9025, WEB www.discovercamping.ca). **Garden City B&B Reservation Service** (✉ 660 Jones Terr., Victoria V8Z 2L7, ☎ 250/479–1986, WEB www.bc-bed-breakfast.com). **Super, Natural British Columbia** (☎ 800/435–5622, WEB www.hellobc.com).

OUTDOORS AND SPORTS

FISHING

Separate licenses are required for saltwater and freshwater fishing in British Columbia. Both are available at sporting-goods stores, government-agency offices, and most fishing lodges and charter-boat companies in the province. A one-day license for nonresidents costs about $15 for freshwater fishing, $7.50 for saltwater fishing, and $14 for saltwater salmon fishing. For information about saltwater-fishing regulations, contact Fisheries and Oceans Canada, or pick up a free *Sport Fishing Guide*, available at most tourist-information centers. Super, Natural British Columbia has a brochure on freshwater fishing.

➤ CONTACTS: **Fisheries and Oceans Canada** (☎ 604/666–2828). **Super, Natural British Columbia** (☎ 800/435–5622).

GOLF

Vancouver Island's mild climate allows most golf courses to stay open all year. Greens fees are about $30–$60, and usually include a cart.

Golf Central offers a transportation and booking service for golfers in southern Vancouver Island. For advance tee-time bookings at courses in Victoria or Parksville, you can try Last Minute Golf.

➤ CONTACTS: **Golf Central** (☎ 250/380–4653 or 866/380–4653). **Last Minute Golf** (☎ 604/878–1833 or 800/684–6344, WEB www.lastminutegolf.net).

HIKING

Ecosummer Expeditions has guided hiking trips along the West Coast and Juan de Fuca trails. Island Outings runs full- and half-day guided hikes in the wilderness areas of southern Vancouver Island. For parks information, contact B.C. Parks.

➤ CONTACTS: **B.C. Parks** (✉ Box 9398, Stn. Prov. Govt., Victoria V8W 9M9, ☎ no phone, WEB www.elp.gov.bc.ca/bcparks). **Ecosummer Expeditions** (☎ 250/674–0102 or 800/465–8884, WEB www.ecosummer.ca). **Island Outings** (☎ 250/386–8817 or 888/345–4469, WEB www.islandoutings.com).

KAYAKING

Several companies offer multiday sea-kayaking trips to the coastal areas of Vancouver Island. Some of the excursions are suitable for beginners, and many trips offer an excellent chance to view orcas. Ecosummer Expeditions runs multiday paddles to Johnstone Strait and the Broken Group Islands. Gabriola Cycle and Kayak has sea-kayaking trips to the Broken Group Islands and other areas off the west coast of Vancouver Island, as well as to the Northern Gulf Islands and Johnstone Strait. Ocean West has three- to six-day paddling, camping, and orca-watching trips in Johnstone Strait. Majestic Ocean Kayaking offers guided half-day harbor tours, day trips, and multiday camping trips to the Broken Group Islands and other areas.

➤ CONTACTS: **Ecosummer Expeditions** (☎ 250/674–0102 or 800/465–8884, WEB www.ecosummer.ca). **Gabriola Cycle and Kayak** (☎ 250/247–8277, WEB www.gck.ca). **Majestic Ocean Kayaking** (☎ 250/726–2868 or 800/889–7644, WEB www.oceankayaking.com). **Ocean West** (☎ 604/898–4979 or 800/660–0051, WEB www.ocean-west.com).

TOURS

The Gourmet Trail offers self-drive and all-inclusive escorted tours linking five hotels and country inns on Vancouver Island and Salt Spring Island that are known for their cuisine. Island Outings runs daylong artisan and winery tours around southern Vancouver Island.

For a guided tour of the backcountry, including the Clayoquot Biosphere Reserve, by chauffeured four-wheel-drive, contact RainCoast Back Road Adventures in Ucluelet.

➤ FEES AND SCHEDULES: **Gourmet Trail** (✉ 304–1913 Sooke Rd., Victoria V9B 1V9, ☎ 250/478–9505 or 800/667–2291). **Island Outings** (☎ 250/386–8817 or 888/345–4469). **RainCoast Back Road Adventures** (☎ 250/726–7625, WEB www.raincoastadventures.com).

TRAIN TRAVEL

VIA Rail's Esquimalt & Nanaimo Rail Liner serves Duncan, Chemainus, Nanaimo, and Courtenay from the Via Rail Station in Victoria.

➤ TRAIN INFORMATION: **Esquimalt & Nanaimo Rail Liner** (☎ 800/561–8630 in Canada; 800/561–3949 in the U.S., WEB www.viarail.ca). **VIA Rail Station** (✉ 450 Pandora Ave., Victoria, ☎ no phone).

VISITOR INFORMATION

➤ TOURIST INFORMATION: **Campbell River Visitor Information Centre** (✉ 1235 Shoppers Row, Box 400, Campbell River V9W 5B6, ☎ 250/287–4636 or 800/463–4386). **Comox Valley Visitor Infocentre** (✉ 2040 Cliffe Ave., Courtenay, WEB www.tourism-comox-valley.bc.ca). **Port Alberni Tourist Infocentre** (✉ 2533 Redford St., off Port Alberni Hwy., Port Alberni, ☎ 250/724–6535). **Port Hardy Visitor Information Centre** (✉ 7520 Market St., Port Hardy, ☎ 250/949–7622, WEB www.ph-chamber.bc.ca). **Super, Natural British Columbia** (☎ 800/435–5622, WEB www.hellobc.com). **Tourism Vancouver Island** (✉ 203–335 Wesley St., Nanaimo V9R 2T5, ☎ 250/754–3500, WEB www.islands.bc.ca).

4 BRITISH COLUMBIA

From rugged mountains to lush valleys, from northern woodlands to lakeside vineyards and forested islands, this western province truly has varied natural beauty. There are plenty of opportunities for wildlife viewing, as well as for skiing, golfing, fishing, hiking, and kayaking—or you can simply relax in a peaceful country inn. Your visit may take you to First Nations villages, luxurious ski resorts, historic towns, and isolated islands.

Revised by Sue
Kernaghan

B RITISH COLUMBIA, CANADA'S WESTERNMOST province, harbors Pacific beaches, verdant islands, year-round skiing, and
world-class fishing—a wealth of outdoor action and beauty. The
citizens are a similarly heterogeneous mix: descendants of original
Native American peoples; 19th-century British, European, and Asian
settlers; and more-recent immigrants from all corners of the Earth.

Canada's third-largest province (only Québec and Ontario are bigger),
British Columbia occupies almost 10% of Canada's total area, stretching from the Pacific Ocean eastward to the province of Alberta, and
from the U.S. border north to the Yukon and Northwest Territories.
It spans almost 1 million square km (about 360,000 square mi), making it larger than every American state except Alaska.

British Columbia's appeal as a vacation destination stems from its status as the most spectacular part of the nation, with abundant coastal
scenery and stretches of snowcapped peaks. Outdoor enthusiasts have
gravitated here for sports including fishing, golfing, kayaking, rafting,
and skiing.

Most of British Columbia's population clusters in two coastal cities.
Vancouver is an international city whose relaxed lifestyle is spiced by
a varied cultural scene embracing large ethnic communities. Victoria,
the provincial capital on Vancouver Island, is a smaller, more subdued
town of 19th-century brick and well-tended gardens, although it, too,
has undergone an international metamorphosis in recent years.

One of the most dramatic changes in British Columbia has been in the
status of the province's native, or First Nations, peoples—the Haida,
Kwakiutl, Nootka, Salish, and others—who occupied the land for
more than 12,000 years before the first Europeans arrived. In 1998
and 1999, two groundbreaking treaties, signed with the Nisga'a people in the north and the Sechelt people in the south, heralded a new
era of native self-government. There has also been a resurgence in First
Nations culture throughout the region, evident in art galleries, restaurants, cultural centers, and re-created villages. Another recent change
has been a decline in the province's traditional industries of forestry,
fishing, and mining, and an increasing reliance on tourism.

Pleasures and Pastimes

Dining
Although Vancouver and Victoria have British Columbia's most varied and cosmopolitan cuisine, some excellent restaurants in smaller towns,
particularly Whistler, and several fine country inns have helped to define a local cuisine based on the best of regional fare, including seafood,
lamb, organic produce, and increasingly good wine. Attire is generally
casual in the region. Almost all restaurants, and many bars and pubs,
ban smoking indoors.

CATEGORY	COST*
$$$$	over $32
$$$	$22–$32
$$	$13–$21
$	under $13

*per person, in Canadian dollars, for a main course at dinner

Lodging
Accommodations range from bed-and-breakfasts and rustic cabins to
deluxe chain hotels, country inns, and remote fishing lodges. In the cities

you'll find an abundance of lodgings, but outside the major centers, especially in summer, it's a good idea to reserve ahead, even for campsites. In winter, many backcountry resorts close, and city hotels drop prices by as much as 50%. Most small inns and B&Bs ban smoking indoors; almost all hotels offer no-smoking rooms.

CATEGORY	COST*
$$$$	over $250
$$$	$170–$250
$$	$90–$170
$	under $90

All prices are in Canadian dollars, for a standard double room, excluding 10% provincial accommodation tax and 7% GST.

Outdoor Activities and Sports

CANOEING AND KAYAKING

The Inside Passage, Queen Charlotte Strait, the Strait of Georgia, and the other island-dotted straits and sounds that border the mainland provide fairly protected sea-going from Washington State to the Alaskan border, with numerous marine parks to explore along the way. BC Ferries' Discovery Coast Passage service gives kayakers direct access to the channels and islands of the midcoast. Two favorites for canoeing are the Powell Forest Canoe Route, an 80-km (50-mi) circuit of seven lakes, and Bowron Lake Park, in the Cariboo region.

FISHING

Miles of coastline and thousands of lakes, rivers, and streams bring more than 750,000 anglers to British Columbia each year. The province's waters hold 74 species of fish (25 of them sport fish), including chinook salmon and rainbow trout.

GOLF

British Columbia has more than 230 golf courses, and the number is growing. The province is an official golf destination of both the Canadian and American PGA tours. The topography tends to be mountainous and forested, and many courses have fine views as well as treacherous approaches to greens.

HIKING

Virtually all the provincial parks have fine hiking-trail networks, and many ski resorts keep their chairlifts running throughout the summer to help hikers and, in some cases, mountain bikers, reach trails. Heli-hiking is also very popular; helicopters deliver you to alpine meadows and verdant mountaintops.

RAFTING

A wide range of rafting trips is available on the many beautiful rivers lacing British Columbia, including the Adams, Chilcotin, Chilliwack, Fraser, and Thompson.

SKIING AND SNOWBOARDING

With more than half the province higher than 4,200 ft above sea level, new downhill areas are constantly opening. More than 60 resorts have downhill skiing and snowboarding facilities. Most of these resorts also have groomed cross-country (Nordic) ski trails, and many of the provincial parks have cross-country trails as well.

Native Culture

Before the arrival of Europeans, the lush landscapes of the Pacific Northwest gave rise to one of the continent's richest and most artistically prolific cultures. There have long been archaeological sites and museums, but newer sights, including the re-created villages at 'Ksan, near Hazelton, and Secwepemc, in Kamloops, are run by First Nations people and offer ways to share a living culture through music, dance, and food.

Exploring British Columbia

Most of the population huddles in a region known as the Lower Mainland, in and around Vancouver in the province's southwest corner. In the mountains about two hours north of Vancouver is the international resort town of Whistler. Beyond the Lower Mainland, three highways and a rail line climb over the Coast Mountains to the rolling high plateau that forms the central interior. To the north are the Cariboo ranch country and, beyond that, the province's vast, sparsely inhabited northern half. To the east are the Okanagan and Shuswap valleys, home to the fruit- and wine-growing region and the lake district. Farther east are the mountainous Kootenays and the foothills of the Rockies.

The southernmost stretch of coastline just north of Vancouver, called the Sunshine Coast, is popular with boaters, artists, and summer vacationers. Farther north is a roadless, fjord-cut wilderness leading to the mist-shrouded Haida Gwaii, or Queen Charlotte Islands, home to the Haida people and to old-growth forest. The gentler, more pastoral Gulf Islands, in the Strait of Georgia, just west of Vancouver, have long attracted escapists of every kind.

The North Coast and the Queen Charlotte Islands can be wet year-round. The interior is drier, with greater extremes, including hot summers and reliably snowy winters. Temperatures here drop below freezing in winter and sometimes reach 90°F in summer.

When you travel by car, keep in mind that more than three-quarters of British Columbia is mountainous terrain. Many areas, including the North Coast, have no roads at all and are accessible only by air or sea.

Numbers in the text correspond to numbers in the margin and on the Southern British Columbia map.

Great Itineraries

British Columbia is about the size of Western Europe, with as much geographical variety and substantially fewer roads. The good news is that many great sights, stunning scenery, and even wilderness lie within a few days' tour of Vancouver or the U.S. border.

IF YOU HAVE 3 DAYS

One option, offering stunning mountain and ocean scenery, is to take the Coast Mountain Circle tour, driving north from Vancouver along the scenic Sea to Sky Highway to ⛺ **Squamish** ② and the resort town of ⛺ **Whistler** ③, then over the scenic Duffy Lake Road to the gold-rush town of **Lillooet** ④. You can then return to Vancouver through the steep gorges of the Fraser Canyon, with stops at Hell's Gate on the Fraser River near **Hope** ⑤ and at ⛺ **Harrison Hot Springs** ⑥.

An alternative is to take a ferry out to one of the Gulf Islands—⛺ **Galiano** ⑪, ⛺ **Mayne** ⑫, or ⛺ **Salt Spring** ⑬—and stay at a romantic country inn for a night. Or, also by ferry, take a brief tour of the Sunshine Coast: **Gibsons Landing** ⑦, **Sechelt** ⑧, **Powell River** ⑨, and **Lund** ⑩.

IF YOU HAVE 6 DAYS

A longer trip allows time to explore the interior. Start with a one- or two-day trip over the mountains via ⛺ **Whistler** ③ and **Lillooet** ④, through the Fraser Canyon, or by the quicker, if less scenic, Coquihalla Highway. On Days 3 through 5, loop through the High Country and the Okanagan Valley. You can make stops in ⛺ **Kamloops** ㉒ to fish or tour the Secwepemc Native Heritage Museum; in **Vernon** ㉔ to visit the mountain resort at Silver Star; or in ⊞ **Kelowna** ㉕, **Summerland and Peachland** ㉖, ⊞ **Penticton** ㉗, or ⊞ **Osoyoos** ㉘ to relax at a beach or tour a vineyard. Any of these towns is fine for an overnight stay.

IF YOU HAVE 10 DAYS
A 10-day trip gives you time to see Vancouver Island and cruise the breathtaking **Inside Passage** ⑭ from Port Hardy, on the island's northern tip, to ⊞ **Prince Rupert** ⑯, where you can catch another ferry to see the old-growth forest and abandoned Haida villages of the ⊞ **Queen Charlotte Islands (Haida Gwaii)** ⑰. From Port Hardy you could also take the scenic **Discovery Coast Passage** ⑮ to Bella Coola. Then complete the circle back to Vancouver by air, ferry, road, or, from Prince Rupert, by train. If you have more time or if you're traveling to or from the Rockies, visit **Nelson** ㉙ and the Kootenays, which are among the most beautiful but least toured parts of southern British Columbia.

When to Tour British Columbia
The Gulf Islands and the Sunshine Coast are enjoyable anytime, but there are fewer ferries and more rain between September and May, and many tourist facilities close in winter. The interior—the Cariboo, High Country, Okanagan Valley, and Kootenays—can be tough to reach in winter, but more ski resorts are making it worth the effort. Spring and fall, with their blossoms and harvest and wine festivals, are attractive, peaceful travel seasons; summer is a great time for most of the interior, although the Okanagan Valley can get hot and crowded in July and August.

COAST MOUNTAIN CIRCLE

A stunning sampler of mainland British Columbia, a drive into the Coast Mountains from Vancouver follows the Sea to Sky Highway (Highway 99) past fjordlike Howe Sound, the town of Squamish, and Whistler Resort, and then continues on a quiet back road to the gold-rush town of Lillooet. From Lillooet, you can continue into the High Country or return to Vancouver on Highways 12 and 1 through the gorges of the Fraser Canyon, stopping for a soak at Harrison Hot Springs on the way. This is a scenic two- to three-day drive; the roads are good but are best avoided in snow, particularly if you plan to travel past Whistler. A BC Rail line also cuts a swath through the mountains from North Vancouver to Lillooet on its way north to Prince George.

Horseshoe Bay

❶ *20 km (12 mi) north of Vancouver, 100 km (62 mi) south of Whistler.*

Tucked into a cove under the Coast Mountains, this little community is the ferry hub for boats to Nanaimo on Vancouver Island, Langdale on the Sunshine Coast, and tiny Bowen Island, a rural retreat 20 minutes across the sound that has pubs, B&Bs, craft shops, and even a winery. Near Horseshoe Bay, off Marine Drive, is **Whytecliff Marine Park,** with a swimming beach, picnic sites, and a rocky little island that's connected to the mainland at low tide.

From Horseshoe Bay, the Sea to Sky Highway (Highway 99) becomes one of British Columbia's most scenic roads, climbing into the mountains along the edge of Howe Sound. Most people on this road are eager to reach the resort town of Whistler, two hours to the north. A number of sights along the way are worth a stop, however.

At the **B.C. Museum of Mining,** once the British Empire's largest copper mine and now a national historic site, the knowledgeable staff offers guided tours of old mine workings and a chance to pan for gold.

Southern British Columbia

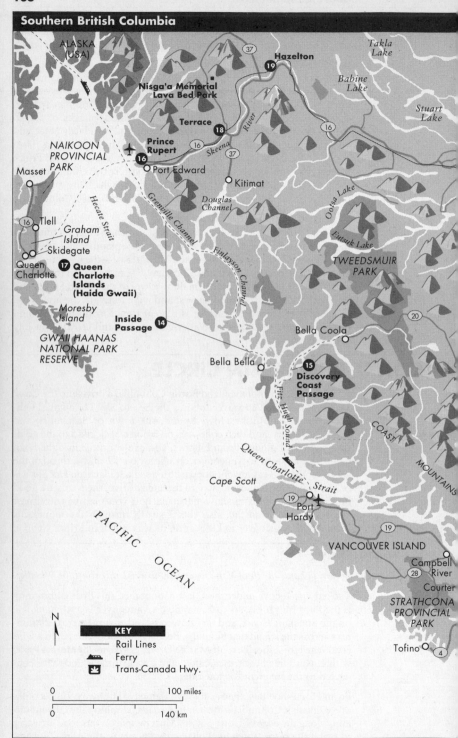

ALASKA (USA)

Takla Lake

(37)

Hazelton
19

Babine Lake

Stuart Lake

Nisga'a Memorial Lava Bed Park

River

Terrace
18

(16)

NAIKOON PROVINCIAL PARK

Prince Rupert
16

Skeena (37)

Oots a Lake

Masset

○ Port Edward

Kitimat

Douglas Channel

Grenville Channel

Eutsuk Lake

(16)
● Tlell

Hecate Strait

Graham Island

Finlayson Channel

TWEEDSMUIR PARK

Skidegate

Queen Charlotte

17 **Queen Charlotte Islands (Haida Gwaii)**

(20)

Moresby Island

Inside Passage
14

Bella Coola

GWAII HAANAS NATIONAL PARK RESERVE

Bella Bella
● **15**

Discovery Coast Passage

Fitz Hugh Sound

PACIFIC OCEAN

Queen Charlotte

Cape Scott

Strait

19
Port Hardy

COAST

MOUNTAINS

(19)

VANCOUVER ISLAND

Campbell River
(28)

Courter

STRATHCONA PROVINCIAL PARK

Tofino ○ (4)

N

KEY
— Rail Lines
⛴ Ferry
⬛ Trans-Canada Hwy.

0 ————————— 100 miles
0 ————————— 140 km

ALBERTA

39

29

43

97

Grande
Cache

27
Vanderhoof

JASPER
NATIONAL
PARK

40

16

20 **Prince
George**

16

16

Wells

BOWRON
LAKE
PARK

26

Barkerville

Valemount

MT.
ROBSON
PARK

93

Quesnel

COLUMBIA

Kinbasket
Lake

97

Quesnel
Lake

21 **Gold Rush Trail**

WELLS GRAY
PARK

MOUNTAINS

FRASER

Williams
Lake

5

MONASHEE
MOUNTAINS

20

PLATEAU

Clearwater

Adams
Lake

Jesmond

Shuswap
Lake

23

Clinton

Sicamous

Cache
Creek

22

Chase

23 **Salmon Arm**

97

4 **Lillooet**

97

Kamloops

24 **Vernon**

12

Okanagan
Lake

6

Pemberton

Lytton

Merritt

Oyama

29

Whistler

3

Yale

Kelowna
Westbank

30

99

GARIBALDI
PARK

1

5A

25

Desolation
Sound

Boston
Bar

Summerland
and
Peachland

26

Powell River

10

Squamish

Hope

Naramata

Lund

9 **Sechelt**

Howe
Sound

Britannia
Beach

5

27 **Penticton**

Gibsons
Landing

8

2

5

3

28 **Osoyoos**

7

Harrison Mills

6

3

CATHEDRAL
PROV. PARK

nay

Horseshoe
Bay

1

7

Harrison Hot
Springs

MANNING
PROVINCIAL
PARK

97

3

19

Nanaimo

Vancouver

CANADA
USA

Port
Alberni

1

Fort Langley

542

1

Gulf Islands

5

NORTH
CASCADES
NATIONAL
PARK

21

Duncan

11 13

9

20

155

Victoria

20

530

153

112

Port
Angeles

101

TO
SEATTLE

Strait of Georgia

The museum is about an hour north of Vancouver. ⊠ *Hwy. 99, Britannia Beach,* ☎ *604/896–2233; 604/688–8735 in Vancouver,* WEB *www.bcmuseumofmining.org.* ⊠ *$9.50.* ⊙ *May–mid-Oct., daily 10–4:30; mid-Oct.–Apr., prebooked group tours only.*

About 42 km (25 mi) north of Horseshoe Bay is **Shannon Falls,** which at 1,105 ft is Canada's third-highest waterfall. You can see it from the highway, or follow a short trail through the woods for a closer look.

Squamish

② *67 km (42 mi) north of Vancouver, 58 km (36 mi) south of Whistler.*

Squamish, or "mother of the winds" in the local First Nations language, has long languished in the shadow of Whistler Resort up the highway. Outdoors enthusiasts have, however, begun to discover its possibilities. The big winds that gave the area its name make it an excellent windsurfing spot. Diving in Howe Sound, kayaking on the sea and in nearby rivers, and hiking are also draws. The **Stawamus Chief,** an enormous rock face on the edge of Highway 99, is the world's second-largest granite monolith (after the Rock of Gibraltar). It attracts rock climbers from all over.

In December and January, one of the world's largest concentrations of bald eagles gathers at the **Brackendale Eagles Park** (⊠ Government Rd. off Hwy. 99, Brackendale, ☎ no phone), about 14 km (8 mi) north of Squamish. The park is open dawn to dusk; admission is free. You can watch the eagles from the banks of the Squamish River, off Government Road in Brackendale or spot the birds from a raft on the Cheakamus River. The **Brackendale Eagle Festival** (☎ 604/898–3333 to Brackendale Art Gallery for information) with music and art events, has sprung up around the annual eagle count, held in January.

The **West Coast Railway Heritage Park,** about a 10-minute drive north of downtown Squamish, has more than 60 pieces of late-19th- and early 20th-century rolling stock. You can ride a minitrain around the site, climb on a caboose, ring the bell on a steam locomotive, and stroll through a restored 1890 first-class business car—the sort of thing railway barons rode in—as well as a 1905 colonists' car that carried settlers to the prairies in minimal comfort. There's also a gift shop and archives in a new, 1915-style station house. ⊠ *39645 Government Rd.,* ☎ *604/898–9336,* WEB *www.wcra.org.* ⊠ *$6.* ⊙ *Daily 10–5.*

Dining and Lodging

$–$$ ✕ **Road House Diner at Klahanie.** A fixture on Highway 99 since the 1970s, this roadhouse across from Shannon Falls offers breakfasts, lunches, and dinners of updated diner classics and Pacific Northwest comfort food. The menu changes seasonally, but highlights have included a starter of sautéed oysters with spinach, black beans, chilis, and cream and such main dishes as baby-back ribs with honey-apple glaze or grilled spring salmon with chili lime butter. Most of the seats inside and on the patio offer views of the mountains, the falls, and the ocean. ⊠ *Shannon Falls, Hwy. 99 (5 km [3 mi] south of Squamish),* ☎ *604/892–5312. MC, V.*

$$ ✕🛏 **Howe Sound Inn & Brewing Company.** This cedar inn near Squamish
★   town center and the Royal Hudson train station covers all the bases. The fireplace in the cozy post-and-beam brew pub is a great place to relax after a day of hiking or rafting. You can also watch climbers tackling Stawamus Chief from the pub's patio, have a go at the inn's climbing wall, or take a brewery tour. The rustic yet elegant restaurant ($–$$) serves Pacific Northwest cuisine and fresh goods from the in-house bakery (try the ale-and-cheddar bread). The rooms upstairs have fur-

niture made of reclaimed fir; most have striking views of Stawamus Chief or the Tantalus Mountains. ✉ *37801 Cleveland Ave., Box 978, V0N 3G0,* ☎ *604/892–2603 or 800/919–2537,* FAX *604/892–2631,* WEB *www.howesound.com. 20 rooms. Restaurant, pub, in-room data ports, sauna, billiards, business services, meeting rooms. AE, MC, V.*

$$ ⊞ **Sunwolf Outdoor Centre.** A highlight of this former fishing lodge on the Cheakamus River, 10 km (6 mi) north of Squamish, is its rafting center, which specializes in class IV (fast-moving rapids) white-water trips, but also offers peaceful floats on slow-moving water. Sunwolf's cabins, tucked in the woods on the 5½-acre property, are attractive and modern, with fir floors, four-poster beds, hand-crafted pine furniture, gas fireplaces, and vaulted ceilings. The cozy lodge has fireplaces and an outdoor deck. In December and January, this is a prime spot for viewing bald eagles. ✉ *70002 Squamish Valley Rd. (4 km [2½ mi] off Hwy. 99), Box 244, Brackendale, V0N 1H0,* ☎ *604/898–1537 or 877/ 806–8046,* FAX *604/898–1634,* WEB *www.mntn.net. 10 cabins. Café, kitchenettes, badminton, croquet, hiking, volleyball, boating, fishing, mountain bikes, meeting rooms. MC, V.*

Outdoor Activities and Sports

Squamish is a major rock-climbing destination, and also a popular spot for hiking, diving, trail riding, sailing, rafting, and kayaking. **Canadian Outback Adventures** (☎ 604/921–7250 or 800/565–8735) offers eagle rafting trips on the Cheakamus River. For a flightseeing tour over area glaciers, a picnic on a glacier, heli-hiking, heli-rafting, or other helicopter-based adventures, contact **Glacier Air Tours** (☎ 604/898–9016 or 800/265–0088, WEB www.glacierair.com).

The challenging 18-hole, par-72 course (open early March–late October) at **Furry Creek Golf and Country Club** (✉ Hwy. 99, Furry Creek, ☎ 604/922–9576 or 888/922–9462), south of Squamish, has striking ocean views and greens fees from $80 to $95, including a mandatory cart. The **Squamish Valley Golf & Country Club** (✉ 2458 Mamquam Rd., ☎ 604/898–9691 or 888/349–3688) is an 18-hole, par-72 course close to town. Greens fees are about $55.

En Route Between Squamish and Whistler on Highway 99 is the 231-ft-high **Brandywine Falls.** A short trail through the woods takes you to a viewing platform.

Whistler

★ ❸ *120 km (74 mi) north of Vancouver, 58 km (36 mi) north of Squamish.*

Whistler and Blackcomb mountains, part of Whistler Resort, are North America's two largest ski mountains and are consistently ranked among the continent's top ski destinations. They offer winter and summer glacier skiing, an extremely long vertical drop, and highly advanced lift systems. In winter, the area buzzes with skiers and snowboarders from all over the world. In summer the pace is more relaxed, as the focus shifts to cycling, hiking, and boating around the Whistler Valley.

At the base of the mountains are Whistler Village, Village North (also called Marketplace), and Upper Village—a rapidly expanding, interconnected community of lodgings, restaurants, pubs, and boutiques. Locals refer to the entire area as Whistler Village. With dozens of hotels and condos within a five-minute walk of the mountains, the site is frenzied. Culinary options range from burgers and deli cuisine to French or Japanese fare. Nightly entertainment runs the gamut from sophisticated piano bars to casual pubs.

Whistler Village is a pedestrian-only community. Anywhere you want to go within the resort is at most five minutes away, and parking lots are just outside the village. The bases of Whistler and Blackcomb mountains are also just at the village edge; in fact, you can ski right into the lower level of the Fairmont Chateau Whistler Hotel.

Dining

Dining at Whistler is informal; casual dress is appropriate everywhere. Many restaurants close for a week or two between late October and late November. In winter and summer, you need dinner reservations in all but the fast-food joints.

$$$-$$$$ ✕ **Val d'Isère.** Chef-owner Roland Pfaff satisfies a skier's craving for fine French food with traditional dishes from his native Alsace and with Gallic takes on Canadian produce. Some specialties served in this elegant room overlooking the Town Plaza are Dungeness crab ravioli with smoked-salmon cream sauce, sea bass fillet baked in a potato crust with a Pinot Noir reduction, and veal tenderloin with Vancouver Island morel mushroom sauce. ☒ *Bear Lodge, Town Plaza, 4314 Main St.,* ☎ *604/932–4666. Reservations essential. AE, DC, MC, V. No lunch Nov.–May.*

$$-$$$$ ✕ **Araxi.** Golden walls, terra-cotta tiles, antiques, and original artwork help create a vibrant atmosphere at one of Whistler's most established restaurants. The chefs work closely with local farmers who produce vegetables and herbs exclusively for Araxi's French and Italian menu. The chefs also makes good use of local cheeses and trout as well as ostrich, salmon, scallops, and venison from the province. Breads and pastries are made in-house each morning. The menu changes seasonally, but dishes have included braised Fraser Valley rabbit and alder-smoked B.C. arctic char with saffron and oyster-mushroom sauce. Wine lovers take note: there's a 12,000-bottle international inventory and three full-time sommeliers. A heated patio is open in summer, and the lounge is a popular après-ski spot. ☒ *4222 Village Sq.,* ☎ *604/932–4540. Reservations essential. AE, MC, V. No lunch Oct.–May.*

$$-$$$$ ✕ **Bearfoot Bistro.** The cutesy name belies the elegance of this acclaimed bistro. The 75-seat dining room has a warm Latin feel with tall leather chairs, dark wood, and live jazz nightly; reservations are essential here. The three- and five-course set menus ($75–$150) feature such starters as whole black and white truffles *en croûte* and, for main dishes, butter-poached Atlantic lobster with fennel and saffron cream. The wild caribou is a specialty; try it when it's available. The wine bar's menu is simpler and less expensive ($$–$$$). Diners in either section can sample from the highly rated 1,100-label wine cellar. ☒ *4121 Village Green,* ☎ *604/932–3433. AE, D, DC, MC, V. No lunch.*

$$-$$$$ ✕ **Il Caminetto di Umberto.** Owner Umberto Menghi offers down-home Italian cooking in a relaxed atmosphere. Il Caminetto has an urban, Florentine style with warm gold walls and terra-cotta tiles. It's known for its grilled veal chops, osso buco, and game dishes. ☒ *4242 Village Stroll,* ☎ *604/932–4442. Reservations essential. AE, DC, MC, V. No lunch.*

$$-$$$$ ✕ **La Rúa.** Reddish flagstone floors and sponge-painted walls, a wine cellar behind a wrought-iron door, modern oil paintings, and sconce lighting give La Rúa an intimate, Mediterranean ambience. Favorites from the Continental menu include charred rare tuna, loin of fallow deer, rack of lamb, baked roulades of pickerel, and Dungeness crab with warm *mizuna* (a peppery herb) vinaigrette. ☒ *4557 Blackcomb Way,* ☎ *604/932–5011. Reservations essential. AE, DC, MC, V. No lunch.*

$$-$$$$ ✕ **Wildflower.** Wooden beams in a lofty ceiling, big picture windows overlooking the ski slopes, leather wall panels, and a limestone and river-rock fireplace give this restaurant, in the Fairmont Château Whistler, the feel of an upscale mountain lodge. The Pacific Northwest menu features local products and changes frequently, but highlights have included wild sockeye salmon braised in Chardonnay with pumpkin and winter thyme spactzle, and rack of Peace River lamb with cauliflower purée and stuffed morel mushrooms. ⊠ *4599 Chateau Blvd.,* ☎ *604/938–2033. Reservations essential. AE, D, DC, MC, V. No lunch some days in spring and fall; call to check.*

$$–$$$ ✕ **Trattoria di Umberto.** Owned by Umberto Menghi, who also owns Il Caminetto di Umberto, this relaxed restaurant specializes in such Tuscan countryside dishes as veal scallopini with Marsala, and cioppino in a saffron, tomato, and fennel broth. ⊠ *4417 Sundial Pl.,* ☎ *604/932–5858. Reservations essential. AE, DC, MC, V.*

$$–$$$ ✕ **Zeuski's.** This friendly taverna in the Town Plaza offers big portions of tasty Greek fare. Wall murals of the Greek islands surround candlelight tables, helping create a Mediterranean atmosphere. It's hard to pass on the spanakopita, souvlakia, and other standards, but the house special, *kotapoulo* (chicken breast rolled in pistachios and roasted), is not to be missed; the tender, delicately herb-battered calamari is also a winner. ⊠ *4314 Main St.,* ☎ *604/932–6009. Reservations essential. AE, DC, MC, V.*

Lodging

Price categories are based on January-to-April ski-season rates; prices can be higher during Christmas and spring break and lower in summer. Many properties require minimum stays, especially during the Christmas season. Also, Whistler Village has some serious nightlife. If peace and quiet are important to you, ask for a room away from the main pedestrian thoroughfares or stay in one of the residential neighborhoods outside the village.

You can book lodgings, including B&Bs, pensions, and hundreds of time-share condos, through **Whistler Central Reservations** (☎ 604/932–4222; 604/664–5625 in Vancouver; 800/944–7853 in the U.S. and Canada, WEB www.tourismwhistler.com).

$$$$ 🏨 **Delta Whistler Resort.** Slate, stone, exposed timbers, and light wood finishes are featured in this resort complex at the base of the Whistler and Blackcomb gondolas. Rooms are so large that most can easily accommodate four people. Many have fireplaces, whirlpool baths, balconies, and kitchens; some suites have saunas. The Delta chain also owns the Delta Whistler Village Suites, an all-suites hotel, in Village North. ⊠ *4050 Whistler Way, V0N 1B4,* ☎ *604/932–1982 or 800/268–1133,* FAX *604/932–7332,* WEB *www.delta-whistler.com. 264 rooms, 24 suites. Restaurant, bar, in-room data ports, in-room safes, minibars, no-smoking rooms, room service, pool, indoor and outdoor hot tubs, massage, steam room, gym, ski shop, ski storage, shops, baby-sitting, concierge, business services, meeting rooms. AE, DC, MC, V.*

$$$$ 🏨 **Fairmont Château Whistler Resort.** This family-friendly fortress just
★   steps from the Blackcomb ski lifts is a self-contained, ski-in, ski-out resort-within-a-resort, with its own shopping arcade, golf course, and spa. The lobby is filled with rustic Canadiana, handmade Mennonite rugs, and enticing overstuffed sofas; there's also a grand stone fireplace. Standard rooms are comfortably furnished and of average size, decorated in burgundies and turquoises, and all have mountain views. Rooms and suites on the Entrée Gold floors have fireplaces, whirlpool tubs, and their own concierge and private lounge. ⊠ *4599 Chateau Blvd., V0N 1B4,* ☎ *604/938–8000 or 800/606–8244,* FAX *604/938–2099,* WEB *www.fairmont.com. 500 rooms, 56 suites. 2 restaurants, lobby lounge, air-conditioning, in-room safes, minibars, no-smoking rooms, room service, indoor-outdoor pool, outdoor lap pool, 2 indoor and 2 outdoor hot tubs, sauna, spa, steam room, 18-hole golf course, 3 tennis courts, health club, ski shop, ski storage, shops, baby-sitting, coin*

laundry, dry cleaning, concierge, concierge floor, convention center, parking (fee). AE, D, DC, MC, V.

$$$$ 🏨 **Pan Pacific Lodge.** Tucked at the base of both mountains, this eight-story lodge is steps from the Whistler and Blackcomb gondolas. Guest quarters include studios with pull-down queen beds or one- and two-bedroom suites. All units are no-smoking and have kitchens, balconies, gas fireplaces, and tall windows that make the most of the mountain or valley views. The use of light colors, natural wood, and granite make the rooms sleek and modern. In the evening, there's excellent Irish cuisine and traditional music at the Dubh Linn Gate Pub downstairs. ✉ *4320 Sundial Crescent, V0N 1B4,* ☎ *604/905–2999 or 888/905–9995,* FAX *604/905–2995,* WEB *www.panpac.com. 76 suites, 45 studios. Pub, in-room data ports, in-room safes, room service, pool, 2 outdoor hot tubs, steam room, gym, ski shop, ski storage, coin laundry, meeting rooms. AE, DC, MC, V.*

$$$$ 🏨 **Westin Resort & Spa.** This luxury hotel has a prime location on the
★   edge of the village. Stone, slate, pine, and cedar are used throughout the two-story lobby. The studio and one- and two-bedroom suites are chic and cozy, with moss-green and rust color schemes, kitchenettes, gas fireplaces, extra-deep tubs, and exceptionally comfortable beds. The 1,400-sq-ft, split-level suites are great for families: each has a full kitchen and a loft bedroom with a whirlpool tub. The spa, with 25 treatment rooms and a mountain-view lounge, offers facials, body wraps, shiatsu, hot-rock massages, and such holistic therapies as herbology and acupuncture. ✉ *4090 Whistler Way, V0N 1B4,* ☎ *604/ 905–5000 or 888/634–5577,* FAX *604/905–5589,* WEB *www.westin-whistler.net. 204 rooms, 215 suites. Restaurant, bar, in-room data ports, in-room safes, kitchenettes, room service, indoor-outdoor pool, hot tub, outdoor hot tub, massage, sauna, spa, steam room, golf privileges, health club, ski shop, ski storage, shops, baby-sitting, children's programs, coin laundry, dry cleaning, laundry service, concierge, business services, meeting rooms, parking (fee). AE, D, DC, MC, V. Entirely no smoking.*

$$$–$$$$ 🏨 **Durlacher Hof.** Custom fir woodwork and doors, exposed ceiling
★   beams, a *kachelofen* (farmhouse fireplace-oven), and antler chandeliers hung over fir benches and tables carry out the rustic Tyrolean theme of this fancy inn a few minutes' walk from the village. The bedrooms, done with Ralph Lauren decor, contain custom-crafted furniture but no phones or TVs to disturb the peace. Four of the rooms are very spacious and have such amenities as whirlpool tubs; smaller rooms have showers rather than tubs. A hearty European breakfast and afternoon tea are included in the rate of this no-smoking inn, and dinner is served occasionally. ✉ *7055 Nesters Rd., Box 1125, V0N 1B0,* ☎ *604/932– 1924,* FAX *604/938–1980,* WEB *www.durlacherhof.com. 8 rooms. Breakfast room, outdoor hot tub, massage, sauna, ski storage, free parking. MC, V. BP.*

$$$ 🏨 **Chalet Luise.** As traditionally Alpine inside as out, Chalet Luise has carved wood furnishings, big sofas, and a gas fireplace in the guest lounge. A hot tub in a whimsical gazebo on the patio is also a great place to unwind. The snug, phone- and TV-free guest rooms have hand-crafted pine furniture and Laura Ashley fabrics. One of the two romantic rooms with bay windows and gas fireplaces is large enough to sleep three people. Attention is paid to details: robes and slippers are on hand, a wooden crib above the staircase to the hot tub holds rolled towels, and the hallway en route to the sauna is lined with racks for ski clothing to be warmed by a woodstove. The chalet has a five-night minimum stay between December and May, and a two-night minimum in summer. ✉ *7461 Ambassador Crescent, Box 352, V0N 1B0,* ☎ *604/932–4187*

or 800/665–1998, FAX 604/938–1531, WEB www.chaletluise.com. 8 rooms. Breakfast room, outdoor hot tub, sauna, ski storage, coin laundry, free parking. MC, V.

$$ ☷ **Edgewater Lodge.** This modern cedar lodge lies along glacier-fed Green Lake on 45 acres of private forested land, about 3 km (2 mi) north of the village. All rooms have private entrances, TVs, phones, and expansive water and mountain views. A bit removed from Whistler's slopes and nightlife, Edgewater is perfectly placed for peace, quiet, and fresh air. The Nicklaus North Golf Course is nearby, and Whistler Outdoor Experience runs an activity center here, offering guests and nonguests fishing, hiking, canoeing, kayaking, and trail rides in summer, and snowshoeing, sleigh rides, and cross-country skiing in winter. Breakfast is included in the rates, and highly rated evening meals are also available. Smoking isn't allowed anywhere in the lodge. ⊠ *8841 Hwy. 99, Box 369, V0N 1B0,* ☎ *604/932–0688 or 888/870–9065,* FAX *604/932–0686,* WEB *www.edgewater-lodge.com. 6 rooms, 6 suites. Restaurant, bar, outdoor hot tub, meeting rooms, free parking. AE, MC, V. CP.*

$ ☷ **Hostelling International Whistler.** One of the nicest hostels in Canada is also the area's cheapest sleep. Beds in men's or women's four-bunk dorms, a shared kitchen, and a game room with a pool table and fireplace make up the basic accommodations of this no-smoking hostel overlooking Alta Lake. It's next to the swimming beach at Rainbow Park and is 7 km (4 mi) by road, or 4 km (2½ mi) by footpath, from the village. About five Buslink buses a day serve the hostel from Whistler Village, and BC Rail will make a request stop here. ⊠ *5678 Alta Lake Rd., V0N 1B0,* ☎ *604/932–5492,* FAX *604/932–4687,* WEB *www.hihostels.bc.ca. 32 beds in 7 dorms, 1 private room (no bath). Sauna, boating, ski storage, free parking. MC, V.*

Nightlife and the Arts

For a small mountain village, Whistler has a surprisingly good choice of nightlife, most of it in the pedestrian-oriented village and within walking distance of the hotels and ski slopes. Most of the pubs, clubs, and bars are open year-round. Dance clubs are open until 2 AM Monday–Saturday and until 1 AM on Sunday (be prepared to line up on weekends); pubs close around 1 AM, midnight on Sunday. Most nightspots serve food, which is often good value compared with Whistler's pricey restaurants, and many of them either ban smoking or have large no-smoking areas. For entertainment listings, pick up a free copy of Whistler's weekly news magazine, *The Pique.*

BARS AND PUBS

Alpenrock. The B.C. drinking age is 19, but there are plenty of options for young people. This enormous complex has all-ages bowling, video games, carnival games, billiards, and a restaurant, as a well as a nightclub and a lounge for the over 19s. ⊠ *100–4295 Blackcomb Way (under the Holiday Inn),* ☎ *604/938–0082.*

Bearfoot Bistro. Oenophiles will love the wine bar, which has a choice of more than 1,000 wines in an elegant setting. ⊠ *4121 Village Green,* ☎ *604/932–3433.*

Black's Pub. Here you'll find Whistler's largest selection of whiskeys (more than 40 varieties) and 95 beers from around the world. ⊠ *4270 Mountain Sq.,* ☎ *604/932–6945.*

Brewhouse. In the village, this place brews six of its own ales and lagers in a big woodsy building with fireplaces and pool tables. The attached restaurant is a good place for casual meals. ⊠ *4355 Blackcomb Way,* ☎ *604/905–2739.*

Citta'. This is a great spot for people-watching and local microbrews. The patio is a good place to sip your pint. ⊠ *Whistler Village Sq.,* ☎ *604/932–4177.*

Dubh Linn Gate Pub. As its name implies, this place has an Irish theme. The staff pours a decent pint of Guinness and serves good Irish food. ✉ *Pan Pacific Hotel, 4320 Sundial Crescent,* ☎ *604/905–4047.*

FILM

Rainbow Theatre. In the Whistler Conference Centre, this theater shows first-run movies twice nightly. ✉ *4010 Whistler Way,* ☎ *604/ 932–2422.*

DANCE CLUBS

Buffalo Bill's Bar & Grill. The DJ's here play mainstream music for an older (over 25) crowd, and well-known bands jam once or twice a month. ✉ *4122 Village Green,* ☎ *604/932–6613.*
Garfinkle's. One of Whistler's largest clubs frequently hosts live bands. ✉ *1-4308 Main St.,* ☎ *604/932–2323.*
Maxx Fish. With its house, hip hop, and theme nights, and occasional live bands, Maxx Fish draws a young crowd. ✉ *Whistler Village Sq.,* ☎ *604/932–1904.*
Tommy Africa's. Here, international guest DJs play alternative and progressive dance music. ✉ *4216 Gateway Dr.,* ☎ *604/932–6090.*

Outdoor Activities and Sports

Adjacent to the Whistler area is the 78,000-acre **Garibaldi Provincial Park** (✉ off Hwy. 99, ☎ 604/898–3678), with dense mountainous forests splashed with hospitable lakes and streams.

The best first stop for any Whistler outdoor activity is the **Whistler Activity and Information Center** (✉ 4010 Whistler Way, ☎ 604/932–2394) in the conference center at the edge of the village, where you can book activities, pick up hiking, biking, and cross-country skiing trail maps, and find out about equipment rentals.

BIKING AND HIKING

The 28-km (45-mi) paved, car-free Valley Trail links the village to lakeside beaches and scenic picnic spots, and there are plenty of challenging, lift-accessed, mountain-bike trails at higher elevations. Ski lifts also whisk hikers up to the alpine, where marked trails are graded by difficulty.

You can rent bikes or arrange for repairs at **Fanatyk Co. Ski and Cycle** (✉ 6–4433 Sundial Pl., ☎ 604/938–9455). **Whistler Outdoor Experience** (✉ Edgewater Lodge, 8841 Hwy. 99, ☎ 604/932–3389 or 877/ 386–1888, WEB www.whistleroutdoor.com) offers guided hikes, nature walks, mountain-bike trips, and bike rentals.

BOATING

Canoe and kayak rentals are available at Alta Lake at both Lakeside Park and Wayside Park. A spot that's perfect for canoeing is the River of Golden Dreams, which connects Alta Lake with Green Lake. For guided canoeing and kayaking trips as well as sailing, call **Whistler Outdoor Experience** (✉ 8841 Hwy. 99, ☎ 604/932–3389 or 877/386–1888, WEB www.whistleroutdoor.com) at the Edgewater Lodge on Green Lake.

CROSS-COUNTRY SKIING

The meandering trail around the Whistler Golf Course in the village is an ideal beginners' route. The 28 km (17 mi) of track-set trails that wind around scenic Lost Lake, Chateau Whistler Golf Course, the Nicklaus North Golf Course, and Green Lake include routes suitable for all levels; 4 km (2½ mi) of trails around Lost Lake are lighted for night skiing 4–10 each evening. On Green Lake, **Whistler Outdoor Experience** (✉ Edgewater Lodge, 8841 Hwy. 99, ☎ 604/932–3389 or 877/ 386–1888) organizes cross-country ski treks.

DOWNHILL SKIING AND SNOWBOARDING

Blackcomb and Whistler mountains (☎ 604/932–3434 or 800/766–0449, WEB www.whistlerblackcomb.com) receive an average of 360 inches of snow a year, and Blackcomb is open June to early August for summer glacier skiing. The mountains' statistics are impressive: the resort covers 7,071 acres of skiable terrain in 12 alpine bowls and on three glaciers; it has more than 200 marked trails and is served by the continent's most advanced high-speed lift system. Blackcomb has a 5,280-ft vertical drop, North America's longest, and a top elevation of 7,494 ft. Whistler's drop comes in second at 5,020 ft, and its top elevation is 7,160 ft.

For a primer on the ski facilities, drop by the resort's free Whistler Welcome Night, held at 6:30 every Sunday evening during ski season at the base of the village gondolas. First-timers at Whistler, whether beginners or experienced skiers or snowboarders, may want to try Ski or Ride Esprit. Run by the resort, these three- to four-day programs combine ski or snowboarding lessons, après-ski activities, and an insider's guide to the mountains.

The **Mountain Adventure Centre** (⊠ Pan Pacific Lodge, 4320 Sundial Crescent, ☎ 604/905–2295) rents high-performance gear and lets you swap equipment during the day. It also has two alpine locations and one at Blackcomb Day Lodge. **Whistler/Blackcomb Ski and Snowboard School** (⊠ 4545 Blackcomb Way, ☎ 604/932–3434 or 800/766–0449) has lessons for skiers of all levels. Equipment rentals are available at the **Whistler Gondola Base** (⊠ 3434 Blackcomb Way, ☎ 604/905–2252) and at several outlets in the village.

FISHING

All five of the lakes around Whistler are stocked with trout. The guides at **Whistler Backcountry Adventures** (⊠ 36–4314 Main St., ☎ 604/932–3474) can take you fly-fishing or spinning in the lakes and rivers around Whistler. Gear is supplied. **Whistler Fishing Guides** (⊠ Whistler Village Gondola Building, 4165 Springs La., ☎ 604/932–3532 or 888/932–3532) offers guided trips on rivers in the area. The staff takes care of everything: equipment, guides, transportation.

GOLF

Golf season runs from May through October; greens fees range from $125 to $185. **Chateau Whistler Golf Club** (⊠ 4612 Blackcomb Way, ☎ 604/938–2092 or 877/938–2092) has an excellent 18-hole, par-72 course designed by Robert Trent Jones Jr. The **Nicklaus North Golf Course** (⊠ 8080 Nicklaus North Blvd., ☎ 604/938–9898 or 800/386–9898) is a challenging 18-hole, par-71 course designed by Jack Nicklaus. Arnold Palmer designed the 18-hole, par-72 championship course at the **Whistler Golf Club** (⊠ 4010 Whistler Way, ☎ 604/932–3280 or 800/376–1777).

HELI-SKIING

Whistler Heli-Skiing (⊠ 3-4241 Village Stroll, ☎ 604/932–4105 or 888/435–4754, WEB www.whistlerheliskiing.com) has guided day trips with up to three glacier runs, or 8,000–10,000 ft of skiing, for intermediate to expert skiers. The cost is about $535.

HORSEBACK RIDING

Sea to Sky Stables (⊠ Paradise Valley Rd. about 3 km, or 2 mi, off Hwy 99, Squamish, ☎ 604/898–3908) south of Whistler offers trail rides for all levels. Guided rides are $35 an hour. **Whistler Outdoor Experience** (⊠ Edgewater Lodge, 8841 Hwy. 99, ☎ 604/932–3389 or 877/386–1888, WEB www.whistleroutdoor.com) on Green Lake runs trail rides ($40 per hour) in the area.

Blackcomb Snowmobiling (⊠ 4599 Château Blvd., ☎ 604/932–8484) runs guided snowmobile trips into the backcountry. **Cougar Mountain Adventures** (⊠ 36–4314 Main St., ☎ 604/932–4086, WEB www.cougar-mountainatwhistler.com) has dogsled trips as well as snowmobiling, snowshoeing, and snowcat tours. **Outdoor Adventures@Whistler** (⊠ Timberline Lodge, 4122 Village Green, ☎ 604/932–0647, WEB www.adventureswhistler.com) can take you for walks in the deep powder on snowshoes. **Whistler Outdoor Experience** (⊠ Edgewater Lodge, 8841 Hwy. 99, ☎ 604/932–3389 or 877/386–1888) runs romantic horse-drawn sleigh rides as well as snowshoeing trips.

Meadow Park Sports Centre (⊠ 8107 Camino Dr., ☎ 604/935–8350), about 6 km (4 mi) north of Whistler Village, has a six-lane indoor pool, a children's wading pool, an ice-skating rink, a hot tub, sauna, steam room, a gym, an aerobics studio, and two squash courts. Day passes are $9.

Shopping

Whistler has almost 200 shops, including chain and designer outlets, art galleries, gift shops, and of course, outdoor clothing and ski shops. Most are clustered in the pedestrian-only Whistler Village Centre; more can be found a short stroll away in Village North, Upper Village, and in the shopping concourses of the major hotels. Whistler remains happily free of malls.

Most of the goods on offer reflect the tastes (and budgets) of the international moneyed set that vacations here, though savvy shoppers can get good deals on ski gear in spring and on summer clothing in fall. Almost anything you buy in British Columbia is subject to a Canada-wide 7% Goods and Services Tax (GST) and a 7% Provincial Sales Tax (PST), and these are added at the register. If you aren't a Canadian resident, you can reclaim the GST on goods you take out of the country. **Maple Leaf GST Refund Services** (⊠ 4299 B Mountain Sq., ☎ 604/905–4977) can give you an immediate refund.

adele-campbell Fine Art Gallery has paintings and sculptures by both established and up-and-coming B.C. artists (many featuring wildlife and wilderness themes), including many affordable pieces. ⊠ *Delta Whistler Resort, 4050 Whistler Way,* ☎ *604/938–0887.*
Black Tusk Gallery offers Northwest Coast native art, including limited-edition silkscreen prints, and such traditional crafts as masks, paddles, bowls, jewelry, and totem poles. ⊠ *101–4359 Main St.,* ☎ *604/905–5540.*
Northwest Connection Gallery of Native Art features the works of Northwest Coast native artists, including prints, masks, and handmade gold and silver jewelry. ⊠ *2–4232 Sunrise Alley,* ☎ *604/932–4646.*
Plaza Galleries showcases the painting efforts of Hollywood stars Tony Curtis, Anthony Quinn, and Red Skelton, as well as works by Canadian visual artists. ⊠ *Whistler Town Plaza, 22–4314 Main St.,* ☎ *604/938–6233.*
Whistler Art Galleries has sculpture, painting, and glassworks by Canadian and international artists, with an impressive collection of B.C. jade sculptures. The Westin Resort & Spa branch features Inuit sculptures. ⊠ *Delta Whistler Resort, 4050 Whistler Way,* ☎ *604/938–3001; Westin Resort & Spa, 4090 Whistler Way,* ☎ *604/935–3999.*

Amos and Andes sells handmade sweaters and dresses in offbeat designs. ⊠ *2–4321 Village Gate Blvd.,* ☎ *604/932–7202.*

Helly Hansen has a good selection of its own brand of Norwegian-made skiing, boarding, and other outdoor wear. ✉ *108–4295 Blackcomb Way, Whistler Village Centre,* ☎ *604/932–0143.*

Horstman Trading Co. specializes in ski togs and accessories, including a good selection of Bogner, Tsunami, and other high-fashion gear. ✉ *4555 Blackcomb Way,* ☎ *604/938–7725;* ✉ *Westin Resort & Spa, 4090 Whistler Way,* ☎ *604/905–2203.*

Roots—the Canadian-owned enterprise known for its leather goods, sweatshirts, and other cozy casuals—is something of a fixture in Whistler, especially now that it outfits both the Canadian and American Olympic teams. ✉ *4229 Village Stroll,* ☎ *604/938–0058.*

SPORTS EQUIPMENT

Can-Ski, operated by Whistler–Blackcomb Resort, has four locations with a good selection of brand-name ski gear, clothes, and accessories. The staff also offers custom boot fitting and repairs. ✉ *Crystal Lodge, Whistler Village,* ☎ *604/938–7755;* ✉ *Deer Lodge, Town Plaza,* ☎ *604/938–7432;* ✉ *Glacier Lodge, Upper Village,* ☎ *604/938–7744;* ✉ *Creekside,* ☎ *604/905–2160.*

Fanatyk Co. Ski and Cycle offers skis, boots, and custom boot fitting in winter. In summer the shop specializes in top-of-the-line mountain bikes as well as bike rentals and repairs. ✉ *6–4433 Sundial Pl.,* ☎ *604/ 938–9455.*

Showcase Snowboards supplies gear to the growing number of snowboarders at Whistler. ✉ *Deer Lodge, Whistler Town Plaza,* ☎ *604/ 938–7432;* ✉ *4340 Sundial Crescent,* ☎ *604/938–7519.*

Snowcovers Ski and Golf carries brand-name ski equipment and outerwear in winter; in summer, it becomes Whistler's only independent golf shop, with brand-name clubs and clothing. ✉ *126–4340 Lorimer Rd.,* ☎ *604/905–4100.*

Lillooet

❹ *131 km (81 mi) northeast of Whistler.*

Beyond Whistler, Highway 99 is much less traveled as it passes lakes and glaciers, through the Mount Currie First Nations reserve, and over the mountains to Lillooet.

The arid gullies and Wild West landscape around Lillooet may come as a surprise after the greenery of the coast and mountains. During the 1850s and 1860s this was Mile Zero of the Cariboo Wagon Road, which took prospectors to the gold fields. There are several motels in Lillooet and a BC Rail station.

Hope

❺ *153 km (95 mi) south of Lillooet, 150 km (93 mi) east of Vancouver.*

Hope is the only sizeable town on Highway 1 between Vancouver and the province's interior; it's also the point where the scenery changes suddenly from the steep gorges of the Fraser Canyon to the wide flat farmland of the Fraser Valley. If you're traveling into the interior from Vancouver, you have a choice of three routes here: Highway 1 through the Fraser Canyon, the Coquihalla (Highway 5), and Highway 3. Highway 1, the Trans-Canada Highway, follows the Fraser River as it cuts through the Coast Mountains to the High Country; the deepest, most dramatic cut is the 38-km (24-mi) gorge between Yale and Boston Bar, north of Hope, where the road and rail line cling to the hillside high above the water. Highway 5 is a fast, high-altitude toll road, and Highway 3 is a quiet back road through Manning Park.

You'll find plenty of facilities for overnight stays in Hope. The Fraser and Thompson Rivers north of town are popular rafting centers. Several operators are based in Lytton and Yale.

At the **Coquihalla Canyon Recreation Area** (☎ 604/824–2300), 6 km (4 mi) northeast of Hope off Highway 5, you can walk through the abandoned tunnels of the old Kettle Valley Railway and catch spectacular views of the Coquihalla Gorge. The tunnels are open dawn to dusk April through mid-October, weather permitting.

At **Hell's Gate,** about 55 km (33 mi) north of Hope on Highway 1, an airtram (cable car) carries you across the foaming canyon above the fishways, where millions of sockeye salmon fight their way upriver to spawning grounds. The lower airtram terminal has displays on the salmon's life cycle as well as a fudge factory, a gift shop, and a restaurant. You can also cross the river for free by taking the footbridge. ⊠ *Hwy. 1, 10 km (6 mi) south of Boston Bar,* ☎ *604/867–9277,* WEB *www.hellsgateairtram.com.* ⊠ *Cable car $11.* ☉ *Apr. and Oct., daily 10–4; May–June and Sept., daily 9–5; July–Aug., daily 9–6.*

En Route   Following Highway 3 east to Princeton and Penticton, you pass through **Manning Provincial Park,** which has campgrounds, hiking trails, swimming, boating, and trail rides, in addition to downhill and cross-country skiing in the winter. Also on Highway 3 are a **visitor center** (☎ 250/840–8836) and **Manning Park Resort** (☎ 250/840–8822 or 800/330–3321), which includes a restaurant.

Harrison Hot Springs

❻ *128 km (79 mi) northeast of Vancouver.*

The small resort community of Harrison Hot Springs lies at the southern tip of picturesque Harrison Lake, off Highway 7 in the Fraser Valley. Mountains surround the 64-km-long (40-mi-long) lake, which is ringed by pretty beaches. Besides the hot springs, boating, windsurfing, and swimming are popular here.

A striking 200-ft-high waterfall is the main attraction at **Bridal Veil Falls Provincial Park** (⊠ off Hwy. 1 about 15 km, or 9 mi, southeast of Harrison Hot Springs, ☎ 604/824–2300), open dawn to dusk. A short path through the forest leads to a viewing platform.

The **Harrison Public Pool,** across from the beach in Harrison Hot Springs, is an indoor hot spring–fed pool. ⊠ *224 Esplanade,* ☎ *604/796–2244.* ⊠ *$7.* ☉ *Daily 9–9.*

☾ Kilby Historic Store and Farm, a 20-minute drive west of Harrison Hot Springs, re-creates a rural B.C. store and farm of the 1920s with farm animals, some original buildings and some replicas, and 1920s-style home cooking in the Harrison River Tearoom. ⊠ *215 Kilby Rd. (off Hwy. 7), Harrison Mills,* ☎ *604/796–9576,* WEB *www.heritage.gov.bc.ca/kilby/kilby.htm.* ⊠ *$5.* ☉ *June–Oct., Thurs.–Mon. 11–5; call for off-season hrs.*

Minter Gardens, 8 km (5 mi) southwest of Harrison Hot Springs, is a 27-acre compound with 11 beautifully presented theme gardens including English, rose, lake, stream gardens, and a giant evergreen maze. ⊠ *Exit 135 off Hwy. 1, 52892 Bunker Rd., Rosedale,* ☎ *604/794–7191 or 888/646–8377,* WEB *www.mintergardens.com.* ⊠ *$12.* ☉ *Apr. and Oct., daily 9–5; May and Sept., daily 9–5:30; June, daily 9–6; July–Aug., daily 9–7.*

Dining and Lodging

$$$–$$$$ ✕☷ **Harrison Hot Springs Resort.** A fixture on Harrison Lake since 1926, the hotel originally was set up to take advantage of the hot springs and

the lake, and it still does. There's a full-service spa, several indoor and outdoor hot-springs–fed pools, and a marina offering such water sports as sturgeon-fishing charters and lake cruises. Rooms have contemporary decor; most have patios or balconies, and those on the north side have striking views over the lake and nearby glacier-topped mountains. The Copper Room Restaurant ($$–$$$) serves beautifully prepared, locally sourced, Continental cuisine and has a live dance band nightly. ✉ *100 Esplanade, V0M 1K0,* ☎ *604/796–2244 or 800/663–2266,* FAX *604/796–3682,* WEB *www.harrisonresort.com. 323 rooms, 11 cottages. 2 restaurants, coffee bar, lounge, no-smoking floor, room service, indoor lap pool, pool, wading pool, massage, mineral baths, steam room, 9-hole golf course, 2 tennis courts, gym, jogging, volleyball, boating, marina, waterskiing, fishing, bicycles, shops, playground, laundry service, concierge, convention center. AE, D, DC, MC, V.*

Outdoor Activities and Sports

The **Hemlock Valley Resort** (✉ Hemlock Valley Rd., off Hwy. 7, Agassiz, ☎ 604/797–4411; 800/665–7080 for snow report), 40 km (24 mi) northwest of Harrison Hot Springs, is a family-oriented ski resort with three chairlifts, 35 runs, and a vertical rise of 1,200 ft. You can also try cross-country skiing and snow tubing here.

En Route From Harrison Hot Springs, two routes lead back to Vancouver. Highway 7 is a scenic back road along the north side of the Fraser River. Highway 1 is the faster, main highway. On Highway 1, you pass the turnoff to **Fort Langley National Historic Site,** a restored 1850s Hudson's Bay trading post about an hour west of Harrison Hot Springs. Costumed docents re-create frontier life, and you can try your hand at gold panning. The nearby village of Fort Langley retains a 19th-century charm. ✉ *23433 Mavis Ave., Fort Langley,* ☎ *604/513–4777,* WEB *www.harbour.com/parkscan/fl.* ☜ *$4.50.* ☉ *Mar.–Oct., daily 10–5.*

SUNSHINE COAST

The stretch of mainland coast north of Vancouver, backed by mountains and accessible only by sea or air, is so deeply cut with fjords that it has the look and feel of an island—or rather, two islands. The Sechelt Peninsula to the south is popular with artists, writers, and Vancouver weekenders. The Malaspina Peninsula, a ferry ride across Jervis Inlet to the north, is wild and densely forested. Highway 101, the one paved road running the length of the coast, forms the last (or the first) 139 km (86 mi) of the Pan-American Highway, connecting the village of Lund, British Columbia, to Puerto Mont, Chile, 24,000 km (14,880 mi) away.

The coast is sunnier than the more exposed coastline to the north (hence its name), and its many provincial parks, marinas, lakes, and walking trails are popular with outdoorspeople and families, though not, as yet, with mass tourism or luxury-resort developers. The Sunshine Coast remains one of the quieter, more affordable places to travel in southern British Columbia.

Gibsons Landing

➐ *5 km (3 mi) plus 12 nautical mi northwest of Vancouver.*

The first stop on the Sunshine Coast, just 5 km (3 mi) north of the Langdale ferry terminal, Gibsons Landing (often just called Gibsons) is an attractive seaside town that's best known as the location of *The Beachcombers,* a long-running Canadian TV show about life on the B.C. coast. Though most of the region's best scenery is farther north, Gibsons is worth a stop for its shops, B&Bs, restaurants, attractive waterfront, and fishing-village air.

Elphinstone Pioneer Museum (✉ 716 Winn Rd., ☎ 604/886–8232, WEB www.gibsonslibrary.bc.ca) has an eclectic collection of pioneer artifacts and rare butterflies. It's open mid-June to Labor Day, Tuesday through Saturday 10:30–4:30; donations are suggested. Call for winter hours. The **Sunshine Coast Maritime Museum** (✉ Molly's La., on waterfront, ☎ 604/886–4114) showcases the region's seafaring history. Hours vary according to volunteer availability; admission is by donation. About 15 minutes north of Gibsons on Highway 101 is the 1930s-era village of **Roberts Creek.** There's a public beach a short stroll from the village.

Dining and Lodging

$$–$$$ ✕ **The Creekhouse.** Set amid gardens 15 minutes north of Gibsons Landing, this restaurant serves classic French cuisine with a touch of Italian. The menu changes seasonally, but there are always good lamb and local seafood options. Hardwood floors, white tablecloths, a fireplace, and outdoor patios create a casual, cozy ambience; many guests like to stroll down to the beach between courses. ✉ *1041 Roberts Creek Rd., Roberts Creek,* ☎ *604/885–9321. Reservations essential. MC, V. Closed Mon.–Thurs. No lunch.*

$–$$ ✕ **Gumboot Garden Café.** Everyone knows everyone else at this funky, kid-friendly, village-center café. It's such an area institution that the sign outside reads simply CAFÉ. The dishes feature, where possible, local and organic ingredients, and the menu includes homemade soups, breads, sauces, and desserts. There's a garden, a fireplace, gum boots (rubber boots) by the door, and an environment that makes it tempting to just hang out. Try the eggs, sausage, and granola breakfasts; the burritos, burgers, and soups on offer at lunch; or the candlelight dinners featuring pizza, pasta, seafood, and vegetarian dishes. ✉ *1057 Roberts Creek Rd., Roberts Creek,* ☎ *604/885–4216. MC, V. June–Sept., no dinner Mon.–Tues.; Oct.–May, no dinner Sun.–Wed.*

$$–$$$ ✕🏠 **Bonniebrook Lodge.** For a romantic place to spend the night, consider this seaside lodge 5 km (3 mi) north of Gibsons. Rooms and suites in the original 1922 building are done in a Victorian style and each has a private deck and a whirlpool tub for two. The three rooms in the 1998 addition have fireplaces, VCRs, minirefrigerators, and whirlpool baths for two. Chez Philippe, a fine French restaurant ($$–$$$), is open to the public for dinner; the $28 four-course set menu is an excellent value. The inn doesn't allow smoking. ✉ *Foot of Gower Point Rd., R.R. 5, 1532 Oceanbeach Esplanade, V0N 1V5,* ☎ *604/886–2887 or 877/290–9916; 604/886–2188 for dinner reservations;* FAX *604/886–8853,* WEB *www.bonnniebrook.com. 5 rooms, 2 suites. Restaurant, hot tubs, beach, camping. AE, DC, MC, V. Restaurant closed Tues.–Thurs. mid-Sept.–mid-May. No lunch. Lodge and restaurant closed Jan. BP.*

$$ 🏠 **Country Cottage Bed & Breakfast.** Loragene and Philip Gaulin have lovingly decorated two private, adult-oriented, no-smoking cottages on their 2-acre farm in the 1930s-vintage village of Roberts Creek. Tiny, romantic Rose Cottage has a woodstove and an antique sideboard. Cedar Lodge, the farm's former barn, is a feast of woodsy Canadiana—from its stone fireplace to its handmade Arts and Crafts furniture. Both cottages have cooking facilities. A full breakfast, delivered to your room, and afternoon tea are included in the rates. ✉ *1183 Roberts Creek Rd., Box 183, Roberts Creek V0N 2W0,* ☎ *604/885–7448. 2 cottages. No credit cards. BP.*

$$ 🏠 **Marina House Bed & Breakfast.** From the street, this seaside home near Gibsons' town center looks like an ordinary house; from the beach side though, it's a striking bright yellow, three-story 1931 house. The rooms (one with a bath across the hall) are small, phone- and TV-

free, and decorated with Victorian antiques. Molly's Room has a view over Shoal Channel and Keats Island. The lounge, the porch, and the breakfast room also overlook the sea. The town is a few minutes' stroll along the beach. ✉ *546 Marine Dr., Box 1696, Gibsons V0N 1V0,* ☎ *604/886–7888 or 888/568–6688,* WEB *www.marinahouse.net. 3 rooms, 2 with bath. Breakfast room, library, beach. MC, V. BP.*

Outdoor Activities and Sports

Sunshine Coast Golf & Country Club (✉ 3206 Hwy. 101, Roberts Creek, ☎ 604/885–9212 or 800/667–5022) is an 18-hole, par-71 course with tree-lined fairways and mountain and ocean views.

Sechelt

❽ *37 km (23 mi) plus 12 nautical mi northwest of Vancouver.*

Sechelt, the largest town on the scenic peninsula of the same name, suffers from sprawl but has several interesting shops and restaurants. It's home to many artists and writers as well as a strong First Nations community, the Sechelt Nation. If you're in Sechelt in mid-August, you can catch readings by internationally acclaimed Canadian writers at the **Sunshine Coast Festival of the Written Arts** (☎ 604/885–9631 or 800/ 565–9631), held at Sechelt's Rockwood Centre.

House of Hewhiwus (✉ 5555 Hwy. 101, ☎ 604/885–4592) includes a small First Nations museum and a gift shop–art gallery. **Porpoise Bay Provincial Park** (☎ 604/898–3678), north of Sechelt on Sechelt Inlet, has a sandy swimming beach. The swimming is good at **Davis Bay,** south of Sechelt on the Georgia Strait.

The coast's best scenery is to the north of Sechelt, around and beyond the little marinas of Madiera Park, Garden Bay, and Irvine's Landing, collectively known as Pender Harbour. Here Highway 101 winds past forests, mountains, and a confusion of freshwater lakes and ocean inlets. In summer, **Pender Harbour Ferries** (☎ 604/883–2561 to Pender Harbour Info Centre) run 1½-hour boat tours of the area.

You can experience a dramatic natural sight at **Skookumchuk Narrows Provincial Park** (✉ Egmont Rd. off Hwy. 101, ☎ 604/898–3678), 5 km (3 mi) inland from the Earls Cove ferry terminal and 45 km (28 mi) northwest of Sechelt. A 4-km (2½-mi) walk through the forest comes out at a viewpoint where, at the turn of the tide, seawater churning through the narrow channel creates thrilling tidal rapids. Tide tables are posted at the trailhead.

Princess Louisa Inlet is a narrow fjord at the top of Jervis Inlet; more than 60 waterfalls tumble down its steep walls. The fjord is accessible only by boat or floatplane; several local tour operators offer summer day trips.

Dining and Lodging

$$ ✕🖾 **Ruby Lake Resort.** The Cogrossi family from Milan chose this seaside cabin resort just off Highway 101 as the place to settle and cook up some of the area's best Italian food ($–$$$$). Diners come from up and down the coast for Aldo Cogrossi's lobster, wild boar, and pasta creations. The salads and vegetarian dishes are often made with produce from the on-site organic garden, and seafood specials are based on what's fresh at the docks that day. The resort has five duplex cabins that overlook a lagoon and a bird sanctuary. The cabins, accessed by a floating bridge over the lagoon, have modern decor and are nosmoking. Canoe rentals are included in the room rates. ✉ *Hwy. 101 (R. R. 1, Site 20, C25), Madeira Park, V0N 2H0,* ☎ *604/883–2269 or 800/717–6611,* FAX *604/883–3602,* WEB *www.rubylakeresort.com. 5* *rooms, 5 suites. Restaurant, kitchenettes, lake, massage, hiking, boating. AE, MC, V. Closed Nov.– mid-Mar.*

$–$$ ⊡ **Sundowner Inn.** An atmospheric, family-run, budget hotel, this 1929 clapboard building perched on a hill overlooking Garden Bay was once a mission hospital. The rooms are basic, with 1950s furniture, but the setting is stunning. You can take a boat trip to Princess Louisa Inlet and Desolation Sound, or a hiking, cycling, or kayaking tour from here. Garden Bay is 7 km (4 mi) off Highway 101, 30 km (19 mi) north of Sechelt. ⊠ *4339 Garden Bay Rd., Box 113, Garden Bay V0N 1S0,* ☎ *604/883–9676 or 888/288–8780,* FAX *604/883–9886,* WEB *www.sundowner-inn.com. 12 rooms, 10 with bath. Restaurant, air-conditioning, fans, outdoor hot tub, dock, boating, fishing, bicycles, chapel, meeting room. MC, V.*

Outdoor Activities and Sports

Pender Harbour and the Sechelt Inlet are spectacular diving spots, especially in the winter, when the water is clearest. An artificial reef has been formed by a scuttled navy ship off Kunechin Point in Sechelt Inlet. **Suncoast Diving and Water Sports** (⊠ 5643 Wharf St., ☎ 604/740–8006 or 866/740–8006, WEB www.suncoastdiving.com) is a PADI dive shop that also rents kayaks and runs boat tours. A 1½-hr evening Zodiac excursion is $30; a one-day dive charter with two dives is $75 per person. Kayak rentals start at $25 a day.

Powell River

❾ *70 km (43 mi) plus 12 nautical mi by ferry northwest of Sechelt, 121 km (75 mi) plus 12½ nautical mi northwest of Vancouver, 17 nautical mi (75-min ferry ride) east across Strait of Georgia from Comox on Vancouver Island.*

The main town on the Malaspina Peninsula, Powell River was established around a pulp-and-paper mill in 1912, and the forestry industry remains a strong presence in the area. Renowned as a year-round salmon-fishing destination, Powell River also has 30 regional lakes with exceptional trout fishing; it's also becoming popular as a winter scuba-diving destination. The town has several B&Bs, restaurants, and parks with oceanfront camping and RV hookups. The Powell River Townsite, one of the province's oldest functioning mill towns, is a national historic site.

Lodging

$ ⊡ **Old Court House Inn and Hostel.** The views are over the neighboring pulp mill, but the low room rates and the refurbished interior of this one-time courthouse make up for such less-than-inspiring vistas. Private rooms, some with baths and all with TVs, are decorated in an early 20th-century style; some have antiques. There are also three dorm rooms ($17 a person) and a shared kitchen that's available to all guests of this no-smoking inn. A shuttle picks you up from the bus station or the Westview (Comox) ferry terminal for $5. ⊠ *6243 Walnut St., V8A 4K4,* ☎ *604/483–4000,* FAX *604/483–4089,* WEB *www.clearlife.net/oldcourt. 8 private rooms, 6 with bath, 1 4-bed dorm room, 2 2-bed dorm rooms. MC, V.*

Outdoor Activities and Sports

BOATING, CANOEING, AND KAYAKING

The 80-km (50-mi) Powell Forest Canoe Route and Desolation Sound Marine Park attract boaters. **Wolfson Creek Adventures** (⊠ 9537 Nassichuk Rd./R.R. 3, Powell River, ☎ 604/487–1699, WEB www.canoeingbc.com) offers canoe and kayak rentals and tours. One-day kayak rentals are $30; canoe rentals cost $27 a day.

HIKING AND BIKING

The Inland Lake Site and Trail System, 12 km (8 mi) inland from Powell River, is a 13-km-long (8-mi-long) hiking and biking trail around Inland Lake that's accessible to people who use wheelchairs. Hikers can also try the Sunshine Coast Trail, which runs 180 km (112 mi) from Sarah Point, north of Lund, to Saltery Bay. BC Ferries sails from Powell River to Texada Island, a rustic, forested island that has accommodations, hiking trails, and campsites.

SCUBA DIVING

Sunken ships, red coral, wolf eels, enormous octopi, and—especially in winter—uncommonly clear water make Powell River one of Canada's leading scuba-diving spots. Local dive outfitters include **Don's Dive Shop** (✉ 4454 Willingdon Ave., ☎ 604/485–6969). Full-gear rental with a dive charter is $50; without a dive charter it's $65. A one-day dive charter is $90 per person and includes two dives and tanks and weights.

Lund

⑩ *27 km (17 mi) north of Powell River.*

Founded by the Swedish Thulin brothers in 1889, the historic boardwalked village of Lund marks the end (or start) of the Pan-American Highway. Lund is the nearest village to **Desolation Sound,** British Columbia's largest marine park and a major draw for boaters and kayakers. You can catch a water taxi from Lund to **Savary Island** and its white-sand beaches.

Dining and Lodging

$–$$$ ✕ **The Laughing Oyster.** All the tables at this pretty, blue restaurant five minutes from Lund have stunning views over Okeover Arm. Though vegetarian, beef, lamb, and poultry dishes are on offer, the focus here is seafood. The namesake laughing oysters are steam shucked and broiled with artichokes, olives, sun-dried tomatoes, hot peppers, and feta cheese. The west-coast seafood harvest for two has salmon, red snapper, oysters, prawns, scallops, and more. Lighter bistro choices include spicy chicken and mushrooms with a ginger-and-garlic sauce over Asian noodles. Boaters can tie up at the dock in front of the restaurant. ✉ *10052 Malaspina Rd., Powell River,* ☎ *604/483–9775. Reservations essential. AE, MC, V.*

$$ 🏨 **Lund Hotel.** This three-story hotel with its dormer windows and wraparound porch was opened by the village's founders in 1889 and was a landmark on this part of the coast for almost a century. Closed for several years, it is once again the life and soul of Lund. The simple, modern rooms are all no-smoking. On site are a post office, a pub, a general store, an art gallery, the Coast Salish Journeys tour operator, and the Good Diving and Kayaking outfitter. ✉ *At end of Hwy. 101 (General Delivery, Lund V0N 2G0),* ☎ *604/414–0474 or 877/ 569–3999,* ℻ *604/414–0476,* 🌐 *www.lundhotel.com. 40 rooms. Restaurant, pub, in-room data ports, in-room VCRs, minibars, room service, outdoor hot tub, dive shop, boating, marina, fishing, shops, coin laundry, business services, meeting rooms. AE, D, DC, MC, V.*

Outdoor Activities and Sports

Coast Salish Journeys (✉ Lund Hotel, at end of Hwy. 101, ☎ 604/ 483–4505 or 800/345–1112, 🌐 www.coastsalishjourneys.com) offers a variety of tours with a cultural or natural-history focus, including guided hikes, kayak tours, lake canoeing, sailing trips, and ocean canoeing in a 31-ft Coast Salish traveling canoe. A two-hour guided hike is $24; a daylong guided canoe tour with gear and a salmon barbecue is $155 per person. **Good Diving and Kayaking** (✉ Lund Hotel, at end

of Hwy. 101, ☎ 604/483–3223 or 877/483–3223) can arrange diving
and kayaking trips and rentals. Dive charters, $120 per person, include
tanks and weights. Kayak day tours, $65 per person, include lunch.
Kayak rentals start at $30 a day. **Powell River Sea Kayaks** (✉ 10676
Crowther Rd., 8 km, or 5 mi, east of Lund on Okeover Inlet, ☎ 604/
483–2160) offers lessons, rentals, and tours of the Lund area. A one-
day kayak rental is $35; a six-hour guided kayak tour is $89, which
includes lunch.

THE GULF ISLANDS

Of the hundreds of islands sprinkled across the Georgia Strait between Vancouver Island and the mainland, the most popular and accessible are Galiano, Mayne, and Salt Spring. A temperate climate
(warmer than Vancouver and with half the rainfall), shell beaches, rolling
pastures, and virgin forests are common to all, but each island has its
unique flavor. Marine birds are numerous, and there's unusual vegetation such as arbutus trees (also known as madrones, a leafy evergreen
with red peeling bark) and Garry oaks.

These islands are rustic (only Salt Spring has a bank machine) but not
undiscovered. Writers, artists, and craftspeople as well as weekend cottagers and retirees from Vancouver and Victoria take full advantage
of them. Make hotel reservations for summer stays. If you're bringing
a car from the B.C. mainland, ferry reservations are highly recommended;
indeed, they're required on some of the busier sailings.

Galiano Island

⑪ *20 nautical mi (almost 2 hrs by ferry due to interisland stops) from*
Swartz Bay (32 km [20 mi] north of Victoria), 13 nautical mi (a 50-
minute ferry ride) from Tsawwassen (39 km [24 mi] south of Vancouver).

Galiano's long, unbroken eastern shore is perfect for leisurely walks,
and the numerous coves and inlets along its western coast make it a
prime area for kayaking. Biological studies show that the straits between Vancouver Island and the B.C. mainland are home to North America's greatest variety of marine life. The frigid waters offer superb
visibility, especially in winter. Alcala Point, Porlier Pass, and Active Pass
are top scuba-diving locations.

Galiano also has miles of trails through Douglas-fir forest that beg for
exploration on foot or by bike. Hikers can climb to the top of Mt.
Galiano for a view of the Olympic Mountains in Washington or trek
the length of Bodega Ridge. The best spots for picnics, bird-watching,
and to view Active Pass and the surrounding islands are Bluffs Park
and Bellhouse Park. Anglers head to the point at Bellhouse Park to spin
cast for salmon from shore, or they go by boat to Porlier Pass and Trin-
comali Channel.

Several local companies offer transportation on the island as well as
land or sea tours. Inquire at the Galiano Island Visitor Information Centre's booth at the Sturdies Bay ferry terminal. It's open daily in July
and August and on weekends the rest of the year. Phone service is available year-round.

Montague Harbour Provincial Marine Park (Montague Park Rd. off Montague Rd., ☎ 250/391–2300) has camping and boating facilities.
Matthew's Point Regional Park (accessed by a footpath across from
556 Bluff's Rd.) has a long sandy beach.

NEED A BREAK?	If all the outdoor activity leaves you longing for human contact, head for the **Hummingbird Inn Pub** (⊠ 47 Sturdies Bay Rd., ☎ 250/539–5472), a friendly local hangout, with live music on summer weekends.

Dining and Lodging

$$–$$$ ★ ✕🛏 **Woodstone Country Inn.** The serene inn is at the edge of a forest overlooking a meadow that's fantastic for bird-watching. Tall windows bring the pastoral setting into spacious bedrooms decorated in green and rose. All guest quarters have fireplaces; most have patios and oversize extra-deep tubs. A hearty gourmet breakfast and afternoon tea are included in the rates. Woodstone's elegant restaurant ($$$$) serves French-influenced Pacific Northwest fare, such as yam soup with toasted almonds or herb-crusted rack of lamb with pear–tomato chutney and mustard sauce. Guests and nonguests can have four-course dinners here; reservations are required. ⊠ *Georgeson Bay Rd., R.R. 1, V0N 1P0,* ☎ *250/539–2022 or 888/339–2022,* FAX *250/539–5198,* WEB *www.gulfislands.com/woodstone. 12 rooms. Restaurant, hiking, piano, library, meeting rooms. AE, MC, V. BP. Closed Dec.–Jan.*

$$–$$$ ★ 🛏 **Bellhouse Inn.** Modeled on an English manor house, this red-and-white clapboard inn sits on 6 seaside acres of farmland next to Bellhouse Park. The interior is decorated in a 19th-century country style, with such antiques as the 1860 farmhouse table where breakfast is served. The peaceful lounge and library has a big fireplace and picture windows overlooking the ocean; on a table here are binoculars for spotting whales and bald eagles in Active Pass. The Kingfisher Room has a whirlpool tub and French doors that open onto a balcony with a full water view. The Eagle Room also has a balcony, with a forest and ocean view, as well as an extra-deep soaking tub and the original hardwood floor. The inn is all no-smoking, and the main house caters to adults; families can stay in one of the 1960s two-bedroom cottages. In summer, the owner takes guests out on his 22-ft cruiser. ⊠ *29 Farmhouse Rd., Box 16, Site 4, V0N 1P0,* ☎ *250/539 5667 or 800/970–7464,* FAX *250/539–5316,* WEB *www.bellhouseinn.com. 3 rooms, 2 cottages. Breakfast room, croquet, hiking, beach. MC, V. CP.*

Outdoor Activities and Sports

BIKING

Bike rentals are available from **Galiano Bicycle** (⊠ 36 Burrill Rd., ☎ 250/539–9906), within walking distance of the Sturdies Bay ferry terminal.

FISHING

Sporades Tours (⊠ 1289 Galiano Way, ☎ 250/539–2278) runs fishing and sightseeing charters. Tours are for a minimum of three hours, at $100 an hour for up to eight people.

GOLF

The **Galiano Golf and Country Club** (⊠ 24 St. Andrew Crescent, ☎ 250/539–5533) is a 9-hole, par-32 course in a forest clearing.

HORSEBACK RIDING

For trail riding, contact **Bodega Resort** (☎ 250/539–2677), which offers trips for all skill levels. A ride of about 70 minutes costs $25 per person.

KAYAKING

Galiano Island Sea Kayaking (⊠ 637 Southwind Rd., ☎ 250/539–2930 or 888/539–2930) has rentals and tours starting at $29 for two hours with a guide. **Gulf Islands Kayaking** (⊠ Montague Harbour Marina, Montague Harbour Rd., ☎ 250/539–2442) has equipment rentals and guided kayak tours (three hours, $38; six hours $68).

For dive charters, contact **Galiano Diving** (☎ 250/539–3109).

Mayne Island

⑫ *28 nautical mi from Swartz Bay (32 km [20 mi] north of Victoria), 22 nautical mi from Tsawwassen (39 km [24 mi] south of Vancouver).*

Middens of clam and oyster shells give evidence that tiny Mayne Island—only 21 square km (8 square mi)—was inhabited as early as 5,000 years ago. It later became the stopover point for miners headed from Victoria to the goldfields of the Fraser River and Barkerville. By the mid-1800s it was the communal center of the inhabited Gulf Islands, with the first school, post office, police lockup, church, and hotel. Farm tracts and orchards, established in the 1930s and 1940s and worked by Japanese farmers until their internment in World War II, still thrive here. Mayne's mild hills and wonderful scenery make it great territory for a vigorous bike ride.

Mount Parke was declared a wilderness park in 1989. A 45-minute hike leads to the island's highest point and a stunning view of the mainland and other gulf islands.

The small town of Miners Bay is home to **Plumper Pass Lockup** (✉ 433 Fernhill Rd., ☎ no phone), built in 1896 as a jail but now a minuscule museum (open July to Labor Day, Friday to Monday 11–3, free) chronicling the island's history. After touring the Plumper Pass Lockup, consider stopping for a drink at the seaside **Springwater Lodge** (✉ 400 Fernhill Rd., Miners Bay, ☎ 250/539–5521), one of the province's oldest hotels. If you're in Miners Bay on a Saturday between July and mid-October, check out the **Farmers' Market** outside the Agricultural Hall. Open 10–1, it sells produce and crafts.

From Miners Bay head north on Georgina Point Road to **St. Mary Magdalene Church,** a pretty stone chapel built in 1898. Active Pass Lighthouse, at the end of Georgina Point Road, north of Miners Bay, is part of **Georgina Point Heritage Park.** It was built in 1855 and still signals ships into the busy waterway. The grassy grounds are great for picnicking. There's a pebble beach for beachcombing at shallow (and therefore warmer) **Campbell Bay.**

Dining and Lodging

$$–$$$$ ✕🅣 **Oceanwood Country Inn.** This Tudor-style house on 10 forested
    ★ acres overlooking Navy Channel has English country decor throughout. Fireplaces, French doors that open onto ocean-view balconies, and whirlpool baths make several rooms deluxe. The waterfront restaurant ($$$$) serves four-course table d'hôte dinners of outstanding regional cuisine. The menu changes daily, but highlights have included roasted Pacific salmon with a ragout of Salt Spring Island mussels, and seared marinated quail with golden pearl onions and bacon and sage tempura. Room rates include afternoon tea and breakfast. ✉ *630 Dinner Bay Rd., Mayne Island V0N 2J0, ☎ 250/539–5074, ℻ 250/539–3002, 🖳 www.oceanwood.com. 12 rooms. Restaurant, hot tub, sauna, hiking, jogging, bicycles, library, meeting rooms. MC, V. Closed late Nov.–early Mar. CP.*

$$ 🅣 **A Coachhouse on Oyster Bay.** Owner Brian Johnston designed this cedar, waterfront house in the style of a turn-of-the-20th-century carriage house. Rooms are elegant, with bold colors, hardwood floors, private entrances, gas fireplaces, and views of Active Pass and Oyster Bay. The Laundau Room, in a former hayloft above the barn, is the most decadent option, with a four-poster bed and a private hot tub on a deck overlooking the ocean. You can swim in the warm, shallow bay

next to the property, watch seals and eagles from the gazebo on the shore, or soak in a hot tub on the ocean's edge. ✉ *511 Bayview Dr., Mayne Island, V0N 2J0,* ☎ *250/539–3368 or 888/629–6322,* FAX *250/ 539–2236,* WEB *www.acoachhouse.com. 3 rooms. Breakfast room, outdoor hot tub, beach, bicycles, piano. MC, V. BP.*

Outdoor Activities and Sports

Bay View Bike Rentals (✉ 764 Steward Rd., Miners Bay, ☎ 250/539– 2924) rents bicycles for $120 a day. **Island Charters** (✉ 263 Laura Point Rd., Mayne Island, ☎ 250/539–5040) offers half- or full-day trips on a crewed 33-ft sailboat. Half-day trips are $135 for two people, $160 for four; full-day trips are $160 and $190, respectively. At **Mayne Island Kayaking** (✉ 359 Maple Dr., Seal Beach, Miners Bay, ☎ 250/ 539–2667), kayak day rentals start at $45.

Salt Spring Island

⑬ *28 nautical mi from Swartz Bay (32 km [20 mi] north of Victoria), 22 nautical mi from Tsawwassen (39 km [24 mi] south of Vancouver).*

Named for the saltwater springs at its north end, Salt Spring is the largest and most developed of the Gulf Islands. Among the first nonnative settlers to arrive in the 1850s were African Americans fleeing repression in California, seafarers from Hawaii, and a small group of Australians. The agrarian tradition they and other immigrants established remains strong (a Fall Fair has been held every September since 1896), but tourism and art now support the local economy.

Ganges, a pedestrian-oriented seaside village about 6 km (4 mi) from the Long Harbour ferry terminal, is the main commercial center for Salt Spring Island's 10,000 residents. It has dozens of smart boutiques, galleries, and restaurants. There are so many artists studios—most are open to the public—that you can actually do a tour that focuses just on them. Pick up a studio tour map at the Ganges Visitor Information Centre on Lower Ganges Road. **Mouat's Trading Company** (✉ Fulford–Ganges Rd., ☎ 250/537–5593), built in 1912, was the original village general store. It's now a hardware store but still houses a display of historical photographs.

At the south end of Salt Spring Island, where the ferries from Victoria arrive, is the tiny village of **Fulford,** which has two cafés, a kayaking outlet, and several offbeat boutiques. Ferries from Crofton, on Vancouver Island, arrive on Salt Spring Island at **Vesuvius,** an even smaller village than Fulford, with a seaside pub, a swimming beach, and craft studios, on the west side of the island.

Near the center of Salt Spring Island, the summit of **Mt. Maxwell Provincial Park** (✉ Mt. Maxwell Rd., off Fulford–Ganges Rd.) has spectacular views of south Salt Spring, Vancouver Island, and other Gulf Islands. The last portion of the drive is steep, winding, and unpaved.

Ruckle Provincial Park (✉ Beaver Point Rd., ☎ 250/391–2300) is the site of an 1872 homestead and extensive fields still farmed by the Ruckle family. The park also has seaside camping and picnic spots, 11 km (7 mi) of coastline, a beach, and 8 km (5 mi) of trails leading to rocky headlands.

There's no public transportation on Salt Spring, so your land travel options are cabs or rental cars. Several establishments also rent bikes and scooters. The tiny *Queen of de Nile* ferry runs from Moby's Marine Pub and Ganges Marina to Ganges town center. There's also water-taxi service to Mayne and Galiano islands.

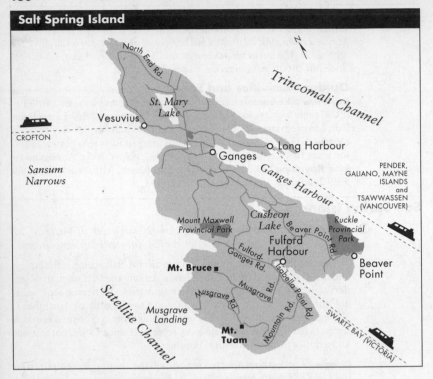

Dining and Lodging

$$$ ✕ **House Piccolo.** This nine-table restaurant in a little blue-and-white house serves beautifully prepared and presented European food. Appetizers feature such classics from the chef–owner's native Finland as gravlax and herring. Favorite main courses include venison with a juniper-and-rowanberry demi-glace, and beef tenderloin with Gorgonzola sauce. For dessert, there's homemade ice cream, lingonberry crêpes with vodka, and chocolate terrine Finlandia, which is rich, delicious, and worth ordering for the presentation alone. The 250-item wine list has won a *Wine Spectator* award of excellence and includes many hard-to-find vintages. The indoor tables are cozy and candlelit; the outdoor patio is a pleasant summer dining spot. ✉ *108 Hereford Ave., Ganges,* ☎ *250/537–1844. Reservations essential. DC, MC, V. No lunch.*

$–$$ ✕ **The Treehouse Café.** Dwarfed by a sprawling plum tree, this tiny 1927 cottage has been a fixture on the Ganges waterfront for generations. Now it's a funky café that serves wholesome breakfasts and rich homemade soups, hefty sandwiches, salads, and chili the rest of the day. Salt Spring lamb, vegetarian burritos, and pastas feature on the dinner menu. There are only three tables; most guests opt for a rustic one under the tree outside, where people gather to hear local musicians on summer evenings. ✉ *106 Purvis La. (next to Mouat's Trading Company),* ☎ *250/537–5379. Reservations not accepted. MC, V. No dinner Oct.–June.*

$ ✕ **Moby's Marine Pub.** Big portions of great food such as warm salmon or scallop salad and lamb burgers, a harborside deck, a cozy room with fireplaces, and Sunday evening jazz make this friendly, no-smoking pub a favorite. Be prepared to wait in line on summer weekends. ✉ *124 Upper Ganges Rd.,* ☎ *250/537–5559. Reservations not accepted. MC, V.*

$$$$ ✕☎ **Hastings House.** The centerpiece of this 25-acre seaside farm estate is a 1940 country house, built in the style of an 11th-century Sussex manor. Guest quarters are in the manor, in renovated outbuildings, in a 1999 hilltop addition overlooking Ganges Harbour, or in a three-bedroom guest house with harbor and property views. Rooms are decorated in an English country style and have antiques, locally crafted woodwork, and fireplaces (gas or wood) or woodstoves. Accommodations in the older buildings are quieter; the newer hillside units have expansive views, but are closer to the main road. In-room spa services are available as is transportation to most island activities and to or from the floatplane dock and ferry terminals. Rates include a full breakfast and afternoon tea. Five-course prix-fixe dinners in the manor house are open to the public ($$$$; reservations essential). The excellent cuisine features local lamb, seafood, and herbs and produce from the inn's gardens. A jacket is required in the formal dining room but not on the veranda. ⊠ *160 Upper Ganges Rd., V8K 2S2,* ☎ *250/537–2362 or 800/661–9255,* ⨍⨯ *250/537–5333,* ⱳⅇⵀ *www.hastingshouse.com. 3 rooms, 14 suites, 1 guest house. Restaurant, in-room data ports, minibars, no-smoking rooms, massage, boccie, croquet, business services. AE, MC, V. BP. Closed mid-Nov.–mid-Mar.*

$$$ ☎ **Anne's Oceanfront Hideaway.** On a steep seaside slope 6 km (4 mi) north of the Vesuvius ferry terminal, this modern home has a cozy library, a sitting room, an elevator, and two verandas. Every room has a hydromassage tub; three have balconies. The Douglas Fir and Garry Oak rooms have the best views. Luxurious amenities—morning coffee brought to your door, robes, and a welcoming bottle of wine—make this a comfortable place to unwind. A lavish hot breakfast is included, and one room is wheelchair accessible. ⊠ *168 Simson Rd., V8K 1E2,* ☎ *250/537–0851 or 888/474–2663,* ⨍⨯ *250/537–0861,* ⱳⅇⵀ *www.annesoceanfront.com. 4 rooms. Breakfast room, air-conditioning, outdoor hot tub, boating, bicycles, library. AE, MC, V. BP.*

$$$ ☎ **Apple Hill Farm.** Francophile Nancy France has filled this weathered hillside farmhouse with local art and whimsical treasures. The guest rooms (one with a sauna), the cozy common room with its big river-rock fireplace, and the nooks and crannies throughout are decorated in a singular European country style and have meadow and sea views. A wide deck, a rustic gazebo, and 43 acres of farmland offer plenty of opportunities for contemplation. Riding stables are just next door. Expect breakfast at this no-smoking inn to include eggs and fruit and vegetables from the farm and bread baked in a brick oven outside. ⊠ *201 Wright Rd., Box 437, Ganges V8K 2W1,* ☎ *250/537–9738,* ⨍⨯ *250/ 538–0217,* ⱳⅇⵀ *www.applehillfarm.net. 3 rooms. Breakfast room, refrigerators, hot tub, sauna, steam room, tennis court, hiking, piano. MC. BP.*

$$–$$$ ☎ **Beddis House.** Emily Beddis and her family built this white clapboard farmhouse overlooking Trincomali Channel in 1900. The original farmhouse is still home to a guest parlor and breakfast room (though with modern decor); a separate 1995 coach house, built in the same style, has three spacious guest rooms. Done in contemporary country pine with a sprinkling of antiques, all rooms have woodstoves, claw-foot tubs, and an ocean-view deck or balcony. The Rose Bower Room is the most romantic option: it takes up most of the top floor and has a four-post, king-size bed and a sofa, as well as sea and garden views. You can stroll in the 1¼-acre garden or step down to the inn's white clamshell beach. Local outfitters will deliver kayaks to the property, too. Beddis House, about a 15-minute drive from Ganges, is completely no-smoking. ⊠ *131 Miles Ave., V8K 2E1,* ☎ *250/537–1028,* ⨍⨯ *250/ 537–9888,* ⱳⅇⵀ *www.saltspring.com/beddishouse. 3 rooms. Breakfast room, fans, beach. MC, V. BP. Closed Dec.–Jan.*

$$ ⚥ **Old Farmhouse Bed and Breakfast.** A registered historic property built in 1894, this white saltbox farmhouse sits in a quiet 3-acre meadow near St. Mary Lake. The style of the main house is echoed in the four-room wing added in 1989, which has comfortable guest rooms furnished with pine bedsteads, down comforters, hardwood floors, and wicker chairs. Each has a balcony or patio. There's also a one-bedroom cottage. The breakfasts of fresh baked goods and hot entrées such as smoked-salmon soufflé are legendary. ⌧ *1077 North End Rd., V8K 1L9,* ☎ *250/537–4113,* FAX *250/537–4969,* WEB *www.bbcanada.com/old-farmhouse. 4 rooms, 1 cottage. Breakfast room. V. BP. Closed Nov.–Feb.*

$ ⚥ **Salt Spring Island Hostel.** In the 10 forested acres behind this hostel near Cusheon Lake are canvas teepees and furnished treehouses (sleeping rooms without baths) reached by a ladder or a staircase. Inside, the main building has private guest rooms, two small dorms, a shared kitchen, and a cozy common room with a fireplace. The hostel is about 5 km (3 mi) from Ganges, and a 25-minute walk from either an ocean beach or a swimming lake. You can rent bicycles and scooters here, and the friendly owners can arrange kayaking, sailing, and a range of other activities. This no-smoking, Hostelling International facility is very popular; reservations are highly recommended. *640 Cusheon Lake Rd., V8K 2C2,* ☎ *250/537–4149,* WEB *www.beacom.com/ssihostel. 2 rooms, 1 with bath, 2 treehouses, 3 teepees, 2 dorms with 4–6 beds. Bicycles. MC. Closed Nov. 1–Mar. 1.*

Nightlife and the Arts

Ganges restaurants are hubs for island nightlife. **Moby's Marine Pub** (⌧ 124 Upper Ganges Rd., ☎ 250/537–5559) is the place to go for live jazz every Sunday night. **The Treehouse Café** (⌧ 106 Purvis La., ☎ 250/537–5379), next to Mouat's Trading Company, features local musicians throughout the summer. Live bands and video nights make **Talons Restaurant** (⌧ Gasoline Alley, on the waterfront, ☎ 250/537–8585) a popular hangout.

If you're looking for music in Fulford, try the **Fulford Inn** (⌧ 2661 Fulford-Ganges Rd., ☎ 250/653–4432). To find out what's happening, see the local weeklies, the *Driftwood* and the *Barnacle*, or contact the Ganges Tourist Info Centre.

You can catch a live music show or a play at **ArtSpring** (⌧ 100 Jackson Ave., ☎ 250/537–2125), a theater and gallery complex in Ganges. ArtSpring is the main venue for July's international **Salt Spring Festival of the Arts,** which features music, theater, and dance.

Outdoor Activities and Sports

For information about hiking trails and beach access, pick up a copy of the Salt Spring Out-of-Doors Map, available at Salt Spring bookstores.

BIKING

Salt Spring Kayak and Cycle (⌧ 2923 Fulford-Ganges Rd., Fulford, ☎ 250/653–4222), on the wharf, rents and repairs bikes.

BOATING, KAYAKING, AND SAILING

Island Escapades (⌧ 163 Fulford-Ganges Rd., Ganges, ☎ 250/537–2537 or 888/529–2567, WEB www.islandescapades.com) has guided kayaking ($35 to $65 for two to five hours) and sailing trips ($40 to $75 per person for three or four hours).

Salt Spring Kayak and Cycle (⌧ 2923 Fulford-Ganges Rd., Fulford, ☎ 250/653–4222) rents kayaks and offers lessons and trips. Guided day paddles are $50 ($30 for two hours at sunset).

Salt Spring Marine Rentals (⌧ head of Ganges Harbour next to Moby's Marine Pub, ☎ 250/537–9100, WEB www.saltspring.com/rentals) rents kayaks and powerboats. Kayaks cost $45 a day, or $12 per hour; power-boats go for $110 a day. It's also a good place to arrange fishing, sailing, and sightseeing charters, buy fishing licenses, and rent scooters ($70 a day).

Sea Otter Kayaking (✉ 149 Lower Ganges Rd., on Ganges Harbour at foot of Rainbow Rd., Ganges, ☎ 250/537–5678 or 877/537–5678, WEB www.seaotterkayaking.com) is a good source for kayak sales, rentals, lessons, and tours. A two-hour introductory lesson is $35.

GOLF

Blackburn Meadows Golf Club (✉ 269 Blackburn Rd., ☎ 250/537–1707) borders a lake. Its 9 holes ($12; $20 for 18) offer you the chance to play on Canada's only organic golf course.

Salt Spring Island Golf and Country Club (✉ 805 Lower Ganges Rd., ☎ 250/537–2121) is a pleasant 9-hole course ($20; $31 for 18 holes) with a restaurant in the clubhouse.

Frisbee Golf Course (✉ end of Seaview Ave., Ganges) in Mouat Park offers the chance to try something a bit different. Players aim to hit a series of 18 targets with Frisbees. It's free (bring your own Frisbee or buy one here).

HIKING

Island Escapades (✉ 163 Fulford-Ganges Rd., Ganges, ☎ 250/537–2537 or 888/529–2567, WEB www.islandescapades.com) organizes hiking and climbing trips as well as outdoor adventure programs for children and teens. A three-hour hike costs about $30; outdoor rock climbing is $65.

HORSEBACK RIDING

You can take small group trail rides with **Salt Spring Guided Rides** (☎ 250/537–5761). Reservations are necessary. The cost is $30 an hour.

SWIMMING

St. Mary Lake, on North End Road, and Cusheon Lake, south of Ganges, are your best bets for warm-water swimming.

Shopping

Ganges's Mahon Hall is the site of **ArtCraft,** a summer-long sale of works by more than 200 artisans. Salt Spring's biggest arts-and-crafts gallery, **Coastal Currents Gallery** (✉ 133 Hereford Ave., Ganges, ☎ 250/537–0070), is in a historic house. Everything at the **Salt Spring Island Saturday Market,** held in Ganges's Centennial Park every Saturday April through October, has been made, baked, or grown on the island. Fresh produce, crafts, clothing, candles, toys, home-canned items, and more are on offer.

NORTH COAST

Gateway to Alaska and the Yukon, this vast, rugged region is marked by soaring, snowcapped mountain ranges, scenic fjords, primordial islands, and towering rain forests. Once the center of a vast trading network, the mid- and north coasts are home to First Nations peoples who have lived here for 10,000 years and to more-recent immigrants drawn by the natural resources of fur, fish, and forest. The region is thin on roads, but you can travel by ferry, sailboat, cruise ship, plane, or kayak to explore the ancient villages of the coast and the Queen Charlotte Islands. The climate of this mist-shrouded region is one of the world's wettest. Winters see torrential rains, and summers are damp; rain gear is essential year-round.

Inside Passage

★ **⑭** *507 km (314 mi), or 274 nautical mi, between Port Hardy on north-*
         ern Vancouver Island and Prince Rupert.

The Inside Passage, a sheltered marine highway, follows a series of natural channels along the green-and-blue-shaded B.C. coast. The undisturbed landscape of rising mountains and humpbacked islands has a
striking, prehistoric look. You can take a ferry cruise along the Inside
Passage or see it on one of the luxury liners that sails from Vancouver
to Alaska.

The comfortable **Queen of the North** ferry carries up to 800 passengers and 157 vehicles, and has cabins, food services, an elevator, children's play areas, and a licensed lounge on board. Between mid-May
and early October, sailings from Port Hardy on Vancouver Island to
Prince Rupert (or vice versa) are direct and take 15 hours, almost entirely in daylight. Sailings are less frequent and longer the rest of the
year, as the ferry makes stops along the way. Reservations are required
for vehicles and recommended for foot passengers. It's also a good idea
to make hotel reservations at Port Hardy and Prince Rupert. ⊠ *BC
Ferries, 1112 Fort St., Victoria, V8V 4V2,* ☎ *250/386–3431 in Victoria and outside B.C.; 888/223–3779 elsewhere in B.C.,* 🖷 *250/381–
5452,* WEB *www.bcferries.com.* 🖃 *One-way summer passage for a car
and driver $324; $106 for each adult passenger; $43–$65 for a day
cabin; $117 for an overnight cabin. Discounts available mid-Sept.–mid-
June.* ⊙ *Mid-May–mid-Oct. departing on alternate days from Port Hardy
and Prince Rupert at 7:30 AM, arriving 10:30 PM.*

Discovery Coast Passage

★ **⑮** *258 km (160 mi), or 138 nautical mi, between Port Hardy on north-*
         ern Vancouver Island and Bella Coola.

This BC Ferries summer-only service travels up the Inside Passage to
the First Nations community of Bella Bella and then turns up Dean
Channel to the mainland town of Bella Coola. The scenery is stunning,
and the route allows passengers to visit communities along the way,
including Namu, Shearwater, Klemtu, and Ocean Falls. It also provides
an alternative route into the Cariboo region, via Highway 20 from Bella
Coola to Williams Lake. Lodging at ports of call varies from luxury
fishing lodges to rough camping, but it is limited and must be booked
in advance.

The **Queen of Chilliwack,** carrying up to 389 passengers and 115 vehicles, takes from 17 to 33 hours (depending on the number of stops)
to travel from Port Hardy on Vancouver Island to Bella Coola. Reservations are required for vehicles and advised for foot passengers. There
aren't any cabins. ⊠ *BC Ferries, 1112 Fort St., Victoria, V8V 4V2,* ☎
*250/386–3431 in Victoria and outside B.C.; 888/223–3779 elsewhere
in B.C.,* 🖷 *250/381–5452,* WEB *www.bcferries.com.* 🖃 *One-way fares
between Port Hardy and Bella Coola $110 for passengers, $220 for
vehicles.* ⊙ *Mid-June–mid-Sept., departs Port Hardy on Tues., Thurs.,
and Sat.; leaves Bella Coola on Mon., Wed., and Fri.*

Prince Rupert

⑯ *1,502 km (931 mi) by highway and 750 km (465 mi) by air northwest
      of Vancouver, 15 hrs by ferry northwest of Port Hardy on Vancouver
      Island.*

The fishing and logging town of Prince Rupert is the largest community on the North Coast. It's the final stop on the BC Ferries route through

the Inside Passage, as well as the base for ferries to the Queen Charlotte Islands and a port of call for Alaska ferries. The terminal is about 2 km (1 mi) from town; in summer, a downtown shuttle bus meets each ferry. Prince Rupert is also the terminus for VIA Rail's Skeena line.

Cow Bay is a historic waterfront area a 10-minute walk from downtown and close to the Museum of Northern British Columbia. Originally the town's fishing hub, it's been revitalized with attractive shops, galleries, and restaurants. While here, you can stop in at Prince Rupert's Visitor Info Centre on Cow Bay Road.

The **Museum of Northern British Columbia,** in a longhouse-style facility overlooking the waterfront, has one of the province's finest collections of coastal First Nations art, with some artifacts that date back 10,000 years. Artisans work on totem poles in the carving shed, and in summer museum staff run walking tours of the town. The museum also operates the **Kwinista Railway Museum**, a five-minute walk away on the waterfront. ⊠ *100 1st Ave. W,* ☎ *250/624–3207,* WEB *www.museumofnorthernbc.com.* ⊠ *$5.* ☉ *Sept.–May, Mon.–Sat. 9–5; June–Aug., Mon.–Sat. 9–8, Sun. 9–5.*

The **North Pacific Historic Fishing Village** in Port Edward, 20 km (12 mi) south of Prince Rupert, is built on stilts where the Skeena River meets the sea and is home to the west coast's oldest salmon cannery. You can tour it and managers' houses, where interpretive displays about the canning process and village life are set up. In summer, be sure to catch the one-person play about the area's history. The old mess hall is now a café, and the former bunkhouse is now a waterfront inn. ⊠ *Off Hwy. 16, Port Edward,* ☎ *250/628–3538,* WEB *www.northpacific.org.* ⊠ *May–mid-Oct. village free, cannery building $7.50; mid-Oct.–May by donation.* ☉ *May–mid.-Oct., daily 9–8:30; mid-Oct.–May, daily 9–5.*

Dining and Lodging

$$ ✕🏨 **Crest Hotel.** Warm and modern, the Crest is close to the town's main shopping areas, but stands on a bluff overlooking the harbor. Many rooms have striking water views, and some have minibars and whirlpool baths. The restaurant ($$–$$$), pleasantly decorated with brass rails and beam ceilings, has a view of the waterfront and specializes in seafood, particularly salmon. You can also book cruises and fishing charters from here. ⊠ *222 1st Ave. W, V8J 1A8,* ☎ *250/624–6771 or 800/663–8150,* FAX *250/627–7666,* WEB *www.cresthotel.bc.ca. 101 rooms, 1 suite. Restaurant, coffee shop, lounge, in-room data ports, no-smoking floor, room service, outdoor hot tub, steam room, gym, fishing, baby-sitting, laundry service, business services, meeting rooms. AE, D, DC, MC, V.*

Outdoor Activities and Sports

Eco-Treks Adventures (⊠ 203 Cow Bay Rd., ☎ 250/624–8311, WEB www.citytel.net/ecotreks) has kayak rentals and kayaking, and Zodiac tours (one- and multiday) of nearby fjords and islands. Itineraries include trips to ancient petroglyphs and pictographs, visits to the edge of the nearby Khutzeymateen grizzly-bear sanctuary, and whale-watching excursions.

Shopping

The historic Cow Bay area on the waterfront has a number of interesting shops. Arts and crafts by local artists are for sale at **Studio 9** (⊠ 105–515 3rd Ave. W, ☎ 250/624–2366).

Queen Charlotte Islands (Haida Gwaii)

★ ⑰ *93 nautical mi southwest of Prince Rupert, 367 nautical mi northwest of Port Hardy.*

The Queen Charlotte Islands, or Haida Gwaii (Islands of the People), have been called the Canadian Galápagos. Their long isolation off the province's North Coast has given rise to subspecies of wildlife found nowhere else in the world. The islands are also the preserve of the Haida people, who make up half the population. Their vibrant culture is undergoing a renaissance, evident throughout the islands. For information about the ancient Haida villages, contact the **Haida Gwaii Watchmen** (⊠ Museum Rd., Skidegate, ☎ 250/559–8225).

Most of the islands' 6,000 permanent residents live on Graham Island—the northernmost and largest of the group of 150 islands—where 108 km (65 mi) of paved road connects the town of Queen Charlotte in the south to Masset in the north. Moresby Island, to the south, is the second-largest of the islands and is largely taken up by the Gwaii Haanas National Park Reserve, an ecological reserve with restricted access. The wildlife (including bears, eagles, and otters), old-growth forest, and stunning scenery make the islands a nature lover's delight, and kayaking enthusiasts from around the world are drawn to waterways here. The islands have most services, including banking, grocery stores, and a range of accommodation and campsites, though public transportation isn't available. It's a good idea to make hotel reservations before arriving.

The 1,470-square-km (570-square-mi) **Gwaii Haanas National Park Reserve/Haida Heritage Site,** managed jointly by the Canadian government and the Council of the Haida Nation, protects a vast tract of wilderness, unique flora and fauna, and many historic and cultural sites. These include the island of SGaang Gwaii (Anthony Island) a UNESCO World Heritage Site, where Nan Sdins is the world's only remaining traditional Northwest Coast First Nations village site. The reserve is on Moresby Island and numerous smaller islands at the archipelago's southern end. The protected area, accessible only by air or sea, is both ecologically and culturally sensitive. One way to visit—and highly recommended for those unfamiliar with wilderness travel—is with a licensed operator. Gwaii Haanas has a list. To visit on your own (without a licensed operator), you must make a reservation, register for each trip, and attend a mandatory orientation session. ⊠ *Parks Canada, Box 37, Queen Charlotte V0T 1S0,* ☎ *250/559–8818; 800/435–5622 for information pack and reservations,* ℻ *250/559–8366,* ⅦⅡⅢ *http://parkscan.harbour.com/gwaii.*

On the southern end of Graham Island, the **Haida Gwaii Museum** has an impressive display of totem poles, masks, and carvings of silver and argillite (hard black slate). A gift shop sells Haida art, and a natural-history exhibit gives interesting background on island wildlife. ⊠ *Off Hwy. 16, Skidegate,* ☎ *250/559–4643.* ⚓ *$5.* ☉ *June–Aug., weekdays 10–5, weekends 1–5; May and Sept., weekdays 10–noon and 1–5, Sat. 1–5; Oct.–Apr., Mon. and Wed.–Fri. 10–noon and 1–5, Sat. 1–5.*

Naikoon Provincial Park (☎ 250/557–4390), in the northeast corner of Graham Island, preserves dramatic sand dunes, pine and cedar forests, lakes, and wildlife. A 5-km (3-mi) walk leads from the Tlell Picnic Site to East Beach and onto the wreck of a 1928 logging vessel, the *Pesuta.* At the park's north end, a climb up 400-ft Tow Hill gives the best views of McIntyre Bay. A 20-km (12-mi) round-trip hike along the Fife Trail will take you from the Tow Hill parking lot to East Beach. The park also has two drive-in campgrounds.

Lodging

$–$$ 🏨 **Alaska View Lodge.** On a clear day, you can see the mountains of Alaska from the large front deck of this B&B, 13 km (8 mi) east of Masset. A 10-km-long (6-mi-long) sandy beach borders the lodge on one side, and there are woods on the other. Eagles are a familiar sight, and in winter you can often catch glimpses of the northern lights. There's also a golf course nearby. Every room in this no-smoking B&B has two queen beds. ✉ *12291 Tow Hill Rd., Box 227, Masset V0T 1M0,* ☎ *250/626–3333 or 800/661–0019,* FAX *250/626–3303,* WEB *www.alaskaviewlodge.com. 4 rooms, 2 with bath. Breakfast room, hiking, beach. MC, V. BP.*

$ 🏨 **Spruce Point Lodge.** This cedar-sided building, encircled by a balcony, is right on the beach, about 5½ km (3½ mi) from the ferry terminal at Skidegate. Like many other Queen Charlotte accommodations, it has pine furnishings and a rustic, down-home feel. The Continental breakfast is delivered to your room. Three rooms have kitchenettes. ✉ *609 6th Ave., Box 735, Queen Charlotte V0T 1S0,* ☎ FAX *250/559–8234,* WEB *www.qcislands.net/sprpoint. 7 rooms. Kitchenettes (some), boating, fishing. MC, V. CP.*

Outdoor Activities and Sports

Parks Canada, Gwaii Haanas (☎ 250/559–8818) has a list of tour companies licensed to operate in Gwaii Haanas.

Moresby Explorers (✉ 469 Alliford Bay Rd., Sandspit, ☎ 250/637–2215 or 800/806–7633, WEB www.moresbyexplorers.com) in Sandspit is a source for kayak rentals, kayak transport, and guided Zodiac tours.

Shopping

The Haida carve valuable figurines from argillite, a variety of hard black slate. Other island specialties are silk-screen prints and silver jewelry. A number of shops in Queen Charlotte City are on 3rd Avenue. In Old Massett, at the islands' north end, **Haida Arts and Jewelry** (✉ 387 Eagle Rd., ☎ 250/626–5560) specializes in local crafts, carvings and jewelry. The **Haida Gwaii Museum** (off Hwy. 16, Skidegate, ☎ 250/559–4643) has an excellent gift shop.

THE CARIBOO AND THE NORTH

This is British Columbia's wild west: a vast, thinly populated region stretching from the snow peaks and dense forests of the north to the rolling, arid ranching country of the south. The Cariboo covers an area roughly bordered by Bella Coola on the west, Lillooet in the south, Wells Gray Park on the east, and Prince George in the north. In the 19th century, thousands came here looking for—and finding—gold. Those times are remembered throughout the region, most vividly at the re-created gold-rush town of Barkerville. You can still pan for gold here, but these days most folks come for ranch getaways, horseback riding, fly-fishing, mountain biking, and cross-country skiing.

Terrace

⑱ *138 km (86 mi) east of Prince Rupert on Hwy. 16, 577 km (346 mi) northwest of Prince George, 1,355 km (813 mi) northwest of Vancouver.*

Traveling into the mountainous interior from Prince Rupert, both Highway 16 and the railway line follow the wide Skeena River. The route passes under snowcapped mountain peaks and by waterfalls. Terrace, the first hub en route, is a logging town and the major commercial center for the Skeena Valley. The region is also home to the

Kitsumkalum and Kitselas peoples. The Terrace Travel Info Centre on Keith Avenue has information about area attractions.

Ferry Island Municipal Park in the Skeena River on the east side of town, and accessed by bridges, has a campground, picnic sites, and hiking trails. **Heritage Park** (⊠ 4113 N. Sparks St., ☎ 250/635–4546) is a re-created turn-of-the-20th-century village, with costumed guides and many original buildings. It's open daily 10–6 May through August; admission is $3.

A 15-minute drive south of Terrace on Highway 37 is the hot-springs complex at **Mt. Layton Resort** (☎ 250/798–2214), which has a swimming pool, slides, and hot spring–fed pools. About 100 km (62 mi) north of Terrace, partly by gravel road, is the **Nisga'a Memorial Lava Bed Park** (☎ 250/798–2277), the site of Canada's most recent volcanic eruption (more than 250 years ago).

About 35 km (21 mi) northwest of Terrace, off Highway 16, is the ski resort at **Shames Mountain** (☎ 250/635–3773; 250/638–8754 for snow report; 877/898–4754, ⓦⒺⒷ www.shamesmountain.com). It has a vertical rise of 1,608 ft, a double chairlift, and 20 trails. The resort also lays claim to the most accumulated snow of any North American ski hill. Anglers flock to the **Skeena River** and its tributaries for some of the province's richest sportfishing (a 92-lb. king salmon, said to be a world-record catch, was caught just west of Terrace).

Hazelton

⑲ *293 km (182 mi) northeast of Prince Rupert, 439 km (272 mi) northwest of Prince George, 1,217 km (755 mi) northwest of Vancouver.*

Hazelton is rich in the culture of the Gitxsan and Wet'suwet'en peoples. ★ **'Ksan Historical Village and Museum,** about 7 km (4 mi) from New Hazelton, is a re-created Gitxsan village. The elaborately painted community of seven longhouses is a replica of the one that stood on the site for thousands of years before European contact. Visitors can watch Gitxsan artists at work in the carving shed, and take a guided tour through several of the longhouses. One has displays about traditional 'Ksan life; another exhibits performing regalia. Song and dance performances are held about once a week in summer (call for times). A restaurant has some traditional Gitxsan dishes on the menu, and a cinema shows documentaries about the area. ⊠ *Hwy. 62,* ☎ *250/842–5544 or 877/842–5518,* ⓦⒺⒷ *www.ksan.org.* 🎫 *$2; $10 with tour.* ☉ *Mid-Apr.–Sept. 30, daily 9–6 tours on the ½ hour; Oct.–mid-Apr. museum and gift shop, weekdays 9–5.*

OFF THE BEATEN PATH **FORT ST. JAMES NATIONAL HISTORIC PARK –** This park, 45 km (27 mi) north of Vanderhoof on Highway 27, on the south shore of Stuart Lake, is a former Hudson's Bay Company fur-trading post and the oldest continually inhabited European settlement west of the Rockies. Careful restoration of the original buildings, costumed staff, and demonstrations of aboriginal arts and food preparation help you experience life as a fur trader in 1896. ☎ *250/996–7191,* ⓦⒺⒷ *http://parkscanada.pch. gc.ca.* 🎫 *$4.* ☉ *Mid-May–Sept. 30, daily 9–5; off-season tours by advance reservation.*

Prince George

⑳ *440 mi (273 mi) southeast of Hazelton, 721 km (447 mi) east of Prince Rupert, 786 km (487 mi) north of Vancouver.*

At the crossroads of two railways and two highways, Prince George has become the capital of northern British Columbia and the province's third-largest city. In Ft. George Park, you can visit **The Exploration Place** to see the fine collection of artifacts illustrating local history; it includes a hands-on gallery for children and a virtual-reality theater. ⊠ *Ft. George Park, off 17th Ave.,* ☎ *250/562–1612,* WEB *www.theexplorationplace.com.* ⊡ *$7.95; $9.95 including theater.* ☉ *Daily 10–5.*

A collection of photos, rail cars, and logging and sawmill equipment at the **Prince George Railway and Forestry Museum** traces the history of the town and the region from the arrival of the railroad. ⊠ *850 River Rd., next to Cottonwood Park,* ☎ *250/563–7351,* WEB *www.pgrfm.bc.ca.* ⊡ *$4.50.* ☉ *May–Oct., daily 10–5.*

Lodging

$$ ⊞ **Coast Inn of the North.** This centrally located, nine-story, full-service hotel has a striking rosewood lobby with a brass fireplace. It connects to a retail concourse with a range of high-end shops. The standard rooms have two double beds, the premium rooms are corner units with balconies, and the suites have fireplaces and large balconies. ⊠ *770 Brunswick St., V2L 2C2,* ☎ *250/563–0121 or 800/663–1144,* FAX *250/563–1948,* WEB *www.coasthotels.com. 155 rooms, 2 suites. 2 restaurants, coffee shop, lounge, pub, air-conditioning, in-room data ports, no-smoking floor, indoor pool, hair salon, hot tub, sauna, gym, shops, meeting rooms, travel services. AE, DC, MC, V.*

Shopping

The **Prince George Native Art Gallery** (⊠ 1600 3rd Ave., ☎ 250/614–7726) sells traditional and contemporary works, including carvings, sculpture, jewelry, and literature.

Gold Rush Trail

㉑ *Begins at Prince George and ends at Lillooet, 170 km (105 mi) west of Kamloops, 131 km (81 mi) northeast of Whistler.*

From Prince George, Highway 97 heads south toward Kamloops and the Okanagan Valley, following the 640-km (397-mi) Gold Rush Trail, along which frontiersmen traveled in search of gold in the 19th and early 20th centuries. The trail goes through Quesnel, Williams Lake, Wells, Barkerville, Cache Creek, and along the Fraser Canyon. Many communities have historic sites that help tell the story of the gold-rush era. The Cariboo, Chilcotin, Coast Tourism Association has information about the trail.

★ The most vivid re-creation of the gold rush is at **Barkerville Historic Town,** 80 km (50 mi) east of Quesnel on Highway 26. Once the biggest town west of Chicago and north of San Francisco, it's now a provincial historic site with more than 120 restored and reconstructed buildings. Actors in period costume, merchants vending 19th-century goods, stagecoach rides, and live musical revues capture the town's heyday. It's open year-round, but most of the theatrical fun happens in summer. There are B&Bs in Barkerville and a campground nearby. ⊠ *Hwy. 26, Barkerville,* ☎ *250/994–3302,* WEB *www.heritage.gov.bc.ca/bark/bark.htm.* ⊡ *Mid-May–mid-June $5.50 for 2-day pass; mid-June–Sept. 9, $8 for 2-day pass; free in winter.* ☉ *Daily 8–8.*

Bowron Lake Provincial Park (⊠ end of Hwy. 26, ☎ 800/435–5622 for canoe trip reservations), 30 km (19 mi) east of Barkerville by gravel road, has a 116-km (72-mi) chain of rivers, lakes, and portages that make up a popular canoe route. Canoeists must reserve ahead and pay a fee of $50 per person.

Lodging

$$$$ 🖫 **Echo Valley Ranch Resort.** At the base of Mt. Bowman, 50 km (31 mi) northwest of Clinton, this adult-oriented ranch makes the most of its scenic setting. Included in the rates are a range of activities and three fine Continental meals using the ranch's own organic produce. You can indulge in spa and beauty treatments or hike, bike, fish, or ride. Tennessee Walker horses and experienced Cariboo cowboys take riders on day and overnight trips. White-water rafting, flightseeing, and staying at a First Nations teepee village can be arranged, too. Winter activities include snowshoeing, cross-country skiing, sleigh rides, and ice fishing. You can stay in comfortable lodge rooms, private cabins, the guest house, or the luxurious suite in the Baan Thai, a traditional Thai-style building that also houses the spa. A four-night minimum stay (2 nights in winter) is required at this no-smoking inn. ⊠ *Box 16, Jesmond V0K 1K0,* ☎ *250/459–2386 or 800/253–8831,* 𝖥𝖠𝖷 *250/459–0086,* 𝖶𝖤𝖡 *www.evranch.com. 15 rooms, 1 suite, 3 cabins, 1 2-bedroom house. Dining room, indoor pool, outdoor hot tub, sauna, spa, steam room, gym, hiking, horseback riding, shuffleboard, fishing, cross-country skiing, sleigh rides, billiards, recreation room, business services, meeting rooms, private airstrip. MC, V. FAP.*

$–$$ 🖫 **Wells Hotel.** The former mining town of Wells, 74 km (46 mi) east of Quesnel on Highway 26, is an atmospheric mountain village of brightly painted false-front buildings. Its Wild West ambience has changed little since the 1930s, but it now has a lively arts scene. The faithfully refurbished 1934 Wells Hotel makes a good base for visiting nearby Barkerville (8 km [5 mi] away) and the Bowron Lake canoeing area and for accessing the 80 km (50 mi) of hiking, biking, and cross-country ski trails nearby. The no-smoking hotel has a country inn ambience. Comfortable rooms and suites are decorated in a 1930s style with hardwood floors, local art, and period photos; in keeping with the historic theme, rooms don't have phones or TVs. The hotel can arrange pickups from Quesnel. ⊠ *2341 Pooley St., Box 39, Wells, V0K 2R0,* ☎ *250/994–3427 or 800/860–2299,* 𝖥𝖠𝖷 *250/994–3494,* 𝖶𝖤𝖡 *www.wellshotel.com. 16 rooms, 9 with bath. Restaurant, pub, hiking. AE, MC, V. CP.*

THE HIGH COUNTRY AND THE OKANAGAN VALLEY

South-central British Columbia (often simply called the "Interior" by Vancouverites) encompasses the high arid plateau between the Coast Mountains on the west and the Monashees on the east. The Okanagan Valley, five hours east of Vancouver by car, or one hour by air, contains the interior's largest concentration of people. The region's sandy lake beaches and hot, dry climate have long made it a family holiday magnet for Vancouverites and Albertans, and rooms and campsites can be hard to come by in summer.

The Okanagan Valley is also the fruit-growing capital of Canada and a major wine-producing area. Many of the region's more than 45 wineries are in scenic spots, and they welcome visitors with tastings, tours, and restaurants. The Wine Museum in Kelowna, and the British Columbia Wine Information Centre in Penticton can help you create a winery tour and can provide details about annual wine festivals.

Throughout the Okanagan you'll see depictions of a smiling green lizard that looks a bit like the Loch Ness Monster without the tartan cap. This is Ogopogo, a harmless, shy, and probably mythical creature said to live in Okanagan Lake.

Kamloops

㉒ *355 km (220 mi) northeast of Vancouver, 163 km (101 mi) northwest of Kelowna.*

Virtually all roads meet at Kamloops, the High Country's sprawling transport hub. From here, highways fan out to Vancouver, the Okanagan, the Cariboo, and Jasper in the Rockies. Kamloops is also the closest town to Sun Peaks, one of the province's leading ski resorts.

The **Kamloops Museum and Archives** has extensive and regularly changing displays about the area's human and natural history. ✉ *207 Seymour St.,* ☎ *250/828–3576,* WEB *www.city.kamloops.bc.ca/parks/index.html.* ⊡ *Free.* ☉ *Tues.–Sat. 9:30–4:30.*

You can see 70 species of local and endangered animals, including zebras, antelope, grizzly bears, and Siberian tigers, in natural settings at the **Kamloops Wildlife Park.** In summer, a miniature train runs around the property. ✉ *Hwy. 1, 15 km (9 mi) east of Kamloops,* ☎ *250/573–3242,* WEB *www.kamloopswildlife.com.* ⊡ *$6.75.* ☉ *Sept.–June, daily 8–4:30; July and Aug., daily 8 AM–9 PM.*

The **Secwepemc Museum and Heritage Park,** a reconstructed village on a traditional gathering site, interprets the culture and lifestyle of the Secwepemc (Shuswap) people, who have lived in this area for thousands of years. Displays in the 12-acre parklike setting include a replica winter pit-house village, a summer lodge, and ethnobotanical gardens showcasing plants used by the Secwepemc. There's also a wildlife marsh, and the museum holds recorded oral history, photographs, and artifacts. ✉ *202–355 Yellowhead Hwy. (Hwy. 5),* ☎ *250/828–9801,* WEB *www.secwepemc.org.* ⊡ *June–Labor Day $6; rest of yr. $5.* ☉ *June 1–Labor Day, weekdays 8:30–8, weekends 10–8; early Sept.–May 31, weekdays 8:30–4:30.*

OFF THE BEATEN PATH

WELLS GRAY PROVINCIAL PARK – This vast wilderness area has great canoeing, fishing, and hiking. About 120 km (74 mi) north of Kamloops on Highway 5 is Clearwater, the major access point to Wells Gray. There's a visitor info center at the junction of Highway 5 and the Clearwater Valley Road. ☎ *250/674–2646; 250/851–3000 to visitor center.*

Dining and Lodging

$–$$$ ✕ **Escapes.** Part of Kamloops's revitalized town center, this erstwhile warehouse is now a five-level restaurant and pub, with river-rock fireplaces, bay windows, and exposed ducts revealing its industrial roots. Each of the levels offers a different kind of venue, including a restaurant, cocktail lounge, and fireside pub, though a menu of full meals and pubs snacks—burgers, quesadillas, and pasta and chicken dishes—as well as microbrews and martinis, are available throughout. Children are welcome in the restaurant area. ✉ *357 Victoria St.,* ☎ *250/377–7700. AE, MC, V.*

$$ ⊞ **Plaza Heritage Hotel.** Built in 1927 as the province's premier hotel, this six-story Spanish mission–style structure in the heart of Kamloops has been restored to its original look; rooms have a period feel with reproduction pine and wicker furniture and 1930s fixtures. ✉ *405 Victoria St., V2C 2A9,* ☎ *250/377–8075 or 877/977–5292,* FAX *250/377–8076,* WEB *www.plazaheritagehotel.com. 66 rooms. Restaurant, lounge, wine shop, air-conditioning, in-room data ports, barbershop, billiards, nightclub, business services, meeting rooms. AE, MC, V.*

$ ✕⊞ **Quilchena Hotel & Resort.** Several movie stars and at least one outlaw have stayed at this three-story white-clapboard inn on the grounds of a large working cattle ranch, 75 km (45 mi) south of Kamloops. Built in 1908 in anticipation of a rail line that never materialized, the hotel has a Victoriana–meets–Wild West ambience, with 19th-century antiques, original woodwork, an elegant parlor, and a saloon with a lovingly preserved bullet hole behind the bar. In keeping with the period, there are no phones or TVs in the rooms. The Ladies' Parlour Room has a private sunporch; Jack's Room (where Jack Nicholson stayed while filming in the area) has views of the lake across the road. A two-bedroom, fully equipped ranch house is also available. The intimate nine-table restaurant ($$–$$$) is worth a trip for the Nicola Valley venison or the filet mignon. ⊠ *Hwy. 5A, Quilchena, 20 km (12 mi) north of Merritt, V0E 2R0,* ☎ *250/378–2611,* FAX *250/378–6091,* WEB *www.quilchena.com. 16 rooms, 5 with bath. Restaurant, coffee shop, pub, fans, lake, 9-hole golf course, tennis court, horseback riding, horseshoes, dock, boating, shop, billiards, piano, meeting rooms, private airstrip. AE, MC, V. Closed Nov.–Mar.*

Outdoor Activities and Sports

GOLF

Rivershore Golf Links (⊠ 330 Rivershore Dr., ☎ 250/573–4211) is an 18-hole, par-72 course designed by Robert Trent Jones Sr. It's about 20 km (12 mi) east of Kamloops on Highway 1. Greens fees are $56 on weekdays, $60 on weekends. There's a 9-hole course ($22 greens fee) at **Sun Peaks Resort** (⊠ 1280 Alpine Rd., Sun Peaks, ☎ 250/578–5484 or 800/807–3257, WEB www.sunpeaksresort.com).

SKIING

With a 2,891-ft vertical drop, 3,408 skiable acres on three mountains, lots of sunshine, powder snow, and a 2,500-ft-long snowboard park, **Sun Peaks Resort** (⊠ 1280 Alpine Rd., Sun Peaks, ☎ 250/578–5484 or 800/807–3257, WEB www.sunpeaksresort.com), 53 km (33 mi) north of Kamloops, is one of B.C.'s leading ski resorts. The compact Tyrolean-theme village has a number of ski-in, ski-out hotels, several restaurants, an ice rink, and a golf course. Ski facilities include 80 downhill runs (the longest is 8 km [5 mi]), five chairlifts, and 20 km (12 mi) of groomed and tracked cross-country trails. A lift ticket goes for about $46. This family-friendly resort also offers a ski school, day care, free mountain tours, snowshoeing, dogsledding, snowmobiling, and sleigh rides. In summer, chairlifts whisk hikers and mountain bikers up to wildflower-strewn meadows.

Salmon Arm

➋➌ *108 km (67 mi) east of Kamloops, 106 km (66 mi) north of Kelowna.*

Salmon Arm is the commercial center of the Shuswap (named for Shuswap Lake), a greener and less visited region than the Okanagan to the south. From Sicamous, 27 km (16 mi) northeast of Salmon Arm, you can take a summer (May to October) 2½–5 hour trip on Shuswap Lake on the **Phoebe Anne** (⊠ Box 9699, 117 Finlayson St., Sicamous, ☎ 250/836–2220), a mini–paddle wheeler. Departure times are 9:30, noon, and 5; prices start at $25.

R. J. Haney Heritage Park and Museum. This 40-acre open-air museum re-creates an early 20th-century North Okanagan village. Most of the buildings, which include a log gas station and a fire hall, a school (where a Miss Hellpenny teaches real kids in a 1914 style) and a manor house, are originals. A 3-km (2-mi) nature trail winds around the site. ⊠ *751 Hwy. 97B, off Hwy. 1, 5 km (3 mi) south of Salmon Arm,* ☎ *250/832–5243,* WEB *www.sjs.sd83.bc.ca.* ☽ *May 1–Sept. 30, daily 10–5.* ☒ *Site free; manor tours $2.*

Roderick Haig-Brown Provincial Park (⊠ off Hwy. 1 at Squilax, ☎ 250/851–3000) is where thousands of salmon come to spawn in the

Adams River in late September and October. The park is about 40 km (25 mi) northwest of Salmon Arm.

Dining and Lodging

$$ ✕⊡ **Quaaout Lodge Resort.** Owned by the Little Shuswap First Nations band, this modern three-story hotel, with its round, 40-ft-high lobby shaped like a traditional winter home, provides the chance to experience the culture of interior native peoples. Some of the large, well-appointed rooms have log furniture, gas fireplaces, and whirlpool baths for two under windows overlooking the lake. The restaurant ($$$–$$$$) serves such First Nations–influenced fare as rainbow trout stuffed with blueberries. On the grounds are a ceremonial sweat lodge and a reconstructed *kekuli*, or winter shelter, as well as a long sandy beach and trails through hundreds of forested acres. The hotel is 43 km (27 mi) northwest of Salmon Arm. ⊠ *Off Hwy. 1, Box 1215, Chase V0E 1M0,* ☎ *250/679–3090 or 800/663–4303,* FAX *250/679–3039,* WEB *www.quaaout.com. 72 rooms. Restaurant, indoor pool, hot tub, steam room, gym, jogging, dock, boating, bicycles, meeting rooms. AE, MC, V.*

Outdoor Activities and Sports

Sicamous on Shuswap Lake is a mecca for houseboat vacationers. **Three Buoys** (⊠ Box 709, 630 Riverside Ave., Sicamous, ☎ 250/836–2403 or 800/663–2333, WEB wwww.threebuoys.com) rents luxurious houseboats ($1,000 to $4,000 a week), many with hot tubs, that sleep 10 to 12. **Twin Anchors** (⊠ 101 Martin St., Box 318, Sicamous, ☎ 250/836–2450 or 800/663–4026, WEB www.twinanchors.com) has a range of fully equipped houseboats that can accommodate 8 to 22 people and rent for $1,000 to $6,000 per week; many have hot tubs.

Vernon

㉔ *117 km (73 mi) southeast of Kamloops.*

Because Vernon has no public access to Okanagan Lake, it's less of a draw than other towns in the area. Nearby are two other lakes and the all-season, gaslight era–theme village resort atop Silver Star Mountain.

The 50-acre **Historic O'Keefe Ranch** provides a window on 19th-century cattle-ranch life. Among the many original and restored ranch buildings are the O'Keefe mansion, a church, and a general store. There's also a restaurant and a gift shop on site. ⊠ *9380 Hwy. 97, 12 km (8 mi) north of Vernon,* ☎ *250/542–7868,* WEB *www.okeeferanch.bc.ca.* ⊡ *$6.50.* ☉ *May 1–mid-Oct., daily 9–5; tours by appointment rest of yr.*

Kalamalka Lake Provincial Park (⊠ Kidston Rd., ☎ 250/494–6500) has warm-water beaches and some of the most scenic viewpoints and hiking trails in the region.

Outdoor Activities and Sports

GOLF

Predator Ridge Golf Resort (⊠ 301 Village Centre Pl., ☎ 250/542–3436 or 888/578–6688) is a 27-hole facility, with a 36 par on each nine. Greens fees for 18 holes are $115 with a cart, $95 without a cart. It's about 15 km (9 mi) south of Vernon on Highway 97.

SKIING

Silver Star Mountain Resort (⊠ Silver Star Rd., Silver Star Mountain, ☎ 250/542–0224; 800/663–4431 reservations), 22 km (13 mi) east of Vernon, has five chairlifts and two T-bars, a vertical drop of 2,500 ft, 85 runs, and night skiing. A one-day lift ticket is $49. The resort also has 35 km (22 mi) of groomed, track-set cross-country trails, as well as hiking and mountain-biking trails open in summer. The resort's Victorian-style village has several hotels, restaurants, and shops, many of which are open all year.

Kelowna

②⑤ *46 km (29 mi) south of Vernon, 68 km (42 mi) north of Penticton.*

The largest town in the Okanagan Valley, Kelowna (pop. 97,000), on the edge of Okanagan Lake, makes a good base for exploring the region's beaches, ski hills, wineries, and golf courses. Although its edges are looking untidily urban these days, the town still has an attractive, walkable core and a restful beachside park. It's also at the heart of British Columbia's wine and fruit-growing district.

The **Wine Museum** (✉ 1304 Ellis St., ☎ 250/868–0441) set in a historic packinghouse, has wine-making exhibits, as well as a wine shop, and information about touring local wineries. Admission is by donation; the museum is open Monday through Saturday 10–5, Sunday noon–5. The **British Columbia Orchard Museum** (✉ 1304 Ellis St., ☎ 250/763–0433), in the same building as the Wine Museum, has displays about the area's other critical industry.

On the **Okanagan Valley Wine Train** (✉ 600 Recreation Ave., ☎ 250/712–9888 or 888/674–8725), you can take a five-hour trip to Vernon along Kalamalka Lake and taste wines on board. The 1950s vintage train runs Friday through Sunday between late June and mid-October. The trip alone is $50; with dinner and entertainment, it's $92.

The **Father Pandosy Mission** (✉ 3685 Benvoulin Rd., ☎ 250/860–8369), the first European settlement in central British Columbia, was founded here by Oblate missionaries in 1859. The 4-acre site has three original mission buildings made of logs (including a tiny chapel) as well as a farmhouse and settler's cabin. The buildings, furnished to look as they did in the late 19th century, are open for viewing (Easter to mid-October, daily 8–8; as weather permits during the rest of the year). Admission is $2.

The **Kelowna Art Gallery** (✉ 1315 Water St., ☎ 250/762–2226) is an elegant public art gallery with a variety of local and international exhibits. It's open Tuesday through Saturday 10–5, Thursday until 9, and Sunday 1–4.

For many Canadians, the Okanagan means apples, and much of the valley is still covered with orchards. One of the largest and oldest (it dates from 1904) is the **Kelowna Land & Orchard Company,** which you can tour on foot or in a tractor-drawn hay wagon. The farm animals are a hit with kids; a tea house serves lunch, dinner, and snacks on a patio with a lake view. ✉ *3002 Dunster Rd. (8 km [5 mi] east of Kelowna),* ☎ *250/763–1091.* ☜ *$5.25.* ☉ *Tours May–June and Sept.–Oct., daily at 11, 1 and 3; July–Aug., daily at 11, 1, 3 and 6:30. Tea house daily 8–8.*

WINERIES

Almost all of the region's wineries offer tastings and tours throughout the summer and during the Okanagan Wine Festivals held in April and October; several have restaurants and most also have wine shops open year-round. The Wine Museum can help you create a winery tour and can provide details about annual wine festivals. Several local operators will act as guides and designated drivers.

The province's oldest winery, and still one of the largest, **Calona Vineyards** (✉ 1125 Richter St., ☎ 250/762–9144 or 888/246–4472) is in central Kelowna. It's within walking distance from most hotels, and offers tours ($5) and tastings (prices vary). Call for tour times.

Cedar Creek Estate Winery (⊠ 5445 Lakeshore Rd., ☎ 250/764–8866 or 800/730–9463), south of Kelowna, has a scenic lakeside location with picnic areas. Free tours are given daily mid-May to mid-October; call for times.

Atop a hill overlooking Okanagan Lake, **Mission Hill Family Estate** was rebuilt in 2000 to look, as the owner describes it, like "a combination of monastery, Tuscan hill village, and French winery," complete with a vaulted cellar blasted from volcanic rock and a 12-story bell tower. Tours—vineyard, cellar, or landscape and architecture—include a video presentation and tastings (prices vary). Snacks and wine by the glass are served on the terrace, which overlooks the vineyard and lake, and an outdoor amphitheater hosts music and theater events on summer evenings. ⊠ *1730 Mission Hill Rd., Westbank, ☎ 250/768–7611 or 800/957–9911. ☎ Tours $10–$15. ۞ July–Aug., daily 9–7, tours 10–5; Sept.–June, open daily, call for tour times.*

Quails' Gate Estate Winery (⊠ 3303 Boucherie Rd., ☎ 250/769–4451 or 800/420–9463), on the edge of Okanagan Lake, gives tours ($5) daily from late April to the middle of October. It has a wine shop in a 19th-century log home and a patio restaurant (open for lunch and dinner late April to mid-October) with views of the vineyard and lake.

Summerhill Estate Winery (⊠ 4870 Chute Lake Rd., ☎ 250/764–8000 or 800/667–3538), south of Kelowna on the east side of the lake, is an organic producer best known for its sparkling and ice wines. What tends to startle visitors, though, is the four-story-high replica of the Great Pyramid at Cheops; it's used to age and store the wine. There's also a wine shop, a restaurant with a veranda overlooking Okanagan Lake (lunch is served daily), a preserved settler's cabin, and a re-created First Nations earth house. Tours are free, as are tastings; call for times.

Dining and Lodging

$$$ ✕ **de Montreuil Restaurant.** This cozy downtown restaurant makes the most of the regional bounty, serving dishes such as duck breast with coronation grape and roast shallot confit, and rack of lamb with rosemary, garlic, and mint, which the owners (two local brothers) have dubbed Cascadian cuisine. The menu, priced by the number of courses rather than by the dish, encourages experimentation; the warm yellow decor encourages lingering. ⊠ *368 Bernard Ave., ☎ 250/860–5508. AE, DC, MC, V. No lunch weekends and May–Sept.*

$$–$$$ ✕ **Guisachan House Restaurant.** Once the summer home of Lord Aberdeen, a former governor general of Canada, this 1891 house on 2½ garden acres is now an attractive restaurant. White cane chairs, pink tablecloths, period furniture, and seating on the glassed-in veranda re-create a Victorian summertime ambience. Chef Georg Rieder, originally from Germany, offers a lengthy menu that features several varieties of schnitzel, risottos, pastas, and seafood, as well as bison, local venison, and such Asian-influenced dishes as Szechuan pork tenderloin. A four-course lunch for less than $9 is an especially good value. ⊠ *1060 Cameron Ave., ☎ 250/862–9368. AE, DC, MC, V. No dinner Mon.–Wed.*

$$$ ✕🏨 **Manteo Resort Waterfront Hotel & Villas.** With a marina, a swimming beach, and a boardwalk, this resort makes the most of its location on the shore of Okanagan Lake. Accommodation choices include rooms and suites (some with kitchenettes, all with balconies) in the Tuscan-style main building and two- and three-bedroom villas with full kitchens. The villas are especially attractive, with gas fireplaces, terracotta tiles, high ceilings, and patios. The restaurant, the Wild Apple

Grill ($–$$$), serves Pacific Northwest cuisine inside and on its big lakeside patio. Smoking isn't allowed throughout the hotel and the villas. ⊠ *3766 Lakeshore Rd., V1W 3L4,* ☎ *250/860–1031 or 800/445–5255,* FAX *250/860–1041,* WEB *www.manteo.com. 48 rooms, 30 suites, 24 villas. Restaurant, lounge, air-conditioning, in-room data ports, kitchenettes (some), room service, 1 indoor and 2 outdoor pools, indoor and outdoor hot tub, massage, sauna, steam room, putting green, tennis court, gym, beach, water park, boating, marina, parasailing, waterskiing, billiards, cinema, baby-sitting, children's programs, playground, dry cleaning, laundry service, concierge, business services, meeting rooms. AE, DC, MC, V.*

$$$–$$$$ 🏨 **Grand Okanagan Lakefront Resort and Conference Centre.** On the shore of Okanagan Lake, this resort is a five-minute stroll from downtown Kelowna, though you may never have to leave the grounds because of all the amenities, including an Internet café, a waterfront park, and so much more. Most standard rooms and suites are spacious, with balconies, sitting areas, and attractive modern decor (the north tower is newer than the south tower). About half the rooms have views over the lake and the surrounding hills. The two-bedroom waterfront condo suites are a good option for families: they have two full baths, full kitchens, washer–dryers, gas fireplaces, and whirlpool baths. ⊠ *1310 Water St., V1Y 9P3,* ☎ *250/763–4500 or 800/465–4651,* FAX *250/763–4565,* WEB *www.grandokanagan.com. 255 rooms, 75 suites. 4 restaurants, café, lounge, pub, air-conditioning, in-room data ports, no-smoking floor, room service, indoor-outdoor pool, hair salon, indoor and outdoor hot tub, sauna, spa, health club, dock, boating, mountain bikes, casino, baby-sitting, laundry service, concierge, business services, convention center, travel services. AE, D, DC, MC, V.*

$$$ 🏨 **Lake Okanagan Resort.** This self-contained, kid-friendly resort 16 km (10 mi) from Kelowna spreads across a 300-acre hill on the undeveloped west side of Okanagan Lake. The attractive modern units, decorated with rich colors and pine furniture, range from one-bedroom suites in the main hotel to three-bedroom chalets. All have lake views and kitchens or kitchenettes, and most have balconies or decks. Activities are plentiful, and a resort shuttle scoots you up and down the hillside. ⊠ *2751 Westside Rd., V1Z 3T1,* ☎ *250/769–3511 or 800/663–3273,* FAX *250/769–6665,* WEB *www.lakeokanagan.com. 92 suites, 16 chalets. Restaurant, bar, café, air-conditioning, kitchenettes, 2 pools, indoor and outdoor hot tub, massage, sauna, 9-hole golf course, 7 tennis courts, gym, hiking, horseback riding, beach, dock, boating, jet skiing, waterskiing, video games, children's programs, playground, coin laundry, meeting rooms, helipad. AE, DC, MC, V.*

Outdoor Activities and Sports

BIKING AND HIKING

Bikers and hikers can try the rail bed of the **Kettle Valley Railway** (☎ 250/861–1515 to visitors bureau) between Penticton and Kelowna. The visitors bureau in Kelowna can provide maps and information.

GOLF

Gallagher's Canyon Golf and Country Club (⊠ 4320 Gallagher's Dr. W, ☎ 250/861–4240 or 800/446–5322), about 15 km (9 mi) southeast of Kelowna, has an 18-hole, par-72 course and a 9-hole, par-32 course; greens fees for the 18-hole course are $80 in high season. Surrounded by orchards (golfers can pick fruit as they play), **Harvest Golf Club** (⊠ 2725 KLO Rd., ☎ 250/862–3103 or 800/257–8577) has 18 holes and is a par-72 course. Greens fees in high season are $85. The Harvest Dining Room, in the clubhouse, has lake views and is open to nongolfers for dinner. The **Okanagan Golf Club** (⊠ 3200 Via Centrale, ☎ 250/765–5955 or 800/446–5322) has two 18-hole, par-72 courses with Okanagan Valley views. The Quail Course is a challenging hillside course with tight tree-lined fairways; the newer Jack Nicklaus Group–designed Bear Course is more forgiving. High-season greens fees are $85 for either course.

SKIING

One of B.C.'s leading ski destinations, **Big White Ski Resort** (✉ Big White Rd., off Hwy. 33 about 1 hr southeast of Kelowna, ☎ 250/765–8888 or 800/663–2772; 250/765–7669 for snow reports, WEB www.big-white.com) is an affordable, family-oriented resort with excellent daycare and children's programs; a ski school; a good mix of more than 100 runs; and up-to-date lift equipment that includes 13 lifts, a gondola, and four high-speed quad chairs. Snow hosts take you out on the mountain for a half day at no charge. A one-day lift ticket is $49. You can ski or walk anywhere in the compact village, which has several restaurants and a total of 10,000 beds in hotels, condos, B&Bs, and hostels. There are 2,165 acres of skiable terrain, a vertical drop of 2,550 ft, average annual snowfall of more than 24 ft, and night skiing five times a week. You'll also find three snowboard parks and 25 km (15 mi) of cross-country trails, as well as snowmobiling, snowshoeing, ice-skating, horse-drawn sleigh rides, Canada's largest snow-tubing park, and even dogsledding.

Summerland and Peachland

㉖ *Summerland 52 km (31 mi) south of Kelowna, Peachland 25 km (15 mi) southwest of Kelowna.*

Between Kelowna and Penticton, Highway 97 winds along the west side of Okanagan Lake, past vineyards, orchards, fruit stands, small resorts, and some of the region's prettiest lake and hill scenery. In Summerland, you can ride the historic **Kettle Valley Steam Railway** (✉ 18404 Bathville Rd., 7 km [4 mi] off Hwy. 97, ☎ 250/494–8422 or 877/494–8424, WEB www.kettlevalleyrail.org), which has trips along 10 km (6 mi) of a 1915 rail line between mid-May and mid-October for $14.

WINERIES

Hainle Vineyards Estate Winery (✉ 5355 Trepanier Bench Rd., Peachland, ☎ 250/767–2525, WEB www.hainle.com), British Columbia's first organic winery and also the first to make ice wines, is a small producer open for tastings (though not tours). The Amphora Bistro ($) has lake views and dishes that incorporate seasonal and organic ingredients. The bistro is open for lunch Thursday through Sunday from late May to mid-October.

Free tours are given daily from May until mid-October at **Sumac Ridge Estate Winery** (✉ 17403 Hwy. 97 N, Summerland, ☎ 250/494–0451, WEB www.sumacridge.com), but you can taste or buy wines here all year. The Cellar Door Bistro ($$–$$$) serves lunches and dinners on a big outdoor deck.

Penticton

㉗ *16 km (10 mi) south of Summerland, 395 km (245 mi) east of Vancouver.*

Penticton, with its long sandy beach backed by motels and cruising pickup trucks, is a nostalgia-inducing family-vacation spot. A growing city extends to the south, but the arid hills around town are full of orchards, vineyards, and small farms. The **SS Sicamous** (✉ 1099 Lakeshore Dr. W, ☎ 250/492–0403), a paddle wheeler moored at the lakeside, is now a museum. It's open April through June and September through December daily 9–6; July and August, daily 9–9. Admission is $4.

The **British Columbia Wine Information Centre** (✉ 888 Westminster Ave. W, ☎ 250/490–2006) will help you plan a self-drive winery tour and can provide details about annual wine festivals, held in spring and fall. It also stocks more than 300 local wines.

WINERY

The **Lake Breeze Vineyards** (✉ 930 Sammet Rd., Naramata, ☎ 250/496–5659) is one of the region's most attractively located wineries. Tours are given May–October daily and by appointment the rest of the year. The **Patio Restaurant** ($$) is open daily for lunch July through September; mid-April through June it's open for lunch Wednesday through Sunday.

Dining and Lodging

$$$$ ✕ **Country Squire.** Plan to spend the evening if you book a meal at this rambling country house in Naramata, 10 km (6 mi) north of Penticton. Diners are asked to choose one of seven or eight main courses when they reserve their table; the chef then designs a five-course meal around it. The options change each evening but have included various treatments of sea bass, duck breast, ostrich, venison, and rack of lamb. There's only one sitting per evening, so lingering over the meal—even taking a stroll along the lake between courses—is very much the thing to do. The wine cellar has hundreds of local and imported labels. ✉ *3950 First St., Naramata,* ☎ *250/496–5416. Reservations essential. MC, V. No lunch. No dinner Mon.–Wed.*

$$–$$$$ ✕ **Historic 1912 Restaurant.** This greenery-draped lakeside restaurant in Kaleden (14 km [8½ mi] south of Penticton) was once the village general store. It still has its original 1912 blue-tin ceiling and hardwood floors, but it's now stocked with 20th-century memorabilia in themed dining areas: there's a *Titanic* corner, a '50s-kitchen corner, and a whole wall filled with the owner's historic record collection. You can also dine in the gardens or the lakeview conservatory. The Pacific Northwest menu changes frequently but has included such entrées as rack of lamb rubbed with rosemary, thyme, and Dijon mustard, and such desserts as chocolate paté with fresh-fruit coulis. The cellar has a large selection of B.C. wines. There's a lakeside B&B room if you want to spend the night, or the restaurant's free shuttle can whisk you to and from Penticton. ✉ *100 Alder Ave. Kaleden,* ☎ *250/497–6868 or 888/633–1912. Reservations essential. AE, MC, V. No lunch. Closed Jan.*

$$$ ▦ **Penticton Lakeside Resort, Convention Centre and Casino.** On the shore of Okanagan Lake, this modern resort is within walking distance of Penticton's beachfront and town center. It has an elegant Italianate lobby and spacious rooms with modern decor, large balconies, and lake or mountain views. The facilities include a health club, a casino, a private beach, and a lakeside café. Magnum's restaurant ($$–$$$) offers Pacific Northwest cuisine and lakeside seating. ✉ *21 Lakeshore Dr. W, V2A 7M5,* ☎ *250/493–8221 or 800/663–9400,* 𝔽𝔸𝕏 *250/493–0607,* 𝕎𝔼𝔹 *www.rpbhotels.com. 197 rooms, 7 suites. Restaurant, bar, in-room data ports, no-smoking floor, room service, indoor pool, hair salon, hot tub, aerobics, health club, beach, dock, shop, casino, baby-sitting, children's programs, dry cleaning, concierge, convention center. AE, D, DC, MC, V.*

$–$$ ▦ **God's Mountain Crest Chalet.** This Mediterranean-style villa sits on 115 acres of empty, arid hilltop overlooking Skaha Lake, 4 km (2½ mi) south of Penticton. The three common rooms are filled with plush cushions and couches, as well as European antiques and theatrical props. The broad patio, poolside bar and gazebo, rooftop hot tub, and several of the guest suites have expansive lake views. Each room or suite has its own veranda or balcony. There's also an elaborate two-story penthouse suite and a two-bedroom cabin in the vineyard. A lavish hot breakfast is included in the rates. ⊠ *4898 Lakeside Rd., V2A 8W4,* ☎ FAX *250/490–4800,* WEB *www.godsmountain.com. 4 rooms, 3 suites, 1 cottage. Dining room, pool, outdoor hot tub, hiking, shop, meeting rooms, helipad. MC, V. BP. Closed Nov.–Feb.*

Outdoor Activities and Sports

For downhill skiing, **Apex Mountain Resort** (⊠ Apex Mountain Rd. off Green Mountain Rd., ☎ 250/292–8222 or 877/777–2739, WEB www.apexresort.com) has 60 trails, two chairlifts, a vertical drop of 2,000 ft, and a peak elevation of 7,187 ft. The resort, known for its intimate ambience and soft powder snow, also has night skiing as well as cross-country trails, a snow-tube park, an outdoor ice rink, a skating trail through the forest, and snowmobile tours. Apex is 32 km (19 mi) northwest of Penticton. A one-day lift ticket is $44. The resort village has a full-service hotel, cabins, condos, restaurants, bars, shops, ski rentals, a ski school, and children's programs.

Osoyoos

㉘ *58 km (36 mi) south of Penticton.*

South of Penticton between the southern tip of Lake Okanagan and the U.S. border, Highway 97 runs along a chain of lakes: Skaha, Vaseaux, and Osoyoos, and through Canada's only desert. The hot, dry climate also makes this a prime wine-producing area; several wineries offer tours and tastings. For information on wine tours and tastings around B.C., contact the **British Columbia Wine Information Centre** (⊠ 888 Westminster Ave. W, ☎ 250/490–2006) in Penticton. Accommodation is available in Osoyoos and other towns in the region.

The northern tip of the Sonoran Desert is home to flora and fauna found nowhere else in the country. You can learn more about the unique local ecology at the **Desert Centre.** There are also guided tours along a boardwalk desert trail. ⊠ *Road 146, off Hwy. 97, 4 km (3 mi) north of Osoyoos,* ☎ *250/495–2470 or 877/899–0897,* WEB *www.desert.org.* ⊒ *$5 (including tour).* ☉ *July–Aug., daily 9–7; Sept.–June, daily 9–6.*

THE KOOTENAYS

Tucked between Highways 1 and 3, along which most travelers rush to and from the Rockies, the Kootenays are an idyllic backwater of mountains, lakes, natural hot springs, ghost towns, and preserved Victorian villages. Kootenay Lake and Lower Arrow Lake define the region. A century ago this area was booming because of the discovery of silver in the hills, and with the prospectors came vestiges of European society: stately homes, an elegant paddle wheeler, and the town of Nelson—built in respectable Victorian brick. These days the Kootenays are filled with fine restaurants, historic country inns, and a wealth of opportunities for outdoor activities amid fantastic scenery.

Nelson

★ **㉙** *321 km (199 mi) east of Penticton, 657 km (407 mi) east of Vancouver.*

Bypassed a little by history, this city of 10,000, with its Victorian architecture, lake and mountain setting, and college-town ambience, is one of British Columbia's most attractive towns. Nelson has a wealth of crafts shops and coffee bars, several B&Bs, a youth hostel, and a restored 1906 streetcar running along the lakeshore. The visitor info center offers self-guided walking or driving tours of many of the town's 355 historic buildings.

About 45 km (30 mi) north of Nelson is **Ainsworth Hot Springs Resort** (⊠ Hwy. 31, Ainsworth Hot Springs, ☎ 250/229–4212 or 800/668–1171), where you can stroll through a network of caves and plunge into hot and cold spring-fed pools.

On the west side of Kootenay Lake, heading north from Nelson on Highway 31, is the pretty village of **Kaslo.** An 1898 stern-wheeler, the SS *Moyie* (☎ 250/353–2525), is moored on the lakeshore, its interior restored to *Titanic*-era opulence. It's open daily mid-May to mid-October. Admission is $5.

If you head west from Kaslo on scenic, winding Highway 31A, you'll pass a number of 19th-century silver-mining towns. Most were abandoned when the ore ran out, but **Sandon,** off Highway 31A, is enjoying a resurgence as a historic site, with several shops and a visitor center. It's also home to Canada's oldest operating power plant; some of the equipment dates to 1890s. **Silversmith Tours** (⊠ Powerhouse Rd., ☎ 250/358–2247, WEB www.sandonbc.com) gives tours of the town and the power plant daily in summer and by appointment off-season.

Dining and Lodging

$–$$$ ✕ **All Seasons Cafe.** Tucked into an alley between Baker and Victoria
★   streets, this former family cottage serves innovative cuisine that its owners have dubbed (because people kept asking) Left Coast Inland Cuisine. In practice, this means a seasonally changing menu that uses fresh, local, often organic produce and lists lots of vegetarian creations. Among the good choices are pan-roasted B.C. halibut with bronze fennel and lemon buerre blanc; and venison sausage, wild mushrooms, and roasted red peppers on penne pasta. The passion fruit and ricotta cheesecake is a popular dessert. ⊠ *620 Herridge La.,* ☎ *250/352–0101. MC, V. No lunch.*

$–$$$ ✕ **Fiddler's Green.** Imaginative Northwest cuisine featuring local organic produce and an exclusively B.C. wine list is featured in this ivy-covered 1920s country house, about 10 km (6 mi) north of Nelson. Dinner is served in the main dining room, in any of three smaller rooms (two have fireplaces), or in the garden. Highlights on the seasonally changing menu have included seafood ravioli, rack of lamb, and rhubarb raspberry strudel with homemade ginger ice cream. ⊠ *2710 Lower Six Mile Rd.,* ☎ *250/825–4466. MC, V. No lunch Mon.– Sat. Closed some evenings in winter.*

$–$$ ▥ **Inn the Garden B&B.** This 1900 painted lady one block from Nelson's restaurants and shopping is adorned with plants, wicker, and antiques. You can relax in the sitting room or on the front porch or the back deck, and a full hot breakfast (the inn caters to special diets if necessary) is included in this no-smoking inn's rates. A two-bedroom suite has a kitchenette and private entrance. The three-bedroom guest house next door, with a full kitchen and private backyard, is a good choice for families. ⊠ *408 Victoria St., V1L 4K5,* ☎ *250/352–3226 or 800/596–2337,* FAX *250/352–3284,* WEB *www.innthegarden.com. 5 rooms, 3 with bath, 1 suite, 1 guest house. Breakfast room, fans. AE, MC, V. BP.*

$–$$ ▥ **Willow Point Lodge.** About 6 km (4 mi) north of Nelson, this three-
★   story 1920 country inn with a broad, covered veranda, is perched on 3½ acres of forested hillside. Three rooms have expansive views of Kootenay Lake and the Selkirk Mountains; the others overlook an extensive garden. A favorite is the Oak Room, with its big stone fireplace, red-velvet bed canopy, and a private entrance. One room has a detached bath. A lavish breakfast is included in the rate, and trails lead from

the property to waterfalls nearby. ⊠ *2211 Taylor Dr. (R.R. 1, S-21, C-31), V1L 5P4,* ☎ *250/825–9411 or 800/949–2211,* FAX *250/825–3432,* WEB *www.pixsell.bc.ca/bb4193.htm. 6 rooms. Breakfast room, outdoor hot tub, hiking. MC, V. BP.*

Outdoor Activities and Sports

HIKING

Kokanee Creek Provincial Park (⊠ north of Nelson, off Hwy. 3A, ☎ 250/422–4200) has lake swimming, walking trails, picnic sites, drive-in camping, and nearby boat rentals. **Kokanee Glacier Provincial Park** (⊠ north of Nelson off Hwy. 3A, ☎ 250/422–4200) is a backcountry park with hike-in campsites and extensive trail networks.

SKIING

Red Mountain Resorts (⊠ 1000 Red Mountain Rd., Rossland, ☎ 250/362–7384 or 800/663–0105, WEB www.ski-red.com), about an hour southwest of Nelson, spans two mountains and three mountain faces, and has 83 marked runs, five lifts, and a vertical drop of 2,900 ft as well as cross-country ski trails. Accommodations, ski rental, and ski lessons are also available. A one-day lift ticket is $43. **Whitewater Ski and Winter Resort** (⊠ Whitewater Ski Rd., off Hwy. 6, ☎ 250/354–4944 or 800/666–9420, WEB www.skiwhitewater.com), about 10 km (6 mi) south of Nelson, has 43 runs, three lifts, a 1,300-ft vertical drop, and plenty of powder skiing. Ski rentals and lessons are available, though the resort doesn't offer lodging. A one-day lift pass goes for $37.

Crawford Bay

㉚ *40 km (25 mi) northeast of Nelson, including ferry ride.*

This peaceful backwater has pastoral scenery framed by snowcapped mountains. It's home to several artisans, including an ironworker and a glassblower, whose workshops are open to the public. On the east side of Kootenay Lake, Crawford Bay can be accessed by a scenic, 45 minute free car ferry from Balfour, north of Nelson. By car, it's off Highway 3 on Route 3A.

Lodging

$–$$
★ **Wedgwood Manor.** Built for the daughter of the famous china magnate, this 1909 country manor with a wide veranda has Edwardian beauty. Rooms are elegant: two have whirlpool baths, and several have canopy beds and fine, original woodwork. Much of the 50-acre estate is forested, walking trails lead through the woods, and the Purcell Mountains form a striking backdrop to croquet games on the lawn. ⊠ *16002 Crawford Creek Rd., Box 135, V0B 1E0,* ☎ FAX *250/227–9233 or 800/862–0022,* WEB *www.bctravel.net/wedgwood. 6 rooms. Breakfast room, badminton, croquet, hiking. MC, V. BP. Closed mid-Oct.–Easter.*

Outdoor Activities and Sports

The 18-hole, par-72 **Kokanee Springs Golf Resort** (⊠ 16082 Woolgar Rd., ☎ 250/227–9226 or 800/979–7999) has views of Kokanee Glacier, accommodations, and a restaurant. Greens fees are $49 on weekdays and $52 on weekends.

BRITISH COLUMBIA A TO Z

To research prices, get advice from other travelers, and book travel arrangements, visit www.fodors.com.

AIR TRAVEL

Air Canada is the dominant carrier. Kenmore Air Harbour has summer floatplane service from Seattle to Pender Harbour and Desolation

Sound. Northwest Seaplanes offers summer floatplane service between Seattle and fishing lodges in the Inside Passage.

Air B.C. (operated by Air Canada) and WestJet serve towns around the province.

Harbour Air Ltd. provides regular service from Victoria, Nanaimo, and Vancouver to Salt Spring, Thetis, Mayne, Saturna, Galiano, and South Pender islands. Pacific Spirit/Tofino Air has scheduled floatplane service from Vancouver International Airport to all southern Gulf Islands. Harbour Air Seaplanes runs scheduled floatplanes between Sandspit, Masset, Queen Charlotte City, and Prince Rupert year-round. It also offers seaplane tours.

➤ AIRLINES AND CONTACTS: **Air Canada** (☎ 888/247–2262). **Harbour Air Ltd.** (☎ 604/688–1277 in Vancouver; 250/385–2203 in Victoria; 800/665–0212 from elsewhere). **Harbour Air Seaplanes** (☎ 250/627–1341 or 800/689–4234, WEB www.harbourair.com). **Kenmore Air Harbour** (☎ 425/486–1257 or 800/543–9595, WEB www.kenmoreair.com). **Northwest Seaplanes** (☎ 800/690–0086, WEB www.nwseaplanes.com). **Pacific Spirit/Tofino Air** (☎ 800/665–2359, WEB www.tofinoair.ca).

AIRPORTS

British Columbia is served by Vancouver International Airport. There are domestic airports in most cities.
➤ AIRPORT INFORMATION: **Vancouver International Airport** (☎ 604/207–7077).

AIRPORT TRANSFERS

LimoJet Gold runs a limousine service from Vancouver Airport to Whistler. Perimeter Whistler Express has daily service from Vancouver International Airport to Whistler (14 times a day in ski season, with slightly fewer trips in the summer). Perimeter has a ticket booth at domestic arrivals Level 2 and one at the airport's international receiving lounge. The fare is around $53 one way; reservations are highly recommended.
➤ TAXIS AND SHUTTLES: **LimoJet Gold** (☎ 604/273–1331 or 800/278–8742, WEB www.limojetgold.com). **Perimeter Whistler Express** (☎ 604/266–5386 in Vancouver; 604/905–0041 in Whistler; WEB www.perimeterbus.com).

BOAT AND FERRY TRAVEL

SUNSHINE COAST

BC Ferries has passenger and vehicle service between Horseshoe Bay north of Vancouver and Langdale on the Sunshine Coast; Earls Cove to Saltery Bay (these towns are about halfway up the coast); and Powell River on the coast to Comox on Vancouver Island. The company also has an excursion to Texada Island off the coast of Powell River. These routes cannot be reserved. If you're planning to combine travel to the Sunshine Coast and Vancouver Island, ask BC Ferries about discount packages.

THE GULF ISLANDS

BC Ferries provides service to Galiano, Mayne, Pender, Saturna, and Salt Spring islands from Tsawwassen (vehicle reservations recommended and are required on some sailings) and from Swartz Bay, on Vancouver Island (reservations not accepted). Salt Spring Island can also be reached from Crofton on Vancouver Island. The Northern Gulf Islands, including Gabriola, Denman, Hornby, Quadra, and Cortes islands, can be reached from ports on Vancouver Island. Dionisio Express runs a summer boat service to Dionisio Marine Park, on Galiano Island's northwestern tip, which doesn't have road access.

On Salt Spring Island the *Queen of de Nile* runs from Moby's Marine Pub and Ganges Marina to Ganges town center. Gulf Islands Water Taxi runs passengers and bicycles between Salt Spring, Mayne, and Galiano islands. The boats run Wednesdays and Saturdays in summer, and on schooldays the rest of the year. Reservations are recommended.

THE NORTH COAST
BC Ferries sails along the Inside Passage from Port Hardy to Prince Rupert (year-round) and from Port Hardy to Bella Coola (summer only). Reservations are required for vehicles and recommended for foot passengers.

QUEEN CHARLOTTE ISLANDS
The *Queen of Prince Rupert,* a BC Ferries ship, sails six times a week from late May through September (three times a week the rest of the year). The crossing from Prince Rupert to Skidegate, near Queen Charlotte on Graham Island, takes about seven hours. Schedules vary and vehicle reservations are required. BC Ferries also connects Skidegate Landing to Alliford Bay on Moresby Island (near the airport at Sandspit). Access to smaller islands is by boat or air; make plans in advance through a travel agent.

THE KOOTENAYS
On the east side of Kootenay Lake, Crawford Bay can be accessed by a scenic, 45-minute free car ferry from Balfour, north of Nelson.
➤ BOAT AND FERRY INFORMATION: **BC Ferries** (☎ 250/386–3431 in Victoria and outside B.C.; 888/223–3779 elsewhere in B.C., WEB www.bc-ferries.com). **Dionisio Express** (☎ 250/539–3109). **Gulf Islands Water Taxi** (☎ 250/537–2510). **Kootenay Lake Ferry** (☎ 250/229–4215). *Queen of de Nile* (☎ 250/537–9100).

BUS TRAVEL
Greyhound Canada connects destinations throughout British Columbia with cities and towns all along the Pacific Northwest Coast. The company has service to Whistler from the downtown Vancouver depot every few hours. West Vancouver Blue Buses provides direct service from downtown Vancouver to Horseshoe Bay.

Whistler Municipality operates a free public transit system that loops throughout the village, and paid public transit serves the whole valley. Malaspina Coach Lines has routes from Vancouver to towns on the Sunshine Coast. Sunshine Coast Transit serves towns between Langdale and Halfmoon Bay on the Sunshine Coast.
➤ BUS INFORMATION: **Downtown Vancouver Depot** (✉ 1150 Station St., ☎ no phone). **Greyhound Canada** (☎ 604/482–8747 or 800/661–8747, WEB www.greyhound.com). **Malaspina Coach Lines** (☎ 877/227–8287). **Sunshine Coast Transit** (☎ 604/885–3234). **West Vancouver Blue Buses** (☎ 604/985–7777). **Whistler Municipality** (☎ 604/932–4020).

CAR RENTAL
Most major agencies, including Avis, Budget, Enterprise, National Tilden, Thrifty, and Hertz serve cities in the province. With Vancouver All-Terrain Adventures you can charter a four-wheel-drive Suburban from the Vancouver airport or Downtown Vancouver to Whistler. The vehicles travel regardless of the weather, and can stop for sightseeing along the way. The cost is $300 one way or $600 round-trip for up to seven passengers.
➤ LOCAL AGENCY: **Vancouver All-Terrain Adventures** (☎ 604/984–2374 or 888/754–5601).

CAR TRAVEL

Driving time from Seattle to Vancouver is about three hours by I–5 and Highway 99. From other Canadian regions, three main routes lead into British Columbia: through Sparwood, in the south, Highway 3; from Jasper and Banff, in the central region, Highways 1 and 5; and through Dawson Creek, in the north, Highways 2 and 97.

Highway 99, also known as the Sea to Sky Highway, connects Vancouver to Whistler and continues to Lillooet in the interior. The Trans-Canada Highway (Highway 1) connects Vancouver with Kamloops and points east via the Fraser Canyon. The Coquihalla Highway (Highway 5), a toll road ($10 for cars and vans) linking Hope and Kamloops, is the fastest route to the interior. Highway 101, the Pan-American Highway, serves the Sunshine Coast from Langdale to Lund.

ROAD CONDITIONS

Major roads, and most secondary roads, are paved and well engineered, although snow tires and chains are needed for winter travel. Many wilderness and park-access roads are unpaved, and there are no roads on the mainland coast once you leave the populated areas of the southwest corner near Vancouver. Before using logging or forestry-service roads, check with the forest-service office in the area where you plan to travel (Inquiry B.C. has a list of addresses and phone numbers) about logging activity. You can also check the Ministry of Forests Web site (www.gov.bc.ca/for/cont).

B.C. Highways has recorded highway reports.

For reports on Whistler area roads, call Mountain FM. Streets in Whistler Village, Village North, and Upper Village are all pedestrian-only; pay parking is available on the village outskirts.
➤ CONTACTS: **B.C. Highways** (☎ 900/565–4997; 75¢ a minute). **Inquiry B.C.** (☎ 800/663–7867 in B.C.; 604/660–2421 in Vancouver and outside B.C.). **Mountain FM** (☎ 888/404–5156).

EMERGENCIES

A few areas do not have 911 service, so if you don't get immediate response, dial 0. British Columbia has many hospitals, including Kelowna General Hospital, Lady Minto Hospital in Ganges on Salt Spring Island, Prince George Regional Hospital, and Royal Inland Hospital in Kamloops.
➤ CONTACTS: **Ambulance, fire, police, poison control** (☎ 911 or 0).
➤ HOSPITALS: **Kelowna General Hospital** (✉ 2268 Pandosy St., ☎ 250/862–4000). **Lady Minto Hospital** (✉ 135 Crofton Rd., Ganges, ☎ 250/538–4800). **Prince George Regional Hospital** (✉ 2000 15th Ave., ☎ 250/565–2000; 250/565–2444 for emergencies). **Royal Inland Hospital** (✉ 311 Columbia St., Kamloops, ☎ 250/374–5111).

OUTDOORS AND SPORTS

FISHING

Separate licenses are required for saltwater and freshwater fishing. Both are available at sporting-goods stores, government-agency offices, and most fishing lodges and charter-boat companies. A one-day license for nonresidents costs $15 for freshwater fishing, $7.50 for saltwater fishing, and $14 for saltwater salmon fishing. For information about saltwater-fishing regulations, contact Fisheries and Oceans Canada or pick up a free *Sport Fishing Guide,* available at most tourist-information centers. Super, Natural British Columbia has a brochure on freshwater fishing.
➤ CONTACTS: **Fisheries and Oceans Canada** (☎ 604/666–2828). **Super, Natural British Columbia** (☎ 800/435–5622).

GOLF

There are courses throughout the region, though Whistler and the Okanagan are the most popular golf destinations. Most courses are open April to mid-October, with greens fees ranging from about $30 to $100, including a cart. Whistler courses, usually open May to late September, are pricier, with greens fees of $125 to $185.

You can arrange advance tee-time bookings at any of 60 courses in British Columbia by calling Last Minute Golf. The company matches golfers and courses, sometimes at substantial greens-fee discounts.
➤ CONTACTS: **Last Minute Golf** (☎ 604/878–1833 or 800/684–6344, WEB www.lastminutegolf.net).

HIKING

➤ CONTACTS: **B.C. Parks** (✉ Box 9398, Station Provincial Government, Victoria, V8W 9M9, ☎ no phone, WEB www.elp.gov.bc.ca/bcparks).

HELI- AND SNOWCAT-SKIING

For a list of helicopter- and snowcat-skiing operators in the province, contact the B.C. Helicopter and Snowcat Skiing Operators Association.
➤ CONTACTS: **B.C. Helicopter and Snowcat Skiing Operators Association** (☎ 250/542–9020).

TAXIS

Go Galiano offers year-round taxi, bus, and ferry pickup services on Galiano Island. For a cab in Whistler, call Sea to Sky Taxi. On Salt Spring Island, Silver Shadow Taxi is a good bet.
➤ TAXI COMPANIES: **Go Galiano** (☎ 250/539–0202). **Sea to Sky Taxi** (☎ 604/932–3333). **Silver Shadow Taxi** (☎ 250/537–3030).

TOURS

ADVENTURE TRIPS

Bluewater Adventures has 8- to 10-day sailboat tours around the Charlottes; trips start and end in Sandspit. Canadian Outback Adventure Company runs rafting day trips on the Elaho River between Squamish and Whistler as well as longer trips on the Babine, Chilcotin, and Tatshenshini in northern British Columbia and the Yukon. Canadian River Expeditions specializes in multiday wilderness rafting expeditions on the Chilcotin, Fraser, Babine, Skeena, and Tatshenshini. Ecosummer Expeditions has guided multiday camping, riding, trekking, canoeing, dogsledding, rafting, sea-kayaking trips and more to the Gulf Islands, the Inside Passage, and Queen Charlotte Islands, as well as an inn-to-inn trip in the Gulf Islands.

Fraser River Raft Expeditions Ltd., with bases in Yale and Lytton in the Fraser Canyon, offers a range of day trips and longer expeditions on several rivers. Fresh Tracks Canada has 55 outdoor-adventure trips around the province, including hiking, kayaking, river rafting, rail journeys, and sailing adventures. Gabriola Cycle and Kayak runs multiday paddles to the Queen Charlottes. Hyak Wilderness Adventures, based in Lytton, picks up at Vancouver hotels for rafting on the Chilliwack and Thompson rivers.

Ocean West Expeditions offers multiday camping and lodge-based kayaking tours to the Gulf Islands, Johnstone Strait, and Desolation Sound. Among their many other activities, Outdoor Adventures@Whistler offers tours to the backcountry on rideable all-terrain vehicles. Queen Charlotte Adventures leads multiday kayak, powerboat, and fishing tours around the Charlotte Islands. Whistler ATV Tours specializes in guided rides through the backcountry on all-terrain vehicles. Whistler River Adventures has both river-rafting and jet-boating trips on rivers near Whistler.

➤ CONTACTS: **Bluewater Adventures** (☎ 604/980–3800 or 888/877–1770). **Canadian Outback Adventure Company** ☎ (604/921–7250 or 800/565–8735). **Canadian River Expeditions** (☎ 250/392–9195 or 800/898–7238, WEB www.canriver.com). **Ecosummer Expeditions** (☎ 250/674–0102 or 800/465–8884, WEB www.ecosummer.ca). **Fraser River Raft Expeditions Ltd.** (☎ 604/863–2336 or 800/363–7238, WEB www.fraser-raft.com). **Fresh Tracks Canada** (☎ 604/737–8743 or 800/667–4744, WEB www.freshtracks.ca). **Gabriola Cycle and Kayak** (☎ 250/247–8277, WEB www.gck.ca). **Hyak Wilderness Adventures** (☎ 800/663–7238, WEB www.hyak.com). **Ocean West Expeditions** (☎ 800/660–0051, WEB www.ocean-west.com). **Outdoor Adventures@Whistler** (☎ 604/932–0647). **Queen Charlotte Adventures** (☎ 250/559–8990 or 800/668–4288, WEB wwwqcislands.net/qciadven). **Whistler ATV Tours** (☎ 604/932–6681). **Whistler River Adventures** (☎ 604/932–3532 or 888/932–3532).

HELICOPTER TOURS

Blackcomb Helicopters flies year-round flightseeing tours over Whistler's stunning mountains and glaciers. In summer, it offers heli-hiking, -biking, -fishing, -picnics, and even heli-weddings.

➤ FEES AND SCHEDULES: **Blackcomb Helicopters** (☎ 604/938–1700 or 800/330–4354).

SIGHTSEEING TOURS

Coast Salish Journeys, in Lund, has cultural and natural-history tours on foot or by kayak, sailboat, and canoe. In summer, Glacier Transportation and Tours offer trolley tours around the Whistler area, with insights into history and ecology and tips on celebrity and wildlife spotting. In winter, it runs day trips to Vancouver for guided city tours and also offers outings to see NHL ice-hockey games in Vancouver. Go Galiano has year-round sightseeing services on Galiano Island.

Gold Safari Tours in Wells offers the chance to pan for gold on a personalized Gold Trail tour, including trips to Barkerville from Quesnel. Sunshine Coast Tours has summer day trips to Princess Louisa Inlet on the Sunshine Coast. With Okanagan Limousine you can tour the wine area in chauffeur-driven style. Okanagan Wine Country Tours gives narrated wine-country tours to small groups. West Coast City and Nature Sightseeing offers a sightseeing tour to Whistler that allows you to stay over and return on your date of choice to Vancouver. The tours run year-round; the cost is about $67.

➤ CONTACTS: **Coast Salish Journeys,** (☎ 604/483–4505 or 800/345–1112, WEB www.coastsalishjourneys.com). **Glacier Transportation and Tours** (☎ 604/932–7565 or 888/287–7488). **Go Galiano** (☎ 250/539–0202). **Gold Safari Tours** (☎ 250/994–3463 or 888/996–4653, WEB www.goldsafaritours.com). **Okanagan Limousine** (☎ 250/717–5466 or 877/295–9373). **Okanagan Wine Country Tours** (☎ 250/868–9463 or 866/689–9463). **Sunshine Coast Tours** (☎ 604/886–7033 or 800/870–9055). **West Coast City and Nature Sightseeing** (☎ 604/451–1600 in Vancouver; 877/451–1777, WEB www.vancouversightseeing.com).

TRAIN TOURS

Rocky Mountaineer RailTours is a luxury, catered train tour that travels across British Columbia from Vancouver to Jasper (in Alberta), and from Vancouver to Calgary via Banff.

BC Rail's luxurious Whistler Northwind train tour travels from North Vancouver to Prince George, between May and October. The train features fine Pacific Northwest cuisine, lounge cars, and domed passenger cars with 180° views. It travels through some of the province's most scenic parts and can be combined with connections to VIA Rail for a circle tour.

BC Rail also operates the Royal Hudson Train, a vintage locomotive that runs between North Vancouver and Squamish, and runs day trips on the Explorer Scenic Tour Train to points north of Whistler that are accessible only by rail.

➤ CONTACTS: **BC Rail** (☎ 604/631–3500 or 800/663–8238, WEB www.bcrail.com). **Rocky Mountaineer RailTours** (☎ 604/606–7200 or 800/665–7245, WEB www.rockymountaineer.com). **VIA Rail** (☎ 800/561–8630 in Canada; 800/561–3949 in U.S., WEB www.viarail.ca). **Whistler Northwind** (☎ 604/631–3500 or 800/663–8238, WEB www.whistlernorthwind.com).

TRAIN TRAVEL

BC Rail has daily service from the North Vancouver BC Rail Station to Whistler. The BC Rail station is about a 30-minute drive from downtown Vancouver; a BC Transit shuttle links the Vancouver bus depot and the train terminal in summer.

BC Rail operates the Cariboo Prospector, a year-round scheduled service between North Vancouver and Prince George, with service to Whistler, Lillooet, Williams Lake, Quesnel, and many smaller centers in the Cariboo region. (BC Rail also offers accommodation, golf, ranch, and spa packages for stops en route, and can arrange circle tours of the province by linking with VIA Rail and with BC Ferries' Inside Passage services.)

VIA Rail offers service between Vancouver and Jasper (in Alberta), and from Prince Rupert to Jasper with an overnight stop in Prince George.

➤ TRAIN INFORMATION: **BC Rail** (☎ 604/631–3500 or 800/663–8238, WEB www.bcrail.com). **BC Transit** (☎ 604/521–0400). **VIA Rail** (☎ 800/561–8630 in Canada; 800/561–3949 in U.S., WEB www.viarail.ca).

VISITOR INFORMATION

Super, Natural British Columbia has information about the province. The principal regional tourist offices are: Cariboo, Chilcotin, Coast Tourism Association; Northern British Columbia Tourism Association, for information on the Queen Charlotte Islands and northern British Columbia; Northern Rockies, Alaska Highway Tourism Association for information on northeastern British Columbia; Thompson Okanagan Tourism Association; Vancouver, Coast & Mountains Tourism Region for information about the Coast Mountain Circle and the Sunshine Coast. Many towns in the region also have visitor information centers, though not all are open year-round.

➤ REGIONAL TOURIST INFORMATION: **Cariboo, Chilcotin, Coast Tourism Association** (✉ 118A N. First Ave., Williams Lake, ☎ 250/392–2226 or 800/663–5885). **Northern British Columbia Tourism Association** (✉ Box 2373, 850 River Rd., Prince George, ☎ 250/561–0432 or 800/663–8843, WEB www.northernbctravel.com). **Northern Rockies, Alaska Highway Tourism Association** (✉ 9923 96th Ave., Fort St. John, ☎ 250/785–2544 or 888/785–2544, WEB www.hellonorth.com). **Super, Natural British Columbia** (☎ 888/435–5622, WEB www.travel.bc.ca). **Thompson Okanagan Tourism Association** (✉ 1332 Water St., Kelowna, ☎ 250/860–5999 or 800/567–2275, WEB www.thompsonokanagan.com). **Vancouver, Coast & Mountains Tourism Region** (✉ 250–1508 W. 2nd Ave., Vancouver, ☎ 604/739–0823 or 800/667–3306, WEB www.coastandmountains.bc.ca).

➤ LOCAL TOURIST INFORMATION: **Galiano Island Visitor Information Centre** (✉ Sturdies Bay ferry terminal, ☎ FAX 250/539–2233, WEB www.galianoisland.com). **Ganges Visitor Information Centre** (✉ 121 Lower Ganges Rd., ☎ 250/537–5252 or 866/216–2936). **Gibsons Landing Tourist Info Centre** (✉ Sunnycrest Mall, 668 Sunnycrest Rd., off Highway 101, ☎ 604/886–2325). **Hope Visitor Info Centre** (✉ 919 Water Ave., off Hwy. 1, ☎ 604/869–2021). **Nelson Visitor Info Centre** (✉ 225 Hall St., ☎ 250/352–3433). **Pender Harbour Info Centre** (Madeira Park, ☎ 604/883–2561). **Penticton Visitors Information Centre** (✉ 888 Westminster Ave. W, ☎ 250/493–4055 or 800/663–5052). **Powell River Visitors Bureau** (✉ 4690 Marine Ave., ☎ 604/485–4701 or 877/817–8669). **Prince Rupert Visitor Info Centre** (✉ 100–215 Cow Bay Rd., ☎ 250/624–5637 or 800/667–1994). **Queen Charlotte Island Visitor Information Centre** (✉ 3220 Wharf St., Queen Charlotte, ☎ 250/559–8316; ✉ 1 Airport Rd., in the airport terminal, Sandspit, ☎ 250/637–5362; ✉ Hwy. 16, Masset, ☎ 250/626–3982. WEB www.qcinfo.com). **Sechelt Visitor Information Centre** (✉ Trail Bay Mall, 45–5755 Cowrie St., ☎ 604/885–0662 or 877/633–2963). **Terrace Travel Info Centre** (✉ 4511 Keith Ave., or Hwy. 16, ☎ 250/635–2063). **Tourism Prince George** (✉ 1198 Victoria St., ☎ 250/562–3700 or 800/668–7646). **Tourism Whistler** (✉ 4010 Whistler Way, ☎ 604/932–4222; 604/664–5625 in Vancouver; 800/944–7853 in U.S. and Canada, WEB www.tourismwhistler.com). **Whistler Activity and Information Center** (✉ 4010 Whistler Way, ☎ 604/932–2394).

5 THE CANADIAN ROCKIES

The ranges that form the rugged Canadian
Rockies arch north-northwest for more than
1,000 mi from the U.S. border in the south
to the Yukon in the north. The majestic
beauty of the Rockies has been preserved in
provincial and national parks that hold some
of the most spectacular drives in the world.
In these mountains you can also fish, ski,
hike, climb, boat, ride, and stay at some of
the best resort facilities anywhere.

Updated by
Monica
Andreeff

COMPARING MOUNTAINS IS A SUBJECTIVE and imprecise business. Yet few would deny that the 640-km (397-mi) stretch
of the Canadian Rockies that marks part of the Alberta–
British Columbia border easily ranks as one of the most extravagantly
beautiful ranges on Earth. Approaching the mountains from the east,
you are struck by the wall of rock on the western horizon, made more
dramatic by the white snowfields that cling to the upper slopes well
into the summer. Near the south end of the range (Waterton Lakes National Park), the view is particularly striking as gently rolling prairie
abruptly butts up against the edge of the mountains. Farther north, in
Banff and Jasper national parks, tree-covered foothills roll out of the
mountains.

It's obvious how the Rockies got their name. Wildly folded sedimen-
tary and metamorphic rocks have been thrust up by awesome forces
of nature to form ragged peaks and high cliffs. Add glaciers and snowfields to the high peaks, carpet the valleys with forests, mix in a generous helping of large mammals, wildflowers, rivers, and lakes, and
you've got the recipe for the Canadian Rockies.

The peaks are aligned in long, closely spaced ranges that run in approximately a north–south direction. From east to west these can be
grouped into the foothills, front ranges, main ranges, and a small area
of west ranges. Apart from forming distinct sets of mountains, these groupings differ somewhat in geology and age—which increases from 40 million to 50 million years in the foothills to 110 million to 120 million
years in the western ranges. The main ranges have the highest peaks.

The Columbia Mountains, a series of parallel ranges just to the west,
are often grouped with the Rockies. Many recreational activities prohibited in most of the national parks of the Rockies (notably power-
and jet-boating, snowmobiling, helicopter-assisted skiing, and heli-
hiking) are allowed in the Columbias. The Columbias were formed about
180 million years ago and consist of four subranges: the Cariboos to
the north and, farther south, the Purcells, Selkirks, and Monashees (from
east to west).

Recognizing early the region's exceptional natural beauty, the Canadian government began shielding the area from human development
and resource exploitation in the 1880s. In 1885, the government created a park preserve around the Cave and Basin Hot Springs in Banff.
Two years later, Canada's first national park, Rocky Mountain Park
(later Banff National Park), was officially established.

Today, about 25,000 square km (roughly 10,000 square mi)—an area
larger than the state of New Hampshire—are protected in seven national parks in the Rockies and the Columbias. The parks of the Rockies—Waterton Lakes, Banff, Kootenay, Yoho, and Jasper—have large
areas that remain untouched by human development and together
they form a UNESCO World Heritage Site. The only significant clusters of human settlement are in the town centers of Banff, Jasper, and
Waterton Park, and the area around Lake Louise. Several thousand more
square kilometers are also protected as wilderness areas and provincial parks, most notably Mt. Robson and Mt. Assiniboine provincial
parks and Kananaskis Country.

Most of the facilities and roads of the Rockies are concentrated in the
valleys, where the elevations are from 3,000 to 4,500 ft, about 1,000
ft higher than in the major prairie cities to the east. Consequently, temperatures in the mountain towns can be 12.2°C (10°F) colder than in

Calgary and Edmonton. The mountains themselves rise to elevations above 10,000 ft, and the alpine areas (above tree line) may be whitened by snowfalls even in midsummer. The Icefields Parkway runs down the heart of the Rockies for 230 km (143 mi) from Jasper to Lake Louise. Although all roads in the Rockies offer stunning scenery, the Icefields Parkway, with more than 100 glaciers along the way, is without doubt the most impressive. Even if you're on a tight schedule, make a point of driving at least part of it.

Pleasures and Pastimes

Dining

Eating out is, for the most part, a casual affair. Given the mix of travelers to the region—families, outdoorspeople, nature lovers, and sightseers—the emphasis is on good, fresh food served in large quantities, at slightly inflated prices. Trout, venison, elk, moose, and quail appear on the menus of even many modest establishments. The Rockies also have a number of top-caliber restaurants. Although Continental and American-style cuisines dominate, ethnic restaurants are becoming more popular.

CATEGORY	COST*
$$$$	over $32
$$$	$22–$32
$$	$13–$21
$	under $13

per person, in Canadian dollars, for a main course at dinner

Lodging

The hotels, inns, and lodges of the Canadian Rockies compose an eclectic list, from rustic, backcountry lodges without electricity or running water to numerous standard roadside motels to hotels of supreme luxury. With just a few exceptions (ski resorts being the main ones) they share one common trait—room rates that are considerably higher in summer than during the rest of the year. The week between Christmas and New Year's often commands a higher rate as well. Flexibility in travel planning can mean considerable savings: a room that goes for $150 a night in summer may well drop to $75 from mid-October through mid-May.

Lodgings are categorized according to their peak-season rates. Low-season discounts are noted within each listing, where applicable. High-season rates generally run from mid-June to late September. Several weeks before and after these dates are the shoulder season, with rates a bit lower than in peak season. Check in advance for off-season rates; the period considered peak season seems to get longer each year.

Bed-and-breakfast accommodations are plentiful in the main towns in the parks. But these aren't the Victorian B&Bs that might normally spring to mind; most are simply ordinary rooms in small, ordinary homes. In fact, few even serve breakfast. The main attractions are price, and you can often find a B&B with a room available if you arrive in town without a reservation. Outside the major towns in the parks, B&Bs are more likely to be in the form of alpine lodges, and a premium rate may apply instead of a discount. This type of accommodation is common in the British Columbia Rockies, and the premium may well be worth it because the towns of the BC Rockies are often geared toward logging and mining, not tourism.

Backcountry lodges have been an integral part of Canadian Rockies travel since the 1920s. They vary considerably in terms of accommodations and accessibility. At the luxurious end are lodges with private rooms, private baths, full electricity, telephones, and restaurant-style dining; at the rugged extreme are lodges with bunk beds, kerosene lamps, and outhouses. A few are accessible by car in summer; some can be reached only by hiking or skiing, or by helicopter. Note that many backcountry lodges are priced on a per-person basis (the price generally includes meals) rather than the double-room rate used for more standard accommodations.

Guest ranches, mainly in the ranching area just east of Kananaskis Country, are another alternative accommodation. These provide comfortable lodging with a definite ranching theme; horseback riding and pack trips are standard activities.

Of the more than 40 public campgrounds within the national parks (not including backcountry sites for backpackers and climbers), most operate on a first-come, first-served basis, though some allow reservations. The season generally runs from mid-May through October, although some campgrounds remain open year-round. Hookups are available at most of the 40 national park campgrounds and at four of the 30 Kananaskis Country campgrounds. Prices for a one-night stay are $18–$22 at hookup sites, $13–$16 at sites without hookups, and $10 at sites with access to pit toilets only. Numerous privately run campgrounds, which usually take reservations, can be found outside park boundaries.

CATEGORY	COST*
$$$$	over $200
$$$	$150–$200
$$	$100–$150
$	under $100

*All prices are for a standard double room, excluding 7% GST (federal tax), a 5% room tax in Alberta, 8% room tax in British Columbia, in Canadian dollars.

Outdoor Activities and Sports

BIKING

Biking is a popular pastime in the Rockies, whether a short spin around town or a multiday guided tour. Around Banff, the Vermilion Lakes loop and the more strenuous loop over Tunnel Mountain are popular half-day bike tours. For a longer ride, Highway 1A between Banff and Lake Louise is a good choice. For a rugged workout, try the steep switchbacks leading up to the Mt. Norquay ski area. Highway 93 is a long and strenuous route for cycling but is becoming increasingly popular because of the wide paved shoulders along most of the way and the spectacular scenery. The Overlander Bike Trail in Jasper National Park passes through four different ecozones: marshland, river, meadow, and mountain.

Mountain biking has become more popular in recent years, but not without controversy. Park officials have reported problems resulting from breakdowns in remote areas, occasionally requiring rescue. Troubles have also been reported when mountain bikers break scent lines between mother bears and cubs. As a result, mountain bikes are restricted to relatively few trails, primarily fire roads in the parks. Check with the nearest park warden or bike store before heading off-road. Mountain bikers may find the more lenient restrictions in Kananaskis Country and the British Columbia Rockies preferable.

CLIMBING

Except for Waterton Lakes, where the rock is generally crumbly, the Canadian Rockies are one of the world's great climbing regions. Among the classic ascents are Mt. Assiniboine, the "Matterhorn of the Rockies"; glacier-cloaked Mt. Athabasca; Mt. Sir Donald, in Glacier National Park; the daunting Mt. Robson; and, in the Purcells, the spires of the Bugaboos. Climbing and mountaineering are year-round activities, although October and November—after the summer and before icefalls are solid enough for winter climbing—are the least desirable months.

FISHING

The principal game fish in the Rockies are trout, with cutthroat and rainbow the most common varieties. Bull trout are catch-and-release only in the mountain parks of Alberta, and in Banff National Park cutthroats are catch-and-release as well. The use of lead sinkers in the national parks is banned; only steel sinkers are permitted. Fishing is generally better outside the national parks because of fish-stocking programs (fish are not stocked in the national parks). The Bow River, the lakes of British Columbia, and the streams of Crowsnest Pass are prime fishing spots outside the national parks.

GOLF

The golf season is short, from about early May through mid-October. Golf courses are generally in excellent playing condition. In Alberta, greens fees range from $50 to $75 at most courses. Cart rentals are mandatory at some courses, where greens fees plus a cart run $100 to $150. Most courses enforce a standard dress code, requiring shirts with collars and Bermuda-length shorts or long pants. In the British Columbia Rockies, greens fees at most courses range from $35 to $50. Carts are mandatory only at Greywolf, where greens fees plus a cart cost $90.

The area between Golden and Cranbrook in British Columbia is growing as a golfing hotbed: golfers can choose from 12 18-hole courses and several 9-hole courses.

HIKING

The four contiguous parks (Banff, Jasper, Kootenay, and Yoho) have 2,900 km (1,800 mi) of hiking trails. In Waterton Lakes there are 183 km (113 mi) of trails, with further access to more than 1,200 km (744 mi) of trails in adjacent Glacier National Park in the United States. Kananaskis Country has numerous hiking and backpacking opportunities, and Revelstoke and Glacier parks in British Columbia are generally best for day hikes.

The snow-free hiking season usually runs from early April to early November for trails in the valleys and mid-June to mid- or late September for trails that extend into alpine areas. Though most trails are restricted to foot traffic, horses and mountain bikes are permitted in some areas; check with the park warden.

HORSEBACK RIDING

Horses are prohibited on many trails within the national parks, but there are still opportunities; among the most attractive areas for pack trips within the parks is Tonquin Valley in Jasper. Outside the national parks, horseback riding is offered in Kananaskis Country, provincial parks, and the British Columbia Rockies region.

RAFTING

Rafting opportunities range from gentle floats along the Bow River near Banff to rollicking white-water rides on the Kicking Horse River near Golden. Most trips are half- or full-day. The season runs from May through October; if you want white water at its frothiest, the best month is usually June, when rivers are swollen with snowmelt, but not dangerously so. Operators may cancel extreme white-water trips if conditions become too hazardous.

SKIING AND SNOWBOARDING

The region has 11 lift-service ski areas. Five are within an hour's drive of Banff; daily lift tickets cost between $30 and $50. Cross-country opportunities are also plentiful, and many backcountry lodges are winterized and offer guide services for backcountry touring. Numerous tour operators have ski packages designed to fit a variety of interests (including heli-skiing), abilities, and budgets.

Snowboarding is accepted at all the ski hills and many of them offer special facilities such as half-pipes and terrain parks. Full rental is available at each area and a lift ticket is the same price as it is for skiers.

WATER SPORTS

Swimmers generally avoid the icy, glacier-fed waters of the Rockies. However, several lakes near Jasper can become comfortable during spells of warm summer weather.

Private motorized craft (including jet skis) are prohibited in most of the waters of the Rockies national parks. The two exceptions to this are Lake Minnewanka (no jet skis) in Banff National Park and Pyramid Lake in Jasper National Park. Lake Minnewanka is a large reservoir near the town of Banff where you can rent aluminum fishing boats with 8-horsepower motors by the hour. Pyramid Lake is a smaller lake near the town of Jasper; you can rent 7-horsepower aluminum fishing boats at the dock, but for sightseeing on the lake it's better to rent one of the nonmotorized craft and enjoy the quiet. (Some commercial motorboat operations are allowed on other lakes—for example, the boat tour operations at Maligne Lake and Upper Waterton Lake.)

Nonmotorized craft are permitted in virtually all waters of the mountain parks. Rentals (by the hour or by the day) are available at numerous lakes, especially as you get closer to the towns of Banff, Jasper, Lake Louise, and Waterton Park. Canoe rentals are most common, but some selection of rowboats, pedal boats, and even kayaks is not unusual.

Outside the national parks, Spray Lakes Reservoir and Kananaskis Lake are the main sites of motorboating activity in Kananaskis Country, where motorized boating is allowed. Lake Windermere, in British Columbia, is popular among sailors, board sailors, and water-skiers and is pleasantly warm for swimming. To the north, the long, dam-controlled Kinbasket and Revelstoke lakes give boaters, canoeists, and anglers more of a wilderness experience. The lakes have several boat ramps but few services. Most motorized boating in Alberta occurs in the lakes and reservoirs east of the Rockies, where restrictions are few and the water generally gets much warmer than in the Rockies, although the water may turn quite green by midsummer.

For sailors and board sailors who like strong winds, Waterton Lakes, with winds often exceeding 50 km (31 mi) per hour, is the place to be. The water is numbingly cold, though, so be sure to wear a wet suit. The Athabasca, Bow, Kicking Horse, and Maligne rivers provide various levels of river-running challenges for canoeists and kayakers—from relatively still water to roaring white water.

Shopping
When shopping in the Rockies, the best selection is found in Banff, with Jasper close behind. Canmore also has some unique shopping opportunities. Given that stores in the mountains are not big-box retailers, and they are paying a resort premium for their location, don't be surprised to see that premium passed on to customers—particularly for souvenirs, sporting gear, and some clothing.

However, the high tourist traffic allows some stores, such as art galleries and quirky shops offering unique and unusual merchandise, to thrive as though they were in a major city. Indeed, you can find items for sale in the Canadian Rockies—local artwork, specially made warm clothes, and jade carvings of wildlife, for example—that you would have difficulty finding anywhere else, at any price. The savvy shopper may find shopping in the Rockies to be quite rewarding.

Exploring the Canadian Rockies

The Canadian Rockies can be divided into four broad regions. The Banff and Lake Louise area is the main hub of tourism and makes a convenient reference point for the other regions. North and west of Banff lie the spectacular Icefields Parkway and Jasper National Park (north), and the smaller Kootenay, Yoho, and Glacier national parks (west). Jasper National Park includes the townsite of Jasper (meaning the town and surrounding cabins and campgrounds). Kootenay, Yoho, and Glacier parks have comparatively few visitor facilities but make good destinations to escape the crowds of Banff and Jasper parks.

The region south of Banff includes Kananaskis Country and Waterton Lakes National Park. Kananaskis Country, adjacent to Banff National Park but outside the national park system, allows many activities— snowmobiling, for example—that are prohibited in the national parks. Waterton, a small national park along the U.S. border contiguous with Glacier National Park in Montana, has smaller mountains and a very unhurried atmosphere, in contrast to the main parks of the Canadian Rockies.

The British Columbia Rockies region, west of the main Rocky Mountains, consists of a series of parallel, somewhat more weathered mountain ranges. The parks here are smaller and more scattered, interspersed with many functional rather than visitor-oriented towns.

Numbers in the text correspond to numbers in the margin and on the Canadian Rockies and Banff maps.

Great Itineraries

The Canadian Rockies are a sizable chunk of real estate, about twice the area of New York State. You could easily spend a month and still just skim the surface. The heart of the Canadian Rockies—the adjoining national parks of Banff, Jasper, Kootenay, and Yoho—puts the major attractions relatively close together. Ten days would allow for a leisurely tour of the main parks, with time left over for hiking or exploring some outlying regions. Five days would be sufficient for a visit to the major attractions in both Banff and Jasper parks, but there wouldn't be much time spent sitting about. A weekend would be time enough to get a feeling for Banff and Lake Louise, the hub of the region.

IF YOU HAVE 2 DAYS

The best option is to visit the Banff–Lake Louise region. One day could be spent in and around ⊠ **Banff,** ①–⑩ exploring, shopping, or just relaxing, perhaps with visits to one or two of the attractions on the outskirts of town: the **Upper Hot Springs** ④, the **Banff Gondola at Sulphur Mountain** ⑤, or the **Cave and Basin National Historic Site** ⑥. Some pleasant short drives are near town, too. On the second day, visit the **Lake Louise** ⑪ area, including scenic Moraine Lake, where you can hike, rent a boat, or just sightsee.

Alternatively, you could choose to make ⊠ **Jasper** ⑭ your destination and spend one day in and around the town (shopping, taking the **Jasper Tramway** ⑮, exploring **Pyramid and Patricia lakes** ⑯). The second day could be filled with a visit to one or two of the scenic attractions within an hour's drive of Jasper: **Mt. Edith Cavell** ⑰, **Athabasca Falls** ⑱, **Maligne Lake** ⑲, **Miette Hot Springs** ⑳, or **Mt. Robson** ㉑.

The Canadian Rockies

IF YOU HAVE 5 DAYS

A few more days allow you to explore a bit farther. If you are feeling energetic, an ideal option would be a two-day visit to the ⊞ **Banff** ①– ⑩ and **Lake Louise** ⑪ areas, a day spent exploring the **Icefields Parkway** between Lake Louise and Jasper, and a two-day visit to the ⊞ **Jasper** ⑭ area.

IF YOU HAVE 10 DAYS

This is enough time to do some serious exploring. You could spend five days touring the ⊞ **Banff** ①–⑩ and **Lake Louise** ⑪ areas, the **Icefields Parkway,** and ⊞ **Jasper** ⑭ and environs. You can spend the additional five days just relaxing, or you can focus on a specific activity such as hiking, which could easily fill up the remaining time.

If you aren't one to sit around in the same spot for too long, spend the extra five days visiting the British Columbia Rockies— ⊞ **Yoho National Park** (perhaps visiting the famous **Burgess Shale Site** ㉕ fossil beds— reservations required), ⊞ **Glacier National Park** ㉜, or **Mt. Revelstoke National Park** ㉝ (overnight in ⊞ **Revelstoke** ㉞). ⊞ **Golden** ㉛ is a destination in itself, and ⊞ **Radium Hot Springs** ㊱ and ⊞ **Kimberley** ㊴ make convenient overnight stops on the British Columbia side of the Rockies.

When to Tour the Canadian Rockies

The main attractions in the Rockies can get crowded in summer, so try to reach them early in the day if you want to avoid the crush. If hiking is your passion, remember that high-altitude trails may be snow-covered until well into June. Animals are more common before the July crowds arrive, although midsummer visitors are still certain to see plenty. Be respectful and keep your distance when encountering wildlife. In winter, although the bears are hibernating, there are still opportunities to see elk and bighorn sheep, which often forage for food near the roads and meadows in the valleys. Wildflowers, especially in the alpine meadows, reach their peak from early July to mid-August.

In the Rockies there's the year-round possibility of snow, although in summer it's usually only at higher altitudes. The weather is best during the mid-June to mid-September period; you can avoid crowds and make substantial savings on lodgings by scheduling your visit outside this period. Check on rates, though, as many hotel operators are now aware that they can keep rates high from mid-May to early October and still fill their rooms.

BANFF AND LAKE LOUISE

Banff, a little more than an hour's drive west of Calgary, is the largest town in the parks and a popular first destination for most visitors to the Canadian Rockies. From Banff, a favorite day trip is to the much smaller, majestic town of Lake Louise, a half-hour's drive north but also within Banff National Park. Other popular excursions are the spectacular drive north along the Icefields Parkway (Highway 93) to Jasper, 280 km (174 mi) away, and the short trip southeast into Kananaskis Country.

Banff National Park

★ *Eastern boundary of park: 113 km (70 mi) west of Calgary.*

Areas of majestic beauty fill the 6,641 square km (2,564 square mi) of Banff National Park, the second-largest of Canada's mountain parks. Bordered by Jasper National Park to the north, Kootenay and Yoho national parks to the west, the Bighorn Wildland Recreation Area to the east, and Kananaskis Country and Peter Lougheed Provincial Park to the south, Banff is at the center of a huge block of protected wilderness.

You can soak up the rugged alpine scenery, hike on more than 1,600 km (1,000 mi) of trails, tour the region by automobile or tour bus, watch wildlife, soak in hot springs, visit historic sites, and enjoy fine dining, lodging, and shopping in the town of Banff. The Banff–Lake Louise hub is not only the geographic center of the park but also the cultural, dining, lodging, and activity center. Expect crowds here but pristine wilderness in the rest of the park.

Outdoor Activities and Sports
The hiking trails of Banff National Park tend to get a lot of traffic in summer. The most interesting hikes are north of the townsite of Banff. Popular day-hiking areas, both accessible and scenic, are around Lake Louise and Moraine Lake.

Banff

128 km (79 mi) west of Calgary.

Banff is a world-renowned tourist destination, and justifiably so, but much of the Canadian Rockies boasts scenery that matches that near the town of Banff. The town came into being at its current location because of the railway that opened this part of the Rockies and because of the hot mineral springs on adjacent Sulphur Mountain.

The original survey for the first Canadian transcontinental railway leaned toward a northerly route, crossing what is now Jasper, where the mountain passes through both the Rockies and the Columbia mountains are least formidable. However, due to concerns that American railways would branch northward and siphon off business, the Canadian Pacific Railway in 1881 chose a more southerly route, through modern-day Banff and across the Rockies via Kicking Horse Pass. The northerly route through Jasper was not constructed until 1911.

With the arrival of the railway in 1883 came the discovery of the hot springs on Sulphur Mountain. Actually, the local people in the area had known of the springs for hundreds, probably thousands of years, and it was these residents who first directed two white hunters to the springs in 1875. One of these newcomers, Peter Younge, recognized the economic potential of the springs and built a rough shack nearby. However, without much money to back him up, he abandoned his new business within a year.

When railway workers "rediscovered" the springs in 1883, they, too, attempted to commercialize the waters. This time, however, the Canadian government also recognized the opportunity. After some wrangling and pressuring, the railworkers were bought out, and in November 1885 the government established a 10-acre preserve around the hot springs. Two years later this was expanded to 416 km (260 square mi), and the newly named Rocky Mountains National Park was born, the third national park in the world at that time. The name was later changed to Banff National Park, and the park was expanded greatly in size.

Meanwhile, eager to promote its new transcontinental line, the Canadian Pacific Railway (CPR) constructed several luxury hotels in the Rockies to advertise its presence. One obvious location was not far from the hot mineral springs of Sulphur Mountain; the Banff Springs Hotel was opened in 1888. The town—named after Banffshire, Scotland, the birthplace of the CPR president of the time, George Stephen—sprang up on the opposite side of the river at about the same time.

Banff was essentially a destination for wealthy tourists from around the world in the early 20th century. The CPR provided train travel to Banff and hired Swiss mountaineering guides to lead wealthy clients to conquer the summits of the innumerable unnamed peaks in the Rockies. In fact, automobiles were prohibited in Banff National Park until 1915, even though a road from Calgary to the park had been built six years previously.

Nowadays, some of that early history remains; altered, no doubt, but not vanquished. Visitors still enjoy the luxury and charm of Banff Springs Hotel, which has modernized its facilities with fine dining, exclusive shops, and a world-class spa, so that it's still a destination unto itself. But it's not in an exclusive club anymore; other luxury hotels, shops, and restaurants have been added to the town and surrounding area through the years. And with easy access on modern highways from all directions, mass tourism with less-expensive hotels, fast-food dining, and ubiquitous gift shops has joined the ranks. But despite—or perhaps because of—these many changes in the past century, Banff is the central depot for almost all travelers to the Canadian Rockies.

This is why unlikely contrasts are the rule in Banff: amid the bustle of commercialism, elk regularly wander into town to graze the lush grass on the town common, and sightseers carrying souvenir-stuffed bags mix with rugged outdoorspeople on Banff Avenue, the main drag. Banff now straddles a thin line between mountain resort town and tourist trap. No quaint little Western outpost, except for the oft-photographed Banff Springs Hotel, it's filled with architecture that is mostly modern, simple, and undistinguished. Although Banff is an autonomous municipality (unlike Jasper to the north), park authorities have placed limits on the town's acreage, and so, instead of expanding, Banff has compressed itself. The result is a hub of hyperactivity, especially in summer.

❶ An amazing number of shops and restaurants have been crammed together on **Banff Avenue.** Clustered in about a half dozen indoor malls and several blocks of street-front stores with modern-alpine architecture are art galleries and clothing, sporting-goods, gift, photo, book, and confectionery stores. Items in the galleries range from trinkets to kitsch to genuine art; price does not necessarily indicate real value.

The Victorian **Banff Park Museum** houses a taxidermy collection of animals indigenous to Banff National Park (some specimens are more than 100 years old) as well as wildlife art and a library on natural history. This is western Canada's oldest natural-history museum, and the rustic building is a National Historic Site. ⊠ *92 Banff Ave.,* ☎ *403/762–1558.* 🖃 *$2.50.* ☉ *Mid-May–Sept., daily 10–6; Oct.–mid-May, daily 1–5.*

The **Whyte Museum** displays art, photography, and historical artifacts, and has exhibits about life in the Canadian Rockies. The museum hosts special events for families in summer. ⊠ *111 Bear St.,* ☎ *403/762–2291,* 𝖶𝖤𝖡 *www.whyte.org.* 🖃 *$7.* ☉ *Daily 10–5.*

❷ For a pleasant after-dinner walk, stroll to the **Parks Administration Building** (⊠ 1 Cave Ave.), with its splendid summertime flower gardens at the rear. It stands at the south end of Banff Avenue, across a stone bridge over the Bow River.

★ ❸ The **Fairmont Banff Springs Hotel** (⊠ 405 Spray Ave., ☎ 403/762–2211 or 800/441–1414, 𝖶𝖤𝖡 www.fairmont.com), 2 km (1 mi) south of downtown Banff, is the town's architectural showpiece and a National Historic Site. Built in 1888, the hotel is easily recognized by its

Banff

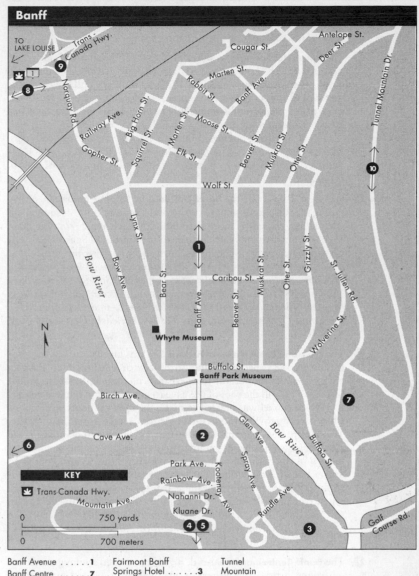

TO LAKE LOUISE

Trans Canada Hwy.

Cougar St.
Antelope St.
Deer St.
Marten St.
Rabbit St.
Banff Ave.
Big Horn St.
Squirrel St.
Marten St.
Moose St.
Beaver St.
Muskrat St.
Otter St.
Elk St.
Railway Ave.
Gopher St.
Norquay Rd.
Tunnel Mountain Dr.

Wolf St.

Lynx St.
Bow River
Bow Ave.

Caribou St.
Bear St.
Banff Ave.
Beaver St.
Muskrat St.
Otter St.
Grizzly St.
St. Julien Rd.
Wolverine St.

Whyte Museum

Buffalo St.
Banff Park Museum

Birch Ave.
Glen Ave.
Bow River
Buffalo St.

Cave Ave.

Park Ave.
Rainbow Ave.
Kootenay Ave.
Spray Ave.
Rundle Ave.

Nahanni Dr.
Mountain Ave.
Kluane Dr.

Golf Course Rd.

N

KEY
⬇ Trans Canada Hwy.

0 ————— 750 yards
0 ————— 700 meters

castlelike exterior. A $50 million renovation has added a new front lobby, restaurants, a museum, and exclusive, upscale retail shops. The shops, restaurants, and spa are open to nonguests.

❹ The **Upper Hot Springs** is a sulfur pool that can be soothing, invigorating, or both. The hot-spring water is especially inviting on a dull, cold day. Lockers, bathing suits (circa 1920s or modern) and towels can be rented, and spa services are available. ⊠ *Mountain Ave., 3 km (2 mi) south of downtown (or 20-minute hike up steep trail from Fairmont Banff Springs Hotel parking area),* ☎ *403/762–1515 or 800/767–1611; 403/ 760–2500 for spa bookings,* WEB *www.parkscanada.gc.ca/hotsprings.* 🎫 *Mid-Oct.–mid-May $5.50, mid-May–mid-Oct. $7.50.* ☉ *Mid-May– mid-Oct., daily 9 AM–11 PM; mid-Oct.–mid-May, Sun.–Thurs. 10–10, Fri.–Sat. 10 AM–11 PM.*

❺ For great vistas, ride the **Banff Gondola at Sulphur Mountain.** Views during the steep eight-minute ride to and from the 7,500-ft summit are spectacular, shared by more than 600,000 each year. From the main deck you can hike the short distance to the summit of Sanson Peak and perhaps catch sight of grazing bighorn sheep, or visit the gift shop or the reasonably priced restaurant. ⊠ *Mountain Ave., 3 km (2 mi) south of downtown (lower terminal next to Upper Hot Springs),* ☎ *403/762– 5438 or 403/762–2523,* WEB *www.banffgondola.com.* 🎫 *$19.* ☉ *Early May–early Sept., daily 7:30 AM–9 PM; early Sept.–mid-Oct., daily 8:30– 6:30; mid-Oct.–early Dec., daily 8:30–4:30; early Dec.–early May, daily 10–4.*

❻ The **Cave and Basin National Historic Site** was given national park protection in 1885, becoming the birthplace of the Canadian Rockies park system. In the earliest years, visitors had to climb down a ladder through a hole in the roof of the cave to get to the hot mineral waters. In 1886, a tunnel was blasted to make the mineral pools more accessible; it now provides modern-day visitors access to this historic site. Two interpretive trails explain the area's geology and plant life. Cave and Basin also has hands-on interpretive displays on the wildlife and history of the national park. The **Cave and Basin Centre Pool** is no longer open for swimming, but you can take a guided tour. A boardwalk leads to a marsh where the warm spring water supports a variety of tropical fish illegally dumped into the waters many years ago. ⊠ *Cave Ave., 2 km (1 mi) west of downtown,* ☎ *403/762–1566,* WEB *www.worldweb.com/parkscanada-banff/cave.html.* 🎫 *$2.50.* ☉ *Weekdays 11–4, weekends 9:30–5.*

❼ The **Banff Centre,** a 69-year-old, highly renowned training center for musicians, artists, and writers, is *the* place in town and in the parks for performances—from poetry readings to rock concerts. The Banff Arts Festival is held here every summer. Within the center, which consists of 16 buildings spread across 43 acres, the **Walter Philips Gallery** (☎ *403/762–6281*) focuses on contemporary works by Canadian and international artists. ⊠ *Main building: St. Julien Rd. (on Tunnel Mountain),* ☎ *403/762–6100 or 800/413–8368,* WEB *www.banffcentre.ca.* 🎫 *Free.* ☉ *Tues.–Sun. noon–5.*

❽ A pleasant, short ride away is **Vermilion Lakes Drive,** off the West Banff exit from Highway 1. Wildlife sightings are excellent: elk, bighorn sheep, muskrat, and the occasional moose. Dawn and dusk are the best times.

❾ The short drive up the steep **Norquay Road** leads to a parking lot with a prize view of Banff townsite and the Bow River valley. Just below, bighorn sheep, deer, goats, elk, and Columbian ground squirrels negotiate their ways on some extremely treacherous slopes.

⑩ **Tunnel Mountain Drive** (east side of Banff) makes a scenic 5-km (3-mi) loop. It's closed in winter, but just off the drive, the **Hoodoos**—fingerlike, eroded rock formations—are accessible year-round.

Dining and Lodging

$$$$ ✗ **Banffshire Club.** The Scottish influence in the region comes to mind when entering the exclusive Banffshire Club. Canadian and international ingredients are featured on the dinner menu. Entrées include roast young partridge with truffles and pecan crusted caribou. Staff members are all sommelier-trained to help make choices from their extensive wine cellar. If you didn't bring a jacket along, the maître d' can lend you one for this adult-only fine dining experience. ⊠ *Fairmont Banff Springs Hotel, 405 Spray Ave.,* ☎ *403/762–6860,* WEB *www.fairmont.com.ca. Reservations essential. Jacket required. AE, D, DC, MC, V. No lunch.*

$$$$ ✗ **Classico.** Set in luxurious decor at the Rimrock Hotel—with magnif-
★ icent mountain views—Classico offers fine cuisine with old- and new-world influences such as Nova Scotia lobster with a delicate, lemon-imbued cream sauce that plays with your tongue. An extensive wine list was carefully crafted by professional sommeliers. There are only two options for dining, but the main courses are constantly changing: the prix-fixe menu includes three courses ($65), and the tasting menu has eight courses with a choice of entrées ($80–$90) and is matched with a Canadian or international wine pairing. There is an elegant private dining room available for as many as 14 guests. ⊠ *Rimrock Resort Hotel, 100 Mountain Ave.,* ☎ *403/762–1865. AE, D, DC, MC, V. No lunch.*

$$$–$$$$ ✗ **Le Beaujolais.** Tapestries on the wall lend a hint of baronial splen-
★ dor to this elegantly decorated restaurant, and the rich food makes a suitable match. Contemporary French preparations of beef, veal, and lamb are menu highlights. Fish and seafood specialties include halibut, salmon, sea bass, and lobster. The wine cellar is lavishly and imaginatively stocked with more than 600 labels. ⊠ *212 Buffalo St., at Banff Ave.,* ☎ *403/762–2712. Reservations essential. MC, V. No lunch.*

$$$–$$$$ ✗ **Bow Valley Grill.** This is probably one of the most popular restaurants in the Fairmont Banff Springs Hotel, serving breakfast, lunch, and dinner in a relaxed atmosphere overlooking the Bow Valley. There's a tantalizing selection of rotisserie-grilled meats, salads, and seafood as well as an on-site bakery and a choice between à la carte or buffet dining. ⊠ *Fairmont Banff Springs Hotel, 405 Spray Ave.,* ☎ *403/762–6860,* WEB *www.fairmont.com.ca. AE, D, DC, MC, V.*

$$–$$$$ ✗ **Buffalo Mountain Lodge.** A large, polished wine cabinet separates the rough-hewn post-and-beam interior into dining and bar areas. On the menu is Rocky Mountain cuisine—fish, meat, and numerous game dishes with sweet nouvelle sauces, supplemented by hearty soups, fresh-baked breads—and an extensive and frequently updated wine list. Choose from entrées of salmon, beef tenderloin, caribou, buffalo steak, and venison. Breakfast offerings include such exotic fare as smoked-salmon Benedict and zucchini-and-carrot French toast. ⊠ *Tunnel Mountain Rd.,* ☎ *403/762–2400 or 800/661–1367. AE, DC, MC, V.*

$–$$$$ ✗ **The Keg and The Keg–Downtown.** The difference between the downtown (117 Banff Avenue) and Caribou Lodge (521 Banff Avenue) locations is that dinner only is available downtown. The Caribou Lodge branch serves up breakfast, a hearty lunch buffet and salad bar. Otherwise, dark-wood tables and chairs, huge wooden beams, and stone fireplaces grace both restaurants, creating a warm, rustic atmosphere. Steak is the dinner specialty, seasoned with The Keg's secret blend of spices and grilled over high heat. Some seafood, pasta, rib, and chicken dishes are also available. ⊠ *117 Banff Ave.,* ☎ *403/760–3030;* ⊠ *521 Banff Ave.,* ☎ *403/762–4442. AE, D, DC, MC, V.*

$–$$$$ ✕ **Miki Japanese Restaurant.** The dining room of one of Banff's best Japanese eateries is bright and cozy, and its second-floor location provides good views along Banff Avenue. Sushi and seafood dishes hold center stage: *sunomona* (cold noodles with vegetables and seafood), *yakizakana* (broiled fish) for appetizers; and hot pots, *shabu-shabu,* (thin slices of beef briefly simmered in broth), and tempura as entrées. ⊠ *Inns of Banff, 600 Banff Ave.,* ☎ *403/762–0600. AE, MC, V. No lunch.*

$$$ ✕ **Cassis Bistro Cafe and Wine Bar.** An intimate, candlelit spot that's popular with the locals, Cassis specializes in a diverse tapas selection available until midnight. The rest of the menu has discernible Californian themes: light pastas, chicken stuffed with fruit, salmon in buerre blanc. Indulge in one of the superb martinis. ⊠ *137 Banff Ave., at Caribou St.,* ☎ *403/762–8289. AE, MC, V.*

$$–$$$ ✕ **Giorgio's Trattoria.** This split-level eatery serves high-quality Italian food, so you might wait a bit during busy hours. Sponge-painted walls, Philippine mahogany tables, and detailed ironwork create an elegant look. The exotic pizzas are cooked in a wood-burning oven—try the pizza *mare* (of the sea), with tiger shrimp, mussels, cilantro, sun-dried tomatoes, and roast-garlic topping. A popular pasta dish is *roselline di pasta* (ham and mozzarella-filled pasta roses in a creamy tomato sauce). ⊠ *219 Banff Ave.,* ☎ *403/762–5114. MC, V. No lunch.*

$$–$$$ ✕ **Golf Clubhouse Restaurant.** One of Banff's best-kept secrets is the Golf Clubhouse Restaurant, with unparalleled mountain views on all sides. The continental menu lists such delights as wild-mushroom terrine with a light chive dressing for an appetizer, and pepper-glazed pork tenderloin as an entrée. The clubhouse is open for lunch and dinner May through October and welcomes nongolfers. ⊠ *Fairmont Banff Springs Hotel, 405 Spray Ave.,* ☎ *403/762–6860,* ⓦⒺⒷ *www.fairmont.com.ca. Reservations essential. AE, D, DC, MC, V. Nov.–Apr.*

$$–$$$ ✕ **Waldhaus.** A raucous, Bavarian-style sing-along sometimes ensues after a meal here. Fondues are a specialty, but the braised beef short ribs, duck with cider sauce, trout, and Wiener schnitzel are also popular. Downstairs in the pub all restaurant menu items are available, except for the fondues. In summer, a barbecue lunch is served on the Red Terrace. The savory barbecued entrées—steaks, salmon, or chicken breast on salad—seem greatly enhanced by the view of Rundle Mountain and the Bow River. ⊠ *Fairmont Banff Springs Hotel, 405 Spray Ave.,* ☎ *403/762–6860,* ⓦⒺⒷ *www.fairmont.com.ca. Reservations essential. Jacket required. AE, D, DC, MC, V. No lunch Sept.–May.*

$–$$$ ✕ **Earls Restaurant.** A fun, casual atmosphere helps make this chain eatery a trendy choice for the younger crowd. The dining area is large and open, and service is prompt and attentive without being overbearing. Popular international dishes on the menu include California shrimp rolls, stir-fry dishes, and pizzas and roast chicken cooked in a wood-burning oven. "Bigger, better" burgers, sandwiches, and salads round out the 50-item menu. Expect serious lines at peak hours. ⊠ *229 Banff Ave.,* ☎ *403/762–4414. Reservations not accepted. AE, MC, V.*

$–$$$ ✕ **Ticino.** Distinctive Swiss dishes show a definite Italian influence in Ticino, the southernmost province of Switzerland. This is evident in the fare at this eponymous, wood-beam and stucco restaurant. Fondue is a house specialty: the *mar-e-mont* (Italian for "ocean and mountain") is a beef-and-shrimp fondue you cook yourself in hot broth. Baked salmon, beef medallions, pan-fried veal, and lamb are other offerings. Ticino is open for breakfast, including a European buffet. ⊠ *High Country Inn, 415 Banff Ave.,* ☎ *403/762–3848. AE, DC, MC, V. No lunch.*

$$$$ ⛻ **Banff Park Lodge Resort Hotel.** On a quiet street downtown, this lodge is within walking distance of shops and restaurants. Rooms are bright, with lots of green and rust colors, and natural oak furniture.

The lobby's high, slanted ceilings, dark cedar paneling, and simple modern style exude a Scandinavian feeling. Ask for a room that doesn't face busy Lynx Street. Rates drop by 40% off-season. ⊠ *Box 2200, 211 Lynx St., T0L 0C0,* ☎ *403/762–4433 or 800/661–9266,* FAX *403/762–3553,* WEB *www.banffparklodge.com. 212 rooms. 2 restaurants, indoor pool, sauna, steam room. AE, DC, MC, V.*

$$$$ 🏨 **Banff Rocky Mountain Resort.** Numerous outdoor facilities are a draw at this resort 5 km (3 mi) east of Banff. Inside the chalet-style building, rooms are bright—with white walls, wall-to-wall carpeting, and blondwood trim. Many have fireplaces and kitchenettes with microwave ovens. Off-season, rates decrease 40%. ⊠ *Box 100, 1029 Banff Ave., at Tunnel Mountain Rd., T0L 0C0,* ☎ *403/762–5531 or 800/661–9563,* FAX *403/762–5166,* WEB *www.rockymountainresort.com. 171 suites. Indoor pool, hot tub, 2 tennis courts, gym, squash. AE, D, DC, MC, V.*

$$$$ 🏨 **Buffalo Mountain Lodge.** Part of the Canadian Rocky Mountain Re-
★ sorts group, along with Emerald Lake Lodge in Yoho National Park and Deer Lodge in Lake Louise, this complex shares their ambience and style. Polished pine, rough-hewn beams, and a stone hearth set the tone in the lobby. There are 48 lodge rooms as well as a hotel-condo cluster. Rooms are dressed in pastel shades and have wood-burning fireplaces, willow chairs, and pine cabinetry. Rates decrease by 25% off-season. ⊠ *Box 1326, Tunnel Mountain Rd., T0L 0C0,* ☎ *403/762–2400 or 800/661–1367,* FAX *403/762–4495,* WEB *www.crmr.com. 88 rooms, 20 suites. 2 restaurants, lobby lounge, hot tub, steam room, gym. AE, DC, MC, V.*

$$$$ 🏨 **Castle Mountain Chalets.** Six different chalet styles satisfy a variety of needs: the smallest have kitchens, bathrooms, and sleeping areas with fireplaces. Although cramped and on the dark side, rooms are clean and quiet. Larger and newer pine-log chalets (which make up the vast majority of the units) have kitchens, fireplaces, two bedrooms, and whirlpool baths, and sleep up to six. Some even larger cabins are available; one cabin is wheelchair accessible. Request a room with a view of Castle Mountain. Rates decrease by 35% off-season; pets are $20 extra each. ⊠ *Box 1655, Hwy. 1A (halfway between Banff and Lake Louise), Banff T0L 0C0,* ☎ *403/522–2783 or 800/661–1315,* FAX *403/762–8629,* WEB *www.castlemountain.com. 22 chalets. Grocery, steam room, gym, coin laundry. AE, MC, V.*

$$$$ 🏨 **Fairmont Banff Springs Hotel.** The building of this massive, castle-
★ like hotel by the Canadian Pacific Railway in 1888 marked the beginning of Banff's tourism boom. More than $33,000 per room was spent in 2001 renovations, adding luxurious amenities, new furniture, decorative lighting, and marble and granite vanities. The hotel's world-class Solace spa is an oasis of modern pampering and luxury, offering massage, hydrotherapy, and aromatherapy wraps among other health and beauty treatments. Heritage Hall, a museum above the Grand Lobby, highlights the natural and cultural history of the area through rotating exhibits. Restaurants, bars, and lounges of varying formality and cuisine—from coffeehouses to a grand dining room—create a small culinary universe in this hotel in the heart of the Rockies. Different room types are available and the gas-burning fireplaces are now ornamental only. In summer about 200 rooms per night are reserved for individual travelers on inclusive resort packages (including use of full hotel facilities, all meals, and gratuities). If the hotel is the focus of your visit to Banff, these packages represent good value. Rates decrease substantially off-season. ⊠ *Box 960, 405 Spray Ave., T0L 0C0,* ☎ *403/762–2211 or 800/441–1414,* FAX *403/762–5755,* WEB *www.fairmont.com.ca. 770 rooms, 70 suites. 10 restaurants, 3 bars, minibars, room service, indoor saltwater pool, outdoor pool, hot tub, massage, mineral baths, outdoor hot tub, sauna, spa, 27-hole golf*

course, 5 tennis courts, bowling, health club, horseback riding, concierge, convention center. AE, D, DC, MC, V.

$$$$ ⊞ **Rimrock Resort Hotel.** Perched on the steep slope of Sulphur Moun-
★ tain, with a gondola and hot springs nearby, this 11-story hotel is where
luxury and natural splendor coexist in harmony. The Grand Lobby has
a 25-ft ceiling, giant windows facing the Rockies, and an oversize
marble fireplace. Nearly all rooms have views of the Bow Valley,
though the views from the lower floors are compromised by trees. Plush
leather and velvet furnishings add to the elegance. Go in the off season for rates that are 50% less. A complimentary shuttle takes you to
and from the Banff townsite. ⊠ *Box 1110, 100 Mountain Ave., T0L
0C0,* ☎ *403/762–3356 or 800/661–1587,* ℻ *403/762–4132,* WEB
*www.rimrockresort.com. 326 rooms, 21 suites. 2 restaurants, 2 lounges,
coffee shop, indoor pool, hot tub, sauna, spa, steam room, gym,
squash, concierge. AE, D, DC, MC, V.*

$$$–$$$$ ⊞ **Brewster Mountain Lodge.** This beautiful wooden lodge is owned by
the Brewster family, which has a 100-year legacy in the tourism and out-
fitting business. Rooms have log furnishings and western ambience, and
the walls are hung with historical photographs. The lodge is in the heart
of downtown Banff where there are dozens of restaurant choices, so it
has no full-service restaurant. There is, however, a daily breakfast buf-
fet. ⊠ *Box 2286, 208 Caribou St., T0L 0C0,* ☎ *403/762–2900 or 888/
762–2900,* ℻ *403/762–3953,* WEB *www.brewsteradventures.com. 57
rooms, 17 suites. Lounge, hot tub, sauna. AE, MC, V.*

$$$ ⊞ **High Country Inn.** There is nothing fancy here—just clean, simple, com-
fortable motel rooms, many with a balcony. Cedar-covered walls give
some rooms a touch of regional character. Ask for a room in the back,
away from the Banff Avenue traffic. Rates decrease by 40% off-season.
⊠ *Box 700, 419 Banff Ave., T0L 0C0,* ☎ *403/762–2236; 800/661–1244
in Canada,* ℻ *403/762–5084,* WEB *www.banffhighcountryinn.com. 70
rooms. Restaurant, indoor pool, 2 hot tubs, gym. AE, MC, V.*

$$$ ⊞ **Shadow Lake Lodge.** Cozy, secluded log cabins for cross-country
skiers or hikers are available at this backcountry lodge. Hike or ski
14 km (9 mi) from the Red Earth parking lot, 19 km (12 mi) west of
Banff on the Highway 1. Gourmet meals are served in the main din-
ing lodge, which is licensed to sell beer and wine. ⊠ *Box 2286, T0L
0C0,* ☎ *403/762–0116 or 888/762–2900,* ℻ *403/760–2866,* WEB
wwww.brewsteradventures.com. 8 cabins. Dining room. V, MC, AE. FAP.

$$ ⊞ **Red Carpet Inn.** Under the same management as the High Country
Inn next door, the no-frills Red Carpet offers quality budget hotel rooms
downtown. Pastel colors fill the rooms, down to pastel-painted wooden
furnishings. The rooms are on the small side, and ones in front, on Banff
Avenue, can be noisy. Rates decrease by 50% off-season. ⊠ *Box 1800,
425 Banff Ave., T0L 0C0,* ☎ *403/762–4184; 800/563–4609 in Canada,*
℻ *403/762–4894. 52 rooms. Hot tub. AE, MC, V.*

Nightlife and the Arts

NIGHTLIFE

Banff's busiest night club, the **Aurora** (⊠ 110 Banff Ave., ☎ 403/760–
5300) has an intimate cigar lounge, and a main bar with Top 40 dance
music. **Barbary Coast** (⊠ 119 Banff Ave., ☎ 403/762–4616) serves up
late-night blues, and good food. If you prefer alternative music with
your cocktails, try **Outa Bounds** (⊠ 137 Banff Ave., ☎ 403/762–
8434). **Wild Bill's** (⊠ Banff Ave. and Caribou St., ☎ 403/762–0333)
is a cowboy bar where two-steppers strut their stuff to live country music.
A late-night Tex-Mex menu is available.

THE ARTS

Most of the cultural activity in the Canadian Rockies takes place in
and around Banff, and the hub of that activity is the **Banff Centre** (⊠

St. Julien Rd., ☎ 403/762–6100; 800/413–8368 in A.B. and B.C.). Presenting a performing-arts grab bag throughout the year—pop and classical music, theater, and dance—the season peaks in summer with the three-month-long Banff Arts Festival.

An annual tradition since 1917, the **Banff–Lake Louise Winter Festival** (☎ 403/762–8421) begins on the third Friday in January and runs for 16 days. Featuring winter sports, outdoor events, nightly bar activities, and a town party, the festival also showcases the work of local artists at **Artventure** (☎ 403/762–8421).

Lux Cinema (✉ Wolf and Bear Mall, 229 Bear St., ☎ 403/762–8595) is a four-screen theater that plays major releases daily.

Outdoor Activities and Sports

BIKING

You can rent mountain bikes and helmets from **Backtrax Bike Rentals** (✉ 337 Banff Ave., ☎ 403/762–8177), which also sells a full range of accessories, clothing, and equipment. There's a repair shop on-site. Backtrax also offers one- to four-hour guided interpretive bike tours on local Banff trails, which are suitable for any age or physical ability. Bicycles are for rent by the hour, the day, and the week at **Performance Ski & Sports** (✉ 208 Bear St., ☎ 403/762–8222). **Unlimited** (✉ 111 Banff Ave., ☎ 403/762–3725) rents bikes and sells a wide range of clothing and accessories for cyclists.

BOATING

Private motorboats are allowed on Lake Minnewanka, near town, the only place in Banff National Park where this is permitted. Aluminum fishing boats with 8-horsepower motors can be rented at the dock (call Lake Minnewanka Boat Tours); if you want something more powerful, you'll have to hook up with a guided fishing tour or bring your own boat.

Lake Minnewanka Boat Tours (☎ 403/762–3473, WEB www.minnewankaboattours.com) offers 1½-hour tours in summer. The cost is $28. **Rocky Mountain Raft Tours** (☎ 403/762–3632) rents canoes at the Banff pier on the Bow River at the end of Wolf Street.

CROSS-COUNTRY SKIING

Banff Alpine Guides (☎ 403/678–6091) leads ski tours into Banff's backcountry. **Michele's Cross Country Ski Tours** (☎ 403/678–2067) leads day tours and weekend getaways to backcountry lodges around Banff, Lake Louise, and Kananaskis country and provides lessons for beginners. **White Mountain Adventures** (☎ 403/678–4099) conducts ski tours and lessons throughout the Bow Valley for beginner and intermediate skiers.

DOWNHILL SKIING

Mike Wiegele Helicopter Skiing (☎ 403/762–5748 or 800/661–9170, WEB www.wiegele.com) serves the Banff region.

Mt. Norquay (✉ Mt. Norquay Rd., ☎ 403/762–4421) runs are generally short and steep with a growing range of intermediate terrain. The vertical drop is 1,650 ft; there are 28 runs and five lifts. At **Sunshine Village** (✉ off Hwy. 1, ☎ 403/762–6500 or 877/542–2633), 8 km (5 mi) west of the town of Banff, the terrain offers plenty of options for beginner, intermediate, and expert skiers. The vertical drop is 3,514 ft, and there are 92 trails and 12 lifts. A good bargain is the $168 three-day pass from **Ski Banff/Lake Louise** (☎ 403/762–4561), which allows you to ski at Sunshine Village and Mt. Norquay and in Lake Louise. It includes free shuttle service to the slopes. You can purchase the pass at the ski areas or at many shops in Banff.

GOLF

The **Fairmont Banff Springs Hotel** (⊠ 405 Spray Ave., ☎ 403/762–6801) has a highly rated, Stanley Thompson–designed, 18-hole, par-71 golf course, as well as an additional 9-hole, par-36 course (advance bookings required). The season runs from early May to mid-October.

HORSEBACK RIDING

Arrangements for hourly or daily rides, as well as lessons, can be made through the concierge at the **Fairmont Banff Springs Hotel** (⊠ 405 Spray Ave., ☎ 403/762–6801). **Holiday on Horseback** (⊠ 132 Banff Ave., ☎ 403/762–4551, WEB www.horseback.com) offers rides in the mountains and foothills—from one hour to six days in length.

RAFTING

Some rafting trips on the Kicking Horse River in Golden, British Columbia, include transportation to and from Banff (1½ hours each way).

Rocky Mountain Raft Tours (☎ 403/762–3632) offers one- to three-hour trips on the Bow River for $24.

SPORTING GEAR

Skis and snowboards can be rented on the slopes, or at many shops in town, concentrated along Bear Street and Banff Avenue.

Monod's (⊠ 129 Banff Ave., ☎ 403/762–3725), part of a chain of sports outfitters, sells and rents a wide array of sports equipment and clothing. **Mountain Magic Equipment** (⊠ 224 Bear St., ☎ 403/762–2591) has three floors of hiking, climbing, skiing, running, and biking equipment for sale or rent—and a 30-ft indoor climbing wall for testing climbing gear.

Shopping

ART AND CRAFTS

Banff Book & Art Den (⊠ 94 Banff Ave., ☎ 403/762–3919) sells art supplies, paper, and paint and has an extensive selection of books on the Rocky Mountains. **Banff Indian Trading Post** (⊠ Birch and Cave Aves., ☎ 403/762–2456) stocks a good selection of local crafts. Handmade jewelry, paintings, sculptures, and fine-art collectibles are available at **Canada House Gallery** (⊠ 201 Bear St., ☎ 403/762–3757). **Freya's North American Native Art** (⊠ Clocktower Mall, 108 Banff Ave., ☎ 403/762–4652) offers Native American art, from clothing to beadwork to dolls. **Freya's Jewelry and Currency Exchange** (⊠ Clocktower Mall, 108 Banff Ave., ☎ 403/762–4652) is the center for Alberta ammolite (a multicolored gemstone) jewelry, a beautiful indigenous stone mounted in 18-karat gold.

Quest Gallery (⊠ 105 Banff Ave., ☎ 403/762–2722) has a good selection of handicrafts and other art principally created by Canadians, including jewelry, and wood and soapstone carvings of wildlife. **The Rock and Fossil Shop** (⊠ Clocktower Mall, 112 Banff Ave., ☎ 403/762–4652) has minerals, gems, and fossils, as well as rocks made into objects such as bookends and clocks. **Rock & Gems Canada** (⊠ 137 Banff Ave., ☎ 403/762–4331) sells fossils, semiprecious and precious stones, jewelry, and rock and gemstone carvings.

Native Canadian art, including moccasins, dream-catchers, and totem poles can be found at **Sleeping Buffalo** (⊠ 111 Banff Ave., ☎ 403/762–8443). **Very Canada** (⊠ 105 Banff Ave., ☎ 403/760–2996) specializes in Canadian crafts, sculptures, jewelry, and paintings.

CLOTHING

Board Walk (⊠ Cascade Plaza, 317 Banff Ave., ☎ 403/760–8755) is Banff's funkiest fashion store with designer streetwear and boardwear (skate not snow). **Canadian Alpaca Store** (⌗ 103 Banff Ave., ☎ 403/760–2511) features a full range of items made from alpaca wool, which is reputedly 10 times stronger and three times warmer than sheep's wool. Some of the garments are from the owner's ranch near Banff; other items are imported. **Great Northern Trading Co.** (⌗ 201 Banff Ave., ☎ 403/762–4166) sells Canadian-designed polar fleece fashions and Cowichan, a Native Canadian style of knitted wool sweater.

Jacques Cartier Clothier (⌗ 131A Banff Ave., ☎ 403/762–5445) deals in exclusive materials such as baby alpaca wool, musk-ox down, and moose leather. **Roots Canada** (⌗ 227 Banff Ave., ☎ 403/762–9434) sells authentic Roots athletic wear and fine leathers. **Rude Girl's** (⌗ 207 Caribou St., ☎ 403/762–4412) has trendy all-female snowboarding and skateboarding clothing.

A good selection of furs, cashmeres, and shearling jackets and coats are available at **Snowflake** (⌗ Sundance Mall, 215 Banff Ave., ☎ 403/762–3633). **Saitoh** (⌗ 115 Banff Ave., ☎ 403/762–8858) sells furs by Nina Ricci and by Canadian designer Paula Lishman, as well as leather clothing.

ECLECTIC

Cows (⌗ 134 Banff Ave., ☎ 403/760–3493) is an eclectic store featuring souvenirs with a cow theme. **Cascade Cigar Co.** (⌗ Cascade Plaza, 317 Banff Ave., ☎ 403/760–5001) has a large selection of Cuban cigars for smoking in Canada. (It's illegal to take them into the U.S.) **Livingstone and Cavell Extraordinary Toys** (⌗ 111 Banff Ave., ☎ 403/762–3755) is the place to look for toys from around the world—handmade toys, wind-up tin toys, puzzles, unusual board games, models, and science toys.

For something a little offbeat (most times of year, anyway), **Spirit of Christmas** (⌗ 133 Banff Ave., ☎ 403/762–2501) has a year-round plethora of Christmas ornaments, figurines, and decorations. **Sundance Gifts** (⌗ Sundance Mall, 215 Banff Ave., ☎ 403/762–3401) sells Anne of Green Gables products (she is one of Canada's favorite fictional daughters) as well as a range of select food items, teas, souvenirs, and collectibles.

Lake Louise

★ ⑪ *56 km (35 mi) northwest of Banff, 184 km (114 mi) west of Calgary.*

Ask people what pops to mind when they think of the Canadian Rockies and they are as likely to say Lake Louise as Banff. What they're really thinking of is the lake itself, with the impressive Victoria Glacier flowing off the mountain at the lake's end, and the classy hotel at the lakeshore—Château Lake Louise. The scenery is among the most spectacular in all of Banff National Park, and the Château Lake Louise is comparable in quality to the Banff Springs Hotel in Banff—both are part of the former Canadian Pacific chain of luxury hotels now under the Fairmont trademark. The town of Lake Louise has a population of only about 1,305 residents. That's not to say there aren't hotels, restaurants, shopping, and other services here—there are, and some very good ones at that. Contact the visitor's center for advice if you're planning a trip in the very busy summer season.

Tom Wilson, a Canadian Pacific Railway packer, was the first nonlocal to see what is now the site of Château Lake Louise. Brought to the area in 1882 by Edwin Hunter, a Stoney Indian guide, Wilson's CPR bosses quickly recognized the tourism potential of the area. A small chalet was built on the lakeshore in 1890. Over the years, the hotel increased in size and splendor, but it was almost entirely burned down in 1924. Most of the present structure is the result of rebuilding soon after the fire.

Most people traveling from Banff to Lake Louise take Highway 1 for about 56 km (35 mi) north along the Bow River. But if you aren't in a hurry, the winding two-lane Highway 1A (the Bow Valley Parkway), running parallel to Highway 1, is the more scenic option. Note that much of this route passes through dense stands of lodgepole pine, a fire succession species (its cones release their seeds when scorched by fire). This area was almost completely burned by accidental fires in the years following rail construction; the even-aged stands of pine along the parkway date from the opening of the West by the railroad.

En Route　　About halfway along the Bow Valley Parkway is a viewpoint for the old mining town of **Silver City**. There isn't much here except an open field today, but for a brief time in the late 19th century, this was the biggest town in the Canadian Rockies.

When the railway came to the area in 1883, and prospectors reported high-grade copper and silver ore in the surrounding mountains, Silver City exploded onto the map. Soon there were 2,000 residents, six hotels, and five general stores. However, there wasn't much silver, just some low-grade copper and lead ore, and by the end of 1885 the ghosts had taken over the now defunct boomtown. One stubborn prospector, Joe Smith, always believed that there were riches to be found, and continued prospecting and living in the former town until his death, 49 years later.

The only sizable metal-ore mines ever developed in the Canadian Rockies were two near the center of Yoho National Park, which produced almost a million tons of lead-silver-zinc ore between 1888 and 1952, when they closed. Most of the successful mines in the Rockies have been coal mines, and several operate outside the national parks today. The Silver City viewpoint is 22.9 km (14.2 mi) from the Bow Valley Parkway turn-off.

In summer you can ride the **Lake Louise Sightseeing Gondola** to an alpine plateau for a stunning view that includes more than a dozen glaciers. In good weather, the deck of the Whitehorn Tea House (open June 1–September 30 for breakfast and lunch), at the top of the lift, is a good place to eat. (In winter, there's a torchlight ski descent.) Free 30- to 90-minute, naturalist-led hikes go to the top of the mountain; schedules vary. ⊠ *Hwy. 1 (Lake Louise exit)*, ☎ *403/522–3555*, WEB *www.skilouise.com.* ⊡ *$17.* ☉ *Open June and Sept. daily 8:30–6; July and Aug., daily 8–6.*

The **Fairmont Château Lake Louise** (⊠ Lake Louise Dr., ☎ 403/522–3511, WEB www.fairmont.com), opened in 1890, overlooks blue-green Lake Louise and the Victoria Glacier at the far end of the lake. The hotel, a Rockies icon, has a setting as scenic as it is popular. Canoe rentals are available at the boathouse. The château is also a departure point for several short, moderately strenuous, well-traveled hiking routes. The most popular hike (about 3½ km, or 2¼ mi) is to Lake Agnes. The tiny lake hangs on a mountain-surrounded shelf that opens to the east with a distant view of the Bow River valley.

Moraine Lake (⊠ Moraine Lake Rd. off Great Divide Hwy., ☎ 403/760–1305 for hiking information, WEB www.morainelake.com), 11 km (7 mi) south of Lake Louise, is a photographic highlight of Banff National Park. Set in the Valley of the Ten Peaks, the lake reflects the snow-clad mountaintops that rise abruptly around it. As beautiful as it is, don't expect an escape from the crowds; it's a major stop for tour buses as well as a popular departure point for hikers. Visit early or late in the day to avoid crowds. A path that runs along the lakeshore takes you beyond much of the parking-lot crush. If you are seeking more solitude, try the moderate hiking trails that lead from the lodge at Moraine Lake into some spectacular alpine country. Hikers should call ahead for special trail restrictions. The best day hike is the 5.8-km (3.6-mi) hike (one way) to Sentinel Pass, at 8,550 ft. After the first 2.4 km (1½ mi), you reach Larch Valley, which is spectacular in fall with the brilliant yellow colors of the larch trees, and popular with photographers for this reason. Past the valley, there are fewer photographers. Strong hikers can head down the other side of Sentinel Pass and back to Moraine Lake Road for a total distance of 16.9 km (10½ mi), plus you need transportation back to your starting point, 10 km (6 mi) down the road. From June through September, you can rent a canoe from the office of **Moraine Lake Lodge** (☎ 403/522–3733).

Dining and Lodging

$$$–$$$$ ✕ **Mount Fairview Dining Room.** Set beneath the high ceilings and inside the log-and-stone framework of Deer Lodge, this fine-dining establishment has large picture windows and a rustic atmosphere. The specialty is Rocky Mountain cuisine, a style based on the principle that foods should only be served together if they grow together, and should only be served in-season. The rather unusual offerings include such dishes as ravioli with dandelions, guinea fowl with birch bark, and sun-dried cranberry sauce on local pork tenderloin. There's also an extensive wine list. ⊠ *109 Lake Louise Dr.,* ☎ *403/522–4202 or 800/661–1595,* 🖷 *403/522–4222. AE, D, MC, DC, V.*

$$$–$$$$ ✕ **Post Hotel.** Here is one of the true epicurean experiences in the Cana-
★ dian Rockies. A low, exposed-beam ceiling and a stone, wood-burning hearth in the corner lend a warm, in-from-the-cold atmosphere; white tablecloths and fanned napkins provide an elegant touch. Daring European cuisine is created with the combination of modern and classic dishes. The house specialty is Alberta rack of lamb; veal and caribou are also good choices. Alternatively, try the house-made pheasant spring rolls with a pickled ginger vinaigrette or salmon with one of the house specialty sauces, which change twice a year. ⊠ *200 Pipestone Rd.,* ☎ *403/522–3989. Reservations essential. AE, MC, V.*

$$$–$$$$ ✕ **Walliser Stube.** For something different, try this Swiss wine bar with warm cherrywood decor and a good selection of fondues. Try pork tenderloin simmered in cider, seafood, or veal in broth or the classic cheese and beef fondues. ⊠ *Fairmont Château Lake Louise, Lake Louise Dr.,* ☎ *403/522–3511 Ext. 1818. Reservations essential. AE, D, DC, MC, V.*

$ ✕ **Laggan's Mountain Bakery and Deli.** This small coffee shop in the Samson Mall is where the local work crews, mountain guides, and park wardens come for an early morning muffin and cup of coffee. Laggan's has excellent baked goods, especially the sweet poppy-seed breads. You may want to pick up a sandwich if you're driving north on the Icefields Parkway. ⊠ *Samson Mall, off Hwy. 1,* ☎ *403/522–2017. No credit cards.*

$$$$ 🛏 **Deer Lodge.** Built in 1921 as a log tea house, this spot quickly became a popular destination, just a 10- or 15-minute walk from the shores of Lake Louise. Guest rooms were added in 1925, and the frequent renovations since then have preserved most of the original rustic charm of the stone-and-log architecture. Rooms have private baths, feather comforters, and tea house–era antiques; the older parts of the lodge are small-but-bright rooms with the most historic charm. In keeping with its heritage, few rooms have phones, and none has TVs. Instead,

many guests prefer to enjoy some quiet time with a book around the central fireplace, in one of the hotel's many nooks and crannies, or in the rooftop hot tub, complete with stunning mountain views. Rates decrease by 40% off-season. ⊠ *Box 100, 109 Lake Louise Dr., T0L 1E0,* ☎ *403/522–3747 or 800/661–1595,* FAX *403/522–4222,* WEB *www.crmr.com. 73 rooms. Restaurant, lounge, hot tub, sauna, recreation room. AE, DC, MC, V.*

$$$$ 🎑 **Fairmont Château Lake Louise.** There's a good chance that no hotel—anywhere—has a more dramatic view out its back door. Terraces and lawns reach to the famous aquamarine lake, backed up by the Victoria Glacier. Inside, off-white walls, polished wood and brass, and burgundy carpeting blend well with the lake view, seen through large, horseshoe-shape windows. Guest rooms have neocolonial furnishings, and some have terraces. The hotel began as a wooden chalet in 1890 but was largely destroyed by fire in 1924. It was soon rebuilt into the present grand stone-facade structure. In late 1999 (though it won't be completed for some time), the Château received approval to add a seven-story convention center, with 80 new rooms, for returning some leasehold land back to the park and for letting some of the lawn-and-garden setting revert to a more natural ecosystem. The many dining choices at the Château range from family dining in the Poppy Room to night-on-the-town elegance in the Edelweiss Dining Room (jacket required for dinner in summer). Afternoon tea is served in the Lakeview Lounge (early June to early September) and in summer you can sample Italian and North American cuisine at Tom Wilson's dining room. Dinner reservations are required for all restaurants except the Poppy Room. ⊠ *Lake Louise Dr., T0L 1E0,* ☎ *403/522–3511 or 800/441–1414,* FAX *403/522–3834,* WEB *www.fairmont.com. 435 rooms, 54 suites. 6 restaurants, 3 lounges, indoor pool, hot tub, steam room, gym, horseback riding, boating, shops. AE, D, DC, MC, V.*

$$$$ 🎑 **Lake Louise Inn.** Five buildings hold a variety of accommodations, from small budget rooms to two-bedroom condo units, some with a balcony, fireplace, and kitchenette. Fifty-five units are equipped with fireplaces and kitchenettes. A shuttle to the mountain and multiday ski packages are winter amenities. Rates decrease by 50% off-season. ⊠ *210 Village Rd., T0L 1E0,* ☎ *403/522–3791 or 800/661–9237,* FAX *403/522–2018,* WEB *www.lakelouiseinn.com. 232 rooms. Restaurant, pizzeria, pub, indoor pool, 2 hot tubs, sauna. AE, DC, MC, V.*

$$$$ 🎑 **Paradise Lodge and Bungalows.** Only 3 km (1.5 mi) up the access road from the town of Lake Louise, this lodge has one- and two-bedroom suites with wood furnishings and oak paneling in the two main log buildings. The two-bedroom units have a balcony, a coffeemaker, and a refrigerator; the one-bedroom units come with a full kitchen and a fireplace. The bungalows, or log-sided cabins (some with kitchenettes), are more rustic on the outside than on the inside. Set in a spruce and pine grove, they can feel somewhat dark and cramped, but they are well maintained. ⊠ *Box 7, 105 Lake Louise Dr., T0L 1E0,* ☎ *403/522–3595,* FAX *403/522–3987,* WEB *www.paradiselodge.com. 24 suites, 21 bungalows. Playground, coin laundry. MC, V. Closed mid-Oct.–mid-May.*

$$$$ 🎑 **Post Hotel.** A bright red roof and log construction make this hotel a
★ model of rustic elegance. Rooms come in 15 configurations, from standard doubles to units that have a sleeping loft, balcony, fireplace, and whirlpool tub. Twenty-six deluxe suites have a king-size bed and a large living room with a river-stone fireplace. For old-fashioned, in-the-mountains romance try one of the three streamside log cabins. Furnishings are solid Canadian pine throughout. The restaurant is regularly rated as one of the best in the Canadian Rockies. Room rates decrease by about 40% off-season. ⊠ *200 Pipestone Rd., T0L 1E0,* ☎ *403/522–3989 or 800/661–1586,* FAX *403/522–3966,* WEB *www.posthotel.com. 69 rooms,*

26 suites, 3 cabins. Restaurant, lounge, pub, indoor pool, steam room, library. AE, MC, V.

$$$ ⛺ **Skoki Lodge.** An 11-km (7-mi) hike or ski jaunt from the Lake Louise ski area, Skoki is the kind of backcountry lodge you must work to get to. The high-alpine scenery of the valley makes the trek well worthwhile, as does the small lodge itself, built in 1930. The log walls and big stone fireplace epitomize coziness, but don't expect private baths, running water, or electricity. However, meals are included. Reserve far in advance. Minimum two-day stay. ⊠ *Box 5, T0L 1E0,* ☎ *403/522–3555,* FAX *403/522–2095,* WEB *www.skilouise.com/skoki. 4 rooms, 3 cabins. Dining room. AE, MC, V. Closed mid-Sept.–mid-Dec., Jan., mid-Apr.–mid-June. FAP.*

Nightlife and the Arts

If you don't want to spend the evening outdoors, Château Lake Louise with its lounges and dining rooms with entertainment and dancing is the place to go.

Although it's quiet during the day, on weekends, **Glacier Saloon** (⊠ Fairmont Château Lake Louise, Lake Louise Dr., ☎ 403/522–3511, WEB www.fairmont.com) has a DJ who plays Top 40 and requests from patrons.

The Outpost (⊠ Fairmont Chateau Lake Louise, Lake Louise Dr., ☎ 403/522–3511, WEB www.fairmont.com) is a relaxing lounge with a fireplace, couches, and a big-screen television. The pub menu features hamburgers, salads, and pizza.

On the weekend beginning the third Friday in January, ice carvers from around the world compete in the annual **Ice Magic** ice-sculpting contest (☎ 403/762–8421), held at various locations in Lake Louise. This free exhibition remains on display until the first of March, weather permitting.

Outdoor Activities and Sports

HORSEBACK RIDING

Lake Louise Stables can arrange for trail rides, from one-hour to half- and full-day rides to an alpine tea house. The stables are a five-minute walk from the Fairmont Château Lake Louise, on the shores of the lake. (☎ 403/762–5454, WEB www.brewsteradventures.com).

SKIING

At **Lake Louise Ski Area** (⊠ off Lake Louise Dr., ☎ 403/522–3555), the downhill terrain is large and varied, with a fairly even spread of novice, intermediate, and expert runs. The vertical drop is 3,257 ft, and there are 105 runs and 11 lifts.

SPORTING GEAR

At **Monod's** (⊠ Fairmont Château Lake Louise, Lake Louise Dr., ☎ 403/522–3837), equipment and clothing sold ranges from hiking and downhill skiing to mountaineering.

Mountain Edge (⊠ Lake Louise Ski Area, ☎ 403/522–3555) offers a full range of equipment and clothing for sale, and you can rent downhill skis, snowboards, and helmets.

Shopping

With Banff only a short drive away, shops in Lake Louise face some pretty stiff competition. Lake Louise has two main shopping areas: Samson Mall and the stores of Château Lake Louise.

Samson Mall (⊠ Village Rd. and Lake Louise Dr., off Hwy. 1, ☎ 403/522–2125) is a mix of about 20 shops selling gifts, books, clothes, sporting goods, groceries, and liquor.

Fairmont Château Lake Louise (✉ Lake Louise Dr., ☎ 403/522–3837) has a promenade with a collection of 34 high-end gift and clothing stores. Here you can find some unique items, such as clothing made with *qiviuk* (the inner down of the Arctic musk ox—reputedly eight times warmer than wool, and softer than cashmere).

NORTH AND WEST OF BANFF

North of Lake Louise, Highways 1 and 93 diverge. Highway 93—the spectacularly scenic Icefields Parkway—continues northward for 230 km (143 mi) to the town of Jasper. Highway 1 bears west over Kicking Horse Pass into Yoho National Park and British Columbia.

The Icefields Parkway

★ ⑫ *230-km long (143-mi long), running from Lake Louise to Jasper.*

Powerfully rugged mountain scenery, glaciers, waterfalls and icefalls, and wildlife: the Icefields Parkway offers all these and more as it snakes its way between Lake Louise and Jasper. The original highway was built during the Great Depression to provide badly needed jobs, but has since been reconstructed. The parkway is now a modern two-lane road, with wide paved shoulders along most of the route. It needs to be: some 4 million people drive it each year.

More than 100 glaciers show off their blue ice along this drive; at the Columbia Icefields, the Athabasca Glacier reaches almost to the roadway (a short walk takes you right up to the ice). Large animals such as elk, moose, deer, and bighorn sheep are fairly common along this route; occasionally you can see bears and mountain goats. In summer, alpine wildflowers carpet Bow Pass and Sunwapta Pass.

There aren't many facilities, so be sure to check the gas gauge and maybe pack some sandwiches. Although you could drive this winding road in three to four hours, it's more likely to be a full-day trip when you add in stops. There are campgrounds, hostels, and four relatively inexpensive motel-cabin facilities along the way (but don't expect anything beyond basic facilities—and book in advance). The road rises to near tree line at several points, and the weather can be chilly and unsettled at these high elevations even in midsummer—bring some warm clothing along.

The most dramatic scenery is in the north end of Banff National Park and the south end of Jasper National Park, where ice fields and glaciers become common on the high mountains flanking the route (ice fields are massive reservoirs of ice; glaciers are the slow-moving rivers of ice that flow from the ice fields). Scenic overlooks and signposted hiking trails of varying lengths abound along the route.

Bow Summit, at 6,787 ft the highest drivable pass in the national parks of the Canadian Rockies, may be covered with snow as late as May and as early as September. On the south side of the pass is Bow Lake, source of the Bow River, which flows through Banff. Around the lake are stubby trees and underbrush—this is where the trees end and high-alpine country begins. Above Bow Lake hangs the Crowfoot Glacier, so-named because of its resemblance to a three-toed crowfoot. At least, that's how it looked when it was named at the beginning of the 20th century. Glaciers in the Canadian Rockies have been receding for at least a century, and the Crowfoot is a good example. The lowest toe completely melted away 50 years ago, and now only the upper two toes remain. On the north side of Bow Pass is **Peyto Lake;** its startlingly deep aqua-blue color comes from the minerals in glacial runoff. ✉ *41 km (25 mi) north of Lake Louise, 190 km (118 mi) south of Jasper.*

The short (2½-km, or 1½-mi), steep **Parker Ridge Trail** is one of the easiest hikes in the national parks to bring you into the alpine world above tree line. There's an excellent view of the Saskatchewan Glacier, where the river of the same name begins, though you've got to make it to the top of the ridge to get the view. Snowbanks can persist into early summer, but sunshine lays intricate carpets of wildflowers across the trail in late July and August. Stay on the path to keep erosion to a minimum. The trailhead is about 4 km (2½ mi) south of the boundary between Banff and Jasper parks; it's signposted on the parkway.

Sunwapta Pass marks the border between Banff and Jasper national parks. Wildlife abounds and is most visible in spring and autumn after a snowfall, when herds of bighorn sheep come to the road to lick up the salt used to melt snow and ice. At 6,675 ft, Sunwapta is the second-highest drivable pass in the national parks of the Canadian Rockies. Be prepared for a series of hairpin turns as you switchback up to the pass summit. ⊠ *122 km (76 mi) north of Lake Louise, 108 km (67 mi) south of Jasper.*

The **Athabasca Glacier** (127 km [79 mi] north of Lake Louise, 103 km [64 mi] south of Jasper) is a 7-km (4½-mi) tongue of ice flowing from the immense Columbia Icefield almost to the highway. A century ago the ice flowed over the current location of the highway; signposts depict the gradual retreat of the ice since that time. Several other glaciers are visible from here; they all originate from the Columbia Icefield—a giant alpine lake of ice covering 325 square km (130 square mi), whose edge is visible from the highway. Hikers can walk up to the toe of the glacier, but venturing far without a trained guide is dangerous because of hidden crevasses and slippery, sharp ice. Athabasca Glacier Ice Walks offers three-, five-, and six-hour guided walks ($28–$32), which can be reserved at the Icefield Center or through Jasper Adventure Centre, in Jasper. You can also take a trip onto the Athabasca Glacier in Brewster Tours' snowcoaches that have been modified to drive on ice (tickets available at the Icefield Center for $21.50).

⑬ The **Icefield Centre,** the interpretive center for the Athabasca Glacier and Columbia Icefield, houses interpretive exhibits, a gift shop, and two dining facilities (one cafeteria style, one buffet style). Keep in mind that the summer midday rush between 11 and 3 can be intense. There are even 32 hotel rooms, available from early May to mid-October (book through **Brewster's Transport** in Banff, ☏ 877/423–7433). ⊠ *Opposite Athabasca Glacier on Hwy. 93, 127 km (79 mi) north of Lake Louise, 103 km (64 mi) south of Jasper,* ☏ *877/423–7433,* WEB *www.brewster.ca.* ☉ *Late May–mid-June and Sept.–early Oct., daily 10–5; mid-June–Aug., daily 10–7.*

Jasper

⑭ *287 km (178 mi) north of Banff, 362 km (224 mi) west of Edmonton.*

The town of Jasper—a smaller, less-hectic version of Banff—is a convenient central location for exploring the sights in Jasper National Park. The town has grown considerably in recent years, as have prices. Still, it remains a relaxed and somewhat less commercialized place to stay in the parks.

In 1811, just across the river from the modern-day town of Jasper, Henry's House became the site of the first outsiders' settlement in what are now the national parks of the Rockies. As with other early settlements in the mountains, it was built as a fur trading post and used also as a stopover for explorers crossing the mountains into British Columbia. It was abandoned several years later when a new fur trading post

(Jasper House) was built near the eastern edge of what is now Jasper National Park. For almost a century following, there was no permanent settlement at the location of present-day Jasper, and the wilderness gradually reclaimed the few scattered buildings of Henry's House.

Early in the 20th century, the nod was given for a railway to cross the mountains on a route that took it up the Athabasca River into the mountains, then across the Yellowhead Pass into British Columbia. In order to protect the newly accessible wilderness, Jasper National Park was created in 1907.

In 1911 the town of Fitzhugh was established to service the new line of the Grand Trunk Pacific Railway. Two years later the town's name was changed to Jasper. A second railway, the Canadian Northern, was added between 1913 and 1915 (later the two were merged into the Canadian National Railway to eliminate obvious redundancy). The town immediately began servicing not only the railways, but also the sudden influx of adventurers who came by rail. The seeds of modern-day Jasper were sown.

Still, the modern era has been relatively slow in coming to Jasper. The first automobile trip from Edmonton to Jasper, in 1922, was a grueling six-day journey along abandoned rail lines, with horses used to pull the cars through the numerous impassible sections. In 1928 a gravel road was built to the park, and pavement finally came to Jasper in 1951. However, it wasn't until 1970 that the blacktop extended west of Jasper into British Columbia, making Jasper an easily accessible destination from both east and west. Today, the drive from Edmonton to Jasper is a leisurely four-hour cruise on a modern four-lane highway with paved shoulders to the park gate; good two-lane pavement continues west into the British Columbia Rockies and beyond.

Jasper is set in one of the preeminent backpacking areas in North America. Multiday loops of more than 160 km (100 mi) are possible on well-maintained trails. Backpacking and horse-packing trips in the northern half of the park offer legitimate wilderness seclusion, if not the dramatic glacial scenery of the park's southern half. However, day trips are much more common, especially around Mt. Edith Cavell, Miette Hot Springs, and Maligne Lake for hiking; and Pyramid Lake and Jasper Park Lodge for horseback riding.

The main drag in Jasper is **Connaught Drive**; railroad tracks border one side of the road, and a dense collection of shops, restaurants, and motels lines the other. One block west of Connaught Drive, **Patricia Street** has shops, restaurants, and services, at a slightly less-hectic pace.

★ ☾ ⑮ The **Jasper Tramway** whisks riders 3,191 vertical ft up the steep flank of Whistlers Mountain to an impressive overlook of the townsite and the surrounding mountains. The seven-minute ride takes you to the upper station, above the tree line (be sure to bring warm clothes). A farther 30- to 45-minute hike takes you to the summit, which is 8,085 ft above sea level. Several unmarked trails lead through the alpine meadows beyond. ⊠ *Whistlers Mountain Rd., 3 km (2 mi) south of Jasper off Hwy. 93,* ☎ *780/852–3093,* ⓦⒺⒷ *www.worldweb.com/JasperTramway.* ⊠ *$16.* ☉ *Apr.–mid-May and Oct., daily 9–4:30; mid-May–early Sept., daily 8:30 AM–10 PM; rest of Sept., daily 9:30–9.*

☾ **Jasper Aquatic Center** pleases children, with a 180-ft indoor water slide, a kids' pool, and a 25-m regular pool. A steam room is also on-site, and towel and suit rentals are available. ⊠ *401 Pyramid Lake Rd.,* ☎ *780/852–3663.* ⊠ *$6.* ☉ *Public swimming: Mon.–Thurs. 6 PM–8:30 PM, Fri. 5 PM–9 PM, Sat. 3–9, Sun. 4:30–8:30.*

🐣 ⑯ Various water-sports options can be found at **Pyramid and Patricia lakes,** 6 km (4 mi) north of Jasper. To get there drive through town to the north side on Cedar Street and take Pyramid Lake Road. Rowboats, canoes, kayaks, and two-seater pedal boats as well as electric and gas-powered boats can be rented from Pyramid Lake Resort from May to October. Pyramid is the only lake in Jasper National Park where boat motors are allowed on private craft. It has picnic tables and a sandy beach, but you're likely to find the water too cold for swimming, except during the hottest summer weather. You can rent from a small selection of canoes and rowboats at Patricia Lake Bungalows.

Dining and Lodging

$$$$ ✕ **Overlander Mountain Lodge.** It's a bit of a drive from town, but this cozy log dining room rewards guests with fine dining in a secluded setting. Weather permitting in summer, the outdoor patio is a nice place to eat. Menu highlights include pecan rack of lamb Dijonese, Atlantic lobster, AAA Alberta beef, and ostrich with peppercorn sauce. Other menu items change frequently to incorporate seasonal ingredients and the chef's latest innovations. Homemade breads and pastries round out the experience. The Overlander also serves breakfast. ⊠ *Hwy. 16, 49 km (30 mi) east of Jasper, 1 km (0.6 mi) from east gate of Jasper National Park,* ☎ *780/866–2330. AE, DC, MC, V.*

$$–$$$$ ✕ **Le Beauvallon Dining Room.** Upholstered chairs, blue tablecloths,
★ and wood-trimmed walls give this dining room an air of elegance that is enhanced by the music of a world-class harpist playing in the nearby lounge Wednesday through Sunday. The menu has some seafood items, but meat and game dishes are the stars, including beef, buffalo, caribou, elk, lamb, and venison. The giant Sunday-brunch buffet ($17) is an epic feast. Le Beauvallon is open for breakfast. ⊠ *Royal Canadian Lodge Jasper, 96 Giekie St.,* ☎ *780/852–5644. Reservations essential. AE, D, DC, MC, V.*

$$–$$$$ ✕ **Moose's Nook.** Inside the Fairmont Jasper Park Lodge, Moose's Nook has intimate dining with a wide range of contemporary Canadian cuisine including wild game and Alberta prime rib of beef. It's open for dinner daily in summer and Saturday through Monday in winter. ⊠ *Off Hwy. 16, 7 km (4 mi) northeast of Jasper,* ☎ *780/852–3301 or 800/441–1414. Reservations essential. AE, D, DC, MC, V.*

$$$ ✕ **Beauvert Room.** The Fairmont Jasper Park Lodge's largest restaurant exudes old-world charm and heritage in the decor and early 20th-century photographs. Menu favorites include warm artichoke pâté with water biscuits and garden crudités, Atlantic salmon, and slow-roasted loin of Alberta pork with apple rhubarb chutney. Open in summer only, the Beauvert Room serves breakfast and dinner. ⊠ *Off Hwy. 16, 7 km (4 mi) northeast of Jasper,* ☎ *780/852–3301 or 800/441–1414. Reservations essential. AE, D, DC, MC, V. No lunch.*

$$–$$$ ✕ **Becker's Gourmet Restaurant.** This fine-dining establishment is
★ often missed by visitors to Jasper because of its out-of-town location. Still, it's popular enough already. Spectacular panoramic views of the Athabasca River and Mt. Kerkeslin from a glass-enclosed dining room are a suitable accompaniment to the food. Try the Brie with Westphalia ham and spinach in puff pastry, the veal with wild mushrooms, or the rack of lamb. There's a breakfast buffet 8 to 11, and a children's menu is available. ⊠ *Beside Becker's Chalets, Hwy. 93, 5 km (3.5 mi) south of Jasper,* ☎ *780/852–3535. AE, MC, V. Closed Nov.–Apr. No lunch.*

$$–$$$ ✕ **Edith Cavell Dining Room.** Catering to adults, this restaurant overlooks the impressive mountain of the same name and has live classical piano music in summer. The menu offers fine regional cuisine with local nuances and signature dishes include arctic char and Alberta rack of lamb. ⊠ *Fairmont Jasper Park Lodge, off Hwy. 16, 7 km (4 mi)*

northeast of Jasper, ☎ *780/852–3301 or 800/441–1414. Reservations essential. AE, D, DC, MC, V. No lunch.*

$–$$$ ✕ **Denjiro Japanese Restaurant.** One of the first Japanese restaurants in Jasper, this remains the most popular. There's an authentic Japanese menu, a sushi bar, and booths for intimate dining. Sushi and sashimi top the menu, but tempura, teriyaki, shabu-shabu, and stir-fry are also available. ✉ *410 Connaught Dr.,* ☎ *780/852–3780. AE, MC, V.*

$–$$$ ✕ **Fiddle River Seafood Company.** Candles, dried flowers, and plenty
★ of wood make this second-floor dining room cozy. Tables facing Connaught Drive have an excellent view of Mt. Tekarra. Seafood is the star, from the relatively simple beer-battered cod with lemon-pepper fries to more exotic choices such as sesame-crusted salmon. Chicken, T-bones, lamb, and pasta dishes are available for landlubbers. ✉ *620 Connaught Drive,* ☎ *780/852–3032. AE, MC, V. No lunch.*

$–$$$ ✕ **Villa Caruso.** Alberta is ranch country, and this steak house is a good place to sample the products of the cattle industry. Entrées include flame-grilled Alberta grain-fed AAA Black Angus beef, from tenderloin to New York steak to prime rib. Pasta, fish, chicken, buffalo, pork tenderloin, lamb, ribs, and pizza round out the menu. (There's also a children's menu.) In summer you can enjoy the mountain views from any of the three outdoor patios; any season you can cozy up for cocktails in the Fireside Lounge. ✉ *640 Connaught Dr.,* ☎ *780/852–3920. AE, MC, V.*

$–$$ ✕ **Earls Restaurant.** Part of a popular chain (with another outlet in Banff), Earls has good food, a campy atmosphere, and efficient service. This is not haute cuisine—dining here is fun and the place draws a young crowd. ✉ *600 Patricia St., 2nd floor,* ☎ *780/852–2393. Reservations not accepted. AE, MC, V.*

$ ✕ **Mountain Foods & Cafe.** This is a good spot to pick up ready-made picnic lunches for a day of touring. A frequently updated menu usually features omelets, waffles, and baked goods in the morning; and assorted quesadillas, tortilla wraps, grilled focaccia sandwiches the rest of the day. The dinner menu changes seasonally. ✉ *606 Connaught Dr.,* ☎ *780/852–4050. MC, V.*

$$$$ ▥ **Fairmont Jasper Park Lodge.** This lakeside resort northeast of town
★ has abundant on-site recreational amenities and is a notable mountain destination in itself, whether or not you stay overnight. Accommodations vary from cedar chalets and heritage log cabins to specialty cabins with up to eight bedrooms. Rooms have homelike comforts including down duvets, and many have a porch, patio, or balcony; some include a fireplace. A year-round outdoor swimming pool (you swim to it from the warm indoors) is heated to 30°C (88°F) in winter—a major draw for winter guests. Rates drop by about one-half October through May, with some outstanding late-winter package deals for budget travelers, often announced in January. ✉ *Box 40, off Hwy. 16, T0E 1E0, 7 km (4 mi) northeast of Jasper,* ☎ *780/852–3301 or 800/441–1414,* 🆋 *780/ 852–5107,* 🕸 *www.jasperparklodge.com. 393 rooms, 58 suites. 4 restaurants, bar, 3 lounges, room service, indoor-outdoor pool, 18-hole golf course, 4 tennis courts, health club, horseback riding, boating, bicycles, ice-skating, rollerblading, sleigh rides. AE, D, DC, MC, V.*

$$$$ ▥ **Jasper Inn.** A few blocks from the main drag in Jasper, this modern, chalet-style hotel is convenient to downtown shopping and dining but feels removed from the constant buzz outside its doors. Slanted cedar ceilings and brick fireplaces warm the angular coolness of the sleek, low-slung furniture. Accommodations vary; living areas in condo-style units are particularly spacious. Most units have kitchenettes and fireplaces. The rooms facing Bonhomme Street have the best views. Rates drop by more than half from October through May. ✉ *Box 879, Giekie St. and Bonhomme Ave., T0E 1E0,* ☎ *780/852–4461 or 800/*

661–1933, FAX 780/852–5916, WEB *www.jasperinn.com. 129 rooms, 14 suites. Restaurant, lobby lounge, indoor pool, sauna, steam room. AE, D, DC, MC, V.*

$$$$ ☎ **Royal Canadian Lodge Jasper.** Large wood beams cantilevered over the front door of this two-story inn suggest a Scandinavian interior, but the large rooms actually have a motel-like decor. The hotel's restaurant, Le Beauvallon, is excellent. Rates drop by more than 50% October through May. ⊠ *96 Giekie St., T0E 1E0,* ☎ *780/852–5644 or 800/661–9323,* FAX *780/852–4860,* WEB *www.charltonresorts.com. 119 rooms. Restaurant, indoor pool, hot tub. AE, DC, MC, V.*

$$$–$$$$ ☎ **Alpine Village.** One of Jasper's few lower-priced options, Alpine Village is south of town. Rooms have pine furnishings, fireplaces, and wood-beam ceilings. Logs in many cabins are left exposed on interior walls, adding to the warm, rustic feeling of this family-run operation. Most units have sun decks; two-bedroom cabins have full kitchens. Mt. Edith Cavell rises in the distance, and the Athabasca River runs nearby—though you must cross a small road to reach it. Rates decrease by almost 50% during the brief time it's open in off-season. ⊠ *Box 610, Hwy. 93A, T0E 1E0, 2 km (1 mi) south of Jasper,* ☎ *780/852–3285,* WEB *www.alpinevillage.com. 41 units. Hot tub. MC, V. Closed mid-Oct.–Apr.*

$–$$$$ ☎ **Patricia Lake Bungalows.** Ten minutes from Jasper, this lodging pro-
★ vides a peaceful retreat on the shores of Patricia Lake. The roomy cabins have basic furnishings: queen-size beds, dressers, and tables, kitchen facilities, and TVs. Shower stalls are the rule here, not bathtubs. This is one of the few remaining bargain accommodations near Jasper. Though the motel rooms are the least expensive accommodation, the cabins—at a 20% premium over the motel units—remain the most popular choice. Rates decrease by 25% off-season. ⊠ *Box 657, Pyramid Lake Rd., T0E 1E0, 5 km (3 mi) from Jasper,* ☎ *780/852–3560,* FAX *780/852–4060. 6 rooms, 29 cabins. Boating, bicycles, playground, coin laundry. AE, MC, V. Closed mid-Oct.–Apr.*

$–$$$ ☎ **Pine Bungalows.** This charming property is minutes from Jasper, off Highway 16 on the shores of the Athabasca River. You can relax, listen to the flowing water and contemplate the breathtaking scenery. Cabins renovated in 2001 are lined with knotty pine, and many have either fireplaces or kitchens—but not telephones or TVs. There's a gift shop, a grocery store, and barbecue grills on-site. ⊠ *Box 7, T0E 1E0,* ☎ *780/852–3491,* FAX *780/852–3432,* WEB *www.jasperadventures.com. 80 rooms. Shop, coin laundry. AE, MC, V. Closed mid-Oct.–May.*

Nightlife and the Arts

NIGHTLIFE

The **Astoria Hotel's Dead Dog Bar & Grill** (⊠ 404 Connaught Dr., ☎ 780/852–3351) is a popular spot where you're sure to meet some colorful local characters on Friday evening. In the Athabasca Hotel, **Atha-B Nightclub** (⊠ 510 Patricia St., ☎ 780/852–3386) has live bands and Top 40 music. **Pete's on Patricia** (⊠ 614 Patricia St., 2nd floor, ☎ 780/852–6262) is a crowded bar that showcases live bands weekly.

Villa Caruso (⊠ 640 Connaught Dr., ☎ 780/852–3920) moves to the sounds of swing, jazz, and blues. Don't miss the martini menu. The **Whistle Stop** (⊠ Whistlers Inn, Connaught Dr., ☎ 780/852–3361) is a local haunt with the ambience of a British pub.

THE ARTS

The **Chaba Movie Theatre** (⊠ 604 Connaught Dr., ☎ 780/852–4749) plays major releases daily. The **Jasper Activity Centre** (⊠ 303 Pyramid Ave., ☎ 780/852–3381) hosts local theater, music, and dance troupe performances throughout the year. The **Jasper Folk Festival** (☎ 780/

852–5781), on the first weekend in August, presents Canadian folk music in the town center and at other venues.

Outdoor Activities and Sports

BIKING

The Boat House (✉ Fairmont Jasper Park Lodge, off Hwy. 16, ☎ 780/852–5708) has adult and children's mountain bikes for rent, as well as paddleboats and canoes. High-performance mountain bikes, bike trailers, and a tandem bicycle can be rented from **Freewheel Cycle** (✉ 618 Patricia St., ☎ 780/852–3898). In the same store, **Wheel Fun** offers interpretive biking tours in the Jasper area. Trips range from two to six hours, and from mild to wild terrain suitable for different ages and abilities. Longer, custom-designed routes are available. All trips include snacks and a guide.

CLIMBING

Gravity Gear (✉ 618A Patricia St., ☎ 780/852–3155 or 888/852–3155) can arrange for ice climbing, backcountry skiing, and mountaineering trips led by certified guides. You can also rent or buy climbing equipment, and arrange for lessons.

GOLF

The **Fairmont Jasper Park Lodge** (✉ off Hwy. 16, ☎ 780/852–6090) has a highly rated championship 18-hole, par-71 course.

GUIDED TOURS

Currie's Guiding (✉ 406 Patricia St., ☎ 780/852–5650) offers four- to six-hour driving tours of scenic highlights in the area, as well as a "wildlife search" tour. Prices begin around $49. They also offer half- to full-day guided fishing tours to Maligne Lake, beginning at $149. **Edge Control Outdoors** (✉ 614D Connaught Dr., ☎ 780/852–4945) has a Walks and Talks Jasper program, with two- to four-hour guided walking programs to Maligne Canyon and Mt. Edith Cavell; a bird- and wildlife-viewing tour; and customized walking tours. Prices begin at $40. The **Jasper Adventure Centre** (✉ 604 Connaught Dr., ☎ 780/852–5595, FAX 780/852–3127, WEB www.jasperadventurecentre.com) provides guided tours of popular sights in Jasper National Park as well as birding trips, ice walks, and snowshoeing tours. Rates start at $45 per adult, with most tours lasting three hours. It also handles bookings for other adventure companies (canoeing, rafting, and other sports). **Sun Dog Tour Company** (✉ 414 Connaught Dr., ☎ 780/852–4056 or 888/786–3641) arranges all types of tours, accommodation, and transportation.

HORSEBACK RIDING

Jasper Backcountry Adventures (c/o On-Line Sport & Tackle, ✉ 600 Patricia St., ☎ 780/852–3630) runs multiday rides along the boundary of Jasper Park, as well as combination pack trip and fishing tours. **Skyline Trail Rides** (✉ Fairmont Jasper Park Lodge, off Hwy. 16, ☎ 780/852–4215, 780/852–3301 Ext. 6189, or 888/852–7787) offers lessons and one-hour to half-day rides. Multiday trips into the backcountry are also available.

SKIING

Marmot Basin (✉ off Hwy. 93A, ☎ 780/852–3816), near Jasper, has a wide mix of downhill skiing terrain, and slopes are a little less crowded than those around Banff. This area has 53 runs and eight lifts; vertical drop is 2,944 ft. Eighteen additional runs are in the works.

SWIMMING

Lakes Annette and Edith (✉ near Fairmont Jasper Park Lodge, off Hwy. 16) have sandy beaches; their water reaches the low 20s°C (low 70s°F) during warm spells. If you swim beyond the stirred-up waters near the shore, the crystal-clear water can trick you into thinking that those rocks 16 ft down are within easy reach of your toes.

Shopping

In Jasper the main shopping streets are Patricia Street and Connaught Drive. Pay attention to price—in some cases, particularly for souvenirs, clothing, and sporting gear, you may pay a resort premium. Other items, such as unique artwork, you may not find anywhere else at any price.

Totem Ski Shop (⊠ 408 Connaught Dr., ☎ 780/852–3078 or 800/363–3078) sells summer and winter sports equipment and clothing.

CLOTHING

Mountain Air Sportswear (⊠ 622 Connaught Dr., ☎ 780/852–3760) sells designer-label clothing, including Tommy Hilfiger, Timberland, and Polo Ralph Lauren. **The Niche** (⊠ 626 Connaught Dr., ☎ 780/852–7234) has classically casual, funky winter and summer clothes, gifts, pottery—and designer furniture hand-crafted by the owner from antiques. At the Fairmont Jasper Park Lodge, **Open Country Sportswear** (⊠ Promenade, Fairmont Jasper Park Lodge, off Hwy. 16, ☎ 780/852–4991) has designer clothes. For quality sportswear, try **Wild Mountain Willy's** (⊠ Patricia Center, 610 Patricia St., ☎ 780/852–5304), selling labels such as Patagonia and Woolrich. A good selection of sportswear can be found at **Mountain Vision Sports** (⊠ Promenade, Fairmont Jasper Park Lodge, off Hwy. 16, ☎ 780/852–5552).

GIFTS

For gifts with a unique flair, try **Christmas in the Rockies** (⊠ Promenade, Jasper Park Lodge, off Hwy. 16, ☎ 780/852–4779), where a large selection of quality Christmas ornaments and decorations is available at any time of the year. For something a bit offbeat, try **Counterclockwise Emporium** (⊠ Jasper Marketplace, Patricia St. and Hazel Ave., ☎ 780/852–3152), with a continually changing gift selection that ranges from home decor to jewelry to gifts for pets. The **Mounted Police Gift Shoppe** (⊠ Patricia Center, 610 Patricia St., ☎ 780/852–2182) sells licensed products of the Canadian Mounted Police Foundation, such as Stetsons and RCMP Beanie Babies.

ARTS AND CRAFTS

Our Native Land (⊠ 601 Patricia St., ☎ 780/852–5592) has one of the largest selections of Canadian Native artwork in the parks. The focus is on western Canadian art, but other regions are also represented. **E&A Studio** (⊠ Maligne Canyon, Maligne Lake Rd., ☎ 780/852–3583) sells arts and crafts. **Jasper Originals** (⊠ Promenade, Fairmont Jasper Park Lodge, off Hwy. 16, ☎ 780/852–5378) offers an extensive selection of regional arts and crafts. **Timber Wolf** (⊠ 609B Patricia St., ☎ 780/852–4082) has a good choice of Canadian Native arts and crafts.

Jasper National Park

South border of park: 178 km (110 mi) north of Banff townsite, 152 km (94 mi) south of Jasper townsite. East border of park: 323 km (200 mi) west of Edmonton, 50 km (31 mi) east of Jasper townsite.

Apart from the innumerable scenic vistas and hiking trails, a number of special attractions in Jasper National Park make for easy half-day trips from Jasper townsite. Most of the lodging in this huge park—almost as large as the entire state of Connecticut—is clustered in the town, but there are 14 outlying accommodations including bungalows and cabins, some set right on the Athabasca River.

★ ⑰ **Mt. Edith Cavell,** the highest mountain in the vicinity of the town of Jasper, towers above the surroundings at 11,033 ft and shows its permanently snow-clad north face to the town. It's named after a World War I British nurse who stayed in Belgium to treat wounded Allied soldiers after Brussels fell to the Germans; she was executed for helping prisoners of war escape. From Highway 93A, a narrow, winding 14½-km (9-mi) road (often closed until the beginning of June) leads to the base of the mountain. Trailers are not permitted on this road, but they can be dropped off at a parking lot near the junction with 93A. This is a very popular spot, and you should head up in early or mid-morning during summer weekends if you hope to avoid parking disasters; the lot can become so crowded between 1 and 4 PM that simply arriving or leaving can be a challenge, let alone finding a parking spot. Several pullouts offer spectacular views, as well as access to trails leading up the **Tonquin Valley,** one of the premier hiking areas in the park.

The mountain itself is arguably the most spectacular site in Jasper National Park reachable by automobile. From the parking lot, a 1-km (½-mi) trail leads to the base of an imposing mile-high, almost vertical cliff. The Angel Glacier drips out of a valley partway up the slope, highlighting the scene. If you feel ambitious, a steep 3-km (2-mi) trail climbs up the valley opposite the mountain, opening into an alpine meadow—**Cavell Meadows.** Wildflowers carpet the meadows from mid-July to mid-August, and there's an excellent view of the Angel Glacier on the opposite slope. ✉ *Off Hwy. 93A, 27 km (17 mi) south of Jasper.*

⑱ At **Athabasca Falls,** the Athabasca River is compressed through a narrow gorge, producing a violent torrent of water. The falls are especially dramatic in early summer, when the river is swollen by snowmelt. Trails and overlooks provide good viewpoints. ✉ *Icefields Pkwy. and Hwy. 93A, 31 km (19 mi) south of Jasper.*

The Maligne River cuts a 165-ft-deep gorge through limestone bedrock at **Maligne Canyon.** An interpretive trail winds its way along the river, switching from side to side over six bridges as the canyon progressively deepens. It's an impressive sight, but the 4-km (2½-mi) trail along the canyon can be crowded, especially near the start of the trail. Just off the path, at the Maligne Canyon tea house, are a restaurant and a good Native Canadian crafts store. ✉ *Maligne Lake Rd., 11 km (7 mi) south of Jasper.*

Medicine Lake has a complex underground drainage system that causes the lake to empty almost completely at times. Early residents suspected that spirits were responsible for the dramatic fluctuations in the level of the placid waters. ✉ *Maligne Lake Rd., 26 km (16 mi) south of Jasper.*

★ ⑲ The remarkably blue, 22-km-long (14-mi-long) **Maligne Lake** (✉ Maligne Lake Rd., 44 km (27 mi) southeast of Jasper, WEB www.malignelake.com/homepage.html) is one of the largest glacier-fed lakes in the world. The first outsider known to visit the lake was Henry MacLeod, a surveyor looking for a possible route for the Canadian Pacific Railway, in 1875. He found only a dead end for the railway, and named the lake Sore-foot Lake. Fortunately, the name didn't stick, and the journey is now just an easy 45-minute car trip. You can explore the lake on a 1½-hour tour with Maligne Lake Scenic Cruises or in a rented canoe. A couple of day hikes (approximately four hours round-trip), with some steep sections, lead to alpine meadows that have panoramic views of the lake and the surrounding mountain ranges. You can also take horseback riding and fishing trips, and there's an excellent cafeteria. In winter Maligne Lake has a range of moderate to challenging lakeside and forest cross-country ski trails. Skiing on the lake is not recommended because the deep snow can keep the ice thin. *Tour reservations:* ✉ *Maligne Lake Scenic Cruises, 627 Patricia St., Jasper,* ☎ *780/852–3370.* 🎫 *Boat tour $32.* ☉ *Early June–early Oct., daily 10–4, every hr on the hr; July–Aug., daily 10–5.*

✋ ⑳ **Miette Hot Springs** is a relaxing spot, especially when the weather turns inclement. You can soak in naturally heated mineral waters originating from three springs that reach 54°C (129°F) and have to be cooled to 40°C (104°F) to allow bathing in the two hot pools. There's also an adjacent cold pool—especially popular with the younger crowd—which is definitely on the cool side, at about 15°C, or 59°F. A short walk leads to the remnants of the original hot-spring facility, where several springs still pour hot sulfurous water into the adjacent creek. Day passes and bathing suit, locker, and towel rentals are available. ✉ *Miette Hot Springs Rd., off Hwy. 16, 58 km (36 mi) northeast of Jasper,* ☎ *780/866–3939,* WEB *www.parkscanada.gc.ca/hotsprings.* 🎫 *$6.* ☉ *Mid-May–late June and early Sept.–early Oct., daily 10:30–9; late June–early Sept., daily 8:30 AM–10:30 PM.*

En Route A scant 4.8 km (3 mi) before Highway 16 from Jasper reaches the turn for Miette Hot Springs, the road passes **Disaster Point Animal Lick.** This is the most easily accessible spot in the park for encountering bighorn sheep; it's a rare summer moment when the sheep haven't descended from the adjacent steep slopes to lick up the mineral-rich mud, wandering back and forth across the road to find the best mineral licks. You are likely to see numerous cars stopped by the side of the road watching the sheep. Obeying the reduced speed limit in this area helps the sheep as well as your car.

The highway threads a narrow ribbon of solid ground between the steep slopes of Disaster Point and the Athabasca River. Before the railway was built, Disaster Point extended right into the river. Early travelers had to ford the river around the slopes or, when the water was high, make a risky climb over Disaster Point. Not everyone made it, hence the name.

Outdoor Activities and Sports

BACKCOUNTRY HIKING AND SKIING

Jasper National Park, with nearly 1,000 km (620 mi) of hiking trails, is popular with hikers who want to go deep into the wilderness for several days at a time. Good day-hiking areas in Jasper are around Maligne Lake, Mt. Edith Cavell, and Miette Hot Springs.

For information on overnight camping quotas on the Skyline and Tonquin Valley trails, or information on any of the hundreds of hiking and mountain biking trails in the area, contact **Jasper National Park Information Centre** (✉ 500 Connaught Dr., ☎ 780/852–6177, WEB www.parkscanada.ga.ca/jasper).

Rocky Mountain Hiking (☎ 780/852–5015) has backcountry guides who take visitors on customized multiday hikes and also offers interpretive programs, day hikes, and some caving.

The **Skyline Trail** wanders for 44 km (27 mi), at or above the tree line, past some of the park's most spectacular scenery. **Tonquin Valley,** near Mt. Edith Cavell, is one of Canada's classic backpacking areas. Its high mountain lakes, bounded by a series of steep, rocky peaks known as the Ramparts, attract many visitors in high summer.

Tonquin Valley Adventures (☎ 780/852–4831) offers hiking, skiing, and horseback trips into the Tonquin Valley. In the winter there's a private cabin with cooking equipment provided, in summer there's a cook. Reservations for backcountry huts in Tonquin Valley can be made through **Tonquin Valley Pack and Ski Trips** (☎ 780/852–3909, WEB www.tonquinvalley.com); call well in advance.

Pyramid Stables (✉ Pyramid Resort, Pyramid Lake Rd., ☎ 780/852–3562) offers one-hour to full-day trips in the hills overlooking Jasper and also has pony rides and carriage rides. Guides from **Ridgeline Riders** (c/o Maligne Tours, ✉ 627 Patricia St., ☎ 780/852–3370) lead 3½-hour horseback tours from the lodge at Maligne Lake into the high country of the Bald Hills.

Jasper Raft Tours (☎ 780/852–3613, WEB www.jasperrafttours.com) runs half-day float trips on the Athabasca. Trips with **Maligne River Adventures** (☎ 780/852–3370, WEB www.mra.ab.ca) include gentle half-day floats on the Athabasca River (mid-May–September; ages 6 and up); half-day intermediate white-water trips on the Sunwapta River (July–September); and three-day advanced trips on the Kakwa River (mid-May–June; ages 13 and up). **Whitewater Rafting (Jasper) Ltd.** (☎ 780/852–7238 or 800/557–7238) offers half-day trips on the Athabasca (Class II white water) and Sunwapta rivers (Class III).

Excellent groomed cross-country trails are at **Pyramid and Patricia lakes** (✉ Pyramid Lake Rd.).

Pyramid Lake (✉ Pyramid Lake Rd.) has a good beach, although it's unusual for the water to warm above 20°C (68°F).

Mt. Robson Provincial Park

80 km (50 mi) west of Jasper.

This provincial park, contiguous with Jasper National Park, makes a pleasant hour-long drive from Jasper townsite on Highway 16. The terrain and scenery are similar to Jasper's, although the vegetation is lusher thanks to the more abundant rainfall on the west side of the Rockies.

㉑ At 12,972 ft, towering **Mt. Robson** is the highest mountain in the Canadian Rockies and was not successfully scaled until 1913. Experienced mountaineers consider certain routes on Robson among the world's most challenging. Mt. Robson's weather is notoriously bad even when the weather elsewhere is perfectly fine, and it's a rare day that clouds do not encircle the summit. A favorite backpacking trip on the mountain is the strenuous 22-km (13½-mi) hike to **Berg Lake,** through the wonderfully named Valley of a Thousand Falls. Berg Lake is no tranquil body of water; the grunts and splashes as Robson's glaciers calve chunks of ice into the lake are regular sounds in summer. It costs $5 per person to camp overnight at Berg Lake, which operates on a reservations and quota system (☎ 800/689–9025). The 5-km (3-mi), mostly level hike to **Kinney Lake,** along the Berg Lake trail, is a good option for day hikers.

The **Mt. Robson Visitor Centre** (✉ Hwy. 16, ☎ 250/566–4325 or 800/689–9025), open mid-May to early October, has a small restaurant, store, gas station, and fine view of Mt. Robson.

Kootenay National Park

34 km (21 mi) west of Banff townsite, 162 km (100 mi) west of Calgary.

When the tourist population of Banff swells in busy summer months, Kootenay National Park remains surprisingly quiet, although not for lack of natural beauty; the scenery certainly matches that of Banff and Jasper parks. Named for the Ktunaxa (or Kootenai) people who have lived in the area for approximately 10,000 years, the park is just over the Alberta border in British Columbia—adjacent to the west side of Banff National Park and the south end of Yoho National Park. Facilities are few here; most people see the park only as they drive south on the busy Highway 93, which traverses the park's length, while on their way to points in British Columbia. Backcountry overnight campers must purchase a Wilderness Pass, available at any national parks visitor center.

㉒ At 5,416 ft, **Vermilion Pass** is not among the highest passes in the Canadian Rockies but it marks the boundary between Alberta and British Columbia, as well as the Continental Divide—rivers east of here flow to the Atlantic Ocean, rivers to the west to the Pacific. The pass is at the boundary of Banff and Kootenay national parks, on Highway 93.

Just beyond the Vermilion Pass summit is the head of the **Stanley Glacier trail,** one of the fine choices for a day hike in the park. The trail climbs easily for 5.5 km (3 mi) through fire remnants and new growth, across rock debris and glacial moraine, ending in the giant amphitheater of the Stanley Glacier basin. ⊠ *3 km (2 mi) from east boundary of Kootenay National Park.*

㉓ **Floe Lake,** at the base of a 3,300-ft-high cliff called the Rockwall, is one of the most popular hiking destinations in Kootenay. The 10-km (6-mi) trail from the highway passes through characteristic Kootenay backcountry terrain. Plan a full day for this one. ⊠ *Trailhead, 22 km (14 mi) from east gate of Kootenay park.*

The trail that best characterizes the hiking in Kootenay is the strenuous **Rockwall Trail,** which runs along the series of steep rock facades that are the park's predominant feature. Floe Lake marks the trail's southern terminus; it then runs north for 28.7 km (19 mi) to join up with the Helmet Creek Trail, which runs for 15 km (10 mi) back to the highway. The total hiking distance, counting the Floe Lake and Helmet Creek trails, is 55.6 km (34 mi). Several other long spurs give hikers the option of doing less than the full distance. ⊠ *Trailheads: Floe Lake trailhead for southern end, 22 km (14 mi) from park's east gate; Helmet Creek trailhead for northern end, 9½ km (6 mi) west of park's east gate.*

Yoho National Park

57 km (35 mi) northwest of Banff townsite, 185 km (115 mi) west of Calgary.

The name Yoho is a Native Canadian word that translates, approximately, to "awe inspiring." Indeed, Yoho National Park contains some of the most outstanding scenery in the Canadian Rockies. The park adjoins Banff National Park to the east, but it's quieter than its neighbor. Highway 1 divides Yoho into the northern half, which includes Takakkaw Falls, the Burgess Shale fossil site, the Yoho River valley, and Emerald Lake; and the southern half, of which Lake O'Hara is the center.

㉔ **Takakkaw Falls,** in the northern half of Yoho park, has a sheer drop of 833 ft—one of the highest waterfalls in Canada. The falls are spectacular in early summer, when melting snow and ice provide ample runoff. The road to the falls is not recommended for vehicles more than 22 ft long; there's a drop-off area for trailers. ⊠ *Yoho Valley Rd., off Hwy. 1, 26 km (16 mi) west of Banff National Park.*

㉕ The **Burgess Shale Site** on a fossil ridge near Field, B.C., was once on the bottom of the ocean and contains the fossilized remains of 120 marine species dating back 515 million years; the area was designated a World Heritage Site in 1981. Guided hikes (maximum 15 people) are the only way to see the actual fossil sites, and they're popular, so make reservations. The hikes ($25–$45) are conducted July through September, from Friday to Monday, trail conditions permitting. Groups meet at the Yoho Brothers Trading Post in Field. The going is fairly strenuous; the round-trip distance is 20 km (12 mi). A shorter, steeper hike leads to the Mt. Stephen trilobite fossil beds. Guided hikes are also offered to extensions of the Burgess Shale fossils in Kootenay and Banff national parks. Allow a full day for any of the hikes. ⊠ *The Yoho-Burgess Shale Foundation, Box 148, Field, BC,* ☏ *800/343–3006,* WEB *www.burgess-shale.bc.ca.*

㉖ At **Emerald Lake,** a vivid turquoise shimmer at the base of the President Range, you can rent a canoe, have a cup of tea at the tea house by Emerald Lake Lodge, or take a stroll around the lake. The lake is a trailhead for hikers, cross-country skiers, and snowshoers. ⊠ *Access from 8-km (5-mi) road off Hwy. 1, 19 km (12 mi) west of Banff National Park.*

㉗ **Lake O'Hara,** in Yoho's southern half, is widely regarded as one of *the* ultimate destinations for outdoor enthusiasts in the Canadian Rockies. In summer, Lake O'Hara Lodge is booked months in advance. Although the forest-lined fire road between Highway 1 and the lake can be hiked, it makes more sense to ride the lodge-run bus (call the lodge for times and space availability). Keep in mind, however, that to protect the fragile alpine area and to ensure an uncrowded experience, there's a quota on overnight and day use. Only 36 spots are available on the bus, which you must reserve in advance (up to three months). Save your legs for hiking any of several moderately strenuous trails that radiate from the lodge into a high-alpine world of small lakes surrounded by escarpments of rock and patches of year-round snow. ⊠ *Lake O'Hara Fire Rd. off Hwy 1, 11-km (7-mi) on fire road, 3 km (2 mi) west of Banff National Park western boundary,* ☏ *250/343–6433,* WEB *www.parkscanada.gc.ca/yoho.*

Dining and Lodging

$$$$ ✕⊞ **Emerald Lake Lodge.** This enchanted place at the edge of a glacier-
★ fed lake is only a 20-minute drive from Lake Louise and an hour from Banff. The log-cabin main lodge has a large stone hearth. The main dining room is a glass-enclosed terrace, with views of the lake through tall stands of evergreens. The menu mixes traditional Canadian and American fare—steaks, game, and fish—with such nouvelle sauces as ginger-tangerine glaze. All guest rooms have fireplaces and balconies, and pleasant though unspectacular interiors. The awe-inspiring setting is what commands premium rates, so be sure to request a lakefront cottage with a balcony overlooking the lake, so you get the full experience. This also attracts a lot of day visitors, so privacy can be compromised; for a more secluded stay, visit off-season, when room rates drop by 40%. ⊠ *Yoho National Park, Box 10, Field, BC V0A 1G0, 9½ km (6 mi) north of Field,* ☏ *250/343–6321 or 800/663–6336,* FAX *250/343–6724,* WEB *www.crmr.com. 85 units in 2- and 4-room cottages. 2 restaurants, bar, outdoor hot tub, sauna, gym, horseback riding, boating, recreation room. AE, DC, MC, V.*

$$$$ ⊞ **Lake O'Hara Lodge.** In summer, guests are ferried by a lodge-operated bus along an 11-km (7-mi) fire road between Highway 1 and the grounds. In winter, guests must ski the distance. The lodge and lakeside cabins offer fairly luxurious backcountry living; cabins have private baths (rooms share baths), and a dining room serves

three meals a day, included in the room rate. Reservations for the high summer season (mid-June–September) should be booked far in advance. The minimum stay is two nights, and rates are based on double-occupancy rooms. ✉ *Yoho National Park, Box 55, off Hwy. 1, Lake Louise, AB T0L 1E0,* ☎ *250/343–6418 in season; 403/678–4110,* WEB *www.lakeohara.com. 23 rooms, 8 without baths. Dining room, hiking, cross-country skiing, boating. No credit cards. Closed mid-Apr.–mid-June and Oct.–mid-Jan. FAP.*

Outdoor Activities and Sports

HIKING

Yoho is divided into two parts: the popular hiking area around Lake O'Hara, dotted with high-alpine lakes; and the less-traveled Yoho River valley, terminating at Yoho Glacier. Entry into the Yoho River valley is from Takakkaw Falls or from Emerald Lake.

HORSEBACK RIDING

The concierge at **Emerald Lake Lodge** (☎ 250/343–6321) can arrange for horseback expeditions and lessons in summer.

SOUTH OF BANFF

The region immediately southeast of Banff—the town of Canmore and the group of provincial parks and recreation areas jointly known as Kananaskis Country—has become increasingly popular since the 1988 Winter Olympics brought many fine new facilities, from ski jumps to hotels, to the area. Farther south, Waterton Lakes National Park marks the meeting of the prairie and the mountains. With Glacier Park in Montana, it forms Waterton-Glacier International Peace Park.

Canmore

28 *24 km (15 mi) southeast of Banff townsite, 106 km (66 mi) west of Calgary.*

Canmore became a modern boomtown with the 1988 Olympics and has never looked back. Just outside of Banff National Park, it attracts a mix of tourists, residents who seek a mountain lifestyle, and commuters from Calgary who feel the hour-long commute is a fair trade-off for living in the mountains. Still, much of the small-town character and charm remain.

Canmore makes a good base for exploring both Kananaskis Country and Banff National Park, without the crowds or cost of Banff. If you want a quieter location with fewer amenities and the remnants of a small-town atmosphere, consider Canmore. But if shopping and dining options, a resort-town atmosphere, or the hustle and bustle of a major tourist destination are important to you, then spend the extra dollars and make Banff your destination.

Dining and Lodging

$$–$$$ ✕ **Musashi Japanese Restaurant.** There's not much in the way of atmosphere at this small, strip mall–style restaurant, but if you want authentic Japanese food in Canmore, this is the place to find it. You can choose tempura, teriyaki, sukiyaki, shabu-shabu, fried seafood, and sushi. ✉ *1306 Bow Valley Trail, No. 7A,* ☎ *403/678–9360. MC, V. Closed Sun.*

$$–$$$ ✕ **Sinclair's.** This restaurant looks remarkably like someone's grand-★ mother's house, complete with white clapboard siding and a white picket fence. The kitchen prides itself on an array of vegetarian dishes, but steak, chicken, buffalo burgers, halibut, salmon, and lamb are available, along with some adventuresome pastas and pizzas. In summer

you can dine on the garden patio. ⊠ *637 Main St.,* ☎ *403/678–5370. AE, DC, MC, V.*

$–$$$ ✕ **Pepper Mill.** The small dining room is simply decorated with off-
★ white walls, green tablecloths, and hanging lamps. This intimate, Eu-
ropean-Swiss dining room is known for its pepper steak but also serves
well-prepared pasta dishes, schnitzels, fish, pork, chicken, and seafood.
⊠ *726 9th St.,* ☎ *403/678–2292. AE, MC, V. Closed Tues. No lunch.*

$–$$ ✕ **Zona's** This funky new restaurant, with local artwork for sale on
the walls, is set in a 100-year-old house. The cuisine is world fusion:
Indonesian pork, Moroccan chicken, Thai lasagna, North African vegetable curry, and New Zealand lamb shanks. There's a large patio for
sunny days. ⊠ *710 9th St.,* ☎ *403/609–2000. AE, MC, V.*

$$$–$$$$ 🏨 **Mt. Assiniboine Lodge.** Built in 1928, this lodge appears to have
changed little through the years. The backcountry setting is classically
alpine—at 7,200 ft, on the edge of 2-km-long (1-mi-long) Lake Magog,
with the rocky pyramid of Mt. Assiniboine in full view. Guests must
hike or ski in 28 km (17 mi), or arrive by helicopter from Canmore
(hikers and skiers can have their luggage flown in). Hearty meals are
served family style. There are cabins that sleep two to four people, as
well as lodge rooms. The lodge has some electricity and running water,
but you should be prepared to use outhouses. The price includes meals
and hiking or skiing guide service. Rates decrease by about 15% off-
season. ⊠ *Box 8128, T1W 2T8,* ☎ *403/678–2883,* 🗎 *403/678–4877,*
🌐 *www.canadianrockies.net/assiniboine. 6 rooms without bath, 6 cab-
ins without bath. Dining room, sauna. MC, V. Closed Oct.–mid-Feb.
and mid-Apr.–late June. FAP.*

$$ 🏨 **Bow Valley Motel.** This two-story, few-frills motel in the center of
Canmore is within easy walking distance of dining and shopping.
Rooms are clean and simply furnished with a bed, dresser, small refrigerator, and TV. Five rooms have kitchens. Rates drop by 50% off-
season. ⊠ *610 8th St., T1W 2B5,* ☎ *403/678–5085 or 800/665–
8189,* 🗎 *403/678–6560,* 🌐 *www.bowvalleymotel.com. 25 rooms. Outdoor hot tub, coin laundry. AE, D, MC, V.*

$$ 🏨 **Rocky Mountain Ski Lodge.** Several motels in Canmore provide
lower-price alternatives to Banff. Of these, Rocky Mountain Ski Lodge
is a notch above the rest. It's really three separate motel properties rolled
into one. Slanting, exposed wood-and-beam ceilings give a chaletlike
feel to otherwise simple decor. Rooms in the older section have kitch-
enettes, but the decor is more '60s American than Swiss chalet. Rates
drop by 40% off-season. ⊠ *Box 8070, 1711 Mountain Ave., at Hwy.
1A, T1W 2T8,* ☎ *403/678–5445; 800/665–6111 in Canada,* 🗎 *403/
678–6484,* 🌐 *www.rockymtnskilodge.com. 82 rooms. Hot tub, sauna,
playground. AE, DC, MC, V.*

Nightlife and the Arts

Locals kick back at **The Drake** (⊠ 909 Railway Ave., ☎ 403/678–5131),
which has live music every weekend. **Sherwood House** (⊠ 838 8th St.,
☎ 403/678–5211) occasionally hosts bands on weekends.

Outdoor Activities and Sports

Many of the outfitters and operators who run tours in Banff National
Park are based in Canmore. These operators provide a wide range of
activities and often have tours in the Canmore region also, primarily
in Kananaskis Country. Equipment (for everything from mountaineering,
hiking, and canoeing, to skiing, snowboarding, ice climbing, and snow-
shoeing) can be rented at most sports shops in Canmore.

GOLF

Canmore Golf Course (⊠ off Hwy. 1, ☎ 403/678–4784) has 18 holes;
par is 71. **Stewart Creek Golf Course** (⊠ 1 Three Sisters Way, ☎ 403/

609–6099 or 877/993–4653, WEB www.stewartcreek.com) is one of two new courses in Canmore (18 holes, par-72). **Silvertip Golf Course** (✉ 1000 Silvertip Tr., ☎ 403/678–1600 or 877/5444) is an 18-hole, par-72 golf course.

Shopping

The Avens Gallery (✉ 709 Main St., ☎ 403/678–4471) sells the works of local artists, from paintings to blown glass to metalwork. **The Corner Gallery** (✉ 7th Ave. and Main St., ☎ 403/678–6090) is one of the largest galleries in town, featuring paintings plus some pottery, sculpture, and Inuit soapstone and jade carvings. **Flux Glassworks International** (✉ 1414 Railway Ave., ☎ 403/678–5051) has a two-ton glass-melt furnace and offers a range of unusual glass items in the gallery. Studio demonstrations take place on Saturdays at 1 PM. **Great Bowls Afire!** (✉ 626 Main St., No. 5, ☎ 403/678–9507) sells ceramics, and has a paint-your-own studio.

For environmentally friendly hemp clothing, lingerie, bathmats, and glass works, among other unique items, check out **P'Lovers** (✉ 817 Main St., No. 101, ☎ 403/609–2339. Bookworms can spend some time browsing **The Second Second Story** (✉ 713 Main St., ☎ 403/609–2368), a used bookstore with a wide range of titles. **Rocky Mountain Soap Company** (✉ retail store: 820 Main St., No. 103, ☎ 403/678–9873 or 877/229–7627, WEB www.canadiansoap.com) is Alberta's largest natural-soap maker, boasting 28 varieties of soap handcrafted on-site.

Kananaskis Country

❷❾ *North entrance: 26 km (16 mi) southeast of Canmore, 80 km (50 mi) west of Calgary.*

Three provincial parks make up the 4,200-square-km (1,600-square-mi) recreational region known as Kananaskis Country, which includes grand mountain scenery, though perhaps not quite a match for that in the adjacent national parks. Visitors to Kananaskis can try the same activities as in the national parks but can also find others that are prohibited within the national park system, such as snowmobiling, motorized boating, off-road driving, and mountain biking.

The main highway through Kananaskis Country is Highway 40, also known as the Kananaskis Trail. It runs north–south through the impressive scenery of the front ranges of the Rockies. Only the northern 40 km (25 mi) of the road remain open from December 1 through June 15, in part because of the extreme conditions of Highwood Pass (at 7,280 ft, the highest drivable pass in Canada), and in part to protect winter wildlife habitat in Peter Lougheed Provincial Park and southward. Highway 40 continues south to join Highway 541, west of Longview. Access to East Kananaskis Country, a popular area for horseback trips, is on Highway 66, which heads west from Priddis.

The **Canmore Nordic Centre,** built for the 1988 Olympic Nordic skiing events, has 70 km (43 mi) of groomed cross-country trails in winter that become mountain biking trails in summer. This state-of-the-art facility is in the northwest corner of Kananaskis Country, south of Canmore. Some trails are lighted for night skiing, and a 1½-km (1-mi) paved trail is open in summer for roller skiing and rollerblading. Skiing and mountain biking lessons and rentals are available. After getting your exercise for the day, stop in at the café for some refreshment. In late January, the annual **Canmore International Dogsled Race**—a two-day event—attracts more than 100 international teams. There are lockers, changing rooms, and showers available. ✉ *1988 Olympic Way,* ☎ *403/678–2400,* WEB *www.gov.ab.ca.* 🖰 *Trails free*

Apr.–Oct.; $5 per day Nov.–Mar. ⊙ *Lodge: daily 9–5:30; some trails illuminated until 9* PM.

Kananaskis Village, a full-service resort complex built for the 1988 Olympics, brings first-class lodging, dining, and golfing to Kananaskis Country. A lodge, a hotel, and an inn cluster next to an attractively landscaped artificial pond on a small plateau between the Nakiska ski area and two 18-hole golf courses. Other facilities include sledding hills, mountain biking trails and bike rental, and an ice-skating pond. Many visitors to the region stay at one of the several campgrounds, most of which can accommodate recreational vehicles.

The **William Watson Lodge** is unique in the Canadian Rockies because it's designed exclusively for senior citizens and people who have disabilities. Access points have been built along Mt. Lorette Ponds north of Kananaskis Village to accommodate anglers using wheelchairs, and many hiking trails near the village have been cut wide and gentle enough for wheelchair travel. Overnight and day-use facilities, including cabins, are available to people with disabilities and Alberta senior citizens. Albertans get preference; people with disabilities from outside the province must book 60 days in advance. ⊠ *Box 130, on Hwy. 40, T0L 2H0, 30 km (19 mi) south of Kananaskis Village,* ☎ *403/591–7227.* ⊙ *Office: weekdays 8* AM–9 PM.

Dining and Lodging

$$$–$$$$ ✕ **Seasons.** The signature dining room of the Delta Lodge at Kananaskis
★ has an intimate atmosphere and attentive service. On the menu are uniquely Canadian dishes such as Brome Lake duck, arctic musk ox, and Yukon char; some desserts are flambéed at the table. Soft, live piano music plays nightly for dancing or relaxing. ⊠ *Delta Lodge at Kananaskis, Hwy. 40, Kananaskis Village,* ☎ *403/591–7711. Reservations essential. AE, D, DC, MC, V. Closed Oct.–May. No lunch.*

$$$$ ⊡ **Delta Lodge at Kananaskis.** Part of the Kananaskis Village built for the 1988 Olympics, this hotel was built as a Canadian Pacific luxury hotel; the lodge was taken over by Delta Hotels in 2000. Six million dollars was spent in recent years on renovations, including improvements to business suites. Rooms are large and lavish—many have fireplaces, hot tubs, and sitting areas. Several restaurants, skewed toward elegance, serve food that ranges from pizza and burgers to haute cuisine. For casual dining, try the Fireweed Grill in the lodge, including a buffet-style breakfast, burgers for lunch, and chicken, salmon, beef tenderloin and lamb chops for dinner. ⊠ *Hwy. 40, Kananaskis Village T0L 2H0, 28 km (17 mi) south of Hwy. 1,* ☎ *403/591–7711 or 888/244–8666,* FAX *403/591–7770,* WEB *www.deltahotels.com. 243 rooms, 78 suites. 3 restaurants, 2 lounges, deli, indoor pool, sauna, spa, steam room, 2 18-hole golf courses, health club. AE, D, DC, MC, V.*

$$$$ ⊡ **Kananaskis Inn & Conference Centre.** This property, part of the Kananaskis Village complex built for the 1988 Olympics, overlooks the resort's pond and has a redwood exterior. Some of the motel-style rooms have private balconies, kitchenettes, or fireplaces. Rooms are bright, with wood furnishings and large windows. Rates drop by 40% off-season. ⊠ *Box 10, Hwy. 40, Kananaskis Village T0L 2H0, 28 km (17 mi) south of Hwy. 1,* ☎ *403/591–7500 or 888/591–7501,* FAX *403/591–7633,* WEB *www.Kananaskisinn.com. 90 rooms. Restaurant, bar, hot tub, coin laundry. AE, D, DC, MC, V.*

$$–$$$ ⊡ **Homeplace Ranch.** This guest ranch east of Kananaskis Country is what its name suggests: homey. From late spring until mid-October, the principal activity is horseback riding in the rolling foothills near

the ranch, which has private rooms and private baths. Multiday pack trips are available and on an overnight trip into the mountains (guests sleep in teepees). Riding is offered to those seven and older. Evening is quiet time; you're left to your own entertainment. Three meals a day, included in the rate, are served family style and range from pork roast and salmon to turkey and steak. South Ranch, 1½ hours away (30 km, or 19 mi, south of Longview), is similar to the main ranch, but accommodation is in bunkhouses without electricity. Rates are based on either a four-day–three-night package ($625), or a seven-day–six-night package ($1,070), which includes all meals plus daily riding. ⊠ *Main Ranch: Box 6, R.R. 1 off Hwy. 2, Priddis T0L 1W0, 10 km (6 mi) west of Priddis,* ☎ FAX *403/931–3245 or 877/931–3245,* WEB *www. homeplaceranch.com. Main Ranch: 7 rooms with bath; South Ranch: 6 bunkhouses without bath. Dining room. No credit cards. FAP.*

$$–$$$ ☉ **Mt. Engadine Lodge.** Hiking and cross-country skiing trails lead out
★   the back door of this backcountry lodge to the mountains and lakes of Kananaskis Country. Rooms (most with shared baths) have a scrubbed simplicity, as do the common areas. Three meals, served family style, are included in the $85–$140 per-person rate. There's about a 30% decrease in off-season rates. The lodge operators are also backcountry guides; hiking packages are available. ⊠ *Box 8239, Spray Trail at Mt. Shark, Canmore T1W 2T9, 38 km (24 mi) south of Canmore,* ☎ *403/678–4080,* FAX *403/678–2109. 10 rooms, 4 with bath; 2 cabins. Restaurant, outdoor hot tub, sauna, hiking. MC, V. Closed May–mid-June, Oct.–Dec. 25, and weekdays Jan.–Apr. FAP.*

Nightlife and the Arts

Nightlife in Kananaskis is mostly of the do-it-yourself variety, but the Delta Lodge at Kananaskis has lounges and dining rooms with entertainment and dancing.

Outdoor Activities and Sports

Rent ski equipment at the Canmore Nordic Centre from **Trail Sports** (⊠ 1995 Olympic Way, ☎ 403/678–6764).

GOLF

Kananaskis Country Golf Course (⊠ off Hwy. 40, ☎ 403/591–7272 in-season; 877/591–2525) has two 18-hole, par-72 links.

HORSEBACK RIDING

Boundary Ranch (⊠ off Hwy. 40, Kananaskis Village, ☎ 403/591–7171, WEB www.boundaryranch.com) has horses to rent for trail rides from May to early October. **Brewster's Kananaskis Guest Ranch** (⊠ off Hwy. 1, ☎ 403/673–3737), on the Bow River 30 minutes east of Banff, offers half- and full-day trips, as well as multiday adventures. Guests stay in small chalets or cabins built in 1923 when the ranch was opened.

SKIING

Nakiska (⊠ off Hwy. 40, Kananaskis Village, ☎ 403/591–7777), 45 minutes southeast of Banff, was the site of the 1988 Olympic alpine events and has wide-trail intermediate skiing and a sophisticated snowmaking system that ensures reliable conditions. The vertical drop is 2,412 ft, and there are 28 trails and four lifts.

Waterton Lakes National Park

   ③⓪   *354 km (219 mi) south of Banff, 267 km (166 mi) south of Calgary.*

The mountains at Waterton Lakes National Park, near the southern end of the Canadian Rockies, seem a bit friendlier—not quite so high, not quite so rugged. This is a small park compared with Jasper or Banff, and you can cover its highlights in a day or two and still have time to relax. Several hundred miles of highway separate Waterton from the other six mountain parks. As a result, the park is a rare side trip from Banff—it's generally a destination in itself or combined with a vacation in the much larger Glacier National Park across the U.S. border.

Waterton is the meeting of two worlds: the flatlands of the prairie and the abrupt upthrust of the mountains. In this juncture of worlds, the park squeezes into a relatively small area (525 square km [200 square mi]) an unusual mix of wildlife, flora, and climate zones.

Politically, too, Waterton represents a meeting of worlds. Established in 1895, it was joined in 1932 with Glacier National Park in Montana to form Waterton-Glacier International Peace Park—a symbol of friendship and peaceful coexistence between Canada and the United States. In fact, some properties in the international park, including the Prince of Wales Hotel—perhaps the park's most recognizable landmark—are owned and operated by the same U.S. company, Glacier Park Incorporated. The most convenient border crossing is at Chief Mountain, to the immediate east of Waterton Lakes National Park. In keeping with the theme of peaceful coexistence, border crossings tend to be swift and efficient. The customs offices at Chief Mountain are open 7 AM–10 PM June–Labor Day; 9–6 from May 15–31, and Labor Day–Sept. 30; and closed in winter. If you want to cross into the U.S. in winter, plan to drive the long way around. In 1995 this park was designated a World Heritage Site by UNESCO.

The townsite of Waterton Park is a decidedly low-key community in roughly the geographical center of the park. In summer it swells with tourists, and the restaurants and shops open to service them. In winter only a few motels are open, and services are largely geared to meet the needs of the several hundred residents. The park contains numerous short hikes for day-trippers and some longer treks for backpackers. Nonmotorized boats can be rented at Cameron Lake in summer; private motorized (no engine size restriction) or nonmotorized craft can be used on Upper and Middle Waterton Lakes. An international boat cruises across Upper Waterton Lake, and the winds that rake across that lake create an exciting ride for windsurfers. Bring a wet suit, though—the water remains numbingly cold throughout the summer.

Because of Waterton's proximity to the U.S. border and its bond with Glacier National Park, many visitors arrive from the south. You can fly into Great Falls or Kalispell, Montana, and drive to Waterton.

Red Rock Canyon is one of the more popular natural attractions in Waterton Park. "Canyon" is stretching the term, as it is little more than a gully carved into the rock by a mountain stream. But "red rock" is appropriate; the exposed rock displays a remarkable red hue. This is a popular spot for a picnic and a stroll along the paths that line the canyon. ⊠ *Red Rock Pkwy. off park access road, watch for signs 10 km (6 mi) north of Waterton Park.*

Cameron Lake, the jewel of Waterton, sits in a land of glacially carved cirques (steep-walled basins). In summer, hundreds of varieties of alpine wildflowers fill the area, including 22 kinds of wild orchids. Canoes and pedal boats can be rented here. ⊠ *Akima Pkwy., 13 km (8 mi) southwest of Waterton Park townsite.*

One of the park's most popular activities is the two-hour cruise on **Upper Waterton Lake** from the Waterton Park townsite south to Goat Haunt Ranger Station, Montana, for $22. From there, several short, easy hikes are possible before you return to Waterton; properly equipped overnighters can also camp out at Goat Haunt. (Because Goat Haunt is in the United States, travelers must clear customs. U.S. stops are only included on the boat trip from June to mid-September.) ✉ *Waterton Internation Shoreline Cruise Company, Box 126, Waterton Park,* ☎ *403/859–2362,* FAX *403/938–5019,* WEB *www.watertoninfo.com.* ☉ *Early May–Oct.*

OFF THE
BEATEN PATH

CROWSNEST PASS – Between Calgary and Fernie (one hour by car northwest of Waterton), lies the town of Frank—buried under an immense pile of rocks. In April 1903, 90 million tons of rock screamed down from Turtle Mountain and buried a portion of this coal-mining town, killing 70 residents. The massive rubble pile still looks as if the disaster happened yesterday. The Frank Slide Interpretive Center documents the story of the slide and the history of coal mining in the region. ✉ *Hwy. 3,* ☎ *403/562–7388,* WEB *www.frankslide.com.* ✆ *$6.50.* ☉ *Mid-May–early Sept., daily 9–6; early Sept.–mid-May, daily 10–5.*

Lodging

$$$$ **⊞ Prince of Wales Hotel.** Perched between two lakes, with a high moun-
★ tain backdrop, this hotel has the best view in town. A high steeple crowns the building, which is fantastically ornamented with eaves, balconies, and turrets. The baronial, dark-paneled interior evokes the feeling of a Scottish hunting lodge. Expect creaks and rattles at night—the old hotel (built in the 1920s) is exposed to rough winds. Rates decrease by about 25% off-season. ✉ *Waterton Lakes National Park, off Hwy. 5 (Glacier Park Inc., 106 Cooperative Way, Suite 104, Kalispell, MT 59901);* ☎ *406/756–2444; 403/859–2231 from mid-May to late Sept.;* FAX *406/257–0384;* WEB *www.glacierparkinc.com. 89 rooms. Restaurant, lounge, tea shop, sauna. AE, MC, V. Closed late Sept.–mid-May.*

$$$–$$$$ **⊞ Bayshore Inn.** This two-story inn is on the lakeshore, and rooms with balconies take full advantage of the setting. Otherwise, the inn's common areas and motel-style rooms are rather ordinary. The lakeside patio is a great spot for light meals and drinks. Rates decrease by 30% off-season. ✉ *Box 38, Main St., Waterton Park T0K 2M0,* ☎ *403/859–2211 in summer; 888/527–9555 year-round,* FAX *403/859–2291,* WEB *www.bayshoreinn.com. 62 rooms, 8 suites. Restaurant, bar, coffee shop, lobby lounge. AE, D, MC, V. Closed mid-Oct.–mid-Apr.*

$$–$$$ **⊞ Kilmorey Lodge.** This 1920s inn with a log-cabin facade sits at the
★ edge of Waterton Park townsite. Rooms are steeped in country-cottage atmosphere, with pine walls, eiderdown comforters, sloped floors, and homespun antique furnishings. Some rooms have additional sleeping or sitting areas. ✉ *Box 100, 117 Evergreen Ave., Waterton Park T0K 2M0,* ☎ *403/859–2334,* FAX *403/859–2342,* WEB *www.watertonparks.com. 23 rooms. Restaurant, café, lounge. AE, D, DC, MC, V.*

Outdoor Activities and Sports

Waterton Golf Course (✉ off Hwy. 5 near Waterton Park, ☎ 403/859–2114) is an 18-hole, par-71 course.

THE BRITISH COLUMBIA ROCKIES

The national and provincial parks of the British Columbia Rockies are a close match for the grandeur found in Alberta's parks to the east. But the parks in British Columbia are smaller, and most of the British Columbia Rockies are not protected within park boundaries. This means that enthusiasts of activities such as snowmobiling, heli-skiing, or heli-hiking can find more opportunities here than elsewhere in the region.

"British Columbia Rockies" is in part a misnomer. The term is often used to refer to the Columbia Mountains of southeastern British Columbia, which flank the western slope of the Rockies but are not geologically a part of the Rockies. The Columbias and the true Rockies are separated by the broad valley of the Columbia River, known colloquially as the Columbia River trench. Four separate ranges form the Columbias themselves: to the north are the Cariboos, west of Jasper and Mt. Robson parks. Reaching south like three long talons from the Cariboos are (west to east) the Monashees, the Selkirks, and the Purcells.

As the first ranges to capture storms moving from the west across the plains of interior British Columbia, the Columbias get much more rain and snow than do the Rockies. In the Monashees, the westernmost of the subranges, annual snowfalls can exceed 65 ft. This precipitation has helped create the large, deep glaciers that add to the high-alpine beauty of the Columbias. Lower down, the moist climate creates lusher forests than those in the Rockies to the east. In winter, the deep snows make the Columbias a magnet for deep-powder and helicopter skiers.

Because only a relatively small portion of the British Columbia Rockies is protected from development, human encroachment from residential and commercial development, farming, mining, and lumbering is rather common in the accessible portions of these ranges. The towns often reflect this. In recent years the natural-resource industries have been hit hard with poor commodity prices, and the towns of the British Columbia Rockies have increasingly looked to tourism to help their economies. Although still no Banff or Jasper, many of these towns now offer an array of amenities for visitors, often at substantially lower prices than in the Alberta Rockies.

From Banff, there are two main routes to the British Columbia Rockies. The first follows the Trans-Canada Highway (Highway 1), northwest from Banff to Lake Louise, then west through Yoho National Park, Golden, Glacier National Park, Mt. Revelstoke National Park, and finally the town of Revelstoke. The second route follows Highway 1 from Banff halfway to Lake Louise, then cuts south on Highway 93 through the southern British Columbia Rockies and Kootenay National Park. It continues through Radium Hot Springs, Invermere, Fairmont Hot Springs, Fort Steele, Cranbrook, Kimberley (a small side trip), and finally through Fernie on a return swing to southern Alberta through the Crowsnest Pass.

Golden

③ *80 km (50 mi) west of Lake Louise, 105 km (65 mi) north of Radium Hot Springs.*

Little more than a truck stop a decade ago, Golden has a new emphasis on tourism. Although the town remains an active service center for the lumber and trucking industries, new hotels, restaurants, and tour operators have sprung up. There's summer sightseeing from the 924-ft gondola ascent, and alpine skiing in the winter. Many fine alpine lodges, most offering hiking and cross-country skiing right out the door, dot the hills and mountains around Golden. You still have to scratch below the surface a bit to get past the industrial history of the town, but the effort is rewarded with some hidden gems, minus the crowds found in the towns of the national parks.

Dining and Lodging

$$–$$$ ✕ **Sisters & Beans.** Local artwork (for sale) adorns the walls of this
  ★   early-20th-century house with numerous cozy dining rooms. The international menu lists appetizers such as hummus and nachos; entrées include Thai curry, bratwurst, pasta, steaks, and seafood. The homemade breads are delectable, as are the fondues served in winter. Garden seating is available in summer. ✉ *1122 10th Ave. S, at Hwy. 95*

and 12th St., ☎ *250/344–2443. MC, V. Closed late Oct.–mid-Nov. and late Apr.–mid-May.*

$–$$$ ✕ **La Cabrina.** Dark brown wood dominates this rustic-yet-elegant restaurant with exposed log beams and walls. The cuisine of 18 different countries, including Greece, Japan, Spain, France, Thailand and Indonesia—is represented on the menu, which changes every two months. ⊠ *1105 9th St. S,* ☎ *250/344–2330. Reservations essential. AE, MC, V.*

$$$$ ⌨ **Kapristo Lodge.** An oasis of pampering service, the Kapristo lies 14
 ★   km (9 mi) south of Golden. From 600 ft above the Columbia River valley, the view is impressive enough, but the lodge's real charm is its unabashed effort to spoil the guests. The rate includes breakfast; lunch and dinner are extra and must be booked in advance. The lodge also sets up a wide variety of tour packages, ranging from 3 to 14 days in length, focusing on any of a variety of activities, from yoga to massage to pottery to golf to outdoor adventure packages (skiing, kayaking, canoeing, mountain biking, hiking, rafting, horseback riding, ATV-ing, and fishing). Reserve well in advance for peak-season accommodation. ⊠ *Box 90, 1297 Campbell Rd., V0A 1H0,* ☎ *250/344–6048,* ℻ *250/344–6755,* 𝖶𝖤𝖡 *www.kapristolodge.com. 3 rooms, 3 suites. Dining room, outdoor hot tub, sauna, travel services. MC, V. BP.*

$$$ ⌨ **Prestige Inn.** Furnishings and amenities make this three-story motel the pick of the lot along Highway 1, just up the hill from the main part of town. Queen-size beds, large rooms, and high ceilings create a very spacious feeling. Ten rooms have kitchenettes, and the suites have whirlpool baths. Ask for a room overlooking town—there's no extra charge, the room faces away from the highway, and the view is far more pleasing. Rates drop by a third off-season. ⊠ *Box 9, 1049 Hwy. 1 N, V0A 1H0,* ☎ *250/344–7990,* ℻ *250/344–7902,* 𝖶𝖤𝖡 *www.prestigeinn.com/golden. 82 rooms, 3 suites. Restaurant, lounge, indoor pool, hot tub, health club, meeting rooms. AE, D, MC, V.*

Outdoor Activities and Sports

The gondola at the **Kicking Horse Mountain Resort** (⊠ Kicking Horse Mountain, ☎ 866/754–5425, 𝖶𝖤𝖡 www.kickinghorseresort.com), a four-season resort formerly known as Whitetooth, transports eight people per car on the 12-minute ride to the summit. There are now four lifts and 38 runs ranging from beginner to expert. Summer sightseers can take the gondola ($17) to Canada's highest restaurant, Eagle's Eye, or sign up for an interpretive hike. Open hours vary.

BACKCOUNTRY HIKING AND SKIING

Golden Alpine Holidays (☎ ℻ 250/344–7273, 𝖶𝖤𝖡 www.goldenalpine-holidays.com) offers alpine hiking and backcountry ski tours in the Selkirk Mountains, with accommodation in three backcountry mountain lodges (propane lights, woodstoves and saunas, full kitchen, no running water or electricity, outhouse toilets) near the tree line. Guests and their gear are helicoptered in to the lodges. You can hire a guide and move between lodges or stay at a single lodge. Backcountry skiing season is from December through April; hiking is offered from early July to mid-September. Packages are three to seven days.

Purcell Heli-Ski/Hiking (☎ 250/344–5410 or 877/435–4754) has two- to seven-day heli-skiing–snowboarding packages in the Purcell Mountains, with day use of a modern mountain lodge. Overnight accommodations are in Golden. Heli-skiing is available from December to mid-May, and half- or full-day heli-hiking from mid-June to September.

RAFTING

The Kicking Horse River has excellent white-water rafting. Half-day excursions run about $50, full-day excursions about $80–$100 per person. Rafting season is generally May–September, but high-water conditions, especially in spring, may force cancellation of the wilder trips. **Alpine Rafting** (☎ 250/344–6778, WEB www.kickinghorseriver.com/alpinerafting) runs mild to extreme white-water trips on the Kicking Horse, including multiday trips. **Glacier Raft Company** (☎ 250/344–6521, WEB www.glacierraft.com) specializes in extreme white water (Class IV) but also runs more serene trips for those of fainter heart. **Rocky Mountain Rafting Co.** (☎ 250/344–6979 or 888/518–7238, WEB www.rocky-mountainadventure.com) runs half- to full-day trips ranging from calm and scenic to wild white water. **Wet 'N' Wild Adventures** (☎ 250/344–6546 or 800/668–9119, WEB www.wetnwild.bc.ca) conducts moderate to wild half- and full-day trips on Kicking Horse white water.

SPORTING GEAR

Selkirk Source for Sports (✉ 504 9th Ave. N, ☎ 250/344–2966) rents and sells bicycles, cross-country skis, kayaks, and canoes. It also has a large selection of sportswear and accessories. **Summit Cycle** (✉ 1007 11th Ave., ☎ 250/344–6600) has bicycle rentals.

Shopping

Canyon Creek Pottery (✉ 917 10th Ave. N, ☎ 250/344–5678) sells a wide range of pottery crafted on-site. You can visit the studio and see future gallery items being created.

En Route   The 105 km (65 mi) south from Golden to Radium Hot Springs, where Highway 93 joins Highway 95, is a pleasant drive, rambling along the rolling floodplain of the Columbia River. To the right are the river and the Purcell Mountains; more immediately to the left are the Rockies, although the major peaks are hidden by the ranges in the foreground. Resorts catering to RVs abound.

Glacier National Park

㉜   *58 km (36 mi) west of Golden, 45 km (28 mi) east of Revelstoke.*

Glacier National Park, not to be confused with the U.S. park of the same name, is known for rugged mountains and, not surprisingly, an abundance of glaciers (more than 400). The glaciers result not because of the exceptionally high elevation—although some peaks here do exceed 10,000 ft—but because of the high winter snowfalls in the park. Many of the glaciers can be seen from the highway, but to appreciate Glacier National Park fully, you must take to the trail.

At **Rogers Pass,** near the center of Glacier National Park along Highway 1, the heavy winter snowfalls made rail and road construction exceedingly difficult. Avalanches claimed the lives of hundreds of railway-construction workers in the early 1900s and continued to be a threat during highway construction in the 1950s.

Today, the Rogers Pass war against avalanches is both active and passive. Heavy artillery—105-mm howitzers—is used to trigger controlled avalanches before they build up to threaten truly dangerous slides. (If you're traveling in the backcountry, always be alert to unexploded howitzer shells that pose a potential hazard.) On the passive side, train tunnels and long snow sheds along the highway shield travelers from major slide paths.

The **Rogers Pass Centre** documents Glacier National Park's history and is well worth a visit even if you're not stopping long. Open year-round, the center has exhibits about geology and wildlife and screens 30-minute movies on such subjects as avalanches and bears. ✉ *Hwy. 1,* ☎ *250/837–7500.* 🖼 *Park pass required.* ☉ *May–mid-June and mid-Sept.– Oct., daily 9–5; mid-June–mid-Sept., daily 7–7; Nov., Thurs.–Mon. 9– 5; Dec.–Apr., daily 7–5.*

Lodging

$$$ ⊞ **Glacier Park Lodge.** This modern, two-story Best Western at the top of Rogers Pass offers ambience in familiar chain style: wood-veneer tables and chairs and pink carpeting. The steep-sloping A-frame roof is a design concession to the heavy winter snows. The lodge accommodates travelers with its 24-hour service station, 24-hour cafeteria, and gift shop. Rates drop 40% off-season. ⊠ *Rogers Pass, Glacier National Park, Hwy. 1, V0E 2S0,* ☎ *250/837–2126 or 800/528–1234,* FAX *250/837–2130,* WEB *www.glacierparklodge.ca. 50 rooms. Restaurant, cafeteria, pool, hot tub, shop. AE, D, DC, MC, V.*

Outdoor Activities and Sports

From the Illecillewaet Campground, a few miles west of the park's Rogers Pass Centre, several trails make good day hikes. One of the best, although fairly strenuous, is the **Asulkan Valley Trail.** This 13-km (8-mi) loop passes waterfalls and yields views of the Asulkan Glacier and three massifs—the Ramparts, the Dome, and Mt. Jupiter. A much easier hike is the 1½-km (1-mi) loop, **Brook Trail,** which starts 6 km (4 mi) west of the Rogers Pass Centre and leads to views of the glaciers of Mt. Bonney.

Mount Revelstoke National Park

③ *Eastern border 20 km (12 mi) west of Glacier National Park; western edge is by town of Revelstoke.*

On the western flanks of the Selkirks, this park has smaller mountains than those in the Rockies to the east, and lusher vegetation, thanks to the additional rain and snow on the west-facing slopes. Conceived primarily as a day-use park, Mount Revelstoke National Park covers just 260 square km (100 square mi). The park's main attraction is the 26-km (16-mi) **Meadows in the Sky Parkway** to the summit of Mount Revelstoke, at 6,395 ft. The paved road begins from Highway 1, 1½ km (1 mi) before the turnoff to the town of Revelstoke. This is a narrow road with many switchbacks, so trailers are not permitted. From the Balsam Lake parking lot, there's a free shuttle bus for the last 2 km (1¼ mi) to the summit area from 10 to 4:20. The road is generally open and snow-free from mid-July to late September. Several easy hikes from the Balsam parking lot meander past small lakes and have excellent views of the Selkirk and Monashee ranges.

Revelstoke

③ *148 km (92 mi) west of Golden, on western edge of Mt. Revelstoke National Park.*

The pretty little town of Revelstoke offers both summer and winter activities for visitors. The downtown district has spruced-up buildings from the late 19th century that house modern shops, restaurants, and businesses.

♨ ③ The two pools at **Canyon Hot Springs,** tucked between Mt. Revelstoke and Glacier national parks about 35 km (22 mi) east of Revelstoke, take advantage of the hot springs and make a good rest stop. A 15,000-gallon hot pool is naturally heated to 42°C (108°F), and a 60,000-gallon pool is mixed with cool water to maintain a temperature of 32°C (90°F). New log cabins—with private baths and kitchenettes—and camping are available. Albert Canyon, a ghost town that was the site of the original hot-spring complex built by railroad workers in the late 1800s, is a short distance south of the present facility. ⊠ *Off Hwy. 1,* ☎ *250/837–2420,* FAX *250/837–6160.* ☞ *$4.50.* ⊙ *May–June, and Sept., daily 9–9; July–Aug., daily 9 AM–10 PM.*

Dining and Lodging

$–$$$ ✕ **One-Twelve.** In the Regent Inn, this restaurant has low cedar ceil-
★   ings and an abundance of historic photos that lend warmth to the atmo-
     sphere. Fine seafood dishes make up about half the menu; Continental
     favorites such as chicken Cordon Bleu and beef brochette complete the
     choices. The blue-ribbon menu selection is lamb broiled with rosemary
     and red wine. ⊠ *112 1st St. E,* ☎ *250/837–2107. Reservations essential.
     AE, MC, V.*

$$ 🏨 **Regent Inn.** This hotel is a Revelstoke landmark, set in the heart
     of downtown. It mixes many styles: Colonial, with its brick-arcade
     facade; true Canadian, in its pine-trimmed lobby area and in One-Twelve
     restaurant; and Scandinavian, in the angular, low-slung wood fur-
     nishings of the guest rooms. Rooms are on the large side but have no
     spectacular views. ⊠ *Box 582, 112 1st St. E, V0E 2S0,* ☎ *250/837–
     2107 or 888/245–5523,* FAX *250/837–9669,* WEB *www.regentinn.com.
     47 rooms. Restaurant, pub, outdoor hot tub, sauna. AE, D, DC,
     MC, V. CP.*

Outdoor Activities and Sports

BIKING

High Country Cycle & Sports (⊠ 118 Mackenzie Ave., ☎ 250/814–0090)
has bikes for rent. **Summit Cycle Tours** (☎ 250/837–3734 or 888/700–
3444, WEB www.compusmart.ab.ca/sumcycle) ferries bike riders (10 years
and older) three times a day to the summit of Mount Revelstoke for
the 26-km (16-mi) coast downhill. Trips range from three to eight hours
depending on the amount of hiking and dining included.

SKIING

Cat Powder Skiing (☎ 250/837–5151) organizes two- to five-day all-
inclusive packages that run into the Selkirks and on the upper slopes
of Mt. MacKenzie in Revelstoke. **Selkirk Tangiers Helicopter Skiing** (☎
250/837–5378 or 800/663–7080, WEB www.selkirk-tangiers.com) runs
three-, five-, and seven-day all-inclusive packages in the Selkirk and
Monashee mountains near Revelstoke.

SNOWMOBILING

Revelstoke Snowmobile Tours (☎ 250/837–5200, FAX 250/837–5210,
WEB www.revelstokecc.bc.ca/rst) offers half- to full-day tours in the
Columbia Mountains that start at $75, and also rents snowmobiles with-
out a guide.

Radium Hot Springs

36 *127 km (79 mi) southwest of Banff, 103 km (64 mi) south of Golden,
     at junction of Highways 93 and 95.*

Radium Hot Springs is little more than a service town for the busy highway traffic passing through, but the town makes a convenient access
point for Kootenay National Park and has lower prices than the national parks.

🖐 **Radium Hot Springs,** the springs that give the town its name, are the
town's longest-standing attraction and the summer lifeblood for the
numerous motels in the area. Two outdoor pools are tucked at the bottom of the spectacular Sinclair Canyon. The hot pool is maintained at
41°C (106°F); in a cooler pool, the hot mineral water is diluted to 28°C
(82°F). Lockers, towels, and suits (period and modern) can be rented.
⊠ *Hwy. 93, 2 km (1 mi) northeast of Hwy. 95* ☎ *250/347–9485 or
800/767–1611,* WEB *www.parkscanada.gc.ca/hotsprings.* 🎫 *$5 per
soak, $7.75 day pass.* ☾ *Hot pool: May–mid-Oct., daily 9 AM–11 PM;
mid-Oct.–Apr., Fri. noon–9 and Sat. noon–10. Cooler pool: schedule
varies with weather.*

Dining and Lodging

$–$$$ ✕ **Black Forest Restaurant.** A Bavarian theme pervades the region, and this is a good place to sample the cuisine. Exposed wood, Bavarian pottery, and big-game trophies decorate the interior, creating something of a cross between a hunting lodge and a Bavarian mountain chalet. Schnitzels are the specialty, but other options are smoked pork with sauerkraut, bratwurst, seafood, chicken, duck, lamb, and steak. Save room for the elaborate cheesecake desserts. ✉ *Hwy 93/95, 5 km (3 mi) west of town,* ☎ *250/342–9417. AE, DC, MC, V. No lunch.*

$–$$$ ✕ **Old Salzburg Restaurant.** This is one of the few restaurants that prepare quality food reflecting the pervasive Bavarian motif of the region, avoiding the greasiness so common in the many low-end Bavarian restaurants nearby. Choose from schnitzels, spaetzle (dumplings), and bratwurst, as well as chicken, beef, and lamb entrées. Steaks, seafood, and pastas are also available. ✉ *4943 Hwy. 93, at Hwys. 95 and 93,* ☎ *250/347–6553. Reservations essential. MC, V. No lunch mid-Sept.–mid-May.*

$$$ ▦ **Radium Resort.** Recreational facilities and activities bring this resort to life. Accommodations are in hotel rooms or one-, two-, or three-bedroom condo units. Rooms are modern, with hardwood furnishings and sponge-painted walls, and each has a sun deck, a mini-refrigerator, and a view overlooking the golf fairways. Condos have full kitchens. Golf is the main attraction (packages are available), along with the proximity to the hot springs. There's a small rate reduction off-season. ✉ *Box 310, 8100 Golf Course Rd., V0A 1M0,* ☎ *250/347–9311 or 800/667–6444,* ℻ *250/347–6299,* 🌐 *www.radiumresort.bc.ca. 90 rooms, 30 condo units. Dining room, indoor pool, hot tub, sauna, 18-hole golf course, 2 tennis courts, health club, racquetball, squash, mountain bikes, cross-country skiing. AE, D, DC, MC, V.*

$$–$$$ ▦ **Chalet Europe.** The hotel sits on a crest above town, and all rooms
★ have expansive views of the Columbia River valley from 300 to 600 ft above the town and valley. Each room comes with a sitting area and kitchenette (microwave oven, refrigerator, sink); all have balconies. Rooms are bright and modern. The best views are from the top floor; deluxe suites even come with telescopes to take full advantage of the vista. Rates drop by a third off-season. ✉ *Box 456, 5063 Madsen Rd., V0A 1M0,* ☎ *250/347–9305 or 888/428–9998,* ℻ *250/347–9306,* 🌐 *www.chaleteurope.com. 17 suites. Kitchenettes, hot tub, sauna, health club, recreation room, coin laundry. AE, D, DC, MC, V. CP.*

Outdoor Activities and Sports

Radium Resort (✉ 8100 Golf Course Rd., ☎ 250/347–9652 or 800/667–6444) has one 18-hole, par-69 golf course and another 18-hole, par-72 course.

Invermere

18 km (11 mi) south of Radium Hot Springs.

Invermere, one of the many highway service towns in the British Columbia Rockies, is the central access point for Windermere Lake, Panorama Resort, and the Purcell Wilderness area.

For summer water sports, **Windermere Lake**—actually an extra-wide stretch of the Columbia River—is popular among swimmers, boaters, and board sailors. There's a good beach on the lake.

One of the best area museums is the **Windermere Valley Pioneer Museum,** which depicts the life of 19th-century settlers through artifacts and other memorabilia in seven pioneer buildings. ✉ *622 3rd St.,* ☎ *250/342–9769.* 🎫 *$2.* ⊙ *June, Tues.–Sat. 1–4; July–early Sept., Tues.–Sat. 10:30–4:30.*

The **Pynelogs Cultural Centre** (✉ 1720 4th Ave., at Kinsmen Beach, ☎ 250/342–4423) showcases and sells all types of local crafts: paintings, pottery, photographs, jewelry, and sculptures. There are occasional evening folk or jazz concerts.

Panorama Mountain Village is a year-round accommodation known best for skiing in winter. Summer visitors (staying at the resort or not) can take advantage of an excellent golf course, tennis courts, outdoor pools, water slides, and hiking and biking trails, including lift-accessed mountain biking.

Dining and Lodging

$$–$$$$ × **Strand's Old House Restaurant.** A gem set amid the usual pizza and
★ burger joints, Strand's seems somewhat out of place in Invermere. The five rooms seat eight to 48 people each, providing varied levels of coziness. In summer there's a large outdoor patio and the gazebo opens for additional seating in an attractive courtyard setting. A deliciously international menu includes dishes such as Thai shrimp salad, snails in garlic butter and red wine, pheasant with shiitake mushroom sauce, and rack of lamb flavored with Dijon mustard and herbs. ✉ *818 12th St.,* ☎ *250/342–6344. Reservations essential. AE, MC, V. No lunch.*

$$–$$$$ × **Toby Creek Dining Lounge.** This ski-lodge restaurant at the Panorama Mountain Village is an elegant fine-dining establishment open from mid-December to late-May for dinner only. The menu showcases superior steaks, chicken, seafood, and fondues, but more adventurous diners may opt for the ostrich, pheasant, venison, caribou, or musk ox. ✉ *Panorama Resort Rd., 18 km (11 mi) west of Invermere* ☎ *250/342–6941. Reservations essential. AE, D, MC, V.*

$$ ⊞ **Best Western Invermere Inn.** The familiar red-and-turquoise decor of this hotel chain means there are few surprises here, although rooms are on the large side. The hotel is conveniently located at a quiet end of the main shopping and dining area in town. It's the nearest major hotel to the town beach, but still about a mile away. Rates drop 20% off-season. ✉ *1310 7th Ave., V0A 1K0,* ☎ *250/342–9246 or 800/661–8911,* FAX *250/342–6079. 46 rooms. Restaurant, lounge, wine shop, outdoor hot tub, health club. AE, D, MC, V.*

$$ ⊞ **Panorama Mountain Village.** Accommodation is either in condo villas (many have fireplaces, patios, or balconies) that resemble part of a mountainside suburb or in a lodge at the base of the ski lift that has a college-dorm atmosphere. Skiing, hiking, biking, and tennis are available, depending on the season. A water park, opened in 2000, features two large year-round outdoor hot pools, two hot tubs, and a 4,000-square-ft swimming pool. In summer the water slides are open. A deluxe golf course, the Greywolf at Panorama, opened in 1999. Summer is still a slower season than winter, however, and some services may be reduced. Rates decrease by 25% off-season. ✉ *Toby Creek Rd., V0A 1T0, 18 km (11 mi) west of Invermere,* ☎ *250/342–6941 or 800/663–2929,* FAX *250/342–3395,* WEB *www.panoramaresort.com. 105 hotel rooms, 350 condo units. 5 restaurants, 3 bars, cafeteria, 3 pools, sauna, 18-hole golf course, 8 tennis courts, hiking, water slide, downhill skiing. AE, D, MC, V.*

Outdoor Activities and Sports

DOWNHILL SKIING

Panorama Mountain Village (✉ Toby Creek Rd., ☎ 800/663–2929, WEB www.panoramaresort.com) has the second-highest lift-served vertical drop (4,300 ft) in Canada; there are more than 100 runs and 10 lifts.

GOLF

Greywolf at Panorama (✉ Toby Creek Rd., ☎ 800/663–2929, WEB www.panoramaresort.com) opened in 1999 and has an 18-hole, par-72 course. The sixth hole requires golfers to play across "Hopeful

Canyon" to a green perched above vertical rock cliffs. *Golf Digest* proclaimed this to be the "best new Canadian golf course in 1999."

HELI-SKIING

R. K. Heli-Ski (☎ 250/342–3889 or 800/661–6060, WEB www. rkheliski.com), based at the Panorama Mountain Village resort, has daily ski tours in winter.

SPORTING GEAR

Columbia Cycle and Motorsports (✉ 375 Laurier St., ☎ 250/342–6164) rents bicycles, snowboards, downhill and cross-country skis, snowshoes, kayaks, and canoes. In summer **D. R. Sports** (✉ 2755 13th St., ☎ 250/342–3517) rents bikes for children and adults (hourly or daily) and snowboards in winter. **Invermere Sales & Rentals** (✉ 403 7th Ave., ☎ 250/342–6336) sells and rents canoes, boats, and personal watercraft.

Fairmont Hot Springs

③⑦ *20 km (12 mi) south of Invermere, 94 km (58 mi) north of Fort Steele.*

Fairmont Hot Springs is named for the hot springs and the resort that has sprouted around it. The "town" is little more than a service strip along the highway, but turn in at the resort and things become more impressive. The town is also close to Columbia Lake, popular with boaters and board sailors. Golf is a growing attraction at several fine courses in the area.

Lodging

$$$ 🏨 ⚠ **Fairmont Hot Springs Resort.** The wide selection of activities from golf to heli-hiking makes vacationing here feel somewhat like being at camp, but don't overlook the hot springs and the spa. Inside the attractive, low-slung bungalow-style structure, rooms are contemporary, many with wood paneling; some are equipped with kitchens and have balconies or patios. The RV sites are popular. Golf, ski, and spa packages are available. Rates decrease by 40% off-season. ✉ *Box 10, Hwy. 93/95, V0B 1L0,* ☎ *250/345–6311; 800/663 4979 in Canada,* FAX *250/345–6616,* WEB *www.fairmontresort.com. 140 rooms, 311 RV sites. 7 restaurants, lobby lounge, snack bar, 4 pools, hot springs, spa, 2 18-hole golf courses, 2 tennis courts, horseback riding, bicycles, private airstrip. AE, D, DC, MC, V.*

Outdoor Activities and Sports

Fairmont Hot Springs Resort (✉ Hwy. 93/95, ☎ 250/345–6514 or 800/663–4979) has two 18-hole courses: a par-72 course at the resort, and a par-71 course along the river in town. New hiking trails have been added and the trail from the hot springs waterfall into the canyon is quite spectacular.

Fort Steele

③⑧ *94 km (58 mi) south of Fairmont Hot Springs.*

Fort Steele and nearby Kimberley were home to many German and Swiss immigrants who arrived in the late 19th century to work as miners and loggers. Southeastern British Columbia was not unlike the Tyrol region they had left, so they found it comfortable to settle here. Later, a demand for experienced alpinists to guide and teach hikers, climbers, and skiers brought more settlers from the Alpine countries, and a Tyrolean influence is evident throughout southeastern British Columbia. Schnitzels and fondues appear on menus as often as burgers and fries.

★ ☾ **Fort Steele Heritage Town,** a reconstructed 1890s boomtown consisting of more than 60 buildings, is a step back to the silver- and lead-mining days of the 1890s. Its theater, period tradesmen, barbershop, and dry-goods store exude the authenticity of a bygone era. Steam-train and wagon rides are available. There's enough to hold the interest of children and adults alike for a half day or more. ⌧ *9851 Hwy. 93/95, 16 km (10 mi) northeast of Cranbrook,* ☎ *250/417–6000,* FAX *250/489–2624,* WEB *www.fortsteele.bc.ca.* ⌧ *Museum: May–Sept. $8.50; grounds: Oct.–Apr. free.* ☉ *Museum: May–Sept., daily 9:30–8; grounds: daily 9:30–dusk.*

Cranbrook

16 km (10 mi) southwest of Fort Steele, 27 km (17 mi) southeast of Kimberley.

Cranbrook is primarily a service center for motorists and the surrounding mining and logging industries. As one of the largest towns in the region, it has more choice in moderately priced basic motels and restaurants.

Kimberley

③⑨ *40 km (25 mi) west of Fort Steele, 98 km (61 mi) south of Fairmont Hot Springs.*

A cross between quaint and kitschy, Kimberley is rich with Tyrolean character. The *Platzl* ("small plaza," in German) is a pedestrian mall of shops and restaurants modeled after a Bavarian village. Chalet-style buildings are as common here as log cabins in the national parks. In summer, Kimberley plays its alpine theme to the hilt: merchants dress up in lederhosen. Gimmicks abound, and the promotion works. The Canadian Rockies are a popular destination for German tourists; Kimberley catches their attention, and sometimes there's as much German as English being spoken in the Platzl.

Dining and Lodging

$$-$$$ ✕ **Chef Bernard's Kitchen.** Eating in this small, homey storefront restau-
★ rant on the Kimberley pedestrian mall is like dining in someone's pantry. Packed into the shelves of the many small rooms in the dining area are the chef's collection of travel memorabilia—license plates, glass figurines, and much more, including a model train that runs on the ceiling in the restaurant. If things aren't too busy, don't be surprised to see cheery Chef Bernard out front in the Platzl, wooing customers inside. The menu is international, ranging from German and Thai to Cajun. Homemade desserts are always a favorite. Breakfast is served in summer. There's also an inn upstairs with a hot tub on the deck. ⌧ *170 Spokane St.,* ☎ *250/427–4820 or 800/905–8338,* WEB *www.chefbernards.com. Reservations essential. AE, D, DC, MC, V.*

$$-$$$ ⊟ **Quality Inn of the Rockies.** In keeping with downtown Kimberley's Bavarian theme, the chain hotel has an exterior of exposed-wood beams and stucco. Large rooms have a small sitting area and are plainly furnished with dark brown wood-veneer furniture. The restaurant serves good, reasonably priced Canadian cuisine including steak and seafood, and the pub features live entertainment on weekends. The only lodging next to the Platzl, this is the best of the mostly plain hotels in Kimberley. There's a small rate decrease during the off-season. ⌧ *300 Wallinger Ave., V1A 1Z4,* ☎ *250/427–2266 or 800/661–7559,* FAX *250/427–7621,* WEB *www.qualityinn.kootenays.com. 43 rooms. Restaurant, lounge, pub, hot tub, coin laundry. AE, DC, D, MC, V.*

Nightlife and the Arts

In summer, Bavarian bands in Kimberley strike up with oompah music on the Platzl, especially when an event such as the **Old Time Accordion**

Championships (☎ 800/667–0871, WEB www.kimberleyvacations.bc.ca) is in full swing (early July).

Outdoor Activities and Sports

Kimberley Ski Resort (✉ Kimberly Ski Area Rd., ☎ 250/427–4881 or 800/258–7669) has a vertical drop of 2,302 ft, 67 runs, 6 lifts, and on-mountain facilities.

Fernie

96 km (60 mi) east of Fort Steele, 331 km (205 mi) southwest of Calgary.

Fernie is primarily a winter destination, serving skiers at the Fernie Alpine Resort ski area. However, mountain biking has become a popular summer attraction in recent years. As one of the largest towns between Cranbrook and Calgary, Fernie has a wider selection of motels and restaurants than other centers along this route.

Outdoor Activities and Sports

Fernie Alpine Resort (✉ Ski Area Rd., ☎ 250/423–4655) has 86 runs, nine lifts, and on-mountain facilities for skiers. In summer a chairlift is kept busy ferrying mountain bikers, and their bikes, up the slopes. Expansion has increased the vertical drop to 2,811 ft with new runs and lifts. The resort now boasts nightclubs, pubs, a grocery and a liquor store, and ski-in, ski-out accommodations.

CANADIAN ROCKIES A TO Z

To research prices, get advice from other travelers, and book travel arrangements, visit www.fodors.com.

AIR TRAVEL

Air Canada has flights to and from many points in southern British Columbia; most of these flights connect with flights through the international airports in Vancouver, Calgary, and Edmonton. Peace Air flies between Jasper and Calgary weekdays.

➤ AIRLINES AND CONTACTS: **Air Canada** (☎ 800/247–2262). **Peace Air** (☎ 780/624–3060 or 800/563–3060, WEB www.peaceair.com).

AIRPORTS

Calgary is the most common gateway for travelers arriving by plane. If you plan to visit only Jasper and northern park regions, you may prefer to use Edmonton as a gateway city. Both cities have international airports served by several major carriers; the Calgary flight schedule is somewhat more extensive.

➤ AIRPORT INFORMATION: **Calgary International Airport** (✉ 2000 Airport Rd. NE, 20 minutes northeast of the city center, ☎ 403/735–1372). **Cranbrook Airport** (✉ 9370 Airport Access Rd., ☎ 250/426–7913). **Edmonton International Airport** (✉ Hwy. 2, 20 km [12 mi] south of downtown Edmonton, ☎ 780/890–8382). **Jasper-Hinton Airport** (✉ Off Hwy. 16, 50 minutes east of Jasper townsite, ☎ 780/865–4474).

BUS TRAVEL

Brewster Transportation and Tours offers service between Calgary International Airport and bus stations in Banff, Jasper, and Lake Louise. Greyhound Lines provides regular service to Calgary, Edmonton, and Vancouver, with connecting service to Jasper and Banff. Taxis are available to get you to your hotel.

Banff Airport Shuttle operates between Calgary International Airport and the Banff–Lake Louise area, dropping you off and picking up at your hotel. The shuttle's information desk is across from baggage carousel four.

➤ Bus Information: **Banff Airport Shuttle** (☎ 403/762–3330 or 888/449–2901). **Brewster Transportation and Tours** (☎ 800/661–1152). **Greyhound Lines** (☎ 800/661–8747; 800/231–2222 in the U.S.).

CAR RENTAL

International car-rental outlets such as Hertz and National are at the Calgary and Edmonton airports, as well as in Banff and Jasper, AB. Banff Rent-A-Car is a local agency in that city. Daily rentals for sightseeing are available but should be reserved well ahead of time, especially in summer.

➤ Major Agencies: **Budget Rent-A-Car** (✉ 208 C Caribou St., Banff, AB, ☎ 403/762–4565; ✉ 1024 Cranbrook St. N, Cranbrook, BC, ☎ 250/489–4371). **Hertz** (✉ 204 Wolf St., Banff, ☎ 403/762–3352; ✉ Cranbrook Municipal Airport, Airport Access Road, Cranbrook, BC, ☎ 250/489–1115; ✉ Jasper VIA Rail Station, 607 Connaught Dr., Jasper, AB, ☎ 780/852–3888). **National Car Rental** (✉ 201 Bear St., Banff, AB, ☎ 403/762–2688; ✉ Cranbrook Municipal Airport, Airport Access Rd., Cranbrook, BC, ☎ 250/489–3689; ✉ Jasper Via Rail Station, 607 Connaught Dr., Jasper, AB, ☎ 780/852–1117).

➤ Local Agencies: **Banff Rent-A-Car** (✉ 204 Wolf Street, Banff, AB, ☎ 403/762–3352).

CAR TRAVEL

Highway 1, the Trans-Canada Highway, is the principal east–west route into the region. Banff is 128 km (79 mi) west of Calgary and 858 km (532 mi) east of Vancouver on Highway 1. The other major east–west routes are Highway 16 to the north, the main highway between Edmonton and Jasper, and Highway 3 to the south. The main routes from the south are U.S. 89 (Highway 2 in Canada), which enters Canada east of Alberta's Waterton Lakes National Park from Montana, and U.S. 93, also from Montana, which provides access to the British Columbia Rockies.

An automobile allows the most flexible travel in the Canadian Rockies, although the sightseeing packages from some tour-bus and train operators can offer almost as leisurely a schedule, with some additional pampering.

ROAD CONDITIONS

Passenger vehicles are fully adequate for travel along the major routes. Keep in mind, however, that snow arrives in early fall and remains until March or April, longer at high elevations. Four-wheel-drive vehicles are popular among the locals, but aren't really needed for most tourist travel, and off-road driving isn't permitted in the national parks. Four-wheel-drives are used mainly for winter travel, and for exploring along logging roads or the backcountry.

When traveling between October and April, stay informed about local road conditions, especially if you're traveling over mountain passes or along the Icefields Parkway (Highway 93). A few roads, such as Highway 40 over Highwood Pass in Kananaskis Country, are closed in winter.

EMERGENCIES

➤ Contacts: **Ambulance, police, and fire** (☎ 911).

LODGING

B&BS

In Alberta, the Bed-and-Breakfast Association of Calgary handles about 42 B&Bs and inspects each property. Alberta's Gem B&B Reservation Agency represents licensed B&Bs and charges a booking fee. For B&Bs in the British Columbia Rockies, contact the British Columbia Bed-and-Breakfast Association.

➤ RESERVATION SERVICES: **Alberta's Gem B&B Reservation Agency** (☎ 780/434–6098, FAX 780/434–6098, WEB www.bbalberta.com). **Bed-and-Breakfast Association of Calgary** (☎ 403/277–0023, FAX 403/237–5433). **British Columbia Bed-and-Breakfast Association** (☎ 604/276–8616).

CAMPING

Campground information is available from Parks Canada and from Kananaskis Country. Contact Super, Natural British Columbia or Travel Alberta for special camping publications.

➤ CONTACTS: **Kananaskis Country** (✉ 3115 12th St. NE, ☎ 403/297–3362 or 403/673–3985, FAX 403/297–2843, WEB www.barriervisitor. infocenter.gov.ab.ca). **Parks Canada** (✉ Canadian Heritage–Parks Canada, Information Services, 220 4th Ave. SE, Room 552, Calgary, ☎ 403/292–4401 or 800/651–7959, FAX 403/292–6004, WEB www.parkscanada.gc.ca).

NATIONAL PARKS

In terms of national-park fees, if you are planning a stay of a week or more, the best option is the Western Canada Annual Pass. The cost is $35 per adult, or $70 per group of two–seven people; the pass is valid one year from the month of purchase for all seven mountain parks (Banff, Jasper, Yoho, Kootenay, Waterton Lakes, Mt. Revelstoke, and Glacier), as well as for Riding Mountain and Prince Albert national parks in Saskatchewan, Elk Island National Park in Alberta, and Pacific Rim National Park in British Columbia. A day pass for Banff, Jasper, Kootenay, and Yoho parks is $5 per adult per day, or $10 per day for a group of two to seven people, and is valid for all four parks. A pass for Mt. Revelstoke and Glacier parks (valid for both parks) is $4 per adult per day or $10 per group in a private vehicle; an annual pass costs $28 per adult, $50 per group. A day pass for Waterton Lakes National Park is $4 per person per day or $8 per day per group in a private vehicle; cost is $28 per adult, $50 per group for an annual pass.

The parks are open daily, 24 hours a day. National historic sites generally charge a $2 or $3 entry fee. If you are planning an extensive tour of such sites, the Alberta Federal and Provincial Historic Sites Pass ($20 per adult for an annual pass, $49.50 per family), which provides entry to four national historic sites and 18 provincial historic sites, is an economical option.

BACKCOUNTRY CAMPING AND HIKING

Backpackers need to register at Parks Canada information centers for backcountry camping permits. This is principally for safety reasons—so that you can be tracked down in case of emergency—as well as for trail-usage records. The fee is $6 per person per night (to a maximum of $30 per person per trip or $42 annually) for the use of backcountry campsites. You can make reservations up to three months in advance ($10 reservation fee) by contacting the park office. These offices can also supply trail and topographical maps and information on current trail conditions.

If you're interested in hiking or backpacking, several good books describe various routes and route combinations. One of the best, *The Canadian Rockies Trail Guide,* by Brian Patton and Bart Robinson, is available in most bookstores in Banff, Lake Louise, and Jasper.

CLIMBING

Safety registrations for climbing can be obtained at park warden office and information centers. Except for very experienced mountaineers, guide and instruction services are essential here. Climbing gear can be rented at outdoor stores in Banff. Banff Alpine Guides, the Canadian School of Mountaineering, and Yamnuska Mountain Adventures lead trips throughout the parks, catering to all ability levels.

Climbers or backpackers interested in extended stays of more than three or four days might consider membership in the Alpine Club of Canada (basic membership $21, including international postage). The club maintains several mountain huts in the parks, and provides other benefits.
➤ CONTACTS: **Alpine Club of Canada** (☎ 403/678–3200, WEB www.alpineclubofcanada.ca). **Banff Alpine Guides** (☎ 403/678–6091). **Canadian School of Mountaineering** (☎ 403/678–4134). **Yamnuska Mountain Adventures** (☎ 403/678–4164, FAX 403/678–4450, WEB www.yamnuska.com).

FISHING

To try your luck at fishing, you need a license, which you can purchase at visitor information centers, sports shops, and many gas stations in the region. A British Columbia license is good only in British Columbia, an Alberta license only in Alberta. If you are fishing in the national parks, you need a national parks license (but not provincial licenses).

In Alberta, the fee for an annual license for nonresident Canadians is $18 and for non-Canadians $36. Non-Canadians can purchase a five-day license for $24. In British Columbia, the fees for one-day, eight-day, and annual licenses for nonresident Canadians are $10, $20, and $28, respectively; for non-Canadians the fees are $10, $25, and $40. A seven-day national park license is $6; an annual license is $13.

Fishing regulations vary between jurisdictions, so ask for a copy of relevant regulations when you purchase a license. In the national parks, all lead weights of less than 50 grams (2 ounces) are banned; steel shot is an acceptable substitute.

SAFETY

Very few of the natural hazards in the Rockies are marked with warning signs. Be wary of slippery rocks and vegetation near rivers and canyons, snow-covered crevasses on glaciers, avalanche conditions in winter, and potentially aggressive animals. Each year there are about a dozen fatalities from natural hazards in the Rockies, with avalanches accounting for the majority of them.

TOURS

AIRPLANE TOURS

Alpenglow Aviation, at the Golden Municipal Airport, runs one- to two-hour tours, mostly of the British Columbia Rockies, with one tour east to the Columbia Icefields.
➤ CONTACTS: **Alpenglow Aviation** (✉ 210 Fisher Rd., Golden, BC, ☎ 250/344–7117 or 888/244–7117).

BIKING TOURS

Rocky Mountain Worldwide Cycle Tours runs seven-day tours in the Banff area and in British Columbia. Prices begin at US$795.
➤ CONTACTS: **Rocky Mountain Worldwide Cycle Tours** (☎ 800/661–2453, WEB www.worldweb.com/RMCT).

BUS TOURS

Brewster Transportation and Tours offers half-, full-, and multiday sightseeing tours of the parks. Prices start at about $48 per person. U.S.-based Tauck Tours conducts multiday bus tours through the region.

➤ CONTACTS: **Brewster Transportation and Tours** (☎ 403/762–6767 in Banff; 780/852–3332 in Jasper; 403/221–8242 in Calgary; 800/661–1152, FAX 403/762–2090, WEB www.brewster.ca). **Tauck Tours** (☎ 800/468–2825, WEB www.tauck.com).

HELICOPTER TOURS

Alpine Helicopters is 20 minutes southeast of Banff and provides year-round guided "flightseeing" tours (25–30 minutes) above the Banff and Kananaskis valleys for $130–$160. It also offers half- and full-day heli-hiking tours. Prices range from $230–$360.

The largest heli-skiing tour operator in the region is Canadian Mountain Holidays. It has heli-skiing (and in summer, heli-hiking) packages in the Cariboo and Purcell ranges in the British Columbia Rockies, with accommodation at remote lodges. Reserve several months in advance.

➤ CONTACTS: **Alpine Helicopters** (☎ 403/678–4802, WEB www.alpine-helicopter.com). **Canadian Mountain Holidays** (☎ 403/762–7100 or 800/661–0252, FAX 403/762–5879, WEB www.cmhmountaineering.com).

HORSEBACK RIDING TOURS

Travel Alberta and Super, Natural British Columbia have listings of pack-trip outfitters. They also have information about guest ranches; riding is generally a major part of a stay. In British Columbia, information is available from the Guide-Outfitters Association.

➤ CONTACTS: **Guide-Outfitters Association** (☎ 250/278–2688, WEB www.goabc.org).

SEASONAL TOURS

Kingmik Expeditions specializes in dogsledding tours through the mountains. Tours range from 35 minutes to five-day outings. Each sled can carry two adults and one small child. Tightline Adventures at Monod Sports offers fly-fishing instruction, guide services, drift-fishing tours including equipment, boat, and meals from $385 for one, or $425 for two people per day. Some of the best brown trout and Rocky Mountain whitefish are caught on this scenic stretch of the Bow River, just outside Banff National Park.

➤ CONTACTS: **Kingmik Expeditions** (☎ 250/344–5298); **Tightline Adventures at Monod Sports** (☎ 403/762–4548).

SELF-GUIDED TOURS

Audiocassette tapes for self-guided tours of the parks are produced by Auto Tape Tours. Canadian Wilderness Videos produces a series of videotapes illustrating highlights along specific routes and across Canada. Both can be purchased at news or gift shops in Banff, Lake Louise, and Jasper.

➤ CONTACTS: **Auto Tape Tours** (☎ 201/236–1666, WEB www.auto-tapetours.com). **Canadian Wilderness Videos** (☎ 403/678–3795, WEB www.crvideo.com).

SNOWMOBILE TOURS

Challenge Enterprises, based in Canmore, specializes in half-day to multiday guided snowmobile tours. Prices start at $120 per person. Great Canadian Snowmobile Tours, based in Revelstoke, runs three-hour to full-week trips in the Columbias, starting at $60 per person. The company also rents snowmobiles.

➤ CONTACTS: **Challenge Enterprises** (☎ 403/678–2628 or 800/892–3429, FAX 403/678–2183). **Great Canadian Snowmobile Tours** (☎

250/837–6500 or 800/668–0330, FAX 250/837–6577, WEB www.snow-mobilerevelstoke.com).

RAIL TOURS

You can start or finish trips with Rocky Mountaineer RailTours in Vancouver, Kamloops, Banff, Jasper, and Calgary—at a premium price. A luxury bi-level dome coach has two spiral staircases, a private dining area (all meals included), an open-air observation platform, and on-board hosts. Two-day, Jasper–Vancouver packages include meals on the rails and lodging in Kamloops so you can travel during the day and see the mountains.

➤ CONTACTS: **Rocky Mountaineer RailTours** (☎ 604/606–7245 or 800/665–7245, FAX 604/606–7201, WEB www.rkymtnrail.com).

TRAIN TRAVEL

VIA Rail trains stop in Jasper en route to and from Edmonton and Vancouver. The train leaves Edmonton at 8:55 AM Monday, Thursday, and Saturday, with a stopover in Jasper from 2:15 PM to 3:30 PM, and arrives in Vancouver at 7:50 the next morning. From Vancouver, the train departs Sunday, Tuesday, and Friday at 5:30 PM, stops in Jasper the next morning from 11:15 AM to 12:25 PM, and arrives in Edmonton at 5:45 PM. Some of the trips through the Rockies are at night, so you lose the views then.

The Jasper VIA Rail Train Station is on Jasper's main street across from the Parks Information Centre.

➤ TRAIN INFORMATION: **Jasper VIA Rail Station** (✉ 607 Connaught Dr., ☎ 800/561–3949 or 800/561–8630, WEB www.viarail.ca).

TRANSPORTATION AROUND THE CANADIAN ROCKIES

It's easy to self-navigate the Rockies by car in summer. Roads are well-maintained and there are many places to pull off that are of historic, geographic, or cultural interest. If you're unfamiliar with snowy and icy winter driving conditions, consider a guided bus tour with an experienced driver in winter. A car may not be necessary in resort towns such as Jasper or Banff, but to explore out-of-the-way spots in the mountains you'll want your own transportation.

VISITOR INFORMATION

The major sources of visitor information are Travel Alberta; Super, Natural British Columbia; Parks Canada; and, in British Columbia, the Rocky Mountain Visitors Association. Individual towns and areas may have their own visitor bureaus as well.

➤ ALBERTA CONTACTS: **Banff Visitor Centre** (✉ 224 Banff Ave., Banff, ☎ 403/762–1550). **Jasper Tourism and Commerce** (✉ 409 Patricia St., Jasper, ☎ 780/852–3858, WEB www.jaspercanadianrockies.com). **Kananaskis Country** (✉ 3115 12th St. NE, Calgary, ☎ 403/297–3362; 403/310–0000 Ext. 673–3985 weekends). **Lake Louise Visitor Centre** (✉ Village Rd. beside Samson Mall, Lake Louise, ☎ 403/522–3833, WEB www.lakelouise.com). **Parks Canada** (✉ Canadian Heritage-Parks Canada, 220 4th St. SE, Room 552, Calgary, ☎ 403/292–4401 or 800/651–7959, FAX 403/292–6004). **Travel Alberta** (✉ 10155 102nd St. NW, Edmonton, ☎ 800/661–8888, WEB www.travel-alberta.com). **Waterton Lakes National Park** (✉ Superintendent, Waterton Park, ☎ 403/859–5133). **Waterton Park Chamber of Commerce** (✉ Box 55, Waterton Park, ☎ 403/859–5133).

➤ BRITISH COLUMBIA CONTACTS: **BC Parks** (✉ 4051 18th Ave., Prince George, ☎ 250/565–6340). **Kootenay National Park Visitor Centre** (✉ Box 220, Radium Hot Springs, ☎ 250/347–9505 in summer; 403/292–4401; 250/347–9615 in winter; WEB www.parkscanada.gc.ca/kootenay). **Mount Revelstoke and Glacier National Parks** (✉ Box

350, Revelstoke, ☎ 250/837–7500). **Rocky Mountain Visitors Association** (✉ Box 10, Kimberley, ☎ 250/427–4838). **Super, Natural British Columbia** (✉ 802–865 Hornby St., Vancouver, ☎ 800/663–6000, WEB www.hellobc.com). **Yoho National Park Visitor Centre** (✉ Hwy. 1, Field exit, Field, ☎ 250/343–6783, WEB wwwparkscanada.gc.ca/yoho).

6 THE PRAIRIE PROVINCES

ALBERTA, SASKATCHEWAN, MANITOBA

Between the eastern slopes of the Rockies and the wilds of western Ontario lie Canada's three prairie provinces: Alberta, Saskatchewan, and Manitoba. Their northern sections are sparsely populated expanses of lakes, rivers, and forests. The fertile southern plains support farms and ranches and five busy cities: Calgary, Edmonton, Saskatoon, Regina, and Winnipeg. Here you also find stunning national parks, dinosaur sites, and attractions that preserve the area's native and frontier heritage.

ALBERTA, SASKATCHEWAN, AND MANITOBA contain Canada's heartland, the principal source of such solid commodities as wheat, oil, and beef. These provinces are also home to a rich stew of ethnic communities that make the area unexpectedly colorful and cosmopolitan. You'll find exceptional outdoor recreational facilities and a spectrum of historical attractions that focus on Mounties, Métis, dinosaurs, and railroads; excellent accommodations and cuisine at reasonable (but not necessarily low) prices; and quiet, crowdless wide-open spaces.

The term "prairie provinces" is a bit of a misnomer, as most of this region—the northern half of Alberta and Saskatchewan, and the northern two-thirds of Manitoba—consists of sparsely populated expanses of lakes, rivers, and forests. Most of northern Saskatchewan and Manitoba belongs to the Canadian Shield, the bedrock core of North America, with a foundation of Precambrian rock that is some of the oldest in the world. On the fertile plains of the south, wheat is still king, but other crops, as well as livestock, help boost the economy. The landscape is quite diverse, with farms and ranches interspersed with wide river valleys, lakes, rolling hills, badlands, and even dry hills of sand.

Early milestones in the history of this region include the period 75 million years ago when dinosaurs roamed what was then semitropical swampland, and the epoch when the first human settlers crossed the Bering Strait from Asia 12,000 years ago. Later, Plains Indians of the Athabascan, Algonquin, and Siouan language groups developed a culture and hunted buffalo here. In the 17th century European fur traders began to arrive, and in 1670 the British Crown granted the Hudson's Bay Company administrative and trading rights to "Rupert's Land," a vast territory whose waters drained into Hudson Bay. A hundred years later, the North West Company went into direct competition by building outposts throughout the area. From this fur-trading tradition arose the Métis mostly French-speaking offspring of native women and European traders who followed the Roman Catholic religion but adhered to a traditional native lifestyle.

By 1873 the North West Mounted Police was established in Manitoba, just six years after the formation of the Canadian federation. In 1874 the Mounties began their march west: their first chores included resolving conflicts between the regional people and American whiskey traders and overseeing the orderly distribution of the free homesteads granted by the Dominion Lands Act of 1872. The Mounties played a role in the Northwest Rebellion—a revolt by Métis, who feared that the encroachment of western settlement would threaten their traditions and freedom. Although the Métis eventually succumbed and their leader, Louis Riel, was hanged in 1885, Riel is now hailed as their martyr. A statue of him stands on the grounds of Manitoba's Legislature Building.

Railroads arrived in the 1880s and with them a torrent of immigrants seeking free government land. An influx of farmers from the British Isles, Scandinavia, Holland, Germany, and Eastern Europe and Russia, and especially Ukraine, plus persecuted religious groups such as the Mennonites, Hutterites, Mormons, and Jews, made the prairies into a rich wheat-growing breadbasket and cultural mosaic that remains in evidence today. In 1947 a big oil strike fueled the transformation of Edmonton and Calgary into gleaming metropolises full of western oil barons.

The people of the prairie provinces are relaxed, reserved, and irascibly independent. They maintain equal suspicion toward "Ottawa" (big government) and "Toronto" (big media and big business). To visitors, the people of this region convey western openness and Canadian-style courtesy: no fawning, but no rudeness. It's an appealing combination.

Pleasures and Pastimes

Dining

Although places specializing in generous helpings of Canadian beef still dominate the scene, restaurants throughout the prairie provinces reflect the region's ethnic makeup and offer a wide variety of cuisines to fit every price range. Dress in the prairie cities tends toward formality in expensive restaurants but is casual in moderately priced and inexpensive restaurants.

CATEGORY	COST*
$$$$	over $32
$$$	$22–$32
$$	$13–$21
$	under $13

per person, in Canadian dollars, for a main course at dinner

Lodging

Perhaps inevitably, prices in the larger metropolitan areas have continued to increase; at luxury properties, they tend to be in line with those in other parts of the country. Smaller centers still offer good value. It's always a good idea to ask about special weekend rates and packages.

CATEGORY	COST*
$$$$	over $200
$$$	$150–$200
$$	$100–$150
$	under $100

All prices are for a standard double room, excluding tax (14% in Manitoba and Saskatchewan, 12% in Alberta), in Canadian dollars.

National and Provincial Parks

Throughout this vast region, some special places have preserved unique landscapes, from Riding Mountain National Park in the rolling hills of Manitoba to the vast wilderness and waterways of Prince Albert National Park in Saskatchewan. You can explore grasslands, badlands, lakes, and forests and participate in a number of activities, including fishing, in the provincial parks.

Regional History

The larger history of these provinces encompasses a number of special elements, from the dinosaurs that roamed here to the native peoples and the fur traders and frontier settlers who came from around the world. Each province has highlights, whether it's the dinosaur sites around Drumheller, Alberta; the Wanuskewin Heritage Park in Saskatoon, which interprets native culture; the Mennonite Heritage Village in Steinbach, Manitoba; the Ukrainian Cultural Heritage Village near Vegreville, Alberta; or the Western Development Museum, a re-created 1920s farming village in North Battleford, Saskatchewan. Together, these distinctly different places present an accurate microcosm of how the region was settled.

Exploring the Prairie Provinces

Compared with the Rockies, the prairie provinces' landscape is dramatically flatter. From the foothills of Alberta to the Great Lakes, you can explore the prairies from west to east, with visits to the region's five major cities: Calgary, Edmonton, Regina, Saskatoon, and Winnipeg.

Numbers in the text correspond to numbers in the margin and on the Alberta, Downtown Calgary, Greater Calgary, Downtown Edmonton, Saskatchewan, Regina, Saskatoon, Manitoba, and Downtown Winnipeg maps.

Great Itineraries

Enormous distances separate many of the region's major attractions. If you're ambitious and want to include all three prairie provinces, you need considerable time. For a shorter visit, pick a major city and the surrounding area to explore.

IF YOU HAVE 2 DAYS

If you're interested in the rich history of the Plains Indians, take the time to delve into the area around Saskatoon known as the Heart of the Old Northwest. Start in ⊞ **Saskatoon** ㊻–㊾ and use it as the base for day trips. On Day 1, you can go to nearby **Wanuskewin Heritage Park** ㊼, a wonderfully cerebral onetime buffalo-hunting ground. Less than an hour's drive away are **Batoche** ㊿ and Batoche National Historic Site, where Louis Riel fought his last battle against the North West Mounted Police. In **Duck Lake** ㊾, 30 minutes north of Batoche along Highway 11, colorful murals on town buildings depict the 1885 Northwest Rebellion. Fort Carlton Provincial Park, another 15 minutes west, is a reconstructed stockade from the fur-trade days. On the second day, go to **North Battleford** ㊱, 138 km (86 mi) northwest of Saskatoon, for the Fort Battleford National Historic Site, which interprets the role of the North West Mounted Police.

IF YOU HAVE 4 DAYS

If you're particularly interested in dinosaurs and fossil hunting, travel from ⊞ **Calgary** ①–⑱, Alberta, to ⊞ **Regina** ㉛–㊲, Saskatchewan, by way of Drumheller, Alberta, and Eastend, Saskatchewan. In ⊞ **Drumheller** ⑲, just over an hour east of Calgary on the Trans-Canada Highway, you can spend an entire day at the world-class Royal Tyrrell Museum of Paleontology. East on the Trans-Canada Highway en route to **Dinosaur Provincial Park** ⑳, you pass through unique badlands areas, where rivers flowed more than 70 million years ago. South along the Trans-Canada, the thriving, oil-rich city of ⊞ **Medicine Hat** ㉑ is a good choice for an overnight stop. Farther east, south of the Trans-Canada, you come to the small community of **Eastend** ㊷, where you can view a fully preserved Tyrannosaurus rex skeleton in a working lab—the T Rex Discovery Center.

IF YOU HAVE 12 DAYS

You can choose between two major routes westward from ⊞ **Winnipeg** ㊾–⑩: northwest on the Yellowhead (Highway 16) to ⊞ **Edmonton** ㉔–㉘ via ⊞ **Saskatoon** ㊻–㊾, or west on the Trans-Canada to ⊞ **Calgary** ①–⑱ via ⊞ **Regina** ㉛–㊲. Either is approximately 1,370 km (850 mi). On the Yellowhead route, you can stop for one or two nights in Riding Mountain National Park, a half hour north of Highway 16 on Highway 10; the town of ⊞ **Wasagaming** ㊴ is inside the park. Here you find forested landscape and sparkling clear lakes, as well as comfortable amenities. Langenburg, just inside the Saskatchewan border, has a provincial tourism-information center. Less than four hours to the northwest you come to Saskatoon, Saskatchewan's largest city. Plan on staying at least two nights. Ninety minutes farther west is the historic community of **North Battleford** ㊱, where the Western Development Museum and Fort Battleford National Historic Site rate as the two must-see attractions. From here it is four hours to Edmonton.

If you take the more southerly Trans-Canada route, you can stop in such major centers as **Brandon** ㊵, ⊞ **Regina** ㉛–㊲, ⊞ **Swift Current** ㊴, and 🖻 **Medicine Hat** ㉑ en route to Calgary. All offer interesting diversions and adequate facilities for dining and lodging.

When to Tour the Prairie Provinces

From June through August you're likely to encounter more festivals and the greatest number of open lodgings (some close seasonally). However, the spring and fall months offer a more tranquil experience for travelers; September can be particularly rewarding, with a combination of warm weather and some autumn foliage. Unless you enjoy bone-chilling cold temperatures, it's best to skip winter.

CALGARY

Updated by
Monica
Andreeff

With the eastern face of the Rockies as its backdrop, the crisp concrete-and-steel skyline of Calgary, Alberta, seems to rise from the plains as if by sheer force of will. Indeed, all the elements in the great saga of the Canadian West—Mounties, native people, railroads, cowboys, cattle, oil—have converged to create a city with a modern face and a surprisingly traditional soul.

Calgary, believed to be derived from the Gaelic phrase meaning "bay farm," was founded in 1875 at the junction of the Bow and Elbow rivers as a North West Mounted Police post. The Canadian Pacific Railway arrived in 1883, and ranchers established major spreads on the plains surrounding the town. Incorporated as a city in 1894, Calgary grew quickly, and by 1911 its population had reached 43,000. More than 40 sandstone buildings constructed during that boom are still in use in the downtown core.

The next major growth came with the oil boom in the 1960s and 1970s, when most Canadian oil companies established their head offices in the city. Today, Calgary is a city of about 850,000 mostly easygoing and downright neighborly people. It's Canada's second-largest center for corporate head offices. Downtown keeps evolving, but Calgary's planners have made life in winter more pleasant by connecting most of the buildings with the Plus 15, a network of enclosed walkways 15 ft above street level. Among the major cities on the prairies, Calgary usually has the most reasonable winter, thanks to the annual series of warm chinook winds that blows in from the nearby Rockies.

Calgary supports professional football and hockey teams, and in July the rodeo events of the Calgary Stampede attract visitors from around the world. Calgary hosted the 1988 Winter Olympics, and the downhill slopes and miles of cross-country ski trails are less than 90 minutes west of town (at Kananaskis). The city is also the perfect starting point for one of the preeminent dinosaur exploration sites in the world, in Drumheller. The Glenbow Museum is one of the top museums in Canada, and the EPCOR Centre for the Performing Arts showcases theater and musical performances.

Downtown Calgary

A walk downtown takes you past some handsome buildings—old and new—and notable cultural venues, besides a number of interesting places to shop. In the Calgary grid pattern, numbered streets run north–south in both directions from Centre Street, and numbered avenues run east–west in both directions from Centre Avenue.

A Good Tour

Start at **Calgary Tower** ① for a bird's-eye view of the city. Take the Plus 15 walkway over 9th Avenue Southeast to the **Glenbow Museum** ②, a major showcase of art and history. Next use the Plus 15 walkway above

1st Street Southeast to get to the **EPCOR Centre for the Performing Arts** ③, a theater complex. You can step outside on **Olympic Plaza** ④, where Olympic medals were presented in 1988. Nearby, you can see the **Municipal Building** ⑤, whose mirror-glass walls reflect other city landmarks. Hop on the C-Train, Calgary's light-rail system, for a free (along 7th Avenue downtown only) ride to the center of the downtown shopping district. Here, the top attraction is **Devonian Gardens** ⑥, an enclosed roof garden above Toronto Dominion Square. On 8th Avenue between Macleod Trail and 4th Street Southwest is **Stephen Avenue Mall** ⑦, a pedestrian-only retail strip with some of the city's oldest buildings. Head north on 1st Street Southwest for several blocks to the ornate **Calgary Chinese Cultural Centre** ⑧ to take in the architecture and the museum. Leaving the center, head west on 2nd Avenue Southwest; a block away are the shops and restaurants of **Eau Claire Market** ⑨.

TIMING

Allow the better part of a day for this tour, for time in the museums and a bit of shopping.

Sights to See

⑧ **Calgary Chinese Cultural Centre.** The focal point of this ornate building in the heart of Chinatown is the Hall of Prayers of the **Temple of Heaven**; the column details and paintings include 561 dragons and 40 phoenixes. It's modeled after the Temple of Heaven in Beijing. The center houses a cultural museum ($2 admission), an art gallery, a crafts store, an herbal-medicine store, and a 330-seat Chinese restaurant. ✉ *197 1st St. SW,* ☎ *403/262–5071,* WEB *www.culturalcentre.ab.ca.* ⊡ *Free.* ☉ *Daily 9:30–9 (11–5 for museum).*

❶ **Calgary Tower.** The views from this 626-ft, scepter-shape edifice are great, taking in the city's layout, the surrounding plains, and the face of the Rockies rising 80 km (50 mi) to the west. A "torch" that crowns the tower is lit for special events and occasions. The tower top also holds the revolving Panorama Room restaurant, which serves all three meals; Tops Bar; and a gift shop. ✉ *9th Ave. and Centre St. S,* ☎ *403/266–7171,* WEB *www.calgarytower.com.* ⊡ *$7.95.* ☉ *May–Sept., Mon.–Sat. 7:30 AM–11 PM; Oct.–Apr., Mon.–Sat. 8 AM–11 PM.*

❻ **Devonian Gardens.** Above Toronto Dominion Square and atop the Toronto Dominion Centre shopping complex, a 2½-acre enclosed roof garden holds 20,000 plants, nearly 2 km (1 mi) of lush walkways, a sculpture court, and a playground. The gardens, which are reached by two glass-enclosed elevators just inside the 7th Avenue LRT (light-rail transit) entrance, have numerous ponds with rainbow trout, koi, goldfish, and turtles. Art exhibitions are held here, and there's a stage for performances. ✉ *317 7th Ave. SW (between 2nd and 3rd Sts.),* ☎ *403/268–3830.* ⊡ *Free.* ☉ *Daily 9–9.*

★ ❾ **Eau Claire Market.** On Barclay Parade next to the entrance to Prince's Island Park, this enclosed 240,000-square-ft area has restaurants (including seven outdoor patios), one-of-a-kind stores, a multiplex cinema and an IMAX theater, and an interactive entertainment center and arcade. The food market sells fresh produce, seafood, range-fed meats, baked goods, and wine. ✉ *2nd St. and 2nd Ave. SW,* ☎ *403/264–6450 or 403/264–6460,* WEB *www.eauclairemarket.com.* ☉ *Summer weekdays 10–8, Sat. 10–6, Sun. noon–5; call for hrs at other times.*

★ ❸ **EPCOR Centre for the Performing Arts.** The complex of four theater spaces and a state-of-the-art concert hall was pieced together in the 1980s incorporating the historic **Calgary Public Building** (1930) and the **Burns Building** (1913). It's one of the largest arts complexes in Canada. ✉ *205 8th Ave. SE,* ☎ *403/294–7455,* WEB *www.theartscentre.org.*

Alberta

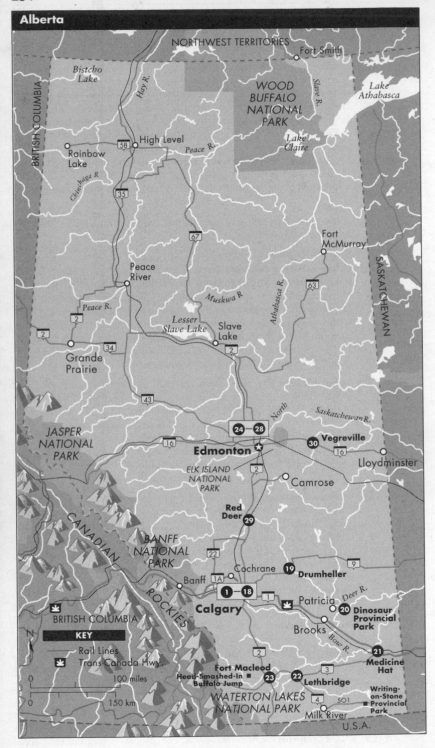

NORTHWEST TERRITORIES

Fort Smith

BRITISH COLUMBIA

Bistcho
Lake

WOOD
BUFFALO
NATIONAL
PARK

Slave R.

Lake
Athabasca

Hay R.

High Level

58

Peace R.

Lake
Claire

Rainbow
Lake

Chinchaga R

35

67

Fort
McMurray

Peace
River

Athabasca R.

63

SASKATCHEWAN

Peace R.

2

Muskwa R

34

Lesser
Slave Lake

Slave
Lake

2

Grande
Prairie

2

43

North

Saskatchewan R.

JASPER
NATIONAL
PARK

24 — 28

30 Vegreville

16

16

Edmonton

Lloydminster

ELK ISLAND
NATIONAL
PARK

2

Camrose

Red
Deer

29

CANADIAN

BANFF
NATIONAL
PARK

22

Cochrane

19 Drumheller

9

Banff

1A

ROCKIES

1 — 18

1

Patricia

Deer R.

BRITISH COLUMBIA

20 Dinosaur
Provincial
Park

KEY

Brooks

Bow R.

N

—— Rail Lines

Trans-Canada Hwy.

21 Medicine
Hat

0   100 miles

2

0   150 km

Fort Macleod

3

Head-Smashed-In
Buffalo Jump

23

22 Lethbridge

Writing-
on-Stone
Provincial
Park

WATERTON LAKES
NATIONAL PARK

4

501

Milk River

U.S.A.

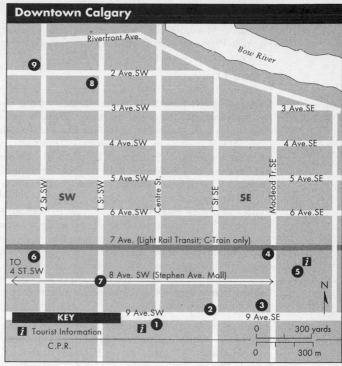

Downtown Calgary

★ ② **Glenbow Museum.** Calgary's premier showcase for both art and history is ranked among the top museums in Canada. Along with traveling exhibits, the Glenbow has comprehensive displays devoted to Alberta's First Nations inhabitants, early European settlers, and latter-day pioneers. One notable exhibit allows visitors to experience being a child in western Canada in the mid-19th to early 20th centuries. The mineralogy collection and the cache of arms and armor are superb. At press time, a permanent gallery dedicated to the Blackfoot Nation was in the works, scheduled to open by 2002. A food area serves quick fresh meals and snacks. ⊠ 130 9th Ave. SE, ☎ 403/268–4100 or 403/237–8988, WEB www.glenbow.org. ☞ $10. ☉ Sat.–Wed. 9–5, Thurs.–Fri. 9–9.

⑤ **Municipal Building.** This angular, mirror-walled building reflects a number of city landmarks, including the stunning City Hall, a stately 1911 sandstone building that still houses the mayor's office and some city offices. The Community and Social Development Information Centre on the main floor has brochures with historical walking tours. ⊠ 800 Macleod Trail SE, ☎ 403/268–2111.

④ **Olympic Plaza.** The site of the 1988 Olympic Games medals presentation, the plaza is a popular venue for festivals and entertainment. The wading pool is turned into a skating rink in winter. ⊠ 7th Ave. SE and Macleod Trail SE, ☎ 403/268–2300.

⑦ **Stephen Avenue Mall.** In this pedestrian-only shopping area, shops, nightclubs, and restaurants occupy the ground floors of Calgary's oldest structures, mostly sandstone buildings erected after an 1886 fire that destroyed almost everything older. ⊠ 8th Ave. between Macleod Trail and 4th St. SW.

Greater Calgary

With a car you can easily visit a number of top Calgary sights, from Heritage Park to the Stampede Park and Canada Olympic Park. Kid favorites such as the Calgary Zoo are here, too.

A Good Drive

From downtown, drive east on 9th Avenue about 1 km (½ mi) to **Fort Calgary Historic Park** ⑩, at the confluence of the Bow and Elbow rivers, to learn the history of the region. Directly across the 9th Avenue Bridge is the **Deane House Historic Site and Restaurant** ⑪, dating from 1906. Continue east on 9th Avenue, turn north on 12th Street, and cross the bridge to St. George's Island and the **Calgary Zoo, Botanical Gardens, and Prehistoric Park** ⑫. From here, head southwest to Olympic Way to reach **Stampede Park** ⑬, where you can tour the grounds and visit the Grain Academy museum. Follow Macleod Trail south and go west on Heritage Drive to get to **Heritage Park** ⑭, where you can see historic structures from all over western Canada. Head west, across Glenmore Reservoir, and turn north on Crowchild Trail to reach the **Museum of the Regiments** ⑮ and the **Naval Museum of Alberta.** Continue north on Crowchild Trail; turn east on 9th Avenue Southwest and then north again on 11th Street Southwest to get to the **Calgary Science Centre** ⑯, which includes a multimedia theater for hands-on exhibits and a star show.

Another drive from downtown takes you west on 6th Avenue, following signs to Crowchild Trail, which you take north to 16th Avenue Northwest (Highway 1). Head west on Highway 1 about 8 km (5 mi) to **Canada Olympic Park** ⑰, site of the 1988 Winter Olympics, where you can visit ski jumps and try the bobsled and luge rides. A 20-minute drive beyond the Olympic Park is **Calaway Park** ⑱, a huge amusement complex.

TIMING

Because of the distances and the size of the sights, you need more than a day to do everything on this tour. Pick attractions based on your interests or location. If you have kids, allow a day with the zoo as the main component in the morning, leaving Calaway Park for the afternoon and evening.

Sights to See

⟲ ⑱ **Calaway Park.** Here in the foothills of the Rockies and about 10 km (6 mi) west of Calgary is western Canada's largest outdoor family amusement park. It includes live entertainment, miniature golf, a fishing pond, shops, and an RV park. ⊠ *Hwy. 1, Springbank Rd. Exit,* ☎ *403/240–3822,* WEB *www.calawaypark.com.* ⊡ *$19.50, includes rides and shows; $9.50 after 5 PM; $60 for family of four.* ☉ *Mid-May–June 24, Fri. 5 PM–10 PM, weekends 10–8; June 29–Sept. 3, daily 10–8; Sept. 3–mid-Oct., weekends 11–6.*

⟲ ⑯ **Calgary Science Centre.** Interactive exhibits present the wonders of science in an entertaining way. Shows at the multimedia Discovery Dome, Alberta's largest indoor theater, combine computer graphics, motion-picture images, slides, and a superb sound system. ⊠ *701 11th St. SW,* ☎ *403/221–3700,* WEB *www.calgaryscience.ca.* ⊡ *$9.* ☉ *Tues.–Thurs. 10–4, Fri.–Sun. 10–5.*

★ ⟲ ⑫ **Calgary Zoo, Botanical Gardens, and Prehistoric Park.** The zoo, on St. George's Island in the middle of Bow River, is one of Canada's five largest, with more than 1,400 animals in natural settings. The House of Night has nocturnal animals and the Canadian Wilds section replicates endangered Canadian ecosystems. Prehistoric Park, a re-created

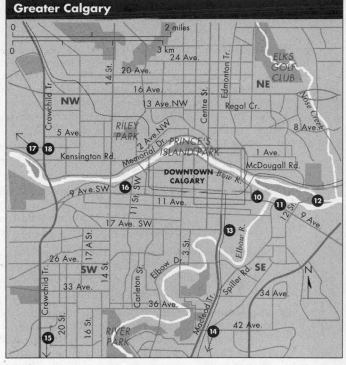

Mesozoic landscape, displays 22 life-size dinosaur replicas. Destination Africa, under construction at press time, is scheduled to open in 2003. ⊠ *1300 Zoo Rd. NE,* ☎ *403/232–9372,* ᵂᴱᴮ *www.calgary-zoo.ab.ca.* ⊠ *About $12.* ⊙ *Daily 9–5.*

⑰ Canada Olympic Park. The premier site of the 1988 Winter Olympics is a year-round attraction. A one-hour bus tour goes over, under, around, and through the 70- and 90-m ski jumps and the bobsled and luge tracks (in summer you have the option of walking down the slopes) and also takes you to the Ice House, a year-round ice-training facility for world-class athletes. In winter the ski slopes are open to the public for skiing and snowboarding; lessons are available. You can try Olympic-size thrills on the one-minute bobsled simulator, the Bobsleigh Bullet ($45), and in summer the Road Rocket ($45). On the premises are a day lodge with a cafeteria and the **Olympic Hall of Fame,** where you can see Olympic memorabilia. ⊠ *88 Olympic Rd. SW,* ☎ *403/ 247–5452,* ᵂᴱᴮ *www.coda.ab.ca.* ⊠ *Free, excluding activities; bus and guided tours $10; self-guided tour $7.* ⊙ *Apr.–mid-May, daily 10–6; mid-May–Sept., daily 8 AM–9 PM.; call for Oct.–Mar. hrs.*

⑪ Deane House Historic Site and Restaurant. Next to Fort Calgary and overlooking the Elbow River, the restored 1906 fort superintendent's house today operates as a lunch restaurant and the Mystery from History Dinner Theatre. The **Hunt House,** just behind it, was built in 1876 for a Hudson's Bay official and is believed to be Calgary's oldest building. ⊠ *806 9th Ave. SE,* ☎ *403/269–7747,* ᵂᴱᴮ *www.fortcalgary.com.*

⑩ Fort Calgary Historic Park. The fort was established in 1875 at the confluence of the Bow and Elbow rivers by the North West Mounted Police, who wanted to stop Montana whiskey traders from selling alcohol to the locals. It remained in operation until 1914. The **Interpretive Centre** here traces the history of the First Nations people, Mounties, and

European settlers with the aid of artifacts, audiovisual displays, and interpretive walks. ⊠ *750 9th Ave. SE,* ☎ *403/290–1875,* WEB *www.fortcalgary.com.* ⊠ *$6.50.* ☉ *May–Oct., daily 9–5.*

☼ ⑭ **Heritage Park.** Set on 66 acres of parkland beside the Glenmore Reservoir, Heritage Park is Canada's largest living-history village. More than 150 exhibits, hundreds of costumed staff and volunteers, and 45,000 artifacts re-create western Canadian life prior to 1914. You can visit an 1850s fur-trading post, a ranch, and an old town; ride on a steam locomotive or horse-drawn wagon; cruise the reservoir on a sternwheeler; and partake of a free pancake breakfast daily at 9 AM. ⊠ *1900 Heritage Dr. SW,* ☎ *403/259–1900,* WEB *www.heritagepark.ab.ca.* ⊠ *$11; $19 with rides and cruise.* ☉ *Mid-May–Labor Day, daily 9–5; early Sept.–mid-Oct., weekends 9–5.*

⑮ **Museum of the Regiments.** Western Canada's largest military museum has a collection of memorabilia that depicts the history of Calgary-based regiments dating back to 1900. ⊠ *4520 Crowchild Trail SW,* ☎ *403/974–2850,* WEB *www.nucleus.com/~regiments.* ⊠ *Free.* ☉ *Daily 10–4.*

Naval Museum of Alberta. Canada's second-largest naval museum focuses on the role of the prairie provinces in the navy. ⊠ *1820 24th St. SW,* ☎ *403/242–0002,* WEB *www.navalmuseum.ab.ca.* ⊠ *$5.* ☉ *Sept.–June, Tues.–Fri. 1–5, weekends 10–5; July–Aug., daily 10–5.*

⑬ **Stampede Park.** International attention focuses here each July for the rodeo events of the Calgary Stampede (WEB www.calgarystampede.com). Throughout the year, the Roundup Centre, Big Four Building, and Agriculture Building host trade shows, and the Grandstand holds thoroughbred and harness racing. You can wander the park grounds and visit the free **Grain Academy** (☎ 403/263–4594), an interesting small museum in Roundup Center that proclaims itself "Canada's only grain interpretive center"; a model-train display depicts the movement of grain from the prairies through the Rockies to Vancouver. There's also a working model of a grain elevator. ⊠ *1410 Olympic Way SE,* ☎ *403/261–0101 or 800/661–1260.* ⊠ *Free.* ☉ *Weekdays 10–4, Sat. noon–4.*

Dining

$$$–$$$$ ✗ **Owl's Nest Dining Room.** Plush armchairs and dark-wood booths
★   are the signature of this venerable restaurant, where Continental cuisine reigns. Tableside preparations are a specialty, as are exclusive and rare-vintage wines offered by the glass. Specialties include Chilean sea bass with wild mushrooms. ⊠ *Westin Calgary Hotel, 320 4th Ave. SW,* ☎ *403/266–1611. Reservations essential. AE, DC, MC, V. Closed Sun.*

$$–$$$$ ✗ **Bistro Jo Jo.** This casual Parisian-style bistro serves excellent traditional French fare in an intimate atmosphere. The house specialty is rack of lamb, with a sauce that changes daily. The wine list is superb, as are the desserts, including chocolate mousse. ⊠ *917 17 Ave. SW,* ☎ *403/245–2382. Reservations essential. AE, DC, MC, V.*

$$–$$$$ ✗ **River Café.** Inspired by the natural surroundings of Prince's Island Park, on Bow River, this restaurant has the look of a fishing lodge and offers a pastoral dining experience. The exquisite regional Canadian cuisine includes Northwest Territories caribou, British Columbia oysters and Pacific salmon, Alberta Black Angus beef, and Alberta lamb. ⊠ *Prince's Island Park (near Eau Claire Market),* ☎ *403/261–7670. Reservations essential. AE, DC, MC, V.*

$$–$$$$ ✗ **Teatro.** The elegant Teatro is in a historic bank building on Olympic Plaza, where a combination of classical features and contemporary decor creates an exquisite setting for fine Italian cuisine. Specialties include numerous antipasti, pizzas from a wood-burning oven, pastas, and risot-

tos, as well as more-exotic items such as rack of elk and a goat-cheese soufflé. ⊠ *200 8th Ave. SE,* ☏ *403/290–1012. AE, DC, MC, V.*

$$–$$$ ✕ **Joey Tomato's.** Italian dishes get a Mediterranean twist at this fun restaurant in Eau Claire Market. Antiques, strands of garlic and chilies, and wine bottles decorate the place. It's popular with the happy-hour and late-night crowds, but families also flock here. The kitchen is open until 1 AM Friday and Saturday nights. ⊠ *Eau Claire Market, 208 Barclay Parade,* ☏ *403/263–6336. AE, MC, V.*

$$–$$$ ✕ **Mescalero.** The fare at this popular dining spot is influenced by the American Southwest and Latin America. The innovative menu changes daily, but a fine tapas menu remains constant. You can sip Margaritas in the Diablo lounge, shop for flowers and collectibles at the Rustica Flowers and Interiors store, or dance in the cantina nightclub, Crazy Horse. ⊠ *1325 1st St. SW,* ☏ *403/266–3339. AE, MC, V.*

$–$$$ ✕ **Buzzard's Cookshack & Waterin' Hole.** A block from the Calgary
★ Tower you can have great Alberta steaks and terrific burgers (or fish and chicken) amid authentic cowboy decor. There's a sunny outdoor patio, and Bottlescrew Bill's Old English Pub next door serves Calgary's largest beer selection, including its Buzzard's Breath Ale house brew. ⊠ *140 10th Ave. SW,* ☏ *403/264–6959. AE, DC, MC, V.*

$–$$ ✕ **Ceili's Irish Pub and Restaurant.** This lively and popular spot is the place for traditional hearty Irish fare, such as lamb stew, kidney pie, and boxty (an Irish pancake served omelette-style). Ceili's has four cozy fireplaces and three patios, including a heated rooftop area, and it offers breakfast in addition to lunch and dinner. Brunch is a Sunday option. ⊠ *126, 513-8th Ave. SW,* ☏ *403/508–9999,* WEB *www.ceilis.com. V.*

Lodging

$$$$ 🏨 **Sheraton Suites Calgary Eau Claire.** This 15-story all-suites hotel has
★ good downtown, river, and park views. An international newsstand and currency exchange are among the amenities. The elegant glass lobby and an outdoor patio adjoin the Eau Claire Market and Prince's Island Park. The Plus 15 indoor walkway leads to downtown, and the nearby outdoor path system follows the Bow River. ⊠ *255 Barclay Parade SW, T2P 5C2,* ☏ *403/266–7200 or 888/784–8370,* FAX *403/266–1300,* WEB *www.sheratonsuites.com. 323 suites. Restaurant, bar, pub, in-room data ports, no-smoking rooms, hair salon, health club, babysitting, dry cleaning, laundry service, concierge, business services, parking (fee). AE, DC, MC, V.*

$$$$ 🏨 **The Westin Calgary.** Calgary's walkway system connects this luxury
★ high-rise in the midst of downtown to most other nearby buildings. Rooms are large, with a cozy country theme in earth colors. The rooftop pool, hot tub, and fitness area is one of this lodging's unique attractions. The Owl's Nest is one of the better dining spots in town. For lighter meals, you can try the Lobby Court, which has buffet breakfasts. ⊠ *320 4th Ave. SW, T2P 2S6,* ☏ *403/266–1611 or 800/228–3000,* FAX *403/265–7908,* WEB *www.westin.com. 469 rooms, 56 suites. 2 restaurants, 2 bars, in-room data ports, no-smoking rooms, indoor pool, hot tub, sauna, health club, dry cleaning, laundry service, concierge, business services, meeting rooms, free parking. AE, DC, MC, V.*

$$$–$$$$ 🏨 **Delta Bow Valley.** The first-class 24-story high-rise is within easy walking distance of the main business district as well as major attractions. Decent-size contemporary rooms have rose-and-green furnishings; those on the upper floors have good views. The sunny lobby—decorated in pink tones and with lush foliage—adds to the already lively setting. ⊠ *209 4th Ave. SE, T2G 0C6,* ☏ *403/266–1980 or 800/268–1133,* FAX *403/266–0007,* WEB *www.deltahotels.com. 337* *rooms, 41 suites. 2 restaurants, bar, no-smoking floor, indoor pool, sauna, health club, concierge, business services, parking (fee). AE, DC, MC, V.*

$$$–$$$$ ☎ **Delta Calgary Airport.** An atrium-style Delta hotel at Calgary International Airport is soundproof and offers many facilities for travelers; you can wheel your luggage into the hotel from the airport. A pleasant, sunlit garden terrace overlooks the pool area. ✉ *2001 Airport Rd. NE, T2E 6Z8,* ☎ *403/291–2600 or 800/268–1133,* FAX *403/250–8722,* WEB *www.deltahotels.com. 296 rooms, 12 suites. 2 restaurants, in-room data ports, no-smoking rooms, indoor pool, health club, baby-sitting, concierge, business services, parking (fee). AE, DC, MC, V.*

$$$–$$$$ ☎ **The Fairmont Palliser.** Built in 1914 as Calgary's grand railroad hotel, ★   the Palliser remains the city's most elegant and historic accommodation. Guest rooms are tastefully appointed with traditional furnishings and have ornate moldings and high ceilings. The Rimrock Room offers excellent dining. A covered walkway connects the hotel to the performing-arts center and the Glenbow Museum. ✉ *133 9th Ave. SW, T2P 2M3,* ☎ *403/262–1234 or 800/441–1414,* FAX *403/260–1260,* WEB *www.fairmont.com. 405 rooms, 17 suites. Restaurant, deli, lounge, no-smoking floor, health club, baby-sitting, concierge, dry cleaning, laundry service, parking (fee). AE, DC, MC, V.*

$$$ ☎ **Calgary Marriott.** This business-class hotel in the heart of downtown is connected to the Telus Convention Centre. Nearby are the Glenbow Museum and the performing arts-center. The warm, inviting lobby sets the tone; rooms are done in pastels and maroons. ✉ *110 9th Ave. SE, T2G 5A6,* ☎ *403/266–7331 or 800/661–7776,* FAX *403/269–1961,* WEB *www.marriott.com. 384 rooms, 10 suites. Restaurant, lounge, in-room data ports, no-smoking floor, indoor pool, sauna, health club, concierge, business services, meeting rooms, parking (fee). AE, DC, MC, V.*

$$$ ☎ **Hyatt Regency Calgary.** Turn-of-the-19th-century buildings combine with a state-of-the-art guest-room tower at this luxury hotel. The $1.4 million of paintings, sculptures, and other artwork in the hotel's public areas and guestrooms showcases 50 Western Canadian artists. A mahogany canoe hangs from the lobby ceiling, and historical photographs and displays convey the pioneer spirit that helped to settle the west. The hotel is linked to the Telus Convention Centre. ✉ *700 Centre St. S, T2G 5P6,* ☎ *403/717–1234,* FAX *403/262–3490,* WEB *www.calgary.hyatt.com. 342 rooms, 13 suites. Restaurant, lounge, in-room data ports, indoor saltwater pool, steam room, gym, meeting rooms, parking (fee). AE, DC, MC, V.*

$$–$$$ ☎ **Best Western Suites Downtown.** Each of the suites at this reasonably priced hotel has a fully equipped kitchenette; you can choose from studio or one- or two-bedroom layouts, and some suites have whirlpool baths. The hotel is within walking distance of downtown and the exclusive shopping and restaurants on 17th Avenue. ✉ *1330 8th St. SW, T2R 1B6,* ☎ *403/228–6900 or 800/981–2555,* FAX *403/228–5535,* WEB *www.bestwesternsuites.com. 123 suites. Restaurant, kitchenettes, gym, laundry service, business services, meeting rooms, free parking. AE, DC, MC, V.*

$–$$$ ☎ **City View Bed and Breakfast.** This charming gem of a B&B is aptly named: its location atop Scotsman's Hill, near downtown, allows for panoramic views of the city, Bow River, and the Rockies beyond. There are balconies upstairs and a fireplace and grand piano in the lounge. The three rooms all have large windows, a couple have fireplaces and private balconies, and one has an old-fashioned claw-foot tub. ✉ *2300 6th St. SE, T2G 4S2,* ☎ *403/870–5640,* FAX *403/235–3393,* WEB *www.calgarycityview.com. 3 rooms. Piano, free parking. MC, V.*

Nightlife and the Arts

Tickets for events at the performing-arts center and Jubilee Auditorium are available at **Ticketmaster** (☎ 403/270–6700 or 403/266–8888) outlets, at the arts center's box office or can be charged over the phone.

The Arts

Calgary's premier performing-arts facility is the **EPCOR Centre for the Performing Arts** (✉ 205 8th Ave. SE, ☎ 403/294–7455), with four modern theaters in two contiguous historic buildings and an 1,800-seat concert hall. Productions by resident Alberta Theatre Projects (ATP) of works by Canadian playwrights are highly recommended, as are performances by the One Yellow Rabbit Performance Theatre. The center also hosts the Calgary Philharmonic Orchestra (☎ 403/571–0270), chamber groups, and a broad spectrum of music shows. The **Southern Alberta Jubilee Auditorium** (✉ 1415 14th Ave. NW, ☎ 403/297–8000) is host to the Alberta Ballet Company as well as classical music, opera, dance, pop, and rock concerts. Concerts and classic and contemporary theater works are staged at the **University of Calgary Theatre** (✉ 2500 University Dr. NW, ☎ 403/220–4900).

Loose Moose (✉ 1229 9th Ave. SE, ☎ 403/265–5682) features competitive "Theatresports" and improvisational fun and games.

Nightlife

BARS AND CLUBS

The **Auburn Saloon** (✉ 712 1st St. SE, ☎ 403/266–6628), an après-theater bar, serves many kinds of martinis and classic drinks. At the **James Joyce Pub** (✉ 114 8th Ave. SW, ☎ 403/262–0708), you can have Guinness stout, which is served at three temperatures at the long antique bar, along with some traditional Irish fare. **Melrose Cafe and Bar** (✉ 730 17th Ave. SW, ☎ 403/228–3566) is a popular spot that broadcasts the National Trivia Network (NTN). **The Mercury** (✉ 801B 17th Ave. SW, ☎ 403/541–1175) is a cool, intimate lounge with excellent food, including seafood risotto and chicken curry.

MUSIC

Cowboys Dance Hall (✉ 826 5th St. SW, ☎ 403/265–0699) includes a bar and a dance hall that plays Top 40 country, dance, and rock tunes, with live entertainment on occasion. It's open Wednesday through Saturday and holds 1,200 people. **Desperados** (✉ 1088 Olympic Way SE, ☎ 403/263–5343) is a restaurant–nightclub with Top 40 DJ music. **The Drink** (✉ 355 10th Ave. SW, ☎ 403/264–0202) plays Top 40 dance music for a mostly under-30 crowd and mixes some of the best martinis around. **The Ranchman's** (✉ 9615 Macleod Trail S, ☎ 403/253–1100) is a legendary honky-tonk restaurant–bar frequented by real local cowboys.

Beat Niq Jazz and Social Club (✉ 811 1st St. SW, ☎ 403/263–1650) is a sexy New York–style jazz club open Wednesday through Saturday. The **King Edward Hotel** (✉ 438 9th Ave. SE, ☎ 403/262–1680) is Calgary's institution for blues and rhythm and blues.

Outdoor Activities and Sports

Participant Sports

BIKING AND JOGGING

Calgary has about 300 km (186 mi) of bicycling and jogging paths, most of which wind along rivers and through city parks. Maps are available at visitor centers and bike shops. You can rent bikes at **Sports Rent** (✉ 4424 16th Ave. NW, ☎ 403/292–0077). **Budget Rent-A-Car** (✉ 140

6th Ave. SE, ☎ 403/264–5212) is a perhaps not-obvious place to rent bikes.

BOATING

Canadian Heritage Tours (☎ 403/241–5275) runs single- and multi-day guided canoe trips on the Bow and Red Deer rivers, and kayaking and white-water rafting trips to northern Saskatchewan.

FISHING

Great Waters Alberta (☎ 403/256–3090) conducts fly-fishing trips for trout on the Bow River and other streams.

HEALTH AND FITNESS CLUBS

The **Eau Claire YMCA** (✉ 101 3rd St. SW, ☎ 403/269–6701) has a 25-m pool, a training pool, a gym, an aerobics studio, four squash courts, two racquetball courts, a running track, and a health club.

Three **Leisure Centre** water parks in Calgary have wave pools and water slides, plus gymnasiums and training facilities; Southland and Family have racquetball and squash courts. *Village Square Leisure Centre,* ✉ *2623 56th St. NE,* ☎ *403/280–9714; Family Leisure Centre,* ✉ *11150 Bonaventure Dr. SE,* ☎ *403/278–7542; Southland Leisure Centre,* ✉ *2000 Southland Dr. SW,* ☎ *403/251–3505.*

HORSEBACK RIDING

Take advantage of Calgary's ranching and cowboy heritage and go horseback riding close to downtown. **Saddle Peak Trail Rides** (✉ off Richards Rd., Cochrane, ☎ 403/932–3299, WEB www.saddle-peak.com) offers trips ranging from one-hour trail rides around the ranch to four-day wilderness pack trips.

Spectator Sports

FOOTBALL

The **Calgary Stampeders,** winners of the 1998 Grey Cup, play home games in McMahon Stadium (✉ 1817 Crowchild Trail NW, ☎ 403/289–0205) from July through November.

HOCKEY

The **Calgary Flames** play National Hockey League matches October through April at the Pengrowth Saddledome (✉ 555 Saddledome Rise SE, ☎ 403/777–2177) in Stampede Park.

HORSE RACING

Spruce Meadows (✉ 18011 14th St. SW, at the corner of Hwy. 22X and Spruce Meadow Trail, ☎ 403/974–4200) is one of the world's finest show-jumping facilities, with major competitions held June through September. **Stampede Park** (✉ 1410 Olympic Way SE, ☎ 403/261–0214) includes a track where thoroughbreds race April through October, trotters July through October.

RODEO

For 10 days each July, rodeo events and chuck-wagon races draw the world's top cowboys and plenty of greenhorns to one of Canada's most popular events, the **Calgary Stampede** (☎ 800/661–1260, WEB www.calgarystampede.com), held in Stampede Park. In addition to rodeo events, there are livestock shows, concerts, and high-spirited western-style entertainment. You should make room and ticket reservations well in advance (at least three months) if you plan to attend.

Shopping

Calgary's major shopping districts include Kensington at Louise Crossing, Uptown 17, 11th Avenue Southwest, 4th Street Southwest, Inglewood, the Eau Claire Market, and Downtown on 8th. There are also several malls, including **Bankers Hall** (✉ 315 8th Ave. SW), **Mount Royal Village** (✉ 16th Ave. and 8th St. SW), with mostly upscale and designer shops, **Scotia Centre and TD Square** (✉ 7th Ave. and 2nd St. SW), and **SouthCentre** (✉ 100 Anderson Rd. SW). The **Stephen Avenue Mall** is really a pedestrian-only stretch of 8th Avenue (between Macleod Trail and 4th Street Southwest) where some of the city's oldest buildings house shops and restaurants.

Specialty Stores

In addition to the familiar chain offerings, Calgary has many unique stores. For authentic cowboy boots, there's Alberta's only Western boot manufacturer, **Alberta Boot** (✉ 614 10th Ave. SW, ☎ 403/263–4623). The **Calgary Shoe Hospital and Boot Company** (✉ 112 8 Ave. SW, ☎ 403/264–4503) can custom-fit you with cowboy boots. **Hudson's Bay Company** (✉ 200 8 Ave. SW, ☎ 403/262–0345), incorporated in 1670, is Calgary's—and Canada's—oldest retailer and is a good source for extra-warm clothing. **Livingstone and Cavell Extraordinary Toys** (✉ 1124 Kensington Rd. NW, ☎ 403/270–4165) carries unique toys and gifts from around the world, including clockwork toys. **Paper Trail** (✉ 820 49 Ave. SW, ☎ 403/243–8888) has a wide array of stationery, invitations, and interesting cards, as well as hand-made paper, giftwear, and flowers. **Primitive** (✉ 3321 10th St. NW, ☎ 403/270–8490) stocks contemporary clothing by up-and-coming Canadian designers. At **Rubaiyat** (✉ 722 17 Ave. SW, ☎ 403/228–7192) the goods range from hand-blown glassworks, silver jewelry, and ironworks to ceramic pots, patio furniture, and French linens. **Rustica Flowers and Interiors** (✉ 1325 1st St. SW, ☎ 403/262–2296) sells extraordinary handcrafted antiquities, artifacts from around the world, and flowers.

Calgary A to Z

AIR TRAVEL TO AND FROM CALGARY
Major airlines serving Calgary include Air Canada, Horizon, Northwest, Canada 3000, American, Continental, Delta, and United.

AIRPORTS AND TRANSFERS
Calgary International Airport is 20 minutes northeast of the city center. Taxis make the trip between the airport and downtown for about $25 to $35.
➤ AIRPORT INFORMATION: **Calgary International Airport** (✉ 2000 Airport Rd. NE, Calgary, ☎ 403/735–1372).

BUS TRAVEL WITHIN CALGARY
Calgary Transit (CT) operates a comprehensive bus system throughout the area. Fares are $1.75. Ten-ticket books are $14.50, five tickets are $7.75. A Calgary Transit Day Pass good for unlimited rides costs $5.
➤ BUS INFORMATION: **Calgary Transit** (CT; ☎ 403/262–1000).

CAR TRAVEL
The Trans-Canada Highway (Highway 1) runs west to southeast across Alberta, through Calgary. Highway 2 passes through Calgary on its way from the U.S. border to Edmonton and points north. Calgary is 690 km (428 mi) northwest of Helena, Montana; it's 670 km (415 mi) northeast of Seattle, via the Trans-Canada Highway.

Within Calgary, although many sights are in the downtown area and can be reached on foot, a car is useful for visiting outlying attractions.

EMERGENCIES
Alberta Children's Hospital, Foothills Hospital, Peter Lougheed Hospital, and Rocky View Hospital all have emergency rooms.

Super Drug Mart is open daily until midnight.

➤ EMERGENCY SERVICES: **Ambulance, fire** (☎ 911). **Police** (☎ 911 or 403/266–1234). **Poison center** (☎ 403/670–1414).

➤ HOSPITALS: **Alberta Children's Hospital** (✉ 1820 Richmond Rd. SW, ☎ 403/229–7211). **Foothills Hospital** (✉ 1403 29th St. NW, ☎ 403/670–1110). **Peter Lougheed Hospital** (✉ 3500 26th Ave. NE, ☎ 403/291–8555). **Rocky View Hospital** (✉ 7007 14th St. SW, ☎ 403/541–3000).

➤ LATE-NIGHT PHARMACIES: **Super Drug Mart** (✉ 504 Elbow Dr. SW, ☎ 403/228–3338).

LRT TRAVEL

Calgary Transit (CT) operates a light-rail transit system (the C-Train or LRT) throughout the area. Fares are $1.75. Ten-ticket books are $14.50, five tickets are $7.75. A Calgary Transit Day Pass good for unlimited rides costs $5. The C-Train has lines running northwest (Brentwood), northeast (Whitehorn), and south (Anderson) from downtown. The C-Train is free within the downtown core.

➤ LRT INFORMATION: **Calgary Transit** (CT; ☎ 403/262–1000).

TAXIS

Taxis are fairly expensive, at $2.50 to start and about $1 for each additional 2 km (1 mi).

➤ TAXI COMPANIES: **Associated Cabs** (☎ 403/299–1111). **Checker** (☎ 403/299–9999), **Co-op** (☎ 403/531–8294), **Red Top** (☎ 403/974–4444), **Yellow Cab** (☎ 403/974–1111).

TOURS

Several companies offer tours of Calgary and environs, although none operate on regular schedules. The Calgary Convention and Visitors Bureau can provide information.

➤ INFORMATION: **Calgary Convention and Visitors Bureau** (☎ 403/263–8510 or 800/661–1678).

TRANSPORTATION AROUND CALGARY

Getting around Calgary on foot or using public transportation is fairly easy, but a car is necessary for visiting outlying areas.

VISITOR INFORMATION

The main visitor information center, part of the Calgary Convention and Visitors Bureau, is in the Riley McCormick western store at 220 8th Street Southwest. There are also walk-in visitor centers on the arrival and departure floors at the airport.

➤ TOURIST INFORMATION: **Calgary Convention and Visitors Bureau** (✉ 200, 238 11th Ave. SE, T2G 0X8, ☎ 403/263–8510 or 800/661–1678, WEB www.tourismcalgary.com).

ELSEWHERE IN SOUTHERN ALBERTA

A number of cities and varied sights in the southern part of the province offer a look at key elements of Alberta's history. You can study the world of the dinosaurs in Drumheller; learn about the role of the locals, settlers, and the North West Mounted Police in Fort Macleod; and explore prosperous, modern Medicine Hat.

Drumheller

🔟 *20 km (12 mi) east of Calgary on Trans-Canada Highway (Highway 1), then 120 km (74 mi) north on Route 9.*

The road to Drumheller takes you through the vast Canadian prairie of seemingly endless expanses of flat country in every direction. Once a coal-mining center, the town lies in the rugged valley of the Red Deer River, where millions of years of wind and water erosion exposed the "strike" that produced what amounts to present-day Drumheller's major industry: dinosaurs. In addition to the excellent Royal Tyrrell Museum, a number of dinosaur-related businesses capitalize on the area's rich paleontological past. The 48-km (30-mi) Dinosaur Trail travels through the Red Deer Valley and surrounding badlands.

The **Homestead Antique Museum** packs about 1,000 native artifacts, medical instruments, pieces of period clothing, and other items of Canadiana into a roadside Quonset hut. ⊠ *Rte. 838,* ☎ *403/823–2600.* ⛁ *$3.* ⊘ *May–mid-June and early Sept.–early Oct., daily 10–5; mid-June–Labor Day, daily 10–8.*

Horseshoe Canyon contains spectacular geological formations, including hoodoos—tall, narrow columns of eroded sandstone topped by mushroomlike caps. Rent an all-terrain vehicle and take a self-guided tour. ⊠ *Hwy. 9, 17 km (11 mi) southwest of Drumheller,* ☎ *403/823–2200.* ⊘ *Mid-May–Sept.*

Reptile World has Canada's largest collection of live reptiles, some of which are available for a "hands-on" experience. Poisonous snakes of several types and anacondas are also in residence. ⊠ *Rte. 9,* ☎ *403/823–8623.* ⛁ *$4.50.* ⊘ *July–Aug., daily 9 AM–10PM; Oct.–June, Thurs.–Mon. 10–5.*

★ The **Royal Tyrrell Museum of Paleontology** in Midland Provincial Park explores the geological and paleontological history of Alberta as far back as the pre-Cambrian period. It holds one of the world's largest collections of complete dinosaur skeletons: more than 40 full-size animals. The barren lunar terrain of stark badlands and eerie hoodoos seems an ideal setting for the dinosaurs that stalked the countryside 75 million years ago; but in fact, when the dinosaurs were here, the area had a semitropical climate and marshlands not unlike those of the Florida Everglades. You can participate in hands-on exhibits and meet the first dinosaur discovered around here, Albertosaurus, a smaller, yet equally as fierce version of Tyrannosaurus rex. ⊠ *Hwy. 838 6 km (4 mi) northwest of Drumheller,* ☎ *403/823–7707 or 800/440–4240,* WEB *www.tyrrellmuseum.com.* ⛁ *$8.50.* ⊘ *Mid-May–early Sept., daily 9–9; early Sept.–early Oct., daily 10–5; early-Oct.–mid-May, Tues.–Sun. 10–5.*

Lodging

$$–$$$$ 🛏 **Best Western Jurassic Inn.** Popcorn is provided nightly at this family-oriented lodging. Rooms have queen-size beds, refrigerators, and microwaves. ⊠ *1103 Hwy. 9 S, T0J 0Y0,* ☎ *403/823–7700 or 888/823–3466,* FAX *403/823–5002,* WEB *www.bestwestern.com/ca/jurassicinn. 46 rooms, 3 suites. Restaurants, in-room data ports, kitchenettes (some), no-smoking rooms, pool, hot tub, gym, coin laundry. AE, D, MC, V.*

$$ 🛏 **Drumheller Inn.** This local standby that opened in 1982 stands on a hillside overlooking the town and surrounding badlands. It has basic but comfortable rooms. ⊠ *100 S. Railway Ave., T0J 0Y0,* ☎ *403/823–8400,* FAX *403/823–5020. 99 rooms, 1 suite. 2 restaurants, pub, pool, hot tub. AE, MC, V.*

Dinosaur Provincial Park

⓴ *190 km (118 mi) south of Drumheller, 240 km (149 mi) southeast of Calgary.*

Dinosaur Provincial Park encompasses 73 square km (28 square mi) of Canada's greatest badlands, as well as prairie and riverside habitats. A United Nations World Heritage Site, the park contains some of the world's richest fossil beds—dating as far back as 75 million years—including many kinds of dinosaurs. Much of the area is a nature preserve with restricted public access. Self-guided trails weave through different habitats, and a public loop road leads to two outdoor fossil displays. The **Royal Tyrrell Museum Field Station** has ongoing fossil excavations. It's open daily from mid-May through August, 8:30 AM–9 PM; September to mid-October daily 9–4; and weekdays 9–4 the rest of the year. Interpretive programs run daily from mid-May to early September and on weekends until mid-October, but many require tickets; call for reservations. You should allow at least two full days for an in-depth experience. The campground has a food-service center. To get here from Drumheller, take Route 56 to the Trans-Canada Highway (Highway 1) east, go north at Brooks on Route 873 and then east on Route 544, and follow signs. ✉ *Rte. 544, Patricia,* ☎ *403/378–4342; 403/378–4344 for bus-tour and interpretive-hike reservations mid-May–Aug.; 403/378–3700 for campground reservations May–Aug.,* WEB *www.gov.ab.ca/env/parks/provparks/dinosaur.* ✉ *Park free; $2.50 for field station; bus tour $4.50.*

Medicine Hat

㉑ *95 km (59 mi) southeast of Patricia (Dinosaur Provincial Park), 293 km (182 mi) southeast of Calgary on Trans-Canada Highway.*

Medicine Hat is a prosperous, scenic city built on high banks overlooking the South Saskatchewan River. Much local lore concerns the origin of its name. One legend tells of a battle between Cree and Blackfoot peoples: the Cree fought bravely until their medicine man deserted, losing his headdress in the South Saskatchewan River. The site's name, Saamis, meaning "medicine man's hat," was later translated by white settlers into Medicine Hat.

Originally settled as a tent town for railroad crews in 1883, Alberta's fifth-largest city has derived wealth from vast deposits of natural gas, some of which is piped up to fuel quaint gas lamps in the turn-of-the-19th-century downtown area. Prosperity is embodied in the striking, glass-sided **Medicine Hat City Hall** (✉ 580 1st St. SE, ☎ 403/529–8115), which won the Canadian Architectural Award in 1986. Guided group and self-guided tours are available. The building is open weekdays 8:30–4:30.

A nice spot to spend an afternoon is alongside the South Saskatchewan River and Seven Persons Creek, a parkland and environmental preserve interconnected by 15 km (9 mi) of walking, biking, and cross-country ski trails. The **Tourist Information Centre** (✉ 8 Gehring Rd. SW, ☎ 403/527–6422) has detailed trail maps of the preserve. Across the road from the preserve is **Sammis Teepee,** a giant tepee built for the Calgary Winter Olympics in recognition of Alberta's First Nations people.

A dozen water slides add up to 1 km (½ mi) of falling water at **Riverside Amusement Park** (✉ Hwy. 1 and Power House Rd., ☎ 403/529–6218). The park also has go-carts, inner tubing, and an 18-hole championship miniature-golf course.

Echodale Regional Park (✉ Holsom Rd., off Hwy. 3, ☎ 403/529–8340) provides a riverside setting for swimming, boating, and fishing; it also has a 1900s farm and a historic coal mine.

Lodging

$$–$$$ 🛏 **Medicine Hat Lodge.** On the edge of town and adjacent to a shopping mall, this hotel has several rooms with atrium views of the indoor pool and the two huge water slides. Mamma's Ristorante serves meals with Italian flair. The cozy Rose and Crown Pub makes excellent pizzas in a wood-fired oven. ✉ *1051 Ross Glen Dr. SE, T1B 3T8,* ☎ *403/529–2222 or 800/661–8095,* WEB *www.medhatlodge.com. 187 rooms. 2 restaurants, 2 bars, in-room data ports, no-smoking rooms, indoor pool, gym, steam room, casino, dry cleaning, business services, meeting rooms. AE, DC, MC, V.*

Lethbridge

㉒ *164 km (102 mi) west of Medicine Hat on Crowsnest Highway, 217 km (135 mi) south of Calgary via Highway 2 and Route 3.*

Alberta's third-largest city, with a population of 73,000, is an 1870s coal boomtown that is now a center of agriculture, oil, and gas. The main attraction in Lethbridge, **Fort Whoop-Up,** part of the **Indian Battle Park,** is a reconstruction of a southern Alberta whiskey fort established in 1869 by desperadoes from Fort Benton, Montana. It became the largest of many similar forts that sprang up illegally on the Canadian prairies. Along with costumed reenactments, weapons, relics, and a 15-minute audiovisual historical presentation, Fort Whoop-Up has horse-drawn wagon tours of the river valley and other points of historical interest. ✉ *West end of 3rd Ave., off Scenic Dr. S in Indian Battle Park,* ☎ *403/329–0444.* ⊡ *$5.* ☉ *Mid-May–Sept., daily 10–6; Oct.– mid-May, Tues.–Fri. and Sun. 1–4.*

Henderson Lake Park, 3 km (2 mi) east of downtown Lethbridge, is filled with lush trees, a golf course, a baseball stadium, a swimming pool, an artificial lake, a year-round ice-skating rink, and tennis courts. The **Nikka Yuko Japanese Gardens** (☎ 403/328–3511, WEB www.japanesegarden.ab.ca) offer a tranquil setting with manicured trees and shrubs, miniature pools and waterfalls, a tea house, and pebble designs originally constructed in Japan and reassembled alongside Henderson Lake. Admission to the gardens is $5; they're open daily 10–4 mid-May to June 22 and early September to early October, daily 9–9 June 23 to early September. ✉ *Mayor Magrath Dr. and N. Parkside Dr. S,* ☎ *403/320–3009.* ⊡ *Free.* ☉ *Dawn–dusk.*

OFF THE BEATEN PATH

WRITING-ON-STONE PROVINCIAL PARK – Here among rock cliffs and hoodoos alongside the Milk River, the park contains the largest concentration of native petroglyphs on the North American plains. Today a campground and restored Mountie outpost are here. You can explore the coulees (gullies) that provided cover for outlaws and illegal whiskey traders. Guided walks explore some of this history. The park is about 100 km (62 mi) southeast of Lethbridge. ✉ *Hwy. 501 about 43 km (26 mi) east of the town of Milk River,* ☎ *403/647–2364.* ⊡ *Free.*

Dining and Lodging

$–$$ ✗ **Coco Pazzo.** Family-owned Coco Pazzo serves authentic Italian cuisine as well as steak and seafood. Imaginative and tasty pizzas are made in a wood-fired oven. A friendly staff adds to the relaxed atmosphere. ✉ *1264 3rd Ave. S,* ☎ *403/329–8979. AE, MC, V.*

$–$$ ✗ **Sven Ericksen's Family Restaurant.** Tasty versions of Canadian prairie standards, including chicken and an especially good prime rib, are cooked up at this homey, colonial-style eatery. "Family Restaurant" label notwithstanding, there's a full bar. ✉ *1715 Mayor Magrath Dr. S,* ☎ *403/328–7756. AE, DC, D, MC, V.*

$$ ▥ **Lethbridge Lodge Hotel.** The city's most upscale hotel has great views of the Oldman River and a tropical indoor courtyard with exotic plants and a pool. The rooms are fairly spacious, with some good options for families. There are two restaurants; at the more formal

Anton's, the waiters wear tuxedos, and reservations are required. ✉ *320 Scenic Dr., T1J 4B4,* ☎ *403/328–1123 or 800/661–1232,* WEB *www.lethbridgelodge.com. 154 rooms, 36 suites. 2 restaurants, bar, lounge, in-room data ports, no-smoking rooms, indoor pool, hot tub, gym, meeting rooms. AE, DC, MC, V.*

$–$$ 🏨 **Best Western Heidelberg.** This nine-story hotel is close to a golf course and within walking distance of Henderson Lake Park and the Nikka Yuko Japanese Gardens. The rooms are tastefully decorated with Thomasville furniture in burgundy and royal blue; rooms facing west have excellent views. ✉ *1303 Mayor Magrath Dr., T1K 2R1,* ☎ *403/ 329–0555 or 800/791–8488,* WEB *www.heidelberginn.com. 66 rooms. Restaurant, lounge, no-smoking rooms, sauna, gym. AE, DC, MC, V.*

Fort Macleod

㉓ *50 km (31 mi) west of Lethbridge on Highway 3, 167 km (104 mi) south of Calgary on Highway 2.*

The pre-1900 wood-frame buildings and the more recent sandstone-and-brick buildings have established Fort Macleod, southern Alberta's oldest town, as the province's first historic area. It was founded by the North West Mounted Police in 1874 to maintain order among the farmers, local people, whiskey sellers, and ranchers. An authentic reconstruction of the 1874 fort, the **Fort Museum** grants almost equal exhibitory weight to settlers, regional people, the old North West Mounted Police, and today's Royal Canadian Mounted Police. ✉ *219 25 St.,* ☎ *403/553–4703,* WEB *www.nwmpmuseum.com.* 🎫 *$5.* ☉ *Mar.–June, daily 9–5; July–Aug., daily 9–8; Sept.–Dec. 24, daily 9–5.*

OFF THE
BEATEN PATH

HEAD-SMASHED-IN BUFFALO JUMP – This UNESCO World Heritage Site has a multilevel interpretive center built into the side of a cliff that provides information about the lifestyle, legends, and history of the Blackfoot people. Exhibits describe the history of the buffalo jump and a film re-creates the event when native peoples herded buffalo over the cliff to their thunderous death. Trails surround the jump, and tours are given by Blackfoot guides. The site is about 18 km (11 mi) west of Fort Macleod. ✉ *Secondary Hwy. 785, off Hwy. 2,* ☎ *403/553–2731,* WEB *www.head-smashed-in.com.* 🎫 *$6.50.* ☉ *May–Aug., daily 9–6; Sept.–Apr., daily 10–5.*

EDMONTON

Lucky Edmonton is a boomtown that never seems to go bust. The first boom arrived in 1795, when the North West Company and Hudson's Bay Company established fur-trading posts in the area. Boom II came in 1897, when Edmonton became the principal outfitter on the overland "All Canadian Route" to the Yukon goldfields; as a result, Edmonton was named capital when the province of Alberta was formed in 1905. The latest boom began on February 13, 1947, when oil was discovered in Leduc, 40 km (25 mi) to the southwest. More than 10,000 wells were eventually drilled within 100 km (62 mi) of the city, and with them came fields of refineries and supply depots. By 1965 Edmonton had solidified its role as the "oil capital of Canada."

More interesting is how wisely Edmonton has spread the wealth to create a beautiful and livable city. Shunning the uncontrolled development of some other oil boomtowns, Edmonton turned its great natural resource, the North Saskatchewan River valley, into a 27-km (17-mi) greenbelt of parks and recreational facilities. With a population approaching 921,000, Edmonton is the fifth-largest city in Canada and also Canada's second-largest city in land area. As the seat of the provincial govern-

ment and home to the University of Alberta, the city has a sophisticated and multiethnic atmosphere that has generated many fine restaurants as well as a thriving arts community that stages a variety of festivals
throughout the year. Another of its attractions, the West Edmonton
Mall, has an amusement park, a hotel, a casino, a cinema complex,
and a water park.

Downtown Edmonton

The city's striking physical feature, where most recreational facilities
are located, is the broad green valley of the North Saskatchewan River,
running diagonally northeast to southwest through the city center.
The downtown area lies just north of the river, between 95th and
109th streets.

The Edmonton street system is a grid with numbered streets running
north–south (numbers decrease as you go east) and numbered avenues
running east–west (numbers decrease as you go south). Edmontoni-
ans often use the last digit or two of large numbers as shorthand for
the complete number: the Inn on 7th is on 107th Street; the 9th Street
Bistro can be found on 109th Street. Edmonton's main drag is Jasper
Avenue, which runs east–west through the center of downtown.

A Good Tour

Start at the **Shaw Conference Centre** ㉔, an architecturally inventive space
built into the riverbank with terraced levels accessed by glass-enclosed
escalators. Walk west along Jasper Avenue and turn north on 99th Street
to **Sir Winston Churchill Square** ㉕ and the Arts District, where you can
find many of the city's major cultural institutions. Across 99th Street
is the **Edmonton Art Gallery** ㉖. Directly west of Churchill Square begins a maze of multilevel shopping malls, department stores, cinemas,
and office buildings—all climate-controlled and interconnected by a
network of tunnels and second-floor walkways. Enter the LRT station
on Jasper Avenue at 103rd or 104th Street for the ride to Grandin Station and the **Alberta Government Centre** ㉗, where you can tour the
Alberta Legislature Building ㉘.

TIMING
You can do this tour in a few hours any day of the week, although you
may choose to linger to explore the cultural institutions or to shop.

Sights to See

㉗ **Alberta Government Centre.** The seat of Alberta's government, this complex encompasses several acres of carefully manicured gardens and fountains. The gardens are open for strolling. ⊠ *109th St. and 97th Ave.,*
☏ *no phone.*

㉘ **Alberta Legislature Building.** The stately 1912 Edwardian structure overlooks the river on the site of an early trading post. Frequent free tours
of the building and an interpretive center help to explain the intricacies of the Albertan and Canadian systems of government. ⊠ *109th
St. and 97th Ave.,* ☏ *780/427–7362,* WEB *www.assembly.ab.ca/visi-
tor/tour_info.htm.* ⊡ *Free.* ☉ *Mid-Oct.–Apr., weekdays 9–4:30, last
tour at 3, weekends noon–5, last tour at 4; May–mid-Oct. weekdays
8:30–5, weekends 9–5, last tour at 4.*

㉖ **Edmonton Art Gallery.** The collection includes more than 4,000 paintings, sculptures, prints, installation works, and photographs by national
and international artists. The gallery mounts more than 30 annual special exhibitions and has a children's section. ⊠ *2 Sir Winston Churchill
Sq.,* ☏ *780/422–6223,* WEB *www.edmontonartgallery.ca.* ⊡ *$5; free
Thurs. after 4.* ☉ *Weekdays 10:30–5, weekends 11–5.*

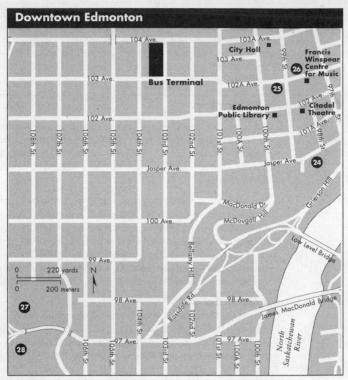

Downtown Edmonton

㉔ Shaw Conference Centre. This most unconventional structure has been built into the banks of the North Saskatchewan River; the terraced levels are reached by glass-enclosed escalators with great views of the river valley. **Edmonton Tourism** (☎ 780/426–4715) operates a visitor-information center on the Pedway (walkway) level. It's open weekdays 8–5. ⊠ 9797 Jasper Ave., ☎ 780/421–9797, WEB www.ede.org.

㉒ Sir Winston Churchill Square. The focus of the Arts District, a six-block area that incorporates many of Edmonton's major institutions, is this square. The **Francis Winspear Centre for Music** (☎ 780/428–1414), has a 1,900-seat concert hall that's home to the Edmonton Symphony Orchestra. The largest theater complex in Canada, the **Citadel Theatre** (⊠ 9828 101A Ave., ☎ 780/425–1820) has five venues—plus workshops and classrooms—and an indoor garden with a waterfall. The Edmonton Public Library's **Stanley Milner Library** (⊠ 7 Sir Winston Churchill Sq., ☎ 780/496–7000) augments books and art exhibits with a lively round of activities in the Children's Department. The **Chinatown Gate** is a symbol of friendship between Edmonton and its sister city, Harbin, China; the gate spans the portal to Edmonton's meager Chinatown. **City Hall** (⊠ 1 Sir Winston Churchill Sq., ☎ 780/496–8200) is more than a place for civic government. This architectural showcase contains a grand stairway, a large art-exhibition space, and a 200-ft tower with an enormous 23-bell carillon.

Greater Edmonton

You can find everything from historical sights and museums to one of the world's largest shopping centers outside downtown Edmonton.

A Good Drive

To make a circuit, start northwest of city center at the **Odyssium,** where you can play with high-tech equipment in hands-on displays.

You can also visit the **West Edmonton Mall,** the world's largest. On the south side of the North Saskatchewan River, just off Whitemud Drive, is **Fort Edmonton Park,** where costumed interpreters take you back in time. On the north side of the river is the **Provincial Museum of Alberta,** which focuses on natural and human history. Back across the river, via the 109th Street High Level Bridge, you come to the **Old Strathcona Historic Area.** On the University of Alberta campus is **Rutherford House Provincial Historic Site,** the spacious, elegant home of the province's first premier, Alexander Cameron Rutherford. To the northeast, but still on the south side of the river, lies **Muttart Conservatory,** an important botanical facility.

TIMING

You can spend a few days taking in these places of interest, depending on how much time you want to devote to shopping or playing in the amusement parks. If you have only one day, choose places based on your interests.

Sights to See

★ **Fort Edmonton Park.** Canada's largest living-history park (158 acres) re-creates the events of white settlement in Edmonton during the 19th century. The park includes a fur press (an apparatus for bundling pelts for shipping) in the 1846 Hudson's Bay Company fort; a blacksmith shop, a saloon, and a jail along 1885 Street; photo studios and a firehouse on 1905 Street; and relatively modern conveniences on 1920 Street. Horse-wagon, streetcar, stagecoach, and pony rides are available, as well as a short trip on a steam-powered train. ⊠ *Whitemud and Fox Drs.,* ☎ *780/496–8787,* WEB *www.gov.edmonton.ab.ca/fort.* ☜ *$7.75.* ☉ *Mid-May–June, weekdays 10–4, weekends 10–6; July–early Sept., daily 10–6.*

Muttart Conservatory. The four spectacular glass-pyramid greenhouses that rise up from Edmonton's river valley are home to one of North America's most important botanical facilities, which includes an extensive collection of orchids and bromeliads. Three pyramids contain flora of different climates (arid, tropical, and temperate), and a show pyramid has seasonal floral displays. The Muttart has a gift shop, an art gallery, and a fine café. ⊠ *9626 96A St.,* ☎ *780/496–8755.* ☜ *$5.* ☉ *Weekdays 9–6, weekends 11–6.*

☾ **Odyssium.** The **Margaret Zeidler Star Theatre** has the largest planetarium dome in North America and presents different laser and star shows hourly. There's an amateur ham radio station and an IMAX theater; renovations in 2001 added four exhibition galleries, featuring forensics, environment, health, and space. ⊠ *11211 142nd St.,* ☎ *780/452–9100,* WEB *www.odyssium.com.* ☜ *$6.95; $7.95 for IMAX; $11.95 for combined ticket.* ☉ *Call for hrs.*

Old Strathcona Historic Area. The area surrounding 104th Street and Whyte (82nd) Avenue on the south side of the river is a district of restored houses and shops built in the 1890s, prior to the amalgamation of Strathcona Town with Edmonton in 1912. Old Strathcona is an attractive shopping district with antiques stores, gift shops, stylish boutiques, music and book stores, theaters, museums, and 75 restaurants and coffeehouses. The Old Strathcona Farmer's Market has fresh produce and crafts. The **Old Strathcona Foundation** (☎ 780/433–5866, WEB www.osf.strathcona.org) can provide information about the Old Strathcona area.

Provincial Museum of Alberta. This innovative natural-history museum in a beautiful park includes the Syncrude Galley of Aboriginal Culture, which spans 11,000 years and 500 generations of native history and displays an impressive collection of artifacts. The Natural History Gallery presents minerals and gems, a "live" bug room, astonishing dinosaur fossils, saber-toothed tigers, and Canada's only complete Columbian mammoth skeleton. The museum also has a shop, a café, and an outdoor sculpture park. ✉ *12845 102nd Ave.,* ☎ *780/453–9100,* WEB *www.pma.edmonton.ab.ca.* 🎟 *$6.50, price may vary with special exhibits.* ⊙ *Daily 9–5.*

Rutherford House Provincial Historic Site. Built in Jacobean Revival style, the 1911 home of Alberta's first premier, Alexander Cameron Rutherford, has been restored to its elegant post-Edwardian charm. Costumed interpreters give tours (included in admission) detailing life in 1915. The gift shop sells reproductions of Edwardian gifts, cards, linens, and jewelry. Lunch and afternoon tea are served at the Arbour Restaurant. ✉ *11153 Saskatchewan Dr., on the University of Alberta campus,* ☎ *780/427–3995,* WEB *www.gov.ab.ca/mcd/mhs/ruther/ruther.htm.* 🎟 *$3.* ⊙ *Early Sept.–mid-May, Tues.–Sun. noon–5; mid-May–early Sept., daily 9–5.*

West Edmonton Mall. Listed in the *Guinness Book of Records* as the world's largest indoor shopping center, Alberta's most popular tourist attraction extends over 5.3 million square ft (48 city blocks). Its sheer magnitude and variety transform it from a mere shopping center to an indoor city with high-rent districts, blue-collar strips, and hidden byways. The more than 800 stores and services include three department stores, 26 movie theaters, and more than 100 places to eat. The mall also contains the world's largest indoor amusement park, with a roller coaster; World Waterpark, the world's largest indoor wave pool; a recreation room with 25 billiard tables, a 25-lane bowling center, and an arcade with the latest interactive games; an National Hockey League–size ice-skating rink; the world's largest indoor artificial lake, which features four seaworthy submarines at the Deep Sea Adventure, a dolphin show, and an exact replica of Columbus's ship the *Santa Maria;* a 64,000-square-ft Las Vegas–style casino; an 18-hole miniature-golf course; a dinner theater; and the Fantasyland Hotel. If you don't feel like walking the mall, rent an electric scooter or hitch a ride on a rickshaw. ✉ *8882 170th St.,* ☎ *780/444–5200 or 800/661–8890,* WEB *www.westedmontonmall.com.* 🎟 *Amusement park day pass $29.95; ride tickets $1.20 (rides cost 1–7 tickets); World Waterpark day pass $29.95; Deep Sea Adventure $12.* ⊙ *Mall, daily 24 hrs; shops weekdays 10–9, Sat. 10–6, Sun. noon–6.*

Dining

$$$–$$$$ ✕ **Hardware Grill.** Casual elegance reigns at this former hardware
★   store, now handsomely refurbished as a well-lit, spacious restaurant. Small alcoves have river-valley views, and several tables overlook the glassed-in kitchen where chef–owner Larry Stewart prepares Ukrainian-influenced regional cuisine made with fresh local produce. Applewood-smoked salmon is served with truffled potato pierogi; beef tenderloin comes smothered in a horseradish–crème fraîche sauce; and the warm gingerbread cake is served with a rhubarb–Saskatoonberry compote. The impressive wine list includes more than 500 choices. ✉ *9698 Jasper Ave.,* ☎ *780/423–0969. AE, DC, MC, V. Closed Sun.*

$$$ ✕ **Il Portico.** Whether it be for a business lunch or a romantic dinner, this downtown restaurant is the place to be seen in Edmonton. You can dine on the beautiful terrace or in the Wine Cellar, a private dining room with 2,000 bottles of wine. Highlights of the innovative Italian cuisine, served from an open kitchen, are sliced beef tenderloin with aged balsamic vinegar and an oregano reduction, and veal scallopini topped with smoked cheese and tomato sauce. ⊠ *10012 107 St.,* ☎ *780/424–0707. AE, DC, MC, V. Closed Sun. No lunch Sat.*

$$–$$$ ✕ **Jack's Grill.** The daddy of all Edmonton grills, this modern bistro consistently wins rave reviews. Highlights of the excellent regional fare include grilled duck breast and smoked duck sausage with a roasted shallot–bacon sauce, potato–goat cheese ravioli, and roasted boneless chicken breast stuffed with chestnut mousse and served with butternut-squash risotto and Calvados cream sauce. Fresh fish and a vegetarian plate are available daily. ⊠ *5842 111 St.,* ☎ *780/434–1113. AE, DC, MC, V. No lunch.*

$$–$$$ ✕ **Packrat Louie Kitchen & Bar.** This affordable Swiss bistro with French, German, and Italian influences serves generous portions of fresh market cuisine in an open, friendly environment. Popular dishes include roast Alberta free-range pork with coffee–sesame spicing served with risotto and tomato chutney, roasted organic lemon–garlic breast of chicken with wild-mushroom compote, and grilled lemon pizza with fontina cheese. The homemade chocolates and desserts are sensational. ⊠ *10335 83rd Ave.,* ☎ *780/433–0123. Reservations essential. AE, MC, V. Closed Sun.–Mon.*

$$ ✕ **Four Rooms.** Each room at this theater-district restaurant decorated
★ like a private home has a different ambience: the "living room" is more formal and no-smoking, while the "library" serves as a cigar bar, with a fully stocked humidor. The "kitchen," where you can sit on stools at the counter and watch the food preparations, is more casual. (The fourth room is a café.) The international tapas menu features everything from latkes to spring rolls, and two or three selections are enough for a light meal. Entrées lean toward seafood, including paella. There's also an extensive wine list. Four Rooms stays open until 1 AM on weekends, drawing a lively crowd. ⊠ *Edmonton Centre, 100th St.,* ☎ *780/426–4767. AE, MC, V. Closed Sun.*

$–$$ ✕ **Da-De-O.** Popular and funky, this 1950s-style diner in Old Strath-
★ cona prides itself on its mix of Cajun and Creole classics. Try the blackened catfish, gumbos, jambalaya, and po'boy sandwiches. On weekends the kitchen is open until midnight. ⊠ *10548A Whyte (82nd) Ave.,* ☎ *780/433–0930. AE, DC, MC, V.*

$–$$ ✕ **High Level Diner.** Named after the High Level Bridge, this southside eatery dishes up the best breakfast in town. Hearty and healthful food is emphasized here. Cinnamon buns and muffins are fabulous, as are the whole wheat–yogurt pancakes, Belgian waffles, and egg dishes. Lunches and dinners feature Middle Eastern specialties (hummus, tabbouleh salad, and souvlaki) as well as Mexican and vegetarian entrées such as spinach pie and black bean chili. The salmon special changes daily. ⊠ *10912 88th Ave.,* ☎ *780/433–0993. AE, DC, MC, V.*

$ ✕ **Zenari's.** A great urban Italian deli, Zenari's is the perfect lunch spot.
★ The original ManuLife Place location combines a lunch counter with specialty housewares and a catering service; the newer restaurant has live jazz in the evenings. Specialties include homemade soups, salads, sandwiches with Italian meats and cheeses, pastas, risottos, and pizza. ⊠ *ManuLife Place, 10180 101 St.,* ☎ *780/423–5409;* ⊠ *10117 101 St.,* ☎ *780/425–6151. AE, DC, MC, V. Closed Sun.*

Lodging

$$$$ 🛏 **Sheraton Grande.** This financial-district luxury high-rise connects by second-level passageways to five office buildings and two shopping centers. Rooms—with bay windows and blue-and-gray color schemes—have a smart look and include marble tabletops, walnut furniture, and brass accents. The Rose and Crown is an English-style pub. ⊠ *10235 101st*

St., T5J 3E9, ☎ *780/428–7111 or 800/263–9030,* FAX *780/441–3098,* WEB *www.sheraton.com. 386 rooms, 27 suites. 3 restaurants, 2 bars, in-room data ports, no-smoking floor, indoor pool, sauna, baby-sitting, concierge, coin laundry, laundry service, parking (fee weekdays). AE, DC, MC, V.*

$$$$ 🏨 **The Varscona.** Its excellent location on Whyte (82nd) Avenue in the Old Strathcona district puts this hotel within walking distance of Edmonton's most unique shops, bars, and restaurants. The comfortable rooms are decorated in a country or classic theme. O'Byrne's Irish Pub and Sorrentino's restaurant offer great atmosphere and food. The business center is open around the clock. ✉ *8208 106 St., T6E 6R9,* ☎ *780/434–6111 or 888/515–3355,* FAX *780/439–1195,* WEB *www.varscona. com. 89 rooms, 4 suites. Restaurant, pub, gym, business services, free parking. AE, DC, MC, V.*

$$$–$$$$ 🏨 **The Fairmont Hotel Macdonald.** The city's landmark 1915 hotel has
★   maintained its original grandeur and offers first-class modern facilities in both the traditionally furnished guest rooms and the ornate public areas. The Royal Suite, in the former attic, is spectacular. There's fine dining in the elegant Harvest Room and Sunday brunch in the Empire Ballroom or the Wedgwood Room. Some rooms have a sweeping view of the river valley. ✉ *10065 100th St., T5J 0N6,* ☎ *780/424–5181 or 800/441–1414,* FAX *780/424–8017,* WEB *www.hotelmacdonald.com. 181 rooms, 17 suites. Restaurant, bar, pool, massage, sauna, whirlpool, steam room, health club, parking (fee). AE, MC, V.*

$$–$$$$ 🏨 **Union Bank Inn.** A 1911 bank building in the center of downtown
★   now houses an upscale boutique hotel. Individually decorated rooms range in style from French country to European modern; all have goose-down duvets. All rooms have fireplaces and a full breakfast is included in the price. ✉ *10053 Jasper Ave., T5J 1S5,* ☎ *780/423–3600 or 888/ 423–3601,* FAX *780/423–4623,* WEB *www.unionbankinn.com. 34 rooms. Restaurant, lounge, meeting rooms, free parking. AE, DC, MC, V. BP.*

$$–$$$$ 🏨 **Westin Edmonton.** In the heart of downtown and the Arts District sits one of Edmonton's finest hotels. Trees and plants fill the luxurious, comfortable atrium lobby, and bright colors and attractive artwork decorate the spacious rooms. The experienced staff speaks a total of 29 languages. The Pradera Café has excellent food. The Westin is connected to the LRT, downtown theaters, art galleries, shopping, and restaurants via the Pedway system of walkways. ✉ *10135 100th St., T5J 0N7,* ☎ *780/426–3636 or 800/937–8461,* FAX *780/428–1454,* WEB *www.westin.com. 413 rooms, 20 suites. Restaurant, bar, no-smoking floor, indoor pool, sauna, gym, parking (fee). AE, DC, MC, V.*

$$$ 🏨 **Fantasyland Hotel.** A component of the West Edmonton Mall, the deluxe Fantasyland has standard and executive rooms as well as 113 theme suites. The latter include Victorian coach rooms where guests sleep in open carriages; Roman rooms with classic round beds; and Polynesian rooms with catamaran beds and waterfalls. All theme rooms have whirlpool baths; other quarters are comfortable and tidy. ✉ *17700 87th Ave., T5T 4V4,* ☎ *780/444–3000 or 800/737–3783,* FAX *780/444–3294,* WEB *www.fantasylandhotel.com. 241 rooms, 113 suites. 2 restaurants, lounge, shops, free parking. AE, DC, MC, V.*

$$ 🏨 **Greenwood Inn.** This affordable family and corporate hotel is 15 minutes from Edmonton International Airport. Ask for rooms in the front of the building, because the railroad runs out back. Some suites have whirlpool baths. ABC Country Restaurant offers home cooking and fresh baked goods, and Dalton's Steak and Seafood prides itself on serving the best Alberta beef. ✉ *4485 Calgary Trail N, T6H 5C3,* ☎ *780/431–1100 or 888/233–6730,* FAX *780/437–3455,* WEB *www.greenwoodinn.ca. 224 rooms, 13 suites. 2 restaurants, lounge, pool, gym, free parking. AE, DC, MC, V.*

$–$$ ⬚ **Glenora Bed & Breakfast Inn.** A historic 1912 apartment building has been converted into a charming inn. Apartments of different sizes have been transformed into grand Victorian bedrooms with old-fashioned wallpaper and antique furniture. Some rooms have full kitchens; others have kitchenettes. A full breakfast is included. The inn is five minutes from downtown, 12 minutes from the West Edmonton Mall, and two blocks from the Provincial Museum of Alberta. ✉ *12327 102 Ave., T5N 0L8,* ☎ *780/488–6766 or 877/453–6672,* FAX *780/488–5168,* WEB *www.glenorabnb.com. 21 suites. Kitchenettes (some), coin laundry, free parking. AE, MC, V. BP.*

Nightlife and the Arts

Tickets for special events and concerts are available from **Ticketmaster** (☎ 780/451–8000, WEB www.ticketmaster.ca), which has various locations. **Tix on the Square** (☎ 780/420–1757), beside the Winspear Theatre in Sir Winston Churchill Square, is run by an arts organization and sells theater and music tickets. To find out what's on, consult www.edmontonarts.ab.ca.

One huge event that encompasses music, shows, and special events is the 10-day **Klondike Days** (☎ 780/479–3500) held in late July. The festivities celebrate the prosperity that the Yukon gold rush brought the city, which was a supply route and stopping point for miners.

The Arts

In August, Old Strathcona hosts the 11-day **Fringe Theatre Festival** (☎ 780/448–9000), showcasing alternative theater, dance, and music.

FILM

The **Edmonton Film Society** screens an ambitious program at a theater in the Provincial Museum of Alberta (✉ 12845 102nd Ave., ☎ 780/453–9100). **Metro Cinema** (✉ Ziedler Hall, Citadel Theatre, 9828 101A Ave., ☎ 780/425–9212) presents local, alternative, and international films and videos Thursday through Sunday. The **Princess Theatre** (✉ 10337 Whyte/82nd Ave., ☎ 780/433–5785), an old-time movie house in Old Strathcona, shows revivals, experiments, and foreign films.

MUSIC AND DANCE

The **Brian Webb Dance Company** (☎ 780/497–4416) presents an annual season of contemporary dance at the John L. Haar Theatre (✉ 10045 156 St.). The **Edmonton Symphony Orchestra** (☎ 780/428–1414) performs in the Francis Winspear Centre for Music on Sir Winston Churchill Square. The **Northern Alberta Jubilee Auditorium** (✉ 87th Ave. and 114th St., ☎ 780/427–2760), at the University of Alberta, hosts the Edmonton Opera (☎ 780/424–4040) and the Alberta Ballet Company (☎ 780/428–6839).

THEATER

Edmonton has 13 professional theater companies. The paramount facility is the glass-clad downtown **Citadel Theatre** complex (✉ 9828 101A Ave., ☎ 780/425–1820), where five theaters present a mix of contemporary works and classics. **Northern Light Theatre** (☎ 780/471–1586) stages avant-garde productions at the Kaasa Theatre in the Northern Alberta Jubilee Auditorium.

Nightlife

BARS AND CLUBS

Ceili's Irish Pub & Restaurant (✉ 10338 109 St., ☎ 780/426–5555) serves up a large variety of beers by the glass; complete breakfast, lunch, and dinner menus; and live entertainment in a friendly pub atmosphere. Smoky cocktail bars are the rage, and **Devlin's** (✉ 10507 Whyte/82nd Ave., ☎ 780/437–7489) has 30 innovative hand-shaken cocktails on the menu. **The Drink** (✉ 2940 Calgary Trail Southbound, ☎ 780/430–4567) caters to the 30-plus suits crowd. Lunch, dinner, and late-night snacks are available in addition to the best mix of martinis around. Top 40 dance music spins nightly.

MUSIC

Blues on Whyte (✉ 10329 Whyte, 82nd Ave., ☎ 780/439–5058), in the Commercial Hotel, is one of the city's best live-music venues; there are jam sessions Saturday afternoon. **Cook County Saloon** (✉ 8010 103rd St., ☎ 780/432–2665) repeatedly has been named Canada's best country club by the Canadian Country Music Association. **Cowboy's Niteclub** (✉ 10102 180 St., ☎ 780/481–8739) holds 1,200 people in the bar and dance hall and plays Top 40 country, dance, and rock Wednesday through Saturday. The top-notch **Sidetrack Cafe** (✉ 10333 112th St., ☎ 780/421–1326) has local and international entertainers, big-screen telecasts of sports events, Variety Night on Sunday, and Blues on Monday. **Yardbird Suite** (✉ 10203 86th Ave., ☎ 780/432–0428) is Edmonton's premier jazz showcase.

Outdoor Activities and Sports

Participant Sports

BICYCLING AND JOGGING

The North Saskatchewan River valley is a lush park system with 97 km (60 mi) of cycling, jogging, and cross-country ski trails. The **River Valley Centre** (✉ 11240 79th St., ☎ 780/496–7275 or 780/496–4999) can provide information about park activities.

HEALTH AND FITNESS CLUBS

The **Kinsmen Sports Centre** (✉ 9100 Walterdale Hill, ☎ 780/496–7300) is open 5:30 AM–10 PM daily. The drop-in fee of $5.50 gives you access to its pools, fitness center, and racquetball, squash, and aerobics facilities. **Mill Woods Recreation Centre** ($5.20 drop-in fee; ✉ 7207 28th Ave., ☎ 780/496–2900) has a wave pool, a gym, racquetball and squash courts, as well as a sauna and hot tub. It's open daily; call for hours.

Spectator Sports

AUTO RACING

Capital Raceway (✉ Rte. 19, 2 km [1 mi] west of Hwy. 2S, on the way to Devon, ☎ 780/462–8901), a multiuse motor-sports complex, has events most weekends from May through October.

BASEBALL

The **Edmonton Trappers** play in the Pacific Coast League (AAA) at Telus Field (✉ 10233 96th Ave., ☎ 780/429–2934) from April to early September.

FOOTBALL

From June through November, the Canadian Football League's **Edmonton Eskimos** team plays at Commonwealth Stadium (✉ 9022 111th Ave., ☎ 780/448–3757 or 780/448–1525).

HOCKEY

The **Edmonton Oilers** of the National Hockey League meet their opponents October through April at the Skyreach Centre (✉ 118th Ave. and 74th St., ☎ 780/414–4625).

HORSE RACING

Northlands Park Spectrum (✉ 116th Ave. and 74th St., ☎ 780/471–7379) hosts harness racing from early March to mid-June. The thoroughbred racing season runs from mid-June through October.

Shopping

The core of downtown, between 100th and 103rd streets, holds a complex of shopping centers and department stores connected by tunnels or second-level walkways. It includes **Commerce Place** (⊠ 102nd St.), **Eaton Centre** (⊠ 102nd Ave.), **Edmonton Centre** (⊠ 100th St.), and **Manu-Life Place** (⊠ 102nd Ave.).

The area along 124th and 125th streets between 102nd and 109th avenues, is full of boutiques, bistros, bookstores, and galleries. **Old Strathcona Historic Area,** the area surrounding 104th Street and Whyte (82nd) Avenue on the south side of the river, has enticing boutiques, antiques shops, and bookstores, as well as a farmers market that also has crafts.

West Edmonton Mall (8882 170th St., ☎ 780/444–5200 or 800/661–8890, WEB www.westedmontonmall.com), the world's largest mall, has more than 800 stores and services. The Bay, Club Monaco, Eddie Bauer, The Museum Company, Banana Republic, Benetton, Champs, Foot Locker, Guess, Speedo, Helly Hansen, Gap, Roots Canada, and Godiva are but a few of the choices. Outside of shopping, the slew of options includes movie theaters, more than 100 places to eat, an amusement park with a roller coaster, billiards, a bowling center, an ice-skating rink, and an indoor wave pool.

The Artworks (☎ 780/420–6311), a gift store in Edmonton Centre, has a nice merchandise mix that includes flowers, designer jewelry, and interesting cards. If you're interested in crafts, the **Alberta Craft Council** (⊠ 10186 106th St., ☎ 780/488–5900) has distinctive Alberta-made items, including pottery and furniture.

Side Trips from Edmonton

Settlers from the Ukraine were among the many European immigrants who made their home in the prairies in the early part of the 20th century by carving farms and homesteads out of the wilderness. Festivals throughout the summer celebrate this cultural history; there are several sights near Edmonton related to Alberta's Ukrainian heritage, and also good day trips to some beautiful natural areas.

Red Deer

㉙ *149 km (92 mi) south of Edmonton, 145 km (90 mi) north of Calgary.*

The railroad boom that began in the late 1800s and later Alberta's oil booms were major driving forces behind the growth of Red Deer, which today has a population of about 68,000. The city, midway between Calgary and Edmonton on Highway 2, is on the Red Deer River. Along the riverbank winds **Waskasoo Park,** with nearly 48 km (30 mi) of pedestrian and bike paths, equestrian trails, and canoeing and fishing.

The **Alberta Sports Hall of Fame and Museum** (⊠ Hwy. 2, on the west edge of town, ☎ 403/341–8614, WEB www.albertasportshalloffame.com) includes interactive and rotating sports-related exhibits. It's open daily 9–6 from late May to early October, 10–5 daily the rest of the year; admission is $3.

At the **Red Deer and District Museum** (⊠ 4525 47A Ave., ☎ 403/343–6844, WEB www.museum.red-deer.ab.ca), where the focus is on the area's immigrant settlers and native peoples, you can see a pioneer home and other historic items. The museum is open 10–5 weekdays (until 9 Wednesday and Thursday) and 1–5 on weekends; donations are welcome.

Elk Island National Park
48 km (30 mi) east of Edmonton on Highway 16.

Elk Island was established in 1906 as Canada's first federal wildlife sanctuary for large mammals. A herd of 600 plains and 350 wood bison roam the park's 194 square km (75 square mi), as do elk, moose, white-tailed deer, and more than 240 species of birds, including herons. The park has hiking and cross-country skiing trails, 80 campsites, a 9-hole golf course, and several lakes. ⊠ *Hwy. 16,* ☎ *780/992–2950,* WEB *www.parcscanada.gc.ca/elk.* ✉ *General entry: $4 May–Oct., $3.50 Nov.–Apr.*

Ukrainian Cultural Heritage Village
3 km (2 mi) east of Elk Island National Park, 50 km (31 mi) east of Edmonton.

The village consists of 34 historic buildings, gathered from around east-central Alberta, which have been assembled in three theme areas to illustrate the culture and lifestyle of pre-1930s Ukrainian settlers. Guides in period dress interpret the displays: the Railway Townsite, Rural Community, and Farmstead. ⊠ *Hwy. 16,* ☎ *780/662–3640,* WEB *www.gov.ab.ca/mcd/mhs/uchv/uchv.htm.* ✉ *$6.50.* ⊙ *May 15–early Sept., daily 10–6; early Sept.–mid-Oct., daily 10–4.*

Vegreville
30 *50 km (31 mi) east of Ukrainian Cultural Heritage Village, 101 km (63 mi) east of Edmonton.*

Vegreville is the center of eastern Alberta's Ukrainian culture and home of the "world's largest Easter egg" (*pysanka*), measuring 31 ft tall, at the east end of the town's main street. The colorfully decorated egg consists of more than 3,500 pieces of aluminum. The **Ukrainian Pysanka Festival** (☎ 780/632–2771) takes place here annually the first weekend in July.

The **Vegreville Regional Museum** (⊠ Hwy. 16A, ☎ 780/632–7650) has an extensive collection of local artifacts.

Edmonton A to Z

AIR TRAVEL TO AND FROM EDMONTON
Delta, Horizon, and Northwest, along with the major Canadian airlines (Air Canada, Air BC), serve Edmonton.

AIRPORTS AND TRANSFERS
Edmonton International Airport, which includes a U.S. Customs pre-clearance facility, is 20 km (12 mi) south of downtown. An airport-improvement fee of $5 is assessed on all flight departures within Alberta, $10 for departures outside Alberta; you pay this at the airport.
➤ AIRPORT INFORMATION: **Edmonton International Airport** (⊠ Hwy. 2, 20 km [12 mi] south of downtown Edmonton, ☎ 780/890–8382).

AIRPORT TRANSFER
Taxi rides from Edmonton International cost approximately $29 to the city center. The Sky Shuttle has frequent service between the airport and major downtown hotels; the fare is $11 one-way, $18 round-trip. ➤ SHUTTLE: **Sky Shuttle** (☎ 780/465–8515).

BUS TRAVEL TO AND FROM EDMONTON
Greyhound has regular bus service from downtown Edmonton to Jasper, Calgary, Red Deer, and Fort MacMurray.
➤ BUS INFORMATION: **Greyhound** (☎ 800/661–8747).

BUS TRAVEL WITHIN EDMONTON

Edmonton Transit operates a comprehensive system of buses throughout the area, as well as a light-rail transit system. The fare is $1.75; transfers are free. Buses operate 5:30 AM to 2 AM. The Edmonton Transit Information Centre, at Churchill Station, is open weekdays 9:30–5.
➤ BUS INFORMATION: **Edmonton Transit** (☎ 780/496–1611). **Edmonton Transit Information Centre** (✉ 102A Ave. and 99th St.).

CAR TRAVEL

Edmonton is on the Yellowhead Highway (Highway 16), which runs from Winnipeg, Manitoba, through the central parts of Saskatchewan and Alberta. This highway has four lanes and is divided through most of Alberta; it intersects with the four-lane divided Highway 2, which runs south to Calgary.

EMERGENCIES

Royal Alexandra Hospital, Misericordia Hospital, Grey Nuns Community Hospital, and University of Alberta Hospital all have emergency rooms. Denta Care offers 24-hour dental care.

Some Shopper's Drug Mart branches are open 24 hours.
➤ DENTISTS: **Denta Care** (✉ 464 Southgate Shopping Centre, 111th St. and 51st Ave., ☎ 780/434–9566).
➤ EMERGENCY SERVICES: **Ambulance, fire, poison center, police** (☎ 911).
➤ HOSPITALS: **Grey Nuns Community Hospital** (✉ 3015 62nd St., ☎ 780/450–7000). **Misericordia Hospital** (✉ 16940 87th Ave., ☎ 780/930–5611). **Royal Alexandra Hospital** (✉ 10240 Kingsway Ave., ☎ 780/477–4111). **University of Alberta Hospital** (✉ 8440 112th St., ☎ 780/492–8822).
➤ 24-HOUR PHARMACIES: **Shopper's Drug Mart** (✉ 11408 Jasper Ave., ☎ 780/482–1171; ✉ 8210 109th St., ☎ 780/433–3121).

LRT TRAVEL

Edmonton Transit operates a light-rail transit (LRT) line from downtown to the northeast side of the city, as well as a comprehensive system of buses throughout the area. The fare is $1.75; transfers are free. The LRT is free in the downtown area (between Churchill and Grandin stations) weekdays 9–3 and Saturday 9–6. The Edmonton Transit Information Centre, at Churchill Station, is open weekdays 9:30–5.
➤ LRT INFORMATION: **Edmonton Transit** (☎ 780/496–1611). **Edmonton Transit Information Centre** (✉ 102A Ave. and 99th St.).

TAXIS

Taxis tend to be costly: $2.50 for the first 105 meters, and 10¢ for each additional 90 meters. Cabs may be hailed on the street, but phoning is recommended.
➤ TAXI COMPANIES: **Alberta Co-op Taxi** (☎ 780/425–8310). **Checker** (☎ 780/484–8888). **Yellow** (☎ 780/462–3456).

TOURS

BOAT TOURS

The *Edmonton Queen* paddlewheeler cruises the North Saskatchewan River from May through September. Some excursions include lunch or dinner and dancing. Klondike Jet Boats ply the North Saskatchewan River May through October.
➤ FEES AND SCHEDULES: *Edmonton Queen* (☎ 780/424–2628). **Klondike Jet Boats** (☎ 780/486–0896).

SIGHTSEEING TOURS

Out an' About Tours and Magic Times Tour & Convention Services offer half- and full-day itineraries that hit the high points of the city or surrounding sights. Day tours can also be scheduled to Jasper, Banff, and the Columbia Icefield.

➤ FEES AND SCHEDULES: **Magic Times Tour & Convention Services** (☎ 780/940–7479). **Out an' About Tours** (☎ 780/909–8687).

VISITOR INFORMATION

The Edmonton Tourism Information Centre is at Gateway Park, on Highway 2 south of downtown.

➤ TOURIST INFORMATION: **Edmonton Tourism Information Centre** (✉ Gateway Park, Hwy. 2, ☎ 780/496–8400 or 800/463–4667, ⓦⒺⒷ www.tourism.ede.org).

REGINA

Updated by
Jens Nielsen

Regina, Saskatchewan, was originally dubbed Pile O'Bones in reference to the remnants left by years of buffalo hunting by native peoples and later European hunters. The city was renamed after the Latin title of Queen Victoria, the reigning monarch in 1883. It was at this time that the railroad arrived and the city became the capital of the Northwest Territories. The Mounties made it their headquarters. When the province of Saskatchewan was formed in 1905, Regina was chosen as its capital. At the beginning of the 20th century, immigrants from the British Isles, Eastern Europe, and East Asia rushed in to claim parcels of river-fed prairie land for $1 per lot. Oil and potash were discovered in the 1950s and 1960s, and Regina became a major agricultural and industrial distribution center as well as the head office of the world's largest grain-handling cooperative.

The centerpiece of this city of nearly 202,000 is Wascana Centre, which was created by expanding meager Wascana Creek into the broad Wascana Lake and surrounding it with 2,000 acres of urban parkland. This unique multipurpose site contains the city's major museums, the Saskatchewan provincial legislature, the University of Regina campus, and all the amenities of a big-city park and natural-habitat waterfowl sanctuary.

Exploring Regina

Museums, government buildings, cultural sites, and a park are highlights of a city tour. Streets in Regina run north–south, avenues east–west. The most important north–south artery is Albert Street (Route 6); Victoria Avenue is the main east–west thoroughfare. The Trans-Canada Highway (Highway 1) bypasses the city to the south and east.

A Good Tour

Begin at the northwest corner of Wascana Centre, at the **Royal Saskatchewan Museum** ③, and check out the Earth Sciences Gallery and the First Nations Gallery. Then head south on Albert Street past Speakers Corner, where, as in London's Hyde Park, free speech is volubly expressed. Turn left onto Legislature Drive to the **Legislative Building** ③ for a tour of its marble interior. Take Saskatchewan Road (west of the Legislative Building) south to the **MacKenzie Art Gallery** ③, which displays European and Canadian art. Continue along Saskatchewan Road, which loops to the right, and turn north onto Avenue G and then east (right) onto Lakeshore Drive until you reach the **Wascana Waterfowl Park Display Ponds** ③, where you can see the many breeds of migratory birds that stop here. Retrace your steps to Broad Street (Wascana Parkway), cross the bridge to Wascana Drive, and turn east on Wascana Drive toward Powerhouse Drive and the **Saskatchewan Science Centre** ③ for hands-on exhibits demonstrating various scientific phenomena. From here, take a car or bike back to Broad Street

Saskatchewan

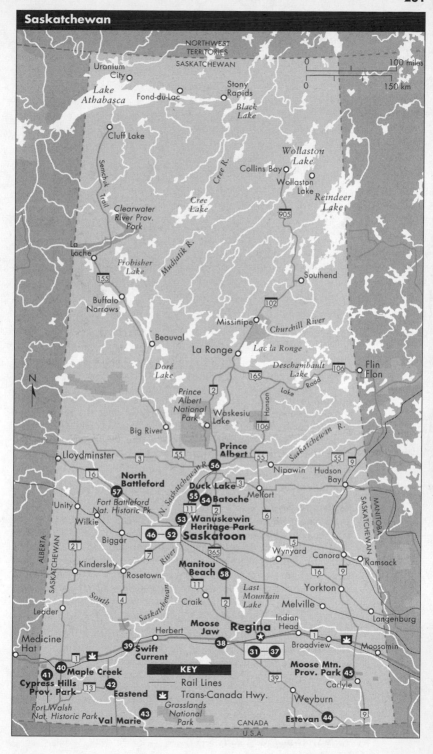

NORTHWEST TERRITORIES

SASKATCHEWAN

0 ——— 100 miles
0 ——— 150 km

Uranium City

Lake Athabasca

Fond-du-Lac

Stony Rapids

Black Lake

Cluff Lake

Wollaston Lake

Collins Bay

Wollaston Lake

Reindeer Lake

Cree R.

Samchuk Trail

Clearwater River Prov. Park

Cree Lake

905

La Loche

Frobisher Lake

Mudiatik R.

Southend

155

Buffalo Narrows

102

Missinipe

Churchill River

Beauval

La Ronge

Lac la Ronge

Deschambault Lake

106

Flin Flon

Doré Lake

165

Hanson Lake Road

N

Prince Albert National Park

2

Waskesiu Lake

106

Hanson

Big River

Saskatchewan R.

Prince Albert

55

Nipawin

Hudson Bay

55

9

Lloydminster

3

55

N. Saskatchewan R.

56

16

North Battleford

57

Duck Lake

3

MANITOBA / SASKATCHEWAN

Unity

Fort Battleford Nat. Historic Pk.

55

54 Batoche

Melfort

11

6

Wilkie

53

Wanuskewin Heritage Park

2

ALBERTA / SASKATCHEWAN

21

Biggar

46 – 52

Saskatoon

5

Wynyard

Canora

Kamsack

Kindersley

7

River

Manitou Beach 58

365

16

9

4

South Saskatchewan River

Rosetown

11

Craik

2

Last Mountain Lake

Yorkton

Melville

Langenburg

Leader

Moose Jaw

Regina

★

Indian Head

1

Broadview

Moosomin

Medicine Hat

1

Herbert

38

31 – 37

39 **Swift Current**

KEY

—— Rail Lines

🛡 Trans-Canada Hwy.

Moose Mtn. Prov. Park 45

41

40 **Maple Creek**

Cypress Hills Prov. Park

13

42

Eastend

Carlyle

39

Weyburn

Fort Walsh Nat. Historic Park

Val Marie

43

Grasslands National Park

CANADA
U.S.A.

Estevan 44

9

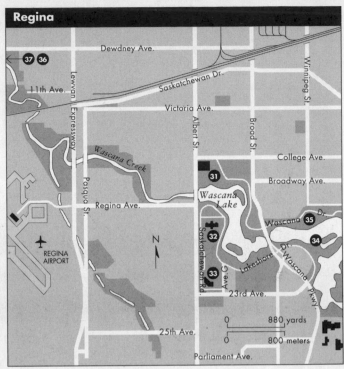

and follow it north to Dewdney Avenue, where you turn left toward the **Government House Heritage Property** ㊱, once the residence of Saskatchewan's lieutenant governors. Continue west on Dewdney Avenue to the **Royal Canadian Mounted Police Depot Division** ㊲, the Mounties' national training center.

TIMING

The tour takes most of the day if you spend some time at each site.

Sights to See

㊱ **Government House Heritage Property.** Between 1891 and 1945 this was the lavish home of Saskatchewan's lieutenant governors. It now serves as the office of the lieutenant governor, and has been restored with period furnishings and mementos of the governors and their families. There are 6 acres of landscaped grounds, and a Victorian tearoom is open on selected weekends; phone ahead. ⊠ *4607 Dewdney Ave.,* ☎ *306/787–5773,* WEB *www.tourismregina.com/government_house.html.* 🎫 *Free.* ☉ *Late May–Labor Day, Tues.–Sun. 10–4; early Sept.–late May, Tues.–Sun. 1–4.*

㊳ **Legislative Building.** Dominating the skyline of the provincial capital is the dome of this quasi-Versailles–style structure. "The Ledge" was built from 1908 to 1912, with Tyndall stone from Manitoba on the exterior and 34 types of marble from all over the world in the interior. As you tour the Legislative Assembly Chamber, note the huge picture of Queen Elizabeth. Tours leave on the half hour. ⊠ *Legislature Dr.,* ☎ *306/787–5357.* 🎫 *Free.* ☉ *Mid-May–Labor Day, daily 8 AM–9 PM; early Sept.–mid-May, daily 8–5.*

㊳ **MacKenzie Art Gallery.** The museum displays 19th- and 20th-century European art and Canadian historical and contemporary works, with a special emphasis on western Canadian art. The popular Prairie Artists

Series allows emerging Saskatchewan artists to display recent work. For three nights a week in July, a stage becomes the courtroom setting for the production of *The Trial of Louis Riel* ($12 for tickets). Riel led rebellions of the Métis against the new Canadian government in the 1870s and 1880s and was tried in Regina, and ultimately hanged, for treason. ⊠ *3475 Albert St.,* ☎ *306/522–4242,* WEB *www.mackenzieartgallery.sk.ca.* ⊠ *Free.* ☉ *Fri.–Tues. 11–6, Wed.–Thurs. 11–10.*

★ ③⑦ **Royal Canadian Mounted Police Depot Division.** At the Mounties' only training center, you can tour the grounds and the nondenominational RCMP Chapel, a converted cookhouse originally built in 1883 and considered Regina's oldest existing building. On the grounds is the **Centennial Museum,** which has exhibits and mementos of the Mounties (originally the North West Mounted Police). The order's proud history is revealed in weaponry, uniforms, photos, and oddities such as Sitting Bull's rifle case and tobacco pouch. ⊠ *11th Ave. W,* ☎ *306/780–5838,* WEB *www.rcmpmuseum.com.* ⊠ *Donations welcome.* ☉ *June–mid-Sept., daily 8–6:45; mid-Sept.–May, daily 10–4:45.*

③ ③① **Royal Saskatchewan Museum.** Here a time line traces local history from before the dinosaur era to today. The Earth Sciences Gallery depicts 2 billion years of Saskatchewan geological history, and the First Nations Gallery highlights aspects of the life and history of Saskatchewan's native peoples. ⊠ *College Ave. and Albert St.,* ☎ *306/787–2815.* ⊠ *Free.* ☉ *May–Labor Day, daily 9–5:30; early Sept.–Apr., daily 9–4:30.*

③ ③⑤ **Saskatchewan Science Centre.** Housed in the refurbished City of Regina powerhouse, the museum has more than 100 hands-on exhibits that encourage visitors to build bubbles and hot-air balloons, make voice prints, and take apart models of human bodies. Demonstrations of biological, geological, and astronomical phenomena begin on the hour. The Kramer IMAX Theatre shows educational films several times daily on a five-story screen. ⊠ *Winnipeg St. and Wascana Dr.,* ☎ *306/522–4629 or 800/667–6300.* ⊠ *$6.50; $11.25 with IMAX.* ☉ *May–Labor Day, daily 9–6; early Sept.–Apr., 9–5.*

③④ **Wascana Waterfowl Park Display Ponds.** At this serene, beautiful park, a boardwalk constructed over a marsh has display panels that identify the more than 60 breeds of migratory waterfowl found here. ⊠ *Lakeshore Dr.,* ☎ *306/522–3661.* ⊠ *Free.* ☉ *Daily 9–9; guided tour, if there's a group, June–Sept., daily at 3.*

Dining

$$–$$$$ ✕ **The Diplomat.** One of Regina's most elegant restaurants is this upscale, traditional steak house in an old brick building downtown. The decor suggests the Victorian era, with paintings of Canada's prime ministers on the walls and dusty-rose cloths and candles on the tables. The Diplomat offers an extensive selection of seafood and steaks and an outstanding rack of lamb, as well as a high-quality wine list. ⊠ *2302 Broad St.,* ☎ *306/359–3366. Reservations essential. AE, D, MC, V.*

$–$$$ ✕ **Danbry's Contemporary Cuisine.** In the center of downtown, this restaurant in the historic Assiniboia Club building serves up a variety of well-prepared Continental fares, including lamb, duck, steak, and seafood. Its reputation is also due to the extensive selection of Scotches, cognacs, and vintage ports, which you can sip as you try Dominican and Cuban cigars. For intimate dining, you can request one of the small dining rooms. ⊠ *1925 Victoria Ave.,* ☎ *306/525–8777. AE, MC, V.*

$–$$$ ✕ **Mediterranean Bistro.** Adam Sperling is a Cordon Bleu chef who specializes in French cuisine and fresh seafood, which can include the likes of Hawaiian tuna or marlin. Desserts change daily and include several warm offerings. The bistro often is mentioned as one of Canada's finest restaurants. ⊠ *2589 Quance St. E,* ☎ *306/757–1666. AE, DC, MC, V.*

$$ ✕ **Harvest Eating House.** There's no shortage of antiques in this family restaurant with an old-time prairie theme. Among the hearty traditional specialties are tasty prime rib and an assortment of seafood, including lobster tail. ⊠ *379 Albert St.,* ☎ *306/545–3777. AE, D, MC, V.*

$–$$ ✕ **Bartleby's.** This good-time downtown "dining emporium and gathering place" is a veritable museum of western memorabilia, musical instruments, and old-time carnival games. Victorian lamp shades and heavy leather armchairs further convey the whimsical tone. Karaoke at night adds a bit of fun, as do medieval feasts. The menu of party-time fare runs to big sandwiches and western beef, especially prime rib. ⊠ *1920 Broad St.,* ☎ *306/565–0040. Reservations essential. AE, DC, MC, V.*

$ ✕ **Brewsters.** The copper kettle and shiny fermentation tanks are proudly prominent in Saskatchewan's first brew pub. This full-mash brewery has 11 in-house concoctions on tap, as well as a large selection of imports and domestic beers, wine, and spirits. The menu consists largely of casual fare, including pasta dishes and burgers, though some more-elaborate options are available, too. ⊠ *Victoria East Plaza, 1832 Victoria Ave. E,* ☎ *306/761–2126;* ⊠ *480 McCarthy Blvd. N,* ☎ *306/522-2739. Reservations not accepted. AE, MC, V.*

$ ✕ **Simply Delicious.** Everything is homemade in this small country-style café. Offerings include cinnamon buns, fresh pies, chicken-noodle and vegetable soups, several salads, and specialty coffees. ⊠ *826 Victoria Ave.,* ☎ *306/352–4929. Reservations not accepted. No credit cards. No dinner.*

Lodging

$$$–$$$$ 🖬 **Radisson Plaza Hotel Saskatchewan.** This former railroad hotel built in 1927 has old-time charm and up-to-date facilities that make it the city's most luxurious lodging. High-ceiling rooms are decorated in an early 1930s style, with lots of wood and lace curtains. For a light lunch or evening cocktails you can visit the cozy and casually elegant Monarch Lounge; the Cortlandt Hall Dining Room offers fine dining. ⊠ *2125 Victoria Ave., S4P 0S3,* ☎ *306/522–7691 or 800/333–3333,* FAX *306/757–5521,* WEB *www.hotelsask.com. 191 rooms, 26 suites. 2 restaurants, bar, no-smoking rooms, health club, parking. AE, DC, MC, V.*

$$ 🖬 **Delta Regina Hotel.** The tallest building in Saskatchewan, this hotel rises 25 stories and is attached to the Saskatchewan Trade and Convention Centre. Rooms are done in subtle pastels. The indoor pool has a three-story water slide. ⊠ *1919 Saskatchewan Dr., S4P 4H2,* ☎ *306/ 525–5255 or 800/268–1133,* FAX *306/781–7188,* WEB *www.deltahotels.com. 248 rooms, 7 suites. 2 restaurants, bar, no-smoking rooms, indoor pool, parking. AE, DC, MC, V.*

$$ 🖬 **Ramada Hotel and Convention Centre.** This modern downtown
★   property has a dramatic, multilevel, sun-filled lobby enhanced by abundant foliage and a charming waterfall. A second-floor oasis is the perfect setting for a soothing soak in the whirlpool or a dip in the kids' or standard pool. The modern rooms are airy and furnished in light colors and dusty-rose tones. Business-class rooms are available on the 14th and 15th floors. ⊠ *1818 Victoria Ave., S4P 0R1,* ☎ *306/569– 1666 or 800/667–6500,* FAX *306/525–3550,* WEB *www.ramada.ca. 237 rooms, 14 suites. 2 restaurants, bar, pub, 2 indoor pools, sauna, parking. AE, DC, MC, V.*

$$ 🖬 **Regina Inn Hotel.** A plant-filled lobby welcomes you into this modern downtown hotel. Rooms on the 10th floor and higher each have one queen-size bed; all rooms have balconies overlooking Broad or Victoria street. Reflections Lounge, on the ground floor, is a local hot spot.

Applause Feast & Folly, a dinner theater, is downstairs in the Catalina Theatre. ⊠ *1975 Broad St., at Victoria Ave., S4P 1Y2,* ☎ *306/525–6767 or 800/667–8162,* FAX *306/352–1858,* WEB *www.reginainn.com. 230 rooms, 5 suites. 2 restaurants, bar, 2 outdoor hot tubs, gym, nightclub, parking. AE, DC, MC, V.*

$–$$ 🛏 **Regina Travelodge Hotel.** The hotel's location, on Regina's main thoroughfare and close to a shopping mall, is its biggest draw. Another plus is the well-known water-slide complex on the property. In the evenings, the Blarney Stone Irish Pub is a cheerful place to grab a beer or soda. ⊠ *4177 Albert St., S4S 3R6,* ☎ *306/586–3443 or 800/578–7878,* FAX *306/586–9311,* WEB *www.travelodge.com. 193 rooms, 7 suites. Restaurant, pub, indoor pool, hot tub, parking. AE, DC, MC, V.*

$ 🛏 **Executive West Harvest Inn.** This five-story, brick 1960s-vintage hotel is dependable. The average-size rooms have low-key beige-patterned drapes and spreads and modern, dark-cherry furniture. ⊠ *4025 Albert St. (Rte. 6), S4S 3R6,* ☎ *306/586–6755 or 800/853–1181,* FAX *306/ 584–1345. 103 rooms, 2 suites. Restaurant, bar, 2 hot tubs, sauna, gym, parking. AE, DC, MC, V.*

Nightlife and the Arts

The Arts

MUSIC AND DANCE

The **Saskatchewan Centre of the Arts** (⊠ Wascana Centre, 200 Lakeshore Dr., ☎ 306/565–0404) is the venue for the Regina Symphony Orchestra, pop concerts, dance performances, and Broadway musicals and plays.

THEATER

On a theater-in-the-round stage inside the old City Hall, the **Globe Theatre** (⊠ 1801 Scarth St., ☎ 306/525–9553) offers classic and contemporary works from October through April. **Regina Little Theatre** (⊠ Regina Performing Arts Centre, 1077 Angus St., ☎ 306/352–5535 or 306/543–7292) presents lighthearted original productions.

Nightlife

BARS

Blarney Stone Irish Pub (⊠ 4177 Albert St., ☎ 306/586–7744), in the Travelodge Hotel, offers more than 30 varieties of ale and beer as well as a good selection of single-malt Scotches. Hearty souls can try a Long Island iced tea in the traditional Yard of Ale. The crowd includes office types and twentysomethings. **The Omega Lounge** (⊠ 1919 Saskatchewan Dr., ☎ 306/525–5255), in the Delta Regina Hotel, is where local movers and shakers mingle with visitors from the convention center next door.

MUSIC

JD's Cafe and Nite Spot (⊠ 1055 Park St., ☎ 306/569–2121) is a casual, trendy downtown establishment. **Pump** (⊠ 641 Victoria Ave. E, ☎ 306/522–0977) presents Canadian and American country-and-western bands on a nightly basis.

Outdoor Activities and Sports

Participant Sports

BIKING AND JOGGING

Wascana Place (⊠ 2900 Wascana Dr., ☎ 306/522–3661) has maps of the many jogging, biking, and hiking trails in Wascana Centre. The Devonian Pathway—8 km (5 mi) of paved trails that follow Wascana Creek and pass through six city parks—is a favorite.

The **Regina Sportplex & Lawson Aquatic Centre** (✉ 1717 Elphinstone St., ☎ 306/777–7156 or 306/777–7323) includes a pool and diving well, a 200-m track, tennis and badminton courts, weight rooms, a sauna, and drop-in aerobic and aqua-exercise sessions.

Spectator Sports

CURLING

You can check out this popular local sport played on ice at the **Caledonian Curling Club** (✉ 2225 Empress Rd., near the airport, ☎ 306/525–8171).

FOOTBALL

The **Saskatchewan Roughriders** (☎ 306/525–2181) of the Canadian Football League play at Taylor Field June through November.

HOCKEY

The **Regina Pats** play other Western Hockey League teams in the Agridome (✉ Exhibition Park, Lewvan Expressway and 11th Ave., ☎ 306/522–5604) from September through April.

HORSE RACING

Queensbury Downs (✉ Exhibition Park, Lewvan Dr. and 11th Ave., ☎ 306/781–9310) hosts standardbred racing in summer and televised racing year-round.

Shopping

Cornwall Centre (✉ 11th Ave. and Saskatchewan Dr.), downtown, is an indoor mall with more than 100 shops. It includes department stores the Bay and Sears, as well as restaurants and coffee shops that are frequented by workers from nearby office towers. **Southland Mall** (✉ 2905 Gordon Rd., at Albert St.) is a suburban mall with more than 80 stores. A Chapters bookstore is here, as is a movie theater and Montana's Cookhouse Salloon.

Affinity's Antiques (✉ 1178 Albert St., ☎ 306/757–4265) sells vintage collectibles, including china, glassware, silver jewelry, and clocks as well as some toys. The **Antique Mall** (✉ 1175 Rose St., ☎ 306/525–9688) encompasses 28 antiques, art, and collectibles sellers. **Basket Cases** (✉ 2445 Quance St. E, ☎ 306/352–3916) offers custom-made gift baskets and distinctive home furnishings. **Sarah's Corner** (✉ 1853 Hamilton St., ☎ 306/565–2200) has artwork, a selection of jewelry, small furniture items, and unique home accessories and crafts. At the **Strathdee Shoppes** (✉ Dewdney Ave. and Cornwall St.), you can peruse (and buy) arts, crafts, and antiques, among other goodies. There's also a food court.

Side Trips from Regina

In and around the modern city of Moose Jaw are attractions that give you a feeling for the area's past and present.

Moose Jaw

❸❽ *71 km (44 mi) west of Regina.*

Saskatchewan's fourth-largest city, Moose Jaw is a prosperous railroad and industrial center, renowned as a wide-open Roaring '20s haven for American gangsters. It is said that Al Capone visited here from Chicago. Nineteen murals on buildings in the downtown business district bring the town's rich history to life. Today Moose Jaw's most prominent citizen stands right on the Trans-Canada Highway: Mac the Moose, an immense sculpture that greets travelers from beside the visitor information center.

The **Western Development Museum,** which focuses on air, land, water, and rail transportation, houses the **Snowbirds Gallery,** filled with memorabilia (including vintage airplanes) of Canada's air demonstration team, the Snowbirds, who are stationed at the nearby Armed Forces base. On weekends the Cinema 180 Theatre shows a film about the Snowbirds. ⊠ *50 Diefenbaker Dr.,* ☎ *306/693–6556.* ⊡ *$5; $7.50 including theater.* ⊙ *Apr.–Sept., daily 9–6; Oct.–Mar., Tues.–Sun. 9–6.*

The **Moose Jaw Art Museum** (⊠ Crescent Park, Athabasca St. and Langdon Crescent, ☎ 306/692–4471) displays regional art and small farm implements. While you're here, pick up *A Walking Tour of Downtown Moose Jaw* ($1.50), a guide to notable and notorious landmarks. The museum is open Tuesday through Sunday noon–5 and Tuesday through Thursday 7 PM–9 PM. Admission is by donation. The **Tunnels of Moose Jaw** (☎ 306/693–7273) are a quirky attraction chronicling aspects of the city's history. You can view these tunnels, rumored to have been built by the Chinese in the late 1800s and later supposedly used by Al Capone to smuggle liquor during Prohibition. Tours cost $8 and depart from 18 Main Street North.

The **Temple Gardens Mineral Spa** (⊠ 108 Main St. N, ☎ 306/694–5055 or 800/718–7727), downtown, has naturally heated indoor and outdoor pools supplied by an artesian well 4,500 ft below the Earth's surface. The four-story geothermal spa adjoins a 96-room hotel. Costs for treatments and massages range from about $16 to $70; general admission is $6.95 on weekdays, $8.95 on weekends.

DINING

$ ✕ **The Pilgrim Restaurant.** Offering home-style cooking, the Pilgrim—actually 19 km (12 mi) west of Moose Jaw, in Caronport—has gained a particular reputation for its wide variety of breakfast fare as well as its substantial Sunday brunch and evening smorgasbord. ⊠ *Trans-Canada Hwy., Caronport,* ☎ *306/756–3335. AE, MC, V.*

Pioneer Village and Museum

13 km (8 mi) south of Moose Jaw, 84 km (52 mi) southwest of Regina.

Besides the old buildings and cars at this offbeat museum, you can see the *Sukanen,* a large, unfinished ship made by a Finnish settler between 1928 and 1941 and patterned after a 17th-century Finnish fishing vessel. ⊠ *Hwy. 2,* ☎ *306/693–7315.* ⊡ *$4.* ⊙ *June–Sept., daily 9–5.*

Regina A to Z

AIR TRAVEL TO AND FROM REGINA

Regina Airport is served by Air Canada, WestJet, Northwest Airlines, and several Canadian commuter airlines.

AIRPORTS AND TRANSFERS

Regina Airport is 8 km (5 mi) southwest of downtown. Taxi cabs charge about $7 for the 10- to 15-minute ride.
➤ AIRPORT INFORMATION: **Regina Airport** (⊠ 1–520 Regina Ave., ☎ 306/780–5750).

BUS TRAVEL WITHIN REGINA

Regina Transit's 19 bus routes serve the metropolitan area every day except Sunday. The fare is $1.55.
➤ BUS INFORMATION: **Regina Transit** (☎ 306/777–7433).

CAR TRAVEL

Regina stands at the crossroads of the Trans-Canada Highway (Highway 1) and Highway 11, which goes north to Saskatoon.

EMERGENCIES

Emergency rooms are located at Pasqua Hospital and Regina General Hospital.

The Shopper's Drug Marts branches at Broad Street and 14th Avenue and at Gordon Road and Albert Street are open daily until midnight.
➤ EMERGENCY SERVICES: **Ambulance, fire, police** (☎ 911).
➤ HOSPITALS: **Pasqua Hospital** (✉ 4101 Dewdney Ave., ☎ 306/766–2222). **Regina General Hospital** (✉ 1140 14th Ave., ☎ 306/766–4444).
➤ LATE-NIGHT PHARMACIES: **Shopper's Drug Marts** (✉ Broad St. and 14th Ave., ☎ 306/757–8100; ✉ Gordon Rd. and Albert St., ☎ 306/777–8040) are open daily until midnight.

TAXIS

Taxis are easy to find outside major hotels, or they can be summoned by phone.
➤ TAXI COMPANIES: **Capital Cab** (☎ 306/781–7777). **Co-op Taxis** (☎ 306/586–6555). **Regina Cabs** (☎ 306/543–3333).

TOURS

Classic Carriage Service offers horse-drawn carriage rides around the city in summer and horse-drawn sleigh rides and hayrides around Wascana Centre in winter. The tours accommodate 15 to 20 people and cost $60 to $75 per hour.
➤ FEES AND SCHEDULES: **Classic Carriage Service** (☎ 306/771–4678).

VISITOR INFORMATION

Tourism Regina has an information center on the Trans-Canada Highway (Highway 1) on the eastern approach to the city and is open Victoria Day (late May) through Labor Day, daily 8–6; Labor Day through Victoria Day, weekdays 8:30–4:30. The Tourism Saskatchewan information center is open weekdays 8–5.
➤ TOURIST INFORMATION: **Tourism Regina** (✉ Box 3355, S4P 3H1, ☎ 306/789–5099). **Tourism Saskatchewan** (✉ 500–1900 Albert St., ☎ 306/787–2300).

ELSEWHERE IN SOUTHERN SASKATCHEWAN

Spread across the southern part of the province are varied attractions, including a fossil research station in Eastend, sites that interpret pioneer and First Nations life, and unique natural areas such as Grasslands National Park in Val Marie.

Swift Current

㊴ *174 km (108 mi) west of Regina on the Trans-Canada Highway.*

West of Regina, the square townships and straight roads of the grain-belt prairie farms gradually give way to the arid rolling hills of the upland plains ranches. The Trans-Canada Highway skirts the edge of the Missouri Coteau—glacial hills that divide the prairie from the dry western plain—on its way west to Swift Current (population 16,000). The town cultivates its western image during the Frontier Days Regional Fair and Rodeo in June. The free **Swift Current Museum** (✉ 105 Chaplin St., ☎ 306/778–2775) displays pioneer and First Nations artifacts and exhibits of local natural history, including fossils. The museum is open 10–5 weekdays and 1–5 weekends June through August, weekdays 1:30–4:30 the rest of the year.

Dining and Lodging

$–$$ ✕ **Wong's Kitchen.** A longtime local favorite serves fine Canadian food and an even better Cantonese menu; dry garlic ribs are the star attraction. Count on live country and western entertainment nightly. ✉ *Hwy. 1, S. Service Rd.,* ☎ *306/773–6244. Reservations essential. AE, MC, V.*

$ ☎ **Days Inn.** This chain property is adjacent to the Trans-Canada Highway and between two major shopping malls. The newer rooms have fine views of the surrounding countryside. The cocktail lounge is a popular meeting spot, and the restaurant offers solid Canadian cooking. ✉ *Mobile Rte. 35, S9H 3X6,* ☎ *306/773–4643,* FAX *306/773–0309. 21 rooms, 2 suites. 2 restaurants, bar, pool. AE, DC, MC, V.*

Maple Creek

40 *128 km (79 mi) west of Swift Current, 302 km (187 mi) west of Regina.*

The Trans-Canada Highway borders the southern edge of the Great Sand Hills. These desertlike remnants of a huge glacial lake abound with such native wildlife as pronghorn, mule deer, coyotes, jackrabbits, and kangaroo rats. Maple Creek, a self-styled "old cow town" just south of the Trans-Canada Highway on Route 21, has a number of preserved Old West storefronts. The **Old Timer's Museum** (✉ 218 Jasper St., ☎ 306/662–2474) is Saskatchewan's oldest museum, displays pictures and artifacts of Mounties, early ranchers and locals. Admission is $3; May through September it's open Tuesday through Saturday 9–5:30 and weekends 1–5 (by appointment the rest of the year).

Cypress Hills Provincial Park

41 *27 km (17 mi) south of Maple Creek, 330 km (205 mi) west of Regina.*

Cypress Hills Provincial Park consists of two sections, a Centre Block and a West Block, which are about 25 km (16 mi) apart and separated by nonpark land. The larger West Block abuts the border with Alberta and is connected to Alberta's Cypress Hills Provincial Park. Within the Centre Block, the Cypress Hills plateau, rising more than 4,000 ft above sea level, is covered with spruce, aspen, and lodgepole pines erroneously identified as cypress by early European explorers. From Lookout Point you have an 80-km (50-mi) view of Maple Creek and the hills beyond. Maps are available at the Administrative Building near the park entrance in the Centre Block. ✉ *Rte. 21,* ☎ *306/662–4411.* ☜ *$6 per day per car.*

In the West Block of Cypress Hills Provincial Park is **Fort Walsh National Historic Park.** The original fort was built by the Mounties in 1875 to establish order between the "wolfers" (whiskey traders) and the Assiniboine. Fort Walsh remained the center of local commerce until its abandonment in 1883. Today, bus service links the Visitor Reception Centre and the reconstructed fort itself, Farwell's Trading Post, and a picnic area. Private vehicles are not permitted beyond the parking area. A rough gravel road connects the Cypress Hills Centre Block plateau with the West Block plateau. In wet weather, take Route 271 southwest from Maple Creek to the West Block. ✉ *Rte. 271, 55 km (34 mi) southwest of Maple Creek,* ☎ *306/662–2645.* ☜ *$6, includes bus trip and tour.* ☉ *Mid-May–mid-Oct., daily 9–5.*

Lodging

$ ☎ **Cypress Four Seasons Resort.** This resort in the Centre Block of Cypress Hills Provincial Park is in a lodgepole-pine forest. Comfortable contemporary rooms are done in pastels or earth tones. The woodsy restaurant has picture windows that overlook the forest; the standard Canadian fare is more successful than the Chinese dishes. Note that this resort is not part of the Four Seasons chain. ⊠ *Hwy. 21 (Box 1480, Maple Creek S0N 1N0),* ☎ *306/662–4477,* FAX *306/662–3238. 31 rooms, 15 cabins, 10 condos. Restaurant, bar, indoor pool. MC, V.*

Eastend

42 *120 km (74 mi) east of Cypress Hills Provincial Park on Route 13, 360 km (223 mi) southwest of Regina.*

In 1994, in this tiny Frenchman River valley town, paleontologists found one of only a dozen Tyrannosaurus rex fossils unearthed thus far anywhere in the world. The T-rex, believed to be 65 million years old, is one of a number of fossils discovered in the area. You can visit an operational laboratory, the **T-Rex Discovery Center** (⊠ 118 Maple Ave. S, ☎ 306/295–4009, WEB www.dinocountry.com), where paleontologists are working on the T-rex fossil. Admission for the center, which has a viewing area and is open weekdays 9–5 (closed for lunch) and weekends 11–5, is $3. The **Eastend Tourism Authority** (☎ 306/295–4144) has information about trips on which you can dig for fossils.

Val Marie

43 *152 km (94 mi) south of Swift Current, 375 km (233 mi) southwest of Regina.*

Val Marie is home to the information center for a unique national park. The 1,554-square-km (600-square-mi) **Grasslands National Park,** between Val Marie and Killdeer in southwestern Saskatchewan, preserves an unusual landscape. The Frenchman River valley, part of which is within Grasslands, was the first portion of mixed-grass prairie in North America to be set aside as a park and is marked by strange land formations and badlands. Colonies of black-tailed prairie dogs are the most numerous of the animals here. Interpretive and visitor services are limited, although there are daily guided hikes during July and August. Tent camping is permitted, and electrical hookups are provided; all sites cost $10 per night. ⊠ *Off Hwys. 4 and 18,* ☎ *306/298–2257.* ☉ *Park office June–Aug., daily 8–5; Sept.–May, weekdays 8–4:30. Information center in Val Marie, late May–early Sept., daily 8–6.*

Estevan

44 *205 km (127 mi) southeast of Regina via Route 39.*

Estevan, within 16 km (10 mi) of the U.S. border, has a rich history dating back to Prohibition days in the United States, when rum-running was popular here. In summer the town hosts popular stage plays in an outdoor tent setting. You can tour nearby megaprojects like the Rafferty and Boundary dams, or take an Energy Tour, which includes visits to area coal mines. An ideal place to picnic is the Estevan Brick Wildlife Display, a 70-acre compound on the south edge of the city where bison, deer, and antelope roam freely. **Estevan Tourism** (☎ 306/634–6044) can provide information about the town and area activities.

Moose Mountain Provincial Park

45 *220 km (136 mi) southeast of Regina via Highway 1 and Route 9.*

Moose Mountain Provincial Park is 401 square km (155 square mi) of rolling poplar and birch forest that forms a natural refuge for moose and elk and a wide variety of birds. A 24-km (15-mi) gravel road leads in to moose and elk grazing areas (best times are early morning and early evening). You can vary the wildlife experiences with beaches, golf, tennis, and horseback riding. One-third of the 330 campsites have electric hookups. The **Kenosee Inn** (✉ Kenosee Village, off Rte. 9, ☎ 306/577–2099) is a 30-room accommodation on the park grounds. ✉ *Rte. 9,* ☎ *306/577–2131; 306/577–2144 for camping reservations.* 💵 *$6 per day per car; camping $14 per night with electricity, $12 without.*

SASKATOON

Saskatchewan's largest city is Saskatoon (population 229,000), nicknamed City of Bridges because it has seven spans across the South Saskatchewan River, which cuts the city in half diagonally. It's considered one of the most beautiful of Canada's midsize cities, in part because a zealous protectionist campaign has allowed the riverbanks to flourish largely in their natural state.

Saskatoon was founded in 1882 when a group of Ontario Methodists was granted 200,000 acres to form a temperance colony. Teetotaling Methodists controlled only half the land, however, and eventually the influence of those who controlled the other half turned the town wet. The coming of the railroad in 1890 made it the major regional transportation hub, but during the 20th century it became known for its three major resources: potash, oil, and wheat. Saskatoon today is the high-tech hub of Saskatchewan's agricultural industry and is also home to the University of Saskatchewan—a major presence in all aspects of local life. The city has a rich cultural life, including a thriving theater scene.

Exploring Saskatoon

Reasonably compact for a western city, Saskatoon proper is easily accessible to drivers and cyclists. Idylwyld Drive divides the city into east and west; 22nd Street divides the city into north and south. The downtown area and Spadina Crescent are on the west side of the South Saskatchewan River.

A Good Drive

Begin exploring at **Meewasin Valley Centre** ㊻, which traces Saskatoon history back to temperance-colony days. Follow Spadina Crescent north along the river to the **Ukrainian Museum of Canada** ㊼. Just north of the museum is **Kinsmen Park** ㊽, with riverside amusements. From Spadina Crescent, head east over the river on the University Bridge to the picturesque **University of Saskatchewan** ㊾ campus. You can detour into the northeastern part of the city, to the **Saskatoon Zoo Forestry Farm Park** ㊿, to see animals and hike. Return to the university campus, head west on College Drive, and then pick up University Drive, lined with grand old houses. University Drive eventually joins Broadway Avenue, the city's oldest business district. Follow Broadway Avenue south to 8th Street; head west to Lorne Avenue and then south to the **Western Development Museum** (51), on the **Saskatoon Prairieland Exhibition Grounds** (52), to see a re-creation of a 1910 boomtown. To return to downtown Saskatoon, take the scenic route: head north a short way on Lorne Avenue, then west on Ruth Street to the river. Follow St. Henry Avenue, Taylor Street, Herman Avenue, and Saskatchewan Crescent past the fine old homes that overlook one of the prettier stretches of the South Saskatchewan River. Cross over the 19th Street Bridge.

TIMING

By car this tour can easily be done without stops in a morning or afternoon. If you want to explore museums or hike, leave more time.

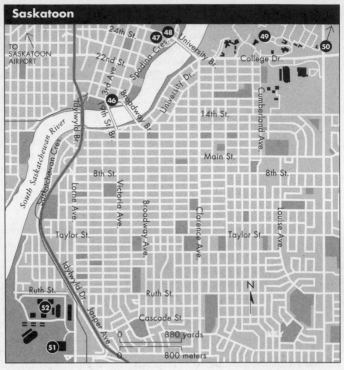

Saskatoon

Sights to See

48 Kinsmen Park. This riverside amusement park includes a children's play village, a merry-go-round, a miniature Ferris wheel, a train, and a paddling pool. ✉ *Spadina Crescent and 25th St.,* ☎ *306/975-3300.* 🖼 *Free; 50¢ for each ride.* ☉ *Late May–Labor Day daily 2–5 and 5:30–9.*

46 Meewasin Valley Centre. The small museum traces Saskatoon history back to the city's beginnings as a Methodist temperance colony. Meewasin is Cree for "beautiful valley," and this is a fitting place to embark upon the **Meewasin Valley Trail,** a 19-km (12-mi) biking and hiking trail along the South Saskatchewan River. ✉ *402 3rd Ave. S,* ☎ *306/665-6888.* 🖼 *Free.* ☉ *Weekdays 9–5, weekends 10:30–5.*

52 Saskatoon Prairieland Exhibition Grounds. A vast plot encompasses the Emerald Casino; space for agricultural shows, rodeos, and horse races; and the ☞ **Western Development Museum.** ✉ *Ruth St. and Lorne Ave.,* ☎ *306/931-7149.*

50 Saskatoon Zoo Forestry Farm Park. More than 300 animals live in the zoo, which focuses on species native to North America, such as deer, wolf, bear, coyote, and fox. The park offers barbecue areas, nature displays, cross-country ski trails, fishing, and sports fields, as well as train rides. ✉ *1903 Forest Rd., off Attridge Dr.,* ☎ *306/975-3382.* 🖼 *May–Labor Day $4.50, early Sept.–Apr. free; vehicle charge $2.* ☉ *May–Labor Day, daily 9–9; early Sept.–Apr., daily 10–4.*

47 Ukrainian Museum of Canada. Through photos, costumes, textiles, and, of course, the famous *pysanky* (Easter eggs), this collection celebrates the rich history of the Ukrainian people who make up 10% of Saskatchewan's population. ✉ *910 Spadina Crescent E,* ☎ *306/244-3800.* 🖼 *$2.* ☉ *July–Aug., Mon.–Sat. 10–5, Sun. 1–5; Sept.–June, Tues.–Sat. 10–5, Sun. 1–5.*

㊾ **University of Saskatchewan.** The parklike riverside campus, among the most picturesque in Canada, occupies a 2,550-acre site on the east bank of the river. The university grounds contain several museums and galleries (all free), including the **Natural Sciences Museum,** the **Little Stone School House,** the **Museum of Antiquities,** the **Biology Museum,** and the **Gordon Snelgrove Gallery.** A highlight is the **Diefenbaker Canada Centre,** a museum, art gallery, and research center in Canadian studies, commemorating Canada's 13th prime minister. The center explores John Diefenbaker's life and times. Two replica rooms represent the Privy Council Chamber and the prime minister's Ottawa office, where he served in the late 1950s and early 1960s. ✉ *Diefenbaker Canada Centre, 101 Diefenbaker Point,* ☏ *306/966–8384.* 🎫 *$2.* 🕘 *Mon. and Fri. 9:30–4:30, Tues.–Thurs. 9:30–8, weekends 12:30–5.*

(51) **Western Development Museum.** One of four such museums in Saskatchewan, the Saskatoon branch is called 1910 Boomtown and re-creates early 20th-century life in western Canada. ✉ *2610 Lorne Ave. S,* ☏ *306/931–1910.* 🎫 *$6.* 🕘 *Daily 9–5.*

Dining

$$–$$$$ ✕ **Samurai Japanese Steak House.** Asian cooking has caught on in a big way in Saskatoon. Excellent food, a tranquil atmosphere, and sheer showmanship are highlights here, and the chef's table-top preparation is a favorite. This restaurant in the Delta Bessborough serves not only steak but also vegetarian stir-fries. ✉ *601 Spadina Crescent E,* ☏ *306/683–6926 or 306/244–5521. AE, DC, MC, V.*

$$ ✕ **R. J. Willoughby's.** Stands of bamboo and other foliage enhance the pink-and-green color scheme of the Quality Hotel's main dining room. Menu highlights are Continental entrées plus theme evenings with specialty buffets (prime rib on Wednesday, pasta on Friday, seafood on Sunday). The wine list is among the city's finest. The very popular Sunday brunch has an impressive array of selections, including custom-made omelets and flambéed fruit. ✉ *90 22nd St. E,* ☏ *306/665–7576. Reservations essential. AE, DC, MC, V.*

$–$$ ✕ **Lydia's.** This neighborhood pub presents a wide selection of international beers and has a full menu, including beef and chicken kebabs as well as Cajun chicken, Caesar salad, and a variety of pasta dishes. There's live music every weekend. ✉ *650 Broadway Ave.,* ☏ *306/652–8595. DC, MC, V.*

$–$$ ✕ **Genesis Family Restaurant.** You can have vegetable and fruit juices freshly squeezed to order at this eatery with a strong emphasis on health foods. Macrobiotic and vegetarian dishes are available, as well as authentic Chinese food, including a popular dim sum lunch. ✉ *901 2nd St. W,* ☏ *306/244–5516. AE, MC, V.*

$–$$ ✕ **Saskatoon Station Place.** The station is not old, but the vintage railroad cars and decorative antiques are authentic and fascinating. The newspaper-style menu headlines Canadian prime rib and steaks, seafood, and Greek specialties, such as Greek ribs and souvlaki. ✉ *221 Idylwyld Dr. N,* ☏ *306/244–7777. Reservations essential. AE, MC, V.*

$ ✕ **Taunte Maria's.** Hearty soups, huge farmer's sausages, potato salad, homemade bread, and noodles steeped in gravy are served up at this Mennonite restaurant. The decor, too, reflects the Mennonite tradition: simple, functional, and comfortable. The Ho-Ho Cake (chocolate cake with cream filling and chocolate icing) and the bread pudding with ice cream are worth saving room for. ✉ *212–2750 Faithful Ave., at 51st St.,* ☏ *306/931–3212. Reservations not accepted. MC, V. Closed Sun.*

Lodging

$$$ ⊞ **Radisson Hotel Saskatoon.** One of Saskatoon's newer luxury properties has a prime riverfront location downtown and 19 floors of classically styled rooms. Guest rooms are large, and the peach, gray, and pastel colors make them bright and airy; some rooms have river views. The elaborate Waterworks Recreation Complex has an indoor pool, a whirlpool, a sauna, and two three-story water slides. ✉ *405 20th St. E, S7K 6X6,* ☎ *306/665–3322 or 800/333–3333,* FAX *306/665–5531,* WEB *www.radisson.com. 277 rooms, 14 suites. Restaurant, bar, in-room data ports, no-smoking rooms, indoor pool, sauna, health club, dry cleaning, business services, meeting rooms, parking. AE, DC, MC, V.*

$$$ ⊞ **Sheraton Cavalier.** Opposite Kiwanis Park downtown, this eight-story property has unusually large rooms that face the city or the river, and an elaborate water-sports complex. Carver's Steak House is the place for elegant dining; the Majestic Grillé is less formal and has a view of the river from every table. Smokers will appreciate Hampton's cigar lounge. ✉ *612 Spadina Crescent E, S7K 3G9,* ☎ *306/652–6770 or 800/325–3535,* FAX *306/244–1739,* WEB *www.sheraton.com. 237 rooms, 12 suites. 2 restaurants, pub, in-room data ports, no-smoking rooms, 2 indoor pools, sauna, gym, dry cleaning, laundry service, concierge, meeting rooms, parking. AE, DC, MC, V.*

$$–$$$ ⊞ **Delta Bessborough.** Saskatoon's majestic old stone landmark, opened
★   in 1935, looks like a castle, complete with gargoyles, and dominates the skyline from its riverfront setting. The hotel has been upgraded with modern amenities, but it retains its grand details. Rooms differ in size; all have traditional furniture. The Samurai Japanese Steak House is excellent. ✉ *601 Spadina Crescent E, S7K 3G8,* ☎ *306/244–5521 or 800/268–1133,* FAX *306/653–2458,* WEB *www.deltahotels.com. 225 rooms, 10 suites. 2 restaurants, 2 bars, lobby lounge, in-room data ports, no-smoking rooms, indoor pool, hair salon, sauna, gym, dry cleaning, laundry service, parking. AE, DC, MC, V.*

$ ⊞ **Quality Hotel Downtown.** Across from Midtown Plaza shopping and Centennial Auditorium, the 15-story Quality Hotel offers some splendid views of the city. Standard rooms are quite spacious with fairly conservative, though pleasant enough, decor. ✉ *90 22nd St. E, S7K 3X6,* ☎ *306/244–2311,* FAX *306/664–2234. 277 rooms, 14 suites. Restaurant, bar, in-room data ports, indoor pool, laundry service, parking (fee). AE, MC.*

$ ⊞ **Saskatoon Travelodge Hotel.** A sprawling property near the airport has two flora-filled indoor pool complexes, and a water slide. Rooms vary in size, and many have balconies overlooking the pool; the executive-style rooms are large, with king-size beds and works areas with desks. The Gardens Terrace Restaurant has informal poolside dining. ✉ *106 Circle Dr. W, S7L 4L6,* ☎ *306/242–8881 or 800/578–7878,* FAX *306/665–7378,* WEB *www.travelodge.com. 269 rooms, 16 suites. 2 restaurants, 2 bars, in-room data ports, no-smoking rooms, 2 indoor pools, sauna, gym, business services, free parking. AE, DC, MC, V.*

$ ⊞ **Colonial Square Motel.** This pink-stucco, two-story motel is east of the river, along a fast-food strip. Rooms are furnished in pastel colors and have two queen-size beds or a double bed plus a pullout sofa. Across the parking lot is the Venice Pizza House and Lounge. ✉ *1301 8th St. E, S7H 0S7,* ☎ *306/343–1676 or 800/667–3939,* FAX *306/956–1313,* WEB *www.colonialsquaremotel.com. 62 rooms, 17 suites. Restaurant, bar, no-smoking rooms, dry cleaning, laundry service, meeting room, free parking. AE, MC, V.*

$ ⊞ **Patricia Hotel.** In the center of downtown, this older hotel is appealing if you're looking for a bargain. Five rooms are also available as a youth hostel ($12). The Karz Kafe and a lounge are on the premises. ✉ *345*

2nd Ave. N, ☎ 306/242–8861, FAX 306/242–8861. 45 rooms. Restaurant, bar, free parking. MC, V.

Nightlife and the Arts

The Arts

MUSIC AND DANCE

The **Mendel Art Gallery** (✉ 950 Spadina Crescent E, ☎ 306/975–7610) has a regular concert program. When the city symphony isn't in concert, the 2,003-seat **Saskatoon Centennial Auditorium** (✉ 35 22nd St. E, ☎ 306/975–7777) hosts ballet, rock and pop concerts, comedians, musical comedies, and opera. The **Saskatoon Jazz Society** performs in the Bassment (✉ 245 3rd Ave. S, ☎ 306/683–2277), its permanent space. The **Saskatoon Symphony** (☎ 306/665–6414) performs October through April at the Saskatoon Centennial Auditorium. From late June to early July Saskatoon hosts the popular **SaskTel Saskatchewan Jazz Festival** (☎ 306/652–1421); jazz musicians from around the world play more than 125 performances throughout the city.

THEATER

Gateway Players (✉ 709 Cumberland St., ☎ 306/653–1200) presents five productions from October through April. **Persephone Theatre** (✉ 2802 Rusholme Rd., ☎ 306/384–7727) stages six plays and musicals a year. **Saskatoon Soaps** has weekly midnight improvisational comedy at the Broadway Theatre (✉ 715 Broadway Ave., ☎ 306/652–6556). A summer tradition, **Shakespeare on the Saskatchewan** (☎ 306/653–2300) is staged in a riverside tent during July and August. Saskatoon's oldest professional theater, **25th Street Theatre Centre** (✉ 616 10th St. E, ☎ 306/664–2239) produces mostly works by Saskatchewan playwrights, as well as the Saskatoon International Fringe Festival every summer.

Nightlife

BARS AND CLUBS

Amigos (✉ 632 10th St. E, ☎ 306/652–4912) is a rock hangout. **The Black Duck Freehouse** (✉ 154 2nd Ave. S, ☎ 306/244–8850) isn't fancy but offers a lively atmosphere, often with a rather diverse crowd. The setting suggests a rural British pub complete with a selection of single-malt Scotch and draft beers. Top rock groups perform at **Bud's on Broadway** (✉ 817 Broadway Ave., ☎ 306/244–4155). You can practice your swing indoors at **Caddy's Golf Club** (✉ 705 Central Ave., ☎ 306/343–2100), which offers the unique combination of a bar with golf simulators. Saskatoon's businesspeople mingle with traveling executives at **Caper's Lounge** (✉ 405 20th St. E, ☎ 306/665–3322), in the Radisson Hotel Saskatoon.

Outdoor Activities and Sports

Participant Sports

BIKING AND JOGGING

The **Meewasin Valley Trail** (☎ 306/665–6888) is a gorgeous 19-km (12-mi) biking and jogging trail along both banks of the South Saskatchewan River in Saskatoon.

HEALTH AND FITNESS CLUBS

The **Riverraquet Athletic Club** (✉ 322 Saguenay Dr., ☎ 306/242–0010) has racquetball and squash courts, a weight room, aerobics classes, miniature golf, and beach volleyball in summer. The **Saskatoon Field House** (✉ University of Saskatchewan, 2020 College Dr., ☎ 306/975–3354) has tennis courts, a weight room, a gymnastics area, an indoor track, a fitness dance area, and drop-in fitness classes.

Spectator Sports

HOCKEY

The Western Hockey League's **Saskatoon Blades** play major junior hockey at Saskatchewan Place (⊠ 3515 Thatcher Ave., ☎ 306/938–7800) from September through March.

HORSE RACING

Marquis Downs Racetrack (⊠ Prairieland Exhibition Centre, enter on Ruth St., ☎ 306/242–6100) has thoroughbred racing from early May through mid-October.

Shopping

Malls and Shopping Districts

If you enjoy funkier, smaller boutiques and restaurants, head to **Broadway Avenue** (⊠ between 8th and 12th Sts. east of river), the city's oldest business district and the location of more than 150 shops and restaurants as well as a cinema. The **Midtown Plaza** mall (⊠ 22nd St. and 1st Ave., ☎ 306/652–9366) has 140 stores, including such well-know chains as The Gap and Eddie Bauer. **Scotia Centre Mall** (⊠ 123 2nd Ave., ☎ 306/665–6120) includes several unique men's and women's clothing stores as well as the popular 2nd Avenue Grill (☎ 306/244–9899).

Specialty Stores

Local crafts, including pottery, woodworking, and weaving, are available at **Handmade House** (⊠ 710 Broadway Ave., ☎ 306/665–5542). The **Homespun Craft Emporium** (⊠ 16–1724 Quebec Ave., ☎ 306/652–3585) specializes in quilting, offering fabrics as well as classes, but also has a variety of crafts materials. The **Trading Post** (⊠ 226 2nd Ave. S, ☎ 306/653–1769) carries First Nations crafts and Canadian foodstuffs—including Saskatoon berry products.

Side Trips from Saskatoon

Day trips to a number of sights outside the city can provide an understanding of native and frontier life, including the heritage of the Métis. Prince Albert National Park may be a bit far for a day trip but it's well worth an overnight stay.

Wanuskewin Heritage Park

★ ❸ *5 km (3 mi) north of Saskatoon.*

The park portrays 6,000 years of Northern Plains native culture. The Interpretive Centre has an archaeological laboratory, displays, films, and hands-on activities. Outside, walking trails take you to archaeological sites, including a medicine wheel, tepee rings, bison kills, habitation sites, and stone cairns. ⊠ *Off Hwy. 11,* ☎ *306/931–6767.* 🖃 *$6.* ☉ *June–Labor Day, daily 9–9; early Sept.–May, daily 9–5.*

Batoche

❺ *100 km (62 mi) northeast of Saskatoon.*

★ This small town is most notable for its historical significance. **Batoche National Historic Site** is a center of Métis' heritage. It was here that the Métis under Louis Riel fought and lost their last battle against the Canadian militia in 1885. The large historical park includes a visitor center, displays, a historic church and rectory, and walking trails that take you by many of the battle sites. ⊠ *Off Hwy. 11, follow signs,* ☎ *306/423–6227.* 🖃 *$4.* ☉ *Daily 9–5.*

Duck Lake

⑤⑤ *20 km (12 mi) north of Batoche, 120 km (74 mi) north of Saskatoon.*

Duck Lake, which lies along Highway 11 between the North and South Saskatchewan rivers, has a number of buildings decorated with life-size murals depicting the area's history, including the 1885 Northwest Rebellion.

The **Regional Interpretive Centre** has more than 2,000 artifacts from the period of the Métis' last rebellion. ⊠ *Hwy. 11,* ☎ *306/467–2057.* ⊠ *$4.* ⊙ *Mid-May–Labor Day, daily 10–5:30; early Sept.–mid-May, by appointment.*

OFF THE
BEATEN PATH

FORT CARLTON PROVINCIAL HISTORIC PARK – This site, 24 km (15 mi) west of Duck Lake, has a reconstructed stockade and buildings from the mid-1800s fur-trade days. The displays include three tepees depicting Plains Cree culture and a replica of a former Hudson's Bay store. ⊠ *Rte. 212,* ☎ *306/467–5205.* ⊠ *$2.50.* ⊙ *Mid-May–Labor Day, daily 10– 5:30.*

Prince Albert

⑤⑥ *141 km (87 mi) north of Saskatoon on Highway 11 and Route 2.*

Prince Albert is Saskatchewan's third-largest city (population 41,000), the center of the lumber industry, and the self-proclaimed "Gateway to the North." The prosperous modern city straddles the North Saskatchewan River; its most interesting attractions are downtown.

The **Prince Albert Historical Museum,** in the old Fire Hall, is mostly devoted to the fur-trade era and includes the first fire-engine pumper used in the Territories. You also can get a walking-tour pamphlet here, or try the tearoom, which overlooks the river. ⊠ *River St. and Central Ave.,* ☎ *306/764–2992.* ⊠ *$1.* ⊙ *Mid-May–Aug., Mon.–Sat. 10–6, Sun. 10–9.*

DINING

$$$–$$$$ ✕ **Amy's on Second Restaurant.** The favorite for locals when they want a special evening out, this small, understated contemporary establishment serves a limited but always interesting menu, from pastas to steak. Fresh pickerel served with wild rice is a good choice. The specialty cheesecakes are decadent, and there are coffee drinks to match. ⊠ *2990 2nd Ave. W,* ☎ *306/763–1515. AE, DC, MC, V. Closed Sun.*

Prince Albert National Park

★ *80 km (50 mi) north of Prince Albert, 221 km (137 mi) north of Saskatoon.*

Prince Albert National Park encompasses nearly a million acres of wilderness and waterways, divided into three landscapes: wide-open fescue grassland, wooded parkland, and dense boreal forest. Besides hiking trails, the park has three major campgrounds with more than 500 sites, plus rustic campgrounds and primitive sites in the backcountry. You can pick up maps and information at the **Waskesiu Lake Visitor Centre** (⊠ Rtes. 263 and 264, ☎ 306/663–5322) in Waskesiu, a town with restaurants, motels, and stores, and a golf course within the park. It's open May through September, daily 8 AM–10 PM, and October through April, weekdays 8–4:30. The **Nature Centre,** inside the visitor center, orients you to the plant and animal life of the area. Hiking along the marked trails, you have a good chance of spotting moose, deer, bear, elk, and red fox. Canoes, rowboats, and powerboats can be rented from Waskesiu Lake Marina. Lodging in Waskesiu includes **Chateau Park Chalets** (☎ 306/663–5556), the **Hawood Inn** (☎ 306/663–5911), and

Waskesiu Lake Lodge (☎ 306/663–6161); all offer year-round accommodation. ⊠ *Off Rte. 2,* ☎ *306/663–5322,* WEB *www.parcscanada.gc.ca/albert.* ☜ *$4.*

North Battleford

57 *138 km (86 mi) northwest of Saskatoon on Highway 16.*

The attractions in this town represent different aspects of the area's history. The **Western Development Museum** presents a re-created 1920s farming village, complete with homes, offices, churches, and a Mountie post. The museum also exhibits vintage farming tools and provides demonstrations of agricultural skills. ⊠ *Hwy. 16 and Rte. 40,* ☎ *306/445–8033,* WEB *www.wdmuseum.sk.ca.* ☜ *$5.* ⊙ *May–Sept. daily 9–5, Oct.–Apr. Wed.–Sun. 12:30–4:30.*

While you're in town, you can visit the **Allen Sapp Gallery,** which displays the paintings of the Cree artist. Allen Sapp has gained a strong following, both in Canada and abroad, for his images of the Northern Plains Cree, including scenes from his childhood on a reserve. ⊠ *1091 100th St.,* ☎ *306/445–1760.* ☜ *Free.* ⊙ *May–Sept., daily 1–5; Oct.–Apr., Wed.–Sun. 1–5.*

Fort Battleford National Historic Site pays tribute to the role of mounted police in the development of the Canadian west. The fort was established in 1876 as the North West Mounted Police headquarters for the District of Saskatchewan. Costumed guides explain day-to-day life at the post, and an interpretive center has exhibits relating to the history of the mounted police and the lives of natives and settlers. ⊠ *Central Ave.,* ☎ *306/937–2621,* WEB *www.parkscanada.pch.gc.ca/parks/saskatchewan/fort_battleford.* ☜ *$4.* ⊙ *Daily 9–5.*

Manitou Beach

58 *124 km (77 mi) southeast of Saskatoon via Highway 16 and Route 365.*

Fifty years ago the town of Manitou Beach was a world-famous spa nicknamed the Carlsbad of Canada. The mineral water in Little Manitou Lake is said to be three times saltier than the ocean and dense enough to make anyone float. Today **Manitou Springs Mineral Spa** (⊠ Rte. 365, ☎ 306/946–2233) attracts vacationers as well as sufferers from arthritis, rheumatism, and skin disorders to the spa resort.

DINING AND LODGING

$ ✕🏠 **Manitou Springs Resort.** This lakeshore resort has rooms and suites with balconies and good views. The rooms are comfortable, with cushy fabrics in muted pastels; the spa is lined with cedar. Continental cuisine, including some seafood, and prairie fare such as steaks and roasts are served in the light, airy Wellington Dining Room ($$), which looks over the lake. ⊠ *Rte. 365, Box 610, Watrous SOK 4TO,* ☎ *306/946–2233; 800/667–7672 in Canada,* WEB *www.manitouspringsspa.sk.ca. 56 rooms, 4 suites. Restaurant, massage, mineral baths, gym, bicycles, meeting rooms. MC, V.*

Saskatoon A to Z

AIR TRAVEL TO AND FROM SASKATOON
Saskatoon Airport is served by Air Canada, WestJet, Canada 3000, Northwest Airlines, and Canadian commuter carriers.

AIRPORTS AND TRANSFERS
Saskatoon Airport is 7 km (4 mi) northwest of downtown. Taxis to downtown cost $10–$12.

➤ AIRPORT INFORMATION: **Saskatoon Airport** (✉ 2625 Airport Dr., ☎ 306/975–4274).

BUS TRAVEL WITHIN SASKATOON

Saskatoon Transit buses offer convenient service to points around the city. Tickets cost $1.60.

➤ BUS INFORMATION: **Saskatoon Transit** (☎ 306/975–3100).

CAR TRAVEL

The two-lane Yellowhead Highway (Highway 16) passes through Saskatoon on its journey from Winnipeg through to Edmonton and west. There's also access to Saskatoon along Highway 11 from Regina.

EMERGENCIES

The Shopper's Drug Mart as Taylor Street East and Broadway Avenue is open daily until midnight; the branch at 2410 22nd Street West is open around the clock.

➤ EMERGENCY SERVICES: **Ambulance, fire, poison center, police** (☎ 911).

➤ HOSPITALS: **City Hospital** (✉ Queen St. and 6th Ave. N, ☎ 306/655–8230). **Royal University Hospital** (✉ University Grounds, ☎ 306/655–1362). **St. Paul's Hospital** (✉ 1702 20th St. W, ☎ 306/665–5113).

➤ LATE-NIGHT PHARMACIES: **Shopper's Drug Mart** (✉ 610 Taylor St. E, at Broadway Ave., ☎ 306/343–1608; ✉ 2410 22nd St. W, ☎ 306/382–5005).

TAXIS

Taxis are plentiful, especially outside downtown hotels, but they are fairly expensive.

➤ TAXI COMPANIES: **Blueline Taxi** (☎ 306/653–3333). **Saskatoon Radio Cab** (☎ 306/242–1221). **United Yellow Cab** (☎ 306/652–2222).

TOURS

The Saskatoon Lady offers one-hour river cruises from May through October. Boats depart hourly from the Mendel Art Gallery Wharf; the cost is $4.

➤ FEES AND SCHEDULES: *The Saskatoon Lady* (☎ 306/549–2400).

VISITOR INFORMATION

Tourism Saskatoon is open weekdays 8:30–5 most of the year, and 8:30–7 mid-May through early September. In summer, visitor-information centers open at various points along Highway 16.

➤ TOURIST INFORMATION: **Tourism Saskatoon** (✉ 6–305 Idylwyld Dr. N, S7L OZ1, ☎ 306/242–1206 or 800/567–2444).

WINNIPEG

Updated by
Randal McIlroy

Winnipeg's geographic isolation and traditionally long, cold winters have fostered an independent spirit among its people. Although its status as a transportation hub and commercial gateway to the West has diminished, the provincial capital of Manitoba has a cultural scene that is the envy of much larger Canadian cities, from a symphony orchestra and ballet company to two major theaters and a strong arts community. Historically, Winnipeg was the funnel for the first great waves of immigration to the West, and ethnic pride remains strong. British and French by colonization, with subsequent arrivals of Ukrainians, Italians, members of the Jewish and Mennonite faiths, and many other groups, the city has seen in recent years the growing pride of the First Nations and Métis people and the members of newer communities, notably from Portugal, Vietnam, and the Philippines.

Recent economic growth has been modest at best, with the population holding at about 620,000. With most of its commercial and business activities concentrated in a compact downtown zone, Winnipeg retains much of its historical charm, evidenced in the many edifices from the turn of the 20th century. Because major residential development has been left generally to its fringes, the city still holds many enclaves of older homes on shady lanes, often set in sudden, surprising contrast to newer structures.

Originally, buffalo-hunting Plains Indians inhabited the area, which was franchised by the British Crown to the Hudson's Bay Company. In 1738, Pierre Gaultier de Varennes established a North West Company fur-trading post at the junction of the Red and Assiniboine rivers. Lord Selkirk, a Scot, brought a permanent agricultural settlement in 1812; Winnipeg was incorporated as a city in 1873; and soon after, in 1886, the Canadian Pacific Railroad arrived, bringing a rush of European immigrants. The "Chicago of the North" boomed as a railroad hub, a center of the livestock and grain industries, and a principal market city of western Canada.

Exploring Winnipeg

With its downtown core packed close to the junction of the Red and Assiniboine rivers, Winnipeg is an excellent city for walkers. However, the necessity of developing streets against the contours of those rivers makes for many diagonal roads and streets that connect at an angle; a map is recommended. Downtown itself is centered on the intersection of Portage Avenue and Main Street. Overhead covered walkways span the length of the central commercial area, taking in a major department store and several shopping malls and offering a welcome break from the elements. Paved paths along stretches of both rivers have handsome views of the city. A vehicle is necessary for reaching more distant sites. Portage Avenue (Highway 1) leads west, while Main Street (Route 52) heads north. Pembina Highway (Route 42) is the main artery to the south. In the historically French-speaking community of St. Boniface, east of the Red River, street signs are labeled in both French and English.

A Good Tour

Begin in downtown Winnipeg at the visitor information center, housed in the **Legislative Building** ⑤⑨. Walk east on Broadway and south on Carlton Street to tour the **Dalnavert Museum** ⑥⓪, the 1895 house built for Manitoba's premier. Back at the Legislature, head north on Osborne Street past the stately store called the Bay (the legacy of the Hudson's Bay Company) to the **Winnipeg Art Gallery** ⑥①, noted for its collection of Inuit art. Turn east (right) onto Portage Avenue for a look at the shopping district. Continue east on Portage Avenue to Main Street and what's reputed to be the windiest intersection in the world. Five floors above the breeze, visit the **Winnipeg Commodity Exchange** ⑥②, the oldest and largest futures exchange in Canada. Below ground is Winnipeg Square, a concourse with shops and fast-food stores. Emerge to street level on the north side of Portage Avenue and head into the **Exchange District** ⑥③—a concentration of renovated warehouses, banks, and insurance companies that today thrives as an arts and nightlife center. Continue north on Main Street to Rupert Avenue and **Manitoba Centennial Centre** ⑥④, site of a concert hall, a natural-history museum, and a planetarium.

The suburb of St. Boniface, about 2½ km (1½ mi) away, can be reached by crossing the Provencher Bridge east over the Red River and turning right onto avenue Taché. Here you can visit the **St. Boniface Cathe-**

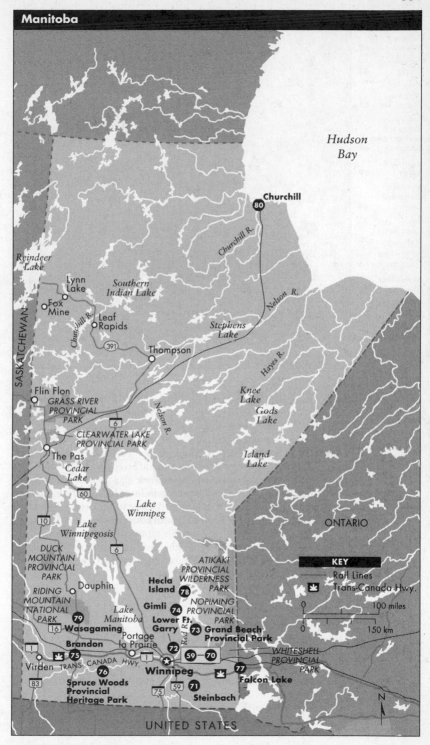

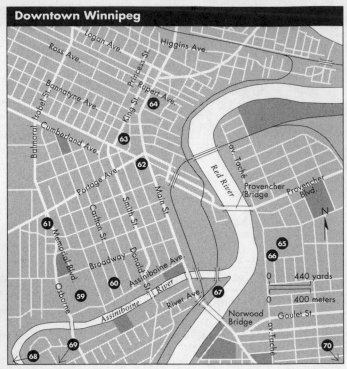

Downtown Winnipeg

dral ⑥⑤, in whose churchyard Louis Riel is buried, and the **St. Boniface Museum** ⑥⑥, which focuses on French and Métis history and culture in Manitoba. Follow avenue Taché south to Goulet Street, turn right, and follow it over Norwood Bridge, which takes you to the **Forks National Historic Site** ⑥⑦, at the junction of the Assiniboine and Red rivers. A longer drive—left on River Avenue, left on Donald Street, and right on Corydon Avenue—brings you to **Assiniboine Park** ⑥⑧, with its zoo and sculpture garden. South of the park, you can follow Shaftesbury Boulevard past Assiniboine Forest across Wilkes Avenue to McCreary Road and the **Fort Whyte Centre for Environmental Education** ⑥⑨, a wildlife sanctuary. To see where some of Canada's money is made, drive 6 km (4 mi) southeast of downtown off Highway 1 or take Bus 50 (available on the south side of Portage Avenue at Fort Street) to the **Royal Canadian Mint** ⑦⓪.

TIMING
This makes for a busy day's tour; you might want to save a few sights for a second day of visiting.

Sights to See

Assiniboine Park. Hugging the river of the same name, the park has 378 acres of rolling fields and dense forest, with picnic areas, a playground, a cricket pitch, and both paved and rugged paths for cyclists. Popular attractions include the **Leo Mol Sculpture Garden,** the only such garden in North America dedicated to a single artist; western Canada's oldest conservatory; and the **Assiniboine Park Pavilion,** an art gallery and restaurant. In warmer weather, you can visit the English garden and the duck pond. The **Assiniboine Zoo,** also on the grounds, houses more than 1,200 species in reasonably natural settings. ⊠ *Park Blvd. and Wellington Crescent,* ☎ *204/986–6921 or 204/986–3130,* WEB *www.city.winnipeg.mb.ca.* ⌑ *Zoo $3; $1 Nov.–Feb.* ☺

Park daily 7 AM–10 PM. Zoo Sept.–late May, daily 10–4; late May–Sept., daily 9–dusk.

60 Dalnavert Museum. This finely detailed style house was built in 1895 for Sir Hugh John Macdonald, who became premier of Manitoba. Guides in period dress escort you around the premises. ⊠ *61 Carlton St.,* ☎ *204/943–2835,* WEB *www.mhs.mb.ca.* ☑ *$4.* ☉ *Jan.–Feb., weekends noon–5; Mar.–May and Sept.–Dec., Tues.–Thurs. and weekends 10–5; June–Aug., Tues.–Thurs. and weekends 10–6.*

63 Exchange District. The original epicenter of Winnipeg's investment and newspaper businesses contains a wealth of architectural history in its surviving offices, warehouses, banks, and hotels. Today, entertainment and the arts dominate the area, with many of the city's vital alternative arts galleries within a small radius. The **Artspace** building (⊠ 100 Arthur St.) includes three galleries and is home to many arts organizations. In spring, **Old Market Square** (⊠ King St. and Bannatyne Ave.) is the site of free concerts, from lunchtime shows to evening events. ⊠ *Between Portage Ave. and Main St.*

★ ☚ **67 Forks National Historic Site.** Winnipeg began here, at the junction of the Red and Assiniboine rivers, with native settlements that date back 6,000 years. You can learn about the region's history through interpretive displays as you stroll the paths of the 9 landscaped acres or rest on benches overlooking the river. The historic site is part of a 56-acre development, the Forks, that combines history, commerce, and entertainment. The **Forks Market** (☎ 204/943–7752) sells fresh produce and specialty foods and contains restaurants in two converted railroad buildings; the attractions of the Johnson Terminal include specialty shops.

The **Manitoba Children's Museum** (☎ 204/956–1888, WEB www.childrensmuseum.com) has a delightful range of hands-on activities; kids can check out the working television studio and a vintage diesel train with Pullman car. The museum is open September through June weekdays 9:30–5 (until 8 Thursday and Friday), Saturday 10–8, and Sunday 10–5; Monday through Saturday 10–8 and Sunday 10–5 the rest of the year. Admission is $4.50.

The best in theater for children and teens is found at the **Manitoba Theatre for Young People** (⊠ CanWest Global Performing Arts Centre, 2 Forks Market Rd., ☎ 204/942–8898); the building's bright colors and dramatic courtyard and balcony provide entertainment in themselves. The **Manitoba Travel Idea Centre** (☎ 800/665–0040) has exhibits about the province and a wealth of information. ⊠ *Forks Market Rd. off Main St.,* ☎ *204/983–2007,* WEB *www.parkscanada.gc.ca/forks.* ☑ *Free.*

☚ **69 Fort Whyte Centre for Environmental Education.** The 200-acre center re-creates the natural habitats of Manitoba's lakes and rivers in and around several former cement quarries. It is home to white-tailed deer, muskrats, foxes, and numerous species of waterfowl. Self-guided nature trails and an interpretive center explain it all. ⊠ *1961 McCreary Rd.,* ☎ *204/989–8355,* WEB *www.fortwhyte.org.* ☑ *$4.* ☉ *Weekdays 9–5, weekends 10–5.*

59 Legislative Building. This classical structure made of local Tyndall stone contains the offices of Manitoba's premier and members of the cabinet, as well as the chamber where the legislature meets. A 240-ft dome supports Manitoba's symbol, the Golden Boy—a 13½-ft gold-sheathed statue with a sheaf of wheat under his left arm and the torch of progress in his right hand. The beautiful rolling grounds ease down to the Assiniboine River at the south, with a fountain plaza leading to a river walk. Statues around the grounds celebrate Manitoba's ethnic diversity. To the east stands Government House, built in 1883 and still the official private residence for the lieutenant governor. ⊠ *450 Broadway, at Osborne St.,* ☎ *204/945–5813.* ۩ *Guided tour July–Labor Day, weekdays 9–6:30; early Sept.–June, by appointment.*

Ⓒ ⓺ **Manitoba Centennial Centre.** The center includes **Centennial Concert Hall,** home to the Winnipeg Symphony Orchestra and the Royal Winnipeg Ballet. The outstanding **Manitoba Museum of Man and Nature** tracks the stories of the province's history and land back to prehistoric times; it has nature dioramas, a miniature prairie town from the 1920s, and a full-size replica of the *Nonesuch,* the ketch that sailed into Hudson's Bay in 1668. Downstairs, the **Planetarium** presents a range of stellar shows; the **Touch the Universe Science Centre** offers interactive exhibits. ⊠ *190 Rupert Ave.,* ☎ *204/956–2830 or 204/943–3139.* ۩ *Museum $5, planetarium $4, science center $4; 3-day all-inclusive Omni pass $11.* ۩ *Mid-May–early Sept., daily 10–6; early Sept.–mid-May, Tues.–Fri. 10–4, weekends 10–5.*

⓻ **Royal Canadian Mint.** At one of only two federal mints in Canada, you can see freshly minted coins produced for general circulation. ⊠ *520 Lagimodière Blvd., at Trans-Canada Hwy.,* ☎ *204/257–3359.* ۩ *$2.* ۩ *Guided tours May–Aug., weekdays 9–5, Sat. noon–5.*

⓺ **St. Boniface Cathedral.** The largest French community in western Canada was founded as Fort Rouge in 1783 and became an important fur-trading outpost for the North West Company. Upon the arrival of Roman Catholic priests, the settlement was renamed St. Boniface. Remnants of a 1908 basilica that survived a 1968 fire can be seen outside the perimeter of the present cathedral, built in 1972. The grave of Louis Riel, the St. Boniface native son who led the Métis rebellion, is in the churchyard. ⊠ *Av. de la Cathédrale and av. Taché,* ☎ *204/233–7304.* ۩ *Free.*

⓺ **St. Boniface Museum.** The history of Manitoba's French and Métis people is examined in the oldest structure in Winnipeg, dating to 1846. Artifacts include an altar crafted from papier-mâché, the first church bell in western Canada, and a host of innovative household gadgets. ⊠ *494 av. Taché,* ☎ *204/237–4500.* ۩ *$2.15.* ۩ *Mid-Feb.–mid-June and Sept., weekdays 9–5, weekends 10–4; mid-June–Aug., weekdays 9–5, Sat. 10–4, Sun. 10–8; Oct.–mid-Feb., weekdays 9–5, weekends noon–4.*

★ ⓺ **Winnipeg Art Gallery.** The city's largest art museum presents a rotating schedule of shows with works from its permanent collection as well as displays of new regional work and traveling exhibitions. It is known for one of the world's most extensive collections of Inuit art. Programming also includes music, films and lectures, and summer concerts on the rooftop plaza. ⊠ *300 Memorial Blvd.,* ☎ *204/786–6641,* WEB *www.wag.mb.ca.* ۩ *$4; free Wed.* ۩ *Tues. and Thurs.–Sun. 11–5, Wed. 11–9.*

⓺ **Winnipeg Commodity Exchange.** At Canada's oldest and largest futures exchange, you can observe the controlled chaos of the people involved in the buying and selling of grains, cooking oils, gold, and silver. Below the exchange is **Winnipeg Square,** with shops and fast-food stores. ⊠ *360 Main St.,* ☎ *204/925–5000.* ۩ *Weekdays 9:30–1:20.*

Dining

$$–$$$$ ✕ **Amici.** The Italian version of nouvelle cuisine extends to lamb, seafood, and imaginative veal dishes in this elegant and bright down-

town restaurant, while the pasta preparations are every bit as artful as you would expect. Downstairs is the more casual Bombolini Wine Bar, with a modified version of the menu at lower prices. The desserts are heavenly. ⊠ *326 Broadway,* ☎ *204/943–4997. Reservations essential. AE, DC, MC, V. Closed Sun.*

$$–$$$$ ★ ✕ **Le Beaujolais.** French cuisine is a perennial draw at this handsome restaurant in St. Boniface, yet Le Beaujolais has also earned raves for such local delicacies as Lake Winnipeg pickerel cheeks, bison tenderloin, and fillet of prairie ostrich with wild-rice pancakes. The warm decor and waiters in black tie add charm. ⊠ *131 Provencher Blvd.,* ☎ *204/237–6306. Reservations essential. AE, DC, MC, V.*

$$–$$$$ ★ ✕ **Restaurant Dubrovnik.** The setting of one of the city's finest restaurants is a charming Victorian home overlooking the Assiniboine River. A must for lovers of contemporary fine dining, Dubrovnik offers an imaginative menu of European and Asian dishes, including its trademark foie gras, chicken stuffed with shrimp mousse, and southern Yugoslavian specialties. The wine list is lengthy. ⊠ *390 Assiniboine Ave.,* ☎ *204/944–0594. Reservations essential. Jacket required. AE, MC, V. Closed Sun.*

$$–$$$ ✕ **The Storm.** Creativity is evident everywhere in this airy downtown restaurant, from the multicolor decor and gorgeous serving arrangements to a border-bending contemporary menu inspired largely by Asian and Jamaican flavors. Try the Asian noodle dishes, served with a generous assortment of spring rolls. Stylish and satisfying sandwiches figure in the less expensive lunch menu. ⊠ *144 Smith St.,* ☎ *204/942–8034. AE, DC, MC, V. Closed Sun.*

$$–$$$ ✕ **Victor's.** This restaurant in the Ramada Marlborough hotel is furnished handsomely with chandeliers and dark wood below vaulted ceilings. Continental dishes include beef, veal, and salmon, with a choice of garnishes and side dishes. ⊠ *331 Smith St.,* ☎ *204/947–2751. AE, DC, MC, V. Closed Sun. No lunch.*

$–$$$ ✕ **Papa George's.** A wide-ranging and eclectic menu spans hefty hamburgers, weighty sandwiches, and distinctively light and crunchy pizza, as well as Greek favorites such as *spanakopita* (spinach-filled pastry) and chicken souvlaki. Bright and busy by day, this large and welcoming restaurant in Osborne Village also serves late-night traffic; from Monday through Saturday the restaurant is open until 4 AM. ⊠ *93 Osborne St.,* ☎ *204/452–6044. AE, DC, MC, V.*

$–$$$ ✕ **Pasta la Vista.** At the southern end of the Eaton Place shopping mall, this large and open contemporary Italian restaurant offers a tantalizing variety of creative pasta dishes and pizzas. The setting is handsome, but the mood is relaxed. The downtown location makes it an afterwork favorite for business types. A large and lively—occasionally extremely lively—bar has a wide selection of wines. ⊠ *66-234 Donald St.,* ☎ *204/956–2229. AE, DC, MC, V.*

$–$$$ ✕ **Picasso's.** It may be named for a Spanish painter, but this is a Portuguese restaurant that serves outstanding seafood. On the street level it's a bustling café; upstairs, white tablecloths, candlelight, and soft music reinforce a subdued atmosphere. Try the salmon or arctic char; Portuguese favorites are paella and octopus stew. ⊠ *615 Sargent Ave.,* ☎ *204/775–2469. Reservations essential. AE, DC, MC, V.*

$–$$ ★ ✕ **Bistro Dansk.** Wood tables, bright red chairs, and strains of classical music convey a cozy European air. Among the dinner entrées are Danish specialties such as *frikadeller* (meat patties of ground veal and pork) and panfried rainbow trout. A less expensive lunch menu lists a variety of open-face sandwiches. ⊠ *63 Sherbrook St.,* ☎ *204/775–5662. Reservations essential. AE, DC, V. Closed Sun.*

$–$$ ✕ **Elephant and Castle.** In the Delta Winnipeg, this magnet for down-town's after-work crowd combines a British-style pub with an airy, well-lit restaurant. Pub standbys such as newspaper-wrapped fish and chips, and steak with thick chips and baked beans share the menu with Cana-dian casual fare. Many stalwart British ales share the shelf with more familiar North American brands. ✉ *350 St. Mary Ave.,* ☎ *204/942–5555. AE, DC, MC, V.*

$–$$ ✕ **Homer's.** This good-time downtown place with a definite Mediter-ranean atmosphere has been one of the city's favorite Greek restau-rants for more than 15 years. Greek specialties include roast leg of lamb and moussaka, but Homer's is also famous for ribs, steak, seafood, pasta, and fresh hot bread. In summer you can eat outdoors. ✉ *520 Ellice Ave.,* ☎ *204/788–4858. Reservations essential. AE, DC, MC, V.*

$–$$ ✕ **Muddy Waters Smokehouse.** Country cooking holds sway in this funky haunt at the Forks National Historic Site. Giant helpings of bar-becue meats, colorful shrimp dishes, daunting burgers and sandwiches, and hot sauces to make a devil sweat are complemented by checkered tablecloths, no-frills furniture, and a perennial soundtrack of swaggering Chicago blues. ✉ *Forks Pavilion, Forks Market Rd. off Main St.,* ☎ *204/947–6653. AE, DC, MC, V.*

$ ✕ **Bangkok Thai.** Imaginative yet inexpensive fish and vegetable dishes take center stage in this elegant second-floor Thai restaurant, where servers wear traditional silks and even the water is served in elaborate metal vessels. The vast menu includes two varieties of the popular *pad Thai* shrimp dish. The view overlooks River Avenue and Osborne Street—the heart of bustling Osborne Village. ✉ *100 Osborne St.,* ☎ *204/474–0908. AE, DC, MC, V.*

$ ✕ **Carlos and Murphy's.** Tex-Mex fare such as chimichanga, taco salad, and a range of nacho dishes are staples at this good-time haunt in funky Osborne Village. The huge hamburgers are also recommended. There's a wide selection of beers on tap. ✉ *129 Osborne St.,* ☎ *204/284–3510. AE, DC, MC, V.*

$ ✕ **Kelekis.** A city institution, this North End favorite—opened in 1931 and still run by the same family—is beloved for its hot dogs, hamburgers, and french fries. Acres of celebrity photos attest to the restaurant's sta-tus as a cornerstone of local culture. ✉ *1100 Main St.,* ☎ *204/582–1786. Reservations not accepted. No credit cards.*

Lodging

$$$–$$$$ 🏨 **Holiday Inn Airport/West.** Bright and pleasant, this modern prop-★ erty stands next to the Trans-Canada Highway's western approach to Winnipeg, near the airport, the racetrack, and shopping areas. Rooms are large and are furnished in shades of blue, burgundy, and green. The atrium is a lush setting for the pool and poolside lounge. ✉ *2520 Portage Ave., R3J 3T6,* ☎ *204/885–4478 or 800/665–0352,* FAX *204/831–5734,* WEB *www.holidayinn.airportwest.com. 208 rooms, 18 suites. Restaurant, no-smoking rooms, indoor pool, sauna, gym, business services, free parking. AE, DC, MC, V.*

$$–$$$$ 🏨 **The Fairmont Winnipeg.** Winnipeg's premier luxury hotel (formerly ★ called The Lombard) presides over downtown's central intersection of Portage and Main. Rooms are spacious, with tasteful furnishings. The Velvet Glove Dining Room provides elegant dining; lighter meals are served in the Velvet Glove Lounge. An underground complex of shops and restaurants connects the hotel to the Winnipeg Square shopping mall and the downtown walkway system. Centennial Concert Hall, Man-itoba Theatre Centre, and the city's major financial institutions are only a few minutes' walk away. ✉ *2 Lombard Pl., R3B 0Y3,* ☎ *204/957–1350 or 800/441–1414,* FAX *204/956–1751,* WEB *www.fairmont.com. 340* *rooms, 20 suites. 2 restaurants, indoor pool, sauna, health club, baby-sitting, dry cleaning, laundry service, concierge, business services, meeting rooms, parking (fee). AE, DC, MC, V.*

$$–$$$ 🏨 **Delta Winnipeg.** In the heart of downtown, Winnipeg's largest hotel is connected by a walkway to the Winnipeg Convention Centre and faces the Eaton Place shopping mall. Rooms are pleasantly modern; some overlook the skylighted pool. The hotel has a cocktail lounge and a lively British-style pub, the Elephant and Castle. ✉ *350 St. Mary Ave., R3C 3J2, ☎ 204/942–0551 or 800/268–1133, FAX 204/943–4627, WEB www.deltahotels.com. 389 rooms, 18 suites. 2 restaurants, bar, in-room data ports, no-smoking rooms, indoor pool, sauna, gym, laundry service, business services, parking (fee). AE, DC, MC, V.*

$$–$$$ 🏨 **Fort Garry Hotel.** Built in 1913 as one of Canada's great railway hotels, this hotel on the southern end of downtown still holds the charm of a bygone era, down to the marble, brass, and crystal in the cavernous lobby. The large guest rooms still have classic dark-wood furnishings and floral wallpapers. An adjoining complex holds shops and services. ✉ *222 Broadway, R3C 0R3, ☎ 204/942–8251 or 800/665–8088, FAX 204/956–2351, WEB www.fortgarryhotel.com. 235 rooms, 16 suites. 2 restaurants, lounge, in-room data ports, no-smoking rooms, baby-sitting, laundry services, concierge, business services, meetings rooms, parking (fee). AE, DC, MC, V.*

$$–$$$ 🏨 **Place Louis Riel.** This luxury-class alternative is a converted apart-
★ ment building that has contemporary suites—studios, one, or two bedrooms—with living rooms, dining areas, and fully equipped kitchens. Though all rooms are up-to-date, the suites on the upper floors facing west are preferable because of their view of the Legislative Building. The excellent downtown location—adjacent to Eaton Place mall and a 10-minute walk from the Forks National Historic Site—is a major advantage. ✉ *190 Smith St., R3C 1J8, ☎ 204/947–6961; 800/665–0569 in Canada, FAX 204/947–3029, WEB www.placelouisriel.com. 283 suites. Restaurant, lounge, in-room data ports, gym, coin laundry, meeting rooms, parking (fee). AE, DC, MC, V.*

$$–$$$ 🏨 **Ramada Marlborough.** Built in 1914, this was once the jewel in Winnipeg's growing financial district. Grace persists in the spacious lobby, with its burnished wood, polished marble, and soft sofas. Joanna's Café is a casual dining spot that's good for before- or after-dinner drinks; Victor's is more formal. Most of downtown's attractions are only a few minutes' walk away. ✉ *331 Smith St., R3B 2G9, ☎ 204/942–6411 or 800/667–7666, FAX 204/942–2017, WEB www.ramada.ca. 148 rooms. 2 restaurants, no-smoking floors, meeting rooms, free parking. AE, DC, MC, V.*

$–$$$ 🏨 **Radisson Winnipeg Downtown.** This downtown hotel is well known for a 12th-floor restaurant, the Peak Bistro, with a panoramic view of the city. Family services include an activity center for children and a package that comes with daily complimentary family movies. The Portage Place shopping mall is nearby. ✉ *288 Portage Ave., R3C OB8, ☎ 204/956–0410 or 800/339–5328, FAX 204/947–1129, WEB www.radisson.ca. 261 rooms, 11 suites. Restaurant, lounge, in-room data ports, indoor pool, sauna, gym, parking (fee). AE, DC, MC, V.*

$–$$ 🏨 **Charter House.** A friendly, reasonably priced restaurant and a convenient downtown location make this low-rise a favorite with families. Business travelers appreciate the corporate floor—where suites are equipped with large desks, task lighting, and other amenities for work—and the setting adjacent to the Winnipeg Convention Centre. ✉ *330 York Ave., R3C 0N9, ☎ 204/942–0101 or 800/782–0175, FAX 204/956–0665. 87 rooms. 2 restaurants, in-room data ports, pool, concierge, meeting rooms, free parking. AE, DC, MC, V.*

$ ⌶ **Travelodge Hotel Downtown Winnipeg.** Part of a Canadian budget chain, this high-rise is at the western edge of downtown, only steps away from the Portage Place shopping mall and the Winnipeg Art Gallery. Rooms on the south side look out on the Legislative Building, and north-side rooms overlook the city. Guest rooms have subdued modern furnishings in neutral or pastel colors. ⊠ *360 Colony St., R3B 2P3,* ☎ *204/786–7011 or 800/578–7878,* FAX *204/772–1443,* WEB *www.travelodge.com. 156 rooms. Restaurant, in-room data ports, no-smoking rooms, indoor pool, parking (fee). AE, DC, MC, V.*

Nightlife and the Arts

The Arts

FILM

A good place to find imports, art films, oldies, and midnight cult classics is **Cinémathèque** (⊠ 100 Arthur St., ☎ 204/925–3457). The **Winnipeg Art Gallery** (⊠ 300 Memorial Blvd., ☎ 204/786–6641, WEB www.wag.mb.ca) has a cinema series.

MUSIC AND DANCE

Winnipeg's principal venue for serious music, dance, and pop concerts is the 2,263-seat Centennial Concert Hall in the **Manitoba Centennial Centre** (⊠ 555 Main St., ☎ 204/956–1360). The **Manitoba Opera** (☎ 204/957–7842) presents two operas a year—in November and April—in Centennial Concert Hall. The acclaimed **Royal Winnipeg Ballet** (☎ 204/956–2792 or 800/667–4792) performs in Centennial Concert Hall in October, December, March, and May; it's a must for dance fans. From September to mid-May, Centennial Centre is the home of the **Winnipeg Symphony Orchestra** (☎ 204/949–3999).

Many smaller performing organizations cater to more-specialized interests. **GroundSwell** (☎ 204/943–5770) explores the most modern music, with concerts in various locations. The **Manitoba Chamber Orchestra** (☎ 204/783–7377) performs eight concerts between September and May at Westminster Church (⊠ 745 Westminster Ave.). **MusikBarock Ensemble** (☎ 204/453–4946) stages six concerts of baroque music annually, at Crescent Fort Rouge United Church (⊠ Wardlaw Ave. and Nassau St. S). Modern dance is championed by several groups, notably **Winnipeg's Contemporary Dancers** (☎ 204/452–0229).

THEATER

One of Canada's most acclaimed regional theaters, the **Manitoba Theatre Centre** (⊠ 174 Market Ave., ☎ 204/942–6537) produces new plays and classics at the 785-seat Mainstage and more experimental work in the MTC Warehouse Theatre (⊠ 140 Rupert Ave., ☎ 204/942–6537). The **Prairie Theatre Exchange** (☎ 204/942–5483) focuses on new Canadian plays in an attractive facility in the Portage Place shopping mall (⊠ Portage Ave. and Carlton St.).

The **Manitoba Theatre for Young People** (⊠ CanWest Global Performing Arts Centre, 2 Forks Market Rd., ☎ 204/942–8898) runs separate seasons for children and teens in a beautiful theater at the Forks National Historic Site. Musicals the whole family can enjoy are staged outdoors every summer in Kildonan Park at **Rainbow Stage** (⊠ 2021 Main St., ☎ 204/780–7328).

Nightlife

BARS AND CLUBS

Bailey's Restaurant and Bar (⊠ 185 Lombard Ave., ☎ 204/944–1180) has a plush lounge that's close to the heart of downtown. The **Toad in the Hole** (⊠ 112 Osborne St., ☎ 204/284–7201) is a chummy British pub well stocked with hearty stouts and ales.

MUSIC

Some of the city's most imaginative jazz players are heard every Tuesday night at the **Franco-Manitoban Cultural Centre** (⊠ 340 Provencher Blvd., ☎ 204/233–8972). Country and rock fans can kick up their heels at the **Palomino Club** (⊠ 1133 Portage Ave., ☎ 204/772–0454). The boldest local and visiting rock bands play for dancers at the **Pyramid Cabaret** (⊠ 176 Fort St., ☎ 204/957–7777). Established and rising talent perform in the relaxed, smoke-free, cabaret-style **West End Cultural Centre** (⊠ 586 Ellice Ave., ☎ 204/783–6918). **Windows Lounge** in the Sheraton Winnipeg Hotel (⊠ 161 Donald St., ☎ 204/942–5300) offers small blues combos on weekends.

Outdoor Activities and Sports

Participant Sports

BIKING AND JOGGING

Many public parks in Winnipeg have marked biking and jogging paths. **Explore Manitoba Centre** (⊠ 21 Forks Market Rd., ☎ 204/945–3777 or 800/665–0040, WEB www.travelmanitoba.com) has maps with information about biking and jogging routes. **Olympia Cycle and Ski** (☎ 204/888–4586) rents bicycles at four city locations.

HEALTH AND FITNESS CLUBS

A full range of equipment and instruction is available at **Fitness City** (⊠ 1119 Nairn Ave., ☎ 204/661–3639). **Shapes Co-Ed** (⊠ 1910 Pembina Hwy., Unit 21, ☎ 204/989–7050) has classes; it also has three centers just for women.

Spectator Sports

BASEBALL

The **Winnipeg Goldeyes** (☎ 204/982–2273) play AA baseball in the Northern League, with games at CanWest Global Park (⊠ 1 Portage Ave. E) from April to early September.

BASKETBALL

The International Basketball League's **Winnipeg Cyclones** (☎ 204/925–4667) play at the Winnipeg Convention Centre (⊠ 375 York Ave.) from November through March.

FOOTBALL

Home games of the **Winnipeg Blue Bombers** (☎ 204/784–2583), of the Canadian Football League, are held at the Winnipeg Stadium (⊠ 1430 Maroons Rd.) from June through November.

HOCKEY

The **Manitoba Moose** (☎ 204/987–7825) of the International Hockey League hit the ice at the Winnipeg Arena (⊠ 1430 Maroons Rd.) from October through April.

HORSE RACING

Assiniboia Downs (⊠ 3975 Portage Ave., at Perimeter Hwy. W, ☎ 204/885–3330) hosts thoroughbred racing from May through October.

Shopping

Art and Crafts

The full breadth of Manitoba crafts, from weaving to ceramics, is displayed at **Craftspace Gallery** (⊠ 390 Academy Rd., ☎ 204/487–6114). **Loch & Mayberry Fine Art Inc.** (⊠ 306 St. Mary's Rd., ☎ 204/237–1622) has exquisite paintings, prints, and sculpture. The **Upstairs Gallery** (⊠ 266 Edmonton St., ☎ 204/943–2734) is one of Canada's greatest sources of Inuit art.

Malls and Shopping Districts

Winnipeg's own global village is found at the **Forks Market** (⊠ 201 Forks Market Rd., ☎ 204/942–6309), enclosing two former railroad buildings beneath a long atrium. Rows of fresh produce jostle with exotic fast-food outlets offering a rainbow of delights from Jamaican roti to Italian gelati. The delicacies at **Fenton's Gourmet Foods–The Cheese Shop** (⊠ Forks Market, 201 Forks Market Rd., ☎ 204/942–8984) range from massive wheels of imported cheese to decadent chocolate. Specialty shops on the second level of Forks Market include **Four Winds Trading Co.** (☎ 204/956–0646), which stocks First Nations clothes, and books and art. Regional artisans are represented at the **Craft Cupboard** (☎ 204/949–1785) in Forks Market.

The **Johnston Terminal** (⊠ 25 Forks Market Rd., ☎ 204/956–5593) has three floors of shops and restaurants. Collectors flock to the Johnston Terminal basement, where the **Johnston Terminal Antique Mall** (☎ 204/947–3952) offers an ever-changing range of vintage attractions sold on consignment, from furniture and musical instruments to sports memorabilia. **Global Connections** (⊠ Johnston Terminal, 25 Forks Market Rd., ☎ 204/989–2173) offers elegant African and Indian clothes and a wide array of ethnic music, resource texts, and ecologically friendly products.

The city's most vivid concentration of boutiques is found in **Osborne Village** (⊠ Osborne St. between River and Corydon Aves.), four short blocks that begin at the southern end of the Osborne Street bridge. A spray of music, book, and design stores attests to the area's bohemian makeup. The high end of local artistry is honored at **David Rice Jewelry and Objects** (⊠ 100 Osborne St., ☎ 204/453–6105). **Giannis Works in Gold** (⊠ 443 Osborne St., ☎ 204/475–8692) has unique jewelry pieces. Custom work is available. At **Leo Boutique** (⊠ B-121 Osborne St., ☎ 204/453–0167), the clothes are European chic. For casual and outdoor wear, head to **Tamarack** (⊠ 472 Stradbrook Ave., ☎ 204/453–6021). Be warned that parking at Osborne Village can be difficult, and traffic is heavy on Saturday.

Polo Park (⊠ 1485 Portage Ave., ☎ 204/784–2500), the city's most popular shopping mall, has three well-stocked department stores as anchors: Eatons, Sears, and Zellers. **Portage Place** (⊠ 393 Portage Ave., ☎ 204/925–4636) stretches across three downtown blocks with more than 150 shops and services. An overhead walkway connects Portage Place to the main outlet of The Bay and the smaller **Eaton Place** (⊠ 333 St. Mary Ave., ☎ 204/989–1800). **St. Vital Centre** (⊠ 1225 St. Mary's Rd., ☎ 204/257–5646) has more than 160 tenants, including The Bay and Wal-Mart, and is a major draw in the south of the city.

Side Trips from Winnipeg

Day trips outside the city offer a closer look at Manitoba's cultural heritage.

Steinbach

71 *48 km (30 mi) southeast of Winnipeg.*

The town of Steinbach is populated with nearly 10,000 descendants of Mennonites who fled religious persecution in late 19th-century Europe. Note all the automobile dealerships: Manitoban car buyers flock here because of the Mennonite reputation for making square deals.

In the **Mennonite Heritage Village,** a 40-acre open-air museum with buildings re-creating a village of the late 1800s (complete with a replica 1877 windmill), guides demonstrate blacksmithing, wheat grinding, and old-time housekeeping. The guides occasionally converse in the Mennonite German dialect. During the Pioneer Days festival in early August, the staff wears costumes and demonstrates homespun crafts. An authentic and economically priced restaurant serves traditional Mennonite specialties, such as borscht, *vereniki* (a cheese-filled perogi), and farmer's sausage. ⊠ *Rte. 12, 2 km (1 mi) north of Steinbach,* ☎ *204/ 326–9661,* WEB *www.mennoniteheritagevillage.mb.ca.* ⊠ *$5.* ☉ *May and Sept., Mon.–Sat. 10–5, Sun. noon–5; June–Aug., Mon.–Sat. 10– 6, Sun. noon–6; Oct. and Apr., weekdays 10–4.*

Selkirk
32 km (20 mi) north of Winnipeg.

The town was founded in 1882 by Scottish and Irish settlers, and Scottish traditions are celebrated each summer at the Manitoba Highland Gathering. **Lower Fort Garry,** built in 1830, is the oldest stone fort remaining from the Hudson's Bay Company fur-trading days. Nowadays, costumed employees describe daily tasks and recount thrilling journeys by York boat, the "boat that won the West." Beaver, raccoon, fox, and wolf pelts hang in the fur loft as a reminder of the bygone days. ⊠ *Rte. 9,* ☎ *204/785–6050,* WEB *www.parkscanada. gc.ca/garry.* ⊠ *$5.50.* ☉ *Grounds daily dawn–dusk; buildings mid-May– early Sept., daily 10–6.*

Grand Beach Provincial Park
73 *87 km (54 mi) northeast of Winnipeg.*

This park on the eastern shore of Lake Winnipeg, the seventh-largest lake in North America, has its charms, but in summer Grand Beach is a hot spot—for the swimming, the gentle 30-ft white sand dunes, and the people-watching. Expect crowds, especially on weekends. For those who prefer birds, the lagoon is the place to go. ⊠ *Rte. 12,* ☎ *888/482– 2267,* WEB *www.manitobaparks.com.* ☉ *May–Sept., daily.*

Gimli
74 *76 km (47 mi) north of Winnipeg.*

The largest Icelandic community outside the homeland, Gimli was once the center of the independent state of New Iceland. It still has an impressive harbor and marina on Lake Winnipeg. A giant Viking statue proclaims allegiance to the far-off island. By far the best choice for a stay here is the **Lakeview Resort** (☎ 204/642–8565), right on the waterfront.

The **New Iceland Heritage Museum** has two sights. The main museum celebrates Gimli's ethnic heritage in vivid displays, including an 18-ft mural. At the Lake Winnipeg Visitor Centre (☎ 204/642–7974), at Gimli Harbour, the tributes to the fishing industry include a 500-gallon tank filled with local fish species. ⊠ *94–1st. Ave.,* ☎ *204/642–4001.* ⊠ *Free.* ☉ *May–June, daily 10–6; July–Aug., daily 10–8.*

Winnipeg A to Z

AIR TRAVEL TO AND FROM WINNIPEG
Winnipeg is served by Northwest, Air Canada, West Jet, CanJet, Canada 3000, Calm Air, First Air, Transwest, Bearskin, and other commuter airlines.

AIRPORTS AND TRANSFERS
Winnipeg International Airport is 8 km (5 mi) from the city. Taxi fare downtown runs about $10–$15. Some airport-area hotels have free airport shuttles.

➤ AIRPORT INFORMATION: **Winnipeg International Airport** (✉ 2000 Wellington Ave., ☎ 204/987–9402, WEB www.waa.ca).

BUS TRAVEL WITHIN WINNIPEG

Winnipeg Transit spans the city. Adult fare is $1.65; exact change is required and transfers are free. Some routes operate on limited hours.
➤ BUS INFORMATION: **Winnipeg Transit** (☎ 204/986–5700 or 204/287–7433, WEB www.winnipegtransit.com).

CAR TRAVEL

Two main east–west highways link Winnipeg with the prairie provinces. The Trans-Canada Highway (Highway 1) runs through Winnipeg, Regina, and Calgary. West of Winnipeg the Yellowhead Highway (Highway 16) branches off the Trans-Canada and heads northwest toward Saskatoon and Edmonton.

Travelers from the United States can reach the Manitoba capital from Minneapolis along I–94 and I–29, connecting to Route 75 at the Canadian border. The driving distance between Minneapolis and Winnipeg is 691 km (428 mi).

EMERGENCIES

Many Winnipeg hospitals have emergency rooms, including the Health Sciences Centre and St. Boniface General Hospital. Misericordia Health Centre has a 24-hour urgent-care service for non-life-threatening conditions.

Two locations of Shopper's Drug Mart are open around the clock.
➤ EMERGENCY SERVICES: **Ambulance, fire, poison center, police** (☎ 911). **Misericordia Health Centre** (✉ 99 Cornish Ave., ☎ 204/788–8200, WEB www.misericordia.mb.ca).
➤ HOSPITALS: **Health Sciences Centre** (✉ 700 William Ave., ☎ 204/774–6511 or 204/787–3167, WEB www.hsc.mb.ca). **St. Boniface General Hospital** (✉ 409 av. Taché, ☎ 204/233–8563 or 204/237–2260, WEB www.sbgh.mb.ca).
➤ 24-HOUR PHARMACIES: **Shopper's Drug Mart** (✉ 43 Osborne St., ☎ 204/958–7000, WEB www.shoppersdrugmart.ca; ✉ 1152 Main St., ☎ 204/989–8700).

TAXIS

Taxi service is available easily by phone, although it is often faster to find one outside a hotel.
➤ TAXI COMPANIES: **Duffy's Taxi** (☎ 204/775–0101 or 204/925–0101). **Unicity Taxi** (☎ 204/925–3131, WEB www.unicitytaxi.mb.ca).

TOURS

Several lines ply the Red and Assiniboine rivers between May and mid-October. The *Paddlewheel River Rouge* has a variety of cruises (dining, dinner-dance, evening), combining sailings with double-decker bus tours. Exchange District Biz conducts summer tours of the Exchange District, offering illuminating descriptions of the region's rich commercial and architectural heritage.
➤ FEES AND SCHEDULES: **Exchange District Biz** (✉ 314-63 Albert St., ☎ 204/942–6716, WEB www.exchangebiz.winnipeg.mb.ca). *Paddlewheel River Rouge* (☎ 204/942–4500).

VISITOR INFORMATION

The Government Tourist Reception Office, in the Manitoba Legislative Building, is open May through Labor Day, daily 8:30 AM–9 PM; Labor Day through April, weekdays 8:30–4:30. Tourism Winnipeg on Portage Avenue is open weekdays 8:30–4:30; an airport location is open

8 AM–9:45 PM.

➤ TOURIST INFORMATION: **Explore Manitoba Centre** (⊠ 21 Forks Market Rd., ☎ 204/945–3777 or 800/665–0040, WEB www.travelmanitoba.com). **Government Tourist Reception Office** (⊠ Broadway and Osborne St., ☎ 204/945–3777 or 800/665–0040). **Tourism Winnipeg** (⊠ 279 Portage Ave., ☎ 204/943–1970 or 800/665–0204, WEB www.tourismwinnipeg.mb.ca; ⊠ 2000 Wellington Ave., ☎ 204/774–0031 or 800/665–0204).

ELSEWHERE IN MANITOBA

A clutch of sites from the city of Brandon to superb parks and the Hudson Bay polar-bear mecca of Churchill are some highlights of this province, which extends from the prairies and deep forests and lakes to the arctic tundra.

Brandon

75 *197 km (122 mi) west of Winnipeg.*

Brandon, Manitoba's second-largest city (population about 40,000), lies west of Winnipeg along the Trans-Canada Highway.

The **Commonwealth Air Training Plan Museum** honors the days when the Royal Canadian Air Force maintained a crucial training school here. It contains excellent examples of pre–World War II aircraft. ⊠ *Brandon Airport, Hangar 1,* ☎ *204/727–2444,* WEB *www.airmuseum.mb.ca.* ⊡ *$3.50.* ⊙ *Mon.–Sat. 10–4, Sun. 1–4.*

Spruce Woods Provincial Heritage Park

76 *180 km (112 mi) west of Winnipeg.*

In the rolling hills covered with spruce and basswood is the desertlike **Spirit Sands,** a 16-square-km (6-square-mi) tract of cactus-filled sand dunes. Walk the self-guided trail through the dunes, but keep your eyes peeled for lizards and snakes. Your final destination is **Devil's Punch Bowl,** a pit dug out by an underground stream. You can also tour the park in a horse-drawn covered wagon. The nearest town is Carberry, north of the park. ⊠ *Rte. 5,* ☎ *204/827–8850 or 204/834–8800,* WEB *www.gov.mb.ca/natres/parks/regions/western/spruce_woods.html.*

Falcon Lake

77 *143 km (89 mi) east of Winnipeg.*

The Falcon Lake development, within a lovely provincial park, has a shopping center, a golf course, tennis courts, a very good beach, a sailing club, and top-grade accommodations in the 40-room **Falcon Lake Resort & Club** (☎ 204/349–8400, WEB www.mbnet.mb.ca/falcon).

Whiteshell Provincial Park, a 2,590-square-km (1,000-square-mi) tract on the edge of the Canadian Shield, has 200 lakes with superb northern-pike, perch, walleye, and lake-trout fishing. Beaver Creek trail is a short walk to such wilderness denizens as beaver and deer. Farther on, West Hawk Lake (or Crater Lake)—formed a few thousand years ago by a falling meteor—is 365 ft deep and full of feisty smallmouth bass. Scuba divers love it. ⊠ *Hwy. 1E,* ☎ *204/369–5232,* WEB *www.whiteshell.mb.ca.* ⊡ *$5 per car (3-day pass).* ⊙ *Daily 8 AM–11 PM.*

Hecla Island

78 *175 km (109 mi) north of Winnipeg.*

Hecla Provincial Park, about a 2½-hour drive from Winnipeg, is a densely wooded archipelago named for the Icelandic volcano that drove the area's original settlers to Canada. The park ($5 per car for a three-day pass) is on the central North American flyway, and 50,000 waterfowl summer here. In early morning and evening the wildlife viewing tower is a good place from which to spot moose and other wildlife. The restored 1880s **Hecla Icelandic Fishing Village** is near Gull Harbour, the tourist center of the park and site of the luxurious **Gull Harbour Resort and Conference Centre** (☎ 204/279–2041 or 800/267–6700, www.gullharbourresort.com), with a marina, hiking trails, and a challenging golf course. ⊠ *Park Rte. 8,* ☎ *204/378–2945,* WEB *www.manitobaparks.com.*

Wasagaming

★ ⓐ *304 km (188 mi) northwest of Winnipeg via Highways 1 and 10.*

The town of Wasagaming is in Manitoba's only national park. **Riding Mountain National Park,** set in the rolling hills south of Dauphin in the western part of the province, covers 3,026 square km (1,168 square mi) and includes forests and grasslands that support a herd of bison. Wasagaming is on Clear Lake, which is popular for fishing and boating and offers supervised swimming. There is also a fine 18-hole golf course. ⊠ *Hwy. 10,* ☎ *204/848–7275 or 800/707–8740,* WEB *http://parkscanada.pch.gc.ca/riding.* 🎟 *$3 per person per day.* ☉ *8 AM–11 PM.*

The **Elkhorn Resort and Conference Centre** (⊠ Rte. 10, Onanole, ☎ 204/848–2802, WEB www.elkhornresort.mb.ca) has a 9-hole golf course, tennis, and trail rides. Camping, as well as other hotels and cabins, are nearby.

Churchill

★ ⓑ *1,600 km (992 mi) north of Winnipeg.*

Churchill, on the shore of Húdson Bay, has towering grain silos that attest to the town's history as Canada's northern port for grain shipping, but the town is known now as the polar-bear capital of the world. The bears congregate throughout October and early November, and many companies offer sightseeing tours in vehicles equipped to withstand both the winter cold and summer's soggy subarctic tundra. **Great White Bear Tours Inc.** (☎ 204/675–2781 or 800/765–8344, WEB www.cancom.net/~gwbt) offers packages for both amateur and professional nature photographers. **Sea North Tours** (☎ 204/675–2195 or 888/348–7591, WEB www.cancom.net/~seanorth) has tours to see seals, the more than 200 species of birds, and the beluga whales that come to bask in the warmer water in early summer. **Tundra Buggy Tours** (☎ 204/675–2121 or 800/544–5049, WEB www.wildlifeadventures.com) has specially designed vehicles that allow for safe and comfortable polar-bear viewing in summer and fall.

THE PRAIRIE PROVINCES A TO Z

To research prices, get advice from other travelers, and book travel arrangements, visit www.fodors.com.

AIR TRAVEL

Air Canada has direct or connecting service from Boston, New York, Chicago, San Francisco, and Los Angeles to Winnipeg, Regina, Saskatoon, Calgary, and Edmonton. Commuter affiliates serve other U.S. and Canadian destinations. U.S. airlines serving the prairie provinces include Northwest to Winnipeg; American, Delta, and United to Calgary; and Delta and Northwest to Edmonton.

Air Canada, WestJet, and Canada 3000 offer flights to cities throughout the prairie provinces.

BUS TRAVEL

Greyhound Lines and local bus companies provide service from the United States, other parts of Canada, and throughout the prairie provinces.

➤ BUS INFORMATION: **Greyhound Lines** (☎ 800/229–9424 in the U.S.; 800/661–8747 in Canada, WEB www.greyhound.ca).

CAR TRAVEL

From the United States, interstate highways cross the Canadian border, and two-lane highways continue on to major cities of the prairie provinces. From Minneapolis, I–94 and then I–29 connect to Route 75 at the Manitoba border south of Winnipeg. A main route to Alberta is I–15 north of Helena, Montana, which connects to Highway 2 and Routes 3 and 4 to Calgary.

Two main east–west highways link the major cities of the prairie provinces. The Trans-Canada Highway (Highway 1), mostly a four-lane divided freeway, runs through Winnipeg, Regina, and Calgary on its nationwide course. The two-lane Yellowhead Highway (Highway 16) branches off the Trans-Canada Highway west of Winnipeg and heads northwest toward Saskatoon, Saskatchewan, and Edmonton, Alberta. Traveling north–south, four-lane divided freeways connect Saskatoon to Regina (Highway 11) and Edmonton to Calgary (Highway 2).

TRAIN TRAVEL

There's no direct rail service between the United States and the prairie provinces. VIA Rail trains connect eastern Canada and the West Coast through Winnipeg–Saskatoon–Edmonton.

➤ TRAIN INFORMATION: **VIA Rail** (☎ 888/842–7245, WEB www.viarail. com).

VISITOR INFORMATION

➤ ALBERTA: **Travel Alberta** (✉ 319 Innovation Business Center, 9797 Jasper Ave., Edmonton T5J 1N9, ☎ 403/427–4321; 800/222–6501 in Alberta; 888/222–7498 in the U.S. and Canada, WEB www.travelalberta.com).

➤ MANITOBA: **Explore Manitoba Centre** (✉ 21 Forks Market Rd., Winnipeg R3C 4T7, ☎ 204/945–3777 or 800/665–0040, WEB www.travelmanitoba.com). **Travel Manitoba** (✉ 155 Carlton St., 7th floor, Winnipeg R3C 3H8, ☎ 204/945–3777 or 800/665–0040, WEB www.travelmanitoba.com).

➤ SASKATCHEWAN: **Tourism Saskatchewan** (✉ 1900 Albert St., Suite 500, Regina S4P 4L9, ☎ 800/667–7191).

7 TORONTO

Toronto's mix of cultures can be experienced through its myriad attractions, which range from the alternately staid and innovative architecture of its abundant bank buildings to the sensual overload of its ethnic markets. High-tone temples of art satisfy the most devoted culture lovers—the Royal Ontario Museum, for example, is one of the best museums in North America—while fun spots such as the CN Tower, Eaton Centre, and Harbourfront Centre keep the seriously frivolous occupied.

Updated by
Bruce Bishop

CANADA'S CENTER OF CULTURE, commerce, and communications, Toronto has enough people and enough money to support a critical mass for each of many special interests. Peter Ustinov is said to have referred to the city as "New York, as run by the Swiss," but proud Torontonians would prefer not to be compared with any one city. This is a multicultural, multiethnic metropolis of over 4.5 million people, with its residents originating from a staggering 170 nations and speaking approximately 100 different languages. What amazes visitors is that even with the multitude of ethnic groups, people seem to get along while retaining their unique cultures, perhaps lending credence to former prime minister Pierre Trudeau's notion of Canada's being much more of a mosaic of cultures and languages than a melting pot. Street signs are commonly in English *and* in the predominant language of the neighborhood. Newspapers are published in many languages weekly and daily. The city is home to Canada's largest gay and lesbian community—the third biggest in North America. Toronto hosts a tremendously successful international film festival every September, it is the second-largest live-theater venue on the continent (after New York), and it even has a pennant-winning baseball team, the Toronto Blue Jays. It's easy to find attractions here to satisfy every taste, whether it be for historic buildings, science museums, or waterfront parks.

The city officially became Toronto on March 6, 1834, but its roots are much more ancient than that. A Frenchman named Etienne Brûlé was sent into the not-yet-Canadian wilderness in the early 1600s by the famous explorer Samuel de Champlain to see what he could discover. And he discovered plenty: the river and portage routes from the St. Lawrence to Lake Huron, possibly Lakes Superior and Michigan, and, eventually, Lake Ontario. Of course the Huron peoples had known about these places for centuries; they had long ago named the area between the Humber and Don rivers "Toronto," which is believed to mean "a place of meetings." Later it developed into a busy village named Teiaiagon, then it was the site of a French trading post and, in 1793, became a British town named York. (If the British hadn't won the Seven Years' War in the late 1700s, you would be reading this in translation from the French). Finally, the city we know today was born, which once again took the original name of Toronto.

The city followed the usual history of colonial towns of the 19th century: it was invaded by the Americans in 1812; there were several devastating fires; there was a rebellion in 1837; and there was a slow but steady increase in its population of white Anglo-Saxon Protestants, from about 9,000 in the 1830s to well over 500,000 before the outbreak of World War II, at which time they outnumbered the non-WASPs by five to two. In the last five decades, Toronto has metamorphosed into a great world city, where colorful ethnic enclaves mix with imposing banks and government buildings—making this a wonderful town to explore.

The most recent alteration to the municipal setup occurred in January 1998, when the six communities that formerly made up the Municipality of Metropolitan Toronto (which itself was created in 1953 to help alleviate growing pains faced by the community with the rapid increase in immigration following the end of World War II) became one large megacity under the name City of Toronto. Visitors, however, will still find reminders of those five cities and one borough from the pre-megacity era (Toronto, Etobicoke, North York, Scarborough, York, and East York, respectively) on shop signs, as part of postal addresses, and in the names of subway stations and newly established Civic Service Centres.

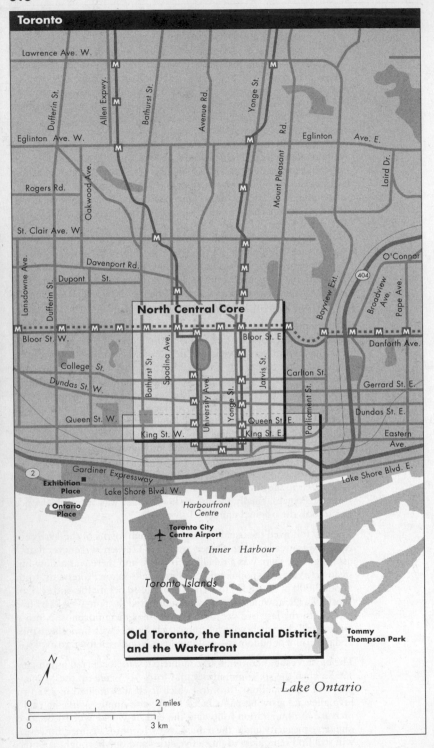

Lawrence Ave. W.

Dufferin St.

Allen Expwy.

Bathurst St.

Avenue Rd.

Yonge St.

Eglinton Ave. W.

Eglinton Ave. E.

Mount Pleasant Rd.

Laird Dr.

Rogers Rd.

Oakwood Ave.

St. Clair Ave. W.

Lansdowne Ave.

Dufferin St.

Davenport Rd.

O'Connor

Dupont St.

Bayview Ext.

404

Broadview Ave.

Pape Ave.

North Central Core

Bloor St. W.

Bloor St. E.

Danforth Ave.

Bathurst St.

Spadina Ave.

College St.

University Ave.

Yonge St.

Jarvis St.

Carlton St.

Gerrard St. E.

Dundas St. W.

Queen St. W.

Queen St. E.

Dundas St. E.

King St. W.

King St. E.

Parliament St.

Eastern Ave.

Gardiner Expressway

2

Exhibition Place

Lake Shore Blvd. E.

Lake Shore Blvd. W.

Ontario Place

Harbourfront Centre

Toronto City Centre Airport

Inner Harbour

Toronto Islands

Old Toronto, the Financial District, and the Waterfront

Tommy Thompson Park

Lake Ontario

N

0		2 miles
0		3 km

Pleasures and Pastimes

Dining

The city's dining scene flourished in the late '90s, providing a huge range of choices. Formal establishments and even steak houses are thriving, but not at the expense of the many new bistros, tapas bars, and noodle parlors. After each of Toronto's immigration waves, an intriguing new batch of restaurants opened. Toronto has been introduced to everything from Hungarian schnitzel after the 1956 revolution to Vietnamese and other Southeast Asian cuisines in the 1970s and beyond. Italian restaurants dominate the city's dining scene, reflecting the locals' long-term passion for this cuisine in all its regional variations, but you can also choose from an abundance of excellent Chinese, French, Greek, Indian, Indonesian, Japanese, Korean, Latin, Thai, seafood, vegetarian, creative contemporary, and, of course, Canadian fare. The wine lists of the finest restaurants include, in addition to international selections, excellent regional wines, while local microbrews provide wonderful accompaniments to more casual meals. If you're visiting in summer, do as the locals do and dine alfresco, a cherished Toronto pastime.

Ethnic Neighborhoods

You can tour the world in Toronto, and encounter markets, clothes, music, newspapers, cuisines, and customs from around the universe. If you walk around long enough, you may hear everything from Hindi to Greek. You can pick up a sari on Gerrard Street East, purchase Chinese herbal medicines on Dundas Street, and browse for French books on Queen Street West.

Little Italy is in the St. Clair Avenue and Bathurst Street area, with lively trattorias and excellent clothing boutiques. The city has three Chinatowns; an Eastern European neighborhood along Roncesvalles Avenue (mainly Polish and Ukrainian); and Estonian, Latvian and Russian wares and dishes can be found along Bloor Street West, from Runnymede Avenue west to Jane Street.

The West Indian community holds a summer festival, Caribana, at the end of every July, which is modeled after Trinidad and Tobago's famous pre-Lenten Carnival. Caribana draws hundreds of thousands of people annually and brings in millions of tourist dollars to the local economy. With more than 300,000 immigrants from 25 island nations, the community has spread to the northern suburbs, but several specialty shops in the Bloor and Bathurst streets area cater to tourists and locals alike. This is where you can find that quintessential spicy Jamaican patty or a bowl of Trinidadian crab and callaloo stew.

The Spanish-speaking community in Toronto is also well represented and spread evenly throughout the city. The first immigrants from Spain arrived in 1913, while many Latin Americans fled their homes for Canada during the turbulent 1960s and 1970s. Chileans and Salvadorans make up the largest number of immigrants, but the Brazilian community is also a visible presence—especially during a World Cup soccer tournament, when Brazilian–Canadians of all ages throng the streets in support of their team.

If you're in the mood to do some cross-cultural traveling in the space of a couple of days, Toronto is your city to do so. Even though many of the immigrants who originally settled Toronto's ethnic enclaves have moved to the suburbs, others have taken their places downtown and kept the old traditions alive.

Lodging

Toronto offers an array of places to lay your head that is commensurate with a city of its size and sophistication. Chain hotels have reliable properties in convenient locations around town. The First Nations inhabitants who came up with the name Toronto, or "place of meetings," certainly had foresight: conventions book huge blocks of hotel rooms year-round. This can mean annoying lobby bustle, but it also tends to ensure that properties in this competitive town have plenty of amenities and high levels of service. The emphasis on business also means that rates sometimes go down drastically on the weekends; many hotels have special packages for couples and families, too.

If you're more of a bed-and-breakfast person, a wide range of options abound, which you can find through the Bed & Breakfast Metropolitan Registry of Toronto (☎ 416/964–2566). There are even several properties in the gay village around Church Street and Wellesley Street East.

Smaller hotels, and apartment-style accommodation in the downtown core, are also moderately priced and therefore very popular in the summer months. If you plan on visiting during the Caribana Festival (late July) or during the Toronto International Film Festival (September), make sure you make your reservations well in advance.

Museums

This metropolis by the lake possesses miles of museums. The Royal Ontario Museum, affectionately known as the ROM, is a sprawling giant that presents a brilliant and wildly diverse collection from mummies and Chinese art to totem poles and musical instruments. Owned by the Government of Ontario, its galleries hold a diverse and eclectic mixture of priceless works, many having been donated by prominent Canadian families and literary figures.

For art lovers, Toronto is the place to explore Canadian art, which is often overlooked by American and European curators. The Art Gallery of Ontario is one place to start, and the McMichael Canadian Art Collection in Kleinburg has a superb collection set in lovely woodland. The former is surrounded by the Ontario College of Art & Design, the trendy neighborhood of Queen Street West to the south, and one of the city's Chinatowns to the west.

Another outstanding institution is the Ontario Science Centre. Then, too, the city has offbeat museums devoted to the study of hockey, design, history, and even shoes.

Parks and Ravines

When Toronto was first settled, it not only had a fine natural port, but also sat at the mouth of two rivers and a handful of streams. While these small streams have either dried up or been covered over by urban development, their valleys and ravines have been retained by the city as parkland. Many parks offer dirt, cinder, or asphalt paths for bikers and joggers. High Park, west of downtown, is lovely, and miniparks throughout the urban core afford good views, public sculpture, historical plaques, and, of course, benches for resting tired feet.

Since 1999, several parking lots off Yonge Street in the downtown core have been turned into mini-parks, with a fusion of florals and greenery in the summer months. This is a bonus for apartment and condominium dwellers with pets to walk (yes, there is a "stoop and scoop" policy!), or office workers needing a quiet refuge from the traffic to enjoy lunch.

Shopping

From haute couture to ethnic markets, Toronto has retail options for every purse and personal taste. Megamalls like the Eaton Centre vie with intimate boutiques on Bloor Street West and in the Yorkville area for shoppers' attention. Unique areas to explore include the St. Lawrence and Kensington markets; funky Queen Street West, with its street-smart shops; Chinatown and Spadina Avenue, loaded with bargains; Queen Street East, with a treasure trove of vintage and antiques stores; and Queen's Quay Terminal, a delightful converted warehouse on the waterfront (the Harbourfront Antique Market is nearby, too).

Spectator Sports

Toronto has venues for American favorites like baseball (the Toronto Blue Jays) and basketball (the Toronto Raptors), as well as for other spectator sports that have a stronger following in Europe. Ice hockey is a national mania; children start out as soon as they're old enough to toddle around on skates, move to league play when they're around 10, and generally keep going as long as their knees hold out. Maple Leaf tickets are a scarce commodity in this town. Amateur leagues sometimes play at 2 AM because there's so much competition for ice time. For a free look at nonprofessional enthusiasts, check out any park with a skating rink on a bright winter's day. U.S. fans may want to sample Canadian football at an Argonauts' game; the play is faster and (locals say) more exciting.

EXPLORING TORONTO

The boundaries of what Torontonians consider downtown, where you'll find most of the sights in this chapter, are subject to debate, but everyone agrees on the southern cutoff—Lake Ontario and the Toronto Islands. The other coordinates of the rectangle that comprise the city core are Bathurst Street to the west, Parliament Street to the east, and Eglinton Avenue to the north. Beyond these borders—to the southeast, southwest, northeast, and northwest are numerous sights that make excellent morning, afternoon, or full-day excursions on their own. An ideal way to get a sense of the city's layout is from one of the observation decks at the CN Tower on a clear day; the view is especially lovely at sunset.

Most city streets are organized on a grid system: with some exceptions, street numbers start at zero from the lake and increase as you go north. On the east–west axis, Yonge Street (pronounced "young"), Toronto's main thoroughfare, is the dividing line: you can expect higher numbers the farther away you get from Yonge.

A tip: traffic is dense and parking expensive within the city core. If you have a car with you, leave it at the hotel and save it for excursions to outlying attractions or to towns like Stratford. In the city, use the excellent Toronto Transit System (TTC) at $2 a ride, or $6.50 for an all-day pass; or take taxis to reach your destination.

Great Itineraries

To see and experience all that is Toronto, you should plan a stay of at least a week (preferably in spring, summer, or fall—winters can be bitter, though no worse than a winter in New York City). If you're here for a short period, you need to plan carefully so you don't miss the must-see sights. The following suggested itineraries will help you structure your visit efficiently.

IF YOU HAVE 1 DAY

The four structures that have become the icons of modern Toronto are grouped close enough together that they can all be visited on a single, albeit busy, day. Start at Queen and Bay streets at the ultramodern New City Hall; then cross the street and explore its quaint predecessor, Old City Hall. Walk south on Bay Street through the heart of the Financial District, with its handsome skyscrapers; head west on Front Street to the spectacular CN Tower. It's not hard to find—just look up at the world's tallest freestanding structure. From the tower's indoor and outdoor observation decks, the city lies spread out before you. Take a lunch break in the tower's 360 Revolving Restaurant.

Continue your day with a visit to the tower's neighbor to the west, the spectacular SkyDome, home of the Toronto Blue Jays baseball team and the Toronto Argonauts of the Canadian Football League. Provided the facility is not in use, you can take a guided tour, complete with a film showing how the retractable roof works. Leaving SkyDome, walk or take a taxi south to Queen's Quay Terminal, part of Harbourfront Centre, the city's lakefront cultural and recreational center. There's plenty to do along Queen's Quay, from shopping to visiting The Pier, a maritime museum. You can spend a comfortable evening strolling along the city's waterfront. The streetcar running along the center of Queen's Quay (make sure the sign in front says Union) will take you back uptown to Union subway station.

IF YOU HAVE 3 DAYS

Visit the classic tourist sights described above on your first day and prepare for a mix of culture, shopping, and relaxation for the next two days. Spend the morning of Day 2 exploring the original Chinatown laid out west along Dundas Street behind New City Hall all the way over to the "new" Chinatown in and around the busy Spadina Avenue–Dundas Street intersection. You'll be near the sights and smells of colorful Kensington Market, too. Walk south on Spadina to Queen Street West (five short blocks) and make a left to check out a funky, stylish new shopping district. You'll find restaurants and cafés here, too. Continue walking east, past the new and old city halls (visited on Day 1) and on a little farther to the the 300 or so shops of Eaton Centre, at Yonge Street. Even people who don't like to shop may be tempted. If you want to skip Eaton Centre or just take a quick look, you can spend the afternoon at the Art Gallery of Ontario (at Dundas and McCaul streets), with its outstanding Henry Moore collection; you can eat here, too. In the evening, pick your favorite ethnic cuisine and head to one of the city's excellent restaurants.

On Day 3, continue your shopping explorations along Bloor Street West, dubbed by some as Toronto's 5th Avenue, between Yonge Street and Avenue Road. Don't forget to explore nearby Yorkville, just to the north, where modern chrome-and-glass-encased shops give way to streets of boutiques nestled within restored former Victorian residences. Yorkville was a real hippie haven in the 1960s, giving birth to emerging musical artists Joni Mitchell and Gordon Lightfoot. Your next stop is the nearby Royal Ontario Museum, at Bloor Street and Queen's Park. Treasures from the worlds of art, archaeology, and science fill this museum; plan to spend two to four hours here. To relax a bit in the afternoon, you have two options. The first is to take the subway south on Yonge and walk to the docks at the foot of Bay Street and Queen's Quay to catch a ferry to the serene Toronto Islands; the view of the city skyline is an added plus. You can also travel 6 km (4 mi) due west of Bloor and Yonge streets (take the subway west to the High Park station and walk south) to large, lovely High Park. In the evening, take in a show or a concert—Toronto is a great city for theater and music.

Follow the itineraries above for your first three days, and venture a bit farther afield on Day 4. You can head in either of two directions to see a number of sights that are accessible by public transportation but are more easily reached by car. The first choices—great family options—are the Ontario Science Centre, with its engaging exhibits and demonstrations, and the sprawling Toronto Zoo. You could truly spend a good day at either, so plan your time and don't be distracted if you want to see both. The Science Center is 11 km (7 mi) northeast of downtown, and the zoo is 35 km (22 mi) northeast. The other choice for Day 4 is to head north of downtown and visit Black Creek Pioneer Village, a living-history museum dedicated to 19th-century life, and the McMichael Canadian Art Collection, an outstanding museum with works by Canadian and First Nations artists. The art museum is set on 100 wooded acres. Black Creek Pioneer Village is 20 km (12 mi) north of downtown; the McMichael is 30 km (19 mi) north. When you're back downtown in the evening, look for a place where you can dine alfresco—patio dining, as the locals say—or head to hip College Street in Little Italy.

On Day 5, you can choose to roam some special neighborhoods in Toronto—even explore the world. Purchase a TTC Day Pass, which allows unlimited use of transit vehicles after 9:30 AM and is available at subway stations. Some areas to the east of downtown are The Beaches, a great place to stroll the lakefront and shop, and The Danforth, with Greek and other restaurants. South of The Danforth is Cabbagetown, which has handsome 19th-century homes. Choices west of the downtown core are the arty Annex community and a number of Italian neighborhoods, including the suddenly hot strip of Little Italy on College Street from Euclid to Grace Street, and, farther north, the area around St. Clair Avenue West from Bathurst Street to Dufferin Street. You'll find intriguing eateries everywhere.

Old Toronto

In this district, which runs from Yonge Street east to Parliament Street and from King Street south to the lake, Toronto got its start as the village of York in 1793. In 1834, the year the little community was "erected" into a city, the area, described as a ward, was renamed in honor of Canada's patron saint, St. Lawrence. A pleasing natural disorder now prevails in this neighborhood, which blends old and new buildings, residential and commercial space. Within the space of a few blocks you can walk past the huge canopy of the 1960s-era Hummingbird Centre, where crowds throng for a ballet, to converted late-19th- and early 20th-century warehouses hosting an array of modern stores, to a hall that has operated continuously as a market since the early 1800s.

Numbers in the text and in the margin correspond to points of interest on the Old Toronto, the Financial District, and Harbourfront map.

A Good Walk

Start your tour at the northwest corner of Yonge and Front streets, where the **Hockey Hall of Fame and Museum** ① is housed in a decommissioned branch of the Bank of Montréal. After having your fill of hockey's golden moments, turn left and walk a short block north on Yonge to Wellington and turn left again. Walk less than half the block, then enter BCE Place, a modern new skyscraper. The reassembled stones of the former 15 Wellington Street West—the oldest building on this walk—are in the BCE Place concourse. The elegant Greek Revival–style bank was one of the earliest (1845) projects of William Thomas, the talented ar-

Old Toronto, the Financial District, and the Harbourfront

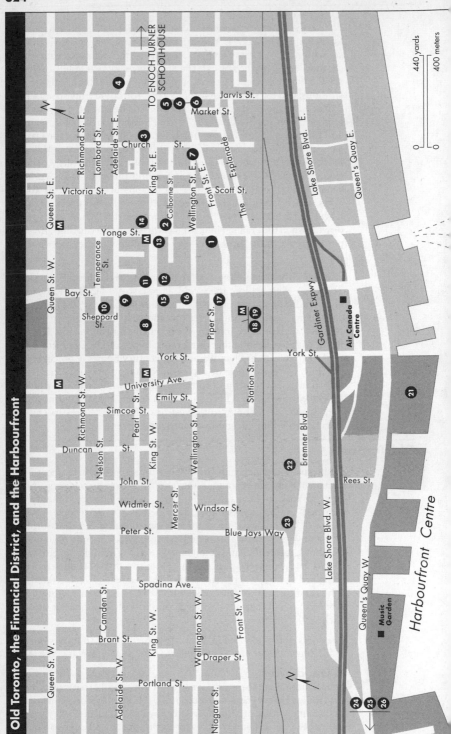

TO ENOCH TURNER SCHOOLHOUSE

Jarvis St.

Market St.

Richmond St. E.

Lombard St.

Adelaide St. E.

Church St.

King St. E.

Colborne St.

Wellington St. E.

Front St. E.

The Esplanade

Scott St.

Victoria St.

Queen St. E.

Yonge St.

Temperance St.

Bay St.

Sheppard St.

Piper St.

Queen St. W.

Lake Shore Blvd. E.

Queen's Quay E.

Gardiner Expwy.

Air Canada Centre

York St.

York St.

University Ave.

Richmond St. W.

Simcoe St.

Pearl St.

Emily St.

Station St.

Duncan St.

Nelson St.

King St. W.

Wellington St. W.

Bremner Blvd.

Rees St.

John St.

Widmer St.

Mercer St.

Windsor St.

Peter St.

Blue Jays Way

Lake Shore Blvd. W.

Spadina Ave.

Camden St.

King St. W.

Queen's Quay W.

Music Garden

Harbourfront Centre

Brant St.

Wellington St. W.

Draper St.

Front St. W.

Queen St. W.

Adelaide St. W.

Portland St.

Niagara St.

440 yards

400 meters

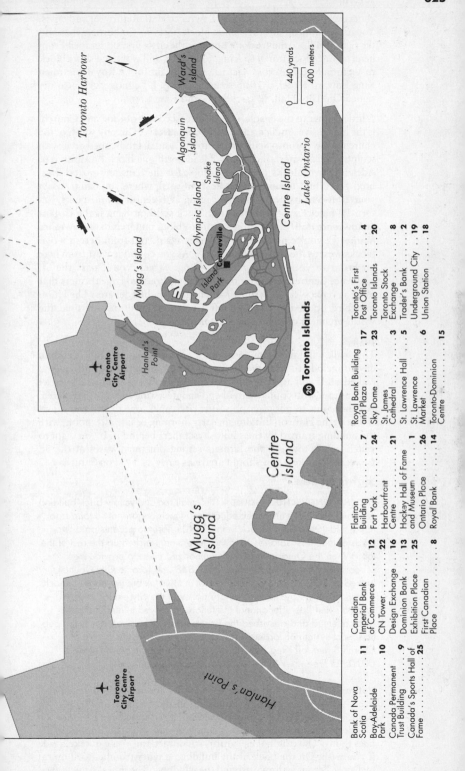

20 Toronto Islands

Bank of Nova
Scotia **11**
Bay-Adelaide
Park **10**
Canada Permanent
Trust Building **9**
Canada's Sports Hall of
Fame **25**

Canadian
Imperial Bank
of Commerce **12**
CN Tower **22**
Design Exchange . . . **16**
Dominion Bank **13**
Exhibition Place . . . **25**
First Canadian
Place **8**

Flatiron
Building **7**
Fort York **24**
Harbourfront
Centre **21**
Hockey Hall of Fame
and Museum **1**
Ontario Plaice **26**
Royal Bank **14**

Royal Bank Building
and Plaza **17**
Sky Dome **23**
St. James
Cathedral **3**
St. Lawrence Hall . . **5**
St. Lawrence
Market **6**
Toronto-Dominion
Centre **15**

Toronto's First
Post Office **4**
Toronto Stock
Exchange **20**
Toronto Stock
Exchange **8**
Trader's Bank **2**
Underground City . . **19**
Union Station **18**

chitect who also designed the St. Lawrence Hall. Return to, and cross, Yonge Street; head another short block north to Colborne, where on the right you'll see the **Trader's Bank** ②, the city's first skyscraper. From here, go one block north to King, turn right, and walk one short block to Victoria Street. Across Victoria is the beautiful Le Royal Meridien King Edward Hotel, a 1903 structure by E. J. Lennox, who also designed Old City Hall, Massey Hall, and Casa Loma.

A little farther to the east, on the northeast corner of King and Church, is the impressive Anglican **St. James Cathedral** ③. Directly south of the church is the Toronto Sculpture Garden, a small landscaped area with sculpture and waterfall displays. Head north one block on Church to Adelaide; two blocks to the east (look for the flags and postal drop box) you'll find **Toronto's First Post Office** ④, where you can transact your 20th-century postal business using 19th-century implements. Return 1½ blocks west to Jarvis; one block south at King is the elegant **St. Lawrence Hall** ⑤. Continue south one block on Jarvis to **St. Lawrence Market** ⑥; you're now on Front Street again, and from here it's two blocks west to the **Flatiron Building** ⑦. As you continue west from here on Front to your starting point, Yonge Street, you'll pass the St. Lawrence Centre and the Hummingbird Centre, two large theaters that serve as venues for everything from ballet to public debates. The Hummingbird opened as the O'Keefe Centre in 1960 and featured the world premiere of the musical *Camelot*.

TIMING

This walk will take from 45 minutes for the buildings alone to a half day to include time at the hockey museum, market, post office, and cathedral. If you add the adjacent Cabbagetown or Financial District to your tour, you could easily spend an interesting full day in the area. For those out to photograph scenic cityscapes, one of the best views is that of the Flatiron building in early morning or late afternoon, with the building framed by the sunlit skyscrapers behind it. If you want to watch or photograph the farmers setting out their wares at the St. Lawrence Market, you should arrive as early as 5 AM on Saturday.

Sights to See

OFF THE
BEATEN PATH

ENOCH TURNER SCHOOLHOUSE – This small red-and-yellow brick building is a reminder that free public education, which began not so long ago in the mid-19th century. Back in the 1840s, Toronto parents paid two-thirds of teachers' salaries, and the government picked up the rest of the tab. When the Ontario legislature authorized cities to provide free schools paid for by property taxes in 1848, the Toronto City Council balked and closed every public school in town. A brewer named Enoch Turner, outraged by the reactionary policy of the city elders, created Toronto's first free educational institution. Three years later, the politicians relented and absorbed the Enoch Turner Schoolhouse into the public school system of Toronto. The schoolhouse is five blocks east of Church Street, off King Street East. ✉ *106 Trinity St.,* ☎ *416/863–0010.* ▧ *Free.* ☉ *Weekdays 9:30–4 (call ahead).*

⑦ **Flatiron Building.** Similarly shaped relatives live in wedge-shape lots all over North America. This building, on the triangle of Wellington, Scott, and Front streets, was erected in 1892 as the head office of the Gooderham and Worts distilling company and still hosts important offices today. The original elevator is still intact and you can take a ride if you wish. On the back of the building, a witty trompe-l'oeil mural by Derek Besant is drawn around the windows. The mural depicts even larger windows, which look like the windows on the south side of Front Street. The illusion? It appears that the whole thing has been tacked up on the wall and is peeling off. ⊠ *Front St., between Church and Scott Sts.*

① **Hockey Hall of Fame and Museum.** Even if you're not a hockey fan, it's worth a trip here to see this shrine to Canada's favorite sport. Relocated to a larger, beautifully ornate building in 1993, the museum has everything from the original Stanley Cup, donated in 1893, to displays of goalie masks, skate and stick collections, jerseys of the great players, video displays of big games, a replica of the Montréal Canadiens' locker room, and chairs from the old Madison Square Garden in New York City. The details of the 1885 building, a former Bank of Montréal branch designed by architects Darling & Curry, have been lovingly preserved: note the richly carved Ohio stone and the Hermés figure supporting the chimney near the back of the building. ⊠ *30 Yonge St.,* ☎ *416/360–7765,* WEB *www.hhof.com.* ⌨ *$12.* ☉ *Weekdays 10– 5, Sat. 9:30–6, Sun. 10:30–5.*

NEED A BREAK?

BCE Place (⊠ 42 Yonge St., between Front and Wellington, Yonge and Bay Sts.), a modern office and retail complex cleverly designed to incorporate the Bank of Montréal building and other older structures under a glass roof, is not only one of the most impressive architectural spaces in Toronto—the atrium is also a pleasant place to sit and enjoy a coffee and baguette.

③ **St. James Cathedral.** Even if bank towers dwarf it now, this Anglican church with noble Gothic spires has the tallest steeple in Canada. Its illuminated spire clock once guided ships into the harbor, which used to be much closer to the church (everything south of Front Street is landfill). This is the fourth St. James Cathedral on this site; the third one burned down in the Great Fire of 1849. As part of the church's bicentennial in 1997, a new peal of 12 bells was installed. Stand near the church most Sundays 30 minutes before the 11 AM service, and you can be rewarded with a glorious concert of ringing bells. ⊠ *65 Church St., at King St., northeast corner,* ☎ *416/364–7865,* WEB *www.stjamescathedral.on.ca.*

⑤ **St. Lawrence Hall.** Standing on the site of Toronto's first town hall, the St. Lawrence Hall, built 1850–51, demonstrates Renaissance Revival architecture at its finest. Erected originally for musical performances and balls, this is where Jenny Lind sang, where antislavery demonstrations were held, and where P. T. Barnum first presented the midget Tom Thumb. Take time to admire the exterior of this architectural gem, now used for everything from small concerts to wedding receptions and graduation parties. ⊠ *157 King St. E,* ☎ *416/392–7130,* WEB *www.stlawrencemarket.com.*

⑥ **St. Lawrence Market.** Built in 1844 as Toronto's first true city hall (for the first 10 years of the city's existence, politicians were forced to use the former town hall up the street), the building now has an exhibition hall upstairs—the Market Gallery—where the council chambers once stood. The building continues to serve the citizens of the city as a food market, which began growing up around the city hall in the early 1900s. Renovated in 1978, the market is renowned for its wide range of foods—from fresh, exotic fruits and vegetables to Ontario cheddar, homemade bread, and conch meat. At the four dozen or so stalls, you can buy lunch fixings for a picnic, or for excursions to the zoo, Canada's Wonderland, or the Toronto Islands, where the excellence of the attractions doesn't guarantee the excellence of the cuisine. Outside the front doors, artisans and stall vendors hawk their wares. The plain brick building across Front Street, on the north side, is open only on Saturday morning as a farmer's market; it's a cornucopia of fine produce and homemade jams, relishes, sauces, and jellies from the farms just north of Toronto. ⊠ *Front and Jarvis Sts.,* ☎ *416/392–7219.* ☉ *Sat. at 5 AM for farmer's market at north bldg.; Tues.–Sat. about 8–6 for permanent stalls at south bldg.*

☙ ❹ **Toronto's First Post Office.** Dating from 1833, when Toronto was still the British colony called Upper Canada, this working post office continues to keep quill pens, ink pots, and sealing wax in use. Exhibits include reproductions of letters from the 1820s and 1830s. It costs $1 to write an old-fashioned letter and affix current postage to it. ⊠ *260 Adelaide St. E,* ☎ *416/865–1833,* ᴡᴇʙ *www.townofyork.com.* ⊡ *Free.* ☉ *Weekdays 9–4, weekends 10–4.*

❷ **Trader's Bank.** It's fun to see the early 20th-century equivalent of the CN Tower. At 15 stories, this was the first "skyscraper" of the city when it went up in 1905–06, complete with an observation deck. The construction of a high-rise next door to the north (at 69 Yonge Street) helped turn the intersection of Yonge and Colborne into a grouping of the tallest buildings in North America outside Manhattan. After nearly a century, the building is still owned by Canadian Pacific, the largest private employer in Canada (planes, trains, hotels, and more). ⊠ *67 Yonge St.*

The Financial District

Those striking, often magnificent high-rises that form the greatest part of Toronto's skyline are banks, banks, and banks. Every one of the major banks of Canada has its headquarters in downtown Toronto, between University Avenue and Yonge Street. The fact that many of the older properties have now been included on the city's Inventory of Buildings of Architectural and Historical Importance proves Toronto is making a concerted effort to preserve its history. Only two cheers though—there was massive destruction of great 19th-century buildings throughout earlier parts of the 20th century.

The most interesting aspect of a Financial District walk is the architectural variety of the skyscrapers—temples to steel construction that reflect the prosperity of the steel industry in Canada. Many banks have more than one building named for them. Most of the towers have bank branches, restaurants, and retail outlets on their ground floors and are also connected to the Underground City of shops and tunnels, so you have many easy choices for a snack or to change money along the way.

Numbers in the text and in the margin correspond to points of interest on the Old Toronto, the Financial District, and Harbourfront map.

A Good Walk

Start the tour at the St. Andrew TTC station on the northeast corner of University and King. Walk one short block east on King past York Street, where you'll see the huge **First Canadian Place** ⑧ complex, which includes the **Toronto Stock Exchange** ⑧. Leave First Canadian Place by the Adelaide Street exit and proceed a half block east on Adelaide to the corner of Bay Street to the **Canada Permanent Trust Building** ⑨ and the **Bay-Adelaide Park** ⑩, tucked in from the street. From here, head one block south on Bay Street to King, where, on the northeast corner, you'll see the **Bank of Nova Scotia** ⑪, with the Scotia Tower just to the east. Cross King to the **Canadian Imperial Bank of Commerce** ⑫ buildings, with their distinct architectural styles, and then go a half block east to Yonge Street, where on the southwest corner of Yonge and King you'll come to the **Dominion Bank** ⑬. At the northeast corner of the same intersection is the original **Royal Bank** ⑭ building.

Now walk back west along King Street to Bay, and the **Toronto-Dominion Centre (TD Centre)** ⑮. A block south on Bay Street is the **Design Exchange** ⑯, the wonderful art deco building that housed the old Toronto Stock Exchange. Continue south on Bay Street for less than a block to reach the modern **Royal Bank Building and Plaza** ⑰; **Union Station** ⑱, where the trains of the national, intercity, and Toronto transit system meet, is just across Front Street from here. You can descend from Union Station into Toronto's vast **Underground City** ⑲, a warren worthy of its own tour.

TIMING

The walk outlined encompasses a little more than 1½ km (1 mi). Stock Market Place at the Toronto Stock Exchange and the Design Exchange exhibits take about 45 minutes each, and if you come between noon and 2 during the summer, you might catch a concert. Taking into account stops for the TSE and Design Exchange and a snack and/or concert, the tour should run two to three hours. This area is adjacent to Old Toronto, and the two tours together would fill a pleasant day.

Sights to See

⑪ **Bank of Nova Scotia.** Built between 1949 and 1951 and partially replaced by the ScotiaBank Tower just to the east, this bank features sculptural panels inspired by Greek mythology above its large windows. In the lobby, bas-reliefs symbolize four regions of Canada; look up to see a brightly colored gilt plaster ceiling. Other interesting details include the original stainless-steel-and-glass stairway with marine motifs and the marble counters and floors. The north wall relief depicts some of the industries and enterprises financed by the bank. ⊠ *44 King St. W, northeast corner, at Bay St.,* ☎ *416/866–6161.*

⑩ **Bay-Adelaide Park.** Originally designed to be a plaza for a building that fell victim to the recession of the early 1990s, the park was nevertheless completed in 1993 as an homage to those who worked on it. The multistory indoor-outdoor space includes a water sculpture, a monument dedicated to construction workers, and a tropical plant collection. ⊠ *Yonge St., between Richmond and Adelaide Sts.*

⑨ **Canada Permanent Trust Building.** Built in the Roaring '20s, just before the 1929 stock-market crash, this skyscraper was designed in New York wedding-cake style. Look up at the ornate stone carvings that grace both the lower and top stories, where stylized faces peer down to the street below. You can walk through the imposing vaulted entrance with its polished brass doors; even the elevator doors in the foyer are embossed. The spacious banking hall has a vaulted ceiling, marble walls and pillars, and a marble floor with mosaic borders. Those were the days—or so the builders thought. ⊠ *320 Bay St., south of Adelaide St.,* ☎ *416/361–8600.*

⑫ **Canadian Imperial Bank of Commerce.** The first of the "twin" Bank of Commerce buildings went up in the two years following the stock-market crash of 1929, but hard times didn't mean stinting on details: the stunning interior has marble floors, limestone walls, and bronze vestibule doors decorated with an array of animals and birds. Murals in the alcoves on either side of the entrance trace the history of transportation. The bronze elevator doors are richly decorated, the vaulted banking hall is lit by chandeliers, and each desk has its own lamp. What a difference from most of the faceless skyscrapers of today! Just south of the old tower, set slightly back around a plaza at 243 Bay Street, is the bank's 57-story stainless-steel counterpart, designed by I. M. Pei in the early 1970s. ⊠ *25 King St.,* ☎ *416/980–2211.*

⑯ Design Exchange. A delightful example of Streamlined Moderne design, a later and more austere version of art deco, this building is clad in polished pink granite and smooth buff limestone, with stainless-steel doors. Between 1937 and 1983, the DX (as it's now known) was the home of the Toronto Stock Exchange. Don't miss the witty stone frieze carved above the doors—a banker in top hat marching behind a laborer and sneaking his hand into the worker's pocket. (Only in Canada, where socialism has always been a strong force, would you find such a political statement on the side of a stock exchange.) In 1994 the building reopened as a nonprofit center devoted to promoting Canadian design. The old trading floor is now used for rotating exhibits—check the local papers for what's on—and the ground floor has a café with good espresso. Special fund-raising events for charities are also held at the DX on a regular basis. ⊠ *234 Bay St.,* ☎ *416/216–2160,* WEB *www.dx.org.* ⊠ *$5.* ◷ *Weekdays 10–6, weekends noon–5.*

⑬ Dominion Bank. Erected in 1913–14 and designed by one of the architects (Frank Darling) responsible for the voluptuous Bank of Montréal branch at Yonge and Front streets, Dominion Bank is a classic Chicago-style skyscraper. You can climb the marble-and-bronze stairway to the opulent banking hall on the second floor and enjoy all the gleaming marble as well as the ornate plaster ceiling, featuring the coats of arms of what were then the nine Canadian provinces (Newfoundland did not join the Confederation until 1949). ⊠ *1 King St. W, corner of Yonge St.,* ☎ *416/982–7748.*

⑧ First Canadian Place. Built in the early 1970s and also known as the Bank of Montréal tower, this building has 72 stories deliberately faced with white marble to contrast with the black of the Toronto-Dominion Centre to the south and with the nearby silver of I. M. Pei's Bank of Commerce tower. This is one of the more attractive office–retail developments in the city. It's also interesting as an early and successful real estate project by the Reichman brothers, who later came to fiscal grief when their Canary Docks project in London failed to capture the imagination—and rental contracts—of that city's financial community. First Canadian Place is best known, however, as the home of the **Toronto Stock Exchange.** ⊠ *100 King St. W,* ☎ *416/363–4669.*

⑭ Royal Bank. The 1913 building that predated the structure of the same name on Bay and Front streets can't quite match the newer building for glitter, but it's no slouch in the decorative department. Note the distinctive cornice, the overhanging roof, the sculpted ox skulls above the ground-floor windows, and the classically detailed leaves at the top of the Corinthian columns. Today the once wide-awake banking floor has been taken over by a company that sells mattresses. ⊠ *2 King St. E, at Yonge St.,* ☎ *416/974–0048.*

⑰ Royal Bank Building and Plaza. Designed by the gifted Torontonian Boris Zerafa, who was also involved in the creation of the Richmond-Adelaide Centre and the ScotiaBank Tower, this 1976 building is a classic of its kind. In this case, all that glitters *is* gold: the exterior is coated with 2,500 ounces of the precious ore to keep the heat in and the cold out (or vice versa, depending on the season). It's "a palette of color and texture as well as mass," in Zerafa's own words. The surface creates gorgeous reflections of sky, clouds, and other buildings; this is the jewel in the crown of the Toronto skyline. The building, dramatic in almost any light, is especially stunning in a full-force sunset. ⊠ *200 Bay St.,* ☎ *416/974–3940.*

⑮ Toronto-Dominion Centre. Mies van der Rohe, a virtuoso of modern architecture, designed this five-building masterwork, even though he died in 1969 before it was fully realized. As with his acclaimed Seagram Building in New York, Mies stripped these buildings to their skin and bones of bronze-color glass and black-metal I-beams. The TD Centre's tallest tower, the Toronto Dominion Bank Tower, reaches 56 stories. The only decoration consists of geometric repetition, and the only extravagance is the use of rich materials, such as marble counters and leather-covered furniture. The setting is far from austere, however. In summer, the plazas and grass are full of office workers eating lunch and listening to one of many free outdoor concerts. Inside the low-rise square banking pavilion at King and Bay streets is a virtually intact Mies interior. Inside the Toronto-Dominion Centre's Maritime Life Tower is the **Gallery of Inuit Art** (⊠ 79 Wellington St., ☎ 416/982–8473), one of the few galleries in North America devoted to Inuit art. The incredible collection, equal to that of the Smithsonian Institution, focuses on Canada's huge and unexplored northern frontier. ⊠ *55 King St. W,* ☎ *416/982–8473.* ☜ *Free.* ☉ *Weekdays 8–6, weekends 10–4.*

NEED A BREAK?

If you like to sit on a bench and watch the world go by, you won't find a better spot than **King Street West** in the theater district. Grab a hot dog, take a seat, and watch theatergoers and maybe even actors walk by. Don't like hot dogs? Don't worry: Italian, Greek, French, and Canadian restaurants and bars all wait anxiously next to the theaters for pre- and postshow action.

⑧ Toronto Stock Exchange. Here beats the pulse of the Canadian economy, and to help the public better understand how it all works, the Toronto Stock Exchange (TSE) has recently opened Stock Market Place, a dynamic state-of-the-art visitor and education center. The history and mystery of stocks and bonds, money markets, and diversified funds are explained through a variety of entertaining and educational interactive displays. ⊠ *Main floor, The Exchange Tower, 130 King St. W, between Bay and York Sts.,* ☎ *416/947–4670,* WEB *www.tse.com.* ☜ *Free.* ☉ *Weekdays 10–5.*

⑲ Underground City. This subterranean universe, which lays claim to being the largest pedestrian walkway in the world, emerged in the mid-1960s partly to replace the retail services in small buildings that were demolished to make way for the latest round of skyscrapers, and partly to protect office workers from the harsh winter weather. As each major building went up, the developers agreed to build and to connect their underground shopping areas with each other and with the subway system. You can walk from beneath Union Station to the Royal York Hotel, the Toronto-Dominion Centre, First Canadian Place, the Sheraton Centre, The Bay, Eaton Centre, New City Hall, and the Atrium on Dundas Street West without ever seeing the light of day. There are nearly 11 km (7 mi) of sparkling clean, well-lit, wheelchair-accessible tunnels altogether—lined wall-to-wall with eateries, shops, banks, and even dental offices and theaters. The 29 tunnels tie together six hotels, nearly 50 office towers, five subway stations, more than 1,000 stores and restaurants, SkyDome, the CN Tower, the 16-screen Cineplex theater, and the intercity bus and rail stations. You'll encounter everything from art exhibitions to buskers (the best are the winners of citywide auditions, licensed to perform throughout the subway system) and walkways, fountains, and trees. There are underground passageways in other parts of the city—one beneath Bloor Street, between Yonge and Bay streets, and another beneath College Street, between Yonge and Bay Streets—but this is the city's most extended subterranean network. PATH maps to guide you through this labyrinth are available in many downtown news and convenience stores.

⑱ Union Station. The popular historian Pierre Berton wrote that the planning of Union Station recalled "the love lavished on medieval churches." Indeed, this train depot that anchors the financial district both visually and historically can be regarded as a cathedral built to serve the god of steam. Designed in 1907 and opened officially in 1927 by the Prince of Wales, it has a 40-ft-high ceiling of Italian tile and 22 pillars weighing 70 tons apiece. The vast main hall, with its lengthy concourse and the light flooding in from arched windows at each end, was designed to evoke the majesty of the country that spread out by rail and imagination from this spot. To this end, too, the names of the towns and cities across Canada that were served by the country's two railway lines, Grand Trunk (which was to become part of today's Canadian National) and Canadian Pacific, are inscribed on a frieze that runs along the inside of the hall. Train travel declined and the building came very near to being demolished in the 1970s, but public opposition eventually proved strong enough to save it, and Union Station is now a vital commuter hub. Commuter, subway, and long-distance trains all arrive and depart from here. ⊠ *65–75 Front St. W, between Bay and York Sts.*

Harbourfront

Before the drastic decline of trucking reduced the Great Lakes trade, Toronto's waterfront was an important center for shipping and warehousing. For a long time after it fell into commercial disuse, the area was sadly neglected. The Gardiner Expressway, Lake Shore Boulevard, and a network of rusty rail yards stood as hideous barriers to the natural beauty of Lake Ontario; the area overflowed with grain silos, warehouses, and malodorous towers of malt, used by local breweries.

Since the early 1980s, however, the city has worked to reclaim this area, now known as Harbourfront, for people-friendly purposes such as residences (some of the city's most expensive real estate can be found here), shops, and parks. The reclaimed lakefront is now appealing for strolls, and myriad recreational and amusement options make it ideal for those traveling with children. As part of the restoration effort, a light rapid transit (LRT) line between Union Station and Harbourfront came into operation in summer 1990. Seven years later the line was combined with another new LRT line constructed on Spadina Avenue. Today the red-and-white streetcars on the 510 Spadina line, which operates between Union Station and the Bloor-Danforth subway, stop at numerous locations along Harbourfront and on colorful Spadina Avenue.

Numbers in the text and in the margin correspond to points of interest on the Old Toronto, the Financial District, and Harbourfront map.

A Good Tour

The waterfront area explored here is roughly 4 km (2½ mi) long; after visits to Harbourfront Centre, SkyDome, or the CN Tower, you might want to proceed by car or taxi because the distances between sights increase and the walking gets a bit more awkward. Start your tour at the Harbourfront stretch between Yonge and Bay streets, south of the Westin Harbour Castle Hotel. The docks here are the embarkation point for ferries to the **Toronto Islands** ⑳, and the surrounding plaza has a festive air, with its balloon sellers and vendors of hot dogs, cotton candy, and ice cream. When you return from the islands, walk west on Queen's Quay West about ½ km (¼ mi) to **Harbourfront Centre** ㉑; along the way you'll see Toronto's amateur sailors taking their boats out on the lake. From here, head north on York Street, then west on Bremner Boulevard about 1¼ km (¾ mi) to the **CN Tower** ㉒ (you'll be going under highway bridges, but persevere). Next to the CN Tower is **SkyDome,** ㉓ which you're more likely to visit when your favorite sport is being played. Not going to a game? Tours of SkyDome are available.

Walk south on Rees Street back to Queen's Quay West, then proceed west 1½ km (1 mi) to Bathurst Street. Walk north on Bathurst about ½ km (¼ mi); under the expressway you'll see the entrance to **Fort York** ㉔ on your left. From Fort York, go south on Bathurst, then west 1 km (½ mi) on Lake Shore Boulevard to **Exhibition Place** ㉕, home to one of the world's largest annual expositions—the Canadian National Exhibition (CNE; mid-August–Labor Day)—and various seasonal events, including a variety of trade and consumer shows in the National Trade Centre. Here you can explore the history of Canadian sports at **Canada's Sports Hall of Fame** ㉕. After Exhibition Place, use the pedestrian bridge to cross Lake Shore Boulevard to **Ontario Place** ㉖, a lakeside amusement park built by the province.

TIMING

All the attractions on this tour are open year-round, but the milder weather from May through October makes exploring them easier and more pleasant; it's also the best time to find the sights in full operation. The walk alone will take about one hour, at a strolling rate. If you're going to the Toronto Islands, add 45 minutes just to cross the bay and return on the same ferry. Depending on your interest in the various sights in the area, you can spend anywhere from a half day to three days here.

Sights to See

㉕ **Canada's Sports Hall of Fame.** This museum in Exhibition Place has three floors devoted to Canadian sports heroes throughout history. Exhibits include touch-screen computers with autobiographies, highlights of famous careers, and sports quizzes. ✉ *Dufferin St. and Lake Shore Blvd., in the center of the CNE grounds,* ☎ *416/260–6789,* WEB *www.city.toronto.on.ca/exhibitionplace.* 🎫 *Free.* ☉ *Weekdays 10–4:30.*

★ ☾ ㉒ **CN Tower.** The tallest freestanding structure in the world at 1,815 ft and 5 inches high—yes, it's listed in the *Guinness Book of World Records*—the CN Tower is tall for a reason. Prior to the opening of this telecommunications tower in summer 1976, so many tall buildings had been built over the previous decades that lower radio and TV transmission towers were having trouble broadcasting. The $63 million building weighs 130,000 tons and contains enough concrete to build a curb along Highway 401 from Toronto to Kingston, some 262 km (162 mi) to the east. It's worth a visit if the weather is clear, despite the steep fee. Six glass-fronted elevators zoom up the outside of the tower. The elevators travel at 20 ft per second and the ride takes less than a minute—a rate of ascent similar to that of a jet-plane takeoff. Each elevator has one floor-to-ceiling glass wall—three opaque walls make the trip easier on anyone prone to vertigo. Also, an elevator attendant chatters away during each ride, putting almost everyone at ease.

There are four observation decks to choose from. The **Glass Floor Level,** some 1,122 ft above the ground, is just what the name describes, and it's like walking on a cloud. This could well be the most photographed indoor location in the city: almost every visitor wants to lie on the transparent floor and have his or her picture taken from above. Beyond the Glass Floor Level are the **Look Out Level,** at 1,136 ft, and ascending one level more, the excellent **360 Revolving Restaurant.** Continuing the climb, and at an elevation of 1,465 ft, is the **Sky Pod,** the world's highest public observation gallery; it's more than 30 stories higher than the other decks and a visit costs about $7.50 more. All the levels provide spectacular panoramic views of Toronto, Lake Ontario, and the Toronto Islands. On really clear days you can often see Lake Simcoe to the north and the mist rising from Niagara Falls to the south.

On the ground level, the **Marketplace at the Tower** has 12,500 square ft of shopping space with quality Canadian sports and travel items and souvenirs, along with a shop selling Inuit art. You can also find the **Fresh Market Cafe,** with seating for 300, the **Maple Leaf Cinema,** which screens the 15-minute documentary, *To the Top,* regarding the building of the Tower, the **Themed Arcade,** with the latest in simulated game experiences, including extreme sports like Alpine Racer, TopSkater, and Indy racing.

One of the most popular attractions at the Tower is **Thrill Zone,** at the observation level near the top of the structure. Digital animation lets you experience the thrill—without the risk—of bungee jumping, hang gliding, or tightrope walking from the top of the CN Tower to nearby office buildings.

Peak visiting hours are 11–4, particularly on weekends; you may wish to work around them. ⊠ *301 Front St. W,* ☎ *416/868–6937; 416/362–5411 restaurant,* WEB *www.cntower.ca.* ⌨ *Observation levels $15.99; concourse attractions and Sky Pod at an additional cost.* ☉ *Sun.–Thurs. 10 AM–10 PM, Fri.–Sat. 10 AM–11 PM; hrs for attractions vary so call ahead.*

㉕ **Exhibition Place.** The Canadian National Exhibition (CNE or "the Ex") draws the most people to this part of Harbourfront, but you'll find many other things happening here year-round. The Ex takes place the last two weeks of August and Labor Day weekend, attracting more than 3 million people each year. It began back in 1879 as primarily an agricultural show, and remnants of that tradition can still be found in the livestock exhibits. Now in its second century, the Ex is a noisy, crowded, often entertaining collection of carnies pushing $5 balloons, plus tummy-turning midway rides, bands, horticultural and technological exhibits, parades, dog swims, horse shows, and (sometimes) top-notch performances. The latter have included grandstand appearances by Elton John, Shania Twain, Bill Cosby, Kenny Rogers, and Whitney Houston. Avoid taking a car to the Ex; the parking is insufficient and always terribly overpriced. Numerous buses and streetcars labeled "Exhibition" travel into the CNE grounds. Also on the grounds is **Canada's Sports Hall of Fame.** ⊠ *Lake Shore Blvd., between Strachan Ave. and Dufferin St.,* ☎ *416/393–6000.*

★ ㉔ **Fort York.** The most historic site in Toronto is a must for anyone interested in the origins of the city. The founding of Toronto occurred in 1793 when the British built Fort York to protect the entrance to the harbor during Anglo-American strife. Twenty years later the fort was the scene of the bloody Battle of York, in which explorer and general Zebulon Pike led U.S. forces against the fort's outnumbered British, Canadian, and First Nations defenders. The Americans won this battle—their first major victory in the War of 1812—and burned down the provincial buildings during a six-day occupation. A year later British forces retaliated when they captured Washington and torched its public buildings, including the Executive Mansion. A tale people love to tell in Toronto is that a subsequent application of whitewash to cover the charred wood gave rise to the sobriquet "White House," a term confirmed on presidential letterhead by Teddy Roosevelt years later. Today Fort York's defensive walls surround Canada's largest collection of original War of 1812 buildings. Exhibits include restored barracks, kitchens, and gunpowder magazines, plus changing museum displays. ✉ *100 Garrison Rd., between Bathurst St. and Strachan Ave., north of Fleet St.,* ☎ *416/392–6907.* ☜ *$5.* ☉ *Hrs vary; call for details.*

★ ☺ ㉑ **Harbourfront Centre.** Stretching from just west of York Street to Spadina Avenue, this culture-and-recreation center is a match for San Francisco's Pier 39 and Baltimore's Inner Harbor and is one of the highlights of a visit to Toronto. A project of the federal government, the original Harbourfront opened in 1974, rejuvenating more than a mile of city waterfront that had deteriorated badly over the years. Today, Harbourfront Centre, a streamlined version of the original concept, draws more than 3 million visitors to the 10-acre site each year.

The **Queen's Quay Terminal** at Harbourfront Centre is a must-see. The former Terminal Warehouse building, where a variety of products shipped to Toronto were stored before being delivered to shops all over the city, was transformed in 1983 into a magnificent, eight-story structure with delightful specialty shops, eateries, and the handsome 450-seat Premiere Dance Theatre. ✉ *204 Queen's Quay W,* ☎ *416/203–0510.*

Contemporary art exhibits of painting and sculpture, architecture and video, photography and design are mounted at the **Power Plant,** which can be spotted by its tall red smokestack. It was built in 1927 as a power station for the Terminal Warehouse's ice-making plant. ✉ *231 Queen's Quay W,* ☎ *416/973–4934,* WEB *www.culturenet.ca/powerplant.* ☜ *$4, free Wed. 5–8.* ☉ *Tues. and Thurs.–Sun. noon–6, Wed. noon–8.*

York Quay Centre offers concerts, live theater, readings, and even skilled artisans at work in open craft studios. A shallow pond at the south end is used for canoe lessons in warmer months and as the largest artificial ice-skating rink in North America in more wintry times. At the nearby Nautical Centre, many private firms give lessons in sailing and canoeing, with vessels for rent. ✉ *235 Queen's Quay W,* ☎ *416/973–3000.*

An ambitious museum dedicated to all things nautical, **The Pier** provides an interactive experience with a wide range of thematic exhibits and changing programs and activities. Highlights include the Discovery Gallery, where you can guide a ship through a set of canal locks or explore a shipwreck; the Boat Shop, in which artisans using mostly forgotten skills and techniques construct traditional watercraft; and the Livery, where you can rent these same traditional craft and explore the harbor. ✉ *245 Queen's Quay W,* ☎ *416/338–7437.* ☜ *$5.* ☉ *July–Aug., daily 10–6; Apr.–June and Sept.–Oct., daily 10–4.*

On the north side of Queen's Quay is the **Harbourfront Antique Market,** the largest antiques exchange in the city. Movie stars shooting films in Toronto are often spotted here in their free time. ✉ *390 Queen's Quay W,* ☎ *416/260–2626.*

Among the seasonal events in Harbourfront Centre are an Ice Canoe Race in late January, Winterfest in February, a jazz festival in June, Canada Day celebrations and a Parade of Lights in July, the Authors' Festival and Harvest Festival in October, and the Swedish Christmas Fair in November. Check the local newspapers or the **Harbourfront Centre Hotline** (☎ 416/973–3000) to see what's happening while you're in town. ✉ *410 Queen's Quay W (Harbourfront administrative offices),* ☎ *416/973–4600 offices; 416/973–3000 events hot line,* WEB *www.harbourfront.on.ca.*

NEED A
BREAK?
There are plenty of places inside **Queen's Quay** for a quick sandwich, freshly squeezed juice, or ice-cream concoctions. You can also check out one of the food trucks outside, selling hot, crispy french fries.

Music Garden. A project developed by renowned cellist Yo-Yo Ma and garden designer Julie Moir Messervy, this park is a recent addition to Toronto's reborn waterfront. Financed through private funding, the project was planned for Boston, but when that venue fell through, Toronto was the pair's next choice. The concept for the park is based on J. S. Bach's *Cello Suite No. 1* (which consists of six movements—Prelude, Allemande, Courante, Sarabande, Minuet, and Gigue), as interpreted by Yo-Yo Ma. Each movement is reflected in the park's elaborate design, using undulating riverscape, a forest grove of wandering trails, a swirling path through a wildflower meadow, a conifer grove, a formal flower parterre, and giant grass steps. The Music Garden is the latest addition to the proposed 40-acre Harbourfront Park system. ⊠ *South side of Queen's Quay W, west of Spadina Ave.*

🖑 ㉖ **Ontario Place.** Highlights of this waterfront complex, built on three man-made islands created out of landfill, include the **Cinesphere,** an enclosed dome that has shows year-round on its six-story movie screen and uses the world's first Canadian-invented IMAX projection system; the 16,000-seat outdoor **Molson Amphitheater,** offering nightly performances by singers and rock groups throughout the summer; and the **Atlantis Pavillions,** a 32,000-square-ft entertainment and dining facility. The **Haida** (☏ 416/314–9755) at Ontario Place, is a World War II and Korean War destroyer turned floating museum. Admission is $2. In addition, the justly popular **Children's Village** has water games, towering tube slides, and a moon walk. It's one of the most creative playgrounds in the world, great for children 3–14. Children's theater, puppet shows, clowns, and magicians are included in the admission price to the park.

The bumper boats, pedal boats, Wilderness Adventure Ride, MARS simulator ride, Rush River Raft Ride, waterslides, miniature golf, and Cinesphere cost extra. ⊠ *955 Lakeshore Blvd. W, south of Lake Shore Blvd., across from Exhibition Place,* ☏ *416/314–9900 recording,* WEB *www.ontarioplace.com.* 🎟 *Gate admission $10; Play-All-Day Pass $24.50; parking rates vary.* ☾ *Late May–Labor Day, daily 10 AM–9 PM.*

🖑 ㉓ **SkyDome.** One of Toronto's newest and most famous landmarks, the SkyDome is home to baseball's Blue Jays, and was the world's first stadium with a fully retractable roof. One way to see the huge 52,000-seat stadium is to buy tickets for a Blue Jays game or one of the many other events that take place here. These may include cricket matches, Wrestlemania, monster truck races, family ice shows, or rock concerts—even the large-scale opera *Aïda* has been performed here. You can also take a one-hour guided walking tour, which includes a 15-minute film. The tours are not available, however, when daytime events are scheduled. ⊠ *1 Blue Jays Way, tour entrance at Front and John Sts., between Gates 1 and 2,* ☏ *416/341–2770 for tours; 416/341–3663 for events and shows; 416/341–1000 for Blue Jays games,* WEB *www.skydome.com.* 🎟 *Tour $12.50.* ☾ *Tours daily; call ahead for times.*

★ 🖑 ⑳ **Toronto Islands.** Though sometimes referred to in the singular, there are actually eight narrow, tree-lined islands plus more than a dozen smaller islets that sit in Lake Ontario just off the city's downtown, providing a welcome touch of greenery. They've been attracting visitors since 1833, and why not? The more than 550 acres of parkland are irresistible, especially in summer when the downtown core seems to be melting as rapidly as the ice-cream cones sold everywhere on the islands. In fact, it's a good idea to bring a sweater to the islands—there's often a wind, and it's usually a few degrees cooler than it is in the city. You'll have spectacular views of Toronto's skyline, especially as the setting sun turns the Royal Bank Tower and other skyscrapers to gold, silver, and bronze.

Sandy beaches fringe the islands, the best ones being those on the southeast tip of Ward's Island, the southernmost edge of Centre Island, and the west side of Hanlan's Island. In summer 1999, a portion of Hanlan's Beach that had long been used by nude bathers was officially declared "clothing-optional" by Toronto's City Council. The declaration passed without protest or incident regarding Ontario's only legal nude beach—perhaps a testament to the truly international flavor of the city. The section frequented by gays and lesbians is at the easterly end; the "straight" section is more westerly. Impromptu beach volleyball games have frequently happened, combining both groups, and there is a nice "live and let live" tolerant attitude here of anyone into a naturist lifestyle. Lake Ontario's water has at times been declared unfit for swimming in past decades, so check reports before you go. There are free changing rooms near each beach, but no facilities for checking your clothes. Swimming in the lagoons and channels is prohibited. The winter can be bitter cold on the islands, but snowshoeing and cross-country skiing with downtown Toronto over your shoulder is appealing to many. In summer, Centre Island has rowboat and canoe rentals. Pack a cooler with picnic fixings or something you can grill on one of the park's barbecue pits. Note that the consumption of alcohol in a public park is illegal in Toronto.

All transportation on these interconnected islands comes to you compliments of your feet: no cars (except for emergency and work vehicles) are permitted anywhere. The boardwalk from Centre to Ward's Island is 2½ km (1½ mi) long. In summer, consider renting a bike for an hour or so—walk south from the Centre Island ferry docks to Avenue of the Islands—and working your way across the islands.

If you're not traveling with children, you might want to avoid Centre Island: it gets so crowded that no bicycles are allowed on its ferry during summer weekends. Those looking to escape the city should take one of the equally frequent ferries to Ward's or Hanlan's, both of which are quiet, delightful places to picnic, sunbathe, or read under a tree.

If you're heading to the Toronto Islands with the kids in tow, Centre Island is the spot to check out first. Signs ask visitors to "Please Walk on the Grass," and a few hundred yards from the ferry docks lies **Centreville** (☏ 416/234–2345 in winter; 416/203–0405 in summer), an amusement park modeled after a children's village from the late 19th century. On the diminutive Main Street you'll find shops, a town hall, a small railroad station, and more than a dozen rides, including a restored 1890s merry-go-round with at least four dozen hand-carved animals. There's no entrance fee to the modest, 14-acre amusement park, although there's a small charge (65¢) for the rides (day passes are $20.75). It's open Victoria Day (late May)–Labor Day, weekdays 10:30–6, weekends 10:30–8; Labor Day–October, weekends 10:30–6, weather permitting.

Perhaps most enjoyable for children is the free **Far Enough Farm**, which is near enough to walk to from Centreville. It has all kinds of animals to pet and feed, ranging from piglets to geese and cows. There are supervised wading pools, baseball diamonds, volleyball and tennis courts—and even a Frisbee course. It's open daylight to dusk.

In summer, the island ferries run between the docks at the bottom of Bay Street and the Ward's Island dock between 6:30 AM and 12:45 AM;

for Centre and Hanlan's islands, they begin at 8 AM. They run roughly at half-hour intervals most of the working day and at quarter-hour intervals during peak times such as summer evenings and weekends. On Canada Day (July 1) the queues are very slow moving. In winter, the ferries run only to Ward's Island on a limited schedule. ✉ *Ferries at foot of Bay St. and Queen's Quay,* ☎ *416/392–8195 for island information; 416/392–8193 for ferry information.* 🚢 *Ferry $5.*

Along Dundas and Queen Streets

This midtown area is full of variety in architecture, purpose, and tone. It includes the town square, two city halls, Eaton Centre, a major art museum, and two ethnic areas that reflect the vitality of Toronto's continuous waves of immigrants.

Numbers in the text and in the margin correspond to points of interest on the North Central Core map.

A Good Walk

Start at the corner of **Spadina Avenue** ㉗ and Nassau Street. Walk two blocks west on Nassau to Bellevue Avenue, turn left, and go south to Denison Square and the Kiever synagogue, a lovely leftover from the early and mid-20th-century immigration of Russian and Polish Jews to this area. Just to the southeast, at the corner of Denison Square and Augusta Avenue, **Bellevue Square** is a pretty little park with shade trees. Take Augusta Avenue one short block north to Baldwin Street, walk two short blocks east to Kensington Avenue and the overflowing stalls of **Kensington Market** ㉘. Continue south one block on Kensington to Dundas, turn left (east) back to Spadina, and head north two short blocks to St. Andrew's Street where, just west of Spadina, you'll see the An-shei Minsk synagogue, another testament to the Jewish influx into the area, but this one with an active congregation. Return to and cross Spadina; on the east side you'll see the Chinese Home for the Aged, which signals the approach to Toronto's original **Chinatown** ㉙ (there are four in the Greater Toronto Area), one block south on Spadina at Dundas.

After exploring this lively area, head east on Dundas for about four blocks to the **Art Gallery of Ontario** ㉚, a large beige building; be sure to visit its annex, the Grange, Toronto's oldest brick building and an earlier home to the gallery's collection. If you want to see more art, across the street is the **Ontario College of Art and Design Gallery** ㉛ and the Rosalie Sharpe Pavillion, which feature contemporary multimedia exhibitions. Head three blocks south from the Grange on McCaul Street to Queen Street, then go three short blocks east to busy University Avenue. At the northwest corner you'll find **Campbell House** ㉜, a restored chief justice's residence.

Cross University, go north one block to Armoury Street, turn right and almost immediately take a left onto Centre Avenue to visit the **Museum for Textiles** ㉝. Now head south on Centre and east on Armory Street, where you'll approach the City Hall complex from behind. Continue along the concrete path, passing on your left a small park with a waterfall, until you reach Bay Street. Walk south on Bay: at the northwest corner of Bay and Queen you'll see the expanse of **Nathan Phillips Square,** the public plaza in front of **New City Hall** ㉞. After visiting the modern building and **Old City Hall** ㉟ diagonally across the square, turn left, walk a short block to Yonge Street, and approach **Eaton Centre** ㊱, a gigantic shopping, office, and hotel complex. Exiting the huge mall at Yonge and Dundas, take Dundas three blocks east to Bond Street and then go south a short distance on Bond to the **Mackenzie House** ㊲.

TIMING

Although it's always nicest to stroll around in warm weather, wintertime brings skating, Christmas caroling, and other festive activities to Nathan Phillips Square. Chinatown is at its busiest (and most fun) on Sunday, but be prepared for very crowded sidewalks, much jostling, and honking car horns. The walk itself is just under 3 km (2 mi) and should take about an hour at a strolling pace. The Campbell and Mackenzie houses merit at least half an hour each, the Art Gallery and the Grange an hour or more. And, of course, Chinatown can gobble up an entire afternoon.

Sights to See

★ ➌ **Art Gallery of Ontario.** From extremely modest beginnings in 1900, the AGO (as it's known) is now in the big leagues in terms of exhibitions and support. A 1992 renovation won international acclaim and put it among North America's top 10 art museums. The **Henry Moore Sculpture Centre** has the largest public collection of Moore's sculpture in the world. The **Canadian Wing** includes major works by such northern lights as Emily Carr, Cornelius Krieghoff, David Milne, and Homer Watson. The AGO also has a growing collection of works by Rembrandt, Hals, Van Dyck, Hogarth, Reynolds, Chardin, Renoir, de Kooning, Rothko, Oldenburg, Picasso, Rodin, Degas, Matisse, and many others. Visitors of any age can drop by the **Anne Tannenbaum Gallery School** on Sunday and explore painting, printmaking, and sculpting in Toronto's most spectacular studio space. The museum arranges numerous other workshops and special activities. All ages can also enjoy climbing in and around Henry Moore's large *Two Forms* sculpture, which sits just outside the AGO, on McCaul Street. Admission to AGO also gains you entrance to **The Grange,** an adjoining Georgian-style house built in 1817–18 and donated to the city in 1911. The columned front and delicately balanced wings only hint at the delightful details of the interior. There are tours, presenters in period costume, brick-oven cooking demonstrations, and special Christmas decorations. ⊠ *317 Dundas St. W,* ☎ *416/979–6648,* WEB *www.ago.net.* ☜ *$6 suggested donation, or pay what you can.* ☉ *Tues. and Thurs.–Fri. 11–6, Wed. 11–8:30, weekends 10–5:30.*

NEED A BREAK?

You can dine in the shadow of two Rodin sculptures at the Art Gallery of Ontario's **Agora Grill** (⊠ 317 Dundas St. W, ☎ 416/979–6612), serving light and healthy cuisine. Weekend brunches, from 11 to 3, are particularly popular here. The restaurant is open for lunch and brunch only.

☟ **Bellevue Square.** This little park with shady trees, benches, and a wading pool and playground is a good place to rest after a visit to Kensington Market. ⊠ *Denison Sq. and Augusta Ave.*

➋ **Campbell House.** The stately Georgian mansion of Sir William Campbell, the sixth chief justice of Upper Canada, is now one of Toronto's most charming house museums. Built in 1822 in another part of town, the Campbell House was moved to this site in 1972. It has been tastefully restored with elegant early 19th-century furniture. Costumed guides detail the social life of the upper class. Note the model of the town of York as it was in the 1820s, and the original kitchen. ⊠ *160 Queen St. W,* ☎ *416/597–0227.* ☜ *$4.50.* ☉ *Oct.–mid-May, weekdays 9:30–4:30; mid-May–Oct., weekdays 9:30–4:30, weekends noon–4:30.*

NEED A BREAK?

Queen Street West is lined with cafés and restaurants. Consider the **Queen Mother Café** (⊠ 206 Queen St. W, ☎ 416/598–4719), a neighborhood favorite for wholesome meals and fabulous desserts at reasonable prices.

340

North Central Core

The Annex

London St.

Albany Ave.

Howland Ave.

Brunswick Ave.

Dalton Rd.

Walmer Rd.

Spadina Rd.

Bathurst

Bloor St. W.

Spadina

Devonshire Pl.

Croft St.

Lennox St.

Sussex Ave.

Glen Morris St.

St. George St.

Huron St.

Herrick St.

Sussex Mews

Harbord St.

Classic Ave.

Univer of Toro

Spadina Ave.

Willcocks St.

Robert St.

Ulster St.

Bancroft Ave.

Bathurst St.

Croft St.

Major St.

Russell St.

Lippincott St.

← TO LITTLE ITALY

College St.

Lillian H. Smith Library

Oxford St.

Glasgow St.

Ross St.

Huron St.

Henry St.

27

Bellevue Ave.

Augusta Ave.

Nassau St.

Cecil St.

Leonard Ave.

Baldwin St.

Bellevue Square

28

St. Andrew St.

Kensington Ave.

D'Arcy St.

Wales Ave.

Glen Baillie Pl.

29

Dundas St. W.

Alexandra Park

Ryerson Ave.

Augusta Ave.

Cameron St.

Grange Ave.

Grange Pl.

Grange Park

Grange

Sullivan St.

Carr St.

Bathurst St.

Denison St.

Spadina Ave.

Phoebe St.

Stephani

Soho St.

Beverley St.

John St.

Wolseley Pl.

Bulwer St.

Queen St. W.

0   440 yards

0   400 meters

Scollard St.

Yorkville Ave.

Collier St.

TO
ROSEDALE

Prince Arthur Ave.

Cumberland St.

Asquith Ave.

Toronto
Reference
Library

Yorkville

Avenue Rd.

Bellair St.

St. Thomas St.

Bay

Bloor

Bloor St. E.

St. George

43

42

44

Park Rd.

Hayden St.

Museum

Queen's Park

Charles St. W.

Bay St.

Balmuto St.

Charles St. E.

St. Mary's St.

Isabella St.

Devonshire Pl.

Massey College

Inkerman St.

St. Nicholas St.

Yonge St.

Gloucester St.

Hoskin Ave.

Irwin Ave.

Dundonald St.

Queen's Park

St. Joseph St.

Phipps St.

Wellesley

iversity of ronto

40

Tower Rd.

Queen's Park Crescent W.

Queen's Park Crescent E.

Wellesley St. W.

Wellesley St. E.

King's St.

College Cir.

Breadalbane St.

Maitland Ter.

Maitland Ave.

39

Grosvenor St.

Alexander St.

King's College Rd.

Grenville St.

Church St.

Wood St.

Queens's Park

College St.

38

College

Carlton St.

Jarvis St.

Orde St.

Bay St.

Granby St.

Henry St.

Murray St.

Laplante Ave.

Elizabeth St.

McGill St.

University Ave.

Gerrard St. W.

Gerrard St. E.

Walton St.

Yonge St.

Elm St.

Mutual St.

Barnaby Pl.

Gould St.

Edward St.

Victoria St.

St. Patrick

**Toronto
Coach Terminal**

Dundas

Chestnut St.

Dundas St. W.

ge

30

31

Centre Ave.

33

Hagerman St.

O'Keefe Ln.

Victoria Ln.

37

ge Rd.

Simcoe St.

34

Bond St.

Shuter St.

McCaul St.

St. Patrick St.

Armoury St.

**Nathan
Phillips
Square**

James St.

36

Dalhousie St.

Church St.

Mutual St.

anie St.

Pullan Pl.

Osgoode

32

35

Queen

W.

Queen St. W.

Queen St. E.

★ **㉙** **Chinatown.** Diverse, exciting, and lively, this is the largest Chinatown in eastern Canada and one of the largest in North America. You'll pass shops selling reasonably priced silk blouses and antique porcelain, silk kimonos for less than half the price elsewhere, lovely sake sets, and women's silk suits. On Sunday, up and down Spadina Avenue and along Dundas Street, Chinese music blasts from storefronts, cash registers ring, abacuses clack, and bakeries, markets, herbalists, and restaurants do their best business of the week.

Spadina and Dundas streets were for years the anchor of Toronto's Chinatown. When a new city hall was built in the 1960s, many of the residents were uprooted from the area behind the old building, and Chinatown began to spread west. Today, Chinatown—which now has to be described as the main or original Chinatown, as three other areas with large Chinese populations have sprung up elsewhere in metropolitan Toronto—covers much of the area of Spadina Avenue from Queen Street to College Street, running along Dundas Street nearly as far east as Bay Street. The population is more than 100,000, which is especially impressive when you consider that just over a century ago there was only a single Chinese resident, Sam Ching, who ran a hand laundry on Adelaide Street. A huge wave of immigration that began some three decades ago still continues today. Most of the newcomers arrive from Hong Kong, adding money and skills to an already burgeoning community. You can start a walk through this lively, interesting area on Elizabeth Street, just north of New City Hall, and walk north to Dundas Street, then either east toward Bay Street or west to Spadina Avenue.

㊱ **Eaton Centre.** Even if you rank shopping with the flu, you may be charmed, possibly dazzled, by this impressive environment, Toronto's top tourist attraction. The 3-million-square-ft building extends along the west side of Yonge Street all the way from Queen Street up to Dundas Street (with subway stops at each end). This is not to say the handsome collection of more than 300 stores and services was not controversial when it was built in the late 1970s; some Torontonians attacked it as "a sterile and artificial environment." Others, like Jane Jacobs, author of *Death and Life of Great American Cities,* wrote that "people like the environment of the Galleria. Its popularity has lessons for Yonge Street."

The mall holds lessons for most cities of the world, as well. From its graceful glass roof, arching 127 ft above the lowest of the mall levels, to Michael Snow's exquisite flock of fiberglass Canada geese floating poetically in the open space of the Galleria, to the glass-enclosed elevators, porthole windows, and nearly two dozen long and graceful escalators, there are plenty of good reasons to visit Eaton Centre.

Such a wide selection of shops and eateries can be confusing, however, so here's a simple rule: Galleria Level 1 contains two food courts; popularly priced fashions; photo, electronics, and record stores; and much "convenience" merchandise. Level 2 is directed to the middle-income shopper, while Level 3, suitably, has the highest elevation, fashion, and prices. A huge branch of eatons, (formerly Eaton's), opened after the family's merchant dynasty came to an end in 1999 and most stores across Canada closed. At the southern end of Level 3 is a skywalk that connects the Centre to the seven floors of The Bay (formerly Simpsons) department store, across Queen Street.

The 17-theater Eaton Centre Cineplex, west of the Dundas Street entrance, provides a cheap break from shopping—admission is only $2.50. Safe, well-lighted parking garages with spaces for some 1,800 cars are sprinkled around Eaton Centre. ✉ *220 Yonge St.,* ☎ *416/598–2322.* ◷ *Weekdays 10–9, Sat. 9:30–7, Sun. noon–6.*

NEED A
BREAK? **The Café at the Church of the Holy Trinity** (✉ 10 Trinity Sq., facing Bay St., ☎ 416/598–4521) is a charming eatery serving sandwiches, soups, pastries, and tea. It's open weekdays 9–5.

28 **Kensington Market.** All your senses will be titillated by this steamy, smelly, raucous, European-style marketplace. Come and explore, especially during warmer weather, when the goods pour out into the narrow streets. On any given day you can find Russian rye breads, barrels of dill pickles, fresh fish on ice, mountains of cheese, and bushels of ripe fruit. Crates of chickens and rabbits can both amuse and horrify.

Kensington Market sprang up in the early 1900s, when Russian, Polish, and Jewish inhabitants set up stalls in front of their houses. Since then, the market—named after the area's major street—has become a United Nations of stores. Unlike the members of the UN, however, these vendors get along well with one another. Jewish and Eastern European shops sit side by side with Portuguese, Caribbean, and East Indian ones, as well as with a sprinkling of Vietnamese, Japanese, and Chinese establishments. Saturday is the best day to go, preferably by public transit; parking is difficult. Kensington's collection of vintage-clothing stores is the best in the city. ✉ *Bordered by College St. on the north, Spadina Ave. on the east, Dundas St. on the south, and Augusta Ave. on the west.* ◷ *Daily 6–6; hrs vary; many stores closed Sun.*

NEED A
BREAK? Hole-in-the-wall eateries flourish around Kensington Market, and plenty of places sell finger foods. **Cafe La Gaffe** (✉ 24 Baldwin St., ☎ 416/596–2397) is filled with people discussing theater, art, and politics over coffee and large portions of chicken brochettes, grilled fish, and fresh veggies. The tiny front patio is great for people-watching in summer, and the ambience is definitely Parisian, though the establishment is owned by a Bermudian-Canadian.

37 **Mackenzie House.** One of a deceptively modest row of houses not far from Eaton Centre, this was once home to journalist William Lyon Mackenzie, who was born in Scotland at the end of the 1700s and emigrated to Canada in 1820. Designated as a National Historic Site, the house is now a museum and library. Mackenzie started up a newspaper that so enraged the powers that be (a clique known as "the Family Compact") that they dumped all his type into Lake Ontario. An undeterred Mackenzie stayed on to be elected the first mayor of Toronto in 1834 and is said to even have designed the coat of arms of his new city; his grandson, William Lyon Mackenzie King, became the longest-serving prime minister in Canadian history.

Mackenzie served only one year as mayor. Upset with the government "big shots" in 1837, he gathered about 700 supporters and marched down Yonge Street to try to overthrow the government. His minions were roundly defeated, and Mackenzie fled to the United States with a price on his head. When the Canadian government granted him amnesty many years later, he was promptly elected to the legislative assembly and began to publish another newspaper. By this time, though, Mackenzie was so down on his luck that some friends bought his family this house. Mackenzie enjoyed the place for but a few sickly and depressing years, and died in 1861. Among the period furnishings preserved here is the fiery Scot's printing press. ✉ *82 Bond St.,* ☎ *416/392–6915.* ▣ *$3.50.* ◷ *Weekends noon–5; call ahead weekdays (times vary).*

③③ **Museum for Textiles.** Ten galleries showcase cross-cultural displays—men's costumes from Northern Nigeria, for example—as well as the latest in contemporary design. Rugs, cloth, and tapestries from around the world are exhibited. ✉ *55 Centre Ave.,* ☎ *416/599–5515,* ⓦⒺⒷ *www.museumfortextiles.on.ca.* ✉ *$5; donation Wednesdays 5–8.* ⊙ *Tues., Thurs., Fri. 11–5, Wed. 11–8, weekends noon–5.*

Nathan Phillips Square. In front of New City Hall, this 9-acre square (named after the mayor who initiated the City Hall project) has become a gathering place for the community, whether for royal visits, protest rallies, picnic lunches, or concerts. The reflecting pool is a delight in summer, and even more so in winter, when office workers come down and skate during lunch. The park also holds a Peace Garden for quiet meditation and Henry Moore's striking bronze sculpture, *The Archer.* ✉ *In front of 100 Queen St. W.*

③④ **New City Hall.** Dubbed "a urinal for the Jolly Green Giant" by some critics, Toronto's latest city hall, the official headquarters of the City of Toronto, was the outgrowth of a 1958 international competition to which some 520 architects from 42 countries submitted designs. The winning presentation by Finnish architect Viljo Revell was controversial—two curved towers of differing height. But there is a logic to it all—an aerial view of the City Hall shows a circular council chamber sitting like an eye between the two tower "eyelids" containing offices. A remarkable mural within the main entrance, *Metropolis,* was constructed by sculptor David Partridge from 100,000 common nails. Revell died before his masterwork was opened to the public in 1965, but within months, the City Hall became a symbol of a thriving city, with a silhouette as recognizable in its own way as the Eiffel Tower. The positive influence that the development of this building has had on Toronto's civic life is detailed in Robert Fulford's 1995 book *Accidental City.*

In front of the building is **Nathan Phillips Square,** a gathering place. Annual events at New City Hall include the Spring Flower Show in late March; the Toronto Outdoor Art Exhibition early each July; and the yearly Cavalcade of Lights from late November through Christmas, when more than 100,000 sparkling lights are illuminated across both city halls. The underground garage holds 2,400 cars. ✉ *100 Queen St. W,* ☎ *416/338–0338; TDD 416/338–0889,* ⓦⒺⒷ *www.city. toronto.on.ca.* ⊙ *Weekdays 8:30–4:30*

③⑤ **Old City Hall.** Standing in marked contrast to the New City Hall structure across Bay Street, this earlier city hall was created in 1899 by E. J. Lennox, who later designed Casa Loma in Forest Hill. The fabulous gargoyles above the front steps were apparently the architect's witty way of mocking certain turn-of-the-20th-century politicians; he also carved his name under the eaves on all four faces of the building. Considered one of North America's most impressive municipal halls in its heyday—note the huge stained-glass window as you enter—it's still going strong as the home of the provincial courts, the county offices, and the marriage bureau. ✉ *60 Queen St. W,* ☎ *416/327–5675.* ⊙ *Weekdays 8:30–5.*

③① **Ontario College of Art and Design Gallery.** The college's gallery, in the Rosalie Sharpe Pavillion, across the street from the Art Gallery of Ontario, shows works by students, faculty, and alumni. OCAD is probably Canada's foremost art and design institution, with a prestigious history—several of Canada's Group of Seven landscape painters taught here at one time—and a vibrant future. The gallery is an important exhibition space for emerging Canadian artists and designers. South of the college, on Queen Street West, you'll find an eclectic assortment of trendy clothing shops, bookstores, pubs, and cafés, as well as the headquarters of a local TV station. ✉ *291 Dundas St. W, entrance on McCaul St.,* ☎ *416/977–6000 Ext. 262,* WEB *www.ocad.on.ca.* 🖭 *Free.* ◷ *Wed.–Sat. noon–6.*

㉗ Spadina Avenue. Spadina, running from the lakeshore north to College Street, has never been fashionable. For decades it has contained a collection of inexpensive stores, factories that sell wholesale if you have connections, ethnic-food and fruit stores, and eateries, including some often first-class, if modest-looking, Chinese restaurants sprinkled throughout the area. Each new wave of immigrants—Jewish, Chinese, Portuguese, East and West Indian, South American—has added its own flavor to the mix, but Spadina-Kensington's basic bill of fare is still bargains galore. Here you'll find gourmet cheeses, fresh (not fresh-frozen) ocean fish, fine European kitchenware at half the prices of stores in the Yorkville area, yards of remnants piled high in bins, designer clothes minus the labels, and the occasional rock-and-roll night spot and interesting greasy spoon. A streetcar line runs down the wide avenue to Front Street.

Toronto's widest street has been pronounced "Spa-*dye*-nah" for a century and a half, and we are too polite to point out that it really should be called "Spa-*dee*-na," as it is derived from a First Nations word with that pronunciation. The history behind Spadina Avenue's width—it is 132 ft wide, double the width of almost every other old street in town—goes back to 1802, when a 27-year-old Irish physician named William Warren Baldwin came to muddy York. He soon married a rich young woman, built a pleasant home where Casa Loma and Spadina House now sit, and decided to cut a giant swath through the forest from Bloor Street down to Queen Street so they could look down, literally and socially, on Lake Ontario. Alas, their view disappeared in 1874, when a thankless granddaughter sold the land at the crescent just above College Street for the site of Knox College. The college vacated the building several decades later and moved to the University of Toronto campus. Now covered with vines, the Victorian building still sits in the crescent, a number of the chestnut trees planted by Dr. Baldwin remaining on the west side. Little else remains of Dr. Baldwin's Spadina, except for a handful of Victorian mansions.

Around Queen's Park

Bounded by College Street to the south, Church Street to the east, Bloor Street to the north, and Spadina Avenue to the west, this midtown area is a political, cultural, and intellectual feast. Its heart is the large oval Queen's Park, south of which is the seat of the Ontario Provincial Legislature, and to the east and west the University of Toronto's main campus, which straddles the park and occupies about 160 acres. It's almost a city unto itself, with a staff and student population of more than 50,000.

The institution dates to 1827, when King George IV signed a charter for a "King's College in the Town of York, Capital of Upper Canada." The Church of England had control then, but by 1850 the college was proclaimed nondenominational, renamed the University of Toronto, and put under the control of the province. Then, in a spirit of Christian competition, the Anglicans started Trinity College, the Methodists began Victoria, and the Roman Catholics begat St. Michael's; by the time the Presbyterians founded Knox College, the whole thing was almost out of hand. Now the nine schools and faculties are united, and they welcome anyone who can meet the admission standards and afford the tuition, which, thanks to government funding, is reasonable. The architecture is interesting, if uneven, as one might expect from a place that's been built in bits and pieces over 150 years.

St. George Street, the major north–south hub of the campus, has suffered from the last four decades of erratic development. The buildings range from the aesthetically successful Innis and Woodsworth colleges to the graceless Sidney Smith Hall. The University has revived the streetscape by adding bike lanes, planting more trees, and adding a café and outdoor plaza in front of Sidney Smith Hall. Another project in the works would include an outdoor amphitheater, skating rink, reflecting pool, and public market. The Visitors Centre at 25 King's College Circle (☎ 416/978–5000) has information and maps; you can ask about summer walking tours. Group tours usually take place from 11 to 2 PM.

Numbers in the text and in the margin correspond to points of interest on the North Central Core map.

A Good Walk

Start out at the northeast corner of University Avenue and College Street (Queen's Park TTC station), where you'll find yourself looking into the green expanse of **Queen's Park.** If you're traveling with kids, you might want to detour two long blocks to the right (east) on College Street until you come to Bay Street and the fascinating **Toronto Police Museum and Discovery Centre** ㊳. Return to University Avenue and go north toward the pink **Ontario Legislative Building** ㊴, on the site originally granted to King's College, the University of Toronto's precursor. University Avenue splits into Queen's Park Circle. Follow Queen's Park Crescent East; when you reach Wellesley Street West you'll find a traffic light and a safe way to cross the stream of four-lane traffic.

After visiting the parliament buildings, return to Wellesley Street West and go left (west) under an overpass onto the University of Toronto; the large green area before you is Front Campus, surrounded by King's College Circle. The circle includes some of the oldest buildings on the campus, such as the domed Convocation Hall, and some of the newest, such as the poured-concrete Medical Sciences building. Take Tower Road north from King's College Circle; almost immediately to your left you'll see the large Romanesque Revival–style University College, the first nonsectarian college. Here the Public Affairs and Alumni Development Building provides visitor information, maps, and guided tours. It's a short block north on Tower Road to **Hart House** ㊵, a Gothic-style student center.

Turn right from Hart House and walk less than a block north along another green area called the Back Campus until you reach Hoskin Avenue, where you'll cross north at the traffic light and take a left. When, after a long block, you get to Devonshire Place, you'll see Massey College, whose handsome buildings and enclosed courtyard were designed by Canadian architect Ron Thom. Past masters have included the late Robertson Davies, one of Canada's finest novelists. Continue west on Hoskin for another block until you reach the corner of St. George Street, where you'll glimpse a linked trio of poured-concrete buildings. The one closest is the library school; the middle one is the Robarts Library, nicknamed "Fort Book" by students, both because of its restrictive loan policies and its slit windows, suitable for shooting arrows or pouring boiling oil on attacking hordes; and the southernmost building houses the **Thomas Fisher Rare Book Library** ㊶.

If you don't want to visit the rare books library, turn right (east) at the traffic light where Tower Road meets Hoskin Avenue; in about a block, Hoskin curves and becomes Queen's Park Crescent. Walk north on the crescent; when the street straightens out again, you'll see on your left the distinctive dome of the **Children's Own Museum** ㊷. Just past it is the TTC's Museum stop and, beyond that, the large stone **Royal Ontario Museum** ⑬, or ROM, one of Canada's finest museums. Across the street from the ROM's main entrance is the **George R. Gardiner Museum of Ceramic Art** ⑭. At this point you are on the edge of **Yorkville,** an elegant shopping district, but don't be distracted (unless you can't resist, of course). On the north end of ROM is Bloor Street; take it west one long block to St. George Street to visit the **Bata Shoe Museum** ⑮. Catercorner from the museum is the York Club, one of the landmarks of the posh neighborhood known as **The Annex.**

TIMING

This Queen's Park walk is good any time of year because many of the attractions bring you indoors. Excluding a stroll around The Annex, the walk alone should take about a half hour at a strolling pace. The walk and a visit to the legislature and one or two of the museums or libraries would make a nice half-day (or more) program; allot at least two hours for the Royal Ontario and Gardiner museums. This area abuts the Yorkville shopping district, the high-end shopping on Bloor Street between Yonge and Avenue Road, the gay- and lesbian-friendly neighborhood of Church and Wellesley, and the Rosedale residential area.

Sights to See

The Annex. Born in 1887, when the burgeoning town of Toronto engulfed the area between Bathurst Street and Avenue Road north from Bloor Street to the Canadian Pacific railroad tracks at what is now Dupont Street, the countrified Annex soon became an enclave for the well-to-do; today it attracts an intellectual set. Timothy Eaton of department store fame built a handsome structure at 182 Lowther Avenue (since demolished) and the Gooderham family (of liquor fame) erected a lovely red castle at the corner of St. George Street and Bloor Street, now the home of the exclusive York Club.

As Queen Victoria gave way to King Edward, the old rich gave way to the new rich and ethnic groups came and went, until the arrival of the ultimate neighborhood wrecker —the developer. Alas, much of St. George Street has been lost to high-rises, and as you near the Spadina subway entrance along Lowther Avenue and Walmer Street, you'll see that many Edwardian mansions have fallen to make room for very ugly 1960s-era apartment buildings.

Still, The Annex, with its hundreds of attractive old homes, can be cited as a prime example of Toronto's success in preserving lovely, safe streets within blocks of the downtown area. Even today, many examples of late-19th-century architecture can be enjoyed on Admiral Road, Lowther Avenue, and Bloor Street, west of University Avenue. Round turrets, pyramid-shape roofs, and conical (some even comical) spires are among the pleasures shared by some 20,000 Torontonians who live in this vibrant community, including professors, students, writers, lawyers, and other professional and artsy types. Bloor Street between Spadina and Palmerston keeps them fed and entertained with its bohemian collection of used-record stores, crafts shops run by eccentrics, and restaurants from elegant Italian to hearty Polish and aromatic Indian. Keep your eyes open, too; you may run into one of Canada's better-known literary types, including Michael Ondatjee, Jane Jacobs, or Daniel Richler (Mordecai's son). ⊠ *Bordered by Bathurst St. to the west, St. George St. to the east, Bloor St. W to the south, and Dupont St. to the north.*

⑮ **Bata Shoe Museum.** Created by Sonja Bata, wife of the founder of the Bata Shoe Company, this collection contains 10,000 varieties of foot coverings and, through the changing fashions, highlights the craft and sociology of making shoes. Some items date back more than 4,000 years. Pressurized sky-diving boots, iron-spiked shoes used for crushing chestnuts, and smugglers' clogs are among the items on display. Elton John's boots have proved wildly popular, but Napoléon's socks give them a run for the money. ⊠ *327 Bloor St. W,* ☎ *416/979–7799,* WEB *www. batashoemuseum.ca.* ⊡ *$6; free first Tues. of every month.* ☉ *Tues.– Wed. and Fri.–Sat. 10–5, Thurs. 10–8, Sun. noon–5.*

㊷ **Children's Own Museum.** This new museum, known as the COM, opened its doors in late 1998 in the former McLaughlin Planetarium building, one door south of the Royal Ontario Museum. It was specifically designed for younger children and incorporates a construction site, workshop, attic, reading nook, and theater, as well as a main street—all just the right size for small children. There are several hands-on, interactive displays. ⊠ *90 Queen's Park,* ☎ *416/542–1492,* WEB *www.childrensownmuseum.org.* ⊡ *$4.75; Sat. by donation.* ☉ *Daily 10–5.*

㊹ **George R. Gardiner Museum of Ceramic Art.** This collection of rare ceramics includes 17th-century English Delftware and 18th-century yellow European porcelain; its pre-Colombian collection dates to Olmec and Maya times. Most popular is the second-floor display of Italian commedia dell'arte figures, especially Harlequin. Don't miss the museum's gift shop, which stocks many unusual items. The restaurant serves a wonderful brunch from 11 to 2 PM. ⊠ *111 Queen's Park,* ☎ *416/586–8080,* WEB *www.gardinermuseum.on.ca.* ⊡ *$10; free first Tues. of every month.* ☉ *Mon. and Wed.–Fri. 10–6, Tues. 10–8, weekends 10–5.*

㊿ **Hart House.** A neo-Gothic-style student center built 1911–19, Hart House represents the single largest gift to the university. Vincent Massey, a student here at the turn of the 20th century, regretted the absence of a meeting place and gym for students and convinced his father to build one. It was named for Vincent's grandfather, Hart, the founder of Massey-Ferguson, once the world's leading supplier of farm equipment. Originally restricted to male students, Hart House has been open to women since 1972. The attached **Soldier's Tower,** with its 51-bell carillon, was erected in 1923 as a memorial to university members who fell in World War I. Names of alumni killed in later wars have been added since then. ⊠ *Hart House Circle,* ☎ *416/978–2452,* WEB *www. utoronto.ca/harthouse.*

NEED A BREAK?   The **Gallery Grill** (⊠ Hart House Circle, ☎ 416/978–2445), in the Great Hall of Hart House, was always worth peeking into for its impressive stained-glass windows, but since the chef of a noted restaurant–jazz bistro took over in 1996, the food is good, too. Stop in during the academic year (September–May) weekdays and Sunday at lunchtime for a bowl of roasted tomato and vegetable soup, East Coast salmon sandwich, or steak salad and a glass of wine.

☙ **Lillian H. Smith Branch of the Toronto Public Library.** Honoring the memory of the city's first children's librarian, this branch maintains nearly 60,000 items in three children's collections, ranging from the 14th century to the present. In addition, the Merril Collection of Science Fiction, Speculation and Fantasy includes about 50,000 items on everything from parapsychology to UFOs. The Electronic Resource Centre offers on-line access to the public (even non-Canadians). ⊠ *239 College St., between Spadina Ave. and St. George St.,* ☎ *416/393–7746.* ⊡ *Free.* ☉ *Library Mon.–Thurs. 10–8:30, Fri. 10–6, Sat. 9–5; children's and Merril collections Sun.–Fri. 10–6, Sat. 9–5; Electronic Resource Centre Mon.–Wed. 10–8:30, Thurs. noon–8:30, Fri. 10–6, Sat. 9–5.*

OFF THE
BEATEN PATH **LITTLE ITALY** – Once a quiet strip of College Street with just a few unfrequented clothing shops and the odd obstinate pizzeria, Little Italy (College Street, west of Bathurst Street between Euclid Avenue and Shaw Street) has suddenly become the hippest place in Toronto. New restaurants open weekly, bars and coffeehouses are packed into the night, and every corner holds fashionable cafés and people dining outdoors. This is the southern edge of the city's Italian community, and though not much remains of this heritage—most people have moved north, toward St. Clair Avenue—the flavor lingers in the menus, food markets, pool halls, and some holdovers from a less glamorous time.

39 **Ontario Legislative Building.** Home of the provincial parliament, this mammoth study in geometric form, with rectangular towers, triangular roofs, and circular glass, was opened in 1893; you can get a taste of Ontario's history and government here. Like New City Hall, it was the product of an international contest among architects, in this case won by a young Briton residing in Buffalo, New York. The Romanesque Revival–style building, made out of pink Ontario sandstone, has a wealth of exterior detail; inside, the huge, lovely halls echo a half millennium of English architecture. The long hallways are hung with hundreds of oils by Canadian artists, most of which capture scenes of the province's natural beauty. Should you choose to take one of the frequent (and free) tours, you will see the chamber where the 130 MPPs (Members of Provincial Parliament) meet on a regular basis. There are two heritage rooms—one each for the parliamentary histories of Britain and Ontario—filled with old newspapers, periodicals, and pictures. The lobby holds a fine collection of minerals and rocks of the province. The many statues that dot the lawn in front of the building, facing College Street, include one of Queen Victoria and one of Canada's first prime minister, Sir John A. Macdonald. The lawn is also the site of Canada Day celebrations and the occasional political protest. These buildings are often referred to simply as Queen's Park, after the park surrounding them, or as the parliament buildings. ⊠ *1 Queen's Park,* ☎ *416/325–7500.* ⊡ *Free.* ☉ *Guided tour mid-May–Labor Day, daily on the hr 9–4, weekends every ½ hr 9–11:30 and 1:30–4; frequent tours rest of the yr on weekdays only.*

Queen's Park. Many visitors consider this to be the soul of Toronto. Surrounding the large oval-shape patch of land are medical facilities to the south, the University of Toronto to the west and east, and the Royal Ontario Museum to the north. To most locals, Queen's Park is chiefly synonymous with politics, as the Ontario Legislative Building sits in the middle of this charming urban oasis. ⊠ *Queen's Park Circle, between College St. and Bloor St. W*

OFF THE
BEATEN PATH **ROSEDALE** – This posh residential neighborhood northeast of Queen's Park repays an hour's walk. Rosedale has the charm of curving roads (it's one of the few neighborhoods to have escaped the city's grid pattern), many small parks and large trees, and a jumble of oversize late-19th-century and early 20th-century houses in Edwardian, Victorian, Georgian, and Tudor styles. In the 1920s, Sheriff William Jarvis and his wife, Mary, settled here on a 200-acre estate in what was then the country. She named her home Rosedale for the wildflowers that bloomed in profusion. Most of the roses are gone now, as are the magnificent trees for which Elm Avenue was named. Morley Callaghan, the Toronto novelist and longtime neighborhood resident (who also boxed with Ernest Hemingway and quarreled with F. Scott Fitzgerald in Paris), called this "a fine and private place." Though some of the fine old houses have been carved up into small apartments, the neighborhood is still the home of old and new wealth and many who wield power and responsi-

bility. The neighborhood is bounded by Yonge Street on the west, the Don Valley Parkway on the east, St. Clair Avenue to the north, and the Rosedale Ravine, just above Bloor Street East, to the south.

★　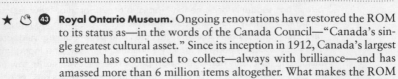 **Royal Ontario Museum.** Ongoing renovations have restored the ROM to its status as—in the words of the Canada Council—"Canada's single greatest cultural asset." Since its inception in 1912, Canada's largest museum has continued to collect—always with brilliance—and has amassed more than 6 million items altogether. What makes the ROM unique is that science, art, and archaeology exhibits are all appealingly presented under one roof. Six new galleries opened in 1999, increasing gallery space by 32,000 square ft and bringing the total public area to 230,000 square ft. This expansion has allowed 3,000 additional objects from the ROM collections to be displayed.

A good place to begin a visit is the restored **Samuel Hall–Currelly Gallery,** with its magnificent glass and mosaic ceiling. The gallery displays some outstanding artifacts and serves as an orientation center.

The new galleries include the **Herman Herzog Levy Gallery,** which exhibits a stunning range of large and colorful textiles, paintings, and prints from the museum's acclaimed Asian collection; the **Asian Sculpture Gallery,** displaying 25 stone Buddhist sculptures dating from the second through 16th centuries; and the **Gallery of Korean Art,** North America's largest permanent gallery devoted to Korean art and culture. With more than 200 exceptional works of fine art and objects, this gallery showcases contributions made to art and science from more than 8,000 years of Korean history.

Also new is the second-floor **Discovery Gallery,** which is great for family members of all ages. Interactive exhibits encourage you to touch museum objects, dig for dinosaur bones, dress up in traditional costumes of armor, and play in an enchanted forest. The 14,000-square-ft **Dynamic Earth Gallery** is the ROM's largest permanent gallery. It showcases the Earth's processes and amazing products, but also tells the story of the planet's formation and evolution. This is another interactive gallery for all ages. Lighting, sound, and visual effects are used to create a dramatic multimedia experience. Finally, the newest gallery is **Hands-on Biodiversity,** which illustrates the natural interdependence of all plants and animals (including humans) in Ontario and the rest of the world. A living stream and a buzzing beehive are two of the many environmental exhibits.

The **Sigmund Samuel Canadiana Collection,** a worthy assemblage of 18th- and 19th-century Canadian furnishings, glassware, silver, and period rooms, is part of the Canadian Heritage gallery. A particular strength of the ROM is the **T. T. Tsui Galleries of Chinese Art,** with stunning sculptures, paintings, and many other artifacts. The **Roman Gallery** has the most extensive collection of Roman artifacts in Canada. The brilliant **Ancient Egypt Gallery** is connected with the newer **Nubia Gallery;** both exhibit artifacts that illuminate the ancient cultures. The **European Musical Instruments Gallery** has a revolutionary audio system and more than 1,200 instruments, some dating from the late 16th century.

The **Evolution Gallery** has an ongoing audiovisual program on Darwin's theories of evolution. A **Bat Cave** contains 4,000 freeze-dried and artificial bats in a lifelike presentation; there's a guided walk through a dimly lit replica of an 8-ft-high limestone tunnel in Jamaica, filled with sounds of dripping water and bat squeaks. Children and adults alike can appreciate the extensive **Dinosaur Collection.** ✉ *100 Queen's*

When you pack your MCI Calling Card, it's like packing your loved ones along too.

Your MCI Calling Card is the easy way to stay in touch when you travel. Use it to call to and from over 125 countries. Plus, every time you call, you can earn frequent flier miles. So wherever your travels take you, call home with your MCI Calling Card. It's even easy to get one. Just visit **www.mci.com/worldphone.**

EASY TO CALL WORLDWIDE

1. Just enter the WorldPhone® access number of the country you're calling from.

2. Enter or give the operator your MCI Calling Card number.

3. Enter or give the number you're calling.

Aruba ⁘	800-888-8
Bahamas ⁘	1-800-888-8000

Barbados ⁘	1-800-888-8000
Bermuda ⁘	1-800-888-8000
British Virgin Islands ⁘	1-800-888-8000
Canada	1-800-800-8000
Mexico	01-800-021-8000
Puerto Rico	1-800-888-8000
United States	1-800-888-8000
U.S. Virgin Islands	1-800-888-8000

⁘ Limited availability.

EARN FREQUENT FLIER MILES

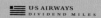

SEE THE WORLD
IN FULL COLOR

Fodor's Exploring Guides bring all the great sights vividly to life with hundreds of photographs, fascinating historical background, and colorful anecdotes. Detailed maps and practical information keep you headed in the right direction.

Pair a **Fodor's** Exploring Guide with your trusted Gold Guide for a complete planning package.

Fodor's EXPLORING GUIDES

At bookstores everywhere.

Park, ☎ 416/586–8000, WEB www.rom.on.ca. ☜ $15; free Fri. after 4:30 and Sat.–Thurs. 1 hr before closing. ☉ Mon.–Sat. 10–6, Fri. 10–9:30, Sun. 11–6.

④ **Thomas Fisher Rare Book Library.** Early writing artifacts such as a Babylonian cuneiform tablet, a 2,000-year-old Egyptian papyrus, and books dating to the beginning of European printing in the 15th century are shown here in rotating exhibits, which changes three times annually. Subjects of these shows might include Shakespeare, Galileo, Italian opera, or contemporary typesetting. ⊠ *120 St. George St., ☎ 416/978–5285, FAX 416/978–1667, WEB www.library.utoronto.ca/fisher. ☜ Free. ☉ Weekdays 9–4:45.*

✋ ㊳ **Toronto Police Museum and Discovery Centre.** Highlights are a replica of a 19th-century police station, an array of firearms, and exhibits of infamous crimes. Interactive displays include everything from information on drugs, computers that help track down missing children, and "Did You Know?" quizzes. You can also study your own fingerprints. Kids can have fun with the 1914 paddy wagon, crash car videos, and, especially, a Harley Davidson they can jump on. They can also enjoy climbing in and out of a car sliced in half and hearing a dispatcher squawk at them. ⊠ *40 College St., ☎ 416/808–7020, WEB www.torontopolice.on.ca. ☜ Free. ☉ Daily 9–9.*

Toronto Reference Library. Designed by one of Canada's most admired architects, Raymond Moriyama, who also created the Ontario Science Centre, this library is arranged around a large atrium, affording a wonderful sense of open space. Among the highlights is a fabric sculpture, *Lyra,* designed by artist Aiko Suzuki; it overhangs the pool and waterfall in the foyer. Glass-enclosed elevators glide swiftly and silently up and down one side of the atrium, allowing you to admire the banners that hang from the ceiling, announcing the collections on each floor. Fully one-third of the more than 4 million items—spread across 45 km (28 mi) of shelves—are open to the public. Audio carrels are available for listening to your choice among the nearly 30,000 music and spoken-word recordings. Open on Saturday from 2 to 4 and by appointment, the **Arthur Conan Doyle Room** will be of special interest to Baker Street regulars. It houses the world's finest public collection of Holmesiana, including records, films, photos, books, manuscripts, letters, and even cartoon books starring Sherlock Hemlock of *Sesame Street.* ⊠ *789 Yonge St., ☎ 416/393–7131, WEB www.tpl.toronto.ca. ☉ Mon.–Thurs. 10–8, Fri.–Sat. 10–5, Sun. 1:30–5.*

NEED A BREAK?	In the heart of the city's gay and lesbian village, **Wilde Oscar's** (⊠ 518 Church St., ☎ 416/921–8142) is a popular restaurant and bar frequented by mostly baby boomers and Gen Xers of every sexual orientation. The outdoor patio provides must-see people-watching from late spring to late fall. The Victorian-inspired two-story interior offers just the right degree of camp, and the menu is international without being overly trendy or pricey. Try one of the local draft beers and a gourmet pizza for two for under $20.

Yorkville. One of the most dynamic and expensive areas of the city is known to some as Toronto's Rodeo Drive; other people call it Toronto's Madison Avenue. One thing is certain: these blocks are packed with restaurants, galleries, specialty shops, and high-price stores specializing in designer clothes, furs, and jewels. It's also the neighborhood where much of the excitement takes place in September during the annual Toronto International Film Festival. This is said by many to be the world's most people-friendly film festival, where the public actually gets to see premieres and hidden gems and attend industry seminars. Klieg lights shine over skyscrapers, bistros serve alcohol until 4 AM, and everyone practices their air kisses. ⊠ *Bordered by Avenue Rd., Yonge and Bloor Sts., and Yorkville Ave.*

Cabbagetown

The area that the late Cabbagetown-born-and-bred novelist and short-story writer Hugh Garner described in his 1950 novel *Cabbagetown* as "the world's largest Anglo-Saxon slum" has turned into one of downtown's most popular neighborhoods. Mockingly named by outsiders for the cabbages that grew on tiny lawns and were cooked in nearly every house, the moniker is used with a combination of inverse pride and almost wistful irony today. Beginning in the 1970s, rehabbers turned houses that sold in the $25,000 range into ones that now fetch $500,000 and more—part of the insistent gentrification of Toronto's downtown. Although there are few tourist attractions per se here, it's fun to stroll around and enjoy its architectural diversity. The enclave extends roughly from Parliament Street on the west—about 1½ km (1 mi) due east of Yonge Street—to the Don River on the east, and from Bloor Street on the north to Queen Street East on the south.

Numbers in the text and in the margin correspond to points of interest on the Metropolitan Toronto map.

A Good Walk

Start at the southeast corner of Carlton and Parliament streets (the latter so named because the first government buildings were built near its foot in the closing years of the 18th century). Walk south, through the busiest part of the **Parliament Street** commercial area. Most of the buildings on the west side date from the 1890s, though the storefronts are more recent.

Turn left at **Spruce Street,** the first block you come to. Of note are No. 35 and No. 41, two buildings that were once part of Trinity College Medical School. Continuing east to the northwest corner of Spruce and Sumach streets, you'll see **Spruce Court,** one of the city's earliest low-income housing projects and now a residential cooperative. Around the corner to the right, on **Sumach Street,** check out No. 289, once the Ontario Women's Medical College. Now turn around and walk north on Sumach Street. After crossing Spruce Street, look to your right at the attractive terrace of workers' cottages at 119–133 Spruce Street.

Continue north on Sumach Street back to **Carlton Street** ㊻, where you'll see some of the area's largest homes. (Note the redbrick surface of the street to the east.) Among the most outstanding are No. 288, No. 286, and No. 295. Continue west on Carlton Street to **Metcalfe Street** ㊼, which, thanks to all its trees, fences, and unbroken rows of terraces, is one of the most beautiful streets in Toronto. Look down on the sidewalk on the east side nearest Carlton Street to see a utility-hole cover from the Victorian era, bearing the date 1889. Proceed north to look at No. 37, a mix of Victorian and Beaux-Arts styles. At the northeast corner of Metcalfe and Winchester streets is the handsome St. Enoch's Presbyterian Church.

Turn left now and head west along **Winchester Street** ㊽ back to Parliament. At the southeast corner of Winchester and Parliament you'll see the most prominent building in the area, the Hotel Winchester, erected in 1881. South of the Hotel Winchester, on Parliament Street, stand Nos. 502–508, an imposing row of large Victorian houses. At the northwest corner of Parliament and Wellesley streets loom the overwhelming apartment towers of St. James Town, built in the 1960s and reviled ever since because they wiped out many attractive older homes. On the east side of Parliament Street, north of Wellesley Street, is the beautiful St. James Cemetery.

From the cemetery, turn left (east) along **Wellesley Street East.** Be sure to take note of No. 314. Farther east, turn north up the lane marked **Wellesley Cottages.** Back on Wellesley Street, walk north up the lane east of No. 402 to see the 1893–94 Owl House, named for the bird on a small terra-cotta plaque under one of its windows. Wellesley Street comes to an end at **Wellesley Park.** Framing the park are parts of the Don Valley, the **Necropolis Cemetery,** and a row of houses to the south. Proceed south through Wellesley Park, and turn right along Amelia Street to Sumach Street. Head south again, past **Winchester Street** ⑭ and make a left (east) into Riverdale Park, which once hosted the city's main zoo and is now home to **Riverdale Farm** ⑭, a living-history farm museum.

TIMING
The Cabbagetown walk covers 2–3 mi and should take an hour or two at a leisurely pace. Because the main reason to explore the neighborhood is its architecture, a clear day in any season is the best time to visit.

Sights to See

⑯ **Carlton Street.** Some of Cabbagetown's largest homes, dating from the late 19th century, are on this street. **No. 288** is a Second Empire–style house built in 1882 of solid brick with white stone trim. **No. 286,** next door, was built in 1883 and has the familiar steep gable and bargeboard trim. Check out the wrought-iron cresting over the round bow window. **No. 295,** an earlier house of Victorian-Gothic design, was originally the home of an executive of Toronto's first telephone company—this wondrous machine was envisioned by Alexander Graham Bell in Brantford, Ontario, just an hour west of Toronto—and had one of the first telephones in the city.

⑰ **Metcalfe Street.** The rows of trees, fences, and terraces along this street make it one of Toronto's most beautiful. Superimposed on the side of the simple but picturesque Victorian No. 37 are 1891 and 1912 additions in Beaux-Arts classical forms. The Romanesque **St. Enoch's Presbyterian Church,** at the northeast corner of Metcalfe and Winchester streets, was erected in 1891.

Parliament Street. This busy commercial and residential Cabbagetown street is particularly noteworthy for its late-19th-century houses. **Nos. 502–508,** erected in 1879, are among the largest and most elaborately decorated Second Empire structures still standing in Toronto. While you're on the street, St. James Town is also worth seeing.

Laid out in the 1840s, **St. James Cemetery** (⊠ Parliament and Wellesley Sts., northeast corner) contains the graves of many of Toronto's prominent citizens from the days when the place was still called the town of York, as well as some of the more interesting burial monuments in Toronto.

While you are at the St. James Cemetery, observe the small yellow-brick Gothic **Chapel of St. James-the-Less,** built in 1858 and considered one of the most beautiful church buildings in the country.

⑲ **Riverdale Farm.** Not only is this museum one of Toronto's most delightful attractions and a special treat for children, but it's also free. The most interesting structure is the original Pennsylvania German–style barn, built in 1858 and moved to the farm in 1975 from suburban Markham, many miles north of the city. Inside are various im-

354

Metropolitan Toronto

Subway Lines

• • • • • • • • Bloor Danforth Line
━━━━━━ Yonge-University Line
═════ Scarborough Rapid Transit
Ⓜ Subway stop
───── Railroad lines

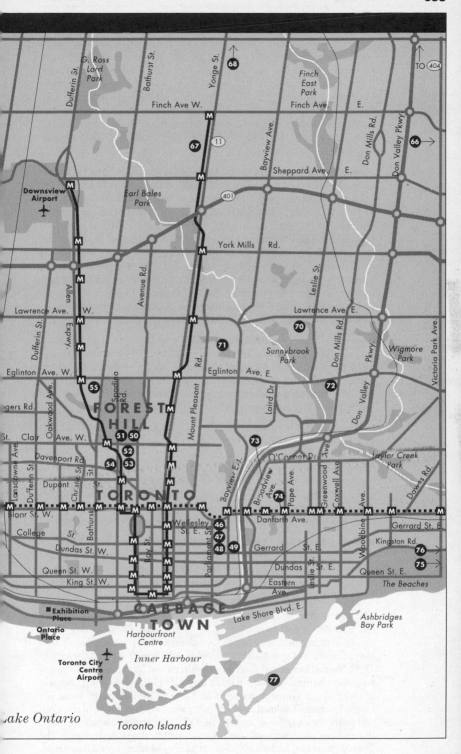

plements such as a light sleigh from the early 20th century and an exact replica of the type of Conestoga wagon used by German-speaking immigrants to this country early in the 19th century. Demonstrations of crafts such as quilting and spinning are offered daily. Riverdale Farm's permanent residents include three Clydesdale horses, cows, sheep, goats, pigs, donkeys, ducks, geese, chickens, and a small assortment of domestic animals. The farm also has a 59-herb garden and a garden of corn and grains. Bring along bathing suits for very young children—the lovely park adjacent to the farm has a wading pool. ⊠ *201 Winchester St.,* ☎ *416/392–6794.* ⊠ *Free.* ☼ *Daily 9–4, crafts demonstrations 10–3.*

Spruce Street. This street in the heart of Cabbagetown is of architectural and historical note. The little brick cottage set far back from the road at **No. 35** was built in 1860–61 and was once home to the dean of Trinity College Medical School. The fence also dates from the 19th century. **No. 41** was built in 1871 and served until 1903 as a medical school; it has now been recycled as part of a residential development. Its history is outlined on the Toronto Historical Board plaque on its front lawn. **Nos. 119–133** on Spruce Street are characteristic of Toronto's residential architecture between 1875 and 1890. These workers' cottages were erected in 1887 in Second Empire style, typified by high mansard roofs punctuated by dormers with marvelous details such as carved wooden brackets and metal decorative devices.

Now a residential cooperative, **Spruce Court** (⊠ Spruce and Sumach Sts., northwest corner) was originally constructed between 1913 and 1926 for the Toronto Housing Company as one of the city's earliest and most attractive low-income housing projects. The individual units not only provided modern conveniences and street access but also opened onto a grassy courtyard.

Sumach Street. Of particular historical importance on this Cabbagetown street is **No. 289.** Now a private residence, this building was once the Ontario Women's Medical College, built in 1889 and a forerunner of Women's College Hospital. Canada's less-than-enlightened attitudes toward women barred them from male-only medical schools and city hospitals. The attractiveness of this brick-and-stone structure demonstrates the success with which Victorian architects and builders managed to integrate institutions into mostly residential streetscapes.

Wellesley Street East. A variety of architectural styles can be found on the Cabbagetown section of this street. **No. 314,** built in 1889–90, has stonework around the windows and carved stone faces above the door and in the keystones. Also on the street are Wellesley Park, Necropolis Cemetery, and the Wellesley Cottages.

The resting place of many of Toronto's pioneers, **Necropolis Cemetery** (⊠ Winchester and Sumach Sts., ☎ 416/923–7911) is a "city of the dead." Among the most famous (and notorious) are Toronto's first mayor, William Lyon Mackenzie, who led a revolt against the city in 1837; Samuel Lount and Peter Matthews, two of Mackenzie's followers, who were hanged for their part in that rebellion; and George Brown, founder of the *Globe* newspaper and one of the fathers of Canada's Confederation. The beautiful chapel, gate, and gatehouse of the nonsectarian burial ground, erected in 1872, constitute one of the most picturesque groupings of small Victorian buildings in Toronto. The Necropolis is also known for its great variety of trees, flowering shrubs, and rare and exotic plants. The cemetery is open mid-May to mid-September daily 8 to 8, and mid-September to mid-May daily 8–5:30.

The simplified Gothic style—faced with wood lath and stucco—of the 1886–87 **Wellesley Cottages** (✉ Off Wellesley St. E, after Parliament St. and before Wellesley Ave.) is typical of much of Toronto's inexpensive housing of the 19th century. Now expensive private homes, the row of cottages were once workers' houses.

From 1848 to 1888 **Wellesley Park** (✉ far east end of Wellesley St. E) was the site of the area's major industry—the P. R. Lamb Glue and Blacking Factory. Today it's a small, pleasant neighborhood park and playground, surrounded by the Don Valley, the Necropolis Cemetery, and a row of houses to the south.

48 **Winchester Street.** As you stroll along this Cabbagetown street, keep an eye out for the repeated sunburst patterns of carved wood in many of the gables and the large amount of stained glass, much of it original and some of it recently installed by lovers of Victoriana. The **Hotel Winchester**, a venerable but sadly decaying building at the southeast corner of Winchester and Parliament, is one of the neighborhood's most prominent structures. It opened in 1888 as the Lake View Hotel, so named because from its roof one could see all the way south to the blue waters of Lake Ontario.

Forest Hill and Beyond

A golden square of about 948 acres, Forest Hill is bounded by Bathurst Street on the west, Avenue Road on the east, Eglinton Avenue on the north, and St. Clair Avenue West on the south. Its major draws for visitors, besides handsome streets and houses, are the Casa Loma and Spadina house museums. The area is home to approximately 25,000 well-heeled people, although it numbered but some 2,100 souls in 1923 when it chose to become a village on its own. Its first reeve (local official) passed a bylaw requiring that a tree be planted in front of every house; you can see the shady results of his campaign today. At that time, there were no paved streets. Eglinton Avenue was a wagon trail, and Old Forest Hill Road was part of a First Nations path that meandered from the Humber River to Lake Ontario.

Forest Hill remained its own little village, with its own police and fire departments and school system, until it was incorporated into Toronto in 1967. A sense of this community can be obtained by considering a 1982 controversy—would the former village of Forest Hill continue to have backyard garbage pickup, or would the villagers have to drag their rubbish out front like everyone else? The City Council finally voted to continue the special service, on the principle that "invisible garbage" was one of the unwritten terms of Forest Hill's amalgamation with Toronto.

Numbers in the text and in the margin correspond to points of interest on the Metropolitan Toronto map.

A Good Walk

The following suggested walk takes you through the heart of Forest Hill and a bit farther south.

Start at Forest Hill Road, just west of Avenue Road and St. Clair Avenue (take the St. Clair streetcar or Avenue Road bus). You are now entering the thick of Forest Hill, with its handsome English manors and splendid Georgian homes. At the northeast corner of Forest Hill and Lonsdale roads is **Upper Canada College** 50, a prominent private boys' school. Several blocks to the west of UCC is **Bishop Strachan School** 51 (pronounced *strawn*), a similar facility for girls. Admire the homes along Old Forest Hill Road, then head up and down the streets that run north–south: Dunvegan, Warren, and Russell Hill. South of St. Clair Avenue, Russell Hill Road becomes a showpiece of impressive mansions.

If you take Spadina Road south from St. Clair Avenue, you'll pass **Winston Churchill Park** ㉒ on your left. Continue farther south on Spadina to reach **Spadina House** ㉓, a magnificently restored Victorian home. Across the street is **Casa Loma** ㉔, a European-style fairy-tale castle.

TIMING

Allow about an hour just to stroll along the area's residential streets. If you want to spend time in Winston Churchill Park, Spadina, or Casa Loma, give yourself at least another hour at each place. You can do this walk in any season. Spring and fall provide the pleasure of extensive gardens and stands of trees blossoming, blooming, and fading. But in winter you'll have a better view of the buildings' architectural details.

Sights to See

㉑ **Bishop Strachan School.** The girls get their shot at success at this much admired, much attended, and very expensive school, a neighborhood counterpart to the boys-only Upper Canada College next door. ✉ *200 Lawnsdale Rd.,* ☎ *416/483–4325,* WEB *www.bss.inforamp.net.*

㉔ **Casa Loma.** An honest-to-goodness 20th-century castle and a great folly with 98 rooms, two towers, creepy passageways, and lots of secret panels, Casa Loma offers some of the best views of Toronto. The European-style castle was built shortly before World War I by Sir Henry Pellatt, who picked ideas and architectural discards from some of the finest houses in England, Scotland, and France to build what he hoped, among other things, would be a home elegant enough to host his king, George V of England, on a visit to Canada. Pellatt, a soldier and financier, spent over $3 million to construct his dream (that's 1913 dollars), only to lose it to the taxman just over a decade later. Today it's owned by the city and operated by the Kiwanis Club of Casa Loma, with all monetary proceeds distributed among a variety of charities or returned to the city for the castle's upkeep. Some impressive features are the giant pipe organ, the reproduction of Windsor Castle's Peacock Alley, the majestic, 60-ft-high ceiling of the Great Hall, and the mahogany and marble stable, reached by a long, underground passage. The rooms are copies of those in English, Spanish, Scottish, and Austrian castles, which Sir Henry had admired during trips across Europe. Its architect, E. J. Lennox, also designed Toronto's Old City Hall and the King Edward Hotel. The entire tour is a good 1½ km (1 mi), so wear sensible shoes. ✉ *1 Austin Terr.,* ☎ *416/923–1171,* WEB *www.casa-loma.org.* 🎫 *$10.* ☉ *Daily 9:30–4.*

㉓ **Spadina House.** Pronounced "spa-*dee*-na," as the avenue should be but never is, this 1866 house is filled with arts and artifacts of the James Austin family, prominent in the natural gas, railroad, and banking businesses. Members of the family lived here from Victorian times until 1982, when it was turned over to public ownership. The 50-room house has been restored with period wallpaper, upholstery, and furniture, and crystal chandeliers burn softly with natural gas. Docents tend the magnificent gardens and the small orchard—they make jam in summer and bread in winter and, additionally, give guided tours. ✉ *285 Spadina Rd.,* ☎ *416/392–6910.* 🎫 *$5.* ☉ *Jan.–Mar., weekends noon–5; Apr.–Dec., weekdays noon–4, weekends and holidays noon–5.*

㉒ **Upper Canada College.** One of the country's most prestigious private boys' schools, UCC has educated both the reverent (the Eatons as well as numerous bankers, mayors, and prime ministers) and the irreverent (humorist Stephen Leacock and the late author Robertson Davies).

The school is for grades 1 through 13—yes, Canada's schools have one more year than those in the States. ⊠ *200 Lonsdale Rd.,* WEB *www.ucc.on.ca.*

☺ ❺❷ **Winston Churchill Park.** In summer, tennis courts and a safe and well-kept playground attract uptown dwellers. Folk-dancing is held on some summer nights. In winter, a serious hill offers the most terrifying—and hence the best—toboggan run in the city. Year-round, it's a favorite of joggers. ⊠ *St. Clair Ave. W and Spadina Rd., southeast corner.*

Southwest Toronto

Ethnic enclaves, parks, and museums make Southwest Toronto an interesting area to visit. High Park is the main green space, but James Gardens and Scarlet Mills Park are two smaller parks also worth a stroll. Area museums include the Beth Tzedec Museum and the restored Montgomery's Inn. You can easily reach all of these sights by mass transit.

Roncesvalles Avenue, east of High Park, is the commercial heart and soul of Toronto's Polish community; this avenue is filled with butcher shops selling homemade sausages just like grandmother should have made if she'd had the skill and time. Consider buying a few to grill in the park. On the west side of High Park is Runnymede Road. Here and along Bloor Street West both German and Ukrainian shops come into view, selling fine food and clothing.

The city's West Indian community is concentrated along Eglinton Avenue east of Dufferin Street, along Bloor Street West near Christie Street, and along Bathurst Street, north of Bloor Street. It's fun to explore and great if you like *roti*, a meat-and-potato or vegetarian wrap that comes from Trinidad, Jamaican meat patties, or spicy jerk chicken.

Numbers in the margin correspond to points of interest on the Metropolitan Toronto map.

Sights to See

❺❺ **Beth Tzedec Museum.** Set in a Conservative synagogue of the same name, the museum houses one of the largest collections of Jewish artifacts in Canada. In addition to displays of ritual objects relating to Jewish celebrations and life cycle, the museum has exhibits that provide a geographic, cultural, and historic view of Jewish life. Highlights of the collection include a treasury of illuminated marriage contracts and a unique circumcision chair from Berlin, dated 1766. Tours can be arranged. ⊠ *1700 Bathurst St., 2 blocks south of Eglinton Ave.,* ☎ *416/ 781–3514 Ext. 32.* ⊠ *Free.* ☉ *Sept.–June, Mon., Wed., Thurs. 11–1, 2–5, Sun. 11–2, and by appointment.*

★ ❺❽ **High Park.** One of North America's loveliest parks, High Park (at one time the privately owned countryside "farm" of John George Howard, Toronto's first city architect) is especially worth visiting in summer, when the many special events include professionally staged Shakespeare productions. Hundreds of Torontonians and guests arrive at suppertime and picnic on blankets before the show. Admission is by donation.

The small **Grenadier Pond** in the southwest corner of High Park is named after the British soldiers who, it is said, crashed through the soft ice while rushing to defend the town against invading American forces in 1813. Today the pond is home to thousands of migrating birds. You can fish in its well-stocked waters, either from the shore or from a rented rowboat. There are Sunday afternoon concerts in summer and supervised skating in winter.

The **High Park Zoo** is more modest than the Toronto Zoo in the northeast quadrant of the city, but it's a lot closer to downtown and it's free. Even young children won't tire walking among the deer, Barbary sheep, peacocks, rabbits, and buffalo.

Colborne Lodge, at the south end of the park, was built more than 150 years ago by John George Howard on a hill overlooking Lake Ontario. This Regency-style "cottage" contains its original fireplace, bake oven, and kitchen, as well as many of Howard's own drawings and paintings. From High Park subway station, enter the park and follow signs for the lodge. It's open weekdays 9:30–4 and weekends noon–5 from April through December; weekends noon–4 from January through March; and holidays noon–5. The cost is $3.50. For more information call (☎ 416/392–6916).

Other highlights of the park are a large swimming pool, tennis courts, fitness trails, and hillside gardens with roses and sculpted hedges. To get here, take the TTC to the High Park station and walk south; you can also take the College Street streetcar to the eastern end of the park and walk west. There's limited parking along Bloor Street north of the park, and along the side streets on the eastern side. ⊠ *Bordered by Bloor St. W, the Gardiner Expwy., Parkside Dr., and Ellis Park Rd., main entrance off Bloor St. W at High Park Ave.,* ☎ *416/392–7291 pool and tennis information; 416/392–1748 walking tours; 416/368–3110 summer plays July–Aug.*

60 **James Gardens.** On the west bank of the Humber River, Fred T. James started his gardens in 1908 and finished in 1948. With a variety of flowers suited to the Canadian climate, stone pathways, and mature trees, James Gardens is a quiet haven at any time of the year. A winterized, fully accessible washroom is on the property. ⊠ *Off Edenbridge Dr., east of Royal York Rd., south of Scarlett Mills Park,* ☎ *416/392–8186.* ☉ *Daily until sunset.*

59 **Montgomery's Inn.** This restored inn, built in the early 1830s by an Irish immigrant, is a good example of the Loyalist architecture—an early American style similar to Georgian—of the time. Costumed staff go about the museum quilting, rug hooking, and cooking traditional foods. There are many tours and a daily afternoon tea. To get here, take the subway to Islington station and then take the Islington bus. ⊠ *4709 Dundas St. W,* ☎ *416/394–8113,* WEB *www.mont-gomerysinn.com.* ☜ *$3.* ☉ *Tues.–Fri. 1–4:30, weekends 1–5.*

61 **Scarlett Mills Park.** An appealing wildflower reserve can be found at this park north of James Gardens on the west bank of the Humber River. The park is ideal for picnics, and attracts cross-country skiers in winter. You can watch golfers at play, as the park overlooks Scarlett Woods Golf Course. Note that there are no washrooms in the park. Pedestrians and cyclists can travel through the park along the Tommy Thompson Trail. ⊠ *Entrance off Edenbridge Dr.* ☉ *Daily to sunset.*

57 **Sir Casimir Gzowski Park.** From this park you have marvelous views of the Toronto Islands, Ontario Place, and the downtown skyline, both from a paved lakeshore-hugging trail—ideal for jogging, biking, and in-line skating—as well as from a boardwalk made of Trex, a product derived from recycled plastic garbage bags. The park is accessible by the 501 Queen and 504 King streetcars and is right next to Sunnyside Park. ⊠ *Along Lakeshore Blvd. W.*

56 **Sunnyside Park.** Once the site of a large, rollicking amusement park, Sunnyside is now a favorite place for a swim in the heated water of the "tank" or a quick snack in the small restaurant inside the handsomely restored 1922 Sunnyside Bathing Pavilion. One of the few remnants of the old amusement park is the Palais Royale dance hall, which still reverberates with the sounds of the big bands most weekends. The park is easily accessible by streetcar from the King, Queen, Roncesvalles, Queensway intersection. Sir Casimir Gzowski Park is a short walk.

Northwest Toronto

Great for a family visit, this primarily residential area encompasses a huge theme park, a conservation center, a pioneer village, a significant art collection, and a large park stretching along the Humber River.

Northwest Toronto is also home to the ever-widening and always vibrant Italian community, which is concentrated in areas that extend from College and Bathurst streets west to Dufferin Street and beyond, and north all the way to the city limits of Steeles Avenue. Its heart is St. Clair Avenue West, running from Bathurst Street to Dufferin Street. On many evenings, especially Sunday, the street is filled with thousands of men and women promenading among the *gelaterias,* people-watching, and generally enjoying their neighbors.

A car is necessary for visiting the Kortright Centre and Paramount Canada's Wonderland, and is helpful for getting to other sights as well.

Numbers in the margin correspond to points of interest on the Metropolitan Toronto map.

Sights to See

Black Creek Pioneer Village. Less than a half hour's drive from downtown Toronto is a rural, mid-19th-century living-history museum village that makes you feel as though you'd gone through a time warp. Black Creek Pioneer Village is a collection of more than three dozen period buildings that have been moved to their current site—a town hall, a weaver's shop, a printing shop, a blacksmith's shop, and a school complete with dunce cap. The mill dates from the 1840s and has a 4-ton wooden waterwheel that still grinds up to a hundred barrels of flour a day (bags are available for purchase).

You can watch men and women in period costumes go about the daily routine of mid-19th-century Ontario life—cutting tin, shearing sheep, tending gardens (weather permitting), fixing and making horseshoes, baking bread, weaving, printing a newspaper, stringing apple slices, and dipping candles. They explain what they're doing and how they do it, and answer all questions about pioneer farm life.

Free wagon rides, a decent restaurant, and many farm animals all contribute to a satisfying outing. In winter, there's also skating, tobogganing, and sleigh rides. An "events pavillion" is set to open in 2002, which will accommodate larger crowds for events like spring and fall fairs, and celebrations of Canada Day, Thanksgiving, and Christmas (beginning in the middle of November). ⊠ *1000 Murray Ross Pkwy., corner of Jane St. and Steeles Ave.,* ☎ *416/736–1733.* ⊡ *$9, parking $5.* ⊙ *May–June, weekdays 9:30–4:30, weekends 10–5; July–Sept., daily 10–5; Oct.–Dec., weekdays 9:30–4, weekends 10–4:30.*

Humber Valley Parkland. This park stretches along the Humber River ravine, from north of the city limits (Steeles Avenue) down to where the Humber flows quietly into Lake Ontario, not far from High Park. Its peaceful location away from traffic makes the park ideal for a hiking, jogging, or biking tour.

Kortright Centre for Conservation. Only 15 minutes north of the city and just a groundhog's shadow away from Paramount Canada's Wonderland, this delightful conservation center holds three aquariums and more than 16 km (10 mi) of hiking trails through forest, meadow, river, and marshland. In winter, some of the trails are reserved for cross-country skiing (bring your own skis or snowshoes and dress warmly). In the magnificent woods, there have been spottings of foxes, coyotes, rabbits, deer, wild turkeys, pheasants, chickadees, finches, and blue jays. Seasonal events include a winter carnival, a spring maple syrup festival, and a Christmas crafts fair. To get to the Kortright Centre, drive 3 km north along Hwy. 400, exit west at Major Mackenzie Drive, continue south 1 km on Pine Valley Drive to the gate. ⊠ *9550 Pine Valley Dr., Woodbridge,* ☎ *905/832–2289,* WEB *www.kortright.org.* ⌖ *$5.* ⊙ *Daily 10–4.*

★ ⑥⑤ **McMichael Canadian Art Collection.** On 100 acres of lovely woodland in Kleinburg, 30 km (19 mi) northwest of downtown Toronto, the McMichael is the only major gallery in the country with the mandate to collect Canadian art exclusively. The museum holds impressive works by Tom Thomson, Emily Carr, and the Group of Seven landscape painters (as well as their contemporaries) from the early 20th century. These artists were inspired by the wilderness and sought to capture it in bold, original styles. First Nations art and prints, drawings, and sculpture by Inuit artists are well represented. Strategically placed windows help you appreciate the scenery as you view art that took its inspiration from the vast outdoors. Inside, wood walls and a fireplace set a country mood. ⊠ *10365 Islington Ave., west of Hwy. 400 and north of Major Mackenzie Dr., Kleinburg,* ☎ *905/893–1121,* WEB *www.mcmichael.on.ca.* ⌖ *$9.* ⊙ *May–Oct., daily 10–5; Nov.–Apr., Tues.–Fri. 10–4, weekends 11–4.*

⟳ ⑥④ **Paramount Canada's Wonderland.** Yogi Bear, Fred Flintstone, and Scooby Doo are part of Canada's first theme park, filled with games, rides, restaurants, and shops. Entertainment ranges from pop and rock musical performances to sea-lion shows. The season runs from May through Labor Day (plus a few weekends on either side of the main season). The park is close to Toronto—it's barely 30 minutes from downtown by car or special GO Transit bus, in good traffic.

Attractions include Kidzville, home of the Rugrats, and the Top Gun looping inverted jet coaster. Splash Works, a 20-acre water park, has an outdoor wave pool called Whitewater Bay; the Black Hole, a fully enclosed water thrill slide; and a children's interactive water play area. Other draws are strolling Star Trek characters, the Paramount Studio Store and memorabilia, cliff divers, minigolf, and batting cages. The high-quality **Kingswood Music Theatre** (☎ 905/832–8131), near the entrance of Canada's Wonderland, has excellent pop and rock acts through the summer. There are 7,000 reserved seats under a covered pavilion and 8,800 additional seats on the sloping lawn.

The park can run up to $48 per adult if you buy the "pay one price passport"—otherwise, grounds admission is $28. Call for information about the day and season passes available and check newspapers, chain stores, and hotels for special discount tickets and coupons. ⊠ *9580 Jane St.,* ☎ *905/832–7000,* WEB *www.canadaswonderland.com.* ⌖ *$28 for grounds admission without rides.* ⊙ *May–Labor Day daily from 10 AM; early Sept.–second Mon. in Oct. weekends from 10 AM; closing times vary.*

⟳ ⑥② **Wild Water Kingdom.** The largest park of its kind in Canada, Wild Water Kingdom has huge water slides, river rapids, giant outdoor hot tubs, a fantastic wave pool, and a delightful area for younger children to splash around in. Right next to it is a sports complex, Emerald Green, which has miniature golf, batting cages, and more. ✉ *Finch Ave. W and Hwy. 427,* ☎ *905/794–0565,* WEB *www.wildwaterkingdom.com.* 🎫 *$21.50; $12 after after 4 PM.* ☉ *Water park: June–Labor Day, daily 10–8; minigolf: Apr.–Oct., daily 10–8.*

Northeast Toronto

Consisting mostly of upper-middle-class residences, this suburban area is popular for its parks and ravines, as well as for the Toronto Zoo and the David Dunlap Observatory. Most of the sights in this part of town can be reached by public transit, but not as easily as those in some parts of the city. Set aside a lot of time to tour Northeast Toronto if you don't have a car.

Numbers in the margin correspond to points of interest on the Metropolitan Toronto map.

Sights to See

68 **David Dunlap Observatory.** Constructed in 1935, this research facility only 24 km (15 mi) north of downtown is both a photo gallery of things astronomical—sunspots, nebulae, and galaxies—and the largest observatory in Canada. Visitors eight years and older are admitted for educational lectures on Wednesday mornings year-round and for stargazing on Saturday nights from mid-April to late September. You can also climb a ladder and peek through the 25-ton telescope to see the planet, star, or moon that is "playing" that night. It can get chilly under the unheated dome, even in midsummer, so dress warmly for your close encounter. From downtown Toronto it takes about an hour by car or mass transit to get to the Observatory. ✉ *123 Hillsview Dr., Richmond Hill,* ☎ *905/884–2112,* WEB *www.ddo.astro.utoronto.ca.* 🎫 *Thurs. lecture free; Sat. evening viewing sessions $5; no children under 8 admitted.* ☉ *Lecture/tour Thurs. 10–11:30 AM; stargazing mid-Apr.– late Sept., Sat. nights from ½ hr after sunset.*

★ ☝ **70** **Edwards Gardens.** The beautiful 35-acre Edwards Gardens (once the private enclave of industrialist Rupert Edwards) flow into one of the city's most visited ravines. Paths wind along colorful floral displays and exquisite rock gardens. Refreshments and picnic facilities are available, but no pets are allowed. A new "teaching garden" helps children learn the pleasures to be found in a garden. For a great ravine walk, start out at the entrance to Edwards Gardens (southwest corner of Leslie Street and Lawrence Avenue East) and head south through **Wilket Creek Park** and the winding Don River valley. Pass beneath the Don Valley Parkway and continue along Massey Creek. After hours of walking (or biking, or jogging) through almost uninterrupted parkland, you'll end up at the southern tip of **Taylor Creek Park** on Victoria Park Avenue, just north of the Danforth. From here you can catch a subway back to your hotel. ✉ *Entrance at southwest corner of Leslie St. and Lawrence Ave. E*

☝ **67** **Gibson House.** It's the Little House in the Suburbs, a 10-room residence built in 1851 by one of the supporters of William Lyon Mackenzie's 1837 rebellion. True, David Gibson's original home was burned to the ground by anti-Mackenzie men while the surveyor was off in a decade-long exile in the United States (when he assisted in constructing the Erie Canal), but when Gibson returned to Toronto, he built this. Men and women in 19th-century costumes demonstrate the cooking and crafts of the pioneers. ✉ *5172 Yonge St., about 1½ km (1 mi) north of Sheppard Ave. and Hwy. 401,* ☎ *416/395–7432.* 🎫 *$2.75.* ☉ *Tues.–Fri. 9:30–4:30, weekends noon–5.*

76 Highland Creek Ravine. The ravines at Highland Creek are considered the most beautiful in Toronto. They are ideal for cross-country skiing, biking, and jogging. Both **Colonel Danforth Park** and **Morningside Park** follow Highland Creek. The **Colonel Danforth Trail** begins south of Kingston Road, on the east side of Highland Creek bridge, and Morningside Park is accessible off Morningside Avenue, between Kingston Road and Ellesmere Avenue. ⊠ *Parks can be entered from the grounds of Scarborough College, 1265 Military Trail.*

71 Sherwood Park. This park is one of the best-kept secrets in Toronto. It has one of the finest children's playgrounds in the city, a lovely wading pool, and a hill that seems to go on forever. A ravine begins at the bottom of the hill; you can follow it across Blythwood Road, all the way to Yonge Street and Lawrence Avenue. There, subways and buses await you—as do the beautiful rose gardens in **Alexander Muir Park.** Or walk or bike southeast to **Sunnybrook Park,** then head 13 km (8 mi) south along the ravine to the lake. ⊠ *Near Lawrence Ave. E and Mount Pleasant Rd.*

★ ⓒ **69 Toronto Zoo.** With its varied terrain, from river valley to dense forest, the Rouge Valley was an inspired choice of site for this 710-acre zoo, in which mammals, birds, reptiles, and fish are grouped according to their natural habitats. In the enclosed, climate-controlled pavilions you'll also find botanical exhibits, such as the Africa pavilion's giant baobab tree. The Events Guide distributed at the Main Entrance will help you plan your day. The "Around the World Tour" takes approximately three hours and includes the Africa, Americas, Australasia, and Indo-Malayan pavilions. The Zoomobile (seasonal operation) glides silently through the outdoor exhibit area without disturbing the animals. A daily program of special events provides opportunities to chat with animal keepers and watch animal and bird demonstrations. Coming with kids? You may want to visit the Children's Web (seasonal attraction) to see displays including "Backyard Bugs," "Backyard Pond," and "Butterfly Garden." This area also has a playground and pony rides. Camel rides are offered in the zoo's Marco Polo area (May through September, daily; October through May, weekends only). The African Savanna is the country's finest walking safari, a dynamic reproduction of "big-game" country that brings rare and beautiful animals and distinctive geological features to the city's doorstep. You can also dine in the Savanna's Safari Lodge and camp overnight in the Bush Camp (reservations required). ⊠ *Meadowvale Rd. north of Hwy. 401, 30-minute drive from downtown, or take Bus 86A from Kennedy subway station,* ☎ *416/392–5900,* WEB *www.torontozoo.com.* ⊠ *$12; parking $5 (free Nov.–Feb.).* ☉ *Summer, daily 9–7:30; winter 9:30–4:30.*

Southeast Toronto

Longtime residents mix with recent immigrants in urbanized Southeast Toronto, which is well served by public transit from downtown. Ethnic neighborhoods include The Danforth (also known as "Greektown") and an Indian community concentrated along Gerard Street East near Greenwood Avenue, called "Little India." Worth a visit in the vicinity of The Danforth is the Todmorden Mills Historic Site, where you can see a number of the city's oldest buildings. A boardwalk in The Beaches and a series of parks flank Lake Ontario in this part of town. The impressive Ontario Science Centre, at the area's northern boundary, could also be combined with a visit to some of the sights in Northeast Toronto.

Numbers in the margin correspond to points of interest on the Metropolitan Toronto map.

Sights to See

The Beaches. Known either as The Beach or The Beaches, this charming section east of downtown has attracted tens of thousands of people who enjoy living in a small town with easy access to Toronto via public transport and even easier access to Lake Ontario. It's easy to spend an afternoon strolling the delightful, safe, and (in summer) often crowded boardwalk, graced by huge, shady trees. Other options are taking a dip in the free Olympic-size Somerville Pool at Woodbine Avenue or window shopping on Queen Street East. Live music is often performed at any of the several public parks, where you're also likely to see artists selling their wares. The neighborhood is also home to an annual jazz festival in July, when all of Queen Street East is closed east of Woodbine Avenue. More than 100 bands participate, and the Kew Gardens Stage features headliners.

A soldier from London, Joseph Williams, first settled the area in 1853, having arrived in Toronto with the 2nd Battalion Rifle Brigade five years earlier. His 25-acre grant was named Kew Farms, after London's Kew Gardens, and it was there that he raised vegetables, selling them at the St. Lawrence Market on Saturday mornings. When Williams chose to turn his property into a park in 1879, he naturally called it Kew Gardens. The youngest son of the paterfamilias, named Kew Williams, built a handsome house of stone with a circular staircase and a tower. Today it serves as home to the park's keeper.

This part of town was soon flooded by hundreds of hot and sticky Torontonians attracted by the advertisements for "innocent amusements" and the prohibition of "spirituous liquors." The cottages that once stood on the lakeshore vanished with the waves in 1932, at which time Kew Gardens, Scarborough Beach Park, and Balmy Beach became one large park called Kew Beach Park. But on a leisurely walk along the thoroughfares that run north from the lake to Queen Street, you'll still find hundreds of New England–style clapboard-and-shingle houses, often standing next door to formal stucco mansions in the Edwardian tradition. ⊠ *Bounded by Kingston Rd., Woodbine and Victoria Park Aves., and the lake.*

❼❹ The Danforth. This area along Danforth Avenue is a dynamic ethnic mix, although it is primarily a Greek community. Once English-settled (although it was named after Asa Danforth, an American contractor who cut a road into the area back in 1799), the neighborhood is now Italian, Greek, East Indian, Latin American, and, increasingly, Chinese. But a large percentage of the 120,000 Greek Canadians in metropolitan Toronto live here, and the area is still referred to as "Greektown." Late-night taverns, all-night fruit markets, and some of the best ethnic restaurants in Toronto abound. Since 1982, 50 English–Greek street signs have been installed. ⊠ *Bounded by the Don Valley Pkwy. to the west, and east to Warden Ave.*

★ ☕ ❼❷ Ontario Science Centre. It has been called a museum of the 21st century, but it's much more than that. Where else can you stand at the edge of a black hole, work hand-in-clamp with a robot, or land on the moon? Even the building itself is extraordinary: three linked pavilions float gracefully down the side of a ravine and overflow with exhibits that make space, technology, and communications fascinating. A dozen theaters show films that bring the natural world to life. Live demonstrations of glassblowing, papermaking, lasers, electricity, and more take place regularly throughout the day; check the schedule when you arrive at the museum. The Human Body, the Information Highway, and the Sport Show are major exhibits, and the domed Omnimax theater (separate charge) shows films on subjects from deep space to deep science. You need at least two hours to scratch the surface, and you may want to spend an entire day. Children love this place, probably more than any other in Toronto, and most adults will be intrigued, too. The museum has a cafeteria, a restaurant, and a gift store with a cornucopia of books and scientific doodads. ⊠ *770 Don Mills Rd., at Eglinton Ave. E; Yonge St. subway from downtown to Eglinton station and No. 34 Eglinton East bus to Don Mills Rd. stop; then walk 1/2 block south,* ☎ *416/429–4100,* WEB *www.osc.on.ca.* ⊠ *$12; Omnimax films $10 each; parking $7.* ☉ *Daily 10–5; extended evening hrs in summer.*

75 **Scarborough Bluffs.** This is the most scenic of the bluff parks along Lake Ontario in the southeastern part of Toronto. It affords wonderful vistas of Lake Ontario, as does **Cathedral Bluffs** at its western edge. ⊠ *From downtown take Kingston Rd. east, past Midland, and right on Brimley Rd.*

73 **Todmorden Mills Museum–Historic Site.** You can bring a picnic to this open parkland, where a number of the city's oldest buildings have been restored on their original sites. Among the structures built by the English settlers are two pioneer houses, a brewery (1821), a paper mill (1825), and the old Don Train Station (1891), designed to serve two once-great railroads, the Canadian National and Canadian Pacific. ⊠ *67 Pottery Rd., off Bayview Ave. Extension,* ☎ *416/396–2819.* ⊠ *$3.* ☉ *May–Sept. Tues.–Fri. 10–4:30, weekends and holidays noon–5; Oct.–Dec. weekdays 10–4.*

77 **Tommy Thompson Park.** This park comprises a peninsula that juts 5 km (3 mi) into Lake Ontario. It was created from the sand dredged for a new port of entry and the landfill of a hundred skyscrapers. It has quickly become one of the best areas in the city for cycling, jogging, walking, sailing, photography, and, especially, bird-watching. The strange, artificial peninsula is home (or stopover) to the largest colony of ring-billed seagulls in the world and for dozens of species of terns, ducks, geese, and snowy egrets. Bird-watching is best mid-May to mid-October. To get here, head east along Queen Street to Leslie Street, then south to the lake. No private vehicles are permitted in the park. ⊠ *Entrance at the foot of Leslie St.,* ☎ *416/661–6600.* ☉ *Daily 9–6.*

DINING

By Sara
Waxman

The Toronto restaurant scene is in a state of perpetual motion. Meeting the demands of a savvy dining public, new restaurants are opening at a vigorous rate, making the search for that perfect restaurant a reachable goal.

Even formal haute cuisine establishments, which had all but faded into Toronto's gastronomic history, are experiencing a renaissance, joining the ever-swelling ranks of bistros, cantinas, tavernas, trattorias, tapas bars, noodle bars, wine bars, and smart cafés. Red meat is making a comeback, and along with steak houses have come cigar and martini lounges. Meanwhile, the cuisines of the world have appeared on Toronto's doorstep. Recipes need no passports to cross borders. Little Italy, a half-dozen individual Chinatowns (urban and suburban), Little India, and, of course, the cooking of Southeast Asia—a tidal wave of Korean, Vietnamese, Laotian, Thai, and Malaysian restaurants—are taking our taste buds by storm with flavors like chili, ginger, lemongrass, coconut, lime, and tamarind.

Toronto's brilliant young chefs recognize that when most customers start requesting "sauce on the side," the public's collective taste is changing.

368

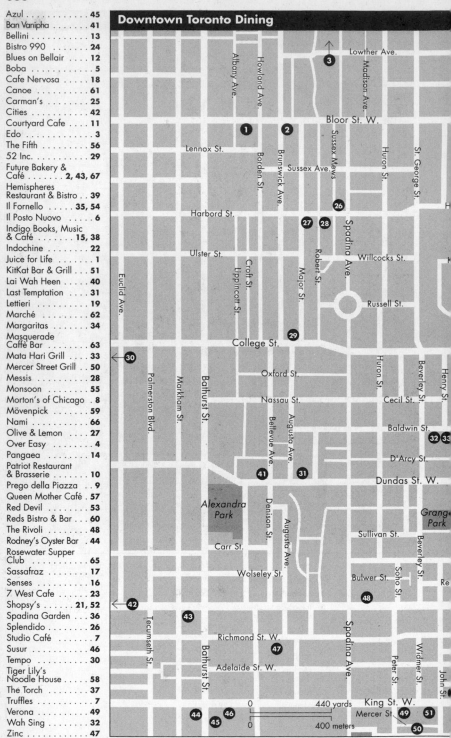

Downtown Toronto Dining

Those with a vision are looking over their shoulders toward California and Asia for a more creative marriage of fresh market ingredients.

Smoking is prohibited in most Toronto restaurants. If this is important to you, call to check on the status of the law.

Servers expect 15% tip on the pre-tax bill. An easy formula is GST (7%) plus PST (8%) equals tip (15%). There's no need to tip on the total after-tax bill.

Unless noted below, dress in Toronto is casual but neat. In the more elegant and expensive restaurants, men are likely to feel more comfortable wearing a jacket.

CATEGORY	COST*
$$$$	over $32
$$$	$22–$32
$$	$13–$21
$	under $13

per person, in Canadian dollars, for a main course at dinner

Old Toronto

Contemporary

$$$–$$$$ ✕ **Rosewater Supper Club.** A historic landmark building with 22-ft-high ceilings, hardwood and marble floors, and thronelike blue velvet banquettes for two or four is a place to go when you're in the party mood. The scintillating appetizers and beautifully presented entrées include roast quail on forest-mushroom risotto to start, and entrées like veal with potato spinach tart and sage fritters. Among the chef's specialties are prime beef tenderloin with shallots and asparagus. Not ready to commit to dinner? A lounge with a baby grand and a slinky torch singer can hold your attention. Or you can relax in luxe comfort in the downstairs cigar lounge. ⊠ *19 Toronto St.,* ☎ *416/214–5888. AE, DC, MC, V. Closed Sun. No lunch Sat.*

Delicatessen

$–$$ ✕ **Shopsy's.** In 1945, when the three Shopsowitz brothers came into the business started by their parents in 1921, you'd pay 8¢ for a corned-beef sandwich. Today Shopsy's belongs to a food conglomerate, and such a sandwich costs $5.75. The corned beef, always freshly cooked and firm, is piled on fresh rye bread slathered with mustard; there's nothing like it. Soups are satisfying, salads are huge, and hot dogs are legendary. All locations are in the heart of the theater and business district. The deli often has a wait at peak hours. ⊠ *33 Yonge St.,* ☎ *416/365–3333;* ⊠ *1535 Yonge St.,* ☎ *416/967–5252;* ⊠ *284-A King St. W,* ☎ *416/599–5464. AE, DC, MC, V.*

Japanese

$$–$$$ ✕ **Megumi.** During the controlled chaos of the busy dinner hour, the sushi chef, wearing the traditional blue-and-white headband of the master, never loses his cool. With fingers flying he makes up platters of Yokozuna, superior sushi sets with 10 pieces of *nigiri* (bite-size rice cakes with cooked or raw fish on top) and 6 pieces of tuna roll. Set meals include miso soup, rice, and a main dish, which can be a breaded chicken cutlet or any number of chef's suggestions. *Nabeyaki udon,* served in a handmade pottery bowl, is steaming broth brimming with slurpy noodles, whole shrimp, crispy tempura chicken, mushrooms, vegetables, and a poached egg. Tatami rooms have neat rows of shoes in front. Behind the door marked "Private Club" is a karaoke bar in full swing. ⊠ *9 Church St.,* ☎ *416/365–0393. AE, DC, MC, V. Closed Mon. No lunch weekends.*

The Financial District

American/Casual

\$\$ ✕ **Marché.** This old-world market square in a downtown office tower
★   is really a self-service restaurant. Herbs grow in pots, fresh fruits and
vegetables are piled high, an enormous snowbank holds bright-eyed
fish and fresh seafood, and fresh pasta spews from pasta makers, ready
to be cooked to order. A rotisserie roasts lacquer-crisp game birds and
European sausages. Bread and croissants are baked before your eyes,
and pizza is prepared to order. Pick up a shopping "credit card" and
a tray and stroll through the marketplace, choosing as much or as little as you want. This high-concept, low-price dining adventure is open
Wednesday through Saturday 7:30 AM–2 AM and Sunday through
Tuesday 7:30 AM–1 AM. There are smaller versions all over town. ⊠
BCE Place, 42 Yonge St., ☎ *416/366–8986. Reservations not accepted. AE, DC, MC, V.*

Canadian

\$\$\$–\$\$\$\$ ✕ **Canoe.** At Canoe, on the 54th floor of the Toronto Dominion Bank
Tower, huge windows let you enjoy the breathtaking view of the Toronto
Islands and Lake Ontario while you dine. Some inspirational dishes here
are seared tuna in the Japanese style, and Québec foie gras with con-
cord grape cruller, cardamom, and onion salad. Canadiana courses
through the menu with entrées such as roast rib eye of organic pork
with spaetzle, roast pumpkin, and collard greens. The adventurous
meat eater might enjoy crusted loin of Yukon caribou with foie gras,
spinach, cashews, and cloudberries. Vegetarian dishes are also available.
⊠ *Toronto-Dominion Center, 66 Wellington St. W, 54th floor,* ☎ *416/
364–0054. Reservations essential. AE, DC, MC, V. Closed weekends.*

\$\$\$–\$\$\$\$ ✕ **360 Revolving Restaurant.** A glassed-in bridge and a glass elevator
carry you to the top of the tallest freestanding structure in the world.
In the distance are New York State and the twinkling lights of Niagara Falls. Curved leather booths and windowside tables circle the core,
which holds the kitchen and the award-winning Wine Cellar in the Sky.
The menu is unabashedly Canadian. The kitchen smokes Prince Edward Island salmon and sets it on a sage-and-onion tart with a splash
of white-truffle vinaigrette. Rack of lamb with sweet-potato frites or
braised lamb shank with buttermilk mashed potatoes shows off fresh
Ontario foods. ⊠ *CN Tower, C301 Front St. W,* ☎ *416/362–5411.
Reservations essential. AE, DC, MC, V.*

Eclectic

\$\$–\$\$\$\$ ✕ **Zoom.** Glass planets, suns, baubles, and lenses are everywhere;
lovely curtains sashed in gold add softness to the hard-edged, steel tables and chairs. The kitchen, as inventive as the setting, composes forest mushrooms and squash into an earthy terrine and sets it on pumpkin
seed and wild rice salad. Fancy edible sculptures are created with lobster and shrimp spiked with seasoned soybeans. Start with ginger-
scented calamari salad, and go to pecan-dusted beef tenderloin or
potato-wrapped Chilean sea bass, or other glitzy choices from a seasonal menu. Zoom isn't everyone's daily bread, but it may be part of
everyone's fantasy. ⊠ *18 King St. E,* ☎ *416/861–9872. AE, DC, MC,
V. Closed Sun. No lunch Sat.*

Japanese

\$–\$\$\$ ✕ **Nami.** In this large, attractive restaurant, diners can choose to eat
★   at the sushi bar, in tatami rooms with nontraditional wells under the
tables, or at the *robatta* (a cooking grill surrounded by an eating
counter). The chef douses soft-shell crabs with a special sauce and puts
them on the grill. Scallops, shrimp, Atlantic salmon, mackerel, and ocean

perch sizzle on skewers. Special dinner combos at a table or booth include soup, salad, tempura, *yakitori* (skewers of chicken) or a beef or salmon teriyaki dish, rice, and dessert. ⊠ *55 Adelaide St. E,* ☎ *416/ 362–7373. AE, DC, MC, V. Closed Sun. No lunch Sat.*

Pan-Asian

$$$ ✕ **Mercer Street Grill.** It's easy to find this funky, bunkerlike, one-step-ahead-of-fusion grill—it's the only restaurant on the block. The decor is smart and spare, but the food is complex, delicious, and entertaining. Start with warm salad of sautéed sea scallops with avocado, roast peppers, and grapefruit in curry–yogurt dressing, or goat cheese and artichoke tempura on lambs lettuce and purple basil with fresh tomato vinaigrette. A simple garden salad becomes exotic with a dressing of wildflower honey and roast ginger. Even commonplace roast loin of lamb is outfitted anew with green spinach curry and parsnip butternut squash pakoras. In summer, enjoy the lovely exotic Japanese garden patio. ⊠ *36 Mercer St.,* ☎ *416/599–3399. Reservations essential. AE, DC, MC, V. No lunch.*

Swiss

$–$$$ ✕ **Mövenpick.** Swiss hospitality makes these downtown restaurants all
★ things to all people. Among the dinner specialties are *Zürcher G'Schnatzlets,* the famous Swiss dish of thinly sliced veal and mushrooms in a creamy white wine sauce served with *rösti* (panfried potatoes); *Kasseler,* a juicy smoked, grilled pork chop served with braised savoy cabbage; and red wine herring from Iceland marinated in wine and spices. The Swiss Farmers Sunday Brunch (York Street location only) is a vast buffet of food stations. The Yorkville location offers a thrilling ice-cream–dessert menu, in addition to the traditional Swiss selections. Downstairs at the seafood dining room, La Pécherie, schools of fish are cooked with respect. ⊠ *165 York St.,* ☎ *416/366–5234;* ⊠ *133 Yorkville Ave.,* ☎ *416/926–9545. AE, DC, MC, V.*

Harbourfront

Steak

$$$–$$$$ ✕ **Harbour Sixty Steakhouse.** Walk up stone steps to the Corinthian columns and the grand neoclassical entrance of the restored and enhanced Harbour Commission building. A baroque-inspired foyer leads to a gold-tone granite bar. Luxury indeed—when you are eating the world's finest basic foodstuffs, an opulent dining room is the only way to go. Beyond the bar is an open kitchen, with a cooler stocked with ruby-red tuna steaks, lobsters on ice, oysters, bright Atlantic salmon, and steaks. Slowly roasted prime rib is delicious. Fresh salmon and tuna are grilled to your taste. Sit in comfortable oversize armchairs or spacious curved and upholstered booths. ⊠ *60 Harbour St.,* ☎ *416/777– 2111. AE, DC, MC, V. No lunch weekends.*

Along Dundas and Queen Streets

American/Casual

$$$ ✕ **Cities.** While some kitchens just play, this tiny café creates symphonies in a space with brown paper–covered tables and hand-painted walls hung with the works of local artists. There's rarely an empty seat in the place. Appetizers such as blue-crab cake on caramelized golden pineapple are the draw. The menu always has a vegetarian entrée among its ever-changing variety of main courses. Dishes have included crispy chicken breast with herb and garlic cream cheese and natural jus, with witty pairings of grilled fruits and vegetables. ⊠ *859 Queen St. W,* ☎ *416/504–3762. Reservations essential. AE, DC, MC, V. No lunch Sat.–Mon.*

Barbecue

$$–$$$ ✗ **Red Devil.** Where there's smoke, there's barbecue. Almost everything on the vast menu of this generous, good family restaurant has a hint of the smoky great outdoors—wood-roasted Portobello mushroom salad, or roasted-garlic Caesar salad textured with crunchy bacon. Cutlery is wrapped in red linen that, unrolled, make nice absorbent napkins, a necessity when digging into a mess of barbecued, jalapeño–mango, pepper-crusted, or smoked prime-rib bones. The waiters know their p's and bbq's. ✉ *14 Duncan St.,* ☎ *416/598–5209. AE, DC, MC, V.*

Chinese

$$–$$$$ ✗ **Lai Wah Heen.** For Cantonese culinary fireworks, phone and pre-
★ order Lustrous Peacock. When it arrives, an explosion of white vapor reveals an arrangement of melon, barbecued duck, chicken, honeyed walnuts, and other exotic ingredients. The mahogany-color lacquer-crisp Peking duck is wheeled in on a trolley and presented with panache. Excellent choices from the 100-dish inventory include wok-fried shredded beef and vegetables in a crisp potato nest. At lunch, the dim sum is divine—translucent dumplings and pouches burst with juicy fillings of shark's fin sprinkled with bright red lobster roe, and shrimp dumplings with green tops look like baby bok choy. The service is French, in an elegant room with a sculptured ceiling, etched-glass turntables, and silver serving dishes. ✉ *Metropolitan Hotel, 118 Chestnut St., 2nd floor,* ☎ *416/977–9899. Reservations essential. AE, DC, MC, V.*

$–$$ ✗ **Wah Sing.** Just one of a jumble of Asian restaurants clustered together on a tiny Kensington Market street, this meticulously clean and spacious restaurant has two-for-the-price-of-one lobsters (in season, which is almost always). With black bean sauce or ginger and green onion, they're scrumptious and tender. You can choose giant shrimps Szechuan-style or one of the lively queen crabs from the tank. Chicken and vegetarian dishes for landlubbers are good, too. ✉ *47 Baldwin St.,* ☎ *416/599–8822. AE, MC, V.*

$ ✗ **Spadina Garden.** The Chen family has owned Spadina Garden for more than a decade, and their dishes are Toronto classics. This is largely the cuisine of northwest China, inland, so there is no tank of finny creatures to peruse. Start with barbecued honey–garlic spareribs or spring rolls before moving on to serious entrées. Orange beef is a dark and delicious saucy dish seasoned with dried orange peel and hot red peppers; sliced beef is served with black mushrooms and oyster sauce. The room itself is calm with standard black lacquer, high-back chairs, and red-paper lanterns hanging from the ceiling. ✉ *116 Dundas St. W,* ☎ *416/977–3413 or 416/977–3414. AE, MC, V.*

$ ✗ **Tiger Lily's Noodle House.** Many come to this clean and bright hand-painted café for real egg rolls and shrimp-and-spinach pot stickers in a light lemony glaze. But most people come for the noodles, cooked in many ways and combinations. Hawaiian duck long-rice soup, redolent with coconut lemongrass, plump with chicken and seafood, is one option. Soups include noodles, wontons, meat or vegetable broth, and garnishes of barbecued pork, Shanghai chicken, or veggies. Black-bean beef is special. If you want your Chinese food steeped in tradition, not grease, you'll find double happiness here. ✉ *257 Queen St. W,* ☎ *416/977–5499. AE, MC, V.*

Contemporary

$$$–$$$$ ✗ **Hemispheres Restaurant & Bistro.** An ordinary hotel facade has been transformed from duckling to beautiful swan by this dazzling restaurant. You can watch the chefs strut their stuff through the window wall of the vast kitchen. An award-winning culinary team puts an exciting East–West spin on the finest local ingredients. Brilliant, clear consommé that hints of duck and morels is poured into a bowl holding patti-pan filled with flavor-rich duck confit and ravioli filled with morels. The chef bakes risotto with chunks of Dungeness crab, crunchy lily root, and baby corn in a hollow, yellow squash. A wine steward does justice to each dish by recommending an appropriate glass of wine from the broad wine selection. A sumptuous, fresh market menu is consistently surprising. ⊠ *Metropolitan Hotel, 110 Chestnut St.,* ☎ *416/ 599–8000. Reservations essential. AE, DC, MC, V.*

French

$$$$ ✕ **The Fifth.** Slip into the lane between two downtown industrial build-
★   ings, enter through The Easy, a main-floor dance club, and take an un-
adorned freight elevator to The Fifth, a very expensive and semiprivate dining club. With its rough beams and exposed pipes, this loft space is deliberately theatrical with the right balance of formality and flirtation. The mood is industrial-strength romantic. In winter sit on a sofa in front of a huge fireplace; in summer dine on a gazebo terrace. The ever-changing seasonal menu is haute French. A thimble of caviar, a slice of foie gras, a fillet of sole, and a cut of beef are all given a classic French interpretation. Try the fragrant Québec lamb served with a classic garnish of anchovy, olive, and tomato purée in a pastry tart shell. ⊠ *225 Richmond St. W,* ☎ *416/979–3005. Reservations essential. AE, DC, MC, V. Closed Sun.–Wed. No lunch.*

Italian

$$–$$$ ✕ **KitKat Bar & Grill.** This eclectic and eccentric Southern Italian eatery is built around a massive tree. A theater-district locale means pre- and post-theater hours are really busy. You can dine at window tables in the front, perch at the long bar, enjoy the privacy of an old-fashioned wooden booth, or sit at a picnic table in the rear. Portions are enormous. An antipasto platter for two is a meal, and pastas, seafood, roast chicken, and grilled steak are all delectable. Owner Al Carbone welcomes everyone like long-lost family. ⊠ *297 King St. W,* ☎ *416/977– 4461. AE, DC, MC, V. No lunch weekends.*

$–$$ ✕ **Masquerade Caffè Bar.** An eclectic array of primary-color furnishings, stoves, and Murano-glass mosaics fills this Fellini-esque environment. The daily-changing Italian menu lists a variety of risottos, divine ravioli, and a choice of *panini*—Italian sandwiches on home-made breads with scrumptious meat, cheese, and veggie fillings. Zabaglione, whipped to a thick, frothy cream and poured over fresh berries, is a knockout dessert. ⊠ *BCE Place, Front and Yonge Sts.,* ☎ *416/363–8971. AE, DC, MC, V. Closed Sun.*

$$–$$$ ✕ **Verona.** The kitchen sends over homemade savories as soon as
★   you're seated—diced marinated vegetables in olive oil, lush olive spread, and a basket of fresh breads. You might start with opulent prosciutto-wrapped warm goat cheese with roasted Portobello, pimento and balsamic glaze, or grilled shrimp and avocado in a toasted flour tortilla. The kitchen tops angel-hair pasta with tiger shrimp, scallops, and woodland mushrooms and graces pork tenderloin with hazelnut crumb crust. A specialty is grilled lamb tenderloin with truffle mashed potato, artichoke, and Portobello mushroom. ⊠ *335 King St. W,* ☎ *416/593– 7771. AE, DC, MC, V. Closed Sun. No lunch Sat.*

Malaysian

$–$$ ✕ **Mata Hari Grill.** Dusky earth tones give this jewel-box interior a calm yet exotic aura, and there's a fresh scent in the room. Sticky rice mixed with shrimp and spices is wrapped in a banana leaf and grilled. Crackling spring rolls filled with shrimp and jicama arrive with little dishes of hot sweet-and-sour sauce. Satays sizzle with the heat of freshly ground spices: sea scallops and red pepper, marinated beef, and chicken speak eloquently with mysterious Malay-Thai flavors. ✉ *39 Baldwin St.,* ☏ *416/596–2832. Reservations essential. AE, DC, MC, V. Closed Mon. No lunch weekends.*

Pan-Asian

$$–$$$$ ✕ **Monsoon.** A fragrant, eclectic consort of Pan-Asian–inspired cuisine is served in a dining-and-lounge environment with a black-brown color scheme that makes for a serene yet dynamic atmosphere. It's hard to pass up any of the raft of incredible small dishes. Tandoori salmon is wrapped in seaweed and rice paper, painted with miso and sesame, and splashed through hot oil to crisp. A covered ceramic bowl holds wok-steamed mussels in a breathtaking pineapple and curry broth. Main courses, such as pan-seared Burmese prawns with *soba* (buckwheat noodles) and golden peanut sauce, excite the palate. Compatible desserts include delicate Chai-spiced crème brûlée. The ambience here is unsnobbish sophistication. ✉ *100 Simcoe St.,* ☏ *416/979–7172. AE, DC, MC, V. No lunch weekends.*

Pizza

$–$$ ✕ **Il Fornello.** Pizza aficionados especially love Il Fornello's 10-inch, thin-crust pie, baked in a wood-burning oven. Orchestrate your own medley from 50 to 60 traditional and exotic toppings that include braised onion, *cappicola* (spicy Italian sausage), provolone, calamari, eggplant, and anchovies. Pasta, veal dishes, and salads are available, too. Wheat-free pizza crust and dairy-free cappuccino are also on the menu. Customer clamor has prompted the opening of more venues. ✉ *214 King St. W,* ☏ *416/977–2855;* ✉ *55 Eglinton Ave. E,* ☏ *416/486–2130;* ✉ *1560 Yonge St.,* ☏ *416/920–8291;* ✉ *35 Elm St.,* ☏ *416/598–1766. AE, MC, V.*

Around Queen's Park

American

$–$$$ ✕ **Blues on Bellair.** A midnight-blue cocoon for grown-ups, the kitchen here sizzles and a groovy rhythm and blues band most nights. To start, try the cilantro-seasoned crab cakes, which come accompanied by creamy chile and sake garlic sauce, or the spicy Jamaican vegetable fritters. New Orleans–style entrées include half rack of beer-and-bourbon soaked pork ribs, Cajun breast of chicken on a bun, or grilled salmon in a hoisin and fresh lime glaze. All entrées come with your choice of mustard-garlic dressed salad or sweet potato fries. Or, if you have the late-night munchies, wings, nachos, and fries are served up til the wee hours. Around 10 PM, the band starts its first set and the room gets jumping. ✉ *25 Bellair St.,* ☏ *416/944–2095. AE, MC, V.*

American/Casual

$ ✕ **7 West Cafe.** It's surprising how many people hunger for pasta primavera, vegetarian chili, or a bagel melt at 3 AM. Luckily, such cravings can be indulged at this 24-hour haven for the hip and hungry. Everything comes with a green salad, and every item is homemade. Soups like Moroccan lentil, carrot, and potato-leek are delicious. Pasta salad is fresh and yummy, and dinner-size sandwiches (grilled honey-and-herb chicken breast, for example) are huge. The ambience on every floor is chic and trendy. ✉ *7 Charles St. W,* ☏ *416/928–9041. AE, MC, V.*

Cafés

$ ✕ **Indigo Books, Music & Café.** Tastemakers and trendsetters, book lovers and gift buyers—all stroll the aisles selecting books and music in a friendly and casual, yet totally efficient ambience. For pre- and post-moviegoing, the café is peerless. From the open kitchen, orders are called out when they're ready. Hand-sliced grilled farmhouse chicken on caraway rye spread with Pommery mustard, grilled Italian vegetarian sandwiches, luscious turkey Reubens, and tuna salad mixed with nonfat yogurt and layered with cucumbers on whole-grain bread are some of your choices. Freshly blended fruit drinks such as Equatorade (mango, pineapple, and banana) lift the spirit. If the soup of the day is chicken noodle, order it. ⊠ *Manulife Centre, 55 Bloor St. W, ☎ 416/925–3536;* ⊠ *Yonge-Eglinton Centre, 2300 Yonge St., ☎ 416/544–0049;* ⊠ *Eaton Centre, 220 Yonge St., ☎ 416/591–3622. AE, D, DC, MC, V.*

Canadian

$$–$$$$ ✕ **Pangaea.** Partners Peter Geary and chef Martin Kouprie use unprocessed, seasonal ingredients and the bounty of produce the world has to offer. Soups—such as wild-rabbit soup with chicken broth, wood ear mushrooms, cattail hearts, and fresh ginger—are unique; salads are creative constructions of organic greens. Grilled mahogany quail comes with crab-apple sauce, and their own sake-cured salmon nestles with shiitake mushrooms and water chestnuts in rice paper. Vegetarians can find bliss in this caring kitchen. And, on the other side of the food chain, rack of lamb gets dolled up with a sunflower mustard crust and delectable variations on root vegetables. Afternoon tea with all the sweet and savory goodies is a joy for Bloor Street shoppers. The tranquil room has an aura of restrained sophistication. ⊠ *1221 Bay St., ☎ 416/920–2323. AE, DC, MC, V.*

$$–$$$ ✕ **Patriot Restaurant & Brasserie.** So what is Canadian cuisine anyway? Just take the elevator to the second floor of The Colonnade shopping complex, ask for a table overlooking the street, and your question will be answered in delicious ways. In a casual ambience of warm woods and subdued tones, enjoy smoked salmon and buckwheat crêpes with crème fraîche and Canadian caviars, or barbecued squab terrine with pickled peaches and blackberry marmalade. With pride in local produce, the kitchen prepares pan-seared Huron whitefish stuffed with seasonal wild mushrooms, potatoes and carrot broth, and rib steak with all the trimmings. Rhubarb crumble with cream-cheese ice cream is a sweet surprise. The wine list is a national treasure; you may be tempted to stand and salute the flag. ⊠ *131 Bloor St. W, 2nd floor, ☎ 416/ 922–0025. AE, MC, V.*

Contemporary

$$$$ ✕ **Courtyard Cafe at the Windsor Arms Hotel.** Now that the Windsor Arms Hotel has burst upon the scene again, a new café has been built over the ghosts of the old. In the '70s and '80s, Cafe Yoo-hoo was the place to be for breakfast, lunch, and dinner. Slowly, the city's social lights are returning to the scene. The vast dining room is impressive; the decor itself makes it worth a visit. Strong architectural details, such as bronze Doric columns, faux windows, balconies, and hedges, give the limestone walls that soar three stories high a more human scale. From the surrounding balconies you can observe huge chandeliers and dramatic paintings by Canadian artist David Bierk. The signature appetizer is foie gras, done two ways. The Caesar salad sets the standard, and the mixed grill combines tender lamb, beef, and chicken. On the mezzanine above the dining room, a pianist adds to the evening fun. ⊠ *Windsor Arms Hotel, 18 St. Thomas St., ☎ 416/971–9666. Reservations essential. AE, DC, MC, V. No dinner Sun.–Mon.*

$$$$ ✕ **Truffles.** Through impressive wrought-iron gates, pale wood walls glow
★   in the reflected soft light of handcrafted candelabra. This restaurant has won the hearts of discerning gastronomes with the true essence of contemporary French cuisine rooted in authentic French flavors. Appetizers include spaghettini with Perigord black gold truffles, Québec foie gras, and marinated venison loin terrine with figs and wine jelly marmalade. Entrées such as Black Angus beef tourenados with smoked bone

marrow, or roasted Ontario red deer loin with rhubarb and pear chutney appear on the menu. The wine list is well worth exploring. Truffles also serves a selection of vegetarian and spa dishes. Leave room for esoteric desserts like a warm soufflé trio of Grand Marnier, chocolate, and cassis, or the Espresso Chocolate Lava Rose, with vanilla bean sauce. ⊠ *Four Seasons Hotel, 21 Avenue Rd.,* ☎ *416/928–7331. Reservations essential. AE, DC, MC, V. Closed Sun. No lunch.*

$$$–$$$$ ✕ **Boba.** Owners Bob Bermann and Barbara Gordon (Boba) are a sophisticated culinary couple who cook in a charming brick house personalized with robust and gorgeous color. The dishes they've dreamed up are original and delicious—rice-paper-wrapped chicken breast on Thai black rice and big-eye tuna grilled rare with coconut noodles, mango and avocado salsa, and black bean sauce are favorites. For a heartier dish, try the traditional grilled Black Angus strip loin with Yukon Gold frites. Vegetable dinners are spontaneously created. Boba has one of the city's prettiest patios for summer dining. ⊠ *90 Avenue Rd.,* ☎ *416/961–2622. AE, MC, V. No lunch.*

$$$–$$$$ ✕ **Senses.** This multipurpose food emporium strokes all the senses. The
★ main-floor displays of caviar, smoked salmon, homemade pastas, gorgeous salads, and exquisite desserts set you up to be pampered in the second-floor dining room. Start with rare seared tuna tataki. Culinary excitement comes in the form of slow-braised beef shortribs with vanilla-roasted sweet potatoes, beet root pesto, and Zinfandel jus. Miso-glazed sea bass is enhanced with chopstick greens and mushroom broth. Even oven roast breast of chicken is all dressed up with a mushroom dumpling, butternut squash, eggplant pickle, and tamarind dressing. Comfort, space, light, and artistic floral arrangements appeal to people who expect to be looked after. There is complimentary valet parking in the evenings. ⊠ *15 Bloor St. W,* ☎ *416/935–0400. AE, DC, MC, V.*

$$–$$$ ✕ **Studio Café.** At this well-lit, comfortable café—a combination hotel coffee shop, restaurant, and contemporary glass-and-art gallery—you can have a full Japanese or Canadian breakfast. Order nutritionally balanced meals, and indulge in trendsetting dishes such as half lobster out of the shell, and risotto with American sauce and melting leeks and tomatoes. Still, sandwiches such as smoked turkey clubhouse with cranberry sauce, and one of the city's best beef burgers with roasted onions, mushrooms, and aged cheddar, are what draw the gourmets. ⊠ *Four Seasons Hotel, 21 Avenue Rd., north of Bloor St.,* ☎ *416/964–0411. AE, DC, MC, V.*

Eclectic

$$–$$$ ✕ **Messis.** The lights on the romantic patio wink an enticing invitation, in stark contrast to the spare, hard-edge dining room. Penne arrives al dente, textured with smoked chicken, mushrooms, zucchini, and roasted peppers in a pesto broth with grated Asiago cheese. The textures and flavors of grilled sage-marinated veal loin with red onion preserve and cognac-soaked currants blessed with a timbale of red potatoes, celery root, and cremini mushrooms unfurl smoothly. Oven-roasted Atlantic salmon, rich and satisfying as a steak, is elevated on a crop of sesame-scented baby bok choy and partnered with strudel of jasmine rice and exotic sun-dried fruit. Menus adapt to the seasons. ⊠ *97 Harbord St.,* ☎ *416/920–2186. AE, DC, MC, V. No lunch.*

French

$$–$$$$ ✕ **Bistro 990.** A superior kitchen combined with bistro informality is
★ the successful recipe here. Start with traditional pâté maison, partnered with quince marmalade, wine preserves, crunchy cornichons, and plenty of homemade croutons. Sea bass baked with wild rice and pine nuts in white wine parsley butter is a treat, and roasted half-chicken with herbed garlic jus crackles with crispness and Provençal flavor. The

purist kitchen uses artesian spring water for all stocks and homemade breads. Faux stone walls stenciled with Cocteau-esque designs, sturdily upholstered chairs, and a tiled floor create a sophisticated but comfortable atmosphere. ⊠ *990 Bay St.,* ☎ *416/921–9990. Reservations essential. AE, DC, MC, V. Closed Sun. No lunch Sat.*

Italian

$$–$$$ ✕ **Bellini.** From the street, it's a few steps down to this comfortable, flower-filled, romantic spot. The beef carpaccio and grilled eggplant are excellent. An antipasto platter for two or more that includes grilled tiger shrimp, seared scallop, charred calamari, smoked salmon, proscuitto and melon, roasted rainbow peppers, marinated Portobello mushrooms and more, will clue you in on what this kitchen is all about. Try the osso buco with garlic mushroom risotto, or the special Bellini chicken with roasted artichokes, wild mushrooms, and baked polenta. While pasta dishes are the kitchen's pride, their delicate ways with classic veal scallopini are what draws a loyal repeat clientele. Service pampers, and a friendly host greets you at the door. ⊠ *101 Yorkville Ave. W,* ☎ *416/929–9111. AE, DC, MC, V. No lunch.*

$$–$$$ ✕ **Sotto Sotto.** A coal cellar in a turn-of-the-20th-century home was
★   dug out, its stone walls and floor polished, and a restaurant created in what has become a dining oasis for locals and international jet-setters alike. The menu gives a tantalizing tug to the taste buds. Of the more than 20 pasta dishes, appetizer or main-course size, *orecchiette* (tiny, disk-shape pasta) with a toss of prosciutto, mushrooms, black olives, and fresh tomatoes is a symphony of textures. Gnocchi are made daily. Cornish hen is marinated, pressed, and grilled to juicy brownness; swordfish and fresh fish of the day are beautifully done on the grill. Lots of nooks and corners and flickering candles cast uneven shadows in these charming, cavelike rooms. ⊠ *116-A Avenue Rd.,* ☎ *416/962–0011. AE, DC, MC, V. No lunch.*

Seafood

$$$–$$$$ ✕ **Joso's.** A two-story midtown restaurant displays sensuous paintings
★   of nudes and the sea, signed celebrity photos, and intriguing wall hangings. The kitchen prepares dishes from the Dalmatian side of the Adriatic Sea, and members of the international artistic community who frequent the place adore the unusual and healthy array of seafood and fish. Leo's award-winning black risotto with squid is a must. Try porgy from Boston, salmon trout from northern Ontario, or baby clams from New Zealand. Grilled prawns, their charred tails pointing skyward, is a dish often carried aloft by speed-walking servers. ⊠ *202 Davenport Rd.,* ☎ *416/925–1903. Reservations essential. AE, DC, MC, V. Closed Sun. No lunch Sat.*

Steak

$$$–$$$$ ✕ **Morton's of Chicago.** A well-rehearsed server rolls up a trolley bearing all the menu's treasures and introduces them with reverence—a 48-ounce porterhouse for two, a veal chop with Sicilian seasonings, a rib eye dry-rubbed with Cajun spices, and a 3- to 5-pound lobster straight from the north Atlantic trying in vain to leap from the stainless-steel tray. Accompanying potatoes can be hash browns or baked Idahos. Morton's has a traditional steak-house atmosphere, right down to the polished wood and white tablecloths. ⊠ *4 Avenue Rd., at Prince Arthur Ave.,* ☎ *416/925–0648. AE, DC, MC, V. No lunch.*

Vegetarian

$ ✕ **52 Inc.** Two young, creative people founded this café on the belief that responsible consumption can be good business. Carefully seasoned gazpacho, Greek salad, grilled vegetables, and extraordinary soups are handcrafted from scratch. Even the espresso is brewed from organically grown beans. Most of the unusual and attractive fixtures were rescued from the demolition of a Victorian house. ⊠ *394 College St.,* ☎ *416/960–0334. V. Closed Mon.*

Cabbagetown

French

$$–$$$ ✕ **Provence.** Antique white walls hung with provocative artwork and
★ plenty of greenery make this pretty villa seem like a little corner of the south of France. In summer the front garden is an especially beautiful place to dine. A classic steak frites fixed-priced three-course dinner is a favorite, as is the six-course gastronomic dinner. A tureen of foie gras is served simply with confit of spiced figs and toast. Traditional fish soup with garlic croutons and rouille is superb. Duck confit, preserved in its own fat and then crisped in the oven and presented with garlic potatoes, sour cherries, and rhubarb and apricot compote, is outstanding. Authentic French patisserie like chocolate marquise or a tart Tatin of luscious brown caramelized apples on a good pastry crust makes a fine ending. Fixed-price Sunday brunch is a real treat. ⊠ *12 Amelia St.,* ☎ *416/924–9901. AE, MC, V.*

Southwest Toronto

American

$$–$$$ **Reds Bistro & Bar.** Country casual with pine beams, etched glass, hanging pots and pans, and cheery prints make this 300-seat oasis in the heart of the financial district a breath of fresh air. The menu sells sizzle, and feeds you on reasonably priced, fancy-sounding dishes that don't shred your credit card. The wine list, heavy on reds (hence the name of the place), is a great read. Each day of the week brings a special— seared rainbow trout with Basque vegetables and potatoes, seared tuna with white bean ragout, and lamb curry with masala spices and basmati rice, to name a few. Sure to please are grilled chicken breast in tomato and sage emulsion with big grain couscous, or seared sea bass with whipped potatoes. Desserts are big enough for sharing. ⊠ *77 Adelaide St. W,* ☎ *416/862–7337. AE, DC, MC, V. Closed Sun. No lunch Sat.*

Cafés

$ ✕ **Future Bakery & Café.** A European-style bakery has blossomed into a small chain of cafeterias supplied by their own dairy. Old European recipes like beef borscht, buckwheat cabbage rolls, and potato cheese *varenycky* (turnovers) slathered with thick sour cream, have remained. This place is beloved by students for its generous portions, by homesick Europeans hungry for goulash and knishes, by the cheesecake-and-coffee crowd, by health-conscious foodies looking for fruit salad with homemade yogurt and honey, and by people-watchers looking for people worth watching from 7 AM to 2 AM. ⊠ *483 Bloor St. W,* ☎ *416/922–5875;* ⊠ *2199 Bloor St. W,* ☎ *416/769–5020;* ⊠ *739 Queen St. W,* ☎ *416/504–8700;* ⊠ *St. Lawrence Market, 95 Front St. E,* ☎ *416/366–7259. Reservations not accepted. MC, V.*

Cajun/Creole

$$–$$$ ✕ **Southern Accent.** This funky Cajun and Creole restaurant fits hand in glove with its neighbors on a street born for browsing, chockablock with antiques shops, bookstores, and galleries. You can perch at the bar, order a martini and hush puppies, and chat with the resident psychic. Whimsical knickknacks adorn every inch of the place. Dining rooms on two floors offer a changing, market-fresh menu. Fortunately there are some constants—bayou chicken, Southern fried with dark and spicy sauce; cracker catfish (a fillet coated with spiced crackers) served with swamp lime tartar sauce; and shrimp étouffée with caramelized vegetables are always on the menu. ⊠ *595 Markham St.,* ☎ *416/536–3211. AE, DC, MC, V. No lunch.*

Canadian–Casual

$–$$ ✕ **Over Easy.** Champions of breakfast adore this all-day-breakfast menu, and with good reason. Fresh-squeezed juice, and coffee in two brightly colored carafes (orange for decaf, blue for regular) are served in a flash. Consider the Eggstro, eggs baked and smothered in three cheese sauce. The Big Breakfast leaves nothing to the imagination—three sunny-side-ups, a pancake in the shape of a maple leaf, a ladle full of baked beans with molasses, chopped garlic and bacon, a grilled tomato, a bowl of home fries with onions, and two big strips of crackling crisp double-smoked bacon. And there's more... wonderful sandwiches and salads, and the best French toast around, prepared with caramelized bananas and pure maple syrup. ⊠ *208 Bloor St. W,* ☎ *416/922–2345. No dinner. Reservations not accepted. AE, DC, MC, V.*

Chinese

$$ ✕ **Mandarin.** Diners may be weak in the knees at the sight of the smorgasbord of Chinese food. First, heap your plate with salad-bar selections and large shrimp in the shell, and then attack the hot-and-sour soup, the wonton soup, or both. The food has no MSG and no preservatives. Servers explain each dish and invite you to come back for seconds of honey-garlic ribs, deep-fried shrimp and chicken wings, breaded chicken, spring rolls, sweet-and-sour dishes, chicken curry, mixed vegetables, seafood stir-fries, and more—even sliced beef with gravy and roast potatoes. Desserts include tarts, cookies, and ice cream. ⊠ *2200 Yonge St.,* ☎ *416/486–2222;* ⊠ *2206 Eglinton Ave. E, Scarborough,* ☎ *416/288–1177.*

Contemporary

$$$$ ✕ **Susur.** Susur Lee, the foodie's darling, returned to Toronto, after a three year hiatus, to open his new restaurant. At first glance, the imposing square room seems cold, white, and stark, until we take note of the subtlety of a wall of recessed mood lighting that changes from pink, blue, green, and shades between. Choose a spacious leather booth or dining table in the center of the room and be prepared for a sometimes unbearable wait between courses. Still, the food is worth it. Soups are complex poetry. An ever-changing menu might offer a delicate rack of baby lamb served whole with a slash from a sharp knife separating meat from bones as juices drizzle into a green curry sauce and feisty, bright green mint chutney. A coil of Szechuan eggplant and a ball of deep-fried string cut potatoes are delectable additions. Desserts include an array of fruit sorbets, dark and white chocolate–coriander mousse, and Peking banana fritters. ⊠ *601 King St. W,* ☎ *416/603–2205. Reservations essential. AE, MC, V. Closed Sun. No lunch.*

Eclectic

$$–$$$$ **Zinc.** To say that Zinc is just cool is like saying that a Lamborghini is just a car. Inside, the heart quickens with the challenge of the avante-garde and the innocent excess. Soothing, spare, but not alienating, this is not a restaurant for everyone. Press a button on a brushed-metal box and the concise menu is illuminated in green. Salad Nicoise features thick slices of seared ahi tuna over the traditional warm potatoes and green beans, along with a few quail eggs and an anchovy fillet bonded by preserved lemon vinaigrette. Light and airy goat's milk Brie is hidden under a small mountain of baby lettuce. Main courses are subtle and masterful—thick beef tenderloin is grilled and set on hearty potato and onion gratin, lamb sirloin is roasted with herbs that leave their lingering scent. Servers are in tune with the restaurant and know how to offer desserts like poached pear in puff pastry with hazelnuts, or chocolate seduction. ✉ *471 Richmond St. W, ☎ 416/504–6013. AE, DC, MC, V. Closed Sun. No lunch.*

$–$$ **Azul.** Way out of the high-rent district, this hand-decorated funky and artistic bistro has a creative menu. Latin and Asian twists to the dishes add distinct charm. Salmon fillet with vanilla tapenade over miso-dressed greens or breast of free-range chicken with spaetzle cream, herbs, mushrooms, and snow peas will put your tastebuds in a tizzy. Vegan dishes such as beet ravioli with fennel, orange zest, and lemongrass coconut sauce, or Dragon Bowl—a choice of organic rice or noodle with chicken, seafood, or vegetables—appeals even to meat eaters. The quality-obsessed chefs prefer to use organic foods. Try unusual vegetable and fruit juices or smoothies. In the evening, sparkly candles light up the room and create an engaging ambience. ✉ *181 Bathurst St., ☎ 416/703–9360. MC, V. Closed Mon.*

French

$$–$$$$ ✗ **Pastis.** Diners may well feel they're in the south of France as they
★ sit surrounded by lush raspberry and violet walls, munching on fresh radishes and slices of baguette and butter, spooning up traditional fish soup with rouille, croutons, and grated cheese. Simply roasted grain-fed chicken is glazed with an intense natural jus and garlic cloves. Cut into four neat sections, it perches on a crisp potato pancake and gives a totally satisfying variety of taste and texture. The adventurous palate will rhapsodize over sweetbreads sautéed with shallots, Madeira, and chanterelles; a sizzling beef steak for two carved tableside; or braised veal cheeks with root vegetables. This place could run on the Gallic charm of owner Georges Gurnon alone. ✉ *1158 Yonge St., ☎ 416/ 928–2212. AE, DC, MC, V. Closed Sun.–Mon. No lunch.*

$$–$$$ ✗ **Le Paradis.** Well-traveled university types, writers, actors, and producers from the surrounding neighborhood come to this authentic French bistro-on-a-budget for the ambience and gently priced wine list. Steak and fries, crisp herb-roasted chicken, and exotic *tajine de volaille* (a Moroccan stew of chicken, prunes, olives, and a shopping list of seasonings) get the creative juices flowing. Pay heed to the daily fixed-price menu. ✉ *166 Bedford Rd., ☎ 416/921–0995. AE, MC, V.*

Italian

$$$–$$$$ ✗ **Mistura.** This place has the buzz that's made it one of the hottest mod-
★ ern Italian restaurants in town. Two hip hospitality professionals have come up with an innovative menu in a space that combines comfort with casual luxury. Choose from more than a dozen delectable starters like caramelized, marinated lamb ribs with cucumber chutney, red-beet risotto, or grilled Portobello arugula caramelized onions with pistachio-nut dressing. Roasted maple-glazed rock Cornish hen, cashew-crusted Atlantic salmon, and seared black sea bass with pommery mustard crust are carefully thought-out triumphs. Vegetarians can find true happiness here, too, with grilled, stuffed, and roasted vegetables. ✉ *265 Davenport Rd., ☎ 416/515–0009. AE, DC, MC, V. Closed Sun. No lunch.*

$$–$$$$ ✗ **Splendido.** Torontonians love the sophisticated ambience here and re-
★ spect chef-owner Arpi Magyar's sparkling contemporary menu. Ricotta and potato are coaxed into plump gnocchi and served splashed with lemon butter, Parmesan, cracked pepper, and sage. Veal is the chef's masterpiece. Oven-baked rack set on garlic mashed potatoes comes with roasted pearl onions and Chinese broccoli, followed a close second by wood-oven roasted sea bass with potato-leek hash browns. Casual good taste meets the eye at every turn. The bar is popular for nightcaps. ✉ *88 Harbord St., ☎ 416/929–7788. Reservations essential. AE, DC, MC, V.*

A BREATH OF FRESH AIR

AT THE FIRST SIGN of warm weather, and until the evenings turn cool in September, Torontonians hit the deck, the patio, the courtyard, and the rooftop terrace. White-plastic tables and chairs sprout around every restaurant that has a patch of frontage to call its own.

In summer, Yorkville lives again—Cumberland Park between Avenue Road and Bellair Street bursts into bloom. Wildflowers, an herb garden, fountains, and groves of trees present a one-word invitation: picnic. The surrounding eateries oblige with pizza, deli sandwiches, salads, and gourmet lunches to go.

Alongside the historic stone edifice of Club Monaco's flagship store is **Club Monaco Cafe & Patio** (⌧ 157 Bloor St. W, ☎ 416/591–8837) serving light, inventive dishes behind a street screening hedge. **Sassafraz** (⌧ 100 Cumberland St., ☎ 416/964–2222) is cool and contemporary. **Lettieri** (⌧ 94 Cumberland St., ☎ 416/515–8764) is an Italian café. **Cafe Nervosa** (⌧ 75 Yorkville Ave., ☎ 416/961–4642) serves up pizza, pasta, and salads. Don't miss the off-street flower-filled terraces of **Il Posto Nuovo** (⌧ 148 Yorkville Ave., ☎ 416/968–0469), **Prego della Piazza** (⌧ 150 Bloor Street W, ☎ 416/920–9900), and **Boba** (⌧ 90 Avenue Rd., ☎ 416/961–2622).

The passage to Indian cuisine (Gerrard Street between Coxwell and Victoria Park avenues) is filled with exciting sights and sounds. Streets are crowded, and everywhere there is food and the scintillating aroma of spices. Sit at an outdoor table at **Madras Express Cafe** (⌧ 1438-A Gerrard St., ☎ 416/461–7470) and eat a *masala dosa*, a folded, foot-long, crunchy rice-flour pancake filled with potato and mustard seed.

Kensington Market (between Dundas and College streets, west of Spadina Avenue), home to melting-pot cuisine, is an area to which immigrants have moved for generations. **Last Temptation** (⌧ 12 Kensington Ave., ☎ 416/599–2551) is great for spicy roti or fresh fruit salad. **Margaritas** (⌧ 14 Baldwin St., ☎ 416/977–5525) is known for great guacamole and fajitas. You can sample Malaysian food at pretty **Mata Hari Grill** (⌧ 39 Baldwin St., ☎ 416/596–2832).

When they're rolling up the sidewalks elsewhere, Greektown (Danforth Avenue between Chester and Jones avenues) is just getting lively. Bouzouki music fills the air, and dozens of Greek restaurants on both sides of the street are filled with night owls nibbling on traditional appetizer platters and warm pita bread. The sidewalk patio of **Lolita's Lust** (⌧ 513 Danforth Ave., ☎ 416/465–1751) is a good place to check out the scene. **Myth** (⌧ 417 Danforth Ave., ☎ 416/461–8383) has a pool as well as a patio.

The Italians practically invented the art of sipping espresso and watching the world go by. Little Italy (College Street between Euclid Avenue and Shaw Street) is packed with trattorias, wine bars, bistrettos, and traditional pool halls. **Giovanna** (⌧ 637 College Ave., ☎ 416/538–2098) serves great roast chicken with Tuscan bread salad. Tasty grilled meats are favored at **Trattoria Giancarlo** (⌧ 41 Clinton St., ☎ 416/533–9619).

Where's everyone going? The Entertainment District (King Street west of University, Duncan, John, Simcoe, and Peter) teems with suited after-work crowds seeking an outdoor terrace and a cool drink. If you see an empty table, take it. Queen Street, between University Avenue and Bathurst Street, is filled with Gen-X dining adventure—pizza, sushi, pad thai, tortillas, pasta. **The Rivoli** (⌧ 322 Queen St. W, ☎ 416/596–1908) is a hot spot. The rear garden at the **Queen Mother Café** (⌧ 208 Queen St. W, ☎ 416/598–4719) is a cool place for East–West dishes.

$$-$$$ ✕ **Olive & Lemon.** The dishes at this casual corner storefront restau-
★ rant are restrained yet have a hint of underlying exuberance. Olives and
lemons, fruits from antiquity, are sautéed with herbs and served with
warm bread. Plump sardines, with a drizzling of organic oil and snip-
pets of mint, are glorious. Grilled squid on a tumble of organic greens
and *crostini* (slices of toast with oil) is delectable. The whole-wheat riga-
toni, with olives, pine nuts, and basil, has a lovely crusty glaze. ⊠ *119
Harbord St.,* ☎ *416/923–3188. Reservations essential. DC, MC, V.*

$$ ✕ **Filippo's Gourmet Pizza.** "Life is like a pizza—the more you put in,
★ the richer it gets" is written on a slate map of Italy that hangs on the
wall in this charming spot. In summer, the large patio is pizza central.
Inside, it's hard to pass by and not stop at the big wooden display table
filled with antipasti—polenta and olives, potato, and fried onion, crisp
green beans, and grilled peppers and eggplant. Home-style bruschetta
is piled high with chopped tomato and fresh basil. The enthusiasm of
owner Filippo DiNatale is transferred to his dishes—rigatoni with fen-
nel, capers, anchovies, and bread crumbs' rich and creamy risottos; and
wonderful pizzas handmade to order. ⊠ *744 St. Clair Ave. W,* ☎ *416/
658–0568. AE, MC, V.*

Japanese

$$-$$$$ ✕ **Edo.** Aficionados of Japanese food may have to stop themselves from
ordering everything on the menu. Even the uninitiated are mesmerized
by the intriguing dishes carried by servers, including plates of *yaki ki-
noko* (grilled mushrooms or thickly sliced eggplant baked to a silken
texture with mildly sweet and sour flavors). If soft-shell crab is on the
menu, it's a worthy choice. The chef is an artist with sushi and sashimi,
but if you can't decide, the set menus give you a balanced and exciting Japanese meal. ⊠ *484 Eglinton Ave. W,* ☎ *416/322–3033;* ⊠ *439
Spadina Rd.,* ☎ *416/482–8973. Reservations essential. AE, DC, MC,
V. No lunch at Eglinton Ave. W*

$$-$$$$ ✕ **Tempo.** The beat at Tempo is buoyant, and it's not just from the high
decibel music, the smoke, or the crowd in the bar. Servers fly about,
adding to the hurly-burly. Behind the counter, three chefs calmly make
hand rolls, sushi, California rolls, and Asian fusion nori-wrapped
cooked lobster, cucumber, and avocado seasoned with truffle oil.
Sashimi is drizzled with olive oil, balsamico, and crispy shallots. Tuna
tataki salad has taken a detour through the peppery hills of Thailand
and even shrimp tempura is high octane on the hot and spicy scale. To
experience the ultimate from Tom Thai, the talented chef, just say
"omakase," which means please create a special meal for us. ⊠ *596
College St.,* ☎ *416/531–2822. Reservations essential. AE, MC, V.
Closed Sun. No lunch Mon.–Sat.*

Pan-Asian

$-$$ ✕ **Indochine.** A century of French colonization influenced Vietnamese
cuisine, and India and China also left an indelible stamp. Indochine
reflects these influences with stunning appetizers like two large west-
coast rock oysters on the half shell poached in a bubbling hot sauce
of butter, garlic, and shallots. Chicken *grandmère* cooks in its own clay
pot; the server lifts the lid, pours in clear and spicy sauce, mixes it through
the chicken and rice, and ladles it onto the plates. Vegetarians go for
noodle soups, fragrant with tamarind and lemongrass. Try Vietnamese
coffee—a filtered mix of milk, sugar, and strong coffee. ⊠ *4 Collier
St.,* ☎ *416/922–5840. AE, MC, V. No lunch weekends.*

Portuguese

$$$-$$$$ ✕ **Chiado.** Service is bilingual (Portuguese and English), and the fish
are flown in from the Azores and Madeira. French doors lead to pol-
ished wood floors, tables set with starched white napery, and plum vel-

vet armchairs. Most days you can find bluefin tuna, piexe aspado, sword-fish, and boca negra, along with monkfish, sardines, squid, and salmon. Traditional Portuguese dishes like *asorda* of seafood, a kind of souf-flé, are served from a silver tureen. There's much for meat eaters to enjoy, too—beef tenderloin blessed with a wild mushroom and tawny port sauce, and roasted rack of lamb that sparkles with Duoro wine sauce. ✉ *864 College St. W, ☎ 416/538–1910. Reservations essential. AE, DC, MC, V. No lunch weekends.*

Thai

$$–$$$ ✕ **Thai Magic.** Bamboo trellises, cascading vines, fish and animal carv-ings, and a shrine to a mermaid goddess make a magical setting for coolly saronged servers and hot-and-spicy Thai food. "Hurricane Ket-tle" is a dramatic presentation of fiery seafood soup. Whole coriander lobster sparkles with flavor, and chicken with cashews and whole dried chilies is for the adventurous. ✉ *1118 Yonge St., ☎ 416/968–7366. Reservations essential. AE, MC, V. Closed Sun. No lunch Sat.*

$ ✕ **Vanipha Lanna.** People can't get enough of the clean and bright fla-
★ vors, grease-free cooking, and lovingly garnished Lao-Thai presenta-tions at this tidy, colorful restaurant. The bamboo steamer of dumplings with minced chicken and seafood, sticky rice in a raffia cylinder, and chicken and green beans stir-fried in lime sauce are exceptional. Rice is served from a huge silver tureen. A sister restaurant, Ban Vanipha (✉ 634–638 Dundas St., ☎ 416/340–0491), is equally accomplished. ✉ *471 Eglinton Ave. W, ☎ 416/484–0895. Reservations essential. AE, MC, V. Closed Sun.*

Vegetarian

$ ✕ **Juice for Life.** There's no gloom that can't be cured by Super Energy Cocktail, Einstein's Theory, or Rocket Fuel Fix, to name just a few of the energy elixirs at this funky gourmet juice bar and vegan café. Sun-day's Feast for Life brunch includes hemp-seed French toast with maple syrup and sliced fruits, grilled corn and potato cakes with warm salsa, and a three-page menu of delicious hot and cold dishes made without dairy, meat, or any animal matter whatsoever. There's a long bar with stools and a whole row of cozy ancient wooden booths. ✉ *521 Bloor St. W, 1½ blocks east of Bathurst, ☎ 416/531–2635. V.*

Northwest Toronto

Contemporary

$$$–$$$$ ✕ **Centro.** Soft and strong natural colors and unique lighting create a
★ subdued, sophisticated ambience. Owners Tony Longo and award-win-ning chef Marc Thuet set city standards of excellence. French-Mediter-ranean style filters through fine regional ingredients in specialties such as fruitwood-smoked Bay of Fundy salmon; pan-seared Québec foie gras; and baked goat cheese with roasted Anjou pears. Pasta dishes—such as pennine with whole roasted garlic, fresh oregano, and olives—surprise and delight. The wine list has an uncommon depth and breadth, and service is urbane and attentive. ✉ *2472 Yonge St., ☎ 416/483–2211. Reservations essential. AE, DC, MC, V. Closed Sun. No lunch.*

Indian

$–$$ ✕ **Cuisine of India.** Civic progress has placed this casual, unassuming restaurant a few blocks away from the magnificent Ford Centre for the Performing Arts. Puffy, crusty, buttery-center naan bread comes from the depths of the tandoor oven. A whole leg of lamb for two, halved chicken breasts, and giant shrimp can all be ordered oven-baked, too. The vegetable dishes are diverse in their seasonings and come with fra-grant basmati rice. ✉ *5222 Yonge St., ☎ 416/229–0377. Reservations essential. AE, DC, MC, V.*

Steak

$$–$$$$ ✕ **House of Chan.** Some people actually come here for the Chinese food, but it's the U.S. prime beef and the huge lobsters filling the tank that are considered by those in the know to be the best in town. Slide into a red-leather booth and order a T-bone, New York strip steak, or fillet in the size you can handle—ditto for the lobster. Best bets are sliced fresh vegetables, crunchy batter-fried onions, and home fries. While you're waiting, have an egg roll. ⊠ *876 Eglinton Ave. W, ☎ 416/781–5575. Reservations not accepted. AE, DC, MC, V. No lunch.*

Northeast Toronto

Contemporary

$$$–$$$$ ✕ **North 44.** Step over the steel compass embedded in the floor of a marble foyer and you are in an urbane, sophisticated environment. A lighting engineer has created a fantasy room with intriguing flares and light-and-shadow patterns on the walls and ceiling to suggest movement. This is the place to awaken your taste buds with appetizers of Parma ham with mascarpone-stuffed figs, frisee salad, and toasted walnuts, or a lobster taco with crisp beet wrapper, jicama salad and scallion. Just try to choose from chef-owner Marc McEwen's creative alchemy, found in his seven-page menu. Exciting main courses include whole roasted Dover sole in brown butter with capers, lemon, and crisp shoestring basket; and braised lamb shank with fried-onion–potato mousse. Pasta and pizzas are other options, and you can choose one of 50 wines sold by the glass to complement any dish. ⊠ *2537 Yonge St., ☎ 416/487–4897. AE, DC, MC, V. Closed Sun. No lunch.*

French

$$–$$$ ✕ **Herbs.** Paintings of lush gardens adorn the walls, while brown butcher
★ paper covers floral-clothed tables. For starters, there's great bread. From the list of superb appetizers, try the silken liver pâté, seasoned with port and cognac, or gravlax and smoked arctic char, twirled on a plate with asparagus vinaigrette. Specialties may include roasted pork tenderloin with a glaze of fresh fig and mint, and breast of free-range pheasant roasted with fruits and berries. The tarte Tatin (caramelized apple cake) will transport you to Paris. The young owner-chef cooks like a dream, but don't expect to eat and run. ⊠ *3187 Yonge St., ☎ 416/322–0487. Reservations essential. AE, MC, V. Closed Sun. No lunch Sat.*

Italian

$–$$ ✕ **Grano.** What started as a bakery and take-out antipasto bar has grown
★ into a cheerful collage of the Martella family's Italy. Come for animated talk, good food, and great bread in lively rooms with faux ancient plaster walls, wooden tables, and bright chairs. Choose, if you are able, from 40 delectable vegetarian dishes and numerous meat and fish antipasti. Lucia's homemade gnocchi and ravioli are divine, as is the white chocolate and raspberry pie. ⊠ *2035 Yonge St., ☎ 416/440–1986. AE, DC, MC, V. Closed Sun.*

Southeast Toronto

Continental

$$–$$$ ✕ **The Torch.** There's a sense of occasion here, amid sumptuous leather booths with rich leather framing and numbered Victorian private dinettes with 8-ft dividing walls windowed with stained glass. (Dinette Number 7 is ventilated for pipe and cigar smoking.) A waiter comes bearing gifts—white crocks filled with tiny gherkins and chicken liver pâté with a basket of sourdough bread. The undisciplined diner could get carried away by the rousing selection of appetizers like grilled quail and roasted wild-mushroom ragout with an edgy balsamic glaze.

Main-course portions are generous. Duck is crisp-skinned, the meat is juicy, falls from the bone, and is lavished with port sauce and a caramelized-tomato tart. Steak frites and bouillabaisse are excellent, but do leave room for extraordinary sticky-toffee pudding with vanilla ice cream. After dinner, it's one flight up to the Top O' The Senator, a late-night jazz club. ⊠ *253 Victoria St.,* ☎ *416/364–7517. AE, DC, MC, V. Closed Mon. No lunch.*

Eclectic

$$–$$$ ✕ **Myth.** Both menu and theme in this Greektown restaurant walk a tightrope between garishness and genuine glamour, taking a nontraditional route to the Mediterranean with a detour through California. Perch at the bar and munch on almond-crusted crisp calamari with zucchini fritters and yogurt dip, or a cold mezze platter—a vast assortment of dips with pita. If table service is more your style, consider an uncomplicated pasta or an adventurous Moroccan grilled Cornish hen. Vegans might appreciate the grapeleaf-wrapped tofu and roasted peppers. Rack 'em and stack 'em at two pool tables—graze, sip, and mingle. ⊠ *417 Danforth Ave.,* ☎ *416/461–8383. AE, DC, MC, V.*

Indian

$ ✕ **Skylark.** Satisfied smiles are reflected time and again in two walls of diamond-shape mirror tiles. One of the oldest, prettiest, and most reliable restaurants in Little India is still at the top. Owner Gurnam Multani extends a jovial welcome and leads you to a blue-clothed table where you must make a decision: buffet or menu. Usually, most people help themselves from the 10-item dinner buffet with vegetable salads, vegetables cooked in sweet cream, and chickpeas and mung beans in a rich onion sauce. Vegans will get the required food groups here. Other dishes on the menu and sometimes on the buffet include lamb curry, tandoori chicken, and chicken muglai with intriguing Indian spices. The bargain of the year gets even better when Mr. Multani strolls by offering hot fresh naan from his tandoor oven. ⊠ *1433 Gerrard St. E,* ☎ *416/469–1500. AE, MC, V.*

Seafood

$–$$ ✕ **Rodney's Oyster Bar.** This playful, basement raw bar is a hotbed of
★ bivalve variety frequented by dine-alones and showbiz and agency types. Among the offerings are salty Aspy Bays from Cape Breton, perfect Malpeques from Rodney Clark's own oyster beds in Prince Edward Island, or New York Pine Islands. A zap of Rodney's own line of condiments or a splash of vodka and freshly grated horseradish are certain eye-openers. Soft-shell steamers, quahogs, and "Oyster Slapjack Chowder" are among the array of oceanic delights. Shared meals and half-orders are okay with Rodney. Be sure to ask about the daily white-plate specials. ⊠ *469 King St. W,* ☎ *416/363–8105. Reservations essential. AE, DC, MC, V. Closed Sun.*

Steak

$$$$ ✕ **Carman's.** The 42-year history of this restaurant unfolds as you walk along the photograph-lined hall. Inside, pewter and copper utensils hang from every inch of the ceiling and fill the shelves. A leather-bound book contains the menu, a five-page wine list, a copy of Abraham Lincoln's work ethic, and great reviews. In the steak-house tradition, Carman's includes plenty of pre-eats—feta-filled phyllo pastries, garlic toast, olives, tsatziki, dill pickles, and cottage cheese. All the right steaks— rib, fillet, slabs of barbecue ribs—come on wooden steak boards. ⊠ *26 Alexander St.,* ☎ *416/924–8558. AE, MC, V. No lunch.*

LODGING

Updated by
Jack Kohane

Places to stay in this cosmopolitan city range from plush palaces to no-frills budget motels. The city once boasted many more charming old lodgings, but only a few, including Le Royal Meridien King Edward, the Fairmont Royal York, and The Windsor Arms have survived. Most other high-quality hotels are part of well-known American, European, or Asian chains. The deluxe Four Seasons chain got its start here and still sets the style and pace for service and amenities. Generally there's a close relationship between price and value, but Toronto has managed to avoid the hefty hotel price inflation of most other cities. In addition, the extremely attractive exchange rate of the Canadian dollar against most other international currencies, makes this world-class metropolis a downright bargain no matter where you decide to set down your luggage.

When planning your trip, take into account that the city draws many conventions and is increasingly popular with leisure travelers, particularly outside the winter months of late November through March. Book well in advance, and—if conventioneers bother you—ask if there will be any large groups in the hotel you're interested in at the time of your stay.

Some hotels cut prices nearly in half over weekends (which sometimes start on Thursday) and during special times of the year; many Toronto hotels drop their rates a full 50% in January and February. When you book, don't forget to ask about family deals and special packages.

If you plan to do plenty of sightseeing, you're best off staying in or near the downtown area, where you can visit Harbourfront Centre, the CN Tower, Eaton Centre, the Toronto Islands, SkyDome, Chinatown, Greektown, Kensington Market, the Art Gallery of Ontario, the Royal Ontario Museum, the Canadian National Exhibition (the world's largest continually running agricultural fair held from mid-August to Labor Day), and most of the finest shopping and restaurants anywhere in the province. If you're staying only a day or two with kids, and are mainly interested in visiting the Metro Toronto Zoo, the Ontario Science Centre, Paramount Canada's Wonderland, or Niagara Falls, look into some of the places along the airport strip or outside the downtown core. Most of these have plenty of rooms on the weekend and frequently offer steep discounts for weekend travelers.

Tourism Toronto (☎ 416/203–2500 or 800/363–1990, WEB www.torontotourism.com) is a good resource for finding any of the city's 35,500-plus hotel rooms in the price range you want, along with pre-ordering tickets to local attractions, sports events, and entertainment venues. More than a dozen private homes, all in and around the downtown core, are affiliated with **Toronto Bed & Breakfast** (✉ 253 College St., Box 269, M5T 1R5, ☎ 705/738–9449, FAX 705/738–0155, WEB www.bbcanada.com/toronto). It's a free registry offering private homes from charming lakeside retreats to Victorian gems close to the heart of the city's action. Most of these homes tend to fall into the less expensive price categories. **Bed & Breakfast Association of Downtown Toronto** (✉ Box 190, Station B, M5T 2W1, ☎ 416/410–3938, FAX 416/368–1653, WEB www.bnbinfo.com) represents 30 fully inspected and privately owned homes scattered throughout the city center, most within 10 minutes of major attractions.

Bridge Street Accommodations (✉ 1000 Yonge St., Suite 301, M4W 2K2, ☎ 416/923–1000 or 800/667–8483, FAX 416/924–2446, WEB www.bridgestreet.com) has furnished apartments for rent in and around

Toronto. Most apartments and condominiums have in-suite laundry facilities and provide play areas for children—all have full kitchens. Pets are welcome at most properties. Fax machines and computers can be arranged at an additional cost. **Apartments International Inc.** (✉ 255 Duncan Mill Rd., Suite 604, M3B 3H9, ☎ 416/410–2400 or 888/410–2400, FAX 416/410–2410) provides furnished apartments throughout the greater Toronto area for short-term and extended-stay rentals. These apartments come with fully equipped kitchens, housekeeping, and more. **Glen Grove Suites** (✉ 2837 Yonge St., M4N 2J6, ☎ 416/489–8441 or 800/565–3024, FAX 416/440–3065, WEB www.glen-grove.com) offers 65 furnished residential-style, one- and two-bedroom suites in a stunning art deco building surrounded by lush parklands and close to everything. **Ontario Farm and Country Accommodations** (✉ R.R. 2, Vankleek Hill, Ontario K0B 1R0, ☎ 613/267–1443, FAX 613/267–1766, WEB www.countryhosts.on.ca) can help if you think you might enjoy staying on a working farm or country home near Toronto. Rates vary from $50 to $75 per person per night including breakfast, with weekly packages also available. Some locations have shared and/or ensuite bathrooms, saunas, hot tubs, cribs for babies (most homes welcome children of all ages), bicycles, and riding stables.

At the hotels listed in the top two price categories, you can expect wheelchair accessibility, room service, twice-daily maid-service, minibars, hair dryers, no-smoking rooms, business services and meeting rooms, and laundry and dry cleaning service. Unless otherwise noted, all hotels have air-conditioning and private baths.

CATEGORY	COST*
$$$$	over $250
$$$	$170–$250
$$	$90–$170
$	under $90

All prices are for a standard double room, excluding 7% GST (Goods and Services Tax), 5% room tax, and optional service charge, in Canadian dollars.

Downtown and Midtown

$$$$ ⊞ **Four Seasons Toronto.** It's hard to imagine a lovelier or more ex-
★ clusive hotel than the elegant Four Seasons. It boasts one of the most ideal locales in the city, in Yorkville, a few yards from the Royal Ontario Museum and the University of Toronto. Rooms are tastefully appointed and come with comfortable bathrobes, oversized towels, and fresh flowers. Ask for upper rooms with views facing downtown and the lake. The Studio Café is one of the best business dining spots in town. The formal dining room, Truffles, has an international reputation and an acclaimed wine list. La Serre is a good place for cocktails, and a lovely afternoon tea service is offered in the lobby. ✉ *21 Avenue Rd., a block north of Bloor St., M5R 2G1,* ☎ *416/964–0411 or 800/268–6282,* FAX *416/964–2301,* WEB *www.fourseasons.com. 210 rooms, 170 suites. 2 restaurants, bar, lobby lounge, in-room data ports, indoor-outdoor pool, health club, bicycles, baby-sitting, business services, parking (fee). AE, D, DC, MC, V.*

$$$$ ⊞ **Inter-Continental Toronto.** Handsome and intimate, this boutique hotel,
★ part of a respected international chain, is just a half block west of the major intersection of Bloor Street and Avenue Road; the Royal Ontario Museum and the Yorkville shopping area are a two-minute walk away. Art deco touches enhance the public areas and the spacious, well-appointed, recently renovated guest rooms. Signatures Restaurant is elegant and comfortably classic. The clublike opulence of the Harmony

Lounge is perfect for light fare, tea, and cocktails after a hard morning of shopping. Service is top-notch. ✉ *220 Bloor St. W, M5S 1T8,* ☎ *416/960–5200 or 800/267–0010,* FAX *416/960–8269,* WEB *www.toronto.interconti.com. 209 rooms, 11 suites. Restaurant, lobby lounge, outdoor café, in-room data ports, indoor lap pool, massage, sauna, gym, parking (fee). AE, DC, MC, V.*

$$$$ 🏨 **Park Hyatt Toronto.** Luxurious Park Hyatt has one of the city's best locations. It's near the Royal Ontario Museum and the upscale Yorkville shopping area, and has windows overlooking Queen's Park and Lake Ontario. The Roof Lounge, a writers' haunt, was once described by novelist Mordecai Richler as "the only civilized place in Toronto," offers attentive service along with sparkling nighttime views of the skyline. With elegantly appointed, spacious rooms, the experience here is *très* New York Park Avenue. ✉ *4 Avenue Rd., at Bloor St. W, M5R 2E8,* ☎ *416/924–5471 or 800/977 4197,* FAX *116/924–4933,* WEB *www. hyatt.com. 346 rooms. 2 restaurants, bar, lounge, in-room data ports, room service, health club, spa, business services, parking (fee). AE, D, DC, MC, V.*

$$$$ 🏨 **Sheraton Centre.** A busy conventioneer's favorite, this hotel is across from New City Hall and just a block from Eaton Centre, which is accessible via an underground passage. The below-ground concourse level is part of Toronto's labyrinth of shop-lined corridors called the Underground City. All guest rooms have marvelous views—to the south are the CN Tower and SkyDome, to the north, both city halls. The Club Level offers upgraded accommodations and amenities such as down-filled duvets, bathrobes, and exclusive access to the luxurious 43rd-floor Club Level Lounge offering a panoramic city view along with complimentary continental breakfast and cocktail hour. Children's programs are only available in summer. ✉ *123 Queen St. W, M5H 2M9,* ☎ *416/361–1000 or 800/325–3535,* FAX *416/947–4874,* WEB *www.sheratontoronto.com. 1,377 rooms. 3 restaurants, coffee shop, lobby lounge, in-room data ports, no-smoking floor, room service, indoor-outdoor pool, hot tub, massage, spa, sauna, gym, children's programs, parking (fee). AE, DC, MC, V.*

$$$$ 🏨 **Sutton Place Hotel.** Elegant and close to the city's bustling heart, the
★ 33-story Sutton Place draws many corporate travelers and visiting film and stage stars because of its commitment to service and privacy. The spacious rooms have comfortable, traditional-style furnishings. Oriental rugs, tapestries, flowers, and plush chairs fill the public areas. Leisure travelers appreciate the proximity to the Royal Ontario Museum, trendy Yorkville shops, the Toronto Eaton Centre, and an expanding array of excellent restaurants. Some suites have full kitchens and whirlpool baths. ✉ *955 Bay St., M5S 2A2,* ☎ *416/324–5621 or 800/268–3790,* FAX *416/924–1778,* WEB *www.suttonplace.com. 230 rooms, 64 suites. Restaurant, in-room data ports, room service, indoor pool, hair salon, health club, business services, parking (fee). AE, DC, MC, V.*

$$$$ 🏨 **Westin Harbour Castle.** Mere steps from Harbourfront and the Toronto Islands ferry, the Westin offers the best views of Lake Ontario of any hotel in the city. A free shuttle bus and the Harbourfront LRT (light rapid transit) provide links to Union Station, the subway, and downtown business and shopping. The hotel is a favorite with conventioneers because of its enclosed bridge to the large convention center across the street. The Toronto Island ferries dock at the plaza in front of the hotel, and all waterfront attractions are accessible within a half-hour's walk or a quick cab ride. Rooms are tastefully modern—all look out onto the lake, but you may want to ask for one of the corner rooms, which look up to the glittering bank skyscrapers and office towers to the north. The renowned Toulà (which means "hayloft") restaurant, perched atop the hotel's revolving 38th floor, serves tradi-

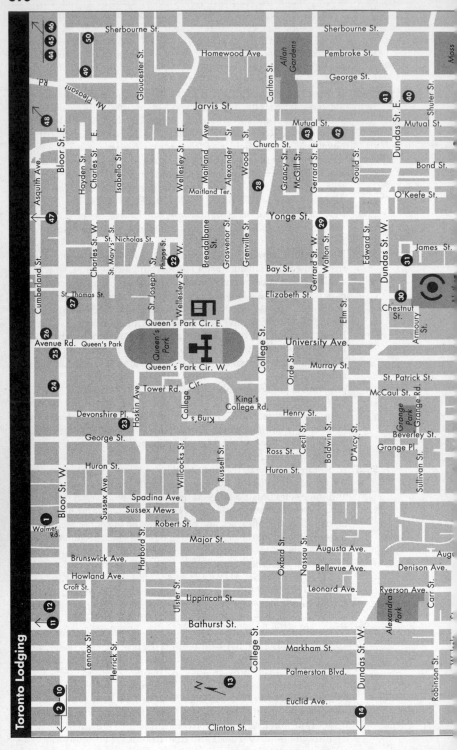

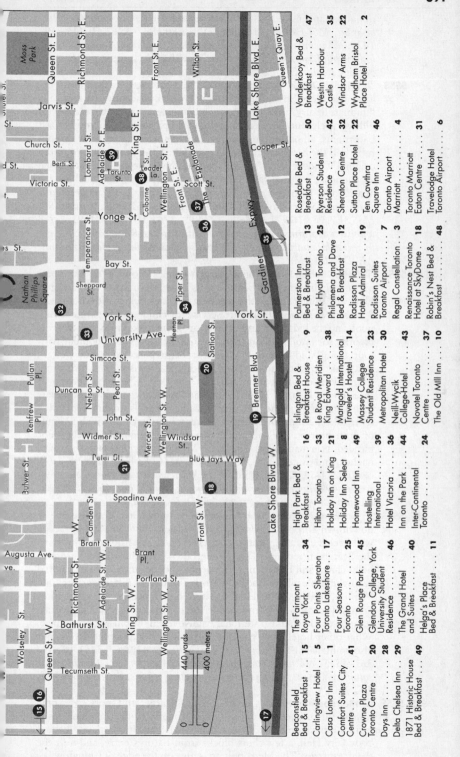

Moss Park

Queen St. E.

Richmond St. E.

Front St. E.

Wilton St.

Jarvis St.

Lake Shore Blvd. E.

Queen's Quay E.

Church St.

Lombard St.

Adelaide St. E.

King St. E.

Cooper St.

Berti St.

Toronto St.

Leader La.

Victoria St.

Colborne

Wellington St. E.

Front St. E.

Scott St.

The Esplanade

Yonge St.

Temperance St.

Bay St.

Piper St.

Gardiner Expwy

Sheppard St.

Nathan Phillips Square

York St.

Heenan Pl.

York St.

University Ave.

Station St.

Simcoe St.

Pearl St.

Nelson St.

Wellington St. W.

Bremner Blvd.

Duncan St.

Pullan Pl.

John St.

Renfrew Pl.

Widmer St.

Mercer St.

Windsor St.

Butler St.

Peter St.

Blue Jays Way

Spadina Ave.

Front St. W.

Lake Shore Blvd. W.

Camden St.

Brant St.

Brant Pl.

Augusta Ave.

Richmond St. W.

Adelaide St. W.

Portland St.

Bathurst St.

King St. W.

Wellington St. W.

Wolseley St.

Queen St. W.

Tecumseth St.

440 yards

400 meters

Beaconsfield
Bed & Breakfast ... **15**
Carlingview Hotel ... **5**
Casa Loma Inn ... **1**
Comfort Suites City
Centre ... **41**
Crowne Plaza
Toronto Centre ... **20**
Days Inn ... **28**
Delta Chelsea Inn ... **29**
1871 Historic House
Bed & Breakfast ... **49**

The Fairmont
Royal York ... **34**
Four Points Sheraton
Toronto Lakeshore ... **17**
Four Seasons
Toronto ... **25**
Glen Rouge Park ... **45**
Glendon College, York
University Student
Residence ... **46**
The Grand Hotel
and Suites ... **40**
Helga's Place
Bed & Breakfast ... **11**

High Park Bed &
Breakfast ... **16**
Hilton Toronto ... **33**
Holiday Inn on King ... **21**
Holiday Inn Select ... **8**
Homewood Inn ... **49**
Hostelling
International ... **39**
Hotel Victoria ... **36**
Inn on the Park ... **44**
Inter-Continental
Toronto ... **24**

Islington Bed &
Breakfast House ... **9**
Le Royal Meridien
King Edward ... **38**
Marigold International
Traveler's Hostel ... **14**
Massey College
Student Residence ... **23**
Metropolitan Hotel ... **30**
Neill-Wycik
College-Hotel ... **43**
Novotel Toronto
Centre ... **37**
The Old Mill Inn ... **10**

Palmerston Inn
Bed & Breakfast ... **13**
Park Hyatt Toronto ... **25**
Philomena and Dave
Bed & Breakfast ... **12**
Radisson Plaza
Hotel Admiral ... **19**
Radisson Suites
Toronto Airport ... **7**
Regal Constellation ... **3**
Renaissance Toronto
Hotel at SkyDome ... **18**
Robin's Nest Bed &
Breakfast ... **48**

Rosedale Bed &
Breakfast ... **50**
Ryerson Student
Residence ... **42**
Sheraton Centre ... **32**
Sutton Place Hotel ... **22**
Ten Cawthra
Square Inn ... **46**
Toronto Airport
Marriott ... **4**
Toronto Marriott
Eaton Centre ... **31**
Travelodge Hotel
Toronto Airport ... **6**

Vanderkooy Bed &
Breakfast ... **47**
Westin Harbour
Castle ... **35**
Windsor Arms ... **22**
Wyndham Bristol
Place Hotel ... **2**

tional Italian cuisine for lunch, dinner, and Sunday brunch. ✉ *1 Harbour Sq., M5J 1A6,* ☎ *416/869–1600 or 800/937–8461,* FAX *416/869–1420,* WEB *www.westin.com. 980 rooms. 2 restaurants, lobby lounge, indoor pool, massage, tennis court, health club, squash, playground, parking (fee). AE, DC, MC, V.*

$$$$ 🖫 **Windsor Arms.** Grand, venerable, and discreetly tucked away be-
★ hind chic Bloor Street, the Windsor Arms aims to offer what it calls "intimate luxury." Its 28 guest rooms combine modern technology with old-world elegance. Several rooms have fireplaces and generously sized bathrooms, all bathrooms have separate shower stalls and whirlpool tubs, and the hotel has butler service. The neo-Gothic exterior of the original Windsor Arms has been painstakingly reconstructed to evoke a bygone age of grace and refinement. Also part of the hotel are the Tea Room, Toronto's only Caviar and Champagne Lounge, and a dance club. Suites have VCRs and CD players. ✉ *18 St. Thomas St., M5S 3E7,* ☎ *416/971–9666 or 877/999–2767,* FAX *416/921–9121,* WEB *www.windsorarmshotel.com. 7 rooms, 21 suites. Restaurant, bar, café, in-room data ports, indoor pool, spa, business services, meeting rooms. AE, DC, MC, V.*

$$$–$$$$ 🖫 **Delta Chelsea Inn.** Toronto's largest hotel is known as the city's premier entertainment hotel because of its close proximity to the Pantages, Elgin, and Winter Garden theaters. You can book tickets with your room. A creative, supervised day-care service for children, a separate family pool, and the kids' stay-and-eat-free program makes the Chelsea a real favorite for families. This friendly hotel has long been popular with tour groups and business travelers, so be prepared for a flurry of activity. Ask for the southeast and southwest rooms in the south wing, overlooking downtown and the lake. The Delta Chelsea is a couple of short blocks north of Eaton Centre, and the College subway station is across the street in the basement of College Park shopping center. Do try to take in Monarchs, a bright, contemporary-style pub with 12 kinds of draft beer on tap and a selection of 15 single-malt scotches (not blended, as in many pubs). The fare at Monarchs includes lasagna, wings, nachos, and oysters. ✉ *33 Gerrard St., M5G 1Z4,* ☎ *416/595–1975 or 800/243–5732,* FAX *416/585–4375,* WEB *www.deltachelsea.com. 1,590 rooms, 49 suites. 3 restaurants, 3 lounges, 2 pools, hot tub, sauna, gym, business services, parking (fee). AE, D, DC, MC, V.*

$$$–$$$$ 🖫 **Le Royal Meridien King Edward.** The undisputed grande dame of
★ downtown Toronto hotels, this stately beauty built in 1903 attracts a well-heeled clientele. (In the past, everyone from Rudyard Kipling to the Beatles stayed here.) The "King Eddy," a member of a European hotel chain, still has an air of opulence and elegance, with its vaulted ceiling, marble pillars, and palm trees. The hotel's restaurant, the Café Victoria, and the Consort Bar (serving a light lunch menu) are favorites among Toronto's corporate and leisure-seeking elite. For a genteel afternoon pastime, take traditional English tea in the plush lobby lounge. What other hotel gives you not only bathrobes and hair dryers, but also umbrellas? ✉ *37 King St. E, M5C 1E9,* ☎ *416/863–3131,* FAX *416/367–5515,* WEB *www.lemeridien.com. 294 rooms. Restaurant, hair salon, spa, gym, business services, meeting rooms, parking (fee). AE, DC, MC, V.*

$$$–$$$$ 🖫 **Metropolitan Hotel.** One of Toronto's larger and more handsome
★ hotels, this contemporary 26-floor property with a glass-enclosed atrium lobby could hardly be more convenient. It's just steps behind New City Hall, a few short blocks from Eaton Centre, and near the theater district. The Metropolitan is also on the edge of Chinatown— one of the most dynamic Chinese communities outside mainland China. The rooms have finely crafted furniture and desks, some have king-size beds, and executive rooms have a work center with printer and

fax. Eight guest rooms are designed for travelers with disabilities. Dining options include the excellent Hemispheres Restaurant & Bistro, and Lai Wah Heen (which means "luxurious meeting place"), a restaurant specializing in Cantonese cuisine. Lai Wah Heen's menu includes "lustrous peacock," and what is reputed to be the best dim sum in Toronto, some say in North America. ⊠ *108 Chestnut St., M5G 1R3,* ☎ *416/977–5000 or 800/668–6600,* ℻ *416/977–9513,* WEB *www.metropolitan.com. 409 rooms, 43 suites. 3 restaurants, 2 bars, in-room data ports, indoor pool, hot tub, sauna, health club, playground, business services, parking (fee). AE, D, DC, MC, V.*

$$$–$$$$ 🏨 **The Old Mill Inn.** The prestige and flawless service of the adjoining Old Mill restaurant (built in 1914), is emulated by the Old Mill Inn, Toronto's latest must-see landmark (completed in 2001) and the only resort within the city. Every exquisitely appointed room has a whirlpool tub, romantic fireplace, and a spectacular view of the picturesque Humber River Valley, an expansive urban forest set along a winding riverbank marked by miles of nature trails just waiting to be explored by foot or bike. The restaurant, which has an international reputation and menu, offers dinner and dancing, luncheon buffets, and traditional afternoon tea. The inn is 15 minutes from both the downtown core and Pearson International Airport. ⊠ *21 Old Mill Rd., M8X 1G5,* ☎ *416/236–2641 or 866/653–6455,* ℻ *416/236–2749,* WEB *www.old-milltoronto.com. 47 rooms, 13 suites. Restaurant, in-room data ports, minibars, spa, gym, tennis courts, business services, free parking. AE, DC, MC, V.*

$$$–$$$$ 🏨 **Renaissance Toronto Hotel at SkyDome.** Billing itself as the "World's Only Sports and Entertainment Hotel," the SkyDome fulfills the fantasies of Torontonians and visitors by providing them with the opportunity to watch their favorite sports team, pop star, or even a monster-truck rally from the comfort of a hotel room. Seventy rooms are built into the north wall of the SkyDome stadium and look right onto the field. The price of those rooms varies with the event. Guests can also book skyboxes for meetings and parties. Unless you want to watch a game, the hotel may not be to your taste—it maintains a very modern look with embossed steel and bare concrete, even in the guest rooms. ⊠ *1 Blue Jays Way, M5V 1J4,* ☎ *416/341–7100 or 800/468–3571,* ℻ *416/341–5090,* WEB *www.renaissancehotels.com. 323 rooms, 23 suites. Restaurant, lobby lounge, indoor pool, health club, business services, parking (fee). AE, DC, MC, V.*

$$$–$$$$ 🏨 **The Fairmont Royal York.** One of Canada's most distinctive and famous railway hotels, this majestic hostelry was built by the Canadian Pacific Railway for the convenience of passengers using nearby Union Station. Although no longer the largest hotel in the British Commonwealth, a title it held for decades, the Fairmont Royal York is still a masterpiece and a monster of a place. The service is efficient, and there's always a convention of some sort going on. Still, it's venerable, comfortable, and close to the financial district, waterfront attractions, and all major downtown theaters. A refurbishment of the hotel has returned the lobby to its classic 1929 decor, with travertine walls and columns. The health club and skylit lap pool feature rich marblework and a stunning hand-painted trompe l'oeil wall mural. You can sample succulent sushi from Benihana's Sushi Bar. The hotel's links to Union Station and the Underground City make it very handy in cold weather. ⊠ *100 Front St. W, M5J 1E3,* ☎ *416/368–2511 or 800/663–7229,* ℻ *416/368–9040,* WEB *www.fairmont.com. 1,365 rooms. 5 restaurants, 3 bars, in-room data ports, indoor lap pool, health club, business services, travel services, parking (fee). AE, D, DC, MC, V.*

$$–$$$$ 🏨 **Ten Cawthra Square Inn.** Combining the genteel essence of Edwardian style with contemporary luxury, Ten Cawthra—once the home of a sergeant in the York Militia—offers travelers accommodations steeped in Toronto history. The owners have lovingly and meticulously restored the inn to its original grace and luster. The breakfast room is large and comfortable, with tin ceilings and access to an adorable private garden complete with a gurgling pond surrounded by dozens of flowering plants and shrubs. A Continental breakfast is made exceptional by a cornucopia of fresh baked goods. Forget the car—you can walk from Cawthra Square to just about anywhere in the downtown area, or the nearby subway can take you wherever you want to go. ✉ *10 Cawthra Sq., M4Y 1K8,* ☎ *416/966–3074 or 800/ 259–5474,* FAX *416/966–4494,* WEB *www.cawthra.com. 6 rooms, 4 with bath. Breakfast room, laundry service, parking (fee). AE, MC, V.*

$$$ 🏨 **The Grand Hotel and Suites.** The Grand is the downtown core's grandest travelers' haven. The entrance with its impressive 30-ft granite facade leads into a soaring lobby of coffee-colored granite pillars and floors accented by plush furniture, splashes of floral arrangements, and regaled by crown moldings. There's tempting local cuisine served at the grandiose Citrus dining room. Each guest room has a marble bathroom and two TVs. The kitchenettes have microwaves and conventional ovens. Two steamy rooftop outdoor hot tubs are open to guests year-round at no additional charge. ✉ *225 Jarvis St., M5B 2C1,* ☎ *416/863–9000 or 877/324–7263,* FAX *416/863–1100,* WEB *www.grandhoteltoronto.com. 117 rooms, 60 suites. Restaurant, kitchenettes, refrigerators, outdoor hot tub, sauna, gym, business services, parking (fee). AE, DC, MC, V.*

$$–$$$ 🏨 **Crowne Plaza Toronto Centre.** Honeymooners swoon over the breathtaking view of the city skyline and lakeside waterfront from this vantage point, and also appreciate the Crowne's short walking distance from the CN Tower, Harbourfront, Air Canada Centre, SkyDome, theaters, and the financial center. The Accolade dining room offers its signature Tasting Menu concept with choices from among four to eight lavish main courses, along with wine pairings and a selection of fine cigars in the adjoining bar. Guests rooms are contemporary and decked in upscale modern decor. Tap your toes to the jazz performances in the early evenings at the Trellis Bistro and Lounge. ✉ *225 Front St. W, M5V 2X3,* ☎ *416/597–1400 or 800/422–7969,* FAX *416/597–8128,* WEB *www.crowneplazatoronto.com. 539 rooms, 48 suites. 2 restaurants, bar, indoor pool, hair salon, spa, health club, business services, parking (fee). AE, DC, MC, V.*

$$$ 🏨 **Holiday Inn on King.** In the heart of the entertainment district, the Holiday Inn is three blocks north of the Metro Toronto Convention Centre, SkyDome, and the CN Tower. Also nearby is Queen Street and its lively club scene. Although the structure is 20 floors high, half of that is office space; the hotel occupies the 9th through 20th floors. You can request views of either Lake Ontario, the downtown skyline, or SkyDome. Executive suites have whirlpool bathtubs. The swimming pool is tiny, but the exercise room is appealing. You get a lot for your money at this chain hotel. ✉ *370 King St. W, M5V 1J9,* ☎ *416/599–4000 or 800/263–6364,* FAX *416/599–7394,* WEB *www.hiok.com. 425 rooms. 2 restaurants, refrigerators, pool, massage, sauna, gym, business services, meeting rooms, parking (fee). AE, D, DC, MC, V.*

$$$ 🏨 **Radisson Plaza Hotel Admiral Toronto–Harbourfront.** The Admiral is a small, personal hotel downtown on the waterfront next to the exciting and always buzzing Harbourfront complex. It's only a short walk to most of the major attractions and sports venues such as the Air Canada Centre, CN Tower, SkyDome, the Harbourfront Antique Market, and Queen's Quay Terminal shopping, and there's a light rail connection to the subway system outside the door. Rooms are handsomely furnished in naval motifs, and the public areas maintain the nautical look with gleaming lacquered wood and polished brass. The hotel affords spectacular views over Lake Ontario to the Toronto Islands, and dramatically impressive views of the city office towers to the north. Commodore's Restaurant has equally stunning views and serves Continental cuisine. ⊠ *249 Queen's Quay W, M5J 2N5,* ☏ *416/203–3333 or 800/ 333–3333,* FAX *416/203–3100,* WEB *www.radisson.com. 157 rooms, 8 suites. 2 restaurants, bar, outdoor pool, squash, parking (fee). AE, D, DC, MC, V.*

$$$ ⊡ **Hilton Toronto.** Proximity to the entertainment and financial districts, SkyDome, Air Canada Centre, and the CN Tower makes the Hilton Toronto a convenient base for many visitors. A recently completed $25 million dollar renovation showcases a glittering, spacious lobby decked in golds and creamy browns, and topped by newly redesigned rooms with wood floors, subtle earth tones, and modern furniture. The indoor-outdoor pool is modest, but the view of the city from the glass-enclosed elevators is a thrill. ⊠ *145 Richmond St. W, M5H 2L2,* ☏ *416/869–3456,* FAX *416/869–1478,* WEB *www.hilton.com. 601 rooms. 4 restaurants, indoor-outdoor pool, hot tub, health club, parking (fee). AE, DC, MC, V.*

$$$ ⊡ **Toronto Marriott Eaton Centre.** A terrific location makes this a tourist and convention lodging favorite. Adjacent to the Eaton Centre shopping complex, this Marriott is within walking distance of SkyDome, the Metro Toronto Convention Centre, and the theater and financial districts. Guest rooms are larger than most you can find in Toronto. An indoor rooftop swimming pool provides a fabulous view of the city. At the airy Parkside Café on the main floor, you can sip your coffee while basking in the light pouring in from the enormous windows, which look out onto the Church of the Holy Trinity. Character's, a sports bar, has TVs and pool tables. ⊠ *525 Bay St., M5G 2L2,* ☏ *416/597–9200 or 800/228–9290,* FAX *416/597–9211,* WEB *www.marriotteatoncentre.com. 435 rooms, 24 suites. 2 restaurants, lobby lounge, sports bar, indoor pool, health club, billiards, business services, parking (fee). AE, DC, MC, V.*

$$–$$$ ⊡ **Comfort Suites City Centre.** An architecturally historic building, this compact seven-story lodging is a former Government edifice. Its stately concrete exterior facade remained untouched when it was converted to hotel use. Lofty guest rooms (many non-smoking) are bright and spacious, exuding an airy feel with creams and plum colors predominating. Its boutiquelike lobby welcomes guests with a fireplace, marble floors, and a cascading waterfall. For honeymooners, there are special suites to spur the romance, with heart-shaped whirlpool spas, fireplaces, and chilled champagne. ⊠ *200 Dundas St. E, M5A 4R6,* ☏ *416/362–7700 or 877/316–9951,* FAX *416/362–7706,* WEB *www.toronto.com/comfortsuites. 151 rooms. Restaurant, lobby lounge, in-room data ports, indoor pool, hot tub, gym, business services, parking (fee). AE, DC, MC, V.*

$$–$$$ ⊡ **Four Points Sheraton Toronto Lakeshore.** Across the street from legendary Sunnyside Beach on the city's western perimeter, the intriguing location off the beaten lakefront path distinguishes this boutique hotel from others in the city core. The creamy-white sandy strand and art deco outdoor pool and restaurant pavilions of Sunnyside Beach have attracted gaggles of geese and sunworshipers for decades. Nearby is High Park, 350 acres of century-old maples, duck ponds, zoo, and miles of jogging paths. Ask for a south-facing guest room for the best view of the beachfront. The C.E.O. Bistro serves up full continental breakfasts, and lunches and dinners are hallmarked by good portions of Italian dishes, gourmet pizzas, and seafoods. ⊠ *1926 Lakeshore Blvd. W, M6S 1A1,* ☏ *416/766–4392 or 800/325–3535,* FAX *416/766–1278,* WEB *www.fourpointstoronto.com. 152 rooms. Restaurant, in-room data ports, sauna, gym, business services, parking (free). AE, DC, MC.*

$$–$$$ ⊞ **Novotel Toronto Centre.** Smack in the middle of the super-trendy Esplanade area in the heart of the city, Novotel is within easy reach of the Financial District, Harbourfront, St. Lawrence Market, SkyDome, the Hockey Hall of Fame, and more. This is a good-value, few-frills hotel. The fitness facilities are extensive for the price range. ⊠ *45 The Esplanade, M5E 1W2,* ☎ *416/367–8900,* ℻ *416/360–8285,* WEB *www.accor.com. 262 rooms. Restaurant, no-smoking floor, indoor pool, hot tub, sauna, gym, meeting rooms, parking (fee). AE, DC, MC, V.*

$$$ ⊞ **Robin's Nest Bed & Breakfast.** A quiet and unhurried reflection of dignified Edwardian Canadian life, Robin's Nest makes the hopeless romantic's heart beat a little faster. The B&B combines elegance with the spirit of an English squire's country home. Lavish touches in the Robin's Nest suite include a fireplace, an adjoining library, a marble whirlpool tub, and a private terrace with a fountain. The Jenny Wren room has antique chairs, bay windows, a small library, and a fireplace. The stately Tree Tops suite has a bird's-eye view of the home's formal gardens. ⊠ *13 Binscarth Rd., M4W 1Y2,* ☎ *416/926–9464,* ℻ *416/ 926–3730,* WEB *www.toronto.com/robinsnest. 3 suites. Dining room, library, free parking. V. BP.*

$$ ⊞ **Days Inn.** Travelers from Canada, the United States, Japan, and Europe frequent this downtown Days Inn. It has resisted the temptation— to which many downtown Toronto hotels have succumbed—to increase rates in light of the booming economy. Within walking distance of the Theater District, the fabulous Eaton Centre and Yorkville, the hotel offers the advantage of being near top attractions without the expense of being right in the thick of them. Most rooms have mini-refrigerators. ⊠ *30 Carlton St., M5B 2E9,* ☎ *416/977–6655 or 800/367– 9601,* ℻ *416/977–0502. 536 rooms. Restaurant, coffee shop, sports bar, indoor pool, hair salon, sauna, meeting rooms, parking (fee). AE, DC, MC, V.*

$$
★ ⊞ **Hotel Victoria.** Travelers on budgets might appreciate this boutique-style Victorian-era hotel with personal service and quiet atmosphere. On Yonge Street, a block east of Union Station, the clean and cozy hotel is a good choice for those who want to be near everything downtown without paying dearly. A complimentary Continental breakfast is served on weekends only. ⊠ *56 Yonge St., M5E 1G5,* ☎ *416/363–1666; 800/363–8228 in Canada and continental U.S.,* ℻ *416/363–7327,* WEB *www.toronto.com/hotelvictoria. 48 rooms. Restaurant, parking (fee). AE, DC, MC, V.*

$–$$ ⊞ **Beaconsfield Bed & Breakfast.** An artist and actress couple owns this unconventional and architecturally distinctive 1882 Victorian B&B in a quiet, multicultural neighborhood in the west end section of downtown Toronto. Walls and ceilings are painted with murals, including a seascape in one bathroom and scenes of rolling hills in other rooms. There's an old-fashioned veranda on the first floor, and the second floor has a deck overlooking a garden. The most popular room, the Mexican Suite, comes complete with colorful paintings, Latin American artifacts, wispy clouds painted on the ceiling, and a private tree-top terrace with hammock—ideal for honeymooners. Creative breakfasts are made with organically grown fruits from the owners' backyard. The eclectic clothing stores and profusion of ethnic restaurants along trendy Queen Street West are within a 10-minute walk. ⊠ *38 Beaconsfield Ave., M6J 3H9,* ☎ *416/535–3338,* ℻ *416/535–3338,* WEB *www.bbcanada.com/beaconsfield. 3 rooms, 1 with bath. Breakfast room, free parking. No credit cards. CP.*

$–$$ ⊞ **Casa Loma Inn.** Hidden within the tree-lined avenues of Toronto's hip Annex neighborhood, the Casa Loma Inn has been welcoming the bed-and-breakfast crowd for years. Rooms in this Victorian mansion built in 1893 are well furnished, if somewhat dated. The inn has an unassuming air—quiet, tidy, and a little old-fashioned—and the owners are kind and garrulous. Breakfast can be brought to your room—there's no central place to dine. Despite being nestled in a quiet residential area, the inn is within walking distance of Yorkville, Casa Loma castle, the Royal Ontario Museum, the venerable University of Toronto, and only five minutes from the subway. All rooms have microwaves and TVs, and four have functioning fireplaces. This is a no-smoking inn. ✉ *21 Walmer Rd., M5R 2W7*, ☎ *416/924–4540*, FAX *416/975–5485*, WEB *www.toronto.com/casalomainn. 23 rooms. Refrigerators, coin laundry, parking (fee). AE, MC, V.*

$–$$ ⊞ **1871 Historic House Bed & Breakfast.** Drift back in time at one of the city's oldest homes. Owners Anita and Danby Wong have painstakingly maintained the home's original graceful Victorian character with an elegant collection of antique furniture and period paintings. Among the inn's legendary guests were Buffalo Bill Cody and his *Wild West Show* entourage of Annie Oakley and Sitting Bull. John Lennon and Yoko Ono also stayed here. The adjoining Coach House accommodates up to three guests in exquisite surroundings. ✉ *65 Huntley St., M4Y 2L2*, ☎ *416/923–6950*, FAX *416/923–1065*, WEB *www.bb-canada.com/3021.html. 6 rooms, 3 with bath. Dining room, free parking. No credit cards. BP.*

$–$$ ⊞ **High Park Bed & Breakfast.** World travelers may especially enjoy the area, which has a friendly European flavor. Both ethnic and unique specialty food stores, crafts shops, and Parisian-style cafés are just minutes away from this B&B's front door. The 1909 house on a quaint tree-lined boulevard is charming and spacious, with marvelous stained-glass windows and attractive gardens. Guest rooms are tastefully decorated with sleigh beds and antiques. A short walk away is High Park, one of North America's largest urban green spaces, which has large duck and wildfowl ponds, botanical gardens, historic Colborne Lodge, a zoo, and lots of quiet spots to have a picnic. ✉ *4 High Park Blvd., M6R 1M4*, ☎ *416/531–7963*, FAX *416/531–7963*, WEB *www.bb-canada.com. 3 rooms, 2 with bath. Dining room, kitchenettes, free parking. No credit cards. BP.*

$–$$ ⊞ **Palmerston Inn Bed & Breakfast.** Capitalizing on her experience as
★ an interior decorator, host Judy Carr has created a classical feel to her 1906 Georgian mansion, a delightful home with something for everyone. Two Grecian-style columns soar to the roof at the front entrance of the inn. Period antiques—some more than a century old—grace each guest room. Two rooms have wood-mantled fireplaces. A covered outdoor patio serves as a breakfast room in the summer. In the winter, a dining room with original stained glass windows, and original fireplaces, bannisters, and wood trims on doors and windows, serves as the breakfast room. Palmerston Boulevard is one of Toronto's most pleasant downtown streets, with attractive gates at either end and iron streetlights. You can stroll down the tree-lined boulevard to bustling Bloor Street or to ultrahip College Street bars and restaurants. ✉ *322 Palmerston Blvd., M5G 2N6*, ☎ *416/920–7842*, FAX *416/960–9529*, WEB *www.toronto.com/palmerstoninn. 8 rooms. Breakfast room, lobby lounge. MC, V.*

$–$$ ⊞ **Rosedale Bed & Breakfast.** History buffs might enjoy this designated Heritage Home in the heart of downtown Toronto. Intimate and homey, the 1887 redbrick town house reflects Toronto's aristocratic past. The French Room, with antiques, French doors, and original fireplace, is a favorite with guests. The Green Room boasts a cozy sleigh bed and wet bar. On display in the parlor is a large collection of rare and unusual books gathered from around the world. ✉ *572 Sherbourne St., M4X 1L3*, ☎ *416/927–0543*, FAX *416/966–0962*, WEB *www.rosedale-bandb.on.ca. 5 rooms, 2 with bath. Dining room, parking (fee). V. CP.*

$ ▦ **Helga's Place Bed & Breakfast.** A spa-like feel makes this spot unique among the city's B&Bs. Helga's Place is modern, with an open-concept style, lots of sunshine streaming in from skylights, a profusion of plants throughout, and a heated indoor pool and solarium. The second floor consists of a common room with sky lights, a deck, a library, and private decks overlooking a splendid flower-filled garden. This is one of the few B&Bs in north Toronto—nearby subway and bus lines can take you downtown quickly. Breakfasts are a three-course affair. One of the rooms has a king-size bed, a fireplace, and a whirlpool bath. The other two have queen-size beds and balconies. ✉ *180 Codsell Ave., M3H 3W7,* ☎ *416/633–5951,* FAX *416/636–3050,* WEB *www.bbcanada.com/3288html. 3 rooms. Dining room, free parking. No credit cards.*

$ ▦ **Hostelling International.** Centrally located and no-frills, this hostel is ideal for adventurers of all ages. Private and dormitory rooms are available. Amenities include a shared kitchenette, a television lounge, roof-top deck, coin Internet access, lockers, linen rental, and discounts on local attractions and restaurants. There are two common washrooms per floor. Most rooms have four beds. You don't have to be a member of Hostelling International to stay here, but nonmembers have to pay a small extra fee. Each floor has six pay phones in a common area. ✉ *76 Church St., M5C 2G1,* ☎ *416/971–4440 or 877/848–8737,* FAX *416/971–4088,* WEB *www.hostellingint-gl.on.ca. 35 rooms, 185 beds Lounge, coin laundry. MC, V.*

$ ▦ **Massey College Student Residence.** The young, hip, and budget-conscious can crash at this student residence at the University of Toronto. The building is modern, with lots of brick and Indiana limestone along with wood, plaster, and bronze. Massey is a stone's throw from Queen's Park and other major attractions. The cafeteria-style lunch and dinner fare, which includes vegetarian dishes, is good, filling, and inexpensive—lunch is $6.50 and dinner is $8.25. Rooms are spartan, but linen, towels, and housekeeping services are provided. Rooms don't have phones, and there's only one pay phone for the entire residence. ✉ *4 Devonshire Pl., M5S 2E1,* ☎ *416/978–2895 or 416/597–0313,* FAX *416/978–1759,* WEB *www.utoronto.ca/massey. 65 rooms. Cafeteria, parking (fee). MC, V.*

$ ▦ **Neill-Wycik College-Hotel.** A perfect lodging option for young peo-
★ ple or families on a tight budget who don't mind sharing bathroom facilities, this college residence near Dundas and Yonge streets becomes Toronto's best hotel value from early May through late August. There is one bathroom with tub and shower for every five guests. Only five guests are allowed per room. The 23rd floor roof deck has barbecues for guest use and a great view of the city. The fifth floor has a terrace. All rooms have phones. ✉ *96 Gerrard St. E, M5B 1G7,* ☎ *416/977–2320 or 800/268–4358,* FAX *416/977–2809,* WEB *www.neill-wycik.com. 300 rooms without bath. Cafeteria, kitchenettes, sauna, coin laundry, parking (fee). MC, V.*

$ ▦ **Philomena and Dave Bed & Breakfast.** Businesspeople and bohemians cross paths in the Annex, the city's avant-garde quarter and the site of this cheerful three-story B&B. Because of the proximity of the University of Toronto, the area attracts a diverse mix of students, academics, and professionals of all pinstripes. The 1910 house retains most of its original finishings. After a hard day of shopping and sightseeing, guests can relax, lemonade in hand, on the third-floor balcony, overlooking a small wooded area. Breakfast is served in a room drenched with morning sunshine. Fashionable Bloor Street is a block away, and about 40 restaurants within a five-block radius serve a kaleidoscope of foods. ✉ *31 Dalton Rd., M5R 2Y8,* ☎ *416/962–2786,* FAX *416/964–8837,* WEB *www.bbcanada.com/2072.html. 3 rooms. Dining room, free parking. No credit cards. BP.*

$ ☷ **Ryerson Student Residence.** Short-term lodging is available in the heart of downtown at Ryerson from early May to late August. Rooms are all single and share bathrooms. TV lounges are on every floor, and each room has a phone. Kitchenettes are shared by up to five rooms. Children under 18 must be accompanied by a chaperone. With prices ranging from about $30 per night and $150 weekly for students (about $50 and $250 for nonstudents), it's hard to do better anywhere else. No pets allowed. ⊠ *160 Mutual St., M5B 2M2,* ☎ *416/979–5296,* FAX *416/979–5212. 450 rooms without bath. Coin laundry. MC, V.*

$ ☷ **Vanderkooy Bed & Breakfast.** Discriminating travelers appreciate this lovely B&B's location, which combines urban convenience with a tranquil upscale neighborhood. An immaculate and cozy house built circa 1910, it has retained many original decorative touches, including excellent examples of Edwardian stained-glass windows, antiques, and a collection of original watercolors. Start your morning with a jog or nature hike through nearby Balfour Park, a practically untouched tract of ravine forest. On nearby Yonge Street, there's a bevy of trendy boutiques, bistros, pubs, and art galleries. A full complimentary breakfast is served on an antique oak table surrounded by fragrant plants and overlooking a colorful garden and miniature waterfall. ⊠ *53 Walker Ave., M4V 1G3,* ☎ *416/925–8765,* FAX *416/925–8557,* WEB *www.bbcanada.com/1107.html. 3 rooms, 1 with bath. Breakfast room, free parking. No credit cards.*

Northeast

$$–$$$ ☷ **Inn on the Park.** Off Don Valley Parkway and about 20 minutes
★ from downtown Toronto, this is the only resort in the city's north. A low-rise unit was built in 1963 as part of the Four Seasons chain, and two larger towers were added in the 1970s. The property became two separate hotels in 1996: the Inn on the Park (in a 23-story building), and a Holiday Inn (☎ 416/446–3700). The two share facilities, but reservations are separate. The hotel is about a 10-minute walk from the Ontario Science Centre and is across the street from 600 acres of parkland that include extensive jogging and cross-country ski trails. From July 1 through Labor Day, children ages 5 to 12 can take advantage of a supervised program with swimming, arts and crafts, and other activities. ⊠ *1100 Eglinton Ave. E, M3C 1H8,* ☎ *416/444–2561,* FAX *416/446–3308,* WEB *www.innontheparktoronto.com. 270 rooms. 2 restaurants, lounge, indoor pool, health club, business services, free parking. AE, DC, MC, V.*

$ ☷ **Glendon College, York University Student Residence.** Monolithic stone gates mark the entrance to Glendon College neighboring the city's posh Bridle Path neighborhood. It's a magnificent campus setting, once the 84-acre estate of a railway magnate, and dominated by its landmark country manor house of rose-colored brick and limestone trim (now in academic use), built in 1902. Its breathtaking rose gardens, accented by stonework terraces, and towering Himalayan pines, are still immaculately preserved, and are a favorite student haunt for quiet meditation. The adjacent student residence is enveloped by accessible woods and the nature trails of the nearby Don River Valley. Bus connections are right at the campus gates. Bathrooms are shared, linen, towels, and light housekeeping services are provided. The cafeteria has $6 lunches and $10 dinners. For a fee, guests can use the recreation center, which has a squash court, an Olympic-sized pool, an indoor driving range, and a gym, weight room, and cycle room. ⊠ *2275 Bayview Ave., M4N 3M6,* ☎ *416/487–6844,* FAX *416/487–6838. 200 rooms without bath. Cafeteria, laundry service, parking (fee). AE, MC, V.*

Southwest

$ ▦ **Islington Bed & Breakfast House.** Nature lovers may feel at home in this tranquil community in the western part of the city, a 20-minute drive from downtown. Abutting the picturesque Humber River valley, this neighborhood offers country scenery—gently undulating hills, an abundance of flora and bird life, and walking trails—in an urban setting. James Gardens, a magnificent formal gardens filled with ponds and rare and indigenous Canadian blooms, is a 10-minute drive from the front door. Host Joey Lopes takes guests on a leisurely walking tour of the valley, describing its history and ecological bounty. The house has solid wood furniture and hardwood floors. Credit cards are accepted for advance reservations only. ⊠ *1407 Islington Ave., M9A 3K5,* ☎ *416/236–2707,* ℻ *416/233–3192. 3 rooms, 1 with bath. Breakfast room, free parking. AE, DC, MC, V. BP.*

$ ▦ **Marigold International Traveler's Hostel.** Popular with international backpackers, this charming private hostel is near High Park in west-central Toronto. It's off the beaten path, but well-connected to downtown by the Dundas and the College Street streetcars. It's also close to Roncesvalles, one of Toronto's most underrated neighborhoods—a mixed community of Poles, Ukrainians, Russians, and yuppies. Some rooms are available for couples, but most have bunk beds and are usually rented as single-sex dormitory rooms or shared by families. The per-person rate is $23. In summer you can lounge on sundecks in the front and back. There are coin lockers and a TV lounge, and free coffee, tea, and doughnuts are set out in the morning. Check-out time is 2 PM. ⊠ *2011 Dundas St. W, M6R 1W7,* ☎ *416/536–8824,* ℻ *416/596–8188. 11 rooms with 2–8 beds. Coin laundry, free parking. No credit cards.*

The Airport Strip

Lester B. Pearson International Airport is 32 km (18 mi) northwest of downtown, so staying near the airport is an option to consider. Keep in mind, however, that in rush hour the drive can take more than an hour. If you don't have a car, taxis and buses provide service into town. All of these hotels are near the Woodbine Race Track and Paramount Canada's Wonderland.

$$$ ▦ **Radisson Suites Toronto Airport.** All-suite hotels such as the Radisson provide an excellent alternative for families or anyone staying for more than a weekend. Suites come with useful extras like umbrellas, two TVs, and a couch that's also a fold-out bed. The affable staff is happy to include a microwave as well. All rooms are decorated in deep, warm neutral tones as are the lobby and lobby lounge. The Fox Bistro serves Continental cuisine in an upscale atmosphere. Plenty of inexpensive restaurants are nearby. ⊠ *640 Dixon Rd., M9W 1J1,* ☎ *416/242–7400,* ℻ *416/242–9888,* 🌐 *www.radisson.com. 215 suites. Restaurant, minibars, gym, free parking. AE, DC, MC, V.*

$$$ ▦ **Wyndham Bristol Place Hotel.** When you've collected your luggage,
★ pick up a phone at the arrival level and call the Wyndham Bristol Place. An airport bus can have you here in about two minutes. This has long been considered the ritziest of the hotels along the airport strip. Bedrooms have mahogany armoires, tables, desks, and minibars. The main lobby has a small waterfall. For an airport hotel, it's fairly quiet—rooms that face east are the quietest of all. ⊠ *950 Dixon Rd., M9W 5N4,* ☎ *416/675–9444 or 800/996–3426,* ℻ *416/675–4426,* 🌐 *www.wyndham.com. 287 rooms, 5 suites. 2 restaurants, lobby lounge, in-room data ports, indoor pool, sauna, health club, playground, parking (fee). AE, DC, MC, V.*

$$–$$$ 🏨 **Regal Constellation.** The Constellation continues to be one of the bright lights at the airport. It has a stunning, six-story, glass-enclosed lobby, a fully equipped health club, and impressive service. It has four types of rooms, from economy to deluxe, in order to cater to all kinds of travelers and their specific needs. ✉ *900 Dixon Rd., M9W 1J7,* ☎ *416/675–1500 or 800/268–4883,* FAX *416/675–1737,* WEB *www.regal-hotel.com. 710 rooms, 18 suites. 4 restaurants, lounge, indoor pool, health club, business services, parking (fee). AE, DC, MC, V.*

$$ 🏨 **Holiday Inn Select.** Pleasant rooms at affordable rates are the mainstays of this chain hotel. Like most hotels along the Dixon Road airport strip, it caters mostly to the business traveler and hosts a large number of conferences. The Metro Bar & Grill provides adequate if unexciting food. ✉ *970 Dixon Rd., M9W 1J9,* ☎ *416/675–7611,* FAX *416/674–4364,* WEB *www.holiday-inn.com. 444 rooms, 8 suites. Restaurant, lobby lounge, indoor pool, sauna, gym, business services, meeting rooms, parking (fee). AE, DC, MC, V.*

$$ 🏨 **Toronto Airport Marriott.** In an attempt to attract the leisure traveler, the Marriott offers substantial weekend discounts of up to 50%. An enormous skylight over the indoor pool, right beside the entrance lobby and breakfast restaurant, ensures that a generous helping of sunshine suffuses the hotel, enhancing the Italian marble floors and rich mahogany wood trims in the public areas. Guest rooms are bright, comfortable, and spacious. ✉ *901 Dixon Rd., M9W 1J5,* ☎ *416/674–9400,* FAX *416/674–8292,* WEB *www.torontoairportmarriott.com. 423 rooms, 12 suites. 2 restaurants, lobby lounge, indoor pool, sauna, health club, parking (fee). AE, DC, MC, V.*

$$ 🏨 **Travelodge Hotel Toronto Airport Dixon Road.** This airport hotel conforms to the chain's overall philosophy and look—pinewood furniture, exposed brick, and a large brass fireplace in the lobby encourage you to leave Toronto's urban sprawl at the door and slip into a rustic oasis. Each room is decorated in the same country spirit. The Royal Host Executive Lounge offers a wide selection of foods and music from around the world. ✉ *925 Dixon Rd., M9W 1J8,* ☎ *416/674–2222 or 888/483–6887,* FAX *416/674–5757,* WEB *www.travelodge.com. 283 rooms. Restaurant, lobby lounge, indoor pool, sauna, gym, meeting rooms, parking (fee). AE, DC, MC, V.*

$–$$ 🏨 **Carlingview Hotel.** If you're looking for basic lodgings, this may be the place for you. This economy hotel off Dixon Road caters to travelers looking for inexpensive accommodations. There are only three floors to this modest place. Rooms are functional and clean. ✉ *221 Carlingview Dr., M9W 5E8,* ☎ *416/675–1176 or 877/675–3303,* FAX *416/675–6524,* WEB *www.atlific.com. 112 rooms. Restaurant, pool, free parking. AE, DC, MC, V.*

Camping

There are 88 serviced campsites with electricity and water and 44 unserviced campsites in **Glen Rouge Park** (✉ Hwy. 2, 1 km [¾ mi] east of Port Union Rd., ☎ 416/392–8186 or 416/392–2541, FAX 416/396–4248), open mid-May–September. The park is in the city's northeast end, near the Toronto Zoo. It's part of the greater Rouge Park, which has thousands of unspoiled acres that include limitless nature trails. Hiking in dense wilderness brush and fishing for trout and salmon are all possible here.

For a list of licensed private campgrounds and trailer parks, write to **Ontario Travel Centre** (✉ Eaton Centre, 230 Yonge St., Level 1, M5B 2H1, ☎ 416/314–5900 or 800/668–2746, WEB www.ontariotravel.net). The **Parks Canada** Web site (WEB www.parkscanada.pch.gc.ca) has links to national parks in the province.

NIGHTLIFE AND THE ARTS

Updated by
Liza Finlay

Toronto's art scene has blossomed in recent years, aided by the introduction of some dazzling new venues and the refurbishing of some magnificent old ones. The influence of the burgeoning film industry has made nightlife in this once-staid town a lot more glamorous, too.

The best places to get information on all the city's cultural events are the free weekly newspapers *NOW* and *eye* and the "What's On" section of *The Toronto Star,* which all appear on Thursday; the Saturday (weekend) *Globe and Mail* and *National Post*; and the monthly magazine *Toronto Life.* On the Web, comprehensive and up-to-the-minute listings are available from *Toronto Life* at www.torontolife.com and *The Toronto Star* at www.torstar.com. You can also check out www.toronto.com and www.canoe.com.

The Arts

Toronto is the capital of the performing arts in English-speaking Canada, but it was not always so. Before 1950, Toronto had no opera company, no ballet, and very little theater worthy of the title "professional." Then came the Massey Report on the Arts, one of those government-sponsored studies that usually helps put sensitive subjects on the back burner for several more years. In this case, however, all heaven broke loose—money began to come from a variety of government grants; two prominent Canadian millionaires passed away, and their death taxes were put toward the creation of a Canada Council, which doled out more money; the Canadian Opera Company, CBC television, and the National Ballet of Canada were born; and a number of little theaters began to pop up, culminating in an artistic explosion throughout the 1970s, in every aspect of the arts.

More than money fueled this arts explosion, though. Other factors were a massive immigration from culturally nourished countries of Eastern and Central Europe, as well as from England; a growing sense of independence from the mother country; a recognition that if Canada did not develop its own arts, then the damned Yankees would do it for them; and, in general, a growing civic and cultural maturity.

Today, Toronto is, after New York and London, the largest center for English-speaking theater in the world. The city's smaller theaters have long been filled with interesting productions of the finest in classic and contemporary Canadian, English, American, and French drama. Since the 1960s the Hummingbird (formerly the O'Keefe Centre) and Royal Alexandra theaters have provided a mix of local, West End, and Broadway productions. Now that Toronto has gained four new performing spaces by restoration (Elgin/Winter Garden complex and the Pantages) and new construction (the Ford Centre and Princess of Wales), it can truly be called "Broadway North"—for better or for worse.

Because of the many movies that have been shot here in recent years, Toronto has also garnered the nickname "Hollywood North." The availability of excellent crews, the variety of locations (Toronto has posed for everything from Paris to Vietnam), and the savings from the exchange rate between U.S. and Canadian dollars are all contributing factors. Toronto has become an excellent venue for "Star Gazers" over the past number of years, with Michael Douglas filming *Don't Say a Word* and Harrison Ford in town for *K19: the Widowmaker. La Femme Nikita* with Peta Wilson continues its shoots along with a number of series including *Blue Murder* and *The Pretenders.*

Sit in the right restaurant or stroll along the tony shopping avenues and you may be lucky enough to run into any number of big-name actors passing through. If you were in Toronto during 2000 or 2001, you may have run into Sylvester Stallone shooting *RPM*, Steven Segal near the set of *Exit Wounds*, Jill Hennessey back home for *The Women of Camelot*, or Jennifer Lopez fresh off the set of *Angel Eyes*. Locals generally let the stars have their privacy, even when spotted in public, which is another reason industry types like working here. For information about productions in town during your visit, phone the **Toronto Film and Television Office** (☎ 416/392–7570).

Tickets

Full-price theater tickets run from as low as $20 to as high as $95. Tickets for pop concerts are usually $35 to $40, although at smaller venues the cost may drop to as low as $20. On certain slow nights and Sundays, many theaters have Pay What You Can (PWYC) entry. Simply phone the venue and ask. Tickets for almost any event in the city can be obtained through **Ticketmaster** (☎ 416/870–8000, WEB www.ticketmaster.ca).

To get half-price tickets on the day of a performance, visit the **Five Star Tickets booth,** on Yonge Street at Dundas Street, open in good weather Monday through Saturday noon to 7:30 and Sunday 11 to 3. All sales are final, credit cards are accepted, and a small service charge is added to the price of each ticket. The booth also gives out piles of superb brochures and pamphlets on the city. You can also call the **Toronto Theatre Alliance** (☎ 416/536–6468) for half-price tickets to certain shows.

Concert Halls

Concert halls tend to focus on music, but many present performances of all types. It's not uncommon for a venue to present modern dance one week, a rock or classical music concert another week, and a theatrical performance the next.

The **Elgin and Winter Garden Theatres** (✉ 189 Yonge St., ☎ 416/872–5555 for tickets; 416/314–2901 for tours) are two jewels in the crown of the Toronto arts scene. The former vaudeville halls are the last operating double-decker theaters in the world. The Elgin, downstairs, has about 1,500 seats, and is more suited for musicals; Winter Garden, upstairs, is somewhat more intimate, with about 1,000 seats. The theaters have put on everything from comedy concerts and jazz to a Mozart opera festival and the Renaissance Theatre Company's productions of *King Lear* and *A Midsummer Night's Dream,* directed by Kenneth Branagh and starring Emma Thompson. A $30-million restoration in 1989 showcased the building's Edwardian charm—original 1913–14 details include a nickelodeon, damask wall coverings, gilt cherubs, and, at Winter Garden, a ceiling canopy with real beech leaves. Both theaters are wheelchair accessible, and both have excellent sight lines. The best Winter Garden seats are mezzanine row A, seats 208–209, or orchestra rows E and F, seats 31–33. At the Elgin, try for orchestra row N, seats 13–14 or 41–42; row J, seats 27–29; or mezzanine row A, seats 207–209. Guided tours are given Thursday at 5 PM and Saturday at 11 AM. The cost is $4.

The **Hummingbird Centre for the Performing Arts** (✉ 1 Front St. E, ☎ 416/872–2262), owned and operated by the city government, was known for 36 years as the O'Keefe Centre but was renamed in 1996 after the Hummingbird Communications software company donated money for renovations and refurbishing. It has long been the home of the Canadian Opera Company and the National Ballet of Canada. The Hummingbird is also home to visiting comedians, rock stars, pre-Broadway shows, and post-Broadway tours. Almost anything but the most lavish opera or musical can be accommodated in the cavernous 3,223-seat hall. The acoustics, however, can be sub-par in certain seats. Try for seats close to A47–48 and avoid very front rows, such as AA, BB.

Roy Thomson Hall (✉ 60 Simcoe St., ☎ 416/872–4255), opened in 1982, is the most important concert hall in Toronto. It was named for the billionaire newspaper magnate known as Lord Thomson of Fleet, after his family donated $4.5 million in his memory. The beautifully designed hall with sensitive acoustics is the home of the Toronto Symphony Orchestra and the Toronto Mendelssohn Choir, and also hosts visiting orchestras and popular entertainers. The best seats are rows H and J in the orchestra and row L upstairs. You can call the volunteer office (☎ 416/593–4822 Ext. 363) to arrange a $4 tour that highlights the acoustic and architectural features of the striking round structure.

The **St. Lawrence Centre for the Arts** (✉ 27 Front St. E, ☎ 416/366–7723) has been presenting theater, music, dance, opera, film, and forums on public issues since 1970. The two main halls are the luxuriously appointed Bluma Appel Theatre and the Jane Mallett Theatre, both venues for recitals and performances by companies like the Toronto Operetta and the Hannaford Street Silver Band. At the Bluma Appel Theatre, try for rows E–N, seats 1–10; the Jane Mallett is small enough for all seats to have good sight lines.

The **Toronto Centre for the Arts** (✉ 5040 Yonge St., ☎ 416/870–8000 or 416/733–9388), opened in 1993, often hosts classical music concerts and franchised megamusicals—past favorites include *Ragtime and Fosse, a Celebration of Song and Dance.* This architecturally impressive complex is less than a half-hour drive north of the waterfront and is close to the North York subway stop. It has a 1,850-seat main stage, a 1,025-seat recital hall, a 250-seat studio theater, and a two-story, 5,000-square-ft art gallery. The George Weston Recital Hall features international artists and a wide array of musical stylings, from classical klezmer to jazz. The best seats in the main stage are center orchestra, especially row H, seats 128–130, and mezzanine row A, seats 230–231.

Dance

The **National Ballet of Canada** (✉ Hummingbird Centre, 1 Front St. E, ☎ 416/345–9686 for information; 416/872–2262 for tickets), Canada's homegrown and internationally recognized classical ballet company, was founded in 1951 by Celia Franca, an English dancer from the Sadler's Wells tradition, and is supported by infusions of dancers trained at its own school. The season runs from November through May. A series of outstanding productions, such as Kenneth MacMillan's *Manon,* John Cranko's *Taming of the Shrew* and *Romeo and Juliet,* Glen Tetley's *Alice,* and James Kudelka's *The Actress* and *The Nutcracker,* have been performed by the company, and many have moved into the permanent repertory. Mr. Kudelka, a Canadian choreographer and the company's artistic director, has directed the National Ballet to a more modern repertoire and is breaking the company's star system by advancing dancers from the corps and soloist ranks. Tickets run $15–$75. Rush tickets at about $15 are available on the same day—for students and seniors, this will buy any unsold seat in the house, for others, it will get a place in the last row on the main floor.

The **Premiere Dance Theatre** (✉ Harbourfront Centre, 235 Queen's Quay W, ☎ 416/973–4000) is a venue for dance performances by local contemporary companies as well as visiting troupes like the internationally renowned LaLa Human Steps.

Toronto Dance Theatre, with roots in the Martha Graham tradition, is the oldest contemporary dance company in the city. Since its beginnings in the 1960s, Toronto Dance Theatre has created close to 100 works, more than a third using original scores commissioned from Canadian composers. It tours Canada and has played major festivals in England, Europe, and the United States. Performances are in the **Premiere Dance Theatre** (✉ Harbourfront Centre, 235 Queen's Quay W, ☎ 416/973–4000).

Film

Toronto has a devoted film audience. The result is a feast of riches—commercial first- and second-run showings, festivals, and lecture series for every taste. A loosely associated group of independent movie theaters, including the Fox, Bloor, The Music Hall Royal, Revue, Kingsway, and Paradise, offers lower-priced screenings of independent productions, old classics, cult films, and new commercial releases; call ☎ 416/690–2600 for schedules at all five theaters.

Created to help address the vast appetite for Canadian and international film, the **Toronto International Film Festival Group** (✉ 2 Carleton St., ☎ 416/967–7371 or 416/968–3456, ⟨WEB⟩ www.bell.ca/filmfest) is the umbrella organization for the Toronto International Film Festival, Cinematheque Ontario, Sprockets, Talk Cinema, and the Film Reference Library.

Carlton Cinemas (✉ 20 Carlton St., ☎ 416/598–2309) presents rarely screened films from around the world. Foreign-language films are shown in the original language with subtitles.

Cinematheque Ontario (✉ 317 Dundas St. W, ☎ 416/968–3456) presents international film programs at the Art Gallery of Ontario, year-round. Series of years past have featured a genre or exceptional director.

The Cinesphere (✉ Ontario Place, 955 Lakeshore Blvd. W, ☎ 416/965–7711) offers 70-mm films—those especially made for the IMAX screen system, and popular films that benefit from the large format and 24-track sound.

The **Film Reference Library**(✉ 2 Carleton St., ☎ 416/967–1517) is the largest collection of English language Canadian film material in the world. The general public is invited to view everything from posters and books to actual screenings from the reference selection. Hours are weekdays noon to 5.

Harbourfront Centre (✉ 235 Queen's Quay W, ☎ 416/973–4000) shows interesting retrospectives. An example of a typical themes would be early 20th-century classic Japanese film. Call for current shows and times.

The **Toronto International Film Festival** (✉ 2 Carlton St., ☎ 416/967–7371 or 416/968–3456, ⟨WEB⟩ www.bell.ca/filmfest) takes over downtown Toronto each September. The 10-day event, the third-largest of its kind in the world, attracts Hollywood's brightest stars to view the latest works of both great international directors and lesser-known independent film directors from Canada and around the world. Unfortunately, most films are sold out at this hugely popular festival except for a few rush tickets, which require enduring long lineups.

Sprockets: The Toronto International Film Festival for Children (✉ 2 Carlton St., ☎ 416/968–3456), is held at the end of April each year and features new works and the classic films aimed at children ages 4 to 14. Call for times and venues.

Talk Cinema (☎ 416/968–3456, ⟨WEB⟩ www.bell.ca/filmfest.) is an interactive cinema experience that takes place Sunday mornings from November to April. Subscribers show up at the York Cinema and are treated to a film and special guest speaker—often a director, producer, or actor—that comments on the feature and answers questions. Tickets are available for individual films or for the entire series. Phone for times.

Music

The **MacMillan Theatre** (✉ University of Toronto Faculty of Music, Edward Johnson Building, 80 Queen's Park Crescent, ☎ 416/978–3744) features the University of Toronto Symphony and Opera School productions. The U of T student newspaper, *The Varsity*, found all around the campus, lists current events.

Massey Hall (✉ 178 Victoria St., ☎ 416/872–4255) has always been cramped, but its near-perfect acoustics and its handsome, U-shape tiers sloping down to the stage have made it a place to enjoy music for nearly 100 years. The nearly 2,800 seats are not terribly comfortable, and a small number are blocked by pillars that hold up the ancient structure, but Massey Hall remains a venerable place to catch the greats and near-greats of the music world. Best seats are in rows G–M, center, and in rows 32–50 in the balcony.

The **Music Gallery** (✉ 219–60 Atlantic Ave., ☎ 416/204–1080, WEB www.musicgallery.org) offers an eclectic selection—new music, world music, atonal, classical, avant-garde jazz—in a relaxed atmosphere. The main venue is St. George the Martyr Church on 197 John Street, but there are several other venues, so call or visit the Music Gallery Web site for times and concert info.

Walter Hall (✉ University of Toronto Faculty of Music, Edward Johnson Building, 80 Queen's Park Crescent, ☎ 416/978–3744) is the place to see avant-garde artists and the stars of the future. The intimate venue is suited to jazz groups, Baroque ensembles, and student recitals. Because it's run by the music faculty of the University of Toronto, serious and experimental jazz bands and baroque chamber orchestras are often presented during the academic year at little or no cost. The acoustics at this small theater are good, as are all sight lines. For concert listings, you can pick up the U of T student newspaper, *The Varsity*, on the university's campus.

CLASSICAL

Glenn Gould Studio (✉ 250 Front St. W, ☎ 416/205–5555) hosts a variety of classical music companies. The box office is open Tuesday through Thursday only.

Tafelmusik (✉ Trinity–St. Paul's United Church, 427 Bloor St. W, ☎ 416/964–6337) presents baroque music on original instruments. The name means "table music."

The Toronto Mendelssohn Choir (✉ Roy Thomson Hall, 60 Simcoe St., ☎ 416/598–0422 or 416/872–4255) often performs with the Toronto Symphony. This group of 180 vocalists was begun in 1894 by Elmer Isler and has since been applauded worldwide. Its yearly *Messiah* is sure to put everyone into the Christmas spirit. Some of the beautiful and heartbreaking music heard in the Academy Award–winning *Schindler's List* was sung by this choir.

The Toronto Symphony Orchestra (✉ Roy Thomson Hall, 60 Simcoe St., ☎ 416/593–4828 or 416/872–4255) doesn't rest on its laurels. Since 1922 it has achieved world acclaim, with conductors of the quality of Seiji Ozawa, Sir Thomas Beecham, and Andrew Davis. The orchestra's director since 1994 has been the young and impressive Jukka-Pekka Saraste, who is doing wonders rejuvenating an already world-class orchestra. When the TSO is home, it presents about three concerts weekly from September through May in Roy Thomson Hall.

OPERA

The Canadian Opera Company (✉ 227 Front St. E, ☎ 416/363–6671), founded in 1950, has grown to be the largest producer of opera in Canada and the fifth-largest company on the continent. From the most popular operas, such as *Carmen* and *Madame Butterfly*, usually performed in the original language, to more modern or rare works, such as *The Cunning Little Vixen* and *Hansel and Gretel,* the COC has proven trustworthy and often daring. Recent versions of Verdi's *La Traviata* and Wagner's *The Flying Dutchman* were considered radical by many. The COC often hosts world-class performers, and it pioneered the use of scrolling subtitles that appear above the performers, which allow the audience to follow the libretto in English in a capsulized translation. Regular performances are at the Hummingbird Centre for the Performing Arts. A number of free performances are held at Harbourfront, by Queen's Quay, usually during the last week of August. Seating is first-come, first-served.

POP AND ROCK

Most major international recording companies have offices in Toronto, so the city is a regular stop for top musical performers, ranging from the Rolling Stones to Shania Twain to the Back Street Boys.

Major Toronto venues for large-scale concerts are: the **SkyDome** (⊠ 1 Blue Jays Way, ☎ 416/341–3663); **Maple Leaf Gardens** (⊠ 60 Carlton St., ☎ 416/977–1641); the **Air Canada Centre** (⊠ 40 Bay St., ☎ 416/815–5500); and the **Hummingbird Centre for the Performing Arts** (⊠ 1 Front St. E, ☎ 416/872–2262).

NorthbyNortheast (⊠ 185A Danforth Ave., 2nd floor, ☎ 416/469–0986), also known as N×NE, is an annual conference and celebration of rock, new music, and more, bringing top-notch talent into town each June. Affiliated with the similar S×SW festival in Austin, Texas, it provides a good opportunity to track new groups, artists, and trends.

The **Molson Amphitheatre** (⊠ Ontario Place, 955 Lakeshore Blvd. W, ☎ 416/870–8000) has pop, rock, and jazz concerts by the lake throughout its summer season at modest prices. The view of the skyline and the summer breezes make this one of the loveliest places to hear music in Toronto.

The **Phoenix Concert Theatre** (⊠ 410 Sherbourne St., ☎ 416/323–1251) presents a wide variety of music in a two room venue. Many nights, music airs live at local radio stations from the Main Room while in the Parlour, every genre from house to retro-rock and live local bands can be enjoyed in a somewhat more intimate setting. Cover charges range from $5 to $8 depending on the night.

Theater

Some of the most entertaining theater in Toronto is free, though donations are always welcome. Every summer, the CanStage theater company presents **Dream in High Park** (⊠ High Park, main entrance off Bloor St. W at High Park Ave., ☎ 416/367–8243 information; 416/368–3110 box office, WEB www.canstage.com), quality productions of Shakespeare and contemporary works in glorious High Park's outdoor amphitheater. The productions are usually a knockout and run from mid-July to late August. In the fall, the natural amphitheater transforms into a picnic ground and family entertainment venue. The plays are under the stars so call ahead if it is drizzling. Call for specific directions to the amphitheater.

COMMERCIAL THEATERS

The Pantages (⊠ 263 Yonge St., ☎ 416/872–2222), a 1920 vaudeville theater that was turned into a movie complex, is now one of the most architecturally and acoustically exciting live theaters in Toronto. In 1988–89, the Cineplex Odeon refurbished the magnificent theater in preparation for the Canadian debut of *The Phantom of the Opera.* The theater itself is one of the most beautiful in the world. Designed by world-renowned theater architect Thomas Lamb, it has Doric, Ionic, and Corinthian columns, a grand staircase, gold-leaf detailing, crystal chandeliers, and working gas lamps. Most sight lines are better than might be expected from a theater with 2,250 seats—the best are, typically, in the middle of the orchestra and the front of the mezzanine. The **Princess of Wales** (✉ 300 King St. W, ☎ 416/872–1212 or 800/461–3333) claims state-of-the-art sound and technical facilities and wonderful wall and ceiling murals by American artist Frank Stella. The producers of *Miss Saigon,* father-and-son team Ed and David Mirvish built this exquisite 2,000-seat theater to accommodate the technically demanding musical when no other venue was available. All levels are accessible to people using wheelchairs and those with mobility problems. If you can, book Row A, seats 29–30 in the dress circle (mezzanine), or Row B, seats 35–36 in the stalls (orchestra).

The **Royal Alexandra** (✉ 260 King St. W, ☎ 416/872–3333 or 800/461–3333) has been the place to be seen in Toronto since 1907. The 1,500 plush red seats, gold brocade, and baroque swirls and flourishes make theatergoing a refined experience. This was Ed Mirvish's first foray into drama and theater production, followed in the 1980s by his purchase of London's Old Vic and in the 1990s by his building of the Princess of Wales theater. Recent programs have been a mix of blockbuster musicals and a variety of dramatic productions, some touring before or after West End and Broadway appearances. The theater is wheelchair-accessible on the first floor only. Avoid rows A and B; try for rows C–L center. For musicals, aim for the front rows of the first balcony.

SMALL THEATERS AND COMPANIES

Buddies In Bad Times (✉ 12 Alexander St., ☎ 416/975–8555) is an alternative theater devoted generally to artistic performances that focus on gay issues.

Factory Theatre (✉ 125 Bathurst St., ☎ 416/504–9971) is an alternative theater devoted to original and experimental work.

Hart House Theatre (✉ 7 Hart House Circle, ☎ 416/978–8668) is the main theater space of the University of Toronto. Amateur, student, and occasional professional productions have been presented here since 1919.

The Rivoli (✉ 332 Queen St. W, ☎ 416/596–1908 or 416/597–0794), along the Queen Street strip, has long been a major showcase for the more daring arts in Toronto. A back room functions as a performance space, with theater happenings, "new music" (progressive rock and jazz), improvisational comedy troupes, and more. Some nights have a cover charge, usually from $5 to $10. Asian-influenced cuisine and good steak is served in the dining room. Dinner for two, without drinks, runs about $25. The walls are lined with artwork (all for sale) by up-and-coming local artists. There's also a bar, and a pool hall upstairs.

The **Tarragon Theatre** (✉ 30 Bridgman Ave., ☎ 416/531–1827), in an old warehouse and railroad district, is the natural habitat for indigenous Canadian theater. Almost anything worthwhile in this country's drama first saw the light of day here.

Le Théâtre Français de Toronto (✉ 26 Berkeley St., 2nd floor, ☎ 416/534–6604) has been providing French-language drama of high quality for many years. Its repertoire ranges from classical to contemporary, from France and French Canada.

Théâtre Passe Muraille (✉ 16 Ryerson Ave., ☎ 416/504–7529) in the unfashionable area of Bathurst and Queen streets, has long been the home of fine Canadian collaborative theater.

The **Young People's Theatre** (✉ 165 Front St. E, ☎ 416/862–2222) is devoted solely to children, but unlike many purveyors of traditional children's fare, this place does not condescend or compromise its dramatic integrity.

Nightlife

Toronto has all kinds of music clubs, as well as lots of places to hang out or dance. Some of these places are hard to characterize, so read the descriptions as well as the headings. Many have the life span of a butterfly, so call before you set out to make sure they're still open and still offering the kind of evening you're searching for. Downtown, Adelaide Street West from University Avenue to Peter Street has spawned numerous clubs of the loud, techno variety. Few places have cover charges anymore—the few that do are mostly after-hours and private clubs, and charge about $10.

The nightlife in The Beaches, home of the Beaches Jazz Festival, is concentrated along Queen Street from Woodbine Avenue east to Victoria Park Avenue. Bars and clubs catering to the casual sporty types who stroll up from beach volleyball and the locals, many of whom work in the performing arts and film trades, dot the streetscape.

The intersection of Yonge Street and Eglinton Avenue—known as "Young and Eligible" by locals—is popular with young professionals. Dance clubs, pool halls, and a variety of bars and pubs are in this business area.

Bars and Pubs

Have a good time in Toronto, but be aware of the strict drinking and driving laws. Police regularly stop cars to check sobriety with a breath analysis test. If you have a blood-alcohol level of higher than .08%, it's the judge or jail, no matter where you're from. Under the city's liquor laws, last call in bars is 2 AM; closing time is 3 AM. The minimum drinking age is 19.

Al Frisco's (⊠ 133 John St., ☎ 416/595–8201) is a landmark in the club district. Any given Thursday or Friday, this retrofitted factory attracts the hi-tech and financial crowd to its restaurant and upstairs bar. Shoulder to shoulder, 25- to 40-year-old singles play pool, dance, and test the draft beer. The line for the sidewalk patio starts at 3:30 PM, and at 9 PM for the upstairs bar.

Allen's (⊠ 143 Danforth Ave., ☎ 416/463–3086) is a quintessential Irish pub—an anomaly on the mostly Greek Danforth Avenue—complete with Irish brews on tap and a dartboard. It's a great place to go for a quick drink or for an entire evening, as the food is better than most pub fare.

Brunswick House (⊠ 481 Bloor St. W, ☎ 416/964–2242) attracts mostly students from the nearby University of Toronto. The saloon atmosphere here is loud, raucous, and fun.

Fiddlers Green (⊠ 27 Wellesley St. E, ☎ 416/967–9442), a Victorian-style Irish pub, attracts a large group of regulars. Multiple taps of ales and lagers, along with a full menu, keep the staff hopping. Drop in for a pint and discover why it claims to have the friendliest atmosphere in town.

Gypsy Co-Op (⊠ 815 Queen St. W, ☎ 416/703–5069), formerly the Squeeze Club, has expanded to two floors to accommodate the artsy crowd of musicians and new bohemians (graphic artists) who hang there. Although the decor has moved from "general store" to upscale, the Co-Op remains an important venue for an eclectic mix of who's who in the performing and visual arts communities.

Hemingway's (⊠ 142 Cumberland St., ☎ 416/968–2828), one of the most crowded singles' bars in Toronto, is homier and less tense than other Yorkville watering holes. The bar has comfortable high-back chairs, mirrors, artsy posters, and real, live books lining one wall. Thursday, Friday, and Saturday evenings the music is live rock and Top 40s. Three-quarters of the middle- to upper-class professionals who frequent this place are regulars.

Madison Avenue Pub (✉ 14–18 Madison Ave., ☎ 416/927–1722), on the edge of the U of T campus, offers six floors of good food and drink with an English pub atmosphere—lots of brass, exposed brick, and dartboards. Sixteen brands of beer are on tap, and there's a large selection of bottled imports. VIP and billiards rooms and a boutique are also part of the scene. The patios are lovely in the summer.

Myth (✉ 417 Danforth Ave., ☎ 416/461–8383), on the Danforth in the middle of the city's Greek area, serves up great Greek food, but the real action starts *après dinner* and centers around the bar and chic rosewood pool tables. The big screens mounted in the vaulted corners play mostly movie classics, but the young, trendy customers are watching each other, not the films.

Wayne Gretzky's (✉ 99 Blue Jays Way, ☎ 416/979–7825), a sports bar and family-style restaurant, is very popular with the pre-game crowds of the Blue Jays and the Maple Leafs and the post-theater crowd that flows in from Second City Comedy Club across the street. When in town, the hockey icon and part owner can often be seen in the crowd. The rooftop patio, open from May through September, is built around a waterfall and is considered one of the best in town.

The **Whistling Oyster** (✉ 11 Duncan St., below, ☎ 416/598–7707) is almost always packed with regulars who crowd around the bar and flirt with the wait staff. Famed for its seafood, the Oyster really rocks during happy hour (between 4 and 7), when the martinis flow and dim sum and other delicacies are offered at invitingly low prices. The crowd is mainly professionals, and a good deal of pick-up business takes place every night. In fact, rumor has it the owner met his wife at the Oyster's bar.

GAY AND LESBIAN

Pegasus on Church (✉ 489B Church St., ☎ 416/927–8832) draws a mostly gay crowd. The attraction? The bartender of the day mixes the music, and each has a loyal following. Patrons come to meet, shoot pool, and above all, play the interactive Internet game NTN Trivia. Pegasus is famous in Toronto for consistently being one of the top scorers on the "wired" trivia game.

Slack Alice (✉ 562 Church St., ☎ 416/696–8742) is one of the oldest gay and lesbian bars in boytown. "The Alice" consistently has a great kitchen for light fare and provides a friendly atmosphere with daily events, themes, and contests.

Woody's (✉ 467 Church St., ☎ 416/972–0887) caters to a predominantly upscale male crowd, with lots of professional types. Check out 'Bad Boy' Tuesdays, 'Best Chest' Thursdays, and the ever-changing entertainment each Sunday.

Comedy Clubs

The Laugh Resort (✉ 370 King St. W, ☎ 416/364–5233) offers stand-up solo acts, and sometimes improvisations, Tuesday through Saturday night. The cover is $7 to $15 for the show only. Ensure a great seat by going early and enjoying a pre-show dinner—with a choice of three entrées—for $23.

Second City (✉ 56 Blue Jays Way, ☎ 416/343–0011 or 800/263–4485, WEB www.secondcity.com) has been providing some of the best comedy in Toronto since it opened in 1973. Many alumni of this troupe have become well known through *Saturday Night Live* and the *SCTV* series. Among those who cut their teeth on the Toronto stage are Mike Myers, Dan Aykroyd, Martin Short, Andrea Martin, and Catherine O'Hara. Recent grads Ryan Stiles and Colin Mochrie appear on *Whose Line Is It Anyway?* Weekend shows tend to sell out in summer. Sundays the troupe performs a "Best of Second City" program. The cost is $14–$27 for shows only, $42–$55 for dinner and show.

Yuk-Yuk's Komedy Kabaret (✉ 2335 Yonge St., ☎ 416/967–6425 for both locations; ✉ 5165 Dixie Rd., Mississauga) has always been a major place to see comedy in Toronto. This is where Jim Carrey got his start and where George Carlin and Robin Williams presented their best routines. Crash and Burn Amateur Night, every Monday beginning at 8:30 PM, is as tough, uneven, and occasionally inspired as it sounds. There's a $5–$15 cover, occasionally more for a huge-name act. Dinner-show packages run $17–$38. The Mississauga location is open Thursday through Sunday, the Toronto Kabaret is open daily.

Dance Clubs

Berlin (✉ 2335 Yonge St., ☎ 416/489–7777) became one of the most popular—and exclusive—spots in Toronto within a year of its opening back in 1987, quickly attracting a rich, twenty- and thirtysomething crowd. It remains the hot and cool place to be. Tuesday there's live Spanish music, Friday and Saturday feature a Top 40 band, playing mostly '70s and '80s sounds. The dress code bans T-shirts and athletic clothes. Crisp, neat blue jeans are allowed any day except Saturday, when jeans of any sort are verboten.

The Courthouse (✉ 57 Adelaide St. E, ☎ 416/214–9379, WEB www.libertygroup.com), with its 12-ft ceilings, plush couches, and roaring fireplaces, more closely approximates a 1940s Hollywood mansion than a courthouse. Fresh market cuisine is served daily in the dining rooms. The cocktail crowd is very modern and upscale. The dance floor is tucked away in the upper reaches, leaving the main floor free for lounging and posing. The cigar bar Cell Bar is in the basement, where you can visit the actual holding cells from the old courthouse days.

The Guvernment (✉ 132 Queen's Quay E, ☎ 416/869–0045) is a huge venue with three lounges and two patios—including the rooftop Skylounge—that plays techno dance and underground music. The week starts on Thursday nights with fashion shows in the Skylounge. Feel Friday features hip-hop, R&B, and house music in the main club. On Sunday morning, the 19- to 35-year-old crowd can watch the sun rise—Saturday night runs until 7 AM. The rooftop patio, heated for chilly fall and spring nights, gives the crowded club breathing room most of the year.

The Joker (✉ 318 Richmond St. W, ☎ 416/598–1313), a three-story dance emporium of brooding and ominous proportions, has a cavelike atmosphere, thanks to its dark decor. Each floor plays different music, but expect high-energy dancing. Saturday night is the most popular night—lines start to form as early as 9 PM. Covers range from $5–$10.

Limelight (✉ 250 Adelaide St. W, ☎ 416/593–6126) is in the vortex of the club scene. It always has a lineup, starting at 10 PM and continuing well past midnight. This is the spot du jour for university types and suburbanites, who drive in for an evening of rave-ish dancing and drinking.

System Sound Bar (✉ 117 Peter St., ☎ 416/408–3996) plays house, techno, and R&B. The basement attracts people in their early twenties. The "older crowd" (23–30) might prefer Tonic (☎ 416/204–9200), upstairs, where the downtown artsy types meet the rave crowd. Tonic plays the same music as System Sound Bar, but is geared to slightly more affluent clients.

The Velvet Underground (✉ 508 Queen St. W, ☎ 416/504–6688) is the most alternative of Toronto's alternative clubs. The dungeon-esque decor and techno music make it popular among the Goth set, especially on Monday nights.

Whiskey Saigon (✉ 250 Richmond St. W, ☎ 416/593–4646) has three gigantic floors, with DJs, laser shows, and everything from rock to funk. One of the most popular clubs of the '90s, it's a very attractive option for the hip crowd. Sunday nights are retro nights, and '80s music fans line up around the block to get in.

GAY AND LESBIAN

At **Boots Warehouse** (✉ 594 McNeil St., ☎ 416/921–0665), gays and straights come to play and gyrate to house, techno, and jungle music from 10 PM to 4 AM. Retro Sunday will have you moving and grooving to sounds of the '70s and '80s, but you can't stay up too late on school nights—closing time is 2:30 AM on Sunday. This is Toronto's largest gay and lesbian dance club.

Pope Joan (✉ 547 Parliament St., ☎ 416/928–1495) is a late-night lesbian gathering place with live music, dancing, DJs, and karaoke.

Entertainment Center

The Docks (✉ 11 Polson St., ☎ 416/469–5655), an enormous center on the lake, provides complete entertainment for partygoers, with video games, six beach volleyball courts, a driving range, a climbing wall, two basketball courts, a swimming pool, 22 outdoor billiard tables, indoor and outdoor dance floors, and even a bungee-jumping platform. There are plenty of places to drink at night. The Docks' terrace has spectacular views of Toronto's skyline.

Latin Dance Clubs

What disco was to the '70s, salsa is to the new millennium. Latin dance clubs have become the hangouts of choice for the club cognoscenti.

Ba-Ba-Lu'U (✉ 136 Yorkville Ave., ☎ 416/515–0587), in the upscale Yorkville area, is truly the best of both worlds, with the luxe of a tony lounge replete with gem-color stools and polished tables, and the sizzle born of the sexy Latin rhythms. The club also offers lessons for novices; call for times.

ChaChaCha (✉ 11 Duncan St., ☎ 416/598–3538) is the place to drag out those red stilettos and ruffled shirts hidden in the back of the closet. Here, dress the part and dance the dance—after all, this is the Copacabana of the 21st century. The sleek bar and stainless-steel dance floor surrounded by marble columns ooze rich Havana. Prime time is 9 to 11, after which funk and disco take over.

El Convento Rico Club (✉ 750 College St., ☎ 416/588–7800) creates a slice of Cuba in the heart of downtown. It's seedy, it's steamy, it's sticky, and it's the real thing. Toronto's Latin community comes here to play, as do many of the city's drag queens and gays.

Lounges

Canoe (✉ 66 Wellington St. W, ☎ 416/364–0054), a stellar restaurant on the 54th floor of the Toronto Dominion Centre, has a magnificent bar with a panoramic view of the lake and the Toronto Islands. The crowd is mostly made up of brokers and financial wizards from the neighboring towers, who suit the swank surroundings.

The **Easy and the Fifth** (✉ 225 Richmond St. W, ☎ 416/979–3000, WEB www.easyandthefifth.com) is what you get when you cross a New York–style loft with a disco. The dark floors, white walls, and high ceilings give the place height, and the crowd of young professionals dressed to the nines in Armani suits and Versace dresses provide the scenery. Couches tucked into corners create cozy conversation areas, while the empty spaces are quickly converted into dance space. The Easy is busiest Thursday through Saturday nights. Covers range from $10 to $12.

La Serre (✉ 21 Avenue Rd., ☎ 416/964–0411), the Four Seasons Hotel's classy lounge, looks like a library in a mansion—plush and green, with lots of brass and dark wood. It has a stand-up piano bar and a pianist worth standing up for. Drinks, coffees, and teas are all pricey, but what can you expect in one of the poshest hotels in the country? Weekdays attract a business crowd, and weekends bring out the couples.

The classy **Roof Lounge** (⊠ Park Hyatt Hotel, 4 Avenue Rd., ☎ 416/925–1234) has been used as a setting in the writings of such Canadian literary luminaries as Margaret Atwood and Mordecai Richler. A clubby bar and marble-top tables are surrounded by books and pictures of Canadian writers. In summer, an adjoining patio affords lovely views of the downtown skyline and lake. This remains an important hangout for the upper-middle class, businesspeople, professionals, and, of course, literary types.

Music Clubs

ECLECTIC

The **Cameron Public House** (⊠ 408 Queen St. W, ☎ 416/703–0811), a small venue with a unique facade that changes with the owners' whims, showcases "alternative" music that ranges from jazz to hard rock and New Wave. Because it's close to the Ontario College of Art, the Cameron draws a creative bunch during the week. The suburbanite scene gets heavy on weekends, as do the crowds.

Free Times Cafe (⊠ 320 College St., ☎ 416/967–1078) is a relatively small space where you'll find, every night of the week, blues and folk singers, along with New Age, jazz, fusion, and other musical forms. A lot of acoustic performers love to put on quality shows here, especially singers and songwriters. This is the place to see the next stars of the Mariposa folk music festival and other happenings.

Horseshoe Tavern (⊠ 370 Queen St. W, ☎ 416/598–4753) was known across the city for more than four decades as the tavern with entertainment, especially country music. Charlie Pride, Tex Ritter, Hank Williams, and Loretta Lynn all played here. Now the music is mostly alternative rock, along with some live roots, blues, and rockabilly. Good new bands perform here six nights a week. No food is served, but there's plenty of booze. The place draws lots of young people in their 20s and 30s.

JAZZ

C'est what? (⊠ 67 Front St. E, ☎ 416/867–9499) offers rotating bands almost every night, along with its own beers, 25 other Ontario microbrews, and plain good cooking.

The **Montreal Restaurant–Bistro & Jazz Club** (⊠ 65 Sherbourne St., ☎ 416/363–0179), a former warehouse, has a large dining room to the right and the jazz club to the left. This is superb for an evening meal with jazz wafting in from the other room or for lounging in the comfortable couches in the club itself for intense listening.

The **Orbit Room** (⊠ 580A College St., ☎ 416/535–0613) is an icon in the heart of funky College Street. Cozy up to one of the lava lamps on the bar or take a turn on the compact dance floor. Either way, you'll be able to enjoy small-club jazz at its finest. Lines form at around 10 PM Thursday through Saturday for the first set, and the second set starts at midnight.

The **Pilot Tavern** (⊠ 22 Cumberland St., ☎ 416/923–5716) serves up modern mainstream jazz Saturday afternoons, and good burgers every day.

Top O' The Senator (⊠ 249 Victoria St., ☎ 416/364–7517), the city's first club devoted exclusively to jazz, sits atop the Torch restaurant. With its long wooden bar and dark blue, towering ceilings, this fabulous room exudes a between-the-wars jazz lounge atmosphere.

REGGAE, CARIBBEAN, AND AFRICAN

BamBoo (✉ 312 Queen St. W, ☎ 416/593–5771), a onetime commercial laundry hidden behind the popular Queen Street strip, serves reasonably priced Thai and Caribbean food along with reggae and world-beat music Monday through Saturday evenings, with an occasional acid jazz group. The sightlines can be terrible, and this is no place for quiet conversation, but it's still popular for its great food and great sounds.

RHYTHM AND BLUES

Chicago's (✉ 335 Queen St. W, ☎ 416/598–3301), on the Queen Street West strip that heads west from University Avenue, is a real charmer. Downstairs are a cowboy-ish bar and good hamburgers. Upstairs, you can see and hear the blues stars of tomorrow every night. Check out the red neon sign in the shape of a beer cap.

Grossman's Tavern (✉ 379 Spadina Ave., ☎ 416/977–7000), old and raunchy, was described in the '80s by one Toronto Star writer as "long established, but never entirely reputable"—which makes it ideal for the blues. There are R&B bands nightly and jazz on Saturday afternoon.

ROCK

Chick 'n Deli (✉ 744 Mount Pleasant Rd., ☎ 416/489–3363), long one of the great jazz places in Toronto, now plays Top 40 music, with cover bands every night. There's a dance floor and dark wood everywhere, and the casual friendliness gives the place a neighborhood bar–type atmosphere.

Hard Rock Cafe at Dundas Square (✉ 283 Yonge St., across from Eaton Centre, ☎ 416/362–3636) features recorded rock most nights and live rock on Sunday. The trademark rock-and-roll memorabilia of this chain decorates the walls. This is a busy hangout for people in their early 20s and those in their 30s who want to hang out with 20-year-olds.

The **Hard Rock SkyDome** (✉ SkyDome, Gate 1, 1 Blue Jays Way, ☎ 416/341–2388), has a DJ on weekends and live rock occasionally. There's a $3.50 cover charge during game events.

Lee's Palace (✉ 529 Bloor St. W, ☎ 416/532–7383), on the edge of the University of Toronto campus, is where rock-and-roll and blues are delivered by local talent. Jams go from 8 PM on. And dig that crazy decor!

The Opera House (✉ 735 Queen St. E, ☎ 416/466–0313 for club and concert line), a venue for live, largely alternative acts, is also a dance club. It's a hot place for ravers.

SUPPER CLUBS

The past few years have witnessed the rebirth of the supper club in Toronto. The places listed below also have active bars, for those who prefer to limit the evening to drinks and dancing.

ChaChaCha (✉ 11 Duncan St., ☎ 416/598–3538) is a sophisticated supper club that turns into a dance club as diners finish their meals and the late-night crowd arrives.

Rosewater Supper Club (✉ 19 Toronto St., ☎ 416/214–5888), with blue velvet banquettes for two, is a lovely place for a festive night on the town. One lounge has a baby grand and a torch singer.

OUTDOOR ACTIVITIES AND SPORTS

Participant Sports

Updated by
Shawna Richer

From Lake Ontario to the hills outside the city and the lakes and parks beyond, a wide range of sports and recreational activities is available for year-round pleasure. As a supplement to the suggestions below, contact the **Ministry of Tourism and Recreation** (✉ Queen's Park M7A 2R2, ☎ 416/327–2422 or 800/267–7329) for pamphlets on various activities. **Tourism Toronto** (☎ 416/203–2500 or 800/363–1990) can provide information on sports and outdoor recreation.

A number of fine conservation areas, including the Kortright Centre, circle the metropolitan Toronto area, many less than a half hour from downtown. Most have large swimming areas, sledding, and cross-country skiing, as well as skating, fishing, and boating. Contact the **Metro Conservation Authority** (☎ 416/661–6600) and ask for their pamphlet, which has information on parks and trails.

Bicycling

More than 29 km (18 mi) of street bike routes cut across the city, and dozens more follow safer paths through Toronto's many parks. Bikes can be rented on the Toronto Islands. The **Martin Goodman Trail** is a 19-km (12-mi) strip that runs along the waterfront all the way from the Balmy Beach Club in the east end out past the western beaches southwest of High Park. Phone the *Toronto Star* (☎ 416/367–2000) for a map.

Toronto Parks and Recreation (✉ 55 John St., ☎ 416/392–8186) has maps that show biking and jogging routes that run through Toronto parkland. **Ontario Cycling** (✉ 1185 Eglinton Ave. E, ☎ 416/426–7242) offers booklets and information as well as maps of trails around the province.

Boating

Grenadier Pond in High Park, Centre Island, Ontario Place, Harbourfront Centre, and most of the conservation areas surrounding Toronto rent canoes, punts, or sailboats.

Bowling

Toronto has five-pin bowling, a marvelous tradition unknown to most Americans. This sport of rolling a tiny ball down an alley at five fat pins—each with a different numerical value, for a possible (impossible) score of 450—is perfect for children, even as young as three or four, and for everyone on a rainy day. **Bowlerama** (✉ 2788 Bathurst St., south of Lawrence Ave. W, ☎ 416/782–1841; ✉ Newtonbrook Plaza, 5837 Yonge St., south of Steeles, ☎ 416/222–4657; ✉ 115 Rexdale Blvd., near Kipling, ☎ 416/743–8388) has lanes all over the city. The Newtonbrook Plaza and Rexdale Boulevard locations are open 24 hours a day.

Golf

The golf season lasts only from April to late October. For information about courses, contact **Toronto Parks and Recreation** (☎ 416/392–8186) or **TraveLinx Ontario** (☎ 416/314–0944 or 800/668–2746). The top course in Canada, a real beauty designed by Jack Nicklaus, is the 18-hole, par-73 **Glen Abbey** (✉ 1333 Dorval Dr., Oakville, ☎ 905/844–1800), where the Canadian Open Championship is held. Cart and greens fees run around $75 on weekends.

The **Don Valley Golf Course** (✉ 4200 Yonge St., south of Hwy. 401, ☎ 416/392–2465) is a moderately challenging course near the heart of the city. The **Flemingdon Park Golf Club** (✉ 155 St. Denis Dr., near Don Mills Rd. and Eglinton Ave., ☎ 416/429–1740) is a fairly standard, no-frills public course. But if you're downtown and looking for a golf fix, this is a good place to get it. A round of 18 holes is $17. The course winds along the Don Valley wall and Taylor Creek, making the city seem far away.

Health and Fitness Facilities
Nearly every major hotel in metropolitan Toronto has a health club or an exercise room, with a track, weight equipment, and some sort of swimming pool. Many private clubs and hotel fitness facilities will sell passes to visitors who want short-term use. The YMCA may honor your membership from another city at one of its local fitness centers.

Horseback Riding
Within the city limits, **Central Don Riding Academy** (⊠ Sunnybrook Park, Park Leslie St. and Eglinton Ave., ☎ 416/444–4044) has an indoor arena, an outdoor ring, and nearly 19 km (12 mi) of bridle trails through the Don Valley.

North of the city, in Richmond Hill, the **Rocking Horse Ranch** (☎ 905/884–3292) offers scenic Western trail rides year-round. For booklets detailing riding establishments across the province, call the **Ontario Equestrian Federation** (☎ 416/426–7232).

Ice-Skating
Toronto operates some 30 outdoor artificial rinks and 100 natural-ice rinks—and all are free. Among the most popular are those in Nathan Phillips Square in front of New City Hall, at Queen and Bay streets, down at Harbourfront Centre (Canada's largest outdoor artificial ice rink), College Park at Yonge and College streets, Grenadier Pond within High Park at Bloor and Keele streets, and inside Hazelton Lanes—the classy shopping mall on the edge of Yorkville—on Avenue Road just above Bloor Street. For details on city rinks, call the **Toronto Parks and Recreation Information Line** ☎ (416/392–1111).

Jogging
Good places to jog are the boardwalk of The Beaches in the city's east end, High Park in the west end, the Toronto Islands, and the ravines or other public parks, many of which have jogging paths and trails. The Martin Goodman Trail is ideal. Many hotels now provide printed copies of interesting routes nearby. Toronto is generally safer than most American cities, but it's still wise to use normal prudence and avoid isolated spots. Check with local people on specific parks or routes.

The **Martin Goodman Trail** offers a 19-km (12-mi) jogging route with an incredible view. The dirt and asphalt trails run along the waterfront from the Balmy Beach Club past the western beaches past High Park. It's a popular place with runners, and is especially busy on weekends. But if you get out in the hours before work and after dinner, you're likely to catch some spectacular sunrises and sunsets. Phone the *Toronto Star* (☎ 416/367–2000) for a map.

Sailing
Sailing on Lake Ontario is especially nice between May and September, but die-hard sailors push the season at both ends. The **Ontario Sailing Association** (⊠ 65 Guise St. E, Hamilton L8L 8B4, ☎ 416/425–7245) is a good resource for sailing on Lake Ontario. The **Royal Canadian Yacht Club** (⊠ 141 St. George St., ☎ 416/967–7245) has its summer headquarters in a beautiful Victorian mansion on Centre Island.

Skiing
CROSS-COUNTRY
Try Toronto's parks and ravines, especially Earl Bales Park, High Park, the lakefront along the southern edge of the city, Tommy Thompson Park,

and best of all, the Toronto Islands. The Kortright Centre, just outside Toronto, has hiking trails, some of which are used for skiing in winter. Most of these places are free. One of the most popular and centrally located places to rent ski equipment is **Play It Again Sports** (✉ 3055 Dundas St. W, Mississauga, ☎ 905/607–2837). **Sports Rent & Sales** (✉ 2137 Bloor St. W, ☎ 416/762–7368) has several locations in Toronto. Check the yellow pages for other ski-equipment rental locations.

DOWNHILL

Most of the area's better hills can be found 30 to 90 minutes north of the city, including **Blue Mountain Resorts** (☎ 705/445–0231, WEB www.bluemountain.ca) in Collingwood, Ontario; the **Caledon Ski Club** (☎ 519/927–5221) in Belfountain, Ontario; **Glen Eden Ski Area** (☎ 905/878–5011) in Milton, Ontario; **Hidden Valley** (☎ 705/789–1773, WEB www.skihiddenvalley.on.ca) in Huntsville, Ontario; **Hockley Valley Resort** (☎ 519/942–0754, WEB www.hockley.com) in Orangeville, Ontario; and **Horseshoe Valley** (☎ 705/835–2790, WEB www.horseshoeresort.com) in Barrie, Ontario. Call ☎ 416/314–0998 for lift and surface conditions in the greater Toronto area.

Sleigh Riding and Tobogganing

The best parks for tobogganing include High Park, in the west end, and a local favorite, Winston Churchill Park, at Spadina Avenue and St. Clair Avenue, just two blocks from Casa Loma. It is sheer terror.

Swimming

Lake Ontario is rarely warm enough for sustained swimming, except in late August, and is often too polluted for any kind of dip. Still, it's fun to relax or take a stroll on one of the city's beaches. In the east end, **Beaches Park,** south of Queen Street and east of Coxwell Avenue, is lovely, thanks to the lengthy boardwalk, local canoe club, and public washrooms. A 20-minute streetcar ride east of downtown, along Queen Street, is **Woodbine Beach Park** and **Ashbridges Bay Park,** both fine for sunbathing and boat-watching. To the west of downtown, a fine area, **Sunnyside Beach,** has a pool, snack bar, jungle gym, and washrooms. The city's most pleasing beaches—and certainly the ones with the best views—are on the **Toronto Islands.**

Public swimming is available at 16 indoor pools, 12 outdoor pools, and 15 community recreation centers—call the **Toronto Department of Parks and Recreation** (☎ 416/392–8186). For the latest information on city pools, call the **Toronto Parks and Recreation Outdoor Pools Hotline** (☎ 416/392–7838). For information about late-night, outdoor swimming, call the **Toronto Late-Night Pool Hotline** ☎ 416/392–1899.

Ontario Place (✉ 955 Lakeshore Blvd. W, ☎ 416/314–9900) has an outstanding water park and slide. This lakefront amusement park has enough other activities and rides, as well as the Cinesphere movie theater, to amuse kids for hours once they tire of the water.

Tennis

The city provides dozens of courts, all free, many of them floodlighted. Parks with courts open from 7 AM to 11 PM, in season, include High Park in the west end; Stanley Park on King Street West, three blocks west of Bathurst Street; and Eglinton Park, on Eglinton Avenue West, just east of Avenue Road. Call the **Ontario Tennis Association** (☎ 416/426–7135).

Windsurfing

Equipment for windsurfing can be rented in various areas of the waterfront. Try along Bloor Street West, near the High Park subway station.

Spectator Sports

The city of Toronto has traditionally enjoyed a love–hate relationship with its professional sports teams, including even the Toronto Blue Jays, who won back-to-back World Series championships in 1992 and 1993. Fans can sometimes be accused of being fair-weather—except when it comes to hockey. In Toronto the national sport attracts rabid, sellout crowds, whether the Maple Leafs win, lose, or draw.

Auto Racing

For the past several years, the **Molson Indy Toronto** (☎ 416/872–4639, FAX 416/351–8560) has been roaring around the Canadian National Exhibition grounds, including the major thoroughfare of Lakeshore Boulevard. Local traffic is diverted for those three days in mid-July. You can book tickets from late February or early March. You'll pay around $100 for a three-day "red" reserved seat, but general admission for the qualification rounds, the practice rounds, and the Indy itself, can be considerably less expensive.

Motorcycle and formula racing are held at **Mosport** (☎ 905/660–7373), about 96 km (60 mi) northeast of Toronto. Take Highway 401 east to Exit 75, then drive north.

Baseball

The **Toronto Blue Jays** (✉ SkyDome, 1 Blue Jays Way, ☎ 416/341–1111; 416/341–1234 ticket and team information, WEB www.bluejays.com) play April through September. Interest in the team has fallen some since they won consecutive World Series championships in 1992–93. They lost some of their more dynamic players to free agency in the seasons following, and crowds also dwindled after the strike-shortened season of 1994. But fans are beginning to come back. The Jays lost one of their best players, star outfielder Shawn Green, to the Los Angeles Dodgers, but they acquired heavy hitter Raul Mondesi and re-signed first baseman Carlos Delgado. The Jays play great baseball and make a run for the wild card each August. Tickets are $16 to $35.

Basketball

The city's NBA franchise, the **Toronto Raptors** (✉ Air Canada Centre, 40 Bay St., ☎ 416/815–5600 tickets, WEB www.raptors.com), opened its first season in 1995. For several years they struggled mightily, both in winning games and fans here in this hockey-mad city. But the Raptors have finally come into their own. Games often sell out, and fans are rabid for high-flying dunkmaster Vince Carter. With the young Carter, and league veterans such as Charles Oakley, Antonio Davis, Chris Childs, and newcomer rookie Morris Peterson, the Raptors field an entertaining and competitive squad. Tickets run from $10.50 to $500 per game and are available beginning in July.

Canoeing and Rowing

Canoe Ontario (☎ 416/426–7170) has information about one of the world's largest canoeing and rowing regattas, held every July 1 on Toronto Island's Long Pond.

Cricket

The British and Commonwealth influence, though waning, is strong enough to support local teams who play in their pristine whites and make moves that those brought up on baseball may find mysterious but fascinating. The **Cricket Association of Ontario** (☎ 416/426–7160) has information about finding a game.

Football

The Canadian Football League (CFL) has a healthy following across most of the country, even in Toronto, where the **Toronto Argonauts** (✉

SkyDome, 1 Blue Jays Way, ☎ 416/341–5151 for tickets and team information) have struggled for fans against the Maple Leafs, Raptors, and Blue Jays. Tickets for home games are a cinch to get. Prices range from $14 to $41. The season runs from June to late November. American football fans who attend a CFL game will discover a faster, more unpredictable and exciting contest than the NFL version. The longer, wider field means quarterbacks have to scramble more, a nifty thing to watch. This season however, the CFL gets some competition, as the Arena Football League joins the crowded Toronto sports scene for a season that runs from April to August. Tickets for the **Toronto Phantoms** (✉ Air Canada Centre, 40 Bay St., ☎ 416/585–2AFL) run from $12 to $50.

Golf

The permanent site of the **Canadian Open** (✉ Glen Abbey, 1333 Dorval Dr., Oakville, ☎ 905/844–1800) is the Jack Nicklaus–designed Glen Abbey, less than 45 minutes west of the city, along the Queen Elizabeth Way (QEW). This tournament is one of golf's Big Five and is always played in late summer.

Hockey

The **Toronto Maple Leafs** (✉ Air Canada Centre, 40 Bay St., ☎ 416/870–8000, WEB www.torontomapleleafs.com) share the Air Canada Centre with the NBA's Raptors. Win or lose, the Leafs are notoriously the toughest ticket to get hold of in the National Hockey League. Availability is always limited, and changes depending on the visiting team. Prices range from $20 to $325—scalpers often demand up to three times the value. If you can, plan ahead and book tickets in advance.

Horse Racing

RACETRACKS

The **Ontario Jockey Club** (☎ 416/675–7223 or 888/675–7223) operates two major racetracks, Woodbine and Mohawk. **Woodbine Race Track** (✉ Hwy. 427 and Rexdale Blvd., ☎ 416/675–7223 or 888/675–7223), 30 minutes northwest of downtown Toronto, near the airport, is the showplace of thoroughbred and harness racing in Canada. Horses run late April–late October. **Mohawk** (✉ Hwy. 401, Campbellville, ☎ 416/675–7223 or 888/675–7223), a 30-minute drive west of Toronto, is in the heart of Ontario's standardbred breeding country. It features a glass-enclosed, climate-controlled grandstand and other attractive facilities.

Nordic Gaming operates **Fort Erie** (✉ 230 Catherine St., Queen Elizabeth Way–Bertie St. exit, Fort Erie, ☎ 905/871–3200 Toronto; 716/856–0293 Buffalo), in the Niagara tourist region. This is one of the most picturesque racetracks in the world, with willows, manicured hedges, and flower-bordered infield lakes. It has racing on the dirt as well as on grass, with the year's highlight being the Prince of Wales Stakes, the second jewel in Canada's Triple Crown of Racing.

ROYAL HORSE SHOW

The Royal Horse Show, a highlight of Canada's equestrian season, is part of the **Royal Winter Fair** (✉ CNE Grounds, Dufferin St., by the waterfront, ☎ 416/263–3400) each November.

Ice Canoe Racing

One of the strangest sports winter has to offer, ice canoeing got its start in Québec more than 100 years ago, when teams competed to deliver the mail over the St. Lawrence River. Today there are 36 ice canoeing teams in Canada. Each January, at the Molson Export Ice Canoe Race, five-member teams row through freezing waters over a 3.5-km course off Harbourfront Centre, stopping at ice floes to haul their vessels to the next stretch of open water. They compete for $2,000 (Canadian) in prize money, and of course, honor.

Soccer

Although Toronto keeps getting and losing a professional soccer team, you can catch this exciting sport, at university and semi-pro levels, in the centrally located **Varsity Stadium** (⌧ Bloor St. W at Bedford, a block west of Royal Ontario Museum and University Ave., ☎ 416/978–7388). The **Soccer Association of Ontario** (☎ 416/426–7300) can provide information about games.

Tennis

The finest players in the world gather each summer at the tennis complex at York University, near Finch Avenue and Keele Street, for the **Rogers and AT&T Canada Cup** (☎ 416/665–9777 tickets).

Wrestling

Exhibitions are sometimes held at **Maple Leaf Gardens** (⌧ 60 Carlton St., one block east of Yonge and College Sts., ☎ 416/977–1641) or at the **SkyDome** (⌧ 1 Blue Jays Way, ☎ 416/341–3663).

SHOPPING

By Liza Finlay

Toronto prides itself on having some of the finest shopping in North America; and, indeed, most of the world's name boutiques can be found here, especially along the Bloor Street strip (between Yonge Street and Avenue Road) and in the Yorkville area, which covers the three streets immediately north of and parallel to the Bloor Street strip.

For those a little leaner of wallet, rest assured that you have come to the right place. In Toronto, bargain hunting is a sport of Olympic proportions, and locals wear those discount threads like badges of honor. Because of the weakness of the Canadian dollar, too, visitors obtain what amounts to an immediate discount on any purchase.

Toronto has a large artistic and crafts community, with many art galleries, custom jewelers, clothing designers, and artisans. From sophisticated glass sculpture to native and Inuit art, the many beautiful objects you'll find are ideal for gifts or for your own home.

Politically incorrect as they may be, fur coats and hats are popular purchases with visitors from outside Canada. You can buy from a high-fashion outlet or directly from a furrier in the Spadina Avenue garment district. Distinctive Hudson Bay wool blankets, available only at The Bay, are an enduring Canadian tradition. The unique Tilley hat, sold by mail order or in the **Tilley Endurables** (Queen's Quay Terminal, Queen's Quay W and York St., ☎ 416/203–0463) boutique, is an ideal present for sailors and adventurers. It's advertised as having been retrieved intact after being eaten by an elephant, and comes with a lifetime guarantee and owner's manual.

The mammoth HMV Music store on Yonge Street, which has listening stations for your prepurchase pleasure and live, in-store performances, makes CD shopping great entertainment. Canadians are proud of their own, and most record stores dedicate shelves to home-grown talent like Celine Dion, Alanis Morissette, The Tragically Hip, Bryan Adams, and Shania Twain, along with a host of smaller pop, rap, hip-hop, folk, opera, and country artists. In a similar bigger-is-better vein, bookstores such as Chapters have lounge areas where you can read while sipping a coffee from the in-store Starbucks, and offer frequent readings by Canadian authors like Barbara Gowdy, Ann-Marie McDonald, and Rohinton Mistry.

When it comes to department stores, all roads lead from Holt Renfrew on Bloor Street West, the epicenter of Toronto's designer mecca. Within a few blocks of this high-end store are virtually all the designer boutiques from Prada to Gucci. A mere block east is the more mid-priced department store The Bay, where you'll find designer collections offset with bridge lines and The Bay's own clothing and houseware lines.

Most stores accept MasterCard and Visa without minimums, though you won't be too popular if you charge a purchase under $5. Major stores also accept American Express. You'll find U.S. cash generally accepted, though not always at the most favorable rate of exchange. On Thursday and Friday most stores downtown stay open until 9 PM; on Sunday many downtown stores open at noon.

The biggest sale day of the year is Boxing Day, the first business day after Christmas, when nearly everything in the city, including furs, is half price. In fact, clothing prices tend to drop even further as winter fades. Summer sales start in late June and continue through August.

Bear in mind that the much hated national 7% Goods and Services Tax (alias the GST, or Grab and Soak Tax) will be added to the cost of your purchases at the cash register, as will the 8% Ontario sales tax. Visitors should save receipts from hotel bills and any major purchases and inquire about rebates on the GST. Ask for the latest refund regulations and forms at Lester B. Pearson International Airport, at visitor information booths like the one outside Eaton Centre, or at stores.

Shopping Districts

The Beaches
Queen Street East, starting at Woodbine Avenue, is a great spot for casual clothing stores, gift and antiques shops, and bars and restaurants, all with a resort atmosphere—a boardwalk along the lake is just to the south. To get to The Beaches, take the Queen Street streetcar to Woodbine and walk east. Parking can be a hassle.

Bloor Street West
Bloor Street West, from Yonge Street to Avenue Road, is a virtual runway for fashion mavens. Two city blocks play host to a world of fashion, with the haute Holt Renfrew department store at the nucleus and the more moderately priced The Bay, Canada's oldest department store, and Club Monaco's flagship store acting as bookends. The cornucopia of couture starts with Emporio Armani to the east; proceeding west, Bloor Street is handily split, with the north side offering more mainstream fare like Gap, Gap Kids, Banana Republic, and The Body Shop, and the south serving up fantasy fashion such as Tiffany & Co., Cartier, Royal De Versailles Jewelers, Chanel, Hermès, and Corbò—a scaled-down department store carrying only upscale merchandise. The Prada store is a must, if only for the inspired interior design. Women should consider parking the guys at Bay Bloor Radio in the Manulife Centre; it's a stereo mecca and only steps from male-fashion bastions like Eddie Bauer for active wear and Harry Rosen for more professional attire. A jolt of java served up at Starbucks in Chapters, a three-story bookstore with lounge areas for adults and a play center for kids, may be just what you'll need after this shopping experience.

Farther west on Bloor Street, between Bathurst Street and Spadina Avenue, near the University of Toronto, is a vibrant mix of cafés, Hungarian restaurants, pubs, specialty groceries, casual-clothing boutiques, and discount bookstores.

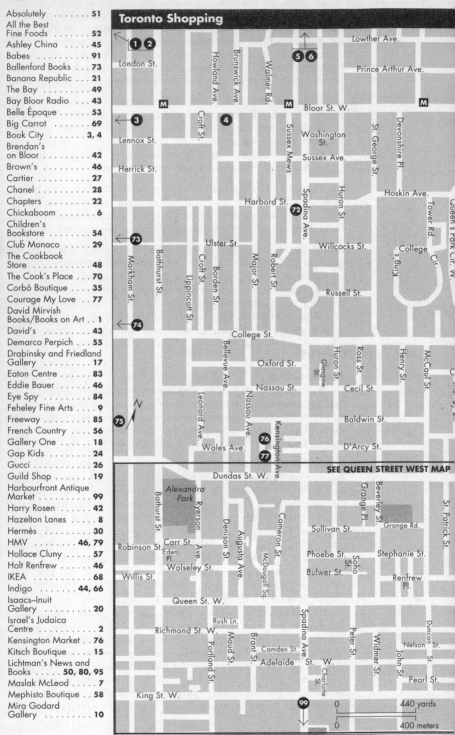

Toronto Shopping

Chinatown

While the Chinese have made Spadina Avenue their own from King Street north to College Street, Spadina's basic bill of fare is still "bargains galore." The street, and the Kensington Market area tucked behind Spadina west to Bathurst Street, between Dundas and College streets, remains a collection of inexpensive vintage clothing stores, Chinese clothing stores, Chinese restaurants, ethnic food and fruit stores, and eateries that give you your money's worth. You'll find gourmet cheeses at gourmet prices, fresh ocean fish, yards of fabric remnants piled high in bins, and designer clothes minus the labels. Start at the southern end of Spadina (south of King Street) where Winners, a discount clothing and home-accessories store, offers designer brands minus the designer prices. Be warned—this area can be extraordinarily crowded on weekends, when smart suburbanites head here for bargains. Park your car at the lot just west of Spadina Avenue on St. Andrew's Street (a long block north of Dundas Street), or take the College or Queen streetcar to Spadina Avenue.

Mirvish Village

Mirvish Village, a one-block assortment of bookstores, antiques shops, and boutiques on Markham Street south of Bloor Street, has an interesting history. Ed Mirvish is an inspired capitalist who, since 1948, has run the truly silly deep-discount store called Honest Ed's, which financed the revival of London's Old Vic theater. When Mirvish tried to tear down all the houses on the block behind his store to build a parking lot, he was prevented by zoning bylaws. No problem: he thought up Mirvish Village. Memory Lane sells vintage movie posters, comic books, and magazines.

Queen Street East

Queen Street East from Pape Street east to Jones Avenue is a bustling young thoroughfare now noted for its antiques and "previously loved" junk shops. With a particular fondness for 1950s memorabilia, Neat Things and Ethel (and the Kitsch Cafe) start the stroll down memory lane. Yesteryear Interior Accents was the best-kept secret of locals who are now being forced to endure the crowds who come here for the exceptional assortment of quality reproduction armoires, bureaus, tables, and garden furnishings. The Tango Palace at the end of antique alley is the hot spot for gourmet coffees and decadent desserts. Parking is at a premium, but the neighborhood is easily accessible via the "Red Rocket"—the Queen Street streetcar, which passes through every 20 minutes or so.

Queen Street West

If it's funky or fun, it's found on Queen West. The best shops are concentrated on both sides of Queen Street West from University Avenue to Spadina Avenue, with some fashionable stores as far west as Bathurst Street. With its collection of vintage stores, Canadian designer boutiques, and bistros, this strip sets the pace of Toronto's street style. City TV's headquarters at the corner of Queen and John streets, with Speaker's Corner (where you can videotape your views to be aired on the station's *Speaker's Corner* show later), is a landmark. On Queen West, the retro stylings of vintage stores like Black Market and Preloved comfortably coexist with Parade, Fashion Crimes, and Sunde, which all stock Canadian designs with a bent for the street beat. To really get into the downtown groove, grab a paper or magazine at Pages and then head into the Second Cup across the street for coffee. Home decor types won't be disappointed on this strip either with Urban Mode and Du Verre. In summer, the stalls of T-shirts and silver jewelry at the Soho Market (at Queen and Soho streets) yield great inexpensive gifts. Finish with a drink on

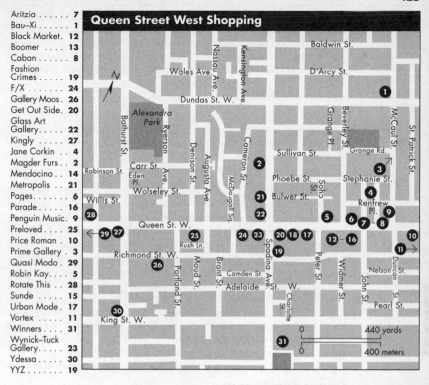

the rooftop patio of BamBoo, a Toronto legend and a likely place to spot the city's Who's Who and any visiting celebrities.

Underground City

Downtown Toronto has a vast underground maze of shopping warrens that burrow in between and underneath the office towers. The tenants of the Underground City are mostly the usual assortment of chain stores, with an occasional surprise. Directions and way-finding have improved somewhat with the introduction of marked PATH walkways. The network runs roughly from the Royal York Hotel near Union Station north to the Atrium at Bay and Dundas, and from Park Road, east of Bloor and Yonge, to Bellair Street and the ManuLife Centre.

Uptown

Yonge Street, the longest road in Canada, begins life at Lake Ontario and takes on a multitude of faces before exiting the city. Uptown is a five-minute walk north of the corner of Yonge and Bloor. The stretch of Yonge Street that runs from the Rosedale subway stop (at Yonge and Crescent streets) north to just past the Summerhill stop (at Yonge and Shaftesbury streets) is the best place to find the most upscale antiques and interiors shops. From the cottage chic of Pack Rat right up to the French Provincial treasures of Absolutely, this area delights. If the thought of freight charges dissuades you from serious spending, you can check out the trinkets at tiny shops like French Country and Word of Mouth, which carry every imaginable kitchen device.

Yorkville

Back in the 1960s, Yorkville was Canada's hippie headquarters, a mecca for runaways and folk musicians. Now this area is the place to find the big fashion names (including about 200 shops for men's and women's designer clothing), fine leather goods, upscale shoe stores, important jewelers, some of the top private art galleries, specialty bookstores, and crafts and home decor shops, as well as eateries from coffee shops to elegant northern Italian restaurants. Streets to explore include Yorkville Avenue and Cumberland Street, running parallel to Bloor Street, and Scollard Street, running north from Yorkville Avenue, east of Avenue Road. These are among the most chichi shopping streets in Canada.

Blitz Tours

Get yourself ready to move around the city by subway and streetcar, and save enough strength to lug all your packages home from these shopping itineraries.

Antiques

While Queen Street East from Pape Street to Jones Avenue is for those who enjoy trinkets and kitsch, you have to go elsewhere for the more upscale antiques. Begin near the lake at the Harbourfront Antique Market (⊠ 390 Queen's Quay W), easily accessible via the LRT from Union Station. Get off at Queen's Quay and walk a block west. About 50 stalls hold everything from big-ticket items like Persian carpets and armoires to smaller finds such as jewelry and china. Take the LRT back to Union Station and pick up the Yonge-University subway. Yonge Street, from the Rosedale subway stop at Crescent Street north to just past the Summerhill stop at Shaftesbury Street, is where you'll find the best pieces, though not at bargain prices. Begin your tour at Pack Rat (⊠ 1062 Yonge St.), across from the Rosedale subway, for items that, while not antiques, look at home in country farms and cottages. French bistros punctuate the trip north and make great stops for coffee and a croissant.

Queen Street Express

One of Toronto's most charming and utilitarian traditions is its streetcars. The Queen Street car, referred to by Torontonians as the "Red Rocket," traverses the city from The Beaches in the east end, through antiques alley on Queen Street East, and on to the trendy Queen Street West. Start the day by scouring one-of-a-kind gift stores, and wind your way east past clothing stores like Freeway. You can grab a latte at a coffee shop or bakery and walk through Kew Beach Park, on the south side of Queen Street, right down to the lake, where a boardwalk winds along the beach. Hop on the streetcar and continue west to Jones Avenue, where a string of quaint antiques stores begins. Be sure to stop at Yesteryear Interior Accents (⊠ 1142 Queen St. E) for the serious stuff. Then head to Eye Spy (⊠ 1100 Queen St. E) and Neat Things (⊠ 1126 Queen St. E) for whimsical '50s nostalgia pieces. Take the streetcar again to Queen Street West, where fashion and funk meet between Simcoe Street (on the east) and Spadina Avenue. It all starts at **Price Roman** (⊠ 267 Queen St. W) and **Noise** (⊠ 275 Queen St. W., at Simcoe St.) and stretches west with groovy vintage and homespun designer shops. Finish your day at any one of the strip's cafés, bistros, or bars.

Department Stores and Shopping Centers

The Bay, (⊠ 44 Bloor St. E, ☎ 416/972–3333; ⊠ 160–184 Yonge St., ☎ 416/861–9111), the modern descendant of the Hudson's Bay Company—which was chartered in 1670 to explore and trade in furs—carries mid-price clothing, furnishings, housewares, and cosmetics, including designer names as well as The Bay's own house lines. The Yonge Street store connects to Eaton Centre by a covered skywalk over Queen Street at the southern end. The Bloor Street store has a huge toy department.

Eaton Centre (☎ 416/598–2322), a block-long complex with an exposed industrial style similar to that of Paris's Beaubourg Center, is anchored at its northern (Dundas Street) end by the main branch of eatons and at its southern end by The Bay. Prices at Eaton Centre increase with altitude—Level 1 offers popularly priced merchandise, Level 2 is directed to the middle-income shopper, and Level 3 sells more expensive fashion and luxury goods. Well-lighted parking garages are sprinkled around the center, with spaces for some 1,800 cars. The complex is bordered by Yonge Street on the east, and James Street and Trinity Square on the west.

eatons (⊠ 290 Yonge St., ☎ 416/343–2111) in Eaton Centre is one of Canada's classic department stores. The store formerly known as Eaton's filed for bankruptcy in 1999, and was bought by Sears and relaunched as "eatons" in fall 2000. Carrying lines such as BCBG, Ralph Lauren, Tommy Hilfiger, and DKNY, the chain is after a more upscale clientele. The store also houses a full-service spa for those who feel like a facial in the middle of shopping.

Hazelton Lanes (⊠ 99 Avenue Rd., ☎ 416/968–8600) is a paean to capitalism. This luxury shopping center's 90 stores offer everything from Teuscher's divine Swiss chocolates to Hermés silks and Giorgio Armani's latest fashions. In winter, the central courtyard café becomes a delightful skating rink.

Holt Renfrew (⊠ 50 Bloor St. W, ☎ 416/922–2333) is filled with high-end clothing and housewares, including couture lines not carried elsewhere in the city and its own product line.

Queen's Quay Terminal (⊠ Queen's Quay W and York St., ☎ 416/ 203–0510), a renovated warehouse, hosts a collection of unique boutiques, crafts stalls, patisseries, and more. It's a great place to buy gifts. A free shuttle bus runs from Union Station, as does the LRT line, but it's a fairly easy walk. Parking is expensive.

Specialty Shops

Antiques and Interiors

Absolutely (⊠ 1132 Yonge St., ☎ 416/324–8351) provides a mixture of solid French antique pieces and whimsical trinkets like stuffed and mounted animals. This store is a famed interiors destination.

Belle Époque (⊠ 1066 Yonge St., ☎ 416/925–0066) sells very French, very *cher* antique and reproduction furnishings, from sleigh beds that look as if they came direct from Versailles, to accents like flirtatious ceramic lamps and candleholders.

Eye Spy (⊠ 1100 Queen St. E, ☎ 416/461–4061) serves up '50s collectibles and furnishings, including the best assortment of colorful '50s tableware in the city.

French Country (⊠ 6 Roxborough St. W, ☎ 416/944–2204) is a quaint shop that stocks mostly French treasures and trinkets, from crystal vases to vintage candelabras. If you need a hostess gift, this is the place to pick up something unique and affordable.

Harbourfront Antique Market (⊠ 390 Queen's Quay W, ☎ 416/260–2626), Canada's largest, provides the most choices for browsers and shoppers, including about 100 to 200 dealers in furniture, dishes, jewelry, art, and carpets. The whole area hops on Sunday, but the market is also open the rest of the week, although some stalls will be closed for hours at a time.

Neat Things (⊠ 1126 Queen St. E, ☎ 416/778–9453) is the destination for kitsch and collectibles from the '50s and '60s. Have a burning desire for a velvet Elvis painting? It can be found here.

Orleans (⊠ 1096A Yonge St., ☎ 416/966–0005) stocks antiques with a Mission twist—solid pieces reminiscent of Frank Lloyd Wright. Most items are mid- to high-priced.

Prince of Serendip (✉ 1073 Yonge St., ☎ 416/925–3760) is a virtual visit to Versailles, with plenty of gilt goodies. The merchandise is pricey, but the pieces are great quality.

Putti (✉ 1104 Yonge St., ☎ 416/972–7652) sells treasures large and small, from France and elsewhere in Europe, for home and summer home. The prices are high, but it's worth the visit for the beauty of the store alone.

Quasi Modo (✉ 789 Queen St. W, ☎ 416/703–8300) has a quirky collection of 20th-century furniture and design. You never know what will be on display—vintage bicycles, Noguchi lamps, a corrugated cardboard table by Frank Gehry. The store will order any (available) lamp for you.

Xit Designs (✉ 1124 Queen St. E, ☎ 416/778–0823) displays high-end, postmodern interior decor from polished chrome chairs to sleek vases.

Zig Zag Collectibles (✉ 1107 Queen St. E, ☎ 416/778–6495) captures the feeling of Grandma's attic, with antiques and trinkets large and small from $20 to $2,000. Shoppers can unearth vintage linens and larger items like late-19th-century iron beds.

Art and Crafts Galleries

Toronto is a cosmopolitan art center, with more than 200 commercial art galleries listed in the yellow pages, offering every kind of art for viewing and sale, from representational to abstract, from Inuit to Indian. The following is a list of some of the best and most respected galleries. The entertainment section of the Saturday *Globe and Mail* has several pages of listings and reviews of current shows, as does *NOW,* a free city newspaper that comes out every Thursday and can be picked up at most restaurants, bars, and hotels. Gallery strolls are fun in either of two major districts—the Yorkville area, and the Queen Street area, west of University Avenue. You can also check out some of the commercial art galleries on the north side of Dundas Street, across from the Art Gallery of Ontario, many of which display classical and contemporary Chinese paintings. Most galleries are open Tuesday through Saturday, 10 AM–5 or 6 PM, but call to be sure.

Bau-Xi Gallery (✉ 340 Dundas St. W, ☎ 416/977–0600), across the street from the Art Gallery of Ontario, was founded by Paul Wong, an artist and dealer from Vancouver. It provides a window on contemporary Canadian West Coast art, though some is from Ontario. Much of it is affordable.

Drabinsky and Friedland Gallery (✉ 122 Scollard St., ☎ 416/324–5766), with attractive, rosy-maple floors, represents such major artists as Harold Town and Alex Colville.

Feheley Fine Arts (✉ 14 Hazelton Ave. in Hazelton Lanes, ☎ 416/323–1373) deals exclusively in Canadian Inuit art with a special emphasis on the contemporary period.

Gallery One (✉ 121 Scollard St., ☎ 416/929–3103) is one of the mainstays for large-format abstract expressionists in Canada and the United States, as well as for representational landscape art from western Ontario and Inuit art. Color-field painters, from Larry Poons to Jules Olitski, are exhibited here.

Gallery Moos (✉ 622 Richmond St. W, ☎ 416/504–5445) was opened by German-born Walter Moos more than 30 years ago to promote Canadian art. He is a discerning, reliable dealer, whose gallery has Picassos, Chagalls, Mirós, and Dufys, as well as such internationally admired Canadians as Gershon Iskowitz, Ken Danby, Sorel Etrog, and Jean-Paul Riopelle.

The Glass Art Gallery (✉ 96 Spadina Ave., ☎ 416/504–1221) is a delightful showroom with stained glass, laminated and crystal sculpture, and other avant-garde work.

Guild Shop (✉ 118 Cumberland St., ☎ 416/921–1721) is an outlet for a variety of Canadian artists. Soapstone carvings from Inuit communities in the Arctic, aboriginal paintings from British Columbia and Ontario, and even woolen ties from Nova Scotia are among the items for sale.

The Isaacs–Inuit Gallery (✉ 9 Prince Arthur Ave., ☎ 416/921–9985) was started by the respected Av Isaacs to showcase fine art and crafts produced in the Canadian Arctic. It is the finest gallery of its kind anywhere. Prints, drawings, sculpture, wall hangings, and antiquities are all beautifully displayed.

Jane Corkin Photographic Gallery (✉ 179 John St., ☎ 416/979–1980) has proven that photography is a major art form. Featuring everyone from André Kertesz to Richard Avedon, this gallery is one of the most fascinating in town, showing hand-painted photos, documentary photos, and fashion photography.

Maslak McLeod (✉ 25 Prince Arthur Ave., ☎ 416/944–2577) offers an assortment of Canadian native and Inuit art.

Mira Godard Gallery (✉ 22 Hazelton Ave., ☎ 416/964–8197), which came from Montréal to Toronto in 1972, carries such major French-Canadian artists as Borduas and Riopelle, as well as established Canadian artists like Alex Colville, Kenneth Lochhead, David Milne, Jean-Paul Lemieux, and Christopher Pratt.

Miriam Shiell Fine Art Ltd. (✉ 16A Hazelton Ave., ☎ 416/925–2461) is a space for displaying 20th-century modern and contemporary fine art.

Nancy Poole's Studio (✉ 16 Hazelton Ave., ☎ 416/964–9050) is a small, intimate space, almost exclusively exhibiting Canadian contemporary painting and sculpture, generally representational. The artists include Jack Chambers, the astonishing First Nations stone carver Joe Jacobs, and the fine contemporary painter John Boyle.

Olga Korper (✉ 17 Morrow Ave., ☎ 416/538–8220), showing art from the 1960s on, is one of the most accessible and knowledgeable dealers in Toronto. She is also a trailblazer who has discovered many important artists. This is a fine place for beginning collectors.

Prime Gallery (✉ 52 McCaul St., ☎ 416/593–5750) has crafts from across Canada, including avant-garde ceramics, functional teapots, wall sculpture, and jewelry.

Sable–Castelli Gallery (✉ 33 Hazelton Ave., ☎ 416/961–0011) is the result of the 1974 amalgamation of Jared Sable's gallery and the renowned Castelli galleries of Manhattan. Since then, it has exhibited established American artists such as Warhol, Oldenburg, Johns, and Rosenquist, as well as innovative young Canadian artists who use strong expressive imagery.

Wynick–Tuck Gallery (✉ 80 Spadina Ave., ☎ 416/504–8716) represents contemporary Canadian artists whose work expresses a wide range of untrendy, often imagistic concerns. Many of them have become well established, attesting to the gallery's influence.

Ydessa Hendeles Art Foundation (✉ 778 King St. W, ☎ 416/413–9400) is a major showcase for contemporary international art.

YYZ Artists' Outlet (✉ 401 Richmond St. W, ☎ 416/598–4546) features performance art, films, and videos, as well as two- and three-dimensional paintings and sculptures. Graduates of the Ontario College of Art frequently have debut exhibitions here.

Auctions

Sotheby's (Canada) Inc. (✉ 9 Hazelton Ave., ☎ 416/926–1774) auctions the rare finds and treasures of past and present, including furnishings, jewels, and art, twice a year—in spring and fall—at the nearby Design Exchange building.

Books

Toronto is rich in stores selling every sort of new and used books.

Book City (⌧ 2350 Bloor St. W, ☎ 416/766–9412; ⌧ 501 Bloor St. W, ☎ 416/961–4496) provides good discounts, even on recently published books and best-sellers, has a knowledgeable staff, and offers a fine choice of magazines. It is usually open late.

Chapters (⌧ 110 Bloor St. W, ☎ 416/920–9299) is the gold standard of chain bookstores. This one is a three-story book lovers' mecca complete with coffee shop and lounge areas for reading. Chapters also has the biggest selection of CD-ROMs in Toronto.

David Mirvish Books and Books on Art (⌧ Mirvish Village, 596 Markham St., ☎ 416/531–9975) overflows with quality books and many remainders. It has the best price in town for the Sunday *New York Times*.

Indigo (⌧ 55 Bloor St. W, ☎ 416/925–3536; ⌧ 2300 Yonge St., ☎ 416/489–2300) offers a huge selection of books, magazines, and CD-ROMs. It has live entertainment and its own café.

Lichtman's News and Books (⌧ 144 Yonge St., ☎ 416/368–7390; ⌧ Atrium on Bay St., north of Dundas, ☎ 416/591–1617; ⌧ 842 Yonge St., ☎ 416/924–4186) has a good assortment of books, but is best known for its selection of magazines and its newspapers from around the world, often only a day old.

Pages Books and Magazines (⌧ 256 Queen St. W, ☎ 416/598–1447) has a wide selection of international and small-press literature, fashion and design books and magazines, and books on film, art, and literary criticism.

This Ain't the Rosedale Library (⌧ 483 Church St., ☎ 416/929–9912) stocks a general selection of magazines and books as well as a number of gay and lesbian titles.

Writers & Co. Booksellers (⌧ 2005 Yonge St., ☎ 416/481–8432) is arguably Canada's finest literary bookstore, with hard-to-find poets, essayists, and novelists. If you have been looking for a rare Caribbean poetry collection, a Swedish play in translation, or an Asian novella, this is the store to visit. The staff will be happy to order any book for you that's not in stock.

SPECIAL-INTEREST BOOKSTORES

Ballenford Books (⌧ 600 Markham St., ☎ 416/588–0800) stocks Canada's largest selection of architecture titles. A gallery in the store usually has interesting exhibits of architectural drawings and related work.

Children's Book Store (⌧ 2532 Yonge St., ☎ 416/480–0233), in a 1930s YMCA building, is simply magical. It frequently holds storytelling sessions and author appearances for new books, especially during March school break and October through December. The staff knows and loves children and the literature they long for. The store also has a superior collection of children's records, many of them Canadian.

The Cookbook Store (⌧ 850 Yonge St., ☎ 416/920–2665 or 800/268–6018) has the city's largest selection of books and magazines on cooking and wine. Book signings are frequently held here.

Israel's Judaica Centre (⌧ 897 Eglinton Ave. W, ☎ 416/256–1010 or 800/449–5918) offers the city's best selection of adult and children's books relating to Judaism in English, Hebrew, and Yiddish. Service is excellent.

Open Air Books and Maps (⌧ 25 Toronto St., ☎ 416/363–0719) offers more than 10,000 travel guides, oodles of atlases and road maps, specialized travel books, and titles on nature and food.

Sleuth of Baker Street (⌧ 1600 Bayview Ave., ☎ 416/483–3111) is the best place for mysteries and detective fiction.

Theatrebooks (⌧ 11 St. Thomas St., ☎ 416/922–7175 or 800/361–3414, FAX 416/922–0739) has an astounding collection of performance-arts books that spans theater, film, opera, jazz, television, and media studies.

Toronto Women's Bookstore (⊠ 73 Harbord St., ☎ 416/922–8744) carries the latest feminist works on women's political and legal issues, divorce, childbirth, lesbian topics, and more. A reading lounge is upstairs.

Clothing

CHILDREN'S CLOTHING

Babes (⊠ 2116A Queen St. E, ☎ 416/699–6110) is known for its snowsuits, but there's tons of cute indoor wear by DKNY Kids, Columbia, Timmy Tom Tom, and much more.

Chickaboom (⊠ 530 Eglinton Ave. W, ☎ 416/486–9991) is aimed at girls 7 to 14 who are particular about what they want. The clothes are cool, but also age appropriate.

Gap Kids (⊠ 80 Bloor St. W, ☎ 416/515–0668) has plenty of pint-size basics in one of the few freestanding Gap Kids stores in Canada.

Kingly (⊠ 922 Queen St. W, ☎ 416/536–2601) embraces the notion that boys' clothes should be as cute as girls' clothes. But that doesn't mean practicality is sacrificed—faux-fur-trimmed cardigans can go in the wash, and cargo pants come waterproofed at the knees and bottom. Sizes run from newborn to 3T.

MEN'S CLOTHING

Boomer (⊠ 309 Queen St. W, ☎ 416/598–0013), one of the best-kept secrets of Toronto men, brings together tasteful yet trendy suitings and separates.

Eddie Bauer (⊠ 50 Bloor St. W, ☎ 416/961–2525) offers casual wear and clothes for sports along with accessories like Swiss Army knives and watches.

Harry Rosen (⊠ 82 Bloor St. W, ☎ 416/972–0556) is a miniature department store dedicated to men's fashion. Rosen brings together the finest menswear designers from Abboud to Boss.

Moore's, the Suit People (⊠ 100 Yonge St., ☎ 416/363–5442; 416/736–7520 for other locations) stocks thousands of Canadian-made men's dress pants, sport coats, and suits, including many famous labels. Sizes range from extra tall to extra short and oversize, at low prices (e.g., all-wool suits that usually cost about $500 may sell for about half that). You'll find solid quality and good service.

At **Tom's Place** (⊠ 190 Baldwin St., ☎ 416/596–0297 or 416/736–7520) you can find bargains galore on brand name suits like Calvin Klein, Fendi, and DKNY. Tom Mihalik has owned the building for 40 years and keeps his prices low.

Perry's (⊠ 131 Bloor St. W, ☎ 416/923–7397) maintains a collection of some of the finest accessories and suitings. This is also one of the best places in town to have a suit custom-made from a broad range of fabrics.

MEN'S AND WOMEN'S CLOTHING

Banana Republic (⊠ 80 Bloor St. W, ☎ 416/515–0018) serves up basic separates, suitings, and casual wear at mid to high prices.

Club Monaco (⊠ 157 Bloor St. W, ☎ 416/591–8837), bought by Ralph Lauren in 1999, is a Canadian fashion success story. An old gymnasium provides the flagship store with a spacious shopping environment for homegrown design basics—mid-priced sportswear and career clothes. They also sell cosmetics, skin care products, housewares, and furniture.

Gucci (⊠ 130 Bloor St. W, ☎ 416/963–5127) sells the label's full range of goods, including ready-to-wear, footwear, and fragrance. This is Canada's first freestanding Gucci boutique.

Roots (⊠ 95-A Bloor St. W, ☎ 416/323–3289) is the manufacturer famous for the Canadian Olympic team's winning uniforms. The flagship store offers the city's favorite leather jackets, bags, and basics.

Urban Outfitters (⊠ 235 Yonge St. W, ☎ 416/214–1466) is for those who want the trendiest piece right now and are willing to pay the price, even if the quality may not be there. Here, you pay for the uniqueness of the item, whether it be clothing or housewares. The stuff is cool, but it's not for those unwilling to shell out $18 for a fuzzy picture frame.

XX XY (⊠ 247 Yonge St., ☎ 416/703–9669) houses the largest selection of the biggest names in denim. The two-level store features the likes of Diesel, DKNY, Silver, and Replay.

Zara (⊠ 50 Bloor St. W, ☎ 416/916–2401), a Spanish chain, has been consistently attracting the crowds. Why? This is where you can get a gorgeous knockoff of the hottest item off the runway at a fraction of the price. If you see something, grab it. It won't be there for long.

WOMEN'S CLOTHING

Aritzia (⊠ 280 Queen St. W, ☎ 416/977–9919) caters to the young urban woman looking for modern funky pieces by lines such as Miss Sixty, the celebrity-coveted Earl, In Wear, and France's Kookai.

Chanel (⊠ 131 Bloor St. W, ☎ 416/925–2577) is a boutique Coco would have loved, especially since it's one of the biggest in the world. The lush surroundings showcase most of the Chanel line, including the double-C'd bags and accessories.

Corbò Boutique (⊠ 131 Bloor St. W, ☎ 416/928–0954) gathers clothes by some of the most tasteful designers under one roof, along with some of the finest footwear in town. It's upscale one-stop shopping.

Fashion Crimes (⊠ 395 Queen St. W, ☎ 416/592–9001) doesn't believe in the less-is-more theory of clothing. With items inspired by the medieval and Victorian ages, the styles are dramatic but still wearable.

Freeway (⊠ 1978 Queen St. E, ☎ 416/693–6670) presents casual clothing that's in line with the Coney Island atmosphere of the store's locale in The Beaches district. Freeway is the place to find lines like Mexx and Dex Brothers—lines that are both sporty and sexy.

F/X (⊠ 515 Queen St. W, ☎ 416/504–0888) embraces the philosophy of fashion as costuming. Some call the crinolined skirts, wild colors, and short skirts masquerade, but the clothes are undeniably fun, especially for evening wear.

Hermès (⊠ 131 Bloor St. W, ☎ 416/968–8626), a tiny boutique, caters to the horse- and hound-loving set with the house's trademark casual wear, accessories, handbags, and luggage.

Kitsch Boutique (⊠ 325 Lonsdale Rd., ☎ 416/481–6712) in Forest Hill offers evening dresses, shoes, suits, and everything funky in between. There's also a basement where slow sellers are relegated until they're scooped up at half price.

Mendocino (⊠ 365 Queen St. W, ☎ 416/593–1011) carries the best of the mid-price funky lines, from Laundry to Daryl K. It's a great stop if you have limited time and want to pack a lot in, since you can peruse the day and evening designs of a number of lines here.

Parade (⊠ 315 Queen St. W, ☎ 416/971–7767), known for Betsey Johnson–esque dresses, specializes in whimsical and flirtatious female fashion.

Plaza Escada (⊠ 110 Bloor St. W, ☎ 416/964–2265) is a spacious store carrying the designer line of chic Italian creations.

At **Prada** (⊠ 131 Bloor St. W, Unit 5, ☎ 416/513–0400), the avant-garde designs are overshadowed only by the brilliant celadon interior of the store and the traffic-stopping window displays.

Price Roman (✉ 267 Queen St. W, ☎ 416/979–7363) sells edgy career wear and separates. Think Jil Sander minimalism combined with Alexander McQueen's sexy cutouts and surprising fabric choices.
San Remo (✉ 23 St. Thomas St., ☎ 416/920–3195), with its lavender walls, is where you can find that ultrafeminine yet funky piece.
Sunde (✉ 55 Bloor St. W, ☎ 416/944–8406) showcases smart and sexy little suits that put a new spin on office wear. If a lavender miniskirted Versace suit is out of your price range, Sunde offers the next-best thing.

VINTAGE CLOTHING
Black Market (✉ 319 Queen St. W, ☎ 416/591–7945), tucked away on the second floor overlooking Queen Street, sells vintage for real aficionados. You have to hunt through racks and bins—very thrift shop—but the bargains are here.
Courage My Love (✉ 14 Kensington St., ☎ 416/979–1992) is probably the best vintage store in Kensington Market. The place is crammed with the coolest retro stuff, from sunglasses to tuxedos. The in-house cats add a nice touch.
Preloved (✉ 611 Queen St. W, ☎ 416/504–8704) was created by former models and fashion insiders who have combed the vintage market for couture pieces from the '50s to be offered at vintage prices. If you want a piece of fashion history, this is the place to find it.

Discount Clothing and Housewares
Winners (✉ 57 Spadina Ave., ☎ 416/585–2052) offers designer lines at rock-bottom prices. This is Toronto's best bargain outlet.

Food Markets
Kensington Market (✉ northwest of Dundas St. and Spadina Ave., ☎ no phone) is an outdoor market with a vibrant ethnic mix. This is where you'll find delightful and exotic Caribbean foods—great cheese, coffee, nuts, and spices, natural foods, South American delicacies, Portuguese bakeries, and charming restaurants. Vintage-clothing lovers will delight in the trove of shops tucked into houses lining the streets. Saturday is the best day to go, preferably by public transit; parking is difficult.
St. Lawrence Market (✉ Front and Jarvis Sts., ☎ 416/392–7219) is best early (from 5 AM) on Saturday, when, in addition to the permanent indoor market on the south side of Front Street, there's a farmer's market in the building on the north side. The historic south market was once Toronto's city hall, and it fronted the lake before extensive landfill projects were undertaken; it's open all week except Monday and has good selections in everything from produce to equipment for make-your-own wine and beer.

Food Shops
All the Best Fine Foods (✉ 1099 Yonge St., ☎ 416/928–3330) provides imported cheeses and good local breads as well as high-quality prepared foods and condiments.
Big Carrot Natural Food Market (✉ 348 Danforth Ave., ☎ 416/466–2129), a large and adventurous health-food supermarket, carries large selections of organic produce, health and beauty aids, and vitamins. There's a café on site and freshly prepared foods for takeout.
Pusateri's (✉ 1539 Avenue Rd., ☎ 416/785–9100) started as a produce stand in Little Italy and today is Toronto's deluxe supermarket, with a wide range of in-house prepared foods, local and imported delicacies, and desserts and breads from the city's best bakers. It's great for putting together a picnic.
Royal Secrets of the World (✉ 100 Front St. W, ☎ 416/368–2511) is where to go for the truly unique items, such as chocolate-covered jalapeño peppers, unique sushi, and marshmallow sandwiches.

Fur

Fur-central is Spadina Avenue, from Queen Street north to Dundas Street.
Magder Furs (✉ 202 Spadina Ave., ☎ 416/504–6077), run by fur king
Paul Magder, is where the ladies who lunch have bought coats and jackets for more than two decades. They also refurbish fur and do alter-
ations while you wait.

Home Decor and Furnishings

Brendan's On Bloor (✉ 60 Bloor St. W, ☎ 416/921–8997) sells high-
end accessories for the bedroom and bathroom, including some of the
best linens in Toronto.

Caban (✉ 262-264 Queen St. W, ☎ 416/596–0386) is Club Monaco's
concept store for the home. The bright, 20,000-square-ft flagship has
themed rooms, a listening booth, a kitchen, and a fireplace. Besides furniture and housewares, you can also buy clothing, books, and music.

Demarco Perpich (✉ 1116 Yonge St., ☎ 416/967–0893) is a floral bounty
with adorable arrangements and garden-inspired accents for the home.

Hollace Cluny (✉ 1070 Yonge St., ☎ 416/968–7894) sells mainly
modern furnishings and accents from chrome pieces to letter holders.

IKEA (✉ 15 Provost Dr., ☎ 416/222–4532) is worth the crowds and
the 45-minute drive from downtown. It offers high-quality items at reasonable prices, from picture frames to living room sets. Most furniture requires assembly.

Pack Rat (✉ 1062 Yonge St., ☎ 416/924–5613) stocks home furnishings
for a chic cottage, or for cottage chic in the city.

Robin Kay (✉ 276 Queen St. W, ☎ 416/585–7731; ✉ 348 Danforth
Ave., ☎ 416/466–1211; ✉ 394 Spadina Rd., ☎ 416/932–2833; ✉ 2599
Yonge St., ☎ 416/485–5097) carries homespun, eco-friendly clothing
in hemp and linen, and products to enliven any interior.

Seagull Classics Ltd. (✉ 1974 Queen St. E, ☎ 416/690–5224) specializes
in unusual lamps, including art deco–inspired brass bases sculpted in
female forms and Tiffany-style light fixtures.

Urban Mode (✉ 389 Queen St. W, ☎ 416/591–8834) carries modern
and trend-oriented home accessories from a high-heel-shaped chair to
funky wine racks and CD stands.

Yesteryear Interior Accents (✉ 1142 Queen St. E, ☎ 416/778–6888)
is the place for quality reproduction pieces with an Indonesian flair.

Jewelry

Cartier (✉ 130 Bloor St. W, ☎ 416/413–4929) caters to Toronto's elite.
The store has the best of the famed jewelry designer's creations.

Royal De Versailles (✉ 101 Bloor St. W, ☎ 416/967–7201) is well
guarded, but don't let the security at the front door scare you away.
The store is noted for having some of the most innovatively classic jewelry designs in town.

Tiffany & Co. (✉ 85 Bloor St. W, ☎ 416/921–3900) makes the grade
for breakfast or anytime. This is still the ultimate for variety and quality in classic jewelry.

Kitchenware and Tabletop

Ashley China (✉ 55 Bloor St. W, ☎ 416/964–2900) has a computer
system capable of tracking almost any china pattern ever made. Crystal and china are beautifully displayed, and prices are decent on expensive names such as Waterford. If Ashley's doesn't stock a pattern,
the staff can find it for you.

The Cook's Place (✉ 488 Danforth Ave., ☎ 416/461–5211), with
everything from baking pans to that hard-to-find gadget or utensil, may
impress even the most cosmopolitan chef.

Word Of Mouth (✉ 1134 Yonge St., ☎ 416/929–6885) sells kitchen
appliances, accessories, and tools at very competitive prices.

Music and Stereo Equipment

Bay Bloor Radio (✉ Manulife Centre, 55 Bloor St. W, ☎ 416/967–1122), a stereo haven, has the latest equipment and has sound-sealed listening rooms that allow the connoisseur to test-drive equipment.

HMV (✉ 50 Bloor St. W, ☎ 416/324–9979; ✉ 333 Yonge St., ☎ 416/596–0333) has the largest selection of CDs of all categories in the city. In-store listening stations allow consumers to sample any CD prior to purchase.

Metropolis (✉ 162-A Spadina Ave. W, ☎ 416/364–0230) carries electronic music of all varieties. This is an especially good spot for people interested in the happenings of Toronto's underground.

Penguin Music (✉ 2 McCaul St. W, ☎ 416/597–1687) is a slender little store that packs a mighty wallop. A comprehensive selection of new and used CDs and LPs from the world of independent music awaits the buyer.

Rotate This (✉ 620 Queen St. W, ☎ 416/504–8447) is something of a mecca among record buyers in the know. It specializes in underground and independent music from Canada, the United States, and beyond. Shoppers will find CDs as well as LPs, T-shirts, magazines, concert tickets, and other treats.

Sam the Record Man (✉ 347 Yonge St., ☎ 416/977–4650) is a Toronto institution, having occupied the corner of Yonge and Gould streets for more than three decades. A wide assortment of music is stocked, and the bargain bins are always overflowing.

Soundscapes (✉ 572 College St., ☎ 416/537–1620) is a new, independent shop that will satisfy the hip and fans of early Americana. It's crammed with pop, rock, jazz, blues, folk, ambient, psychedelic, and electronic titles. Selections and organization reflect a love of music and its ever-expanding history.

Vortex (✉ 229 Queen St. W, ☎ 416/598–4039), well known and well frequented, is revered as the best used-CD store in the city.

Shoes

Brown's (✉ Eaton Centre, ☎ 416/979–9270; ✉ Holt Renfrew, 50 Bloor St. W, ☎ 416/960–4925) has an excellent selection of shoes, including the latest designer models from Manolo Blahnik to Steve Madden. Brown's also carries a broad range of handbags and boots.

David's (✉ 66 Bloor St. W, ☎ 416/920–1000) has a somewhat subdued but always elegant collection.

Get Out Side (✉ 437 Queen St. W, ☎ 416/593–5598) carries funky street wear and footwear for men and women, including an entire wall of sneakers.

Mephisto Boutique (✉ 1177 Yonge St., ☎ 416/968–7026) has been making its fine walking shoes since the 1960s—all from natural materials. Passionate walkers swear by these shoes and claim they never, ever wear out—even in cross-Europe treks.

Pegabo (✉ 91 Bloor St. W, ☎ 416/323–3722) sells knockoff versions of designer shoes.

Zola (✉ 1726 Avenue Rd., ☎ 416/783–8688) is tiny, but it's what's inside—a selection of women's shoes that includes the likes of Sigerson Morrison and Emma Hope—that counts.

Sporting Goods

Nike (✉ 110 Bloor St. W, ☎ 416/921–6453) has two floors of everything the famous brand name has to offer, from athletic equipment to sneakers.

Sporting Life (✉ 2665 Yonge St., ☎ 416/485–1611), in Toronto's north end, has become the ultimate place for sports equipment and apparel. The first off-the-mark with the latest sports trends, this is the place to get snowboard gear and advice on where to go to use it.

Trailhead (✉ 61 Front St. E, ☎ 416/862–0881) started life catering to camp and canoe enthusiasts but has grown to include sporting equipment for activities from racquetball to rock climbing. Still, this store's specialty is rugged outdoor sports, and the staff consists of real experts who can offer great advice on the best gear.

TORONTO A TO Z

To research prices, get advice from other travelers, and book travel arrangements, visit www.fodors.com.

AIR TRAVEL TO AND FROM TORONTO

Toronto is served by American, Delta, Northwest, United, US Airways, Air Canada, and Canadian Airlines International, as well as more than a dozen European and Asian carriers with easy connections to many U.S. cities. Air Ontario, affiliated with Air Canada, flies between the small, downtown Island Airport and Ottawa, Montréal, and London, Ontario. (☞ Air Travel *in* Smart Travel Tips A to Z for airline telephone numbers.)

AIRPORTS AND TRANSFERS

Flights into Toronto land at the Lester B. Pearson International Airport, commonly called the Toronto airport, 32 km (20 mi) northwest of downtown. Island Airport, in downtown Toronto, can be a convenient alternative to Pearson International.

➤ AIRPORT INFORMATION: **Lester B. Pearson International Airport** (✉ Airport Rd., ☎ 416/247–7678). **Island Airport** (✉ take the ferry from the foot of Bay St., ☎ 888/247–2262 Air Ontario).

AIRPORT TRANSFER

Although Pearson International Airport is not far from downtown, the drive can take well over an hour during weekday rush hours. Taxis and limos to a hotel or attraction near the lake can cost $40 or more. Airport cabs have fixed rates to different parts of the city. You must pay the full fare from the airport, but it's often possible to negotiate a lower fare from downtown, where airport cabs compete with regular city cabs. It's illegal for city cabs to pick up passengers at the airport, unless they are called—a time-consuming process, but sometimes worth the wait. Some airport and downtown hotels offer free shuttle bus service from the airport.

If you rent a car at the airport, ask for a street map of the city. Highway 427 runs south some 6 km (4 mi) to the lakeshore. Here you pick up the Queen Elizabeth Way (QEW) east to the Gardiner Expressway, which runs east into the heart of downtown. If you take the QEW west, you'll find yourself swinging around Lake Ontario, toward Hamilton, Niagara-on-the-Lake, and Niagara Falls.

Pacific Western Transportation Service offers express coach service linking the airport to three subway stops in the southwest and north-central areas of the city. Buses depart several times each hour from 8 AM to 11:30 PM. Fares average $6–$9. The service to and from several downtown hotels operates every 20 minutes from 6:25 AM to at least 10:45 PM daily and costs approximately $13.75.

➤ TAXIS AND SHUTTLES: **Pacific Western Transportation Service** (☎ 905/564–6333 automated; 905/564–3232 administration).

BUS TRAVEL TO AND FROM TORONTO

The Toronto Coach Terminal serves a number of lines, including Greyhound, Trentway-Wagar, Trantario Coachlines, Ontario Northland,

Penetang-Midland Coach Lines (PMCL), and Can-AR. Greyhound Lines has regular bus service into Toronto from the United States and Canada. From Detroit the trip takes five hours, from Buffalo two to three hours, and from Chicago and New York City 11 hours.

➤ Bus Information: **Toronto Coach Terminal** (✉ 610 Bay St., north of Dundas St., ☎ 416/393–7911). **Greyhound Lines** (☎ 416/367–8747; 800/231–2222 in the U.S.).

BUS TRAVEL WITHIN TORONTO

All buses accept exact change, tickets, or tokens. Paper transfers are free; pick one up from the driver when you pay your fare.

➤ Bus Information: **Toronto Transit Commission** (TTC; ☎ 416/393–4636, WEB www.ttc.ca).

CAR TRAVEL

Detroit–Windsor and Buffalo–Fort Erie crossings can be slow, especially on weekends and holidays. The wide Highway 401—reaching up to 16 lanes as it slashes across metro Toronto from the airport on the west almost as far as the zoo on the east—is the major link between Windsor, Ontario (and Detroit), and Montréal. It's also known as the Macdonald-Cartier Freeway but is generally called simply the 401. There are no tolls, but be warned: in weekday rush hour the 401 can become dreadfully crowded, even stop-and-go.

From Buffalo or Niagara Falls, take the Queen Elizabeth Way (QEW), which curves up along the western shore of Lake Ontario, eventually turns into the Gardiner Expressway, and flows right into the downtown core. Last year, parts of the Gardiner were being removed, and this highway "improvement" will continue throughout 2002.

Yonge Street, which begins at the lakefront, is called Highway 11 once you get north of Toronto and continues all the way to the Ontario–Minnesota border, at Rainy River. At 1,896 km (1,176 mi), it's the longest street in the world.

EMERGENCY SERVICES

The Canadian Automobile Association has 24-hour road service; membership benefits are extended to U.S. AAA members.

➤ Contacts: **Canadian Automobile Association** (☎ 416/222–5222).

RULES OF THE ROAD

Pedestrian crosswalks are sprinkled throughout the city; they are marked clearly by yellow overhead signs and very large painted Xs. All a pedestrian has to do is stick out a hand, and cars (you hope!) screech to a halt in both directions. Right turns on red lights, after a complete stop, are nearly always permitted, except where otherwise posted.

CONSULATES

➤ United Kingdom: **British Consulate General** (✉ 777 Bay St., at College St., M56 2G2, ☎ 416/593–1267).

➤ United States: **Consulate General of the United States** (✉ 360 University Ave., north of Queen St., M56 1S4, ☎ 416/595–1700, WEB www.usembassycanada.gov).

EMERGENCIES

The Dental Emergency Service operates from 8 AM to midnight. Concierges at hotel desks can recommend doctors.

➤ Doctors and Dentists: **Dental Emergency Service** (✉ 1650 Yonge St., ☎ 416/485–7121).

➤ Hospitals: **St. Michael's Hospital** (✉ 30 Bond St., ☎ 416/360–4000). **Toronto General Hospital** (✉ 200 Elizabeth St., ☎ 416/598–9135).

➤ Hot Lines: **Ambulance, fire, and police** (☎ 911).

➤ LATE-NIGHT PHARMACIES: **Pharma Plus Drugmart** (✉ Church St. and Wellesley St. E, ☎ 416/924–7769) is open daily from 8 AM to midnight. Some locations of the **Shoppers Drug Mart** (✉ 700 Bay St., ☎ 416/979–2424; ✉ 2500 Hurontario St., Mississauga, ☎ 905/896–2500) are open 24 hours.

LODGING

Some 10 homes in various parts of the city have signed up with Bed and Breakfast Homes of Toronto; write for a brochure detailing individual homes. Bed & Breakfast Metropolitan Registry of Toronto registry service has about 30 city and suburban homes on its books. More than two dozen private homes in downtown Toronto are affiliated with Toronto Bed & Breakfast.

➤ RESERVATION SERVICES: **Bed and Breakfast Homes of Toronto** (✉ Box 46093, College Park Postal Station, M5B 2L8, ☎ 416/363–6362); **Bed & Breakfast Metropolitan Registry of Toronto** (✉ 650 Dupont St., Suite 113, M6G 4B1, ☎ 416/964–2566, FAX 416/960–9529); **Toronto Bed & Breakfast** (✉ 253 College St., Box 269 M5T 1R5, ☎ 705/738–9449, FAX 705/738–0155, WEB www.torontobandb.com).

MEDIA

The *Toronto Star,* the *Toronto Sun,* the *Globe and Mail,* and the *National Post* are all daily newspapers. *NOW* and *eye* are free newspapers with entertainment listings, printed every Thursday.

SUBWAY TRAVEL

The Toronto Transit Commission runs one of the safest, cleanest, most trustworthy systems of its kind anywhere. There are two subway lines, with 60 stations along the way: the Bloor/Danforth line, which crosses Toronto about 5 km (3 mi) north of the lakefront, from east to west, and the Yonge/University line, which loops north and south, like a giant "U," with the bottom of the "U" at Union Station. A light rapid transit (LRT) line extends service to Harbourfront along Queen's Quay. Tokens and tickets are sold in subway stations and at hundreds of convenience stores along the many routes of the TTC. Get your transfers just after you pay your fare and enter the subway; you'll find them in machines on your way down to the trains.

TAXIS

The meter begins at $2.50 and includes the first .2 km (.1 mi). Each additional .235 km (.146 mi) is 25¢—as is each passenger in excess of four. The waiting time "while under engagement" is 25¢ for every 33 seconds—and in a traffic jam, this could add up. Still, it's possible to take a cab across downtown Toronto for $8–$9. The largest companies are Beck, Co-op, Diamond, Metro, and Royal. For more information, call the Metro Licensing Commission.

➤ TAXI COMPANIES: **Beck** (☎ 416/751–5555); **Co-op** (☎ 416/504–2667); **Diamond** (☎ 416/366–6868); **Metro** (☎ 416/504–8294); **Royal** (☎ 416/785–3322); **Metro Licensing Commission** (☎ 416/392–3000).

TOURS

BOAT TOURS

You can take tours of the Toronto harbor and islands on comfortably equipped Toronto Tours boats for about $15. The hourly tour passes the Toronto Islands, with lovely city views. Boats leave from the Pier Six Building next to Queen's Quay Terminal early May–mid-October, daily 10–6. Tours leave as late as 7:15 PM in summer. Other boats depart from the Westin Harbour Castle hotel at the foot of Yonge Street.

➤ FEES AND SCHEDULES: **Toronto Tours** (☎ 416/869–1372, WEB www.torontotours.com).

BUS TOURS

Gray Line Sightseeing Bus Tours has tours April through November. The two-hour tours start at the **Toronto Coach Terminal** (✉ 610 Bay St., north of Dundas St.) and include Eaton Centre, the Old and New City Halls, Queen's Park, the University of Toronto, Yorkville, Ontario Place, and Casa Loma. The fare is $29 and the tour departs every day at 10 AM from the Toronto Coach Terminal.

Olde Town Toronto Tours has hop-on, hop-off tours on London-style double-decker buses and trolleys. Both take you around the city on a two-hour loop and cost $29; your ticket is good for 24 hours, so you can get on and off. Tours leave every 20 minutes in summer. Call for a winter schedule. The company also has tours to Niagara Falls.
➤ FEES AND SCHEDULES: **Gray Line Sightseeing Bus Tours** (☎ 416/594–3310); **Olde Town Toronto Tours** (☎ 416/614–0999, WEB www.old-etown.toronto.on.ca).

HIKING TOURS

The Bruce Trail Association arranges day and overnight hikes around Toronto and its environs.
➤ FEES AND SCHEDULES: **Bruce Trail Association** (☎ 800/665–4453, WEB www.brucetrail.org).

WALKING TOURS

Heritage Toronto has free guided walking tours on weekends and occasional holiday Mondays from mid-April to early October. They last 1½ to 2 hours and cover one neighborhood or topic, such as the historic theater block.
➤ FEES AND SCHEDULES: **Heritage Toronto** (☎ 416/392–6827 Ext. 265).

TRAIN TRAVEL

Amtrak runs a daily train to Toronto from Chicago (a 12-hour trip) and another from New York City (12 hours). Canada's VIA Rail runs trains to most major cities in Canada; travel along the Windsor–Québec City corridor is particularly well-served. Substantial discounts are available on VIA Rail if you book at least five days in advance or if you have an International Student Identity Card. Amtrak and VIA Rail operate from Union Station. You can walk underground to many hotels—a real boon in inclement weather. There's a cab stand outside the main entrance of the station.
➤ TRAIN INFORMATION: **Amtrak** (☎ 800/872–7245); **VIA Rail** (☎ 416/366–8411); **Union Station** (✉ 65–75 Front St., between Bay and York Sts.).

TRANSPORTATION AROUND TORONTO

Much of Toronto is laid out on a grid. Yonge (pronounced "young") Street is the main north–south artery. Most major cross streets are numbered east and west of Yonge Street. If you're looking for 180 St. Clair Avenue West, you want a building a few blocks *west* of Yonge Street; 75 Queen Street East is a block or so *east* of Yonge Street. You can call the TTC from 7 AM to 11:30 PM for information on how to take public transit to any street or attraction in the city. The Toronto Transit Commission (TTC) publishes a useful *Ride Guide* that shows nearly every major place of interest and how to reach it by public transit. These guides are available in most subways and many other places around the city.

Riding the city's streetcars is a great way to capture the flavor of the city, because you pass through many neighborhoods. The main streetcar lines running east–west are College, Queen, King, and Dundas, following those streets. The new Spadina line runs north–south. All of them, especially the King line, are interesting rides with frequent service.

FARES AND SCHEDULES

At press time the fare for buses, streetcars, and trolleys was $2.25 for adults in exact change. Five-fare tickets are available for $8.50, and you can buy tokens at subway stations. The subways stop running at 2 AM, but the TTC has bus service from 1 AM to 5:30 AM on many major streets, including Queen, College, Bloor, Yonge, part of Dufferin, and as far north as Finch and Eglinton. The Day Pass costs $7 and is good for unlimited travel for one person, weekdays after 9:30 AM, and all day Saturday. On Sunday and holidays, it's good for up to six persons (maximum two adults) for unlimited travel. If you plan to stay in Toronto for a month or longer, consider the Metropass, a photo-identity card ($88.50 for adults plus $3.25 extra for the photo), which allows unlimited rides in one calendar month. Tokens, tickets, and passes can be purchased at subway stations and convenience stores.

➤ CONTACTS: **Toronto Transit Commission** (TTC; ☎ 416/393–4636 or 416/393–8663).

VISITOR INFORMATION

Tourism Toronto has its office at Queen's Quay Terminal. Traveller's Aid Society recommends restaurants and hotels and distributes subway maps and Ontario sales-tax rebate forms.

➤ TOURIST INFORMATION: **Tourism Toronto** (✉ 207 Queen's Quay W, Suite 509, Box 106, M5J 1A7, ☎ 416/203–2600 or 800/363–1990, WEB www.torontotourism.com); **Traveller's Aid Society** (✉ Union Station, arrivals level and basement level, Room B23, ☎ 416/366–7788; ✉ Pearson Airport, Terminal I, arrivals level, past Customs, near Area B, ☎ 905/676–2868; ✉ Pearson Airport, Terminal 2, between international and domestic arrivals, ☎ 905/676–2869; ✉ Pearson Airport, Terminal 3, arrivals level, near international side, ☎ 905/612–5890).

8 PROVINCE OF ONTARIO

OTTAWA, ALGONQUIN PROVINCIAL PARK, WINDSOR, NIAGARA, LONDON

With shorelines on four of the five Great Lakes, Ontario is Canada's second-largest and most urbanized province, containing both the nation's capital, Ottawa, and its biggest city, Toronto. Of Ontario's 11 million people, 90% live within a narrow strip just north of the U.S. border. Beyond this busy region lie rolling farmlands, quiet towns and villages, woodland lakes and rivers, and the vast wilderness of the Canadian Shield.

Updated by
Rosemary
Allerston

ONTARIO IS AN IROQUOIAN WORD often interpreted as "beautiful lake" or "glittering waters." It's an apt name for a province whose vastness (more than a million square km or 412,582 square mi) contains 177,388 square km (68,490 square mi) of fresh water—one-fourth of all there is in the world.

More than half of this huge province's population lives in a small fraction of its geographical area: the four cities of the "Golden Horseshoe," at the western end of Lake Ontario. Dominant is the megacity of Toronto, with more than 4.5 million people. Farther east, 280,000 Ontarians live in Oshawa and its heavily populated suburbs. Southwest of Toronto are Hamilton and Wentworth, with 650,000 people, and St. Catharines, with 290,000.

The towns and cities of northern Ontario, on the other hand, are farther apart, strung along the railway lines that first brought them into being. The discovery of gold, silver, uranium, and other minerals by railroad construction gangs sparked mining booms that established such communities as Sudbury, Cobalt, and Timmins.

Ontario has the most varied landscape of any Canadian province. Its most conspicuous topographical feature is the Niagara Escarpment, which runs from Niagara to Tobermory at the tip of the Bruce Peninsula in Lake Huron. The northern 90% of Ontario is part of the Canadian Shield—worn-down mountain ranges of the world's oldest rock, pitted with lakes and cloaked in boreal forest.

The province's climate ranges from subarctic along Hudson and James bays, to humid-continental in its most southerly latitudes, which parallel those of northern California. Toward Niagara Falls, in a partial rain shadow of the Escarpment, the gentle climate allows the growing of tender fruits and grapes, making it Canada's largest wine-producing area.

Pleasures and Pastimes

The Arts

By combining public and private resources, Ontario has fostered one of North America's most supportive environments for the arts. Each year thousands flock to see great Shakespeare at the Stratford Festival and top-notch plays at Niagara-on-the-Lake's Shaw Festival. Toronto is the world's third-largest center for English-language theater, but smaller cities have their artistic treasures, too, including fine music festivals. Hamilton has Ontario's third-largest art gallery, and Ottawa's National Arts Centre is the biggest performing-arts complex in the country.

Dining

The cuisine of this vast province runs the gamut from fresh-caught fish in Cottage Country to French-influenced dishes in Ottawa and great home-style Canadian fare such as maple-syrup pie in southern Ontario. Given the enormous British influence here, there's plenty of roast beef, shepherd's pie, and rice pudding, especially in the English-dominated enclaves of London, Stratford, and Hamilton. Ontarians crave Tim Horton's doughnuts, found at franchise shops in virtually every city.

CATEGORY	COST*
$$$$	over $32
$$$	$22–$32
$$	$13–$21
$	under $13

*per person, in Canadian dollars, for a main course at dinner

Lodging

Reservations are strongly recommended anywhere in Ontario during summer months, and most importantly in Ottawa, Toronto, and Niagara Falls. Generally, you get what you pay for at Ontario hotels and motels. Taxes are seldom included in quoted prices, but rates sometimes include food, especially in areas such as Muskoka and Haliburton, where many resorts offer meal plans.

Most major cities have bed-and-breakfast associations. Prices vary according to the location and facilities but are comparable to those found south of the border. All types of accommodations tend to be more expensive in tourist venues. In Niagara Falls, for example, hotel and motel rates are determined by proximity to the famous waterfall.

CATEGORY	COST*
$$$$	over $200
$$$	$150–$200
$$	$100–$150
$	under $100

*All prices are in Canadian dollars, for a standard double room, excluding 7% GST and 5% room tax.

Museums

The museums of Canada's most populous province document Ontario's evolution from a pioneer outpost to a lively urban society. Living-history museums, such as Upper Canada Village, Fort Henry, and Old Fort William, re-create life in earlier centuries. The story of the country's development can also be traced through paintings, carvings, and artifacts—the legacy of European, Canadian, and native artists—that are on display at the National Gallery of Canada in Ottawa and at regional museums like the McMichael Canadian Art Collection in Kleinburg, near Toronto. Numerous institutions document the War of 1812.

Outdoor Activities and Sports

CAMPING

Many of Ontario's 272 provincial parks and all its national parks (except Point Pelee) offer a variety of services for campers, from electrical outlets and sturdy, covered picnic shelters to laundry facilities and camp stores for provisions. Some also have cottages for rent. Additionally, many sponsor educational programs that teach children about wilderness survival techniques and nature.

In southern Ontario, most parks operate from mid-May until Labor Day weekend; in northern Ontario they are open from early June until Labor Day, though increasing interest in winter sports like cross-country skiing and dogsledding means more parks are staying open year-round. Even when "closed," however, the parks never completely shut down, and visitors are welcome in the off-season, although few facilities are maintained. Some parks may be gated to prevent vehicular entry, but all are accessible to pedestrians from sunrise to sunset. Vault privies are open, fireplace grates are typically available, and fees are collected through self-serve registration. Winter camping is allowed in some provincial parks, although most are unsupervised and facilities are limited. During fall and winter months reservations are not required at most parks, but call ahead to make sure.

FISHING

Ontario has about 250,000 lakes and 150,000 rivers, which contain myriad species of fish. The favorite trophies are salmon and trout, but many anglers lust after pike or muskie whereas others swear that battling a black bass on light tackle is life's ultimate piscatorial challenge.

SKIING

This province is rich with cross-country and downhill ski trails. Nordic ski trails exist just about everywhere you find snow and accommodations for skiers. Ontario has hundreds of alpine slopes, although most have vertical drops of less than 660 ft. All major Ontario ski centers have high-tech snowmaking equipment, which ensures good skiing from late November through early April.

Shopping

Visitors from the United States often relish Ontario's handsome inventory of things British, scooping up everything from china teacups to crumpet tins. Others marvel at the province's rich handicraft tradition. Ottawa, Sault Ste. Marie, Midland, and Thunder Bay have museum shops and galleries that specialize in First Nations crafts, including Inuit carvings and prints. Antiques stores abound; some of the best are in small towns like Cobourg, Peterborough, and St. Jacobs.

Exploring Ontario

You could spend several months exploring this enormous province and still not see it all. But if your time is limited, consider one of these linked itineraries covering the southern part of the province. You might choose one or all of these excursions, depending on how many days you have. You can take in most of the major sights in just a few days, plus see some special little corners that even many Ontarians don't know about.

Numbers in the text correspond to numbers in the margin and on the Southern Ontario, Downtown Ottawa, Greater Ottawa and Hull, Niagara Falls, and Northern Ontario maps.

Great Itineraries

IF YOU HAVE 3 DAYS

Spend two days and nights in Canada's capital city, 🖈 **Ottawa** ①–⑲, beginning at the Parliament Buildings, where a variety of indoor sights and outdoor events could keep you occupied for an afternoon. Ottawa's colorful downtown and excursions to neighboring Hull offer numerous historical and cultural activities. On Day 3, drive to Morrisburg and **Upper Canada Village** ⑳, a superbly re-created pre-Confederation community of the 1860s. Then set out for **Prescott** ㉑, where you can rediscover the War of 1812 at Fort Wellington National Historic Site. You can easily return to Ottawa the same day.

IF YOU HAVE 5 DAYS

Spend Day 1 in historic 🖈 **Kingston** ㉒, Upper Canada's capital from 1841 to 1844. The city is famous for its well-preserved limestone architecture and lively waterfront facing the St. Lawrence River. Your explorations might include massive Fort Henry or the Marine Museum of the Great Lakes. You can also enjoy a few hours touring the scenic Thousand Islands aboard a well-appointed cruise boat. On Day 2, set out along the Heritage Highway route through **Prince Edward County** ㉓, a Loyalist enclave with strong ties to Sir John A. Macdonald, Canada's first prime minister. Quinte's Isle, as locals call it, juts into Lake Ontario; it's dotted with picturesque waterside towns. When the Heritage Highway rejoins Highway 2 on the mainland, turn west toward **Cobourg** ㉔, where you can investigate the town's lovely centerpiece, Victoria Hall. You'll still have plenty of time to drive on to 🖈 **Peterborough** ㉖. Day 3 can be devoted to a number of adventures in and around this small city and the Kawartha Lakes. You might visit the Trent Canal Locks, then drive to Serpent Mounds Park at **Keene** ㉕ and perhaps to Lang Pioneer Village. You shouldn't miss the ancient rock

carvings preserved at **Petroglyphs Provincial Park** ㉗, northeast of Peterborough on Highway 28. On Day 4, head through cottage country
on Highways 115 and 35 to the northern reaches of Lake Simcoe and
Orillia ㉛, home of Casino Rama and the quieter delights of the Stephen
Leacock Museum. Your next destination is ▣ **Penetanguishene and
Midland** ㉙ on Georgian Bay. Along the way, stop at Ste-Marie among
the Hurons and the Martyrs' Shrine, both on Highway 12. On Day 5,
there's time to visit the Huronia Museum and Ouendat Village in
downtown Midland before you embark on a scenic, three-hour cruise
to Georgian Bay's 30,000 Islands, a memorable excursion on some of
Canada's loveliest waters.

IF YOU HAVE 7 DAYS

Make Day 1 a Saturday so you can visit the **Kitchener and Waterloo** ㉊
Farmer's Market. You have to arrive early (the market opens at 6 AM)
to have your choice of fresh produce, homemade sausages, pastries,
and preserves. In the afternoon, drive a few kilometers north to ▣ **St.
Jacobs** ㉑, in the heart of Mennonite country, where attractions include
a huge flea market, several restaurants, and lots of interesting little shops.
On Day 2, travel on to ▣ **Stratford** ㉒, home of the acclaimed Stratford Festival and a centerpiece of Canada's rich artistic landscape. You
can take in some of the world's best theater, shop to your heart's content, and dine in style at some of the province's very best restaurants.
It's best to stay here at least two nights (Days 2 and 3). On Day 4 drive
southeast to the Queen Elizabeth Way then aim for ▣ **Niagara-on-the-
Lake** ㉗, also a town where you may want to spend at least two days
to take everything in. There are historic sites and heritage buildings
galore, plus a horde of interesting shops. Several of the famous old inns
have been renovated to luxury standards, complete with spas and
sumptuous cuisine. The Shaw Festival provides excellent entertainment
in summer. Spend the evening of Day 4 plus Day 5 in town, enjoy a
play, and set out on Day 6 to tour the vineyards and wineries of the
flourishing Niagara Peninsula. You could catch another play in Niagara-on-the-Lake the night of Day 6, or head straight on to the hustle
and excitement of ▣ **Niagara Falls** ㊿–㊻, a short drive and a world
away. Plan to spend Day 7 here; this doesn't mean you can take in all
the essentials, but you can come close. Park your car and hop aboard
the People Mover, an inexpensive shuttle run by the Niagara Parks Commission. It stops where you catch the major tours, from Journey Behind the Falls to the Spanish Aerocar and *Maid of the Mist*. You can
also fly over the gorge in a helicopter, check out the wax museums on
Clifton Hill, and ride to the top of a viewing tower. If you long for respite,
drop into the Butterfly Conservatory. On the last night of your seven-
day tour, fall asleep to the thunder of the Falls, knowing you've almost
seen it all.

When to Tour the Province of Ontario

In winter Ontario's weather veers toward the severe, making road travel
difficult away from major highways, and many museums and attractions are closed or have limited hours. Still, if you like to ski, skate,
snowmobile, or ice fish, you may want to visit during the cold months:
the province offers some of the world's best winter recreation opportunities. Otherwise, it's best to visit from April through October, when
most sights are open longer. Try to avoid the highways over the busy
July 1 Canada Day weekend. The warm months also offer travelers
the chance to catch some cultural highlights, especially the Stratford
and Shaw festivals, as well as to enjoy outdoor action, such as boating and hiking—or even just resting on a beach.

Southern Ontario

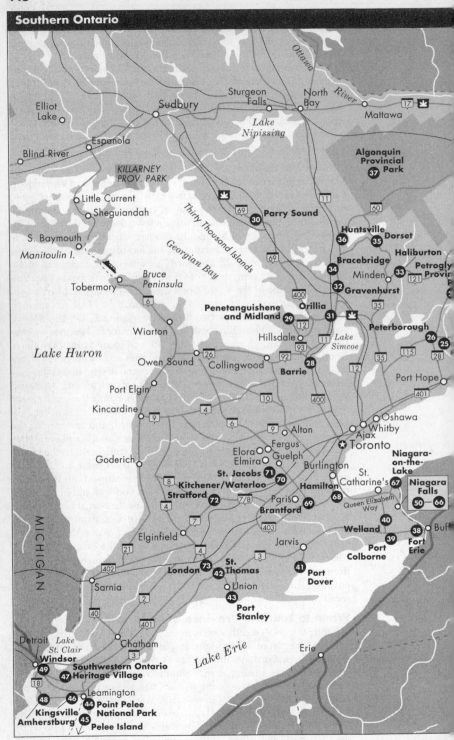

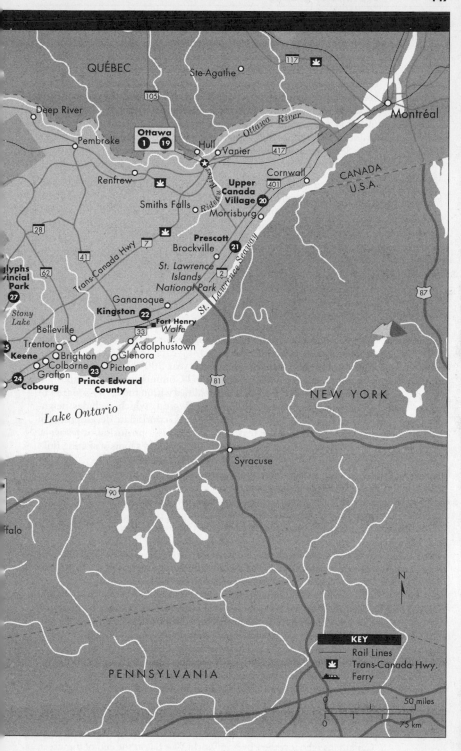

OTTAWA

Only a few scattered settlers lived in what is now Ottawa in 1826, when Colonel John By and his Royal Engineers arrived to build the Rideau Canal, which links the Ottawa River to Lake Ontario. By's headquarters fast became a rowdy backwoods settlement as hordes arrived seeking employment on the largest construction project on the continent. The canal, completed in 1832, was hacked through 200 km (124 mi) of swamp, rock, and lakes whose different levels were overcome by locks. Bytown, as the settlement was called, officially became a city in 1855, when the population had reached 10,000. It was renamed Ottawa, after the Algonquin-speaking First Nation of the region.

Canadians are taught in school that it was Queen Victoria's fault their capital is inconveniently situated off the main east–west route along the Great Lakes. From 1841 to 1857, politicians dithered over several towns vying to be the capital of Canada and finally asked Her Majesty to decide. Victoria chose prosperous Ottawa because its beautiful setting—at the confluence of the Ottawa and Rideau rivers—was centrally located between Upper and Lower Canada (present-day Ontario and Québec). It was also reassuringly remote from the hostile United States. With the big decision finally made, construction began on the magnificent neo-Gothic Parliament Buildings that earned Ottawa the nickname "Westminster in the Wilderness."

Today's Parliament Buildings no longer stand in wilderness and have evolved considerably over the past 140 years. Indeed, the towers and spires received a face-lift to mark the year 2000. The buildings' dignity is assured by the National Capital Commission (NCC), an organization that works with all municipalities within the 2,903-square-km (1,121-square-mi) National Capital Region, which includes neighboring Hull and a big chunk of Québec, to coordinate development in the best interests of the region. The result is a profusion of festivals, parks, bicycle paths, jogging trails, and the world's longest skating rink, on an 8-km (5-mi) stretch of the Rideau Canal.

Downtown Ottawa

Given Ottawa's architectural beauty and the fact that parking is at a premium here, one of the best ways to see many of the gems in this metropolis of 720,000 is on foot.

A Good Walk

Begin your walk at the **Parliament Buildings** ①. The Centre Block and the Peace Tower are surrounded by 29 acres of lawn interspersed with statues of celebrated Canadians. Turn right onto Wellington Street and walk past Bank Street to the Bank of Canada. On Sparks Street, a block south of Wellington, you can enter the **Bank of Canada Currency Museum** ②, where seven galleries chronicle the evolution of notes and coins within the context of Canadian history. North of Wellington, on Kent Street, is the **Supreme Court** ③, housed in a stunning art deco edifice. The **Garden of the Provinces** ④ is at the western end of Wellington Street. Across from the park are the **National Archives of Canada and the National Library of Canada** ⑤, two centers of Canadian history.

Head back toward Parliament Hill via the friendly **Sparks Street Pedestrian Mall** ⑥. **Confederation Square** ⑦, where homage is paid to those Canadians who lost their lives in World War I, is at the end of the street. Adjacent to the square stands the **National Arts Centre** ⑧, a huge complex that's home to a fine orchestra plus English and French theater and dance performances. The Rideau Canal is close to the center, and

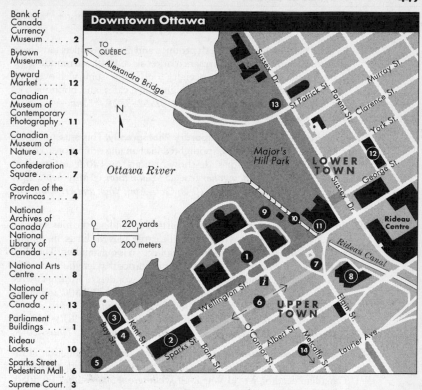

Downtown Ottawa

you can walk north along it to Ottawa's older buildings, including the **Bytown Museum** ⑨, which houses a collection of 3,500 artifacts that once belonged to Colonel By. The **Rideau Locks** ⑩ are next door, and farther down the canal, back toward Wellington Street, is the **Canadian Museum of Contemporary Photography** ⑪. The **Byward Market** ⑫, with food shops that date back a century, is several blocks east. From the market, walk west on York Street for a block and turn right on Sussex Drive. It's a five-minute stroll to the **National Gallery of Canada** ⑬, which reflects the Parliament Buildings in its modern mirror-and-granite facade. The **Canadian Museum of Nature** ⑭ is a brisk 20-minute walk or short car ride south of the Parliament Buildings, on Metcalfe Street at McLeod Street. The museum has a fabulous dinosaur display.

TIMING

You'll need at least a day to visit the sights downtown; allow more time if you wish to tour the National Gallery and the other museums. Most museums are closed Monday, but the staff at the Capital Infocentre (☎ 613/239–5000) can help you locate the ones that are open.

Sights to See

② **Bank of Canada Currency Museum.** The ancestors of the credit card are all here: bracelets made from elephant hair, cowrie shells, whales' teeth, and what is believed to be the world's largest coin (measuring 6½ ft tall and weighing 3 tons). Here, too, of course, is the country's most complete collection of Canadian notes and coins. ⊠ 245 Sparks St., ☎ 613/782–8914. ☐ Free. ☉ Tues.–Sat. 10:30–5, Sun. 1–5.

⑨ **Bytown Museum.** In the former commissariat used by the Royal Engineers and Colonel John By during the building of the Rideau Canal—the oldest stone masonry building in the city—are exhibits that record the life and times of Bytown and Ottawa. ⊠ 540 Wellington St., at *bottom of Ottawa Locks, behind Chateau Laurier Hotel,* ☎ *613/ 234–4570.* 💲 *$2.50.* ⊙ *Mon., Wed.–Fri. 10–2.*

⓬ **Byward Market.** Excellent fresh produce and maple products have been attracting shoppers to this farmers market since 1840. Surrounding the market stalls are permanent specialty food shops, some well over 100 years old, as well as restaurants, nightclubs, cafés, and boutiques. ⊠ *Between George and York Sts.,* ☎ *613/562–3325.* ⊙ *Sun.–Wed. 8–6, Thurs.–Sat. 8 AM–9 PM.*

⓫ **Canadian Museum of Contemporary Photography.** This museum holds more than 158,000 images, spotlighted in changing exhibitions. There's also a 50-seat theater for slide-show exhibits. ⊠ *1 Rideau Canal,* ☎ *613/990–8257,* WEB *cmcp.gallery.ca.* 💲 *$2 donation.* ⊙ *May–Sept., Sat.– Tues. 10–5, Wed. 4–8, Thurs. 10–8; Oct.–Apr., Wed. and Fri.–Sun. 10– 5, Thurs. 10–8.*

🐣 ⓮ **Canadian Museum of Nature.** In a castlelike building, the museum and its exhibits explore the evolution of the earth, plus the birds, mammals, and plants of Canada. The dinosaur collection is outstanding. The High Definition Cinema shows nature documentaries that let you swim with the whales in the Sea of Cortez or explore the wonders of African deserts. ⊠ *240 McLeod St., at Metcalfe St.,* ☎ *613/566–4700; 800/263–4433 in North America,* WEB *www.nature.ca.* 💲 *$5; half price Thurs. until 5, free Thurs. 5–8, cinema free.* ⊙ *May–early Sept., Fri.–Wed. 9:30–5, Thurs. 9:30–8; early Sept.–Apr., Tues.–Wed and Fri.–Sun. 10–5, Thurs. 10–8.*

➐ **Confederation Square.** In the center of this triangular junction in the heart of the city stands the **National War Memorial,** honoring the 66,651 Canadian dead of World War I. ⊠ *Wellington, Sparks, and Elgin Sts.*

➍ **Garden of the Provinces.** Two fountains and the arms and floral emblems of Canada's 10 provinces and three territories commemorate Confederation in this park. ⊠ *Southwest corner of Bay and Wellington Sts.*

➎ **National Archives of Canada and National Library of Canada.** The archives contain more than 60 million manuscripts and government records, 1 million maps, and about 11 million photographs. The National Library collects, preserves, and promotes the published heritage of Canada and exhibits books, paintings, maps, and photographs. Both institutions mount exhibitions regularly. ⊠ *395 Wellington St., at Bay St.,* ☎ *613/995–5138 Archives; 613/995–9988 Library;* WEB *www.archives.ca.* 💲 *Free.* ⊙ *Daily 9–9.*

➑ **National Arts Centre.** This complex includes an opera hall, a theater, a studio theater, and a salon for readings and concerts. The grounds are populated with sculptures by Canadian artists. The popular canal-side Le Café (☎ 613/594–5127) spills outside in warm weather. In winter it's a cozy vantage spot from which to watch skaters on the canal. ⊠ *53 Elgin St.,* ☎ *613/947–7000,* WEB *www.nac.cna.ca.*

★ ⓭ **National Gallery of Canada.** A magnificent glass-tower structure engineered by Canadian architect Moshe Safdie holds the premier collection of Canadian art in the world. In addition, it houses important collections of European and American art and hosts major traveling exhibits from around the world. Inside is the reconstructed **Rideau Convent Chapel,** a classic example of French Canadian 19th-century architecture with the only neo-Gothic fan-vaulted ceiling on the continent. The building has three restaurants and a large bookstore with publications on the arts. ⊠ *380 Sussex Dr.,* ☎ *613/990–1985 or 800/319– 2787,* WEB *national.gallery.ca.* 💲 *Free, except special exhibits.* ⊙ *May– mid-Oct., daily 10–6 (Thurs. until 8); mid-Oct–Apr., Wed.–Sun. 10– 5 (Thurs. until 8).*

★ ☙ ❶ **Parliament Buildings.** Three beloved Gothic-style buildings with copper roofs dominate the nation's capital from Parliament Hill, overlooking the Ottawa River. Originally built between 1859 and 1877, they were destroyed by fire in 1916 and rebuilt by 1917. The **Centre Block** is where the Senate and House of Commons, the two houses of Parliament, work to shape the laws of the land. The wonderfully detailed stone frieze in the foyer, which depicts Canadian history, and the masterfully carved stone pillars and provincial emblems in stained glass in the House of Commons are all works of the nationally renowned artist Eleanor Milne.

The central **Peace Tower** houses a Memorial Chamber with an Altar of Sacrifice, which bears the names of the 66,651 Canadians killed during service in World War I and the 44,895 Canadians who died in World War II. Also in the Tower is the 53-bell carillon; concerts are performed daily in summer by the Dominion Carillonneur. Outside on the lawn, there's plenty of room to observe the colorful **Changing of the Guard ceremony,** which takes place daily, late June to late August, weather permitting. The Ceremonial Guard brings together two of Canada's most historic regiments, the Canadian Grenadier Guards and the Governor General's Foot Guards.

North of the Centre Block and reached via its corridors is the **Library of Parliament,** the only part of the original Parliament Buildings saved from the fire of 1916. A statue of the young Queen Victoria is the centerpiece of the octagonal chamber, which is surrounded by ornately carved pine galleries lined with books, many of them priceless.

In front of and on either side of the Centre Block are the **East Block** and the **West Block.** The East Block has four historic rooms open to the public: the original Governor General's office restored to the period of Lord Dufferin, 1872–78; the offices of Sir John A. Macdonald and Sir Georges Étienne Cartier, Fathers of Confederation in 1867; and the Privy Council Chamber. The West Block contains offices for parliamentarians and is not open to the public.

Against the backdrop of the imposing Parliament Buildings, a free half-hour laser **Sound and Light Show** (late May–early Sept., twice nightly, one in English, one in French) highlights Canada's history. Parliament Hill is also the place to be every summer on Canada Day, July 1, for concerts, fireworks, cultural exhibitions, and free performances by top Canadian entertainers. ⊠ *Parliament Hill,* ☎ *613/992–4793 or 613/239–5000,* WEB *parliamenthill.gc.ca.* 🎦 *Free.* ☉ *Late May–early Sept., daily 9–8:30; early Sept.–late May, daily 9–4:30; 20-min tours in English or French every ½ hr; same-day reservations for tours available at the Visitor Welcome Centre, inside entrance to the Centre Block.*

❿ **Rideau Locks.** On the Rideau Canal, which runs southward through the city from the Ottawa River, the locks are a downtown landmark. ⊠ *Junction of Rideau Canal and Wellington St., where Wellington becomes Rideau St.*

❻ **Sparks Street Pedestrian Mall.** Here, the automobile has been banished, and shoppers and browsers can wander carefree in warm weather among fountains, rock gardens, sculptures, and outdoor cafés. ⊠ *1 block south of Wellington St., between Confederation Sq. and Kent St.*

❸ **Supreme Court.** Established in 1875, this body became the ultimate court of appeal in the land in 1949. The nine judges sit in their stately art deco building for three sessions each year. ⊠ *Kent and Wellington Sts.,* ☎ *613/995–4330 or 613/995–5361.* 🎦 *Free.* ☉ *Tours May–Aug., daily 9–5; Sept.–Apr., by appointment.*

Greater Ottawa and Hull

A car, taxi, or bus is needed to visit some of the other major attractions and outstanding museums in the area.

A Good Drive

Sussex Drive is Ottawa's embassy row. Take a glimpse at the entrance to 24 Sussex Drive—the **Residence of the Prime Minister** ⑮—across from **Rideau Hall** ⑯, the Governor General's home, at 1 Sussex Drive. Continue north on Sussex Drive to the Rockcliffe Driveway and watch for the signs that mark the 4 km (2½ mi) to the **National Aviation Museum** ⑰. A 10-minute drive from the National Aviation Museum takes you to the **Canada Science and Technology Museum** ⑱, where children, in particular, enjoy the institution's hands-on exhibits. Across the Ottawa River in Hull, Québec, the **Canadian Museum of Civilization** ⑲ has an IMAX/Omnimax theater and stunning collections documenting the country's history in a fresh, interactive way.

TIMING

You'll need a full day to see the sights and museums on this drive; plan your time according to your interests. Note that many museums are closed Monday.

Sights to See

⑱ **Canada Science and Technology Museum.** Canada's largest science museum has permanent displays of printing presses, antique cars, steam locomotives, and agricultural machinery, as well as ever-changing exhibits, many of which are hands-on, or "minds-on." The evening "Discover the Universe" program uses the largest refracting telescope in Canada to stargaze into the world of astronomy. ⊠ *1867 St. Laurent Blvd.,* ☎ *613/991–3044,* WEB *www.science-tech.nmstc.ca.* ⊡ *$6.* ☺ *May–Aug., daily 9–5 (Fri. until 9); Sept.–Apr., Tues.–Sun. 9–5.*

★ ⑲ **Canadian Museum of Civilization.** Across the Ottawa River in Hull, Québec, is one of the area's most architecturally stunning buildings, with striking, curved lines that appear to have been molded more by natural forces than by human design. Exhibits trace Canada's history from prehistoric times to the present. Six West Coast longhouses, towering totem poles, and life-size reconstructions of an archaeological dig are in the Grand Hall. Kids can enjoy hands-on activities in the Children's Museum. The Cineplus holds the larger-than-life IMAX and Omnimax. ⊠ *100 Laurier St., Hull,* ☎ *819/776–7000 or 800/555–5621; 819/776–7010 Cineplus,* WEB *www.civilization.ca.* ⊡ *Museum Oct.– Apr. $5, free Thurs. 5–9; May–Sept. $8; free Sun. 9–noon year-round. Cineplus $8.50 (varies with show).* ☺ *May–early Oct., Tues.–Sun. 9– 6 (Thurs. until 9; Fri. 9–9 July–early Sept.); mid-Oct.–Apr., Tues.–Sun. 9–5 (Thurs. 9–9).*

⑰ **National Aviation Museum.** This museum holds Canada's most comprehensive collection of vintage aircraft, including a replica of the model that made the country's first powered flight. Engines, propellers, and aeronautical antiques complete the collection. ⊠ *Rockcliffe and Aviation Pkwys.,* ☎ *613/993–2010 or 800/463–2038,* WEB *www.aviation.nmstc.ca.* ⊡ *$6; free Thurs. 5–9.* ☺ *Tues.–Sun. 10–5 (Thurs. 10–9).*

⑮ **Residence of the Prime Minister.** It has been home to men named Laurier, Pearson, and Trudeau, among others. Unlike the White House, it's not open for public inspection. Lacking an invitation, you can hope only for a drive-by glimpse of a couple of roof gables. Don't even try parking near the mansion; security is tight. ⊠ *24 Sussex Dr.*

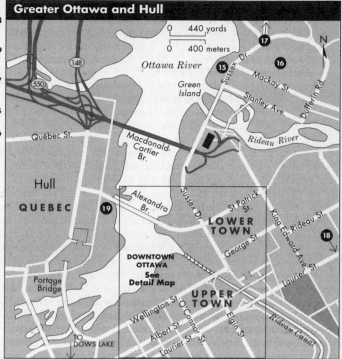

Greater Ottawa and Hull

0   440 yards
0   400 meters

Ottawa River

Green
Island

Hull

QUEBEC

Québec St.

Macdonald-
Cartier
Br.

Rideau River

Sussex Dr.

Mackay St.

Stanley Ave.

Dufferin Rd.

Alexandra
Br.

Sussex Dr.

St. Patrick
St.

**LOWER
TOWN**

George St.

King Edward Ave.

Rideau St.

**DOWNTOWN
OTTAWA
See
Detail Map**

Portage
Bridge

**UPPER
TOWN**

Wellington St.

O'Connor St.

Albert St.

Elgin St.

Laurier St.

Rideau Canal

TO
DOWS LAKE

Laurier St.

---

16 Rideau Hall. The official residence of the Governor General of Canada since 1865 is where Britain's official representative welcomes visiting heads of state and royalty. The 1830 mansion has a ballroom, skating rink, and cricket pitch. Canadian Grenadier Guards and the Governor General's Foot Guards are posted outside the main gate in summer. Free guided tours of the public rooms and grounds are available; call ahead for tour information. ⊠ *1 Sussex Dr.,* ☎ *613/998 7113 or 800/468–6890.*

Dining

The residents of Canada's bilingual capital include politicians, bureaucrats, and diplomats from around the world. The demand for ethnic food is reflected in dining places that range from the eclectic cafés and bistros around lively Byward Market and along trendy Elgin Street to the elegant dining rooms favored by ambassadors and those who work in the upper echelons of government. In this city, as elsewhere in Canada, Italian cuisine is extremely popular.

$$$–$$$$ ✕ **Le Jardin.** If only the very best will do, this top-drawer French es-
★ tablishment may be for you. The menu is varied, the execution virtually flawless. Begin with an appetizer of spinach-stuffed ravioli in *sauce Americaine* (crab flambéed in cognac and simmered in white wine with crushed tomatoes and spices) or lobster–mushroom salad in mayonnaise. Entrées include pan-seared sweetbreads with cassis sauce and tender beef fillet served with plump snails in a red wine sauce. Despite its lofty reputation, Le Jardin has formal but friendly service. ⊠ *127 York St.,* ☎ *613/241–1424. Reservations essential. AE, DC, MC, V.*

$$–$$$ ✕ **Chez Jean Pierre.** Owner Jean Pierre Muller was a chef at the U.S. Embassy for 17 years, and his experience serving diplomats has stood him in good stead. The elegantly furnished dining room is lighted by candelabras, and patrons are treated to fine linen, silver cutlery, and freshly cut flowers. Jean Pierre prepares traditional French cuisine—escargots flavored with garlic, tournedos Rossini (fillet of beef with foie gras and truffles), veal kidneys sautéed in Madeira, and the like. ✉ *210 Somerset St. W, ☎ 613/235–9711. AE, DC, MC, V.*

$$–$$$ ✕ **Courtyard Restaurant.** Fine French cuisine is served in this historic limestone building on a quiet cul-de-sac near the Parliament Buildings. The forerunner of today's elegant dining establishment was a log tavern built in 1827. The humble tavern was replaced by the limestone Ottawa Hotel a decade later. Extensive renovations created the Courtyard Restaurant, and its cuisine—carefully prepared classics such as beef Wellington, rack of lamb, and fresh salmon—and ambience have attracted a dedicated following. ✉ *21 George St., ☎ 613/241–1516. Reservations essential. AE, MC, V.*

$$–$$$ ✕ **Domus Café.** Conscientious use of all-Canadian ingredients is a grand and daunting mission for any restaurant, but the Domus Café makes it work. Here, says the menu, the foie gras and goat cheese come from Québec, the asparagus, tomatoes, and organic leeks from local farms. Ontario wines are offered as a matter of course. And what could be more Canadian than fiddlehead soup, poached quail eggs, and woodland chanterelles? The chefs apply a certain flair to these products of the land: dashes of red wine, fresh thyme, and crème fraîche leaven the risottos; buerre blanc with chives bathes the delicate Arctic char. Prairie-bred beef tenderloin is glazed with red wine and balsamic vinegar and served with small, sweet, very Canadian potatoes. Domus pays strict attention to detail, and the results are eminently satisfying. ✉ *85 Murray St., ☎ 613/241–6007. AE, MC, V. No dinner Sun.*

$$–$$$ ✕ **Empire Grill.** Evening jazz adds flair to this popular restaurant, and the eclectic menu offers diners a melting pot of tempting fare: Mediterranean, Thai, Mexican, and East Indian are among the influences. Lamb strudel is stuffed with spinach, wild mushrooms, and goat cheese; West Coast crab cakes are served with chipotle. Cocoa-grilled duck breast is served on risotto, accompanied by a tart red-currant reduction. In summer you can dine on the patio and enjoy Byward Market's passing parade. ✉ *47 Clarence St., Byward Market, ☎ 613/241–1343. AE, DC, MC, V.*

$–$$ ✕ **Fresco.** This cozy Italian restaurant's dominant feature is the mural of mountains in Tuscany on the back wall, although the dizzying number of food options is impressive, too. You can choose from 10 sauces to accompany such house specialties as pasta, rack of lamb, and veal. ✉ *354 Elgin St., ☎ 613/235–7541. AE, DC, MC, V.*

$$ ✕ **The Ritz.** This small but hugely popular Italian bistro is the original of three Ritz restaurants in Ottawa. The pasta, made on the premises, is teamed with interesting blends of vegetables and seafood. Spinach linguine with smoked salmon, rye whiskey, capers, plum tomatoes, and cream is a typical creation. The Ritz also serves veal and chicken dishes. ✉ *274 Elgin St., ☎ 613/235–7027. Reservations essential. AE, DC, MC, V.*

Lodging

$$$$ ⊞ **Château Laurier Hotel.** Ottawa may have posh and glitzy new ho-
★ tels, but this grand hotel is an institution. The Château, as it's known, is one of Canada's greatest railroad hotels, built in 1912 and named for Sir Wilfrid Laurier, who served as prime minister from 1896 to 1911. Rooms that were formerly on the small side have been combined into several types of suites, from deluxe to family. Zoe's, the conservatory lounge, serves afternoon tea and coffee and Sunday brunch. ✉ *1*

Rideau St., K1N 8S7, ☎ *613/241–1414 or 800/441–1414,* FAX *613/562–7030,* WEB *www.chateaulaurier.com. 385 rooms, 40 suites. Restaurant, bar, lounge, indoor pool, health club. AE, D, DC, MC, V.*

$$$$ 🏨 **Novotel Ottawa.** The rooms in this modern hotel are freshly decorated, and works by local artists hang in the spruced-up lobby. (The paintings are for sale.) Across the street from Rideau Centre, Ottawa's main downtown shopping mall, the Novotel is a few minutes' walk from Parliament Hill, the National Gallery of Canada, and the Rideau Canal. ✉ *33 Nicholas St., K1N 9M7,* ☎ *613/230–3033 or 800/668–6835,* FAX *613/230–7865,* WEB *www.novotel.com. 282 rooms. Restaurant, bar, indoor pool, sauna, steam room, gym. AE, D, DC, MC, V.*

$$$$ 🏨 **Westin Ottawa.** Attached to the Rideau Centre shopping mall and convention hall, this 24-story hotel is in the heart of the city. All guestrooms have plush carpeting and elegant furniture. Floor-to-ceiling windows provide some of the best views in Ottawa ($20 extra for rooms facing the Rideau Canal and the Parliament Buildings). ✉ *11 Colonel By Dr., K1N 9H4,* ☎ *613/560–7000 or 800/228–3000,* FAX *613/560–7359,* WEB *www.westin.com. 484 rooms. Restaurant, lounge, indoor pool, hot tub, sauna, gym, squash, nightclub. AE, D, DC, MC, V.*

$$$–$$$$ 🏨 **Albert at Bay.** One- and two-bedroom suites with fully equipped kitchens and laundry facilities make up this 12-story hotel close to the Sparks Street Mall. All the suites were renovated in 2001, with new carpets and drapes, ceramics, and granite countertops in the kitchens and baths, and two televisions per suite. Most have balconies, as well. ✉ *435 Albert St., at Bay St., K1R 7X4,* ☎ *613/238–8858 or 800/267–6644,* FAX *613/238–1433,* WEB *www.albertatbay.com. 198 suites. Restaurant, grocery, kitchenettes, hot tub, sauna, gym, coin laundry, dry cleaning. AE, D, DC, MC, V.*

$$$ 🏨 **Carmichael Inn & Spa.** Open since 1996, this hostelry in a century-
★   old brick mansion is particularly popular with single women (including politicians), who come to get back on track at the spa. Treatments include Swedish massage, herbal body wraps, and reflexology. A full breakfast is included in the rate, and the inn is near the restaurants and cafés along fashionable Elgin Street. ✉ *46 Cartier St., K2P 1J3,* ☎ *613/236–4667 or 877/416-2417,* FAX *613/563–7529,* WEB *www.carmichaelinn. com. 10 rooms. Spa. AE, DC, MC, V. BP.*

Nightlife and the Arts

The Arts

The Corel Centre (✉ 1000 Palladium Dr., Kanata, K2V 1A4, ☎ 613/599–0100) is 15 minutes from downtown. Complete with several pubs, chain restaurants, and souvenir shops, it's a huge venue where NHL hockey is played (the home team, of course, is the Ottawa Senators). But it's also the setting for concerts by big-name artists like Bon Jovi and Celine Dion. Ice shows featuring international champions are perennial favorites, too. All events are announced well in advance, so you can purchase tickets before you come to Ottawa.

More than 900 performances are showcased annually at the **National Arts Centre** (✉ 53 Elgin St., ☎ 613/947–7000), and it's the home of the National Arts Centre Orchestra. In summer the center is one of the hosts of the Ottawa International Jazz Festival Canada and Festival Canada (opera, choral works, cabaret).

Nightlife

Barrymore's Music Hall (✉ 323 Bank St., ☎ 613/233–0307) has transformed the Imperial Theatre of 1914 into one of the city's liveliest nightclubs. It draws a 20s-to-30s crowd. Musicians take center stage

Wednesday through Saturday until midnight, after which dance music thumps through the three-tier hall until 2 AM.

Outdoor Activities and Sports

Biking

Ottawa has 150 km (93 mi) of bicycle paths. On Sunday, Queen Elizabeth Drive and Colonel By Drive are closed to traffic until noon for cyclists. **Rent A Bike** (☎ 613/241–4140), in the Château Laurier Hotel, rents bicycles, including tandems, for riders of all ages.

Hiking

The **Rideau Trail** runs 406 km (252 mi) along the Rideau Canal from Kingston to Ottawa. Access points from the highway are marked with orange triangles. For information, contact the Rideau Trail Association (✉ Box 15, Kingston K7L 4V6, ☎ 613/545–0823, WEB www.ncf.ca/rta).

Ice-Skating

In winter the **Rideau Canal** becomes the longest skating rink in the world, stretching from the National Arts Centre to Dows Lake. Skates can be rented and sharpened across from the National Arts Centre, where wooden sleds for towing children can also be rented. Along the route are a few warm-up changing shelters and food concessions. Call the NCC (☎ 613/239–5000 or 800/465–1867) for daily skating conditions.

Shopping

John Coles at the **Astrolabe Gallery** (✉ 112 Sparks St., ☎ 613/234–2348) is a good source for 19th-century prints of Ottawa scenes or antique maps of North America.

Rideau Centre (✉ Rideau St. and Colonel By Dr., ☎ 613/236–6565) has more than 200 stores, including The Bay department store. At **Sparks Street Pedestrian Mall** (✉ 240 Sparks St.) you can comb the racks for high fashion at tony Holt Renfrew or browse through some 50 other shops. **Westboro Village,** a neighborhood west of the downtown hustle—along Richmond Road from Island Park Drive to Windermere Avenue—is a fine place to browse interesting shops. Classy restaurants and coffee bars are plentiful, too.

Ottawa A to Z

AIR TRAVEL TO AND FROM OTTAWA

Ottawa International Airport, 18 km (11 mi) from downtown, is served by Air Canada, First Air, Delta Airlines, and US Airways. Cab fare from the airport to downtown Ottawa is about $20.
➤ AIRPORT INFORMATION: **Ottawa International Airport** (✉ 50 Airport Rd., Gloucester, ☎ 613/248–2000).

BUS TRAVEL TO AND FROM OTTAWA

Voyageur Colonial Bus Lines offers frequent service from Montréal and Toronto to Ottawa, including some express buses.
➤ BUS INFORMATION: **Voyageur Colonial Bus Lines** (✉ 265 Catherine St., ☎ 613/238–5900, WEB www.voyageur.com).

BUS TRAVEL WITHIN OTTAWA

OC Transpo serves the Ottawa–Carleton region on the Ontario side of the Ottawa River. It operates buses on city streets and on the Transitway, a system of bus-only roads. All bus routes in downtown Ottawa meet at the Rideau Centre.

➤ Bus Information: **OC Transpo** (☎ 613/741–4390, WEB www.octranspo.com). **Rideau Centre** (✉ Rideau St. between Nicholas and Sussex and the Mackenzie King Bridge).

CAR TRAVEL

Highway 417 links Ottawa to Québec from the east; Highway 16 connects Ottawa with Highway 401 to the south.

EMERGENCIES

Ottawa has one of the largest acute-care hospitals in Canada, divided into three separate centers, or campuses. If you are sick or injured, all have emergency rooms where you can be assessed and treated.

➤ Emergency Services: **Ambulance, fire, police** (☎ 911).

➤ Hospitals: **Ottawa Civic Hospital** (☎ 613/761–4000). **Ottawa General Hospital** (☎ 613/737–6111). **Riverside Outpatients' Centre** (☎ 613/738–7100).

➤ 24-Hour Pharmacies: **Shoppers Drug Mart** (✉ 1460 Merivale Rd., ☎ 613/224–7270).

TAXIS

➤ Taxi Companies: **Blue Line** (☎ 613/238–1111). **Capital** (☎ 613/744–3333).

TOURS

BOAT TOURS

Paul's Boat Lines Limited offers seven 75-minute cruises daily on the Rideau Canal and four 90-minute cruises daily on the Ottawa River from mid-May to mid-October. Canal boats dock across from the National Arts Centre; river cruise boats dock at the Bytown Museum at the foot of the Ottawa Locks on the Rideau Canal. Ottawa Riverboat Company operates two-hour sight-seeing boat tours on the Ottawa River May through October.

➤ Fees and Schedules: **Ottawa Riverboat Company** (☎ 613/562–4888, WEB www.ottawariverboat.ca). **Paul's Boat Lines Limited** (☎ 613/235–8409).

BUS TOURS

Gray Line operates two-hour, 50-km (31-mi) orientation bus tours mid-May through October. From April through November, Capital Double-Decker and Trolley Tours has a regular schedule of two-hour tours in London buses to Ottawa's major sights.

➤ Fees and Schedules: **Capital Double-Decker and Trolley Tours** (☎ 613/749–3666 or 800/823–6147). **Gray Line** (☎ 613/725–1441 or 800/297–6422, WEB www.grayline.ca/ottawa).

TRAIN TRAVEL

Trans-Canada VIA Rail serves the Ottawa Rail Station at the southeastern end of town. It's a $12 taxi ride to downtown.

➤ Train Information: **VIA Rail** (✉ 200 Tremblay Rd., ☎ 613/244–8289, WEB www.viarail.ca).

VISITOR INFORMATION

The Capital Infocentre can provide you with detailed information about the city and the Capital Region.

➤ Tourist Information: **Capital Infocentre** (✉ 90 Wellington St., ☎ 613/239–5000 or 800/465–1867, WEB www.capcan.ca).

THE HERITAGE HIGHWAYS

Most of Ontario's first French, English, and Loyalist settlers entered the province from the southeast. You can retrace some of their routes on southern Ontario's Heritage Highways. Highway 2, parallel to Highway 401, is smaller than the cross-Ontario freeway and more picturesque. It's the original 19th-century route that linked Québec and Kingston to "Muddy York" (Toronto) in the west. With appropriate detours it provides a good glimpse into this area's attractions.

Upper Canada Village

★ ⑳   *86 km (53 mi) southeast of Ottawa on Hwy. 2.*

Eight villages disappeared under rising waters when the St. Lawrence Seaway opened in 1959, but their best historic buildings were moved to a new site called Upper Canada Village, a re-creation of an Ontario community of the 1860s. The village occupies 66 acres of the 2,000-acre Crysler's Farm Battlefield Park, which figured in the War of 1812. A tour takes three to four hours. Staff members in period costume answer visitors' questions as they work with authentic tools at the mills and farms. Willard's Hotel serves lunches, full-course meals, and teas. ✉ *Hwy. 2E, Morrisburg,* ☎ *613/543–3704 or 800/437–2233,* WEB *www.uppercanadavillage.com.* 🎟 *$15.95.* ☉ *Mid-May–mid-Oct., daily 9:30–5; group tours can be arranged year-round.*

Prescott

★ ㉑   *35 km (22 mi) west of Morrisburg on Hwy. 2.*

Both Prescott's Fort Wellington and the Windmill Historic Site saw action in the War of 1812, and both have been restored and are open to the public. **Fort Wellington National Historic Site** was built by the British in 1813 to protect goods and troops moving between Mont-réal and Upper Canada after the outbreak of the War of 1812. The Rideau Canal eliminated the need for the fort, and it was abandoned. In 1837, when rebellion broke out in Upper and Lower Canada, the British built a stronger Fort Wellington on the same site. The restored buildings are furnished in 1846 period style. Canadian rebels and their American allies tried to capture the nearby **Battle of the Windmill National Historic Site** in 1838. In the 1870s it was converted into a lighthouse and served as one for over a century, until it was restored to a windmill again in 1996. ✉ *370 Vankoughnet St.,* ☎ *613/925–2896 or 800/230–0016,* WEB *www.parkscanada.pch.gc.ca/wellington.* 🎟 *$3.* ☉ *Mid-May–Sept., daily 10–5; Oct.–mid-May, by reservation only.*

Ontario's oldest barracks building, the 1810 **Stockade Barracks,** one block west of Fort Wellington, serves historic dinners by candlelight Friday and Saturday evenings. By prior arrangement, groups of 15–40 can have five- or six-course meals of 1812-style dishes served by mess waiters in military uniforms. ✉ *356 East St.,* ☎ *613/925–4894.* ☉ *Year-round, Fri. and Sat. 6 PM–10 PM. AE, MC, V.*

Kingston

㉒   *105 km (65 mi) southwest of Prescott on Hwy. 401.*

Kingston's architecture has been amazing visitors since 1673, when Governor Frontenac built a stockaded fort to impress the Iroquois and thus tap into the fur trade. The city occupied a strategic site at the junction of the St. Lawrence River and the Rideau Canal system, making it a major military site. Kingston survived the War of 1812 almost unscathed; many of its beautiful limestone buildings remain in mint condition today. The appealing waterfront is filled with sailboats and serves as the jumping-off point for cruises around the scenic Thousand Islands.

From 1841 to 1844, Kingston was the national capital; today the gorgeous, cut-limestone **City Hall** (✉ 216 Ontario St., ☎ 613/546–4291) dominates the downtown core, facing a riverfront park. Tours are given weekdays in summer, but you can visit the lobby anytime.

The **Royal Military College of Canada** was founded at Point Frederick in 1876, on the site of the old British Navy dockyard; the dockyard's relics can still be seen on the college grounds. Of particular note is the **Royal Military College Museum,** housed in the largest of four Martello towers that guarded the Kingston harborfront. The museum contains the well-known Douglas Arms Collection. ✉ *Off Hwy. 2, east of Kingston,* ☎ *613/541–6000 Ext. 6664,* ⓦⒺⒷ *www.rmc.ca.* ⌲ *Free.* ☉ *Last weekend in June–early Sept., daily 10–5.*

★ The massive **Fort Henry** was built between 1832 and 1834 to repel an American invasion that never came. Today, it's a living-history museum of early military life in which people in period costume guide visitors and hold parades. ✉ *Hwys. 2 and 15,* ☎ *613/542–7388 or 800/437–2233,* ⓦⒺⒷ *www.parks.on.ca/fort.* ⌲ *$10.75.* ☉ *Late May–early Oct., daily 10–5; mid-Oct.–late May by reservation only.*

Locals have nicknamed it "Tea Caddy Castle," but Canada's first prime minister, Sir John A. Macdonald, who lived in the house for a year, called it **Bellevue** because of its view of the St. Lawrence River. Today the 1840 house is a National Historic Site, restored and furnished in the style of 1848, when Macdonald lived here. ✉ *35 Centre St.,* ☎ *613/545–8666,* ⓦⒺⒷ *www.parkscanada.pch.gc.ca.* ⌲ *$2.75.* ☉ *June–early Sept., daily 9–6; Apr.–May and early Sept.–Oct., daily 10–5.*

The **Pump House Steam Museum,** a Victorian-style 1849 municipal water-pumping station, is maintained by the Marine Museum of the Great Lakes. All exhibits run on steam; models range from miniatures to an 1897 engine with a 9-ton flywheel. ✉ *23 Ontario St.,* ☎ *613/546–4696 or 613/542–2261.* ⌲ *$4.25; Pump House and Marine Museum $5.75.* ☉ *June–Labor Day, daily 10–5.*

The rambling display area at the **Marine Museum of the Great Lakes,** at the historic former Kingston dry dock, traces Great Lakes shipping since 1678. The *Alexander Henry,* a 3,000-ton, 210-ft retired icebreaker, is open for tours in summer; you can even rent a stateroom and sleep aboard. ✉ *55 Ontario St.,* ☎ *613/542–2261,* ⓦⒺⒷ *www.marmus.ca.* ⌲ *$4.25; Marine Museum and Pump House $5.75.* ☉ *May–Oct., daily 10–5; Nov.–Apr., weekdays 10–4.*

Dining and Lodging

$$–$$$ ✕ **Clark's on King.** Stylish cuisine is served in an upstairs room with tall windows, yellow walls, and lots of flowers. Asian, Italian, and Canadian culinary traditions fuse handsomely on a menu that changes with the seasons. Openers might include fresh tuna marinated in tamarind and sesame oil, or crispy quail flavored with lime and ginger. There's a table d'hôte special every evening ($40), but you may be tempted by entrées like house-made lobster-and-crab ravioli topped with shrimp and scallops and bathed in a delicate lobster–cream sauce; smoked salmon with dill-infused risotto; and succulent rack of lamb in a Stilton and port sauce. ✉ *300 King St. E,* ☎ *613/542–2761. Reservations essential. AE, DC, MC, V. Closed Sun.*

$$ ✕ **Chez Piggy.** Kingston diners rate Piggy's very highly indeed, maybe because it's an energetic, upbeat kind of place where you can expect the unexpected. Owner Zal Yanofsky (who was once a Canadian rock star) has scoured the planet for inspiration, and his menu has inflections of diverse cultures: appetizers like frites mayonnaise, Stilton pâté, and carpaccio with capers share space with Asian delicacies. Entrées

might include seared sea scallops with lemongrass and coconut milk, or monkfish in coriander sauce with preserved lemons and olives. There's also a corn-crusted chicken breast with chipotle–black bean cakes, salsa, and avocado slices to remind you of Mexico. Overwhelmed by all the choices? You can't go wrong with a steak, accompanied by horseradish or peppercorn butters. ✉ *68-R (rear) Princess St.,* ☎ *613/549–7673. AE, DC, MC, V.*

$$–$$$$ 🛏 **Rosemount Bed & Breakfast Inn.** This atmospheric, Tuscan-style villa recalls its 1850s origins with period furnishings and fabrics. Rooms are lavish, but cozy, with colorful prints and Victorian antiques. The complimentary Continental breakfast might include the inn's trademark Welsh toast (the owner's unique version of French toast). At teatime, the fireplace crackles in the Victorian sitting room. The Rosemount is in Kingston's Old Stones neighborhood, a short walk from the waterfront, galleries, museums, and downtown shops. ✉ *46 Sydenham St. S, K7L 3H1,* ☎ *613/531–8844 or 888/871–8844,* ℻ *613/531–9722,* 𝚆𝙴𝙱 *www. rosemountinn.com. 8 rooms, 1 suite. Dining room, massage, spa. AE, MC, V. Closed Dec. 10–Jan. 10. CP.*

$$–$$$ 🛏 **Hochelaga Inn.** Built more than a century ago, this Victorian inn is in a quiet residential and historic neighborhood, a five-minute walk from downtown. All the rooms have private baths, and all but one have a queen-size bed. ✉ *24 Sydenham St. S, K7L 3G9,* ☎ *613/549–5534 or 877/933–9433,* ℻ *613/549–5534,* 𝚆𝙴𝙱 *www.someplacesdifferent. com. 23 rooms. Restaurant, meeting room. AE, DC, MC, V. CP.*

$$–$$$ 🛏 **Hotel Belvedere.** This Victorian gem, with its mansard roof, airy rooms, and proximity to the waterfront, is steeped in restful charm. Expertly chosen antiques, from plush Persian carpets to Regency tables, furnish the inn's rooms, each of which has a private bath and high ceilings. A complimentary Continental breakfast can be served in your room, by the fireplace in the living room, or on the shady terrace in summer. ✉ *141 King St. E, K7L 2Z9,* ☎ *613/548–1565 or 800/559– 0584,* ℻ *613/546–4692,* 𝚆𝙴𝙱 *www.hotelbelvedere.com. 20 rooms, 1 suite. Meeting room. AE, D, DC, MC, V. CP.*

Prince Edward County

❷❸ *80 km (50 mi) southwest of Kingston.*

New Englanders wandering the island county of Prince Edward may find themselves wondering if they've ever left home—so similar are the scenery and the pages of history that brought both regions into being. The island was one of the earliest parts of Ontario to be settled after the American Revolution, and a Loyalist influence remained dominant for generations. The Loyalist church erected in 1822 is still used as a parish meeting hall. Although Prince Edward County can be reached by car via Highway 33, a free, 10-minute ride on a car ferry, which departs from Adolphustown every 15 minutes in summer, is another option.

Picton, the island's capital of sorts, is a serene town of 4,300 with fine old buildings and strong associations with Sir John A. Macdonald, Canada's first prime minister, who practiced law at the 1834 county courthouse. The **Macaulay Heritage Park** is here. It sits on about 15 acres of land and includes picnic facilities, the **Macaulay House,** and the **County Museum.** Tours of the park and the town's attractions are available by prior arrangement and may include a visit to the jail, where a double gallows is kept handy (although it hasn't been used since 1884). ✉ *1 block south of Hwy. 33 at Union and Church Sts.,* ☎ *613/476– 3833,* 𝚆𝙴𝙱 *www.pec.on.ca/macaulay.* 🎟 *House $2, museum $2; $3 for both.* ☉ *House and museum June–early Sept., weekdays 10–4, weekends 1–4.*

Dining and Lodging

$$$ ✗⊡ **Isaiah Tubbs Inn and Resort.** A dozen kilometers (7 mi) west of Picton, this posh property is set on 500 acres of gardens and woodlands on the shore of West Lake. The main inn is a beautifully restored 1820s farmhouse complete with fireplaces and authentic beamed ceilings. There's a fully integrated two-story annex and contemporary cottages. At the casual Restaurant on the Knoll, you can try four-onion soup or baked Brie with a triple-berry compote. Other influences, from Asian to Californian, give the traditional menu an interesting edge. ⊠ *R.R. 1 West Lake Rd., K0K 2T0,* ☎ *613/393–2090; 800/724–2393 in Canada,* ℻ *613/393–2912,* WEB *www.someplacesdifferent.com. 40 rooms, 24 suites, 14 cottages. Restaurant, indoor pool, hot tub, sauna, tennis court, gym. AE, DC, MC, V.*

$–$$$ ⊡ **Merrill Inn.** This beautiful, 1870 redbrick house near the heart of downtown Picton was converted to an inn with antiques and modern amenities. It is an excellent example of restored Victorian architecture, with 12 tall gables, iron filigree, and carpenter's gingerbread. Rooms have period furniture and are spacious; many have high ceilings. The atmospheric pub has reasonably priced traditional fare like bangers and mash and steak-and-kidney pie. A golf course and health club are nearby. ⊠ *343 Main St. E, K0K 2T0,* ☎ *613/476–7451 or 800/567–5969,* WEB *www.pgs.com/merrill. 12 rooms, 1 suite. Pub. AE, MC, V. CP.*

Cobourg

㉔ *90 km (56 mi) west of Picton on Hwy. 401 or Hwy. 2.*

Cobourg once expected to be chosen as the provincial capital, but it was passed over. The town nearly went bankrupt building the magnificent **Victoria Hall,** officially opened in 1860 by the young Prince of Wales, later King Edward VII. A courtroom modeled after London's Old Bailey was on the ground floor, and town council meetings and concerts were held on the second floor. Today you can tour some of the 41 rooms. ⊠ *55 King St. W,* ☎ *905/372–5481 or 888/262–6874,* ℻ *905/372–1306.* ⛶ *Free.* ☉ *Guided tours in summer or by prior arrangement.*

Lodging

$$$$ ⊡ **Ste. Anne's Country Inn & Spa.** Soothing New Age music and the scent of eucalyptus greet you at this fine old fieldstone inn, now dedicated to pampering tired city types. Ste. Anne's, in the lovely Northumberland Hills, offers everything from massage and hydrotherapy to hot mud baths. Guest rooms relax you in uncluttered country comfort, with a mix of Ontario antiques and quality modern furnishings, upscale linens, and Oriental carpets on gleaming hardwood floors. Most rooms have fireplaces and whirlpool baths. Health-minded dishes served in the dining room include Mandarin orange salad and poached chicken breast, or citrus-marinated tuna. The inn is a few miles east of Cobourg north of Highway 2. Book well ahead. Prices include meals and spa credits. ⊠ *R.R. 1, Grafton, K0K 2G0,* ☎ *905/349–2493 or 888/346–6772,* ℻ *905/349–3531,* WEB *www.steannes.com. 5 rooms, 5 suites, 7 guest houses. Dining room, indoor lap pool, pool, sauna, spa, steam room, 2 tennis courts, gym. AE, D, DC, MC, V. MAP.*

Keene

㉕ *67 km (42 mi) north of Cobourg via Hwys. 28 and 2.*

Keene's most noteworthy attraction is an unusual grave site. A native burial ground is preserved in **Serpent Mounds Park.** About 2,000 years ago a nomadic tribe buried its dead in nine earth mounds, the largest of which is shaped like a 200-ft-long serpent. An interpretation center explains the site and displays artifacts. ✉ *R.R. 2,* ☎ *705/295–6879,* WEB *www.serpentmoundspark.com.* 🎟 *$7 per vehicle.* ☉ *Mid-Apr.–early Sept., daily 8 AM–10 PM.*

The well-signed **Lang Pioneer Village,** about 3 km (2 mi) north of Keene, has a museum and 26 pioneer buildings. In summer you can see displays and demonstrations of pioneer arts and crafts. ✉ *Off County Rd. 34, Lang,* ☎ *705/295–6694,* WEB *www.county.peterborough. on.ca/lang.htm.* 🎟 *$6.* ☉ *Mid-May–early Sept., weekdays and Sun. noon–5, Sat. 1–4.*

Peterborough

🔵 26 *13 km (8 mi) northwest of Keene via Hwys. 34 and 7.*

The small city of Peterborough is home to Trent University. The lift locks, built in 1904 on the **Trent-Severn Waterway** are among the world's highest and are in operation mid-May through October. The locks have floated boats straight up 65 ft in less than 10 minutes. Slides and films at the **Peterborough Lift Lock Visitor Centre** can help you learn more about how the locks work. ✉ *Hunter St. E,* ☎ *705/750–4950,* WEB *www.parkscanada.pch.gc.ca.* 🎟 *$2 donation, $2 parking.* ☉ *Apr.– mid-Oct., daily 10–5.*

The **Canadian Canoe Museum** houses the world's largest collection of canoes, honored here as the greatest gift of the First Nations people. Exhibits also include kayaks, a Nootka (West Coast) whaling dugout, and a huge freighter canoe touted as the largest birchbark vessel in the world at 33 ft long. ✉ *910 Monaghan Rd.,* ☎ *705/748–9153,* WEB *www.canoemuseum.net.* 🎟 *$5 donation.* ☉ *Daily 10–4.*

Lodging

$$ 🏨 **Holiday Inn.** The location is hard to beat. Surrounded by a marina in the heart of the downtown area, the Holiday Inn overlooks the Trent-Severn Waterway. (The other hotels are on the shopping mall strip on the way into town.) If you come by boat, as many guests do, you won't be charged for docking. ✉ *150 George St. N, K9J 3G5,* ☎ *705/743– 1144 or 800/465–4329,* FAX *705/740–6559,* WEB *www.sixcontinentshotels. com. 150 rooms, 4 suites. Restaurant, indoor/outdoor pool, sauna, gym, recreation room. AE, D, DC, MC, V.*

Petroglyphs Provincial Park

🔵 27 *55 km (34 mi) northeast of Peterborough on Hwy. 28.*

Canada's largest concentration of native rock carvings was found at the east end of Stony Lake, outside the hamlet of Stonyridge in 1954. The site is now within Petroglyphs Provincial Park. The well-preserved symbols and figures are carved on a flat expanse of white marble almost 70 ft wide, which is sheltered in a protective building. The more than 900 carvings are believed to be Algonquin spirit figures. ✉ *East of Hwy. 28 on Northey's Bay Rd., Stonyridge,* ☎ *705/877–2552,* WEB *www.on- tarioparks.com.* 🎟 *$8 per vehicle.* ☉ *May–mid-Oct., daily 10–5.*

NORTH OF TORONTO TO THE LAKES

There are several ways to explore this picturesque area, known to Torontonians as Cottage Country. You can take a day trip from Toronto, driving through the area and perhaps stopping for a picnic lunch at one of the lakes or at one of numerous roadside restaurants. Alternatively, spend up to a week exploring the district from one of many lakeside resorts near towns such as Orillia, Gravenhurst, Bracebridge, and

Huntsville. A cheaper—but equally satisfying—choice is to rent a cottage for a week or two. "Cottages" range from log cabins to palatial homes that would not look out of place in a wealthy urban neighborhood. Rentals are available through local real estate agents or by consulting **Tyler's Cottage Rental Directory** (⊠ 124 Brock St., Barrie L4N 2M2, ☏ 705/726–6015 or 800/461–7585, ⛛ www.cottagerentals.com). The directory is also available in local bookstores.

Barrie

❷❽ *90 km (56 mi) north of Toronto on Hwy. 400.*

Barrie is on the shore of Lake Simcoe. The town's annual **Winterfest** (☏ 705/739–4285, ⛛ www.barrietourism.on.ca) in early February has ice fishing, dogsledding, ice motorcycling, and other colorful attractions. From late June through Labor Day, there's informal drama in Barrie's **Gryphon Theatre** (☏ 705/728–4613) at Georgian College. You can watch harness racing at **Barrie Raceway** (☏ 705/726–9400). On the August 1 long weekend, Barrie's waterside arts and crafts festival, **Kempenfest** (☏ 705/739–4223, ⛛ www.kempenfest.com), draws up to 250,000 visitors.

Dining and Lodging

$$$ ✕⬚ **Inn at Horseshoe.** This top-drawer lodge has modern guest rooms with down comforters. Many suites have sunken living rooms, fireplaces, and whirlpool baths. Dining options range from the distinctive Continental menu of the formal Silks restaurant ($$$) to the informal Santa Fe–style Go West Grill ($). ⊠ *Horseshoe Valley Rd.; Box 10, R.R. 1, L4M 4Y8,* ☏ *705/835–2790 or 800/461–5627,* ⛛ *705/835–6352,* ⛛ *www.horseshoeresort.com. 54 rooms, 48 suites. 2 restaurants, lounge, indoor pool, hot tub, 2 golf courses, 2 tennis courts, gym, squash, mountain bikes, downhill skiing. AE, DC, MC, V.*

$$–$$$ ✕⬚ **Blue Mountain Inn.** In addition to being the largest ski resort in Ontario, this acclaimed lodge 71 km (44 mi) outside of Barrie has an outstanding 18-hole golf course. Rooms are fairly standard, and suites as well as condominium units have kitchens and fireplaces. The Pottery dining room ($$–$$$$) serves Continental interpretations of Canadian standards, or you can opt for the Mexican-influenced Monterra Bar & Grill ($–$$). ⊠ *R.R. 3, Collingwood, L9Y 3Z2,* ☏ *705/445–0231 or 416/869–3799,* ⛛ *705/444–1751,* ⛛ *www.bluemountain.ca. 95 rooms, 2 suites, 100 condominiums. 2 restaurants, lounge, indoor pool, outdoor hot tub, massage, sauna, 18-hole golf course, 9 tennis courts, gym, squash, beach. AE, DC, MC, V.*

Outdoor Activities and Sports

Blue Mountain, near Collingwood on Highway 26, is Ontario's most extensively developed and heavily used ski area, with a vertical drop of 720 ft. It has 32 pistes served by a high-speed quad lift, three triple chairs, eight double chairs, two pomas, and a rope tow. **Horseshoe Valley Resort** is among the few resorts that offer cross-country and downhill skiing and snowboarding facilities, plus a new, specially designed snow-tubing run. It has 22 alpine runs, 14 of which are lit at night, served by seven lifts. The vertical drop is only 309 ft, but several of the runs are rated for advanced skiers.

Penetanguishene and Midland

❷❾ *47 km (29 mi) north of Barrie on Hwys. 400 and 93.*

The quiet towns of Penetanguishene (known locally as Penetang) and Midland occupy a small corner of northern Simcoe County known as

Huronia. Both towns sit on a snug, safe harbor at the foot of Georgian Bay's Severn Sound.

Ste-Marie among the Hurons, 5 km (3 mi) east of Midland on Highway 12, is a complete reconstruction of the Jesuit mission that was originally built on this spot in 1639. The village, which was once home to a fifth of the European population of New France, was the site of the European settlers' first hospital, farm, school, and social service center in Ontario. Villagers also constructed a canal from the Wye River. A combination of disease and Iroquois attacks led to the mission's demise. Twenty-two structures, including a native longhouse and wigwam, have been faithfully reproduced from a scientific excavation. The canal is working again, and staff members in period costume saw timber, repair shoes, sew clothes, and grow vegetables. ⊠ *Hwy. 12 E,* ☎ *705/ 526–7838,* WEB *www.saintemarieamongthehurons.on.ca.* ☎ *$9.75.* ☉ *Mid-May–mid-Oct., daily 10–5 (last entry at 4:45).*

On a hill overlooking Ste-Marie among the Hurons is the **Martyrs' Shrine,** a twin-spired stone cathedral built in 1926 to honor the eight missionaries who died in Huronia; in 1930, five of the priests were canonized by the Roman Catholic Church. The grounds include a theater, a souvenir shop, a cafeteria, and a picnic area. ⊠ *Off Hwy. 12 E,* ☎ *705/526– 3788,* WEB *www.jesuits.ca/martyrs-shrine.* ☎ *$3.* ☉ *Mid-May–mid-Oct., daily 8:30 AM–9 PM.*

The best artifacts from several hundred archaeological digs in the area are displayed at **Huronia Museum** in Little Lake Park, Midland. Behind the museum and gallery building is **Huron-Ouendat Village,** a full-scale replica of a 16th-century Huron settlement. ⊠ *Little Lake Park,* ☎ *705/526–2844 or 800/263–7745.* ☎ *Museum and village $6.* ☉ *May–June, daily 9–5; July–Aug. daily 9–6; Sept.–Apr., Mon.–Sat. 9–5.*

Cruises leave from the town docks of both Midland and Penetang to explore the 30,000 Islands region of Georgian Bay from May through October. The 300-passenger **MS *Miss Midland*** (☎ 705/526–0161; 888/ 833–2628 in ON), which leaves from the Midland town dock, offers 2½-hour sightseeing cruises daily. From the Penetang town dock, the 200-passenger **MS *Georgian Queen*** (☎ 705/549–7795 or 800/363– 7447, WEB www.georgianbaycruises.com) takes passengers on three-hour tours of the islands.These cruises leave one to three times daily, from mid-May to mid-October; call ahead for times.

Lodging

$$ ☷ **Best Western Highland Inn.** An enormous atrium anchors this completely self-contained hotel–motel–resort. Honeymoon suites have heart-shape tubs or sunken Jacuzzis. Sunday brunches by the pool in the Garden Cafe are popular; there are three other dining areas (reserve ahead) as well. ⊠ *924 King St. and Hwy. 12, Midland L4R 4L3,* ☎ *705/526–9307 or 800/461–4265,* FAX *705/526–0099,* WEB *www.bwhighlandinn.on.ca. 113 rooms, 17 suites. 2 restaurants, indoor pool, sauna, gym. AE, D, DC, MC, V.*

Parry Sound

③⓪ *117 km (73 mi) north of Penetanguishene and Midland on Hwys. 400 or 12 and 69.*

Parry Sound is home to Canada's largest sightseeing cruise ship. The ***Island Queen*** offers an extensive three-hour cruise of Georgian Bay once or twice daily, depending on the season. There's free parking at the town dock. ⊠ *9 Bay St.,* ☎ *705/746–2311 or 800/506–2628.* ☎ *$17.* ☉ *June–mid-Oct., daily; call for cruise times.*

From mid-July to mid-August, the **Festival of the Sound** (☎ 705/746–2410) fills the auditorium of Parry Sound High School and the decks of the *Island Queen* with jazz, folk, and classical music daily.

Orillia

③① *98 km (61 mi) southeast of Parry Sound on Hwy. 69, 35 km (22 mi) northeast of Barrie on Hwy. 11.*

Readers of Canada's great humorist Stephen Leacock may recognize Orillia as "Mariposa," the town he described in *Sunshine Sketches of a Little Town.* Leacock's former summer home is now the **Stephen Leacock Museum.** In the Mariposa Room, characters from the book are matched with the Orillia residents who inspired them. ⊠ *50 Museum Dr., off Hwy. 12B,* ☎ *705/329–1908.* ☞ *$7.* ☉ *Mid-June–early Sept., daily 10–7; Labor Day–mid-June, weekdays 10–7.*

For the past few years, **Casino Rama,** the largest First Nation–run gambling emporium in Canada, has lured thousands of visitors to Orillia. The huge complex (195,000 square ft) just outside town has 2,300 slot machines, more than 110 gambling tables, three restaurants, an entertainment lounge, and a gift shop where you can buy crafts. ⊠ *R.R. 6, Rama, 5 km (3 mi) north of Orillia,* ☎ *705/329–3325 or 888/817–7262,* WEB *www.casino-rama.com.*

Gravenhurst

③② *38 km (24 mi) north of Orillia on Hwy. 11.*

North along Highway 11, rolling farmland suddenly changes to lakes and pine trees amid granite outcrops of the Canadian Shield. This region, called Muskoka, is a favorite playground of people who live in the highly urbanized areas around Toronto. Gravenhurst is a town of approximately 6,000 and the birthplace of a Canadian hero. The **Bethune Memorial House,** an 1880-vintage frame structure, is a National Historic Site that honors the heroic efforts of field surgeon and medical educator Norman Bethune, who worked in China during the 1930s. It has become a shrine of sorts for Chinese diplomats visiting North America. ⊠ *235 John St. N, P1P 1G4,* ☎ *705/687–4261.* ☞ *$2.50.* ☉ *Late May–mid-Oct., daily 10–5; mid-Oct.–late May, weekdays 1–4.*

The **RMS *Segwun*** (the initials stand for Royal Mail Ship) is the sole survivor of a fleet of steamships that once provided transportation through the Muskoka Lakes. The 128-ft boat carries 99 passengers on cruises from mid-June to mid-October. Cruises range from 90 minutes to two days in length (passengers dine aboard but sleep in one of Muskoka's grand resorts). ⊠ *Muskoka Lakes Navigation and Hotel Company Ltd., 820 Bay St., Sagamo Park, P1P 1G7,* ☎ *705/687–6667.*

Dining and Lodging

$$$$ ✗🏨 **Muskoka Sands.** This upscale year-round resort, surrounded by a magnificent landscape of rocky outcrops and windswept trees typical of the Muskoka region, has all kinds of diversions, from squash to ice-skating. Gourmet food is served in the Winewood Dining Room ($$–$$$). Condos are available as well. ⊠ *Muskoka Beach Rd., P1P 1R1,* ☎ *705/687–2233 or 800/461–0236,* FAX *705/687–7474,* WEB *www.muskokasands.com. 83 rooms, 22 suites, 26 condos. 2 restaurants, indoor pool, outdoor pool, 9-hole golf course, 5 tennis courts, gym, hiking, horseback riding, squash, mountain bikes, ice-skating, cross-country skiing, snowmobiling, playground. AE, DC, MC, V.*

$$–$$$ ⊞ **Bayview-Wildwood Resort.** This century-old resort complex, a 15-minute drive south of Gravenhurst, is particularly geared to outdoor types and families. Canoeing and kayaking are popular; floatplane excursions and golf can also be arranged. Some rooms have fireplaces, whirlpool baths, and views over the lake. Bayview-Wildwood offers only all-inclusive two-, five-, and seven-day packages. ⊠ *1500 Port Stanton Pkwy., R.R. 1, Severn Bridge P0E 1N0,* ☎ *705/689–2338 or 800/461–0243,* ℻ *705/689–8042,* WEB *www.bayviewwildwood.com. 48 rooms, 27 cottages. Dining room, indoor pool, gym, boating, fishing, mountain bikes, cross-country skiing, snowmobiling. AE, DC, MC, V. AP.*

Haliburton

㉝ *90 km (56 mi) northeast of Gravenhurst via Hwy. 11 and Hwy. 118, 250 km (155 mi) northeast of Toronto.*

Close to huge Algonquin Provincial Park, Haliburton is a cross-country skiing and winter sports base. In summer the self-guided trails of **Leslie M. Frost Natural Resources Center** (⊠ Hwy. 35 at St. Nora's Lake, Minden K0M 2K0, ☎ 705/766–2451) offer a great introduction to Ontario's wildlife.

Lodging

$$$ ⊞ **Domain of Killien.** Step inside and breathe the scent of pine and rich aromas from the kitchen: you have entered the domain of peace and quiet, a haven of year-round relaxation amid 800 acres of private forest near Algonquin Provincial Park. Rooms in the main lodge have whirlpool tubs, cedar dressing rooms, and views of the lake. Cabins have fireplaces and decks overlooking the lake. Fine wines are served with sophisticated dishes that showcase local ingredients: wild game in fall, new herbs and vegetables in spring, house-smoked duck and salmon year-round. The trout and bass are fresh from local lakes, and even the maple syrup is homemade. ⊠ *Carrol Rd., Box 810, K0M 1S0,* ☎ *705/457–1100,* ℻ *705/457–3853,* WEB *www.domainofkillien. on.ca. 5 lodge rooms, 9 lakeside cabins. Restaurant, 2 tennis courts, hiking, boating, ice-skating, cross-country skiing. AE, DC, MC, V. MAP.*

Outdoor Activities and Sports

SKIING LODGE-TO-LODGE

Three- and four-night guided lodge-to-lodge cross-country ski packages are available along the Haliburton Nordic Trail system. There are groups for skiers of all levels, and the trips cover 8–25 km (5–16 mi) per day, depending on the group's abilities. Six lodges participate in the program, and skiers stay and dine at a different lodge each night. Packages include all meals, trail passes, and a guide. For information about ski packages, contact **Haliburton Highlands Trails and Tours** (⊠ Box 147, Minden K0M 2K0, ☎ 800/461–7677, WEB www.trailsand-tours.on.ca).

SNOWMOBILING

C Mac Snow Tours (☎ 519/887–6686 or 800/225–4258) has three- and five-night all-inclusive excursions in Haliburton Highlands–Algonquin Provincial Park. In the 50,000-acre privately owned **Haliburton Forest** (⊠ R.R. 1, K0M 1S0, ☎ 705/754–2198, WEB www.haliburtonfor-est.com) there are 300 km (186 mi) of snowmobile trails, plus a shelter system. The day-use trail fee is $20. Machine and cottage rentals are available; call for rates.

Bracebridge

③④ *23 km (14 mi) north of Gravenhurst on Hwy. 11.*

Holiday cheer brightens Bracebridge in summer with Christmas-oriented amusements. The Bracebridge Falls on the Muskoka River are a good option for those who prefer a more peaceful excursion. After letting Santa know what they'd like to find under the Christmas tree, youngsters can ride the Kris Kringle Riverboat, the Candy Cane Express Train, minibikes, bumper boats, paddleboats, ponies, and more ♻ at **Santa's Village.** At the same location, **Sportsland** (⌨ $2.75 per ticket, rides cost 1 or 2 tickets each; ☉ mid-June–early Sept., Mon.–Sat. 9–9, Sun. 9–6), for children 12 and older, offers go-carts, batting cages, in-line skating, 18-hole miniature golf, laser tag, and an indoor activity center with video games. ⊠ *Santa's Village Rd. (west of Bracebridge)*, ☎ *705/645–2512*, WEB *www.santasvillage.on.ca.* ⌨ *$16.95.* ☉ *Mid-June–early Sept., daily 9–9.*

Dining and Lodging

$$ ✕▥ **Inn at the Falls.** This Victorian inn and its annex of motel-style
★ rooms command a magnificent view of pretty Bracebridge Falls. Accommodations include rooms and cottages; six of the units have fireplaces. The outdoor pool is heated. The main dining room ($$-$$$) and pub–lounge offer food and live entertainment; there's an outdoor patio as well. Try the steak-and-kidney pie. ⊠ *1 Dominion St., Box 1139, P1L 1V3,* ☎ *705/645–2245,* FAX *705/645–5093,* WEB *www. innatthefalls.net. 37 rooms, 2 cottages. Restaurant, pub, pool. AE, DC, MC, V.*

Dorset

③⑤ *48 km (30 mi) northeast of Bracebridge via Hwys. 11 and 117.*

Dorset is a pretty village on Lake of Bays; a lookout tower allows you to see for miles across the lake and over the forested landscape. It's home to **Robinson's General Store** (⊠ Main St., ☎ 705/766–2415), which has been in business since 1921. You'll find everything here from moose-fur hats to stoves and pine furniture. You can circle back to Toronto on scenic Highway 35 or make Dorset a stop on a tour from Huntsville around Lake of Bays.

Huntsville

③⑥ *34 km (21 mi) north of Bracebridge on Hwy. 11, 215 km (133 mi) north of Toronto on Hwys. 400 and 11.*

The Huntsville region is filled with lakes and streams, strands of virgin birch and pine, and deer that browse along the trails. Because the area is part of Toronto's Muskoka playground, there's no shortage of year-round resorts.

Dining and Lodging

$$$–$$$$ ✕▥ **Deerhurst Resort.** This spectacular, ultradeluxe resort at Peninsula Lake is a self-contained community on 800 acres. The flavor is largely modern, although the main lodge dates from 1886 and is appointed with a rustic flair. The historic part of the resort is home to Steamers restaurant ($$–$$$), which specializes in steaks prepared with a choice of marinades and imaginative sauces. The resort's spectacular, $15 million new wing (2000) is four stories high and embellished with an octagonal tower and decorative gables; it contains 102 warmly decorated guestrooms where large windows offer views of the 800-acre grounds and lakefront. While in the new wing, be sure to stop in at the Eclipse

Dining Room ($$–$$$), which serves Canadian specialties, such as Ontario lamb, Alberta beef, and rainbow trout, as well as more-exotic fare like baked grouper with blueberry-citrus essence. ⊠ *1235 Deerhurst Dr., P1H 2E8,* ☎ *705/789–6411 or 800/461–4393,* FAX *705/789–2431,* WEB *www.deerhurst.on.ca. 425 rooms. 3 restaurants, 2 lounges, indoor pool, 2 18-hole golf courses, tennis court, gym, racquetball, squash, windsurfing, boating, cross-country skiing, snowmobiling. AE, D, DC, MC, V.*

$$$ ✕🏨 **The Norsemen Restaurant and Resort.** Steeped in Old Muskoka ambience, this place is even more famous for its dining room than for its rustic cottages (rented by the week only) overlooking Walker Lake. The Norsemen Restaurant has earned generations of devotees by serving up a tempting Canadian harvest—from fresh Atlantic salmon and breast of pheasant to medallions of caribou—prepared with European flair. It's open for dinner only (seatings from 6 to 8:30 PM) Tuesday through Sunday in summer, and Thursday through Sunday in winter. ⊠ *1040 Walker Lake Dr., R.R. 4, P1H 2J6,* ☎ *705/635–2473; 800/565–3856 in Canada;* FAX *705/635–9370,* WEB *www.muskoka.com/norsemen. 7 cottages. Restaurant, kitchenettes, boating, fishing, cross-country skiing. AE, MC, V.*

$$$–$$$$ 🏨 **Grandview Inn.** This modern lakeside resort, a five-minute drive east of Huntsville, has a health spa where guests can relax with facials, massages, and other treatments. The numerous outdoor activities include excursions led by a resident naturalist into nearby Algonquin Provincial Park. You can try bird-watching and explore forested hiking and biking trails. ⊠ *939 Hwy. 60, P1H 1Z4,* ☎ *705/789–4417; 800/461–4454 in Canada;* FAX *705/789–6882,* WEB *www. grandviewinn.com. 98 rooms, 74 suites. 2 restaurants, indoor/outdoor pool, spa, 9-hole golf course, windsurfing, waterskiing, cross-country skiing. AE, DC, MC, V.*

Outdoor Activities and Sports

In southern Ontario the Huntsville area is usually the cross-country skier's best bet for an abundance of natural snow. Deerhurst, Grandview, and Norsemen resorts all have trails.

Algonquin Provincial Park

★ ㊲ *50 km (31 mi) northeast of Huntsville on Hwy. 60.*

Algonquin Provincial Park stretches across 7,725 square km (2,983 square mi) of lakes, forests, rivers, and cliffs. It's a hiker's, canoeist's, and camper's paradise. But don't be put off if you're not the athletic or rough-outdoors sort. About a third of all visitors to Algonquin come for the day to walk one of the 16 interpretive trails, or enjoy a swim or a picnic. Swimming is especially good at the Lake of Two Rivers, halfway between the west and east gates along Highway 60. A morning drive through the park in May or June is often rewarded by a moose sighting. Park naturalists give talks on wildflowers, animals, and birds of the area, and you can book a guided hike or canoe trip. Wolf-howling expeditions take place in autumn. Complete information about the park can be found at the gates.

Two attractions near the east side of the park are the **visitor center,** which includes a bookstore, a restaurant, and a panoramic-viewing deck, and the **Algonquin Logging Museum** (☉ May–late Oct., daily 10–6), which depicts life at an early Canadian logging camp. ⊠ *Box 219, Whitney K0J 2M0,* ☎ *705/633–5572,* WEB *www.algonquinpark.on.ca.* 🖼 *$10 per vehicle.* ☉ *Park daily 8* AM–*10* PM.

Dining and Lodging

$$$–$$$$
★ ✗▣ **Arowhon Pines.** Arowhon, a family-run resort in the heart of Algonquin Provincial Park, is known for unpretentious luxury and superb dining. Two- to twelve-bedroom log cabins are decorated with antique pine furnishings and have central lounges. The waterside suites have fireplaces and private decks. Room rates include three meals a day in the six-sided dining hall. Breakfast might include pancakes with maple syrup or Welsh rarebit with Canadian bacon; lunch could be a lakeside barbecue. At dinner, the chef emphasizes Ontario's seasonal ingredients: grilled pickerel in orange–ginger sauce, salmon with sorrel, spring lamb with fresh mint sauce. The menu changes daily. A sinful array of made-from-scratch desserts follows. Nonlodgers can reserve prix-fixe meals. If you'd like wine with dinner, you'll have to bring your own: park restrictions prohibit its sale here. Servers are happy to uncork it for you. Swimming, sailing, hiking, and birding are all possible, or you can choose to do nothing but enjoy the peace and quiet. ✉ *Off Hwy. 60, Box 10001, Algonquin Park, Huntsville P1H 2G5,* ☎ *705/633–5661 or 416/483–4393,* ℻ *705/633–5795,* ⟨WEB⟩ *www.arowhonpines.ca. 50 rooms in 13 cabins. Dining room, sauna, 2 tennis courts, hiking, boating. MC, V. Closed mid-Oct.–May. AP.*

$$$ ✗▣ **Bartlett Lodge.** A short boat ride on Cache Lake, about halfway through Algonquin Provincial Park along Highway 60, carries you to this venerable resort, founded in 1917. Bartlett Lodge is simple in design, offering both housekeeping cabins where you cook your own meals and accommodations with two meals included in the rate. The immaculate cabins have gleaming hardwood floors and king-size beds or two singles. Quiet reigns: no waterskiing, jet skiing, or motors over 10 horsepower are allowed on Cache Lake; and you won't find radios or TVs in the cabins. The Algonquin-style dining room offers a choice of table d'hôte menus that might include broiled rainbow trout with four-onion marmalade. Nonlodgers are welcome for dinner. No wine is sold, but you're welcome to bring your own. ✉ *Box 10004, Algonquin Park, Huntsville P1H 2G8,* ☎ *705/633–5543; 905/338–8908 in winter;* ℻ *705/633–5746,* ⟨WEB⟩ *www.bartlettlodge.com. 12 cabins. Dining room, kitchenettes (some), boating, mountain bikes. MC, V. Closed mid-Oct.–May. MAP.*

CAMPING

Camping is available in three categories, from the eight organized campgrounds along the Park Corridor, a 56-km (35-mi) stretch of Highway 60, to the vast interior, where there are no organized campsites at all (and the purists love it that way). In between are the lesser-known peripheral campgrounds in the western part of the park—Kiosk, Brent, and Achray—which you reach by long, dusty roads. These have only firewood and privies; the organized campsites have showers, picnic tables, and in some cases RV hookups. All organized campsites must be reserved; call **Ontario Parks** (☎ 800/688–7275, ⟨WEB⟩ www.ontarioparks.com). You need permits for interior camping, available at the Canoe Centre adjacent to the Portage Store or from Ontario Parks.

Outdoor Activities and Sports

If you plan to camp in the park, you may want to contact **The Portage Store** (✉ Hwy. 60, Box 10009, Huntsville P1H 2H4, ☎ 705/663–5622 in summer; 705/789–3645 in winter; ⟨WEB⟩ www.portagestore.com), which provides extensive outfitting services, from packages that might include permits, canoes, and food supplies to maps and detailed information about routes and wildlife.

Radcliffe Hills ski area (✉ Box 188, Barry's Bay K0J 1B0, ☎ 613/756–2931 or 800/668–8249), south of the park on Highway 60, has a vertical drop of 450 ft and a tubing run with a tube lift.

FORT ERIE AND WEST TO WINDSOR

The southernmost region of Canada is home to nature havens like Point Pelee National Park, mecca for birders from all over North America, historic sites like Fort Malden, and the glittering nightlife of Casino Windsor. The towns along Lake Erie tend to have histories in fishing and Great Lakes shipping. This is pretty farm country, too—once famous for tobacco, now a source of fruit and vegetables, including the grapes from which respectable wines are made on Pelee Island.

Fort Erie

㊳ *155 km (96 mi) south of Toronto via the Queen Elizabeth Way.*

Fort Erie, at the extreme southeast tip of the Niagara Peninsula, opposite Buffalo, New York, may be a drab town, but it's also the gateway to the scenic Niagara Parkway. This road along the Niagara River is lined with picnic tables and bicycle paths. The Peace Bridge, which links Fort Erie to its southern neighbor, is one of the busiest crossings along the Canada–U.S. border.

Historic Fort Erie, built in 1764 at what is now the south end of town, has been reconstructed to look as it did during the War of 1812, when thousands of soldiers lost their lives within sight of the earthworks, drawbridges, and palisades. Visitors are conducted through the display rooms by guards in period British army uniforms. In summer the guards stand sentry duty, fire the cannon, and demonstrate drill and musket practice. ⊠ *350 Lakeshore Rd.,* ☎ *905/871–0540 or 877/642-7275,* WEB *www.niagaraparks.com/historical/71-idx.html.* ☎ *$3.75.* ⊙ *May–Sept. 2, daily 10–6; Sept. 3–Oct., daily 10–4; Nov., weekdays 9:30–4.*

Although it dates from 1897, **Fort Erie Race Track** is one of the most modern, and picturesque, tracks in North America. Glass-enclosed dining lounges overlook a 2-km (1-mi) dirt track and a seven-furlong turf course. Also in view are gardens, ponds, and waterways. ⊠ *Bertie St. and Queen Elizabeth Way,* ☎ *905/871–3200 or 800/295–3770,* WEB *www.forterieracing.com.* ⊙ *May–Sept., Fri.–Mon., races at 12:45; Oct., Fri.–Sun., races at 12:45.*

Port Colborne

㊴ *30 km (19 mi) west of Fort Erie on Hwy. 3.*

Port Colborne, a shipping center on Lake Erie, is at the southern end of the 44-km-long (27-mi-long) Welland Canal, which connects Lake Ontario to Lake Erie, bypassing Niagara Falls. You can view **Lock 8** from a platform. The town (population 18,800) remains an enclave for descendants of United Empire Loyalist stock. Chronicling the town's rich history and development is the **Port Colborne Historical and Marine Museum,** a six-building complex. ⊠ *280 King St.,* ☎ *905/834–7604.* ☎ *Free.* ⊙ *May–Dec., daily noon–5.*

Welland

㊵ *10 km (6 mi) north of Port Colborne on Hwy. 58 or 140.*

In 1988 Welland staged a Festival of Arts Murals to attract some of the 14–16 million tourists who were bypassing the town on their way to Niagara Falls. Today nearly 30 giant murals depicting the city's multicultural history decorate downtown buildings; the longest spans 130 ft, and the tallest is three stories high. You can pick up a free mural tour map from **Welland-Niagara Tourism** (⊠ 800 Niagara St. N, Seaway Mall, ☎ 905/735–8696) or from brochure racks at City Hall and in local restaurants and hotels. Welland is also the home of the annual **Niagara Food Festival.** Held on the first weekend in October, the festival brings together an array of local farmers, wineries, and restaurants to present regional foods to crowds of visitors.

OFF THE
BEATEN PATH

WELLAND CANAL – At St. Catharines, about 25 km (16 mi) north of Welland, you may see a ship pass through Lock 3 of the Welland Canal, which joins Lake Erie and Lake Ontario. Also on the site, the St. Catharines Museum (☎ 905/984–8880, ☎ $3) has historical exhibits and displays about the construction of the canal, now part of the St. Lawrence Seaway. To get here from Welland, take Highway 406 north to the Queen Elizabeth Way and head west to St. Catharines; Lock 3 is at 1932 Government Road, near the Queen Elizabeth Way.

Port Dover

❹❶ *120 km (74 mi) west of Welland via Hwys. 58, 23, 3, and 6.*

Port Dover is the home of the world's largest fleet of freshwater fishing boats. It's a pretty beach resort town where freshwater fish is served up steamy and golden at a number of restaurants.

St. Thomas

❹❷ *99 km (61 mi) west of Port Dover on Hwy. 3 and 30 km (19 mi) east of London on Hwy. 3.*

St. Thomas has been associated with the railway industry since 1856. As a result, it has a number of railway-related shops, buildings, and preservation societies. St. Thomas's first buildings went up in 1810, more than a decade and a half ahead of the first building in London, Ontario. However, whereas London's population has hit 320,000, St. Thomas's leveled out at 30,000. The town has a **statue of Jumbo** (⊠ 555 Talbot St.), the Barnum and Bailey circus elephant killed here in a freak railway accident in 1885. The monument is a 10%-larger-than-life-size statue of the largest elephant ever in captivity. The **St. Thomas–Elgin Tourist Association** (⊠ 450 Sunset Dr., ☎ 519/631–8188 or 877/463–5446, WEB www.elgintourist.com), open May through Labor Day, is adjacent to the Jumbo monument and an antique railway caboose.

Port Stanley

❹❸ *15 km (9 mi) south of St. Thomas on Hwy. 4.*

The fishing village of Port Stanley has the largest natural harbor on the north shore of Lake Erie. Its fine brown-sand beach, boutiques, snack bars, and kitsch stands make for a lively summer destination.

☙ The **Port Stanley Terminal Railway,** built in 1856, survived on excursion traffic until 1957. Railroad buffs have restored passenger cars to their original 19th-century style and have repaired the line as far as Union, extending it to St. Thomas. You can take a round-trip excursion to Union (45 minutes) or St. Thomas (90 minutes). ⊠ *Port Stanley Railway Station,* ☎ *519/782–3730 or 877/244–4478.* ☎ *Round-trip fare to Union $9.50, to St. Thomas $11.50.* ☉ *July–Aug., daily; Sept.–Nov. and May–June, weekends; Dec.–Apr., Sun.; call for times.*

Dining and Lodging

$$–$$$ ✕🛏 **Kettle Creek Inn.** All the rooms and suites in this small, elegant
★   country inn and its modern annex have views of a landscaped court-

yard and gazebo. Some rooms have whirlpool baths and gas fireplaces. There are other nice touches, such as old-fashioned pedestal sinks and interesting local artwork. The three-room restaurant in the original inn (reserve ahead) offers daily specials, including fresh Lake Erie fish and Ontario venison, lamb, and pork. A two-night stay is mandatory on weekends in summer. ✉ *216 Joseph St., N5L 1C4,* ☎ *519/782–3388,* FAX *519/782–4747,* WEB *www.kettlecreekinn.com. 10 rooms, 5 suites. Restaurant. AE, D, DC, MC, V. CP.*

Point Pelee National Park

★ ❹❹ *150 km (93 mi) west of Port Stanley–St. Thomas on Hwy. 401 or Hwy. 3, near Leamington on Hwy. 33.*

The southernmost tip of mainland Canada, Point Pelee National Park has the smallest dry land area of any Canadian national park, yet it draws more than a half-million visitors every year. At the park's visitor center you'll find exhibits, slide shows, and a knowledgeable staff ready to answer questions. Some 700 kinds of plants and 347 species of birds have been recorded here, including a number of endangered species. A tram operates seasonally to "the tip." September is the best time to see monarch butterflies resting in Pelee before they head to Mexico's Sierra Madres. The park is also renowned for bird-watching, especially during spring and fall migrations. This is a day-use park only. ✉ *R.R. 1, Leamington N8H 3V4,* ☎ *519/322–2365,* WEB *www.parkscanada. pch.gc.ca.* 🔳 *$3.25 Apr.–Oct.; $2.25 Nov.–Mar.* ☉ *Late May–mid-Oct., daily 6 AM–9:30 PM; mid-Oct.–Mar., daily 7 AM–6:30 PM; Apr. 1–27, daily 6 AM–9:30 PM; Apr. 28–May 27, daily 5 AM–9:30 PM.*

Pelee Island

❹❺ *25 km (16 mi) and 90 min by ferry from Point Pelee via Hwy. 33 and Leamington ferry.*

Pelee is a small, flat island, roughly 13 by 6 km (8 by 4 mi), at the west end of Lake Erie. This is Canada's southernmost inhabited point, on the same latitude as northern California and northern Spain. In winter there are scheduled flights from Windsor. The island's permanent population is fewer than 300, but in summer that quadruples as vacationers cram into private cottages. Still, Pelee maintains its island pace. You can enjoy the beaches, cycle around the island, tour the Wine Pavilion (wine tastings $5), or visit the ruins of Vin Villa winery, which dates from the mid-1800s.

Kingsville

❹❻ *15 km (9 mi) west of Point Pelee National Park on Hwy. 18.*

Kingsville, one of the southernmost towns in Ontario, is best known for **Jack Miner's Bird Sanctuary,** started in 1904 as a wintering spot for Canada geese by hunter-turned-conservationist Jack Miner. About 50,000 Canada geese now winter here—up from the original four introduced by Miner. No admission is charged and nothing is sold on the grounds. A museum (closed Sunday) in the former stables has a wealth of Miner memorabilia. You can also feed far-from-shy geese and ducks. At 4 PM daily, the birds are flushed for "air shows" and circle overhead. The best times to view migrations are late March, October, and November. ✉ *Essex County Rd. 29, 5 km (3 mi) north of Kingsville,* ☎ *519/733–4034.* 🔳 *Free.* ☉ *Mid-Mar.–Dec., Mon.–Sat. 9–5.*

The **John R. Park Homestead and Conservation Area,** 8 km (5 mi) west of Kingsville, is a pioneer village anchored by one of Ontario's few examples of American Greek Revival architecture, an 1842 home. The village's 10 buildings include the house of John R. Park, a shed built without nails, a smokehouse, an icehouse, an outhouse, and a sawmill. ⊠ *County Rd. 50 at Iler Rd., Colchester,* ☎ *519/738–2029,* WEB *www.erca.org.* ⌧ *$3.* ☉ *May–Oct., Sun.–Thurs. 11–4; Nov.–Apr., Tues.–Thurs. 11–4.*

Southwestern Ontario Heritage Village

47 *About 10 km (6 mi) north of Kingsville on Hwy. 23.*

The Southwestern Ontario Heritage Village has 14 historic buildings spread across 54 wooded acres. Volunteers in period dress show visitors how pioneers baked, operated looms, and dipped candles. The **Transportation Museum** of the Historic Vehicle Society of Ontario, Windsor Branch, also on the grounds, displays a fine collection of travel artifacts, from snowshoes to buggies to vintage automobiles. ⊠ *6155 Arner Townline, Harrow N0R 1G0,* ☎ *519/776–6909.* ⌧ *$3.* ☉ *Village and museum Apr.–June and Sept.–Nov., Wed.–Sun. 10–5; July–Aug., daily 10–5.*

Amherstburg

48 *38 km (24 mi) west of Kingsville on Hwy. 18.*

The riverside parks in the quiet town of Amherstburg are great places to watch the procession of Great Lakes shipping. **Navy Yard Park,** with flower beds ringed by old anchor chains, has benches overlooking Bois Blanc Island and the narrow main shipping channel.

Fort Malden was the British base from which Detroit was captured in the War of 1812, although the site dates from 1727, when Jesuits founded a mission here. Now the fort is an 11-acre National Historic Park, with original earthworks, restored barracks, a military pensioner's cottage, two exhibit buildings, and picnic facilities. ⊠ *100 Laird Ave.,* ☎ *519/ 736–5416,* WEB *www.parkscanada.pch.gc.ca.* ⌧ *$2.75.* ☉ *May–Oct., daily 10–5; Nov.–Apr., call for times.*

The **North American Black Historical Museum** commemorates the Underground Railroad system many U.S. slaves used to flee to Canada. Between 1800 and 1860, an estimated 30,000 to 50,000 slaves made the journey to Canada; many crossed the Detroit River at Amherstburg because it was the narrowest point. An 1848 church and log cabin contain artifacts and biographies. ⊠ *277 King St.,* ☎ *519/736–5433.* ⌧ *$4.50.* ☉ *Mid-Apr.–Oct., Wed.–Fri. 10–5, weekends 1–5.*

Windsor

49 *24 km (15 mi) north of Amherstburg on Hwy. 18, 190 km (118 mi) west of London on Hwy. 401.*

Long an unattractive industrial city that hosted Ford, General Motors, and Chrysler manufacturing plants, Windsor has become a pleasant place to visit. The riverfront has pretty parks, some with fountains and statues, all overlooking the dramatic Detroit skyline. Windsor and Detroit are linked by the Ambassador Bridge and the Windsor–Detroit Tunnel. For many visitors, a major attraction is the spectacular **Windsor Casino** (⊠ 377 Riverside Dr. E, ☎ 800/991–7777), with 3,000 slot machines and 130 gambling tables. If you're traveling by car, start your Windsor visit at the **Convention & Visitors Bureau** (⊠ 333 Riverside Dr. W, Suite 103, ☎ 800/265–3633, WEB www.city.windsor.on.ca/cvb).

The **Art Gallery of Windsor** mounts displays of contemporary and historic Canadian art, and hosts traveling shows. After eight years at Devonshire Mall, the gallery has returned to the city center, in a gleaming facility facing the Detroit River. ⊠ *401 Riverside Dr.,* ☎ *519/977–0013.* ⊠ *Free, except for special exhibits.* ⊙ *Tues.–Thurs. 11–7, Fri. 11–9, Sat. 10–5, Sun. noon–5.*

The **Windsor Community Museum** holds a collection of area artifacts in the 1812 house where the Battle of Windsor, the final incident in the Upper Canada Rebellion, was fought in 1838. ⊠ *254 Pitt St. W,* ☎ *519/253–1812.* ⊠ *Free.* ⊙ *Tues.–Sat. 10–5, Sun. 2–5.*

Willistead Manor is the former home of Edward Chandler Walker, second son of Hiram, who founded Walker's Distillery in 1858. The 15-acre estate is now a city park. Each September, the Manor hosts an antique car show, one of the most prestigious in Canada. ⊠ *1899 Niagara St. at Kildare Rd.,* ☎ *519/253–2365.* ⊠ *Manor $3.50.* ⊙ *House tours Sept.–June, 1st and 3rd Sun. of each month 1–4; July and Aug., Sun. and Wed., 1–4; call for hrs.*

Since 1959, Windsor and Detroit have combined their national birthday parties (Canada Day, July 1, and Independence Day, July 4) into a massive bash called the **International Freedom Festival** (☎ 519/252–7264). The two-week party includes nonstop entertainment with more than 100 special events on both sides of the river and a spectacular fireworks display, billed as the largest in North America.

Dining and Lodging

$$–$$$ ✕ **Brigantino's.** This popular establishment serves traditional home-style Italian cooking with original twists, such as veal with cognac and Portobello mushrooms, or pasta stuffed with ricotta cheese and spinach and smothered in your choice of pesto, hot red, or cream sauce. Nightly entertainment adds festivity to the atmosphere, especially when accordion players are scheduled. ⊠ *1063 Erie St. E,* ☎ *519/254–7041. Reservations essential. AE, D, DC, MC, V.*

$$–$$$ 🖼 **Hilton Windsor.** Each of the guest rooms in this downtown riverbank hotel has a view of Detroit's skyline and the shipping activity on the world's busiest inland waterway. The Park Terrace Restaurant and Lounge offers a wide menu and a spectacular river view. There's music and dancing in the River Runner Bar and Grill. ⊠ *277 Riverside Dr. W, N9A 5K4,* ☎ *519/973–5555 or 800/445–8667,* FAX *519/973–1600,* WEB *www.hilton.com. 303 rooms. 2 restaurants, bar, room service, indoor pool, hot tub, sauna, meeting rooms. AE, DC, MC, V.*

THE NIAGARA PENINSULA

The two most-visited towns on the Niagara peninsula have very different flavors. Home to a wildly popular natural attraction, Niagara Falls can have a certain kitschy quality, whereas Niagara-on-the-Lake, which draws theatergoers to its annual Shaw festival, is a more tasteful, serene town. Still, Niagara Falls has something for everyone, from water slides and wax museums to honeymoon certificates. Niagara is one of the three best regions for wine production in Canada—Point Pelee and British Columbia are the others. More than 20 small, reputable vineyards produce fine wines, and most of them offer tastings and tours.

Niagara Falls

50—66 *130 km (81 mi) south of Toronto via the Queen Elizabeth Way.*

The town of Niagara Falls has attractions of all kinds, from the high-minded (a botanical garden) to the frankly commercial (the "museums" on Clifton Hill); the falls themselves are a one-of-a-kind reason to come here, though, in spite of the distractions. Although cynics have had a ★ field day with **Niagara Falls**—calling it everything from "water on the rocks" to "the second major disappointment of American married life" (Oscar Wilde)—most visitors are truly impressed. Missionary and explorer Louis Hennepin, whose books were widely read across Europe, first described the falls in 1678 as "an incredible Cataract or Waterfall which has no equal." Nearly two centuries later, Charles Dickens declared, "I seemed to be lifted from the earth and to be looking into Heaven." Henry James recorded in 1883 how one stands there "gazing your fill at the most beautiful object in the world."

These rave reviews lured countless daredevils to the falls. In 1859, 100,000 spectators watched as the French tightrope walker Blondin successfully crossed Niagara Gorge, from the American to the Canadian side, on a 3-inch-thick rope. From the early 18th century, dozens went over in boats and barrels. Nobody survived until 1901, when schoolteacher Annie Taylor emerged from her barrel and asked, "Did I go over the falls yet?" The stunts were finally outlawed in 1912.

The waterfall's colorful history began more than 10,000 years ago as a group of glaciers receded, diverting the waters of Lake Erie northward into Lake Ontario. The force and volume of the water as it flowed over the Niagara Escarpment created the thundering cataracts we know so well. Their turbulence didn't stop settlers on both sides of the river from killing one another in the War of 1812, most notably at the battle of Lundy's Lane. Today, however, relations are friendly between the two modest cities named Niagara Falls—one in the United States, the other in Canada.

The Niagara Parks Commission (NPC) was formed in 1885 to preserve the area around the falls, and in 1887, Ontario created Queen Victoria Park—the first provincial park in all of Canada. Since then the NPC has gradually acquired most of the land fronting the Canadian side of the Niagara River, from Niagara-on-the-Lake to Fort Erie. The Niagara Parkway, a 56-km (35-mi) riverside drive, is a 3,000-acre ribbon of parkland lined with parking overlooks, picnic tables, and barbecue pits; the public is welcome to use the facilities at no charge.

Winter shouldn't discourage you from coming: the **Winter Festival of Lights** is a real stunner. Seventy trees are illuminated with 34,000 lights in the parklands near the Rainbow Bridge; there's also "The Enchantment of Disney," lighted displays based on Disney characters. The falls are illuminated nightly from 5 to 10 PM, late November–mid-January.

50 The **Niagara Parks Botanical Gardens and School of Horticulture** has been graduating professional gardeners since 1936. The art of horticulture is celebrated by its students with 100 acres of immaculately maintained gardens. Within the Botanical Gardens is the **Niagara Parks Butterfly Conservatory** (☎ 905/371–0254; 💲 $8.50), home to one of North America's largest collections of free-flying butterflies—at least 2,000 are protected in a lush rain-forest setting by a glass-enclosed conservatory. The climate-controlled conservatory operates year-round and contains 50 species from around the world, each with its own colorful markings. ✉ 2565 N. Niagara Pkwy., ☎ 905/371–0254 or 877/642–7275. 💲 Botanical Gardens free. ☉ Year-round dawn–dusk.

Niagara Falls

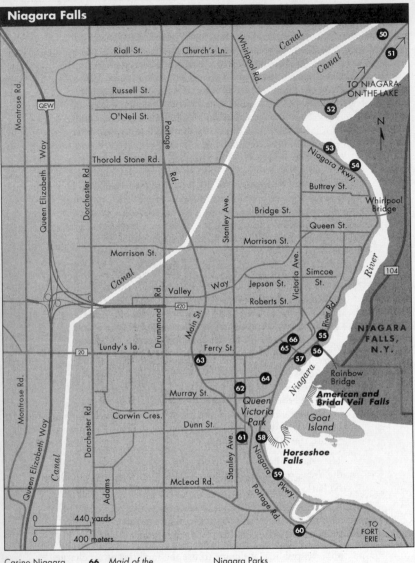

(51) A short distance (downriver) from the Botanical Gardens and School of Horticulture on the Niagara Parkway is a **floral clock,** one of the world's largest; its 39-ft "living" face is planted in a different design twice every season.

(52) There are trails maintained by the NPC in the **Niagara Glen.** A bicycle trail that parallels the Niagara Parkway from Fort Erie to Niagara-on-the-Lake winds between beautiful homes on one side and the river, with its abundant bird life, on the other.

(53) The **Niagara Spanish Aero Car,** in operation since 1916, is a cable car that crosses the Whirlpool Basin in the Niagara Gorge. This trip is not for the fainthearted; when you're high above the roiling whirlpool, those cables seem awfully thin. ✉ *Niagara Pkwy., 4½ km (3 mi) north of the falls,* ☎ *905/371–0254 or 877/642–7275.* 🎫 *$6.* ⏲ *Mid-June–early Sept., daily 9–9; early Sept.–Nov., shorter hours, weather permitting.*

(54) The **Great Gorge Adventure** involves taking an elevator to the bottom of the Niagara Gorge, where you can walk on a boardwalk beside the torrent of the Niagara River. The gorge is rimmed by sheer cliffs as it enters the giant whirlpool. ✉ *Niagara Pkwy., 3 km (2 mi) north of falls,* ☎ *905/371–0254 or 877/642–7275.* 🎫 *$5.75.* ⏲ *Late Apr.–mid-June, Sun.–Fri. 9–5, Sat. 9–6; mid-June–early Sept., daily 9–8; early Sept.–late Oct., daily 9–5.*

(55) The **Niagara Falls Museum,** founded in 1827, claims to be North America's oldest museum. It contains everything from stuffed birds and Egyptian mummies to the **Daredevil Hall of Fame,** where the barrels and other contraptions in which people have gone over the falls pay tribute to two centuries of Niagara Falls rebels. There are 26 galleries on four floors and 700,000 artifacts, so gauge your time accordingly—this museum is well worth two hours of browsing. ✉ *5651 River Rd.,* ☎ *905/356–2151.* 🎫 *$6.75.* ⏲ *May–Sept., daily 9 AM–11 PM; Oct.–Apr., daily 10–5.*

(56) **Ride Niagara** is divided into three portions: a theater presentation, an elevator ride down to the tunnel, and the shuttle that simulates plunging over the falls and down the rapids in a barrel. The entire event takes about 20–25 minutes. Children under three are not admitted. ✉ *5755 River Rd.,* ☎ *905/374–7433,* WEB *www.rideniagara.com.* 🎫 *$8.95.* ⏲ *June–early Sept., daily 8:30 AM–10:30 PM; call for off-season hrs.*

(57) ***Maid of the Mist*** boats have been operating since 1846, when they were wooden-hulled, coal-fired steamboats. Today, boats tow fun-loving passengers on 30-minute journeys to the foot of the falls, where the spray is so heavy that raincoats must be distributed. ✉ *Boats leave from foot of Clifton Hill,* ☎ *905/358–0311.* 🎫 *$12.25.* ⏲ *Apr.–June and early Sept.–Dec., daily 9–5 (weekends until 6), every 15 min; July–early Sept., daily 9–6, every 15 min.*

(58) At **Journey Behind the Falls** your admission ticket includes use of rubber boots and a hooded rain slicker. An elevator takes you to an observation deck that provides a fish's-eye view of the Canadian Horseshoe Falls and the Niagara River. From there a walk through three tunnels cut into the rock takes you behind the wall of crashing water. ✉ *Tours begin at Table Rock House, Queen Victoria Park,* ☎ *905/371–0254 or 877/642–7275.* 🎫 *$7.* ⏲ *Mid-June–early Sept., daily 9 AM–11 PM; early Sept.–mid-June, daily 9–5.*

(59) At the NPC's enormous **Greenhouse and Plant Conservatory,** south of Horseshoe Falls, you can see myriad plants and flowers year-round. ✉ *Niagara Pkwy.,* ☎ *905/371–0254 or 877/642–7275.* 🎫 *Free; parking $3 per hr.* ⏲ *Sun.–Thurs. 9:30–6, Fri.–Sat. 9:30–8.*

ⓒ ⑥⓪ **Marineland,** a theme park with a marine show, wildlife displays, and rides, is 1½ km (1 mi) south of the falls. The daily marine show includes performing killer whales, dolphins, harbor seals, and sea lions. Children can pet and feed members of a herd of 500 deer and get nose-to-nose with North American freshwater fish. Among the many rides is Dragon Mountain, the world's largest steel roller coaster. Marineland is signposted from Niagara Parkway or reached from the Queen Elizabeth Way by exiting at McLeod Road (Exit 27). ⊠ *8375 Stanley Ave.,* ☎ *905/356–9565,* ⓦⒺⒷ *www.marinelandcanada.com.* 🎫 *$16.95–$29.95, depending on season.* ⊙ *May–June and Sept., daily 10–5; Oct., daily 10–4:30; July–Aug., daily 9–6.*

⑥① **Minolta Tower Centre,** 525 ft above the base of the falls, affords panoramic views of Horseshoe Falls and the area. Renovations in 2001 did away with the "Cybermind" thrill-ride simulators, but made room for more shopping and dining opportunities. ⊠ *6732 Oakes Dr.,* ☎ *905/356–1501 or 800/461–2492.* 🎫 *$6.95.* ⊙ *9 AM until lights go off at the falls (as late as midnight in summer).*

⑥② **Niagara Falls IMAX Theatre/The Daredevil Adventure Gallery.** You can see the wonder of the falls up close and travel back in time for a glimpse of its 12,000-year-old history with *Niagara: Miracles, Myths and Magic.* The movie screen, Canada's largest, is more than six stories high. The Daredevil Adventure Gallery chronicles the expeditions of those who have tackled the falls. ⊠ *6170 Buchanan Ave.,* ☎ *905/358–3611.* 🎫 *$10.* ⊙ *Daily 11–8; movies run every hr on the hr.*

⑥③ **Lundy's Lane Historical Museum,** dating from 1874, is on the site of a savage battle in the War of 1812. There are displays of the lives of settlers of that era, as well as military artifacts. ⊠ *5810 Ferry St.,* ☎ *905/358–5082.* 🎫 *$1.60.* ⊙ *May–Nov., daily 9–4; Dec.–Apr., weekdays noon–4.*

⑥④ Rising 775 ft above the falls, **Skylon Tower** offers the best view of both the great Niagara gorge and the entire city. An indoor-outdoor observation deck facilitates the view. Amusements for children plus a revolving dining room are other reasons to visit. ⊠ *5200 Robinson St.,* ☎ *905/356–2651 or 877/475–9566.* 🎫 *$8.50.* ⊙ *Mid-June–early Sept., daily 8 AM–midnight; early Sept.–early June, daily 10–10.*

ⓒ ⑥⑤ **Clifton Hill,** opposite the American falls, is the most crassly commercial district of Niagara Falls. Sometimes referred to as "Museum Alley," this area encompasses the **Guinness Museum of World Records** (☎ 905/356–2299, 905/356–2238, 905/374–6601, or 905/358–3061), **Ripley's Believe It or Not Museum** (☎ 905/356–2299, 905/356–2238, 905/374–6601, or 905/358–3061), **Movieland Wax Museum** (☎ 905/356–2299, 905/356–2238, 905/374–6601, or 905/358–3061), and much more. Admission for most attractions runs from about $7 to $10.

⑥⑥ **Casino Niagara,** set in an architectural design reminiscent of the 1920s, has a total of 3,000 slot machines and 123 gambling tables, such as blackjack, roulette, baccarat, Caribbean stud poker, Let It Ride, Pai Gow poker, and Big Six. Within the casino are several restaurants and lounges. ⊠ *5705 Falls Ave.,* ☎ *888/946–3255 or 905/374–3598.* ⊙ *Daily 24 hrs.*

Dining and Lodging

$$$–$$$$ ✕ **Skylon Tower.** Don't come here for surprises—this tower is owned by the same people who own the local Holiday Inn—but for the view from the Revolving Dining Room, which rotates at one revolution per hour. Traditionally prepared rack-of-lamb, baked salmon, steak, and chicken make up the list of entrées. It's an eclectic crowd, with people

in cocktail wear and casual clothes seated side-by-side. Even with a reservation, there may be a short wait. ⊠ *5200 Robinson St.,* ☎ *905/356–2651. AE, DC, MC, V.*

$$$–$$$$ ✕ **21 Club.** Whether you come to the casino for baccarat or the slots, dining at this elegant restaurant is no gamble. The menu has solid high-end American steak-house fare and some Italian specialties. The room, totally insulated and away from the crowds, is a great setting in which to appreciate classic shrimp cocktail or lobster lasagnetta—fresh pasta wrapped around sautéed lobster, shallots, and basil. You'd have to search far to find a more delectably grilled 24-ounce Canadian porterhouse steak. ⊠ *Casino Niagara, 5705 Falls Ave.,* ☎ *905/374–3598. AE, DC, MC, V.*

$$–$$$$ ✕ **Casa d'Oro.** It looks a little like a Disney version of a Venetian castle, but ornate wall sconces, fireplaces, wine casks, and huge faux-marble and bronze sculptures are somehow not out of place in Niagara Falls. The Roberto family has been serving steak, seafood, and traditional Italian specialties here for 30 years. Folks come not only for the gigantic portions of prime rib, T-bones, and fillets, but also for the experience. After dinner, you can cross a painted bridge that spans a water-filled moat to the Rialto nightclub's raised dance floor. ⊠ *5875 Victoria Ave.,* ☎ *905/356–5646. AE, D, DC, MC, V.*

$$–$$$ ✕ **Casa Mia.** Casa Mia, a lovely off-the-tourist-track Italian villa 10
★ minutes from the center of town, is truly a special place. All the pasta is kitchen-made. Fresh-grated beets impart a shocking pink color to the gnocchi, divine with fresh Gorgonzola sauce. If you've ever wondered what real cannelloni is like, try these light pasta pancakes, filled with coarse-ground veal and spinach. The veal chop, pan seared with sage and truffle oil, is a thing of beauty. Heart-smart menu selections are indicated, and even the desserts, particularly cassata (a light cake with homemade ice-cream terrine) are not overly heavy. You can dine in the wine cellar or in the airy and modern dining room. Weekends there's live music in the piano lounge. ⊠ *3518 Portage Rd.,* ☎ *905/356–5410. AE, MC, V.*

$$–$$$ ✕ **Table Rock.** Run by Niagara Parks, Table Rock serves inoffensive, standard U.S.–Canadian fare in an amazing setting: as it loves to advertise, "If you were any closer, you'd go over the Falls." The dining room, in the rear of a two-story souvenir shop, offers tourist comfort food such as Caesar salads, baked salmon, pasta primavera, and beef and chicken burritos. ⊠ *Just above Scenic Tunnels,* ☎ *905/354–3631. AE, DC, MC, V.*

$$–$$$ ✕ **Victoria Park.** What you see is what you get at this middle-of-the-road kitchen, run by Niagara Parks. A salmon is a salmon. Chicken is chicken. But who's looking at the plates when the Falls are right outside? Pass on the cake on Sunday; it's often a bit dry by the end of the week. The restaurant is open for breakfast. ⊠ *River Rd. and Murray St.,* ☎ *905/356–2217 or 877/642–7275. AE, MC, V.*

$–$$ ✕ **Capri.** This family-owned restaurant serves huge, Italian-style plat-
★ ters such as linguine with chicken cacciatore. The three separate dining rooms, decorated in dark-wood paneling, draw families daily because of the half dozen specially priced children's dishes and a something-for-everyone menu. ⊠ *5438 Ferry St. (Hwy. 20), about ½ mi from Falls,* ☎ *905/354–7519. AE, DC, MC, V.*

$–$$ ✕ **Yukiguni.** Excellent Japanese food is served up in what might have been a country-and-western restaurant in a previous life. Yukiguni is popular with locals and Japanese tourists because of its reasonable lunch specials, which include miso soup, fresh salad, and such entrées as juicy pepper-flavored chicken skewers. Other menu options include tempura soba, thin buckwheat noodles that come with shrimp and vegetable tempura; and steamed smoked eel, served on rice in a round stacked lacquer box. Chicken and salmon teriyaki leave an aromatic trail as they are carried aloft on sizzling iron plates. ⊠ *5980 Buchanan Ave.,* ☏ *905/354–4440. AE, DC, MC, V.*

$ ✕ **Simon's Newsstand and Restaurant.** This large, bustling room, run by the Simon family for more than 100 years, has a few Formica tables with vinyl-and-chrome chairs, as well as decades of license plates, duck decoys, and a hodgepodge of Canadian memorabilia. You can take out such staples as bread, milk, and soda pop, or sit down at the long counter and enjoy a hearty all-day breakfast. Simon's makes super grilled-cheese sandwiches, BLTs, and tuna salads, and the meat loaf dinner has its die-hard fans. ⊠ *4116 Bridge St.,* ☏ *905/356–5310. Reservations not accepted. No credit cards.*

$$$$ ✕☷ **Sheraton Fallsview Hotel and Conference Centre.** This high-rise hotel has oversize guest rooms and suites, most with breathtaking views of the falls. Business facilities are excellent; the hotel provides high-quality teleconferencing. The fine dining room ($$–$$$) has snagged the best view in town, and the kitchen does its part with a French Continental menu that might include tournedos with a three-peppercorn sauce. There's a two-night minimum stay on weekends. ⊠ *6755 Fallsview Blvd., L2G 3W7,* ☏ *905/374–1077 or 800/267–8439,* FAX *905/374–6224,* WEB *www.fallsview.com. 295 rooms. 2 restaurants, lobby lounge, pool, hot tub, sauna, spa, convention center, meeting rooms. AE, D, DC, MC, V.*

$$$$ ☷ **Renaissance Fallsview Hotel.** Many rooms overlook the falls at this luxuriously appointed hotel, about ½ km (⅓ mi) from the mighty cataracts. In Mulberry's Dining Room, you can sample the artistry of executive chef Michael Heeb. There are lots of recreational facilities on the premises and golf and fishing nearby. ⊠ *6455 Buchanan Ave., L2G 3V9,* ☏ *905/357–5200 or 800/363–3255,* FAX *905/357–3422,* WEB *www.renaissancefallsview.com. 262 rooms. 2 restaurants, lounge, indoor pool, hot tub, sauna, gym, racquetball, squash, business services, meeting rooms. AE, D, DC, MC, V.*

$$$–$$$$ ☷ **Brock Plaza Hotel.** Since its opening in the 1920s, this grande dame of Niagara hotels has hosted royalty, prime ministers, and Hollywood stars. Now completely renovated but with glamorous details intact, the imposing, stone-walled Brock is part of the Casino Niagara complex, with indoor access to gaming facilities, the Hard Rock Café, and the Rainbow Room restaurant overlooking the falls. Rooms offer the elegance and comfort suggested by a first-class, four-star rating. Classic 1920s details like white wainscoting and brass fixtures blend with expansive windows that offer views of the falls from nearly every room. ⊠ *5685 Falls Ave., L2E 6W7,* ☏ *905/374–4444 or 800/263–7135,* FAX *905/371–8347,* WEB *www.niagarafallshotels.com. 236 rooms. 2 restaurants, coffee shop, dining room, lounge, indoor pool, hot tub, sauna, spa. AE, D, DC, MC, V.*

$$–$$$$ ☷ **Fallsway Quality Inn.** Very near the falls and not far from a golf course, the inn is on nicely landscaped grounds, which can be viewed from a pleasant patio. Rooms range from opulent, with plush furnishings and hot tubs, to clean, comfortable, and affordable family suites, some at poolside. ⊠ *4946 Clifton Hill, Box 60, L2E 6S8,* ☏ *905/358–3601 or 800/263–7137,* WEB *www.fallswayresort.com. 275 rooms. Restaurant, lobby lounge, 2 pools, hot tub, playground. AE, MC, V.*

$$–$$$$ ☷ **Lincoln Motor Inn.** A pleasant landscaped courtyard gives this motor inn, within walking distance of the falls, an intimate feeling. Connecting family suites sleep up to a dozen. Facilities include an extra-large heated pool and an outdoor heated whirlpool. A golf course is nearby. ⊠ *6417 Main St., L2G 5Y3,* ☏ *905/356–1748 or 800/263–2575,* FAX *905/356–7531,* WEB *www.lincolnmotorinn.com. 57 rooms. Restaurant, pool, hot tub. AE, MC, V.*

$–$$ ☑ **Candlelight Motor Inn.** This two-story motel offers good, basic accommodations. Some rooms have whirlpool tubs and slightly fancier decor; the two efficiency suites have small kitchens. ✉ *7600 Lundy's La., L2H 1H1,* ☎ *905/354–2211 (reservations); 905/374–7010 or 800/ 572–0308;* FAX *905/358–0696,* WEB *www.candlelightniagara.com. 50 rooms. Restaurant, pool. AE, DC, MC, V.*

Nightlife and the Arts
There are free band concerts on summer Sundays at Queenston Heights Park, Queen Victoria Park, and Historic Fort Erie, as well as Rainbow Bridge Carillon recitals.

Guided Tours
Double Deck Tours (☎ 905/295–3051) operates 4½- to 5-hour tours in double-decker English buses. The tours operate daily from mid-May through October and include most of the major sights of Niagara Falls. The $44 fare includes admission to Journey Behind the Falls, *Maid of the Mist,* and a trip in the Niagara Spanish Aero Car. Tours depart from the *Maid of the Mist* building. From late April to mid-October, the NPC operates a **People Mover System** in which air-conditioned buses travel on a loop route between its public parking lot above the falls at Rapids View Terminal (well marked) and the Niagara Spanish Aero Car parking lot about 8 km (5 mi) downriver. With a day's pass (available at any booth on the system for $5.50) you can get on and off as many times as you wish at the well-marked stops along the route. **Executive Coach Services** (☎ 416/740–3339) has year-round guided day trips from Toronto to Niagara. These include a buffet lunch overlooking the Falls year-round; in summer, a ride on the *Maid of the Mist* boat under the Falls is added, and in winter the IMAX film *Miracles, Myths, and Magic of Niagara* is part of the package. Cost is about $110.

Niagara Helicopters Ltd. (☎ 905/357–5672 or 800/281–8034, WEB www.niagara-helicopter.com) takes you on a nine-minute flight over the Giant Whirlpool, up the Niagara Gorge, and past the American falls and then banks around the curve of the Horseshoe Falls for a thrill. The cost is $85 per person.

Outdoor Activities and Sports
The Niagara Parks Commission (☎ 905/371–0254 or 877/642–7275, WEB www.niagaraparks.com) maintains 56 km (30 mi) of **bicycle trails** along the Niagara River between Fort Erie and Niagara-on-the-Lake.

Wine Region
Some of the Niagara Peninsula's 30 wineries are on the Niagara Parkway between Niagara Falls and Niagara-on-the-Lake, or on Highway 55 from the Queen Elizabeth Way. As the quality of Ontario wines has improved in recent years, wine makers have stepped up their marketing and promotional activities. Several wineries offer wine tasting and tours; call ahead for exact times.

For a map of the wine region, including locations of individual wineries and details of summer events, contact the **Wine Council of Ontario** (✉ 110 Hanover Dr., Suite B205, St. Catharines L2W 1A4, ☎ 905/ 684–8070). **Château des Charmes Wines Ltd.** (☎ 905/262–4219), one of Ontario's most respected wineries, is about halfway between Niagara Falls and Niagara-on-the-Lake. **Hillebrand Estates Winery** (☎ 905/ 468–7123 or 800/582–8412) is close to town on Highway 55. **Inniskillin Wines** (☎ 905/468–3554) has won a name for itself internationally. **Konzelmann Winery** (☎ 905/935–2866) overlooks Lake Ontario. **Reif Estates Winery** (☎ 905/468–7738) overlooks the Niagara River.

Niagara-on-the-Lake

⑥⑦ *15 km (9 mi) north of (downriver from) Niagara Falls.*

Since 1962 Niagara-on-the-Lake has been considered the southern outpost of fine summer theater in Ontario because of its acclaimed Shaw Festival. But it offers far more than Stratford, its older theatrical sister to the west: this city is a jewel of Canadian history, architectural marvels, remarkable beauty, and, of course, quality theater. Though the town of 14,000 is worth a visit at any time of the year, its most attractive period is from April through October, when both the Shaw Festival and the flowers are in full bloom.

Being located where the Niagara River enters Lake Ontario has both advantages and disadvantages. Because of its ideal placement, the area was settled by Loyalists to the British Crown, who found it a haven during the American Revolution. Soon after, it was made the capital of Upper Canada by John Graves Simcoe, a soldier–statesman who settled here after fighting in the war. For a time the town was the site of the provincial capital, but its proximity to the border made it subject to easy attack. As a result, Simcoe moved the capital to a more remote outpost, York—today's Toronto. Simcoe was also unimpressed with the name Niagara (roughly translated as "thundering waters"), so he changed the town's name to Newark (it was a new ark of safety for the Loyalists fleeing the upheaval south of the border). Eventually the original name returned, but following years of confusion with the Niagara with the falls to the south, in 1906 it was renamed once again, to the present Niagara-on-the-Lake.

Simcoe's decision to move the capital was vindicated during the War of 1812 when the upstart Americans came calling, but not as tourists. They captured nearby Fort George in 1813, occupied the town that summer, and burned it to the ground that December. Some of Niagara-on-the-Lake's best days were in the late 1800s to early 1900s, when it was connected to Toronto by steamer and the town became a prominent summer retreat for sweltering Torontonians. A passenger boat service connecting the town with Toronto has recently been reintroduced.

Following the transfer of the county seat to nearby St. Catharines and the arrival of the automobile and four-lane highways, the town slipped into relative obscurity. It remained a sleepy town until 1962, when local lawyer Brian Doherty organized eight weekend performances of two George Bernard Shaw plays, *Don Juan in Hell* and *Candida*. The next year he helped found the festival, whose mission is to perform the works of Shaw and his contemporaries.

The three theaters used by the Shaw Festival present quality performances, but what's also special are the abundant orchards and flower gardens, sailboats, and the utterly charming town of Niagara-on-the-Lake itself. This is one of the best-preserved 19th-century towns on the continent, with many neoclassical and Georgian homes still standing proudly—and lived in, too.

This is a very small town that can easily be explored on foot. **Queen Street** is the core of the commercial portion; walking east along that single street, with Lake Ontario to your north, you get a glimpse of the town's architectural history. At No. 209 is the handsome Richardson-Kiely House, built about 1832 for a member of Parliament, with later additions at the end of the 19th century. No. 187 dates from 1822, with later Greek Revival improvements. A veteran of the 1814 Battle of Lundy's Lane in Niagara Falls once occupied No. 165, an 1820 beauty. For decades, No. 157, built in 1823, was occupied by descendants of the Rogers-Harrison family, prominent since the early 19th century in church and town affairs. McClelland's, a store at No. 106, has been in business in Niagara-on-the-Lake since the War of 1812. The huge "T" sign means "provisioner."

Grace United Church, built in 1852, is a collage of architectural styles, including Italianate and Norman. Stained-glass windows dedicated to the memory of Canadians killed in World War I were installed in the 1920s. The church was originally commissioned by a congregation of "Free Kirk" Presbyterians, but was later sold to Methodists and now serves a congregation of the United Church (a merger of Presbyterians, Methodists, and Congregationalists). In summer the Shaw Festival often uses the church as a rehearsal space. ⊠ *222 Victoria St.,* ☎ *905/468–4044.*

The **Niagara Apothecary** was built in 1866 and restored in 1971. The museum has exquisite walnut and butternut fixtures, crystal pieces, and a rare collection of apothecary glasses. ⊠ *5 Queen St.,* ☎ *905/468–3845.* ▭ *Free.* ☉ *Mid-May–early Sept., daily noon–6.*

The **Niagara Historical Society Museum,** one of the oldest and most complete museums of its kind in Ontario, has an extensive collection relating to the often colorful history of the Niagara Peninsula from the earliest times through the 19th century. The museum has a gift shop and also offers guided tours of the town. ⊠ *43 Castlereagh St.,* ☎ *905/468–3912.* ▭ *$3.* ☉ *May–Oct., daily 10–5; Nov.–Dec. and Mar.–Apr., daily 1–5; Jan.–Feb. weekends 1–5.*

☾ On a wide stretch of parkland south of town sits **Fort George National Historic Park.** The fort was built in the 1790s to replace Fort Niagara, but was lost to the Yankees during the War of 1812. It was recaptured after the burning of the town in 1813, and largely survived the war, only to fall into ruins by the 1830s. It was reconstructed a century later, and you can explore the officers' quarters, barracks rooms of the common soldiers, the kitchen, and more. Like many other historic sites in Ontario, the town is staffed by people in period uniform who conduct tours and reenact 19th-century infantry and artillery drills. ⊠ *Queens Parade, Niagara Pkwy.,* ☎ *905/468–4257,* ⊞ *www.niagara.com/~parkscan.* ▭ *$6.* ☉ *Apr.–Oct., daily 10–5.*

Dining and Lodging
The area has some lovely restaurants and inns, both within town and outside it; a number of wineries in the area have restaurants and inns as well.

$$$–$$$$ ✕ **Hillebrands Vineyard Café.** After a complimentary winery tour and tasting, you can settle down to a superb meal that focuses on the freshest local produce. Chef Tony di Luca creates dishes such as grilled salmon and fennel on vegetable risotto, juicy venison burger with onion, sage, and Dijon mustard relish, and hearty pasta tossed with a luscious peppery-edged beef ragout. Tossed salad is a beautiful relationship between organic greens, sun-dried blueberries, and roasted crisp garlic. The pastry chef composes incredible desserts: bittersweet chocolate nut tart molded in a cup is filled with vanilla ice cream and topped with candied hazelnuts. ⊠ *Hwy. 55, Niagara Stone Rd.,* ☎ *905/468–3201. AE, D, MC, V.*

$$$–$$$$ ✕ **Ristorante Giardino.** Italian marble combines with stainless steel and rich colors to create a contemporary Italian ambience on 19th-century Queen Street. Chefs recruited from Italy produce antipasti such as Parma ham served with melon, smoked salmon terrine, or marinated swordfish with herbs. There's always grilled fresh fish or oven roasted chicken and lamb. Make time to indulge in the kitchen's classic Italian desserts

and fresh Niagara fruits. The long wine list is worth a careful read. ⊠ *Gate House Hotel, 142 Queen St.,* ☎ *905/468–3263. AE, DC, MC, V. Closed Jan.–Feb.*

$$$–$$$$ ✕ **Vineland Estates Winery Restaurant.** Exquisite Italian food and award-winning wines are served by an enthusiastic staff on the wine deck or in the glassed-in restaurant, with a panoramic view of the vineyard and lake. The fresh lemon poppyseed baguette is served warm, and the pasta is homemade (try the pappardelle tossed with Niagara hazelnuts, arugula, cremini mushrooms, and Montasio cheese). Feeling carnivorous? The chef pan roasts local venison and partners it with parsnip–potato puree, leeks, and blueberry jus. Desserts are a happy marriage of local fruits and an imaginative pastry chef. ⊠ *3620 Moyer Rd., Vineland,* ☎ *905/562–7088. AE, D, MC, V.*

$$ ✕ **Buttery Theatre Restaurant.** At Margaret Niemann's authentic British pub–café, the wood-beam ceiling, beaten copper tabletops, and china and pewter all bear the patina of age. Lively Tudor banquets and feasts are held every Friday and Saturday, and the tavern menu includes good pâtés and Cornish pasties (a beef-filled pastry envelope). The chef bakes chicken with fresh lemons and roasts leg of lamb in the manner of Henry VIII. After-theater dinners (10 PM–midnight) are offered on Friday and Saturday, and there's afternoon tea daily from 2 to 5. ⊠ *19 Queen St.,* ☎ *905/468–2564. AE, MC, V.*

$$ ✕ **Fans Court.** Delicate Cantonese cuisine is prepared in a lovely, antiques-filled restaurant in a courtyard between an art gallery and a greenhouse. Mature jade trees in urns stand at the entrance. In summer you can sit outdoors and sample such favorites as fried rice served in a pineapple, lemon chicken, and black-pepper-and-garlic beef. ⊠ *135 Queen St.,* ☎ *905/468–4511. AE, MC, V.*

$$$$ ✕▥ **Inn on the Twenty.** The inn is part of Leonard Pennachetti's Cave Spring Cellars winery in the village of Jordan, 10 minutes from Niagara-on-the-Lake. Rooms have elegant antiques, whirlpool baths, and fireplaces. The sophisticated restaurant On the Twenty ($$–$$$) has a reputation for top-notch cuisine that emphasizes the bounty of the region. Dine on quail grilled with shiitake mushrooms, trout baked in parchment with Riesling and leeks, or Ontario rack of lamb with mashed potatoes. You are welcome to tour and sample the wines of Cave Spring Cellars across the street. The restaurant is closed some days from January through April, so call ahead. ⊠ *3845 Main St., Jordan L0R 1S0,* ☎ *905/562–5336 or 800/701–8074; 905/562–1313 for restaurant;* ℻ *905/562–0009;* ⍟ *www.innonthetwenty.on.ca. 19 rooms. Restaurant. AE, DC, MC, V. CP.*

$$$$ ✕▥ **Oban Inn.** This elegant, historic country inn has a view of Lake Ontario. Each room is distinct, embellished with antiques in an Old World English tone; some have fireplaces. While away the day on broad verandas or in beautifully manicured gardens. The popular dining room ($$–$$$) spotlights Canadian beef with fresh vegetables and fruits; the poached salmon is a favorite in summer. The lounge offers an all-day menu of traditional fish-and-chips, steak-and-kidney pie, and a variety of sandwiches and appetizers. On Sunday, a brunch of whole turkey, ham, and prime rib brings out the locals. ⊠ *160 Front St., L0S 1J0,* ☎ *905/468–2165 or 888/669–5566,* ℻ *905/468–4165,* ⍟ *www.vintageinns.com. 22 rooms. Restaurant, pub, library, baby-sitting. AE, D, DC, MC, V.*

$$$$ ✕▥ **Pillar and Post Inn, Spa and Conference Center.** This hotel, six long blocks from the heart of town, has been a cannery, barracks, and basket factory. Most rooms have handcrafted early American pine furniture, patchwork quilts, and such modern amenities as hair dryers. The 100 Fountain Spa has a variety of soothing body treatments. The casual Vintages Wine Bar and Lounge serves regional cuisine and wines.

The Cannery is a terrific casual steak house and the Carriages Dining Room menu is inspired by what the market has to offer: four-peppercorn liver pâté with fig-and-onion marmalade, perhaps, or stuffed chicken breast with herb-crusted goat cheese on roasted eggplant. ⊠ *48 John St., L0S 1J0,* ☏ *905/468–2123 or 888/669–5566,* FAX *905/468–3551,* WEB *www.vintageinns.com. 123 rooms, 7 suites. 2 restaurants, lobby lounge, indoor pool, sauna, spa, health club, business services. AE, D, DC, MC, V.*

$$$$ ✕⌂ **Prince of Wales Hotel.** A visit from the Prince of Wales in the early
★ 1900s inspired the name of this venerable hostelry. A lot has changed since then. The improved Prince of Wales has been designed in the style of an upper-crust English manor house, Victorian in flavor and complete with its own tearoom (where the Queen herself might feel at home). Exquisite wall treatments, antique furnishings, and fresh flowers meet the eye at every turn. Renowned chef Lee Parsons presides at the Escabechè restaurant; his haute French cuisine changes at whim. *Ballotine* (boned, stuffed, and rolled meat) of duck confit and foie gras with lentil salad, roast lamb with garlic shallot purée, and brilliant sauces are all possibilities. At the Churchill Lounge, lighter and less expensive meals such as beef Stroganoff, wild-mushroom risotto, and salads are served. ⊠ *6 Picton St., Box 46, L0S 1J0,* ☏ *905/468–3246 or 888/669–5566,* FAX *905/468–5521. 108 rooms. Dining room, tea shop, indoor pool, health club. AE, D, DC, MC, V.*

$$$$ ✕⌂ **Queen's Landing Inn.** This hotel has knockout views of historic
★ Fort George. Rooms are nicely decorated with antiques, including canopy beds; many have working fireplaces and modern whirlpool baths. The Tiara Dining Room offers an outstanding regional Canadian menu in a room flattered by stained glass and a full view of the lake. The kitchen provides a blend of Asian spicing and excellent local meats and produce. Don't miss the rosemary-grilled quail with Japanese greens and Niagara peach preserves, or the pan-seared foie gras with wild raspberries. Main courses such as cinnamon-roasted veal tenderloin and parsley-crusted breast of chicken with buckwheat risotto show the skill and imagination of the chef. The menu also lists vegetarian choices. ⊠ *155 Byron St., Box 1180, L0S 1J0,* ☏ *905/468–2195 or 888/669–5566,* FAX *905/468–2227,* WEB *www.vintageinns.com. 142 rooms. Dining room, lounge, indoor pool, hot tub, sauna, gym, baby-sitting. AE, D, DC, MC, V.*

$$$$ ⌂ **White Oaks Conference Resort & Spa.** Close to town, this luxury resort has a full range of activities—squash, racquetball, and tennis, as well as aerobics classes. A video arcade keeps kids occupied. ⊠ *253 Taylor Rd., L0S 1J0,* ☏ *905/688–2550 or 800/263–5766,* FAX *905/688–2220,* WEB *www.whiteoaksresort.com. 126 rooms, 24 suites. 2 restaurants, lobby lounge, indoor pool, hot tub, sauna, 12 tennis courts, health club, racquetball, squash, baby-sitting, business services. AE, D, MC, V.*

$$–$$$ ✕⌂ **Olde Angel Inn.** The War of 1812 saw much action around this inn, a charming lemon-yellow coach house with green shutters that was established circa 1779. A resident ghost—some say he's a soldier who had gone AWOL and was killed here—is believed to walk the cellar. Rooms have antiques and canopy beds. The tavern sets out pub fare such as steak, Guinness, and oyster pie on antique wooden refectory tables. Entrées on the dining room menu include prime rib of beef au jus, rack of lamb with mint sauce, or *trois amours*—shrimp, scallops, and crab baked in a supreme sauce with Swiss and Parmesan cheese. Even if you don't stay here, be sure to stop in for a meal. ⊠ *224 Regent St., L0S 1J0,* ☏ *905/468–3411,* WEB *www.angel-inn.com. 5 rooms, 2 cottages. Restaurant, pub. AE, D, DC, MC, V.*

$–$$ **⊞ Moffat Inn.** This charmer has individually appointed rooms, some with original 1835 fireplaces, outdoor patios, brass beds, and wicker furniture. Enjoy breakfast fritters on the outdoor patio. All guest rooms and common areas except the pub are no-smoking. ⊠ *60 Picton St., L0S 1J0,* ☎ *905/468–4116,* WEB *www.moffatinn.com. 22 rooms. Restaurant. AE, MC, V.*

Nightlife and the Arts

The **Shaw Festival** began modestly back in the early 1960s with a single play and a premise: to perform the plays of George Bernard Shaw and his contemporaries, who include Noël Coward, Bertolt Brecht, J. M. Barrie, and J. M. Synge. The season now runs from April through October, staging close to a dozen plays. The festival operates in three buildings within a few blocks of one another. The handsome **Festival Theatre,** the largest of the three, stands on Queen's Parade near Wellington Street and houses the box office. The **Court House Theatre,** on Queen Street between King and Regent streets, served as the town's municipal offices until 1969. At the corner of Queen and Victoria streets is the slightly smaller **Royal George Theater,** the most intimate of the three. Tickets range from $25 to $75. ⊠ *Shaw Festival Box Office, Box 774, L0S 1J0,* ☎ *905/468–2172 or 800/511–7429,* FAX *905/468–3804,* WEB *www.shawfest.com.*

En Route   The Niagara Peninsula is Ontario's fruit basket. From mid-summer to late fall, fruit and vegetable stands proliferate along the highways and byways, and there are several farmers' markets along the Queen Elizabeth Way between Niagara Falls and Hamilton. Some of the best displays of fruits and vegetables are on Highway 55, between Niagara-on-the-Lake and the Queen Elizabeth Way. **Harvest Barn Market** (⊠ Hwy. 55, Niagara-on-the-Lake, ☎ 905/468–3224), marked by a red-and-white-stripe awning, not only sells regional fruits and vegetables but also tempts with a bakery offering sausage rolls, tiny loaves of bread, and fruit pies. You can test the market's wares at the picnic tables, where knowledgeable locals have lunch.

HAMILTON AND FESTIVAL COUNTRY

A combination of rural pleasures and sophisticated theater draws visitors to this region. Stratford has made a name for itself with its Shakespeare festival; Kitchener and Waterloo attract thousands with an annual Oktoberfest. Once you're in these areas, you can also enjoy the less famous lures—parks, gardens, and country trails. Hamilton, known for its exceptionally productive iron and steel mills, maintains acre upon acre of lush gardens, and London has handsome riverside parks.

Hamilton

68   *70 km (43 mi) west of Niagara Falls on the Queen Elizabeth Way.*

Hamilton is Canada's steel capital—not exactly the sort of city where you'd expect to find 2,700 acres of gardens and exotic plants, a symphony orchestra, a modern and active theater, 45 parks, and a developed waterfront. But they're all here in Ontario's second-largest city and Canada's third-busiest port. Downtown Hamilton, between the harbor and the base of "the mountain" (a 250-ft-high section of the Niagara Escarpment), is a potpourri of glass-walled high-rises, century-old mansions, a convention center, a coliseum, and a shopping complex.

With 176 stalls spread over more than 20,000 square ft, **Hamilton Farmers' Market** is Canada's largest. The Market, a Hamilton tradition since

1837, is a down-home haven in the very core of the city, with fresh produce, sausage, cheese, home-baked bread, and more. ⊠ *55 York Blvd., adjoining Jackson Sq. and Eaton Centre,* ☎ *905/546–2096.* ⊙ *Tues. and Thurs. 7–6, Fri. 9–6, Sat. 6–6.*

The **Art Gallery of Hamilton** houses 7,500 works of art, both Canadian and international, in an acclaimed three-level modern structure in the central business district. ⊠ *123 King St. W,* ☎ *905/527–6610,* WEB *www.artgalleryofhamilton.com.* ⌑ *Free.* ⊙ *Tues.–Sun. 11–5 (Thurs. 11–9).*

★ The **Royal Botanical Gardens,** opened in 1932, encompass five major gardens and 50 km (31 mi) of trails, which wind across marshes and ravines, past the world's largest collection of lilacs, 2 acres of roses, and all manner of shrubs, trees, plants, hedges, and flowers. Two tea houses are open May to mid-October. The Mediterranean Greenhouse, best visited November through May, displays plant species from warm climates. ⊠ *Plains Rd. (Hwy. 2), Burlington, accessible from Queen Elizabeth Way and Hwys. 6 and 403,* ☎ *905/527–1158.* ⌑ *$7; greenhouse $2.* ⊙ *Gardens daily 9:30–dusk; greenhouse daily 9:30–6.*

Gage Park, with 70 acres of botanical greens, is a beautiful oasis in the center of the city. Its rose garden, with more than 30 varieties, is especially stunning. ⊠ *Main St. E and Gage Ave., east of downtown.*

Sir Allan Napier MacNab, a War of 1812 hero and a pre-Confederation prime minister of Upper Canada, built a 35-room mansion called ★ **Dundurn Castle** from 1832 to 1835. It's been furnished to reflect the opulence in which MacNab lived at the height of his political career. ⊠ *Dundurn Park and York Blvd.,* ☎ *905/546–2872,* WEB *www.city.hamilton.on.ca/cultureandrecreation.* ⌑ *$6.* ⊙ *Late May– early Sept., daily 10–4:30; early Sept.–late May, Tues.–Sun. noon–4.*

Flamboro Downs harness-racing track, west of Hamilton, has matinee and evening races year-round, although not on a daily basis. The clubhouse has two dining areas that overlook the track. ⊠ *967 Hwy. 5,* ☎ *905/627–3561.*

☺ At **African Lion Safari,** lions, tigers, cheetahs, elephants, and zebras abound. You can drive your own car or take an air-conditioned tram over a 9-km (6-mi) safari trail through the wildlife park. ⊠ *Safari Rd., off Hwy. 8 south of Cambridge, Rockton,* ☎ *519/623–2620 or 800/ 461–9453,* WEB *www.lionsafari.com.* ⌑ *$19.95.* ⊙ *Grounds late Apr.– June and Sept.–Oct., weekdays 10–4, weekends 10–5; July–Aug., daily 9–5:30.*

Dining and Lodging

$$–$$$ ✕ **Ancaster Old Mill.** Just outside Hamilton, this historic mill is worth
★ the trip if only to sample the bread, baked daily with flour ground on millstones installed in 1863. Main dishes might include roast Muscovy duck with potato–fennel gratin, rack of venison with braised purple cabbage, or mushroom-celeriac ravioli. The dining rooms are light and bright with hanging plants. Try to get a table overlooking the mill stream and a waterfall. ⊠ *548 Old Dundas Rd., Ancaster,* ☎ *905/648–1827. Reservations essential. AE, DC, MC, V.*

$$ ✕▥ **Royal Connaught Howard Johnson Plaza Hotel.** This venerable 1916 hotel in the heart of downtown Hamilton is a grand old place complete with a ballroom. The 11-story landmark has recently undergone improvements to guest rooms, meeting rooms, the lobby, and the mezzanine. The recreation center has an indoor swimming pool with a two-story water slide, plus a whirlpool spa and exercise equipment. Fran's, the hotel's popular restaurant, serves family-style meals 24 hours a day.

The old gazebo houses Last Minute Larry's, a lounge serving pub-style food, and on weekends, Yuk-Yuk's Comedy Club. ⊠ *112 King St. E, L8N 1A8,* ☎ *905/546–8111 or 800/446–4656,* FAX *905/546–8144,* WEB *www.infoniagara.com/d-hotel-hojo-ham.html. 206 rooms, 11 suites. Restaurant, lounge, indoor pool, hot tub, sauna, gym, comedy club, meeting rooms. AE, D, DC, MC, V.*

Nightlife and the Arts

The Great Hall at **Hamilton Place** (⊠ 10 MacNab St., ☎ 905/546–3100) can accommodate more than 2,000 people. Opera Hamilton holds performances here from September through April. Its repertoire includes works from *Aïda* to *Nixon in China.*

Outdoor Activities and Sports

The 800-km (496-mi) **Bruce Trail** stretches northwest along the Niagara Escarpment from the orchards of the Niagara Peninsula to the cliffs and bluffs at Tobermory, at the end of the Bruce Peninsula. You can access the Bruce Trail at just about any point along the route, so your hike can be any length you wish. Contact the Bruce Trail Association (⊠ Box 857, L8N 3N9, ☎ 905/529–6821 or 800/665–4453, WEB www.brucetrail.org).

Brantford

69 *40 km (25 mi) west of Hamilton on Hwy. 403.*

Brantford is named for Joseph Brant, the Loyalist Mohawk chief who brought members of the Six Nations Confederacy into Canada after the American Revolution. King George III showed gratitude to Chief Brant by building the **Mohawk Chapel.** In 1904, by royal assent, it was given the name His Majesty's Chapel of the Mohawks (now changed to Her Majesty's). This simple, white-painted frame building with eight stained-glass windows depicting the colorful history of the Six Nations people is the oldest Protestant church in Ontario. ⊠ *291 Mohawk St.,* ☎ *519/756–0240,* WEB *www.city.brantford.on.ca.* ✉ *Donations requested for individual visitors; $3 per person for groups.* ☉ *July–early Sept., daily 10–6; early Sept.–mid-Oct., Wed.–Sun. 10–6; late May–June, Wed.–Sun. 1–5:30.*

Woodland Cultural Centre aims to preserve and promote the culture and heritage of First Nation peoples. The modern building contains displays and exhibits showing early Woodland Native American culture. ⊠ *184 Mohawk St., near Mohawk Chapel,* ☎ *519/759–2650,* WEB *www.museumat.woodland-centre.ca.* ✉ *$4.* ☉ *Weekdays 9–4:30, weekends 10–5.*

Although Brantford is the hometown of hockey star Wayne Gretzky, it's better known as the Telephone City: Alexander Graham Bell invented the device here and made the first long-distance call from his parents' home to nearby Paris, Ontario, in 1874. The **Bell Homestead,** where Bell spent his early years before moving to the United States, is now a National Historic Site. Also part of the site is the house of the Reverend Thomas Henderson, who left his Baptist church when he recognized the profit potential in telephones. His home served as the first telephone office and is now a museum of telephone artifacts and displays. Guided tours can be arranged. ⊠ *94 Tutela Heights Rd.,* ☎ *519/756–6220 or 800/265–6299.* ✉ *$3.* ☉ *Tues.–Sun. 9:30–4:30.*

Outdoor Activities and Sports

BIKING

Brantford is protected by a flood-control dam, on top of which is a bicycle trail that passes many attractions.

HIKING

The **Grand Valley Trail** runs 128 km (79 mi) between Elora and Brantford. Contact the Grand River Conservation Authority (✉ Box 729, 400 Clyde Rd., Cambridge N1R 5W6, ☎ 519/621–2761, WEB www.grandriver.on.ca) for more information.

Kitchener and Waterloo

70 *Approximately 40 km (25 mi) north of Brantford on Hwy. 24.*

Kitchener and Waterloo, which merge into one another, are usually referred to as K–W. Swiss-German Mennonites from Pennsylvania settled here around 1800, and the region's German origins remain obvious: there's a huge glockenspiel downtown by Speakers' Corner, and each October since 1967 the city has hosted Oktoberfest. The event now draws more than 700,000 people, who swarm to more than a dozen festival halls where they dance, gorge on German-style food, listen to oompah bands, and drink with a fervor that seems driven by fear that all Canadian breweries are about to go on strike.

Kitchener Farmers' Market has stalls with eggs, home-canned fruit, fresh herbs, vegetables, sausages, flowers, and crafts. This Saturday-morning tradition began in 1869, and since 1986 has operated in spacious quarters at Market Square, under the shadow of a 90-ft clock tower. It's adjacent to dozens of shops and snack bars. ✉ *Frederick and Duke Sts.,* ☎ *519/741–2287,* WEB *www.city.kitchener.on.ca.* ☉ *Sat. 6 AM–2 PM.*

William Lyon Mackenzie King, prime minister of Canada for almost 22 years between 1921 and 1948, spent part of his childhood living in a rented 10-room house, now **Woodside National Historic Site.** There's no particular imprint here of the bachelor prime minister, whose diaries reveal his belief in mysticism, portents, and communications with the dead, but the house has been furnished to reflect the Victorian period of the King family's occupancy. ✉ *528 Wellington St. N,* ☎ *519/571–5684 or 800/839–8221,* WEB *www.parkscanada.pch.gc.ca/parks/ontario/woodside.* ▨ *$2.50.* ☉ *Late May–mid-Dec., daily 10–5.*

Doon Heritage Crossroads is a complete living-history site with a restored 1914 village and two farms. The village recalls the tranquillity of rural lifestyles in the early 1900s. You can cross a covered bridge and wander tree-shaded roads to visit with costumed staff members who perform authentic period trades and activities. ✉ *North of Hwy. 401, exit Homer Watson Blvd. N,* ☎ *519/748–1914,* WEB *www.region.waterloo.on.ca/doon.* ▨ *$6.* ☉ *May–early Sept., daily 10–4:30; early Sept.–Dec., weekdays 10–4:30.*

Dining and Lodging

$$$$ ✕▥ **Langdon Hall Country House Hotel.** This magnificent Colonial Re-
★ vival–style mansion on 200 acres of gardens and woodlands has grand public rooms and huge fireplaces. Built in 1898 as a summer home for a great-granddaughter of John Jacob Astor, it has 13 guest rooms in the original building and 30 in a modern annex. A member of Relais & Châteaux, the hotel also offers a billiard room, conservatory, and drawing room. The restaurant (reserve ahead) specializes in regional cuisine such as Waterloo County pork tenderloin and Woolwich goat cheese in phyllo pastry. Call for directions. ✉ *R.R. 33, Cambridge N3H 4R8,* ☎ *519/740–2100 or 800/268–1898,* FAX *519/740–8161,* WEB *www.countryinns.org./inn-langdonhall. 43 rooms. Restaurant, room service, pool, hot tub, sauna, spa, tennis court, croquet, gym, billiards, meeting rooms. AE, DC, MC, V.*

$$–$$$ ▣ **Four Points Sheraton.** This modern hotel across the street from Market Square has a major sports complex downstairs. Guest rooms are decorated in beige and burgundy and have blond-wood furnishings. Bistro 105 serves reliable fare such as beef tenderloin and rack of lamb. Appetizers might include salmon napoleon or goat cheese with roasted vegetables. ⊠ *105 King St. E, Kitchener N2G 2K8,* ☎ *519/ 744–4141 or 800/483–7812,* FAX *519/578–6889,* WEB *www.four-points.com. 201 rooms. Restaurant, café, lounge, indoor pool, hot tub, sauna, miniature golf, bowling. AE, DC, MC, V.*

St. Jacobs

★ ㉑ *12 km (7 mi) north of Kitchener and Waterloo on Hwy. 8.*

The villages of St. Jacobs and Elmira (10 km, or 6 mi, north of St. Jacobs via Route 86 and County Road 21) are in the heart of Mennonite and Hutterite country. The **Mennonite Visitor Centre** (☎ 519/664–3518, WEB www.stjacobs.com) in St. Jacobs offers visitors a chance to learn more about the Old Order Mennonite community in the area. St. Jacobs is also a unique shopping destination with more than 100 shops that run the gamut from antiques to fashion wear. The St. Jacobs **Farmers' Market and Flea Market** has more than 350 vendors selling fresh produce and crafts on Thursday and Saturday from 7 to 3:30 year-round and on Tuesday 8 to 3 June through August.

Dining and Lodging

$$$$ ✕▣ **Millcroft Inn.** This 19th-century stone knitting mill has been con-
★ verted to an exquisite full-service country inn beside the millpond. About 40 km (25 mi) northeast of Elmira (80 km, or 50 mi, northwest of Toronto) in Alton, it's one of Canada's finest hostelries. Some larger rooms have fireplaces. Rooms are available in both the older inn and a more modern annex, where they tend to be more spacious. A spa was added in 1997. The dining room ($$$–$$$$; reserve ahead) uses Canadian and imported ingredients to create an imaginative variety of dishes such as grilled caribou medallions with cranberry thyme sauce, or pan-seared quail with foie gras. ⊠ *55 John St., Alton L0N 1A0,* ☎ *519/941–8111 or 800/383–3976,* FAX *519/941–9192,* WEB *www.millcroft.com. 52 rooms. Restaurant, pool, hot tub, sauna, spa, 2 tennis courts, croquet, gym, volleyball, cross-country skiing, recreation room. AE, DC, MC, V. CP.*

$$–$$$ ✕▣ **Elora Mill.** One of Canada's few remaining five-story gristmills has
★ been converted to luxury accommodations and a superb restaurant. There are 16 guest rooms in the 1859 mill building and 15 more in three other historic stone buildings in the immediate vicinity of the mill. The inn is in the heart of Elora, a village about 15 km (9 mi) north of Elmira full of stone buildings that could have been lifted from England's Cotswolds or southern France. The restaurant ($$–$$$$; reserve ahead) serves a mix of imaginative Canadian and European dishes such as trout stuffed with crab and slivered almonds, and chicken breast served with fruit compote and a cranberry and red currant sauce. ⊠ *77 Mill St. W, Elora N0B 1S0,* ☎ *519/846–5356,* FAX *519/846–9180,* WEB *www.eloramill.com. 31 rooms. Restaurant. AE, DC, MC, V.*

$–$$ ✕▣ **Benjamin's.** This is a lovely re-creation of the original 1852 Farmer's Inn. Nine guest rooms on the second floor are furnished with antiques, and every bed is covered with a locally made Mennonite quilt. The 120-seat restaurant ($$–$$$$; reserve ahead) has pine ceiling beams, an open-hearth fireplace, lots of greenery, and imaginative cuisine. ⊠ *17 King St., N0B 2N0,* ☎ *519/664–3731,* FAX *519/664–2218,* WEB *www.stjacobs.com/benjamins. 9 rooms. Restaurant. AE, DC, MC, V. CP.*

Outdoor Activities and Sports
BIKING

Two popular **bike routes** can be reached from Fergus, 18 km (11 mi) northwest of Elmira: one is a 32-km (20-mi) tour around Lake Belwood, the other a 40-km (25-mi) loop around Eramosa Township. There is little traffic on these scenic routes. Restaurants are few and far between, so take a picnic lunch.

HIKING

The 5-km (3-mi) **pathway** along the Elora Gorge between Fergus and Elora, 15 km (9 mi) north of Elmira, is a great minihike. You'll pass a whirlpool at Templin Gardens, and a restored English garden, and then cross a bridge at Mirror Basin.

Stratford

⑫ *45 km (28 mi) west of Kitchener on Hwys. 7 and 8.*

Ever since July 1953, when one of the world's greatest actors, Alec Guinness, joined with probably the world's greatest Shakespearean director, Tyrone Guthrie, beneath a hot, stuffy tent in a backward little town about 145 km (90 mi) and 90 minutes from Toronto, the Stratford Festival has been one of the most successful, most widely admired theaters of its kind in the world—and the town has been ensured a place on the map of Canada.

The origins of Ontario's Stratford are modest. After the War of 1812, the British government granted a million acres of land along Lake Huron to the Canada Company, headed by a Scottish businessman. When the surveyors came to a marshy creek surrounded by a thick forest, they named it "Little Thames" and noted that it might make "a good millsite." It was Thomas Mercer Jones, a director of the Canada Company, who decided to rename the river the Avon, and the town Stratford. The year was 1832, 121 years before the concept of a theater festival would take flight and change Canadian culture.

For many years Stratford was considered a backwoods hamlet. Then came the first of two saviors of the city, both of them (undoubting) Thomases. In 1904 an insurance broker named Tom Orr transformed Stratford's riverfront into a park. He also built a formal English garden, where every flower mentioned in the plays of Shakespeare—monkshood to sneezewort, bee balm to bachelor's button—blooms grandly to this day.

Next, Tom Patterson, a fourth-generation Stratfordian born in 1920, looked around, saw that the town wards and schools had names like Hamlet, Falstaff, and Romeo, and felt that some kind of drama festival might save his community from becoming a ghost town. The astonishing story of how he began in 1952 with $125 (a "generous" grant from the Stratford City Council), tracked down the directorial genius Tyrone Guthrie and the inspired stage and screen star Alec Guinness, obtained the services of the brilliant stage designer Tanya Moiseiwitsch, and somehow pasted together a world-class theater festival in a little over one year is recounted in Patterson's memoirs, *First Stage— The Making of the Stratford Festival.*

The festival is now moving into middle age and it has had its ups and downs. Soon after it opened and wowed critics from around the world with its professionalism, costumes, and daring thrust stage, the air was filled with superlatives that had not been heard in Canada since the Great Blondin walked across Niagara Falls on a tightrope.

The early years brought giants of world theater to the tiny town of some 20,000: James Mason, Siobhan McKenna, Alan Bates, Christopher Plummer, Jason Robards Jr., and Maggie Smith. But the years also saw an unevenness in productions and a tendency to go for flash and glitter over substance. Many never lost faith in the festival; others, such as Canada's greatest theater critic, the late Nathan Cohen of the *Toronto Star,* once bemoaned the fact that "Stratford has become Canada's most sacred cow."

Sacred or not, Stratford's offerings are still among the best of their kind in the world, with at least a handful of productions every year that put most other summer arts festivals to shame. The secret of deciding which ones to see, of course, is to try to catch the reviews of the plays, which have their debuts in May, June, July, and August in the festival's three theaters, and then book as early as you can. (The *New York Times* always runs major write-ups, as do newspapers and magazines in many American and Canadian cities.)

There are quieter things to do in Stratford when the theaters close. Art galleries remain open throughout winter. Shopping is great off-season, and those who love peaceful walks can stroll along the Avon. Many concerts are scheduled in the off-season, too.

Gallery Stratford has regular exhibits of Canadian visual art in a variety of media (some for sale) and, in summer, of theater arts. ⊠ *54 Romeo St.,* ☎ *519/271–5271.* 🎟 *Free.* ☉ *Tues.–Fri. and Sun. 1–4, Sat. 10–4.*

The **Stratford Perth Museum** interprets the history of Stratford and Perth County with displays that cover everything from the settlement of the area in the early 1800s to some of Canada's firsts, including the story of Dr. Jenny Trout, Canada's first female physician. Hockey in Stratford, Stratford's railroad history, children's activities, and a working printing press are other exhibits. ⊠ *270 Water St.,* ☎ *519/271–5311.* 🎟 *$3.75.* ☉ *May–Oct., Tues.–Sat. 10–5, Sun. and Mon. noon–5; call for reduced hrs Nov.–Apr.*

Dining and Lodging

$$$$ ✕ **Rundles Restaurant.** The look here is Venetian, in a theatrical Stratford way. Flowing white silk scarves hang from a series of primitive stone masks in this sophisticated, calm restaurant. Several prix-fixe menus with three courses each and a wine-with-dinner menu offer plenty of choices. Seared foie gras with caramelized endive on garlic fried potatoes; marinated mushroom salad strewn with fresh nasturtium blossoms and a scattering of asparagus and just-picked peas; and crisp, potato-wrapped duck ravioli are worthy of applause. Chicken is roasted with a whole range of vegetables, and the peppered rib-eye steak is set on goose fat–fried potatoes. ⊠ *9 Cobourg St.,* ☎ *519/271–6442. AE, DC, MC, V. Closed Nov.–mid-May. No lunch Mon.–Tues. and Thurs.–Fri.*

$$$–$$$$ ✕ **Church Restaurant and Belfry.** It was constructed in 1873 as a Con-
★ gregational church, but today white cloths gleam in the afternoon light that pours through the stained-glass windows, and greenery thrives. Prix-fixe or à la carte, the meals here are production numbers. Tea-smoked salmon comes with sea scallops and shrimp; warm salad of spiced veal sweetbreads is lively with a cherry-tomato compote. The roast Ontario lamb with garlic custard and eggplant flan is outstanding. Upstairs, The Belfry uses the same excellent kitchen, but the ambience is casual, and the dishes are lighter. ⊠ *70 Brunswick St.,* ☎ *519/273–3424. Reservations essential. AE, DC, MC, V. Closed Sun.–Mon. and Jan.–Mar.*

$$$–$$$$ ✕ **Old Prune.** A converted Victorian house holds a number of charm-
★ ing dining rooms and a glass-enclosed conservatory surrounded by a
tidy sunken garden. The kitchen coaxes fresh local ingredients into in-
novative dishes: smoked rainbow trout with apple radish and curry oil,
vegetable lasagna with roasted tomato sauce, or, with a nod to the East,
chicken seasoned with coriander and cumin. Desserts are baked fresh
for each meal and come straight from the oven. ⊠ *151 Albert St.,* ☎
519/271–5052. AE, MC, V. Closed Nov.–Apr. and Mon. No lunch Tues.

$$ ✕ **Down the Street Bar and Café.** Funky and informal, this bistro with
live jazz and food by Stratford Chefs School graduates is the hottest
place in town. Thrilling grills of chicken, salmon, and rib eye, as well
as grilled stacked tomato salad and herb-crusted pizza, make for de
licious casual dining. An inspirational late-night menu includes everything from spicy spring rolls and steamed Prince Edward Island mussels
to a classic cheeseburger with the works. ⊠ *30 Ontario St.,* ☎ *519/
273–5886. AE, MC, V. No lunch Mon.*

$$ ✕ **Theatrical Picnics** Sumptuous three-course picnics including spring
★ water and dinner roll are prepared for you by the chefs of the Festival
Theater's green room (where the actors eat). Dine on the banks of the
Avon or the Festival Theatre terraces. Falstaff's Feast consists of cru-
dites with aioli; a roast beef and roast tomato sandwich on a baguette
with balsamic, red onion, and horseradish dressing; and Kahlua choco-
late mousse with biscotti. Or try the lighter Coward's Cuisine: curried
mango soup, poached Atlantic salmon and salads, and strawberry
shortcake. Order 24 hours in advance from June 5 to Sept. 1. ⊠ *Fes-
tival Theatre, 55 Queen St.,* ☎ *519/273–1600. Reservations essential.
AE, MC, V. Closed Nov.–May.*

$–$$ ✕ **Bentley's Inn.** At this long and narrow British-style pub that's part
★ of an inn, the well-stocked bar divides the room into two equal halves.
There's an unspoken tradition: the actors have claimed one side, and
the locals the other. Darts are played here, seriously, and getting a
bull's-eye is the norm. The menu consists of pub fare such as good fish-
and-chips, grilled steak and fries, and steak-and-mushroom pie. The ul
timate club sandwich on homemade multigrain bread hits the spot for
lunch or dinner, while the sturdy dessert of fruit crumble and ice cream
is big enough for two. The regulars say they come for the imported, domestic, and microdraft beers—the easygoing ambience and camaraderie
are bonuses. ⊠ *99 Ontario St.,* ☎ *519/271–1121. AE, MC, V.*

$–$$ ✕ **Pazzo Ristorante Bar and Pizzeria.** The decor in the cheery main-floor
★ dining room brings to mind harlequins and Punch and Judy. The careful kitchen, however, is no joke. Dishes include hearty vegetable soups,
dewy fresh salads accompanied by roasted free-range chicken, and inspired pasta dishes that change weekly. Dessert, particularly the lemon
fruit tart, is not to be missed. Downstairs they have dreamed up 30 different kinds of pizza. ⊠ *70 Ontario St.,* ☎ *519/273–6666. MC, V.*

$ ✕ **Anna Banana's Cheesecakes and Cones.** The beautiful garden patio
is a fine place to indulge in frozen yogurt, ice cream, cheesecakes, muffins,
and a gourmet barbecue with four kinds of natural 100% all-beef hot
dogs. ⊠ *39 George St.,* ☎ *519/272–0065. Reservations not accepted.
No credit cards. Closed mid-Oct.–Mar.*

$ ✕ **Boomer's Gourmet Fries.** No time for leisurely dining? Boomer's
★ quickly serves up a fabulous variety of gourmet fries (no preservatives,
cooked in canola oil) and scrumptious fish-and-chips. ⊠ *26 Erie St.,*
☎ *519/275–3147. MC, V.*

$$ ✕▥ **Queen's Inn at Stratford.** This country-style inn dating from 1850
has large, curved windows and cheerful furnishings in Victorian and
Ontario country styles. The restaurant, Soltar, serves flavorful Santa
Fe cuisine at reasonable prices. The Boar's Head is a popular pub-lounge
with light snacks and a great variety of brews. ⊠ *161 Ontario St., N5A*

3H3, ☎ 519/271–1400 or 800/461–6450, FAX 519/271–7373. 32 rooms. Restaurant, lounge. AE, MC, V.

$$–$$$$ ⌂ **Stone Maiden Inn.** This beautiful spot near the city center is decorated with a Victorian theme. Some rooms have canopy beds and fireplaces. It's now totally no-smoking. Rates include a full buffet breakfast and afternoon refreshments. ⊠ *123 Church St., N5A 2R3, ☎ 519/271–7129,* WEB *www.stonemaideninn.com. 14 rooms. Lobby lounge. AE, MC, V. CP.*

$$–$$$$ ⌂ **Woods Villa Bed and Breakfast.** The public rooms in this elegant 1875 home hold an astonishing collection of restored vintage jukeboxes, music boxes, and player pianos. Five of the six guest rooms have fireplaces. You can start the day on the right foot with a grand complimentary breakfast accompanied by full table service. Woods Villa does not accept children or pets, either of which might ruffle the feathers of the owner's five tropical birds. Note that although credit cards are accepted, cash is preferred. ⊠ *62 John St. N, N5A 6K7, ☎ 519/271–4576,* WEB *www.woodsvilla.orc.ca. 6 rooms. Breakfast room, pool. MC, V. BP.*

$$–$$$ ⌂ **Festival Inn.** An old-English atmosphere has survived modernization of this hotel on the eastern outskirts of town, only a short drive from the theaters. All rooms have refrigerators, some have coffeemakers, and four rooms have double whirlpools. ⊠ *1144 Ontario St., Box 811, N5A 6W1, ☎ 519/273–1150 or 800/463–3581,* FAX *519/273–2111,* WEB *www.festivalinnstratford.com. 182 rooms. Restaurant, lobby lounge, indoor pool, hot tub, sauna, gym. AE, MC, V.*

$–$$$ ⌂ **23 Albert Place.** Since this three-story, brick-front building was opened in 1876 as the Windsor Arms hotel, it has been refurbished a few times; no elevator was ever installed, however, so you'll have to walk up one or two flights to your room. The hotel is at the heart of the downtown shopping area, just a few hundred yards from the Avon Theatre. Some of the suites offer mini-refrigerators and VCRs. ⊠ *23 Albert St., N5A 3K2, ☎ 519/273–5800,* FAX *519/273–5008. 29 rooms, 5 suites. Restaurant, lobby lounge. AE, MC, V.*

$–$$ ⌂ **Swan Motel.** This unassuming brick motel, 3 km (2 mi) south of the Avon Theatre, is known for the flower beds set on its generous grounds. Free coffee and muffins await guests in the morning. The Swan is happy to book guests at nearby public and private golf courses. ⊠ *959 Downie St. S, N5A 6S3, ☎ 519/271–6376,* FAX *519/271–0682,* WEB *www.swanmotel.on.ca. 24 rooms. Refrigerators, pool. Closed Dec.– late Apr. MC, V.*

$ ⌂ **Stratford General Hospital Residence.** Groups traveling on a tight budget may appreciate this modern, bright residence, rented out in the summer like a university residence. Rates include a full, cooked breakfast. Tour groups only. ⊠ *Housekeeping Supervisor, Stratford General Hospital Residence, 130 Youngs St., N5A 1J7, ☎ 519/271–5084,* WEB *www.sgh.stratford.on.ca. 167 rooms with shared baths. Cafeteria, pool, coin laundry. Closed Dec.–Apr. No credit cards. BP.*

Nightlife and the Arts

The **Stratford Festival** performances—now a mix of Shakespeare, works by other dramatists, and popular musicals—take place in three theaters, each in its own building and each with particular physical aspects (size, stage configuration, technical support) that favor different types of productions. This also means that at the height of the season you may have the flexibility of choosing among three simultaneous performances, and a weekend menu including up to 10 different productions.

The Festival Theatre, the original and, with nearly 1,850 seats, the largest, has a thrust stage that brings the action deep into the audience space. Try for fairly central seats in this theater. The Avon has about 1,100 seats and a traditional proscenium stage. The Tom Patterson Theatre, with about 500 seats, is the most intimate. It has a modified thrust stage.

The Festival and the Avon theaters are open from late April to early November. The Tom Patterson Theatre and the Festival Fringe (a variety of special events and performances) start up in late June, with the Patterson productions going through September and the Fringe's continuing into October. There are matinee and evening performances Tuesday through Saturday, matinees only on Sunday; the theaters are dark on Monday.

For tickets and information, contact the Stratford Festival (✉ Box Office, Box 520, N5A 6V2, ☎ 416/364–8355 in Toronto; 519/273–1600 or 800/567–1600, WEB www.stratfordfestival.ca).

Regular tickets are $48.90–$79.15, but there are many special plans. The festival has an accommodations bureau that can help you book a room if you're buying tickets. Rush seats, when available, may be bought the day of the performance in person at the Stratford box office at 55 Queen Street, beginning at 9 AM, or by telephone beginning at 9:30 AM; prices range from $19.50 to $40. Students can get seats for $27. "Two for One" tickets are available for selected performances in June, September, October, and November at both the Festival and Avon theaters.

Events surrounding the plays include "Meet the Festival," a free series of informal discussions with members of the company, held at the Tom Patterson Theatre from July through August on Wednesday and Friday mornings 9:30 AM–10:30 AM. At the same time and place on Thursday mornings, Stratford Festival personnel host discussions about production issues and the current season's themes. On designated Thursday nights from early July through late August there are also half-hour post-performance question-and-answer sessions with the actors at the Festival Theatre. Meet the usher at Aisle 2, Orchestra Level, immediately after the performance. Contact the theater for confirmation of events.

Shopping

Stratford's downtown area invites browsing with numerous fashion boutiques, antiques stores, garden shops, music stores, fine furniture and tableware shops, arts-and-crafts studios, galleries, and bookshops. The Theatre Stores, in the lobbies of the Festival and Avon theaters and at 100 Downie Street, offer exclusive Festival-related gifts, as well as original costume sketches, play-related books and music, plus art books, literature, and children's classics.

London

🔞 *60 km (37 mi) southwest of Stratford on Hwys. 7 and 4.*

Nicknamed Forest City, quiet and provincial London has more than 50,000 trees and 1,500 acres of parks. London has been called a microcosm of Canadian life; it is so "typically Canadian" that the city is often used as a test market for new products—if something sells in London, it will probably sell anywhere in Canada.

From mid-May through October you can view London from the Thames River in a 60-passenger boat: **Afternoon cruises** (✉ Springbank Park, ☎ 519/661–5000) depart from Storybook Gardens. Call for times and rates. The easiest way to get an overview of the town is to take a two-hour **bus tour** (☎ 800/265–2602, 🎫 $8) on a big, red double-decker—what else?—London bus. Buses leave daily from City Hall, July–Labor Day at 10 and 2.

Because **Storybook Gardens** is owned and operated by the city's Public Utility Commission, it's one of the least expensive children's theme parks in the country. It's on the Thames River in the 281-acre Springbank Park. You'll see a castle, storybook characters, and a zoo. There are rides, too, including a merry-go-round and miniature trains. ✉ 929 *Springbank Dr. W,* ☎ *519/661–5770.* ☑ *$5.25.* ⊙ *May–early Sept., daily 10–8; early Sept.–mid-Oct., weekdays 10–5, weekends 10–6.*

London Regional Art and Historical Museum is as interesting from the outside as its exhibits are on the inside. The gallery is contained in six joined, glass-covered structures whose ends are the shape of croquet hoops. An impressive collection of fine art and artifacts plus regularly changing exhibitions are complemented by films, lectures, music, and live performances. ✉ *Forks of the Thames, 421 Ridout St. N,* ☎ *519/ 672–4580.* ☑ *Donation requested.* ⊙ *Tues.–Sun. noon–5.*

The **London Museum of Archaeology** maintains more than 40,000 native artifacts plus a gallery of artists' conceptions of the lives of the Attawandaron native people who inhabited the Lawson site, a nearby archaeological dig, 500 years ago. Nearby is a reconstructed multifamily longhouse on its original site. ✉ *1600 Attawandaron Rd., south of Hwy. 22,* ☎ *519/473–1360,* ⦿ *www.uwo.ca/museum.* ☑ *$3.50.* ⊙ *May– Labor Day, daily 10–4:30; Sept. 3–Dec., Wed.–Sun. 10–4:30; Jan.–Apr., weekends 1–4.*

London's oldest building is also one of its most impressive. The wrecker's ball came awfully close to the **Old Courthouse Building,** and it got one wall of the former Middlesex County Gaol. But a citizens' group prevailed, and the Old Courthouse, modeled after Malahide Castle in England, reopened as the home of the Middlesex County council. ✉ *399 Ridout St. N,* ☎ *519/434–7321.* ☑ *Free.* ⊙ *Weekdays; call for hrs.*

Dining and Lodging

$–$$ ✕ **Marienbad and Chaucer's Pub.** The reasonably priced Czech fare served here includes popular favorites such as goulash, schnitzels, chicken paprika, and Carlsbad roulade (rolled beef stuffed with ham and egg). Forget the diet: most dishes come with rib-sticking dumplings. ✉ *122 Carling St.,* ☎ *519/679–9940. AE, MC, V.*

$–$$ ✕ **Michael's on the Thames.** This popular lunch and dinner spot overlooks the Thames River. The Canadian and Continental cuisine includes flambéed dishes, fresh seafood, chateaubriand, and flaming desserts and coffees. ✉ *1 York St., at Thames River,* ☎ *519/672–0111. Reservations essential. AE, DC, MC, V.*

$$–$$$$ 🏠 **Idlewyld Inn.** Although an elevator was installed in this converted 1878 mansion, the architects succeeded in preserving the house's original details. Complimentary breakfast, snacks, and parking are included in your room rate. ✉ *36 Grand Ave., N6C 1K8,* ☎ 🖷 *519/ 433–2891 or 877/435–3466,* ⦿ *www.someplacesdifferent.com/ idlewyld. 17 rooms, 10 suites. Breakfast room. AE, DC, MC, V.*

$$–$$$ 🏠 **Delta London Armouries Hotel.** This 20-story, silver-mirrored tower rises from the center of the 1905 London Armoury. The lobby is a greenhouse of vines, trees, plants, and fountains, wrapped in marble and accented by rich woods and old yellow brick. The architects left as much of the original armory intact as possible. A set of steps through manicured jungle takes you to the indoor pool, sauna, and whirlpool. Guest rooms are spacious and decorated in pastel shades. Suites vary in size and grandeur: the Middlesex Suite has a grand piano. ✉ *325 Dundas St., N6B 1T9,* ☎ *519/679–6111 or 800/668–9999,* 🖷 *519/679–3957,* ⦿ *www.deltahotels.com. 242 rooms, 8 suites. Restaurant, lounge, indoor pool, sauna, racquetball, squash. AE, D, DC, MC, V.*

SAULT STE. MARIE AND WEST TO THUNDER BAY

Trans-Canada Highway 17 hugs the northeastern shore of Lake Superior as it connects the towns of this region. Several provincial parks and the amazing Ouimet Canyon are here.

Sault Ste. Marie

㉔ *690 km (428 mi) northwest of Toronto.*

Sault Ste. Marie has always been a natural meeting place and cultural melting pot. Long before Etienne Brulé "discovered" the rapids in 1622, Ojibwa tribes gathered here. Whitefish, their staple food, could easily be caught year-round, and the rapids in the St. Mary's River linking Lakes Huron and Superior were often the only sources of open water for miles in winter. When Father Jacques Marquette opened a mission in 1668, he named it Sainte Marie de Sault. *Sault* is French for "rapids," which help generate hydroelectric power for the city. Today locals call the city simply "the Sault," pronounced "the Soo."

Hiawathaland Tours (☎ 705/759–6200) operates three city tours by double-decker bus and a wilderness tour by minivan to Aubrey Falls from June 15 through October 15. There's also a 75-minute evening tour.

The elegant **Ermatinger/Clergue Heritage Site,** a house built by Montréal fur trader Charles Oakes Ermatinger in 1814, is the oldest stone building in Canada west of Toronto. Ermatinger married a daughter of the influential Indian chief Katawebeda, a move that didn't hurt his business. Costumed interpreters guide visitors through the house. ⊠ *831 Queen St. E,* ☎ *705/759–5443.* ☞ *$2.* ☉ *Apr.–May, weekdays 10–5; June–Sept., daily 10–5; Oct.–Nov., weekdays 1–5.*

Lock Tours Canada runs two-hour excursions through the 21-ft-high **Soo Locks,** the 16th and final lift for ships bound for Lake Superior from the St. Lawrence River. Tours aboard the 200-passenger MV *Chief Shingwauk* leave at least twice a day from the Roberta Bondar Dock next door to the Holiday Inn, from late May through October 15, and up to four times daily in peak season, July 1 through Labor Day. ⊠ *Roberta Bondar Park dock off Foster Dr.,* ☎ *705/253–9850 or 877/ 226–3665,* WEB *www.locktours.com.* ☞ *$20.*

★ **Agawa Canyon Train Tours** runs day trips to and from scenic Agawa Canyon, a deep river valley with 800-ft-high cliff walls. In summer the Agawa Canyon Train makes a two-hour stopover in the canyon. Passengers can lunch in a park, hike to their choice of three waterfalls, or climb to a lookout 250 ft above the train. In colder months, the Snow Train makes the same trip, minus the layover. ⊠ *129 Bay St.,* ☎ *705/ 946–7300 or 800/242–9287,* WEB *www.agawacanyontourtrain.com.* ☞ *Agawa Canyon Train $56 in summer, $75 in autumn; Snow Train $56.* ☉ *Agawa Canyon Train June–mid-Oct., daily; Snow Train late Dec.– mid-Mar., weekends; trains depart at 8 AM and return at 5 PM in warmer seasons and 4 PM in cooler weather.*

Lodging

$$–$$$ 🏨 **Bay Front Quality Inn.** If you're planning to take an Agawa Canyon Train Tour, book a room at this popular hotel. Rooms and suites are clean and modern with many comforts, including a sauna and in-house movies. Most important—because the train leaves at 8 AM and you should be at the station by 7:30 AM at the latest—the hotel is across the street from the Algoma Central Railroad station. When you return at night,

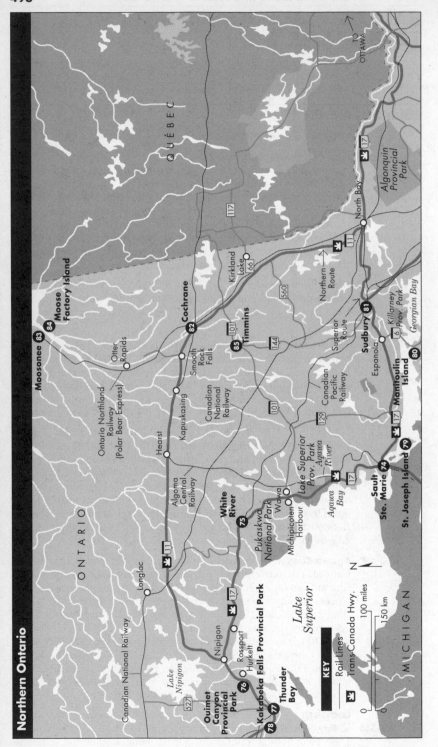

Northern Ontario

KEY
Rail Lines
Trans-Canada Hwy.

N

0   100 miles
0   150 km

the hotel's swimming pool and dining room await you. The hotel's Gran Sesta Ristorante, bright and airy with lots of brass and greenery, serves southern Italian dishes garnished with edible flowers. ✉ *180 Bay St., P6A 6S2*, ☎ *705/945–9264 or 800/228–5151,* FAX *705/945–9766,* WEB *www.soonet.ca/bayfront. 109 rooms, 13 suites. Restaurant, indoor pool, hot tub, sauna, gym, meeting rooms. AE, DC, MC, V.*

En Route **Wawa,** 225 km (140 mi) north of Sault Ste. Marie on Trans-Canada Highway 17, is the first town north of Lake Superior Provincial Park. Its name is derived from the Ojibwa word meaning "wild goose." Accordingly, a 30-ft-tall Canada goose stands guard at the entrance to town, next door to the log-cabin tourist information office.

White River

⓻ *93 km (58 mi) northwest of Wawa on Trans-Canada Hwy. 17.*

This town is marked by a huge thermometer indicating 72°F below zero and a sign that advises: "White River—coldest place in Canada." But it has another claim to fame as the actual birthplace of the bear cub that went to England to become immortalized as Winnie-the-Pooh in the children's stories by A. A. Milne. A 25-ft-tall statue honors Pooh, and each August the town holds a three-day Winnie's Hometown Festival, with parades, street dances, and a community barbecue.

Dining and Lodging

$ ✕⊞ **Rossport Inn.** The hamlet of Rossport, about 200 km (124 mi) west of White River on a harbor off Lake Superior, is about as close as you can get to an unspoiled outpost on the Great Lakes. The inn, built in 1884 as a railroad hotel, has seven small guest rooms. One of the nicest country inns in the province, the Rossport is cozy and down-home— the nightlife consists of swapping lies with the innkeepers and other guests about the fish that got away. Breakfast is included in the room rate. The dining room's ($$) home-style cuisine, which includes Lake Superior trout and whitefish, as well as steak, chicken, pork chops, and lobster, is irresistible. Reservations are essential. ✉ *Rossport Loop, ½ mi from Trans-Canada Hwy. 17, 6 Bowman St., P0T 2R0,* ☎ *807/824–3213 or 877/824–1032,* FAX *807/824–3217,* WEB *www.rossportinn.on.ca. 7 rooms, 1 with bath; 7 cottages. Restaurant. MC, V. Closed Nov.– Apr. BP.*

Ouimet Canyon Provincial Park

★ ⓻ *315 km (195 mi) west of White River on Trans-Canada Hwy. 17.*

Steep, narrow Ouimet Canyon cuts so deeply into the volcanic rock of Lake Superior's north shore that botanists have discovered Arctic plants growing on its sunless floor. A walking path stops short at the edge of the 2½-km-long (1½-mi-long) chasm, where viewing platforms allow you to look 350 ft straight down; the far wall is only 492 ft away. Geologists believe the canyon could be a gigantic fault in the earth's surface or the result of glacial action. (Note: access to the canyon floor is restricted due to its fragile nature.) To get here, watch for signs to Ouimet Canyon, just past the town of Hurkett, west of Nipigon. ✉ *11 km (7 mi) off Trans-Canada Hwy. 17, 10 km (6 mi) west of Hurkett,* ☎ *807/977–2526 or 888/668–7275,* WEB *www.ontarioparks.com/ ouimet.htm.* ▣ *Day use $6 per vehicle.* ☉ *Mid-May–mid-Oct., daily 9–5.*

En Route Ontario's official mineral is amethyst, an imperfect quartz tinted violet or purple. There are five amethyst mines and an agate mine between Sleeping Giant Provincial Park and Ouimet Canyon, a distance of 50 km (31 mi) along Highways 11 and 17 east of Thunder Bay. All are signposted from the highway, and each offers the opportunity to hand-pick some samples (paid for by the pound). The **Amethyst Mine Panorama** is closest to Thunder Bay. Mine tours run four times daily, at 11, 12:30, 3, and 5. Follow East Loon Road from Highways 11 and 17; 40 km (25 mi) east of Thunder Bay. ⊠ *400 E. Victoria Ave.,* ☎ *807/622–6908,* WEB *www.amethystmine.com.* ☒ *$3.* ☼ *Mid-May–June and Sept.–mid-Oct., daily 10–5; July–Aug., daily 10–7.*

Thunder Bay

🄬 *65 km (40 mi) southwest of Ouimet Canyon on Trans-Canada Hwy. 17.*

Thunder Bay, the world's biggest freshwater port, has an extraordinary ethnic mix of 42 nationalities, including the largest Finnish population outside Finland. Gateway to the fabled country north of Lake Superior and within easy reach of four provincial parks, Thunder Bay has Ontario's best alpine and cross-country skiing (and the longest ski season), superb fishing, great camping and hiking, unlimited canoe and boating routes, and even ice climbing. Several amethyst mines have shops in the city. There are also dozens of good restaurants, a growing number of B&Bs, an art gallery, and nine shopping malls.

At **Old Fort William,** one of the largest living-history sites in North America, with 42 historic buildings on a 125-acre site, interpreters re-create an early 1800s fur-trading fort. ⊠ *Broadway Ave. to King Rd.,* ☎ *807/473–2344,* WEB *www.oldfortwilliam.on.ca.* ☒ *$10.* ☼ *Mid-May–mid-Oct., daily 9–6.*

Dining and Lodging

$$ ✕🏨 **Valhalla Inn.** The warm lobby is based on an old Scandinavian design and has plenty of wood and brass. Guest rooms are large, with queen-size beds and local art. The Nordic dining room ($$) tempts visitors with imaginative fare, from poached salmon in sorrel butter to medallions of beef tenderloin grilled with whiskey. ⊠ *1 Valhalla Inn Rd., P7E 6J1,* ☎ *807/577–1121 or 800/964–1121,* FAX *807/475–4723,* WEB *www.valhallainn.com. 267 rooms. Restaurant, indoor pool, hot tub, sauna, gym. AE, D, DC, MC, V.*

Outdoor Activities and Sports

North of Superior Climbing Company (⊠ Trail's End Resort, Montreal River Harbour, P0S 1H0, ☎ 705/882–1032, WEB www.northofsuperiorclimbing.com) offers ice-climbing lessons, professionally led climbs, and two-day packages. Accommodations in rustic cabins or motels are provided, but meals are not included.

Kakabeka Falls Provincial Park

🄭 *32 km (20 mi) west of Thunder Bay off Hwys. 11 and 17.*

In this park, Kakabeka Falls on the Kaministiquia River drops 128 ft over a limestone ledge. Paths lead around the falls, and there are large, free parking lots. ☎ 807/473–9231, WEB *www.ontarioparks.com.*

EAST ALONG GEORGIAN BAY AND SOUTH TO MANITOULIN ISLAND

On a half-day journey by car from Sault Ste. Marie you can see the stunning beauty of Georgian Bay. Highlights include the wildflowers of St. Joseph Island, the rugged simplicity of Manitoulin Island, and educational fun at Science North in Sudbury.

St. Joseph Island

㉙ *90 km (56 mi) southeast of Sault Ste. Marie on Hwy. 17.*

St. Joseph Island is a sparsely settled bit of land about 24 by 30 km (15 by 19 mi) in the mouth of the St. Mary's River, connected by causeway and bridge to the mainland. In spring the island is a scented riot of wild lilac, and you're likely to see moose and deer along the quiet side roads.

In fur-trading days, **Fort St. Joseph,** established by the British at the southeast tip of the island in 1789, guarded the trade route from Montréal to the upper Great Lakes. Today you can wander through this National Historic Site where the fort once stood and see the outlines and a few above-ground stone ruins of the 42 building sites that have been identified. Free walking tours and a booklet are available at the visitor center, about 30 minutes by car southeast of the Gilbertson Bridge. Call ahead for directions. ⊠ *Richards Landing,* ☎ *705/246–1796 or 800/839–8221,* WEB *www.stjosephisland.net.* ☞ *$2.25.* ⊙ *Late May–mid-Oct., daily 10–5.*

Manitoulin Island

㉘ *235 km (146 mi) east of St. Joseph Island and south of Espanola via Trans-Canada Hwy. 17 and Hwy. 6.*

Manitoulin, the world's largest freshwater island, sits at the top of Lake Huron. The island, with a total area of 2,800 square km (1,081 square mi), is pretty and rugged, with granite outcrops, forests, meadows, rivers, and rolling countryside. Yachters rate these waters among the best in the world, and anglers have taken advantage of the island's riches for generations. Hikes and exploration could easily turn this "side trip" into a weeklong stay. For the most part, the island has not been ravaged by time and human incursions. Archaeological digs have unearthed traces of human habitation more than 30,000 years old. There is no interim record of people living here until explorer Samuel de Champlain met some island residents in 1650. Island towns such as Little Current (closest to the mainland), Sheguiandah, and Wikwemikong are simple and picturesque.

The **MS *Chi-Cheemaun*** connects the picturesque town of Tobermory, at the northern tip of the Bruce Peninsula, with South Baymouth on Manitoulin Island. The ferry is a convenient alternative to driving if you are heading to the island from southern Ontario (rather than from Sault Ste. Marie). The trip takes an hour and 45 minutes each way. There are four sailings in each direction daily between late June and Labor Day, and three during spring and fall. Reservations are advised. ⊠ *Owen Sound Transportation Company, 343 8th St. E, Owen Sound N4K 1L3,* ☎ *519/376–6601 or 800/265–3163,* WEB *www.manitoulin-tourist.com.* ☞ *One-way: passengers $11.20, plus $24.50 and up per vehicle, depending on size.*

Little Current–Howland Centennial Museum, in the village of Sheguiandah about 11 km (7 mi) south of Little Current, displays local native and pioneer artifacts. ⊠ *Hwy. 6,* ☎ *705/368–2367.* ☞ *$3.* ⊙ *Mid-May–mid-Oct., daily 10–4:30.*

Wikwemikong Unceded Indian Reserve encompasses the entire southeastern peninsula of Manitoulin Island. One of Manitoulin's most colorful events is the Wikwemikong Pow Wow, held on Civic Holiday (the first weekend in August). Dancers accompanied by drummers and singers compete while performing the steps of their ancestors. For details contact the Wikwemikong Heritage Organization (☎ 705/859–2385, WEB www.wiky.net).

Sudbury

㉑ *70 km (43 mi) east of Espanola on Trans-Canada Hwy. 17.*

The mining town of Sudbury used to bear the brunt of frequent un-kind jokes. After all, didn't the U.S. astronauts go there to train in the type of terrain they were likely to encounter on the moon? Today, the greening of Sudbury, an ongoing reclamation project, has revived much of the landscape that suffered from years of logging, smelter emissions, and soil erosion. What you see today is typical Canadian Shield coun-try with beautiful lakes, rocky outcroppings, and trees. The town has outdoor concerts, art centers, museums, and cruises on Ramsey Lake, the largest freshwater lake inside city limits in North America.

Science North is northern Ontario's largest tourist attraction, encom-passing a science museum, a giant-screen IMAX theater, and the Vir-tual Voyages Motion Theatre. The museum explores science in the everyday world; you can touch live animals, gaze at the stars, test your senses, play with technology, watch a 3-D film, and more. Friendly staff scientists are available to share their knowledge. The museum's fre-quent special events may affect ticket prices. ⊠ *100 Ramsey Lake Rd.,* ☎ *705/522–3700 or 800/461–4898,* ᵂᴱᴮ *sciencenorth.on.ca.* ⊠ *Mu-seum $13, IMAX theater $12.* ☉ *Apr.–late June, daily 9–5; late June–Sept., daily 9–6; Oct.–Mar., daily 10–4.*

The **Big Nickel,** a 30-ft replica of the 1951 Canadian commemorative coin, has been synonymous with Sudbury for almost three decades. It stands on a hillside, overlooking the smokestacks of Inco, one of the world's largest nickel producers. In spring 2002 a major Dynamic Earth exhibit by Science North was to open nearby, allowing visitors to learn about the history of nickel mining and the geology of North-ern Ontario. Plans also include an underground simulated mine.

FROM COCHRANE TO MOOSONEE AND MOOSE FACTORY ISLAND

For many people, these northern outposts are simply fly-over land, but you can find undiscovered Canada here. The terrain is densely packed with spruce trees, and moose and bear are common. Nearby lies the expansive, awe-inspiring James Bay.

Cochrane

㉒ *380 km (236 mi) north of Sudbury via Trans-Canada Hwys. 17 east and 11 north.*

Cochrane is Ontario's gateway to the Arctic, Moose Factory, and Moosonee at the southern end of James Bay, but don't expect a road to the far north—you need to take a train or fly to those areas. There's train service to Cochrane from Toronto and North Bay. You can fly to Moosonee from Timmins via Air Creebec. Ontario Northland's fa-

★ mous *Polar Bear Express* train (⊠ 555 Oak St. E., North Bay P1B 8L3, ☎ 705/472–4500 or 800/268–9281, ᵂᴱᴮ www.ontc.on.ca) is the most memorable way to go. Every day except Friday from late June through Labor Day, the *Polar Bear* leaves Cochrane at 8:30 AM, arrives at Moosonee just before 1 PM, departs Moosonee at 6 PM, and returns to Cochrane by 10:10 PM. The fare is $55. Meals, light lunches, and snacks are available in the snack car.

Lodging

If you plan to take the *Polar Bear Express* train, you'll probably need to overnight in Cochrane. There are 10 motels in and around town. Not all have restaurant facilities, but they are geared to early wake-up calls for guests taking the train and late check-ins for those returning from the excursion. All are reasonably priced ($). ⊡ The **Chimo Motel** (✉ Box 2326, P0L 1C0, ☎ 705/272–6555, FAX 705/272–5666, WEB www.motelsontario.on.ca/region10.htm) on Highway 11 offers snowmobile rentals in winter. *29 rooms. AE, MC, V.*

⊡ The **Station Inn** (✉ 200 Railway St., Box 1926, P0L 1C0, ☎ 705/272–3500 or 800/265–2356, FAX 705/272–5713, WEB www.ontc.on.ca) is at the center of town near Ontario Northland's railway Station. *23 rooms. AE, MC, V.*

⊡ The **Westway Motor Hotel** (✉ 21 1st St., P0L 1C0, ☎ 705/272–4285, FAX 705/272–4429, WEB www.motelsontario.on.ca/region10.htm) is close to several restaurants and stores. *42 rooms. AE, MC, V.*

Moosonee

83 *300 km (186 mi) north of Cochrane by train.*

Moosonee, Ontario's only tidal port, came into existence in 1903 when Revillon Frères Trading Company established a post to compete with the Hudson's Bay Company in Moose Factory. It wasn't until the Ontario Northland Railway arrived in 1932 that the region's population began to catch up to that of Moose Factory. Now about 2,500 people live here, many of them Mushkegowuk Cree, whose ancestors lived in the region for centuries before fur traders created settlements. During tourist season, locals open stalls on Revillon Road to sell First Nations handicrafts ranging from moccasins and buckskin vests to jewelry, beadwork, and wood and stone carvings.

The **Moosonee visitor center** (✉ Ferguson Rd. at 1st St., ☎ 705/336–2238, FAX 705/336–3899) is in a small, one-story office building. In the modern **James Bay Education Centre** (✉ 1st Avenue, Box 130, P0L 1Y0, ☎ 705/336–2913) Northern College operates interpretive programs where you can see exhibits of regional wildlife and the area's geological and geographical history.

Dining and Lodging

$ ✕⊡ **Polar Bear Lodge, Moosonee Lodge.** Both of these lodges face the Moose River. Their rates may seem high for the caliber of accommodation offered, but there's little else to choose from. Both hotels serve meals, but alcohol is available only to those having dinner at the hotel. ✉ *Polar Bear Lodge, Box 305, P0L 1Y0,* ☎ *705/336–2345; winter 416/244–1495;* FAX *705/336–2185,* WEB *www.polarbearlodge.com. 27 rooms. Restaurant. MC, V;* ✉ *Moosonee Lodge, Revillon St., P0L 1Y0,* ☎ *705/336–2351; winter 416/244–1495;* FAX *705/336–2185. 21 rooms. Restaurant. MC, V.*

Moose Factory Island

84 *2½ km (1½ mi) from Moosonee by boat.*

One of a number of islands in the delta of the Moose River, historic Moose Factory Island was the site of the Hudson's Bay Company's second trading post, established in 1673. You can reach the island by water taxi—a freighter canoe from Moosonee ($6 each way; canoes line up at the Moosonee dock)—or take a 20-minute boat ride aboard the *Polar Princess,* a 100-passenger cruise vessel operated by **TwoBay Tours** (☎ 705/336–2944, WEB www.twobay.com). The company's $20 day-trip fare includes a bus tour of the island with stops at historic sites. *Polar Princess* gets back to Moosonee in time for day-trippers to board the Polar Bear Express for the return journey to Cochrane.

Contrary to popular myth, **St. Thomas Anglican Church** (✉ Front Rd., ☎ 705/658–4800) never floated away. Holes in the floor are to let flood-water out and to ventilate the foundation. When the church was being built in 1864, the foundation floated a short distance in a spring flood, but the church itself has never floated anywhere. The altar cloths and lectern hangings are of moose hide decorated with beads.

The Hudson's Bay post, now known as the North West Company, is a modern building, but beside it is the 1850 **Hudson's Bay Staff House** (✉ River Rd., ☎ 705/272–5338), in which animal pelts, carvings, snow-shoes, gloves, slippers, and beadwork are sold.

The **Blacksmith's Shop** in Moose Factory Centennial Park Museum isn't the oldest wooden building in Ontario, but the stone forge inside it may be the oldest "structure" in the province. The original shop was built in the late 1600s but moved back from the riverbank in 1820. The forge stones had to be transported a long distance and were dis-assembled and rebuilt at the present location. In summer an appren-tice smith runs the forge.

Timmins

85 *90 km (56 mi) southwest of Cochrane on Hwys. 11 and 101.*

The mining center of Timmins prides itself on being the largest city in Canada—geographically, that is. Timmins gained a lot of territory when it amalgamated with neighboring townships a few decades ago, but its population is a modest 50,000. Despite its vastness, there's not much to see here, except for one of Canada's few underground mine tours. From Timmins you can fly to Moosonee via **Air Creebec** (✉ Tim-mins Airport, R.R. 2, Timmins P4N 7C3, ☎ 705/264–9521 or 800/567–6567).

At the **Timmins Gold Mine Tour and Museum,** visitors dress in full min-ing attire for the 2½-hour tour of the old Hollinger gold workings. Sur-face attractions include a headframe, a prospector's trail with a view of mineral outcrops and ore samples, and a refurbished miner's house. The road to the tour site near downtown Timmins is well marked. A new attraction at the same site is the **Shania Twain Centre**, opened in summer 2001 and devoted to the country superstar, whose hometown is Timmins, as well as to several past and present Canadian hockey stars who also hail from the area. ✉ *Park Rd. off Hwy. 101,* ☎ *705/360–8510 or 800/387–8466,* WEB *www.timminsgoldminetour.com.* ✉ *Tour $17, Shania Twain Centre $8.* ◷ *Tours May–June and Sept.–Oct., Wed.–Sun. at 10:30 and 1:30; July–Aug., daily at 9:30, 10:30, noon, 1:30, and 3.*

ONTARIO A TO Z

To research prices, get advice from other travelers, and book travel ar-rangements, visit www.fodors.com.

AIRPORTS

Toronto, the province's largest city, is served by most major interna-tional airlines. Ottawa International Airport is the gateway to Ontario's capital region. The Niagara Falls International Airport in Niagara Falls, New York, is the closest air link to Niagara Falls, Ontario, and its popular attractions.

➤ AIRPORT INFORMATION: **Niagara Falls International Airport** (☎ 716/ 297–4494). **Ottawa International Airport** (☎ 613/248–2000).

BUS TRAVEL

About 20 intercity bus lines connect communities all over Ontario. Ontario Tourism can provide details on intercity bus routes, contacts and schedules.

➤ BUS INFORMATION: **Ontario Tourism** (☎ 800/668–2746, WEB www.ontariotravel.net).

CAR TRAVEL

The Macdonald–Cartier Freeway, known as Highway 401, is Ontario's major highway link. It runs from Windsor in the southwest through Toronto, along the north shore of Lake Ontario, and along the north shore of the St. Lawrence River to the Québec border west of Montréal. The Trans-Canada Highway follows the west bank of the Ottawa River from Montréal to Ottawa and on to the town of North Bay. From North Bay to Nipigon at the northern tip of Lake Superior, there are two branches of the Trans-Canada (Highways 11 and 17), and from just west of Thunder Bay to Kenora, near the Manitoba border, another two (Highways 11 and 17).

Highway 400 is the main north–south route between Toronto and the Cottage Country.

ROAD CONDITIONS

Call for 24-hour road-condition information anywhere in Ontario.
➤ CONTACTS: **Road-condition information** (☎ 416/235–1110 or 800/ 268–1376).

RULES OF THE ROAD

Ontario is a no-fault province, and minimum liability insurance is $200,000. If you're driving across the Ontario border, bring the policy or the vehicle registration forms and a free Canadian Non-Resident Insurance Card from your insurance agent. If you're driving a borrowed car, also bring a letter of permission signed by the owner.

Driving motorized vehicles while impaired by alcohol is taken seriously in Ontario and results in heavy fines, imprisonment, or both. You can be convicted for refusing to take a Breathalyzer test. Radar warning devices are not permitted in Ontario even if they are turned off. Police can seize them on the spot, and heavy fines may be imposed.

Studded tires and window coatings that do not allow a clear view of the vehicle interior are forbidden in Ontario. Right turns on red lights are permitted unless otherwise noted. Pedestrians crossing at designated crosswalks have the right of way.

LODGING

B&BS

Some cities and towns have local bed-and-breakfast associations; ask regional and municipal visitor-information offices for more information. A comprehensive B&B guide listing about 200 establishments is published by the Federation of Ontario Bed and Breakfast Accommodations. The Ontario Bed and Breakfast Reservation Service can help you locate a B&B and reserve a room.

➤ RESERVATION SERVICES: **Federation of Ontario Bed and Breakfast Accommodations** (☎ 416/515–1293, WEB www.fobba.com). **Ontario Bed and Breakfast Reservation Service** (☎ 877/477–5827, WEB www.bbreservationsontario.com).

OUTDOORS AND SPORTS

CAMPING

You can find out everything you need to know about camping in provincial parks by contacting Ontario Parks. Peak season in Ontario's parks is June through August, and it is advised that you reserve a campsite if reservations are accepted; sites can be guaranteed by phone, by mail, or in person by using a Visa or MasterCard. All provincial parks that offer organized camping have some sites available on a first-come, first-served basis. In an effort to avoid overcrowding on canoe routes and hiking or backpacking trails, daily quotas have been established governing the number of people permitted in the parks. Permits can be reserved ahead of time. For detailed information on both provincial and privately operated parks and campgrounds in Ontario, contact Ontario Tourism, which has a free outdoor-adventure guide.

➤ CONTACTS: **Ontario Parks** (☎ 800/668–2746, WEB www.ontarioparks.com). **Ontario Tourism** (✉ 181 Bay St., Suite 350, Toronto M5J 2T3, ☎ 416/314–0944 or 800/668–2746, WEB www.ontariotravel.net).

DOGSLEDDING

Burton Penner of Vermilion Bay, 91 km (56 mi) east of Kenora (480 km, or 298 mi, west of Thunder Bay), offers guided dogsled tours into the wilderness, overnighting in an outpost cabin or heated wall tent. Winterdance Dogsled Tours take you on afternoon or multi-day adventures in Haliburton and Algonquin Park.

➤ CONTACTS: **Burton Penner** (☎ 807/227–2203). **Winterdance Dogsled Tours** (☎ 705/457–5281, WEB www.winterdance.com).

FISHING

Licenses are required for fishing in Ontario and may be purchased from Ministry of Natural Resources regional and community offices and from most sporting goods stores, outfitters, and resorts. Seasons and catch limits change annually, and some districts impose closed seasons. Restrictions are published in *Recreational Fishing Regulations Summary,* free from the Ministry of Natural Resources.

There are about 500 fishing resorts and lodges listed in the current catalogue of fishing packages available free from Ontario Tourism. The establishments are not hotels near bodies of water that contain fish but businesses designed to make sport fishing available to their guests. Each offers all the accoutrements, including boats, motors, guides, floatplanes, and freezers. Rates at these lodges are hefty.

➤ CONTACTS: **Ministry of Natural Resources** (300 Water St., Peterborough K9J 8M5, ☎ 705/755–2001 or 800/667–1940, WEB www.mnr.gov.on.ca/mnr/fishing). **Ontario Tourism** (✉ 181 Bay St., Suite 350, Toronto M5J 2T3, ☎ 416/314–0944 or 800/668–2746, WEB www.ontariotravel.net).

HIKING

➤ CONTACTS: **Hike Ontario** (☎ 416/426–7362, WEB www.hikeontario.com).

MULTIACTIVITY

Call of the Wild offers guided trips of different lengths—dogsledding and cross-country skiing in winter, canoeing and hiking in summer—in Algonquin Provincial Park and other areas in southern Ontario. Prices include transportation from Toronto.

➤ CONTACTS: **Call of the Wild** (☎ 905/471–9453 or 800/776–9453, WEB www.callofthewild.ca).

RAFTING

A growing number of companies in eastern Ontario offers packages ranging from half-day to weeklong trips from May through September. Esprit Rafting Adventures offers trips on the Ottawa River, canoeing in Algonquin Provincial Park, or mountain biking in the Upper Ottawa Valley. Owl Rafting conducts half-day excursions on the nearby Ottawa and Madawaska rivers. RiverRun, in Beachburg, a 90-minute drive north of Ottawa, has a one-day tour on the Ottawa River.

➤ CONTACTS: **Esprit Rafting Adventures** (☎ 819/683–3241 or 800/596–7238, WEB www.espritrafting.com). **Owl Rafting** (☎ 613/646–2263, 613/238–7238, or 800/461–7238, WEB www.owl-mkc.ca). **RiverRun** (☎ 613/646–2501 or 800/267–8504, WEB www.riverrunners.com).

SKIING

➤ CONTACTS: **Snow report** (☎ 416/314–0998 or 800/668–2746).

SNOWMOBILING

Ontario has 49,000 km (30,380 mi) of trails, and many outfitters and guided excursions are available from Haliburton Highlands–Algonquin Provincial Park to Kenora in the province's far northwest. Halley's Camps has guided excursions on wilderness trails to outpost camps for three to six nights.

➤ CONTACTS: **Halley's Camps** (☎ 807/224–6531; 800/465–3325 in ON and MB; WEB www.halleyscamps.com).

TRAIN TRAVEL

Ontario is served by cross-Canada VIA Rail, which stops in towns and cities across the southern sector of the province. VIA Rail connects with Amtrak service at Niagara Falls (Niagara Falls, NY) and Fort Erie (Buffalo, NY).

➤ TRAIN INFORMATION: **Amtrak** (☎ 800/872–7245, WEB www.amtrak.com). **VIA Rail** (☎ 888/842–7245 or 416/236–2029, WEB www.viarail.ca).

VISITOR INFORMATION

Ontario has a wealth of excellent and free tourist information. Ontario Tourism provides detailed guides about a variety of travel interests, from cruising rivers and lakes, to big-city adventures.

Ontario's principal regional tourist offices are also excellent information sources. Algoma Country Travel Association provides complete information on the Sault Ste. Marie region. Contact the James Bay Frontier Tourism Association with your queries about the Timmins, Cochrane, and Moosonee areas. Get in touch with Kawartha Lakes Tourism for information on Peterborough and the many nearby parks and lakes. Contact Kingston Area Tourist Information Office for key information about this historic city and its environs. Kitchener-Waterloo Tourism will answer your questions about touring these twin cities and surrounding villages. Midland-Penetanguishene Tourism provides details about traveling in and around these lakeside towns. Muskoka Tourism has all the facts about one of Ontario's most popular destinations. Tourism Niagara is the official source for information on the cities of Niagara Falls, Niagara-on-the-Lake, and the wine region of the Niagara Peninsula. Ontario East Tourism Association is a comprehensive resource if you're planning a trip to the regions south of Ottawa and along the St. Lawrence corridor. North of Superior Tourism provides travel information on this vast region, including the city of Thunder Bay. The Convention and Visitors Bureau of Windsor, Essex County, and Pelee Island has helpful information about touring those areas.

➤ TOURIST INFORMATION: **Algoma Country Travel Association** (✉ 485 Queen St. E, Suite 204, Sault Ste. Marie P6A 1Z9, ☎ 705/254–4293 or 800/263–2546, WEB www.algomacountry.com). **Convention and Visitors Bureau of Windsor, Essex County, and Pelee Island** (✉ 333 Riverside Dr. W, Suite 103, Windsor N9A 5K4, ☎ 519/255–6530 or

800/265–3633, WEB www.city.windsor.on.ca/cvb/tourismlinks.asp). **James Bay Frontier Travel Association** (✉ Bag 920, Schumacher P0N 1G0, ☎ 705/360–1980 or 800/461–3766, WEB www.jamesbayfrontier. com). **Kawartha Lakes Tourism** (✉ 175 George St. N, Peterborough K9J 3G6, ☎ 705/742–2201 or 800/461–6424, WEB www.thekawarthas. net). **Kingston Area Tourist Information Office** (✉ 209 Ontario St., Kingston K7L 2Z1, ☎ 613/548–4415 or 888/855–5455, WEB www. kingstonarea.on.ca/tourism). **Kitchener-Waterloo Tourism** (✉ 80 Queen St. N, Kitchener N2H 2H3, ☎ 519/745–3536 or 800/265–6959, WEB www.kw-visitor.on.ca). **Midland-Penetanguishene Tourism** (✉ 208 King St., Midland L4R 4K8, ☎ 705/549–3811 or 800/263–7745, WEB www.georgianbaytourism.on.ca). **Muskoka Tourism** (✉ R.R. 2, Kilworthy P0E 1G0, ☎ 705/689–0660 or 800/267–9700, WEB www. muskoka-tourism.on.ca). **North of Superior Tourism** (✉ 1119 Victoria Ave. E, Thunder Bay P7C 1B7, ☎ 807/626–9420 or 800/265–3951, WEB www.nosta.on.ca). **Ontario East Tourism Association** (✉ 108 St. Lawrence St., Merrickville K0G 1N0, ☎ 613/269–3999 or 800/576–3278, WEB www.ontarioeast.com). **Ontario Tourism** (✉ 181 Bay St., Suite 350, Toronto M5J 2T3, ☎ 416/314–0944 or 800/668–2746, WEB www.ontariotravel.net). **Tourism Niagara** (✉ 2201 St. David's Road, Thorold L2V 4T8, ☎ 905/685–1308 or 800/263–2988, WEB www. tourismniagara.com).

9 MONTRÉAL

Traces of this island city's long history are found everywhere, from the 17th-century buildings in Vieux-Montréal to grand churches and verdant parks such as Mont-Royal. But Montréal, with its romantically elegant atmosphere, is also full of very modern pleasures: fine dining, whether you want French cuisine or any kind of ethnic fare; good shopping for everything from antiques to high fashion; and nightlife, arts events, and festivals that provide diversions year-round.

MONTRÉAL IS CANADA'S most romantic metropolis, an island city that seems to favor grace and elegance over order and even prosperity, a city full of music, art, and joie de vivre. It is rather like the European capital Vienna—past its peak of power and glory, perhaps, but still a vibrant and beautiful place full of memories, dreams, and festivals.

By Paul and Julie Waters

That's not to say Montréal is ready to fade away. It may not be so young anymore—2002 marks its 360th birthday—but it remains Québec's largest city and an important port and financial center. Its office towers are full of young Québécois entrepreneurs, members of a new breed who are ready and eager to take on the world. The city's four universities—two English and two French—and a host of junior colleges add to that youthful zest. In fact, a 1999 study by local McGill University showed that Montréal's population had the highest proportion of students of any city in North America—3.48 per hundred, just a whisker ahead of Boston with 3.47.

Montréal is the only French-speaking metropolis in North America and the second-largest French-speaking city in the world, but it's a tolerant place that over the years has made room for millions of immigrants who speak dozens of languages. Today about 15% of the 3.1 million people who live in the metropolitan area claim English as their mother tongue, and another 15% claim a language that's neither English nor French. The city's gentle acceptance has made it one of the world's most livable cities.

The city's grace, however, has been sorely tested. Since 1976, Montréal has endured the election (twice) of a separatist provincial government, a law banning all languages but French on virtually all public signs and billboards, and four referenda on the future of Québec and Canada. The latest chapter in this long constitutional drama was the cliff-hanger referendum on Québec independence on October 30, 1995. In that showdown Québécois voters chose to remain part of Canada, but by the thinnest of possible margins. More than 98% of eligible voters participated, and the final province-wide result was 49.42% in favor of independence and 50.58% against. In fact, 60% of the province's Francophones voted in favor of establishing an independent Québec. But Montréal, where most of the province's Anglophones and immigrants live, bucked the separatist trend and voted nearly 70% against independence. The drama has cooled; since 1998 the separatist government has turned its attention to the economy, and Montréal has prospered accordingly.

But if politics can be hard, the weather can be harder. Montréal got a reminder in January 1998 of just how vulnerable to the elements it is, when a freak storm buried the city under a glittering carapace of ice. The *verglas*, as it was called in French, created scenes of unspeakable beauty, but the weight of all that ice destroyed many of the city's hardwood trees and crushed the lines and pylons that carried the city's electrical supply from power stations in the north. Much of the city was without heat or light for more than a week, and parts of the surrounding area endured the darkness for as long as a month. But it wasn't as bleak as it sounds. Shared hardship brought people together and tested their ingenuity and generosity. Neighbors shared generators, food, and shelter, and their children—shorn of television and video games—learned the simpler joys of charades, board games, and storytelling.

If anything, Montréal emerged stronger and more optimistic. And why not? It's a city that's used to turmoil. It was founded by the

French, conquered by the British, and occupied by the Americans. It has a long history of reconciling contradictions and even today is a city of contrasts. The glass office tower of La Maison des Coopérants, for example, soars above a Gothic-style Anglican cathedral that squats gracefully in its shadow. The neo-Gothic facade of the Basilique Notre-Dame-de-Montréal glares across Place d'Armes at the pagan temple that's the head office of the Bank of Montréal. And while pilgrims still crawl up the steps of the Oratoire St-Joseph on one side of Mont-Royal, thousands of their fellow Catholics line up to get into the very chic Casino de Montréal on the other side—certainly not what the earnest French settlers who founded Montréal envisioned when they landed on the island in May 1642.

Those 54 pious men and women under the leadership of Paul de Chomedey, sieur de Maisonneuve, hoped to do nothing less than create a new Christian society. They named their settlement Ville-Marie in honor of the mother of Christ and set out to convert the natives. The heroism of two women—Jeanne Mance, a French noblewoman who arrived with de Maisonneuve, and Marguerite Bourgeoys, who came 11 years later—marked those early years. Jeanne Mance, working alone, established the Hôpital Hôtel-Dieu de St-Joseph, still one of the city's major hospitals. In 1659 she invited members of a French order of nuns to help her in her efforts. That order, the Religieuses Hospitalières de St-Joseph, now has its motherhouse in Montréal and is the oldest nursing group in the Americas. Marguerite Bourgeoys, with Jeanne Mance's help, established the colony's first school and taught both French and native children how to read and write. Bourgeoys founded the Congrégation de Notre Dame, a teaching order that still has schools in Montréal, across Canada, and around the world. She was canonized by the Roman Catholic Church in 1982.

Piety wasn't the settlement's only raison d'être, however. Ville-Marie was ideally located to be a commercial success as well. It was at the confluence of two major transportation routes—the St. Lawrence and Ottawa rivers—and fur trappers used the town as a staging point for their expeditions. But the city's religious roots were never forgotten. Until 1854, long after the French lost possession of the city, the island of Montréal remained the property of the Sulpicians, an aristocratic order of French priests. The Sulpicians were responsible for administering the colony and for recruiting colonists. They still run the Basilique Notre-Dame-de-Montréal and are still responsible for training priests for the Roman Catholic archdiocese.

The French regime in Canada ended with the Seven Years' War—what Americans call the French and Indian War. British troops took Québec City in 1759, and Montréal fell less than a year later. The Treaty of Paris ceded all New France to Britain in 1763, and soon English and Scottish settlers poured into Montréal to take advantage of the city's geography and economic potential. By 1832, Montréal was a leading colonial capital of business, finance, and transportation and had grown far beyond the walls of the old settlement. Much of that business and financial leadership has since moved to Toronto, the upstream rival Montrealers love to hate.

Pleasures and Pastimes

Dining

Montrealers are passionate about food. They love to dine on classic dishes in restaurants such as Les Halles and Chez La Mère Michel, or swoon over culinary innovations in places like Toqué! and La Chronique, but they can get equally passionate about humbler fare. They'll argue

Montréal

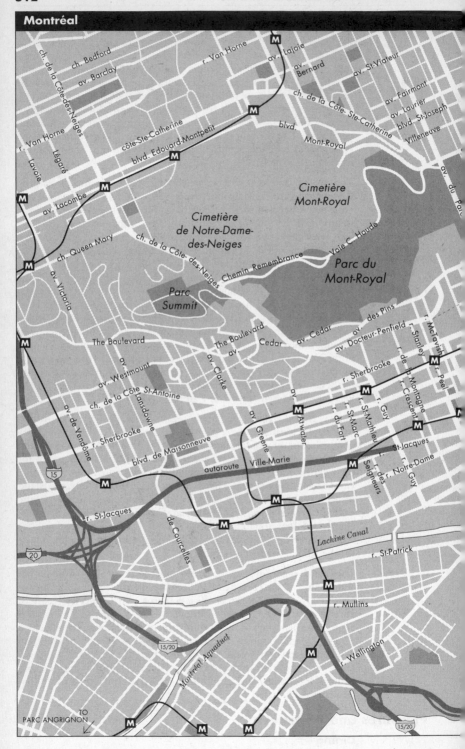

ch. Bedford
ch. de la Côte-des-Neiges
av. Barclay
r. Van Horne
av. Lajoie
av. Bernard
av. St-Viateur
av. Fairmont
av. Laurier
ch. de la Côte-Ste-Catherine
blvd. St-Joseph
Villeneuve
r. Van Horne
côte-Ste-Catherine
blvd. Edouard-Montpetit
ch. de la Côte-Ste-Catherine
blvd.
Mont-Royal
av. du Parc
Lavoie
Légaré
av. Lacombe
Cimetière
Mont-Royal
ch. Queen Mary
ch. de la Côte-des-Neiges
Cimetière
de Notre-Dame-
des-Neiges
Voie C. Houde
Parc du
Mont-Royal
av. Victoria
Parc
Summit
Chemin Remembrance
The Boulevard
The Boulevard
Cedar
av. Cedar
av. des Pins
av. Docteur-Penfield
r. McTavish
r. Peel
av. Westmount
av.
av. Clarke
r. Sherbrooke
r. de la Montagne
r. Stanley
ch. de la Côte St-Antoine
Lansdowne
av. Greene
av. Atwater
r. Guy
r. St-Mathieu
r. Crescent
av. de Vendôme
r. Sherbrooke
r. St-Marc
r. du Fort
St-Jacques
blvd. de Maisonneuve
autoroute Ville-Marie
r. des Seigneurs
r. Notre-Dame
r. Guy
15
r. St-Jacques
de Courcelles
Lachine Canal
r. St-Patrick
20
Montréal Aquaduct
15/20
r. Mullins
r. Wellington
TO
PARC ANGRIGNON
15/20

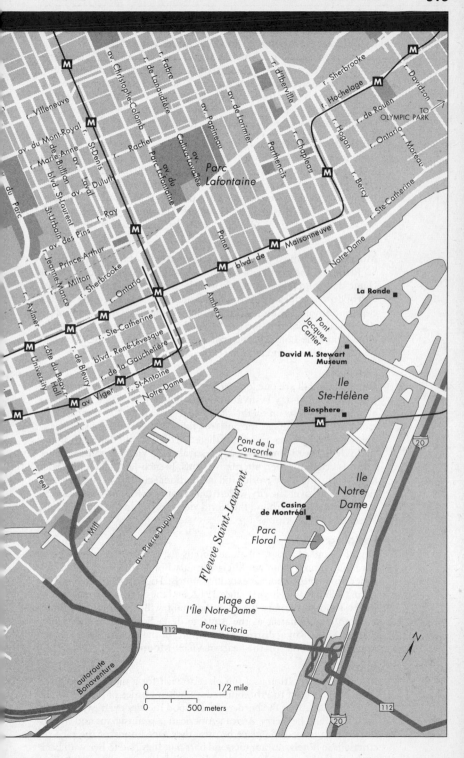

with some heat about where to get the juiciest smoked meat (the city's beloved version of corned beef), the crispiest barbecued chicken, and the soggiest *stimés* (steamed hot dogs). There's great French food here, but also some of North America's most innovative chefs, who seamlessly blend French discipline, Asian and Latin flavors, and the freshest of local ingredients. Over the years, immigrants from all over the world—notably Jews from Eastern Europe, Greeks, Thais, Chinese, Portuguese, and especially Italians—have added to the mix; the city's restaurants represent more than 75 ethnic groups.

Faith and History

Reminders of the city's long history are found everywhere, including in its churches. Some buildings in Vieux-Montréal date from the 17th century. Other parts of the city are full of wonderful examples of Victorian architecture. Museums such as the Musée McCord de l'Histoire Canadienne, the Musée d'Archéologie de la Pointe-à-Callière, and the Stewart Museum in the Old Fort on Île Ste-Hélène attest to the city's fascination with its past.

Montréal's two most popular attractions are the oratory dedicated to St. Joseph on the north side of Mont-Royal and the Basilique Notre-Dame-de-Montréal dedicated to his wife in the old city. These are just two of dozens of beautiful churches built in the days when the Québécois were among the most devout Roman Catholics. Other gems of ecclesiastical architecture include St. Patrick's Basilica and the Chapelle Notre-Dame-de-Lourdes. Even parish churches in working-class neighborhoods are as grand as some cathedrals.

Festivals

Summer and fall are one long succession of festivals, beginning in late June with the 10-day Festival International de Jazz, when as many as a million fans descend on the city to hear more than 1,000 musicians, including such giants as the guitarist John Scofield and the tenor saxophonist Joe Lovano. In August there are the World Film Festival and the lively Just for Laughs Comedy Festival in the Vieux-Port area. Other festivals celebrate beer, alternative films, French-language music and song from around the world, and international cuisine. In late June and July the skies over the city waterfront erupt in color and flame as fireworks teams from around the world vie for prizes in the International Fireworks Competition.

Lodging

On the island of Montréal alone, rooms are available in every type of accommodation, from world-class luxury hotels to hostels, from student dormitories to budget executive motels. The Ritz-Carlton has been setting standards of luxury since 1912, and the nearby Omni is one of the best modern luxury hotels in the country. But the city also offers more intimate charm, at the Auberge de la Fontaine in the trendy Plateau Mont-Royal district, for example, or the tiny Auberge les Passants du Sans Soucy in the heart of Vieux-Montréal.

Nightlife

Montréal's reputation as a fun place to visit for a night on the town dates back at least to Prohibition days, when hordes of thirsty Americans from south of the border would flood the city every weekend to eat, drink, and be merry. African-American jazz musicians and singers in particular loved the place because they faced none of the race restrictions in hotels, restaurants, and bars that they had to live with back in the United States. The city has dozens of dance and jazz clubs and bistros, not to mention hundreds of bars where you can go to argue about sports, politics, and religion until the early hours of the morning. Much of the action takes place along rue St-Denis and adjacent streets in the eastern part of the city or on rues Bishop, Crescent, and de la Montagne in the downtown area. The night scene is constantly shifting—last year's hot spot can quickly become this year's has-been. The best and easiest way to figure out what's in is to stroll down rue St-Denis or rue Bishop at about 10:30 and look for the place with the longest line and the rudest doorman.

Shopping

The development of the Underground City has made shopping a year-round sport in Montréal. That vast complex—heated in winter, air-conditioned in summer—is linked by underground passageways and the Métro and includes two major department stores, at least a dozen huge shopping malls, and more than 1,000 boutiques. Add to this Montréal's status as one of the fur capitals of the world, and you have a city that was born to be shopped.

EXPLORING MONTRÉAL

The Île de Montréal is an island in the St. Lawrence River, 51 km (32 mi) long and 14 km (9 mi) wide. The only rise in the landscape is the 764-ft-high Mont-Royal, which gave the island its name and which residents call simply "the mountain." The city of Montréal is the oldest and by far the largest of the island's 24 municipalities, which are melting into one huge megacity—much to the dismay of many proud suburbanites. There's a belt of off-island suburbs on the south shore of the St. Lawrence, and just to the north across the narrow Rivière-des-Prairies, on an island of its own, is Laval, a suburb that has grown to be the second-largest city in the province. But the countryside is never far away. The pastoral Eastern Townships, first settled by Loyalists fleeing the American Revolution, are less than an hour's drive away, and the Laurentians, an all-season playground full of lakes and ski hills, are even closer.

For a good overview of the city, head for the lookout at the Chalet du Mont-Royal. You can drive most of the way, park, and walk ½ km (¼ mi), or hike all the way up from chemin de la Côte-des-Neiges or avenue des Pins. If you look directly out—southeast—from the belvedere, at the foot of the hill is the McGill University campus and, surrounding it, the skyscrapers of downtown Montréal. Just beyond, along the bank of the river, are the stone houses of Vieux-Montréal. Hugging the south shore on the other side of the river are the l'Îles Ste-Hélène and Notre-Dame; sites of La Ronde amusement park, the Biosphere, and the Casino de Montréal; acres of parkland; and the Lac de l'Île Notre-Dame public beach—all popular excursions. To the east are rue St-Denis and the Quartier Latin, with its rows of French and ethnic restaurants, bistros, chess hangouts, designer boutiques, antiques shops, and art galleries. Even farther east you can see the flying-saucer–shape Olympic Stadium with its leaning tower.

Montréal is easy to explore. Streets, subways, and bus lines are clearly marked. The city is divided by a grid of streets roughly aligned east–west and north–south. (Montréal takes its directions from the flow of the river rather than the compass, so this grid is tilted about 40 degrees off—to the left of—true north, meaning that west is actually southwest and so on.) North–south street numbers begin at the St. Lawrence River and increase as you head north; east–west street numbers begin at boulevard St-Laurent, which divides Montréal into east and west halves. The city is not so large that seasoned walkers can't see all the districts around the base of Mont-Royal on foot. Nearly everything else is easily accessible by the city's clean and quiet bus and Métro (subway) system. If you're planning to visit a number of museums, look into the city's museum pass (available at museums and Centre Info-Touriste).

Numbers in the text correspond to numbers in the margin and on the Vieux-Montréal, Downtown Montréal (Centre-Ville) and Golden Square Mile, Quartier Latin and Parc du Mont-Royal, and Olympic Park and Botanical Garden maps.

Great Itineraries

Getting a real feel for this bilingual, multicultural city takes some time. An ideal stay is seven days, but even three days of walking and soaking up the atmosphere gives you enough time to visit Mont-Royal, explore Vieux-Montréal, do some shopping, and perhaps visit the Parc Olympique. It also includes enough nights for an evening of bar-hopping on rue St-Denis or rue Crescent and another for a long, luxurious dinner at one of the city's excellent restaurants.

IF YOU HAVE 3 DAYS

Any visit to Montréal should start with Mont-Royal, Montréal's most enduring symbol. Afterward wander down to avenue des Pins and then through McGill University to downtown. Make an effort to stop at the Musée des Beaux-Arts and St. Patrick's Basilica. On Day 2, explore Vieux-Montréal, with special emphasis on the Basilique Notre-Dame-de-Montréal and the Musée d'Archéologie Pointe-à-Callière. On Day 3 you can either visit the Parc Olympique (recommended for children) or stroll through the Quartier Latin.

IF YOU HAVE 5 DAYS

Start with a visit to Parc du Mont-Royal. After viewing the city from the Chalet du Mont-Royal, visit the Oratoire St-Joseph. You should still have enough time to visit the Musée des Beaux-Arts before dinner. That leaves time on Day 2 to get in some shopping as you explore downtown, with perhaps a visit to the Centre Canadien d'Architecture. Spend all of Day 3 in Vieux-Montréal, and on Day 4 stroll through the Quartier Latin. On Day 5, visit the Parc Olympique and then do one of three things: visit the islands, take a ride on the Lachine Rapids, or revisit some of the sights you missed in Vieux-Montréal or downtown.

IF YOU HAVE 7 DAYS

A week gives you enough time for the five-day itinerary while expanding your Vieux-Montréal explorations to two days and adding a shopping spree on rue Chabanel and a visit to the Casino de Montréal.

Vieux-Montréal

When Montréal's first European settlers arrived by river in 1642, they stopped to build their houses just below the treacherous Lachine Rapids that blocked the way upstream. They picked a site near an old Iroquois settlement on the bank of the river nearest Mont-Royal. In the mid-17th century, Montréal consisted of a handful of wood houses clustered around a pair of stone buildings, all flimsily fortified by a wooden stockade. For almost three centuries this district—bounded by rues Berri and McGill on the east and west, rue St-Jacques on the north, and the river to the south—was the financial and political heart of the city. Government buildings, the largest church, the stock exchange, the main market, and the port were here. The narrow but relatively straight cobblestone streets were lined with solid, occasionally elegant houses, office buildings, and warehouses—also made of stone. In the early days a thick stone wall with four gates protected the city against native people and marauding European powers. Montréal quickly grew beyond the bounds of its fortifications, however, and by World War I the center of the city had moved toward Mont-Royal. The new heart of Montréal became Dominion Square (now Square Dorchester). For the next two decades Vieux-Montréal (Old Montréal), as it became known, was gradually abandoned, the warehouses and offices emptied. In 1962 the city began studying ways to revitalize Vieux-Montréal, and a decade of renovations and restorations began.

Today Vieux-Montréal is a center of cultural life and municipal government. Most of the summer activities revolve around Place Jacques-Cartier, which becomes a pedestrian mall with street performers and outdoor cafés, and the Vieux-Port, one of the city's most popular recreation spots. The Orchestre Symphonique de Montréal performs summer concerts at Basilique Notre-Dame-de-Montréal, and English-language plays are staged in the Centaur Theatre in the old stock-exchange building. This district has museums devoted to history, religion, and the arts. It also has a growing number of hotel beds. A decade ago it was impossible to find a place to stay in the old city; now there are half a dozen fine inns and boutique hotels and new ones opening all the time.

A Good Walk

Take the Métro to the Square-Victoria station and follow the signs to the **Centre de Commerce Mondial de Montréal** ①, one of the city's more appealing enclosed spaces, with a fountain and frequent art exhibits. Exit on the east side of the complex and turn right on rue St-Pierre, walk south to **rue St-Jacques** and turn left. Walking east, you see the Victorian office buildings of the country's former financial center. This area can seem tomblike on weekends when the business and legal offices close down, but things get livelier closer to the waterfront.

Stop at **Place d'Armes** ②, a square that was the site of battles with the Iroquois in the 1600s and later became the center of Montréal's Haute-Ville, or Upper Town. Calèches are available at the south end of the square; on the north side is the **Bank of Montréal** ③, an impressive building with Corinthian columns. The **Basilique Notre-Dame-de-Montréal** ④, one of the most beautiful churches in North America, dominates the south end of Place d'Armes. The low, more retiring stone building behind a wall to the west of the basilica is the **Vieux Séminaire** ⑤, Montréal's oldest building. Unlike the basilica, it is closed to the public. To the east of the basilica is **rue St-Sulpice,** one of the first streets in Montréal, and catercorner from it is the art deco Aldred Building. Next to that is Montréal's first skyscraper, a nine-story red-stone tower built by the now defunct Québec Bank in 1888. One block farther east on rue Notre-Dame, just past boulevard St-Laurent on the left, rises the black glass–sheathed **Palais de Justice** ⑥ (1971), the courthouse. The large domed building at 155 rue Notre-Dame Est is the **Vieux Palais de Justice** ⑦ (1857). Across the street, at 160 rue Notre-Dame Est, is the Maison de la Sauvegarde, one of the city's oldest houses. The Old Courthouse abuts the small **Place Vauquelin** ⑧, named after an 18th-century naval hero. North of this square is Champs-de-Mars, a former military parade ground and now a public park crisscrossed by archaeologists' trenches. The ornate building on the east side of Place Vauquelin is the Second Empire–style **Hôtel de Ville** ⑨, or City Hall, built in 1878.

You are in a perfect spot to explore **Place Jacques-Cartier** ⑩, the square that is the heart of Vieux-Montréal. At the western corner of rue Notre-Dame is the **Office des Congrès et du Tourisme du Grand Montréal** ⑪, an information center. Both sides of the square are lined with

518

Vieux-Montréal

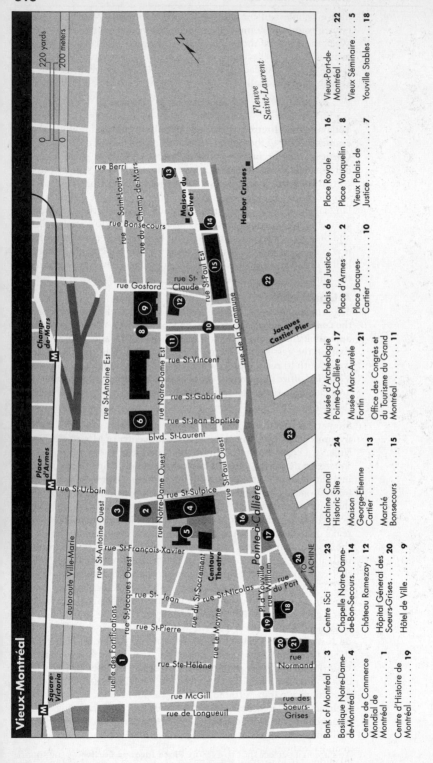

two- and three-story stone buildings that were originally homes or hotels. In summer, the one-block rue St-Amable, near the bottom of the square, becomes a marketplace for local jewelers, artists, and other craftspeople.

Retrace your steps to the north end of Place Jacques-Cartier and continue east on rue Notre-Dame. On the right, at the corner of rue St-Claude, is **Château Ramezay** ⑫, built as the residence of the 11th governor of Montréal, Claude de Ramezay, and now a museum. Continue east to rue Berri. On the corner are two houses from the mid-19th century that have been transformed into the **Maison George-Étienne Cartier** ⑬, a museum honoring one of the leading figures in the founding of the Canadian federation in 1867.

When you come out of the museum, walk south on rue Berri to rue St-Paul and then start walking west again toward the center of the city. The first street on your right is rue Bonsecours, one of the oldest in the city. On the corner is the charming Maison du Calvet, now a restaurant and small but opulent bed-and-breakfast. Opposite it is the charming **Chapelle Notre-Dame-de-Bon-Secours** ⑭, founded by St. Marguerite Bourgeoys, Montréal's first schoolteacher. The long, domed building to the west of the chapel is the **Marché Bonsecours** ⑮, a public market transformed into a center with both cultural and commercial goals—there are exhibits on Montréal in the hall upstairs and boutiques specializing in regional crafts and Québec fashions downstairs.

Restaurants, shops filled with Québécois handicrafts, and nightclubs line rue St-Paul, the most fashionable street in Vieux-Montréal, for almost 20 blocks. Eight blocks west of Place Jacques-Cartier, rue St-Paul leads to **Place Royale** ⑯, the oldest public square in Montréal. Behind the Old Customs House on the square are the **Pointe-à-Callière**, a small park that commemorates the settlers' first landing, and the **Musée d'Archéologie Pointe-à-Callière** ⑰, Montréal's dazzling museum of history and archaeology. A 1½-block walk down rue William takes you to the **Youville Stables** ⑱, on the left. These low stone buildings enclosing a garden now hold offices, shops, and a restaurant.

Across rue William from the stables is the old fire station that houses the **Centre d'Histoire de Montréal** ⑲, a museum that chronicles the day-to-day life of Montrealers throughout the years. Now walk south on rue St-Pierre toward the harbor. You pass the ruins of the **Hôpital Général des Soeurs-Grises** ⑳, which served as a shelter for homeless children in the 18th and 19th centuries. Just south of the ruins is the charming **Musée Marc-Aurèle Fortin** ㉑, a gallery dedicated to the works of one of Québec's most distinctive landscape artists. Just south of the museum, rue St-Pierre ends at rue de la Commune, across the street from the **Vieux-Port-de-Montréal** ㉒, a pleasant and popular waterfront park that makes a fitting close to any walk in Vieux-Montréal. If you have time, you can arrange for a harbor excursion or a daring ride on the Lachine Rapids. The Vieux-Port is also home to the **Centre iSci** ㉓, Montréal's state-of-the-art science center. At the western end of the port area is the entrance to the **Lachine Canal Historic Site** ㉔, a canal-turned-park that has the city's most popular bicycle path.

TIMING

If you walk briskly and don't stop, you could get through this route in under an hour. A more realistic and leisurely pace would take about 90 minutes (still without stopping), or longer in winter when the streets are icy. Comfortable shoes are a must for the cobblestone streets. The Basilique Notre-Dame is one of Montréal's most famous landmarks and deserves at least a 45-minute visit; Château Ramezay deserves the same. The Pointe-à-Callière museum could keep an enthusiastic history buff occupied for a whole day, so give it at least two hours. If you do visit any museums, check ahead for seasonal hours.

Sights to See

❸ Bank of Montréal. The head office of Canada's oldest chartered bank is a temple to business and finance. It's housed in a neoclassical structure built on Place d'Armes in 1847 and remodeled by the renowned New York architectural firm McKim, Mead & White in 1905. The central dome and Corinthian columns give it the air of an ancient Greek or Roman sanctuary, a stark contrast to the Gothic glory of the Catholic Basilique Notre-Dame-de-Montréal across the square. If anything, the bank's interior is even more templelike. In the main entrance, a 20-ft statue stands like an ancient goddess amid a forest of dark marble columns supporting an intricate coffered ceiling. She actually represents Patria—or "homeland"—and stands as a memorial to the war dead of 1914–18. The bank's tellers work in an immense room surrounded by more marble columns. A one-room museum recounts the early history of banking in Canada. ⊠ *119 rue St-Jacques Ouest,* ☎ *514/877–7373.* ▣ *Free.* ☉ *Weekdays 10–4. Métro: Place-d'Armes.*

★ **❹ Basilique Notre-Dame-de-Montréal** (Notre-Dame Basilica). The first church called Notre-Dame was a bark-covered structure built in 1642. Three times it was torn down and rebuilt, each time larger and more ornate. The present church is an enormous (3,800-seat) neo-Gothic structure that opened in 1829. Its architect was an American Protestant named James O'Donnell, who converted to Catholicism during its construction and is buried in the church crypt. The twin towers are 228 ft high, and the western one holds one of North America's largest bells. The interior is not so much Gothic as neo-Romanesque, with stained-glass windows, pine and walnut carvings, and a blue vaulted ceiling studded with thousands of 24-karat gold stars. Life-size wooden carvings of Ezekiel and Jeremiah sit under the opulently decorated pulpit with its intricately twisting staircase. The stained-glass windows from Limoges commemorate episodes of Montréal's history and were installed to mark the church's 100th birthday. Side altars honor—among others— St. Marguerite d'Youville, Canada's first native-born saint; St. Marguerite Bourgeoys, Canada's first schoolteacher; and a group of Sulpician priests who were martyred in Paris during the French Revolution.

As the northwest corner of the church has been glassed off to make a small prayer room away from the noise of the visiting hordes, the magnificent baptistery, decorated with frescoes by Ozias Leduc, is difficult to see. With more than 7,000 pipes, the Cassavant pipe organ is one of the largest on the continent. If you just want to hear the organ roar, drop in for the 11 AM solemn Mass on Sunday and pay special attention to the recessional. Behind the main altar is the **Sacré-Coeur Chapel,** destroyed by fire in 1978 and rebuilt in five different styles. Its dominant feature is the huge and very modern bronze sculpture that forms the backdrop for the Plexiglass altar. The chapel is often called the Wedding Chapel, because hundreds of Montrealers get married in it every year. Pop diva Céline Dion's wedding to her manager in 1994, however, filled the main church, as did the state funeral of former Prime Minister Pierre Elliot-Trudeau in 2000. The basilica's museum includes a collection of vestments, religious artifacts, art, and old documents and titles.

Notre-Dame is an active house of worship and visitors are asked to dress accordingly (i.e., no shorts or bare midriffs). Also, it's advisable to plan your visit around the daily 12:15 PM mass in the chapel and the 5 PM mass in the main church. ⊠ *116 rue Notre-Dame Ouest,* ☎ *514/849–1070 basilica; 514/842–2925 museum.* ⊡ *$2, including guided tour.* ☉ *Basilica: early Sept.–June 24, daily 8:30–6; June 25– early Sept., daily 8:30–8. Guided tour, except Sun. morning: May–June 24, daily 9–4; June 25–early Sept., daily 8:30–4:30. Métro: Place-d'Armes.*

❶ Centre de Commerce Mondial de Montréal (Montréal World Trade Center). One of the nicest enclosed spaces in Montréal, this narrow, soaring atrium houses a growing number of boutiques, a food court, frequent art exhibits, and Montréal's own chunk of the Berlin Wall, complete with colorful graffiti. Photographers often use the fountain and reflecting pond at the west end as a backdrop for fashion shoots and wedding groups. The semi-reclining statue of Amphitrite (Poseidon's wife) overlooking the fountain is an 18th-century piece and comes from the municipal fountain of St-Mihiel-de-la-Meuse in France. The complex covers a block of the run-down ruelle des Fortifications, a narrow lane that marks the place where the city walls stood. Developers glassed it in and sandblasted and restored 11 of the 19th-century buildings that lined it. One of them—the **Nordheimer,** at the southeastern end of the complex—is worth a look. It now forms part of the Hôtel Inter-Continental Montréal. To see it, climb the stairs to the hotel lobby and cross the footbridge. The building's dark woodwork and suggestive Celtic-style mosaics reflect the romantic tastes of the Scottish businessmen who ran Victorian Montréal. The building also once housed a small concert hall where such luminaries as Sarah Bernhardt and Maurice Ravel performed. ⊠ *747 Sq. Victoria,* ☎ *514/982–9888. Métro: Square-Victoria.*

☺ ⓵⑨ Centre d'Histoire de Montréal. Video games, sound tracks, and more than 300 artifacts re-create the day-to-day life of the ordinary men and women who have lived in Montréal from pre-colonial to modern times. Some of the most touching exhibits depict family life in Montréal's working-class tenements in the 20th century. You can sit in a period-furnished living room and listen to a 1940s radio broadcast that includes the play-by-play of a hockey game and the recitation of the rosary, or you can step into a phone booth and eavesdrop on a young working-class couple arranging a date. ⊠ *335 pl. d'Youville,* ☎ *514/ 872–3207,* WEB *www.ville.montreal.qc.ca/chm/engl.* ⊡ *$6.50.* ☉ *Tues.– Sun. 10–5. Métro: Place-d'Armes or Square-Victoria.*

☺ ㉓ Centre iSci. The "i" stands for interactive, the "Sci" for science, and together they spell the name of Montréal's science center, which fills more than 600,000 square ft on the old King Edward Pier. The center has three main exhibition halls—the Life Lab, the Information Studio, and Matter Works. Each uses puzzles, quizzes, games of strategy and skill, and hands-on experiments, as well as lectures and demonstrations, to explore various aspects of such scientific and technological themes as medicine, aerospace, computers, communications and media, natural resources, and engineering. The center also encompasses three IMAX film theaters and the giant-screen, interactive Immersion Studios theater, complete with digital projection system and "surround sound," where audience members use touch screens to vote on the twists and turns of the story. And Montréal being the dining capital of Canada, the center also includes Porto Fiorentino, a 1,000-seat family restaurant with interactive culinary activities and piano concerts overlooking the harbor. Even the neighboring food court teaches lessons about nutrition and agriculture. In summer, ship containers serve as boutiques with a science message—for example, the watch boutique demonstrates the use of liquid quartz, and the jewelry boutique might explain the formation of amber. ⊠ *Quai King Edward,* ☎ *514/496–4724 or 877/496–4724,* WEB *www.isci.ca.* ⊡ *$9.95 for exhibit halls, $9.95 for IMAX, $5.50 for Immersion Studios, $16.95 for IMAX and exhibit halls.* ⏱ *June 24–Labor Day, daily 10–9; early Sept.–June 23, Fri.–Sat. 10–9, Sun.–Thurs. 10–6. Métro: Place-d'Armes or Champ-de-Mars.*

⑭   **Chapelle Notre-Dame-de-Bon-Secours.** St. Marguerite Bourgeoys dedicated the original waterfront chapel on this site to the Virgin Mary in 1657. (Montréal's founder, Paul de Chomedey, sieur de Maisonneuve, apparently helped cut the timber.) Fire destroyed that structure and the present stone chapel dates to 1771. A renovation project in 1998 revealed some beautiful 18th-century murals that had been covered up with more-recent pictures. The chapel has always had a special place in the hearts of mariners. It was built to house a statue of Notre-Dame-de-Bon-Secours (Our Lady of Good Hope), credited with the rescue of those in peril at sea. A larger-than-life statue of the Virgin graces the steeple of the present building, facing the river with arms outstretched in welcome. Mariners who survived the perils of ocean crossings in the 18th and 19th centuries often came to the church to thank the Virgin for her help and to leave votive lamps in the shape of small model ships as tokens of appreciation. Many of them still hang from the ceiling, and the chapel is usually referred to simply as the Église des Matelots, or the Sailors' Church. Visitors can climb the steeple to the "aerial," a tiny chapel where mariners came to pray for safe passage. The attached **Musée Marguerite Bourgeoys** explores the life of the saint and the history of Montréal, with an emphasis on education. ⊠ *400 rue St-Paul Est,* ☎ *514/282–8670,* ⊡ *Chapel free; museum $5.* ⏱ *Chapel: May–Oct., daily 10–5; Nov.–mid-Jan. and mid-Mar.–Apr., daily 11–3:30. Museum: May–Oct., Tues.–Sun. 10–4:30; Nov.–mid-Jan. and mid-Mar.–Apr., Tues.–Sun. 11–3:30. Métro: Champ-de-Mars.*

⌣ **⑫**   **Château Ramezay.** This colonial building was constructed in 1702 as the residence of the 11th governor of Montréal, Claude de Ramezay. The Compagnie des Indes Occidentales (the French West Indies Company) took it over in 1745 and stored precious furs in the basement vaults. The British used it as headquarters after their conquest in 1760, and so did the American commanders Richard Montgomery and Benedict Arnold, whose troops occupied the city during their 1775–76 campaign to conquer Canada. Benjamin Franklin, who came north in a failed attempt to persuade the Québécois to join the American Revolution, stayed here during that winter adventure. With its thick stone walls, steeply pitched roof, and dormer windows, the château has the air of a Norman castle. Two squat stone towers added in the late 18th century contribute to the effect. The building became a museum of city and provincial history in 1895 and has been restored to the style of Governor de Ramezay's day. The public rooms on the ground floor are gracefully elegant. Of particular interest is the Salon Nantes, with 18th-century Louis XV–style mahogany paneling carved by the French architect Germain Boffrand and imported from the Compagnie des Indes's head office in Nantes about 1750. The main-floor displays are somewhat staid—uniforms, documents, and furniture—but a series of tableaux in the basement vividly depicts the everyday lives of the city's early European settlers, and the château's garden has been planted in a typical colonial fashion. The museum's collection is fairly eclectic, however. One of its most prized possessions, for example, is a bright-red automobile that was produced at the turn of the 20th century by the De Dion-Bouton company for the city's first motorist. ⊠ *280 rue Notre-Dame Est,* ☎ *514/861–3708,* WEB *www.chateauramezay.qc.ca.* ⊡ *$6.* ⏱ *June–Sept., daily 10–6; Oct.–May, Tues.–Sun. 10–4:30. Métro: Champ-de-Mars.*

In summer, few places are lovelier and livelier than **Place Jacques-Cartier.** You can stop at a *terasse* (sidewalk café) for a beer or a coffee, or just sit on a bench amid the flower vendors and listen to the street musicians. If you're really daring, you might try *poutine*, Québec's contribution to junk-food culture. It consists of french fries covered with cheese curds and smothered in gravy—an acquired taste.

㉕ Hôpital Géneral des Soeurs-Grises. The ruins of this old hospital—established in 1694 by the Frères Charon—have been lovingly preserved as a memorial to Canada's first native-born saint, Marguerite d'Youville, who took over the hospital in 1747 and ran it until it burned down in 1765. The bare stone walls once formed the west wing and the transept of the chapel. The gold script on the one facing the street is a re-creation of the letters patent signed by Louis XIV establishing the hospital. St. Marguerite founded the Soeurs de la Charité, better known as the Soeurs Grises, or gray nuns. In the shadow of the walls is the Maison de Mère d'Youville, which houses a small retreat operated by the nuns as well as some remarkable reminders of St. Marguerite's days, such as the old kitchen where she worked, with its enormous fireplace and big stone sink, the stone floor of the room that served as North America's first external clinic or outpatients' department, and the room where St. Marguerite died. The house is not open to the general public, but guided tours can be arranged. ⊠ *138 rue St-Pierre,* ☎ *514/842–9411 (ask for Sr. Marguerite D'Aoust). Métro: Square-Victoria.*

❾ Hôtel de Ville. Montréal's ornate City Hall, built in 1878 in the Second Empire style, was modeled on the city hall in Tours, France. On July 24, 1967, at the height of Canada's centennial celebrations, President Charles de Gaulle of France stood on the central balcony here and made his famous "*Vive le Québec libre*" ("Long live free Québec") speech, much to the delight of the fledgling separatist movement. Free guided tours are available in June, July, and August, and the main hall is used for occasional exhibitions. ⊠ *275 rue Notre-Dame Est,* ☎ *514/872–3355. Métro: Champ-de-Mars.*

OFF THE
BEATEN PATH **LACHINE –** This suburb has a long history; it gets its name from the antics of the first seigneur to hold land west of the Lachine Rapids, Robert Cavalier de La Salle. He was obsessed with finding a westward passage to the Orient, and his persistent and unsuccessful attempts led his fellow colonists to refer to his lands derisively as La Chine, or China.

Lachine has the oldest standing house on the Île de Montréal—the Mayson LeBer–LeMoyne, built by the Montréal merchants Jacques LeBer and Charles LeMoyne between 1669 and 1685. Now the **Musée de la Ville de Lachine,** the city's museum, it houses Lachine's historical collections, including artifacts and documents dating from colonial times. It and its outbuildings also serve as a showcase for local and regional artists. ⊠ *110 chemin LaSalle, Lachine,* ☎ *514/634–3471 Ext. 346,* FAX *514/637–6784,* WEB *parkscanada.pch.gc.ca/fourrure.* ⊠ *Free.* ☉ *Wed.–Sun., 11:30–4:30.*

An old stone warehouse on the Lachine waterfront that dates from 1802 is now the **Fur Trade in Lachine National Historic Site.** The museum recalls the city's salad days when its position upstream from the rapids made it an important center in the fur trade with the interior: the site is stocked with bales of pelts ready for shipment to England and trade goods—blankets, flour, tea, axes, firearms—for the area trappers. ⊠ *1255 blvd. St-Joseph, Lachine,* ☎ *514/637–7433 or 514/283–6054.* ⊠ *$2.50.* ☉ *Apr.–mid-Oct., daily 10–12:30 and 1–6 (closed Mon. AM); mid-Oct.–late Nov., Wed.–Sun. 9:30–12:30 and 1–5.*

👋 ㉔ **Lachine Canal Historic Site.** It was a group of prescient French priests who first tried to dig a canal to move cargo around the treacherous Lachine Rapids, but they had neither the royal approval nor the money to finish the job. That didn't happen until 1825, when the Lachine Canal opened, linking Montréal's harbor to Lac St-Louis and the Ottawa River. For more than 150 years, the canal was one of Canada's most vital waterways, but it was rendered obsolete in 1959 when the St. Lawrence Seaway opened, making it possible for large cargo ships to move freely from the sea to the Great Lakes. The Lachine Canal was subsequently closed to navigation and became an illicit dumping ground for old cars and the victims of underworld killings, while the area around it degenerated into an industrial slum.

In 1988, however, the federal government planted lawns and trees along the old route and transformed it into a long, thin park linking the Vieux-Port to the city of Lachine, one of the island's oldest municipalities and the spot where the St. Lawrence widens to become Lac St-Louis. In spring, summer, and fall, hundreds of Montrealers ride or skate the 9-mi bicycle path to picnic in Lachine's lakefront park or dine in one of the century-old buildings along the waterfront. (At press time, the canal was scheduled for pleasure craft in the summer of 2002.) In winter, the path becomes a cross-country ski trail. The canalside factories and warehouses—most now abandoned or converted into offices or housing—provide an insight into the city's early industrial development. The trail is the first link in the more than 60 mi of bike trails that constitute the **Pôle des Rapides.** A permanent exhibition at the small **Lachine Canal Interpretation Centre** explains the history and construction of the canal. The center, on the western end of the canal, is free and open daily (except Monday morning) mid-May to Labor Day, 10–noon and 1–6. ☎ *514/637–7433; 514/732–7303 for Pôle des Rapides,* ⬛ *parkscanada.pch.gc.ca/canallachine.* ⬛ *Free.* ☉ *Sunrise–sunset.*

⑬ **Maison George-Étienne Cartier.** Two houses make up this museum, which honors one of the architects of the 1867 Canadian federation. The east house focuses on the political career of Cartier, one of the most important French-Canadian statesmen of his day. You can listen to recordings of him and his contemporaries argue the pros and cons of confederation or learn about the importance of Cartier's role in the building of the colony's first railways. The house on the west, where the Cartier family lived in the 1860s, is furnished in the opulently fussy style favored by prosperous 19th-century bourgeois leaders. Costumed guides act out the roles of the Cartiers' friends and servants, and you can listen to portions of taped conversation from "servants" gossiping about the lives of their master and mistress. From mid-November to mid-December, Victorian decorations festoon the home. ⊠ *458 rue Notre-Dame Est,* ☎ *514/283–2282 or 800/463–6769,* ⬛ *parkscanada.pch.gc.ca/cartier.* ⬛ *$3.25.* ☉ *Late May–early Sept., daily 10–6; early Sept.–mid-Dec. and Apr.–late May, Wed.–Sun. 10–noon and 1–5. Métro: Champ-de-Mars.*

OFF THE
BEATEN PATH
MAISON ST-GABRIEL – This fine and rare example of 17th-century rural architecture, and one of the city's most touching and most overlooked museums, is lost among the tenements and low-rise apartment buildings of working-class Pointe-St-Charles. St. Marguerite Bourgeoys and her religious order used the farm as a place to train the *filles du roy* to be the wives and mothers of New France. These were young orphan girls (literally "daughters of the king") sent from France to find husbands and help populate the colony. The two-story stone structure with its complex roof beams—one of the few authentic 17th-century roofs in North America—and huge attics has been carefully restored to show the kind of life these young girls faced

and the kind of training they got in cooking and child-rearing from their devout instructors. The kitchen is equipped with a rare black-stone sink and an ingenious waste-water disposal system. Several items that belonged to St. Marguerite are also on display, including a writing desk she used. ⊠ *2146 pl. Dublin,* ☎ *514/935–8136,* WEB *www.maisonsaint-gabriel.qc.ca.* 🖭 *$5.* ⊙ *June 24–Labor Day, Tues.–Sun. 11–5 (guided tours every hour); early Sept.–June 23, Tues.–Sat. 1:30–3:30, Sun. 1–5.*

⑮ Marché Bonsecours. The graceful, neoclassical building dominates the waterfront of Vieux-Montréal. It was built of gray stone in the 1840s to serve as the city's main market. Its main entrance, on rue St-Paul, has a stately portico supported by six cast-iron Doric columns imported from England. Two rows of meticulously even, sashed windows and a silvery dome complete the building's distinctive features; because of the slope of the land, the building's waterfront side has a more massive look than the long, low frontage along rue St-Paul. A market until the early 1960s, the building was then converted into municipal offices. A 1998 refurbishing transformed it into a charming public space with an exhibition hall on the second floor for history and culture displays, and shops and boutiques on the bright, airy ground floor that focus on local crafts and fashions. ⊠ *350 rue St-Paul Est,* ☎ *514/872–7730,* WEB *www.marchebonsecours.qc.ca. Métro: Champ-de-Mars.*

★ 🖐 ⑰ Musée d'Archéologie Pointe-à-Callière. One of the finest historical museums in Canada is housed in this imposing, shiplike building near the Pointe-à-Callière park. Its exhibits take you quite literally right to the foundations of New France—it's built over the excavated remains of structures dating to Montréal's beginnings. Visits usually start with an audio-visual show that gives an overview of the area's history from the Ice Age to the present. But as soon as that's over, you descend deep below street level to the bank of the Rivière St-Pierre that once flowed past the site and was where the first settlers built their homes and traded with the local natives. One of the most impressive finds the archaeologists unearthed was the city's first Catholic cemetery, with some tombstones still intact. From there, you wander through the stone foundations of an 18th-century tavern and a 19th-century insurance building. Filmed figures from the past appear on ghostly screens. The museum's excellent gift shop, full of interesting books on Montréal's history as well as pictures and reproductions of old maps, engravings, and other artifacts, is in the Old Customs House, a lovely, neoclassical gray-stone building erected in 1836. An industrial exhibit is housed in the 1915 Youville Pumping House, across the street from the main building. ⊠ *350 pl. Royale,* ☎ *514/872–9150,* WEB *musee-pointe-a-calliere.qc.ca.* 🖭 *$9.50.* ⊙ *June 24–Sept. 4, Tues.–Sun. 10–6; Sept. 5–June 23, Tues.–Fri. 10–5, Sun. 11–5. Métro: Place-d'Armes.*

★ ㉑ Musée Marc-Aurèle Fortin. Marc-Aurèle Fortin (1888–1970) was one of the great pioneers of modern art in Québec. He created his own style of landscape painting marked by heavy clouds, higgledy-piggledy villages, and lush, fantastic trees—and experimented wildly with different techniques. For example, he painted some of his works on canvases that he'd prepainted with gray to emphasize the warm light of the countryside, and others he painted on black backgrounds to create dramatic contrasts. He highlighted his watercolors with pencil strokes and by smearing on pastels with his thumb. Fortin painted some cityscapes, usually focusing on the working-class areas of the east end, but he is best known for his rich and bountiful landscapes of the Laurentians, the Gaspé, and the Charlevoix region. This little three-room museum is dedicated to his work. ⊠ *118 rue St-Pierre,* ☎ *514/845–6108.* 🖭 *$4.* ⊙ *Tues.–Sun. 11–5. Métro: Square-Victoria.*

⑪ **Office des Congrès et du Tourisme du Grand Montréal.** This small building (1811) was the site of the old Silver Dollar Saloon, so named because it had 350 silver dollars nailed to its floor. Today it's one of two visitor-information offices operated by Info-Touriste; the other is at 1001 Square Dorchester. ⊠ *174 rue Notre-Dame Est,* ☎ *514/873–2015.* ☉ *Mid-Oct.–mid-May, daily 9–5; mid-May–mid-Oct., daily 9–7. Métro: Champ-de-Mars.*

⑥ **Palais de Justice.** Built in 1971, this black-glass building is the main courthouse for the judicial district of Montréal. Criminal law in Canada falls under federal jurisdiction and is based on British common law, but civil law is a provincial matter, and Québec's is based on France's Napoleonic Code, which governs all the minutiae of private life—from setting up a company and negotiating a mortgage to drawing up a marriage contract and registering the names of children. Although the building does not offer tours, you can drop in to any courtrooms and see how justice is dispensed in Montréal. Proceedings are usually in French—defendants in criminal cases can choose which official language they wish to be tried in—and the lawyers wear the same elaborate robes and cravats as their English counterparts, but not the wigs. Judges wear robes trimmed in scarlet and tricorn hats. ⊠ *1 rue Notre-Dame Est. Métro: Place-d'Armes or Champ-de-Mars.*

❷ **Place d'Armes.** Montréal's founder, Paul de Chomedey, slew an Iroquois chief in a battle here in 1644 and was wounded in return. His statue stands in a fountain in the middle of the square. Tunnels beneath the square protected the colonists from the winter weather and provided an escape route; unfortunately they are too small and dangerous to visit. ⊠ *Bordered by rues Notre-Dame Ouest, St-Jacques, St-Sulpice. Métro: Place-d'Armes.*

★ ⑩ **Place Jacques-Cartier.** This two-block-long square at the heart of Vieux-Montréal opened in 1804 as a municipal market, and every summer it is transformed into a flower market. The 1809 monument at the top of the square celebrates Lord Nelson's victory over Napoléon Bonaparte's French navy at Trafalgar. It was the first monument in the British Empire erected in Nelson's honor; the campaign to raise money for it was led not by patriotic British residents of Montréal but by the Sulpician priests, who didn't have much love for the Corsican emperor either, and who were engaged in delicate land negotiations with the British government at the time and eager to show what good subjects they were. ⊠ *Bordered by rues Notre-Dame Est and de la Commune. Métro: Champ-de-Mars.*

⑯ **Place Royale.** The oldest public square in Montréal served as a public market during the French regime and later became a Victorian garden. The neoclassical Vielle Douane (Old Customs House) on its south side serves as the gift shop for the Musée d'Archéologie Pointe-à-Callière. ⊠ *Bordered by rues St-Paul Ouest and de la Commune. Métro: Place-d'Armes.*

❽ **Place Vauquelin.** The statue in this little square is of Admiral Jacques Vauquelin, a naval hero of the French regime. ⊠ *Between rues St-Antoine Est and Notre-Dame Est near rue Gosford. Métro: Champ-de-Mars.*

Pointe-à-Callière. This small park commemorates the European settlers' first landing. A little stream used to flow into the St. Lawrence here, and it was on the point of land between the two waters that the colonists landed their four boats on May 17, 1642. A flood almost washed away the settlement the next Christmas. When it was spared,

Paul de Chomedey, Sieur de Maisonneuve, placed a cross on top of Mont-Royal as thanks to God. ✉ *Bordered by rues de la Commune and William. Métro: Place-d'Armes.*

Rue St-Jacques. This was once the financial heart not only of Montréal but of Canada. As you walk here, note the fine, decorative stone flourishes—grapevines, nymphs, angels, and goddesses—on the Victorian office buildings. Popular with filmmakers, the stretch of rue St-Jacques between rue McGill and boulevard St-Laurent is often decked out as Main Street U.S.A., complete with American flags, English signs, and period cars.

Rue St-Sulpice. A plaque on the eastern side of rue St-Sulpice—one of the oldest streets in Montréal—marks the spot, at No. 445 (near St-Paul), where in 1644 Jeanne Mance built the Hôpital Hôtel-Dieu de St-Joseph, the city's first hospital.

❼ Vieux Palais de Justice. The old courthouse, a domed building in the Classical Revival style, was built in 1857. It once housed the civil courts but is now a warren of city offices. ✉ *155 rue Notre-Dame Est,* ☎ *no phone. Métro: Champ-de-Mars.*

㉒ Vieux-Port-de-Montréal. Montréal is 1,000 mi from the sea, but it has been a major North American port since the earliest days of European settlement. The city was built just below the Lachine Rapids, which marked the westernmost limit for oceangoing ships sailing up the St. Lawrence River, and all cargo bound for the interior had to be unloaded at the Vieux-Port for transhipment. The St. Lawrence Seaway, which opened in 1959, diminished the port's importance, and by the mid-1970s it was just too small for modern megaships. Most of the harbor operations moved downriver, and the old harbor decayed. Then, in the 1980s, the federal government cleared away the decaying warehouses and planted the waterfront with grass and trees to create one of the most popular parks in Montréal. In summer, skateboarders, strollers, cyclists, and street performers crowd the promenade that runs the length of the waterfront, and private operators offer harbor cruises and raft rides on the Lachine Rapids (bicycles and in-line skates are for rent at shops along rue de la Commune). A ferry takes foot passengers to the park on Île-Ste-Hélène. In winter, visitors can skate on a huge outdoor rink. The **King Edward Pier** is the home of iSci, Montréal's innovative science center. At the eastern end of the harbor is the **Clock Tower**, erected in memory of merchant mariners killed during World War I. If you feel up to it, you can climb the 192 steps to the top for a good view of the waterfront and the islands. ☎ *514/496–7678 or 800/971-7678,* WEB *www.oldportofmontreal.com. Métro: Place-d'Armes or Champ-de-Mars.*

❺ Vieux Séminaire. Montréal's oldest building is considered the finest, most elegant example of 17th-century Québec architecture. It was built in 1685 as a headquarters for the Sulpician priests who owned the island of Montréal until 1854, and it is still a residence for the Sulpicians who administer the basilica. The clock on the roof over the main doorway is the oldest (pre-1701) public timepiece in North America. Behind the seminary building is a garden that is closed to the public, as is the seminary itself. ✉ *116 rue Notre-Dame Ouest, behind wall west of Basilique Notre-Dame-de-Montréal. Métro: Place-d'Armes.*

❿⑧ Youville Stables. These low stone buildings enclosing a garden were originally built as warehouses in 1825 (they never were stables). They now house offices, shops, and Gibby's restaurant. ✉ *298 Pl. d'Youville. Métro: Square-Victoria or Place-d'Armes.*

Downtown

On the surface, Montréal's downtown, or *centre-ville,* is much like the downtown core of many other major cities—full of life and noisy traffic, its streets lined with department stores, boutiques, bars, restaurants, strip clubs, amusement arcades, and bookstores. In fact, however, much of the area's activity goes on beneath the surface, in Montréal's Cité Souterrain (Underground City). Development of this unique endeavor began in 1966 when the Métro opened. Now it includes (at last count) seven hotels, more than 1,500 offices and 1,600 boutiques, 30 movie theaters, 200 restaurants, three universities, two colleges, two train stations, a skating rink, 40 banks, a bus terminal, an art museum, a complex of concert halls, the home ice arena of the Montréal Canadiens, and a cathedral. All this is linked by Métro lines and more than 30 km (19 mi) of well-lighted, boutique-lined passages that protect shoppers and workers from the hardships of winter and the heat of summer. A traveler arriving by train could book into a fine hotel and spend a week shopping, dining, and going to a long list of movies, plays, concerts, sports events, and discos without once stepping outside.

A Good Walk

The start of this walk is designed for moles—it's underground—but it gives you an idea of the extent of the Underground City. Start at the McGill Métro station, one of the central points in the Underground City. It's linked to office towers and two of the "Big Three" department stores, Simons and La Baie (the other is Ogilvy). Passages also link the station to major shopping malls such as Le Centre Eaton, Les Promenades de la Cathédrale, and Place Montréal Trust.

Follow the signs from the station to Le Centre Eaton and then descend yet another floor to the tunnel that leads to **Place Ville-Marie** ㉕. The mall complex underneath this cruciform skyscraper was the first link in the Underground City. From here head south via the passageways toward **Le Reine Elizabeth** ㉖, which straddles the entrance to the Gare Centrale (Central Station). Walk through the station and follow the signs marked MÉTRO/PLACE BONAVENTURE until you see a sign for Le 1000 rue de la Gauchetière, a skyscraper that's home to the **Atrium le Mille de la Gauchetière** ㉗, an indoor ice rink. Return to the tunnels and again follow signs to the Bonaventure Métro station and then to the Canadian Pacific Railway Company's **Windsor Station** ㉘, with its massive stone exterior. The rail station and the Place Bonaventure Métro station below it are all linked to **Centre Molson** ㉙, the home of the Montréal Canadiens.

By now—having covered 10 city blocks and visited two train stations, a couple of malls, a major hotel, an office tower, and the city's most important sports shrine without once emerging from cover—you are probably ready for some fresh air. Exit the Underground City at the north end of Windsor Station and cross rue de la Gauchetière to **St. George's** ㉚, the prettiest Anglican church in the city. Just to the east across rue Peel is **Place du Canada** ㉛, a park. Cross the park and rue de la Cathédrale to **Cathédrale Marie-Reine-du-Monde** ㉜, which is modeled after St. Peter's Basilica in Rome. People sometimes call the gray granite building across boulevard René-Lévesque from the cathedral the Wedding Cake, because it rises in tiers of decreasing size and has lots of columns, but its real name is the **Sun Life Building** ㉝. The park that faces the Sun Life Building just north of boulevard René-Lévesque is **Square Dorchester** ㉞, for years the heart of Montréal. Backtrack across the park to rue Peel and walk north to rue Ste-Catherine. Many regard this intersection as the heart of downtown.

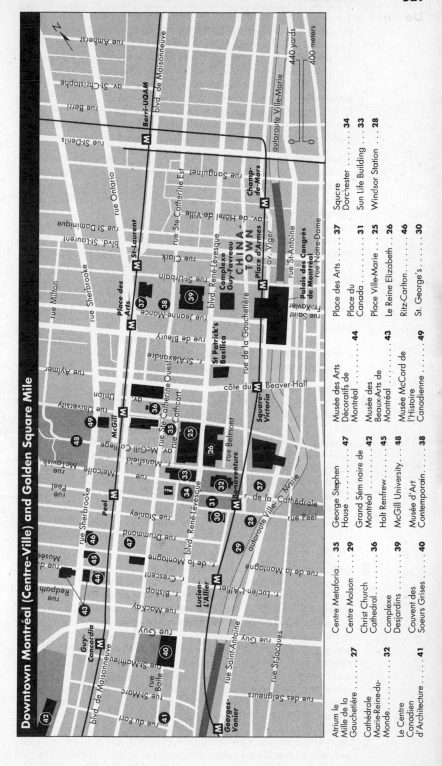

Downtown Montréal (Centre-Ville) and Golden Square Mile

Turn right and walk east along rue Ste-Catherine, pausing to admire the view at the corner of avenue McGill College. Look north up this broad boulevard and you can see the Victorian-era buildings of the McGill University campus, with Mont-Royal looming in the background. The grim-looking gray castle high on the slope to the right is the Royal Victoria Hospital. On the south side of rue Ste-Catherine is **Centre Metaforia** ㉟, which offers visitors a "virtual voyage" to the bottom of the sea. One block more brings you to the Eaton department store, where this whole adventure started, and next to that is **Christ Church Cathedral** ㊱, the main church of the Anglican diocese of Montréal.

You can end your stroll here or continue six blocks farther east on rue Ste-Catherine to **Place des Arts** ㊲, Montréal's main theater complex. The **Musée d'Art Contemporain** ㊳, the modern-art museum, is also part of the complex. While still in Place des Arts, follow the signs to the **Complexe Desjardins** ㊴, an office building, hotel, and mall along the lines of Place Ville-Marie. The next development south is the Complexe Guy-Favreau, a huge federal office building named after the Canadian minister of justice in the early 1960s. Continue in a straight line to hit the Palais des Congrès de Montréal, the city's convention center, above the Place d'Armes Métro stop. However, a left out of Guy-Favreau onto rue de la Gauchetière takes you into **Chinatown,** a relief after all that enclosed retail space.

TIMING

Just walking this route briskly takes a minimum of an hour, even on a fine day. The Musée d'Art Contemporain is worthy of at least two hours by itself, so plan on a half day.

Sights to See

㉗ **Atrium le Mille de la Gauchetière.** Skating is a passion in Montréal, and you can do it year-round in this indoor ice rink on the ground floor of a skyscraper. The rink is bathed in natural light and surrounded by cafés, a food court, and a winter garden. It's open to skaters of all levels of ability; skate rentals and lockers are available. There are also skating lessons Friday and Saturday, and Saturday-night disco skating, and scheduled ice shows. To find the rink once you're inside the building, it might help to remember the French word for skating rink, *patinoire*. ⊠ *1000 rue de la Gauchetière,* ☎ *514/395–0555.* ☞ *$5; skate rental $4.50.* ☉ *Sun.–Thurs. 11:30–9, Fri.–Sat. 11:30–7 for all ages; Fri.–Sat. 7 PM–midnight for those 16 and older, Sat. 10–11 AM for those under 12. Métro: Bonaventure.*

㉜ **Cathédrale Marie-Reine-du-Monde** (Mary Queen of the World Cathedral). When Roman Catholic Bishop Ignace Bourget (1799–1885) picked this site in the heart of the city's Protestant neighborhood as the site for his new cathedral, many of his co-religionists thought he was mad. But the bishop was determined to assert the Church's authority—and its loyalty to Rome—in the British-ruled city. So he built a quarter-scale replica of St. Peter's Basilica, complete with a quite magnificent reproduction of Bernini's ornate baldachin over the main altar and a series of figures on the roof. These do not, as many think, represent the apostles, but rather the patrons of the Montréal parishes that contributed to the construction. Victor Bourgeau, the architect who created the interior of Basilique Notre-Dame in Vieux-Montréal, thought the idea of the cathedral's design terrible but completed it after the original architect proved incompetent. All the bishops and archbishops of Montréal are entombed in the mortuary chapel on the east side of the nave, where a reclining figure of Bishop Bourget holds the place of honor. One last symbol of the bishop's loyalty to the Roman pontiff is a plaque on a pillar in the northeast corner honoring local residents who went to Italy to defend the Papal States from Garibaldi. A huge accompanying painting shows the Papal Zouaves fighting off a nationalist attack. ✉ *1071 rue de la Cathédral (enter through main doors on blvd. René-Lévesque)*, ☎ *514/866–1661.* ⌦ *Free.* ☉ *Mass weekdays at 7, 7:30, 8, 12:10, and 5; also at 7 PM on Mon.; Sat. at 8, 12:10, 5, and 7:30; Sun. at 9:30, 11 with choir, 12:15, and 5. Métro: Bonaventure or Peel.*

Ⓒ ㉟ **Centre Metaforia.** Metaforia Inc. has used the prizewinning technology it developed for Lisbon's 1998 World's Fair to re-create and update its wildly popular Oceania experience—a 45-minute voyage to an underwater base to explore the ruins of an ancient civilization. Participants make the journey via computer-generated effects, including group and individual interaction segments, 3-D images, vibrating seats, and stereo-display helmets. The center, in a converted theater, also includes a wide array of computer games, restaurants, interactive displays, and boutiques, as well as a climbing wall. ✉ *698 rue Ste-Catherine Ouest*, ☎ *514/878–6382*, WEB *www.metaforia.com/an.* ⌦ *$16 weekdays, $20 weekends.* ☉ *Mon.–Wed., 11–11; Thurs. and Sun. 10 AM–midnight; Fri. and Sat. 10 AM–1 AM.*

㉙ **Centre Molson.** This arena is the home of the Montréal Canadiens, the hockey team fans call simply *les Glorieux.* The 1996 brown-brick building replaced the old Forum that had been the Canadiens' home since 1917. The name refers to the Molson family, who established Montréal's first brewery in the 18th century and whose company, Molson-O'Keefe, owned the hockey team until 2001, when it sold it to U.S. businessman George Gillett. ✉ *1260 rue de la Gauchetière Ouest*, ☎ *514/932–2582; 514/925–5656 for tours.* ⌦ *Tour $8.* ☉ *Tours daily at 11:15 and 2:45 in English, and 9:45 and 1:15 in French. Métro: Bonaventure or Lucien-L'Allier.*

Chinatown. The Chinese first came to Montréal in large numbers after 1880, following the construction of the transcontinental railroad. They settled in an 18-block area between boulevard René-Lévesque and avenue Viger to the north and south, and near rues Hôtel de Ville and de Bleury on the west and east, an area now full of mainly Chinese and Southeast Asian restaurants, food stores, and gift shops. If you have enough energy, stroll south on rue St-Urbain for a block to rue St-Antoine. A half block east is **Steve's Music Store** (✉ 51 rue St-Antoine Ouest, ☎ 514/878–2216), a shabby warren of five storefronts jammed with just about everything you need to be a rock star. *Métro: Place-d'Armes.*

NEED A BREAK?   **Pho Bang New York** (✉ 970 blvd. St-Laurent, ☎ 514/954–2032) is the best of the small Vietnamese restaurants on the edge of Chinatown that specialize in traditional noodle soups, a tasty treat. For less than $5 (cash only), you get soup, a plate of crispy vegetables, and a small pot of tea. The iced coffee with condensed milk is worth trying.

㊱ **Christ Church Cathedral.** The gargoyles and grand Gothic entrance of the seat of Montréal's Anglican bishop make a welcome break in the unrelenting strip of commercial rue Ste-Catherine. The church, built in 1859 and patterned on Snettisham Parish Church in Norfolk, England, is the architectural sister of the cathedral in Fredericton, New Brunswick. The church has had its problems: it was built on unstable ground, and in 1927 the community had to pull down the stone steeple because it was too heavy and sinking fast. Thirteen years later, the church leaders replaced it with a much lighter structure with aluminium plates molded to simulate stone. In 1988 the diocese assured the stability of both soil and finances by leasing its land and air rights to developers,

who then built **La Maison des Coopérants,** a 34-story office tower behind the cathedral, and a huge retail complex, **Les Promenades de la
Cathédrale,** below it. Inside, the pillars that support the cathedral's Gothic
arches are crowned with carvings of all the different types of foliage
to be found on Mont-Royal at the time the church was built. At the
four corners of the nave are sculpted heads representing the four Evan-
gelists. The stained-glass windows behind the main altar were installed
in the early 1920s as a memorial to the dead of World War I and show
scenes from the life of Christ in the lower part of the stone screen, topped
by vivid portraits of St. George, St. Martin of Tours (on whose day the
1918 Armistice was signed), St. Lawrence (on whose day Jacques
Cartier entered the river that he named after the saint), Christ the King,
St. John the Baptist (patron saint of French Canada), St. Nicholas of
Myra (patron saint of sailors), and St. Michael the Archangel (patron
saint of airmen). On the wall just above and to the left of the pulpit is
the Coventry Cross; it's made of nails taken from the ruins of Britain's
Coventry Cathedral, destroyed by bombing in 1940. The church has
a quiet, graceful interior and hosts frequent organ recitals and concerts.
✉ *635 rue Ste-Catherine Ouest,* ☏ *514/843–6577,* WEB *www.montreal.
anglican.org/cathedral.* 🎟 *Free.* ☉ *Daily 8–6. Métro: McGill.*

㊲ Complexe Desjardins. The large galleria space in this boutique-rich mall
hosts all types of events, from lectures on Japanese massage techniques
to pop-music performances. ✉ *Bordered by rues Ste-Catherine, Jeanne-
Mance, and St-Urbain and blvd. René-Lévesque.* ☏ *514/845–4636 or
514/281–1870. Métro: Place d'Armes or Place des Arts.*

㊳ Musée d'Art Contemporain. The Museum of Modern Art's large permanent collection (more than 5,000 works) of modern art contains works
by Québécois, Canadian, and international artists in every medium and
reflecting all the major movements, but it focuses on the works of Québec
artists. It has, for example, 72 paintings, 32 works on paper, and a sculpture by Paul-Émile Borduas (1905–60), one of Canada's most important artists. The museum often has weekend programs, with many
child-oriented activities, and almost all are free. The hours for guided
tours vary. ✉ *185 rue Ste-Catherine Ouest,* ☏ *514/847–6226,* WEB
www.macm.org. 🎟 *$6; free after 6* PM *Wed.* ☉ *Tues. and Thurs.–Sun.
11–6, Wed. 11–9. Métro: Place des Arts.*

㊲ Place des Arts. The Place des Arts is a government-subsidized complex
of five very modern theaters. Guided tours of the halls and backstage
are available for groups of at least 15. ✉ *175 rue Ste-Catherine Ouest,*
☏ *514/842–2112 for tickets; 514/285–4270 for information; 514/285–
4200 for guided tours,* WEB *www.pda.qc.ca. Métro: Place des Arts.*

㉛ Place du Canada. This park has a statue of Sir John A. Macdonald,
Canada's first prime minister. In October 1995 the park was the site
of a rally for Canadian unity that drew more than 300,000 participants
from across the country. That patriotic demonstration was at least partly
responsible for preserving a slim victory for the pro-unity forces in the
subsequent referendum on independence for Québec. At the south
end of Place du Canada is Le Marriott Château Champlain, often called
"the Cheese Grater" because of its rows and rows of half-moon-shape
windows. ✉ *Bordered by blvd. René-Lévesque and rues de la Gauchetière, Peel, and de la Cathédrale. Métro: Bonaventure.*

㉕ Place Ville-Marie. The cross-shape 1962 office tower was Montréal's first
modern skyscraper; the mall complex underneath it was the first link in
the Underground City. ✉ *Bordered by blvd. René-Lévesque and rues
Mansfield, Cathcart, and University. Métro: McGill or Bonaventure.*

NEED A
BREAK?

The once grim passageways at the back of Gare Centrale just below the escalators leading to Place Ville-Marie today house a trendy food court, **Les Halles de la Gare.** The food available includes some of the city's best bread and pastries, salads, and sandwiches made with fresh terrines and pâtés. If it's nice out, you can take your snack up the escalator to the mall under Place Ville-Marie and then up the stairs in the middle of its food court to the terrace, a wide area with a fine view.

㉖ Le Reine Elizabeth. One of the city's major hotels, The Queen Elizabeth straddles the Gare Centrale (Central Station), where most trains from the United States and the rest of Canada arrive. ⊠ *900 blvd. René-Lévesque,* ☎ *514/861–3511. Métro: Bonaventure or Square-Victoria.*

㉚ St. George's. The original St. George's was built in 1843 on rue Notre-Dame to accommodate the overflow from Christ Church Cathedral. The present structure, a jewel of neo-Gothic architecture built in 1872, is the prettiest Anglican church in the city. Its dimly reverent interior is reminiscent of a medieval sanctuary in a prosperous English merchant town, with its magnificent double hammer-beam roof (one of the largest of its type in the world). The unique column-free interior, which combines elements of both English and French Gothic styles, is decorated with superb English wood-carving and illuminated with fine stained-glass windows. ⊠ *1101 rue Stanley,* ☎ *514/866–7113.* 🎟 *Free.* ☉ *Tues.– Sun. 8:30–4:30; Sun. services at 9 and 10:30 AM. Métro: Bonaventure.*

St. Patrick's Basilica. Rarely visited by tourists, this magnificent 1847 church is one of the purest examples of the Gothic Revival style in Canada. It is to Montréal's English-speaking Catholics what the Basilique Notre-Dame is to the city's French-speaking Catholics. The church's colors are soft, and the vaulted ceiling glows with green and gold mosaics. The old pulpit has panels depicting the apostles, and a huge lamp decorated with six 6-ft angels hangs over the main altar. The tall, slender columns that support the roof are actually pine logs lashed together and decorated to look like marble. The Canadian poet Emile Nelligan (1879–1941) was baptized in the beautiful font installed in front of the side altar on the east side of the sanctuary. The pew used by Thomas Darcy McGee—a Father of confederation who was assassinated in 1868—is marked with a small Canadian flag. Visitors named after some obscure saint might well be able to find their namesake's portrait in the 156 painted panels on the walls of the nave. The church is three blocks east of Place Ville-Marie. ⊠ *460 blvd. René-Lévesque Ouest,* ☎ *514/866–7379,* 🌐 *www.sympatico.ca/stpatricksmtl.* 🎟 *Free.* ☉ *Daily 8:30–6. Métro: Square-Victoria.*

㉞ Square Dorchester. Until 1870, a Catholic burial ground occupied this downtown park, and there are still bodies buried beneath the grass. The statuary includes a monument to the Boer War and statues of the Scottish poet Robert Burns and Sir Wilfrid Laurier, Canada's first French-speaking prime minister. ⊠ *Bordered by rues Peel, Metcalfe, and McTavish and blvd. René Lévesque. Métro: Bonaventure or Peel.*

㉝ Sun Life Building. At one time this was the largest building in the British Commonwealth. During World War II, much of England's financial reserves and national treasure was stored in Sun Life's vaults. ⊠ *1155 rue Metcalfe. Métro: Bonaventure.*

㉘ Windsor Station. This magnificent building with its massive stone exterior and steel-and-glass roof was once the eastern passenger terminus for the Canadian Pacific Railway, Canada's first transcontinental link. Alas, today it is a trainless shell. ⊠ *1100 rue de la Gauchetière. Métro: Bonaventure.*

Golden Square Mile

As Montréal grew in confidence and economic might in the 19th century, the city's prosperous merchant class moved north, building lavish stone homes on Mont-Royal. In fact, at the turn of the 20th century, the people who lived here (mostly of Scottish descent) controlled 70% of the country's wealth. Their baronial homes and handsome churches—Protestant, of course—covered the mountain north of rue Sherbrooke roughly between avenue Côte-des-Neiges and rue University.

Humbler residents south of rue Sherbrooke referred to the area simply as the Square Mile, a name immortalized in novelist Hugh MacLennan's *Two Solitudes* (1945). The Square Mile was eventually gilded by the newspaper columnist Al Palmer in the 1950s, long after its golden age had passed. (Proud Square Milers like the actor Christopher Plummer still bridle at the extra adjective.) Many of the area's palatial homes have been leveled to make way for high-rises and office towers, but it is still studded with architectural gems, and rue Sherbrooke remains the city's most elegant street.

This walk takes in much of the Square Mile along with an area named Shaughnessy Village, to the southwest (bounded roughly by rues Atwater and Guy to the west and east and rue Sherbrooke and boulevard René-Lévesque to the north and south). The village takes its name from the very lush Shaughnessy Mansion on boulevard René-Lévesque, a house that would fit in quite comfortably up the hill in the Square Mile. But whereas most of the Shaughnessy family's 19th-century neighbors were well-off businesspeople and professionals who lived in elegantly comfortable homes, they certainly weren't wealthy enough to make it into the Square Mile.

A Good Walk

Start at the Guy-Concordia Métro station at the rue Guy exit. The statue just north of the station on the little triangular slice of land in the middle of boulevard de Maisonneuve portrays Norman Bethune, a McGill University–trained doctor from Gravenhurst, Ontario, who served with the Loyalists in the Spanish civil war and died in China in 1939 while serving with Mao's Red Army. Walk south on rue Guy to rue Ste-Catherine and turn right. The long building on the south side of the street used to be a car dealership and bowling alley until it was transformed into the Faubourg Ste-Catherine, an enclosed market selling specialty and ethnic foods, pastries, and bagels.

At rue St-Mathieu, turn left and head south. The huge gray building on the left side of the street is **Couvent des Soeurs Grises** ㊵, the motherhouse of an order of nuns founded by St. Marguerite d'Youville, Canada's first native-born saint. Across from the convent, turn right onto rue Baile and into the heart of Shaughnessy Village. The family mansion the area is named for now forms part of **Le Centre Canadien d'Architecture** ㊶. Many of the area's town houses and mansions were torn down during the philistine 1960s to make way for boxy high-rises, but a few remain. Note, for example, the fine row of stone town houses just across rue Baile from Le Centre Canadien d'Architecture.

Turn right on rue du Fort and walk north four blocks to rue Sherbrooke. On the north side of the street is a complex of fine neoclassical buildings in a shady garden. This is the **Grand Séminaire de Montréal** ㊷, which trains priests for Montréal's Roman Catholic parishes. The two stone towers on the property are among the oldest buildings on the island. In 1928, the anticlerical Freemasons built the grandly Greek Masonic Temple right across the street at No. 1859.

Walk east along stately rue Sherbrooke past rows of exclusive shops and galleries housed in old town houses to the **Musée des Beaux-Arts de Montréal** ㊸, at rues Sherbrooke and du Musée. The museum houses the city's main art collection, which includes works from around the world. Behind it is the **Musée des Arts Déoratifs** ㊹, with its fine collection of furniture, hangings and decorations. Farther east on rue Sherbrooke is the small and exclusive **Holt Renfrew** ㊺ department store, at the corner of rue de la Montagne. Dozens of popular bars, restaurants, and bistros are ensconced in the old row houses that line rue de la Montagne and the two streets just west of it, rues Crescent and Bishop, between boulevard René-Lévesque and rue Sherbrooke. The area once encompassed the playing fields of the Montréal Lacrosse and Cricket Grounds and later became an exclusive suburb lined with millionaires' row houses.

One block farther east on the south side of rue Sherbrooke at rue Drummond stands the **Ritz-Carlton** ㊻, the grande dame of Montréal hotels. Directly across from the Ritz is Le Château (1926), a huge, copper-roofed apartment building that looks somewhat like a cross between a French Renaissance château and a Scots castle. It's one of the few samples of gracious living left west of rue Atwater. Others worth looking at are the Corby House and the Maison Louis-Joseph Forget, at 1201 and 1195 rue Sherbrooke Ouest, respectively. One of the area's most magnificent homes, however, is on rue Drummond a couple of blocks south of Sherbrooke. The **George Stephen House** ㊼ was built for the founder of the Canadian Pacific Railway and is now the private Mount Stephen Club.

The campus of **McGill University** ㊽ is on the north side of rue Sherbrooke three blocks east of the Ritz-Carlton. Opposite its main gate is the Banque Commerciale Italienne (✉ 888 rue Sherbrooke Ouest), housed in a beautiful neo-Elizabethan house built in 1906 for Dr. William Alexander Molson, a scion of Montréal's most famous brewing family. Another block east is the **Musée McCord de l'Histoire Canadienne** ㊾, one of the best history museums in Canada.

TIMING

To walk this route briskly takes a minimum of 90 minutes, but the area is rich in places—the Musée des Beaux-Arts, the Musée des Art Décoratifs, the Musée McCord de l'Histoire Canadienne—that all deserve longer visits. It's easy to spend a day or more here.

Sights to See

㊶ **Le Centre Canadien d'Architecture** (Canadian Center for Architecture). Phyllis Lambert, an heiress to the Seagram liquor fortune and an architect of some note, was the genius behind this temple to the art of building. She had a hand in designing the ultramodern U-shaped structure of gray limestone and filled it with her vast collection of drawings, photographs, plans, books, documents, and models; the library alone has more than 165,000 volumes. The center's six large and well-lit exhibition rooms present a series of rotating exhibits that focus on the work of a particular architect or on a particular style. Some can be forbiddingly academic, but more-playful exhibits have looked at such subjects as dollhouses and American lawn culture. The two arms of the center are wrapped around a grandly ornate mansion built in 1874 for the family of the president of the Canadian Pacific Railway, Sir Thomas Shaughnessy. It has a remarkable art nouveau conservatory with an intricately decorated ceiling. On a tiny piece of land across the street is an amusing sculpture garden. ✉ *1920 rue Baile*, ☏ *514/939–7000*, WEB *cca.qc.ca.* ✆ *$6.* ☉ *Oct.–May, Wed., Fri., and weekends 11–*

6, Thurs. 11–8; June–Sept., Tues.–Sun. 11–5, Thurs. until 9. Métro: Guy-Concordia or Georges-Vanier.

④⓪ Couvent des Soeurs Grises. *Soeurs grises* translates as "gray nuns," but the name originally had nothing to do with the color of the good sisters' habits. Their founder, St. Marguerite d'Youville (1701–71), started looking after the city's down-and-outs after her unhappy marriage to a whiskey trader ended in widowhood. Her late husband's profession and the condition of many of her clients earned her and her colleagues the sobriquet "soeurs grises," which is slang for tipsy nuns. The order ran a public hospital, opened the city's first nursing schools, operated shelters for abandoned children, and, indeed, adopted gray habits. The order, which still administers hospitals, shelters for battered women, halfway houses, and nursing homes, moved to this vast, gray-stone convent in 1874. ⊠ *1185 rue St-Mathieu,* ☎ *514/937–9501. Métro: Guy-Concordia or Georges-Vanier.*

④⑦ George Stephen House. Scottish-born George Stephen, founder of the Canadian Pacific Railway, spent $600,000 to build this impressive home in 1883—an almost unimaginable sum at the time. He imported artisans from all over the world to panel its ceilings with Cuban mahogany, Indian lemon tree, and English oak and to adorn its walls with marble, onyx, and gold. The house is a private club now (the Mount Stephen Club), but most Sundays visitors can drop in for a guided tour or, with reservations, a sumptuous brunch ($25) of braised duck or roast beef served to the accompaniment of live music. ⊠ *1440 rue Drummond,* ☎ *514/849–7338.* ⊘ *Sun. by reservation. Closed to nonmembers mid-July–Aug. Métro: Peel or Guy-Concordia.*

④② Grand Séminaire de Montréal. The Montréal Roman Catholic archdiocese trains its priests here in buildings that date from 1860. Two squat towers in the gardens date from the 17th century, and it was in one of these that St. Marguerite Bourgeoys set up her first school for Native American girls. The towers, among the oldest buildings on the island, are visible from the street; a little area by the gates has three plaques that explain the towers' history in French. The seminary is private, but September through June you can attend Sunday morning mass at 10:30 in the lovely neoclassical chapel. ⊠ *2065 rue Sherbrooke Ouest,* ☎ *no phone. Métro: Guy-Concordia.*

④⑤ Holt Renfrew. This is perhaps the city's fanciest department store. ⊠ *1300 rue Sherbrooke Ouest,* ☎ *514/842–5111.* ⊘ *Mon.–Wed. 10–6, Thurs.–Fri. 10–9, Sat. 9:30–5, Sun. noon–5. Métro: Guy-Concordia.*

④⑧ McGill University. James McGill, a wealthy Scottish fur trader and merchant, bequeathed the money and the land for this institution, which opened in 1828 and is perhaps the finest English-language university in the nation. The student body numbers 15,000, and the university is best known for its medical and engineering schools. A tree-lined road leads from the Greek Revival Roddick Gates to the austerely beautiful neoclassical Arts Building—the university's original building—at the northern end of the campus. The templelike building to the west of the Arts Building houses McGill University's delightful **Redpath Museum of Natural History** (⊠ 845 rue Sherbrooke Ouest, ☎ 514/398–4086), with an eclectic collection of dinosaur bones, old coins, African art, and shrunken heads. Admission to the museum, which is open weekdays 9–5 (except June through August, when it's closed Friday) and Sunday 1–5, is free. Under the trees to the east of the main drive, a bronze James McGill hurries across campus holding his tricorn hat against the wind. ⊠ *845 rue Sherbrooke Ouest,* ☎ *514/398–4455,* 🕸 *www.mcgill.ca. Métro: McGill or Peel.*

The campus of **McGill University** (✉ 845 rue Sherbrooke Ouest, ☎
514/398–4455, WEB www.mcgill.ca) is an island of green in a sea of
traffic and skyscrapers. On a fine day you can sit on the grass in the
shade of a 100-year-old tree and just let the world drift by.

★ ⓴ **Musée des Arts Décoratifs** Homey things take on a very stylish allure
in this ultramodern display space just behind the Musée des Beaux-
Arts de Montréal, which took over the museum's collection in 2000.
Highlights of the collection include the prototypes of Frank Gehry's
bentwood furniture for Knoll, designs by Charles and Ray Eames, furniture and ceramics by Ettore Sottsass, Alessi prototypes for coffeepots,
and contemporary Canadian glass. ✉ *2200 rue Crescent,* ☎ *514/
285–2000,* WEB *www.mbam.qc.ca.* ⌧ *$5.* ⊙ *Tues. and Thurs.–Sun. 11–
6, Wed. 11–9 for special exhibitions. Métro: Guy-Concordia.*

★ ⓳ **Musée des Beaux-Arts de Montréal** (Museum of Fine Arts). The oldest museum in the country was founded by a group of English-speaking Montrealers in 1860. The art collection is housed in two
buildings—the older **Benaiah-Gibb Pavilion,** on the north side of rue
Sherbrooke, and the glittering glass-fronted **Pavilion Jean-Noël-Des-
marais,** across the street. The two buildings, connected by underground tunnels, hold a large collection of European and North American
fine and decorative art; ancient treasures from Europe, the Near East,
Asia, Africa, and America; art from Québec and Canada; and Native
American and Inuit artifacts. The museum is particularly strong in 19th-
century works and has one of the finest collections of Canadian paintings, prints, and drawings. It also has a gift shop, an art-book store,
a restaurant, a cafeteria, and a gallery from which you can buy or rent
paintings by local artists. ✉ *1380 rue Sherbrooke Ouest,* ☎ *514/285-
2000,* WEB *www.mbam.qc.ca.* ⌧ *Permanent collection free, special exhibitions $12.* ⊙ *Tues. and Thurs.–Sun. 11–6; Wed. 11–9 for special
exhibitions. Métro: Guy-Concordia.*

★ ☕ ⓸ **Musée McCord de l'Histoire Canadienne.** A grand, eclectic attic of a
museum, the McCord documents the life of ordinary Canadians, using
costumes and textiles, decorative arts, paintings, prints and drawings,
and the 450,000 print-and-negative Notman Photographic Archives,
which highlight 19th-century life in Montréal. One series of photographs, for example, portrays the prosperous members of the posh
Montréal Athletic Association posing in snowshoes on the slopes of
Mont-Royal all decked out in Hudson Bay coats and woolen hats. Each
of the hundreds of portraits was shot individually in a studio and then
painstakingly mounted on a picture of the snowy mountain to give the
impression of a winter outing. The McCord is the only museum in
Canada with a permanent costume gallery. There are guided tours (call
for times), a reading room and documentation center, a gift shop and
bookstore, and a café. ✉ *690 rue Sherbrooke Ouest,* ☎ *514/398-7100,*
WEB *www.musee-mccord.qc.ca.* ⌧ *$8.50.* ⊙ *Tues.–Fri. 10–6, weekends
10–5. Métro: McGill.*

⓴ **Ritz-Carlton.** The grande dame of Montréal hotels has been in business
since 1912. ✉ *1228 rue Sherbrooke Ouest,* ☎ *514/842–4212,* WEB
www.ritzcarlton.com. Métro: Guy-Concordia.

Quartier Latin and Plateau Mont-Royal

Early in the 20th century, rue St-Denis cut through a bourgeois neighborhood of large, comfortable residences. The Université de Montréal
was established here in 1893, and the students and academics who moved
into the area dubbed it the Quartier Latin, or Latin Quarter. The university eventually moved to a larger campus on the north side of Mont-

Royal, and the area went into decline. It revived in the early 1970s, largely as a result of the 1969 opening of the Université du Québec à Montréal and the launch of the International Jazz Festival in the summer of 1980. Plateau Mont-Royal, the trendy neighborhood just north of the Quartier Latin, shared in this revival. Residents are now a mix of immigrants, working-class Francophones, and young professionals eager to find a home they can renovate close to the city center. The Quartier Latin and Plateau Mont-Royal are home to rows of French and ethnic restaurants, charming bistros, coffee shops, designer boutiques, antiques shops, and art galleries. When night falls, these streets are always full of omnilingual hordes—young and not so young, rich and poor, established and still studying.

Many of the older residences in this area have graceful wrought-iron balconies and twisting staircases that are typical of Montréal. They were built that way for practical reasons. The buildings are what Montrealers call duplexes or triplexes, that is, two or three residences stacked one atop the other. To save interior space, the stairs to reach the upper floors were put outside. The stairs and balconies are treacherous in winter, but in summer they are often full of families and couples gossiping, picnicking, and partying. If Montrealers tell you they spend the summer in Balconville, they mean they don't have the money or the time to leave town and won't get any farther than their balcony.

A Good Walk

Begin at the Berri-UQAM Métro stop. The "UQAM" in the subway name is pronounced "oo-kam" by local Francophones and "you-kwam" by local Anglophones. It refers to the **Université du Québec à Montréal** ⑤⓪, whose drab brick campus fills up much of three city blocks between rues Sanguinet and Berri, with a few splendid fragments of the old Église St-Jacques poking up. A more substantial religious monument that has survived intact right in UQAM's resolutely secularist heart is the ornate **Chapelle Notre-Dame-de-Lourdes** ⑤①, on rue Ste-Catherine.

Just west of rue St-Denis is the **Cinémathèque Québécoise** ⑤②, which houses one of the largest cinematic reference libraries in the world. Around the corner on rue St-Denis is the headquarters of the **National Film Board of Canada** ⑤③, home of a robot-serviced screening room. A half block north on rue St-Denis stands the 2,500-seat **Théâtre St-Denis** ⑤④, the city's second-largest auditorium. On the next block north is the **Bibliothèque Nationale du Québec** ⑤⑤.

Continue north on rue St-Denis until you reach Sherbrooke. Turn left and then left again on boulevard St-Laurent for the **Musée Juste pour Rire** ⑤⑥, one of the few museums in the world dedicated to humor. Backtrack east on rue Sherbrooke, turn left on rue St-Denis, and walk north to **Square St-Louis** ⑤⑦, a lovely green space.

The stretch of **rue Prince-Arthur** ⑤⑧ beginning at the western end of Square St-Louis and continuing several blocks west is a center of youth culture. When you reach **boulevard St-Laurent,** take a right and stroll north through Montréal's ethnic diversity. This area was still partly rural in the mid-19th century, with lots of fresh air, which made it healthier than overcrowded Vieux-Montréal. So in 1861 the Hôpital Hôtel-Dieu, the hospital Jeanne Mance founded in the 17th century, moved into a building at what is now the corner of avenue des Pins and rue St-Urbain, two blocks west of boulevard St-Laurent. Hôtel-Dieu, one of the city's major hospitals, is still here, and next to it is the **Musée des Hospitalières de l'Hôtel-Dieu** ⑤⑨, which gives a remarkable picture of the early days of colonization.

Quartier Latin and Parc du Mont-Royal

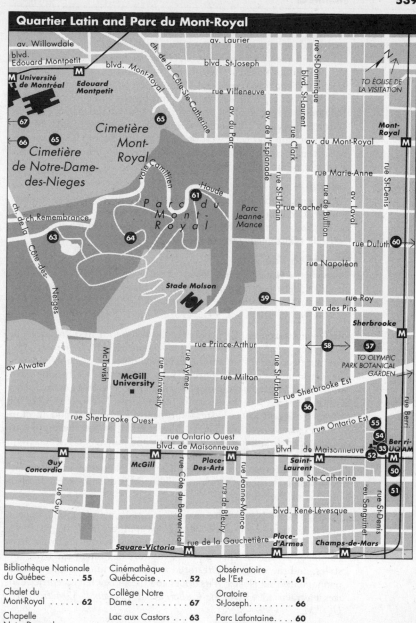

av. Willowdale
blvd. Edouard Montpetit
Université de Montréal
Edouard Montpetit
blvd. Mont-Royal
ch. de la Côte-Ste-Catherine
av. Laurier
blvd. St-Joseph
rue Villeneuve
rue St-Dominique
TO ÉGLISE DE LA VISITATION
Cimetière Mont-Royal
Cimetière de Notre-Dame-des-Nieges
av. du Parc
av. de l'Esplanade
rue Clark
blvd. St-Laurent
av. du Mont-Royal
rue Marie-Anne
av. Laval
rue St-Denis
Mont-Royal
voie Camillien
Houde
Parc du Mont-Royal
rue St-Urbain
rue Rachel
rue Bullion
Parc Jeanne-Mance
ch. Remembrance
ch. de la Côte-des-Neiges
Stade Molson
rue Duluth
rue Napoléon
rue Roy
av. des Pins
Sherbrooke
McTavish
McGill University
rue University
rue Aylmer
rue Prince-Arthur
rue Milton
rue St-Urbain
rue Sherbrooke Est
TO OLYMPIC PARK BOTANICAL GARDEN
rue Berri
av Atwater
av. des Pins
rue Sherbrooke Ouest
rue Ontario Est
Benri-UQAM
rue Ontario Ouest
blvd. de Maisonneuve
Guy Concordia
McGill
Place-Des-Arts
rue Côte du Beaver-Hall
rue de Bleury
rue Jeanne-Mance
blvd. de Maisonneuve
Saint-Laurent
rue Ste-Catherine
rue St-Denis
rue Sanguinet
rue Guy
blvd. René-Lévesque
Square-Victoria
rue de la Gauchetière
Place-d'Armes
Champs-de-Mars

A few blocks to the north, merchants have been attempting to re-create rue Prince-Arthur on rue Duluth; modest little ethnic restaurants with outdoor terraces have sprouted along the street, as have crafts boutiques and a few shops selling collectibles such as cookie jars and bottles. Turn right onto rue Duluth and walk east back to rue St-Denis, where you can find Greek and Vietnamese restaurants and boutiques and art galleries. Walk east another nine blocks and you come to **Parc Lafontaine** ⑥⓪, the smallest of Montréal's three major parks. After exploring the park's 100 acres, walk south to rue Sherbrooke Est and then turn right and walk west on rues Sherbrooke and Cherrier to the Sherbrooke Métro station to complete the walk. Or head farther west to explore Parc du Mont-Royal.

TIMING

This is a comfortable afternoon walk, lasting perhaps two hours, longer if you linger for an hour or so in the Musée des Hospitalières and spend some time shopping. There's a bit of a climb from boulevard de Maisonneuve to rue Sherbrooke.

Sights to See

⑤⑤ **Bibliothèque Nationale du Québec.** This Beaux-Arts library built in 1915 houses Québec's official archives. It also plays host to numerous artistic, cultural, and literary exhibitions. ✉ *1700 rue St-Denis,* ☎ *514/ 873–1100.* ☉ *Tues.–Sat. 9–5. Métro: Berri-UQAM.*

Boulevard St-Laurent. Depending on how you look at it, this street divides the city into east and west or it's where east and west meet. After the first electric tramway was installed on boulevard St-Laurent, working-class families began to move in. In the 1880s the first of many waves of Jewish immigrants escaping pogroms in Eastern Europe arrived. They called the street The Main, as in "Main Street." The Jews were followed by Greeks, other Eastern Europeans, Portuguese, and, most recently, Latin Americans. The 10 blocks north of rue Sherbrooke are filled with delis, junk stores, restaurants and luncheonettes, and clothing stores, as well as fashionable boutiques, bistros, cafés, bars, nightclubs, bookstores, and galleries. The block between rues Roy and Napoléon is particularly rich in delights. Métro: Saint-Laurent, Sherbrooke, or Mount-Royal.

⑤① **Chapelle Notre-Dame-de-Lourdes.** This tiny Roman Catholic chapel is one of the most ornate pieces of religious architecture in the city. It was built in 1876 and decorated with brightly colored murals by the artist Napoléon Bourassa. The chapel is a mixture of Roman and Byzantine styles, and the beautifully restored interior is a must-see, despite the panhandlers that cluster at its doors and the somewhat eccentric devotees it attracts. ✉ *430 rue Ste-Catherine Est.* ☉ *Daily 8–5. Métro: Berri-UQAM.*

⑤② **Cinémathèque Québécoise.** One of Montréal's great bargains is this museum and repertory movie house. For $5 you can visit the permanent exhibition on the history of filmmaking equipment and see two movies. There's also a TV-documentary center. ✉ *335 blvd. de Maisonneuve Est,* ☎ *514/842–9763,* 🕸 *www.cinematheque.qc.ca.* 🎟 *$5.* ☉ *Tues.–Sun. 11–8:30. Métro: Berri-UQAM.*

OFF THE BEATEN PATH

ÉGLISE DE LA VISITATION DE LA BIENHEUREUSE VIERGE MARIE – Far to the north on the banks of Rivière des Prairies is the oldest extant church on the island of Montréal, the Church of the Visitation of the Blessed Virgin Mary. Its stone walls were raised in the 1750s, and the beautifully proportioned Palladian front was added in 1850. The task of decorating lasted from 1764 until 1837, with simply stunning results. The altar and the pulpit are as ornate as wedding cakes and as delicate as starlight. The church's most notable treasure is a rendering of the Visitation attributed to Pierre Mignard, a painter in the 17th-century court of Louis XIV. The church is a 15-minute walk from the Henri Bourassa Métro station, but the trek is worth it. Parkland surrounds the church, and the nearby Îles de la Visitation (reachable by footbridge) make a delightful walk. ✉ *1847 blvd. Gouin Est,* ☎ *514/388–4050.* ▧ *Free.* ⊙ *Daily 10–11:30 and 2–4. Métro: Henri Bourassa.*

59 **Musée des Hospitalières de l'Hôtel-Dieu.** More than just a fascinating exhibit on the history of medicine and nursing, this museum captures the spirit of an age. France in the 17th century was consumed with religious fervor, and aristocratic men and women often built hospitals, schools, and churches in distant lands. The nuns of the Religieuses Hospitalières de St-Joseph who came to Montréal in the mid-17th century to help Jeanne Mance run the Hôpital Hôtel-Dieu were good examples of this fervor, and much of their spirit is evident in the letters, books, and religious artifacts displayed here. Pay special attention to the beautiful wooden stairway in the museum's entrance hall. ✉ *201 av. des Pins Ouest,* ☎ *514/849–2919.* ▧ *$5.* ⊙ *Mid-June–mid-Oct., Tues.–Fri. 10–5, weekends 1–5; mid-Oct.–mid-June, Wed.–Sun. 1–5. Métro: Sherbrooke.*

NEED A BREAK? The homey **Café Santropol** (✉ 3990 rue St-Urbain, ☎ 514/842–3110) serves hearty soups, cake, salads, and unusual high-rise sandwiches garnished with fruit (the Jeanne Mance mixes pineapples and chives in cream cheese). One percent of the profits goes to charity, and the staff runs a meals-on-wheels program. Credit cards are not accepted.

56 **Musée Juste pour Rire** (Just for Laughs Museum). Here's one of the few museums in the world to be dedicated to laughter. Its multimedia exhibits explore and celebrate humor by drawing you into their plots. Some visiting exhibits have a serious side, too. There's a large collection of humor videos, a cabaret where budding comics can test their material, and a restaurant where you can watch old tapes while you eat. ✉ *2111 blvd. St-Laurent,* ☎ *514/845–5105.* ▧ *$5.* ⊙ *Thurs.–Fri. 9:30–3:30, weekends 10–5. Métro: Sherbrooke or Berri-UQAM.*

53 **National Film Board of Canada.** Canada's government-financed film board is known worldwide for the thousands of documentaries, dramas, and groundbreaking animated features it has produced in both French and English since it was founded in 1944. Visitors can rent a booth for two in the CinéRobothèque and use a computer terminal to order one of more than 6,000 videotapes; a robot in another room retrieves it from the archives and plays it. The center also sponsors filmmaking and animation programs and workshops, some for children. ✉ *1564 rue St-Denis,* ☎ *514/496–6887,* 🌐 *www.nfb.ca.* ▧ *Free; booth rental $5 for 3 hrs.* ⊙ *Tues.–Sun. noon–9. Métro: Berri-UQAM.*

60 **Parc Lafontaine.** Montréal's two main cultures are reflected in the layout of this very popular park: the eastern half is pure French, with paths, gardens, and lawns laid out in geometric shapes; the western half is very English, with meandering paths and irregularly shaped ponds that follow the natural contours of the land. In summer there are bowling greens, tennis courts, an open-air theater with free arts events, and two artificial lakes with paddleboats. In winter the two lakes form a large skating rink. ✉ *3933 av. Parc Lafontaine,* ☎ *514/872–9800.* ⊙ *Daily 9 AM–10 PM. Métro: Sherbrooke or Mont-Royal.*

58 **Rue Prince-Arthur.** In the 1960s, the young people who moved to the neighborhood transformed this street into a small hippie bazaar of clothing, leather, and smoke shops. It remains a center of youth culture, although it's now much tamer and more commercial. The city turned the blocks between avenue Laval and boulevard St-Laurent into a pedestrian mall. Hippie shops have metamorphosed into inexpensive Greek, Vietnamese, Italian, Polish, and Chinese restaurants and little neighborhood bars. *Métro: Sherbrooke.*

⑤⑦ Square St-Louis. This graceful square has a fountain, benches, and trees and is surrounded by 19th-century homes built in the large, comfortable style of the Second Empire. Originally a reservoir, these blocks became a park in 1879 and attracted upper-middle-class families and artists. French-Canadian poets were among the most famous creative people to occupy the houses back then, and the neighborhood is now home to painters, filmmakers, musicians, and writers. On the wall of 336 Square St-Louis you can see—and read, if your French is good—a long poem by Michel Bujold. ⊠ *Bordered by av. Laval and rue St-Denis between rue Sherbrooke Est and av. des Pins Est. Métro: Sherbrooke.*

⑤④ Théâtre St-Denis. With 2,500 seats, this is the second-largest auditorium in Montréal (after Salle Wilfrid Pelletier in Place des Arts). Sarah Bernhardt is one of the many famous performers who have graced its stage. ⊠ *1594 rue St-Denis,* ☎ *514/849–4211. Métro: Berri-UQAM.*

⑤⓪ Université du Québec à Montréal. Part of a network of provincial campuses set up by the provincial government in 1969, UQAM is housed in a series of massive, modern brick buildings clogging much of the three city blocks bordered by rues Sanguinet and Berri and boulevards de Maisonneuve and René-Lévesque. The splendid fragments of Gothic grandeur sprouting up like flowers among the modern brick hulks in a swamp are all that's left of Église St-Jacques. ⊠ *Bordered by rues Sanguinet and Berri and blvds. de Maisonneuve and René-Lévesque,* ☎ *514/987–3000. Métro: Berri-UQAM.*

Parc du Mont-Royal

Frederick Law Olmsted, the codesigner of New York City's Central Park, designed Parc du Mont-Royal, 494 acres of forest and paths in the heart of Montréal. Olmsted believed that communion with nature could cure body and soul, and the park follows the natural topography and accentuates its features, in the English style. You can jog, cycle, or stroll the miles of paths, or just scan the horizon from one of two lookouts. Horse-drawn transport is popular year-round: sleigh rides in winter and calèche rides in summer. On the eastern side of the hill stands the 100-ft steel cross that is the symbol of the city. Not far away from the park and perched on a neighboring crest of the same mountain is the Oratoire St-Joseph, a shrine that draws millions every year.

A Good Tour

Begin by taking the Métro's Orange Line to the Mont-Royal station and transfer to Bus 11 (be sure to get a transfer—*correspondence* in French—from a machine before you get on the Métro). The No. 11 drives right through the Parc du Mont-Royal on the Voie Camillien Houde. Get off at the **Obsérvatoire de l'Est** ⑥①, a lookout. Climb the stone staircase at the end of the parking lot and follow the trails to the **Chalet du Mont-Royal** ⑥②, a baronial building with a terrace that overlooks downtown Montréal. The next stop is **Lac aux Castors** ⑥③, and there are at least three ways to get to this lake. You can take the long way and walk down the steep flight of stairs at the east end of the terrace and then turn right to follow the gravel road that circles the mountain. The shortest way is to leave the terrace at the west end and follow the crowds along the road. The middle way is to leave at the east end, but then to turn off the main road and follow one of the shaded paths that lead through the woods and along the southern ridge of the mountain.

Across chemin Remembrance from Lac aux Castors is what looks like one vast cemetery. It is in fact two cemeteries—one Protestant and one Catholic. The **Cimetière Mont-Royal** ⑭ is toward the east in a little valley that cuts off the noise of the city; it's the final resting place of Anna Leonowens, the real-life heroine of *The King and I*. The yellow-brick buildings and tower on the north side of the mountain beyond the cemetery belong to the Université de Montréal, the second-largest French-language university in the world, with nearly 60,000 students. If you're now humming "Getting to Know You," you'll probably change your tune to Canada's national anthem when you enter the **Cimetière de Notre-Dame-des-Neiges** ⑮; the composer of "O Canada," Calixa Lavallée, is buried here.

Wander northwest through the two cemeteries, and you eventually emerge on chemin Queen Mary on the edge of a decidedly lively area of street vendors, ethnic restaurants, and boutiques. Walk west on Queen Mary across chemin Côte-des-Neiges, and you come to Montréal's most grandiose religious monument, the **Oratoire St-Joseph** ⑯. Across the street is the ivy-covered **Collège Notre Dame** ⑰, where the oratory's founder, Brother André, worked as a porter. After visiting the church, retrace your steps to chemin Côte-des-Neiges and walk to the Côte-des-Neiges station to catch the Métro.

TIMING

Allot the better part of a day for this tour, longer if you plan on catching some rays or ice-skating in the park.

Sights to See

★ ㊽ **Chalet du Mont-Royal.** The view here overlooks downtown Montréal. In the distance you can see Mont-Royal's sister mountains—Mont St-Bruno, Mont St-Hilaire, and Mont St-Grégoire. These isolated peaks—called the Montérégies, or Mountains of the King—rise dramatically from the flat countryside. Be sure to take a look inside the chalet, especially at the murals depicting scenes from Canadian history. There's a snack bar in the back. ⊠ *Off voie Camillien-Houde.* ☉ *Daily 9–5.*

㊺ **Cimetière de Notre-Dame-des-Neiges.** The largest Catholic graveyard in the city is the final resting place of hundreds of prominent artists, poets, intellectuals, politicians, and clerics. Among them is Calixa Lavallée (1842–91), who wrote "O Canada." Many of the monuments and mausoleums—scattered along 55 km (34 mi) of paths and roadways—are the work of leading artists. There are no tours of the cemetery, but a book at the reception gates lists locations of certain graves. ⊠ *4601 chemin Côte-des-Neiges,* ☎ *514/735–1361. Métro: Université de Montréal.*

㊽ **Cimetière Mont-Royal.** This cemetery was established in 1852 by the Anglican, Presbyterian, Unitarian, and Baptist churches and was laid out like a landscaped garden with monuments that are genuine works of art. The cemetery's most famous permanent guest is Anna Leonowens, who was governess to the children of the King of Siam and the real-life model for the heroine of the musical *The King and I*. There are no tours of the cemetery. ⊠ *1297 chemin de la Forêt,* ☎ *514/279–7358.* ☉ *Daily 10–6. Métro: Edouard Montpetit.*

㊿ **Collège Notre Dame.** Brother André, founder of the Oratoire St-Joseph, worked as a porter here. It's an important private school and one of the few in the city that still accept boarders. Its students these days, however, include girls, a situation that would have shocked Brother André. ✉ *3791 chemin Queen Mary. Métro: Côte-des-Neiges.*

OFF THE
BEATEN PATH

COSMODOME – The adventure of space exploration is the focus of this interactive center in suburban Laval, about a 30-minute drive from downtown. It's loaded with such kid-pleasing exhibits as replicas of rockets and space ships and a full-size mock-up of the space shuttle Endeavor. There are films—some of them shown on a 360-degree screen—demonstrations, and games. Next door to the Cosmodome is the **Space Camp** (☎ 800/565–2267), a training center for amateur astronauts 9 or older that is affiliated with the U.S. Space Camp in Georgia. ✉ *2150 autoroute des Laurentides, Laval,* ☎ *450/978–3600,* WEB *www.designc.com/cosmodom.htm.* 🎟 *$9.75.* ⏲ *June 24–Aug., daily 10–6; Sept.–June 23, Tues.–Sun. 10–6.*

🦫 ㉓ **Lac aux Castors** (Beaver Lake). In summer, children can float boats in this lake reclaimed from boggy ground. It makes a fine skating rink in winter. ✉ *Off chemin Remembrance. Métro: Edouard Montpetit.*

㉑ **Observatoire de l'Est.** This lookout gives a spectacular view of the east end of the city and the St. Lawrence River. ✉ *Voie Camillien-Houde.*

㉖ **Oratoire St-Joseph.** St. Joseph's Oratory, a huge domed church perched high on a ridge of Mont-Royal, is the largest shrine in the world dedicated to the earthly father of Jesus. It is the result of the persistence of a remarkable little man named Brother André Besette, who was a porter in the school run by his religious order. The son of very poor farmers, he dreamed of building a shrine dedicated to St. Joseph—Canada's patron saint—and began in 1904 by building a little chapel. Miraculous cures were reported and attributed to St. Joseph's intercession, and Brother André's project caught the imagination of Montréal. The result is one of the most important shrines in North America.

The octagonal copper dome on top of the church is one of the biggest in the world—146 ft tall and 125 ft in diameter—and the church has a magnificent mountainside setting with sweeping views over the north of the city and the Laurentian foothills in the distance. It's also home to Les Petits Chanteurs de Mont-Royal, the city's finest boys' choir. But alas, the starkly modern concrete interior is oppressive and drab: a soaring dim cave full of rows of folding metal chairs and not much in the way of art or color except for some striking stained-glass windows made by Marius Plamondon. The Montréal sculptor Henri Charlier is responsible for the elongated wooden statues of the apostles in the transepts, the main altar, and the huge crucifix.

There's a more modest and quite undistinguished crypt church at the bottom of the structure, and right behind it is a room that glitters with hundreds of votive candles lighted in honor of St. Joseph. The walls are festooned with crutches discarded by the cured. Right behind that is the simple tomb of Brother André, who was beatified in 1982. Brother André's heart is displayed in a glass case upstairs in a small museum depicting events in his life.

From early December through February, the oratory has a display of crèches (nativity scenes) from all over the world. High on the mountain beside the main church is a beautiful garden, commemorating the Passion of Christ with life-size representations of the 14 traditional Stations of the Cross. Carillon, choral, and organ concerts are held weekly at the oratory in summer. To visit the church you can either climb the more than 300 steps to the front door (many pilgrims do so on their knees, pausing to pray at each step) or take the shuttle bus that runs

from the front gate. ⊠ *3800 chemin Queen Mary,* ☏ *514/733–8211,*
WEB *www.saint-joseph.org.* ☏ *Free.* ☉ *Mid-Sept.–mid-May, daily 7–*
5:30; mid-May–mid-Sept., daily 7 AM–9 PM. Métro: Côte-des-Neiges.

Olympic Park and Botanical Garden

The Parc Olympique (Olympic Park) and the Jardin Botanique (Botanical Garden) are in the city's east end. You can reach them via the Pie-
IX or Viau Métro stations (the latter is nearer the stadium entrance).
The giant Stade Olympique and the leaning tower that supports the
stadium's roof dominate the skyline of the eastern part of town. But
the area has more to recommend it than the stadium complex; there's
the city's botanical garden, the world's largest museum dedicated to
bugs, and Parc Maisonneuve, which is an ideal place for a stroll or a
picnic. A free shuttle links the Jardin Botanique, Biodôme, Parc
Olympique, and the Viau Métro station.

A Good Tour

Start with a ride on the Métro's Green Line and get off at the Viau station, which is only a few steps from the main entrance to the 70,000-
seat **Stade Olympique** ⑱, a stadium built for the 1976 summer games.
A trip to the top of the **Tour Olympique** ⑲, the world's tallest tilting
structure, gives you a view up to 80 km (50 mi) on a clear day. The
six pools of the **Centre Aquatique** ⑳ are under the tower.

Next to the tower is the **Biodôme** ㉑, where you can explore both a rain
forest and an arctic landscape. Continuing your back-to-nature experience, cross rue Sherbrooke to the north of the park (or take the free
shuttle bus) to reach the enormous **Jardin Botanique** ㉒. The botanical complex includes the **Insectarium** ㉓ and the 5-acre Montréal-
Shanghai Lac de Rêve, an elegant Ming-style garden.

After you've looked at the flowers, return to boulevard Pie-IX, which
runs along the western border of the gardens. The name of this traffic artery (and the adjoining Métro station) puzzles thousands of visitors every year. The street is named for the 19th-century pope Pius IX,
or Pie IX in French. It's pronounced Pee-neuf, however, which isn't at
all how it looks to English speakers. At rue Sherbrooke cross boulevard Pie-IX and walk east to rue Jeanne-d'Arc past the lavish **Château
Dufresne,** ㉔ a pair of attached mansions built as family homes by two
brothers in 1916.

TIMING
To see all the sights at a leisurely pace, you need a full day.

Sights to See

☺ ㉑ **Biodôme.** Not everyone thought it was a great idea to change an
Olympic bicycle-racing stadium into a natural-history exhibit, but the
result is one of the city's most popular attractions. It combines four
ecosystems—the boreal forest, tropical forest, polar world, and St.
Lawrence River—under one climate-controlled dome. You follow protected pathways through each environment, observing flora and fauna
of each ecosystem. A word of warning: the tropical forest really is tropical. If you want to stay comfortable, dress in layers. ⊠ *4777 av.
Pierre-de-Coubertin,* ☏ *514/868–3000,* WEB *www.ville.montreal.
qc.ca/biodome.* ☏ *$10.* ☉ *Daily 9–5. Métro: Viau.*

☺ ㉒ **Centre Aquatique.** Olympic swimmers competed here in 1976, but now
anyone can use four of the six pools: one for games such as water polo,
the others for laps. Volleyball courts also are available. ⊠ *4141 av. Pierre-
de-Coubertin,* ☏ *514/252–4622.* ☏ *$3.30.* ☉ *Weekdays 2–9, week-
ends 1–4. Métro: Pie-IX or Viau.*

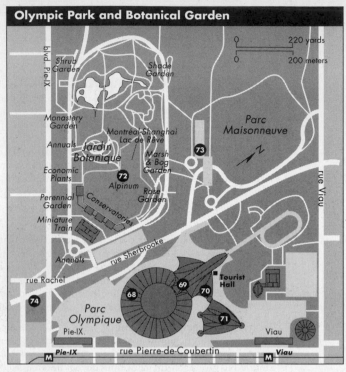

Olympic Park and Botanical Garden

🎴 **Château Dufresne.** Two wealthy brothers, Oscar and Marius Dufresne, lived with their families in this splendid Beaux-Arts palace inspired by the Petit-Trianon in Paris—Oscar in the eastern half and Marius in the western half. The ground floors of both residences are open to the public and provide an unequalled glimpse into the lives of Montréal Francophone bourgeoisie in the early 20th century. The lavish decor includes oak staircases with gilded rails, marble-tile floors, stained-glass windows, and coffered ceilings. Many of the walls have murals by Guido Nincheri, an artist who also decorated many of the city's most beautiful churches. Of particular charm are the delicate domestic scenes on the walls of the Petit Salon, a room in which Madame Oscar Dufresne would entertain her friends. Her brother-in-law, on the other side of the house, relaxed with his male friends in a smoking room decorated like a Turkish lounge. During the house's incarnation as a boys' school, the Eudist priests, who ran the place, covered the room's frieze of gamboling nymphs and satyrs with a modest curtain that their charges lifted at every opportunity. The ornate table in Marius's front hall hints at the brothers' political sympathies: it's decorated with portraits of Napoléon and his marshals. ✉ 2929 rue Jeanne-d'Arc, ☎ 514/256–4636. 💲 $5. ⊙ Tues.–Fri. 9:30–noon and 1:30–4:30, weekends 10–5. Métro: Pie-IX.

🐛 🎴 **Insectarium.** A bug-shape building in the ☞ **Jardin Botanique** houses more than 250,000 insect specimens. Most are mounted, but colorful butterflies fly free in the butterfly room, and there are ant and bee exhibits, too. In February you can taste such delicacies as deep-fried bumblebees. ✉ 4581 rue Sherbrooke Est, ☎ 514/872–1400, 🌐 www.ville.montreal.qc.ca/insectarium. 💲 May–Oct. $10, Nov.–Apr. $7.50; includes Jardin Botanique admission. ⊙ May–mid-June and Sept. 10–Apr., daily 9–5; mid-June–Sept. 9, daily 9–7. Métro: Pie-IX or Viau.

★ ⊙ ⑫ **Jardin Botanique.** This botanical garden, with 181 acres of plantings in summer and 10 exhibition greenhouses open all year, is the second-largest attraction of its kind in the world (after England's Kew Gardens). Founded in 1931, the garden has more than 26,000 species of plants. Among the 30 thematic gardens are a rose garden and an alpine garden; the poisonous-plant garden is a favorite. Traditional tea ceremonies are held in the Japanese Garden, which also has one of the best bonsai collections in the West. The Tree House exhibit center in the arboretum explores the world of the forest. In 2001, in celebration of the 300th anniversary of the signing of the Great Peace Treaty of Montréal between the French settlers and the natives of the region, the Jardin Botanique opened the Jardin des Premier Nations, or the First Nations Garden. It includes such indigenous plants and trees as silver birch, maples, Labrador, and tea and jack-in-the-pulpit. Other highlights are the 5-acre Montréal-Shanghai Lac de Rêve, the largest Ming-style Chinese garden outside Asia, with seven elegant pavilions and a 30-ft rock garden built around a pool, and the **Insectarium.** ✉ *4101 rue Sherbrooke Est,* ☎ *514/872–1400,* 🆆🅴🅱 *www.ville.montreal.qc.ca/jardin.* 🎫 *May–Oct. $10, Nov.–Apr. $7.50.* ⊙ *May–Oct. 9–7, Nov.–Apr. 9–5. Métro: Pie-IX or Viau.*

OFF THE
BEATEN PATH

MAISONNEUVE – Olympic organizers weren't the first dream-makers to have big plans for this socially cohesive but economically depressed neighborhood. At the beginning of the 20th century, when the district was a hard-working, booming industrial center with its own municipal government, civic leaders wanted to transform it into a model city with broad boulevards, grandiose public buildings, and fine homes. World War I and the Depression soon killed those plans, but a few fine fragments of the grand dream survive, just three blocks south of the Olympic site. The magnificent Beaux-Arts public market with its 20-ft-tall bronze statue of a farm woman stands at the northern end of tree-lined avenue Morgan. Farmers and butchers have moved into a modern building next door; the old market is now a community center and the site of shows and concerts in the summer. The public baths across the street are decorated with monumental staircases and a heroic rooftop sculpture; the **Théâtre Denise Pelletier,** at the corner of rue Ste-Catherine Est, has a lavish Italianate interior; **Fire Station No. 1,** at 4300 rue Notre-Dame Est, was inspired by Frank Lloyd Wright's Unity Temple in suburban Chicago; and the sumptuously decorated **Église Très-Saint-Nom-de-Jésus** has one of the most powerful organs in North America. **Tourisme Maisonneuve** (✉ 4375 rue Ontario Est, ☎ 514/256–4636) has information about the area. *Métro: Pie-IX or Viau.*

---

⑥⑧ **Stade Olympique.** The stadium, built for the 1976 Summer Olympics, is beautiful to look at but not very practical. It's hard to heat, and the retractable fabric roof, supported by the tower, has never worked properly. Nevertheless, it's home to the Expos of baseball's National League and is used for events like Montréal's annual car show. ✉ *4141 av. Pierre-de-Coubertin,* ☎ *514/252–8687,* 🆆🅴🅱 *www.rio.gouv.qc.ca. Métro: Pie-IX or Viau.*

⑥⑨ **Tour Olympique.** A trip to the top of this tower, the world's tallest tilting structure, is very popular; a two-level cable car can whisk 90 people up the exterior of the 890-ft tower. On a clear day you can see up to 80 km (50 mi) from the tower-top observatory. Daily guided tours of the Olympic complex leave from the **Tourist Hall** (☎ 514/252–8687) in the base of the tower. Tours at 12:40 and 3:40 are in English and tours at 11 and 2 are in French; cost is $5.25. ✉ *Av. Pierre-de-Coubertin,* ☎ *514/252–4141 Ext. 5246 for tour and tower-ride arrange-*

ments. ✉ *$9; $12 including tour of Olympic complex. Métro: Pie-IX or Viau.*

The Islands

Expo '67—the world's fair staged to celebrate the centennial of the Canadian federation—was the biggest party in Montréal's history, and it marked a defining moment in the city's evolution as a modern metropolis. That party was held on two islands in the middle of the St. Lawrence River—Île Ste-Hélène, which was formed by nature, and Île Notre-Dame, which was created with the stone rubble excavated from Montréal's Métro. The two islands are still a playground. Together they form **Parc Jean-Drapeau** (☎ 514/872–4537, WEB www.parcjeandrapeau.com/en) named for the visionary mayor who brought the world's fair to Montréal, and encompass a major amusement park, acres of flower gardens, a beach with clean filtered water, and the Casino de Montréal. There's history, too, at the Old Fort, where soldiers in colonial uniforms display the military skills of ancient wars. In winter you can skate on the old Olympic rowing basin or slide down iced trails on an inner tube.

A Good Walk

Start at the Parc Jean-Drapeau station on the Métro's Yellow Line. The first thing you see when you emerge is the huge geodesic dome that houses **Biosphère,** an environmental exhibition center. From the Biosphere walk to the northern shore and then east to the Old Fort, now the **Stewart Museum.** Just east of the Old Fort past the Pont Jacques-Cartier (Jacques Cartier Bridge) is **La Ronde,** an amusement park.

Now cross over to the island's southern shore and walk back along the waterfront to the Cosmos Footbridge, which leads to Île Notre-Dame. On the way you pass the Hélène de Champlain restaurant, which probably has the prettiest setting of any restaurant in Montréal, and the military cemetery of the British garrison stationed on Île Ste-Hélène from 1828 to 1870.

Île Notre-Dame is laced with a network of canals and ponds, and the grounds are brilliant with flower gardens left from the 1980 Floralies Internationales flower show. Most of the Expo '67 buildings are gone, the victims of time and weather. One that has remained, however, is the fanciful French Pavilion. It and the neighboring Québec Pavilion have been turned into the **Casino de Montréal.** A five-minute walk west of the casino is the Lac de l'Île Notre-Dame, site of **Plage de l'Île Notre-Dame,** Montréal's only beach. In mid-June Île Notre-Dame is the site of the Player's Grand Prix du Canada, a top Formula 1 international auto race at the **Circuit Gilles Villeneuve.**

After your walk you can return to the Métro or walk back to the city via the Pont de la Concorde and the Parc de la Cité du Havre to Vieux-Montréal. If you walk, you can see Habitat '67, an irregular pile of concrete blocks on avenue Pierre-Dupuy that was designed by Moshe Safdie and built as an experiment in housing for Expo '67. The private apartment complex resembles an updated version of a Hopi cliff dwelling.

TIMING
This is a comfortable two-hour stroll, but the Biosphere and the Old Fort (try to time your visit to coincide with a drill display) deserve at least an hour each, and you should leave another half hour to admire the flowers. Children are likely to want to spend a whole day at La Ronde, but in summer the best time to go is in the evening, when it's cooler. Try to visit the casino on a weekday when the crowds are thinnest.

Sights to See

Biosphere. An environmental center in the huge geodesic dome designed by Buckminster Fuller as the American Pavilion at Expo '67 successfully brings fun to an earnest project—heightening awareness of the St. Lawrence River system and its problems. ⊠ *Île St-Hélène,* ☎ *514/ 496–8300,* WEB *biosphere.ec.gc.ca/bio.* 🎫 *Nov.–Apr. $8.50.* ☉ *June– Sept., daily 10–6; Oct.–May, Tues.–Sat. 10–4. Métro: Parc Jean-Drapeau.*

★ **Casino de Montréal.** The government has tried to capture the elegance of Monte Carlo here, one of the biggest gambling palaces in the world. This stunning complex—originally the French Pavilion for Expo '67, Montréal's world's fair—glitters with glass and murals and offers stunning city views. The casino, which is open around the clock, has a strict dress code and houses four restaurants, including Nuances, and a bilingual cabaret theater. ⊠ *1 av. du Casino, Île Notre-Dame.* ☎ *514/392– 2746 or 800/665–2274. Métro: Parc Jean-Drapeau (then Bus 167).*

Circuit Gilles Villeneuve. All the big names in motor sports gather at this track every summer for the Air Canada Grand Prix, one of the racing season's most important Formula 1 events. One of the veterans of the Formula 1 circuit is local hero Jacques Villeneuve, who won the world championship in 1997. The track is named for his father, Gilles, who was killed in a racing crash in Belgium in 1982. At press time, the track was also to play host to the Molson Indy of Montréal, part of the CART FedEx Championship Series in automobile racing (starting in late summer of 2002). ⊠ *Île Notre-Dame,* ☎ *800/797–4537. Métro: Parc Jean-Drapeau.*

Ⓒ **Plage de l'Île Notre-Dame.** The swimming beach is an oasis, with clear, filtered lake water and an inviting stretch of lawn and trees; it's often filled to capacity in summer, however. Lifeguards are on duty, a shop rents swimming and boating paraphernalia, and there are picnic areas and a restaurant. ⊠ *West side of Île Notre-Dame,* ☎ *514/872–4537.* 🎫 *$7.50. Métro: Parc Jean-Drapeau.*

Ⓒ **La Ronde.** This world-class amusement park has Ferris wheels, boat rides, simulator-style rides, and the second-highest roller coaster in the world. U.S. company Six Flags, which purchased the park in 2000, plans to spend $90 million in the next few years adding to the inventory of rides. The popular **International Fireworks Competition** (☎ *514/935–5161 or 800/678–5440; 800/361–4595 in Canada),* which takes place weekends in late June and July, is held here. ⊠ *Île Ste-Hélène,* ☎ *514/872–6222.* 🎫 *$24.75; grounds only $13.* ☉ *May, weekends 10–9; June 1–20, daily 10–9; June 21–Sept. 2, daily 11–11. Métro: Parc Jean-Drapeau.*

Ⓒ **Stewart Museum at the Fort.** In summer the grassy parade square of the fine stone Old Fort comes alive with the crackle of colonial musket fire. The French are represented by the Compagnie Franche de la Marine and the British by the kilted 78th Fraser Highlanders, one of the regiments that participated in the conquest of Québec in 1759. The fort itself, built to protect Montréal from American invasion, is now a museum that tells the story of colonial life in Montréal through displays of old firearms, maps, and uniforms. The two companies of colonial soldiers raise the flag every day at 11, practice their maneuvers at 1, put on a combined display of precision drilling and musket fire at 2:30, and lower the flag at 5. Children can participate. ⊠ *Île Ste-Hélène,* ☎ *514/861–6701,* WEB *www.stewart-museum.org.* 🎫 *Early May–mid-Oct. $7, mid-Oct.–early May $6.* ☉ *Early May–mid-Oct., daily 10–6; mid-Oct.–early May, Wed.–Mon. 10–5. Métro: Parc Jean-Drapeau.*

DINING

Montréal has more than 4,500 restaurants of every price range, representing dozens of ethnic groups. When you dine out, you can, of course, order à la carte, but be sure to look for the table d'hôte, a two- to four-course package deal. It's usually more economical, often offers interesting special dishes, and may also take less time to prepare. If you want to splurge with your time and money, indulge yourself with the *menu dégustation,* a five- to seven-course tasting menu executed by the chef. It generally includes soup, salad, fish, sherbet (to refresh the taste buds), a meat dish, dessert, and coffee or tea. At the city's finest restaurants, such a meal for two, along with a good bottle of wine, can cost more than $200 and last four hours; it's worth every cent and every second.

A word about language: menus in many restaurants are bilingual, but some are in French only. If you don't understand what a dish is, don't be shy about asking; a good server will be delighted to explain. If you feel brave enough to order in French, remember that in French an entrée is an appetizer and what English speakers call an entrée is a *plat principal,* or main dish.

CATEGORY	COST*
$$$$	over $32
$$$	$22–$32
$$	$13–$21
$	under $13

per person, in Canadian dollars, for a main course at dinner

Cafés

$ ✕ **Brioche Lyonnaise.** The quintessential Quartier-Latin café—it opened
★ in 1980—is in a charmingly decorated semibasement across the street from the Théatre St-Denis. It still serves some of the city's finest pastries, all loaded with butter, cream, pure fruit, and a dusting of sugar. The butter brioche and a bowl of steaming café au lait make for one of the city's finest breakfasts. ⊠ *1593 rue St-Denis,* ☎ *514/842–7017. MC, V.*

$ ✕ **Café Toman.** This Czech pastry shop perched in a second-floor lo-
★ cation near Concordia University has been a downtown favorite since it opened in 1975. The family that runs it serves up cakes made with pralines and hazelnut cream, Sacher torte, apple strudel, and generous cups of Viennese coffee topped with whipped cream. Its soups and light lunches are particularly popular with weekend shoppers and Concordia students. The shop usually closes for four weeks in summer when local tastes run to ice cream rather than pastries. ⊠ *1421 rue MacKay,* ☎ *514/844–1605. No credit cards. Closed Sun.–Mon. and mid-July–mid-Aug. No dinner.*

$ ✕ **Les Gâteries.** The revered Montréal playwright Michel Tremblay is reputed to be among the writers and artists who take their morning espresso in this comfortable little café facing Square St-Louis. The menu is decidedly more Montréalais than European with such local favorites as bagels, muffins, maple-syrup pie, and toast with *cretons* (a coarse, fatty kind of pâté made with pork) sharing space with baguettes and croissants. ⊠ *3443 rue St-Denis,* ☎ *514/843–6235. MC, V.*

Canadian

$ ✕ **Binerie Mont-Royal.** This tiny restaurant specializes in that rarest of the city's culinary finds—authentic Québécois food. That includes stews made with meatballs and pigs' feet, various kinds of *tourtière* (meat pie), and, of course, pork and beans. It's cheap, filling, and charming. ⊠ *367 av. Mont Royal Est,* ☎ *514/285–9078. No credit cards. No dinner weekends.*

$ ✕ **Chalet Barbecue.** In the early 1950s, Swiss-born Marcel Mauron and French-born Jean Detanne built a large brick oven in this west-end location and pioneered a Montréal tradition: crispy, spit-barbecued chicken served with a slightly spicy, gravylike sauce and mountains of french fries. There are literally dozens of imitators all over the city, but no one does it better. Many of the restaurant's customers order their meals to go. ⊠ *5456 rue Sherbrooke Ouest,* ☎ *514/489–7235. MC, V.*

$ ✕ **Chez Clo.** Here, deep in east-end Montréal, where seldom is heard an English word, is authentic Québécois food. A meal in this unpretentious neighborhood diner could start with a bowl of the best pea soup in the city, followed by a slab of tourtière, mounds of mashed potatoes, carrots, and turnips, and a bowl of gravy on the side. The dessert specialty is *pudding au chomeur* (literally, pudding for the unemployed), a kind of shortcake smothered in a thick brown-sugar sauce. The service is noisy and friendly and the clientele mostly local. ⊠ *3199 rue Ontario Est,* ☎ *514/522–5348. No credit cards.*

Chinese

$$–$$$$ ✕ **Orchidée de Chine.** Diners feast on such delectables as baby bok choy with mushrooms, perfumed spareribs, feather-light fried soft-shell crabs with black-bean sauce, and steamed, gingery grouper in an elegant, glassed-in dining room with a great view on a busy, fashionable sidewalk. There's a more intimate room in the back. ⊠ *2017 rue Peel,* ☎ *514/287–1878. Reservations essential. AE, DC, MC, V. Closed Sun.*

$$–$$$ ✕ **Piment Rouge.** High ceilings, crystal chandeliers, and floor-to-ceiling windows serve as an elegant Edwardian backdrop for excellent Szechuan and northern Chinese food. Starters include beef and banana rolls and sliced kidneys in hot sauce. Crispy shrimp with honeyed walnuts, shredded lamb in spiced sauce, and steamed fish in ginger are among the main dishes. Prices are high, but servings are generous. ⊠ *Le Windsor, 1170 rue Peel,* ☎ *514/866–7816. AE, DC, MC, V.*

$–$$ ✕ **Maison Kam Fung.** This bright, airy restaurant serves the most reliable dim sum lunch in Chinatown. Every day from 10 to 3, waiters push a parade of trolleys through the restaurant, carting treats such as firm dumplings stuffed with pork and chicken, stir-fried squid, and delicate shrimp-filled pastry envelopes. ⊠ *1008 rue Clark,* ☎ *514/878–2888. AE, DC, MC, V.*

$ ✕ **Bon Blé Riz.** The food in this little restaurant is flamboyantly Chinese, but the prices are as modest as its unpretentious decor. Sizzling shrimp with onion, green pepper, and carrot, and finely chopped lamb served with celery and bamboo shoots in a peppery anise-flavored sauce are two of the intriguing dishes. The Beijing-style dumplings are good starters. ⊠ *1437 blvd. St-Laurent,* ☎ *514/844–1447. AE, DC, MC, V.*

Contemporary

$$–$$$$ ✕ **Toqué!** The name means "a bit crazy." Its innovative co-owner and
★ chef, Normand Laprise, has achieved a level of celebrity in Montréal equaled only by the captain of the Canadiens hockey team and the conductor of the Orchéstre Symphonique de Montréal. His restaurant whips market-fresh ingredients into dazzling combinations and colors, the menu changing constantly depending on whim and availability. Summer's opening cold soup of fresh green tomatoes might be replaced in winter by a fluffy cake of bronzed potatoes, goat cheese, and spinach. Main courses could range from sautéed scallops to butter-bean stew with cumin and jalapeño peppers. The portions don't look big but are surprisingly filling. And the desserts—crème brûlée, almond-crusted blueberry pie,

552

Montréal Dining

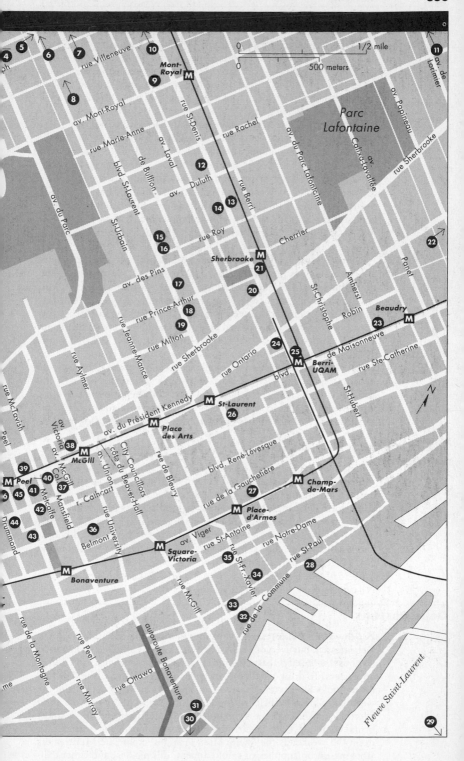

rue Villeneuve

Mont-Royal
[M]

9

10

av. de Lorimier

11

0   1/2 mile

0   500 meters

4 **5** **6** **7** **8**

av. Mont-Royal

rue Marie-Anne

blvd. St-Laurent

de Bullion

av. Laval

rue St-Denis

rue Rachel

rue Duluth

Parc
Lafontaine

av. du Parc Lafontaine

av. Calixa-Lavallée

av. Papineau

rue Sherbrooke

12

14 **13**

rue Berri

rue Roy

15
16

St-Urbain

av. du Parc

av. des Pins

Cherrier

22

17

rue Prince-Arthur

18

rue Milton

19

rue Jeanne-Mance

rue Sherbrooke

Sherbrooke
[M]
21

20

St-Christophe

Amherst

Robin

Beaudry
[M]
23

Panet

rue Aylmer

rue McTavish

av. Victoria

av. du Président Kennedy

rue Ontario

24

25
Berri-
UQAM
[M]

de Maisonneuve

rue Ste-Catherine

rue St-Hubert

blvd.

[M] St-Laurent

26

Place
des Arts
[M]

McGill
[M]
38

Peel
[M]
39

40

37

av. McGill College

r. Cathcart

côte du Beaver-Hall

City Councillors

av. Union

rue de Bleury

blvd. René-Lévesque

rue de la Gauchetière

Champ-
de-Mars
[M]

Place-
d'Armes
[M]

St-Hubert

6 **45** **41**

42

Metcalfe

44

43

Belmont

rue University

36

Mansfield

27

Peel

Drummond

Square-
Victoria
[M]

Bonaventure
[M]

av. Viger

rue St-Antoine

rue Notre-Dame

rue St-Paul

rue de la Commune

35

34

28

rue de la Montagne

rue Peel

rue Ottawa

autoroute Bonaventure

rue McGill

rue St-François-Xavier

33

32

31

30

Fleuve Saint-Laurent

29

rue Murray

chocolate mille-feuille—are worth saving space for. ⊠ *3842 rue St-Denis,* ☎ *514/499–2084. Reservations essential. AE, DC, MC, V.*

$$–$$$ ✕ **Bazou.** The name means "jalopy," and a car theme appears in the decor and menu of this charming little eatery. To start, for example, you can have crevettes Thais Suzuki, shrimp cooked with peanut butter, coriander, chili, and fried spinach; one main dish is rabbit cooked in a "Mustang sauce" of cream, white wine, and mushrooms. ⊠ *1310 blvd. de Maisonneuve Est,* ☎ *514/526–4940. AE, MC, V.*

$$–$$$ ✕ **La Chronique.** The storefront bistro with yellow walls and minimalist
★ decor makes a perfectly understated backdrop for some of Montréal's most adventurous cooking. Owner–chef Marc de Canck seamlessly blends lightened French with Japanese, Chinese, and creole flashes. Scallops tempura on swirls of fried yam and spiced salmon sashimi are among the openers on a constantly changing menu. Main dishes are equally daring—blackened duck breast with shrimp, for example, or bokchoy calf sweetbreads with coconut-milk polenta. ⊠ *99 av. Laurier Est,* ☎ *514/271–3095. Reservations essential. AE, DC, MC, V. Closed Sun.–Mon.*

$$–$$$ ✕ **Globe.** Frosted lighting fixtures, potted palms, and red-velvet banquettes adorn this very fashionable haunt of successful thirtysomethings—and the cuisine matches the decor in daring. Home-grown chef David McMillan thinks nothing of tossing a few Szechuan peppercorns into a dessert or serving a reduced plum wine with a dish of pan-seared Québec foie gras. For dessert, try the roasted pineapple crumble if it's on the menu. ⊠ *3455 blvd. St-Laurent,* ☎ *514/284–3823. AE, DC, MC, V.*

$$–$$$ ✕ **Mediterraneo.** Sandstone floors, a space-age metallic ceiling, and huge windows that wrap around two walls set off some of the trendiest food in Montréal. Dinner could start with tuna sashimi or spring rolls stuffed with chicken, spinach, and ricotta, and then move on to duck with sweet potatoes, dried cranberries, and a marmalade of pears and exotic fruits. ⊠ *3500 blvd. St-Laurent,* ☎ *514/844–0027. Reservations essential. AE, MC, V.*

Continental

$$$$ ✕ **Beaver Club.** This grand old institution traces its roots to a 19th-century social club for the trading and banking elite, and its wood paneling, formal settings, and starched, veteran servers give it the air of an exclusive men's club. It's not the place for daring dining, however, and you'd do well to stick to the classics—roast beef, grilled chops, and maybe the poached salmon. The bar serves the best martini in the city. ⊠ *Hôtel Reine Elizabeth, 900 blvd. René-Lévesque Ouest,* ☎ *514/ 861–3511. Jacket and tie. AE, D, DC, MC, V. Closed Sun. and July. No dinner Mon.; no lunch July–Aug.*

Delicatessens

$–$$ ✕ **Schwartz's Delicatessen.** Its proper name is the Montréal Hebrew Delicatessen, but everyone calls it Schwartz's. The smoked meat (cured in-house) is the city's best, and the tender steaks come with grilled-liver appetizers. To drink you'll find nothing stronger than a Coke. The furniture looks like it was rescued from a Salvation Army depot, and the waiters are briskly efficient. Don't ask for a menu (there isn't one) and avoid the lunch hour unless you don't mind long lines; even on the most brutal winter days, the lunch line stretches well outside the frosted front door. On weekends the lineup often includes expatriate Montrealers stocking up on supplies of smoked meat, dill pickles, and other delicacies to take back to Toronto, Vancouver, or Boston. ⊠ *3895 blvd. St-Laurent,* ☎ *514/842–4813. Reservations not accepted. No credit cards.*

$ ✗ **Bens.** This big, brassy deli is a Montréal institution, with 1950s decor and photos of celebrity customers on green and yellow walls. Sadly, the food is not what it once was, though this is still a good place for a late-night snack. ⊠ *990 blvd. de Maisonneuve Ouest,* ☎ *514/844–1000. Reservations not accepted. MC, V.*

$ ✗ **Wilensky's Light Lunch.** Since 1932, the Wilensky family has served up its special: salami and bologna on a "Jewish" (kaiser) roll, slathered with mustard. You can also get a cherry or pineapple cola from the fountain (there's no liquor license). This neighborhood haunt was a setting for the film *The Apprenticeship of Duddy Kravitz,* starring Richard Dreyfuss and based on the novel by Mordecai Richler. ⊠ *34 rue Fairmount Ouest,* ☎ *514/271–0247. Reservations not accepted. No credit cards. Closed weekends.*

French

$$$$ ✗ **Les Halles.** Main dishes such as grapefruit Marie-Louise with scallops and lobster or roasted duck with pears sit comfortably beside the chef's ventures into nouvelle cuisine, such as his lobster with herbs and butter. The desserts are classic—the Paris-Brest, a puff pastry with praline cream inside, is one of the best in town. Mirrors, murals, and light colors are part of the Paris-market decor. ⊠ *1450 rue Crescent,* ☎ *514/844–2328. Reservations essential. AE, DC, MC, V. Closed Sun.*

$$$$ ✗ **Les Trois Tilleuls.** About an hour southeast of Montréal, you can lunch or dine on delectable food next to the Rivière Richelieu. This small, romantic inn, one of the prestigious Relais & Châteaux chain, has a terrace and a large, airy dining room with beautiful sunset views. The chef's specialties include cream of onion soup, sweetbreads, and game dishes. ⊠ *290 rue Richelieu, St-Marc sur Richelieu,* ☎ *450/584–2231. Reservations essential. AE, DC, MC, V.*

$$$–$$$$ ✗ **Caprices de Nicholas.** Antique furniture, plush seats, stained-glass
★ lamps, and dainty china make this restaurant one of Montréal's most luxurious. Its two Art Nouveau–inspired rooms are magnificent, but the most romantic tables are in the soaring, three-story atrium filled with tropical plants (reserved for nonsmokers). The poached sea bass is exquisite, as is the salmon pavé with onion preserves and currants. Meatier dishes include Alberta beef with an herb crust and pistachio gravy. ⊠ *2072 rue Drummond,* ☎ *514/282–9790. Reservations essential. AE, DC, MC, V. Closed Sun.*

$$$–$$$$ ✗ **Chez la Mère Michel.** A fine gray-stone town house provides a staid front for one of the city's most elegant dining rooms: big, well-spaced tables; large, comfy chairs; and bright paintings and murals. Chef–owner Micheline Delbuguet—the Mère Michel of the name—presides over a kitchen that turns out such flawlessly executed examples of classic French cuisine as Dover sole meunière and coq au vin (made with a rooster— not a chicken). Save room for such desserts as soufflé Grand Marnier and poached pears in an almond basket. ⊠ *1209 rue Guy,* ☎ *514/934–0473. Reservations essential. AE, DC, MC, V.*

$$$–$$$$ ✗ **Les Remparts.** A stone-walled cellar under the Auberge du Vieux-Port showcases innovative French cooking in an atmosphere redolent of Nouvelle France. The restaurant gets its name from an ancient lump of gray stone unearthed during renovations to the building in 1994— it once formed part of the city wall. Wild-mushroom soup with walnut croutons and quail with squash and sage gnocchi are some of the enticing appetizers, fitting preparation for main courses such as venison steak with parsley, salsify root, and juniper berries or Atlantic salmon cooked with endives, shallots, and red wine. ⊠ *93 rue de la Commune Est,* ☎ *514/392–1649. AE, DC, MC, V.*

$$-$$$$ ✕ **Guy and Dodo Morali.** Pale yellow walls and lots of art decorate this comfortable restaurant in the Cours Mont-Royal shopping plaza. In summer, dining spills out onto a little terrace on rue Metcalfe. The daily table d'hôte menu is the best bet, with openers such as lobster bisque followed by *agneau en croûte* (lamb in a pastry) with thyme sauce, or fillet of halibut with leeks. For dessert try the *tatan,* apples and caramel with crème anglaise. ⊠ *Les Cours Mont-Royal, 1444 rue Metcalfe,* ☎ *514/842–3636. Reservations essential. AE, D, DC, MC, V.*

$$-$$$$ ✕ **Nuances.** You can sit amid rosewood paneling and take in the magnificent view of the city at the simply stunning main restaurant of the Casino de Montréal, on Île Notre-Dame. You might start with sautéed duck foie gras with exotic fruits and progress to lightly grilled red tuna with vegetables marinated in balsamic vinegar and olive oil. Even dishes that have been approved by the Québec Heart and Stroke Foundation sound exciting, like the saddle of rabbit pot-au-feu served with mushrooms. ⊠ *1 av. de Casino,* ☎ *514/392–2708. Reservations essential. AE, DC, MC, V. No lunch.*

$$$ ✕ **Le Passe-Partout.** The bread made by the York–born chef James
★ MacGuire might be the best in Montréal. (He and his wife, Suzanne Baron-Lafrenière, sell it, along with homemade pâtés and terrines, in a bakery next door to their restaurant.) The short, handwritten menu changes according to mood and availability. You might start with smoked salmon, a potage of curried sweet potatoes, or perhaps a venison terrine. Dishes include swordfish steak served with a puree of red cabbage, or the signature dish—rosy slices of crisp-skinned duck with lightly browned pineapple pieces and tangy orange sauce. ⊠ *3857 blvd. Décarie (5-minute walk south from Villa Maria Métro),* ☎ *514/487– 7750. Reservations essential. AE, DC, MC, V. No lunch Sat.–Wed., no dinner Sun.–Wed. Groups only Mon.–Wed.*

$$-$$$ ✕ **Bistro Gourmet.** At chef Gabriel Ohana's tiny but richly atmospheric bistro, you can try such classics as rack of lamb with garlic, roasted shallot, and a stuffed broiled tomato; fillet of beef in a sauce spiked with blue cheese; and crispy-skinned breast of duck on a wine-stewed pear. ⊠ *2100 rue St-Mathieu,* ☎ *514/846–1553. AE, D, DC, MC, V.*

$$-$$$ ✕ **Bonaparte.** A cheerful fireplace and walls richly trimmed in impe-
★ rial purple and hung with sketches of Napoleonic soldiers set the tone at this wonderful little restaurant in the heart of Vieux-Montréal. The menu features traditional French dishes served with a light touch. You could start with a wild-mushroom ravioli seasoned with fresh sage and move on to a lobster stew flavored with vanilla and served with a spinach fondue, or a roast rack of lamb in a port sauce. Lunch is a good value. Upstairs, there's a little auberge. ⊠ *443 rue St-François-Xavier,* ☎ *514/ 844–4368. AE, D, DC, MC, V. No lunch weekends.*

$$-$$$ ✕ **Le Caveau.** Lost among the towers of downtown is an eccentric Victorian house where buttery sauces, creamy desserts, and fairly reasonable prices have survived the onslaught of inflation and nouvelle cuisine. The restaurant gets its name from its warm and comfortable low-ceiling cellar, but claustrophobes can dine on the upper two floors amid sculptures and paintings. Appetizers include sautéed brains with a caper mousseline; a main course might be rabbit cooked with sweet wine, spices, and raisins, or rack of lamb crusted with bread crumbs, mustard, garlic, and herbs. A children's menu—rare in restaurants of Le Caveau's caliber—is available. ⊠ *2063 av. Victoria,* ☎ *514/844– 1624. AE, DC, MC, V.*

$$-$$$ ✕ **Jongleux Café.** The delightful split-level café–restaurant south of Square St-Louis has survived the untimely death of its visionary founder, Nicolas Jongleux, in 2000. Protegé Thierry Baron has taken over the kitchen, and the roasted venison with prunes and pureed parsnips is still a delight. Some of the best dishes are at the lower end of the price list: melt-in-your-mouth pig's cheeks, for example, with Camembert ravioli, or the beef equivalent with escargot ravioli and sun-dried tomatoes. Chocolate soufflé is the signature dessert. ⊠ *2424 rue St-Denis*, ☎ *514/841–8080. Reservations essential. AE, DC, MC, V. Closed Sun.*

$–$$$ ✕ **Le Paris.** Every city should have a Le Paris. Its crowded dining
★ room, with big tables and age-dimmed paint, is as comfortable as the reasonably priced bourgeois fare that streams out of the kitchen. The *brandade de morue*—salt cod, potatoes, garlic, and cream—is famous, and American foodies have been known to time their visits to Montréal so they can indulge in the herb-roasted chicken served on Saturday. Desserts range from creamy pastries to such comfort dishes as stewed rhubarb. ⊠ *1812 rue Ste-Catherine Ouest*, ☎ *514/937–4898. AE, DC, MC, V.*

$–$$ ✕ **L'Express.** This Paris-style bistro has mirrored walls, a smoky atmosphere, and noise levels that are close to painful on weekends. But the food is good (even if the tiny crowded tables barely have room to accommodate it), the service fast, and the prices reasonable. The steak tartare with french fries, the salmon with sorrel, and the calves' liver with tarragon are marvelous. Jars of gherkins, fresh baguettes, and cheeses aged to perfection make the pleasure last longer. L'Express has one of the best and most original wine cellars in town. ⊠ *3927 rue St-Denis*, ☎ *514/845–5333. Reservations essential. AE, DC, MC, V.*

Greek

$$$$ ✕ **Milos.** Despite the nets and floats hanging from the ceiling, this isn't a simple neighborhood taverna but rather a first-class Greek restaurant of international stature. Indeed, Paul Newman and Bette Midler are among the admirers who enjoyed Milos so much that they persuaded its eponymous owner to open a branch in New York City. The real display is in the refrigerated cases and on the beds of ice in the back by the kitchen—octopus, squid, shrimp, crabs, oysters, and sea urchins. The main dish is usually fish grilled over charcoal and seasoned with parsley, capers, and lemon juice. It's done to perfection and is achingly delicious. The fish are priced by the pound, and you can order one large fish to serve two or more. You can also find lamb and veal chops, cheeses, and olives. Milos is a healthy walk from Métro Laurier. ⊠ *5357 av. du Parc*, ☎ *514/272–3522. Reservations essential. AE, D, DC, MC, V.*

$$–$$$ ✕ **Mythos Ouzerie.** Scores of incipient Zorbas come to this brick-lined semibasement every weekend to eat, drink, dance, and make merry in a Pan-inspired atmosphere of chaos and frenzy. The food is good every night—unctuous moussaka, plump stuffed vine leaves, grilled mushrooms, braised lamb, grilled squid—but go on Thursday, Friday, or Saturday night when the live and very infectious bouzouki music makes it impossible to remain seated. If you want to burn those calories before you have a chance to digest them, this is the place. ⊠ *5318 av. Park*, ☎ *514/270–0235. AE, MC, V.*

$–$$ ✕ **Rotisserie Panama.** No one seems to know why this big, noisy Greek taverna is named for a Latin American country, but who cares? It offers some of the best grilled meat in Montréal at startlingly reasonable prices. The chicken and crispy lamb chops are excellent and on weekends you can order roasted baby lamb. The more adventurous might try the *kokoretsi* (various organ meats wrapped in intestines and grilled on a spit) or the *patsas,* a full-flavored tripe soup. And although the chefs specialize in meats, they have a deft hand with grilled fish and octopus as well. ⊠ *789 rue Jean-Talon Ouest*, ☎ *514/276–5223. AE, MC, V.*

Indian

$ ✕ **Le Taj.** The cuisine of the north of India, less spicy and more refined than that of the south, is showcased here. The tandoori ovens seal in the flavors of the grilled meat and fish. Among the vegetarian dishes are the *taj-thali,* which includes lentils, basmati rice, and *saag panir,* spicy white cheese with spinach. A nine-course lunch buffet is less than $10, and at night there's an "Indian feast" for $20. The desserts—pistachio ice cream or mangoes—are often decorated with pure silver leaves. ✉ *2077 rue Stanley,* ☎ *514/845–9015. AE, MC, V.*

Italian

$$–$$$ ✕ **Da Emma.** Massive stone pillars and wooden beams give this family-run restaurant on the Vieux-Port a genuinely Roman feel. So does the food. Seafood antipasto (squid, mussels, shrimp, and octopus drizzled with olive oil), fettuccine with porcini mushrooms, and suckling pig roasted with garlic and rosemary are among the highlights. ✉ *777 rue de la Commune Ouest,* ☎ *514/392–1568. AE, D, DC, MC, V.*

$$–$$$ ✕ **Il Mulino.** Nothing about the decor or the location of this family-
★   run restaurant in Little Italy hints of the delights within. The antipasti alone—grilled mushrooms, stuffed eggplant, pizza, broiled scallops— are worth the trip. The pasta, too, is excellent, especially the agnolotti and the gnocchi. Main dishes include simply prepared lamb chops, veal, and excellent fish. ✉ *236 rue St-Zotique Est,* ☎ *514/273–5776. Reservations essential. AE, DC, MC, V. Closed Sun.–Mon.*

$–$$$ ✕ **Bocca d'Oro.** This restaurant next to the Guy-Concordia Métro station has a huge menu. One pasta specialty is *tritico di pasta*: one helping each of spinach ravioli with salmon and caviar, shellfish marinara, and spaghetti primavera. With dessert and coffee, the waiters bring out a bowl of walnuts for you to crack at your table. The two-floor dining area is inexplicably decorated with golf pictures, and Italian pop songs play in the background. The staff is friendly and professional; if you're in a hurry, they can serve your meal in record time. ✉ *1448 rue St-Mathieu,* ☎ *514/933–8414. Reservations essential. AE, DC, MC, V. Closed Sun.*

$–$$ ✕ **Pizzaiole.** Pizzaiole brought the first wood-fired pizza ovens to Montréal, and it's still the best in the field. Whether you choose a simple tomato-cheese, a ratatouille on a whole-wheat crust, or another of the approximately 30 possible combinations, all the pizzas are made to order and brought to your table piping hot. The calzone, with its rich, generous filling, is particularly satisfying. ✉ *1446A rue Crescent,* ☎ *514/845–4158;* ✉ *5100 rue Hutchison,* ☎ *514/274–9349. AE, DC, MC, V.*

Japanese

$$–$$$ ✕ **Katsura.** The sushi chefs in this elegant Japanese restaurant create an assortment of raw seafood delicacies, as well as their own delicious invention, the cone-shaped Canada roll (smoked salmon and salmon caviar). Other Japanese dishes are available as well. Service is excellent, but if you sample all the sushi, the tab can be exorbitant. ✉ *2170 rue de la Montagne,* ☎ *514/849–1172. Reservations essential. AE, DC, MC, V. No lunch weekends.*

Peruvian

$–$$ ✕ **Pucapuca.** Dark-green walls and Latin music give this bargain restaurant a vaguely junglelike atmosphere, and its mostly young aficionados give it a cheery air. But it's the Peruvian cooking and the great value that keep crowds coming back. The owner, Ciro Wong, serves up a particularly fine version of the classic Peruvian *papa huancaina,* a boiled potato covered with a spicy cheese sauce. Other items on the menu include grilled beef heart, rabbit with roasted peanuts, and grilled shark. ⊠ *5400 blvd. St-Laurent,* ☏ *514/272–8029. No credit cards. Closed Sun. and Mon.*

Polish

$–$$ ✕ **Café Stash.** On chilly nights many Montrealers turn to Café Stash in Vieux-Montréal for sustenance—for pork chops or duck, hot borscht, pierogi, or cabbage and sausage—in short, for all the hearty specialties of a Polish kitchen. Diners sit on pews from an old chapel at refectory tables from an old convent. ⊠ *200 rue St-Paul Ouest,* ☏ *514/ 845–6611. AE, MC, V.*

Portuguese

$$–$$$ ✕ **Café Ferriera.** This high-ceilinged room with pale-yellow walls is decorated with antique pottery and bottles of aged port. It makes an elegant setting for the "haute" version of Portuguese cuisine. The traditional *caldo verde,* or green soup, shares space on the menu with grilled fresh sardines, baked salt cod topped with tomato–onion–pepper salsa, and *arroz di marisco,* a paella-like dish rich with seafood, garlic, and onions. *1446 rue Peel,* ☏ *514/848–0988. AE, MC, V.*

Seafood

$$–$$$$ ✕ **Chez Delmo.** The long, shiny wooden bar is crammed at lunchtime with lawyers and businesspeople gobbling oysters and fish. In the back is a more relaxed and cheerful dining room. The poached salmon with hollandaise is a nice slab of perfectly cooked fish served with potatoes and broccoli. Also excellent are the arctic char and the Dover sole. ⊠ *211–215 rue Notre-Dame Ouest,* ☏ *514/849–4061. Reservations essential. AE, DC, MC, V. No dinner Mon. Closed Sun., 3 wks in midsummer, and 3 wks at Christmas.*

$$–$$$$ ✕ **Maestro S.V.P.** Posters, wine-red walls, etched glass, and a chalked menu board give this seafood spot a real bistro ambience. The dark-blue ceilings, matching glassware, and musical instruments displayed on the walls match the playfulness of the cooking. Oysters are the house specialty (dozens of different kinds from all over the world are always in stock), but the rest of the menu is impressive, too—a half-dozen variations on the mussels-and-fries theme, an excellent poached salmon with mango butter, and a truly bountiful fish and seafood pot-au-feu cooked in a tomato-basil sauce. Appetizers include meltingly tender calamari as well as shrimp dipped in beer batter, rolled in shredded coconut, and served with a marmalade and horseradish sauce. ⊠ *3615 blvd. St-Laurent,* ☏ *514/842–6447. AE, DC, MC, V.*

$$$ ✕ **Bleu Marin.** Fish here comes with an Italian touch. Antipasto Bleu Marin, for example, includes little plates of baby clams, mussels, and oysters with a light gratinée of crumbs and cheese. All fish are baked or steamed; a main course could be fillets of sea bass baked with olive oil, lemon juice, white wine, and capers. ⊠ *1437A rue Crescent,* ☏ *514/847–1123. AE, D, DC, MC, V.*

$–$$$ ✕ **La Sirène de la Mer.** You pick your fish at the fishmonger's next door, pay a modest, fixed price to have it cooked to your taste—panfried, deep-fried, grilled, poached, etc.—and then eat it at your table in this large, family-friendly restaurant. But don't let the freshness of the seafood lead you to overlook the excellent Lebanese lamb and goat dishes or the endless selection of excellent mezze. ⊠ *1805 rue Sauvé Ouest,* ☏ *514/332–2255. AE, DC, MC, V.*

Steak

$$$–$$$$ ✕ **Gibby's.** Although the extensive menu is rich in items such as broiled lobster and Cajun-blackened grouper, it was Gibby's first-class steaks—some say the best in the city—that made this restaurant famous. Gibby's also boasts an on-site bakery and makes its own ice cream. The thick gray-stone walls here date from 1825, and the attention to service and detail also seems to belong to another age. ✉ *298 pl. d'Youville,* ☎ *514/282–1837. AE, D, DC, MC, V.*

$$$–$$$$ ✕ **Moishe's.** The Lighter brothers still age their big, marbled steaks in their own cold rooms for 21 days before charcoal-grilling them, just the way their father did when he opened Moishe's in 1938. There are other things on the menu, such as lamb and grilled arctic char—but people come for the beef. The selection of single-malt Scotches is exquisite. ✉ *3961 blvd. St-Laurent,* ☎ *514/845–3509. AE, DC, MC, V. No lunch.*

$–$$ ✕ **Magnan.** The atmosphere in this tavern in working-class Pointe St-Charles is defiantly masculine. In fact, women didn't get full run of the place until 1988; before that they were tolerated only in a small, coed dining room. The decor is upscale warehouse, with a half-dozen television sets noisily stuck on professional sports. You can't beat the roast beef, though, and the steaks that range from 6 to 22 ounces; everyone from dock workers to corporate executives comes here. Other delicacies on the menu include salmon pie, a delightfully stodgy filler that makes great picnic fare, pigs' feet (*pattes de cochon*), and such soul-satisfying desserts as sugar pie. In summer the tavern adds Québec lobster to its menu and turns its parking lot into an outdoor dining area. It also has excellent beer from several local microbreweries on tap. ✉ *2602 rue St-Patrick,* ☎ *514/935–9647. AE, DC, MC, V.*

$–$$ ✕ **Mr. Steer.** This unpretentious restaurant with vinyl booths and plain beige walls has several things going for it: a great location in the heart of the downtown shopping district, friendly if brisk service, and the best hamburgers in Montréal. The thick, juicy, almost globular patties, discretely seasoned and served slightly *saignant* (rare) with a wide choice of almost unnecessary dressings and garnishes, are a worthy replacement for steak—although that's available, too, at reasonable prices. ✉ *1198 rue Ste-Catherine Ouest,* ☎ *514/866–3233. MC, V.*

Thai

$–$$ ✕ **Chao Phraya.** The huge front window of this bright, airy restaurant with its subtle flashes of Oriental decor overlooks fashionable rue Laurier, from which it draws many of its upscale customers. They come to feast on such classics as crunchy, multiflavored *poe pia* (imperial rolls), *pha koung* (grilled-shrimp salad), and fried halibut in red curry with lime juice. ✉ *50 rue Laurier Ouest,* ☎ *514/272–5339. Reservations essential. AE, DC, MC, V. No lunch.*

$–$$ ✕ **Salsa Thai.** It began as a tiny hole in the wall in Chinatown, but Salsa Thai's popularity enabled the owners to move into plusher digs on Square Dorchester. Prices are still reasonable, though, and portions are generous. Some appealing choices are hot-and-sour seafood soup with coconut milk; squid salad with onion, hot chilies, and mint leaves; and deep-fried whole pomfret (butterfish). Frogs' legs are fried with pepper, garlic, and sesame seeds; beef with *satay* sauce (a peanut-based sauce) comes on a sizzling-hot plate. ✉ *1237 rue Metcalfe,* ☎ *514/874–9047. MC, V.*

Vegetarian

$–$$ ✕ **Chu Chai.** Vegetarians can usually dine well in any Thai restaurant, even one that serves plenty of meat and fish dishes. But the chefs at

Chu Chai—rigorously vegan in their cooking—see no reason vegetarians shouldn't be able to enjoy the same classic Thai dishes as their meat-eating compatriots. So they cook up such delicacies as "duck" salad with pepper and mint leaves, "fish" with three hot sauces, and "beef" with yellow curry and coconut milk, substituting soy and seitan (a firm, chewy food made from wheat gluten) for the offending flesh. ✉ *4088 rue St-Denis,* ☎ *514/843–4194. Reservations essential. AE, DC, MC, V.*

$–$$ ✕ **Le Commensal.** The food at this Montréal-grown chain of vegetarian restaurants—heavy on salads, sandwiches, couscous, and delightfully "meaty" bean dishes—is served buffet style and sold by weight. There are at least seven outlets on the island, all of them big and bright with modern furniture; the nicest is on the second floor of a downtown building with big windows overlooking busy, fashionable rue McGill College. There's also one on rue St-Denis in the heart of the busy nightclub and shopping district and another on chemin Queen-Mary near the Oratoire St-Joseph. ✉ *1205 rue McGill College,* ☎ *514/871–1480;* ✉ *1720 rue St-Denis,* ☎ *514/845–2627;* ✉ *3715 chemin Queen Mary,* ☎ *514/733–9755. AE, DC, MC, V.*

LODGING

Keep in mind that during peak season (May through August) it may be difficult to find a bed without reserving, and most, but not all, hotels raise their prices. Rates often drop from mid-November to early April. Throughout the year a number of the better hotels have two-night, three-day double-occupancy packages that offer substantial discounts.

CATEGORY	COST*
$$$$	over $160
$$$	$120–$160
$$	$85–$120
$	under $85

All prices are for a standard double room, excluding 7.5% provincial sales tax, 7% goods-and-services tax (GST), and $2.30, in Canadian dollars.

$$$$ ▦ **Bonaventure Hilton International.** The large Hilton occupies the top
★ three floors of the Place Bonaventure exhibition center. From the outside, the massive building is uninviting, but you step off the elevator into an attractive reception area flanked by an outdoor swimming pool (heated year-round) and 2½ acres of rooftop gardens. The rooms have sleek modern furniture and pastel walls. The Bonaventure has excellent access to the Métro and the Underground City. ✉ *1 pl. Bonaventure, H5A 1E4,* ☎ *514/878–2332 or 800/267–2575,* FAX *514/028–1442,* WEB *www.hilton.com. 30 rooms, 1 suite. Restaurant, bar, in-room data ports, minibars, room service, pool, shops, meeting rooms, business services, parking. AE, D, DC, MC, V.*

$$$$ ▦ **Le Centre Sheraton.** This huge 37-story complex is well placed between the downtown business district and the restaurant-lined Crescent and Bishop streets. It offers services to both the business and tourist crowds. Rooms have coffeemakers, irons, and ironing boards. The 10-story Club section is geared toward business travelers, and there are lots of meeting rooms for conventions. The bar in the busy lobby is in a pleasant forest of potted trees, some of them 30 ft tall. ✉ *1201 blvd. René-Lévesque Ouest, H3B 2L7,* ☎ *514/878–2000 or 888/627–7102,* FAX *514/878–3958,* WEB *www.sheraton.com. 784 rooms, 25 suites. Restaurant, 2 bars, indoor pool, hair salon, health club, baby-sitting, business services, meeting rooms, parking. AE, D, DC, MC, V.*

Montréal Lodging

Ⓜ Édouard-Montpetit

blvd.

ch. de la Côte-Ste-Catherine

av. Laurier

blvd. St-Joseph

Villeneuve

Mont-Royal

Cimetière Mont-Royal

voie C. Houde

Parc du Mont-Royal

chemin Remembrance

av. des Pins

rue McTavish

av. Docteur-Penfield

rue Peel

av. Cedar

av. Cedar

rue du Musée

rue Redpath

rue Stanley

rue Drummond

rue de la Montagne

rue Simpson

Peel

Ⓜ

av. Atwater

rue Sherbrooke

rue Crescent

rue Bishop

rue Mackay

rue Guy

rue St-Mathieu

rue St-Marc

rue du Fort

Guy-Concordia

Ⓜ

Atwater

Ⓜ

Maisonneuve

Forum

blvd. de

rue Ste-Catherine

Lucien-L'Allier

Ⓜ

Bonave

P

blvd. Dorchester

blvd. René-Lévesque

rue St-Antoine

autoroute Ville-Marie

Georges-Vanier

Ⓜ

rue des Seigneurs

rue St-Jacques

rue Notre-Dame

rue Guy

rue de la N.

Lionel-Groulx

Ⓜ

Mont-Royal M

0   1/2 mile
0   500 meters

rue Villeneuve

av. du Mont-Royal

rue Marie-Anne

blvd. St-Laurent

de Bullion

av. Duluth

av. Laval

rue St-Denis

St-Urbain

rue Roy

av. des Pins

rue Prince-Arthur

rue Milton

rue Jeanne-Mance

av. du Parc

rue Aylmer

av. du Parc

rue Rachel

rue Berri

30

Parc
Lafontaine

av. du Parc Lafontaine

av. Calixa-Lavallée

rue Sherbrooke

av. de Lorimier

av. Papineau

Cherrier

Sherbrooke M
29

31

rue Ontario

Berri-
UQAM
M

St-Christophe

Amherst

Robin

Panet

M Beaudry

de Maisonneuve

rue Ste-Catherine

Université
Concordia Univesity

Université du
Québec à
Montréal

32

St-Hubert

18

19

rue Sherbrooke

20

av. du Président Kennedy

M St-Laurent

M McGill
17

av. McGill Col.

r. Cathca

av. Union

City Councillors
côte du Beaver Hall

rue de Bleury

28

Place
des Arts

blvd. René-Lévesque

Champ-
de-Mars
M

27

rue St-Antoine

rue de la Gauchetière

Place-
d'Armes
M

26

Nouveau Palais
de Justice

33

rue Bonsecours

Post Office

15

Belmont

rue University

av. Viger

Palais des
Congrès
de Montréal

25

Square
Victoria
M

21

rue Notre-Dame

23

24

rue St-Paul

rue St-Fr.-
Xavier

22

Place Bonaventure

rue Mansfield

rue Metcalfe

aventure M

13

14

rue de la Commune

autoroute Bonaventure

de la Montagne

rue Peel

rue Ottawa

rue Murray

Pont de la
Concorde

Fleuve Saint-Laurent

$$$$ ⊞ **Château Versailles.** The four turn-of-the-20th-century mansions that make up this property have shed their somewhat dowdy image to become a smart and trendy boutique hotel. The row of houses, in the Golden Square Mile, was built for some of the city's leading families. The rich decor and sumptuous furnishings now reflect the Beaux-Arts style of the architecture, with its high ceilings and plaster moldings. The ornate marble fireplaces in many of the guest rooms and public rooms are not just decorative—they actually work. ⊠ *1659 rue Sherbrooke Ouest, H3H 1E3,* ☎ *514/933–3611 or 800/933–8111,* ℻ *514/933–8401,* WEB *www.versailleshotels.com. 63 rooms, 2 suites. Restaurant, bar, breakfast room, in-room data ports, minibars, room service, sauna, gym, baby-sitting, dry cleaning, laundry service, concierge, business services, parking (fee). AE, DC, MC, V. CP.*

$$$$ ⊞ **Delta Montréal.** The Delta has the city's most complete exercise and pool facility and an extensive business center. The hotel's public areas spread over two stories and are decorated to look a bit like a French château, with a huge baronial chandelier and gold patterned carpets. Rooms are big, with plush broadloom, pastel walls, mahogany-veneer furniture, and windows that overlook the mountain or downtown. The Cordial Music bar serves lunch on weekdays. ⊠ *475 av. du Président-Kennedy, H3A 1J7,* ☎ *514/286–1986 or 800/268–1133,* ℻ *514/284–4306,* WEB *www.deltamontreal.com. 453 rooms, 8 suites. Restaurant, bar, 1 indoor and 1 outdoor pool, hot tub, sauna, aerobics, health club, squash, recreation room, video games, baby-sitting, business services, meeting rooms, parking. AE, D, DC, MC, V.*

$$$$ ⊞ **Fairmont Le Reine Elizabeth.** In the center of the city, this Canadian Pacific/Fairmont hotel sits on top of the Gare Centrale train station. The lobby is a bit too much like a railroad station—hordes march this way and that—but upstairs the rooms are modern, spacious, and spotless, with lush pale carpets, striped Regency wallpapers, and chintz bedspreads. The Penthouse floors—20 and 21—have business services, and the Gold Floor is a hotel within a hotel with its own elevator, check-in, and concierge. The hotel is home to the grand old Beaver Club. The hotel hosts many conventions. ⊠ *900 blvd. René-Lévesque Ouest, H3B 4A5,* ☎ *514/861–3511 or 800/441–1414,* ℻ *514/954–2256,* WEB *www.cphotels.ca. 1,064 rooms. 2 restaurants, 3 bars, indoor pool, hair salon, health club, baby-sitting, concierge floors, parking (fee). AE, D, DC, MC, V.*

$$$$ ⊞ **Hôtel le Germain.** The hotelier Christiane Germain turned a dowdy, outdated, downtown office building into a sleekly luxurious boutique hotel that includes two huge two-story apartments. The earth-tone rooms showcase Québec-designed bed and bathroom furnishings in dark, dense tropical woods. All rooms have individual sound systems, three phones, and an iron and ironing board; some have grand views of the skyscrapers along avenue du Président-Kennedy or of Mont-Royal. ⊠ *2050 rue Mansfield, H3A 1Y9,* ☎ *514/849–2050 or 877/333–2050,* ℻ *514/849–1437,* WEB *www.hotelgermain.com. 99 rooms, 2 apartments. Bar, breakfast room, in-room data ports, gym, meeting rooms, parking. AE, DC, MC, V. CP.*

$$$$ ⊞ **Hotel Inter-Continental Montréal.** On the edge of Vieux-Montréal, this luxury hotel is part of the Montréal World Trade Center, a block-long retail and office development. Rooms are in a modern 26-story brick tower with fanciful turrets and pointed roofs. They're large, with lush carpets, pastel walls, heavy drapes, and big windows overlooking downtown or Vieux-Montréal and the waterfront. The main lobby is home to Le Continent, which serves fine international cuisine. A footbridge across the Trade Center's mall links the hotel with the 18th-century Nordheimer Building, which houses many of the hotel's public rooms. ⊠ *360 rue St-Antoine Ouest, H2Y 3X4,* ☎ *514/987–9900 or 800/827–0200,* ℻ *514/847–8730,* WEB *montreal.interconti.com.*

334 rooms, 23 suites. 3 restaurants, bar, room service, indoor pool, sauna, health club, meeting rooms, parking. AE, D, DC, MC, V.

$$$$ 🔲 **Hôtel Place d'Armes.** Whether you're here for business or pleasure,
★ you couldn't ask for a better location. The Basilique Notre-Dame-de-Montréal is just across the square and the Palais de Congrès, the convention center, is 100 yards to the north. The building itself, once the Canadian headquarters of the Great Scottish Life Insurance Co., is a charmingly ornate example of Victorian business architecture. It has been converted into a comfortable boutique hotel with a fireplace and a bar in the lobby. Furnishings are contemporary, but some of the rooms have brick or stone walls. The bathrooms are tiled in black granite and white marble, and there are four duplex suites. A rooftop terrace with a view of Chinatown and the old city adds a crowning touch. ✉ *701 Côte de la Place d'Armes, H2Y 2X6,* ☎ *514/842–1887 or 888/450–1887,* FAX *514/842–6469,* WEB *www.hotelplacedarmes.com. 44 rooms, 4 suites. Restaurant, bar, room service, gym, parking. AE, DC, MC, V.*

$$$$ 🔲 **Hôtel Versailles.** In a modern 15-story building, this boutique hotel caters primarily to business travelers. The decor includes lots of wood paneling, rich mahogany trim, and textured earth-tone walls. ✉ *1808 rue Sherbrooke Ouest, H3H 1E5,* ☎ *514/933–8111 or 888/933–8111,* FAX *514/933–7102,* WEB *www.versailleshotels.com. 105 rooms, 2 suites. Restaurant, bar, breakfast room, in-room data ports, minibars, room service, gym, sauna, parking (fee). AE, DC, MC, V. CP.*

$$$$ 🔲 **Loews Hôtel Vogue.** Tall windows and a facade of polished rose gran-
★ ite grace this chic hotel in the heart of downtown. The lobby's focal point, L'Opéra Bar, has an expansive bay window overlooking the trendy rue de la Montagne. Room furnishings are upholstered with striped silk, and the beds are draped with lacy duvets. The bathrooms have whirlpool baths, televisions, and phones. ✉ *1425 rue de la Montagne, H3G 1Z3,* ☎ *514/285–5555 or 800/465–6654,* FAX *514/849–8903,* WEB *www.loewshotel.com. 126 rooms, 16 suites. Restaurant, bar, gym, parking (fee). AE, D, DC, MC, V.*

$$$$ 🔲 **Omni.** Color, flair, and marble bathrooms have been added to this
★ hotel's large, sunny rooms. Public rooms also have been refurbished. Opus II, a contemporary French restaurant, occupies a street-level atrium, which gives it the air of an upscale sidewalk café. A Chinese restaurant, the Zen, is in the basement. ✉ *1050 rue Sherbrooke Est, H3A 2R6,* ☎ *514/284–1110 or 800/843–6664,* FAX *514/845–3025,* WEB *www.omnihotels.com. 275 rooms, 25 suites. 2 restaurants, lobby lounge, minibars, room service, pool, hot tub, 2 saunas, health club, parking (fee). AE, D, DC, MC, V.*

$$$$ 🔲 **Pierre du Calvet** AD **1725.** Merchant Pierre du Calvet—a notorious
★ republican and Freemason—entertained Benjamin Franklin behind the stone walls of this 18th-century home in Vieux-Montréal. Today it's a bed-and-breakfast lavishly decorated with antique furniture and Oriental rugs. The French restaurant is first-rate, and the garden, filled with flowers and potted plants, is lovely. ✉ *405 rue Bonsecours, H2Y 3C3,* ☎ *514/282–1725,* FAX *514/282–0546,* WEB *www.pierreducalvet.com. 9 rooms. Dining room, parking. AE, D, DC, MC, V. BP.*

$$$$ 🔲 **Ritz-Carlton.** The guest rooms at Montréal's grandest hotel are a suc-
★ cessful blend of Edwardian style—some suites have working fireplaces—and such modern accessories as electronic safes. Careful and personal attention are hallmarks of the Ritz-Carlton's service: your shoes are shined, there's fresh fruit in your room, and everyone calls you by name. Power meals are the rule at Le Café de Paris, which also serves a formal afternoon tea. ✉ *1228 rue Sherbrooke Ouest, H3G 1H6,* ☎ *514/842–4212, 800/363–0366, 800/241–3333,* FAX *514/842–3383,* WEB *www.ritz-carlton.montreal.com. 201 rooms, 39 suites. Restaurant, bar, in-room safes, room service, barbershop, parking (fee). AE, DC, MC, V.*

$$$-$$$$ ⊞ **Auberge Bonaparte.** One of the finest restaurants in Vieux-Mont-
★ réal—Bonaparte—has converted the upper floors of its 19th-century
building into an inn. The rooms are decorated in pastels with wrought-
iron or Louis Philippe–style furniture. Some rooms have double whirl-
pool baths, and the back rooms (some with balconies) have views over
the private gardens of the Basilique Notre-Dame-de-Montréal. Break-
fast, included in the price, is served in your room, and you can order
dinner, too. ⊠ 447 rue St-François-Xavier, H2Y 2T1, ☎ 514/844–1448,
FAX 514/844–0272, WEB www.bonaparte.ca. 30 rooms, 1 suite. Restau-
rant, bar, meeting room, parking. AE, D, DC, MC, V. BP.

$$$-$$$$ ⊞ **Auberge de la Place Royale.** A 19th-century stone rooming house
has been converted into a charming waterfront bed-and-breakfast
overlooking the Vieux-Port. The 11 very spacious rooms are linked by
a magnificent old wooden staircase. The rooms are furnished with an-
tiques and antique reproductions, and some have whirlpool baths. Guests
are served a full breakfast on a sidewalk terrace in summer and in their
rooms in winter. The service is very attentive. ⊠ 115 rue de la Com-
mune Ouest, H2Y 2C7, ☎ 514/287–0522, FAX 514/287–1209, WEB
www.aubergeplaceroyale.com. 11 rooms. Café, parking. AE, DC, MC,
V. BP.

$$$-$$$$ ⊞ **Holiday Inn Select.** This Chinatown hotel is full of surprises, from
the two pagodas on the roof to the Chinese garden in the lobby. Its
restaurant, Chez Chine, is excellent. An executive floor has all the usual
business facilities. The hotel has a pool and a small gym, but guests
also have access to a plush private health and leisure club downstairs
with a whirlpool, saunas, a billiard room, and a bar. The hotel sits cater-
corner to the Palais des Congrès convention center and is a five-minute
walk from the World Trade Center. ⊠ 99 av. Viger Ouest, H2Z 1E9,
☎ 514/878–9888 or 888/878–9888, FAX 514/878–6341, WEB www.his-
elect-yul.com. 235 rooms. Restaurant, bar, indoor pool, gym, business
services, parking. AE, D, DC, MC, V.

$$$-$$$$ ⊞ **Hôtel du Fort.** All rooms here have good views of the city, the river,
or the mountain. The hotel is in the west end of downtown in a resi-
dential neighborhood known as Shaughnessy Village, close to shop-
ping at the Faubourg Ste-Catherine and Square Westmount, and just
around the corner from the Canadian Center for Architecture. Rates
include Continental breakfast served in a charming Louis XV lounge.
⊠ 1390 rue du Fort, H3H 2R7, ☎ 514/938–8333 or 800/565–6333,
FAX 514/938–2078, WEB www.hoteldufort.com. 127 rooms. Bar, gym,
parking. AE, DC, MC, V. CP.

$$$-$$$$ ⊞ **Hôtel de la Montagne.** A naked nymph rises out of the fountain in
the lobby, and an enormous crystal chandelier hangs from the ceiling.
The rooms are tamer, large, and comfortable. There's a piano bar and
a rooftop terrace, and a tunnel connects the hotel to Thursdays/Les Beaux
Jeudis, a popular singles bar, restaurant, and dance club. ⊠ 1430 rue
de la Montagne, H3G 1Z5, ☎ 514/288–5656 or 800/361–6262, FAX
514/288–9658, WEB www.hoteldelamontagne.com. 135 rooms. 2 restau-
rants, bar, piano bar, pool, concierge, parking. AE, D, DC, MC, V.

$$$ ⊞ **Le Marriott Château Champlain.** At the southern end of Place du
Canada is this 36-floor skyscraper with distinctive half-moon-shape
windows that give the rooms a Moorish feeling. The furniture is elegant and French and the bedspreads are brightly patterned. Underground passageways connect the Champlain with the Bonaventure
Métro station and Place Ville-Marie. ⊠ 1050 rue de la Gauchetière
Ouest, H3B 4C9, ☎ 514/878–9000 or 800/200–5909, FAX 514/878–
6761, WEB www.marriott.com. 611 rooms, 33 suites. Restaurant, bar,
no-smoking rooms, indoor pool, sauna, health club, parking. AE, DC,
MC, V.

$$–$$$ ⊡ **Auberge de la Fontaine.** The decor of this small hotel in the heart
★ of the trendy Plateau Mont-Royal district sounds wild—contrasting
purple and bare-brick walls, red molding, yellow walls, green ceilings—
but the hotel is delightful. Its rooms are in two adjoining turn-of-the-
20th-century residences; some have whirlpool baths and a few have
private balconies. Guests can use the little ground-floor kitchen and
take whatever they like from its refrigerator full of snacks. The hotel
is on one of the city's bicycle paths and across the street from Parc Lafontaine. ⊠ *1301 rue Rachel Est, H2J 2K1,* ☎ *514/597–0166 or 800/
597–0597,* ℻ *514/597–0496,* ⟦WEB⟧ *www.aubergedelafontaine.com. 21
rooms. Meeting rooms, parking. AE, DC, MC, V. BP.*

$$–$$$ ⊡ **Auberge du Vieux-Port.** A splendid little hotel—27 rooms over five
★ floors—backs onto fashionable rue St-Paul and overlooks the Vieux-
Port. The Vieux-Montréal building dates to the 1880s. Rooms have
stone or brick walls, tall casement windows, brass beds, and massive
exposed beams; many have whirlpool tubs. In summer, guests can
watch the fireworks competitions from a rooftop terrace. Rates include
a full breakfast in Les Remparts, the hotel's French restaurant. ⊠ *97
rue de la Commune Est, H2Y 1J1,* ☎ *514/876–0081,* ℻ *514/876–8923,*
⟦WEB⟧ *www.aubergeduvieuxport.com. 27 rooms. Restaurant. AE, DC, MC,
V. BP.*

$$–$$$ ⊡ **Auberge les Passants du Sans Soucy.** A little gem on rue St-Paul,
★ this is one of the most romantic city hostelries you'll find anywhere,
with brass beds, stone walls, exposed beams, soft lighting, whirlpool
baths, and lots of fresh-cut flowers. The inn is a former fur warehouse
that dates from 1836; the foundations date from 1684. The lobby doubles as an art gallery that opens onto the street. Behind it are a living
room and a breakfast room separated by a fireplace that crackles with
burning hardwood in winter. ⊠ *171 rue St-Paul Ouest, H2Y 1Z5,* ☎
514/842–2634, ℻ *514/842–2912. 9 rooms, 1 suite. Breakfast room.
AE, MC, V. BP.*

$$–$$$ ⊡ **Le Nouvel Hôtel.** This hotel has brightly colored and functional stu-
dios and 2½-room apartments. It's near the restaurants and bars on
rues Crescent, de la Montagne, and Bishop and is two blocks from the
Guy-Concordia Métro station. ⊠ *1740 blvd. René-Lévesque Ouest,
H3H 1R3,* ☎ *514/931–8841 or 800/363–6063,* ℻ *514/931–3233,* ⟦WEB⟧
*www.lenouvelhotel.com. 126 rooms. Restaurant, bar, pool, comedy club.
AE, DC, MC, V.*

$$–$$$ ⊡ **Renaissance Montréal.** The L-shaped brick tower has large, bright
rooms decorated in modern earth tones, a comfortable lobby bar, and
a good restaurant, but it's the location that sets it apart. It overlooks
Parc du Mont-Royal, which is close enough for athletic guests to consider jogging on its trails. The McGill University campus is a five-minute
walk to the west and downtown is not much farther. ⊠ *3625 av. du
Parc, H2X 3P8,* ☎ *514/288–6666 or 800/363–0735,* ℻ *514/288–2469,*
⟦WEB⟧ *www.renaissancehotels.com. 455 rooms. Restaurant, bar, café,
no-smoking floor, parking. AE, D, DC, MC, V.*

$$ ⊡ **Hôtel de l'Institut.** The upper floors of Québec's leading hotel
school—the Institut de Tourisme et d'Hôtellerie du Québec—house hotel
rooms where students can learn how to pamper guests. The building
is gracelessly modern, but it overlooks charming Square St-Louis. The
Restaurant Salle Gérard-Delage is staffed by student waiters and chefs.
⊠ *3535 rue St-Denis, H2X 3P1,* ☎ *514/282–5120 or 800/361–5111,*
℻ *514/873–9893,* ⟦WEB⟧ *www.hotel.ithq.qc.ca. 42 rooms. Restaurant,
parking. AE, MC, V.*

$–$$ ⊡ **Hôtel Lord Berri.** Rooms in this hotel near the restaurants and
nightlife of rue St-Denis have brightly colored bedspreads, modern fur-
niture, and in-room movies. The restaurant, Il Cavaliere, serves Italian food and is popular with locals. ⊠ *1199 rue Berri, H2L 4C6,* ☎

514/845–9236 or 888/363–0363, FAX *514/849–9855,* WEB *www.lord-berri.com. 154 rooms. Restaurant, no-smoking floor, meeting rooms, parking. AE, DC, MC, V.*

$ ☷ **Hostelling International.** This hostel in the heart of downtown has same-sex dorms that sleep 4, 6, or 10 people. Members pay $19 for a bed, and nonmembers $24.16 (tax included). Some rooms are available for couples and families. There are kitchen facilities and lockers for valuables. Reserve early during summer. ✉ *1030 rue MacKay, H3G 2H1,* ☎ *514/843–3317,* FAX *514/934–3251,* WEB *www.hostelling-montreals.com. 243 beds. Café, coin laundry. AE, DC, MC, V.*

$ ☷ **Hôtel l'Abri du Voyageur.** Price and location are this hotel's main selling points, but it also manages to squeeze in some unassuming charm: high ceilings, bare-brick walls, original pine and maple floors, and paintings by local artists. The hotel's three floors are over a restaurant in a pre–World War I commercial building. Each room has a TV and a sink. ✉ *9 rue Ste-Catherine Ouest, H2X 1Z5,* ☎ *514/849–2922,* FAX *514/499–0151,* WEB *www.abri-voyageur.ca. 30 rooms with shared bath. Parking. AE, MC, V.*

$ ☷ **Hôtel Tajmahal.** The Tajmahal is adjacent to the Terminus Voyageur bus station (buses park directly beneath one wing of the hotel), and some of the bus-station aura has rubbed off on the place: it's a little dingy. But if you're stumbling after a long bus ride and want somewhere to stay *now*, the rooms are large and clean, the service is friendly, and the price is right. It's also handy to the Berri-UQAM Métro station. ✉ *1600 rue St-Hubert, H2L 3Z3,* ☎ *514/849–3214 or 800/363–5260,* FAX *514/849–9812. 147 rooms. Restaurant, parking. AE, MC, V.*

$ ☷ **McGill Student Apartments.** From mid-May to mid-August, when McGill is on summer recess, you can stay in its dorms on the grassy, quiet campus in the heart of the city. Nightly rates are $32 for students, $38 for nonstudents (single rooms only); some more-expensive rooms include a kitchenette. As a visitor, you may use the campus swimming pool and gym facilities for a fee. The university cafeteria is also open during the week, serving breakfast and lunch. Be sure to book early. ✉ *3935 rue University, H3A 2B4,* ☎ *514/398–6367,* FAX *514/398–6770. 1,000 rooms with shared bath. Kitchenettes (some). MC, V.*

$ ☷ **Université de Montréal Residence.** The university's student housing accepts visitors from early May to late August. It's on the other side of Mont-Royal from downtown and Vieux-Montréal but next to the Edouard-Monpetit Métro station. The rooms have phones for local calls; common lounges have microwaves and TVs. For a fee you may use the campus sports facilities. Rates are $23 per night or $141 per week—$87.50 a week if you book for at least three weeks. ✉ *2350 blvd. Edouard-Montpetit, H3T 1J4,* ☎ *514/343–6531,* FAX *514/343–2353. 1,119 rooms with shared bath. MC, V.*

$ ☷ **YMCA.** This clean Y is downtown, next to Peel Métro station. Men should book at least two days in advance; women should book seven days ahead, because there are fewer rooms with showers for them. Anyone staying summer weekends must book at least a week ahead. There is a full gym facility and a typical Y cafeteria. ✉ *1450 rue Stanley, H3A 2W6,* ☎ *514/849–8393,* FAX *514/849–7821. 353 rooms, 3 with bath. Cafeteria, gym. AE, MC, V.*

$ ☷ **YWCA.** Very close to dozens of restaurants, the Y is downtown, one block from rue Ste-Catherine. Men can use the overnight facilities and gym, too. If you want a room with any amenities, you must book in advance; not all the rooms come with a sink and bath. There are single, double, and triple rooms. ✉ *1355 blvd. René-Lévesque Ouest, H3G 1T3,* ☎ *514/866–9941,* FAX *514/861–1603. 63 rooms. Café, indoor pool, sauna, aerobics, gym. MC, V.*

NIGHTLIFE AND THE ARTS

The Friday Preview section of the *Gazette*, the English-language daily paper, has an especially good list of all events at the city's concert halls, theaters, clubs, dance spaces, and movie houses. Other publications listing what's on include the *Mirror, Hour, Scope,* and *Voir* (in French), distributed free at restaurants and other public places.

For tickets to major pop and rock concerts, shows, festivals, and hockey and baseball games, you can go to the individual box offices or call **Admission** (☎ 514/790–1245 or 800/361–4595). Tickets to Théâtre St-Denis and other venues are available via **Ticketmaster** (☎ 514/790–1111).

The Arts

Cinema

Newly released movies are shown in both English and French in several multiscreen complexes. Montréal's main repertory cinema theater is **Cinéma du Parc** (⊠ 3575 av. du Parc, ☎ 514/281–1900). The **Cinémathèque Québécoise** (⊠ 335 blvd. de Maisonneuve Est, ☎ 514/842–9763) has a collection of 25,000 Québec, Canadian, and foreign films, as well as a display of equipment dating from the early days of film. Cinephiles can browse through the national Film Board of Canada collection of 6,000 documentaries, dramas, short features, and animated flicks at the **CinéRobothèque** (⊠ 1564 rue St-Denis, ☎ 514/496–6887). At the **Ciné Express Café** (⊠ 1926 rue Ste-Catherine Ouest, ☎ 514/939–CINE), you can drop in for a drink, a bistro-style meal, and an old flick. The tiny, 83-seat **Cinéma Parallèle** (⊠ 3682 blvd. St-Laurent, ☎ 514/847–9272) opened in 1978 to show *cinéma d'auteur* to dyed-in-the-wool film buffs. The most elaborate of Montréal's cinemas is the **Famous Players Paramount** (⊠ 707 rue Ste-Catherine Ouest, ☎ 514/842–5828), in the old Simpson building. It has two IMAX theaters in addition to 15 rooms with regular screens.

Circus

The **Cirque du Soleil** (☎ 800/361–4595) is one of Montréal's great success stories. The company began revolutionizing the ancient art of circus when it opened in a blue-and-yellow striped tent on the Montréal waterfront in 1984. Since then it has become an international phenomenon—its combination of dance, acrobatics, glorious costumes, and dramatic presentation filling multimillion-dollar permanent theaters in Las Vegas and at Disney World in Florida, while touring companies attract adoring crowds all over North America, Europe, and Asia. Every second summer (in odd-numbered years), the circus sets up its tent in the city of its birth. It no longer plays on the waterfront, however, but on the grounds around its corporate headquarters and training school in a rather bleak neighborhood in northeast Montréal.

Dance

Traditional and contemporary dance companies thrive in Montréal, though many take to the road or are on hiatus in the summer. **Ballets Classiques de Montréal** (☎ 514/866–1771) performs mostly classical programs. **Les Ballets Jazz de Montréal** (☎ 514/982–6771) experiments with new musical forms. The leading Québec company is **Les Grands Ballets Canadiens** (☎ 514/849–0269). **LaLaLa Human Steps** (☎ 514/277–9090) is an avant-garde, exciting powerhouse of a group. **Margie Gillis Fondation de Danse** (☎ 514/845–3115) gives young dancers and choreographers opportunities to develop their art. **Montréal Danse** (☎ 514/871–4005) is a contemporary dance repertory company. **Ouest Vertigo Danse** (☎ 514/251–9177) stages innovative, postmodern performances. **Tangente** (☎ 514/525–5584) is a nucleus for many of the more avant-garde dance troupes.

Montréal's dancers have a downtown performance and rehearsal space, the **Agora Dance Theatre** (✉ 840 rue Chérrier Est, ☎ 514/525–1500), affiliated with the Université du Québec à Montréal dance faculty. Every other September (in odd-numbered years), the **Festival International de Nouvelle Danse** (☎ 514/287–1423 for tickets) brings "new" dance to various venues around town. Tickets for this event always sell quickly. When not on tour, many dancers can be seen at Place des Arts or at any of the **Maisons de la Culture** (☎ 514/872–6211) performance spaces around town.

Music

The city is home to one of the best chamber orchestras in Canada, I **Musici de Montréal** (☎ 514/982–6037). McGill University's Pollack Concert Hall (☎ 514/398–4535) presents concerts, notably by the **McGill Chamber Orchestra.** The **Orchestre Métropolitain de Montréal** (☎ 514/598–0870) stars at Place des Arts most weeks during the October–April season. The **Orchestre Symphonique de Montréal** (☎ 514/842–9951) has gained world renown under the baton of Charles Dutoit. When the group is not on tour, its regular venue is the Salle Wilfrid-Pelletier at the Place des Arts. The orchestra also gives Christmas and summer concerts in Basilique Notre-Dame-de-Montréal and pop concerts at the Arena Maurice Richard in Olympic Park. Also check the *Gazette* listings for its free summertime concerts in Montréal's city parks.

The **Spectrum** (✉ 318 rue Ste-Catherine Ouest, ☎ 514/861–5851) is an intimate concert hall. **Stade Olympique** (✉ Olympic Park, 4141 av. Pierre-de-Coubertin, ☎ 514/252–8687) hosts rock and pop concerts. The 2,500-seat **Théâtre St-Denis** (✉ 1594 rue St-Denis, ☎ 514/849–4211), the second-largest auditorium in Montréal, stages a wide range of pop-music concerts performed in both languages, from Maritime folk singer Rita MacNeil to Québécois heartthrob Roch Voisine.

Opera

L'Opéra de Montréal (☎ 514/985–2258) stages four productions a year at Place des Arts.

Theater

French speakers can find a wealth of dramatic productions. There are at least 10 major companies in town, some of which have an international reputation. The choices for Anglophones are more limited. **Théâtre Denise Pelletier** (✉ 4353 rue Ste-Catherine Est, ☎ 514/253–8974) puts on a wide range of productions in a beautifully restored Italianate hall. Named for one of Québec's best loved actors, the **Théâtre Jean Duceppe** (☎ 514/842–2112) stages major productions in the Place des Arts. **Théâtre de Quat'Sous** (✉ 100 av. des Pins Est, ☎ 514/845–7277) performs modern, experimental, and cerebral plays. **Théâtre du Nouveau Monde** (✉ 84 rue Ste-Catherine Ouest, ☎ 514/866–8667) is the North American temple of French classics. Modern French repertoire is the specialty at **Théâtre du Rideau Vert** (✉ 4664 rue St-Denis, ☎ 514/844–1793).

The **Centaur Theatre** (✉ 453 rue St-François-Xavier, ☎ 514/288–3161), the best-known English theatrical company, stages everything from musical revues to Eugène Ionesco works in the former stock-exchange building in Vieux-Montréal. **Infinitheatre** (☎ 514/288–3161) stages contemporary and experimental plays and shows in various venues around the city. **Place des Arts** (✉ 175 rue Ste-Catherine Ouest, ☎ 514/842–2112, WEB www.pda.qc.ca) is a favorite venue for visiting productions. English-language plays can be seen at the **Saidye Bronfman Centre** (✉

5170 chemin de la Côte Ste-Catherine, ☏ 514/739–2301 or 514/739–7944), a multidisciplinary institution that is a focus of cultural activity for Montréal as a whole and for the Jewish community in particular. Many activities, such as gallery exhibits, lectures, performances, and concerts, are free. The center is home to the Yiddish Theatre Group. Touring Broadway productions can often be seen at the **Théâtre St-Denis** (✉ 1594 rue St-Denis, ☏ 514/849–4211), especially in summer.

Festivals

Montréal loves a party, and every summer festivals are held to celebrate everything from beer to Yiddish theater; here are some of the largest.

At the **Concours d'Art International Pyrotechnique** (International Fireworks Competition; ☏ 514/935–5161 or 800/678 5440; 800/361–4595 in Canada), held weekends in late June and July (call for exact dates), teams from around the world compete to see who can best light up the sky in a show that combines fireworks and music. Their launch site is La Ronde, on Île Ste-Hélène, and you can buy a ticket, which includes an amusement-park pass and a reserved seat with a view, but thousands of Montrealers fill the Jacques-Cartier Bridge to watch the show for nothing, and hundreds more take their lawn chairs and blankets down to the Vieux-Port or across the river to the park along the south shore and watch the show. They bring radios to pick up the musical accompaniment for the fireworks.

Such international stars as Denzel Washington, Bette Midler, Ben Kingsley, and Charlie Sheen show up for the **Festival International des Films du Monde** (World Film Festival; ☏ 514/848–3883) at the end of August and the beginning of September. They compete for the Grand Prix of the Americas. This is the only competitive North American film festival recognized by the International Federation of Film Producers' Associations and usually screens about 400 films in a dozen ventures, some of them outdoors.

The **Festival International de Jazz de Montréal** (tickets: ☏ 514/790–1245 or 800/678–5440; 800/361–4595 in Canada), the world's biggest jazz festival, brings together 2,000 musicians for more than 400 concerts over a period of 11 days, from the end of June to the beginning of July. Big names who have appeared in the past include Chick Corea, Count Basie, Ella Fitzgerald, France's Orchéstre National de Barbes, and Canada's hottest singer–pianist, Diana Krall. About three-fourths of the concerts are presented free on outdoor stages for lively audiences who sing, clap, and dance to the music. You can also hear blues, Latin rhythms, gospel, Cajun, and world music. **Bell Info-Jazz** (☏ 514/871–1881 or 888/515–0515) answers all queries about the Festival International de Jazz de Montréal and about travel packages.

The **Festival Juste pour Rire** (Just for Laughs Comedy Festival; ☏ 514/790–4242) begins in early July; the comics show up for a 12-day festival that attracts about 650 performers and 350,000 spectators. Big names in the past have included Jerry Seinfeld, Drew Carey, Marcel Marceau, and Sandra Bernhard. Canadian comics including Mike McDonald and Bowser and Blue also got their start at this festival.

The **FrancoFolies** (☏ 514/876–8989) celebrates the art of French songwriting and is one of the most important festivals of its type in the world. Such major French stars as Isabelle Boulay and Michel Rivard play to packed concert halls while lesser-known artists from all over the world play free outdoor concerts on the plaza at the Place des Arts. Performers come from just about every country and region where French is spoken—and sung—as well as from the other Canadian provinces. In all, more than 1,000 musicians perform in dozens of different styles, including rock, hip-hop, jazz, funk, and Latin.

Montréal en Lumière (Montréal Highlights festival; ☎ 514/288–9955) is designed to brighten the the bleak days of February, both literally and figuratively. One of the main aspects of this multifaceted mid-winter festival, which began in 2000, is the art of illumination. For every festival, experts artfully illuminate a few historic buildings. Food, too, is a major ingredient in the fun. Such leading world chefs as Paul Bocuse of France come to town to give lessons and demonstrations and to take over the kitchens of some of the leading restaurants. Outdoor and indoor concerts, ice-sculpture displays, plays, dance recitals, and other cultural events are also scheduled during the festival.

Nightlife

Club Med World (✉ 954 rue Ste-Catherine Ouest, ☎ 514/393–3003), at press time, was scheduled to open in mid-2001 in a refurbished classic movie theater. The international resort company's second "urban resort" (the first is in Paris), it encompasses bars and bistros, shows, concerts, dancing spots, and circus acts.

When the Montréal Canadiens hockey team moved to the Centre Molson in 1996—abandoning the old Forum, which had been their home for more than 70 years and a shrine for hockey fans everywhere—developers gutted the old place and re-opened it as the **Forum Entertainment Centre** (✉ 2313 rue Ste-Catherine Ouest, ☎ 514/933–6786 or 888/933–6786), a one-stop entertainment center with cinemas, restaurants, high-tech games, free shows, and dance bars.

Bars

Professionals and journalists who work in Vieux Montréal keep **Bistro Au Cépage** (✉ 212 rue Notre-Dame Ouest, ☎ 514/845–5436) lively with talk and debate all week. There's good food, too. Rich wood decor and an impressive selection of single-malt whiskies make the **Ile Noir** (✉ 342 rue Ontario Est, ☎ 514/982–0866) one of the more exclusive bars in town. As the name suggests, **Sofa** (✉ 451 rue Rachel Est, ☎ 514/285–1011) is a comfortable place to sip a port or a Scotch. You can argue about anything you like at **Stogie's Café and Cigars** (✉ 2015 rue Crescent, ☎ 514/848–0069), except the merits of smoking. The cleverly named **Le Swimming** (✉ 3643 blvd. St-Laurent, ☎ 514/ 282–7665) is a vast upscale pool lounge ("pool hall" just isn't genteel enough) that's very popular with the young and fashionable. **Winnie's** (✉ 1455 rue Crescent, ☎ 514/288–0623) gets its name from Winston Churchill and draws its clientele from the young and ambitious professionals and entrepreneurs who work downtown. **Ziggy's Pub** (✉ 1470 rue Crescent, ☎ 514/285–8855) bills itself as the place "where nobody knows your name," but it's actually quite friendly in a brusque way.

Casino

The **Casino de Montréal** (✉ 1 av. du Casino, ☎ 514/392–2746 or 800/ 665–2274), on Île Notre-Dame in the St. Lawrence River, is one of the world's 10 biggest, with 3,000 slot machines and 120 tables for baccarat, blackjack, and roulette. The casino has a strict dress code, and croupiers are trained in politeness as well as math. There are some oddities for those used to Vegas: no drinking on the floor, and no tipping the croupiers. Craps wasn't introduced until summer 2000, because dice games had been illegal in Canada. The casino, which is open 24 hours, is a $10 cab ride from downtown, or you can take the Métro to the Île Ste-Hélène station and transfer to Bus 167. Driving here is a hassle.

Comedy

The **Comedy Nest** (✉ 4020 rue Ste-Catherine Ouest, ☎ 514/932–6378) has shows by name performers and up-and-comers, and offers dinner-

and-show packages. Both amateurs and professionals work **Comedy-works** (⊠ 1238 rue Bishop ☎ 514/398–9661), and the acts tend to be a little more risqué than the ones at the Comedy Nest.

Dance Clubs

Montréal's love affair with Latin dance is one of long standing; even before the current craze, the Québecois took dancing seriously. Serious dancers of all ages and ethnic backgrounds head for **Cactus** (⊠ 4461 rue St-Denis, ☎ 514/849–0349), where the music is rigorously authentic and the floor is always packed. One of the most popular Latin clubs in Montréal is **Salsathèque** (⊠ 1220 rue Peel, ☎ 514/875–0016).

House, pop, retro, and salsa play the night away in the crowded **Bar Minuit** (⊠ 115 rue Laurier Ouest, ☎ 514/271–2110) on fashionable rue Laurier. **Club 737** (⊠ 1 Place Ville-Marie, ☎ 514/397–0737), on top of Place Ville-Marie, does the disco number every Thursday, Friday, and Saturday night. This has become very popular with the upscale, mid-twenties to mid-thirties crowd. The view is magnificent and there's an open-air rooftop bar. **Hard Rock Cafe** (⊠ 1458 rue Crescent, ☎ 514/987–1420) is Montréal's branch of the chain. For something on the funky side, try the **Jello Bar** (⊠ 151 rue Ontario Est, ☎ 514/285–2621); the furnishings (chairs, sofas, lamps, and decorations) are from 1960s suburban living rooms, and the music varies from night to night—salsa, swing, jazz—with live performances on weekends. **Kokino** (⊠ 3556 blvd. St-Laurent, ☎ 514/848–6398) is *the* place for the beautiful people, with jazz, Brazilian, and house music. **Thursdays/Les Beaux Jeudis** (⊠ 1449 rue Crescent, ☎ 514/288–5656) is a popular dance club that doesn't open until 10 PM.

Folk Music

An enthusiastic crowd sings along with Québécois performers at **Boîte à Chansons Aux Deux Pierrots** (⊠ 104 rue St-Paul Est, ☎ 514/861–1270). **Hurley's Irish Pub** (⊠ 1225 rue Crescent, ☎ 514/861–4111) attracts some of the city's best Celtic musicians and dancers. Celtic fiddlers from all over Canada and indeed the world put in appearances at **McKibbin's Irish Pub** (⊠ 1426 rue Bishop, ☎ 514/288–1580).

Jazz

Downtown, duck into **Biddle's** (⊠ 2060 rue Aylmer, ☎ 514/842–8656), where bassist Charles Biddle holds forth most evenings. Biddle's serves pretty good ribs and chicken. The best-known jazz club in the city is Vieux-Montréal's **L'Air du Temps** (⊠ 191 rue St-Paul Ouest, ☎ 514/842–2003). The small, smoky club presents 90% local talent and 10% international acts from 5 PM on into the night.

Rock

Rock clubs seem to spring up, flourish, then fizzle out overnight. **Club Soda** (⊠ 1225 blvd. St-Laurent, ☎ 514/286–1010), the granddaddy of all city rock clubs, moved to bigger digs in 2000: a high narrow concert hall with high-tech decor and 500 seats—all of them good. The club is open only for shows; phone the box office to find out what's on. The busy, smoky **Le Balattou** (⊠ 4372 blvd. St-Laurent, ☎ 514/845–5447) specializes in African and Caribbean music. Pushing the envelope with its music and its performances is what **Foufounes Electriques** (⊠ 87 rue Ste-Catherine Est, ☎ 514/844–5539) does best, which is just about what you'd expect from a club whose name means "electric buttocks." **L'Ours Qui Fume** (⊠ 2019 rue St-Denis, ☎ 514/845–6998), or the Smoking Bear, is loud, raucous, and very Francophone. You might try the **Quai des Brumes Dancing** (⊠ 4481 rue St-Denis, ☎ 514/499–0467) for house and techno-rave music. The most popular performance venue for rock bands in Montréal is **Spectrum** (⊠ 318 rue Ste-Catherine Ouest, ☎ 514/861–5851).

OUTDOOR ACTIVITIES AND SPORTS

Most Montrealers would probably claim they hate winter, but the city is rich in cold-weather activities—skating rinks, cross-country ski trails, and toboggan runs. In summer there are tennis courts, miles of bicycle trails, golf courses, and two lakes for boating and swimming.

Participant Sports

Biking

Despite the bitter winters (or perhaps because of them), Montréal has fallen in love with the bicycle. On the first Sunday of every June, more than 45,000 cyclists of all ages and sizes celebrate the arrival of summer by taking part in the **Tour de l'Île de Montréal,** a 70-km (43-mi) bike ride through the city streets. More than 350 km (217 mi) of cycling paths crisscross the metropolitan area, and bikes are welcome on the first and last cars of Métro trains during non–rush hours. Ferries at the Vieux-Port take cyclists to Île Ste-Hélène and the south shore of the St. Lawrence River, where they can connect to hundreds of miles of trails in the Montérégie region.

The most popular trail on the island begins at the Vieux-Port and follows the 1825 **Lachine Canal** from Vieux-Montréal to the shores of Lac St-Louis in suburban Lachine. Along the way you can stop at the bustling Atwater Farmer's Market (⌷ 110 av. Atwater) to buy the makings of a picnic. **Parks Canada** (☏ 514/283–6054 or 514/637–7433) conducts guided cycling tours along the Lachine Canal every summer weekend. The Lachine Canal is part of the **Pôle des Rapides** (☏ 514/732–7303), a network of more than 96 km (60 mi) of nearby bicycle trails that follow lakefronts, canals, and aqueducts.

You can rent bicycles at **Vélo Aventure** (☏ 514/847–0666), on the grounds of the Vieux-Port. At the **Maison des Cyclistes** (⌷ 1251 rue Rachel Est, ☏ 514/521–8356), you can drop in to sip a coffee in the Bicicletta café or to browse the maps in the adjoining boutique.

Boating

In Montréal you can get in a boat at a downtown wharf and be crashing through Class V white water minutes later. Jack Kowalski of **Lachine Rapids Tours Ltd.** (⌷ 47 rue de la Commune, or quai de l'Horloge, ☏ 514/284–9607) takes thrill seekers on a one-hour voyage through the rapids in big aluminum jet boats. He supplies heavy-water gear. You can also choose a half-hour trip around the islands in 10-passenger boats that can go about 100 kph (62 mph). Reservations are required; trips are narrated in French and English. There are five trips daily through the rapids from May through September; the cost is $53. Rafting trips are also available.

Golf

For a complete listing of the many golf courses in the Montréal area, call **Tourisme Québec** (☏ 514/873–2015 or 800/363–7777).

Ice-Skating

The city has at least 195 outdoor and 21 indoor rinks. There are huge ones on Île Ste-Hélène and at the Vieux-Port. Call the **Parks and Recreation Department** (☏ 514/872–6211) for information. You can skate year-round in the **Atrium le Mille de la Gauchetière** (⌷ 1000 rue de la Gauchetière, ☏ 514/395–0555 Ext. 237).

Jogging

There are paths in most city parks, but for running with a panoramic view, head to the dirt track in **Parc du Mont-Royal** (take rue Peel, then the steps up to the track).

Skiing

Trails crisscross most city parks, including Parc des Îles, Maisonneuve, and Mont-Royal, but the best are probably the 46 km (29 mi) in the 900-acre **Cap St-Jacques Regional Park** (⊠ off blvd. Gouin, ☎ 514/280–6871) in Pierrefonds, on the west end of Montréal Island. The **Lachine Canal** trail also is used by cross-country skiers in winter.

DOWNHILL

Northwest of the city are the Laurentian Mountains, a winter and summer playground for Montrealers. The closest, decent-size Laurentian ski hill is **Mont St-Sauveur** (☎ 514/871–0101), with a vertical drop of 700 ft; it's about an hour's drive from Montréal. Skiers travel to the Eastern Townships southeast of the city, to ski on the Appalachians. The closest hill—about a 1¼-hr drive from the Champlain Bridge—is **Bromont** (☎ 450/534–2200), with a vertical drop of 1,329 ft. There's a small ski slope in Parc du Mont-Royal. **Mont St-Bruno** (☎ 450/653–3441), on the south shore, has a modest vertical drop of 443 ft, but it has Québec's biggest ski school, a high-speed chairlift, and offers night skiing. A "Ski-Québec" brochure is available from **Tourisme Québec** (☎ 514/873–2015 or 800/363–7777).

Swimming

Four indoor pools at Olympic Park's **Centre Aquatique** (⊠ 4141 av. Pierre-de-Coubertin, ☎ 514/252–4622) are public. **Centre Sportif et des Loisirs Claude-Robillard** (⊠ 1000 av. Emile-Journault, ☎ 514/872–6900) has a big indoor pool. The outdoor pool on Île Ste-Hélène is a popular (and crowded) gathering place, open June to early September. **Plage de l'Île Notre-Dame** is the only natural swimming hole in Montréal.

Tennis

The Jeanne-Mance, Kent, Lafontaine, and Somerled parks have public courts. For details call the **Parks and Recreation Department** (☎ 514/872–6211).

Windsurfing and Sailing

Sailboards and small sailboats can be rented at **L'École de Voile de Lachine** (⊠ 2105 blvd. St-Joseph, Lachine, ☎ 514/634–4326).

Spectator Sports

Baseball

The National League's **Montréal Expos** (☎ 514/253–3434 or 800/463–9767) play at Olympic Stadium April through September.

Football

The **Montréal Alouettes** (☎ 514/871–2266 for information; 514/871–2255 for tickets) of the Canadian Football League plays the Canadian version of the game—bigger field, just three downs, and a more wide-open style—under open skies at McGill University's Molson Stadium June through October. It's one of the best sporting deals in town.

Grand Prix

The annual **Air Canada Grand Prix du Canada** (☎ 514/350–4731; 514/350–0000 for tickets), which draws top Formula 1 racers from around the world, takes place every June at Circuit Gilles Villeneuve on Île Notre-Dame. Starting in late summer 2002, the course is also to host the Molson Indy of Montréal, a race sanctioned by the CART FedEx Championship Series.

Hockey

The **Montréal Canadiens** (⊠ 1250 rue de la Gauchetière Ouest, ☎ 514/932–2582), winners of 23 Stanley Cups, meet National Hockey League rivals at the Centre Molson October through April. Buy tickets in advance.

SHOPPING

Montrealers *magasinent* (go shopping) with a vengeance, so it's no surprise that the city has 160 multifaceted retail areas encompassing some 7,000 stores. The law allows shops to stay open weekdays 9–9 and weekends 9–5. However, many merchants close evenings Monday through Wednesday and on Sunday. Many specialty service shops are closed on Monday, too. Just about all stores, with the exception of some bargain outlets and a few selective art and antiques galleries, accept major credit cards. Most purchases are subject to a federal goods and services tax (GST) of 7% as well as a provincial tax of 8%. International visitors can claim a refund of some of these taxes, however.

If you think you might be buying fur, it's wise to check with your country's customs officials before your trip to find out which animals are considered endangered and cannot be imported. Do the same if you think you might be buying Inuit carvings, many of which are made of whalebone and ivory and cannot be brought into the United States.

Department Stores

La Baie (the Bay; ⊠ 585 rue Ste-Catherine Ouest, ☎ 514/281–4422) has been a department store since 1891. It's known for its duffel coats and Hudson Bay red-green-and-white striped blankets. La Baie also sells the typical department-store goods.

At exclusive **Holt Renfrew** (⊠ 1300 rue Sherbrooke Ouest, ☎ 514/842–5111), furs and fashions are the specialty. It has supplied coats to four generations of British royalty, and when Queen Elizabeth II got married in 1947, Holt gave her a priceless Labrador mink. The store carries the pricey line of furs by Denmark's Birger Christensen, as well as the haute couture and prêt-à-porter collections of Giorgio Armani, Calvin Klein, and Chanel.

A kilted piper regales shoppers at **Ogilvy** (⊠ 1307 rue Ste-Catherine Ouest, ☎ 514/842–7711) every day at noon. Founded in 1865, the department store still stocks traditional apparel by retailers such as Aquascutum and Jaeger. The store is divided into individual designer boutiques that sell pricier lines than La Baie. The name used to be Ogilvy's before Québec's French-only sign laws made apostrophes illegal.

Simons (⊠ 977 rue Ste-Catherine Ouest, ☎ 514/282–1840), in elegant 19th-century digs, is one of the swankiest department stores on Ste-Catherine. The Québec City–based chain specializes almost exclusively in high-quality clothes for men and women, including its own highly respected house label. Simons shares its address with a 12-screen Paramount theater, an IMAX theater, a bar, and a coffee shop.

Shopping Centers and Malls

Centre Eaton (⊠ 705 rue Ste-Catherine Ouest ☎ 514/288–3708) has a definite youthful edge, with a huge Levi's store and some trendy sporting-goods stores. The five-story mall—the largest in the downtown core, with 175 boutiques and shops, is linked to the McGill Métro station.

Complexe Desjardins (⊠ blvd. René-Lévesque and rue Jeanne Mance ☎ 514/845–4636) gets its relaxed feel from splashing fountains and exotic plants. The roughly 80 stores vary in price range, from budget clothing outlets to the exclusive Jonathan Roche Monsieur for men's fashions. To get here, take the Métro to the Place des Arts and then follow the tunnels to the multitiered atrium mall.

Les Cours Mont-Royal (⊠ 1455 rue Peel, ☎ 514/842–7777) is *très élégant*. This mall linked to the Peel and McGill Métro stations caters to expensive tastes, but even bargain hunters find it an intriguing spot for window shopping. The more than 80 shops include DKNY and Harry Rosen. Beware: the interior layout can be disorienting.

The **Faubourg Ste-Catherine** (⌧ 1616 rue Ste-Catherine Ouest, at rue Guy, ☎ 514/939–3663) is a vast indoor bazaar abutting the Couvent des Soeurs Grises. It includes clothing and crafts boutiques, but it's best known as a wonderful source of quality foods—fresh bagels, pastries, fruits and vegetables, gourmet meats, and some of the city's spiciest and best Chinese takeout. A dozen or so very reasonably priced lunch counters sell ethnic foods.

The **Marché Bonsecours** (⌧ 350 rue St-Paul Est ☎ 514/872–7730), in-augurated in the 1840s in the Vieux-Montréal area, has seen many in-carnations over the years. Although mainly known as Montréal's principal public market for more than 100 years the market also en-joyed a stint as Montréal's city hall. Completely restored it now houses boutiques that exclusively showcase Québecois, Canadian, and First Nation's artwork, clothing, and furniture.

The **Place Montréal Trust** (⌧ 1500 rue McGill College, at rue Ste-Cather-ine Ouest, ☎ 514/843–8000) serves as a lively entrance to Place Mont-réal Trust's imposing glass office tower as well as a gateway to Montréal's vast Underground City. With its aqua and pastel decor and its interior access to the Métro system, the mall offers a welcome refuge from Montréal's winter chills. Its shops tend to specialize in high-end fashion. Indigo, one of the city's better bookstores, and the local branch of the Planet Hollywood chain are also here.

Weatherproof indoor shopping began here in 1962 with the con-struction of the 42-story cruciform towers of **Place Ville-Marie** (⌧ blvd. René-Lévesque and rue University, ☎ 514/866–6666). It was also the start of the underground shopping network that Montréal now enjoys. Stylish shoppers head to the 100-plus retail outlets for lunchtime sprees. When you're ready for a food break, consider the Mövenpick marché restaurant. Offerings range from salads and sandwiches to stir-fries and sushi. Fresh juices, pastries, and wonderful coffees make it a good breakfast choice.

The 50-plus shops of **Les Promenades de la Cathédrale** (⌧ 625 rue Ste-Catherine Ouest, ☎ 514/849–9925) are directly beneath Christ Church Cathedral. Connected to the McGill Métro station, Les Promenades in-cludes Canada's largest Linen Chest outlet, with hundreds of bedspreads and duvets, plus aisles of china, crystal, linen, and silver. It's also home to the Anglican Church's Diocesan Book Room, which sells an unusu-ally good and ecumenical selection of books as well as religious objects.

Square Westmount (⌧ rue Ste-Catherine Ouest and av. Greene, ☎ 514/ 932–0211) serves the mountainside suburb of Westmount, home to wealthy Montréalers including executives and former prime ministers, so it's hardly surprising that the city's finest shops are here. With more than 50 boutiques as well as a gourmet market and the exclusive Spa de Westmount, the opportunities for self indulgence are endless. To get here, take the Métro to the Atwater station and follow the tunnel.

Shopping Districts

Downtown is Montréal's largest retail district. It takes in rue Sherbrooke, boulevard de Maisonneuve, rue Ste-Catherine, and the side streets be-tween them. Because of the proximity and variety of shops, it's the best shopping bet if you're in town overnight or for a weekend. The area bounded by rues Sherbrooke and Ste-Catherine, and rues de la Mon-tagne and Crescent has antiques and art galleries in addition to designer salons. Fashion boutiques and art and antiques galleries line rue Sher-brooke. Rue Crescent holds a tempting blend of antiques, fashions, and jewelry displayed beneath colorful awnings.

Avenue Laurier Ouest, from boulevard St-Laurent to chemin de la Côte-Ste-Catherine, is roughly an eight-block stretch dotted with fashionable and trendy shops that carry everything from crafts and clothing to books and paintings.

Rue St. Denis, perhaps Montréal's trendiest area, includes shops of all descriptions and some of the best restaurants in town. People-watching is a popular pastime as this is where the beautiful people go to see and be seen. Cutting-edge fashions can be found both in the shops and on the shoppers.

Boulevard St-Laurent, affectionately known as The Main, is enjoying a renewed popularity. Its restaurants, boutiques, and nightclubs cater mostly to the upscale visitor. Still, the area has managed to retain its working-class immigrant roots and vitality, resulting in a unique melding of businesses: high-fashion shops are interspersed with ethnic food stores, secondhand bookshops, and hardware stores. Indeed, a trip up this street takes you from Chinatown to Little Italy. Shoppers flock to the two blocks of avenue Mont-Royal just east of boulevard St-Laurent for secondhand and recycled clothes.

Rue Chabanel, in the city's north end, is the soul of Montréal's extensive garment industry. Every Saturday, from about 8:30 to 1, many of the manufacturers and importers in the area open their doors to the general public. At least they do if they feel like it. What results is part bazaar, part circus, and often all chaos—but friendly chaos. When Montrealers say "Chabanel," they mean the eight-block stretch just west of boulevard St-Laurent. The factories and shops here are tiny—dozens of them are crammed into each building. The goods seem to get more stylish and more expensive the farther west you go. For really inexpensive leather goods, sportswear, children's togs, and linens, try the shops at 99 rue Chabanel; 555 rue Chabanel offers more-deluxe options. The manufacturers and importers at 555 have their work areas on the upper floors and have transformed the mezzanine into a glitzy mall with bargains in men's suits, winter coats, knitted goods, and stylish leather jackets. A few places on Chabanel accept credit cards, but bring cash anyway. It's easier to bargain if you can flash bills, and if you pay cash, the price will often "include the tax."

Though **Vieux-Montréal** seems choked with garish souvenir shops, shopping here can be worthwhile. Fashion boutiques and shoe stores with low to moderate prices line both rues Notre-Dame and St-Jacques, from rue McGill to Place Jacques-Cartier. Rue St-Paul also has some interesting shops. During the warm-weather months, sidewalk cafés are everywhere. Street performers are a favorite with the kids.

The fashionable place for antiquing is a formerly run-down five-block strip of **rue Notre-Dame Ouest** between rue Guy and avenue Atwater, a five-minute walk south from the Lionel-Groulx Métro station. Antiques stores have been popping up along **rue Amherst** between rues Ste-Catherine and Ontario (a five-minute walk west of the Beaudry Métro station). The area is shabbier than rue Notre-Dame but a lot less expensive. The more affluent antiques hunter might want to try her luck in **Westmount,** where the shops cater to the tastes of the executives who live in the upscale suburb.

Specialty Shops

Antiques

Art Deco furnishings and decorations get top billing at **L'Antiquaire Joyal** (✉ 1475 rue Amherst, ☎ 514/524–0057).

Antiquité Landry (✉ 1726 rue Notre-Dame Ouest, ☎ 514/937–7040) has French and English furniture in pine, mahogany, walnut, and maple.

At **Antiquités Curiosités** (⊠ 1769 rue Amherst, ☎ 514/525–8772), you can find well-priced Victorian-era tables and tallboys.

In the downtown area, **Antiquités Phyllis Friedman** (⊠ 1476 rue Sherbrooke Ouest, ☎ 514/935–1991) specializes in high-quality antique English furniture and decorative accessories—Anglo-Irish glass, ceramics, crystal, and the like.

Antiquités Pour La Table (⊠ 2679 rue Notre-Dame Ouest, ☎ 514/989–8945) has an extensive selection of antique china, crystal, and linens of only the finest quality—all impeccably preserved and beautifully displayed. This is not the place to replace your missing pieces, however, as the pieces are mostly in complete sets.

For **Cité Déco** (⊠ 1761 rue Amherst, ☎ 514/528–0659), the focus is furnishings of the 1930s, '40s, and '50s, with lots of chrome and blonde wood.

The **Coach House** (⊠ 1325 av. Greene, ☎ 514/937–6191) is a source for antique silverware.

Galerie Tansu (⊠ 1622 rue Sherbrooke Ouest, ☎ 514/846–1039) offers 18th- and 19th-century porcelain and ceramic objects, furnishings from Japan and China, and Tibetan chests and carpets.

Hélène Holden (⊠ 2691 rue Notre-Dame Ouest, ☎ 514/989–9542) specializes in porcelain dolls and accessories.

In **Héritage Antique Métropolitain** (⊠ 1646 rue Notre-Dame Ouest, ☎ 514/931–5517), you almost can't turn your head without spotting another beautiful object. The store has a wide variety of clocks and lamps as well as elegant English and French furniture.

Much of the stock at **Lapidarius** (⊠ 1312 av. Greene, ☎ 514/935–2717 or 800/267–0373) is made up of watches, jewelry, and silverware.

Ruth Stalker (⊠ 4447 rue Ste-Catherine Ouest, ☎ 514/931–0822) is the place for high-quality Canadian furniture and exquisitely carved hunting decoys.

Several dealers share **Le Village Antiquaires** (⊠ 1708 rue Notre-Dame Ouest, ☎ 514/931–5121), including specialists in furniture, jewelry, books, and vintage clothing. Galerie du Louvre merits a special visit for its beautiful antique stained glass.

At **Viva Gallery** (⊠ 1970 rue Notre-Dame Ouest, ☎ 514/932–3200), Asian antique furniture and art take center stage. A wide selection of carved tables, benches, and armoirs is available.

Art

Montréal brims with art galleries that present work by local luminaries as well as international artists. The Downtown area has a wide choice; Vieux-Montréal is also rich in galleries, which usually specialize in Québecois and First Nations work.

The nondescript **Edifice Belago** (⊠ 372 rue Ste-Catherine Ouest) is in essence a mall for art galleries showing established and upcoming artists. Two of the best for contemporary art are Galerie René Blouin (☎ 514/393–9969) and Galerie Trois Points (☎ 514/866–8008), both on the fifth floor.

Canadian landscapes are the focus at the **Galerie Art & Culture** (⊠ 227 rue St-Paul Ouest, ☎ 514/843–5980).

Galerie des Arts Relais des Époques (⊠ 234 rue St-Paul Ouest, ☎ 514/844–2133) sells modern and abstract works by contemporary Montréal painters.

The **Galerie de Bellefeuille** (⊠ 1367 av. Greene, Westmount, ☎ 514/933–4406), in the upscale suburb of Westmount, has a knack for discovering important new talents.

At **Galerie de Chariot** (⊠ 446 Place Jacques-Cartier, ☎ 514/875–6134), the selection of Inuit carvings and drawings is truly spectacular.

The **Galerie Elena Lee Verre** (⊠ 1460 rue Sherbrooke Ouest, ☎ 514/844–6009 is the city's leading dealer in glassworks.

Galerie Walter Klinkhof (⊠ 1200 rue Sherbrooke Ouest ☎ 514/288–7306) shows established artists.

La Guilde Graphique (⊠ 9 rue St-Paul Ouest ☎ 514/844–3438) has an exceptional selection of original prints, engravings, and etchings.

Books and Stationery

Bibliomania (⊠ 460 rue Ste-Catherine Ouest, ☎ 514/933–8156) includes some out-of-print gems among its extensive shelves of secondhand books. It also has engravings, postcards, and other printed collectibles.

Chapters (⊠ 1171 rue Ste-Catherine Ouest, ☎ 514/849–8825) stocks one of the largest selections of books and magazines in the city, as well as CD-ROMs and stationery, and has a Starbucks café. Book signings are a frequent occurrence here.

Since 1974, **Double Hook** (⊠ 1235A av. Greene, ☎ 514/932–5093) has been selling Canadian books—from fiction and poetry, to children's books, cookbooks, and business tomes.

With its selection of imported and handmade papers, **L'Essence du Papier** (⊠ 4160 rue St. Denis, ☎ 514/288–9691) is a reminder that letter-writing can be an art form. Here are pens suited to all tastes and budgets as well as waxes and stamps with which to seal any romantic prose that you might be inspired to produce. It also offers a wide selection of placecards, invitations, and journals.

Ex Libris (⊠ 1628B rue Sherbrooke Ouest, ☎ 514/932–1689) houses a fine collection of secondhand books in an elegant, gray stone building.

Indigo (⊠ 1500 rue McGill College, ☎ 514/281–5549) is mainly about books and magazines, but the chain has branched into CD-ROMs, videos, cards, gifts, and housewares. This location also has a large section devoted to children and their education.

Paragraphe (⊠ 2220 av. McGill College, ☎ 514/845–5811) is the biggest and most successful independent bookstore in the city.

The wide selection of old books at **S. W. Welch** (⊠ 3878 blvd. St-Laurent, ☎ 514/848–9358) ranges from religion and philosophy to mysteries and science fiction.

The Word (⊠ 469 rue Milton, ☎ 514/845–5640), deep in the McGill University neighborhood, is a timeless shop with sagging shelves that specializes in books on art, philosophy, and literature. (Leave your credit cards at home—the owner here tallies his bills by hand.)

Clothes

Aime Com Moi (⊠ 150 av. Mont-Royal Est, ☎ 514/982–0088) sells exclusive men's and women's clothing created by Québec designers.

Brisson et Brisson (⊠ 1472 rue Sherbrooke Ouest, ☎ 514/937–7456), established in the 1950s, is perhaps Montréal's most exclusive men's store. Renowned for attentive service, Brisson et Brisson makes sure that every piece of your wardrobe, even your pajamas, is a perfect fit.

Kiltless Highlanders can remedy their sad state at **Chas. Johnson & Sons** (⊠ 1184 Phillips Place, ☎ 514/878–1931), which has on hand three expert kilt makers who can cut any tartan to any size; this downtown shop also rents Highland formal gear for all occasions and sells sporrans, skean-dhus, dirks, doublets, and day jackets, as well as a full line of classic British menswear.

At **Diffusion Griff 3000** (⊠ 350 rue St-Paul Est, ☎ 514/398–0761), Anne de Shalla has created a showcase for leading Québecois fashion designers.

Kanuk (⊠ 485 rue Rachel Est, ☎ 514/527–4494) has developed a line of coats and sleeping bags that could keep an arctic explorer warm. But it also sells elegant winter clothes that are designed for layering and are suitable for any city or town where the temperature dips below freezing. The company's logo—a stylized owl, usually displayed on the collar—has become something of a status symbol among the shivering urban masses. Many fine retailers carry Kanuk coats, but you can also buy them at the display room over the factory.

For something exotically tropical, try **Mains Folles** (⊠ 4427 rue St-Denis, ☏ 514/284–6854), which sells dresses, skirts, and blouses imported from Bali.

Women can find well-crafted original fashions by Québecois designers at **Revenge** (⊠ 3852 rue St-Denis, ☏ 514/843–4379).

Scandale (⊠ 3639 blvd. St-Laurent, ☏ 514/842–4707) has cutting-edge fashions, each piece an original by Québecois designer Georges Lévesque and created on site. Here also is one of the most lurid window displays in the city.

Tilley Endurables (⊠ 1050 av. Laurier Ouest, ☏ 514/272–7791) sells the famous, Canadian-designed Tilley hat and other easy-care travel wear.

CHILDREN'S

Oink Oink (⊠ 1343 av. Greene, ☏ 514/939–2634) carries the latest fashions as well as toys for infants and children. It's fun to hear how the staff answers the phone.

FURS

Montréal is one of the fur capitals of the world. Close to 85% of Canada's fur manufacturers are based in the city, as are many of their retail outlets. Many of them are clustered along rue Mayor and blvd. de Maisonneuve between rue de Bleury and rue Aylmer.

The storefront showroom of **Alexandor** (⊠ 2055 rue Peel, ☏ 514/288–1119), nine blocks west of the main fur-trade area, caters to the downtown trade.

Birger Christensen at Holt Renfrew (⊠ 1300 rue Sherbrooke Ouest, ☏ 514/842–5111) is perhaps the most exclusive showroom in the city, with prices to match.

Marcel Jodoin Fourrures (⊠ 1228 rue St-Denis, ☏ 514/288–1683) has a wide selection of nearly new (under five years old), previously owned fur coats, jackets, and stoles, most of which go for less than the cost of an imitation.

Two of the biggest merchants—**McComber Grosvenor** (⊠ 402 blvd. de Maisonneuve Ouest, ☏ 514/288–1255)—share a showroom filled with beautiful mink coats and jackets.

LINGERIE

The lacy goods at **Collange** (⊠ 1 Westmount Square, ☏ 514/933–4634) are of the designer variety.

As its name suggests, **Deuxième Peau** (Second Skin; ⊠ 4457 rue St-Denis, ☏ 514/842–0811) sells lingerie so fine you don't notice you're wearing it.

For seductively lacy lingerie, try **Lyla** (⊠ 1087 av. Laurier Ouest, ☏ 514/271–0763).

VINTAGE

Boutique Encore (⊠ 2165 rue Crescent, ☏ 514/849–0092), in business for about 50 years, retains its popularity by maintaining a good selection of designer labels. Although best known for its nearly new women's fashions, it now includes the big names for men.

At **Eva B** (⊠ 2013 blvd. St-Laurent, ☏ 514/849–8246), which has a vast collection of clothes that spans the decades, you can turn back the clock and perk up your wardrobe. Maybe being a flapper is your fantasy, or you miss the '60s.

Cigars

Casa del Habano (✉ 1434 rue Sherbrooke Ouest, ☎ 514/849–0037) stocks the finest cigars Cuba produces. (Note: U.S. law forbids its citizens to buy Cuban products.)

Davidoff (✉ 1458 Sherbrooke Ouest, ☎ 514/289–9118) stocks the best names in cigars as well as a fine collection of smoking accessories and humidors.

H. Poupart (✉ 1385 Ste-Catherine Ouest, ☎ 514/842–5794) has been supplying Montréalers with the best tobacco the world has to offer for almost 100 years. Be it cigars, cigarettes, chewing and pipe tobaccos, or snuff, you can find a large selection here.

Crafts

A'Anowara (✉ 350 rue St-Paul Est, ☎ 514/398–0710), the only Montréal crafts shop owned and run entirely by native people, sells First Nations crafts.

L'Empreinte Coopérative (✉ 272 rue St-Paul Est, ☎ 514/861–4427) has fine Québec handicrafts.

Eclectic

Creations Nicole Moisan (✉ 4324 rue St-Denis, ☎ 514/284–9506) has miles and miles of lace, with thousands of patterns to choose from, all from Europe. Custom orders are available.

Desmarais et Robitaille (✉ 60 rue Notre-Dame Ouest, ☎ 514/845–3194), a Vieux-Montréal store that supplies churches with vestments and liturgical items, also has Québecois carvings and handicrafts as well as tasteful religious articles.

Food

The family-owned and -operated **Charcuterie/Boucherie Hongroise** (✉ 3843 blvd. St-Laurent, ☎ 514/844–6734) smokes and cures its own bacon and hams, as well as a wide selection of German, Polish, and Hungarian sausages.

Marché de Westmount (✉ 1 Westmount Sq., ☎ no phone) includes an array of gourmet boutiques selling pastries, cheeses, pâtés, fruits, cakes, and chocolates. You can assemble your own picnic and eat it at one of the little tables scattered among the stalls.

Milano (✉ 6862 blvd. St-Laurent, ☎ 514/273–8558), in the heart of Little Italy, offers one of the largest cheese selections in the city as well as fresh pasta of all kinds. An entire wall is devoted to olive oils and vinegars; there are also a butcher and a big produce section.

On weekends, shoppers pack the narrow aisles of **Nino** (✉ 3667 blvd. St-Laurent, ☎ 514/844–7630), scanning the shelves for spices, pickles, hams, and kitchen gadgets of all sorts, from enormous stock pots to tiny cheese graters for shredding garlic buds.

Since before World War II, immigrant communities have relied on the **Warshaw Supermarket** (✉ 3863 blvd. St-Laurent, ☎ 514/842–5251) groceries and other goods; the store also sells kitchen gadgets and furniture.

Home Furnishings

Students at the **Institut de Design de Montréal** (✉ 350 rue St-Paul Est, ☎ 514/866–2436) offer an amusingly innovative collection of kitchen brushes, buckets, CD-storage racks, clocks, bathroom equipment, and so forth.

Jeunes d'Ici (✉ 134 av. Laurier Ouest, ☎ 514/270–5512) has furniture and decorating accessories for children of all ages.

MDI Multi Design (✉ 273 av. Laurier Ouest, ☎ 514/277–0052) designs and sells funky decor and unusual gadgets for the well-equipped home.

Rita R. Giroux (✉ 206 rue St-Paul Ouest, ☎ 514/844–4714) makes flamboyant creations with fresh, dried, and silk flowers.

Canadian-down comforters are made at the **Ungava Factory Outlet** (⊠ 10 av. des Pins Ouest, Suite 112, ☎ 514/287–9276), where they are offered at wholesale prices. Custom orders are accepted, but if you don't want to part with your current comforter, you can have it restuffed here.

Jewelry

Since 1879, **Birks** (⊠ 1240 Phillips Sq., ☎ 514/397–2511) has helped shoppers mark their special occasions. Be it an engagement ring or a wedding or retirement gift, a blue Birks box is a welcome sight for its recipient.

The craftspeople at **Kaufmann de Suisse** (⊠ 2195 rue Crescent, ☎ 514/848–0595) make finely wrought jewelry.

Music

Good secondhand CDs are available at **Cheap Thrills** (⊠ 2044 Metcalfe, ☎ 514/844–8988). There's also a wide selection of secondhand books at bargain prices.

Sporting Goods and Clothing

At the **Boutique Classique Angler** (⊠ 414 rue McGill, ☎ 514/878–3474), anglers can find everything they need, from rods and reels to feathers for tying flies. Owner Peter Ferago has advice on where to fish and also sells packets of exquisitely smoked Atlantic salmon at reasonable prices.

The **Canadiens Boutique Centre Molson** (⊠ 1250 rue de la Gauchetière, ☎ 514/989–2836) offers sticks, posters, pucks, authentic jerseys, and other memorabilia, all bearing the emblem of the world's most storied hockey team.

If you're trying to assemble your own sports hall of fame, **Lucie Favreau Sports Memorabilia** (⊠ 1904 rue Notre-Dame Ouest, ☎ 514/989–5117) might just have the autographed hockey stick or 1950s football poster you're looking for.

MONTRÉAL A TO Z

To research prices, get advice from other travelers, and book travel arrangements, visit www.fodors.com.

AIR TRAVEL TO AND FROM MONTRÉAL

Major airlines serving Montréal include Air Canada, American Airlines, British Airways, Delta, El Al, Sabena, Swissair, and US Airways.

Note that when you depart by plane, you must pay a $10 airport tax (for capital improvements); you can pay cash or with a credit card.

AIRPORTS AND TRANSFERS

Dorval International, 22½ km (14 mi) west of the city, handles all scheduled flights foreign and domestic and some charter operations. Mirabel International, 54½ km (34 mi) northwest of the city, serves most charter traffic.

➤ AIRPORT INFORMATION: **Dorval International** (⊠ 975 blvd. René-Vachon, Dorval, ☎ 514/394–7377). **Mirabel International** (⊠ 12600 rue Aérogare, Mirabel, ☎ 514/394–7377).

AIRPORT TRANSFER
A taxi from Dorval International to downtown costs about $28; from Mirabel, about $56. All taxi companies in Montréal must charge the same rates by law. L'Aerobus is a much cheaper alternative into town from Mirabel and Dorval. Shuttle service from Mirabel to the terminal next to the Gare Centrale, at 777 rue de la Gauchetière, is frequent and costs only $20 ($30 round-trip). The shuttle from Dorval runs about

every half hour and stops at Le Centre Sheraton, the Marriott, Le Reine Elizabeth, and the central bus terminal. It costs $11 ($19.75 round-trip).
➤ SHUTTLE: **L'Aerobus** (☎ 514/931–9002).

BUS TRAVEL TO AND FROM MONTRÉAL

Greyhound Lines and its subsidiaries provide service to Montréal from various U.S. cities; Greyhound Canada has service from Toronto and points west in Canada. SMT & Acadian Lines arrives from eastern Canada. All buses arrive at and depart from the city's downtown bus terminal, the Station Central d'Autobus Montréal, which connects with the Berri-UQAM Métro station. Terminal staff have schedule and fare information for all bus service from Montréal, including the patchwork of independent companies that provide service to all Québec and some Ontario destinations.
➤ BUS INFORMATION: **Greyhound Canada** (☎ 800/661–8747). **Greyhound Lines** (☎ 800/231–2222). **SMT & Acadian Lines** (☎ 800/567–5151). **Station Central d'Autobus Montréal** (✉ 505 blvd. de Maisonneuve Est, ☎ 514/842–2281).

BUS TRAVEL WITHIN MONTRÉAL

STCUM (Société de Transport de la Communauté Urbaine de Montréal) administers the buses as well as the Métro, so the same tickets and transfers (free) are valid on either service. You should be able to get within a few blocks of anywhere in the city on one fare. At press time rates were single ticket $2, six tickets $8.50, and monthly pass $48.50. Visitors can buy a day pass for $7 or a three-day pass for $14. They're available at some major hotels and at Berri-UQAM and some other downtown stations.
➤ BUS INFORMATION: **Société de Transport de la Communauté Urbaine de Montréal** (STCUM; ☎ 514/288–6287).

CAR RENTAL

➤ MAJOR AGENCIES: **Alamo** (✉ Dorval International, ☎ 514/633–1222). **Avis** (☎ 800/879–2847; ✉ Dorval International, ☎ 514/636–1902; ✉ 1225 rue Metcalfe, ☎ 514/866–7906; ✉ Mirabel International, ☎ 450/476–3481). **Budget** (☎ 800/268–8900; ✉ Dorval International, ☎ 514/636–0052; ✉ Mirabel International, ☎ 450/476–2687). **Discount** (☎ 514/286–1554 or 800/263–2355). **Dollar** (✉ Mirabel International, ☎ 514/633–4467; ✉ 1155 rue Guy, ☎ 514/344–5858). **Enterprise** (☎ 800/562–2886; ✉ 1005 rue Guy, ☎ 514/931–3722; ✉ Dorval International, ☎ 514/633–1433). **Hertz** (☎ 800/263–0600 or 514/842–8537; ✉ Mirabel International, ☎ 450/476–3385; ✉ Dorval International, ☎ 514/636–9530). **National Car Rental** (☎ 514/878–2771 or 800/387–4747). **National Tilden** (☎ 514/878–2771 or 800/387–4747). **Thrifty** (✉ Dorval International, ☎ 514/631–5567; ✉ Mirabel International, ☎ 450/476–0496; ✉ 845 rue Ste-Catherine Est, ☎ 514/845–5954). **Via Route** (☎ 514/521–5221 or 888/842–7388).

CAR TRAVEL

Montréal is accessible from the rest of Canada via the Trans-Canada Highway (Highway 1), which enters the city from the east and west via Routes 20 and 40. The New York State Thruway (I–87) becomes Route 15 at the Canadian border, and then it's 47 km (29 mi) to the outskirts of Montréal. U.S. I–89 becomes two-lane Route 133, which eventually joins Route 10, at the border. From I–91 from Massachusetts via New Hampshire and Vermont, you must take Routes 55 and 10 to reach Montréal. At the border you must clear Canadian Customs, so be prepared with proof of citizenship and your vehicle's ownership papers. On holidays and during the peak summer season, expect waits of a half hour or more at the major crossings.

In winter, remember that your car may not start on extra-cold mornings unless it has been kept in a heated garage.

➤ CONTACTS: **Touring Club de Montréal–AAA, CAA, RAC** (☎ 514/861–7111).

GASOLINE

Gasoline is sold in liters (3¾ liters equal 1 U.S. gallon), and lead-free is called *sans plomb*.

PARKING

Montréal police have a diligent tow-away and fine system for cars double-parked or stopped in no-stopping zones downtown during rush hours and business hours. A parking ticket usually costs between $35 and $40. All Montréal parking signs are in French, so brush up on your *gauche* (left), *droit* (right), *ouest* (west), and *est* (east). If your car is towed while illegally parked, it will cost an additional $35 to retrieve it. Be especially alert in winter: Montréal's street plowers are ruthless in dealing with any parked cars in their way. If they don't tow them, they'll bury them.

RULES OF THE ROAD

Once you're in Québec, the road signs are in French, but they're designed for everyone to understand them. The speed limit is posted in kilometers; on highways the limit is 100 kph (about 62 mph), and the use of radar-detection devices is prohibited. There are heavy penalties for driving while intoxicated, and drivers and front-seat passengers must wear over-the-shoulder seat belts. New York, Maine, and Ontario residents should drive with extra care in Québec: traffic violations in the province are entered on their driving records back home (and vice versa).

If you drive in the city, remember two things: Québec law forbids you to turn right on a red light, and Montrealers are notorious jaywalkers.

CONSULATES

The U.S. consulate is open weekdays 8:30–noon and Wednesday also 2–4; the U.K. consulate is open weekdays 9–5.

➤ UNITED KINGDOM: (✉ 1000 rue de la Gauchetière Ouest, ☎ 514/866–5863).

➤ UNITED STATES: (✉ 1155 rue St-Alexandre, ☎ 514/398–9695).

DISCOUNTS AND DEALS

The Montréal museum pass allows access to 19 major museums. A day pass costs $15, a three-day pass $28; family passes are $30 for one day and $60 for three days. They are available at museums or Centre Info-Touriste (1001 Sq. Dorchester).

EMERGENCIES

The U.S. Consulate has a list of various medical specialists in the Montréal area. (Call ☎ 514/398–9695 in advance to make sure the consulate is open.) There's a dental clinic on avenue Van Horne that's open 24 hours; Sunday appointments are for emergencies only.

Many pharmacies are open until midnight, including Jean Coutu and Pharmaprix locations. Some are open around the clock, including the Pharmaprix on chemin de la Côte-des-Neiges.

➤ DENTISTS: **Dental clinic** (✉ 3546 av. Van Horne, ☎ 514/342–4444).

➤ EMERGENCY SERVICES: **Ambulance, fire, police** (☎ 911). **Québec Poison Control Centre** (☎ 800/463–5060).

➤ HOSPITALS: **Montréal General Hospital** (✉ 1650 av. Cedar, ☎ 514/937–6011).

➤ LATE-NIGHT PHARMACIES: **Jean Coutu** (✉ 501 rue Mont-Royal Est, ☎ 514/521–1058; ✉ 5510 chemin de la Côte-des-Neiges, ☎ 514/344–

8338). **Pharmaprix** (✉ 1500 rue Ste-Catherine Ouest, ☎ 514/933–4744; ✉ 5157 rue Sherbrooke Ouest, ☎ 514/484–3531; ✉ 901 rue Ste-Catherine Est, ☎ 514/842–4915; (✉ 5122 chemin de la Côte-des-Neiges, ☎ 514/738–8464).

LODGING

The room-reservation service of Hospitality Canada can help you find you a room in one of 80 hotels, motels, and B&Bs. Tourisme Québec also operates a room-booking service.

➤ TOLL-FREE NUMBERS: **Hospitality Canada** (☎ 800/665–1528). **Tourisme Québec** (☎ 877/266–5687, WEB www.bonjourquebec.com).

B&BS

Bed and Breakfast à Montréal represents more than 50 homes in downtown and in the elegant neighborhoods of Westmount and Outremont. Downtown B&B Network represents 75 homes and apartments, mostly around the downtown core and along rue Sherbrooke, that have one or more rooms available for visitors.

➤ RESERVATION SERVICES: **Bed and Breakfast à Montréal** (✉ Marian Kahn, Box 575, Snowdon Station, H3X 3T8, ☎ 514/738–9410 or 800/ 738–4338, FAX 514/735–7493, WEB www.bbmontreal.com). **Downtown B&B Network** (✉ Bob Finkelstein, 3458 av. Laval, H2X 3C8, ☎ 514/ 289–9749 or 800/267–5180, WEB www.bbmontreal.qc.ca).

SUBWAY TRAVEL

The Métro, or subway, is clean, quiet (it runs on rubber wheels), and safe, and it's heated in winter and cooled in summer. As in any city, visitors should be alert and attentive to personal property such as purses and wallets. The Métro is also connected to the 29 km (18 mi) of the Underground City. Each of the 65 Métro stops has been individually designed and decorated; Berri-UQAM has stained glass, and at Place d'Armes a small collection of archaeological artifacts is exhibited. The stations between Snowdon and Jean-Talon on the Blue Line are worth a visit, particularly Outremont, with its glass-block design. Each station connects with one or more bus routes, which cover the rest of the island.

Free maps may be obtained at Métro ticket booths. Try to get the *Carte Réseau* (system map); it's the most complete. Transfers from Métro to buses are available from the dispenser just beyond the ticket booth inside the station. Bus-to-bus and bus-to-Métro transfers may be obtained from the bus driver. The Société de Transport de la Communauté Urbaine de Montréal does operate an automated line for information on bus and Métro schedules, but in French only.

FARES AND SCHEDULES

Métro hours on the Orange, Green, and Yellow lines are weekdays 5:30 AM–12:58 AM, Saturday 5:30 AM–1:28 AM, and Sunday 5:30 AM–1:58 AM. The Blue Line runs daily 5:30 AM–11 PM. Trains run as often as every three minutes on the most crowded lines—Orange and Green— at rush hours.

The STCUM, or Société de Transport de la Communauté Urbaine de Montréal, administers both the Métro and the buses, so the same tickets and transfers, which are free, are valid on either service. You should be able to get within a few blocks of anywhere in the city on one fare. At press time rates were single ticket $2, six tickets $8.50, monthly pass $48.50, day pass $7, and three-day pass $14. They're available at some of the bigger hotels, at Berri-UQAM, and at some other downtown stations.

➤ SUBWAY INFORMATION: **Société de Transport de la Communauté Urbaine de Montréal** (STCUM; ☎ 514/288–6287).

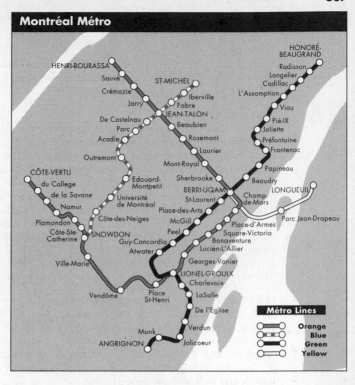

Montréal Métro

HONORÉ-BEAUGRAND
Radisson
Langelier
Cadillac
L'Assomption
Viau
Pié-IX
Joliette
Préfontaine
Frontenac
Papineau
Beaudry
LONGUEUIL
Champ-de-Mars
Parc Jean-Drapeau
Place-d'Armes
Square-Victoria
Bonaventure
Lucien-L'Allier
Georges-Vanier
LIONEL-GROULX
Charlevoix
LaSalle
De l'Église
Verdun
Jolicoeur
HENRI-BOURASSA
Sauvé
Crémazie
Jarry
De Castelnau
Parc
Acadie
Outremont
ST-MICHEL
Iberville
Fabre
JEAN-TALON
Beaubien
Rosemont
Laurier
Mont-Royal
Sherbrooke
BERRI-UQAM
St-Laurent
Place-des-Arts
McGill
Peel
CÔTE-VERTU
du Collège
de la Savane
Namur
Plamondon
Côte-Ste-Catherine
SNOWDON
Guy-Concordia
Atwater
Ville-Marie
Edouard-Montpetit
Université de Montréal
Côte-des-Neiges
Vendôme
Place St-Henri
Monk
ANGRIGNON

Métro Lines
Orange
Blue
Green
Yellow

TAXES

A $10 airport tax (for capital improvements) is charged when you leave. You can pay cash or with a credit card.

TAXIS

Taxis in Montréal all run on the same rate: $2.50 minimum and $1.10 per km (½ mi). They're usually reliable, although they may be difficult to find on rainy nights after the Métro has closed. Each has on its roof a white or orange plastic sign that is lit when available and off when occupied.

TOURS

BOAT TOURS

From May through October, Amphi Tour offers a unique one-hour tour of Vieux-Montréal and the Vieux-Port on both land and water in an amphibious bus. Bateau-Mouche runs four harbor excursions and an evening supper cruise daily May through October. The boats are reminiscent of the ones that cruise the canals of the Netherlands—wide-beamed and low-slung, with a glassed-in passenger deck. Boats leave from the Jacques Cartier Pier at the foot of Place Jacques-Cartier in the Vieux-Port.

➤ FEES AND SCHEDULES: **Amphi Tour** (☎ 514/849–5181 or 514/386–1298. **Bateau-Mouche** (☎ 514/849–9952).

BUS TOURS

Gray Line offers nine different tours of Montréal from June to October and one tour during the other months. It has pickup service at the major hotels and at Info-Touriste (1001 Sq. Dorchester).

Imperial Tours' double-decker buses follow a nine-stop circuit of the city. You can get off and on as often as you like and stay at each stop as long as you like. There's pickup service at major hotels.

➤ FEES AND SCHEDULES: **Gray Line** (☎ 514/934–1222). **Imperial Tours** (☎ 514/871–4733).

CALÈCHE RIDES
Open horse-drawn carriages—fleece-lined in winter—leave from Place Jacques-Cartier, Square Dorchester, Place d'Armes, and rue de la Commune. An hour-long ride costs about $50.

TRAIN TRAVEL
The Gare Centrale, on rue de la Gauchetière between rues University and Mansfield (behind Le Reine Elizabeth), is the rail terminus for all trains from the United States and from other Canadian provinces. It is connected underground to the Bonaventure Métro station. The Amtrak *Adirondack* leaves New York's Penn Station every morning for the 10½-hour trip through scenic upstate New York to Montréal. Amtrak also has bus connections with the *Vermonter* in St. Albans, Vermont. VIA Rail connects Montréal with all the major cities of Canada, including Québec City, Halifax, Ottawa, Toronto, Winnipeg, Edmonton, and Vancouver.
➤ TRAIN INFORMATION: **Amtrak** (☎ 800/872–7245). **VIA Rail** (☎ 514/989–2626 or 888/842–7245; 800/361–5390 in Québec).

TRANSPORTATION AROUND MONTRÉAL
Public transportation is easily the best and cheapest way to get around. Finding your way around Montréal by car is not difficult, as the streets are laid out in a fairly straightforward grid and one-way streets are clearly marked. But parking isn't easy, and the narrow cobbled streets of Vieux-Montréal can be a trial. It's much easier to park near a Métro station and walk and use public transit.

TRAVEL AGENCIES
➤ LOCAL AGENTS: **American Express** (✉ 1141 blvd. de Maisonneuve Ouest, ☎ 514/284–3300). **Canadian Automobile Club** (✉ 1180 rue Drummond, ☎ 514/861–5111). **Vacances Tourbec** (✉ 595 blvd. de Maisonneuve Ouest, ☎ 514/842–1400). **Voyages Campus** (✉ McGill University, 3480 rue McTavish, ☎ 514/398–0647).

VISITOR INFORMATION
Centre Info-Touriste, on Square Dorchester, has extensive tourist information on Montréal and the rest of the province of Québec. It's open June 1 to early September, daily 7:30–8, and early September to June 9, daily 9–6. The Vieux-Montréal branch is open mid-October to mid-May, daily 9–5, and daily 9–7 the rest of the year.

Tourisme-Montréal has information on city attractions and events. The very trendy Plateau Mont-Royal district has its own tourist association. The Hochelaga-Maisonneuve tourist association has information on attractions and events in the colorful district around the Stade Olympique.
➤ TOURIST INFORMATION: **Centre Info-Touriste** (✉ 1001 Sq. Dorchester, ☎ 514/873–2015 or 800/363–7777; ✉ 174 rue Notre-Dame Est, at pl. Jacques-Cartier, ☎ 514/873–2015). **Hochelaga-Maisonneuve tourist association** (☎ 514/256–4636, WEB www.tourismemaisonneuve.qc.ca). **Plateau Mont-Royal tourist association** (☎ 514/840–0926 or 888/449–9944, FAX 514/524–4848, WEB www.tpmr.qc.ca). **Tourisme-Montréal** (☎ 514/844–5400, WEB www.tourism-montreal.org).

10 QUÉBEC CITY

Whether you're strolling along the Plains of Abraham or exploring the Vieux-Port, Québec City will give you a feeling for centuries of history and French civilization. The city, which has one of the most spectacular settings in North America, is perched on a cliff above a narrow point in the St. Lawrence River. It is the capital of, as well as the oldest municipality in, the province of Québec.

Updated by
Elizabeth
Thompson

N O EXCURSION TO FRENCH-SPEAKING Canada is complete without a visit to exuberant, romantic Québec City, which can claim one of the most beautiful natural settings in North America. The well-preserved Vieux-Québec (Old Québec) is small and dense, steeped in four centuries of history and French tradition. The ramparts that once protected the city, 17th- and 18th-century buildings, and numerous parks and monuments are here. The government of Québec has completely restored many of the centuries-old buildings of Place Royale, one of the oldest districts on the continent. Because of the site's immaculate preservation as the only fortified city remaining in North America north of Mexico, UNESCO has designated Vieux-Québec a World Heritage Site.

Perched on a cliff above a narrow point in the St. Lawrence River, Québec City is the oldest municipality in Québec province. In the 17th century the first French explorers, fur trappers, and missionaries came here to establish the colony of New France. Today it still resembles a French provincial town in many ways; its family-oriented residents have strong ties to their past. An estimated 96% of the Québec City region's population of more than 650,000 list French as their mother tongue.

In 1535 French explorer Jacques Cartier first came upon what the Algonquin people called Kebec, meaning "where the river narrows." New France, however, was not actually founded in the vicinity of what is now Québec City until 1608, when another French explorer, Samuel de Champlain, recognized the military advantages of the location and set up a fort. On the banks of the St. Lawrence, on the spot now called Place Royale, this fort developed into an economic center for fur trade and shipbuilding. Twelve years later, Champlain realized the French colony's vulnerability to attacks from above and expanded its boundaries to the top of the cliff, where he built the fort Château St-Louis on the site of the present-day Château Frontenac.

During the early days of New France, the French and British fought for control of the region. In 1690, when an expedition led by Admiral Sir William Phipps arrived from England, Comte de Frontenac, New France's most illustrious governor, defied him with the statement, "Tell your lord that I will reply with the mouth of my cannons."

The French, preoccupied with scandals at the courts of Louis XV and Louis XVI, gave only grudging help to their possessions in the New World. The French colonists built walls and other military structures and had the strong defensive position on top of the cliff, but they still had to contend with Britain's naval supremacy. On September 13, 1759, the British army, led by General James Wolfe, scaled the colony's cliff and took the French troops led by General Louis-Joseph Montcalm by surprise. The British defeated the French in a 20-minute battle on the Plains of Abraham, and New France came under British rule.

The British brought their mastery of trade to the region. During the 18th century, Québec City's economy prospered because of the success of the fishing, fur-trading, shipbuilding, and timber industries. Wary of new invasions, the British continued to expand upon the fortifications left by the French. They built a wall encircling the city and a star-shaped citadel, both of which mark the city's urban landscape today. The constitution of 1791 established Québec City as the capital of Lower Canada until the 1840 Act of Union united Upper and Lower Canada and made Montréal the capital. Québec City remained under British rule until 1867, when the Act of Confederation united several Canadian provinces (Québec, Ontario, New Brunswick, and

Nova Scotia) and established Québec City as capital of the province of Québec.

In the mid-19th century the economic center of eastern Canada shifted west from Québec City to Montréal and Toronto. Today, government is Québec City's main business: about 27,000 full- or part-time civil-service employees work and live in the area. Office complexes continue to spring up outside the older part of town; modern malls, convention centers, and imposing hotels now cater to a business clientele.

Pleasures and Pastimes

Dining

Gone are the days when Québec City dining consisted mostly of classic French and hearty Québécois cuisine served in restaurants in the downtown core. Nowadays the city's finest eateries, found both inside and outside the city's walls, offer lighter contemporary fare, often with Asian or Italian as well as French and Québécois influences. There are still fine French restaurants, though, and visitors can sample French-Canadian cuisine composed of robust, uncomplicated dishes that make use of the region's bounty of foods, including fowl and wild game (quail, caribou, venison), maple syrup, and various berries and nuts. Other specialties include *cretons* (pâtés), *tourtière* (meat pie), and *tarte au sucre* (maple-syrup pie).

Lodging

With more than 35 hotels within its walls and an abundance of family-run bed-and-breakfasts, Québec City has a range of lodging options. Landmark hotels stand as prominent as the city's most historic sites; modern high-rises outside the ramparts have spectacular views of the old city. Another choice is to immerse yourself in the city's historic charm by staying in an old-fashioned inn where no two rooms are alike.

Walking

Québec City is a wonderful place to wander on foot. Impressive vistas of the Laurentian Mountains and the St. Lawrence River are revealed on a walk along the city walls or a climb to the city's highest point, Cap Diamant, near the Citadelle. It's possible to spend days investigating the narrow cobblestone streets of Vieux-Québec, visiting historic sites, or browsing for local arts and crafts in the boutiques of quartier Petit-Champlain. A stroll on the Promenade des Gouverneurs and the Plains of Abraham provides a view of the river as well as the Laurentian foothills and the Appalachian Mountains.

EXPLORING QUÉBEC CITY

Québec City's split-level landscape divides Upper Town on the cape from Lower Town, along the shores of the St. Lawrence. If you look out from the Terrasse Dufferin boardwalk in Upper Town, you will see the rooftops of Lower Town buildings directly below. Separating these two sections of the city is steep and precipitous rock, against which were built more than 25 *escaliers* (staircases). A *funiculaire* (funicular) climbs and descends the cliff between Terrasse Dufferin and the Maison Louis-Jolliet in Lower Town. There's plenty to see in the oldest sections of town, as well as in the modern city beyond the walls.

Numbers in the text correspond to numbers in the margin and on the Upper and Lower Towns (Haute-Ville, Basse-Ville), Outside the Walls, and Ile d'Orléans maps.

Metropolitan Québec City

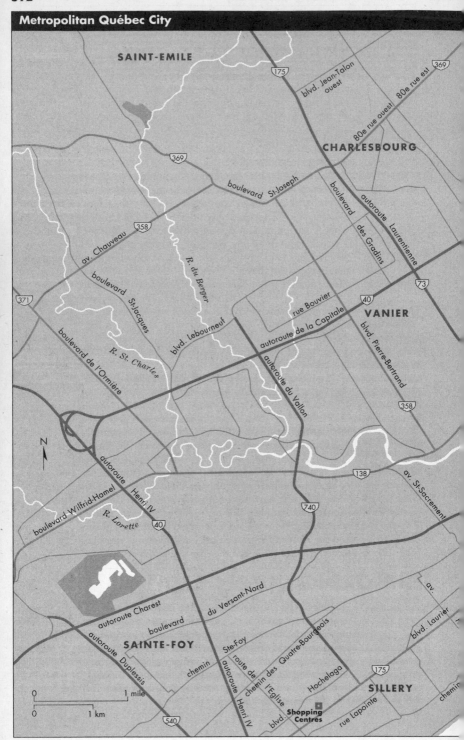

SAINT-EMILE

175

blvd. Jean-Talon
ouest

80e rue ouest

80e rue est

369

CHARLESBOURG

369

boulevard St-Joseph

boulevard des Gradins

autoroute Laurentienne

358

av. Chauveau

boulevard St-Jacques

R. du Berger

73

371

rue Bouvier

40

VANIER

boulevard de l'Ormière

R. St. Charles

blvd. Lebourneuf

autoroute de la Capitale

autoroute du Vallon

blvd. Pierre-Bertrand

358

N

autoroute Henri IV

138

av. St-Sacrement

boulevard Wilfrid-Hamel

R. Lorette

40

740

av.

du Versant-Nord

blvd. Laurier

autoroute Charest

boulevard

Ste-Foy

chemin des Quatre-Bourgeois

175

SAINTE-FOY

autoroute Duplessis

chemin

route de

chemin de l'Église

Hochelaga

SILLERY

autoroute Henri IV

rue Lapointe

chemin

540

blvd.

Shopping
Centres

0   1 mile

0   1 km

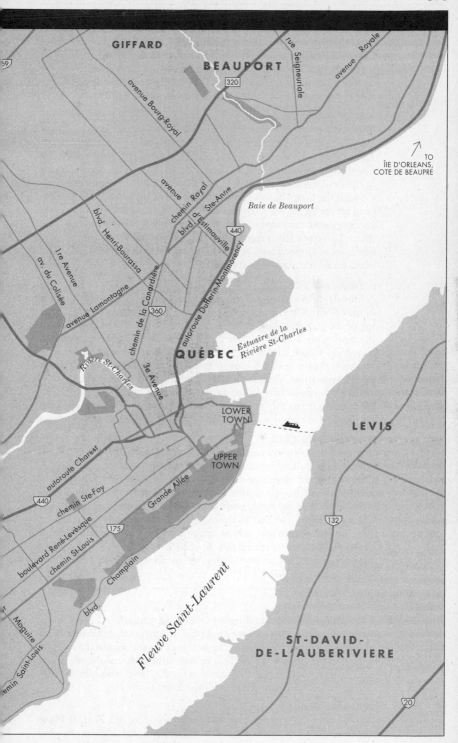

GIFFARD

BEAUPORT

rue Seigneuriale

avenue Royale

avenue Bourg-Royal

320

avenue

chemin Royal

blvd. Henri-Bourassa

blvd. d'Estimauville

Ste-Anne

TO
ÎLE D'ORLEANS,
COTE DE BEAUPRE

Baie de Beauport

440

1re Avenue

av. du Colisée

avenue Lamontagne

chemin de la Canardière

360

autoroute Dufferin-Montmorency

QUÉBEC

*Estuaire de la
Rivière St-Charles*

Rivière St-Charles

3e Avenue

LOWER
TOWN

LEVIS

autoroute Charest

UPPER
TOWN

440

chemin Ste-Foy

Grande Allée

132

175

boulevard René-Lévesque

chemin St-Louis

Champlain

Fleuve Saint-Laurent

Maguire

blvd.

chemin Saint-Louis

**ST-DAVID-
DE-L'AUBERIVIERE**

20

Great Itineraries

Whether you take a weekend or almost a week, there's enough history, scenery, and entertainment for even the most seasoned traveler. On a weekend or four-day trip, you can take in the historic sites of Vieux-Québec, walking along ancient streets and the boardwalk by the river before dining at some of the city's fine restaurants. A longer stay allows you to explore some lovely places beyond the city.

IF YOU HAVE 2 DAYS

With only a couple of days, you should devote one day to Lower Town, where you can view the earliest site of French civilization in North America, and the second day to Upper Town, where more of the later British influence can be seen. On Day 1, stroll through the narrow streets of the Petit-Champlain, visiting the Maison Chevalier and browsing through the many handicraft boutiques. Moving on to Place Royale, head for the Église Notre-Dame-des-Victoires; in summer there's a wide variety of entertainment in the square. On Day 2, take the time to view the St. Lawrence River from Terrasse Dufferin and visit the impressive buildings of Upper Town, where 17th- and 18th-century religious and educational institutions predominate.

IF YOU HAVE 4 DAYS

A four-day trip allows you to wander farther afield, outside the walls of the old city. On Day 3, watch the pomp and ceremony of the changing of the guard at the Citadelle; roam the Plains of Abraham, site of the battle that decided the fate of New France; and tour the National Assembly, where battles for power are still being waged. On Day 4, you can take an in-depth look at the Musée du Québec or the Musée de la Civilisation. Then see the city from a different vantage point—aboard a horse-drawn *calèche* or from a walk atop the ramparts. In summer, do what the locals do—grab a seat on an outdoor *terrasse,* sip a cool drink, and watch the world go by.

IF YOU HAVE 6 DAYS

A trip this length gives you time to experience some of Québec's scenic countryside. Follow the itinerary above for a four-day trip. On Day 5, you could spend more time exploring Vieux-Québec. Or you could take historic avenue Royale (Route 360) east to Montmorency Falls, higher than Niagara. Afterward, you can explore the farms and woodlands of Ile d'Orléans. On Day 6, do something you've never done before. In summer, you can take a boat cruise along the St. Lawrence or raft down the Jacques Cartier River. In winter, strap on skis and head to Mont Ste-Anne. Try snowmobiling, dogsledding, or even ice climbing at Montmorency Falls.

Upper Town

The most prominent buildings of Québec City's earliest European inhabitants, who set up the city's political, educational, and religious institutions, stand here. Haute-Ville, or Upper Town, became the political capital of the colony of New France and, later, of British North America. Historic buildings with thick stone walls, large wood doors, copper roofs, and majestic steeples fill the heart of the city.

A Good Walk

Begin your walk where rue St-Louis meets rue du Fort at **Place d'Armes** ①, a large plaza bordered by government buildings. To your right is the colony's former treasury building, **Maison Maillou,** interesting for its 18th-century architecture. Maison Kent, where the terms of the surrender of Québec to the British were signed in 1759, is a little farther along, at 25 rue St-Louis. Québec City's most celebrated landmark, **Château Frontenac** ②, an impressive green-turreted hotel, stands south of Place d'Armes. As you head to the boardwalk behind the Frontenac, notice the glorious bronze statue of Champlain, standing where he built his residence.

Walk south along the boardwalk called the **Terrasse Dufferin** ③, where street performers provide a lively atmosphere in summer, for a panoramic view of the city and its surroundings. As you pass to the southern side of the Frontenac, you arrive at a small park called **Jardin des Gouverneurs** ④. From the north side of the park, follow rue Haldimand and turn left on rue St-Louis, past the **Musée d'Art Inuit Brousseau**; then make a right and follow rue du Parloir until it intersects with tiny rue Donnacona. Here stands the **Couvent des Ursulines** ⑤, a private school that houses a museum and has a lovely chapel next door.

Take rue Donnacona to rue des Jardins and visit the **Holy Trinity Anglican Cathedral** ⑥, a dignified church with precious objects on display. Next come two buildings interesting for their art deco details: the **Hôtel Clarendon** ⑦, on the corner of rue des Jardins and rue Ste-Anne, and, next door, the **Edifice Price** ⑧. Continue along rue Ste-Anne up to rue St-Stanislas and **Morrin College** ⑨, which now houses the Literary and Historical Society library. Walk along rue St-Stanislas and turn left onto rue Dauphine, to the **Chapelle des Jésuites** ⑩ at the corner of rues Dauphine and d'Auteuil. Turn right on rue d'Auteuil and head down the hill to rue St-Jean and the entrance to the **Parc de l'Artillerie** ⑪, a complex of 20 military, industrial, and civilian buildings.

On your way out of Artillery Park, turn left, away from the walls, and walk along rue St-Jean, one of Québec City's most colorful thoroughfares; turn left on rue Collins. The cluster of stone buildings at the end of the street is the **Monastère des Augustines de l'Hôtel-Dieu de Québec** ⑫, which can be toured. Turn right onto rue Charlevoix, then left on rue Hamel to rue des Remparts. **Maison Montcalm** ⑬, the famous general's former home, is to the right, on rue des Remparts between rues Hamel and St-Flavien.

Continue along rue des Remparts and then turn right on rue Ste-Famille. When you reach côte de la Fabrique, look for the iron entrance gates of the **Séminaire du Québec** ⑭. Head west across the courtyard to the **Musée de l'Amérique Française** ⑮. Next, visit the seminary's Chapelle Extérieure, at its west entrance.

The historic **Basilique Notre-Dame-de-Québec** ⑯, which has an ornate interior, is nearby at the corner of rues Ste-Famille and de Buade. Turn left on rue de Buade, then cross the street halfway down the block and wander through the outdoor art gallery of **rue du Trésor** ⑰. At the end of the alley, turn left on rue Ste-Anne and wind up your walk (and rest your feet) with a 30-minute recap of the six sieges of Québec City at the **Musée du Fort** ⑱.

TIMING

Plan on spending at least a day visiting the sites and museums in Upper Town. Lunchtime should find you around Parc de l'Artillerie and rue St-Jean, where there is a good selection of restaurants. Those who prefer a leisurely pace could take two days, stopping to watch street performers and enjoying long lunches. May through October are the best months for walking, July and August being the busiest.

Sights to See

⑯ **Basilique Notre-Dame-de-Québec.** This basilica has the oldest parish in North America, dating from 1647. It's been rebuilt three times: in the early 1700s, when François de Montmorency Laval was the first

596

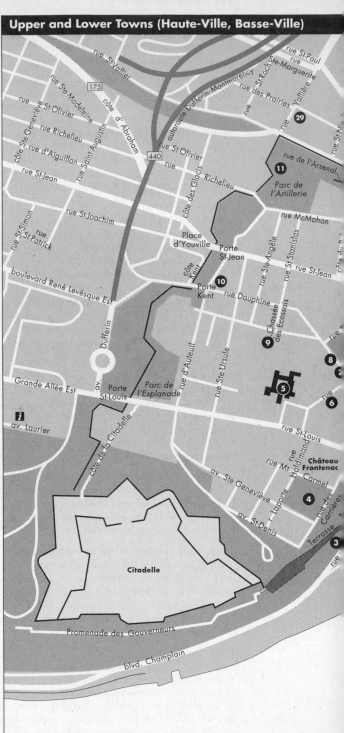

Upper and Lower Towns (Haute-Ville, Basse-Ville)

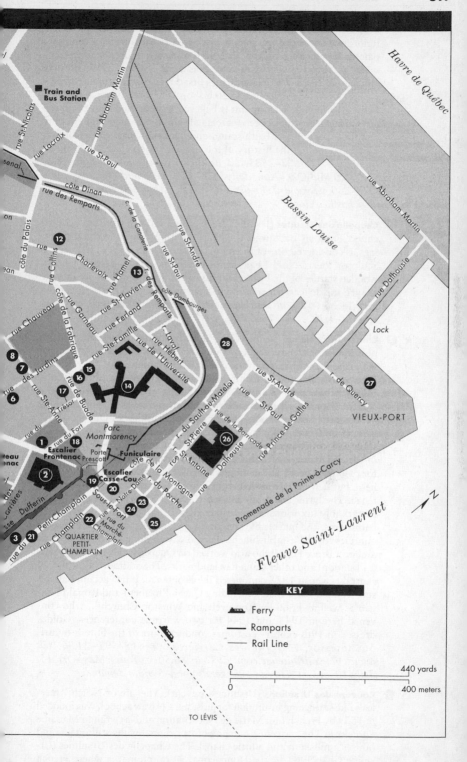

Train and Bus Station

Havre de Québec

rue St-Nicolas
rue Lacroix
rue St-Paul
rue Abraham Martin

rsenal

côte Dinan
rue des Remparts

on

côte du Palais
rue
rue Collins
rue Chauveau
côte de la Fabrique

Charlevoix
rue Garneau
rue St-Flavien
rue Ferland
rue Ste-Famille

rue Hamel
r. des Remparts
côte Dambourges
r. Lavol
rue Hébert
rue de l'Université

rue St-André
rue St-Paul

Bassin Louise

rue Abraham Martin

rue Dalhousie

Lock

8
7
rue des Jardins
6
rue Ste-Anne
rue du
16
15
17
rue de Buade
rue Trésor
14

Parc Montmorency

1
rue du Fort
18
Porte Prescott
Funiculaire

Escalier Frontenac

2

rue des Carrières
Dufferin
sse
19
Escalier Casse-Cou
20
Sous-le-Fort
côte de la Montagne
r. Notre-Dame
r. du Porche

r. du Sault-au-Matelot
rue St-Pierre
rue St-Antoine
r. de la Barricade
rue St-Paul
rue Prince-de-Galles
rue Dalhousie

28

r. St-Paul

rue St-André

r. de Quercy

27

VIEUX-PORT

26

Promenade de la Pointe-à-Carcy

3
21
Petit-Champlain
rue Champlain
22
rue du Marché
r. rue du Champlain
23
24
25

QUARTIER PETIT-CHAMPLAIN

Fleuve Saint-Laurent

N

KEY

Ferry
Ramparts
Rail Line

0   440 yards
0   400 meters

TO LÉVIS

bishop; in 1759, after cannons at Lévis fired upon it during the siege of Québec; and in 1922, after a fire. The basilica's somberly ornate interior includes a canopy dais over the episcopal throne, a ceiling of painted clouds decorated with gold leaf, richly colored stained-glass windows, and a chancel lamp that was a gift of Louis XIV. The large and famous crypt was Québec City's first cemetery; more than 900 people are interred here, including 20 bishops and four governors of New France. Samuel de Champlain is believed to be buried near the basilica: archaeologists have been searching for his tomb since 1950. In summer the indoor Act of Faith sound-and-light show uses the basilica as a backdrop to tell the history of the city and the basilica. ⊠ *16 rue de Buade,* ☎ *418/692–2533.* ⊡ *Basilica free, sound-and-light show $7.50.* ☉ *Mid-Oct.–Apr., daily 7:30–4:30; May–mid-Oct., weekdays 7:30–2:30, weekends 7:30–6; sound-and-light show late Apr.–early Oct., after basilica closes.*

🔟 **Chapelle des Jésuites** (Jesuits' Chapel). Built in 1820 from plans by architect François Baillairgé, the chapel, with its sculptures and paintings, is considered one of the monuments of Québec art of the period. Sculptor Pierre-Noël Levasseur contributed the mid-18th-century wooden statues of the Blessed Virgin and St. Joseph, which predate the chapel; the delicately carved high altar was designed by architect Eugène Taché. ⊠ *20 rue Dauphine,* ☎ *418/694–9616.* ⊡ *Free.* ☉ *Weekdays 11–1:30.*

★ ❷ **Château Frontenac.** Québec City's most celebrated landmark, this imposing green-turreted castle with its copper roof stands on the site of what was the administrative and military headquarters of New France. It owes its name to the Comte de Frontenac, governor of the French colony between 1672 and 1698. Looking at the magnificence of the château's location, you can see why Frontenac said, "For me, there is no site more beautiful nor more grandiose than that of Québec City." Samuel de Champlain, who founded Québec City in 1608, was responsible for Château St-Louis, the first structure to appear on the site of the Frontenac; it was built between 1620 and 1624 as a residence for colonial governors. In 1784 Château Haldimand was constructed here, but it was demolished in 1892 to make way for Château Frontenac. The latter was built as a hotel in 1893, and it was considered remarkably luxurious at that time: guest rooms contained fireplaces, bathrooms, and marble fixtures, and a special commissioner purchased antiques for the establishment. The hotel was designed by New York architect Bruce Price, who also worked on Québec City's Gare du Palais (rail station) and other Canadian landmarks. The addition of a 20-story central tower in 1925 completed the Frontenac. It has accumulated a star-studded guest roster, including Queen Elizabeth and Ronald Reagan as well as Franklin Roosevelt and Winston Churchill, who convened here in 1943 and 1944 for two wartime conferences. Guides dressed in 19th-century costumes conduct tours of the hotel's luxurious interior. ⊠ *1 rue des Carrières,* ☎ *418/691–2166,* WEB *www.chateaufrontenac.com.* ⊡ *Tours $6.50.* ☉ *Tours: May–Oct. 15, daily 10–6; Oct. 16–Apr., weekends noon–5 or on demand.*

❺ **Couvent des Ursulines** (Ursuline Convent). The site of North America's oldest teaching institution for girls, still a private school, was founded in 1639 by French nun Marie de l'Incarnation and laywoman Madame La Peltrie. The convent has many of its original walls still intact, and houses a museum and a little chapel. The **Chapelle des Ursulines** (Ursuline Chapel; ⊠ 12 rue Donnacona, ☎ no phone) is where French general Louis-Joseph Montcalm was buried after he died in the 1759 battle that decided the fate of New France. The exterior was rebuilt in

1902, but the interior contains the original chapel, which took sculptor Pierre-Noël Levasseur from 1726 to 1736 to complete. The votive lamp was lit in 1717 and has never been extinguished. The chapel is open May–October, Tuesday through Saturday 10–11:30 and 1:30–4:30, Sunday 1:30–4:30. Admission is free. The **Musée des Ursulines** (✉ 12 rue Donnacona, ☎ 418/694–0694) is the former residence of one of the convent's founders, Madame de la Peltrie. It provides an informative perspective on 120 years of the Ursulines' life under the French regime, from 1639 to 1759. It took an Ursuline nun nine years of training to attain the level of a professional embroiderer; the museum contains magnificent pieces of ornate embroidery, such as altar frontals with gold and silver threads intertwined with semi-precious jewels. Admission is $4. May through September the museum is open Tuesday through Saturday 10–noon and 1–5, Sunday 1–5; in October and November and February through April it's open Tuesday through Sunday 1–4:30. Next door to the museum is the **Centre Marie-de-l'Incarnation** (✉ 10 rue Donnacona, ☎ 418/694–0413), a center with an exhibit and books for sale on the life of the Ursulines' first superior, who came from France and cofounded the convent. The center is open March–October, Tuesday through Saturday 10–11:30 and 1:30–4:30, Sunday 1:30–4:30; in February and November, it's open Tuesday through Sunday 1:30–4:30. ✉ *18 rue Donnacona.*

★ ❽ **Edifice Price** (Price Building). The city's first skyscraper, a 15-story art-deco structure, was built in 1929 and served as headquarters of the Price Brothers Company, the lumber firm founded in Canada by Sir William Price. Don't miss the interior: exquisite copper plaques depict scenes of the company's early pulp and paper activities, and the two maple-wood elevators are '30s classics. Only the lobby is open to the public. ✉ *65 rue Ste-Anne.*

❻ **Holy Trinity Anglican Cathedral.** This stone church dates from 1804 and was one of the first Anglican cathedrals built outside the British Isles. Its simple, dignified facade is reminiscent of London's St. Martin-in-the-Fields. The cathedral's land was originally given to the Recollet fathers (Franciscan monks from France) in 1681 by the king of France for a church and monastery. When Québec came under British rule, the Recollets made the church available to the Anglicans for services. Later, King George III of England ordered construction of the present cathedral, with an area set aside for members of the royal family. A portion of the north balcony still remains exclusively for the use of the reigning sovereign or her representative. The church houses precious objects donated by George III; wood for the oak benches was imported from the Royal Forest at Windsor. The cathedral's impressive rear organ has more than 2,500 pipes. ✉ *31 rue des Jardins,* ☎ *418/692–2193.* 🎟 *Free.* ☉ *Mid-May–June, daily 9–5; July–Aug., daily 9–9; Sept.–Oct., weekdays 10–6; Nov.–mid-May, services only; Sun. services in English at 11 AM, in French at 9:30 AM.*

❼ **Hôtel Clarendon.** One of the city's finest art-deco structures is the Clarendon, Québec's oldest hotel. Although the hotel dates from 1866, it was reconstructed in its current style, with geometric patterns of stone and wrought iron decorating its interior, in 1930. ✉ *57 rue Ste-Anne, at rue des Jardins,* ☎ *418/692–2480.*

❹ **Jardin des Gouverneurs** (Governors' Park). This small park on the south side of the Château Frontenac is home to the **Wolfe-Montcalm Monument,** a 50-ft obelisk that is unique because it pays tribute to both a winning (English) and a losing (French) general. The monument recalls the 1759 battle on the Plains of Abraham, which ended French rule of New France. British general James Wolfe lived only long enough to hear of his victory; French general Louis-Joseph Montcalm died shortly after Wolfe with the knowledge that the city was lost. During the French regime the public area served as a garden for the governors who resided in Château St-Louis. On the south side of the park is **avenue Ste-Geneviève**, lined with well-preserved Victorian houses dating from 1850 to 1900. Several have been converted to old-fashioned inns.

Maison Maillou. The colony's former treasury building typifies the architecture of New France with its sharply slanted roof, dormer windows, concrete chimneys, shutters with iron hinges, and limestone walls. Built between 1736 and 1753, it stands at the end of **rue du Trésor**. Maison Maillou now houses the Québec City Chamber of Commerce and is not open for tours. ✉ *17 rue St-Louis.*

⑬ Maison Montcalm. This was the home of French general Louis-Joseph Montcalm from 1758 until the capitulation of New France. A plaque dedicated to the general is on the right side of the house. ✉ *Rue des Remparts between rues Hamel and St-Flavien. Closed to public.*

⑫ Monastère des Augustines de l'Hôtel-Dieu de Québec (Augustine Monastery). Augustine nuns arrived from Dieppe, France, in 1639 with a mission to care for the sick in the new colony. They established the first hospital north of Mexico, the **Hôtel-Dieu**, the large building west of the monastery. The **Musée des Augustines** (Augustine Museum) is in hospital-like quarters with large sterile corridors leading into a ward that has a small exhibit of antique medical instruments, such as a pill-making device. Upon request the Augustines also offer guided tours of the **chapel** (1800) and the cellars used by the nuns as a shelter, beginning in 1659, during bombardments by the British. During the Second World War, the cellars hid national treasures that had been smuggled out of Poland for safekeeping. ✉ *32 rue Charlevoix,* ☎ *418/692–2492.* 🎟 *Museum free, guided tour $3.* ⊙ *Tues.–Sat. 9:30–noon and 1:30–5, Sun. 1:30–5.*

★ ⑨ Morrin College. This stately gray stone building was once Québec City's first prison (the cells are still in the basement), where wrongdoers were hanged outside the front door. In 1868 it was turned into one of the city's early private schools, Morrin College. The **Literary and Historical Society library** has been on the site since then. Its superb collection includes some of the earliest books printed in North America, and the librarian's desk once belonged to Sir Georges-Étienne Cartier, one of Canada's fathers of Confederation. A statue of Gen. James Wolfe, on the second-floor balcony that wraps around the interior of the library, dates from 1779. The society, founded in 1824, is the oldest of its kind in North America and a forerunner to Canada's National Archives. ✉ *44 rue Chausée des Ecossais,* ☎ *418/694–9147.* 🎟 *Free.* ⊙ *Tues., Thurs.–Fri. 9:30–4:30, Wed. 9:30–6:30, weekends 10–4.*

Musée d'Art Inuit Brousseau. The first museum south of the Arctic circle to be dedicated exclusively to Inuit art and culture includes some surviving examples of Inuit art from more than 200 years ago and shows how the art has evolved following contact with white people. The collection includes Inuit artifacts and a wide range of works by Inuit artists, illustrating different styles and using materials such as walrus tusks, bone, caribou antlers, soapstone, basalt, and serpentine. ✉ *39 rue St-Louis,* ☎ *418/694–1828.* 🎟 *$6.* ⊙ *Daily 9:30–5:30.*

⑮ Musée de l'Amérique Française. Housed in a former student residence of the Québec Seminary, Laval University, this museum focuses on the history of the French in North America. You can view about 20 of the museum's 400 landscape and still-life paintings, some from as early as the 15th century, rare Canadian money from colonial times, a 3,500-

year-old mummy, and scientific instruments acquired for the purposes of research and teaching. The museum uses historical documents and movies to tell the story as well. A former chapel is used for exhibits, conferences, and cultural activities. ⊠ *2 côte de la Fabrique,* ☎ *418/ 692–2843.* 🖾 *$4, free Tues. early Sept.–June 23.* ◷ *June 24–early Sept., daily 9:30–5; early Sept.–June 23, Tues.–Sun. 10–5.*

<table>
<tr><td>NEED A
BREAK?</td><td>The stone-walled **Bistro Le Figaro** (⊠ 32 rue St-Louis, ☎ 418/692–4191), on the corner of rues des Jardins and St-Louis, is a good place to sample delicious salads, pastries, and desserts.</td></tr>
</table>

⑱ **Musée du Fort.** This museum's sole exhibit is a sound-and-light show that reenacts the area's important battles, including the battle of the Plains of Abraham and the 1775 attack by American generals Arnold and Montgomery. ⊠ *10 rue Ste-Anne,* ☎ *418/692–1759.* 🖾 *$6.25.* ◷ *Apr. 1–Oct. 31, daily 10–5; Nov.–Jan., by reservation; Feb.–Mar., Thurs.–Sun. noon–4.*

★ ⑪ **Parc de l'Artillerie** (Artillery Park). This national historic park is a complex of 20 military, industrial, and civilian buildings that were situated to guard the St. Charles River and the Old Port. Its earliest buildings served as headquarters for the French garrison and were taken over in 1759 by the British Royal Artillery soldiers. The defense complex was used as a fortress, barracks, and cartridge factory during the American siege of Québec in 1775–76. The area served as an industrial complex providing ammunition for the Canadian army from 1879 until 1964. One of the three buildings open is a former **powder magazine,** which in 1903 became a shell foundry. It houses a detailed model of the buildings, streets, and military structures of Québec City in 1808, rendered by two surveyors in the office of the Royal Engineers Corps. Sent to Britain in 1813, the model was intended to show officials the strategic importance of Québec so that more money would be provided to expand the city's fortifications. The **Dauphin Redoubt,** named in honor of the son of Louis XIV (the heir apparent), was constructed from 1712 to 1748. It served as a barracks for the French garrison until 1760, when it became an officers' mess for the Royal Artillery Regiment. The **Officers' Quarters,** a dwelling for Royal Artillery officers until 1871 when the British army departed, has an exhibit on military life during the British regime. A former cannon warehouse now houses **Les Dames de Soie** (☎ 418/692–1516), an economuseum devoted to dolls where visitors can watch porcelain dolls being made (admission is free). From June 24 to early September, it's open Monday through Saturday 9:30–6 and Sunday noon–6; the rest of the year it's open Tuesday through Saturday 11–5. ⊠ *2 rue d'Auteuil,* ☎ *418/648–4205,* 🖳 *www. parcscanada.risq.qc.ca/artillery.* 🖾 *$3.50.* ◷ *Apr.–Oct., daily 10–5.*

❶ **Place d'Armes.** For centuries, this square atop a cliff has been used for parades and military events. Upper Town's most central location, the plaza is bordered by government buildings; at its west side is the majestic **Ancien Palais de Justice** (Old Courthouse), a Renaissance-style building from 1887. The plaza is on land that was occupied by a church and convent of the Recollet missionaries (Franciscan monks), who in 1615 were the first order of priests to arrive in New France. The Gothic-style **fountain** at the center of Place d'Armes pays tribute to their arrival. ⊠ *Rues St-Louis and du Fort.*

⑰ **Rue du Trésor.** The road that colonists took on their way to pay rent to the king's officials is now a narrow alley where colorful prints, paintings, and other artworks are on display. You won't necessarily find masterpieces, but this walkway is a good stop for a souvenir sketch or two.

In summer, activity on this street and nearby rue Ste-Anne, lined with eateries and boutiques, starts early in the morning and continues until late at night. Stores stay open, artists paint, and street musicians perform as long as there is an audience, even if it's 1 AM. At 8 rue du Trésor is the **Québec Experience** (☎ 418/694–4000), a multimedia sound-and-light show that traces Québec's history from the first explorers until modern days; cost is $6.75.

⓮ Séminaire du Québec. Behind these gates lies a tranquil courtyard surrounded by austere stone buildings with rising steeples; these structures have housed classrooms and student residences since 1663. François de Montmorency Laval, the first bishop of New France, founded Québec Seminary to train priests in the new colony. In 1852 the seminary became Université Laval, the first Catholic university in North America. In 1946 the university moved to a larger campus in suburban Ste-Foy. Today priests live on the premises, and Laval's architecture school occupies part of the building. The on-site **Musée de l'Amerique Francaise** gives tours ($4) of the seminary grounds in summer. The small Second Empire–style chapel, **Chapelle Extérieure** (Outer Chapel), at the west entrance of Québec Seminary, was built in 1888 after fire destroyed the original 1750 chapel. Joseph-Ferdinand Peachy designed the chapel; its interior decor is patterned after that of the Église de la Trinité in Paris. ⊠ *1 côte de la Fabrique,* ☎ *418/692–3981.* ☉ *Tours Jun. 24–early Sept., daily 9:45–3:45.*

❸ Terrasse Dufferin. This wide boardwalk with an intricate wrought-iron guardrail has a panoramic view of the St. Lawrence River, the town of Lévis on the opposite shore, Ile d'Orléans, and the Laurentian Mountains. It was named for Lord Dufferin, governor of Canada between 1872 and 1878, who had this walkway constructed in 1878. The **Promenade des Gouverneurs,** which skirts the cliff and leads up to Québec's highest point, Cap Diamant, and also to the Citadelle, begins at its western end.

Lower Town

New France first began to flourish in the streets of the Basse-Ville, or Lower Town, along the banks of the St. Lawrence River. These streets became the colony's economic crossroads, where furs were traded, ships came in, and merchants established their residences. Despite the status of Lower Town as the oldest neighborhood in North America, its narrow and time-worn thoroughfares have a new and polished look. In the 1960s, after a century of decay as the commercial boom moved west and left the area abandoned, the Québec government committed millions of dollars to restore the district to the way it had been during the days of New France. Today the area is undergoing a renaissance. Modern boutiques, restaurants, galleries, and shops catering to visitors occupy the former warehouses and residences.

A Good Walk

Begin this walk on the northern end of rue du Petit-Champlain, at **Maison Louis-Jolliet** ⑲ at the foot of the **Escalier Casse-Cou.** The **Verrerie La Mailloche** ⑳ is across the street, where master glassblowers create contemporary works of art. Heading south on **rue du Petit-Champlain** ㉑, the city's oldest street, notice the cliff on the right that borders this narrow thoroughfare, with Upper Town on the heights above. At the point where rue du Petit-Champlain intersects with boulevard Champlain, make a U-turn to head back north on rue Champlain. One block farther, at the corner of rue du Marché-Champlain, is **Maison Chevalier** ㉒, a stone house in the style of urban New France. Walk east to rue Notre-Dame, which leads directly to **Place Royale** ㉓, formerly the heart of New France. The interpretation center here features exhibits on life in the colony. The small stone church at the south side of Place Royale is the **Église Notre-Dame-des-Victoires** ㉔, the oldest church in Québec.

On the east side of Place Royale, take rue de la Place, which leads to an open square, **Place de Paris** ㉕. Head north on rue Dalhousie until you come to the **Musée de la Civilisation** ㉖, devoted to Québécois culture and civilization. Walk east toward the river to the **Vieux-Port de Québec** ㉗, at one time the busiest port on the continent. The breezes from the St. Lawrence provide a cool reprieve on a hot summer's day, and you can browse through a farmers' market here. You are now in the ideal spot to explore Québec City's **antiques district** ㉘.

In summer walk west along rue St-Paul, all the way past the train station built in 1915 in the style of the castles in France's Loire Valley, and turn left on rue Vallière to **L'Ilot des Palais** ㉙, an archaeological museum that has the remnants of the first two palaces of the French colonial intendants (administrators).

TIMING

This is a good day of sightseeing. A morning stroll takes you to two of the city's most famous squares, Place Royale and Place de Paris. You can see the city from the Lévis ferry, if you wish, or pause for lunch before touring the Musée de la Civilisation and the antiques district. After browsing along rue St-Paul, explore L'Ilot des Palais, open in summer.

Sights to See

㉘ **Antiques district.** Antiques shops cluster around rues St-Pierre and St-Paul. Rue St-Paul was once part of a business district where warehouses, stores, and businesses abounded. After World War I, shipping and commercial activities plummeted; low rents attracted antiques dealers. Today numerous cafés, restaurants, and art galleries have turned this area into one of the town's more fashionable sections.

㉔ **Église Notre-Dame-des-Victoires** (Our Lady of Victory Church). The oldest church in Québec stands on the site of Samuel de Champlain's first residence, which also served as a fort and trading post. The church was built in 1688 and has been restored twice. Its name comes from two French victories against the British: one in 1690 against Admiral William Phipps and another in 1711 against Sir Hovendon Walker. The interior contains copies of paintings by European masters such as Van Dyck, Rubens, and Boyermans; its altar resembles the shape of a fort. A scale model suspended from the ceiling represents *Le Brezé*, the boat that transported French soldiers to New France in 1664. The side chapel is dedicated to Ste-Geneviève, the patron saint of Paris. ⊠ *Pl. Royale,* ☎ *418/692–1650.* ☜ *Free.* ☺ *Mid-May–mid-Oct., daily 9– 5, except during mass (Sun. at 10:30 and noon), marriages, and funerals; mid-Oct.–mid-May, daily 10–4, except during mass, marriages, and funerals.*

Escalier Casse-Cou. The steepness of the city's first iron stairway, an ambitious 1893 design by city architect and engineer Charles Baillairgé, is ample evidence of how it got its name: Breakneck Steps. The 170 steps were built on the site of the original 17th-century stairway that linked the Upper Town and Lower Town during the French regime. Today shops and restaurants can be found at various levels.

㉙ **L'Ilot des Palais.** More than 300 years of history have been laid bare at this archaeological museum on the site of the first two palaces of New France's colonial intendants. The first palace, erected as a brewery by Jean Talon in 1669, was turned into the intendant's residence in 1685 and destroyed by fire in 1713. In 1716, a second palace was built facing the first. It was later turned into a modern brewery, but the basement vaults remain and now feature an archaeology exhibit and a multimedia display. ✉ *8 rue Vallière,* ☏ *418/691–6092.* 🎫 *$3.* ⏲ *June 24–early Sept., daily 10–5.*

OFF THE BEATEN PATH

LÉVIS–QUÉBEC FERRY – En route to the opposite shore of the St. Lawrence River, you get a striking view of Québec City's skyline, with the Château Frontenac and the Québec Seminary high atop the cliff. The view is even more impressive at night. ✉ *Rue Dalhousie, 1 block south of Place de Paris,* ☏ *418/644–3704.* 🎫 *Winter $1.80, summer $2.25.*

22 **Maison Chevalier.** This old stone house was built in 1752 for shipowner Jean-Baptiste Chevalier. The house's style, of classic French inspiration, clearly reflects the urban architecture of New France. The fire walls, chimneys, vaulted cellars, and original wood beams and stone fireplaces are noteworthy. ✉ *50 rue du Marché-Champlain,* ☏ *418/643–2158.* 🎫 *Free.* ⏲ *May–June 23, Tues.–Sun. 10–5; June 24–Oct. 21, daily 9:30–5; Oct. 22–Apr., weekends 10–5.*

19 **Maison Louis-Jolliet.** The first settlers of New France used this house, built in 1683, as a base for further westward explorations. Today it's the lower station of the funicular. A monument commemorating Louis Jolliet's discovery of the Mississippi River in 1672 stands in the park next to the house. The **Escalier Casse-Cou** is at the north side of the house. ✉ *16 rue du Petit-Champlain.*

★ 26 **Musée de la Civilisation** (Museum of Civilization). Wedged into the foot of the cliff, this spacious museum with a striking limestone-and-glass facade has been artfully designed by architect Moshe Safdie to blend into the landscape. Its campanile echoes the shape of the city's church steeples. The museum's innovative exhibits explore aspects of Québec's culture. Some tell the story of how the first settlers lived, and how they survived such harsh winters. Others illustrate the extent to which the Roman Catholic Church dominated the people and explain the evolution of Québec nationalism. *Encounter with the First Nations* looks at the 11 aboriginal nations that inhabit Québec. Several of the shows, with their imaginative use of artwork, video screens, computers, and sound, appeal to both adults and children. The museum's thematic, interactive approach also extends to exhibits of an international nature. From Dec. 2001 to Sept. 2002 the museum is to host an exhibit featuring treasures from the Chinese city of Xi'an, including life-size terracotta warriors buried for 2,200 years. ✉ *85 rue Dalhousie,* ☏ *418/643–2158,* WEB *www.mcq.org.* 🎫 *$7, free Tues. Labor Day–June 23.* ⏲ *June 24–Labor Day, daily 9:30–6:30; Sept.–June 23, Tues.–Sun. 10–5.*

25 **Place de Paris.** A black-and-white geometric sculpture, *Dialogue avec l'Histoire* (*Dialogue with History*) dominates this square and is a newcomer (1987) to these historic quarters. A gift from France, the sculpture is on the site where the first French settlers landed. ✉ *Rue Dalhousie.*

NEED A BREAK?

Beer has been brewed in Québec since the early 17th century and **L'Inox** (✉ 37 quai St-André, ☏ 418/692–2877) carries on the tradition with a combination brew pub and beer museum. The decor is a blend of the old and the new: cherry-red columns and a stainless-steel bar contrasting with exposed stone and brick walls. Outside, there's a large sunny terrace that's open in summer. L'Inox offers a wide variety of its own beers brewed on site as well as most other beverages, both alcoholic and not. Food is limited to European-style hot dogs served in baguettes or plates of

Québec cheeses. If you reserve in advance, you can also take a guided tour of the brewery ($5) and partake in a taste test.

★ ⬭ ㉓ **Place Royale.** Formerly the homes of wealthy merchants, houses with steep Normandy-style roofs, dormer windows, and several chimneys encircle this cobblestone square. Until 1686 the area was called Place du Marché, but its name changed when a bust of Louis XIV was erected at its center. During the late 1600s and early 1700s, when Place Royale was continually under threat of attacks from the British, the colonists progressively moved to higher and safer quarters atop the cliff in Upper Town. Yet after the French colony fell to British rule in 1759, Place Royale flourished again with shipbuilding, logging, fishing, and fur trading. The Fresque des Québécois, a 420-square-meter trompe-l'oeil mural depicting 400 years of Quebec's history, is to the east of the square, at the corner of rue Notre-Dame and côte de la Montagne. An information center, the **Centre d'Interpretation de Place Royale** (✉ 27 rue Notre-Dame, ☎ 418/646–3167) includes exhibits, a multimedia show, and a Discovery Hall with a replica of a 19th-century home where children can try on period costumes. Admission is $3, free on Tuesday from early September to June 23. It's open daily 9:30–5 June 24 to early September. The rest of the year it's open 10–5, closed on Monday.

㉑ **Rue du Petit-Champlain.** The oldest street in the city was the main street of a former harbor village, with trading posts and the homes of rich merchants. Today it has pleasant boutiques and cafés. Natural-fiber weaving, Inuit carvings, hand-painted silks, and enameled copper crafts are some of the local specialties that are good buys here.

⬭ ⑳ **Verrerie La Mailloche.** The glassblowing techniques used in this combination workshop, boutique, and museum are as old as Ancient Egypt, but the results are contemporary. In the workshop, master glassblower Jean Vallières and his assistants turn 1,092°C (2,000°F) molten glass into works of art and answer questions. Examples of Vallières' work have been presented by the Canadian government to visiting dignitaries such as Queen Elizabeth and former president Ronald Reagan. ✉ 58 rue Sous-le-Fort, ☎ 418/694–0445. 🎟 Free. ☉ Workshop June–Oct., Wed.–Sun. 10–4:30; Nov.–May, weekdays 10–4:30. Boutique regular store hrs in winter, daily 9 AM–10 PM in summer.

㉗ **Vieux-Port de Québec** (Old Port of Québec). Today this historic 72-acre area encompasses several parks. The old harbor dates from the 17th century, when ships first arrived from Europe bringing supplies and settlers to the new colony. At one time this port was among the busiest on the continent: between 1797 and 1897, Québec shipyards turned out more than 2,500 ships, many of which passed the 1,000-ton mark. The port saw a rapid decline after steel and steam replaced wood and the channel to Montréal was deepened to allow larger boats to reach a good port upstream. You can stroll along the riverside promenade, where merchant and cruise ships dock. At the port's northern end, where the St. Charles meets the St. Lawrence, a lock protects the marina in the Louise Basin from the generous Atlantic tides that reach even this far up the St. Lawrence. In the northwest section of the port, the **Old Port of Québec Interpretation Center** (✉ 100 quai St-André, ☎ 418/648–3300) presents the history of the port in relation to the lumber trade and shipbuilding. Admission to the center is $3; it's open daily May to Labor Day 10–5, early September to October 6 1–5, and by reservation only October 7 through April. From June 22 through August 31, guides in 19th-century costume conduct walking tours of the port ($8). The **Marché du Vieux-Port** (Old Port Market), where farmers sell their fresh produce and cheese, as well as handicrafts, is at the port's northwestern tip. The market, near quai St-André, is open daily 8–8 in summer. Some of the stalls stay open in winter, 9–4.

The Fortifications

In the 20th century, Québec City grew into a modern metropolis outside the confines of the city walls. Beyond the walls lies a great deal of the city's military history, in the form of its fortifications and battlements, as well as a number of museums and other attractions.

A Good Walk

Start close to Porte St-Louis (St-Louis Gate) at the **Parc de l'Esplanade** ㉚, the site of a former military parade ground. From here you can tour the walls of the old city, North America's only walled city north of Mexico. From the powder magazine in the park, head south on côte de la Citadelle, which leads directly to **La Citadelle** ㉛, a historic fortified base. Retrace your steps on côte de la Citadelle to **Grande Allée** ㉜. Once you pass through the Porte St-Louis, turn left on avenue Georges VI past the concrete building that houses the premier's offices to the historic and scenic **Parc des Champs-de-Bataille** ㉝. Head up the hill to the Cap Diamant. Here at the observation point you have a spectacular view of the St. Lawrence River and the cliff that British general James Wolfe and his troops scaled to win the 1759 battle that decided the fate of New France. The exact point where Wolfe's forces made the ascent is just to the west of the plains at Gilmour Hill. Retrace your steps down the hill and turn left along avenue Georges VI.

Look left as you walk along avenue Georges VI to see the **Plains of Abraham** ㉞, site of the famous battle. The neatly tended garden **Parc Jeanne d'Arc** ㉟ is a little farther along, on the right. To the left, toward the south end of the park, stands **Tour Martello No. 1** ㊱, a stone defense tower. Continue along avenue Georges VI past where it turns into avenue de Bernières. Tour Martello No. 2 is to the right, up avenue Taché. Continue heading west along avenue de Bernières to avenue Wolfe-Montcalm, where you come to the tall **Wolfe Monument** ㊲, which marks the place where the British general died.

Turn left on avenue Wolfe-Montcalm to visit the **Musée de Québec** ㊳. Attached to the museum, the Centre d'interpretation du Parc des Champs-de-Bataille has a multimedia show on the battles that took place on the site.

From the museum, head north on avenue Wolfe-Montcalm, turning right on Grande Allée and walking a block to **avenue Cartier** ㊴. Across the street, at the corner of avenue Cartier, is the **Henry Stuart House** ㊵, which once marked the city's outskirts. Near the corner of avenue Cartier and Grande Allée, note the simple white house with green trim that was once the home of the well-known painter Cornelius Krieghoff. Today it's a private home, not open to the public. Continue east along Grande Allée to Cours du Général-de Montcalm, where you arrive at the **Montcalm Monument** ㊶. Farther along the Grande Allée, past the bars and restaurants, is the Manège Militaire, a turreted armory built in 1888 that is still a drill hall for the Royal 22nd Regiment. You can return on Grande Allée to your starting point or cross the street to begin the walk outside the walls.

TIMING

This walk takes a half day, or a full day if you begin by walking the walls of the city. In summer you should try to catch the colorful 10 AM changing of the guard at the Citadelle. For lunch try one of the many restaurants around avenue Cartier or bring a picnic and eat on the Plains of Abraham.

Outside the Walls

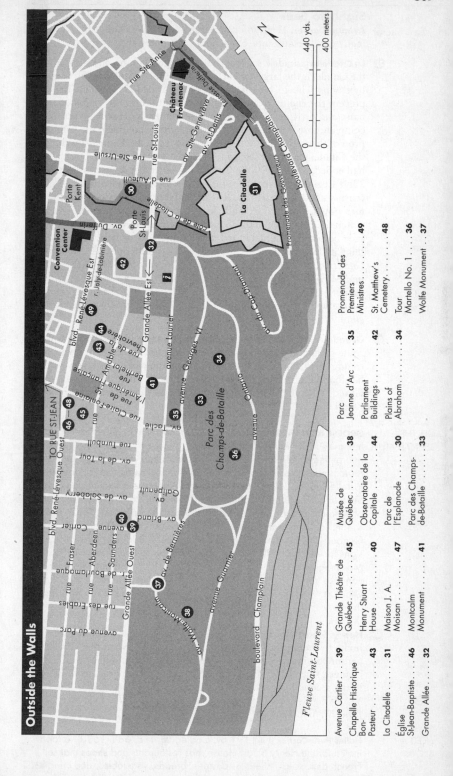

Avenue Cartier.... **39**

Chapelle Historique Bon-Pasteur **43**

La Citadelle **31**

Église St-Jean-Baptiste.... **46**

Grande Allée **32**

Grande Théâtre de Québec........ **45**

Henry Stuart House **40**

Maison J. A. Moisan **47**

Montcalm Monument **41**

Musée de Québec........ **38**

Observatoire de la Capitale **44**

Parc de l'Esplanade **30**

Parc des Champs-de-Bataille **33**

Parc Jeanne d'Arc **35**

Parliament Buildings ... **42**

Plains of Abraham........ **34**

Promenade des Premiers Ministres........ **49**

St. Matthew's Cemetery........ **48**

Tour Martello No. 1.... **36**

Wolfe Monument ... **37**

Sights to See

㉟ Avenue Cartier. Here you can indulge in the pleasures offered by the many good restaurants, clubs, and cafés lining the street.

㉛ La Citadelle (Citadel). Built at the city's highest point, on Cap Diamant, the Citadel is the largest fortified base in North America still occupied by troops. The 25-building fortress was intended to protect the port, prevent the enemy from taking up a position on the Plains of Abraham, and provide a refuge in case of an attack. Having inherited incomplete fortifications, the British sought to complete the Citadel to protect themselves against retaliations from the French. By the time the Citadel was completed in 1832, the attacks against Québec City had ended. Since 1920 the Citadel has served as a base for the Royal 22nd Regiment. Firearms, uniforms, and decorations from the 17th century are displayed in the **Royal 22nd Regiment Museum,** in the former powder magazine, built in 1750. If weather permits, you can watch the Changing of the Guard, a ceremony in which the troops parade before the Citadel in red coats and black fur hats. Admission to the Citadel and the museum is by guided tour only. ⊠ *1 côte de la Citadelle,* ☎ *418/694–2815.* ☞ *$6.* ☉ *Apr.–mid-May, daily 10–4; mid-May–June, daily 9–5; July–Labor Day, daily 9–6; Sept., daily 9– 4; Oct., daily 10–3; Nov.–Mar., groups only (reservations required). Changing of the guard June 24–Labor Day, daily 10 AM. Retreat ceremony July–Aug., Wed.–Sat. 6 PM.*

㉜ Grande Allée. One of the city's oldest streets, Grande Allée was the route people took from outlying areas to sell their furs in town. Now trendy cafés, clubs, and restaurants line the road. The street actually has four names: inside the city walls it's rue St-Louis; outside the walls, Grande Allée; farther west, chemin St-Louis; and farther still, boulevard Laurier.

OFF THE **GROSSE ILE NATIONAL PARK –** For thousands of immigrants from Europe
BEATEN PATH in the 1800s, the first glimpse of North America was the hastily erected quarantine station at Grosse Ile—Canada's equivalent of Ellis Island. For far too many passengers on the plague-racked ships, particularly the Irish fleeing the potato famine, Grosse Ile became a final resting place. Several buildings have been restored to tell the story of the tragic period of Irish immigration. During the time Grosse Ile operated (1832–1937), 4.3 million immigrants passed through the port of Québec. From Québec City, head south on the Pierre Laporte Bridge and follow the signs for Autoroute 20 East for about an hour to Berthier-sur-Mer or Montmagny. In either town, follow the signs to the marina where ferries can take you across to the island. Tours also depart from Québec City's Old Port. ☎ *418/248–8888 or 800/463–6769.* ☞ *$26–$48, including ferry.* ☉ *May–Oct., daily 9–6.*

㊵ Henry Stuart House. Built in 1849, this Regency-style cottage was home to the Stuart family from 1918 to 1987, when the Ministry of Culture designated it a historic monument. Its decor has remained unchanged since 1930. Most of the furniture was imported from England in the second half of the 19th century. ⊠ *82 Grande Allée Ouest,* ☎ *418/647–4347.* ☞ *$5.* ☉ *June 24–Labor Day, daily 11–5; early Sept.– June 23, Sun. 1–5.*

NEED A **Halles Petit-Cartier** (⊠ 1191 av. Cartier, ☎ 418/688–1630), a food
BREAK? mall near the Henry Stuart House, has restaurants and shops that sell French delicacies—cheeses, pastries, breads, vegetables, and candies.

㊵ **Montcalm Monument.** France and Canada joined together to erect this monument honoring Louis-Joseph Montcalm, the general who claimed his fame by winning four major battles in North America. His most famous battle, however, was the one he lost, when the British conquered New France on September 13, 1759. Montcalm was north of Québec City at Beauport when he learned that the British attack was imminent. He quickly assembled his troops to meet the enemy and was wounded in battle in the leg and stomach. Montcalm was carried into the walled city, where he died the next morning. ⊠ *Pl. Montcalm.*

★ ㊳ **Musée de Québec** (Québec Museum). A neoclassical Beaux-Arts showcase, the museum has more than 23,000 traditional and contemporary pieces of Québec art. The portraits by artists well known in the area, such as Jean-Paul Riopelle (1923-), and Horatio Walker (1858–1938), are particularly notable. The museum's very formal, dignified building in Parc des Champs-de-Bataille was designed by Wilfrid Lacroix and erected in 1933 to commemorate the tercentennial of the founding of Québec. The museum renovated the original building, incorporating the space of an abandoned prison dating from 1867. A hallway of cells, with the iron bars and courtyard still intact, has been preserved as part of a permanent exhibition on the prison's history. ⊠ *1 av. Wolfe-Montcalm,* ☎ *418/643–2150,* WEB *www.mdq.org.* ⊡ *$7, free Wed. Sept.–mid-May.* ☉ *Sept.–mid-May, Tues. and Thurs.–Sun. 10–5, Wed. 10–9; mid-May–Aug., Thurs.–Tues. 10–6, Wed. 10–9.*

㉚ **Parc de l'Esplanade** (Esplanade Park). In the early 19th century, this was a clear space surrounded by a picket fence and poplar trees. Today you'll find the **Poudrière de l'Esplanade** (⊠ 100 rue St-Louis, ☎ 418/648–7016), the powder magazine that the British constructed in 1820; it houses a model depicting the evolution of the wall surrounding Vieux-Québec. There's a $2.75 charge to enter the magazine, which is open 10–5 daily mid-May to October 6. The French began building ramparts along the city's natural cliff as early as 1690 to protect themselves from British invaders. However, the colonists had trouble convincing the French government back home to take the threat of invasion seriously, and by 1759, when the British invaded for control of New France, the walls were still incomplete. The British, despite attacks by the Americans during the War of Independence and the War of 1812, took a century to finish them. In summer the park can also be the starting point for walking the city's 4½ km (3 mi) of walls; guided tours begin at Terrasse Dufferin.

㉝ **Parc des Champs-de-Bataille** (Battlefields Park). One of North America's largest and most scenic parks, this 250-acre area of gently rolling slopes has unparalleled views of the St. Lawrence River. Within the park and west of the Citadel are the **Plains of Abraham**, the site of the famous 1759 battle that decided the fate of New France.

㉟ **Parc Jeanne d'Arc.** An equestrian statue of Joan of Arc is the focus of this park, which is bright with colorful flowers in summer. A symbol of courage, the statue stands in tribute to the heroes of 1759 near the place where New France was lost to the British. The park also commemorates the Canadian national anthem, "O Canada"; it was played here for the first time on June 24, 1880. ⊠ *Avs. Laurier and Taché.*

★ ㉞ **Plains of Abraham.** This park, named after the river pilot Abraham Martin, is the site of the famous 1759 battle that decided the fate of New France. People cross-country ski here in winter and in-line skate in summer. The interpretation center, attached to the Musée de Québec, is open year-round; in summer a bus driven by a guide portraying Abraham Martin provides an entertaining tour—with commentary in French

and English—around the Plains of Abraham. Call the Maison de Dé-
couverte (☎ 418/648–4071) for departure times. ⊠ *Tour $3.50.* ◷
Tours mid-June–mid-Oct., daily 10–5:30.

36 Tour Martello No. 1 (Martello Tower No. 1). Of the 16 Martello towers in Canada, four were built in Québec City because the British government feared an invasion after the American Revolution. Tour
Martello No. 1, which exhibits the history of the four structures, was
built between 1802 and 1810. **Tour Martello No. 2,** at avenues Taché
and Laurier, features Council of War, a mystery dinner show with a
military theme. Tour No. 3 guarded westward entry to the city, but it
was demolished in 1904. Tour No. 4 is on rue Lavigueur overlooking
the St. Charles River but is not open to the public. ⊠ *South end of
Parc Jeanne d'Arc.* ⊠ *$3.50.* ◷ *Mid-June–Sept., daily 10–5:30.*

37 Wolfe Monument. This tall monument marks the place where the
British general James Wolfe died in 1759. Wolfe landed his troops about
3 km (2 mi) from the city's walls; 4,500 English soldiers scaled the cliff
and opened fire on the Plains of Abraham. Wolfe was mortally wounded
in battle and was carried behind the lines to this spot. ⊠ *Rue de
Bernières and av. Wolfe-Montcalm.*

Outside the Walls

Although its economy is slowly diversifying, Québec City continues
to revolve around the provincial government and the provincial government revolves around the National Assembly, one of the oldest par-
liaments in the world. One of the city's trendiest neighborhoods is down
the hill on St. Jean Street.

A Good Walk

Start at the **Parliament Buildings** ㊷, home of the National Assembly,
headquarters of the provincial government. As you leave the legislature, turn right and then right again onto the Grande Allée. The modern concrete building across the street holds the offices of Québec's
premier and the Treasury Board, which controls the government's
purse strings. As you walk along the Grande Allée, look to the right
to see a statue of former Québec premier Maurice Duplessis, who ruled
the province with an iron fist from 1936 to 1939 and again from 1944
to 1959. At the corner of Grande Allée and Des Parlementaires sits the
Parc de la Francophonie, dedicated to French-speaking countries
around the world. Turn right on rue de la Chevrotière and walk past
rue St-Amable. The **Chapelle Historique Bon-Pasteur** ㊸, a church surrounded by office buildings, is on the west side of the street. The entrance to Edifice Marie-Guyart is across the street; its observation
tower, **Observatoire de la Capitale** ㊹, provides a spectacular view.

Turn left on boulevard René-Lévesque Est and walk two blocks past the
Parc de l'Amérique-Française, dedicated to places in North America with
a French-speaking population. At the corner, the modern concrete building is the **Grande Théâtre de Québec** ㊺, a performing-arts center. Turn
right at rue Claire-Fontaine, cross the street and walk down the hill to
rue St-Jean, where the **Église St-Jean-Baptiste** ㊻ dominates the neighborhood. Turn right and stroll down rue St-Jean past trendy shops in
century-old buildings to **Maison J. A. Moisan** ㊼, which claims the title
of the oldest grocery store in North America. Farther down the street
you arrive at **St. Matthew's Cemetery** ㊽, the city's oldest remaining
graveyard. Cut through the cemetery to rue St-Simon, walk up the hill,
cross the street, and turn right on boulevard René-Lévesque. In summer
you can end your walk by crossing the street and strolling along the raised
Promenade des Premiers Ministres ㊾, which tells the stories of Québec's

premiers. Past the National Assembly, at the end of the promenade is a life-size statue of René Lévesque, the diminutive late premier who is considered the father of Québec's independence movement.

TIMING

This walk should take a half day. From March through June and from October through December, you should pause to listen to the cut and thrust of debates or Question Period in the National Assembly. For lunch, dine among decision-makers at the legislature's Le Parlementaire restaurant or in one of the many interesting and affordable restaurants along rue St-Jean.

Sights to See

☼ **Aquarium du Québec.** The aquarium, about 10 km (6 mi) from the city center, is closed for renovations in 2002. It's scheduled to re-open in 2003, with a focus on Nordic fish and marine mammals, including a replica of a sub-arctic ocean. When open, a wooded picnic ground makes this spot ideal for a family outing. ⊠ *1675 av. des Hôtels, Ste-Foy,* ☏ *418/659–5264 or 418/659–5266.*

⓸ **Chapelle Historique Bon-Pasteur.** Charles Baillargé designed this slender church with a steep sloping roof in 1868. Its ornate Baroque-style interior has carved-wood designs elaborately highlighted in gold leaf. The chapel houses 32 religious paintings created by the nuns of the community from 1868 to 1910. Classical concerts are performed here year-round. ⊠ *1080 rue de la Chevrotière,* ☏ *418/648–9710.* ▨ *Free.* ◷ *July–Aug., weekdays 1:30–4:30, Sun. 9–1; Sept.–June on request; musical artists' mass Sun. 10:45.*

★ ⓴ **Église St-Jean-Baptiste.** Architect Joseph-Ferdinand Peachy's crowning glory, this church was inspired by the facade of the Église de la Trinité in Paris and rivals the Basilique Notre-Dame-de-Québec in beauty and size. The first church on the site, built in 1847, burned in the 1881 fire that destroyed much of the neighborhood. Seven varieties of Italian marble were used in the soaring columns, statues, and pulpit of the present church, which dates from 1884. Its 36 stained-glass windows consist of 30 sections each, and the organ, like the church, is classified as a historic monument. October to June 23 and outside regular opening hours, knock at the **presbytery** (⊠ 490 rue St-Jean) to see the church. ⊠ *410 rue St-Jean,* ☏ *418/525–7188.* ◷ *June 24–Sept., weekdays 10–4:30, Sun. 9–4.*

⓯ **Grande Théâtre de Québec.** Opened in 1971, the theater incorporates two main halls, named for 19th-century Canadian poets. Louis Frechette was the first Québec poet and writer to be honored by the French Academy; Octave Crémazie stirred the rise of Québec nationalism in the mid-19th century. A three-wall mural by Québec sculptor Jordi Bonet depicts Death, Life, and Liberty. Bonet wrote "La Liberté" on one wall to symbolize the Québécois' struggle for freedom and cultural distinction. ⊠ *269 blvd. René-Lévesque Est,* ☏ *418/646–0609.*

OFF THE
BEATEN PATH

ICE HOTEL – You can tour the art gallery of ice sculptures, watch a movie in a theater made of ice, have a drink at the bar made of ice, or nestle into a sleeping bag on a bed lined with caribou skins for a night's sleep in this hotel constructed entirely of ice and snow. The first of its kind in North America, the hotel is open January 1 to March 31. A night's stay, including equipment (like an extra-insulated sleeping bag), supper, breakfast, and a welcome cocktail is around $170 per person. ⊠ *Duchesnay Ecotourism Station, 143 route Duchesnay, Ste Catherine de la Jacques Cartier (about 20 minutes west of Québec City),* ☏ *418/661–4522 or 877/505–0423.*

☾ **Jardin Zoologique du Québec.** This zoo is especially scenic because of the DuBerger River, which traverses the grounds. It's closed in 2002 for renovations. It plans to re-open in 2003, when it will specialize in birds. ⊠ *9300 rue de la Faune, Charlesbourg,* ☎ *418/622–0313.*

㊼ **Maison J. A. Moisan.** Founded in 1871 by Jean-Alfred Moisan, this store claims the title of the oldest grocery store in North America. The original display cases, woodwork, tin ceilings, and antiques preserve that old-time feel. The store stocks a wide variety of products, including difficult-to-find delicacies from other regions of Québec. ⊠ *699 rue St-Jean,* ☎ *418/522–0685.*

NEED A   **La Piazzeta** (⊠ 707 rue St-Jean, ☎ 418/529–7489), with its delicious
BREAK?   thin-crust square pizzas, is just one of the many good and affordable
          restaurants along this stretch of rue St-Jean.

㊺ **Observatoire de la Capitale.** This observation gallery is atop Edifice Marie-Guyart, Québec City's tallest office building. The gray, modern concrete tower, 31 stories tall, has by far the best view of the city and the environs. There's an express elevator. ⊠ *1037 rue de la Chevrotière,* ☎ *418/644–9841.* ⊡ *$4.* ☉ *Daily 10–5; closed Mon. Oct. 15–June 24.*

★ ㊷ **Parliament Buildings.** These buildings, erected between 1877 and 1884, are the seat of L'Assemblée Nationale (the National Assembly) of 125 provincial representatives. Québec architect Eugène-Étienne Taché designed the stately buildings in the late-17th-century Renaissance style of Louis XIV, with four wings set in a square around an interior court. In front of the Parliament, statues pay tribute to important figures of Québec history: Cartier, Champlain, Frontenac, Wolfe, and Montcalm. There's a 30-minute tour (in English or French) of the President's Gallery, the Legislative Council Chamber, and the National Assembly Chamber, which is blue, white, and gold. ⊠ *Av. Honoré-Mercier and Grande Allée, Door 3,* ☎ *418/643–7239,* ⓦⒺⒷ *www.assnat.qc.ca.* ⊡ *Free.* ☉ *Guided tours weekdays 9–4:30; late June–early Sept. also open weekends 10–4:30.*

㊾ **Promenade des Premiers Ministres.** Inaugurated in 1997, the promenade has a series of panels that tell the story (in French) of the premiers who have led the province and their contributions to its development. ⊠ *Parallel to blvd. René-Lévesque Est between rue de la Chevrotière and the Parliament Buildings. Closed in winter.*

㊽ **St. Matthew's Cemetery.** The burial place of many of the earliest English settlers in Canada was established in 1771 and is the oldest cemetery remaining in Québec City. Closed in 1860, it has been turned into a park. Next door, St. Matthew's Anglican Church is now a public library. It has a book listing most of the original tombstone inscriptions, including those that disappeared to make way for the city's modern convention center. ⊠ *755 rue St-Jean,* ☎ *no phone.*

DINING

Most restaurants have a selection of dishes à la carte, but more creative specialties are often found on the table d'hôte, a two- to four-course meal chosen daily by the chef. This can also be an economical way to order a full meal. At dinner many restaurants will offer a *menu dégustation* (tasting menu), a five- to seven-course dinner of the chef's finest creations. In French-speaking Québec City, an *entrée,* as the name suggests, is an entry into a meal, or an appetizer. It is followed by a *plat principal,* which is the main dish. Note that lunch generally costs about 30% less than dinner, and many of the same dishes are available. Lunch is usually served 11:30 to 2:30, dinner 6:30 until about 11. You should tip at least 15% of the bill.

CATEGORY	COST*
$$$$	over $32
$$$	$22–$32
$$	$13–$21
$	under $13

per person, in Canadian dollars, for a main course at dinner

Upper Town

$$$$ ✕ **La Maison Gastronomique Serge Bruyère.** The maison, serving classic French cuisine with a Québec twist and plenty of crystal and silver, put Québec City on the map of great gastronomic cities. Opened in 1980 by the late Serge Bruyère, a native of Lyon, France, it continues to benefit from his reputation. One highlight is the *menu découvert* (literally "discovery menu"), an eight-course meal for about $85. Chef Martin Còté was a student of Bruyère's. Among his dishes are *aiguillettes* (thin strips) of roasted duck with foie gras or loin of veal from Charlevoix with Parma ham. The adjacent bistro **Chez Livernois** shares the kitchen but is less formal and less expensive, with such dishes as roasted chicken breast in a blueberry and fresh mint sauce. ✉ *1200 rue St-Jean,* ☎ *418/694–0618. AE, D, DC, MC, V.*

$$$–$$$$ ✕ **Le Saint-Amour.** Here are all the makings of a true haute-cuisine establishment without the pretentious atmosphere. The light and airy
★ atrium creates a relaxed dining ambience at this restaurant, which was renovated in 2000. Award-winning chef Jean-Luc Boulay travels the world for inspiration; his studies pay off in such creations as caribou steak grilled with wild berries and served with poached pears in red wine, and beef tenderloin grilled with peppercorns, red wine, and Roquefort sauce. Sauces are generally light, with no flour or butter. The $72 menu découvert has nine courses, and the table d'hôte has five. For dessert, try the crème brûlée with maple sugar and blackberries. An extensive wine list, given an award of excellence by Wine Spectator magazine, has 650 choices ranging from $27 to $4,500 a bottle. ✉ *48 rue Ste-Ursule,* ☎ *418/694–0667. Reservations essential. AE, DC, MC, V.*

$$–$$$$ ✕ **Aux Anciens Canadiens.** This establishment is named for a book by Philippe-Aubert de Gaspé, who once resided here. The house, dating from 1675, has five dining rooms with different themes. For example, the *vaisselier* (dish room) is bright and cheerful, with colorful antique dishes and a fireplace. People come for the authentic French-Canadian cooking; hearty specialties include duck in maple glaze, Lac St-Jean meat pie, and maple-syrup pie with fresh cream. The restaurant also serves the best caribou drink (a local beverage known for its kick) in town, using its own special mix of sherry and vodka. ✉ *34 rue St-Louis,* ☎ *418/692–1627. AE, DC, MC, V.*

$$–$$$$ ✕ **Le Continental.** If Québec City had a dining Hall of Fame, Le Continental would be there among the best. Since 1956, the Sgobba family has been serving award-winning Continental cuisine. Deep-blue walls, mahogany paneling, and crisp white tablecloths create a stately ambience, and house specialties such as orange duckling and filet mignon Continental are flambéed at your table. ✉ *26 rue St-Louis,* ☎ *418/ 694–9995. AE, D, DC, MC, V.*

$–$$$ ✕ **Portofino Bistro Italiano.** By joining two 18th-century houses, owner James Monti has created a cozy Italian restaurant with a bistro flavor. The room is distinctive: burnt-sienna walls, soccer flags hanging from

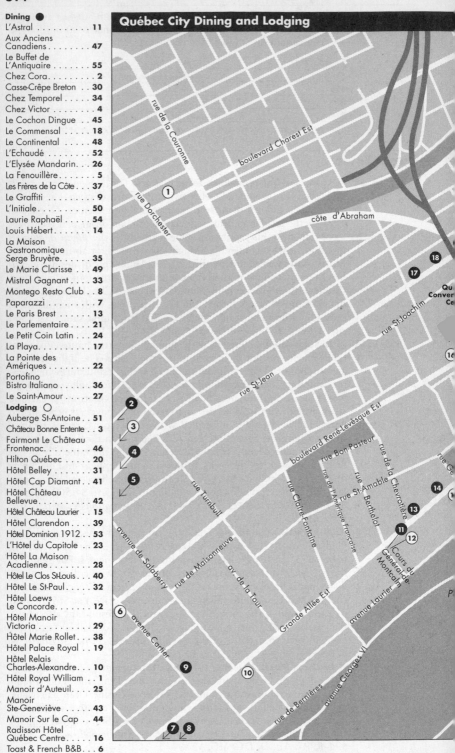

Québec City Dining and Lodging

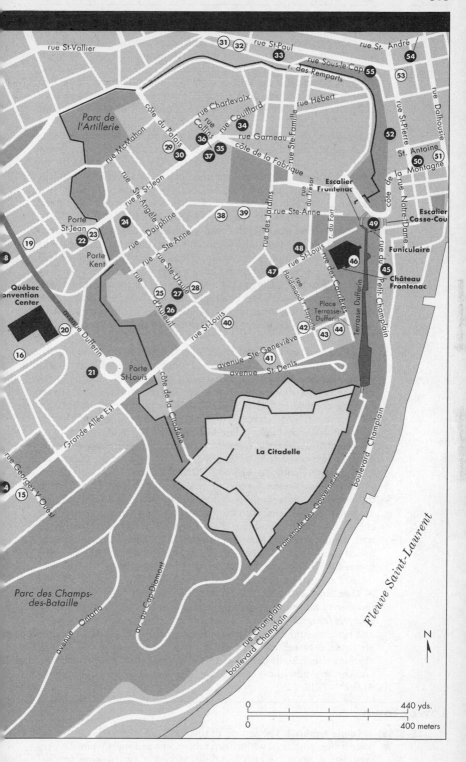

rue St-Vallier
rue St-Paul
rue St-André
31 32
33 54
rue Sous-le-Cap
f. des Remparts 55 53
Parc de
l'Artillerie
côte du Palais
rue Charlevoix
rue Couillard
rue Hébert
rue St-Pierre
rue Dalhousie
52
rue Collins
rue Garneau
St. Antoine
34
36
29 35
30 37
côte de la Fabrique
rue Ste-Famille
50 51
de la Montagne
Escalier
Frontenac
St-Jean
rue Ste-Anne
côte de la Notre-Dame
rue Garneau
rue McMahon
rue Ste-Angèle
Porte
St-Jean 23
22
38 39
rue des Jardins
rue du Trésor
Escalier
Casse-Cou
19
Porte
Kent
rue Dauphine
rue Ste-Anne
49
Funiculaire
8
rue St-Louis
48
46
45 Château
Frontenac
Québec
Convention
Center
24
rue Ste-Ursule
28
47
rue Hamel-Lagacé
rue des Carrières
20
25 27
rue d'Auteuil
26
Place
Terrasse
Dufferin
16
40
rue St-Louis
42
43 44
avenue Dufferin
21
Porte
St-Louis
avenue Ste-Geneviève
41
avenue St-Denis
Terrasse Dufferin
Grande Allée Est
côte de la Citadelle
La Citadelle
boulevard Champlain
4
15
rue Georges V Ouest
Promenade des Gouverneurs
Parc des Champs-
des-Bataille
avenue Ontario
avenue Cap-Diamont
rue Champlain
boulevard Champlain
Fleuve Saint-Laurent
N
0   440 yds.
0   400 meters

the ceiling, a wood pizza oven set behind a semicircular bar, deep-blue tablecloths and chairs. Not to be missed are the thin-crust pizza and its accompaniment of oils flavored with pepper and oregano, and *pennini al'arrabiata*—tubular pasta with a spicy tomato sauce. Save room for the homemade tiramisu—ladyfingers dipped in espresso with a whipped-cream and mascarpone-cheese filling. There's a prix-fixe meal of the day, and from 3 PM to 7 PM the restaurant serves a beer and pizza meal for about $11. ⊠ *54 rue Couillard,* ☎ *418/692–8888. AE, D, DC, MC, V.*

$–$$ ✗ **Les Frères de la Côte.** With its central location, Mediterranean influence, and reasonable prices, this busy bistro is a favorite among politicians and the journalists who cover them. The menu, inspired by the south of France, changes constantly, but among the regular features are osso bucco and a tender leg of lamb. If you sit near the back, you can watch the chefs at work. This kitchen is often among those open the latest. ⊠ *1190 rue St-Jean,* ☎ *418/692–5445. AE, D, MC, V.*

$–$$ ✗ **L'Elysée Mandarin.** A 19th-century home has been transformed into an elegant Chinese mandarin's garden where diners sip jasmine tea to the strains of soothing Asian music. Owner David Tsui uses rosewood and even imported stones from China to reproduce the atmosphere of his native Yanchao, a city near Shanghai known for training great chefs. Among the restaurant's Szechuan specialties are beef fillets with orange flavoring and crispy chicken with ginger sauce. The crispy duck with five spices is also delicious. ⊠ *65 rue d'Auteuil,* ☎ *418/692–0909. AE, DC, MC, V.*

$–$$ ✗ **Le Petit Coin Latin.** Tucked into a quiet street off bustling rue St-Jean, Le Petit Coin Latin, with its dark-wood furniture, stone walls, and background music of French *chansonniers,* has the look and feel of a Parisian neighborhood café. Low prices and generous portions attract a diverse clientele, including many students. In summer there's a sunny, secluded courtyard terrace. The menu ranges from morning croissants, *chocolatines* (a chocolate-filled pastry), or eggs Benedict, to all you-can-eat raclette, the restaurant's specialty. In between, there are plenty of low-cost options, including sandwiches, quiches, and salads. ⊠ *8½ rue Ste-Ursule,* ☎ *418/692-2022. MC, V.*

$ ✗ **Casse-Crêpe Breton.** Crepes in generous proportions are served in
★ this café-style restaurant. From a menu of more than 20 fillings, pick your own chocolate or fruit combinations; design a larger meal with cheese, ham, and vegetables; or sip a bowl of Viennese coffee topped with whipped cream. Many tables surround three round griddles at which you watch your creations being made. Crepes made with two to five fillings cost less than $6.15. ⊠ *1136 rue St-Jean,* ☎ *418/692–0438. Reservations not accepted. No credit cards.*

$ ✗ **Chez Temporel.** Tucked behind rue St-Jean and côte de la Fabrique, this smoky café perfumed with the aroma of fresh coffee is an experience *très français.* The rustic decor incorporates wooden tables, chairs, and benches, and a tiny staircase leads to an upper level. Croissants are made in-house; the staff will fill them with Gruyère and ham or anything else. Equally delicious are the *croques monsieur* (grilled ham-and-cheese sandwiches) and quiche Lorraine. ⊠ *25 rue Couillard,* ☎ *418/694–1813. V.*

Lower Town

$$–$$$$ ✗ **Laurie Raphaël.** The setting of this local hot spot is classic yet un-
★ pretentious, with cool white linen tablecloths and sheer white drapery contrasting against warm burgundy accents. Award-winning chef Daniel Vezina, a star of Québec cuisine, is known for innovative recipes that mix classic French cuisine with international flavors. Among his

creations are roulade of caribou and duck foie gras with cranberry juice and port served with apple puree and grilled Portobello, and an Australian rack of lamb that comes with a shallot sauce, blue potatoes from Charlevoix, and goat cheese. There's a seven-course menu dégustation for $79, with wines to complement each course available by the glass. The wine list ranges from $25 to $400 a bottle. ⊠ *117 rue Dalhousie,* ☏ *418/692–4555. Reservations essential. AE, D, DC, MC, V.*

$$$ ✕ **L'Initiale.** With its sophisticated ambience and gracious service, L'Ini-
★ tiale sets out to rival the great tables of Europe. Its modern decor of simple lines and light colors blends with its historic setting, and widely spaced tables lend themselves to intimate dining. Chef Yvan Lebrun has brought a spit over from his native France and uses it to produce a unique taste, particularly with lamb. The constantly changing menu follows the whims of the chef and the season. There's also an eight-course menu gastronomique for $72. Try the cream of barley with truffles, rabbit, and calf sweetbreads, or the grilled tuna with horseradish. For dessert there's a variety of small treats attractively presented on a single plate. The restaurant is one of only three in Québec City chosen by the prestigious Chaine des Rotisseurs, a gastronomic society. ⊠ *54 rue St-Pierre,* ☏ *418/694–1818. AE, DC, MC, V.*

$$$ ✕ **Le Marie Clarisse.** This restaurant at the bottom of Escalier Casse-Cou near Place Royale is known for unique seafood dishes, such as halibut with nuts and honey and scallops with port and paprika. The menu usually lists a good game dish, such as the deer and beef duo with berries and sweet garlic. The *menu du jour* has about seven entrées; dinner includes soup, salad, dessert, and coffee. Wood-beam ceilings, stone walls, sea-blue decor, and a fireplace make this one of the coziest spots in town. ⊠ *12 rue du Petit-Champlain,* ☏ *418/692–0857. Reservations essential. AE, DC, MC, V. No lunch weekends Oct.–Apr.*

$$–$$$ ✕ **L'Echaudé.** A chic beige-and-green bistro, L'Echaudé attracts a mix
★ of business and tourist clientele because of its location between the financial and antiques districts. Lunch offerings include *cuisse de canard confit* (duck confit) with french fries and fresh salad. Highlights of the three-course brunch for Sunday antiques shoppers are eggs Benedict and tantalizing desserts. The modern decor features hardwood floors, a mirrored wall, and a stainless-steel bar where you dine atop high stools. ⊠ *73 Sault-au-Matelot,* ☏ *418/692–1299. AE, DC, MC, V. No Sun. brunch mid-Oct.–mid-May.*

$$–$$$ ✕ **Mistral Gagnant.** Don't be surprised if the pottery bowl on your table or the antique armoire you're sitting beside is sold midway through your meal: much of what you see in this sunny restaurant comes from Provence and is for sale. The aromas of Provence also waft through the menu in dishes such as bouillabaisse or the lamb duo—grilled rack and eggplant charlotte with braised shoulder. With an appetizer and a main course comes dessert, such as the restaurant's famous lemon meringue pie or crème brûlée with lavender. ⊠ *160 rue St-Paul,* ☏ *418/ 692–4260. AE, MC, V. Closed Sun.–Mon. in winter; call ahead.*

$–$$ ✕ **Le Cochon Dingue.** The boulevard Champlain location of this chain, a cheerful café whose name translates to The Crazy Pig, is across the street from the ferry in Lower Town. Sidewalk tables and indoor dining rooms artfully blend the chic and the antique; black-and-white checkerboard floors contrast with ancient stone walls. Café fare includes delicious mussels, *steak-frites* (steak with french fries), thick soups, and apple pie with maple cream. ⊠ *46 blvd. Champlain,* ☏ *418/692–2013;* ⊠ *46 blvd. René-Lévesque Ouest,* ☏ *418/523–2013;* ⊠ *1326 av. Maguire, Sillery,* ☏ *418/684–2013. AE, DC, MC, V.*

$ ✕ **Le Buffet de L'Antiquaire.** Hearty home cooking, generous portions, and rock-bottom prices have made this no-frills, diner-style eatery a Lower Town institution. As the name suggests, it's in the heart of the antiques district. In summer it has a small sidewalk terrace where you can sit and watch the shoppers stroll by. It's also a good place to sample traditional Québécois dishes such as tourtière, and its soupe à l'oignon gratinée (onion soup with melted cheese) has been praised by the New York Post. Desserts, such as the triple-layer orange cake, are homemade and delicious. ✉ *95 rue St-Paul,* ☎ *418/692–2661. AE, MC, V.*

Outside the Walls

$$–$$$$ ✕ **L'Astral.** A spectacular view of Québec City is still the chief attraction at this revolving restaurant atop the Hôtel Loews Le Concorde, but the cuisine has made great strides in recent years: L'Astral has wooed well-known chefs such as Jean-Claude Crouzet away from other restaurants and introduced a constantly evolving menu promoting local products—fillet of Breton pork from the Beauce with polenta, Parmesan, and a garden herb sauce, for example, or rack of Charlevoix lamb with cabbage, dried fruits, and cumin sauce. ✉ *1225 Cours du Général-de Montcalm,* ☎ *418/647–2222. AE, D, DC, MC, V.*

$$–$$$ ✕ **La Fenouillère.** Although this award-winning restaurant is con-
   ★   nected to a standard chain hotel, inside there's an elegant, spacious dining room, with a view of the Pierre Laporte bridge. Chefs Yvon Godbout and Bernard St. Pierre serve a constantly rotating table d'hôte, going out of their way to offer seasonal products. The house specialty is salmon, but lamb is done to a turn and is very popular among the restaurant's regular customers. ✉ *Hotel Best Western Aristocrate, 3100 chemin St-Louis, Ste-Foy,* ☎ *418/653–3886. AE, DC, MC, V.*

$$–$$$ ✕ **Le Graffiti.** A good alternative to Vieux-Québec dining, this French restaurant is housed in an upscale food mall. The colorful setting has bright gold, red, and royal-blue accents and large bay windows that look out onto avenue Cartier. The distinctive seasonal menu features such dishes as *escalope de veau Graffiti* (thin slices of veal) with white wine, cream, and crushed tomatoes, or angel-hair pasta with pesto, pine nuts, black olives, and sun-dried tomatoes. The table d'hôte is reasonably priced. ✉ *1191 av. Cartier,* ☎ *418/529–4949. AE, DC, MC, V.*

$$–$$$ ✕ **Le Paris Brest.** This busy restaurant on Grande Allée serves a gregarious crowd attracted to its tastefully prepared French dishes. Traditional fare, such as a warm salad with escargots and sweet breads, and steak tartare, are presented artistically. Some popular choices are lamb with *herbes de Provence* and beef Wellington. A generous side platter of vegetables accompanies à la carte and main-course dishes; wine prices range from $22 to $700. Angular halogen lighting and soft yellow walls add a fresh, modern touch to the historic building. ✉ *590 Grande Allée Est,* ☎ *418/529–2243. AE, DC, MC, V.*

$$–$$$ ✕ **Louis Hébert.** With its fine French cuisine and convenient location on the bustling Grande Allée, this restaurant has long been popular with many of the Québec government's top decision-makers. There's a variety of dining areas, from the very public summer terrace to discreet second-floor meeting rooms. There's also a solarium with bamboo chairs as well as a cozy dining room with exposed stone walls and warm wood accents. In winter, chef Hervé Toussaint's roast lamb in a nut crust with Stilton and port is a favorite. In summer, seafood dishes, such as lobster and fresh pasta with a white-wine and basil cream sauce, are favored. ✉ *668 Grande Allée Est,* ☎ *418/525–7812. AE, D, DC, MC, V.*

$$–$$$ ✕ **Paparazzi.** The food at this Italian restaurant competes with that of many of the finer dining establishments in town, but without the high prices. Paparazzi has a sleek bistro ambience—bare wood tables, halogen lighting, and wrought-iron accents. Manicotti stuffed with smoked salmon is one appealing choice; calf sweetbreads with port and blackberries is another. The restaurant is a 10-minute drive west of Vieux-Québec. ⊠ *1365 av. Maguire, Sillery,* ☎ *418/683–8111. AE, DC, MC, V.*

$–$$$ ✕ **Montego Resto Club.** The sun shines year-round at this trendy bistro where Californian, Italian, French, and Szechuan cuisine share the bill. The red-and-yellow Sante Fe decor pays close attention to detail; each rainbow-colored light is a work of art. Every dish is presented with a creative twist, as well. The inventive menu lists escalope of veal with mushrooms and hazelnuts or Californian filet of beef with salsa, morello cherries and cantaloupe. Montego Resto Club is a 10-minute drive west of Vieux-Québec. ⊠ *1460 av. Maguire, Sillery,* ☎ *418/688–7991. AE, D, DC, MC, V.*

$–$$ ✕ **Le Parlementaire.** With its magnificent Beaux-Arts interior and
★ some of the most reasonable prices in town, the National Assembly's restaurant is nevertheless one of the best-kept secrets in Québec City. Chef Réal Therrien prepares contemporary cuisine that employs products from Québec's various regions. Although the restaurant is usually open Tuesday through Friday for breakfast and a three-course table d'hôte lunch, hours follow the National Assembly's schedule and can vary (it's sometimes open for dinner during the legislature's intensive sessions in June and December). It is wise to call ahead. ⊠ *Av. Honoré-Mercier and Grande Allée Est, Door 3,* ☎ *418/643–6640. AE, MC, V. Closed Sat.–Mon.; usually no dinner.*

$–$$ ✕ **La Playa.** More than 75 different martinis and a brick-walled courtyard terrace that's heated in spring and fall make this restaurant on trendy rue St-Jean a popular choice. The restaurant has a West Coast influence in both its decor and its cuisine. Choose a pasta and then combine it with any one of 38 sauces, including the Bangkok, with shrimp, chicken, peanut, and coconut sauce, or the Ile d'Orléans, with smoked duck. ⊠ *780 rue St-Jean,* ☎ *418/522–3989. AE, D, DC, MC, V. Closed Mondays in winter.*

$–$$ ✕ **La Pointe des Amériques.** Adventurous pizza lovers should explore the fare at this bistro, where the original brick walls of the century-old building just outside the St-Jean Gate contrast boldly with modern mirrors and artsy wrought-iron lighting. Some pizza combos (marinated alligator, smoked Gouda, Cajun sauce, and hot peppers) are strange. But don't worry—there are more than 27 different pizzas as well as meat and pasta dishes, soups, salads, and Southwest cuisine. Connected to the downtown restaurant is the **Canyon Bar and Grill,** which has the same menu. ⊠ *964 rue St-Jean,* ☎ *418/694–1199;* ⊠ *2815 blvd. Laurier, Ste-Foy,* ☎ *418/658–2583. AE, DC, MC, V.*

$ ✕ **Chez Cora.** Spectacular breakfasts decorated with mounds of fresh
★ fruit are the specialty at this sunny chain restaurant in the trendier part of the St. Roch neighborhood. Whimsy is everywhere, from the plastic chicken decorations to the inventive dishes, often named after the customers and family members who inspired them. Try the Eggs Ben et Dictine, which has smoked salmon, or the Gargantua—two eggs, sausage, ham, pancakes, *cretons* (pâtés), and baked beans. Kids love the Banana Surprise, a banana wrapped in a pancake with peanut butter and honey. For years the restaurant was open only for breakfast, but now it's open for lunch as well, serving light fare such as salads and sandwiches. ⊠ *545 rue de l'Église,* ☎ *418/524–3232. AE, DC, MC, V. No dinner.*

$ ✕ **Chez Victor.** It's no ordinary burger joint: this cozy café with brick walls attracts an arty crowd to trendy rue St-Jean. Lettuce, tomatoes, onions, mushrooms, pickles, hot mustard, mayonnaise, and a choice of cheeses (mozzarella, Swiss, blue, goat, and cream) top hearty burgers. French fries are served with a dollop of mayo and poppy seeds. Salads, sandwiches, and a daily dessert also are available. ⊠ *145 rue St-Jean,* ☎ *418/529–7702. MC, V.*

$ ✕ **Le Commensal.** At a kind of upscale cafeteria, diners serve themselves from an outstanding informal vegetarian buffet and then grab a table in the vast dining room, where brick walls and green plants add a touch of class. Plates are weighed to determine the price. Hot and cold dishes run the gamut of health-conscious cooking and include stir-fry tofu and ratatouille with couscous. ⊠ *860 rue St-Jean,* ☎ *418/647–3733. AE, DC, MC, V.*

LODGING

Be sure to make a reservation if you visit during peak season (May through September) or during the Winter Carnival, in February. During busy times, hotel rates usually rise 30%. From November through April, many lodgings offer weekend discounts and other promotions.

CATEGORY	COST*
$$$$	over $200
$$$	$150–$200
$$	$100–$150
$	under $100

All prices are in Canadian dollars, for a standard double room, excluding 7% GST, 7.5% provincial sales tax, and an optional service charge.

Upper Town

$$$$ ▥ **Fairmont Le Château Frontenac.** Towering above the St. Lawrence
★   River, the Château Frontenac is Québec City's most renowned landmark. Its public rooms—from the intimate piano bar to the 700-seat ballroom reminiscent of the Hall of Mirrors at Versailles—have the opulence of years gone by. Reserve well in advance, especially late June to mid-October. More expensive deluxe or Frontenac premier rooms have views of the river, but all rooms are elegantly furnished and well maintained. At Le Champlain, classic French cuisine is served by waiters in traditional French costumes. Because the hotel is a tourist attraction, the lobby can be quite busy. ⊠ *1 rue des Carrières, G1R 4P5,* ☎ *418/692–3861 or 800/441–1414,* ℻ *418/692–1751,* Ⅶⅅ *www.fairmont.com. 581 rooms, 37 suites. 2 restaurants, piano bar, snack bar, indoor pool, hair salon, health club. AE, DC, MC, V.*

$$$$ ▥ **Hôtel Palace Royal.** A soaring indoor atrium with balconies overlooking a tropical garden, swimming pool, and jacuzzi lend a dramatic air to this luxury hotel, opened in 2001. The decor is eclectic, blending everything from Asian to art deco. Elegant yet functional rooms with antique gold accents have views of either Old Town or the atrium. Views of the river can be had from rooms on the 7th floor and up. Four rooms are adapted for clients with disabilities. ⊠ *775 Dufferin Montmorency, G1R 6A5,* ☎ *418/694–2000 or 800/567–JARO,* ℻ *418/380–2553,* Ⅶⅅ *www.jaro.qc.ca. 74 rooms, 160 suites. Restaurant, bar, refrigerators, data ports, indoor pool, health club, meeting rooms. AE, DC, MC, V.*

$$$ ▥ **L'Hôtel du Capitole.** In 1992 this turn-of-the-century theater just outside the St-Jean Gate was transformed into an exclusive lodging, an Italian bistro, and a 1920s cabaret-style dinner theater, Théâtre Capitole. The glitzy showbiz theme, with stars on carpets and doors, has attracted celebrities such as Céline Dion and Claudia Schiffer. Rooms are small and simple, highlighted with a few rich details. Painted ceilings have a blue-and-white sky motif, and white down-filled comforters dress the beds. ⊠ *972 rue St-Jean, G1R 1R5,* ☎ *418/694–4040 or 800/363–4040,* ℻ *418/694–1916,* Ⅶⅅ *www.lecapitole.com. 37 rooms, 3 suites. Restaurant, 2 theaters, meeting rooms. AE, DC, MC, V.*

$$–$$$ ⚅ **Hôtel Clarendon.** Built in 1866 and considered the oldest hotel in Québec, the Clarendon was refurbished in its original art deco and Art Nouveau styles, most notably in the public areas. Some guest rooms have period touches, while others are more modern. About half the rooms have excellent views of Old Québec, and others look out onto a courtyard. ⊠ *57 rue Ste-Anne, G1R 3X4,* ☎ *418/692–2480 or 888/554–6001,* ℻ *418/692–4652,* ⊞ *www.hotelclarendon.com. 140 rooms. Restaurant, bar, meeting rooms. AE, D, DC, MC, V.*

$$–$$$ ⚅ **Hôtel Manoir Victoria.** This European-style hotel with a good fitness center is well situated near the train station. Its discreet, old-fashioned entrance gives way to a large, wood-paneled foyer. Typical rooms have red floral or blue-gray bedspreads. A substantial buffet breakfast is included in some packages. ⊠ *44 côte du Palais, G1R 4H8,* ☎ *418/692–1030 or 800/463–6283,* ℻ *418/692–3822,* ⊞ *www.manoir-victoria.com. 143 rooms, 2 suites. 2 restaurants, indoor pool, hair salon, sauna, health club, meeting rooms. AE, D, DC, MC, V.*

$$–$$$ ⚅ **Manoir Sur le Cap.** No two rooms are alike in this elegant 19th-century inn with picturesque views of Governors' Park and the St. Lawrence River. Built in 1837 as a private home, it was severely damaged in 1849 by a fire that razed the neighborhood. It was rebuilt the same year by George Mellis Douglas, the medical superintendent at Grosse Ile. Rooms are light and airy with antiques and hardwood floors. Some have brass beds, exposed brick walls, or small balconies. A two-story condo apartment at the rear includes a double whirlpool tub and a small balcony with a view of the river. Rooms have no phones and smoking isn't allowed. ⊠ *9 av. Ste-Geneviève, G1R 4A7,* ☎ *418/694–1987,* ℻ *418/627–7405,* ⊞ *www.manoir-sur-le-cap.com. 13 rooms, one apartment. AE, MC, V.*

$–$$$ ⚅ **Hôtel Le Clos St-Louis.** Winding staircases and crystal chandeliers add to the Victorian elegance of this centrally located inn, which was formed by combining two houses built around 1845. All the rooms have antiques or antique reproductions, and six have decorative fireplaces. Nine rooms have romantic four-poster beds, and seven have whirlpool baths. The small but attractive rooms with shared baths on the top floor are less expensive. ⊠ *69 rue St-Louis, G1R 3Z2,* ☎ *418/694–1311 or 800/461–1311,* ℻ *418/694–9411,* ⊞ *www.quebecweb.com/csl. 25 rooms, 21 with bath. Breakfast room, in-room data ports. AE, DC, MC, V. CP.*

$$ ⚅ **Hôtel Cap Diamant.** An antique lover's paradise, this hotel is perched
★ on a quiet side street overlooking Upper Town. An eclectic collection of vintage furniture, ecclesiastical accents such as stained glass from a church and a confessional door, and even the odd angel complement decorative marble fireplaces, stone walls, and hardwood floors, giving each room a distinct personality. A sunroom overlooks one of the old city's few gardens with a small waterfall (it flows in summer only). Note that rooms do not have phones. Rates include a buffet-style Continental breakfast. Smoking is not allowed. ⊠ *39 av. Ste-Geneviève, G1R 4B3,* ☎ *418/694–0313,* ℻ *418/694–1187,* ⊞ *www.hcapdiamant.qc.ca. 12 rooms. Air-conditioning, refrigerators. MC, V. CP.*

$$ ⚅ **Hôtel Château Bellevue.** Behind the Château Frontenac, this hotel offers comfortable accommodations at reasonable prices in a good location. Guest rooms are modern, with standard hotel furnishings; many have a view of the St. Lawrence River. The rooms vary considerably in size (many are a bit cramped), and package deals are available in winter. ⊠ *16 rue de la Porte, G1R 4M9,* ☎ *418/692–2573 or 800/463–2617,* ℻ *418/692–4876,* ⊞ *www.old-quebec.com/bellevue. 58 rooms. Meeting rooms. AE, D, DC, MC, V.*

$–$$ ⚅ **Hôtel La Maison Acadienne.** Period decor and exposed brick walls combine with modern comforts to make this a good centrally located, low-cost option. The romantic, more expensive suites have double whirlpool tubs—and sparkling wine. In summer, breakfast is served on a rooftop terrace. ✉ *43 rue Ste-Ursule, G1R 4E4,* ☎ *418/694–0280 or 800/463–0280,* FAX *418/694–0458,* WEB *www.maison-acadienne.com. 37 rooms, 33 with bath; 3 suites. Breakfast room. AE, D, DC, MC, V.*

$–$$ 🖥 **Hôtel Marie Rollet.** This intimate little inn in the heart of Vieux-Québec, built in 1876 by the Ursuline Order, has warm woodwork and antique charm. The rooms lack phones, but two have working fireplaces. A rooftop terrace has a garden view. ✉ *81 rue Ste-Anne, G1R 3X4,* ☎ *418/694–9271 or 800/275–0338,* WEB *www.hotelmarierollet.com. 10 rooms. MC, V.*

$–$$ 🖥 **Manoir d'Auteuil.** Originally a private home, this lodging is one of the more lavish manors in town. A major renovation in 1957 reinstated many of its art deco and Art Nouveau details. An ornate sculpted iron banister wraps around four floors, and guest rooms blend modern design with the art deco structure. Each room is different; one was formerly a chapel, and another has a tiny staircase leading to its bathroom. Two rooms have showers with seven showerheads. Some rooms look out onto the wall between the St-Louis and St-Jean gates. Note that rooms on the fourth floor are smaller, and thus less expensive. Smoking isn't permitted. ✉ *49 rue d'Auteuil, G1R 4C2,* ☎ *418/694–1173,* FAX *418/694–0081,* WEB *www.quebecweb.com/dauteuil. 16 rooms. Breakfast room, air-conditioning. AE, D, DC, MC, V. CP.*

$–$$ 🖥 **Manoir Ste-Geneviève.** Quaint and elaborately decorated, this hotel dating from 1880 stands near the Château Frontenac, on the southwest corner of Governors' Park. A plush Victorian ambience is created with fanciful wallpaper and stately English manor furnishings, such as marble lamps, large wooden bedposts, and velvet upholstery. Front rooms have views of the park and the St. Lawrence River. Three rooms have kitchenettes; none have phones. ✉ *13 av. Ste-Geneviève, G1R 4A7,* ☎ FAX *418/694–1666 or* ☎ *877/694–1666,* WEB *www.quebecweb.com/msg. 9 rooms. Air-conditioning, kitchenettes (some). AE, MC, V.*

Lower Town

$$$–$$$$ 🖥 **Auberge St-Antoine.** This charming little find is within comfortable walking distance of all Vieux-Québec's attractions. The hotel, which opened in 1992, seems much older than it is because of its location in an old maritime warehouse and the generally rustic atmosphere. Each room is styled differently, but all have a combination of antiques and contemporary pieces. Some rooms have river views; some have terraces. Rates include an extensive buffet-style Continental breakfast. ✉ *10 rue St-Antoine, G1K 4C9,* ☎ *418/692–2211 or 888/692–2211,* FAX *418/ 692–1177,* WEB *www.saint-antoine.com. 24 rooms, 7 suites. AE, DC, MC, V. CP.*

$$$–$$$$ 🖥 **Hotel Dominion 1912.** Sophistication and attention to the smallest detail prevail at this boutique hotel—from the custom-designed swing-out night tables in the modern rooms to the white goose-down duvets and the custom umbrellas in each room. Built in 1912 as a warehouse, the hotel offers views of either the St. Lawrence River or of the Old Town from rooms on higher floors. Rates include a substantial buffet-style Continental breakfast. ✉ *126 rue St-Pierre, G1K 4A8,* ☎ *418/692–2224 or 888/833–5253,* FAX *418/692–4403,* WEB *www.hoteldominion.com. 60 rooms. In-room data ports, meeting rooms. AE, DC, MC, V. CP.*

$$–$$$ 🖥 **Hôtel Le Saint-Paul.** Perched at the edge of the antiques district, near art galleries and the train station, this European-style hotel was transformed from a 19th-century office building in 1998. Comfortable rooms feature hunter-green carpeting, standard hotel furnishings, and bedspreads with a Renaissance motif of characters in period dress. Some rooms have exposed brick walls. ✉ *229½ rue St-Paul, G1K 3W3,* ☎ *418/694–4414* *or 888/794–4414,* FAX *418/694–0889,* WEB *www.lesaint-paul.qc.ca. 23 rooms, 3 suites. Restaurant, in-room data ports, meeting rooms. AE, DC, MC, V.*

$–$$ 🖬 **Hôtel Belley.** Modern artwork by local artists is everywhere in this modest little hotel tucked above the Belley Tavern, a stone's throw from the train station and the antiques district. Built as a private home around 1842, the building has housed various taverns uninterrupted since 1868. The current hotel was added in 1987. Ikea-style furniture in the simple rooms blends with the exposed brick walls and beamed ceilings of the historic building. Downstairs, the old-fashioned tin ceilings and modern furniture attract a café crowd. Five apartments are also available in a separate building. ⊠ *249 rue St-Paul, G1K 3W5,* ☎ *418/692–1694 or 888/692–1694,* FAX *418/692–1696,* WEB *www.oricom.ca/belley. 8 rooms, 5 apartments. Restaurant. AE, D, MC, V.*

Outside the Walls

$$$–$$$$ 🖬 **Hilton Québec.** Just opposite the National Assembly, the spacious Hilton rises from the shadow of Parliament Hill. The lobby, which can be chaotic at times, has a bar and an open-air restaurant. The hotel is next to the Parliament Buildings and connected to the convention center and a mall, Place Québec, which has more than 30 shops and restaurants. Standard yet modern rooms have tall windows; those on upper floors have fine views of Vieux-Québec. Guests on executive floors are offered a free breakfast and an open bar from 5 to 10 PM. ⊠ *1100 blvd. René-Lévesque Est, G1K 7M9,* ☎ *418/647–2411; 800/447–2411 in Canada;* FAX *418/647–6488,* WEB *www.hilton.com. 535 rooms, 36 suites. Restaurant, bar, pool, sauna, health club. AE, D, DC, MC, V.*

$$–$$$$ 🖬 **Hôtel Loews Le Concorde.** When Le Concorde was built in 1974,
★ the shockingly tall concrete structure aroused controversy because it supplanted 19th-century Victorian homes. Still, visitors love its location on Grande Allée, where cafés, restaurants, and bars dot the street. Rooms have good views of Battlefields Park and the St. Lawrence River, and nearly all have been redone in a combination of modern and traditional furnishings. This hotel is one of the few in the city that allows guests to bring their pets. ⊠ *1225 Cours du Général-de Montcalm, G1R 4W6,* ☎ *418/647–2222 or 800/463–5256,* FAX *418/647–4710,* WEB *www.loewshotels.com. 422 rooms. 2 restaurants, bar, pool, sauna, health club, business services. AE, D, DC, MC, V.*

$$–$$$$ 🖬 **Radisson Hôtel Québec Centre.** The rooms in this large establishment opposite the Parliament Buildings were renovated in 2000 in a motif of olive green, gold, and blue stripes with wood furniture. VIP floors were designed for the business traveler. The hotel occupies the first 12 floors of a tall office complex; views of Vieux-Québec are limited to the higher floors. ⊠ *690 blvd. René-Lévesque Est, G1R 5A8,* ☎ *418/647–1717, 888/884–7777, or 800/333–3333,* FAX *418/647–2146,* WEB *www.radisson.com. 371 rooms, 6 suites. Restaurant, outdoor pool, sauna, health club. AE, D, DC, MC, V.*

$$$ 🖬 **Château Bonne Entente.** In a grassy parkland with a duck pond in
★ a residential neighborhood, this English-style country inn is off the beaten path but worth the trip. Wings were added to what was originally a private home. In keeping with the hotel's English roots, many rooms are decorated in hunter greens and burgundies, and tea and biscuits are served every afternoon near the fireplace in the wood-paneled tearoom. A wing added in 2000 features a blue and beige decor, multijet showers, and two suites with fireplaces. A separate, motel-style building has 25 rooms with utilitarian furnishings, including an in-room rack for hanging clothes (no closets). The hotel is 20 minutes from down-

town, with a shuttle service. ✉ *3400 chemin Ste-Foy, Ste-Foy G1X 1S6,* ☎ *418/653–5221 or 800/463–4390,* FAX *418/653–3098,* WEB *www.chateaubonneentente.com. 151 rooms, 15 suites. Restaurant, bar, outdoor pool, spa, tennis court, badminton, health club, volleyball, ice-skating, baby-sitting, nursery, playground, meeting rooms. AE, D, DC, MC, V.*

$$–$$$ 🏨 **Hôtel Royal William.** The *Royal William* was considered to be at the forefront of technology and innovation when the Québec City–built vessel became the first Canadian steamship to cross the Atlantic in 1833. Its namesake, opened in 1998, brings that spirit of technology and innovation to this hotel designed with the business traveler in mind. All rooms have two phone lines, a fax connection, plus a high-speed Internet port. The meeting rooms on each floor have Internet connections and several are equipped for videoconferencing. Throughout, the style is art deco with a modern twist in shades of sable and rich hunter green. About five minutes from Vieux-Québec, the hotel is also at the forefront of the transformation of the low-rent St-Roch district, where hip young artists, academics, and techies are rapidly taking the place of panhandlers. ✉ *360 blvd. Charest Est, G1K 3H4,* ☎ *418/521–4488 or 888/541–0405,* FAX *418/521–6868,* WEB *www.royalwilliam.com. 44 rooms. Restaurant, in-room data ports, in-room safes, library, meeting rooms. AE, D, DC, MC, V.*

$–$$$ 🏨 **Hôtel Château Laurier.** A 1999 expansion has left few traces of the hotel's origins as a private home. The spacious lobby has brown-leather sofas and easy chairs and wrought-iron and wood chandeliers. All rooms have sleigh beds with paisley-inspired bedspreads in green, beige, or blue. Rooms in the new section are a bit larger than those in the old; deluxe rooms have fireplaces and double whirlpool baths. Some rooms look out on the Plains of Abraham; more have a view of the National Assembly and the Upper Town. Busy Grande Allée is crowded with popular restaurants and trendy bars. ✉ *1220 pl. Georges V Ouest, G1R 5B8,* ☎ *418/522–8108 or 800/463–4453,* FAX *418/524–8768,* WEB *www.old-quebec.com/laurier. 151 rooms, 3 suites. Restaurant, meeting rooms. AE, D, DC, MC, V.*

$$ 🏨 **Hôtel Relais Charles-Alexandre.** Sunny bay windows, hardwood
★ floors, and furniture handmade by Québec artisans combine to make you feel as if you're staying in a family home. The hotel's elegant atmosphere and low prices, as well as its convenient location (a 10-minute walk from the old city), make it advisable to reserve several weeks in advance for stays from May through October. Rates include a Continental breakfast served in a small art gallery. Rooms do not have phones. ✉ *91 Grande Allée Est, G1R 2H5,* ☎ *418/523–1220,* FAX *418/523–9556,* WEB *www.quebecweb.com/rca. 23 rooms, 19 with bath. Breakfast room. AE, MC, V. CP.*

$ 🏨 **Toast & French Bed & Breakfast.** If you would like to take advantage of your visit to Québec City to learn French, then this is the place to stay. In addition to large, comfortable rooms, owner France Levasseur, a certified French teacher, offers breakfast as well as tailor-made, on-site French lessons. Tours can be arranged to help you discover Québec City and introduce you to the neighborhood. Rooms in this centrally located third-floor home have hardwood floors and are tastefully decorated; two have private bathrooms. Ms. Levasseur can also arrange rooms with host families. Canadian tax receipts are available for French lessons, which aren't included in room rates. ✉ *1020 av. Cartier, G1R 2S4,* ☎ *418/523–9365,* FAX *418/523–6706,* WEB *www. quebecweb.com/toast&french. 4 rooms. AE, DC, MC, V. CP.*

NIGHTLIFE AND THE ARTS

Considering its size, Québec City has a wide variety of cultural institutions, from the renowned Québec Symphony Orchestra to several small theater companies. The arts scene changes significantly depending on the season. From September through May, a steady repertory of concerts, plays, and performances is presented in theaters and halls. In summer, indoor theaters close to make room for outdoor stages. For arts and entertainment listings in English, consult the *Québec Chronicle-Telegraph,* published on Wednesday. The French-language daily newspaper *Le Soleil* has listings on a page called "Agenda." Also, *Voir,* a weekly devoted to arts listings and reviews, appears on the street every Thursday.

Tickets for most shows can be purchased through **Billetech,** with outlets at the Bibliothèque Gabrielle-Roy (✉ 350 rue St-Joseph Est, ☎ 418/691–7400), Colisée Pepsi (✉ Parc de l'Expocité, 250 blvd. Wilfrid-Hamel, ☎ 418/691–7211), Comptoir postal Le Soleil (✉ Pl. Laurier, 2nd floor, ☎ 418/656–6095), Grand Théâtre de Québec (✉ 269 blvd. René-Lévesque Est, ☎ 418/643–8131 or 877/643–8131), Palais Montcalm (✉ 995 Pl. d'Youville, ☎ 418/670–9011), Salle Albert-Rousseau (✉ 2410 chemin Ste-Foy, Ste-Foy, ☎ 418/659–6710), and Théâtre Capitole (✉ 972 rue St-Jean, ☎ 418/694–4444). Hours vary, and in some cases tickets must be bought at the outlet.

The Arts

Dance

Dancers appear at Bibliothèque Gabrielle-Roy, Salle Albert-Rousseau, and the Palais Montcalm. **Grand Théâtre de Québec** (✉ 269 blvd. René-Lévesque Est, ☎ 418/643–8131) presents a dance series with Canadian and international companies.

Film

Most theaters present French and American films dubbed into French. **Cinéma Galeries de la Capitale** (✉ 5401 blvd. des Galeries, ☎ 418/628–2455) almost always shows some films in English. **Cinéma Place Charest** (✉ 500 rue du Pont, ☎ 418/529–9745) is close to downtown. **IMAX Theatre** (✉ Galeries de la Capitale, 5401 blvd. des Galeries, ☎ 418/627–4629, 418/627–4688, or 800/643–4629) has extra-large screen movies (educational fare on scientific, historical, and adventure topics) and translation headsets. **Le Clap** (✉ 2360 chemin Ste-Foy, Ste-Foy, ☎ 418/650–2527) has a repertoire of foreign, offbeat, and art films.

Music

L'Orchestre Symphonique de Québec (Québec Symphony Orchestra) is Canada's oldest. It performs at Louis-Frechette Hall in the Grand Théâtre de Québec (✉ 269 blvd. René-Lévesque Est, ☎ 418/643–8131).

Tickets for children's concerts at the **Joseph Lavergne auditorium** must be purchased in advance at the **Bibliothèque Gabrielle-Roy** (✉ 350 rue St-Joseph Est, ☎ 418/691–7400). For classical concerts at the **Salle de l'Institut Canadien** (✉ 42 Chaussée des Ecossais), buy tickets in advance at the Palais Montcalm.

Maison de la Chanson (✉ Théâtre Petit Champlain, 68 rue du Petit-Champlain, ☎ 418/692–4744) is a fine spot to hear contemporary Francophone music.

Popular music concerts are often booked at the **Colisée Pepsi** (✉ Parc de l'Expocité, 250 blvd. Wilfrid-Hamel, ☎ 418/691–7211).

An annual highlight is the July **Festival d'Eté International de Québec** (☎ 418/523–4540, WEB www.infofestival.com), an 11-day music festival with more than 400 shows and concerts (most of them free), from classical music to Francophone song. Events are held in more than 10 locations, including outdoor stages and public squares. Dates for 2002 are July 4–14.

During the **Québec City International Festival of Military Bands** (☎ 418/694–5757) in August, the streets of Old Québec resound with military airs. Bands from several countries participate in the four-day festival, which includes a gala parade. Shows, most of them free, are held in Vieux-Québec or just outside the walls. Dates for 2002 are August 22–25.

Theater

Most theater productions are in French. The following theaters schedule shows September to April: **Grand Théâtre de Québec** (✉ 269 blvd. René-Lévesque Est, ☎ 418/643–8131) offers classic and contemporary plays staged by the leading local company, le Théâtre du Trident (☎ 418/643–5873). **Palais Montcalm** (✉ 995 Pl. d'Youville, ☎ 418/670–9011), a municipal theater outside St-Jean Gate, presents a broad range of productions. A diverse repertoire, from classic to comedy, is staged at **Salle Albert-Rousseau** (✉ 2410 chemin Ste-Foy, Ste-Foy, ☎ 418/659–6710).**Théâtre Le Capitole** (✉ 972 rue St-Jean, ☎ 418/694–4444), a restored cabaret-style theater, schedules pop music and musical comedy shows. **Théâtre Périscope** (✉ 2 rue Crémazie Est, ☎ 418/529–2183), a multipurpose theater, stages about 125 shows a year, including performances for children.

In summer, **open-air concerts** are presented at Place d'Youville (just outside St-Jean Gate) and on the Plains of Abraham.

Nightlife

Québec City nightlife centers on the clubs and cafés of rue St-Jean, avenue Cartier, and Grande Allée. In winter, evening activity becomes livelier as the week nears its end, beginning on Wednesday. As warmer temperatures set in, the café-terrace crowd emerges, and bars are active seven days a week. Most bars and clubs stay open until 3 AM.

Bars and Lounges

One of the city's most romantic spots is the Château Frontenac's **Bar St-Laurent** (✉ 1 rue des Carrières, ☎ 418/692–3861), with soft lights, a panoramic view of the St. Lawrence, and a fireplace. The rhythms at **Chez Maurice** (✉ 575 Grande Allée Est, 2nd floor, ☎ 418/647–2000) have attracted stars such as Mick Jagger and the Backstreet Boys. **Cosmos Café** (✉ 575 Grande Allée Est, ☎ 418/640–0606) is a lively club and restaurant. **L'Inox** (✉ 37 quai St-André, ☎ 418/692–2877) is a popular Lower Town brew pub where patrons can sample a wide variety of beers brewed on site. Some of them, like Transat and Viking, were developed to mark special events. Inside are billiard tables; outside there's a summer terrace. **Le Pub Saint-Alexandre** (✉ 1087 rue St-Jean, ☎ 418/694–0015), a popular English-style pub, was a men-only tavern until the 1990s. It serves 200 kinds of beer, 20 on tap.

Dance Clubs

Patrons at **Absolute Nightclub** (✉ 1170 rue d'Artigny, ☎ 418/529–9973) move to techno beats at the second-story dance club. There's a little bit of everything—live rock bands to loud disco—at **Chez Dagobert** (✉ 600 Grande Allée Est, ☎ 418/522–0393), a large and popular club. **La Fourmi Atomik** (✉ 33 rue d'Auteuil, ☎ 418/694–1473), in a converted prayer hall across from the Kent Gate, features alternative music, including techno, heavy metal, and punk.

Folk, Jazz, and Blues

French-Canadian folk songs fill **Chez Son Père** (✉ 24 rue St-Stanislas, ☎ 418/692–5308), a smoky pub on the second floor of an old building in the Latin Quarter. Singers perform nightly. The first jazz bar in Québec City, **L'Emprise at Hôtel Clarendon** (✉ 57 rue Ste-Anne, ☎ 418/692–2480), is the preferred spot for enthusiasts. The art-deco decor sets the mood for Jazz Age rhythms.

OUTDOOR ACTIVITIES AND SPORTS

Two parks are central to Québec City. The 250-acre Battlefields Park has panoramic views of the St. Lawrence River. Cartier-Brébeuf Park runs along the St. Charles River. Both are favorites for jogging, biking, and cross-country skiing. Scenic rivers and mountains close by (no more than 30 minutes by car) make this city ideal for the sporting life. For information about sports and fitness, contact the **Québec City Tourist Information Office** (✉ 835 av. Laurier, G1R 2L3, ☎ 418/649–2608). The **Québec City Bureau of Culture, Recreation and Community Life** (✉ 275 rue de l'Eglise, 4ᵉ, G1K 6G7, ☎ 418/691–6284) has information about municipal facilities.

Participant Sports and Outdoor Activities

Biking

The number of bike paths and trails in the Québec City area has mushroomed in recent years; detailed maps are available at tourism offices. Bike paths along rolling hills traverse Battlefields Park at the south side of the city. The more ambitious can head for the 22-km-long (14-mi-long) Corridor des Cheminots, which runs from Limoilou near Vieux-Québec to the picturesque community of Shannon. Paths along the côte de Beaupré, beginning at the confluence of the St. Charles and St. Lawrence rivers, are especially scenic. They begin northeast of the city at rue de la Verandrye and boulevard Montmorency or rue Abraham-Martin and Pont Samson (Samson Bridge) and continue 10 km (6 mi) along the coast to Montmorency Falls. **Mont Ste-Anne,** site of the 1998 world mountain-biking championship and annual World Cup races, has 200 km (124 mi) of mountain-bike trails, 14 downhill runs, and a gondola.

From the end of March to mid-October, you can rent bicycles, including helmets and locks, for $25 a day or $17 for four hours at **Vélo Passe-Sport** (✉ 22 Côte du Palais, ☎ 418/692–3643).

Boating

Lakes in the Québec City area have facilities for boating. **Manoir St-Castin** (✉ 99 chemin du Tour du Lac, ☎ 418/841–4949), at Lac Beauport, has canoes, kayaks, and pedal boats. Follow Route 73 north of the city to Lac Beauport and then take Exit 157, boulevard du Lac. Just west of Québec City, on the St. Lawrence River, canoes, pedal boats, and small sailboats can be rented at **Parc Nautique du Cap-Rouge** (✉ 4155 chemin de la Plage Jacques Cartier, Cap-Rouge, ☎ 418/650–7770).

Dogsledding

Aventure Nord-Bec (✉ 665 rue St-Aimé, St-Lambert de Lévis, ☎ 418/889–8001), 30 minutes from the bridges south of the city, teaches people how to mush in the forest. A half day—including initiation, dogsledding, and a snack—is $79. Overnight camping trips are available.

Fishing

Permits are needed for fishing in Québec. Most sporting-goods stores and all Canadian Tire stores sell permits. **Latulippe** (✉ 637 rue St-Vallier Ouest, ☎ 418/529–0024) sells permits and also stocks a wide selection of hunting and fishing equipment. The **Société de la Faune et Parcs** (✉ 675 blvd. René-Lévesque Est, ☎ 418/521–3830, 🌐 www.fapaq.gouv.qc.ca) publishes a pamphlet on fishing regulations and is available at ministry offices and where permits are sold.

Réserve Faunique des Laurentides (☎ 418/528–6868; 418/890–6527 for fishing reservations; FAX 418/528–8833), a wildlife reserve with good lakes for fishing, is approximately 48 km (30 mi) north of Québec City via Route 73. It's advisable to reserve a slot 48 hours ahead by phone or fax.

Golf

The Québec City region has 18 golf courses, and most are open to the public. Reservations are essential in summer. The 18-hole, par-72 course at **Club de Golf de Cap-Rouge** (✉ 4600 rue St-Felix, Cap-Rouge, ☎ 418/653–9381) is one of the closest courses to Québec City. **Club de Golf de Mont Tourbillon** (✉ 55 montée du Golf, Lac Beauport, ☎ 418/849–4418), a par-70, 18-hole course, is 20 minutes from the city by car via Route 73 North (Lac Beauport exit). **Le Grand Vallon** (✉ 100 rue Beaumont, Beaupré, ☎ 418/827–4653), a half-hour drive north of Québec City, has one of the best 18-hole, par-72 courses in the region.

Health and Fitness Clubs

One of the city's most popular health clubs is **Club Entrain** (✉ Pl. de la Cité, 2600 blvd. Laurier, ☎ 418/658–7771). Facilities, available for a daily fee of $11.50, include a weight room with Nautilus, sauna, whirlpool, aerobics classes, and squash courts. **Hilton Québec** (✉ 1100 blvd. René-Lévesque Est, ☎ 418/525–9909) has a health club with weights, exercise machines, a sauna, and a year-round heated outdoor pool available to nonguests for a $10 fee. Nonguests can use the health-club facilities at **Radisson Hôtel Québec Centre** (✉ 690 blvd. René-Lévesque Est, ☎ 418/649–7273), including weights, sauna, whirlpool, and an outdoor heated pool (in summer), for $5. The pool at the **YMCA du Vieux-Québec** (✉ 650 av. Wilfred Laurier, ☎ 418/522–0800) is open to nonmembers for a $2.30 fee. Use of the weight room with Nautilus equipment is $8 while aerobics cost $11.50. At the **YWCA** (✉ 855 av. Holland, ☎ 418/683–2155), pool facilities cost $2.50 for nonmembers.

Hiking and Jogging

Parc Cartier-Brébeuf (✉ 175 rue de l'Espinay, ☎ 418/648–4038), north of Vieux-Québec along the banks of the St. Charles River, is connected to about 13 km (8 mi) of hiking trails. It's also a historic site with a reconstruction of a native longhouse. For mountainous terrain, head 19 km (12 mi) north on Route 73 to **Lac Beauport. Battlefields Park, Parc Cartier-Brébeuf,** and **Bois-de-Coulonge** park (✉ 1215 chemin St-Louis, ☎ 418/528–0773) in Sillery are the most popular places for jogging.

Horseback Riding

Jacques Cartier Excursions (✉ 978 av. Jacques-Cartier Nord, Tewkesbury, ☎ 418/848–7238), also known for rafting, offers summer and winter horseback riding. A summer excursion includes an hour of instruction and three hours of riding; the cost is $35–$50.

Ice-Skating

The ice-skating season is usually December through March. There's a 1.6-km (1-mi) stretch for skating alongside the **St. Charles River,** between the Drouin and Lavigeur bridges; the season runs January through March, depending on the ice. Changing rooms are nearby. For information, contact ☎ 418/691–6284.

From December through March, try the **Patinoire de la Terrasse** adjacent to the Château Frontenac (☎ 418/692–2955), open 11–11; it costs $2 to skate and skates can be rented for $5 daily. **Place d'Youville,** outside St-Jean Gate, has an outdoor rink that's open November through April. Nighttime skating is an option at **Village Vacances Valcartier** (✉ 1860 blvd. Valcartier, St-Gabriel-de-Valcartier, ☎ 418/844–2200).

Outfitters

Outdoor enthusiasts flock to **Latulippe** (✉ 637 rue St-Vallier Ouest, ☎ 418/529–0024) for its wide selection of clothing and equipment for such open-air pursuits as hiking, camping, snowmobiling, hunting, and fishing.

Rafting

The Jacques Cartier River, about 48 km (30 mi) northwest of Québec City, provides good rafting. **Jacques Cartier Excursions** (✉ 978 av. Jacques-Cartier Nord, Tewkesbury, ☎ 418/848–7238) runs rafting trips on the river from May through October. Tours originate from Tewkesbury, a half-hour drive from Québec City. A half-day tour costs less than $40; wet suits are $16. In winter, you can slide on inner tubes for about $16 a day.

Village Vacances Valcartier (✉ 1860 blvd. Valcartier, St-Gabriel-de-Valcartier, ☎ 418/844–2200) has excursions on the Jacques Cartier River from mid-May through mid-October. A three-hour excursion costs $42.95. It also offers hydro speeding—running the rapids on surfboards—and quieter family river tours.

Skiing

Brochures about ski centers in Québec are available at the **Québec Tourism and Convention Bureau** or by calling ☎ 877/BON–JOUR. The **Hiver Express** (☎ 418/525–5191) winter shuttle is a taxi service between major hotels in Vieux-Québec, Ste-Foy, ski centers, and the Village Vacances Valcartier. It leaves hotels in Ste-Foy at 8 AM and in Vieux Québec at 8:30 for the ski hills, 9 for Valcartier; the shuttle returns at 2:30 and 4:30 PM. The cost is $22 from Québec City or Ste-Foy; reserve and pay in advance at hotels.

CROSS-COUNTRY

You can ski cross-country on many trails. **Battlefields Park,** which you can reach from Place Montcalm, has scenic marked trails. Thirty ski centers in the Québec area offer 2,000 km (1,240 mi) of groomed trails and heated shelters; for information, call **Regroupement des Stations de Ski de Fond** (☎ 418/653–5875, WEB www.rssfrq.qc.ca). **Le Centre de Randonnée à Skis de Duchesnay** (✉ 143 rue de Duchesnay, St-Catherine-de-Jacques-Cartier, ☎ 418/875–2147), north of Québec City, has marked trails totaling 150 km (93 mi). **Mont Ste-Anne** (☎ 418/827–4561), 40 km (25 mi) northeast of Québec City, is the second-largest cross-country ski center in North America, with 21 trails totaling 224 km (139 mi). Lac Beauport, 19 km (12 mi) north of the city, has more than 20 marked trails (150 km, or 93 mi); contact **Les Sentiers du Moulin** (✉ 99 chemin du Moulin, Lac Beauport, ☎ 418/849–9652).

DOWNHILL

Three downhill ski resorts, all with night skiing, are within a 30-minute drive of Québec City. There are 25 trails and a vertical drop of 734 ft at the relatively small **Le Relais** (✉ 1084 blvd. du Lac, Lac Beauport, ☎ 418/849–1851), where you can buy lift tickets by the hour. **Mont Ste-Anne** (✉ 2000 blvd. Beaupré, Beaupré, ☎ 418/827–4561; 800/463–1568 for lodging) is one of the largest resorts in eastern Canada, with a vertical drop of 2,050 ft, 56 downhill trails, two half-

pipes for snowboarders, a terrain park, and 13 lifts including a gondola. **Station Touristique Stoneham** (✉ 1420 av. du Hibou, Stoneham,
☎ 418/848–2411), with a vertical drop of 1,380 ft, is known for its
long, easy slopes. It has 30 downhill runs and 10 lifts as well as a terrain park and two halfpipes.

Snowmobiling

Québec is the birthplace of the snowmobile, and with 30,000 km
(18,600 mi) of trails it is one of the best places in the world to practice this activity. Two major trails, the Trans-Québec Snowmobile Trail
and the 1,300-km (806-mi) Fur Traders Tour, run just north of Québec
City. Trail maps are available at tourist offices. Snowmobiles can be
rented near Mont Ste-Anne, a half-hour drive north of the city, at **Centre de Location de Motoneiges du Québec** (15 blvd. Beaupré, Beaupré,
☎ 418/827–8478), starting at $40 for an hour or $100 a day plus taxes,
insurance, and gas. **SM Sport** (113 blvd. Valcartier, Loretteville, ☎ 418/
842–2703) will pick you up from several downtown hotels for $25 per
person. It rents snowmobiles starting at $45 plus tax for an hour. A
day starts at $135, plus $15 insurance and cost of gas.

Snow Slides

At **Glissades de la Terrasse** (☎ 418/692–2955), adjacent to the Château
Frontenac, a wooden toboggan takes you down a 700-ft snow slide.
Cost is $1.50 per ride per adult, $1 for children under 10.

Visitors to **Village Vacances Valcartier** can use inner tubes or carpets
on the 30 snow slides, or join 6–12 others for a snow-raft ride down
one of six groomed trails. ✉ *1860 blvd. Valcartier, St-Gabriel-de-Valcartier,* ☎ *418/844–2200.* ✑ *Rafting and sliding $20 per day; $22 with
skating.* ◷ *Daily 10–10.*

Tennis and Racquet Sports

At **Montcalm Tennis Club** (✉ 901 blvd. Champlain, Sillery, ☎ 418/687–
1250), southwest of Québec City, four indoor and seven outdoor
courts are open weekdays from 7 AM and weekends from 8 AM to midnight. **Tennisport** (✉ 6280 blvd. Hamel, Ancienne Lorette, ☎ 418/872–
0111) has nine indoor tennis courts, two squash courts, two racquetball courts, and eight badminton courts.

Water Parks

Village Vacances Valcartier (✉ 1860 blvd. Valcartier, St-Gabriel-de-
Valcartier, ☎ 418/844–2200) has one of the largest water parks in
Canada, with 23 water slides, a wave pool, and the Amazon, a tropical river adventure. On Everest, one of the highest slides in North America, bathers shoot down at speeds of up to 50 mph. Admission is $25
a day for those at least 52 inches tall, $16 for those under 52 inches.

Winter Carnival

One winter highlight is the **Québec Winter Carnaval** (✉ 290 rue Joly,
GIL 1N8, ☎ 418/626–3716, 🌐 www.carnaval.qc.ca). The whirl of
activities over three weekends in January and/or February includes night
parades, a snow-sculpture competition, and a canoe race across the St.
Lawrence River. You can participate in or watch every activity imaginable in the snow from dogsledding to ice climbing. Dates for 2002
are Feb. 1–17.

Spectator Sports

Tickets for sporting events can be purchased at **Colisée Pepsi** (✉ Parc
de l'Expocité, 250 blvd. Wilfrid-Hamel, ☎ 418/691–7211). You can
order tickets through Billetech.

Baseball

The **Capitales de Québec** (⊠ 100 rue du Cardinal Maurice-Roy, ☎ 418/521–2255 or 877/521–2244), part of the Northern League, play Single A professional baseball from May 24 through September.

Harness Racing

There's horse racing at **Hippodrome de Québec** (⊠ Parc de l'Expocité, 250 blvd. Wilfrid-Hamel, ☎ 418/524–5283).

SHOPPING

Shopping is European-style on the fashionable streets of Québec City. The boutiques and specialty shops clustered along narrow streets such as rue du Petit-Champlain, and rues de Buade and St-Jean in the Latin Quarter, have one of the most striking historic settings on the continent. Prices in Québec City tend to be on a par with those in Montréal and other North American cities. The city's attractions for shoppers traditionally have been antiques, furs, and works by local artisans rather than bargains, but the exchange rate for the U.S. dollar and sales-tax rebates available to international visitors make shopping particularly tempting. When sales occur, they are usually listed in the French daily newspaper *Le Soleil*.

Stores are generally open Monday through Wednesday 9:30–5:30, Thursday and Friday until 9, Saturday until 5, and Sunday noon–5. In summer, shops may be open seven days, and most have later evening hours.

Department Stores

Most large department stores can be found in the malls of suburban Ste-Foy. **La Baie** (⊠ Pl. Laurier, Ste-Foy, ☎ 418/627–5959) is Québec's version of the Canadian Hudson's Bay Company conglomerate, founded in 1670 by Montréal trappers Pierre Radisson and Médard Chouart des Groseilliers. Today La Baie carries clothing for the entire family and household wares. **Holt Renfrew & Co., Ltd.** (⊠ Pl. Ste-Foy, Ste-Foy, ☎ 418/656–6783), one of the country's more exclusive stores, carries furs in winter, perfume, and tailored designer collections for men and women. **Simons** (⊠ 20 côte de la Fabrique, ☎ 418/692–3630; ⊠ Pl. Ste-Foy, Ste-Foy, ☎ 418/692–3630), one of Québec City's oldest family stores, used to be its only source for fine British woolens and tweeds; now the store also has a large selection of designer clothing, linens, and other household items.

Shopping Malls

An indoor amusement park with a roller coaster and an IMAX theater attracts families to the **Galeries de la Capitale** (⊠ 5401 blvd. des Galeries, ☎ 418/627–5800), with 250 stores about a 20-minute drive from Vieux-Québec. **Place Québec** (⊠ 880 autoroute Dufferin-Montmorency, ☎ 418/529–0551), the mall closest to the old city, is a multilevel shopping complex and convention center with more than 30 stores and restaurants; it's connected to the Hilton Québec.

The following shopping centers are approximately a 15-minute drive west along Grande Allée. **Place de la Cité** (⊠ 2600 blvd. Laurier, Ste-Foy, ☎ 418/657–6920) has 150 boutiques, services, and restaurants. With 350 stores and a wide variety, the massive **Place Laurier** (⊠ 2700 blvd. Laurier, Ste-Foy, ☎ 418/653–9318) is your best bet for one-stop shopping. Designer labels and upscale clothing are easy to find at **Place Ste-Foy** (⊠ 2450 blvd. Laurier, Ste-Foy, ☎ 418/653–4184), which has 130 stores.

Quartier Petit-Champlain (☎ 418/692–2613) in Lower Town is a pedestrian mall with some 45 boutiques, local businesses, and restaurants. This popular district is the best area for native Québec arts and crafts, such as wood sculptures, weavings, ceramics, and jewelry. **Pauline Pelletier** (✉ 38 rue du Petit-Champlain, ☎ 418/692–4871) specializes in porcelain. **Pot-en-Ciel** (✉ 27 rue du Petit-Champlain, ☎ 418/692–1743) carries ceramics and tablewares.

Specialty Stores

Antiques

Québec City's antiques district is centered on rues St-Paul and St-Pierre, across from the Old Port. French-Canadian, Victorian, and art deco furniture along with clocks, silverware, and porcelain are some of the rare collectibles found here. Authentic Québec pine furniture, characterized by simple forms and lines, is rare and costly.

Engravings, maps and prints of Québec and Canada, and white ironstone are the specialties at **Les Antiquités du Matelot** (✉ 55 Sault-au-Matelot, ☎ 418/694–9585). **Antiquités Marcel Bolduc** (✉ 74 rue St-Paul, ☎ 418/694–9558) is the largest antiques store on rue St-Paul. Antique books, most of them in French, can be found at **Argus Livres Anciens** (✉ 160 rue St-Paul, ☎ 418/694–2122). **Boutique Aux Mémoires Antiquités** (✉ 105 rue St-Paul, ☎ 418/692–2180) has a good selection of Regency, Victorian, and Edwardian pieces, silver, porcelain, curiosities, and bronzes. You're not likely to find any bargains but you will find the best selection of authentic 18th- and 19th-century Québec pine furniture at **Gérard Bourguet Antiquaire** (✉ 97 rue St-Paul, ☎ 418/694–0896). **L'Héritage Antiquité** (✉ 110 rue St-Paul, ☎ 418/692–1681) is probably the best place in the neighborhood to find good Québécois furniture, clocks, oil lamps, porcelain, and ceramics.

Art

Aux Multiples Collections (✉ 43 rue de Buade, ☎ 418/692–4298) has Inuit art and antique wood collectibles. **Galerie Brousseau et Brousseau** (✉ 35 rue St-Louis, ☎ 418/694–1828) has fine Inuit art. In Lower Town, **Galerie Madeleine Lacerte** (✉ 1 côte Dinan, ☎ 418/692–1566) sells contemporary art and sculpture. A source for less expensive artwork or work by promising young artists is **Rue du Trésor,** where local artists display their sketches, paintings, and etchings. Good portraits of Québec City and the region are plentiful.

Books

English-language books are difficult to find in Québec City. **Librairie du Nouveau-Monde** (✉ 103 rue St-Pierre, ☎ 418/694–9475) stocks titles in French and some in English. **Librairie Smith** (✉ 2700 blvd. Laurier, ☎ 418/653–8683), in the Place Laurier mall, has both English and French books. In the Place de la Cité mall, **La Maison Anglaise** (✉ 2600 blvd. Laurier, Ste-Foy, ☎ 418/654–9523) carries English-language titles only, specializing in fiction.

Clothing

Le Blanc Mouton (✉ 51 Sous le Fort, ☎ 418/692–2880), in Quartier Petit-Champlain, specializes in unique creations for women by Québec designers, including accessories and handcrafted jewelry. **François Côté Collection** (✉ 1200 Germain des Prés, Ste-Foy, ☎ 418/657–1760) is a chic boutique with fashions for men. **Louis Laflamme** (✉ 1192 rue St-Jean, ☎ 418/692–3774) has a large selection of stylish men's clothes. **La Maison Darlington** (✉ 7 rue de Buade, ☎ 418/692–2268) carries well-made woolens, dresses, and suits for men, women, and children by fine names in couture.

Crafts

The variety of crafts by Québec artisans at **Regard d'Ici** (⊠ Pl. Québec, 880 autoroute Dufferin-Montmorency, ☎ 418/522–0360) includes jewelry, clothing, leather goods, and decorative items. **Les Trois Colombes Inc.** (⊠ 46 rue St-Louis, ☎ 418/694–1114) sells handmade items, including clothing made from handwoven fabric, native and Inuit carvings, jewelry, and ceramics.

Food

Chocolate becomes a work of art at **Choco-Musée Érico** (⊠ 634 rue St-Jean, ☎ 418/524–2122), where *chocolatier* Éric Normand will handcraft whatever you like out of chocolate within a few days.

Fur

The fur trade has been an important industry here for centuries. Québec City is a good place to purchase high-quality furs at fairly reasonable prices. The department store **J. B. Laliberté** (⊠ 595 rue St-Joseph Est, ☎ 418/525–4841) carries furs. Since 1894, one of the best furriers in town has been **Richard Robitaille Fourrures** (⊠ 1500 rue des Taneurs, Suite 200, ☎ 418/681–7297).

Gifts

Collection Lazuli (⊠ 774 rue St-Jean, ☎ 418/525–6528; ⊠ Pl. de la Cité, 2600 blvd. Laurier, Ste-Foy, ☎ 418/652–3732) offers a good choice of unusual art objects and jewelry from around the world.

Jewelry

Joaillier Louis Perrier (⊠ 48 rue du Petit-Champlain, ☎ 418/692–4633) has Québec-made gold and silver jewelry. Exclusive handmade jewelry can be found at **Zimmermann** (⊠ 46 côte de la Fabrique, ☎ 418/692–2672).

SIDE TRIPS FROM QUÉBEC CITY

Several easy excursions show you another side of the province and provide more insight into its past. The spectacular Montmorency Falls can be seen in a day trip. A drive around the Ile d'Orléans, east of the city, is an easy way to experience rural Québec. The farms, markets, and churches here evoke the island's long history. The island can be toured in an energetic day, though rural inns make it tempting to extend a visit.

Côte de Beaupré and Montmorency Falls

As legend tells it, when explorer Jacques Cartier first caught sight of the north shore of the St. Lawrence River in 1535, he exclaimed, *"Quel beau pré!"* ("What a lovely meadow!"), because the area was the first inviting piece of land he had spotted since leaving France. Today this fertile meadow, first settled by French farmers, is known as Côte de Beaupré (Beaupré Coast), stretching 40 km (25 mi) east from Québec City to the famous pilgrimage site of Ste-Anne-de-Beaupré. Historic Route 360, or avenue Royal, winds its way from Beauport to St-Joachim, east of Ste-Anne-de-Beaupré. The impressive Montmorency Falls are midway between Québec City and Ste-Anne-de-Beaupré.

Montmorency Falls

50 *10 km (6 mi) east of Québec City.*

As it cascades over a cliff into the St. Lawrence River, the Montmorency River (named for Charles de Montmorency, who was a governor of New France) is one of the most beautiful sights in the province. The falls, at 274 ft, are 50% higher than Niagara Falls. A cable car runs to the top of the falls in **Parc de la Chute-Montmorency** (Mont-

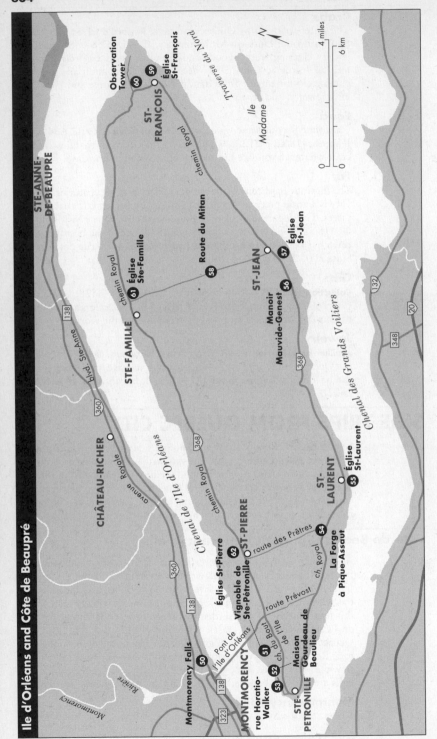

Île d'Orléans and Côte de Beaupré

morency Falls Park) from late April to early November. During very cold weather, the falls' heavy spray freezes and forms a giant loaf-shape ice cone known to Québécois as the Pain du Sucre (Sugarloaf); this phenomenon attracts sledders and sliders from Québec City. Ice climbers come to scale the falls; from late December through mid-March, a school trains novices to make the ascent. In the warmer months, you can visit an observation tower in the river's gorge that is continuously sprayed by a fine drizzle from water pounding onto the cliff rocks. The top of the falls can be observed from avenue Royale. In late July and early August, the skies above the falls light up with **Les Grands Feux Loto-Québec** (WEB www.lesgrandsfeux.com), an international competition with fireworks set to music.

The park is also historic. The British general Wolfe, on his way to conquer New France, set up camp here in 1759. In 1780, Sir Frederick Haldimand, then the governor of Canada, built a summer home—now a good restaurant called Manoir Montmorency—on top of the cliff. Prince Edward, Queen Victoria's father, rented this villa from 1791 to 1794. Unfortunately, the structure burned down several years ago; what stands is a re-creation. ✉ *2490 av. Royale, Beauport,* ☎ *418/663–3330,* WEB *www.chutemontmorency.qc.ca.* ✉ *Cable car $7.50 round-trip, car parking $7.50.* ☉ *Cable car Apr. 14–June 16 and Aug. 26–Oct. 20, daily 8:30–7; June 17–Aug. 25, daily 8:30 AM–9 PM; Dec. 26–Jan.6, daily 9–4; Jan. 27–Apr. 13, weekends 9–4, for the Sugarloaf slide.*

OFF THE BEATEN PATH

MUSÉE DE L'ABEILLE – Things are buzzing at this economuseum devoted to bees and honey. A giant glassed-in hive with a tube leading outdoors allows you to get a close look at life inside a beehive. On the bee safari, guides take a hive apart, explaining how it works and how bees behave, before taking you indoors to taste a variety of honey wines. You can also taste honey made from different kinds of flowers, from clover to blueberry. ✉ *8862 blvd. Ste-Anne, Château-Richer,* ☎ *418/824– 4411; 877/499–4411 in Canada.* ✉ *Museum free, bee safari $2.*

Côte de Beaupré and Montmorency Falls A to Z

CAR TRAVEL

To reach Montmorency Falls, take Route 440 (Autoroute Dufferin–Montmorency) east from Québec City approximately 9½ km (6 mi) to the exit for Montmorency Falls.

TOURS

Autocar Dupont-Gray Line leads day excursions along the Côte de Beaupré, with stops at Montmorency Falls and the Ste-Anne-de-Beaupré basilica. The cost is about $35 per person.
➤ FEES AND SCHEDULES: **Autocar Dupont-Gray Line** (☎ 418/649–9226).

VISITOR INFORMATION

At the Beaupré Coast Interpretation Center, in the old mill Petit-Pré built in 1695, guides in New France costumes explain displays on the history of the region. Admission is $2.50. The Center is open from mid-June to mid-October, daily 10–5. During the rest of the year, the Center is open by reservation only. Québec City Tourist Information has a bureau in Beauport, in Montmorency Falls Park. It's open June 5 to mid-October, daily 9–5.
➤ TOURIST INFORMATION: **Beaupré Coast Interpretation Center** (✉ 7007 av. Royale, Château-Richer, ☎ 418/824–3677). **Québec City Tourist Information** (✉ 4300 blvd. Ste-Anne, Rte. 138).

Ile d'Orléans

The Algonquins called it Minigo, the "Bewitched Place," and over the years the island's tranquil rural beauty has inspired poets and painters. The Ile d'Orléans is only 15 minutes from downtown Québec City, but a visit here is one of the best ways to get a feel for traditional life in rural Québec. Centuries-old homes and some of the oldest churches in the region dot the road that rings the island. Ile d'Orléans is at its best in summer when the boughs of trees in lush orchards bend under the weight of apples, plums, or pears, and the fields are bursting with strawberries and raspberries. Roadside stands sell woven articles, maple syrup, baked goods, jams, fruits, and vegetables. You can also pick your own produce at about two dozen farms. The island, immortalized by one of its most famous residents, the late poet and songwriter Félix Leclerc, is still fertile ground for artists and artisans.

The island was discovered at about the same time as Québec City, in 1535. Explorer Jacques Cartier noticed an abundance of vines and called it the Island of Bacchus, after the Greek god of wine. (Today, native Québec vines are being crossbred with European varieties at Ste-Pétronille's fledgling vineyard.) In 1536 Cartier renamed the island in honor of the duke of Orléans, son of the French king François I. Its fertile soil and abundant fishing made it so attractive to settlers that its population once exceeded Québec City's.

Ile d'Orléans, about 8 km (5 mi) wide and 34 km (21 mi) long, is composed of six small villages that have sought over the years to retain their identities. The island's bridge to the mainland was built in 1935, and in 1970 the island was declared a historic area to protect it from urban development.

Ste-Pétronille

17 km (10½ mi) northeast of Québec City.

The lovely village of Ste-Pétronille, the first to be settled on Ile d'Orléans, lies to the west of the bridge to the island. Founded in 1648, the community was chosen in 1759 by British general James Wolfe for his headquarters. With 40,000 soldiers and a hundred ships, the English bombarded French-occupied Québec City and Côte de Beaupré.

In the late 19th century, the English population of Québec developed Ste-Pétronille into a resort village. This area is considered to be the island's most beautiful, not only because of its spectacular views of Montmorency Falls and Québec City but also for the Regency-style English villas and exquisitely tended gardens.

51 At the **Vignoble de Ste-Pétronille,** hardy native Québec vines have been crossbred with three types of European grapes to produce a surprisingly good dry white wine. A guided tour of the vineyard includes a tasting. ⊠ *1A chemin du Bout de l'Ile,* ☎ *418/828–9554.* 🖾 *Guided tour $2.50.* ☉ *June–mid-Oct., daily 10–6; mid-Apr.–May and Nov.–Dec., weekends 11–5.*

At the **Plante family farm** (⊠ 20 chemin du Bout de l'Ile, ☎ 418/828–9603) you can stop to pick apples and strawberries (in season) or buy fresh fruits, vegetables, and apple cider.

52 The island's first home, the **Maison Gourdeau de Beaulieu** (⊠ 137 chemin du Bout de l'Ile) was built in 1648 for Jacques Gourdeau de Beaulieu, who was the first *seigneur* (a landholder who distributed lots to tenant farmers) of Ste-Pétronille. Remodeled over the years, this white house with blue shutters now incorporates both French and Québécois styles. Its thick walls and dormer windows are characteristic of Breton architecture, but its sloping bell-shape roof, designed to protect buildings from large amounts of snow, is typically Québécois. The house is not open to the public.

53 The tiny street called **rue Horatio-Walker,** off chemin Royal, was named after the early-19th-century painter known for his landscapes of the island. Walker lived on this street from 1904 until his death in 1938. At 11 and 13 rue Horatio-Walker are his home and workshop, but they are not open to the public.

DINING AND LODGING

$$ ✕🏨 **La Goéliche.** This English-style country manor, rebuilt in 1996–97 following a fire, stands steps away from the St. Lawrence River. Antiques decorate the cozy, elegant rooms, all with river views. Sinks are in the rooms instead of the baths to maximize space. Classic French cuisine includes calf sweetbreads with honey and lime sauce, garnished with hazelnuts, and quail baked in a creamy pear and celery sauce. The romantic dining room overlooks the river; a heated outdoor terrace is open from April to November. ✉ *22 chemin du Quai,* ☎ *418/828–2248 or 888/511–2248,* FAX *418/828–2745,* WEB *www.goeliche.ca. 18 rooms. Restaurant. AE, DC, MC, V.*

SHOPPING

Chocolaterie de l'Ile d'Orléans (✉ 150 chemin du Bout de l'Ile, ☎ 418/828–2252) combines Belgian chocolate with local ingredients to create handmade treats. Some choices are chocolates filled with maple butter or the *framboisette* made from raspberries. In summer try the homemade ice creams and sherbets.

St-Laurent

9 km (5½ mi) northeast of Ste-Pétronille.

Founded in 1679, St-Laurent is one of the island's maritime villages. Until as late as 1935, residents here used boats as their main means of
54 transportation. **La Forge à Pique-Assaut** (✉ 2200 chemin Royal, ☎ 418/828–9300) belongs to the talented and well-known local artisan Guy Bel, who has done ironwork restoration for Québec City. He was born in Lyon, France, and studied there at the École des Beaux Arts. From June to mid-October, daily 9–5, you can watch him work; his stylish candlesticks, chandeliers, fireplace tools, and other ironwork are for sale. Call ahead for reservations in winter.

The **Parc Maritime de St-Laurent,** at a former boatyard, is where craftspeople specializing in boatbuilding practiced their trade. Now you can picnic here and visit the Chalouperie Godbout (Godbout Longboat), which houses a complete collection of tools used during the golden era of boatbuilding. ✉ *120 chemin de la Chalouperie,* ☎ *418/828–9672.* 🎫 *$3.* ⏲ *Mid-June–Aug., daily 10–5; Sept.–early Oct., weekends 10–4 or by reservation; mid-May–mid-June by reservation.*

55 The tall, inspiring **Église St-Laurent,** which stands next to the village marina on chemin Royal, was built in 1860 on the site of an 18th-century church that had to be torn down. One of the church's procession chapels is a miniature stone replica of the original. ✉ *1532 chemin Royal,* ☎ *418/828–2551.* 🎫 *Free.* ⏲ *Summer, daily 9–5.*

DINING AND LODGING

$$ ✕ **Moulin de St- Laurent.** This is an early 18th-century stone mill where you can dine in the herb-and-flower garden out back. Scrumptious snacks, such as quiches, bagels, and salads, are available at the café-terrace. Evening dishes include local game such as stuffed rabbit. ✉ *754 chemin Royal,* ☎ *418/829–3888 or 888/629–3888. AE, DC, MC, V. Closed mid-Oct.–mid-Apr.*

$$ ✕🍴 **Le Canard Huppé.** As the inn's name suggests, its contemporary
★ cuisine usually showcases at least one dish with duck, such as duck
paté with stewed vanilla pears or confit of duck with blueberry and
maple sauce. Chef François Blais also offers dishes such as venison with
foie gras and asparagus, or Iles de la Madeleine scallops with somen
noodles in a mushroom and ginger sauce. Upstairs, each of the inn's
rooms has its own personality. They have original paintings by Québec
City area artists and unusual antiques. Deluxe rooms in a separate build-
ing have fireplaces, whirlpool tubs, and a view of the river. ✉ *2198
chemin Royal,* ☎ *418/828–2292 or 800/838–2292,* 🅵🅰🅷 *418/828–0966,*
🆆🅴🅱 *www.canard-huppe.qc.ca. 17 rooms. AE, DC, MC, V. CP.*

St-Jean
12 km (7 mi) northeast of St-Laurent.

The southernmost point of the island, St-Jean is a village whose in-
habitants were once river pilots and navigators. Most of its small, ho-
mogeneous row homes were built between 1840 and 1860. Being at
sea most of the time, the sailors didn't need large homes and plots of
land, as did the farmers.

56 St-Jean's beautiful Normandy-style manor, **Manoir Mauvide-Genest,**
was built in 1734 for Jean Mauvide (surgeon to Louis XV) and his wife,
Marie-Anne Genest. Most notable about this house, which still has its
original thick walls, ceiling beams, and fireplaces, is the degree to
which it has held up over the years. English guns targeted the house
during the 1759 siege of Québec City, and the facade still has inden-
tations left by cannonballs. At press time the building was closed but
exterior tours were being given. It is to reopen in mid-2002 as an in-
terpretation center dealing with the seigneurial regime. ✉ *1451 chemin
Royal,* ☎ *418/829–2630.*

57 At the eastern end of the village is **Église St-Jean,** a massive granite struc-
ture with large red doors and a towering steeple built in 1749. The church
resembles a ship; it's big and round and appears to be sitting right on
the river. Paintings of the patron saints of seamen line the interior walls.
The church's cemetery is also intriguing, especially if you can read French.
Back in the 18th century, piloting the St. Lawrence was a dangerous
profession; the cemetery tombstones recall the tragedies of lives lost
in these harsh waters. ✉ *2001 chemin Royal,* ☎ *418/828–2551.* 🖼
Free. ☉ *Summer, daily 10–5.*

58 Outside St-Jean, chemin Royal crosses **route du Mitan,** the most beau-
tiful on the island. In old French, *mitan* means "halfway." This road,
dividing the island in half, has views of acres of tended farmland,
apple orchards, and maple groves. If you need to end your circuit of
the island here, take route du Mitan, which brings you to Ste-Famille;
head west on chemin Royal to return to the bridge to the mainland.

St-François
12 km (7 mi) northeast of St-Jean.

Sprawling open fields separate 17th-century farmhouses in St-François,
the island's least-toured and most rustic village. This community at the
eastern tip of the island was originally settled mainly by farmers. St-
François is also the perfect place to visit one of the island's *cabanes à
sucre* (maple-sugaring shacks), found along chemin Royal. Stop at a hut
for a tasting tour; sap is gathered from the maple groves and boiled until
it turns to syrup. When it's poured on ice, it tastes like a delicious tof-
fee. The maple syrup season is from late March through April.

59 **Église St-François** (✉ 341 chemin Royal, ☎ 419/828–2551), built in
1734, is one of eight provincial churches dating from the French

regime. At the time the English seized Québec City in 1759, General James Wolfe knew St-François to be a strategic point along the St. Lawrence. Consequently, he stationed British troops here and used the church as a military hospital. In 1988 a car crash set the church on fire and most of the interior treasures were lost. A separate children's cemetery stands as a silent witness to the difficult life of early residents.

60 A picnic area with a wood **observation tower** is perfectly situated for viewing the majestic St. Lawrence. In spring and fall, wild Canada geese can be seen here. The area is about 2 km (1 mi) north on chemin Royal from St-François Church.

Ste-Famille
14 km (9 mi) west of St-François.

The village of Ste-Famille, founded in 1661, has exquisite scenery, including abundant apple orchards and strawberry fields with views of Côte de Beaupré and Mont Ste-Anne in the distance. But it also has plenty of historic charm, claiming the area's highest concentration of stone houses dating from the French regime.

61 The impressive **Église Ste-Famille,** constructed in 1749, is the only church in Québec province to have three bell towers at the front. Its ceiling was redone in the mid-19th century with elaborate designs in wood and gold. The church also holds a famous painting, *L'Enfant Jésus Voyant la Croix (Baby Jesus Looking at the Cross)*, done in 1670 by Frère Luc (Father Luc), who was sent from France to decorate churches in the area. ⊠ *3915 chemin Royal,* ☎ *419/828–2656.* ⊡ *Free.* ☺ *Summer, daily 11–5.*

St-Pierre
14 km (9 mi) southwest of St-Famille.

St-Pierre, established in 1679, is set on a plateau that has the island's most fertile land. The town has long been the center of traditional farming industries. The best products grown here are potatoes, asparagus, and corn, and the many dairy farms have given the village a reputation for butter and other dairy products. If you continue west on chemin Royal, just up ahead is the bridge back to the mainland and Route 440.

62 **Église St-Pierre,** the oldest on the island, dates from 1717. It's no longer open for worship, but it was restored during the 1960s and is open to visitors. Many original components are still intact, such as benches with compartments below where hot bricks and stones were placed to keep people warm in winter. Félix Leclerc (1914–88), the first Québécois singer to make his mark in Europe, is buried in the cemetery nearby. ⊠ *1243 chemin Royal,* ☎ *419/828–2656.* ⊡ *Free.* ☺ *Summer, daily 9–6.*

La Ferme Monna has won international awards for its crème de cassis de l'Ile d'Orléans, a liqueur made from black currants. The farm offers free samples of the strong, sweet cassis or one of its black-currant wines; the tour explains how they are made. ⊠ *723 chemin Royal,* ☎ *418/828–1057.* ⊡ *Free; guided tours $4.* ☺ *Mid-June–Sept., daily 10–6; Mar. and Oct.–Dec., weekends 10–5.*

Ile d'Orléans A to Z

CAR TRAVEL
From Québec City, take Route 440 (Autoroute Dufferin–Montmorency) northeast. After a drive of about 10 km (6 mi) take the Pont de l'Ile d'Orléans (a bridge) to the island. The main road, chemin Royal (Route 368), extends 67 km (42 mi) through the island's six villages, turning into chemin du Bout de l'Ile in Ste-Pétronille.

Parking can sometimes be a problem, but you can leave your car in the church parking lot and explore each village on foot.

EMERGENCIES
Centre Médical Prévost is the principal medical clinic on the island.
➤ HOSPITALS: **Centre Médical Prévost** (✉ 1015 Rte. Prévost, St-Pierre, ☎ 418/828–2213).

LODGING
Reservations are necessary at the island's 50 B&Bs, which cost about $55–$100 per night for a double-occupancy room. The Chamber of Commerce has a referral service for B&Bs.
➤ RESERVATION SERVICES: **Chamber of Commerce** (☎ 418/828–9411).

TOURS
The island's Chamber of Commerce rents a cassette tape or compact disc for $10 with an interesting 108-minute tour of the island by car; it's available at the tourist kiosk.

Québec City tour companies, including Autocar Dupont-Gray Line, run bus tours of the western tip of the island, combined with sightseeing along the Côte de Beaupré.
➤ FEES AND SCHEDULES: **Autocar Dupont-Gray Line** (☎ 418/649–9226).

VISITOR INFORMATION
Any of the offices of the Québec City Region Tourism and Convention Bureau can provide information on tours and accommodations on the island. The island's Chamber of Commerce operates a tourist-information kiosk at the west corner of côte du Pont and chemin Royal in St-Pierre.
➤ TOURIST INFORMATION: **Chamber of Commerce** (✉ 490 côte du Pont, ☎ 418/828–9411, WEB www.iledorleans.qc.ca).

QUÉBEC CITY A TO Z

To research prices, get advice from other travelers, and book travel arrangements, visit www.fodors.com.

AIR TRAVEL TO AND FROM QUÉBEC CITY
Two U.S. airlines fly directly to Québec City. American Eagle has flights from Boston, while Continental flies from Newark. You can also stop in Montréal, Toronto, or Ottawa and take a regional or commuter airline, such as Air Canada's Air Nova.

AIRPORTS AND TRANSFERS
Jean Lesage International Airport is about 19 km (12 mi) from downtown.
➤ AIRPORT INFORMATION: **Jean Lesage International Airport** (✉ 500 rue Principale, Ste-Foy, ☎ 418/640–2600).

AIRPORT TRANSFERS
The ride from the airport into town should be no longer than 30 minutes. Most hotels do not have an airport shuttle, but they will make a reservation for you with a bus company. If you're not in a rush, a shuttle bus offered by Autobus La Québécoise Inc. is convenient and half the price of a taxi.

If you're driving from the airport, take Route 540 (Autoroute Duplessis) to Route 175 (blvd. Laurier), which becomes Grande Allée and leads right to Vieux-Québec. The ride is about 30 minutes and may be only slightly longer (45 minutes or so) during rush hours (7:30–8:30 AM into town and 4–5:30 PM leaving town).

Autobus La Québécoise Inc. has a shuttle bus from the airport to hotels; the cost is less than $10 one way. Reservations are advised for the trip to the airport. Private limo service is expensive, starting at $50 for the ride from the airport into Québec City. Try Groupe Limousine A-1. Taxis are available immediately outside the airport exit near the baggage-claim area. A ride into the city costs about $24.50. Two local taxi firms are Taxi Québec and Taxi Coop de Québec, the largest company in the city.

➤ TAXIS AND SHUTTLES: **Autobus La Québécoise Inc.** (✉ 5480 rue Rideau, ☎ 418/872–5525). **Groupe Limousine A-1** (✉ 361 rue des Commissaires Est, ☎ 418/523–5059). **Taxi Coop de Québec** (✉ 496 2e av., ☎ 418/525–5191). **Taxi Québec** (✉ 975 8e av., ☎ 418/522–2001).

BOAT AND FERRY TRAVEL

The Québec–Lévis ferry crosses the St. Lawrence River to the town of Lévis. Although the crossing takes 15 minutes, waiting time can increase that to an hour. The cost is $1.80 in winter and $2.25 in summer. The first ferry from Québec City leaves daily at 6:30 AM from the pier at rue Dalhousie, across from Place Royale. Crossings run every half hour from 7:30 AM until 6:30 PM, then hourly until 2:20 AM. From May through November, the ferry adds extra service every 20 minutes during rush hours: 7:20–9 AM and 4–6 PM.

➤ BOAT AND FERRY INFORMATION: **Québec–Lévis ferry** (☎ 418/644–3704).

BUS TRAVEL TO AND FROM QUÉBEC CITY

Orléans Express Inc. provides service between Montréal and Québec City daily.

Buses depart hourly from both cities Monday through Saturday 6 AM–8 PM and Sunday 7 AM–8 PM. Additional buses run at 9:30 and 11 PM from Québec City and 9:30 PM, 10:30, and midnight from Montréal. The three-hour one-way ride costs $39.57; a round-trip is $59.35 if you return within 10 days and do not travel on Friday or certain days during holiday periods, but otherwise it's double the one-way price. You can purchase tickets only at one of the terminals.

➤ TERMINALS: **Québec City Terminal** (✉ 3020 rue Abraham Martin, ☎ 418/525–3000). **Ste-Foy Terminal** (✉ 3001 chemin Quatre Bourgeois, Ste-Foy, ☎ 418/650–0087). **Terminus Voyageur** (✉ 505 blvd. de Maisonneuve Est, Montréal, ☎ 514/842–2281).

BUS TRAVEL WITHIN QUÉBEC CITY

The city's transit system, Société de Transport de la Communauté Urbaine de Québec, runs buses approximately every 10 minutes to an hour, stopping at major points around town.

The cost is $2.25; you need exact change. For a discount on your fare, buy bus tickets at a major convenience store for $1.75 ($4.70 for a day pass). Terminals are in Lower Town at Place Jacques-Cartier and outside St-Jean Gate at Place d'Youville in Upper Town. Timetables are available at visitor information offices and at Place Jacques Cartier.

➤ BUS INFORMATION: **Société de Transport de la Communauté Urbaine de Québec** (STCUQ; ☎ 418/627–2511).

BUSINESS HOURS

In winter, many attractions and shops change their hours; visitors are advised to call ahead. Most banks are open Monday through Wednesday 10–3 and close later on Thursday and Friday.

Museum hours are typically 10–5, with longer evening hours in summer. Most are closed on Monday.

CAR RENTAL

➤ MAJOR AGENCIES: **Hertz Canada** (✉ Jean Lesage International Airport, ☎ 418/871–1571; ✉ 44 Côte du Palais, ☎ 418/694–1224; 800/263–0600 in English; 800/263–0678 in French). **National** (✉ Jean Lesage International Airport, ☎ 418/871–1224; ✉ 295 rue St-Paul, ☎ 418/694–1727). **Via Route** (✉ 2605 blvd. Wilfrid-Hamel, ☎ 418/682–2660).

CAR TRAVEL

Montréal and Québec City are linked by Autoroute 20 on the south shore of the St. Lawrence River and by Autoroute 40 on the north shore. On both highways, the ride between the two cities is about 240 km (149 mi) and takes about three hours. U.S. I–87 in New York, U.S. I–89 in Vermont, and U.S. I–91 in New Hampshire connect with Autoroute 20. Highway 401 from Toronto links up with Autoroute 20.

Driving northeast from Montréal on Autoroute 20, follow signs for Pont Pierre-Laporte (Pierre Laporte Bridge) as you approach Québec City. After you've crossed the bridge, turn right onto boulevard Laurier (Route 175), which becomes the Grande Allée leading into Québec City.

A car is necessary only if you plan to visit outlying areas. Automated seasonal information about roads is available November through April by calling ☎ 418/684–2363.

PARKING

The narrow streets of the old city leave few two-hour metered parking spaces available. However, several parking garages at central locations charge about $12 a day on weekdays or $6 for 12 hours on weekends. Main garages are at City Hall, Place d'Youville, Edifice Marie-Guyart, Place Québec, Château Frontenac, rue St-Paul, and the Old Port.

CONSULATES

The U.S. Consulate faces Governors' Park near Château Frontenac.
➤ UNITED STATES: ✉ 2 pl. Terrasse Dufferin, ☎ 418/692–2095 for recorded information; 418/692–2096 for an operator.

EMERGENCIES

Centre Hospitalier Universitaire de Québec is a hospital in Ste-Foy. Pavillon Hôtel-Dieu is the main hospital in Vieux-Québec.

If you don't have an emergency but require medical assistance, you can avoid long hospital waits at the Clinique Médecine de Famille. The walk-in clinic is open weekdays 8 AM–9 PM and weekends 9 AM–1 PM.

Clinique Dentaire Darveau, De Blois, and Tardif is open for dental services Monday and Tuesday 8–8, Wednesday 8–5, Thursday 8–6, and Friday 8–4. Pharmacie Brunet, north of Québec City in Charlesbourg, is open 8 AM–1 AM daily.
➤ DOCTORS AND DENTISTS: **Clinique Dentaire Darveau, De Blois, and Tardif** (✉ 1175 rue Lavigerie, Edifice Iberville 2, Room 100, Ste-Foy, ☎ 418/653–5412). **Clinique Médecine de Famille** (✉ 1000 chemin Ste-Foy, ☎ 418/688–1385).
➤ EMERGENCY SERVICES: **Distress Center** (☎ 418/686–2433). **Fire or police** (☎ 911 or 418/691–7722). **Poison Center** (☎ 418/656–8090). **Provincial police** (☎ 418/310–4141).
➤ HOSPITALS: **Centre Hospitalier Universitaire de Québec** (✉ 2705 blvd. Laurier, ☎ 418/656–4141). **Pavillon Hôtel-Dieu** (✉ 11 côte du Palais, ☎ 418/691–5151; 418/691–5042 for emergencies).
➤ LATE-NIGHT PHARMACIES: **Pharmacie Brunet** (✉ Les Galeries Charlesbourg, 4250 1ʳᵉ av., Charlesbourg, ☎ 418/623–1571).

ENGLISH-LANGUAGE MEDIA
BOOKS
➤ BOOKSTORES: **La Maison Anglaise** (✉ Pl. de la Cité, 2600 blvd. Laurier, Ste-Foy, ☎ 418/654–9523).

LODGING
B&BS
Québec City has many accommodations in hostels and B&Bs, which increasingly are known as Couette & Cafés. To guarantee a room during the peak season, reserve in advance. Québec City Tourist Information has B&B listings.
➤ RESERVATION SERVICES: **Québec City Tourist Information** (✉ 835 av. Laurier, G1R 2L3, ☎ 418/649–2608).

MONEY MATTERS
ATMs, or *guichets automatiques,* are widely available throughout Québec City and technical difficulties or running out of cash are rare. ATMs accept a wide variety of bank cards and are generally linked to international banking networks such as Cirrus.

BANKS
From May through September, Caisse Populaire Desjardins de Québec is open weekends 9–6, in addition to weekday hours.
➤ CONTACTS: **Caisse Populaire Desjardins de Québec** (✉ 19 rue des Jardins, ☎ 418/694–1774).

CURRENCY EXCHANGE
Echange de Devises Montréal is open September to mid-June, daily 9–5, and mid-June to early September, daily 8:30–7:30.
➤ EXCHANGE SERVICES: **Echange de Devises Montréal** (✉ 12 rue Ste-Anne, ☎ 418/694–1014).

TAXIS AND LIMOUSINES
Taxis are stationed in front of major hotels and the Hôtel de Ville (City Hall), along rue des Jardins, and at Place d'Youville outside St-Jean Gate. Passengers are charged an initial $2.50, plus $1.20 for each kilometer (½ mi). For radio-dispatched cars, try Taxi Coop de Québec or Taxi Québec.

Limousines are another option. Groupe Limousine A-1 has 24-hour service.
➤ TAXI AND LIMOUSINE COMPANIES: **Groupe Limousine A-1** (✉ 361 rue des Commissaires Est, ☎ 418/523–5059). **Taxi Coop de Québec** (☎ 418/525–5191). **Taxi Québec** (☎ 418/522–2001).

TOURS
Tours can include Montmorency Falls, whale-watching, and Ste-Anne-de-Beaupré in addition to sights in Québec City; combination city and harbor-cruise tours are also available. Québec City tours operate year-round; excursions to outlying areas may operate only in summer.

BOAT TOURS
Croisières AML Inc. runs cruises on the St. Lawrence River aboard the MV *Louis-Jolliet.* The 1½- to 3-hour cruises run from May through mid-October and start at $23 plus tax.
➤ FEES AND SCHEDULES: **Croisières AML Inc.** (✉ Pier Chouinard, 10 rue Dalhousie, beside the Québec–Lévis ferry terminal, ☎ 418/692–1159).

BUS TOURS
Tickets for Autocar Dupont–Gray Line bus tours can be purchased at most major hotels. Tours depart across the square from the Château

Laurier Hotel (⌂ 1230 place Georges V). The company also offers guided tours in a minibus or trolley. Tours run year-round and cost $25–$100. Call for a reservation and the company will pick you up at your hotel.
➤ FEES AND SCHEDULES: **Autocar Dupont–Gray Line** (☎ 418/649–9226 or 888/558–7668).

Adlard Tours leads walking tours of the old city through the narrow streets that buses cannot enter. The $14 cost includes a refreshment break; unilingual tours are available in many languages. Tours leave from 12 rue Ste-Anne.
➤ FEES AND SCHEDULES: **Adlard Tours** (⌂ 13 rue Ste-Famille, ☎ 418/692–2358).

TRAIN TRAVEL

VIA Rail, Canada's passenger rail service, runs daily trains from Montréal to Québec City. The train arrives at the 19th-century Gare du Palais, in the heart of the old city.

Trains from Montréal to Québec City and from Québec City to Montréal run four times daily on weekdays, three times daily on weekends. The trip takes less than three hours, with a stop in Ste-Foy. Tickets can be purchased in advance at any VIA Rail office, travel agent, or at the station before departure. The basic one-way fare, including taxes, is $60.96.

First-class service costs $112.23 each way and includes early boarding, seat selection, and a three-course meal with wine. One of the best deals, subject to availability, is the round-trip ticket bought 10 days in advance for $78.22.
➤ TRAIN INFORMATION: **Gare du Palais** (⌂ 450 rue de la Gare du Palais, ☎ no phone). **VIA Rail** (☎ 418/692–3940; 800/561–3949 in the U.S.; 800/361–5390 in Québec).

TRANSPORTATION AROUND QUÉBEC CITY

Walking is the best way to explore the city. Vieux-Québec measures 11 square km (about 4 square mi), and most historic sites, hotels, and restaurants are within the walls or a short distance outside. City maps are available at visitor information offices.

La Belle Epoque, Balades en Calèche et Diligence, and Les Calèches du Vieux-Québec are three calèche companies. You can hire a calèche at Place d'Armes near the Chateau Frontenac, at the St. Louis gate, or on rue d'Auteuil between the St-Louis and Kent gates. If you call ahead, some companies can also pick you up at your hotel. Some drivers talk about Québec's history and others don't; if you want a storyteller, ask for one in advance. The cost is about $60 including all taxes for a 45-minute tour of Vieux-Québec.
➤ FEES AND SCHEDULES: **Balades en Calèche et Diligence** (☎ 418/624–3062). **La Belle Epoque** (☎ 418/687–6653). **Les Calèches du Vieux-Québec** (☎ 418/683–9222).

TRAVEL AGENCIES

➤ LOCAL AGENTS: **American Express** (⌂ Pl. Laurier, 2700 blvd. Laurier, ☎ 418/658–8820). **Inter Voyage** (⌂ 1095 rue de l'Amérique Française, ☎ 418/524–1414).

VISITOR INFORMATION

The Québec City Region Tourism and Convention Bureau has two visitor information centers that are open year-round and a mobile information service that operates between mid-June and September 7 (look for the mopeds with a big question mark). The Québec City information center is open June 24 to early September, daily 8:30–7:30; early September to mid-October, daily 8:30–6:30; and mid-October through June 23, Monday through Thursday and Saturday 9–5, Friday 9–6, and Sunday 10–4. The Ste-Foy information center is open the same hours; look for big question marks as signage. The Québec Government Tourism Department has a center that is open daily 9–5 from September 4 to June 20, and 8:30–7:30 June 21 to September 3.

➤ TOURIST INFORMATION: **Québec City Tourist Information** (✉ 835 av. Laurier, Québec City G1R 2L3, ☎ 418/649–2608, WEB www.quebec-region.com). **Québec Government Tourism Department** (✉ 12 rue Ste-Anne, Pl. d'Armes, ☎ 877/BON–JOUR or 877/266–5687, WEB www. bonjour-quebec.com). **Ste-Foy** (✉ 3300 av. des Hôtels, Ste-Foy G1W 5A8, ☎ 418/651–2891).

11 PROVINCE OF QUÉBEC

THE LAURENTIANS, THE EASTERN TOWNSHIPS, CHARLEVOIX, THE GASPÉ PENINSULA

Québec has a distinct personality forged by its French heritage and culture. The land, too, is memorable: within its boundaries lie thousands of lakes and rivers—the highways for intrepid explorers, fur traders, and pioneers. The Laurentians with their ski resorts and the forested coastline of the Gulf of St. Lawrence are the playground of La Belle Province. Echoes of the past remain in the charming rural communities of the Eastern Townships and Charlevoix, and the rugged beauty and isolation of Gaspé are unsurpassed in the province.

Updated by
Helga
Loverseed

A MONG THE PROVINCES OF CANADA, Québec is set apart by its strong French heritage, a matter not only of language but of customs, religion, and political structure. Québec covers a vast area—almost one-sixth of Canada's total—although the upper three-quarters is only sparsely inhabited. Outside Montréal and Québec City, serenity and natural beauty abound in the province's innumerable lakes, streams, and rivers; in its farmlands and villages; in its great mountains and deep forests; and in its rugged coastline along the Gulf of St. Lawrence. Though the winters are long, activities from skiing to snowmobiling lure residents and visitors outdoors.

The first European to arrive in Québec was French explorer Jacques Cartier in 1534; another Frenchman, Samuel de Champlain, arrived in 1603 to build French settlements in the region, and Jesuit missionaries followed. In 1663 Louis XIV of France proclaimed Canada a crown colony—New France, and the land was allotted to French aristocrats and administrators in large grants called *seigniories*.

Tenants, known as *habitants*, settled on the farms belonging to those who received the grants, *seigneurs*. The Roman Catholic Church took on an importance that went beyond religion. Priests and nuns acted as doctors, educators, and arbiters among the habitants, and liaisons between French-speaking fur traders and English-speaking merchants. An important church priority in Québec, one emphasized after the British conquest of 1759, was *survivance*—the survival of the French people and their culture. Couples were encouraged to have large families, and they did; up to the 1950s, families with 10 or 12 children were common.

Québec's threats to secede from the Canadian union are part of a long-standing tradition of independence. Although the British won control of Canada in the French and Indian War in 1763, Parliament passed the Québec Act in 1774. The act ensured the continuation of French civil law in Québec and left provincial authority in the hands of the Roman Catholic Church. In general the law preserved the traditional French-Canadian way of life. Tensions between French- and English-speaking Canada continued throughout the 20th century, however, and in 1974 the province proclaimed French its sole official language, much the same way the provinces of Manitoba and Alberta had taken steps earlier in the century to make English their sole official language. Québec is part of the Canadian union and a signatory to its original constitution, but it has not accepted the changes made in that document during the 1980s. Two attempts to get Québec to sign the revised constitution in the 1990s failed.

Being able to speak French can make a visit to the province more pleasant—many locals, at least in rural areas, do not speak English. If you don't speak French, arm yourself with a phrase book or at least a knowledge of some basic phrases. It's also worth your while to sample the regional Québécois cuisine, for this is a province where food is taken seriously.

Pleasures and Pastimes

Dining

Whether you choose a mixed-game pie such as *cipaille* or a sweet–salty dish like ham with maple syrup, you won't soon forget your meals here. Cooking in the province tends to be hearty: cassoulet, *tourtières* (meat pies), onion soup, and apple pie head up menus. Maple syrup, much of it produced locally, is a mainstay of Québécois dishes. In addition, cloves, nutmeg, cinnamon, and pepper—spices used by the first settlers—have never gone out of style.

Lower Québec

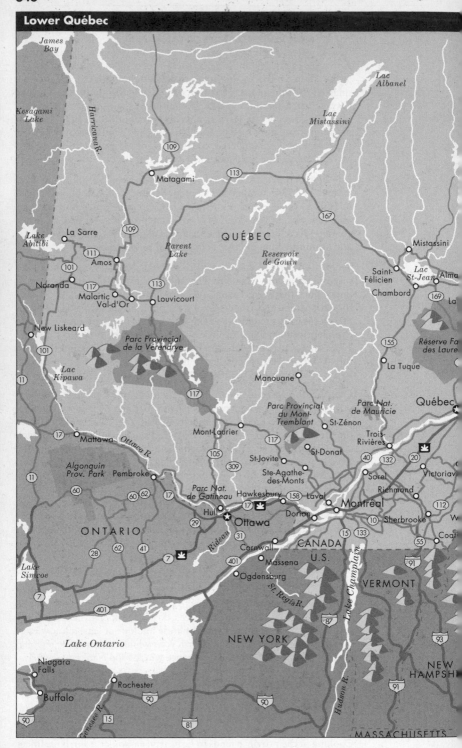

James Bay

Kesagami Lake

Harricana R.

Lac Albanel

Lac Mistassini

109

Matagami

113

QUÉBEC

167

La Sarre

109

Parent Lake

Reservoir de Gouin

Mistassini

111

Amos

Saint-Félicien

Lac St-Jean

Alma

101

113

Chambord

La

Noranda

117

169

Malartic

Val-d'Or

Louvicourt

New Liskeard

101

Parc Provincial de la Verendrye

155

Réserve Fa des Laure

La Tuque

Lac Kipawa

117

Manouane

11

Parc Provincial du Mont-Tremblant

Parc Nat. de Mauricie

Québec

17

Mattawa

Ottawa R.

Mont-Laurier

117

St-Zénon

Trois-Rivières

Algonquin Prov. Park

11

105

309

St-Jovite

St-Donat

40

132

20

60

Pembroke

Parc Nat. de Gatineau

Ste-Agathe-des-Monts

Sorel

Victoriav

60

62

17

Richmond

112

28

62

41

29

Hawkesbury

158

Laval

Montréal

Sherbrooke

ONTARIO

Hull

17

Dorion

10

Coal

7

Bideau

31

Cornwall

CANADA

15

133

55

Lake Simcoe

401

Massena

U.S.

91

7

Ogdensburg

VERMONT

201

St. Regis R.

87

Lake Champlain

Lake Ontario

NEW YORK

93

NEW HAMPSH

Niagara Falls

Hudson R.

91

Buffalo

Rochester

90

90

90

Genesee R.

15

81

MASSACHUSETTS

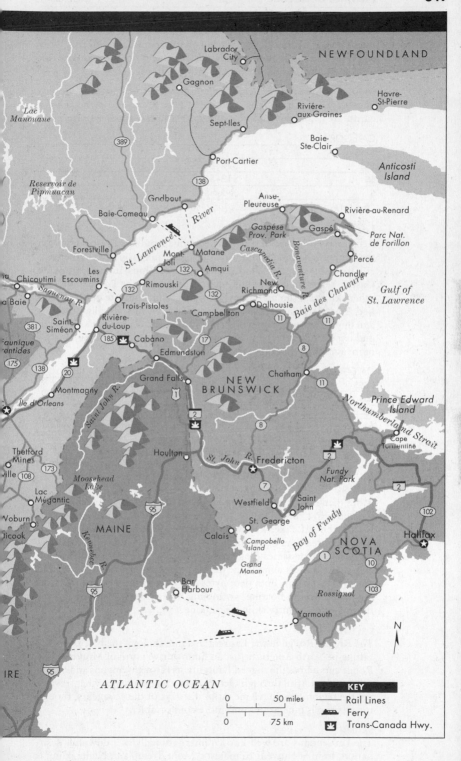

NEWFOUNDLAND

Labrador City

Gagnon

Havre-St-Pierre

Rivière-aux-Graines

Sept-Iles

Baie-Ste-Clair

Lac Manouane

389

Port-Cartier

Anticosti Island

138

Reservoir de Pipmuacan

Godbout

St. Lawrence River

Anse-Pleureuse

Rivière-au-Renard

Gaspése Prov. Park

Gaspé

Baie-Comeau

Parc Nat. de Forillon

Forestville

Mont-Joli

Matane

Cascapedia R.

Percé

132

Amqui

Chandler

Les Escoumins

Chicoutimi

132

Rimouski

New Richmond

Bonaventure R.

Gulf of St. Lawrence

Saguenay R.

132

a Baie

Trois-Pistoles

Dalhousie

Baie des Chaleurs

Campbellton

11

11

Rivière-du-Loup

381

Saint-Siméon

185

Cabano

17

8

aunique entides

Edmundston

175

138

20

Grand Falls

NEW BRUNSWICK

Chatham

11

Prince Edward Island

Northumberland Strait

Montmagny

1

Ile d'Orleans

2

Cape Tormentine

Houlton

St. John R.

8

Fredericton

2

Thetford Mines

St. John R.

Fundy Nat. Park

108

173

7

2

ville

Moosehead Lake

Lac Mégantic

95

Westfield

Saint John

102

Voburn

St. George

Bay of Fundy

Halifax

ticook

Calais

NOVA SCOTIA

MAINE

Campobello Island

1

10

Kennebec R.

Grand Manan

Rossignol

103

95

Bar Harbour

Yarmouth

N

IRE

95

ATLANTIC OCEAN

KEY
—— Rail Lines
Ferry
Trans-Canada Hwy.

0   50 miles

0   75 km

Restaurants are an integral slice of Québec life. The Eastern Townships are one of Québec's foremost regions for fine cuisine and chefs at the finer Laurentian inns have attracted an international following. Early reservations are essential. Monday or Tuesday is not too soon to book weekend tables at the best provincial restaurants.

More casual fare such as a croissant and an espresso, or *poutine*, a heaped plate of *frites* (french fries) smothered with gravy and melted cheese curds, are available from sidewalk cafés and fast-food emporiums.

CATEGORY	COST*
$$$$	over $32
$$$	$22–$32
$$	$13–$21
$	under $13

per person, in Canadian dollars, for a main course at dinner

Lodging

Accommodation options in Québec range from large resort hotels in the Laurentians and elegant Relais & Châteaux properties in the Eastern Townships to simple motels and *auberges* (inns) in the heart of the Gaspé. Year-round or in high season (winter in the Laurentians and other ski areas, summer elsewhere), many inns operate on the Modified American Plan (MAP) and include two meals, usually breakfast and dinner, in the cost of a night's stay. Be sure to ask what's included, and expect prices to be lower off-season. In addition, some inns require a minimum two-night stay; always ask.

CATEGORY	COST*
$$$$	over $160
$$$	$120–$160
$$	$85–$120
$	under $85

All prices are for a standard double room, excluding optional service charge, 7% GST, and 7.5% provincial tax, in Canadian dollars.

Outdoor Activities and Sports

FISHING

More than 60 outfitters (some of whom are also innkeepers) work in the northern Laurentians area, where provincial parks and game sanctuaries abound. Pike, walleye, and lake and speckled trout are plentiful just a three-hour drive north of Montréal. Open year-round in most cases, lodging facilities range from luxurious, first-class resorts to log cabins. As well as supplying trained guides, all provide services and equipment to allow both neophytes and experts the best possible fishing in addition to boating, swimming, river rafting, windsurfing, ice fishing, cross-country skiing, or hiking.

RAFTING

The Rivière Rouge in the Laurentians rates among the best rivers for rafting in North America. Just an hour's drive north of Montréal, the Rouge cuts across the rugged Laurentians through canyons and alongside beaches. April through October you can experience what traversing the region must have meant in the days of the voyageurs, though today's trip is much safer and more comfortable.

SKIING

The Laurentians are well known internationally as a downhill destination, from St-Sauveur to majestic Mont-Tremblant. Night skiing is available on some slopes. Cross-country skiing is popular throughout the area from December to the end of March, especially at Val David,

Val Morin, and Estérel. Each has a cross-country ski center and at least a dozen groomed trails.

The Eastern Townships have more than 1,000 km (620 mi) of cross-country trails. Three inns here offer a week-long package of cross-country treks from one inn to another. The area is also popular as a downhill ski center, with ski hills on four mountains that dwarf anything the Laurentians have to offer, with the exception of Mont-Tremblant.

Charlevoix has three main ski areas with excellent facilities for both downhill and cross-country skiers.

Lift ticket prices vary by resort, and the cost is often included in hotel packages. Expect to pay about $40 per day. Road names near ski areas are seldom labeled (they're up the mountain, where else?) but the signage is extremely good, with ski symbols and distance clearly marked.

Sugar Shacks

Every March the combination of sunny days and cold nights causes the sap to run in the maple trees. *Cabanes à sucre* (sugar shacks) go into operation, boiling the sap collected from the trees in buckets (now, at some places, complicated tubing and vats do the job). The many commercial enterprises scattered over the area host "sugaring offs" and tours of the process, including tapping the maple trees, boiling the sap in vats, and *tire sur la neige,* pouring hot syrup over cold snow to give it a taffy consistency just right for "pulling" and eating. A number of cabanes serve hearty meals of ham, baked beans, and pancakes, all drowned in maple syrup.

Exploring Québec

Two major recreational areas attract stressed-out urbanites and anyone else who wants to relax: The Laurentians are a resort area with fine ski hills and thousands of miles of wilderness beginning only 60 km (37 mi) north of Montréal. The Eastern Townships, in a southern corner of the province, have outdoor activities on ski slopes and lakes and in provincial parks. Cultural attractions are other pleasures in the Townships, which start just 80 km (50 mi) east of Montréal.

Charlevoix is often called the Switzerland of Québec because of its landscape, which includes mountains, valleys, streams, and waterfalls. Charming villages line the north shore of the St. Lawrence River for about 200 km (124 mi)—from Ste-Anne-de-Beaupré, east of Québec City, to the Saguenay River. The knobby Gaspé Peninsula is where the St. Lawrence River meets the Gulf of St. Lawrence. This isolated peninsula, which begins about 200 km (124 mi) east of Québec City, has a wild beauty all its own: mountains and cliffs tower above its beaches. The drive around the Gaspé is 848 km (526 mi).

Numbers in the text correspond to numbers in the margin and on the Laurentians (les Laurentides), Eastern Townships (les Cantons de l'Est) and Montérégie, Charlevoix, and Gaspé Peninsula (Gaspésie) maps.

Great Itineraries

IF YOU HAVE 2 DAYS

If you have only a few days for a visit, you'll need to concentrate on one area, and the Laurentians, outside Montréal, are a good choice. This resort area has recreational options (depending on the season) that include golf, hiking, and great skiing. Pick a resort town to stay in, whether it's 🔲 **St-Sauveur-des-Monts** ④, 🔲 **Ste-Adèle** ⑥, or 🔲 **Mont-Tremblant** ⑩ near the vast **Parc Provincial du Mont-Tremblant,** and use that as a base to visit some of the surrounding towns. There's good eating and shopping here—and even a reconstructed historic village in Ste-Adèle.

If your starting point is Québec City, you could take two days to explore the towns of Charlevoix east of the city, with an overnight in the elegant resort town ⊞ **La Malbaie** ㉕.

IF YOU HAVE 5 DAYS

You can combine a taste of the Eastern Townships with a two-day visit to the Laurentians. Get a feeling for the Laurentians by staying overnight in ⊞ **St-Sauveur-des-Monts** ④ or ⊞ **Ste-Adèle** ⑥ and exploring surrounding towns such as **St-Jérôme** ③ and **Morin Heights** ⑤. Then head back south of Montréal to the Townships, which extend to the east along the border with New England. Overnight in ⊞ **Granby** ⑪ or ⊞ **Bromont** ⑫: Granby has a zoo and Bromont is known for its factory outlets. The next day, you can shop in pretty **Knowlton** ⑭ and explore regional history in such towns as **Valcourt** ⑮, where a museum is dedicated to the inventor of the snowmobile. Spend a night or two in the appealing resort town of ⊞ **Magog** ⑱, along Lac Memphrémagog, or the quieter ⊞ **North Hatley** ⑲, on Lac Massawippi. You'll have good dining in either. Save a day for some outdoor activity, whether it's golfing, skiing, biking on former railroad lines, or hiking.

IF YOU HAVE 10–12 DAYS

A longer visit can show you a number of regions in Québec, but you must do some driving between them. You can spend a few days in either the Laurentians or the Eastern Townships before heading east to Québec City and historic Charlevoix, the heart of what was New France, along the St. Lawrence River. The drive from Montréal or Sherbrooke to Québec City is more than 240 km (149 mi); Charlevoix begins 33 km (20 mi) to the east, at **Ste-Anne-de-Beaupré** ㉒, with its famous basilica. Colonial-era homes and farmhouses dot several villages; some are still homes, and others are now theaters, museums, or restaurants. Spend time in ⊞ **Baie St-Paul** ㉓ and ⊞ **La Malbaie** ㉕, or just drive lovely roads such as Route 362. In season you can whale-watch in **Tadoussac** ㉖. To get to the Gaspé Peninsula, you have to cross the St. Lawrence River. An hourlong ferry ride from St-Siméon, between La Malbaie and Tadoussac, takes you to Rivière-du-Loup. From there it's a day to get to ⊞ **Carleton** ㉗ on the Gaspé's southern shore. The peninsula offers one of the most scenic drives in North America; you can stop in ⊞ **Percé** ㉘ and spend a day visiting **l'Ile Bonaventure** ㉙ with its fascinating bird colony.

When to Tour Québec

The Laurentians are mainly a winter ski destination, but you can drive up from Montréal to enjoy the fall foliage; to hike, bike, or play golf; or to engage in spring skiing—and still get back to the city before dark. The only slow periods are early November, when there is not much to do, and June, when there is plenty to do but the area is plagued by black-flies (admittedly less of a problem thanks to effective biological-control programs).

The Eastern Townships are best in fall, when the foliage is at its peak. The region borders Vermont and has the same dramatic colors. It's possible to visit wineries at this time, although you should call ahead to see if visitors are welcome during the harvest, which can be busy. Charlevoix is lovely in fall, but winter is particularly magical—although the roads aren't great. In summer there is a special silvery light, born of the mountains and the proximity of the sea, which attracts many painters.

Summer is really the only time to tour the Gaspé. Some attractions have already closed by Labor Day, and few hotels are open during winter. The weather can be harsh, too, and driving the coast road can be difficult.

THE LAURENTIANS

The Laurentians (les Laurentides) are divided into two major regions: the Lower Laurentians (les Basses Laurentides) and the Upper Laurentians (les Hautes Laurentides). But don't be fooled by the designations; they don't signify great driving distances. Just 45 minutes to the north, avid skiers might call Montréal a bedroom community for the Laurentians. The range dates to the Precambrian era (more than 600 million years ago). These rocky hills are relatively low, but they include eminently skiable hills, with a few peaks above 2,500 ft. World-famous Mont-Tremblant, at 3,150 ft, is the tallest.

The P'tit Train du Nord—the former railroad line that is now a 200-km (124-mi) linear park used by cyclists, hikers, skiers, and snowmobilers—made it possible to transport settlers and cargo easily to the Upper Laurentians. It also opened the area up to skiing by the early 20th century. Before long, trainloads of skiers replaced settlers and cargo as the railway's major trade. Initially a winter weekend getaway for Montrealers who stayed at boardinghouses and fledgling resorts and skied its hills, the Upper Laurentians soon began attracting international visitors.

Ski lodges and private family cottages for wealthy city dwellers were accessible only by train until the 1930s when Route 117 was built. Today there is an uneasy peace between the longtime cottagers who want to restrict development and resort entrepreneurs who want to expand. At the moment, commercial interests seem to be prevailing. A number of large hotels have added indoor pools and spa facilities, and efficient highways have brought the country even closer to the city—45 minutes to St-Sauveur, 1½–2 hours to Mont-Tremblant.

The Lower Laurentians start almost immediately outside Montréal and are rich in historic and architectural landmarks. Towns such as St-Eustache and Oka are home to the manors, mills, churches, and public buildings seigneurs built for themselves and their habitants.

The resort area truly begins at St-Sauveur-des-Monts (Exit 60 on Autoroute 15) and extends as far north as Mont-Tremblant, where it turns into a wilderness of lakes and forests best visited with an outfitter. Guides that offer fishing trips are concentrated around Parc Provincial du Mont-Tremblant. To the first-time visitor, the hills and resorts around St-Sauveur, Ste-Adèle, Morin Heights, Val Morin, and Val David up to Ste-Agathe-des-Monts, form a pleasant hodgepodge of villages, hotels, and inns that seem to blend one into another.

Oka

❶ *40 km (25 mi) west of Montréal.*

To promote piety among the native people, the Sulpicians erected the **Calvaire d'Oka** (Oka Calvary; ✉ Rte. 344), representing the Stations of the Cross, between 1740 and 1742. Three of the seven chapels are still maintained, and every September 14 since 1870 Québécois pilgrims have congregated here to participate in the half-hour ceremony that proceeds on foot to the calvary's summit. A sense of the divine is inspired as much by the magnificent view of Lac des Deux-Montagnes as by religious fervor.

The **Abbaye Cistercienne d'Oka** is one of the oldest North American abbeys. In 1887 the Sulpicians donated about 865 acres of their property near the Oka Calvary to the Trappist monks, who had arrived in New France in 1880 from Bellefontaine Abbey in France. Within 10

The Laurentians (les Laurentides)

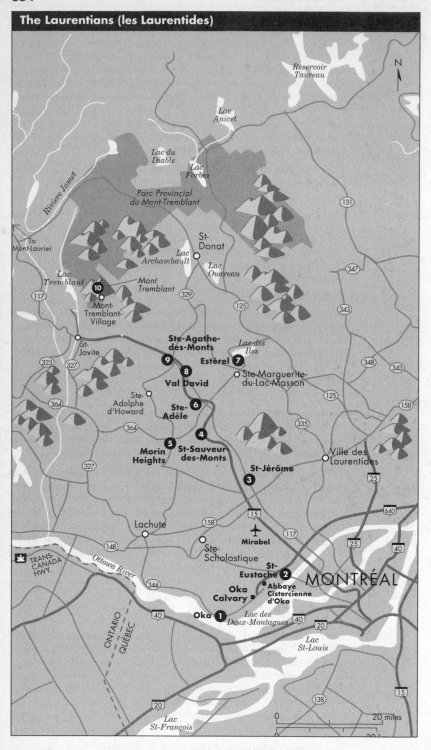

N

Reservoir Taureau

Lac Anicet

Lac du Diable

Lac Forbes

Rivière Jamet

Parc Provincial du Mont-Tremblant

131

To Mont-Laurier

St-Donat

Lac Archambault

Lac Ouareau

347

117

Lac Tremblant

10 Mont Tremblant

Mont-Tremblant-Village

343

329

125

St-Jovite

Ste-Agathe-des-Monts

Lac des Îles

348

343

9

8

Esterel 7

Ste-Marguerite-du-Lac-Masson

323

327

Val David

Ste-Adolphe d'Howard

6

Ste-Adèle

125

158

364

364

5

4

335

327

Morin Heights

St-Sauveur-des-Monts

Ville des Laurentides

327

3 St-Jérôme

25

Lachute

158

15

640

148

Mirabel

117

25

40

TRANS-CANADA HWY.

Ottawa River

Ste-Scholastique

St-Eustache 2

MONTRÉAL

344

Oka Calvary

Abbaye Cistercienne d'Oka

ONTARIO QUÉBEC

40

Oka 1

Lac des Deux-Montagnes

40

20

Lac St-Louis

20

138

15

0   20 miles

Lac St-François

years they had built their monastery and transformed this land. Trappists established the Oka School of Agriculture, which operated until 1960, and are still famous for making Oka cheese today. The monastery is a noted prayer retreat. The gardens and chapel are open to visitors. ⊠ *1600 chemin d'Oka,* ☎ *450/479–8361.* ☞ *Free.* ☉ *Chapel Mon.–Sat. 4 AM–9 PM; gardens and boutique weekdays 9:30–11:30 and 1–4:30, Sat. 9–4.*

Parc Provincial d'Oka, surrounded by rolling hills, has a lake fringed by a sandy beach with picnic areas and hiking and biking trails. There are 800 camp sites here and this is a good place for kayaking, canoeing, fishing, and, in winter, snowshoeing and cross-country skiing. ⊠ *2020 chemin Oka,* ☎ *450/479–8365; 450/479–8337 for activities.* ☞ *$3.50 plus $5 per car.* ☉ *Daily 8–8.*

If you're traveling with children, take a quick detour on the ferry across Lac des Deux Montagnes to **Hudson,** an attractive hamlet where the fire hydrants are decorated with human "faces." In winter, when there is an ice "bridge" across the water—it's even more fun for youngsters from warmer climes who may never have experienced this characteristically Canadian way of crossing a frozen lake.

Lodging

$$$$ ▣ **Hotel du Lac Carling.** This modern, but classically furnished hotel near Lachute (about 40 km [25 mi] northwest of Oka) caters to an upmarket clientele. Besides a large sports center, a spa, and 20 km (12 mi) of cross-country ski trails, there's an excellent par-72 golf course. On the doorstep to 5,000 acres of wilderness, the hotel is owned by a real-estate magnate with 23 manor houses in his native Germany. The rooms have oil paintings and priceless antiques shipped over from his various estates, and his daughter, Janet Hildebrand, runs the property. Rates include breakfast and dinner. ⊠ *2255 Rte. 327, Pinehill, J0V 1A0,* ☎ *450/533–9211 or 800/661–9211,* FAX *450/533–4495,* WEB *www.laccarling.com. 97 rooms. Restaurant, bar, pool, sauna, spa, 18-hole golf course, gym, racquetball, squash, cross-country skiing. AE, DC, MC, V. MAP.*

St-Eustache

❷ *25 km (16 mi) northeast of Oka, 15 km (9 mi) north of Montréal.*

St-Eustache is a must for history buffs. One of the most important and tragic battles in Canadian history was fought here during the 1837 Rebellion. After the British conquest of 1759, French Canadians had been confined to preexisting territories and the new townships were allotted exclusively to the English. Adding to this insult was the government's decision to tax all imported products from England, which made them prohibitively expensive. The result? In 1834 the French Canadian Patriot party defeated the British party locally. Lower Canada, as it was then known, became a hotbed of tension between the French and English.

Rumors of rebellion were rife, and in December 1837, some 2,000 English soldiers led by General Colborne were sent in to put down the "army" of North Shore patriots by surrounding St-Eustache. Jean-Olivier Chénier and his 200 patriots took refuge in the local church, which Colborne's cannons bombed. Chénier and 80 of his followers were killed during the battle, and more than 100 of the town's buildings were looted and burned by Colborne's soldiers. Traces of shots fired by the English army cannons are visible on the facade of Église St-Eustache (St-Eustache Church) at 123 rue St-Louis.

Most of the town's period buildings are open to the public. The oldest structure is the **Moulin Légaré** (✉ 232 rue St-Eustache, ☎ 450/472–9529), a flour mill that dates back to 1762. Designated a National Historic Site, it's the oldest working mill in Canada. Wheat and buckwheat are still ground on the premises.

The **Manoir Globensky** (✉ 235 rue St-Eustache, ☎ 450/974–5166), a handsome white manor house built in 1903 (once a private residence), includes exhibits about the Rebellion. The museum is open from late June until early September, with guided tours at 1 and 3. There's also a free brochure that can be used for a good self-guided tour.

St-Jérôme

❸ *25 km (16 mi) north of St-Eustache, 48 km (30 mi) north of Montréal.*

Rivaling St-Eustache in Québec's historic significance is St-Jérôme. Founded in 1834, it is today a thriving economic center and cultural hub. The town first gained prominence in 1868 when Curé Antoine Labelle became pastor of this parish on the shores of the Rivière du Nord. Curé Labelle devoted himself to opening up northern Québec to French Canadians. Between 1868 and 1890, he founded 20 parish towns—an impressive achievement given the harsh conditions of this vast wilderness. But his most important legacy was the famous P'tit Train du Nord railroad line, which he persuaded the government to build in order to open St-Jérôme to travel and trade.

Le P'tit Train du Nord, immortalized by singer Felix Leclerc, spurred settlement into what was then virgin wilderness. In the 1920s and '30s, it also boosted the just-emerging tourist industry. "Snow trains" used to carry Montrealers into the hinterland to enjoy what was then a trendy new sport. By the beginning of the 1940s, some 10,000 skiers were wending their way northward every weekend—nothing compared with today's numbers, of course, but a record at the time.

Le P'tit Train du Nord no longer exists, but in 1996 the track was transformed into the 200-km (124-mi) **Linear Park.** From the moment it opened, the park proved hugely popular. By the end of 1997, it had already attracted more than 1 million visitors. The well-signposted trail starts at the former railway station (1 place de la Gare) in St-Jérôme and is used mostly by cyclists (walkers use it at their peril, because the bikers fairly hurtle along). The path runs all the way to Mont-Laurier in the north. It's flanked by mileage markers, so that cyclists can track their progress (or ride just parts of the trail) and along the route, some of the old railway stations and historic landmarks have been converted into places where *velo-touristes* (bike tourists) can stop for a snack. In winter, the trail is used by cross-country skiers and snowmobilers.

St-Jérôme's **promenade,** a 4-km-long (2½-mi-long) boardwalk, follows the Rivière du Nord from rue de Martigny bridge to rue St-Joseph bridge, providing a walk through the town's history. Descriptive plaques en route highlight episodes of the Battle of 1837, a French–Canadian uprising.

Centre d'Exposition du Vieux-Palais, housed in the old courthouse, has changing exhibits of contemporary art and mostly features artists from Québec. ✉ *185 rue du Palais,* ☎ *450/432–7171.* 🖼 *Free.* ☉ *Tues. noon–8, Wed.–Sun. noon–5.*

Parc Régional de la Rivière-du-Nord was created as a nature retreat. Trails through the park lead to the spectacular **Wilson Falls.** The **Pavillon Marie-Victorin** has summer weekend displays and workshops devoted to nature, culture, and history. You can hike, bike, cross-country ski, snowshoe, or snow slide here. ⊠ *1051 blvd. International,* ☎ *450/431–1676.* ⌨ *$5 per vehicle.* ⊙ *Labor Day–late May, daily 9–5; late May–Labor Day, daily 9–7.*

Outdoor Activities and Sports

Para Vision (⊠ C.P. 95, Bellefeuille J7Z 5T7, ☎ 450/438–0855, WEB www.para-vision.qc.ca), a parachute school with a flying center in Bellefeuille, 15 minutes from St-Jérôme, caters to novices and seasoned flyers alike. Courses are limited to ages 16 and up ($265 per person).

St-Sauveur-des-Monts

❹ *25 km (16 mi) north of St-Jérôme, 63 km (39 mi) north of Montréal.*

A focal point for area resorts, during the past 20 years St-Sauveur-des-Monts has changed from a sleepy Laurentian village of 4,000 residents to a thriving year-round town attracting some 30,000 cottagers and visitors on weekends. Its main street, rue Principale, once dotted with quaint French restaurants, now has dozens of eateries at all price levels; they serve everything from lamb brochettes to spicy Thai cuisine. The narrow strip is so choked with cars and tourists in summer that it has earned the sobriquet Crescent Street of the North, after the action-filled street in Montréal. Despite all this development, St-Sauveur has maintained some of its charming, rural character.

For those who like their vacations activity-filled, St-Sauveur is *the* place. In winter, skiing is the main event. Mont-St-Sauveur, Mont-Avila, Mont-Gabriel, and Mont-Olympia all offer special season passes and programs, and some ski-center passes can be used at more than one center in the region. Blue signs on Route 117 and Autoroute 15 indicate where the ski hills are.

ⓒ Just outside St-Sauveur, the **Mont-St-Sauveur Water Park** and tourist center will keep children occupied with slides, a giant wave pool, a shallow wading pool, snack bars, and more. The rafting river attracts the older, braver crowd; the nine-minute ride follows the natural contours of steep hills and requires about 12,000 gallons of water to be pumped per minute. On the tandem slides, plumes of water flow through figure-eight tubes. ⊠ *350 rue St-Denis,* ☎ *514/871–0101 or 800/363–2426,* WEB *www.montsaintsauveur.com.* ⌨ *Full day $27, half-day $22, after 5 PM $14.* ⊙ *Early June–early Sept., daily 10–7.*

Outdoor Activities and Sports

La Vallée de Saint-Sauveur (⊠ 350 rue St-Denis, ☎ 800/363–2426) is the collective name for the ski area with 93 downhill runs, crowned by five peaks north of the village of St-Sauveur-des-Monts. Mont St-Sauveur has nine lifts; the vertical drop is 762 ft and the runs are linked to Mont-Avila. **Ski Mont-Gabriel** (⊠ 1501 Montée Gabriel, ☎ 450/227–1100) has a vertical drop of 660 ft, 13 runs, and eight lifts. With a vertical drop of 660 ft, **Station de Ski Mont-Habitant** (⊠ 12 blvd. des Skieurs, ☎ 450/393–1821, WEB www.montsaintsauveur.com) has 11 runs and three lifts.

Shopping

Factorerie St-Sauveur (⊠ 100 rue Guindon; Autoroute 15, Exit 60; ☎ 450/227–1074) is a factory outlet mall with 28 stores. Canadian, American, and European manufacturers sell goods at reduced prices, from designer clothing to household items. **Rue Principale** has shops, fashion boutiques, and café terraces with bright awnings and flowers. Housed in a former bank, **Solo Mode** (⊠ 239B rue Principale, ☎ 450/227–1234) carries international fashion labels such as Byblos.

Morin Heights

❺ *10 km (6 mi) west of St-Sauveur-des-Monts, 73 km (45 mi) northwest of Montréal.*

The town's architecture and population reflect its Anglo settler's heritage: most residents are English-speaking. Morin Heights has escaped the overdevelopment of St-Sauveur but still provides a range of restaurants, bookstores, boutiques, and craft shops to explore.

In summer, windsurfing, swimming, and canoeing on the area's two lakes are popular. You can also head for the region's golf courses (including the 18-hole links at Mont-Gabriel), campgrounds at Val David, Lacs Claude, and Lafontaine, and beaches. In fall and winter, come for the foliage and the alpine and Nordic skiing.

Dining and Lodging

$$$$ ✕🏠 **Auberge le Clos Joli.** This farmhouse turned country inn—only
★ two minutes from the ski slopes—is considered one of the top hostelries in the Laurentians. The cozy, intimate auberge run by the Roux family is decorated with original art by Québécois painters. The dining room has a fireplace. The menu highlights French cuisine with local touches, such as soufflé of wild mushrooms with port, homemade duck or rabbit paté, and layers of smoked salmon and trout flavored with warm goat cheese. ⊠ *19 chemin du Clos Joli, J0R 1H0,* ☎ *450/ 226–5401. 9 rooms. Restaurant, cross-country skiing. AE, MC, V. MAP.*

Outdoor Activities and Sports

At **Ski Morin Heights** (⊠ Autoroute 15 N, Exit 60, ☎ 450/227–2020), snowboarding has been increasing in popularity. The vertical drop at this downhill skiing center is 660 ft, and there are six lifts. Although it doesn't have overnight accommodations, Ski Morin Heights has a 44,000-square-ft chalet with eateries, a pub, a day-care center, and equipment rental. Ages two and up can join ski lessons.

Ste-Adèle

❻ *12 km (7 mi) north of Morin Heights, 85 km (53 mi) north of Montréal.*

Busy Ste-Adèle, with a permanent population of more than 9,000, is the largest community in the lower part of the Laurentians and the service center for the region. A number of government offices and facilities for local residents are here: cinemas, modern retail malls, and summer theater (in French). Of interest to visitors are the sports shops, boutiques, restaurants, and family-oriented amusements.

☺ **Au Pay des Merveilles** bills itself as "Walt Disney World in the Laurentians" but it's a far cry from the sophisticated theme park in Florida. Fairy-tale characters such as Snow White, Little Red Riding Hood, and Alice in Wonderland wander the grounds, playing games with children. Small fry will also enjoy the petting zoo, wading pool, puppet theater, and several rides. ⊠ *3595 rue de la Savane,* ☎ *450/229–3141,* 🌐 *www.paysmerveilles.com.* ⊡ *$9.* ☉ *Early June and early Sept., weekends 10–6; June 24–Aug. 26, daily 10–6.*

The Laurentian region has more than its share of water parks; Sainte-
☺ Adèle started the trend with **Super Splash Sainte-Adèle.** On hot, humid weekends, the water park is extremely popular among Montrealers with families. Super Splash has water slides, a wading pool, and the requisite wave pool. ⊠ *1791 blvd. Sainte-Adèle,* ☎ *450/ 229–2909,* 🌐 *www.supersplash.qc.ca.* ⊡ *$13.00.* ☉ *late June–late Aug., daily 10–5.*

Dining and Lodging

$$$–$$$$ ✕ **La Clef des Champs.** Tucked away among trees facing a mountain, this family-owned restaurant is known for its superior French cuisine (the owners come from France) and its cozy, romantic atmosphere. Game dishes are a specialty, including farm-raised rabbit with mustard, medallions of roasted ostrich in a port-infused sauce, and caribou served with a pungent, red-currant marinade. Good dessert choices are *gâteaux aux deux chocolats* (two-chocolate cake) and crème brulée. ⊠ *875 chemin Ste-Marguerite,* ☎ *450/229–2857. AE, DC, MC, V. Closed Mon. Oct.–May.*

$$$$ ✕▥ **Hotel Mont-Gabriel.** At this deluxe resort spread out on a 1,200-acre estate, you can relax in a cozy, modern room with a valley view or be close to nature in a log cabin with a fireplace. The hotel was completely refurbished (for $7 million) in 1999. The French cuisine is superb, with entrées such as pork with ginger and orange, or salmon with braised leeks. Tennis, golf, and ski packages are available. On Jewish holidays, kosher meals can be served if you call in advance. ⊠ *Autoroute 15, Exit 64, Mont-Rolland J0R 1G0,* ☎ *450/229–3547 or 800/668–5253,* ℻ *450/229–7034,* ⟨WEB⟩ *www.montgabriel.com. 129 rooms, 6 suites. Restaurant, 1 indoor and 1 outdoor pool, 18-hole golf course, 6 tennis courts. AE, DC, MC, V. EP, MAP.*

$$–$$$$ ✕▥ **L'Eau à la Bouche.** Superb service, stunning rooms awash with color, ★ and a terrace with a flower garden are highlights of this elegant inn. Facing Le Chantecler's slopes, skiing is literally at the door. Tennis, sailing, horseback riding, and a golf course are nearby. This property belongs to the Relais & Chateaux chain and in 2001, it was designated a "Relais Gourmand"—one of only three hotels in North America to be thus-honored by the exacting, Paris-based organization. The highly recommended restaurant marries nouvelle cuisine and traditional Québécois cooking. The care and inventiveness of chef proprietor Anne Desjardins are extraordinary: she uses local ingredients whenever possible. Her menus change with the seasons, but have included dishes such as foie gras with apple-cider sauce and red wine–marinated venison. ⊠ *3003 blvd. Ste-Adèle, J0R 1L0,* ☎ *450/229–2991,* ℻ *450/229–7573,* ⟨WEB⟩ *www.relaischateaux.fr. 25 rooms. Restaurant, pool. AE, DC, MC, V. EP, MAP.*

$$$$ ▥ **Le Chantecler.** This Montrealer favorite on Lac Ste-Adèle is nestled at the base of a mountain with 22 downhill ski runs. Skiing is the obvious draw—trails begin almost at the hotel entrance. The rooms and chalets, furnished with Canadian pine, have a rustic appeal. ⊠ *1474 chemin Chantecler, J0B 1A2,* ☎ *450/229–3555; 800/363–2420 in Québec,* ℻ *450/229–5593,* ⟨WEB⟩ *www.lechantecler.com. 200 rooms, 18 suites. Restaurant, indoor pool, spa, 18-hole golf course, tennis court, beach, boating, downhill skiing. AE, D, DC, MC, V. EP, MAP.*

Outdoor Activities and Sports

GOLF

The par-72 **Club de Golf Chantecler** (⊠ 2520 chemin du Golf, Autoroute 15, Exit 67, ☎ 450/229–3742) has 18 holes.

SKIING

Ski Chantecler (⊠ Mont-Chantecler, ☎ 450/229–3555) has a vertical drop of 663 ft, six lifts, and 23 runs. There are 50 km (31 mi) of cross-country trails, too. **Station de Ski Côtes** (⊠ Mont-Côtes, ☎ 450/229–2700) has six runs and a vertical drop of 392 ft.

Ski Mont-Gabriel (⊠ Monté Mont-Gabriel, ☎ 450/227–1100 or 800/363–2426), 19 km (12 mi) northeast of Ste-Adèle, has eight lifts and 13 superb downhill trails—primarily for intermediate and advanced skiers. The vertical drop is 660 ft. The most popular runs are the

Tamarack and the O'Connell trails for advanced skiers and Obergurgl for intermediates.

Estérel

❼ *15 km (9 mi) north of Ste-Adèle, 100 km (62 mi) north of Montréal.*

The permanent population of Estérel is a mere 95 souls, but visitors to Hôtel l'Estérel—a resort off Route 370, at Exit 69 near Ste-Marguerite Station—swell that number into the thousands throughout the year. Founded in 1959 on the shores of Lac Dupuis, Baron Louis Empain named the 5,000-acre estate Estérel because it evoked memories of his native village in Provence. Fridolin Simard bought the property and Hôtel l'Estérel soon became a household word for vacationers in search of a first-class resort area.

Dining and Lodging

$$$-$$$$ ✕ **Bistro à Champlain.** An astonishing selection of wines—some 2,000 ★ vintages are represented—has made the bistro famous. You can tour the cellars, where 35,000 bottles (at last count) had prices from $28 to $25,000. The restaurant is in a former general store built in 1864; paintings of Jean-Paul Riopelle adorn the walls. Next to the 150-seat dining room is a comfy lounge for cigar smokers. The *menu dégustation* (tasting menu) includes a different wine with each of several courses for $69. Typical dishes are marinated Atlantic smoked salmon and roast duckling with rosemary. ✉ *75 chemin Masson, Ste-Marguerite du Lac Masson, J0T 1L0,* ☎ *450/228–4988,* 🌐 *www.bistrochamplain.qc.ca. AE, DC, MC, V.*

$$-$$$ 🏨 **Hôtel l'Estérel.** Given the nonstop activities, if this all-inclusive resort were in the Caribbean, it would probably be run by Club Med. Dogsledding and an ice-skating disco are two of the more unusual options, a spa was added to the resort in 2000, and there are buses to nearby downhill resorts. Comfortable air-conditioned rooms have a view of either the lake or the beautiful flower gardens. ✉ *39 blvd. Fridolin Simard, J0T 1E0,* ☎ *450/228–2571 or 888/378–3735,* 🆕 *450/ 228–4977,* 🌐 *www.esterel.com. 124 rooms. Restaurant, indoor pool, spa, 18-hole golf course, tennis court, gym, beach, dock, cross-country skiing, snowmobiling. AE, DC, MC, V. MAP.*

Val David

❽ *18 km (11 mi) west of Estérel, 82 km (51 mi) north of Montréal.*

Val David is a rendezvous for mountain climbers, hikers, and campers, besides being a center for arts and crafts. Children know Val David because of ♻ **Santa Claus Village.** At Santa Claus's summer residence kids can sit on Santa's knee and speak to him in French or English. On the grounds is a petting zoo (with goats, sheep, horses, and colorful birds), games, and bumper boats. ✉ *987 rue Morin,* ☎ *819/322–2146 or 800/287–6635.* 🎟 *$9.* ☼ *Late May–early June, weekends 10–6; early June–late Aug., daily 10–6.*

Dining and Lodging

$$$$ 🏨 **Hôtel La Sapinière.** This homey, dark-brown wood-frame hotel overlooks a fir-fringed lake ("sapin" is fir tree in French). Built by Léonidas Dufresne—father of the present owner—in 1936, the property has been modernized several times. Rooms, with country-style furnishings and pastel floral accents, come with such luxurious extras as thick terry bathrobes. You can relax in front of a blazing fire in one of several lounges. The property is best known for the French nouvelle cuisine in its fine dining room. The minimum stay is two nights. ✉ *1244 chemin de la Sapinière, J0T 2N0,* ☎ *819/322–2020 or 800/*

567–6635, FAX 819/322–6510, WEB *www.sapiniere.com. 70 rooms. Restaurant. AE, DC, MC, V. MAP.*

Outdoor Activities and Sports
Mont-Alta (✉ Rte. 117, ☎ 819/322–3206) has 22 runs and two lifts; the vertical drop is 587 ft. **Station de Ski Vallée-Bleue** (✉ 1418 chemin Vallée-Bleue, ☎ 819/322–3427) has 17 runs and three lifts.

Shopping
Val David is a haven for artists, many of whom open their studios to the public.

Atelier Bernard Chaudron, Inc. (✉ 2449 chemin de l'Ile, ☎ 819/322–3944) sells hand-shaped lead-free pewter objets d'art.

Ste-Agathe-des-Monts

❾ *5 km (3 mi) north of Val David, 96 km (60 mi) northwest of Montréal.*

The sandy beaches of Lac des Sables are the most surprising feature of Ste-Agathe-des-Monts, a tourist town best known for its ski hills. Waterbound activities include canoeing, kayaking, swimming, and fishing. Ste-Agathe is also a stopover point on the Linear Park, the bike trail between St-Jérôme and Mont-Laurier.

Dining and Lodging
$$$–$$$$ ✕ **Chatel Vienna.** This venerable Viennese eatery, in a century-old building that was once a private home, is now owned by Claudine and Clement Martins, who hail from Grenoble, France. They've spiffed up the decor a bit but still serve the popular Austrian and Continental fare that put this lakeside restaurant on the map way back in 1966. You may want to try the home-smoked trout, served with an herb-and-spice butter and garden-fresh vegetables. Other options on the prix fixe menu are schnitzels, a sauerkraut plate, and venison. Hot spiced wine, Czech pilsner beer, and dry Austrian and other international white wines are some of the beverage choices. In summer, sit on the patio and enjoy the lake view. ✉ *6 rue Ste-Lucie,* ☎ *819/326–1485,* WEB *www.chatelvienna.com. Reservations essential. MC, V.*

$$ ⛴ **Auberge du Lac des Sables.** A favorite with couples, this inn provides a quiet, relaxed atmosphere in a country setting with a magnificent view of Lac des Sables. All rooms have contemporary decor; suites have fireplaces and whirlpool baths. ✉ *230 St-Venant, J8C 2Z7,* ☎ *819/326–3994 or 800/567–8329,* FAX *819/326–9159,* WEB *www.aubergedulac.com. 18 rooms, 5 suites. MC, V. CP.*

$ ⛺ **Au Parc des Campeurs.** This spacious campground is near a lively resort area. Thirty sites have hook-ups for RVs. You can also rent canoes and kayaks here. ✉ *Tour du Lac and Rte. 329, J8C 1M9,* ☎ *819/324–0482. 556 sites. Miniature golf, tennis court, volleyball, bicycles, coin laundry. MC, V.*

Outdoor Activities and Sports
Sailing is the favorite summer sport, especially during the **24 Heures de la Voile** (☎ 819/326–0457), a weekend sailing competition that takes place each year in June. The sightseeing boat *Alouette* (✉ municipal dock, rue Principale, ☎ 819/326–3656) offers guided tours of Lac des Sables.

Mont-Tremblant

❿ *25 km (16 mi) north of Ste-Agathe-des-Monts, 100 km (62 mi) north of Montréal.*

Mont-Tremblant, at more than 3,000 ft, is the highest peak in the Laurentians and a major center for skiing. It's also the name of the village. The resort area at the foot of the mountain, simply called Tremblant, has accommodations and restaurants, bars, and shops.

The mountain, and the hundreds of square miles of wilderness beyond, constitute the **Parc Provincial du Mont-Tremblant** (☏ 819/688–2281). Created in 1894, the park was once the home of the Algonquin people, who called this area Manitonga Soutana, meaning "mountain of the spirits." Today it's a vast wildlife sanctuary of more than 400 lakes and rivers protecting about 230 species of birds and animals, including moose, deer, bear, and beaver. In winter its trails are used by cross-country skiers, snowshoers, and snowmobile enthusiasts. Moose hunting is allowed in season, and camping and canoeing are the main summer activities. Entrance to the park is free, and the main entry point is through the hamlet of St-Donat.

Dining and Lodging

$$$$ ✕🏨 **Club Tremblant.** Built as a private retreat in the 1930s by a wealthy American, this hotel is across the lake from the ski station at Mont-Tremblant. The original large log-cabin lodge is furnished in colonial style, with wooden staircases and huge stone fireplaces. The rustic but comfortable accommodation has excellent facilities, including a spa and an outstanding restaurant that serves French cuisine. On Saturday nights there's a buffet ($42.50 per person) featuring a wide selection of seafood. Both the main lodge and the deluxe condominium complex (with fireplaces, private balconies, kitchenettes, and split-level design), up the hill from the lodge, have magnificent views of Mont-Tremblant. There's a golf course nearby. ✉ *121 rue Cuttle, J0T 1Z0,* ☏ *819/425–2731,* 🅵🅰🆇 *819/425–9903,* 🆆🅴🅱 *www.clubtremblant.com. 113 rooms. Restaurant, indoor pool, tennis court, gym. AE, MC, V. EP, MAP.*

$$ ✕🏨 **Auberge du Coq de Montagne.** Owners Nino and Kay Faragalli have earned a favorable reputation for their auberge on Lac Moore. The cozy, family-run inn is touted for its friendly service, hospitality, and modern accommodations. Year-round facilities and activities— on-site or nearby—include canoeing, kayaking, sailboarding, fishing, badminton, tennis, horseback riding, skating, and skiing. Kudos have also been garnered for the Italian cuisine served up nightly, which draws a local crowd. Menu offerings include tried-and-tested favorites such as veal marsala, veal *fiorentina* (cooked with spinach and cheese), and veal with tangy mushroom and pepper sauce. The chef also makes great homemade pasta. Reservations are essential. ✉ *2151 chemin Principal, C.P. 208, J0T 1Z0,* ☏ *819/425–3380 or 800/895–3380,* 🅵🅰🆇 *819/ 425–7846,* 🆆🅴🅱 *www.recreation-tremblant.com. 13 rooms. Restaurant, sauna, gym, beach. AE, MC, V. MAP in winter; EP, MAP in summer.*

$$$–$$$$ 🏨 **Fairmont Tremblant.** The attractive centerpiece of the Tremblant re-
   ★   sort area was built by Canadian Pacific Hotels (now under the prestigious Fairmont banner). Similar in style to the historic railroad "castles" scattered throughout Canada, the hotel has wood paneling, copper details, stained glass, stone fireplaces, and wrought-iron lamps with parchment shades. The ambience is elegant but sporty. Skiers can zoom off the mountain right into the ground-level deli or opt for a more formal meal in the restaurant. The cuisine is mostly French (several of the chefs come from France) though less "gourmet" than at some other establishments. Menu offerings have included smoked salmon flavored with local maple syrup, three-pepper steak, and trout in a subtle lemon sauce. ✉ *Box 100, 3045 chemin Principal, J0T 1Z0,* ☏ *819/*

681–7000, WEB *www.fairmont.ca. 316 rooms. Restaurant, deli, 1 indoor and 1 outdoor pool, sauna, spa, gym. AE, DC, MC, V.*

\$\$\$–\$\$\$\$ 🏨 **Le Grand Lodge.** No expense has been spared at this Scandinavian-style log cabin all-suites hotel on 13½ acres on Lac Ouimet, where the old Villa Bellevue once stood. The accommodations, from studios to two-bedroom suites, are spacious, with kitchenettes, stone fireplaces, and balconies that overlook the water. The indoor–outdoor café, which serves light fare, also looks out on the lake. The more formal Chez Borivage, which has a good wine cellar (try a vintage port), specializes in French cuisine. Although the resort attracts a sizeable corporate clientele, it caters to families as well, with day-care facilities and a game room for teens. There's also a spa with steam rooms and a 21-meter indoor lap pool. ⊠ *845 chemin Principal, J0T 1Z0,* ☎ *819/425–2734 or 800/567–6763,* FAX *819/425–9725,* WEB *www.legrandlodge.com. 112 suites. Restaurant, café, indoor lap pool, spa, 4 18-hole golf courses, badminton, shuffleboard, volleyball, boating, bicycles, meeting rooms. AE, MC, V.*

\$\$–\$\$\$\$ 🏨 **Tremblant.** *Ski* magazine has selected this world-class resort, spread around 14-km-long (9-mi-long) Lac Tremblant, as among the top ski resorts in eastern North America for several years, and Tremblant has become the most fashionable vacation venue in Québec among sporty types. The resort area's hub is a pedestrian-only village that looks a bit like a displaced Québec City. The buildings—constructed in the style of New France, with dormer windows and steep roofs—hold pubs, restaurants, boutiques, sports shops, a cinema, and accommodations ranging from hotels to self-catering condominiums. An indoor water-recreation complex includes pools, water slides, and whirlpool baths. Some of the newer lodgings are the 139-suite Le Lodge de la Montagne, the 219-suite La Tour des Voyageurs, and the 120-suite Westin Resort Tremblant. The Fairmont Tremblant is also a part of this complex. Reservations can be made through the individual properties or through central reservations. ⊠ *3005 chemin Principal, J0T 1Z0,* ☎ *819/425–8711 or 800/461–8711; 800/567–6760 (central reservations),* FAX *819/425–9604,* WEB *www.tremblant.com. 1,345 units. Indoor lap pool, indoor-outdoor pool, wading pool, 2 18-hole golf courses, 13 tennis courts, hiking, horseback riding, beach, windsurfing, boating, mountain bikes, video games. AE, MC, V.*

Outdoor Activities and Sports

With a 2,131-ft vertical drop, **Mont-Tremblant** (☎ 819/425–8711 or 819/681–2000) offers 77 downhill trails, 11 lifts, and 90 km (56 mi) of cross-country trails. Downhill beginners favor the 6-km (4-mi) Nansen trail; intermediate skiers head for the Beauchemin run. Experts choose the Flying Mile on the south side and Duncan and Expo runs on the mountain's north side. The speedy Duncan Express is a quadruple chairlift; there's also a heated, high-speed gondola.

On the other side of the mountain is the **Versant Soleil** (sunny slope). The area has a vertical drop of 1,905 ft and 15 runs (including much sought-after glade skiing) served by a state-of-the-art, high-speed quad chair that's capable of moving 2,250 people to the summit every hour. Sixty percent of the trails are for advanced skiers and 7% are classified for expert skiers only. The remainder are for skiers who consider themselves intermediate.

THE EASTERN TOWNSHIPS

The Eastern Townships (also known as les Cantons de l'Est, and formerly as l'Estrie) refers to the area in the southwest corner of the province of Québec—bordering Vermont, New Hampshire, and Maine.

Its northern Appalachian hills, rolling down to placid lakeshores, were first home to the Abenaki natives, long before "summer people" built their cottages and horse paddocks. The Abenaki are gone, but the names they gave to the region's recreational lakes remain: Memphrémagog, Massawippi, Mégantic.

The Townships, as locals call them, were populated by United Empire Loyalists fleeing the Revolutionary War and, later, the newly created United States of America. They wanted to continue living under the English king in British North America. It's not surprising that the covered bridges, village greens, white church steeples, and country inns are reminiscent of New England. The Loyalists were followed, around 1820, by the first wave of Irish immigrants (ironically, Catholics fleeing their country's union with Protestant England). Some 20 years later the potato famine sent more Irish pioneers to the Townships.

The area became more Francophone after 1850 as French Canadians moved in to work on the railroad and in the lumber industry. During the late 19th century, English families from Montréal and Americans from the border states began summering at cottages along the lakes. During Prohibition the area attracted even more cottagers from the United States. Lac Massawippi became a favorite summer resort of wealthy families, and those homes have since been converted into gracious inns and upscale bed-and-breakfasts.

Today the summer communities fill up with equal parts French and English visitors, though the year-round residents are primarily French. The locals are proud of their multi-ethnic heritage. They boast of "Loyalist tours" and Victorian gingerbread homes, and in the next breath direct visitors to the snowmobile museum in Valcourt, where in 1937, native French son Joseph-Armand Bombardier built the first *moto-neige* (snowmobile) in his garage. (Bombardier's other inventions became the basis for one of Canada's biggest industries—supplying New York City and Mexico City with subway cars and other rolling stock.)

Since the 1980s, the Townships have developed from a series of quiet farm communities and wood-frame summer homes to a thriving all-season resort area. In winter, skiers flock to seven downhill centers and more than 1,000 km (622 mi) of cross-country trails. Three inns—Manoir Hovey, Auberge Hatley, and the Ripplecove Inn—offer cross-country packages. Skiers can ski between the inns on a challenging trail that meanders through the woods for 32 km (20 mi). Still less crowded and commercialized than the Laurentians, the area has ski hills on four mountains that dwarf anything the Laurentians have to offer, with the exception of Mont-Tremblant. And compared to Vermont, ski-pass rates are still a bargain. Owl's Head, Mont-Orford, and Mont-Sutton have interchangeable lift tickets.

By early spring, the sugar shacks are busy with the new maple syrup. In summer, boating, swimming, sailing, golfing, rollerblading, hiking, and bicycling take over. And every fall the inns are booked solid with leaf peepers eager to take in the brilliant foliage.

The fall is also a good time to visit the wineries (though most are open all year). Because of its mild micro-climate, the Townships area has become one of the fastest-developing wine regions in Canada, with a dozen of the more than 30 wineries in Québec province. The wines don't quite measure up to the standards of Ontario's Niagara Peninsula or British Columbia's Okanagan Valley—at least not yet, as the industry is fairly young here—but wine makers produce some good hearty reds and sparkling whites that go well with the regional cuisine. Wine makers are also making some inroads with ice wine, a sweet dessert wine made—as the name suggests—from frozen grapes (they have a very high sugar content).

Granby

⑪ *80 km (50 mi) east of Montréal.*

Granby is the western gateway to the Eastern Townships and home to a notable zoo. It also hosts a number of annual festivals: the Festival of Mascots and Cartoon Characters (July), a great favorite with youngsters and families, and the Granby International, an antique-car competition held at the Granby Autodrome (also in July). The Festival International de la Chanson, a songfest of budding composers and performers that has launched several of Québec's current megastars, is a nine-day event in mid-September.

★ ⓒ The **Jardin Zoologique de Granby** (Granby Zoo), one of the biggest attractions in the area, houses some 1,000 animals representing 225 species in a naturally landscaped setting. The Afrika pavilion, with its gorillas, lions, and birds, is a favorite with youngsters; they also love the Amazoo—an aquatic park with turbulent wave pools and rides. At certain times of the day, keepers demonstrate the acrobatic skills of the birds of prey. The complex includes amusement rides and souvenir shops, as well as a playground and picnic area. ✉ *347 rue Bourget,* ☎ *450/372–9113.* ☞ *$19.95.* ☉ *Mid-May–early Sept., daily 10–6; late Sept., weekends 10–6.*

Outdoor Activities and Sports

Biking is big here. The quiet back roads lend themselves to exploring the region on two wheels, as does the network of off-road trails. There are 450 km (279 mi) of bike-friendly trails, some linked to La Route Verte (The Green Route), a province-wide network that is being expanded by leaps and bounds. For details and a map, contact Vélo Québec. Mountain biking is also popular in the Townships.

One of the most popular (and flattest) bike trails is the paved **l'Estriade,** which links Granby to Waterloo. The **Montérégiade** bike trail between Granby and Farnham is 21 km (13 mi) long. The mountain-biking season kicks off in late May with the **Tour de la Montagne** (☎ 450/534–2453 for information), a 25-km (15-mi) rally. Competitions for serious mountain bikers are held in summer.

Bromont

⑫ *78 km (48 mi) east of Montréal.*

The town of Bromont has the only night skiing in the Eastern Townships and a slope-side disco, Le Bromontais, where the après-ski action continues. Bromont is a *station touristique* (tourist center); it offers a wide range of activities in all seasons—boating, camping, golf, horseback riding, swimming, tennis, biking, canoeing, fishing, hiking, cross-country and downhill skiing, and snowshoeing. Bromont has more than 100 km (62 mi) of maintained trails for mountain bikers.

A former Olympic equestrian site, Bromont is horse country, and every year in late June it hosts the **International Bromont Equestrian Competition** (☎ 450/534–3255).

ⓒ **Bromont Aquatic Park** is a water park with 15 different rides and games, including the Corkscrew (self-explanatory) and the Elephant's Trunk (where kids shoot out of a model of an elephant's head). Slides are divided into four degrees of difficulty from easy to extreme, which is recommended for adults and older children only. Admission in-

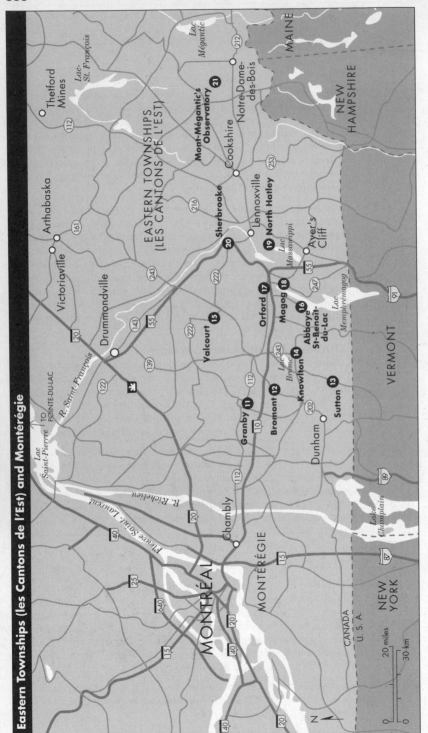

Eastern Townships (les Cantons de l'Est) and Montérégie

cludes a chairlift ride to the top of the ski hill. ✉ *Autoroute 10, Exit 78,* ☎ *450/534–2200.* ⊡ *$23.* ☉ *Late May–Aug. 10–6, Sept.–late Oct. 10–4.*

<table>
<tr><td>OFF THE
BEATEN PATH</td><td>

SAFARI AVENTURE LOOWAK – The brainchild of butterfly collector Serge Poirier, this park sprawls over 500 acres of wooded land, 10 km (6 mi) from Bromont. It's a kind of Indiana Jones–theme guided tour where you head off into the bush to hunt for treasure and to look for downed planes. It's a great hit with little ones, but parents get caught up in the fantasy, too. Reservations are recommended. ✉ *475 Horizon Blvd., Autoroute 10, Exit 88, Waterloo,* ☎ *450/539–0501,* WEB *www.safariloowak.qc.ca.* ⊡ *Trips begin at $10 per person, minimum 4 people.*

DUNHAM – At least three wineries near the town of Dunham, about 20 km (12 mi) from Bromont on Route 202, offer tastings and tours. Call ahead for business hours, which can be erratic, especially in the autumn, when they're set around harvesting. **Vignoble Domaine Côtes d'Ardoise** (✉ 879 Rte. 202, Dunham, ☎ 450/295–2020) was one of the first wineries to set up shop, more than 20 years ago. The original, French owner encountered a lot of skepticism, but in time he proved that vines could be grown successfully in the region. Before walking through the vineyard at **Vignoble de l'Orpailleur** (✉ 1086 Rte. 202, Dunham, ☎ 450/295–2763), stop by the ecomuseum (opened in 2001) to learn everything you ever wanted to know about the production of wine, from the growing of the grapes right up to the bottling process. There's also a gift shop and patio restaurant. The name **Vignoble Les Arpents de Neige** (✉ 4042 Principale, Dunham, ☎ 450/295–3383) means "a few arpents of snow" (arpent is an old French measurement used before acres). The vineyard's premier wine—a white and fruity drink—is appropriately named Premier Neige, or first snow. The winery also produces a pleasant rosé.

</td></tr>
</table>

Lodging

$$$–$$$$ 🏨 **Le Château Bromont Hotel Spa.** Massages, electropuncture, algae wraps, facials, and aromatherapy are just a few of the pampering services at this European-style resort spa. Rooms are large and comfortable, with contemporary furniture. Sunny Mediterranean colors dress the atrium walls, and central-facing rooms have balconies and window boxes. Greenery and patio furniture surround the swimming pool in the middle of the atrium. L'Equestre Bar, named for Bromont's equestrian interests, has a pianist who plays background music on Sunday evenings. ✉ *90 rue Stanstead, J0E 1L0,* ☎ *450/534–3433 or 800/304–3433,* FAX *450/534–0514,* WEB *www.chateaubromont.com. 152 rooms. Restaurant, bar, indoor pool, hot tub, sauna, spa, badminton, racquetball, squash. AE, D, DC, MC, V. EP, MAP.*

Outdoor Activities and Sports

The **Royal Bromont** (✉ 400 chemin Compton, ☎ 450/534–4653, WEB www.royalbromont.com) is an 18-hole, par-72 course.

Station de Ski Bromont (✉ 150rue Champlain, ☎ 450/534–2200, WEB www.skibromont.com), with 25 trails for downhill skiing, was the site of the 1986 World Cup Slalom. The vertical drop is 1,336 ft, and there are four lifts.

Shopping

Shopping for bargains is a popular weekend activity in the Townships; the **Bromont Flea Market** is the largest. (You can't miss the HUGE sign on Autoroute 10.) More than 350 vendors sell their wares—everything from T-shirts to household gadgets—from May to the end of October, and shoppers come from as far afield as Montréal and Vermont, just over the border.

Sutton

⑬ *106 km (66 mi) southeast of Montréal.*

Sutton is a well-established community with crafts shops, cozy eateries, and bars (La Paimpolaise is a favorite among skiers). **Arts Sutton** (✉ 7 rue Academy, ☎ 450/538–2563), an art gallery with works for sale, is a long-established mecca for the visual arts.

Lodging

$$ 🏨 **Auberge la Paimpolaise.** This alpine-style auberge on Mont-Sutton is 50 ft from the ski trails. It's nothing fancy, but the location is hard to beat. Rooms are simple, comfortable, and clean, with a woodsy appeal. All-inclusive weekend ski packages are available. ✉ *615 rue Maple, J0E 2K0,* ☎ *450/538–3213 or 800/263–3213,* FAX *450/538–3970,* WEB *www.paimpolaise.com. 28 rooms. Dining room. AE, MC, V. EP, FAP.*

Outdoor Activities and Sports

GOLF

Reservations must be made in advance at **Les Rochers Bleus** (✉ 550 Rte. 139, ☎ 450/538–2324), a par-72, 18-hole course.

HIKING

Au Diable Vert (✉ 160 chemin Staines, Glen Sutton J0E 2K0, ☎ 450/538–5639 or 888/779–9090, WEB www.audiablevert.qc.ca) is a 200-acre mountainside site, 15 minutes from the village of Sutton, where the hiking trails look out over spectacular mountain scenery. Glen Sutton is between the Appalachians and Vermont's Green Mountains and the Missisquoi River runs through the middle. The centerpiece of Au Diable Vert is a rustic lodge, a converted, early-20th-century farmhouse with three bedrooms and a dormitory. (The lodge can accommodate 17 hikers.)

SKIING

Mont-Sutton (✉ Rte. 139 S, Autoroute 10, Exit 68, ☎ 450/538–2339, WEB www.montsutton.com), where skiers pay by the hour, has 53 downhill trails, a vertical drop of 1,518 ft, and nine lifts. This ski area—one of the region's largest—attracts a die-hard crowd of mostly Anglophone skiers from Québec. Trails plunge and meander through pine, maple, and birch trees.

Knowlton

⑭ *101 km (63 mi) southeast of Montréal.*

Along the shore of Lac Brome, picturesque Knowlton makes a great stop for antiques, clothes, and gifts. The village is a treasure trove: trendy stores, art galleries, and interesting little eateries fill renovated clapboard buildings painted every shade of the rainbow. Distinctive Lake Brome duck is found on local menus.

Dining and Lodging

$$ ✕🏨 **Auberge Knowlton.** At the main intersection in Knowlton, within walking distance of boutiques and factory outlets, this 12-room inn has been a local landmark since 1849, when it was a stagecoach stop on the road between Bolton Pass and Gilman's Corner. The owners, husband-and-wife team Michel Gabereau and Signy Stephenson, have gutted the building and renovated the rooms, but retained the historic exterior. The inn attracts a corporate clientele (the rooms have Internet access) as well as tourists and locals who like coming to the old, familiar hotel to celebrate special occasions. The on-site bistro, Le Relais, offers a wide range of duck dishes such as roast breast of duck and warm duck salad served with gizzards. Confit du canard is made

with the leg of duck, roasted slowly in the oven, then marinated in its own juices for several days before being reheated. The result is tender, tasty meat. ⊠ *286 chemin Knowlton, J0E 1V0,* ☎ *450/242–6886,* FAX *450/242–1055,* WEB *www.cclacbrome.qc.ca/ak. 12 rooms. Restaurant, in-room data ports. AE, MC, V.*

Nightlife and the Arts

Théâtre Lac Brome (⊠ 267 rue Knowlton, ☎ 450/242–2270 or 450/242–1395) stages plays, musicals, and productions of classic Broadway and West End hits. The company specializes in English productions but also has dabbled in bilingual productions and some new Canadian works. The 175-seat, air-conditioned theater is behind Knowlton's popular pub of the same name.

Outdoor Activities and Sports

Not far from Knowlton is **Golf Inverness** (⊠ 511 chemin Bondville/Rte. 215, ☎ 450/242–1595 or 800/468–1595), an 18-hole, par-71 course.

Many Montrealers come for the downhill skiing at **Mont-Glen** (⊠ off Rte. 243, ☎ 450/243–6142, WEB www.glen.qc.ca). The area has 32 trails, four lifts, and a vertical drop of 1,099 ft.

Valcourt

⑮ *158 km (98 mi) east of Montréal.*

Valcourt is the birthplace of the inventor of the snowmobile, and the Eastern Townships are a world center for the sport, with more than 2,000 km (1,240 mi) of paths cutting through the woods and meadows. In February Valcourt hosts the **Valcourt Snowmobiling Grand Prix** (☎ 450/532–3443), a five-day event with competitions and festivities. The **Musée Joseph-Armand Bombardier** displays innovator Bombardier's many inventions, including the snowmobile. ⊠ *1001 av. Joseph-Armand Bombardier,* ☎ *450/532–5300.* ☷ *$5.* ☉ *May–Sept., daily 10–5; Sept.–Apr., Tues.–Sun. 10–5.*

Abbaye St-Benoît-du-Lac

★ **⑯** *132 km (82 mi) southeast of Montréal.*

This abbey's slender bell tower juts up above the trees like a fairy-tale castle. Built by the Benedictines in 1912 on a wooded peninsula on Lac Memphrémagog, the abbey is home to some 60 monks who sell apples and sparkling apple wine from their orchards as well as distinctive cheeses: Ermite, St-Benoît, and ricotta. Gregorian prayers are sung daily and some masses are open to the public; call for schedule. Dress modestly if you plan to attend vespers or other rituals, and avoid shorts. The monks might be traditionalists but they've joined the modern world with a comprehensive Web site that explains their way of life and spiritual practices. To get to the abbey from Magog, take Route 112 and follow the signs for the side road (Rural Route 2, or rue des Pères) to the abbey. Call for mass schedule. ⊠ *R.R. 2,* ☎ *819/843–4080,* WEB *www.st-benoit.com.* ☉ *Store open daily between services.*

Orford

⑰ *115 km (72 mi) east of Montréal.*

Orford is the township where the **Parc Provincial du Mont-Orford** (⊠ chemin du Parc, ☎ 819/843–6548 or 800/567–2772) lies. The park is in use year-round, whether for skiing, camping, or hiking. An annual arts festival, Festival Orford, highlights classical music and chamber-orchestra concerts.

Since 1951, thousands of students have come to the **Orford Arts Centre** (☎ 819/843–3981; 800/567–6155 in Canada May–Aug., WEB www.arts-orford.org) to study and perform classical music in summer. Canada's internationally celebrated Orford String Quartet originated here.

Lodging

$$$ 🏨 **Auberge Estrimont.** An exclusive complex built of cedar, Auberge Estrimont has hotel rooms, condos, and larger chalets close to ski hills, riding stables, and golf courses. Every room in the hotel or in an adjoining condo unit has a fireplace and a private balcony. The attractive dining room serves Continental cuisine. The table d'hôte menu, priced at $28.95 per person, features such specialties as smoked salmon, braised veal kidneys in port, and chicken breast marinated with mead. ✉ 44 av. de l'Auberge, C.P. 98, Orford-Magog J1X 3W7, ☎ 819/843–1616 or 800/567–7320, FAX 819/843–4909, WEB www.estrimont.qc.ca. 76 rooms, 7 suites. Restaurant, bar, 1 indoor and 1 outdoor pool, hot tub, sauna, 2 tennis courts, gym, racquetball, squash. AE, DC, MC, V.

Outdoor Activities and Sports

Mont-Orford Ski Area (✉ Rte. 141, ☎ 819/843–6548 or 800/567–2772), at the center of the provincial park, has plenty of challenges for alpine and cross-country skiers, from novices to veterans. It has 52 runs, a vertical drop of 1,782 ft, and eight lifts, as well as 56 km (35 mi) of cross-country trails.

Magog

⑱   *118 km (74 mi) east of Montréal.*

At the northern tip of Lac Memphrémagog, a large body of water that reaches into northern Vermont, lies the bustling town of Magog, with bed-and-breakfasts, hotels, and restaurants. It has sandy beaches as well as activities that include boating, bird-watching, sailboarding, horseback riding, dogsledding, rollerblading, and snowmobiling. (You might even see the lake's legendary sea dragon, said to have been sighted about 90 times since 1816.)

The streets downtown are lined with century-old homes that have been converted into boutiques, stores, and dozens of eating places—from fast-food outlets to bistros serving Italian and French fare.

People can stroll or picnic (skate or cross-country ski in winter) in the scenic Linear Park. A trail for cyclists, walkers, and cross-country skiers hugs the lake, then parallels Route 112 before turning into an off-road recreational trail that leads into the Parc Provincial du Mont-Orford, 13½ km (8 mi) from town.

Magog is the site of one of the largest wineries in the province, **Le Cep d'Argent** (✉ 1257 chemin de la Rivière, R.R. 5, ☎ 819/864–4441). The sparkling white wine is particularly good, and the dessert wine, which is similar to a port and flavored with a soupçon of maple syrup, makes a wonderful accompaniment to a plate of local cheese. This winery plays a leading role in the annual wine festival that's held in Magog in early September.

Dining and Lodging

$$–$$$$ ✕🏨 **Ripplecove Inn.** The Ripplecove, 11 km (7 mi) south of Magog, vies with the Hatley and Hovey inns in North Hatley for best in the region. Its accommodations, service, and restaurant are consistently excellent. The chef, Marco Guay, who trained in Europe, has designed a delicious Eastern Townships set menu: pan-sautéed veal kidneys, spicy breast of duck in green-peppercorn sauce, a goat-cheese salad, and crème brûlée with a crust of local maple syrup—for $59 per person. A seven-

course gourmet menu is also available. ⊠ *700 chemin Ripplecove, C.P. 246, Ayer's Cliff J0B 1CO,* ☎ *819/838–4296 or 800/668–4296,* FAX *819/838–5541,* WEB *www.ripplecove.com. 25 rooms. Restaurant, pool, 2 beaches, windsurfing, boating, cross-country skiing, meeting room. AE, MC, V. MAP.*

$$–$$$ ✕🄷 **Auberge l'Étoile Sur-le-Lac.** This popular hotel and restaurant is right on Magog's waterfront. All 38 rooms are modern; half were built in 2000 and the existing rooms were renovated in the same year. Some rooms have whirlpools and fireplaces. Large windows overlooking mountain-ringed Lac Memphrémagog make the restaurant bright and airy. In summer you can sit outside and take in the smells and sounds, as well as the beautiful view. House specialties include wild game and Swiss fondue. ⊠ *1150 rue Principale Ouest,* ☎ *819/843–6521 or 800/567– 2727,* WEB *www.etoile-sur-le-lac.com. 38 rooms. Restaurant, spa, hiking, boating, bicycles, ice-skating, rollerblading. AE, DC, MC, V.*

$$ 🄷 **Centre de Santé d'Eastman.** The oldest spa in Québec has evolved
★ from a simple health center into a bucolic haven for anyone seeking rest and therapeutic treatments. In Eastman, 15 km (9 mi) west of Magog, owner Jocelyna Dubuc has opened a new complex, but the wooden exterior evokes the earlier, rustic buildings it has replaced. Surrounded by 350 acres of rolling, wooded land, the spa is an elegant, simple structure with mustard and pale-green walls and tile floors that bring to mind the soothing calm of a Japanese garden. Some of the bedrooms have fireplaces, large balconies (you can have your massage here instead of in the treatment area), and views of Mont-Orford. The restaurant, which, unlike many spas, has a wine license, is flooded with light from its large windows. Vegetarian dishes predominate, but innovative seafood, rabbit, and chicken courses are also served from time to time. You can rejuvenate your body and mind through walking programs, massages, and various treatments. You can also take a brisk walk into nearby Eastman, an attractive hamlet with antiques and gift shops. ⊠ *895 chemin Diligence, Eastman J0E 1P0,* ☎ *450/297–3009 or 800/665– 5272,* FAX *450/297–3370,* WEB *www.spa-eastman.com. 45 rooms. Dining room, spa, cross-country skiing. AE, MC, V. FAP.*

Nightlife and the Arts

NIGHTLIFE

Magog is lively after dark, with bars, cafés, bistros, and restaurants to suit every taste and pocketbook. A patio bar at **Auberge Orford** (⊠ 20 rue Merry Sud, ☎ 819/843–9361) overlooks the Magog River (you can moor your boat alongside it). Sometimes there's live entertainment. **Café St-Michel** (⊠ 503 rue Principale Ouest, ☎ 819/868– 1062), in a century-old building on the northeastern corner of the main street, is a cheery pub that serves Tex-Mex food and imported and local beers. *Chansonniers* (singers) belt out popular hits for a full house every weekend. **Le Chat du Mouliner** (⊠ 101 rue Du Moulin, ☎ 819/868– 5678) is a hot newcomer in a cool location: a former factory on the waterfront. The jazz club (it also serves food) has exposed beams, exposed-brick walls with climbing vines, and a concrete dance floor with a grand piano in the center. **La Grosse Pomme** (⊠ 270 rue Principale Ouest, ☎ 819/843–9365) is a multilevel complex with huge video screens, dance floors, and restaurant service. The **Liquor Store** (⊠ 101 rue Du Moulin, ☎ 819/686–0841), a dance club below Le Chat du Mouliner jazz club, has live entertainment. The huge windows, which illuminated the former factory building, give panoramic views of Lac Memphrémagog.

THE ARTS

Le Vieux Clocher (⊠ 64 rue Merry Nord, ☎ 819/847–0470) is one of two former churches converted into theaters by local impresario

Bernard Caza. It headlines well-known comedians and singers. Most performances are in French, but big names, such as Jim Corcoran and Michel Rivard, perform here from time to time.

Outdoor Activities and Sports

GOLF

Golf du Mont Orford (⊠ chemin de Parc Orford, ☎ 819/843–5688, WEB www.mt-orford.com) is a venerable course—it was laid out in 1939. The 18-hole, 6,061-yard (18,183-ft) course winds around un-dulating, forested land; and from many of the greens you can see the peak of Mont-Orford.

Golf Owl's Head (⊠ 181 chemin Owl's Head, Mansonville, ☎ 450/292–3666), close to the Vermont border, offers spectacular views. Laid out with undulating greens and 64 sand bunkers, the 6,705-yard (20,115-ft), 18-hole course (par 71), designed by Graham Cooke, is surrounded by mountain scenery. It's considered to be one of the best courses in Canada, and its club house, a stunning timber and fieldstone structure with five fireplaces, is a favorite watering hole for locals and visitors alike.

The **Manoir des Sables golf course** (⊠ 90 av. des Jardins, Magog-Orford, ☎ 819/847–4299) is a 6,120-yard (18,360-ft), 18-hole course built on a sandy base.

SKIING

Owl's Head Ski Area (⊠ Rte. 243 S; Autoroute 10, Exit 106; ☎ 450/292–3342, WEB www.owlshead.com), on the Knowlton side of Lake Memphrémagog, is a mecca for skiers looking for fewer crowds. It has seven lifts, a 1,782-ft vertical drop, and 27 trails, including a 4-km (2½-mi) intermediate run, the longest in the Eastern Townships. From the trails you can see nearby Vermont and Lac Memphrémagog.

North Hatley

⑲ *134 km (83 mi) east of Montréal.*

North Hatley, the small resort town on the tip of lovely Lac Massawippi, has a theater and a number of excellent inns and restaurants. Set among hills and farms, it was discovered by well-to-do vacationers early in the 20th century and has been drawing people ever since. A number of events such as "The Springtime in Music" series (early April–mid-June), concerts held in Ste-Elizabeth church, and the North Hatley Antique Show (early July) are additional attractions.

Dining and Lodging

$-$$ ✕ **Café de Lafontaine.** This is more of a neighborhood café than a restaurant, but it has a great atmosphere and attracts an artsy clientele. The food is on the light side—soups, salads, pastas, and the like—but on Saturday nights October through May, more-formal dinners are served and live entertainers (mostly from Montréal) come to play for the locals. The music is eclectic. Recent lineups have included a Cuban trio, a Celtic group, and a jazz duo that played piano and double bass. ⊠ *35 rue Principale,* ☎ *819/842–4242. MC, V.*

$-$$ ✕ **The Pilsen.** Québec's earliest microbrewery no longer brews beer on-site, but Massawippi pale ale and brown ale are still on tap at this lively spot. Good pub food—pasta, homemade soups, burgers, and the like—is served in the upstairs restaurant and in the tavern, both of which overlook the water. ⊠ *55 rue Principale,* ☎ *819/842–2971. AE, MC, V.*

$$$$ ✕▥ **Auberge Hatley.** As befits a member of the prestigious Relais & ★ Chateaux chain, the service at this elegant country inn is consistently good. Some guest rooms in the 1903 country manor have whirlpool

baths and fireplaces. The color schemes are lively, French Provincial: tailored floral curtains in mustard yellow and bright reds and oranges compliment the matching floral duvets. Chef Alain Labrie specializes in regional dishes and has won numerous awards. The menu changes seasonally: the rich foie gras and venison are recommended when available. Herbs and vegetables are grown in the inn's hydroponic greenhouse. The dining room has a panoramic view of Lake Massawippi, or you can dine in a corner of the kitchen, at the "chef's table," and watch the goings-on behind the scenes. The wine cellar has been expanded to accommodate diners who want to eat in a cozy, intimate ambience reminiscent of the great "caves" of France. Wine tastings are also offered. The man in charge of the more than 1,400 wines here— Alain Bélanger—is highly respected worldwide. ✉ *325 chemin Virgin, C.P. 330, J0B 2C0,* ☎ *819/842–2451,* FAX *819/842–2907,* WEB *www.relaischateaux.fr/hatley. 25 rooms. Restaurant, massage, hiking, boating, bicycles. AE, DC, MC, V. Closed last 2 wks Nov. MAP.*

$$$$ ✕🏠 **Manoir Hovey.** Overlooking Lac Massawippi, this retreat main-
★ tains the ambience of a private estate and provides the activities of a resort. Built in 1900, it resembles George Washington's home at Mount Vernon. Each wallpapered room has a mix of antiques and newer wood furniture, richly printed fabrics, and lace trimmings; many have fireplaces and private balconies. The restaurant serves exquisite Continental and French cuisine; try the endive salad with braised fennel, apples, Barlett pears, and cheese from the Benedictine Abbey, or stewed rabbit flavored with mustard and cumin seeds. Even more exotic than the local fare are the grilled caribou cutlets from far flung Nunavik, served in a peppercorn sauce laced with tequila. Dinner, breakfast, and most sports are included in room rates. ✉ *575 chemin Hovey, C.P. 60, J0B 2C0,* ☎ *819/842–2421 or 800/661–2421,* FAX *819/842–2248,* WEB *www.manoirhovey.com. 39 rooms, 2 suites, 1 4-bedroom cottage. 2 bars, dining room, pool, tennis court, 2 beaches, mountain bikes, cross-country skiing, library, meeting rooms. AE, DC, MC, V. MAP.*

$$ ✕🏠 **Auberge Le Saint-Amant.** This cozy, 19th-century home is perched on a hill overlooking Lac Massawippi. The rooms of this bed-and-breakfast with a full restaurant are hung with plants and furnished with antiques. The dining room, which has a fireplace, seats about 50 people, but the food would do justice to a much bigger and fancier establishment. Jean-Claude, the chef–owner, whips up sophisticated fare at reasonable prices: rabbit terrine, sorrel-flavored salmon, sweetbreads in raspberry-vinegar sauce, and venison (in season) served with blackberries. ✉ *3 chemin Côte Minton, J0B 2C0,* ☎ *819/842–1211. 3 rooms. Restaurant. MC, V. MAP.*

Nightlife and the Arts

The **Piggery** (✉ Rte. 108, ☎ 819/842–2432 or 819/842–2431, WEB www.piggery@piggery.com), a theater that was once a pig barn, reigns supreme in the Townships' cultural life. The venue often presents new plays by Canadian playwrights and experiments with bilingual productions. The season runs July through August.

L'Association du Festival du Lac Massawippi (☎ 819/563–4141) presents an annual antiques and folk-art show in July. The association also sponsors classical-music concerts at the Église Ste-Elizabeth in North Hatley on Sunday starting in late April and continuing through June. The biennial **Naive Arts Contest** (✉ Galerie Jeannine-Blais, 100 rue Main, ☎ 819/842–2784) shows the work of more than 100 painters of art naïf from 15 countries; the next show is in 2002.

Sherbrooke

20 *130 km (81 mi) east of Montréal.*

The region's unofficial capital and largest city is Sherbrooke, named in 1818 for Canadian governor general Sir John Coape Sherbrooke. It was founded by Loyalists in the 1790s along the St-François River.

Sherbrooke has a number of art galleries and museums, including the **Musée des Beaux-Arts de Sherbrooke.** This fine-arts museum has a permanent exhibit tracing the history of art in the region from 1800 to the present. Changing shows display the works of regional artists. ⊠ *241 rue Dufferin, J1H 4M3,* ☎ *819/821–2115.* ⊡ *$4.* ☉ *Tues. and Thurs.–Sun. 1–5, Wed. 1–9.*

The **Sherbrooke Tourist Information Center** (⊠ 3010 King St. W, ☎ 819/821–1919) conducts city tours for groups from late June through early September. Call for reservations.

Sugar shacks near Sherbrooke give tours of their maple-syrup producing operations in spring (call before visiting). **La Ferme Martinette** (⊠ 1728 chemin Martineau, Coaticook, ☎ 819/849–7089 or 888/881–4561) in the heart of Québec's dairy country, hosts "sugaring off" parties with traditional menus in March and April. Lisa Nadeau and her husband, Gérald Martineau, have 2,500 maple trees as well as a herd of 50 Holsteins. You can tour the farm in a trailer pulled by the tractor that belonged to Gérald's grandfather.

One of the oldest, most traditional maple-syrup operations in the Eastern Townships is **Sucerie des Normand** (⊠ 426 George Bonnalie, Eastman, ☎ 450/297–2659), run by a third-generation farmer, Richard Normand. In Eastman, about a half-hour drive west of Sherbrooke, the farm is spread over 250 acres of wooded land (there are 9,000 maple trees). Visitors who tour the property in horse-drawn carriages can watch the "sugaring off" process—from the tapping of trees to the rendering down of the sweet liquid into this syrup and sugar. After the tour, Richard and his wife, Marlene, serve traditional Québécois food in a wood cabin, to the sounds of the harmonica and spoons.

Dining and Lodging

$$–$$$$ ✕ **La Falaise St-Michel.** A warmly decorated redbrick and wood room takes off any chill even before you sit down. Chef, and part-owner, Patrick Laigniel serves up superb French cuisine. A large selection of wines complements the table d'hôte. Menu offerings at this award-winning restaurant, considered to be one of the best in town, include lamb, salmon, and Barbary duck. ⊠ *Rues Webster and Wellington N, behind Banque Nationale,* ☎ *819/346–6339. AE, DC, MC, V.*

$–$$$ ✕ **Restaurant au P'tit Sabot.** The chef–owner of this establishment is a woman (still an uncommon occurrence in this part of the country); Anne-Marie Eloy designs adventurous menus using local ingredients such as wild boar, quail, and bison. The emphasis is on French cuisine; Anne-Marie is yet another local chef who hails from France. The serene blue decor and small dining area (it seats around 35 people) create an intimate, romantic atmosphere—a pleasant refuge from the busy and not very attractive shopping strip. ⊠ *1410 rue King Ouest,* ☎ *819/563–0262. AE, DC, MC, V.*

$ ⊞ **Bishop's University.** If you're on a budget, the students' residences, 5 km (3 mi) south of Sherbrooke, are a great place to stay in summer. The prices can't be beat, and the location near Sherbrooke is good for touring. The university's lovely grounds have architecture reminiscent of stately New England campuses. The 1857 Gothic-style chapel, paneled with richly carved ash, shows fine local craftsmanship. Reservations for summer guests are accepted as early as September, so book in advance. ✉ *rue College, Lennoxville J1M 1Z7,* ☎ *819/822–9651,* FAX *819/822–9615. 564 beds in single or double rooms. Indoor pool, 18-hole golf course, tennis court, gym. MC, V. Closed Sept.–mid-May.*

Nightlife and the Arts

The **Centennial Theatre** (✉ rue College, ☎ 819/822–9692) at Bishop's University in Lennoxville, 5 km (3 mi) south of Sherbrooke, presents a roster of jazz, classical, and rock concerts, as well as opera, dance, mime, and children's theater. **Le Vieux Clocher de Sherbrooke** (✉ 1590 rue Galt Ouest, ☎ 819/822–2102), in a converted church, presents music, from classical to jazz, and a variety of theater.

Mont-Mégantic's Observatory

㉑ *204 km (127 mi) east of Montréal.*

Both amateur stargazers and serious astronomers are drawn to this site, in a beautifully wild and mountainous area. The observatory (known as the Astrolab du Mont-Mégantic in French) is at the summit of the Townships' second-highest mountain (3,601 ft), whose northern face records annual snowfalls rivaling any other in North America. A joint venture by the University of Montréal and Laval University, the observatory has a powerful telescope that allows scientists to observe celestial bodies 10 million times smaller than the human eye can detect. At the welcome center on the mountain's base, you can view an exhibition and a multimedia show to learn about the night sky. ✉ *189 Rte. du Parc, Notre-Dame-des-Bois,* ☎ *819/888–2941,* WEB *www.astrolab.qc.ca.* ✉ *$10, summit tour $10.* ☉ *Mid May–early Sept., daily 10–6; summit tour: late June–early Sept., daily 8 PM.*

Dining and Lodging

$$ ✕▥ **Aux Berges de l'Aurore.** Although this tiny B&B has attractive furnishings and spectacular views (it sits at the foot of Mont-Mégantic), the draw is the inn's cuisine. The restaurant ($$) serves a five-course meal using ingredients from the inn's huge fruit, vegetable, and herb garden, as well as local wild game: boar, fish, hare, and quail. ✉ *51 chemin de l'Observatoire, Notre-Dame-des-Bois,* ☎ *819/888–2715. 4 rooms. Restaurant. MC, V. Closed Jan.–May.*

CHARLEVOIX

Stretching along the St. Lawrence River's north shore, east of Québec City from Ste-Anne-de-Beaupré to the Saguenay River, Charlevoix embraces mountains rising from the sea and a succession of valleys, plateaus, and cliffs cut by waterfalls, brooks, and streams. The roads wind into villages of picturesque houses and huge tin-roof churches. The area has long been popular both as a summer retreat and as a haven for artists and craftspeople. In winter there are opportunities for both downhill and cross-country skiing.

New France's first historian, the Jesuit priest François-Xavier de Charlevoix, gave his name to the region. Charlevoix (pronounced sharle-*vwah*) was first explored by Jacques Cartier, who landed in 1535, although the first colonists didn't arrive until well into the 17th century. They developed a thriving shipbuilding industry, specializing in the sturdy schooner called a *goélette,* which they used to haul everything from logs to lobsters up and down the coast in the days before rail and paved roads. Shipbuilding was a vital part of the provincial economy until recently; today wrecked and forgotten goélettes lie along beaches in the region.

Ste-Anne-de-Beaupré

㉒   *33 km (20 mi) east of Québec City.*

Charlevoix begins in the tiny town Ste-Anne-de-Beaupré, named for Québec's patron saint. Each year more than a million pilgrims visit the region's most famous religious site, the **Basilique Ste-Anne-de-Beaupré,** ★ dedicated to the mother of the Virgin Mary. The basilica is surrounded by aged, modest homes and tacky souvenir shops that emphasize its grandeur.

The French brought their devotion to St. Anne (the patron saint of those in shipwrecks) with them when they sailed across the Atlantic to New France. In 1650 Breton sailors caught in a storm vowed to erect a chapel in honor of this patron saint at the exact spot where they landed. The present-day neo-Roman basilica constructed in 1923 was the fifth to be built on the site where the sailors first touched ground. According to local legend, St. Anne was responsible over the years for saving voyagers from shipwrecks in the harsh waters of the St. Lawrence. Tributes to her miraculous powers can be seen in the shrine's various mosaics, murals, altars, and ceilings. A bas-relief at the entrance depicts St. Anne welcoming her pilgrims, and ceiling mosaics represent her life. Numerous crutches and braces posted on the back pillars have been left by those who have felt the saint's healing powers.

The basilica, in the shape of a Latin cross, has two granite steeples jutting from its gigantic structure. Its interior has 22 chapels and 18 altars, as well as round arches and numerous ornaments in the Romanesque style. The 214 stained-glass windows, completed in 1949 by Frenchmen Auguste Labouret and Pierre Chaudière, tell a story of salvation through personages who were believed to be instruments of God over the centuries. Other features of the shrine are intricately carved wood pews decorated with various animals and several smaller altars (behind the main altar) dedicated to different saints.

The original, 17th-century wood chapel was built too close to the St. Lawrence and was swept away by river flooding. In 1676 the chapel was replaced by a stone church that was visited by pilgrims for more than a century, but this structure was demolished in 1872. The first basilica, which replaced the stone church, was destroyed by a fire in 1922. The following year architects Maxime Rosin from Paris and Louis N. Audet from Québec province designed the basilica that now stands. ✉ *10018 av. Royale,* ☎ *418/827–3781.* 🎟 *Free.* ☉ *Reception booth May–mid-Oct., daily 8:30–5:30; mid-Oct.–Apr., daily 8:30–4:30. Guided tours daily at 1 in summer; Sept.–mid-May, call in advance to arrange a tour.*

At the **Rèserve Faunique du Cap Tourmente** (Cap Tourmente Wildlife Reserve) about 8 km (5 mi) northeast of Ste-Anne-de-Beaupré, more than 800,000 greater snow geese gather every October and May (with an average of 100,000 per day). The park harbors hundreds of kinds of birds and mammals and more than 700 plant species. This enclave on the north shore of the St. Lawrence River has 14 hiking trails; naturalists give guided tours. ✉ *St-Joachim,* ☎ *418/827–4591 Apr.–Oct.; 418/827–3776 Nov.–Mar.* 🎟 *$5.* ☉ *Daily 8:30–5.*

Dining

$$–$$$ ✕ **Auberge Baker.** This restaurant in a 150-year-old French-Canadian farmhouse blends the best of old and new. Antiques and old-fashioned woodstoves decorate the dining rooms, where you can sample traditional Québécois fare such as tourtière, pork hocks, meatball

Charlevoix

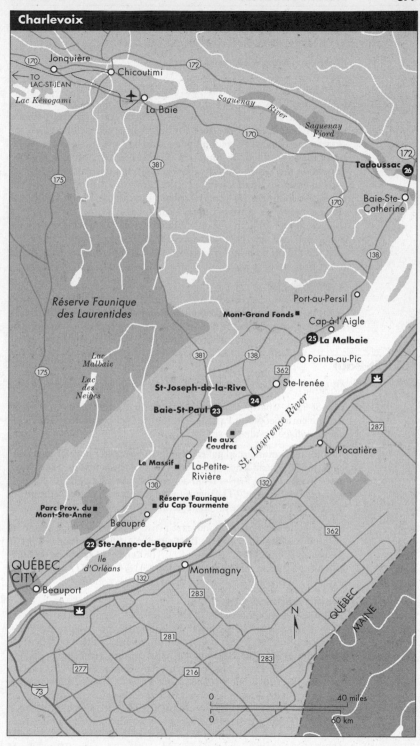

170 Jonquière

172

← TO LAC-ST-JEAN

Lac Kénogami

Chicoutimi

La Baie

Saguenay River

170

Saguenay Fjord

172

Tadoussac 26

Baie-Ste-Catherine

170

381

175

138

Port-au-Persil

Réserve Faunique des Laurentides

Mont-Grand Fonds ■

Cap-à-l'Aigle

25 **La Malbaie**

Lac Malbaie

381

138

362

Pointe-au-Pic

Lac des Neiges

175

Ste-Irenée

St-Joseph-de-la-Rive

24

St. Lawrence River

Baie-St-Paul 23

Ile aux Coudres ■

287

Le Massif ■

La-Petite-Rivière

La Pocatière

132

130

Réserve Faunique du Cap Tourmente ■

Parc Prov. du Mont-Ste-Anne ■

Beaupré

362

22 **Ste-Anne-de-Beaupré**

Ile d'Orléans

QUÉBEC CITY

132

Montmagny

Beauport

283

N

QUÉBEC

MAINE

281

73

277

216

283

0 ——— 40 miles

0 ——— 60 km

stew, and maple-sugar pie. The adventurous can opt for more-exotic dishes, including grilled ostrich with fir sauce. ⊠ *8790 av. Royale*, ☎ *418/824–4478 or 866/824–4478. AE, MC, V.*

Outdoor Activities and Sports

SKIING

Le Massif (⊠ 1350 rue Principale, Petite Rivière St-François, ☎ 418/632–5876, WEB www.lemassif.com) is a three-peak ski resort that has the province's longest vertical drop—2,500 ft. The 20 trails (there are three lifts) are divided into runs for different levels, including one for extremely advanced skiers. Equipment can be rented on-site. **Mont-Ste-Anne** (⊠ 2000 blvd. Beaupré, ☎ 418/827–4561), outside Québec City, is on the World Cup downhill circuit. It's one of the largest resorts in eastern Canada, with a vertical drop of 2,050 ft, 56 downhill trails, two halfpipes for snowboarders, a terrain park, and 13 lifts including a gondola. Cross-country skiing is also a draw here, with 21 trails totaling 224 km (139 mi). When the weather warms, mountain biking becomes the sport of choice. Enthusiasts can choose from 200 km (124 mi) of mountain-bike trails, 14 downhill runs (and a gondola to get back up to the top).

SNOWMOBILING

Snowmobiles can be rented near Mont Ste-Anne, a half-hour drive north of the city, at **Centre de Location de Motoneiges du Québec** (15 blvd. Beaupré, Beaupré, ☎ 418/827–8478), starting at $40 for an hour or $100 a day plus taxes, insurance, and gas.

Baie-St-Paul

㉓ *60 km (37 mi) northeast of Ste-Anne-de-Beaupré.*

Baie-St-Paul, Charlevoix's earliest settlement after Beaupré, is popular with craftspeople and artists. The high hills circle a wide plain, holding the village beside the sea.

A handful of commercial galleries in the town center have original artwork for sale. In addition, from late July to early September each year, more than a dozen artists from across Canada take part in "Symposium of New Painting." The themes are different each time and the artists work together to create a giant canvas.

Many of Québec's greatest landscape artists depicted the area, and some of these works are for sale at the **Centre d'Art Baie-St-Paul** (⊠ 4 rue Ambroise-Fafard, ☎ 418/435–3681). The **Centre d'Exposition de Baie-St-Paul** (⊠ 23 rue Ambroise-Fafard, ☎ 418/435–3681) displays the work of various artists, some of them from the region.

Dining and Lodging

$$$$ ✕🍴 **Auberge la Maison Otis.** The calm and romantic accommoda-
★   tions of this inn are housed in three buildings (the restaurant is in an old stone house) in the center of the village. Some country-style rooms have whirlpools, fireplaces, and antique furnishings. Skiing and ice-skating are available nearby. The restaurant serves creative Québec-oriented French cuisine such as *ballotine de faisan*, pheasant stuffed with quail and served in a venison sauce, followed by an assortment of cheeses. The Norman-style house, which dates back to the mid-1850s, is elegantly decorated in pink, and has a huge fireplace. ⊠ *23 rue St-Jean-Baptiste, G0A 1B0*, ☎ *418/435–2255*, FAX *418/435–2464*, WEB *www.quebecweb.com/maisonotis. 30 rooms, 4 suites. Restaurant, lounge, piano bar, indoor pool, sauna, health club. AE, MC, V. MAP.*

St-Joseph-de-la-Rive

㉔ *15 km (9 mi) northeast of Baie-St-Paul.*

A secondary road leads sharply down into St-Joseph-de-la-Rive, with its line of old houses hugging the mountain base on the narrow shore road. The town has a number of peaceful inns and inviting restaurants. The small **Exposition Maritime** (Maritime Museum) commemorates the days of the St. Lawrence goélettes, the feisty little steamships that, until the 1950s, were the lifeblood of the region. Fifty years ago, the roads through Charlevoix were little more than rugged tracks. (Indeed, they are still narrow and winding and are being upgraded). Entire, very large, families lived in cramped conditions aboard the boats. To modern eyes, it wasn't a comfortable existence, but the folklore of the goélettes celebrated in poetry, paintings, and song is part of the strong cultural identity of the region. ⊠ *305 place de l'Église,* ☎ *418/635–1131.* ⌨ *$2.* ☉ *Mid-May–mid-June, weekdays 9–5, weekends 11–4; mid-June to Labor Day, daily 9–5.*

A free, government-run ferry takes you on the 15-minute trip to **Ile aux Coudres** (☎ 418/438–2743 ferry information), an island where Jacques Cartier's men gathered *coudres* (hazelnuts) in 1535. Since then, the island has produced many a goélette, and the families of former captains now run several small inns. Larger inns have folk-dance evenings. You can bike around the island and see windmills and water mills, or stop at boutiques selling paintings and handicrafts such as household linens.

Lodging

$$–$$$$ **⊞ Hôtel Cap-aux-Pierres.** This hotel provides comfortable accommo-
★ dations in a traditionally Canadian main building as well as a motel section that's open in summer only. It's one of several properties in the region run by the large, entrepreneurial Dufour family. The family has been in the business since the 1930s, when Louis Dufour and his wife, Alvine Desmeules, started taking in paying guests as a way to raise money to help support their 17 children. About a third of the rooms have river views. The restaurant serves a mix of Québec standards and French cuisine, and summer entertainment includes folk dancing on Saturday evening. ⊠ *246 rue Principale, La Baleine, Ile aux Coudres G0A 2A0,* ☎ *418/438–2711 or 800/463–5250,* 𝔽𝔸𝕏 *418/438–2127,* 𝕎𝔼𝔹 *www.familledufour.com. 98 rooms. Restaurant, bar, indoor-outdoor pool, spa. AE, DC, MC, V. MAP.*

Shopping

Papeterie St-Gilles (⊠ 304 rue F. A. Savard, ☎ 418/635–2430) produces unusual handcrafted stationery, using a 17th-century process. The paper factory, which is also a small museum, explains through photographs and demonstrations how paper is manufactured the old-fashioned way. Slivers of wood and flower petals are pressed into the paper sheets, which are as thick as the covers of a paperback book. The finished products—made into writing paper, greeting cards, and one-page poems or quotations—make beautiful, if pricey, gifts.

La Malbaie

㉕ *35 km (22 mi) northeast of St-Joseph-de-la-Rive.*

La Malbaie, one of the province's most elegant and historically interesting resort towns, was known as Murray Bay in an earlier era when wealthy Anglophones summered here and in the neighboring villages: Pointe-au-Pic, 3 km (2 mi) to the south, and Cap-à-l'Aigle, 3 km (2 mi) to the north. This area became popular with both American and

Canadian politicians in the late 1800s when Ottawa Liberals and Washington Republicans partied decorously through the summer with members of the Québec judiciary. Once called the "summer White House," William Howard Taft built the first of three summer residences in Pointe-au-Pic in 1894, when he was the American civil governor of the Philippines. He became the 27th president of the United States in 1908.

Now many Taft-era homes serve as handsome inns, guaranteeing an old-fashioned coddling, with such extras as breakfast in bed, whirl-pool baths, and free shuttles to the ski areas in winter. Many serve lunch and dinner to nonresidents, so you can tour the area going from one gourmet delight to the next. The cuisine, as elsewhere in Québec, is genuine French or regional fare.

Musée de Charlevoix traces the region's history as a vacation spot in a series of exhibits and is developing an excellent collection of local paintings and folk art. The museum's mission statement: "one museum, one passion: the people of this place," pretty much sums up this sight. ⊠ *1 chemin du Havre, Pointe-au-Pic,* ☎ *418/665–4411.* ⌦ *$4.* ☉ *Late June–early Sept., Tues.–Fri. 10–6; early Sept.–late June, weekends and Tues.–Fri. 10–5.*

The **Casino de Charlevoix,** one of three highly profitable gaming halls (the others are in Montréal and Hull), is operated by Loto-Québec, a province-owned lottery corporation. Expanded in 1999, this is the small-est of the casinos, but it still hauls in almost 1 million visitors a year—some of them tourists from Japan and Germany who stay at the Fairmont Le Manoir Richelieu. There are 21 gaming tables and 780 slot machines. Minimum age is 18. ⊠ *Fairmont Le Manoir Richelieu, 183 rue Richelieu,* ☎ *418/665–5353 or 800/665–2274.* ☉ *Sun.–Thurs. 10 AM–midnight, Fri.–Sat. 10 AM–3 AM.*

Dining and Lodging

$$$–$$$$ ✕🏠 **Auberge des 3 Canards.** The inn has made a name for itself in the region, not only for its accommodations but also for its fine restau-rant. Rooms in a rustic-chic style have wicker furniture, brass beds, pine dressers, and chintz curtains; all have views over the St. Lawrence. Maple syrup and sugar flavor many regional dishes. Boneless guinea fowl comes with a maple syrup and spicy mustard sauce; maple-sugar pie and maple-flavored mousse are sweet dessert treats. ⊠ *49 côte Belle-vue, Pointe-au-Pic G5A 1Y2,* ☎ *418/665–3761,* FAX *418/665–4727,* WEB *www.aubergedes3canards.com. 40 rooms. Restaurant, pool, putting green, tennis court. AE, MC, V. CP, MAP.*

$$$–$$$$ ✕🏠 **Auberge la Pinsonnière.** An atmosphere of country luxury pre-
★ vails at this Relais & Châteaux inn. Each room is decorated individ-ually; some have fireplaces, whirlpools, and king-size four-poster beds. The rooms overlook Murray Bay on the St. Lawrence River. The haute cuisine is excellent, and the auberge has one of the largest wine cellars in North America. The food doesn't come cheap. The appetizers here—duck ravioli, warm smoked salmon salad, braised sweetbreads and the like—cost as much as the entrées in other establishments but the din-ing experience is well worth the money. ⊠ *124 rue St-Raphael, Cap-à-l'Aigle G0T 1B0,* ☎ *418/665–4431,* FAX *418/665–7156,* WEB *www.lapinsonniere.com. 26 rooms, 1 suite. 2 restaurants, 3 lounges, indoor pool, spa, tennis court, beach. AE, MC, V. MAP.*

$$$–$$$$ 🏠 **Fairmont Le Manoir Richelieu.** The Richelieu, an imposing castle-
★ like building sitting amid trees on a cliff overlooking the St. Lawrence River, has been offering first-class accommodations for 100 years. The hotel was constructed in 1929 on the site of an earlier property. It re-tains a classically elegant feel. A full-service spa, La Relaxarium, has

22 treatment rooms. There is a clubby after-dinner lounge where guests can smoke cigars and drink single malts or vintage ports, and the restaurants offer a wide range of food—from family fare to haute cuisine. While the children have fun at the kid's club, adults can enjoy some golf on the links-style course—similar to those in Scotland—overlooking the St. Lawrence. ⊠ *181 rue Richelieu, Pointe-au-Pic, G5A 1X7,* ☎ *418/665–3703 or 800/463–2613,* FAX *418/665–3093,* WEB *www.fairmont.com. 405 rooms. 3 restaurants, 1 indoor and 1 outdoor pool, sauna, spa, 18-hole golf course, tennis court, cross-country skiing, snowmobiling, casino. AE, DC, MC, V.*

Nightlife and the Arts

Domaine Forget is a music and dance academy with a 600-seat hall in Ste-Irenée, 15 km (9 mi) south of La Malbaie. Summer evening concerts are given by fine musicians from around the world, many of whom are teaching or learning at the school. The Domaine also functions as a stopover for traveling musicians, who take advantage of its rental studios. ⊠ *5 St-Antoine, Ste-Irenée,* ☎ *418/452–8111, 418/452–2535, or 888/336–7438,* WEB *www.domaineforget.com.* ☉ *Concerts May–Aug.*

Outdoor Activities and Sports

Club de Golf de Manoir Richelieu (⊠ 181 rue Richelieu, Pointe-au-Pic, ☎ 418/665–2526 or 800/463–2613) is a par-71, 18-hole course. One of Canada's top-10 courses, it's been awarded the Gold Medal by Golf International magazine.

Mont-Grand Fonds (⊠ 1000 chemin des Loisirs, ☎ 418/665–0095, WEB www.quebecweb.com/montgrandfonds), 10 km (6 mi) north of La Malbaie, has 14 downhill slopes, a 1,105-ft vertical drop, and two lifts. It also has 160 km (99 mi) of cross-country trails. Two trails meet International Ski Federation standards, and the resort hosts major competitions occasionally. Other sports available are dogsledding, sleigh riding, skating, and tobogganing.

Tadoussac

26 *71 km (44 mi) north of La Malbaie.*

The small town of Tadoussac shares the view up the magnificent Saguenay Fjord with Baie-Ste-Catherine across the river. The drive here from La Malbaie, along Route 138, leads past lovely villages and views along the St. Lawrence. Jacques Cartier made a stop at this point in 1535, and it became an important meeting site for fur traders until the mid-19th century. Whale-watching excursions and cruises of the fjord now depart from Tadoussac, as well as from Chicoutimi, farther up the deep fjord.

As the Saguenay River flows from Lac St-Jean south toward the St. Lawrence, it has a dual character: Between Alma and Chicoutimi, the once rapidly flowing river has been harnessed for hydroelectric power; in its lower section, it becomes wider and deeper and flows by steep mountains and cliffs en route to the St. Lawrence. The white beluga whale breeds in the lower portion of the Saguenay in summer. The many marine species that live in the confluence of the fjord and the seaway attract other whales, too, such as pilots, finbacks, humpbacks, and blues.

Sadly, the beluga is an endangered species; the whales, with 27 other species of mammals and birds and 17 species of fish, are being threatened by pollution in the St. Lawrence River. This has inspired a $100 million project funded by both the federal and provincial governments. The 800-square-km (309-square-mi) **Parc Marine du Saguenay–St-Laurent** (⊠ park office: 182 rue de l'Église, ☎ 418/235–4703 or 800/463–6769), a marine park at the confluence of the Saguenay and St. Lawrence rivers, has been created to protect the latter's fragile ecosystem.

You can learn more about the whales and their habitat at the **Centre d'Interprétation des Mammifères Marin.** The interpretation center is run by members of a locally based research team and they're on hand to answer questions. In addition, explanatory videos and exhibits (including a collection of whale skeletons) tell you everything there is to know about the mighty cetaceans. ⊠ *108 rue Cale-Sèche,* ☎ *418/235–4701.* ☎ *$5.50.* ☼ *In summer, daily 9–8; winter, daily noon–5.*

Outdoor Activities and Sports

Croisières AML (☎ 418/692–4643; 800/463–1292 in season) has three-hour whale-watching tours ($35). Cruises depart from Baie-Ste-Catherine, Tadoussac, and Rivière du Loup (the departure from Rivière du Loup costs an additional $3). The best months for seeing whales are July, August, and September, although some operators extend the season at either end if whales are around.

THE GASPÉ PENINSULA

Jutting into the stormy Gulf of St. Lawrence like the battered prow of a ship, the Gaspé Peninsula (Gaspésie in French) remains an isolated region of unsurpassed wild beauty. Sheer cliffs tower above broad beaches, and tiny coastal fishing communities cling to the shoreline. Inland rise the Chic-Choc Mountains, eastern Canada's highest, the realm of woodland caribou, black bear, and moose. Townspeople in some areas speak mainly English.

The Gaspé was on Jacques Cartier's itinerary—he first stepped ashore in North America in the town of Gaspé in 1534—but Vikings, Basques, and Portuguese fishermen had come before. The area's history is told in countless towns en route. Acadians, displaced by the British from New Brunswick in 1755, settled Bonaventure; Paspébiac still has a gunpowder shed built in the 1770s to help defend the peninsula from American ships; and United Empire Loyalists settled New Carlisle in 1784.

Today the area still seems unspoiled and timeless, a blessing for anyone dipping and soaring along the spectacular coastal highways or venturing on river-valley roads to the interior. Geographically, the peninsula is among the oldest lands on earth. A vast, mainly uninhabited forest covers the hilly hinterland. Local tourist officials can be helpful in locating outfitters and guides for fishing. The Gaspé has many parks, nature trails, and wildlife sanctuaries. The most accessible include Parc de l'Ile-Bonaventure-et-du-Rocher-Percé (Bonaventure Island is a sanctuary for 250,000 birds); Parc National Forillon at the tip of the peninsula, with 50 km (31 mi) of trails and an interesting boardwalk; and the Parc Provincial de la Gaspésie. The provincial park includes the Chic-Choc Mountains and has terrain ranging from tundra to subalpine forest.

Carleton

🕗 *574 km (357 mi) northeast of Québec City.*

Windsurfers and sailors enjoy the breezes around the Gaspé; there are windsurfing marathons in the Baie des Chaleurs each summer.

The **Oratoire Notre-Dame-du-Mont Saint-Joseph** (Notre Dame Oratory), a chapel on Mont-St-Joseph, dominates this French-speaking city. There are lookout points and hiking trails around the site. The views, almost 2,000 ft above Baie des Chaleurs, are lovely.

Dining and Lodging

$–$$$ ✕🏨 **Motel Hostelerie Baie-Bleue.** This motel snuggles up against a mountain beside the Baie des Chaleurs and has great views. Daily guided

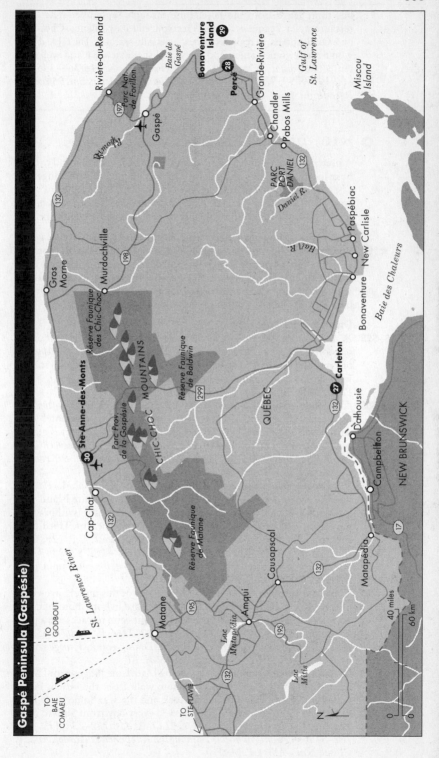

Gaspé Peninsula (Gaspésie)

Bonaventure Island **29**

Bonaventure **28**
Percé
Grande-Rivière

Gulf of
St. Lawrence

Miscou
Island

Rivière-au-Renard
Parc Natl. de Forillon
197
Gaspé
Baie de Gaspé

Chandler
Pabos Mills
132

PARC
PORT
DANIEL
Daniel R.

Gros
Morne
198
Murdochville

Paspébiac
New Carlisle

Bonaventure
Baie des Chaleurs

Réserve Faunique
des Chic-Choc

CHIC-CHOC MOUNTAINS

Réserve Faunique
de Baldwin
299

Ste-Anne-des-Monts
Parc Prov.
de la Gaspésie

Carleton **27**

QUÉBEC

132
Dalhousie

30 Cap-Chat
132

Réserve Faunique
de Matane

Campbellton

NEW BRUNSWICK

St. Lawrence River

TO
GODBOUT

Causapscal
132
17

Matane
195
Amqui

Lac
Matapédia

Lac
Mitis

Matapédia

195

132

TO
BAIE
COMEAU

TO
STE-FLAVIE

N

40 miles

60 km

0
0

bus tours leave from the hotel June through September. The large restaurant, La Seignerie, has been recognized for excellence. Chef Yannick Ouillet prepares regional dishes, especially seafood. The table d'hôte won't break your budget, and the wine list is extensive and well chosen. ⊠ *482 blvd. Perron (Rte. 132), G0C 1J0,* ☎ *418/364–3355 or 800/463–9099,* FAX *418/364–6165,* WEB *www.baiebleue.com. 95 rooms. Restaurant, pool, tennis court, beach. AE, MC, V.*

Percé

㉘ *193 km (120 mi) east of Carleton.*

A pretty fishing village, Percé has a number of attractions and can get busy in summer. The most famous sight in the region is the huge fossil-embedded rock offshore that the sea "pierced" thousands of years ago. There are many pleasant places to walk and hike near town, and it's also possible to do some fishing or take a whale-watching cruise.

★ **㉙** The largest colony of gannets (large, fish-eating seabirds) in the world summers off Percé on **l'Ile Bonaventure** (Bonaventure Island). From the wharf at Percé, you can join an organized tour to the island and walk the trails. Take binoculars and a camera; there are many kinds of seabirds. Several companies offer trips from Percé to Bonaventure Island.

Dining and Lodging

$–$$$ ✕ **La Sieur de Pabos.** This rustic restaurant serving some of the best seafood in the province overlooks Pabos Bay, about 40 km (25 mi) south of Percé. Try the *casserole aux fruits de mer* (seafood casserole) stuffed with shrimps and scallops and encased in potatoes. ⊠ *325 Rte. 132, Pabos Mills,* ☎ *418/689–4741. AE, MC, V.*

$$–$$$ ▣ **La Bonaventure-sur-Mer Hotel.** The waterfront location with views of Percé Rock and Bonaventure Island makes up for the motel-standard decor. Some units have kitchenettes. The restaurant serves mainly beef and seafood dishes. ⊠ *Rte. 132, C.P. 339, G0C 2L0,* ☎ *418/782–2166,* FAX *418/782–5323,* WEB *www.quebectel.com/rest. 90 rooms. Restaurant, beach. AE, DC, MC, V. Closed Nov.–May.*

$$–$$$ ▣ **La Normandie Hotel/Motel.** All but four rooms of this split-level motel face the ocean, with views of Percé Rock and Bonaventure Island. The location in the center of town puts shops and restaurants within walking distance; a beach and a municipal pool are also nearby. Third-floor rooms are the most spacious. ⊠ *221 Rte. 132 Ouest, C.P. 129, G0C 2L0,* ☎ *418/782–2112 or 800/463–0820,* FAX *418/782–2337,* WEB *www.normandieperce.com. 45 rooms. Restaurant, lounge, sauna, gym. AE, DC, MC, V. Closed Nov.–Apr. EP, MAP.*

$$ ▣ **La Côte Surprise Motor Hotel.** Most rooms at this motel have views of Percé Rock and the village. Decor is standard in both motel and second-floor hotel units, but the private balconies and terraces are a plus. ⊠ *Rte. 132, C.P. 339, G0C 2L0,* ☎ *418/782–2166,* FAX *418/782–5323,* WEB *www.quebectel.com/rest. 36 rooms. Dining room, lounge, snack bar. AE, D, DC, MC, V. Closed Oct.–May. BP.*

$ ▣ **Hôtel-Motel Rocher Percé.** Owned by Madeleine Pidgeon and Marc Bourdages, this hostelry is a 10-minute walk from the beach. Picnic tables and chairs overlook Percé Rock and the sea. Some units have kitchenettes and sea views. Tea is served every day from 5:30 to 8. ⊠ *111 Rte. 132 Ouest, C.P. 34, G0C 2L0,* ☎ *418/782–2330,* FAX *418/ 782–5136. 4 rooms in hotel, 14 in motel. Kitchenettes (some). MC, V. Closed Nov.–Apr. CP, MAP.*

Ste-Anne-des-Monts

③⓪ *282 km (175 mi) northwest of Percé.*

The area south of this coastal town has Québec's highest peaks, the Chic-Choc Mountains. **Parc Provincial de la Gaspésie** (Gaspé Peninsula Provincial Park; ✉ Rte. 299, ☎ 418/763–3301, WEB www.sepaq. com) has climbing, heli-skiing, mountain hiking, and nature interpretation programs such as moose-watching.

There's backcountry skiing at **Club du Grand Yétis** (✉ 85 blvd. Ste-Anne Ouest, ☎ 418/763–7782 or 800/665–6527). Overnight accommodation is also available in cabins heated by wood-burning stoves. (Hardier types can opt for camping out.)

Lodging

$$ 🏨 **Gîte du Mont-Albert.** In the middle of the Chic-Choc Mountains, this property is 40 km (25 mi) south of Ste-Anne-des-Monts, in the Parc Provinçial de la Gaspésie. It's a perfect retreat for hiking, bicycling, horseback riding, or salmon fishing on the Ste-Anne River. The rooms are similar to a European mountain lodge: basic and modern, but comfortable. ✉ *Rte. 299, C.P. 1150, G0E 2G0,* ☎ *418/763–2288 or 888/ 270–4483,* WEB *www.sepaq.com. 48 rooms, 19 cottages. Restaurant, bar. AE, MC, V. MAP.*

$–$$ 🏨 **Riôtel Monaco des Monts.** This small hotel is near the entrance to the Parc Provinçial de la Gaspésie and all its activities, from cross-country skiing to biking (packages including some of the outdoor activities are available). Half the rooms are motel-style; the rest are plain-but-comfortable standard hotel rooms. The air-conditioned restaurant is open 24 hours. ✉ *90 blvd. Ste-Anne, G0E 2G0,* ☎ *418/763–3321,* WEB *www.riotel.com. 46 rooms. Restaurant. AE, DC, MC, V. EP, MAP.*

PROVINCE OF QUÉBEC A TO Z

To research prices, get advice from other travelers, and book travel arrangements, visit www.fodors.com.

AIR TRAVEL

Most airlines fly into Montréal or Québec City. Air Canada dominates about 90% of the market since its takeover of Canadian Airlines.

BIKE TRAVEL

The Green Route, a 4,000-km (2,480-mi) path that will run from northern Québec to the Gaspé and will also link up with trails in New England and New York, is scheduled to be completed by 2005. More than half of the marked bikeways are already open. For information and a map, contact Vélo Québec.

➤ CONTACT: **Vélo Québec** (☎ 514/521–8356, WEB www.routeverte.com).

BUS TRAVEL

Frequent bus service for the province is available from the central bus station in downtown Montréal. Daily service to Granby, Lac-Mégantic, Magog, and Sherbrooke in the Eastern Townships leaves from the Montréal central bus station.

Voyageur is a province-wide bus line. Several smaller private companies also serve the regions and connect with Voyageur. The trip to Gaspé Peninsula takes 13 hours.

Limocar Laurentides service departs for the Laurentians: L'Annonciation, Mont-Laurier, Ste-Adèle, Ste-Agathe-des-Monts, and St-Jovite, among other stops. Limocar also has a service to the Lower Lauren-

tians region (including St-Jérôme), departing from the Laval bus terminal at the Métro Henri-Bourassa stop in north Montréal.
➤ CONTACTS: **Limocar Laurentides** (☏ 450/435–8899). **Montréal central bus station** (✉ 505 blvd. de Maisonneuve Est, Montréal, ☏ 514/842–2281). **Québec bus terminal** (✉ 320 rue Abraham-Martin, Québec City, ☏ 418/525–3000). **Voyageur** (☏ 514/842–2281, WEB www.voyageur.com).

CAR TRAVEL

Major entry points are Ottawa/Hull, U.S. 87 from New York State south of Montréal, U.S. 91 from Vermont into the Eastern Townships area, and the Trans-Canada Highway (Highway 1) just west of Montréal.

Québec has fine roads, and speedy drivers. The major highways are Autoroute des Laurentides 15, a six-lane highway from Montréal to the Laurentians; Autoroute 10 East from Montréal to the Eastern Townships; U.S. 91 from New England, which becomes Autoroute 55 as it crosses the border to the Eastern Townships; and Route 138, which runs from Montréal along the north shore of the St. Lawrence River. Road maps are available at Québec tourist offices.

Autoroute des Laurentides 15 and Route 117—a slower but more scenic secondary road at its northern end—lead to the Laurentians. Exit numbers on Autoroute 15 are the distance in kilometers from Montréal. Try to avoid traveling to and from the region Friday evening or Sunday afternoon, as you're likely to sit in traffic for hours.

Autoroute 10 East heads from Montréal through the Eastern Townships; from New England, U.S. 91 becomes Autoroute 55, a major road.

The main roads through the Charlevoix region are the scenic Route 362 and the faster Route 138.

On the Gaspé Peninsula, the Trans-Canada Highway (Highway 1) runs northeast along the southern shore of the St. Lawrence River to just south of Rivière-du-Loup, where the 270-km (167-mi) Route 132 hugs the dramatic coastline. At Ste-Flavie, follow the southern leg of Route 132. The entire distance around the peninsula is 848 km (526 mi).

EMERGENCIES

➤ CONTACTS: **Ambulance, fire, police** (☏ 911).
➤ HOSPITALS: **Centre Hospitalier de Charlevoix** (✉ 74 rue Ambroise-Fafard, Baie-Saint-Paul, ☏ 418/435–5150). **Centre Hospitalier de Gaspé** (✉ 215 blvd. York Ouest, Gaspé, ☏ 418/368–3301). **Centre Hospitalier Laurentien** (✉ 234 rue Saint-Vincent, Sainte-Agathe-des-Monts, ☏ 819/324–4000). **Centre Universitaire de Santé de l'Estrie** (**CUSE;** ✉ 560 rue Bowen Sud, Sherbrooke, ☏ 819/346–1110).

LODGING

`CAMPING`

Inquiries about camping in Québec's national parks should be directed to Canadian Heritage Parks Canada. Contact the individual park administration for camping in provincial parks. For information on camping in the province's private trailer parks and campgrounds, write for the free publication "Québec Camping," available from Tourisme Québec.
➤ CONTACTS: **Canadian Heritage Parks Canada** (✉Box 6060, Passage du Chien d'Or, Québec City G1R 4V7, ☏ 418/648–4177 or 800/463–6769, WEB www.parkscanada.pch.gc.ca). **Tourisme Québec** (✉ Box 979, Montréal H3C 2W3, ☏ 514/873–2015 or 800/363–7777, WEB www.tourisme.gouv.qc.ca).

Agricotours, the Québec farm-vacation association, can provide lists of guest farms in the province.

➤ CONTACTS: **Agricotours** (✉ 4545 av. Pierre-de-Coubertin, C.P. 1000, Succursale M, Montréal H1V 3R2, ☎ 514/252–3138, WEB www.agricotours.qc.ca).

OUTDOORS AND SPORTS

FISHING

Twenty outfitters are members of the Laurentian tourist association. The Fédération des Pourvoyeurs du Québec (Québec Outfitters Federation) has a list of outfitters that is available through tourist offices. Fishing requires a permit, available from the regional offices of the Ministère de l'Environnement et de la Faune (Ministry of the Environment and Wildlife), or at regional sporting-goods stores displaying an "authorized agent" sticker.

➤ CONTACTS: **Fédération des Pourvoyeurs du Québec** (✉ 5237 blvd. Hamel, Bureau 270, Québec City G2P 2H2, ☎ 418/877–5191, WEB www.fpq.com). **Ministère de l'Environnement et de la Faune** (✉ 675 blvd. René-Lévesque Est, Québec City G1R 5V7, ☎ 418/643–3127 or 800/561–1616, WEB www.menv.gouv.qc.ca).

MOUNTAIN CLIMBING

The Fédération Québécoise de la Montagne (Québec Mountain-Climbing Federation) has information about climbing, as do the province's tourist offices.

➤ CONTACTS: **Fédération Québécoise de la Montagne** (✉ 4545 rue Pierre-de-Coubertin, C.P. 1000, Succursale M, Montréal H1V 3R2, ☎ 514/252–3004).

RIVER RAFTING

Aventure en Eau Vive, Nouveau Monde, and Aventure Rivière Rouge —specializing in white-water rafting at Rivière Rouge—are on-site at the trip's departure point near Calumet. (To get here, take Route 148 past Calumet; turn onto chemin de la Rivière Rouge until you see the signs for the access road to each rafter's headquarters.) All offer four-to five-hour rafting trips and provide transportation to and from the river site, as well as guides, helmets, life jackets, and, at the end of the trip, a much-anticipated meal. Most have facilities on-site or nearby for dining, drinking, camping, bathing, swimming, hiking, and horseback riding.

➤ CONTACTS: **Aventure en Eau Vive** (☎ 819/242–6084 or 800/567–6881). **Aventure Rivière Rouge** (☎ 450/533–6996 or 888/723–8484). **Nouveau Monde** (☎ 819/242–7238 or 800/361–5033, WEB www.newworld.ca).

SKIING

Lift tickets range from $34 to $52. For information about ski conditions, you can call Tourisme Québec and ask for the ski report.

➤ CONTACTS: **Tourisme Québec** (☎ 800/363–7777).

SNOWMOBILING

Regional tourist offices have information about snowmobiling in their area, including snowmobile maps and lists of essential services. Snowmobilers who use trails in Québec must obtain an access pass or day user's pass for the trails. This increasingly popular activity is regulated by the Québec Federation of Snowmobiling Clubs.

Jonview Canada offers snowmobile tours in the Laurentians, in Charlevoix, and as far north as the James Bay region. Other week-long packages may include dogsledding and ice fishing.

➤ CONTACTS: **Jonview Canada** (✉ 1134 rue Ste-Catherine Ouest, 12th floor, Montréal, ☎ 514/861–9190). **Québec Federation of Snowmobiling Clubs** (✉ Box 1000, 4545 av. Pierre-de-Coubertin, Montréal H1V 3R2, ☎ 514/252–3076, WEB www.fcmq.qc.ca).

TOURS

The Montréal Zoological Society is a nature-oriented group that runs lectures, field trips, and weekend excursions. Tours include whale-watching in the St. Lawrence estuary and hiking and bird-watching in national parks throughout Québec, Canada, and the northern United States.

Autocar Dupont-Gray Line leads day excursions along the Côte de Beaupré, with stops at Montmorency Falls and the Ste-Anne-de-Beaupré basilica. The cost is about $35 per person.

Trips from Percé to Bonaventure Island off the Gaspé Peninsula are offered by Croisières Baie de Gaspé, Agences Touristiques de Gaspé, and Les Bateliers de Percé.
➤ CONTACTS: **Agences Touristiques de Gaspé** (☎ 418/892–5629). **Autocar Dupont-Gray Line** (☎ 418/649–9226). **Les Bateliers de Percé** (☎ 418/782–2974). **Croisières Baie de Gaspé** (☎ 418/892–5500). **Montréal Zoological Society** (☎ 514/845–8317).

TRAIN TRAVEL

The railway line follows the coast. On the south shore, VIA trains stop at Rimouski, Mont-Joli, Matapédia, Carleton, Gaspé, and Percé.
➤ TRAIN INFORMATION: **VIA Rail** (☎ 514/989–2626; 800/361–5390 in Québec; 888/842–7245 outside Québec, WEB www.viarail.ca).

VISITOR INFORMATION

Tourisme Québec can provide information on specific towns' tourist bureaus.

In the Laurentians, the major tourist office is the Association Touristique des Laurentides, just off the Autoroute des Laurentides 15 at Exit 39. The office is open mid-June through August, daily 8:30–8; September to mid-June, Saturday through Thursday 9–5, Friday 9–7. The towns of L'Annonciation, Labelle, Mont-Tremblant, St-Jovite, Ste-Agathe-des-Monts, St-Eustache, St-Adolphe-d'Howard, and Val David have year-round regional tourist offices. Seasonal tourist offices (open mid-June to early September) are in Grenville, Lachute, St-Jérôme, Oka, Notre-Dame-du-Laus, Saint-Sauveur, Sainte-Marguerite-du-Lac-Masson, Nominique, Lac-du-Cerf, and Ferme Neuve.

In the Eastern Townships, year-round regional provincial tourist offices are in Bromont, Granby, Lac Mégantic, Magog-Orford, Sherbrooke, Sutton, Ulverton, La Patrie, and Exit 68 off Autoroute 10. Seasonal tourist offices (open June to early September) are in Coaticook, Danville, Dunham, Eastman, Frelighsburg, Granby, Lambton, Masonsville, Birchton, Cowansville, Dudswell, Lac-Brome (Foster), Waterloo, and Pike River. The schedules of seasonal bureaus are irregular, so it's a good idea to contact the Association Touristique des Cantons de l'Est before visiting. This association also provides lodging information.

On the way from Québec City to Charlevoix, look for the Beaupré Coast Interpretation Center off Highway 360 in Château-Richer. The old mill Petit-Pré (built in 1695) serves as the backdrop for guides in New France costumes to explain displays on the history of the region. Admission is $2.50. The center is open from mid-June to mid-October, daily 10–5 (by reservation only the rest of the year).
➤ TOURIST INFORMATION: **Association Touristique des Cantons de l'Est** (✉ 20 rue Don Bosco Sud, Sherbrooke, ☎ 819/820–2020 or 800/355–

5755, WEB www.tourisme-cantons.qc.ca). **Association Touristique de la Gaspésie** (✉ 357 rte. de la Mer, Ste-Flavie, ☎ 418/775–2223 or 800/ 463–0323, WEB www.tourisme-gaspesie.com). **Association Touristique des Laurentides** (✉ 14142 rue de la Chapelle, Mirabel, ☎ 450/436– 8532 or 800/561–6673, WEB www.laurentides.com). **Association Touris-tique Régionale de Charlevoix** (✉ 630 blvd. de Comporté, C.P. 275, La Malbaie, ☎ 418/665–4454, WEB www.tourisme-charlevoix.com). **Beaupré Coast Interpretation Center** (✉ 7007 av. Royale, Château-Richer, ☎ 418/824–3677). **Tourisme Québec** (✉ C.P. 979, Montréal, ☎ 800/363–7777).

12 NEW BRUNSWICK

With the highest tides in the world carving a rugged coast and feeding more whales than you can imagine, New Brunswick can be a phenomenal adventure. White sandy beaches, lobsters in the pot, and cozy inns steeped in history make it easy to have a relaxing interlude, too. And with fine art galleries, museums, and a dual Acadian and Loyalist heritage, the province is an intriguing cultural destination.

By Ana Watts

NEW BRUNSWICK IS WHERE the great Canadian forest, sliced by sweeping river valleys and modern highways, meets the sea. It's an old place in New World terms, and the remains of a turbulent past are still evident in some of its quiet nooks. Near Moncton, for instance, wild strawberries perfume the air of the grassy slopes of Fort Beauséjour, where, in 1755, one of the last battles for possession of Acadia took place—the English finally overcoming the French. The dual heritage of New Brunswick (35% of its population is Acadian French) provides added spice. Other areas of the province were settled by the British and by Loyalists, American colonists who chose to live under British rule after the American Revolution. If you stay in both Acadian and Loyalist regions, a trip to New Brunswick can seem like two vacations in one.

In fact, a wide range of experience is possible in Canada's only officially bilingual province. For every gesture as grand as the giant rock formations carved by the Bay of Fundy tides, there is one as subtle as the gifted touch of a sculptor in her studio. For every experience as colorful as salmon and fiddleheads served at a church supper, there is another as low-key as the gentle waves of the Baie des Chaleurs. New Brunswick is the luxury of an inn with five stars, or the tranquillity of camping under a million.

At the heart of New Brunswick is the forest, which covers 85% of the province's entire area—nearly all its interior. The forest drives the economy, defines the landscape, and delights hikers, anglers, campers, and bird-watchers.

But New Brunswick's soul is the sea. The largest of Canada's three maritime provinces, New Brunswick is largely surrounded by coastline. The warm waters of the Baie des Chaleurs, Gulf of St. Lawrence, and Northumberland Strait lure swimmers to their sandy beaches. The chilly Bay of Fundy, with its monumental tides, draws breaching whales, whale-watchers, and kayakers.

In this part of the country traditions endure and family ties are strong. It is a strength born of adversity. Rich forests and oceans notwithstanding, the economy here is not robust. Over the years some of the best and the brightest have gone down the road to central and western Canada to make their marks. Now many bright young New Brunswickers are traveling down another road—the Information Highway, with its ever-expanding opportunities for them to stay at home and work "virtually" anywhere.

Pleasures and Pastimes

Beaches

There are two kinds of saltwater beaches in New Brunswick: warm and c-c-c-cold. The warm beaches are along the east coast. At Parlee it's sand castles, sunscreen, and a little beach volleyball on the side. If sand and solitude are more your style, try Kouchibouguac National Park and its 26 km (16 mi) of beaches and dunes.

The cold beaches are on the Bay of Fundy, on the province's southern coast. The highest tides in the world (a *vertical* difference of as much as 48 ft) have carved some spectacular caves, crevices, and cliffs. There are some sandy beaches, and hardy souls do swim in the "invigorating" salt water. The extreme tides make it possible to explore rich tidal pools and walk on the flats at low tide. Beaches like Cape Enrage combine salt air and opportunities for thrilling adventures such as rappeling. Others, like the beach at Marys Point, where you can see thousands of semipalmated plovers take flight, allow you to observe awesome natural sights.

Dining

Cast your line just about anywhere in New Brunswick and you catch some kind of fish-and-chips. Just about any restaurant in any coastal community has its own great chowder, but catching fresh seafood usually means a trip to a better restaurant. New Brunswick's oysters, scallops, clams, crabs, mussels, lobsters, and salmon are worth it. Some seafood is available seasonally, but now that salmon is farmed extensively, this taste of heaven is available anytime, and the price is very reasonable. What New Brunswick serves best and most often is comfort food. Ham and scalloped potatoes, turkey dinners, pork chops, and even liver and onions are staples on many menus. The beer of choice is Moosehead, brewed in Saint John.

A spring delicacy is fiddleheads—emerging ostrich ferns that look like the curl at the end of a violin neck. These emerald gems are picked along riverbanks as the freshet recedes, then boiled and sprinkled with lemon juice or vinegar and butter, salt, and pepper. Summer ends with wild blueberries—delicately flavored dark pearls—sprinkled on cereal, baked in muffins, or stewed with dumplings in a grunt. New Brunswickers also eat dulse, a dried purple seaweed, as salty as potato chips and as compelling as peanuts, whenever the mood hits. You'll find it on Grand Manan Island, in the Old Saint John City Market, and in barrels for tasting at some seafood restaurants.

CATEGORY	COST*
$$$$	over $32
$$$	$22–$32
$$	$13–$21
$	under $13

per person, in Canadian dollars, for a main course at dinner

Lodging

Among its more interesting options, New Brunswick has a number of officially designated Heritage Inns. These historically significant establishments run the gamut from elegant to homey; many have antique china and furnishings. Cottage clusters are springing up in coastal communities, and Saint John, Moncton, and Fredericton each have a link in first-rate hotel chains. Accommodations are at a premium in summer, so reserve ahead.

CATEGORY	COST*
$$$$	over $200
$$$	$150–$200
$$	$100–$150
$	under $100

All prices are for a standard double room, excluding 15% harmonized sales tax (HST), in Canadian dollars.

Outdoor Activities and Sports

BIKING

Byroads, lanes, and an emerging network of multiuse trails run through small towns, along the ocean, and into the forest. Bikers can set out on their own or try a guided adventure.

FISHING

Dotted with freshwater lakes, crisscrossed with fish-laden rivers, and bordered by 1,129 km (700 mi) of seacoast, this province is one of Canada's natural treasures. Anglers are drawn by the bass fishing and such world-famous salmon rivers as the Miramichi. Commercial fishers often take visitors line fishing for groundfish.

GOLF

Golf is an increasingly popular sport, and a continuing program to upgrade even the best courses to championship and signature status, and to construct new courses, has enjoyed great success.

WHALE-WATCHING

One unforgettable New Brunswick experience is the sighting of a huge humpback, right whale, finback, or minke. Outfitters along the Bay of Fundy take people to see a variety of whales. Most trips run from May through September.

WINTER SPORTS

New Brunswick can get as much as 16 ft of snow each year, so winter fun often lasts well into spring. Dogsledding is taking off, ice-fishing communities pop up on many rivers, and tobogganing, skating, and snowshoeing are popular. Snowmobiling has boomed: there are more than 9,000 km (5,580 mi) of groomed, marked, and serviced snowmobile trails and dozens of snowmobile clubs hosting special events.

For cross-country skiers, New Brunswick has groomed trails at Mactaquac Provincial Park near Fredericton, Fundy National Park in Alma, and Kouchibouguac National Park between Moncton and Miramichi. Many communities and small hotels offer groomed trails, but skiers can also set off on their own. New Brunswick downhill ski areas usually operate mid-December through April. There are four ski hills—Farlagne, Crabbe, Poley, and Sugarloaf.

Shopping

Fine art galleries display and sell local artists' paintings and sculptures. Crafts galleries, shops, and fairs brim with jewelry, glass, pottery, clothing, furniture, and leather goods. Some of the province's better bookstores have sections devoted to New Brunswick authors. Saint John, Fredericton, and Moncton all have their share of fine art and crafts studios, galleries, and farmers' markets. Saint John has wonderful antiques, Fredericton can claim a bit of haute couture, and the Moncton area has the biggest malls. The shops in the resort town of St. Andrews are artistic, eclectic, and sophisticated.

Exploring New Brunswick

In recent years high-tech companies in New Brunswick have helped lead much of the world onto the Information Highway, but all that has done little to change settlement patterns. The population still clings to the original highways—rivers and ocean. In fact, the St. John River in the west and the Fundy and Acadian coasts in the south and east essentially encompass the province.

The Fundy Coast is phenomenal. Yachts, fishing boats, and tankers bob on the waves at high tide, then sit high and dry on the ocean floor when the tide goes out. The same tides force the mighty St. John River to reverse its flow in the old city of Saint John. The southwestern shores have spawned more than their share of world-class artists, authors, actors, and musicians. Maybe it's the Celtic influence; maybe it's the fog.

Along the Acadian Coast the water is warm, the sand is fine, and the accent is French—except in the middle. Where the Miramichi River meets the sea, there is an island of First Nations, English, Irish, and Scottish tradition that is unto itself, rich in folklore and legend. Many people here find their livelihood in the forests, in the mines, and on the sea.

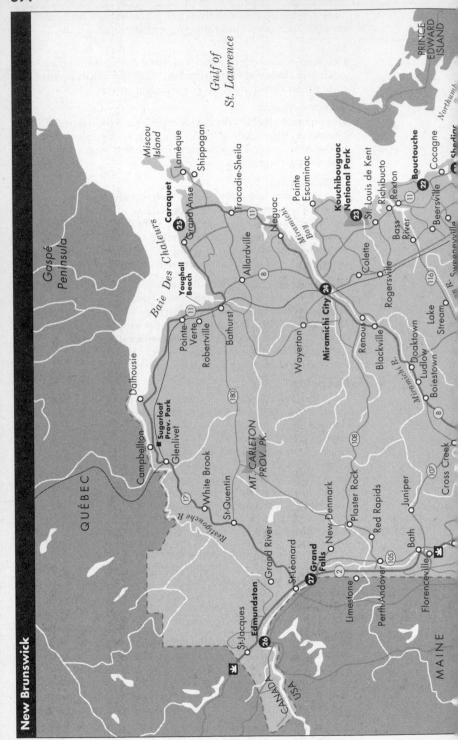

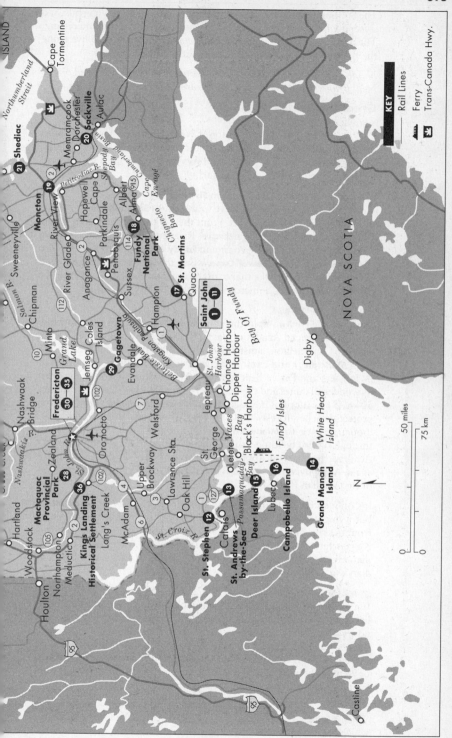

KEY
—— Rail Lines
🚢 Ferry
🛡 Trans-Canada Hwy.

NOVA SCOTIA

Bay Of Fundy

N

50 miles
75 km

ISLAND

Cape Tormentine
Northumberland Strait
21 Shediac
19 Moncton
River View
20 Sackville
Memramcook
Dorchester
Aulac
Petitcodiac R.
Sweeneyville
Salmon R.
Chipman
Minto
Grand Lake
10
Hopewell Cape
Parkindale
Penobsquis
18 Albert
Alma 915
Fundy National Park
Cape Enrage
Chignecto Bay
Shepody Bay
Cumberland Basin
River Glade
Anagance
Sussex
114
112
Jemseg
Coles Island
29 Gagetown
Evandale
Belleisle Bay
Hampton
1
17 St. Martins
Quaco
Saint John 1 - 11
St. John Harbour
Chance Harbour
Dipper Harbour
Lepreau
Maces Bay
Black's Harbour
Olette
Dipper Harbour
Fundy Isles
White Head Island
Digby
Kingston Peninsula
7
Welsford
Fredericton 30 - 35
Nashwaak
Zealand
Nashwaaksis R. Bridge
28
36
Mactaquac Provincial Park
Kings Landing Historical Settlement
Oromocto
Upper Brockway
Lawrence Sta.
Oak Hill
St. George
Passamaquoddy Bay
13
15 Deer Island
16 Lubec
Campobello Island
14 Grand Manan Island
Hartland
Woodstock
Northampton
Meductic
105
2
Long's Creek
McAdam
4
3
127
1
St. Croix R.
St. Stephen 12
Calais
St. Andrews by-the-Sea
Houlton
Castine
9
9
102
102
2
6

The St. John River valley scenery is panoramic—gently rolling hills and sweeping forests, with just enough rocky gorges to keep it interesting. The native peoples, French, English, Scots, and Danes who live along the river, ensure its culture is equally intriguing.

Numbers in the text correspond to numbers in the margin and on the New Brunswick, Downtown Saint John, and Fredericton maps.

Great Itineraries

IF YOU HAVE 4 DAYS

Plan to concentrate on one region if you have only a few days. Start on the Fundy Coastal Route. Art, history, nature, and seafood abound in the resort community of **St. Andrews by-the-Sea** ⑬. Whale-watching tours leave from the town wharf.

The Fundy Coastal Drive begins in **St. Stephen** ⑫ and winds about 100 km (62 mi) along the shore to the venerable city of **Saint John** ①–⑪, steeped in English and Irish traditions. From the Fundy Coastal Drive, Route 121 moves inland, up the Kennebecasis River past Sussex and meets Route 114; that leads back to the coast and **Fundy National Park** ⑱. Head up to **Cape Enrage** and **Hopewell Cape,** where the Fundy tides have sculpted gigantic flower-pot rocks that turn into islands at high tide. Finish the trip with **Moncton** ⑲, a microcosm of New Brunswick culture.

IF YOU HAVE 7 DAYS

With seven days for exploring you can add an Acadian Coastal experience. The official Acadian Coastal Drive Route is well marked from Aulac to Campbellton, a distance of about 400 km (248 mi). Head north from **Moncton** ⑲ and explore the area around **Shediac** ㉑, famous for its lobsters and Parlee Beach. **Bouctouche** ㉒ is just beyond that, with its wonderful dunes and the make-believe land of La Sagouine. Another 50 km (31 mi) north is unspoiled **Kouchibouguac National Park** ㉓, which protects beaches, forests, and peat bogs. The coastal drive from Kouchibouguac Park to **Miramichi City** ㉔, about 75 km (47 mi), passes through several bustling fishing villages. Most of the communities are Acadian, but as you approach Miramichi City, English dominates again. A stopover here positions you perfectly to begin your exploration of the Acadian Peninsula.

It's only about 120 km (74 mi) from Miramichi City to **Caraquet** ㉕, but it might as well be a million. The entire peninsula is so different from the rest of the province it's like a trip to a foreign country: this is a romantic land with a dramatic history and an artistic flair. The Acadian Historical Village is a careful re-creation of the traditional Acadian way of life.

IF YOU HAVE 10 DAYS

With 10 days to explore New Brunswick you can hit most of the highlights. Your explorations of the Acadian Peninsula end in Bathurst, and now you begin the ride over to the western edge of the province. Drive the coast (114 km, or 71 mi) to Campbellton and nearby Sugarloaf Provincial Park. Route 17 from Campbellton to St-Léonard (159 km, or 99 mi) is breathtaking in the autumn, and the detour to Mount Carleton Provincial Park (with the highest peak in the Maritimes) is a must for those who value a wilderness experience.

When you reach St-Léonard, you are on the River Valley Scenic Drive, which begins upriver in St-Jacques and runs all the way down the St. John River valley and back to the city of Saint John. Begin with the New Brunswick Botanical Gardens in **St-Jacques,** just outside **Edmundston** ㉖. The drive from here to **Fredericton** ㉚–㉟ is about 275 km (171 mi) of panoramic pastoral and river scenery, including a dramatic gorge and waterfall at **Grand Falls** ㉗. With its Gothic cathedral, Victorian architecture, museums, and riverfront pathways, Fredericton is a beautiful, historic, and cultural stopping place. Nearby **Kings Landing Historical Settlement** ㊱ provides a faithful depiction of life on the river in the last century. The drive from Fredericton to Saint John is just over 100 km (62 mi); about halfway between the two is the village of **Gagetown** ㉙, a must-see for those who love art and history.

When to Tour New Brunswick

Late spring through fall are lovely times to visit, although winter sports lovers have plenty of options. Whales are more plentiful in the Bay of Fundy after the first of August. Festivals celebrating everything from jazz to salmon are held from late spring until early fall. Many communities have festivities for Canada Day (July 1), and on the Acadian Peninsula many festivals, including the unique Blessing of the Fleet, are clustered around the August 15 Acadian national holiday. Fall colors are at their peak from mid-September through mid- or late October. The **Autumn Colours Line** (☎ 800/268–3255) provides daily information on where fall foliage is at its best.

SAINT JOHN

Like any seaport worth its salt, Saint John is a welcoming place. The natives welcomed Samuel de Champlain and Sieur de Monts when they landed here on St. John the Baptist Day in 1604. Nearly two centuries later, in May 1783, 3,000 British Loyalists—fleeing the aftermath of the American Revolutionary War—poured off a fleet of ships to make a home amid the rocks and forests. Two years later (1785) the city of Saint John was incorporated, the first in Canada.

Although most of the Loyalists were English, there were some Irish among them. Following the Napoleonic Wars in 1815, thousands more Irish workers found their way to Saint John. It was the potato famine that spawned the largest influx of Irish immigrants though; a 20-ft Celtic Cross on Partridge Island at the entrance to Saint John Harbor stands as a reminder of the hardships and suffering they endured. Their descendants make Saint John Canada's most Irish city, an undisputed fact that is celebrated in grand style each March, with a weeklong St. Patrick's festival.

Saint John remains a welcoming place—just ask the thousands of visitors who stream ashore from the dozens of cruise ships that dock at downtown Pugsley Wharf each year. They are greeted with music, flowers and cheerful people ready and willing to help in any way they can.

All the comings and goings over the centuries have exposed Saint Johners to a wide variety of cultures and ideas, and made it a sophisticated city in a friendly Maritime way. Major provincial artists like Jack Humphrey, Millar Brittain, Fred Ross, and Herzl Kashetsky were born here, as were Hollywood notables like Louis B. Mayer, Donald Sutherland, and Walter Pidgeon.

Industry and salt air have combined to give parts of this city a weatherbeaten quality, but you can also find lovingly restored redbrick homes as well as modern office buildings, hotels, and shops.

Downtown Saint John

An ambitious urban renewal program undertaken in the early 1980s spruced up the waterfront and converted old warehouses into trendy restaurants and shops. Underground and overhead walkways connect several attractions and shops in the area.

A Good Walk

Saint John is a city on hills, and **King Street** ①, its main street, slopes steeply to the harbor. A system of escalators, elevators, and skywalks inside buildings means you can climb to the top and take in some of the more memorable spots without effort; you can also walk outside if you wish. Start at the foot of King, **Market Slip** ②. This is where the Loyalists landed in 1783 and is the site of **Barbour's General Store** and the Little Red Schoolhouse. At Market Square, restored waterfront buildings house historic exhibits, shops, restaurants, and cafés. Also here are the Saint John Regional Library, a year-round visitor information center, and the fine **New Brunswick Museum** ③.

From the second level of Market Square, a skywalk crosses St. Patrick Street, and an escalator takes you up into the City Hall shopping concourse. Here, if you wish, you can branch off to the Canada Games Aquatic Centre and its pools and fitness facilities, or to Harbor Station, with its busy schedule of concerts, sporting events, and trade shows. Once you are through City Hall, another skywalk takes you across Chipman Hill and into the Brunswick Square Complex of shops, offices, and a hotel. To visit historic **Loyalist House** ④, exit onto Germain Street and turn left; it's on the corner at the top of the hill. Continue on for a block to see the venerable **St. John's (Stone) Church** ⑤. In the flavorful **Old City Market** ⑥, across from Brunswick Square, make your way past fish- and cheesemongers, butchers, greengrocers, sandwich makers, and craftspeople. When you leave by the door at the top of the market, you arrive at the head of King Street and right across Charlotte Street from **King's Square** ⑦. Take a walk through the square, past the statues and bandstand, to Sydney Street. Cross Sydney and you're in the **Loyalist's Old Burial Ground** ⑧. Make your way back to Sydney Street and then cross King Street East to the **Old Courthouse** ⑨ with its spiral staircase. Head south on Sydney; turn right on King's Square South and you're at the handsome Imperial Theatre. Follow King's Square South and cross Charlotte Street to reach the back door of historic **Trinity Church** ⑩.

To end your walk, make your way back to King Street and walk down the hill toward the water. Notice the plaque near the corner of Canterbury Street (at 20 King Street) that identifies a site where Benedict Arnold operated a coffeehouse. **Prince William Street** ⑪ is at the foot of the hill, just steps from where you began at Market Slip. Turn left for antiques shops, galleries, and historic architecture.

TIMING

Allow the better part of a day for this walk, if you include a few hours for the New Brunswick Museum and some time for shopping. You can walk the route in a couple of hours, though. On Sunday some of the indoor walkways are closed, as is the City Market.

Sights to See

Barbour's General Store. This 19th-century shop, now a museum, is filled with the aromas of tobacco, smoked fish, peppermint sticks, and dulse, an edible seaweed. There's an old post office and barber shop, too. ⊠ *Market Slip,* ☎ *506/658–2939.*

❶ **King Street.** The steep main street of the city is lined with solid Victorian redbrick buildings filled with a variety of shops.

❼ **King's Square.** Laid out in a Union Jack pattern, this green refuge has a two-story bandstand and a number of monuments. The mass of metal on the ground in its northeast corner is actually a great lump of melted stock from a neighboring hardware store that burnt down in Saint John's Great Fire of 1877, in which hundreds of buildings were destroyed. ⊠ *Between Charlotte and Sydney Sts.*

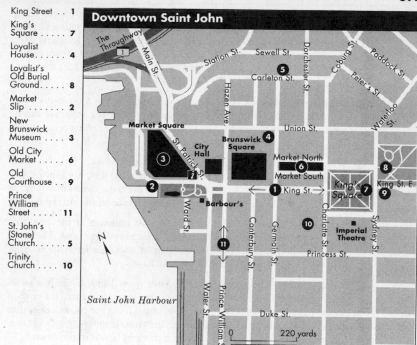

Downtown Saint John

④ **Loyalist House.** David Daniel Merritt, a wealthy Loyalist merchant, built this imposing Georgian structure in 1810. It is distinguished by its authentic period furniture and eight fireplaces. July through August the mayor hosts a tea party here each Wednesday afternoon. ✉ *120 Union St.,* ☎ *506/652-3590.* ✇ *$3.* ⏰ *June, weekdays 10–5; July–Aug., daily 10–5; Sept.–May, by appointment.*

⑧ **Loyalist's Old Burial Ground.** This cemetery, now a landscaped park, is like a history book published in stone. Brick walkways, gardens, and a beaver-pond fountain make it a delightful spot. ✉ *Off Sydney St., between King and E. Union Sts.*

② **Market Slip.** The waterfront area at the foot of King Street is where the Loyalists landed in 1783. Today it's the site of the Saint John Hilton, an amphitheater, restaurants, and Market Square, but it still conveys a sense of the city's maritime heritage. A floating wharf accommodates boating visitors to the city and those waiting for the tides to be right so they can sail up the St. John River.

★ ☾ ③ **New Brunswick Museum.** Delilah, a suspended full-size right whale skeleton, is on the natural-history level of this fine museum. You can hike along a geologic trail and watch the phenomenal Bay of Fundy tides rise and fall in a glass tube. The province's industrial, social, and artistic history is creatively displayed, and outstanding local, regional, and international art work hangs in fine galleries. The Family Discovery Gallery, with lots of fun and educational games, and a gift shop are also here. ✉ *Market Sq.,* ☎ *506/643-2300,* WEB *www.gov.nb.ca/nbmuseum.* ✇ *$6.* ⏰ *Mid-May–Oct., Mon.–Wed. and Fri. 9–5, Thurs. 9–9, weekends noon–5; Nov.–mid-May, Tues., Wed. and Fri. 9–5, Thurs. 9–9, weekends noon–5.*

6 **Old City Market.** The 1876 inverted ship's–keel ceiling of this handsome market occupies a city block between Germain and Charlotte Streets. Its temptations include live and fresh-cooked lobsters, great cheeses, dulse, and tasty, inexpensive snacks, along with plenty of souvenir and crafts items. ⊠ *47 Charlotte St.,* ☎ *506/658–2820.* ☉ *Mon.– Thurs. 7:30–6, Fri. 7:30–7, Sat. 7:30–5.*

9 **Old Courthouse.** This 1829 neoclassical building has a three-story spiral staircase built of tons of unsupported stones. The staircase can be seen year-round during business hours, except when court is in session. ⊠ *King St. E and Sydney St.* ☜ *Free.*

11 **Prince William Street.** South of King Street near Market Slip, this street is full of historic bank and business buildings that now hold shops, galleries and restaurants. At the foot of the street is the lamp known as the Three Sisters, which was erected in 1848 to guide ships into the harbor.

5 **St. John's (Stone) Church.** The first stone building in the city, this church was built for the garrison posted at nearby Fort Howe. The stone was brought from England as ships' ballast. ⊠ *87 Carleton St.,* ☎ *506/ 634–1474.* ☉ *Guided tours weekdays 10–4.*

10 **Trinity Church.** The present church dates from 1880, when it was rebuilt after the Great Fire. Inside, over the west door, there's a coat of arms—a symbol of the monarchy—rescued from the council chamber in Boston by a British colonel during the American Revolution. It was deemed a worthy refugee and given a place of honor in the church. ⊠ *115 Charlotte St.,* ☎ *506/693–8558 for hours.*

Greater Saint John

This may be the largest city in New Brunswick, but you can be on a secluded beach, talking to the harbor seals and listening to the birds, within 10 minutes of getting into your car on a downtown street. And you'll still be within the city limits.

A Good Drive

From Market Square in downtown Saint John, head west in your car (or on any westbound bus) to see the **Reversing Falls.** Go up St. Patrick Street, cross the viaduct, and you are on Main Street. Drive to the top of the hill and turn left on Douglas Avenue, with its grand old homes. A right off Douglas Avenue onto Fallsview Drive takes you to a Reversing Falls lookout and the Reversing Falls Jet Boat Ride. Return to Douglas Avenue, turn right, and keep right to cross the Reversing Falls Bridge. At the end of the bridge, on your left, is the Reversing Falls Tourist Bureau. The west side is home to **Carleton Martello Tower.** Turn left from the Reversing Falls Tourist Bureau, past the Simms Brush Factory, and bear left when the road splits. The rest of the way is well marked. You're also near **Irving Nature Park** (off Route 1 at Catherwood Drive if you're on the highway), 600 acres of volcanic rock and forest that are a haven for wildlife and hikers. There's more exotic wildlife at **Cherry Brook Zoo,** northeast of downtown. The zoo is part of **Rockwood Park,** the largest in-city park in Canada.

TIMING

To appreciate the Reversing Falls fully takes time; you need to visit at high, slack, and low tides. Check with any visitor information office for these times to help you plan a visit.

Sights to See

Carleton Martello Tower. The tower, a great place from which to survey the harbor and Partridge Island, was built during the War of 1812 as a precaution against an American attack. Guides tell you about the spartan life of a soldier living in the stone fort, and an audiovisual presentation outlines its role in the defense of Saint John during World War II. ⊠ *Whipple St. at Fundy Dr.,* ☎ *506/636–4011.* ☞ *$2.50.* ☉ *June–Labor Day daily 9–5; early–Sept.–mid-Oct. by appointment.*

⚬ **Cherry Brook Zoo.** An entertaining monkey house, wildebeests, and other exotic species are highlights of this small zoo. There's a trail featuring extinct-animal exhibits. ⊠ *901 Foster Thurston Dr.,* ☎ *506/634–1440.* ☞ *$6.* ☉ *Daily 10–dusk.*

Irving Nature Park. The ecosystems of the southern New Brunswick coast are preserved in this lovely 600-acre park on a peninsula close to downtown. Roads and seven walking trails (up to several kilometers long) make bird- and nature-watching easy. From downtown take Route 1 west to Exit 107 (Catherwood Road) south; follow Sand Cove Road 4½ km (3 mi) to the park. ⊠ *Sand Cove Rd.,* ☎ *506/634–7135 for seasonal access.* ☞ *Free.*

Reversing Falls. The strong Fundy tides rise faster than the river can empty twice daily at the Reversing Falls rapids, and the tide water pushes the river water back upstream. When the tide ebbs, the river once again pours over the rock ledges and the rapids appear to reverse themselves. To learn more about the phenomenon, watch the film shown at the Reversing Falls Tourist Bureau. There's a restaurant here, too. A jet boat provides a closer (and wetter) look. A pulp mill on the bank is less scenic, and the smell it occasionally emits is a less charming part of a visit. ⊠ *Rte. 100, Reversing Falls Bridge,* ☎ *506/658–2937.*

Rockwood Park. Encompassing 2,000 acres, this is the largest in-city park in Canada. There are hiking trails through the forest, 13 lakes, several sandy beaches, a campground, a golf course with an aquatic driving range, the Cherry Brook Zoo, and a unique play park for people of all ages. ⊠ *main entrance off Crown St.,* ☎ *506/658–2883.* ☉ *Daily 10–dusk.*

Dining and Lodging

$$–$$$ ✕ **Beatty and the Beastro.** Quaint, quirky (check out the specially made plates), and next to the Imperial Theatre, this place hops at lunchtime as well as before and after the theater. The frequently changing menu, with its distinctive European accent, takes advantage of local and seasonal meat, seafood, and produce. Breads and soups are specialties, with lines on Scotch broth day (the last stop for the local spring lamb). ⊠ *60 Charlotte St., at King's Sq.,* ☎ *506/652–3888. AE, DC, MC, V.*

$$–$$$ ✕ **Billy's Seafood Company.** It's a restaurant, it's an oyster bar, it's a fish market—it's lots of fun, too, with jazzy background music and funny, fishy paintings. The oysters Rockefeller are served with a hint of Pernod. Billy's Seafood Splash is a lobster surrounded by sautéed scallops, steamed clams, and mussels. Live and cooked lobsters can be packed to go. ⊠ *Old City Market, Charlotte St. entrance,* ☎ *506/672–3474 or 888/933–3474. AE, DC, MC, V.*

$$–$$$ ✕ **Suwanna Restaurant.** If you're lucky, Thai duck will be on the menu the night you try this authentic Thai restaurant. The wine cellar is outstanding, and green and yellow curries are always available. The signature dish, Suwanna chicken, is a stir-fry of chicken, sweet peppers, and hot peppers drizzled with dark sauce. The flavor is delicate and unique (and not too spicy, unless you actually eat one of the hot peppers). ⊠ *325 Lancaster Ave.,* ☎ *506/637–9015. MC, V. No lunch.*

$–$$$ ✕ **Grannan's.** Seafood brochette with scallops, shrimp, and lobster tail, sautéed at your table in a white wine and mushroom sauce, is a favorite in this nautically decorated restaurant. The desserts, including bananas Foster flambéed at your table, are memorable. Dining spills over onto the sidewalk in summer. ✉ *1 Market Sq.,* ☎ *506/634–1555. AE, DC, MC, V.*

$–$$$ ✗ **Incredible Edibles.** Here you can enjoy down-to-earth food—biscuits, garlic-laden hummus, salads, pastas, and desserts—in cozy rooms or, in summer, on the outdoor terrace. The menu also includes classic French, vegetarian, and seafood dishes. ✉ *42 Princess St.,* ☎ *506/633–7554. AE, DC, MC, V. Closed Sun.*

$–$$$ ✗ **Steamer's Lobster Company.** This rustic spot is close to Market Square and across from Pugsley Terminal where the cruise ships dock. Servers dress like fishermen, and the décor is all about fishnets and lobster traps. Lobsters, mussels, and clams are steamed outside on the patio. Kids love it. ✉ *110 Water St.,* ☎ *506/648–2325. AE, DC, MC, V.*

$–$$ ✗ **Taco Pica.** This modest place is a slice of home for the Guatemalan refugees who run it as a worker's co-op. The atmosphere is colorful— ornamental parrots rule in the dining room—and the recipes are authentic: garlic, mint, coriander seeds, and cilantro rule in the kitchen. Frequently, a guitarist entertains on Friday and Saturday evenings. ✉ *96 Germain St.,* ☎ *506/633–8492. AE, DC, MC, V.*

$–$$ ✗ **Vito's.** The former pizza take-out joint now offers much more. The pizzas in this uptown location are still robust, with lots of fresh toppings, but many pasta choices as well as chicken, seafood, and veal dishes have been added to the menu. The setting is roadhouse meets Mediterranean. Weekends are busy. ✉ *1 Hazen Ave.,* ☎ *506/634–3900. AE, DC, MC, V.*

$$$ ✗▥ **Delta Brunswick Hotel.** Part of Brunswick Square, this hotel is in the heart of downtown Saint John. MRA's, a venerable department store that presided over the mercantile life of generations of Saint Johners, used to stand here. The hotel honors the old store in the names of some of its function rooms and in its courtly service. Rooms are large, modern, and comfortable. The entire hotel was renovated and refurbished in 2001. Shucker's Restaurant specializes in New Brunswick's best, including dishes made with local seafood, fiddleheads, and blueberries. This property is connected to shopping and entertainment facilities by the walkway that runs through much of Saint John. ✉ *39 King St., E2L 4W3,* ☎ *506/648–1981,* ℻ *506/658–0914,* 🌐 *www.deltahotels.com. 255 rooms. Restaurant, bar, pool, gym. AE, D, DC, MC, V.*

$$$ ✗▥ **Saint John Hilton.** In this Hilton, furnished in Loyalist décor, guest rooms overlook the harbor or the town. A pedestrian walkway system connects the 10-story property to uptown shops, restaurants, a library, a museum, an aquatic center, and a civic center. The large Turn of the Tide restaurant has terrific views of the harbor. Although the dining, with seafood and meat dishes, is pleasant at all times, the best meal is the Sunday brunch, with a long table full of dishes from the exotic to the tried-and-true. ✉ *1 Market Sq., E2L 4Z6,* ☎ *506/693–8484; 800/ 561–8282 in Canada,* ℻ *506/657–6610,* 🌐 *www.hilton.com. 197 rooms. Restaurant, bar, pool, gym. AE, D, DC, MC, V.*

$–$$$ ✗▥ **Shadow Lawn Inn.** Ten minutes from Saint John, this charming inn
★ is in an affluent suburb with tree-lined streets, palatial homes, tennis, golf, and a yacht club. With its clapboards and columns, antiques and amenities, this property fits right into the neighborhood. Some of the bedrooms have fireplaces; one suite has a whirlpool bath. The chef honed his skills in some of the finest upper-Canadian kitchens. His creative ideas are reflected in the dining room's Continental and seafood dishes. ✉ *3180 Rothesay Rd., Rothesay E2E 5V7,* ☎ *506/847–7539 or 800/561–4166,* ℻ *506/849–9238. 9 rooms, 2 suites. Restaurant. AE, DC, MC, V. CP.*

$$ ▥ **Inn on the Cove and Day Spa.** Near Irving Nature Park, and with
★ its back lawn terraced down to the ocean, this inn has as much character as its owners, who tape their delightful cooking show in the kitchen.

Bedrooms are furnished with local antiques, and several bathrooms include whirlpool tubs with ocean views and electric fireplaces. Dinner, available with advance reservations, is served in the informal Tide's Table dining room, with its massive fireplace and walls of windows overlooking the Bay of Fundy. Guests and nonguests can also, with reservations, receive health and beauty treatments at the inn's spa. ⊠ *1371 Sand Cove Rd. (Box 3113, Station B), E2M 4X7,* ☎ *506/672–7799 or 877/257–8080,* FAX *506/635–5455,* WEB *www.innonthecove.com. 3 rooms, 3 suites. Dining room, spa. MC, V. BP.*

$–$$ ☷ **Homeport Historic Inn c1858.** Graceful arches, fine antiques, Italian marble fireplaces, oriental carpets, and a maritime theme are all at home in these 19th-century twin mansions built by a prominent Saint John shipbuilding family. Together the two buildings make a large inn that commands stunning harbor views and is close to both downtown and the Reversing Falls. Each oversize room is elegant, unique, and equipped with modern amenities. One even has a skeleton in the closet. The hearty Rise & Dine Breakfast, included in the room rate, sets you up nicely for the day. ⊠ *60–80 Douglas Ave., E2K 1E4,* ☎ *506/672–7255 or 888/678–7678,* FAX *506/672–7250,* WEB *www.homeport.nb.ca. 6 rooms, 4 suites. Breakfast room, in-room VCRs. AE, MC, V. BP.*

$ ☷ **Earle of Leinster B&B.** This 1877 three-story brick home in the heart of one of the city's oldest residential areas is within easy walking distance of theaters, restaurants, and more. The in-house rooms are Victorian; rooms in the converted coachhouse in the courtyard include kitchenettes. Families, and some small pets (call ahead to see if yours qualifies) can be accommodated. Access to laundry facilities and a games room is included in the room rate. ⊠ *96 Leinster St., E2L 1J3,* ☎ *506/ 652–3275. 7 rooms. Breakfast room, kitchenettes (some), in-room VCRs, billiards, laundry. AE, MC, V. BP.*

Nightlife and the Arts

The Arts

Aitken Bicentennial Exhibition Centre (ABEC; ⊠ 20 Hazen Ave., ☎ 506/ 633–4870), in a former Carnegie library, has several galleries displaying the work of local artists and artisans as well as a hands-on science gallery for children. Admission is free. The **Imperial Theatre** (⊠ King's Sq., ☎ 506/633–9494), a beautifully restored 1913 vaudeville theater, is home to Saint John's theater, opera, ballet, and symphony productions as well as road shows. Summer tours ($2) are available Monday through Saturday, 10–6; winter tours are free, but must be arranged in advance.

Nightlife

Taverns and lounges, usually with music of some kind, provide lively nightlife. **D'Arcy Farrow's Pub** (⊠ 43 Princess St., ☎ 506/657–8939) has five rooms and a main stage area that regularly features live Celtic, jazz, and blues music. Top musical groups and other performers regularly appear at **Harbour Station** (⊠ 99 Station St., ☎ 506/657–1234). **O'Leary's Pub** (⊠ 46 Princess St., ☎ 506/634–7135), in the middle of the Trinity Royal Preservation Area, specializes in old-time Irish fun complete with Celtic performers; on Wednesday, Brent Mason, a well-known neofolk artist, starts the evening and then turns the mike over to the audience. **Tapps Brew Pub and Steak House** (⊠ 78 King St., ☎ 506/634–1957) pleases the over-30 population with jazz and blues.

Outdoor Activities and Sports

Boat Tours

The **Reversing Falls Jet Boat** (⊠ Fallsview Park, off Fallsview Dr., ☎ 506/634–8987 or 888/634–8987, WEB www.jetboatrides.com) offers you a choice of a 20-minute thrill ride in the heart of the Reversing Falls or a more sedate sightseeing tour along the falls and in through the port. Some age and size restrictions apply on certain rides. The cost is about $25 per person; child and family rates are available.

Kayaking

Kayaking along the Fundy coast is popular. **Eastern Outdoors** (⊠ Brunswick Square, King and Germain Sts., ☎ 506/634–1530 or 800/565–2925, WEB www.easternoutdoors.com) has single and double kayaks and offers lessons, tours, and white-water rafting. You can make arrangements over the phone or at the Eastern Outdoors retail store in Brunswick Square in downtown Saint John.

GOLF

The **Westfield Golf Club** (⊠ Exit 177 off Route 7, ☎ 506/757–2907 or 877/833–4662) is a venerable 18-hole course about 20 minutes outside the city.

Shopping

Brunswick Square (⊠ King and Germain Sts., ☎ 506/658–1000), a vertical mall, has many top-quality boutiques. **Handworks Gallery** (⊠ 12 King St., ☎ 506/652–9787) carries the best of professional crafts and fine art made in New Brunswick. **House of Tara** (⊠ 72 Prince William St., ☎ 506/634–8272) is wonderful for fine Irish linens and woolens. **Peter Buckland Gallery** (⊠ 80 Prince William St., ☎ 506/693–9721), open Wednesday through Saturday or by appointment, is an exceptionally fine gallery that carries paintings, drawings, and sculpture by Canadian artists. **Tim Isaac Antiques** (⊠ 97 Prince William St., ☎ 506/652–3222) has fine furniture, glass, china, Oriental rugs, and a well-informed staff; unique sales are often advertised in local papers. **Trinity Galleries** (⊠ 128 Germain St., ☎ 506/634–1611) represents fine Maritime and Canadian artists.

THE FUNDY COAST

Bordering the chilly and powerful tidal Bay of Fundy is some of New Brunswick's most dramatic coastline. This area extends from the border town of St. Stephen and the lovely resort village of St. Andrews, past tiny fishing villages and rocky coves, through Saint John and on to Fundy National Park, where the world's most extreme tides rise and fall twice daily. The Fundy Isles—Grand Manan Island, Deer Island, and Campobello—are havens of peace that have lured harried mainlanders for generations. Some of the impressive 50-km (31-mi) stretch of coastline between St. Martins and Fundy National Park is now accessible by the new Fundy Parkway, the Fundy Footpath (for hikers), and the Fundy Trail (multiuse, but not for motorized vehicles).

St. Stephen

⑫ *107 km (66 mi) west of Saint John.*

St. Stephen is across the St. Croix River from Calais, Maine. The small town is a mecca for chocoholics, who converge here during the Chocolate Festival held early in August. "Choctails," chocolate puddings and cakes, and even complete chocolate meals should come as no surprise when you learn that the chocolate bar was invented here. There's a provincial **visitor information center** (⊠ 5 King St., ☎ 506/466–7390) on King Street.

Ganong's famed, hand-dipped chocolates are available at the factory store, **Ganong Chocolatier.** ⊠ *73 Milltown Blvd.,* ☎ *506/465–5611.*

⊙ *Jan.–Apr., Mon.–Sat. 10–5; May, daily 9–5; June–Aug., weekdays 8–8, weekends 9–5; Sept.–Dec., daily 9–5.*

The Chocolate Museum, behind Ganong Chocolatier, explores the sweet history of candy making with hand-dipping demonstrations and hands-on exhibits. ⊠ *73 Milltown Blvd.,* ☎ *506/466–7848.* ⊡ *$4.* ⊙ *Nov.–Apr., Tues.–Sat. 9–5; May–Oct., Mon.–Sat. 10–8, Sun. 1–5.*

St. Andrews by-the-Sea

★ ⑬ *29 km (18 mi) southeast of St. Stephen.*

On Passamaquoddy Bay, St. Andrews by-the-Sea, a designated National Historic District, is one of North America's prettiest resort towns. It has long been a summer retreat of the affluent (mansions ring the town). Of the town's 550 buildings, 280 were erected before 1880, and 14 of those have survived from the 1700s. Some Loyalists even brought their homes with them piece by piece from Castile, Maine, across the bay, when the American Revolution didn't go their way.

Knowledgeable costumed guides from **Heritage Discovery Tours** (☎ 506/529–4011) conduct historical walking tours of St. Andrews. You can also take ghost tours in summer.

If you'd like to take a self-guided tour, pick up a walking-tour map at the visitor information center at 46 Reed Avenue (next to the arena) and follow it through the pleasant streets. A particular gem is the **Court House** (⊠ 123 Frederick St., ☎ 506/529–4248), which is still active. Within these old stone walls is the **Old Gaol**, home of the county's archives. In summer, tours are given weekdays 9–5. **Greenock Church,** at the corner of Montague and Edward Streets, owes its existence to a remark someone made at an 1822 dinner party about the "poor" Presbyterians not having a church of their own. Captain Christopher Scott, who took exception to the slur, spared no expense on the building, which is decorated with a carving of a green oak tree in honor of Scott's birthplace, Greenock, Scotland. **Water Street,** down by the harbor, has an assortment of eateries, gift and crafts shops, and artists' studios.

The **Ross Memorial Museum** is a monument to an American family, summer residents of St. Andrews, who appreciated beautiful things. Lovely 19th-century New Brunswick furniture and objets d'art fill the rooms. ⊠ *188 Montague St.,* ☎ *506/529–5124.* ⊡ *Donation.* ⊙ *Late June–Aug., Mon.–Sat. 10–4:30; Sept.–mid-Oct., Tues.–Sat. 10–4:30.*

With more than 40,000 plants on site, **Kingsbrae Gardens** is one of Canada's top 10 public gardens. It incorporates 27 acres of mature cedar hedges and rare Acadian old-growth forest from several fine estates with creative new plantings. Unusual and exotic flowers border the pathways—the rose and daylily collections are amazing—and towering trees line the woodland trail. There are gardens to attract butterflies, birds, and children; demonstration gardens that reveal the secrets of successful horticulture; and a garden maze. An art gallery and gift shop are housed in a stately mansion along with a café that serves light meals and decadent desserts. ⊠ *220 King St.,* ☎ *506/529–3335.* ⊡ *$7.* ⊙ *May–Oct., daily 9–6.*

Ⓒ The **Huntsman Aquarium and Museum** houses marine life and displays, including a teeming touch tank and some very entertaining seals fed at 11 and 4 daily. ⊠ *1 Lower Campus Rd.,* ☎ *506/529–1202.* ⊡ *$5.25.* ⊙ *May–June, daily 10–4:30; July–Aug., daily 10–6; Sept.–Oct., Mon.–Tues. noon–4:30, Wed.–Sun. 10–4:30.*

Dining and Lodging

$-$$$ ✕ **The Gables.** Salads, fish, and seafood as well as fresh-made desserts are served in this casual harborside eatery. The owner's art decorates the walls, and there's a deck for alfresco dining in summer. ⊠ *143 Water St.,* ☎ *506/529–3440. MC, V.*

$ ✕ **Sweet Harvest Market.** Known for its natural products and made-on-site breads, cookies, cakes, cheesecakes, and preserves, this is a casual bakery–deli that is always experimenting. At press time it was considering dinner items, too. ⊠ *182 Water St.,* ☎ *506/529–6249.*

$$$$ ✕⊞ **The Fairmont Algonquin.** This grand old resort hotel, where the
★   bellhops wear kilts and dinner is served on the wraparound veranda in fine weather, presides over town like an elegant dowager. The rooms have a feeling of relaxed refinement; the ones in the newer Prince of Wales wing are especially comfortable. In 2001 most of the rooms got a spruce-up, including new drapes, carpets and duvets; the traditional bathrooms were also modernized. The Passamaquoddy Dining Room is noted for its seafood and for regional dishes such as seared pork loin with local blueberry–balsamic vinegar sauce. The Right Whale Pub is a casual lunch and dinner option. The Library Lounge and Bistro is a year-round restaurant. ⊠ *184 Adolphus St., E0G 2X0,* ☎ *506/529–8823,* FAX *506/529–7162,* WEB *www.cphotels.ca. 238 rooms. 3 restaurants, 2 bars, pool, hair salon, massage, sauna, 18-hole golf course, 4 tennis courts, health club, racquetball, beach, bicycles, children's programs, meeting rooms. AE, DC, MC, V.*

$$$$ ✕⊞ **Windsor House.** The rooms in this restored 1798 Georgian home are exquisite, with antiques and fabrics true to the period. Note the fine art collection, unusual lighting fixtures, and attention to detail as you wander about the house. The food is amazing—especially the rack of lamb. The menus are built around locally grown produce and freshly baked goods. A good wine cellar, two quiet dining rooms, and a garden courtyard complete the experience. ⊠ *132 Water St., E5B 1A8,* ☎ *506/529–3330 or 888/890–9463,* FAX *506/529–4063,* WEB *www.townsearch.com/windsorhouse. 4 rooms, 2 suites. Dining room, bar, billiards. AE, D, DC, MC, V. BP.*

$$$-$$$$ ✕⊞ **Pansy Patch.** A visit to this B&B, a 1912 Normandy-style farm-
★   house with an art gallery, is a bit like a close encounter with landed gentry who are patrons of the arts and who like their gardens as rich and formal as their meals. Four rooms are in the Corey Cottage next door. All rooms have period furniture and are individually decorated. Afternoon tea and cookies are served wherever you like—in the dining room, in your room, in the garden, or on the deck overlooking the water. Non-lodgers are welcome for lunch and dinner. Entrées include seafood paella, beef tenderloin, and lobster. The price of a room here entitles you to use the pool and tennis courts of the Fairmont–Algonquin Hotel next door. ⊠ *59 Carleton St., E5B 1M8,* ☎ *506/529–3834 or 888/726–7972,* FAX *506/529–9042,* WEB *www.pansypatch.com. 9 rooms. Restaurant, concierge. MC, V. Closed mid-Oct.–mid-May. BP.*

$$$$ ⊞ **A. Hiram Walker Estate Heritage Inn.** This restored mansion, built for the Hiram Walker Distillery family in 1912, is gracious, elegant, and welcoming. All rooms have fireplaces; most have whirlpool baths. You can ask the owner about everything from the mustard she serves with your breakfast ham to the chandelier over the dining table. A converted carriage house has two additional rooms and an apartment. ⊠ *109 Reed Ave., E5B 2J6,* ☎ *506/529–4210 or 800/470–4088,* FAX *506/ 529–4311,* WEB *www.walkerestate.com. 9 rooms. Dining room, pool, library. AE, MC, V.*

$$$$ ⊞ **Kingsbrae Arms.** A member of Relais & Châteaux, this restored 1897
★   estate is an experience as much as it is a property. Eclectic and entertaining antique furnishings contribute to the classy décor. Pampering

touches are plentiful—roses and Belgian chocolates in the rooms, plush robes, a pantry stocked with biscotti, daily afternoon tea, and farewell gifts from local shops. The owners are gregarious, and you can expect excellent service. Guests celebrating a honeymoon or anniversary get champagne and red roses, as well as tickets to Kingsbrae Garden next door. In high season, breakfast and dinner are included in the room rate. The wine cellar is outstanding. ⊠ *219 King St., E5B 1Y1,* ☎ *506/ 529–1897,* FAX *506/529–1197,* WEB *www.kingsbrae.com. 5 rooms, 3 suites. Dining room, pool. MC, V.*

$–$$$ 🏠 **Treadwell Inn.** Gardens, a huge deck, and balconies all overlook the ocean at this gracious old inn. Built by a ships chandler about 1820, the inn has been faithfully restored and furnished to reflect the era. All the rooms are lovely, though the less expensive ones overlook the street. A healthy, hearty breakfast (included in the rate) is served in the big kitchen, which also has an ocean view. ⊠ *129 Water St., E5B 1A7,* ☎ *506/529–1011 or 888/529–1011,* FAX *506/529–4826,* WEB *www. townsearch.com/treadwell. 6 rooms. Kitchenettes (some), laundry service. AE, MC, V.*

$ 🏠 **Seaside Beach Resort.** If the click of a closing screen door sounds like summer at the beach to you, this waterfront cluster of cottages is your kind of place. At one end of the town's main street, it's close to all the action and a beach. The efficiency units are simple but comfortable and well equipped, right down to big pots for boiling lobsters. This is a terrific, casual spot for kids and dogs. ⊠ *339 Water St., E5B 2R2,* ☎ *506/529–3846 or 800/506–8677,* FAX *506/529–4479,* WEB *www.seaside.nb.ca. 24 cottages. Coin laundry. AE, MC, V.*

Outdoor Activities and Sports

St. Andrews Creative Playground (⊠ 168 Frederick St.) is an amazing wooden structure for climbing, swinging, performing, making music, and playing games. The **Sunbury Shores Arts & Nature Centre** (⊠ 139 Water St., ☎ 506/529–3386) offers art workshops in drawing, etching, painting, pottery, and many other media, in conjunction with environmental excursions.

GOLF

The **Algonquin Golf Club** (⊠ Off Rte. 127, ☎ 506/529–7124) has an 18-hole, par-72 signature course.

WATER SPORTS

The **Day Adventure Centre** (☎ 506/529–2600), open May through early September, can arrange explorations of Passamaquoddy Bay on various kinds of boats. **Fundy Tide Runners** (☎ 506/529–4481) uses a 24-ft Zodiac to search for whales, seals, and marine birds. The clipper **MV Corey** (☎ 506/529–8116) is an elegant vessel for whale-watching. **Seascape Kayak Tours** (☎ 506/529–4866) provides instruction as well as trips around the area from a half day to a week.

Shopping

Cottage Craft (⊠ Town Sq., ☎ 506/529–3190) employs knitters year-round to make mittens and sweaters from its specially dyed wool. **Garden by the Sea** (⊠ 217 Water St., ☎ 506/529–8905) is an aromatic shop whose owners made a name for themselves with natural, vegetarian soap. You can buy the soap, along with herbal shampoos, rinses, masks, even "Sea Spirit" balls for the bath. Attached to the store is the Garden Party herbal tearoom. **Jon Sawyer's Studio** (⊠ 719 Mowat Dr., ☎ 506/529–3012) has exquisite glass. The **Sea Captain's Loft** (⊠ 211 Water St., ☎ 506/529–3190) specializes in English and New Brunswick woolens, English bone china, and marvelous wool yarn. The **Seacoast Gallery** (⊠ 174 Water St., ☎ 506/529–0005) carries fine arts and crafts by eminent New Brunswick artists. **Serendipin' Art** (⊠ 168 Water St.,

☏ 506/529–3327) sells blown glass, hand-painted silks, jewelry, and other crafts by New Brunswick artists. **Steven Smith Designs/The Crocker Hill Store** (✉ 45 King St., ☏ 506/529–4303), is a special place for those who love gardens, birds, and art. Top-notch Canadian, American, and English antiques—including furniture, rugs, silver, china, paintings, and drawings—can be found at **Windsor House Art & Antiques** (✉ 136 Water St., ☏ 506/529–3026), which is next door to and affiliated with the Windsor House inn.

Grand Manan Island

⑭ *35 km (22 mi) east of St. Andrews by-the-Sea to Black's Harbour, 2 hrs by car ferry from Black's Harbour.*

Grand Manan, the largest of the three Fundy Islands, is also the farthest from the mainland; it's possible to see spouting whales, sunning seals, or a rare puffin on the way over. Circular herring weirs dot the island's coastal waters, and fish sheds and smoke houses lie beside long wharfs that reach out to bobbing fishing boats. Place names are evocative—Swallowtail, Southern Head, Seven Days Work, and Dark Harbour. It's easy to get around; only about 32 km (20 mi) of road lead from the lighthouse at Southern Head to the one at North Head. Grand Manan attracted John James Audubon, that human encyclopedia of birds, in 1831. More than 240 species of seabirds nest on the island, making it a haven for bird-watchers. The puffin may be the island's symbol, but whales are its visitors' passion. Giant finbacks, right whales, minkes, and humpbacks feed in the rich waters here. A day trip is possible, but your car might not make the infrequent ferry both ways. It's this limited access, however, that keeps the island authentic and relaxing, so you might as well plan to stay a while. Ferry service is provided by **Coastal Transport** (☏ 506/662–3724), which leaves the mainland from Black's Harbour, off Route 1, and docks at North Head on Grand Manan Island.

Dining and Lodging

$ ✕🗔 **Compass Rose.** Two old houses on the water combine to make this small, English-style country inn. The floral-theme guest rooms are bright and comfortable. Morning and afternoon teas, lunch (the lobster rolls are amazing), and dinner are served in a dining room that overlooks the busy fishing wharf. A full English breakfast is included in the rate, and all rooms overlook the water. ✉ *North Head, E0G 2M0,* ☏ FAX *506/662–8570. 7 rooms. Restaurant. MC, V. BP.*

$ ✕🗔 **The Inn at Whale Cove Cottages.** This secluded waterfront compound with beach access combines rustic surroundings with elegant furnishings. It includes a lodge with three rooms and three separate cottages, two of which are rented by the week. Full breakfast is included for guests of the lodge and the smaller cottage. The dining room ($$–$$$; reserve ahead) serves everything from local seafood to chicken Oscar (breaded chicken breast stuffed with lobster and cheddar cheese) from 6 to 8:30 every evening. An on-site food shop offers meals, desserts, bread, tabbouleh, hummus, and sauces to go. ✉ *26 Whale Cove Cottage Rd., E5G 2B5,* ☏ *506/662–3181,* WEB *www.holidayjunction.com/whalecove. 3 rooms, 3 cottages. Dining room, beach, library. MC, V. Closed Nov.–Apr.*

$ 🗔 **Marathon Inn.** This gracious mansion built by a sea captain sits on a hill overlooking the harbor. The Marathon has been an inn since 1871, and many of its original furnishings can still be found in the guest rooms. The dining room specializes in seafood; it does not serve lunch but can pack lunches for guests. ✉ *19 Marathon La., North Head, E5G 3A4,* ☏ *506/662–8488,* WEB *www.angelfire.com/biz2/marathon. 28 rooms, 15 with bath. Restaurant, 2 lounges, pool, tennis court. MC, V.*

Outdoor Activities and Sports

For complete information on bird-watching, nature photography, hiking, cycling, horseback riding, sea kayaking, and whale-watching, contact **Tourism New Brunswick** (⊠ Box 12345, Fredericton E3B 5C3, ☎ 800/561–0123).

WHALE-WATCHING

A whale-watching cruise from Grand Manan takes you well out into the bay. When the cruise operator tells you to dress warmly, he means it. Some of the boats have winter jackets, hats and mittens on board for the customers who don't believe him. Most of the operators guarantee sightings. **Island Coast Boat Tours** (☎ 506/662–8181) has been around for many years and has a great reputation. **Sea Land Adventure** (☎ 506/662–8997) has the only whale-watching schooner in the Bay of Fundy. Interpreters on **Sea Watch Tours** (☎ 877/662–8552 or 506/662–1081) are very knowledgable about the birds you might encounter on your cruise, as well as the whales.

Deer Island

⑮ *50 km (31 mi) east of St. Andrews by-the-Sea to Letete, 40 min by free ferry from Letete.*

One of the pleasures of Deer Island is walking around the fishing wharves like those at Chocolate Cove. Exploring the island takes only a few hours; it's 12 km (7 mi) long, varying in width from almost 5 km (3 mi) to a few hundred feet at some points. At **Deer Point** you can walk through a small nature park while waiting for the ferry to Campobello Island. If you listen carefully, you may be able to hear the sighing and snorting of the **Old Sow,** the second largest whirlpool in the world. If you can't hear it, you'll be able to see it, just a few feet offshore in the Western Passage off Point Park.

Dining and Lodging

$ 🏠 **Sunset Beach Cottage & Suites.** A modern property surrounded by natural beauty, this complex is right on a secluded cove. Watch the porpoises and bald eagles during the day, and in the evening enjoy a rare east-coast treat—an ocean sunset. ⊠ *21 Cedar Grove Rd., Fairhaven E5V 1N3,* ☎ *506/747–2972 or 888/576–9990,* WEB *www.cottageandsuites.com. 5 suites, 1 cottage. Pool, laundry service. V.*

$ 🏠 **West Isles World B&B.** This white frame house overlooks the cove and has two snug rooms with an informal country feel—the big upstairs suite has a water view. The owners arrange whale-watching cruises and kayaking for guests. ⊠ *3 Mountain Side Dr., Lambert's Cove E5V 1G3,* ☎ FAX *506/747–2946. 2 rooms. Hiking, library. No credit cards. BP.*

Outdoor Activities and Sports

Cline Marine Tours (⊠ Richardson Wharf, 91 Richardson Rd., Richardson, ☎ 506/529–2287 or 800/567–5880) offers scenic and whale-watching tours. **Sparky Too Scuba Dive Charters** (⊠ 108 Richardson Rd., ☎ 506/747–1988) offers whale-watching tours, and scuba excursions for certified divers.

Campobello Island

★ **⑯** *40 min by ferry (summer only) from Deer Island; 90 km (56 mi) southeast of St. Stephen via bridge from Lubec, Maine.*

Neatly manicured, preening itself in the bay, Campobello Island has always had a special appeal to the wealthy and the famous. It was here that the Roosevelt family spent its summers. The 34-room rustic summer cottage of the family of President Franklin Delano Roosevelt is now part of a nature preserve, **Roosevelt Campobello International Park,** a joint project of the Canadian and U.S. governments. The miles of trails here make for pleasant strolling. President Roosevelt's boyhood home was also the setting for the movie *Sunrise at Campobello.* To drive here from St. Stephen, cross the border to Maine, drive about 80 km (50 mi) down Route 1, and take Route 189 to Lubec, Maine, and a bridge. ⊠ *Roosevelt Park Rd.,* ☎ *506/752–2922.* ☎ *Free.* ⊙ *House late May–mid-Oct., daily 10–6; grounds daily year-round.*

The island's **Herring Cove Activity Destination** (⊠ Welshpool, ☎ 506/ 752–7010) has camping facilities; a 9-hole, par-36 Geoffrey Cornish golf course; a sandy beach; and miles of hiking trails.

Dining and Lodging

$ ✕🖬 **Lupine Lodge.** Originally a vacation home built by the Adams family (friends of the Roosevelts) in the early 1900s, these three attractive log cabins set on a bluff overlooking the Bay of Fundy are now a modern guest lodge. Nature trails connect Lupine Lodge to Herring Cove Activity Destination. Two of the cabins contain the guest rooms, which are rustic, with modern furniture and homemade quilts. The third cabin houses the dining room ($$–$$$), which specializes in simple but well-prepared local seafood. A deck overlooking the bay connects the three buildings. ⊠ *610 Rt. 774, Welshpool E5E 1A5,* ☎ *506/752–2555,* WEB *www.lupinlodge.com. 10 rooms, 1 suite. Restaurant, lounge. MC, V.*

$$$ 🖬 **Water's Edge Villas.** Watch the sun set over the water from the deck of a modern, two-bedroom cottage with all the comforts of home, including a lobster pot and a barbecue. The kitchen appliances are full-size, and the living room couch is a pullout so six can sleep comfortably. The water is just across the road, and the rocky beach is great for explorers. ⊠ *37 Hutchins Rd., Welshpool E5E 1H1,* ☎ *506/752–2359 or 800/836–7648. 3 villas. In-room VCRs, laundry service. V.*

St. Martins

⑰   *45 km (28 mi) east of Saint John.*

The fishing village of St. Martins has a rich shipbuilding heritage, whispering caves, miles of lovely beaches, spectacular tides, and a cluster of covered bridges, as well as several Heritage Inns and a couple of restaurants right on the beach. It's also the gateway to the Fundy Parkway. The scenic drive portion of this linear road extends to a new interpretation center at Salmon River. The road closely parallels the cycling–walking Fundy Trail along the shore. There are lots of places to park and many accessible scenic lookouts. The Fundy Parkway, only partially complete at press time, does not extend through Fundy National Park; the Fundy Trail and an expert hiking trail called the Fundy Footpath do, however, continue through to the park.

Some of New Brunswick's finest artists and craftspeople welcome visitors to their galleries and studios. Several of them live and work around St. Martins. Call ahead to arrange a visit. Among the green and rolling hills between St. Martins and Sussex is **Powning Design** (⊠ 610 Markhamville Rd., ☎ 506/433–1188), a studio–gallery operated by Peter and Beth Powning. He has won many awards for his work in clay, cast bronze, and other media. She is a writer and photographer whose work is found in galleries and books throughout North America.

Dining and Lodging

$$ ✕🖬 **Weslan Inn.** Fireplaces, antiques, and lots of floral prints give the rooms in this Heritage Inn an English country feel. Breakfast, served in the rooms, is included in the overnight rate. The dining room (reser-

vations required) specializes in seafood; lobster pie is a hot item. ⊠ *45 Main St., E5R 1B4,* ☎ *506/833–2351,* WEB *www.weslaninn.com. 3 rooms. Restaurant. MC, V.*

$–$$ ✕⌑ **St. Martins Country Inn.** High on a hill overlooking the Bay of Fundy, this restored sea captain's home is furnished with Victorian antiques. Breakfast is served in the Country Dining Room; formal dinners in the Candlelight Dining Room are excellent. Children are welcome to stay in the carriage house, though not the main inn. ⊠ *303 Main St., E5R 1C1,* ☎ *506/833–4534 or 800/565–5257,* FAX *506/833–4725,* WEB *www.stmartinscountryinn.com. 16 rooms (4 in carriage house). Restaurant. MC, V.*

Alma

135 km (84 mi) northeast of Saint John.

The small seaside town of Alma services Fundy National Park and has some motels as well as restaurants that serve good lobster and sticky buns. Around this area, much of it in Albert County, there's plenty to do outdoors—from bird-watching to spelunking. The **Albert County Tourism Association** (⊠ Hopewell Cape E0A 1Y0, ☎ 888/228–0444 or 506/882–2004) can provide information by phone or mail.

★ ⑱ **Fundy National Park** is an awesome 206-square-km (80-square-mi) microcosm of New Brunswick's inland and coastal climates. The influence of the Bay of Fundy has also created some climatic conditions not found anywhere else in the region. This has led to a fascinating biological evolution that can clearly be seen in its protected forests. The park has 110 km (68 mi) of varied hiking and mountain-biking trails, some gravel-surface auto trails, year-round camping, golf, tennis, a heated Bay of Fundy saltwater pool, and a restaurant. Park naturalists offer regular programs throughout the summer. Its more than 600 campsites range from full-service to wilderness. ⊠ *Hwy. 114 (Box 1001), E4H 1B4,* ☎ *506/887–6000,* WEB *www.parkscanada.pch.gc.ca.* ⛵ *$3.50 per person late May–mid-Oct.; free rest of year.* ☉ *Daily 24 hrs.*

Salem & Hillsborough Railroad Inc. (⊠ 197 Main St., Hillsborough, ☎ 506/734–3195 seasonal) offers one-hour train excursions on Sunday and some Wednesdays mid-June through Labor Day. The train skirts the Petitcodiac River and travels near scenic marshlands and wooded areas. The cost is $8.

OFF THE BEATEN PATH

CRAFTS STUDIOS AND GALLERIES – Along Routes 915 and 114 from Alma to Hillsborough are dozens of talented artists and craftspeople, many of whom open their studios and galleries to visitors. Pick up a Fundy Studio Tour pamphlet at visitor information centers for more information and a map. **Cornucopia Great Gifts and Fine Art** (⊠ 2816 Main St., Hillsborough, ☎ 506/734–1118), stocks New Brunswick's finest crafts, including pottery, glass, wood, metal, and jewelry. Lynne Saintonge, an owner of **Joie de Vivre Contemporary Arts & Craft Gallery** (⊠ Rte. 114, Riverside-Albert, ☎ 506/882–2276), is a painter–visual artist who uses computer and sound to enhance her images. Her fascinating work is created in a studio upstairs from the gallery. **Kindred Spirits Stained Glass Studio** (⊠ 2831 Main St., Hillsborough, ☎ 506/734–2342) is where Diana Boudreau creates unique patterns with glass carefully chosen for its color and texture. Brian Blakney's **Lonesome Rose Pottery** (⊠ Waterside Rd., ☎ 506/882–2770) is east of Fundy National Park. At **Oval Door Manor Arts** (⊠ 2666 Main St., Hillsborough, ☎ 506/734–3382), Paul and Elsie Nowlan create wonderful, highly detailed oil and ink works that are cherished in collections throughout North America and Europe. **Samphire Casuals** (⊠ Albert Mines Rd., off

Rte. 2114 near Hopewell, ☎ 506/734–2851) is a converted one-room schoolhouse where Judy Tait silk-screens her unique designs on T-shirts, sweatshirts, and even mugs. Lars Larsen's **Studio on the Marsh** (✉ Mary's Point Rd., off Rte. 915, ☎ 506/882–2917) is the perfect setting for his wildlife art. Many of **Tim Isaac and Karin Bach's** (✉ Rte. 915, between Alma and Riverside-Albert, ☎ 506/882–2166) wildlife clay sculptures and fountains are on display in a garden outside their studio. **Wendy Johnston's Pottery** (✉ behind the post office on Main St., Hillsborough, ☎ 506/734–2046) is contemporary, functional, and brightly colored with abstract designs.

Dining

$$ ✕ **Adair's Wilderness Lodge.** All of the food at this cedar lodge in the woods is made from scratch in the kitchen; you'll be served hearty portions of just about anything you like, including arctic char, rainbow trout, and sirloin steak. If you want fresh lobster, call ahead. ✉ *Creek Rd., 12 km (7 mi) past Poley Mountain*, ☎ *506/432–6687. AE, DC, MC, V.*

Outdoor Activities and Sports

BIRD-WATCHING

The bit of shoreline at **Marys Point** (✉ Watch for signs off Rte. 915) draws tens of thousands of migrating birds, including semipalmated sandpipers and other shore birds, each summer. The area, now a bird sanctuary and interpretive center, is near Riverside-Albert.

CAVING

Baymount Outdoor Adventures (✉ 17 Elwin Jay Dr., Hillsborough, ☎ 506/734–2660, ꟿWEB www.baymountadventures.com) has trained interpreters who lead expeditions into the White Caves near the Bay of Fundy. The caving experience is great fun, but not for the faint of heart, as it requires crawling on cave floors and slithering through narrow openings at some points. You can also arrange interpretive walks around Hopewell Rocks and Marys Point.

GOLF

The **Fundy National Park Golf Club** (✉ Fundy National Park, near the Alma entrance, ☎ 506/887–2970) is near cliffs overlooking the restless Bay of Fundy; it's one of the province's most beautiful and challenging 9-hole courses.

HORSEBACK RIDING

Broadleaf Guest Ranch (✉ 5526 Rte. 114, Hopewell Hill, ☎ 506/882–2349 or 800/226–5405) can provide an overnight adventure or a short trail ride. The short excursions are through the lowland marsh; longer rides take the high road into the forest.

SEA KAYAKING

Baymount Outdoor Adventures (✉ 17 Elvin Jay Dr., Hillsborough, ☎ 506/734–2660) offers sea kayaking around the Hopewell Rocks. **Fresh Air Adventure** (✉ 16 Fundy View Dr., Alma, ☎ 506/887–2249 or 800/545–0020, ꟿWEB www.freshairadventure.com) conducts Bay of Fundy sea-kayaking excursions that last from two hours to three days. Guides, instruction, and equipment are provided.

SKIING AND SNOWMOBILING

Poley Mountain Resort (✉ Waterford Rd. [Box 4466], Sussex E4E 5L6, ☎ 506/433–7653), 10 km (6 mi) from Sussex on Waterford Road, has a vertical drop of 660 ft, 23 trails, a snowboard park, and a tubing park with four trails and its own lift that converts to a water-based thrill ride in summer. Poley is also on the groomed Fundy Snowmobile Trail between Saint John and Moncton.

Cape Enrage

15 km (9 mi) east of Alma.

Route 915 takes you to the wild driftwood-cluttered beach at Cape Enrage, which juts out into the bay. A lighthouse, restaurant, gift shop, and some spectacular views can be found here. You can arrange for rappeling and other adventures.

Outdoor Activities and Sports

Cape Enrage Adventures (⊠ off Rte. 114, ☎ 506/887–2273 mid-May–mid-Sept.; 506/856–6081 off-season) offers rappeling and rock-climbing ($49.50 per person for two hours), kayaking ($54.50 per person for four hours), and hiking, including a particularly challenging five-day coastal hike.

Hopewell Cape

40 km (25 mi) north of Alma.

The coastal road (Route 114) from Alma to Moncton winds through covered bridges and along rocky coasts. **Hopewell Rocks** is home to the famous Giant Flowerpots—rock formations carved by the Bay of Fundy tides. They're topped with vegetation and are uncovered only at low tide, when you can climb down for a closer study. There are also trails, an interactive visitor center, and a children's play area. ⊠ *131 Discovery Rd.,* ☎ *877/734–3429.* ⌨ *$5.* ☉ *Late May–June, Sept.–Oct, daily 8–5; July–Aug., daily 8–8; closing hrs vary slightly, so call ahead.*

Dining and Lodging

$–$$ ✕⊡ **Aubergine & Spa.** The young couple that bought and converted this 1854 home (he's a chef, she's a massage therapist) added a section for the spa in 1999, which includes a cedar sauna. The rooms are all named for local flowers, and the key fobs are miniature hand-painted replicas of the floral paintings that identify each room. The furniture is antique, and many of the paintings are by young Acadian artists—the combination works amazingly well. A Continental breakfast is included in the rate. The intimate dining room, which features Thai and Indian food in addition to Indonesian specialties, is open to the public. ⊠ *5 Maple St., Riverside-Albert (24 km, or 15 mi, outside of Hopewell Cape) E4H 3X1,* ☎ *506/882–1800 or 877/873–1800,* FAX *506/882–1801,* WEB *www.aubergine-spa.com. 4 rooms. Restaurant, in-room data ports, spa, sauna, laundry service. AE, MC, V. CP.*

$–$$ ⊡ **Florentine Manor Heritage Inn.** With silver candlesticks on the dining-room table and handmade quilts on the beds, this restored old shipbuilder's house is a haven for honeymooners and romantics. All the rooms have at least two windows, the better to hear the birds in the trees outside. Two rooms have fireplaces and two have whirlpool baths. Dinner is served by request. ⊠ *356 Rte. 915, Harvey on the Bay E4H 2M2,* ☎ *506/882–2271 or 800/665–2271,* FAX *506/882–2936. 9 rooms. Dining room, bicycles. MC, V. BP.*

Moncton

⓳ *80 km (50 mi) north of Alma.*

A friendly city, often called the Gateway to Acadia because of its mix of English and French and its proximity to the Acadian shore, Moncton has a renovated downtown, where wisely placed malls do a booming business. A walking-tour brochure, available at the tourist information centers at both Magnetic Hill on Route 126, and at City Hall on Main Street, indicates the city's historic highlights.

This city has long touted two natural attractions: the Tidal Bore and the Magnetic Hill. You may be disappointed if you've read too much tourist hype, though. In days gone by, before the harbor mouth filled with silt, the **Tidal Bore** was an incredible sight, a high wall of water that surged in through the narrow opening of the river to fill red mud banks to the brim. It still moves up the river, and is worth seeing, but it's no longer a raging torrent. Bore Park on Main Street is the best vantage point; viewing times are posted there.

☺ **Magnetic Hill** creates a bizarre optical illusion. If you park your car in neutral at the designated spot, you'll seem to be coasting uphill without power. Shops, an amusement park, a zoo, a golf course, and a small railroad are part of the larger complex here; there are extra charges for the attractions. ✉ *North of Moncton off Trans-Canada Hwy. (watch for signs).* ☞ *$2.* ☉ *May–early Sept., daily 8–8.*

☺ An excellent family water-theme park, **Magic Mountain** is adjacent to Magnetic Hill. ✉ *North of Moncton off Trans-Canada Hwy.,* ☎ *506/857–9283; 800/331–9283 in Canada.* ☞ *$19.50.* ☉ *Mid–late June and mid-Aug.–early Sept., daily 10–6; July–mid-Aug., daily 10–8.*

☺ The award-winning **Magnetic Hill Zoo,** the largest zoo in Atlantic Canada, has no shortage of exotic species: lemurs, lions, macaques, muntjacs, and more. At Old MacDonald's Barnyard, children can pet domestic animals or ride a pony in summer. ✉ *North of Moncton off Trans-Canada Hwy.,* ☎ *506/384–0303.* ☞ *$6.* ☉ *Apr.–mid-June, daily 10–6; mid-June–early Sept., daily 9–8; early Sept.–Oct., weekdays 10–6, weekends 9–7; Jan.–Mar., Sun. 11–4.*

A restored 1920s vaudeville theater, the opulent **Capitol Theatre** is a beautiful attraction in itself as well as a venue for plays, musicals, ballets, and concerts. Free tours are available. ✉ *811 Main St.,* ☎ *506/856–4379; 800/567–1922 in Canada.*

The **Thomas Williams Heritage House,** a neo-Gothic structure built in 1883 by the treasurer of the Intercolonial Railway, is elegantly furnished and contains several original family pieces. The Veranda Tea Room is open in July and August. ✉ *103 Park St.,* ☎ *506/857–0590.* ☞ *By donation.* ☉ *May and Sept., Mon., Wed., and Fri. 10–3; June, Tues.–Sat. 9–5, Sun. 1–5; July–Aug., Mon.–Sat. 9–5, Sun. 1–5.*

The 1821 **Free Meeting House,** a simple and austere National Historic Site operated by the Moncton Museum, is Moncton's oldest standing building. It was built as a gathering place for all religious denominations without their own places of worship. ✉ *100 Steadman St.,* ☎ *506/856–4383.* ☞ *By donation.* ☉ *Mon.–Sat. 9–4:30.*

Comprehensive exhibits trace the city's history from the days of the Mi'Kmaq people to the present at the **Moncton Museum.** ✉ *20 Mountain Rd.,* ☎ *506/856–4383.* ☞ *By donation.* ☉ *Mon.–Sat. 9–4:30.*

The halls of the **Aberdeen Cultural Centre,** a converted schoolhouse, ring with music and chatter. This is home to theater and dance companies, a framing shop, and several galleries. **Galerie 12** represents leading contemporary Acadian artists. **Galerie Sans Nom** is an artist-run co-op supporting avant-garde artists from throughout Canada. The English, artist-run **IMAGO Inc.** is the only print production shop in the province. Guided tours are available by appointment. ✉ *140 Botsford St.,* ☎ *506/857–9597.* ☉ *Weekdays 10–4.*

At **Lutz Mountain Heritage Museum** you can find genealogical records of the area's non-Acadian pioneer settlers from as far back as 1766.

It's also a hands-on museum. ⊠ *3143 Mountain Rd.,* ☎ *506/384–7719.* 🖼 *Free.* ☉ *Mon.–Sat. 10–6.*

The **Acadian Museum,** at the University of Moncton, has a remarkable collection of artifacts reflecting 300 years of Acadian life in the Maritimes. There's also a fine gallery showcasing contemporary art by local and Canadian artists. ⊠ *Clement Cormier Bldg., Universite Ave.,* ☎ *506/858–4088.* 🖼 *$2.* ☉ *June–Sept., weekdays 10–5, weekends 1–5; Oct.–May, Tues.–Fri. 1–4:30, weekends 1–4.*

Dining and Lodging

$$–$$$$ ✕ **Fisherman's Paradise.** The enormous dining area at this restaurant seats more than 350 people. Memorable à la carte seafood dishes are served in an atmosphere of candlelight and wood furnishings. ⊠ *375 Dieppe Blvd.,* ☎ *506/859–4388. AE, DC, MC, V.*

$$–$$$ ✕ **Le Château à Pape.** This riverside restaurant in an old Victorian home has it all—crisp white linen, romantic atmosphere, and a well-stocked wine cellar (you go down and select your own). The chef is third generation in a French-Acadian tradition. He prepares everything from steak to seafood with an Acadian flare. Traditional Acadian dishes include *fricot* (stew) and *poutine à trou* (apple pastry). ⊠ *2 Steadman St.,* ☎ *506/855–7273. AE, DC, MC, V. No lunch.*

$ ✕ **Pump House Brewery.** Metal fermentation tanks and bags of hops are proudly displayed in the laid-back atmosphere of the Pump House. Seasonal ales, such as pumpkin ale for Halloween, are served in addition to the regular house brews. Try the blueberry ale, complete with floating blueberries. A limited menu includes snack foods, burgers, and single-serving pizzas. The veggie pizza is loaded with fresh vegetables. ⊠ *5 Orange La.,* ☎ *506/855–2337. AE, MC, V.*

$ ✕ **Vito's.** This restaurant is the original in what is now a small but successful family chain. The pizza toppings are fresh and generous. Pasta, chicken dishes, seafood, and veal round out the selection. The Mediterranean décor completes the mood. Vito's can be busy on weekends, so reserve ahead. ⊠ *726 Mountain Rd.,* ☎ *506/858–5000. AE, DC, MC, V.*

$$–$$$ ✕⊞ **Delta Beauséjour.** Moncton's finest hotel is conveniently located
★ downtown and has friendly service. The décor of the guest rooms echoes the city's Loyalist and Acadian roots. L'Auberge, the main hotel restaurant ($–$$$), has a distinct Acadian flavor. The more formal Windjammer dining room ($$$) is modeled after the opulent luxury liners of the early 1900s. ⊠ *750 Main St.,* ☎ *506/854–4344,* 🅵🅰🆇 *506/858–0957,* 🆆🅴🅱 *www.deltahotels.com. 299 rooms, 11 suites. 2 restaurants, bar, café, indoor pool, gym. AE, D, DC, MC, V.*

$$–$$$ ⊞ **Best Western Crystal Palace.** Part of an amusement complex, this hotel keeps the fun coming with theme rooms devoted to rock and roll, the Victorian era, and more. The hotel also has movie theaters, a giant bookstore, an indoor pool, and an indoor amusement park. Pets are welcome. Champlain Mall is just across the parking lot. ⊠ *499 Paul St., Dieppe E1A 6S5,* ☎ *506/858–8584 or 800/561–7108,* 🅵🅰🆇 *506/858–5486,* 🆆🅴🅱 *www.m2000.nb.ca/bestwestern. 92 rooms, 23 suites. Restaurant, indoor pool, gym. AE, D, DC, MC, V.*

$$ ⊞ **Château Moncton Hotel & Suites.** This modern chateaulike hotel stretches along the Petitcodiac River. The décor is European with custom-made cherry-wood furniture. Some rooms overlooking the water have decks with great views of the Tidal Bore. Continental breakfast is included in the room rate, but no other meals are served here. ⊠ *100 Main St., E1C 1B9,* ☎ *506/870–4444 or 800/576–4040,* 🅵🅰🆇 *506/870–4445,* 🆆🅴🅱 *www.chateau-moncton.nb.ca. 106 rooms, 12 suites. In-room data ports, minibars, gym. AE, DC, MC, V. CP.*

$ ⚏ **Victoria B & B.** This historic home in the heart of downtown has antiques-furnished rooms with amenities such as terry robes and aromatic bath gels. The full complimentary breakfast, served in the dining room, often includes chocolate pecan and orange-brandy French toast. ✉ *71 Park St., E1C 2B2,* ☎ *506/389–8296,* FAX *506/389–8296,* WEB *www.sn2000.nb.ca/comp/victoria-b&b. 3 rooms. Dining room, inroom VCRs. MC, V. BP.*

Nightlife and the Arts

THE ARTS

Top musicians and other performers appear at the **Colosseum** (✉ 377 Killam Dr., ☎ 506/857–4100).

NIGHTLIFE

Moncton rocks at night. **Club Cosmopolitan** (✉ 700 Main St., ☎ 506/ 857–9117) is open Wednesday through Saturday for dancing, rock, jazz, or the blues. It's billed as one cool club with four different atmospheres. **Club Mystique** (✉ 939 Mountain Rd., ☎ 506/858–5861) features major Canadian rock and alternative artists a couple of times a month. **Rockin Rodeo** (✉ 415 Elmwood Dr., ☎ 506/384–4324) is the biggest country-and-western bar in the province. **Voodoo** (✉ 938 Mountain Rd., ☎ 506/858–8844) has lots of room for dancing and caters to the 25-plus crowd.

Shopping

Five spacious malls, retail stores, and numerous pockets of shops make Moncton and nearby suburban Dieppe two of the best places to shop in New Brunswick. This city is also the province's fashion trendsetter, a reputation upheld by several downtown boutiques. Moncton has its share of fine crafts as well. **La Difference Fine Craft and Art** (✉ 181 Main St., ☎ 506/861–1800) specializes in Atlantic Canadian woodwork, jewelry, and pottery, and also features paintings and photographs. **The Moncton Market** (✉ 120 Westmorland St., ☎ 506/383– 1749) brims with fresh produce, baked goods, ethnic cuisine, and crafts every Saturday morning 7–1.

Outdoor Activities and Sports

The **All World Super Play Park** (✉ Cleveland Ave., Riverview), across the river from Moncton, is a giant wooden structure with plenty of room for children to exercise their bodies and imaginations.

GOLF

Royal Oaks Golf Club (✉ 1746 Elmwood Dr., ☎ 506/384–3330) is an 18-hole, par-72 PGA Championship course, the first Canadian course designed by Rees Jones.

TANTRAMAR REGION

History and nature meet on the Tantramar salt marshes east of Moncton. Bounded by the upper reaches of the Bay of Fundy, the province of Nova Scotia, and the Northumberland Strait, the region is rich in history and culture and is teeming with birds. The marshes provide a highly productive wetland habitat, and this region is along one of North America's major migratory bird routes.

Dorchester and Memramcook

40 km (25 mi) from Moncton.

Acadian roots run deep in Memramcook; on the other side of a marsh, Dorchester was a center of British culture and industry long before the Loyalists landed. Dorchester is home to some of the province's oldest buildings, including **The Bell Inn** on the village square. Now a restaurant, The Bell Inn was built in 1811 as a stagecoach stop; it is reputed to be the oldest stone structure in New Brunswick.

Keillor House & Coach House Museum and Saint James Church is a cluster of historic properties turned into museums. The restored 1813 Keillor House has 16 rooms and nine fireplaces. Saint James Church is home to the Beachkirk textile collection and is a working textile museum. ⊠ *4974 Main St., Dorchester,* ☎ *506/379–6633 (seasonal).* ▣ *$2 (each property).* ☉ *June–mid-Sept., Mon.–Sat. 10–5, Sun. 1–5.*

The **Monument Lefebvre National Historic Site** in Memramcook explores the turbulent history of the Acadian people in passionate detail. ⊠ *480 Central St.,* ☎ *506/758–9808.* ▣ *$2.* ☉ *June–mid-Oct., daily 9–5; rest of year by appointment.*

Outdoor Activities and Sports

Along the beaches at **Johnson's Mills** (⊠ Rte. 935, about 8 km [5 mi] south of Dorchester) is part of the internationally recognized staging area for migratory shorebirds like semipalmated sandpipers. The numbers are most impressive in July and August.

Sackville

㉒ *22 km (14 mi) from Dorchester and Memramcook.*

Sackville is an idyllic university town complete with a swan-filled pond. Its stately homes and ivy-clad university buildings are all shaded by venerable trees, and there's a waterfowl park right in the town. It makes for a rich blend of history, culture, and nature. The **Sackville Waterfowl Park** in the heart of the town has more than 3 km (2 mi) of boardwalk and trails. The area is dotted with rest benches, viewing areas, and interpretive signs throughout the marsh that reveal the rare waterfowl species that nest here. There's an interpretation center, and guided tours are available in French and English June through August. ⊠ *Main St.,* ☎ *506/364–4968.* ▣ *Park free, tour $4.* ☉ *Daily 24 hrs.*

The sophisticated **Owens Art Gallery** is on the Mt. Allison University campus. One of the oldest and largest university art galleries in the country, it houses 19th- and 20th-century European, American, and Canadian artwork. ⊠ *61 York St.,* ☎ *506/364–2574.* ▣ *Free.* ☉ *Weekdays 10–5, weekends 1–5.*

Near the Nova Scotia border in Aulac and 12 km (7 mi) outside of Sackville, the **Fort Beauséjour National Historic Site** holds the ruins of a star-shape fort that played a part in the 18th-century struggle between the French and English. The fort has indoor and outdoor exhibits as well as fine views of the marshes at the head of the Bay of Fundy. ⊠ *Rte. 106,* ☎ *506/364–5080 in summer; 506/876–2443 off-season.* ▣ *$2.50.* ☉ *June–mid-Oct., daily 9–5.*

Dining and Lodging

$–$$ ✕ **Schnitzel Haus.** This unpretentious roadside restaurant is refreshingly authentic. The German owners make everything from schnitzel and bratwurst to spaetzle. ⊠ *153 Aulac Rd., Aulac (12 km [7 mi] outside of Sackville),* ☎ *506/364–0888. MC, V.*

$$–$$$ ✕▥ **Marshlands Inn.** In this white clapboard inn, a welcoming dou-
★ ble parlor with fireplace sets the comfortable country atmosphere. Bedrooms are furnished with sleigh beds or four-posters. The chefs offer traditional and modern dishes; seafood, pork, and lamb are specialties ($$–$$$). In summer most of the vegetables come from the organic garden in the backyard. ⊠ *55 Bridge St., E4L 3N8,* ☎ *506/536–0170*

*or 800/561–1266, FAX 506/536–0721, WEB www.marshlands.nb.ca. 20
rooms. Restaurant. AE, DC, MC, V.*

Outdoor Activities and Sports

Without a doubt, bird-watching is the pastime of choice in this region.
Several locations around Sackville allow you to observe a variety of
species. For information on bird-watching in the area, contact the
Canadian Wildlife Service (⊠ 17 Waterfowl La., ☎ 506/364–5044).
Cape Jourimain Nature Centre (⊠ Exit 51 off Rt. 16, at the foot of
Confederation Bridge, Bayfield, ☎ 506/538–2220), at the Cape Jourimain National Wildlife Area, covers 1,800 acres of salt and brackish
marshes. Large numbers of waterfowl, shorebirds, and other species
can be seen here. It includes a fine nature interpretation center, nature
store, restaurant, viewing tower, and a 13 km (8 mi) trail network. **Good-
win's Pond** (⊠ off Rte. 970), near the Red-Wing Blackbird Trail in Baie
Verte, allows for easy viewing of wetland birds and boasts more birds
per acre than anywhere else in the province. The **Port Elgin Rotary Pond
and Fort Gaspereaux Trail** (⊠ 30 km [19 mi] from Sackville via Rte.
16) offer a diverse coastal landscape that attracts migrating waterfowl,
bald eagles, and osprey. At the **Tantramar Marshes** (⊠ High Marsh
Rd., between Sackville and Point de Bute) you may be able to spot marsh
hawks. The **Tintamarre National Wildlife Area** (⊠ Goose Lake Rd.,
off High Marsh Rd., ☎ 506/364–5044) consists of 5,000 acres of protected land ideal for sighting several species of ducks, rails, pied-billed
grebes, and American bittern.

Shopping

Fog Forest Gallery (⊠ 14 Bridge St., ☎ 506/536–9000) is a small, friendly,
and reputable commercial gallery representing Atlantic Canadian artists.
The **Sackville Harness Shop** (⊠ 39 Main St., ☎ 506/536–0642) still
actually makes harnesses for horses. You can also pick up fine leather
belts, wallets, bags, and jewelry. **Tidewater Books** (⊠ 4 Bridge St., ☎
506/536–0404) offers old-fashioned service and all the latest titles.

THE ACADIAN COAST AND PENINSULA

The white sands and gentle tides of the Northumberland Strait and Baie
des Chaleurs are as different from the rocky cliffs and powerful tides
of the Bay of Fundy as the Acadians are from the Loyalists. In the Acadian Peninsula, fishing boats and churches define this land where a
French-language culture survives. You're not likely to run into any language barriers in stores, restaurants, and attractions along the beaten
path, but down the side roads it's a different story altogether.

Shediac

㉑ *25 km (16 mi) east of Moncton.*

Shediac is the self-proclaimed Lobster Capital of the World. It even has
a giant lobster sculpture to prove it. But this is not what draws people
to this fishing village–resort town. The magnet is **Parlee Beach,** a 3-km
(2-mi) stretch of glistening sand. Surveys have named it the best beach
in Canada, making it a popular vacation spot for families. It also plays
host to beach-volleyball and touch-football tournaments; an annual sand-
sculpture contest and a triathlon are held here as well. Services include
canteens and a licensed restaurant. ⊠ *off Rte. 133,* ☎ *506/533–3363.*
🎫 *$5 per vehicle.* ☉ *Mid-May–mid-Sept., 7 AM–9 PM.*

Parc de L'Aboiteau, on the western end of Cap-Pelé, has a fine, sandy
beach as well as a boardwalk that runs through salt marshes where
waterfowl nest. The beach complex includes a restaurant and lounge

with live music in the evening. Cottages are available for rent. ⊠ *Rte. 15, Exit 53,* ☎ *506/577–2005.* ⊠ *$4 per vehicle.* ☉ *Beach complex June–Sept., daily dawn–dusk; cottages year-round.*

Dining and Lodging

$–$$$ ✕ **Lobster Deck.** Don't bother trying to wipe the sand off your table at this casual restaurant; it's here to stay. But don't worry—it won't get into your chowder. Lobster is the specialty here, but a platter that includes a half lobster with scallops, haddock, shrimp, and mussels is wonderful. On nice evenings you can eat on the front deck and watch people passing by, or you can dine on the back deck and watch gulls soaring over the water. Reservations are recommended in July and August. ⊠ *312 Main St.,* ☎ *506/532–8737. AE, MC, V. Closed Dec.–Apr.*

$–$$$ ✕ **Paturel Shorehouse Restaurant.** This big "cottage" on the beach is quite cozy, and because it's right next door to a fish-processing plant, you can get nearly anything you want—even a 5-pound lobster. The chef has a way with salmon and sole. Reservations are recommended for July and August. ⊠ *corner of Cap Bimet and Legere,* ☎ *506/532–4774. AE, DC, MC, V. Closed mid-Sept.–mid-May. No lunch.*

$–$$$ ✕🏠 **Little Shemogue Country Inn.** The unusual name (pronounced shim-o-*gwee*; it means "good feed for geese") is not nearly as surprising as the inn itself, a jewel in the rough along a rural coastal road. The main inn is a restored country home, exquisitely furnished and decorated with antiques. (One of the common rooms has an African motif: in another life the owner was an engineer who often worked on that continent.) A three-story wall of windows in the common area of the modern Log Point annex overlooks the ocean; the rooms here are large and have ocean views and whirlpool tubs. The 200-acre property has its own white-sand beach, canoes, and trails along a salt marsh. Breakfast (not included in the rate) and a set five-course dinner, for guests and the public, are served in three dining rooms ($$$) by reservation. ⊠ *2361 Rte. 955, Little Shemogue (40 km [25 mi] outside of Shediac), E4M 3K4,* ☎ *506/538–2320,* ☒ *506/538–7494,* 🌐 *www.little-inn.nb.ca. 9 rooms. Dining room, outdoor hot tub, beach, boating, bicycles. AE, MC, V.*

$–$$ ✕🏠 **Le Gourmand Country Inn.** The dining room ($$$), with its table d'hôte menu, is the most outstanding feature of this fine renovated home near the beach. The chef understands and appreciates Maritime flavors, so you're assured an extra fine dining experience. Rooms in the inn are modern and comfortable. The property also includes 10 two-bedroom cottages with cedar walls, cathedral ceilings, gas fireplaces, and fully equipped kitchens. ⊠ *562 Main St., E4P 2H1,* ☎ *506/532–4351 or 888/532–2585,* ☒ *506/532–1025. 6 rooms, 10 cottages. Restaurant. AE, DC, MC, V.*

$$ 🏠 **Auberge Belcourt Inn.** This elegant Heritage Inn was built around 1912 and has been carefully restored and furnished with lovely period furniture. In summer the front veranda is an ideal spot for a drink before dinner at the Lobster Deck restaurant next door. The inn doesn't serve dinner in the summer, but in September through May offers authentic Chinese dinners to guests and the public ($45). ⊠ *310 Main St., E4P 2E3,* ☎ *506/532–6098,* ☒ *506/533–9398,* 🌐 *www.sn2000. nb.ca/comp/auberge-belcourt. 7 rooms. Dining room, air-conditioning, laundry service. AE, DC, MC, V. Closed Jan. BP.*

Bouctouche

㉒ *35 km (22 km) north of Shediac.*

Bouctouche is a coastal town with a number of attractions. **Le Pays de la Sagouine** is a theme park with a make-believe island community that comes to life in French in day-long musical and theatrical performances and dinner theater–musical evenings July through September. La Sagouine is an old charwoman–philosopher created by award-winning author Antonine Maillet. ⊠ *Hwy. 11, Exit 32,* ☎ *506/743–1400 or 800/561–9188.* 🎫 *$12.* ☉ *Mid-June–Labor Day, daily 10–6; Sept., daily 10:30–4.*

★ **Irving Eco-Centre, La Dune de Bouctouche** is a superb example of a coastal ecosystem that protects the exceptionally fertile oyster beds in Bouctouche Bay. Hiking trails and boardwalks to the beach make it possible to explore sensitive areas without disrupting the environment of one of the few remaining great dunes on the northwest coast of North America. An outstanding interpretive center puts the ecosystem in perspective. Swimming and clam digging are allowed. ⊠ *Rte. 475,* ☎ *506/743–2600.* 🎫 *Free.* ☉ *Visitor center May–June, daily noon–8; July–Sept., daily 10–8; Sept.–Oct., weekdays noon–5, weekends 10–6.*

Dining and Lodging

$ ✕🏠 **Auberge le Vieux Presbytère de Bouctouche.** This inn, formerly a rectory and then a retreat house complete with chapel (now a conference room), has a courtly staff and is brimming with wonderful New Brunswick art and fascinating collections of antiques and books. The dining room ($$–$$$) is open to the public, serves seafood and Acadian fare, and is supported by a substantial wine cellar. ⊠ *157 chemin du Couvent, E4S 3B8,* ☎ *506/743–5568,* FAX *506/743–5566,* WEB *www.sn2000.nb.ca/comp/presbytere. 19 rooms, 3 suites. Restaurant. AE, MC, V. Closed Oct.–June.*

Kouchibouguac National Park

★ ㉓   *40 km (25 mi) north of Bouctouche, 100 km (62 mi) north of Moncton.*

The park's white, dune-edged beaches, some of the finest on the continent, are preserved here. Kellys Beach is supervised and has facilities. The park also protects forests and peat bogs, which can be explored along its 10 nature trails. There are lots of nature interpretation programs and you can bicycle, canoe, kayak, and picnic, too. Reservations are strongly recommended for the 311 campsites. ⊠ *186 Rt. 117, Kouchibouguac,* ☎ *506/876–2443,* WEB *www.parkscanada.pch.gc.ca.* 🎫 *Late May–mid-Sept., $3.50 per person; free rest of year.* ☉ *Year-round.*

Outdoor Activities and Sports

Kouchibouguac National Park conducts **Voyager Canoe Day Adventures** (☎ 506/876–2443), which take you to offshore sandbars to meet grey seals and common terns and to discuss the Mi'Kmaq and Acadian culture in the area. The cost is $28, and outings take place four times a week, twice in English and twice in French. **Kayakouch, Inc.** (☎ 506/876–1199) offers guided, interpretive tours, ranging anywhere from four hours to five days, through the waters of Kouchibouguac National Park.

Miramichi City

㉔   *40 km (25 mi) north of Kouchibouguac, 150 km (93 mi) north of Moncton.*

The fabled Miramichi region is one of lumberjacks and fisherfolk. Celebrated for salmon rivers that reach into some of the province's richest forests, and the ebullient nature of its residents (Scottish, English, Irish, and a smattering of First Nations and French), this is a land of ghost stories, folklore, and lumber kings.

Sturdy wood homes dot the banks of Miramichi Bay at Miramichi City, which in 1995 incorporated the former towns of Chatham and New-castle and several small villages. This is also where the politician and British media mogul Lord Beaverbrook grew up and is buried.

Dare the Dark for the Headless Nun! (☎ 800/459–3131) is a tragic tale best told in the dark while exploring one of the city's most infamous haunts. Costumed guides meet participants at French Fort Cove (watch for signs along the King George Highway through the city) at 9 PM Monday, Wednesday, and Friday from mid-June through August; the cost is $5.

The **Atlantic Salmon Museum and Aquarium** provides a look at the en-dangered Atlantic salmon and at life in noted fishing camps along the rivers. ⊠ *263 Main St., Doaktown (80 km [50 mi] southwest of Mi-ramichi City),* ☎ *506/365–7787.* ☜ *$4.* ☉ *June–early Oct., daily 9–5.*

The **Central New Brunswick Woodmen's Museum,** with artifacts that date from the 1700s to the present, is in what looks like two giant logs set on more than 60 acres of land. The museum portrays a lumber-jack's life through displays, but its tranquil grounds are excuse enough to visit. The Whooper, a 10-passenger amusement train ($2) is a 1½ km (1 mi) woodland adventure. There are picnic facilities and camp-ing sites. ⊠ *6342 Rte. 8, Boiestown (110 km [68 mi] southwest of Mi-ramichi City),* ☎ *506/369–7214.* ☜ *$5.* ☉ *May–Sept., daily 9–5.*

Dining and Lodging

$$ ✕🏨 **Rodd Miramichi River.** This grand riverside hotel, with warm nat-ural wood and earth-tone interior, manages to feel like a fishing lodge. The rooms are comfortable, with lots of fishing prints on the walls. One room is specially equipped for guests with disabilities, and has a wheel-chair-accessible shower stall. The Angler's Reel Restaurant is dedicated to fresh salmon. ⊠ *1809 Water St., E1N 1B2,* ☎ *506/773–3111,* 𝗙𝗔𝗫 *506/773–3110,* 𝖶𝖤𝖡 *www.rodd-hotels.ca. 76 rooms, 4 suites. Restaurant, bar, indoor pool, hot tub, gym. AE, DC, MC, V.*

$ 🏨 **Pond's Chalet Resort.** You'll get a traditional fishing-camp experi-ence in this lodge and chalets, 100 km (62 mi) outside of Miramichi, set among trees overlooking a salmon river. The accommodations in Ludlow, 15 km (9 mi) northwest of Boiestown, are comfortable but not luxurious. You can canoe and bicycle here, too. The dining room turns out reliable but undistinguished food. ⊠ *91 Porter Cove Rd., Ludlow E9C 2J3 (watch for signs on Rte. 8),* ☎ *506/369–2612,* 𝗙𝗔𝗫 *506/369–2293,* 𝖶𝖤𝖡 *www.pondsresort.com. 10 rooms, 5-bedroom lodge, 14 cabins. Bar, dining room, tennis court, volleyball, snowmo-biling. AE, D, DC, MC, V.*

Shippagan

37 km (23 mi) from Tracadie-Sheila.

Shippagan is an important commercial fishing and marine education center as well as a bustling, modern town with lots of amenities. It's also the gateway to the idyllic islands of Lamèque and Miscou. The wonderful **Aquarium and Marine Centre** has a serious and a fun side. The labs here are the backbone of marine research in the province, and the marine museum houses more than 3,000 specimens. A family of seals in the aquarium puts on a great show in the pool at feeding time. There's a touch tank for making the acquaintance of various sea crea-tures, and during the fisheries and aquaculture festival in July, there are fish races in a special tank with numbered racing lanes. Place a bet on your favorite fish, and you could win a prize. ⊠ *100 rue de l'Aquar-ium,* ☎ *506/336–3013.* ☜ *$6.* ☉ *May–Sept., daily 10–6.*

Across a causeway from Shippagan is Île Lamèque and the **Sainte–Cécile church** (⊠ Rte. 113 at Petite-Rivière-de-l'Île). Although the church is plain on the outside, every inch of it is decorated on the inside. Each July, the **International Festival of Baroque Music** (☎ 506/344–5846) takes place here.

Île Miscou, accessible by bridge from Île Lamèque, has white sandy beaches.

Caraquet

㉕   *40 km (25 mi) from Shippagan.*

Perched along the Baie des Chaleurs, with Québec's Gaspé Peninsula beckoning across the inlet, Caraquet is rich in French flavor and is the acknowledged Acadian capital. Beaches are another draw. The two-week **Acadian Festival** (☎ 506/727–6515) held here in August includes the Tintamarre, in which costumed participants noisily parade through the streets; and the Blessing of the Fleet, a colorful and moving ceremony that eloquently expresses the importance of fishing to the Acadian economy and way of life.

★ ℭ   A highlight of the Acadian Peninsula is **Acadian Historical Village,** 10 km (6 mi) west of Caraquet. The more than 40 restored buildings recreate Acadian communities between 1770 and 1939. There are modest homes, a church, a school, and a village shop, as well as an industrial area that includes a working hotel with barbershop, a bar and restaurant, a lobster hatchery, a cooper, and tinsmith shops. ⊠ *Rte. 11,* ☎ *506/726–2600,* WEB *www.gov.nb.ca/vha.* ☒ *$12.* ☉ *June–mid-Sept., daily 10–6. Guided tours through mid-Oct.*

With 86 figures in 23 scenes, the **Acadian Wax Museum** traces the history of the Acadians between 1604 and 1761. ⊠ *Rte. 11, outside the Acadian Historical Village,* ☎ *506/727–6424.* ☒ *$6.* ☉ *June and Sept., daily 9–6; July–Aug., daily 9–7.*

The **Pope's Museum,** 7 km (4 mi) outside of Caraquet, is the only museum in North America dedicated to papal history. It includes replicas of Saint Peter's Basilica, the cathedral in Florence, and even an Egyptian pyramid. ⊠ *184 Acadie St., Grand-Anse,* ☎ *506/732–3003,* WEB *www.museedespapes.com.* ☒ *$5.* ☉ *Mid-June–Aug., daily 10–6.*

Dining and Lodging

$$–$$$$ ✕ **La Fine Grobe-Sur-Mer.** North of Bathurst in Nigadoo, about 80 km
★   (50 mi) outside of Caraquet, is one of New Brunswick's finest restaurants. The French cuisine, seafood, and wine are outstanding because the chef–owner never compromises. Sample dishes include seafood crepes, bouillabaisse, and roast leg of lamb. The dining room is small, but has a cozy fireplace and three walls of windows overlooking the ocean. Lunch is available only by special arrangement. ⊠ *289 rue Principal,* ☎ *506/783–3138,* WEB *www.finegrobe.com. Reservations essential. AE, DC, MC, V. No lunch.*

$ ✕☷ **Hotel Paulin.** Each pretty room of this quaint property has its own unique look, with old pine dressers and brass beds. An excellent small dining room, open to the public, specializes in fresh fish cooked to perfection, Acadian style. ⊠ *143 blvd. St-Pierre W, E1W 1B6,* ☎ *506/727–9981,* FAX *506/727–4808. 4 rooms, 4 suites. Restaurant, in-room data ports. MC, V.*

The Arts

Caraquet is home to **Théâtre Populaire d'Acadie** (⊠ 276 blvd. St-Pierre W, ☎ 506/727–0920), a professional theater that mounts original productions by Acadian playwrights.

ACADIAN CULTURE, PAST AND PRESENT

CULTURE IS OFTEN DEFINED by geographical boundaries. Acadian culture, however, defines Acadia, because it isn't so much a place as it is an enduring French society. In New Brunswick it abides (although not exclusively) above an imaginary line drawn from Edmundston to Moncton. In the heartland you can hear remnants of Norman-French. Around Moncton you're just as apt to hear a melodious Acadian dialect called Chiac, a tweedy kind of French with flecks of English.

French settlers arrived in the early 1600s and brought with them an efficient system of dykes called aboiteaux that allowed them to farm the salt marshes. In the 1700s they were joined by Jesuit missionaries who brought the music of Bach, Vivaldi, and Scarlatti along with their zeal. In 1713 England took possession of the region, and authorities demanded Acadians swear an oath to the English crown. Some did, others didn't. By 1755 it didn't seem to matter. Only those who fled into the forests escaped Le Grand Dérangement—The Expulsion of the Acadians, which dispersed them to Québec, the eastern seaboard, Louisiana (where they became known as Cajuns), France, and even as far as the Falkland Islands. It was a devastating event that probably should have eradicated French language and culture in the Maritimes. It didn't. It did, however, profoundly affect Acadian expression—mobility remains a pervasive theme in the art, literature, and music of Acadian people.

Whether they were hiding deep in Maritime forests or living in exile, Acadians clung tenaciously to their language and traditions. Within 10 years of their deportation, Acadians began to return. They built new communities along coasts and waterways remote from English settlement. In the 1850s Acadians began

to think "nationally." By 1884 there was an Acadian national anthem and a flag.

The Acadian National Holiday on August 15 provides an official reason to celebrate Acadian culture. Le Festival Acadien de Caraquet stretches the celebration out for two weeks. Caraquet is also home to Théâtre Populaire d'Acadie, which mounts original productions for French communities throughout the Maritimes and encourages contemporary Acadian playwrights. Books by Acadian authors, including internationally renowned Antonine Maillet, circulate in Québec, France, and Belgium. Conceptual artist Herménégilde Chiasson pushes the envelope with his poetry and painting, and Paulette Foulem Lanteigne's palette contains the bright colors that have traditionally defined the Acadian spirit.

The earliest Acadian settlers made pine furniture that was elegant in its simplicity. Modern Acadian artisans continue to make functional things, such as pottery and baskets, beautiful. Handmade wooden spoons are doubly beautiful—in pairs they keep time to the music at kitchen parties, where Acadian families have traditionally sung their history around the kitchen fire. But it isn't necessary to have a party to enjoy "music de cuisine." Today, folk singer Edith Butler of Paquetville takes some of that history back to her French cousins in Paris. A lively pop band called Mechants Maquereaux (roughly translated that's "Naughty Mackeral") carries the same messages with a modern spin.

Clearly, the love of music endures here: it rings clear in churches, the cotillion and quadrille are danced at Saturday-night soirées, Acadian sopranos and jazz artists enjoy international renown, and a world-class Baroque Music Festival in Lamèque still celebrates Bach, Vivaldi, and Scarlatti.

—Ana Watts

Outdoor Activities and Sports

Sugarloaf Provincial Park (✉ 596 Val d'Amour Rd., Atholville E3N 4C9, ☏ 506/789–2366) is in Atholville, 180 km (112 mi) north of Caraquet. The eight trails on this 507-ft vertical drop accommodate skiers of all levels. There are also 25 km (16 mi) of cross-country ski trails. Instruction and equipment rentals are available. In summer an Alpine Slide offers fun on the ski hill, and there's lots of space for camping and hiking. The park has a lounge and cafeteria.

ST. JOHN RIVER VALLEY

The St. John River forms 120 km (74 mi) of the border with Maine, then swings inland. Eventually it cuts through the heart of Fredericton and rolls down to Saint John. Gentle hills of rich farmland and the blue sweep of the water make this a lovely area to drive through. The Trans-Canada Highway (Route 2) follows the banks of the river for most of its winding, 403-km (250-mi) course. New highway construction has left Route 102 (the old Route 2) above Fredericton as a quiet scenic drive. In the early 1800s the narrow wedge of land at the northern end of the valley was coveted by Québec and New Brunswick; the United States claimed it as well. To settle the issue, New Brunswick governor Sir Thomas Carleton rolled dice with the governor of British North America at Québec. Sir Thomas won—by one point. Settling the border with the Americans was more difficult; even the lumberjacks engaged in combat. Finally, in 1842, the British flag was hoisted over Madawaska county. One old-timer, tired of being asked to which country he belonged, replied, "I am a citizen of the Republic of Madawaska." So began the mythical republic, which exists today with its own flag (an eagle on a field of white) and a coat of arms.

St-Jacques

280 km (174 mi) north of Fredericton.

This town near the Québec border contains Les Jardins de la République Provincial Park, with recreational facilities, the Antique Auto Museum, and a botanical garden. At the **New Brunswick Botanical Garden,** roses, rhododendrons, alpine flowers, and dozens of other annuals and perennials bloom in eight gardens. The music of Mozart, Handel, Bach, or Vivaldi often plays in the background. Two arboretums have coniferous and deciduous trees and shrubs. ✉ *Main St.,* ☏ *506/737–5383.* ☞ *$4.75.* ☉ *June and Sept., daily 9–6; July and Aug., daily 9–8.*

Outdoor Activities and Sports

Mont Farlagne (✉ 360 Mont Farlagne Rd., E7B 2X1, ☏ 506/735–8401) has 20 trails for downhill skiing on a vertical drop of 600 ft. Its four lifts can handle 4,000 skiers per hour, and there's night skiing on eight trails. Snowboarding and tube sliding add to the fun. Equipment rentals are available, and there is a cafeteria and a bar.

Edmundston

㉖ *5 km (3 mi) south of St-Jacques, 275 km (171 mi) northwest of Fredericton.*

Edmundston, the unofficial capital of Madawaska, has always depended on the wealth of the deep forest around it. Even today, the town looks to the Fraser Papers pulp mills as the major source of employment. In these woods the legend of Paul Bunyan was born; tales spread to Maine and beyond. The annual **Foire Brayonne** (☏ 506/739–6608), held over the New Brunswick Day (first Monday in August) long weekend, is the biggest Francophone festival outside of Québec. It's also one of the liveliest and most vibrant cultural events in New Brunswick, with concerts by acclaimed artists as well as local musicians and entertainers.

Lodging

$$ 🏨 **Howard Johnson Hotel & Convention Centre.** Its downtown location within a shopping complex near the town's riverside walking trail and a small restaurant with talented chefs, make this chain worth visiting. ⊠ *100 Rice St., E3V 1T4,* ☎ *506/739–7321 or 800/576–4656,* 𝖥𝖠𝖷 *506/735–9101. 99 rooms, 4 suites. Restaurant, indoor pool, hot tub, sauna, meeting rooms. AE, D, DC, MC, V.*

Grand Falls

㉗ *50 km (31 mi) south of Edmundston.*

At Grand Falls, the St. John River rushes over a high cliff, squeezes through a narrow rocky gorge, and emerges as a wider river. The result is a magnificent cascade, whose force has worn strange round wells in the rocky bed, some as large as 16 ft in circumference and 30 ft deep. A **pontoon boat** operates June through early September at the lower end of the gorge and offers an entirely new perspective of the cliffs and wells. Tickets are available at the LaRochelle Tourist Information Centre. ⊠ *2 Chapel St.,* ☎ *506/475–7760.* 🎫 *$10.* ☉ *Hourly boat trips daily 10–7.*

The **Gorge Walk,** which starts at the Malabeam Tourist Information Center (⊠ 24 Madawaska Rd., ☎ 506/475–7788) and covers the full length of the gorge, is dotted with interpretation panels and monuments. There's no charge for the walk, unless you descend to the wells ($3). Guided walking tours are also available ($6). According to native legend, a young maiden named Malabeam led her Iroquois captors to their deaths over the foaming cataract rather than guide them to her village.

The **Grand Falls Historical Museum** depicts local history. ⊠ *142 Court 209, Suite 103,* ☎ *506/473–5265.* 🎫 *Free.* ☉ *July–Aug., Mon.–Fri. 9–5.*

En Route   About 75 km (47 mi) south of Grand Falls, stop in Florenceville for a look at the small but reputable **Andrew and Laura McCain Gallery** (⊠ McCain St., Florenceville, ☎ 506/392–6769), which has launched the career of many New Brunswick artists. The Trans-Canada Highway is intriguingly scenic, but if you're looking for less-crowded highways and typical small communities, cross the river to Route 105 at Hartland (about 20 km [12 mi] south of Florenceville), via the **longest covered bridge** in the world: 1,282 ft in length.

Mactaquac Provincial Park

🐾 **㉘** *197 km (122 mi) south of Grand Falls.*

Surrounding the giant pond created by the Mactaquac Hydroelectric Dam on the St. John River is Mactaquac Provincial Park. Its facilities include an 18-hole championship golf course, two beaches with lifeguards, two marinas (one for power boats and the other for sailboats), supervised crafts activities, myriad nature and hiking trails, and a restaurant. Reservations are advised for the 300 campsites in summer. Winter is fun, too: there are lots of trails for cross-country skiing, and snowshoeing and sleigh rides are available by appointment. The toboggan hills and skating–ice hockey ponds are even lit in the evening. ⊠ *Rte. 105 at Mactaquac Dam,* ☎ *506/363–4747.* 🎫 *$5 per vehicle in summer, free Sept.–June.* ☉ *Daily; overnight camping mid-May–mid-Oct.*

En Route   Oromocto, along Route 102 from Mactaquac Provincial Park, is the site of the Canadian Armed Forces Base, **Camp Gagetown,** the largest military base in Canada (not to be confused with the pretty village of Gagetown farther downriver). Prince Charles completed his helicopter training here. The base has an interesting military museum. ⊠ *Museum, Bldg. A5, off Tilley St.,* ☎ *506/422–1304.* ⊠ *Museum free.* ⊙ *June–Aug., weekdays 8–4, weekends noon–4; Sept.–May, weekdays 8–4.*

Gagetown

㉙   *265 km (164 mi) southeast of Grand Falls, 50 km (31 mi) southeast of Fredericton.*

Historic Gagetown bustles with artisans and the summer sailors who tie up at the marina. The **Queens County Museum** is growing by leaps and bounds. Its original building, **Tilley House,** was the birthplace of Sir Leonard Tilley, one of the Fathers of Confederation. It displays loyalist and First Nations artifacts, early 20th-century medical equipment, Victorian glassware, and more. The museum now also includes the nearby old **Queens County Court House,** which holds county archival material and court house furniture. It also hosts changing exhibits throughout the season. ⊠ *Museum: Front St.; Court House: Court House Rd.,* ☎ *506/488–2966.* ⊠ *$2 per building, $3 for both.* ⊙ *June–mid-Sept., daily 10–5.*

Lodging

$ 🏨 **Steamers Stop Inn.** This grand old waterside inn has a screened veranda, antiques, and an art gallery on the premises. Continental breakfast is included in the rate. Dinner is served by reservation from 6 to 9 each evening. ⊠ *74 Front St., E5M 1A1,* ☎ *506/488–2903,* FAX *506/488–1116,* WEB *www.heritageinns.com/steamers. 6 rooms. Dining room, outdoor hot tub, boating. AE, MC, V. Closed Oct.–Apr.*

Shopping

Beamsley's Coffee House (⊠ 44 Front St., ☎ 506/488–3164) sells lunches, big cookies, sticky buns, and coffee in pottery cups. **Grimcross Crafts** (⊠ 17 Mill Rd., ☎ 506/488–2832) represents 30 area craftspeople. **Flo Grieg's** (⊠ 36 Front St., ☎ 506/488–2074) carries superior pottery made on the premises. **Juggler's Cove** (⊠ 32 Tilley Rd., ☎ 506/488–2574) is a studio-gallery featuring pottery, paintings, and woodwork. **Loomcrofters** (⊠ Loomcroft La., off Main St., ☎ 506/488–2400) is a good choice for handwoven items.

FREDERICTON

The small inland city of Fredericton spreads itself on a broad point of land jutting into the St. John River. Its predecessor, the early French settlement of St. Anne's Point, was established in 1642 during the reign of the French governor Villebon, who made his headquarters at the junction of the Nashwaak and the St. John rivers. Settled by Loyalists and named for Frederick, second son of George III, the city serves as the seat of government for New Brunswick's 753,000 residents. Wealthy and scholarly Loyalists set out to create a gracious and beautiful place, and thus even before the establishment of the University of New Brunswick, in 1785, the town served as a center for liberal arts and sciences. It remains a gracious and beautiful place as well as a center of education, arts, and culture. The river, once the only highway to Fredericton, is now a focus of recreation.

Exploring Fredericton

Downtown Queen Street runs parallel with the river, and its blocks enclose historic sights and attractions. Most major sights are within walking distance of one another. An excursion to Kings Landing Historical Settlement, a reconstructed village, can bring alive the province's history.

Dressed in 18th-century costume, actors from the **Calithumpians** theater company (☎ 506/457–1975) conduct free historical walks several times a day in summer and an after-dark Haunted Hike ($12) several evenings a week.

A Good Walk

Start at City Hall, formerly a farmers' market and opera house, on Phoenix Square, at the corner of York and Queen streets. Its modern council chambers are decorated with tapestries that illustrate Fredericton's history. Walk down (as the river flows) Queen Street to Carleton Street to the **Military Compound** ㉚, which includes the New Brunswick Sports Hall of Fame and the **York-Sunbury Museum** ㉛, the latter occupying what used to be the Officers' Quarters in Officers' Square. Here the Calithumpians offer outdoor comedy theater at lunchtime. On a rainy day the show goes on in the nearby Carleton Street Armory. The next stop down the river side of Queen Street is the **Beaverbrook Art Gallery** ㉜, with its sculpture garden outside. Turn right on Church Street and walk to **Christ Church Cathedral** ㉝. Once you have had your fill of its exquisite architecture and stained glass, turn right and start walking back up Queen. The **Provincial Legislature** ㉞ is on your left. Restaurants and cafés along Queen Street provide opportunities for refreshment. Turn left on St. John Street and then take the second right onto Brunswick Street, where the wonders of **Science East** ㉟ await you. If you make your way back to York Street (across from where you started at City Hall), turn left to visit a chic block of shops. One variation to this walk: if you're touring on Saturday, start in the morning with the **Boyce Farmers' Market,** off George and Brunswick Streets, to get a real taste of the city.

TIMING

The distances are not great, so the time you spend depends on how much you like history, science, art, and churches. You could do it all in an afternoon, but start in the morning at the Boyce Farmers' Market on Saturday.

Sights to See

❸❷ **Beaverbrook Art Gallery.** A lasting gift of the late Lord Beaverbrook, this gallery could hold its head high in the company of some smaller European galleries. Salvador Dali's gigantic *Santiago el Grande* has always been the star, but a rotation of avant-garde Canadian paintings now shares pride of place. The McCain "gallery-within-a-gallery" is devoted to the finest Atlantic Canadian artists. ⊠ *703 Queen St.,* ☎ *506/458–8545.* 🖘 *$5.* ☉ *June–Sept., weekdays 9–6, weekends 10–5; Oct.–May, Tues.–Fri. 9–5, Sat. 10–5, Sun. noon–5.*

Boyce Farmers' Market. It's hard to miss this Saturday-morning market because of the crowds. There are lots of local meat and produce, baked goods, crafts, and seasonal items like wreaths and maple syrup. The market sells good ready-to-eat food, from German sausages to tasty sandwiches. ⊠ *Bounded by Regent, Brunswick, and George Sts.*

❸❸ **Christ Church Cathedral.** One of Fredericton's prides, this gray stone building, completed in 1853, is an excellent example of decorated neo-Gothic architecture. The cathedral's design was based on an ac-

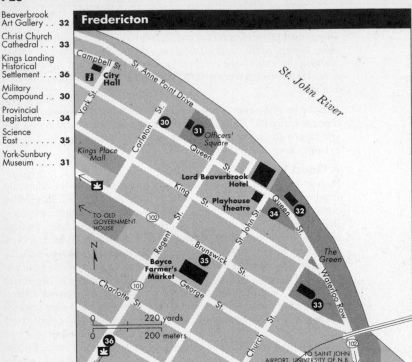

tual medieval prototype in England, and it became a model for many American churches. Inside you'll see a clock known as "Big Ben's little brother," the test run for London's famous timepiece, designed by Lord Grimthorpe. ⊠ *Church St.,* ☎ *506/450–8500.* ☉ *Self-guided tours available year-round. Free guided tours mid-June–Aug., weekdays 9–6, Sat. 10–5, Sun. 1–5.*

OFF THE **MARYSVILLE –** A National Historic Region, Marysville is one of Canada's
BEATEN PATH best-preserved examples of a 19th-century mill town. Its architecture and social history are amazing and can be appreciated with the help of a self-guided walking-tour booklet available at the York-Sunbury Museum and at Westminster Books on King Street. Marysville itself is on the north side of the St. John River, about 10 km (6 mi) from downtown via Route 8.

30 **Military Compound.** The restored buildings of this British and Canadian post, which extends two blocks along Queen Street, include soldiers' barracks, a guardhouse, and a cell block. Local artisans operate studios in the casemates below the soldiers' barracks. In July and August free guided tours run throughout the day and there are outdoor concerts in Officers' Square Tuesday and Thursday evenings. Red Coat soldiers have long stood guard in Officers' Square, and a formal changing-of-the-guard ceremony takes place in summer at 11 and 7. It's even possible for children of all ages to live a soldier's life for a while: each summer afternoon at 2, would-be red coats get their own uniforms and practice drilling ($12 per person, $40 per family). ⊠ *Queen St. at Carleton St.,* ☎ *506/460–2129.* ☑ *Free.*

Old Government House. This imposing 1828 Palladian mansion has been restored as the official seat of office for the province's lieutenant governor. A hands-on interpretation center with multimedia presentations spans 12,000 years of history. Guided tours take in elegantly restored state rooms and art galleries. The 11-acre grounds include a 17th-century Acadian settlement and border an early Maliseet burial ground. ⊠ *Woodstock Rd.,* ☏ *506/453–2505.* 🎫 *Free.* ☉ *June–Oct., daily 10–5 (last hourly tour begins at 4); Nov.–May, weekdays by appointment.*

㉞ Provincial Legislature. The interior chamber of the legislature, where the premier and elected members govern the province, reflects the taste of the late Victorians. The chandeliers are brass, and the prisms are Waterford. Replicas of portraits by Sir Joshua Reynolds of King George III and Queen Charlotte hang here. There's a freestanding circular staircase, and a volume of Audubon's *Birds of America* is on display. ⊠ *Queen St.,* ☏ *506/453–2527.* 🎫 *Free.* ☉ *Legislature tours June–Aug., daily 9–6; Sept.–May, weekdays 9–4; library weekdays 8:15–5.*

㉟ Science East. This hands-on science center, in what was once the York County Jail, has family fun locked up. The more than 70 exhibits include a giant kaleidoscope you can walk inside, a pattern-making laser beam, and a place where you can create a minitornado. ⊠ *668 Brunswick St.,* ☏ *506/457–2340.* 🎫 *$2.* ☉ *June–Sept., Mon.–Sat. 10–5, Sun. 1–4; Oct.–May, Tues.–Fri. noon–5, Sat. 10–5.*

York Street. Here is the city's high-fashion block, with designer shops, a hairdresser-cum-art dealer, an incense-burning boutique, and a general store with an eclectic assortment of gifts and housewares. At the middle of the upriver side of the block is Mazucca's Alley, with more shops and the gateway to several more stores and restaurants in Piper's Lane. King and Queen streets, at either end of the block, have some fun shops, too.

㉛ York-Sunbury Museum. The Officers' Quarters houses a museum that offers a living picture of the community from the time when only First Nations peoples inhabited the area, through the Acadian and Loyalist days, to the immediate past. Its World War I trench puts you in the thick of battle, and the shellacked remains of the giant Coleman Frog, a Fredericton legend, still inspire controversy. ⊠ *Officers' Sq., Queen St.,* ☏ *506/455–6041.* 🎫 *$2.* ☉ *May–early Sept., Mon.–Sat. 10–6; July–Aug., Mon. and Fri. til 9, Sun. noon–6; early Sept.–mid-Oct., weekdays 9–5, Sat. noon–4; mid-Oct.–Apr., Mon., Wed., and Fri. 11–3, or by appointment.*

Dining and Lodging

$$–$$$$ ✕ **Lobster Hut.** A 200-gallon tank stocked with 1- to 2-pound lobsters adds the finishing touch to the nautical décor of this popular spot. The high end of the price range depends on the market price of lobster. ⊠ *City Motel, 1216 Regent St.,* ☏ *506/455–4413. AE, DC, MC, V.*

$–$$$ ✕ **Brewbaker's.** With an old-world Italian atmosphere, California and eclectic cuisine, and a rooftop garden patio, Brewbaker's is downtown's most popular casual lunch and dinner spot. Dishes include fabulous salads, authentic pastas, and thin-crust pizzas baked in a wood-fired brick oven. ⊠ *546 King St.,* ☏ *506/459–0067. Reservations essential. AE, DC, MC, V.*

$–$$ ✕ **Dimitri Souvlaki.** Chicken souvlaki reigns supreme in this downtown authentic Greek eatery, but lots of people make a meal of the appetizers, especially the *pikilia* (hors d'oeuvres) platters and *saganaki* (sautéed goat's milk cheese with lemon juice). ⊠ *349 King St., at Piper's La.,* ☏ *506/452–8882. AE, DC, MC, V.*

$–$$ ✕ **El Burrito Loco.** With cooking experience on his hands, family recipes in his head, and love in his heart, Perez Huerta moved to his wife's home in Fredericton from his home in Jalisco, Mexico. His authentic Mexican dishes—even huevos rancheros for breakfast—caught on like wildfire up north. Everything is made on the spot, from the burritos and tacos to the guacamole and salsa. There's a patio for summer, and occasionally local Spanish guitarists or mariachi players from Montréal entertain. ⊠ *304 King St.*, ☎ *506/459–5626. Reservations essential. AE, MC, V.*

$$$$ ⊞ **Sheraton Fredericton Hotel.** This stately riverside property is within walking distance of downtown. The elegant country décor is almost as delightful as the sunset views over the river from the patio restaurant and many of the modern rooms. The gift shop carries top-notch crafts. Bruno's Cafe serves legendary buffets, seafood on Friday evening, and brunch on Sunday. ⊠ *225 Woodstock Rd., E3B 2H8*, ☎ *506/457–7000, FAX 506/457–4000, WEB www.sheraton.com. 208 rooms, 15 suites. Restaurant, bar, 1 indoor and 1 outdoor pool, hot tub, sauna, gym. AE, DC, MC, V.*

$$$ ⊞ **Holiday Inn Hotel and Resort Fredericton.** Outside the city and overlooking the Mactaquac Headpond, this modern hotel offers luxurious appointments in a relaxed, country atmosphere. There's a fireplace in the lobby, and the suites have electric fireplaces. Some of the rooms with water views have cathedral ceilings. The cottages are ideal for boating and skiing families. ⊠ *35 Mactaquac Rd., off Rte. 102, French Village E3E 1L2*, ☎ *506/363–5111 or 800/561–5111, FAX 506/363–3000, WEB www.holidayinnfredericton.com. 72 rooms, 4 suites, 6 cottages. Dining room, lounge, in-room data ports, indoor pool, hot tub, tennis court, gym, dock. AE, D, DC, MC, V.*

$$ ⊞ **On the Pond Lodge.** This woodland, European-style lodge near the river offers several opportunities for relaxation and rejuvenation, including full spa packages, canoeing, kayaking, and hiking. Everything about the place is elegant yet hearty, from the big stone fireplace and exposed beams in the great room to the well-appointed bedrooms. Dinner in the dining room can be as decadent or as nutritious as you like. ⊠ *20 Rte. 615, Mactaquac E6L 1M2*, ☎ *506/363–3420, FAX 506/363–3479, WEB www.onthepond.com. 8 rooms. Dining room, sauna, bicycles. MC, V.*

$ ⊞ **Carriage House Inn.** The lovely bedrooms in this venerable mansion are furnished with Victorian antiques. A complimentary breakfast, complete with homemade maple syrup for the fluffy pancakes, is served in the solarium. ⊠ *230 University Ave. E3B 4H7*, ☎ *506/452–9924 or 800/267–6068, FAX 506/458–0799, WEB www.bbcanada.com/4658.html. 11 rooms. Solarium. AE, DC, MC, V.*

$ ⊞ **The Very Best—A Victorian B&B.** This elegant home, with its fine antiques and original artwork, is in the downtown Heritage Preservation Area. The smoked-salmon omelette is an outstanding breakfast choice. ⊠ *806 George St., E3B 1K7*, ☎ *506/451–1499, FAX 506/454–1454, WEB www.bbcanada.com/2330.html. 3 rooms. Dining room, pool, sauna. AE, MC, V. BP.*

Nightlife and the Arts

The Arts

The **Calithumpians** (☎ 506/457–1975) offer free summer outdoor theater daily (12:15 weekdays, 2 PM weekends) in Officers' Square and an evening Haunted Hike ($12) through a historic haunted neighborhood and ghostly graveyards. The **Playhouse** (⊠ 686 Queen St., ☎ 506/458–8344) is the venue for theater and most other cultural performances, including Symphony New Brunswick, Theatre New Brunswick, and traveling ballet and dance companies.

Nightlife

Fredericton has a lively nightlife, with lots of live music in downtown pubs, especially on the weekends. King Street and Piper's Lane, off the

300 block of King Street, have a number of spots. **Bugaboo Creek** (✉ 422 Queen St., ☎ 506/453–0582) features R&B and blues. **The Capital** (✉ 362 Queen St., ☎ 506/459–3558) offers an eclectic collection of good acts—jazz, blues, oldies, and folk. **Dolan's Pub** (✉ 349 King St., ☎ 506/454–7474) features Maritime acts every weekend. The **Lunar Rogue** (✉ 625 King St., ☎ 506/450–2065) has an old-world pub atmosphere and occasionally showcases acoustic folk, rock, and Celtic music. **Moe's Garage** (✉ 375 King St., ☎ 506/458–1254) is a venue for rock, blues, folk, and pretty much anything other than country. **Rye's Deli&Pub** (✉ 73 Carleton St., ☎ 506/472–7937) goes for cozy and romantic with leather booths and soft lights. There's live jazz and blues every weekend.

Outdoor Activities and Sports

Boat Tours

The 80-passenger **Carleton II** (✉ Departs from Regent Street Wharf, ☎ 506/454–2628) is used for sightseeing river cruises. **The Wood Duck** (☎ 506/444–9180 or 506/447–7494), a little water taxi complete with a canopy, offers nature and exploration tours. It departs from the Sheraton Hotel and Regent Street Wharf.

Canoeing and Kayaking

Shells, canoes, and kayaks can be rented by the hour, day, or week at the **Small Craft Aquatic Center** (✉ behind Victoria Health Centre, where Brunswick St. becomes Woodstock Rd., ☎ 506/460–2260), which also arranges guided tours and instruction.

Golf

The Lynx At Kingswood Park (✉ 31 Kingswood Park, ☎ 506/443–3333 or 877/666–0001), opened in 2001, is the first major course to open in many years. It's an 18-hole, par-72 championship course designed by Cooke–Huxham International.

Skiing

Ski Crabbe Mountain (✉ 50 Crabbe Mountain Rd., Central Hainesville E6E 1E3, ☎ 506/463–8311) is about 55 km (34 mi) west of Fredericton. There are 17 trails, a vertical drop of 853 ft, snowboard and ski rentals, instruction, a skating pond, baby-sitting, and a lounge and restaurant.

Many of Fredericton's 70 km (44 mi) of walking trails, especially those along the river and in Odell and Wilmot parks, are groomed for cross-country skiing. Other trails are broken and useful for skate-skiing.

Walking

Fredericton has a fine network of walking trails, one of which follows the river from the Green, past the Victorian mansions on Waterloo Row, behind the Beaverbrook Art Gallery, and along the riverbank to the Sheraton. The **visitor information center** in City Hall (✉ Queen St., at York, ☎ 506/460–2129) has a trail map.

Shopping

Indoor mammoth crafts markets are held in the fall; a Labor Day–weekend outdoor craft fair is held in Officers' Square. You can find pottery, blown glass, pressed flowers, turned wood, leather, and other items, all made by members of the New Brunswick Craft Council.

Aitkens Pewter (✉ 65 Regent St., ☎ 506/453–9474) makes its own pewter goblets, belt buckles, candlesticks, and jewelry. **Botinicals Gift Shop** (✉ 65 Shore St. ☎ 506/454–7361) sells crafts by juried Maritime

artisans only. **Carrington&Co.** (✉ 225 Woodstock Rd., ☎ 506/450–8415)
in the Sheraton is a gem for crafts and Tilley Endurables clothing. **Eloise**
(✉ 83 York St., ☎ 506/453–7715) carries kinder, gentler women's fashions. **Gallery 78** (✉ 96 Queen St., ☎ 506/454–5192) has original
works by local artists. **Marba Gallery** (✉ 1565 Woodstock Rd., ☎ 506/
454–4862) offers fine art and crafts, antiques, and even oriental carpets. **The New Brunswick Fine Craft Gallery** (✉ 87 Regent St., ☎ 506/
450–8989) exhibits and sells juried crafts. **Table for Two** (✉ Kings Place
Mall, 440 King St., ☎ 506/455–1401) specializes in New Brunswick
crafts and offers fine imported glass and tableware. **The Urban Almanac
General Store** (✉ 59 York St., ☎ 506/450–4334) has an eclectic collection of unique housewares and other items of exemplary design.

Kings Landing Historical Settlement

★ ☺ ➌➏ *30 km (19 mi) west of Fredericton.*

The Kings Landing Historical Settlement was built by moving period
buildings to a new shore. The drive from Fredricton takes less than a
half hour; to appreciate the museum, plan to spend at least a half day.
Route 102 passes through some spectacular river and hill scenery on
the way, including the Mactaquac Dam—turn off here if you want to
visit Mactaquac Provincial Park.

This excellent outdoor living-history museum on the St. John River
evokes the sights, sounds, and society of rural New Brunswick between
1790 and 1900. The winding country lanes and meticulously restored
homes pull you back a century or more, and programs are available
to let you cane a chair at the carpenter shop or bake bread on an open
hearth. There are daily dramas in the theater, barn dances, and strolling
minstrels. You can see how the wealthy owner of the sawmill lived and
just how different things were for the immigrant farmer. Hearty meals
are served at the Kings Head Inn. ✉ *Exit 253, Trans-Canada Hwy.
(near Prince William),* ☎ 506/363–4999, WEB *www.kingslanding.nb.ca.*
🖾 *$12.* ☺ *June–mid-Oct., daily 10–5.*

NEW BRUNSWICK A TO Z

*To research prices, get advice from other travelers, and book travel ar-
rangements, visit www.fodors.com.*

AIR TRAVEL

Air Canada serves the three major airports in the area. Moncton Airport is also served by Canada 3000 and WestJet.

➤ AIRLINES AND CONTACTS: **Air Canada** (☎ 800/776–3000). **airNova**
(☎ 888/247–2262). **Canada 3000 Airlines** (☎ 877/973–3000). **West-
Jet Airlines** (☎ 800/538–5696).

AIRPORTS

New Brunswick has three major airports. Saint John Airport is in the
east end of the city; Moncton Airport is on Champlain Road; and Fredericton Airport is minutes from downtown on Lincoln Road.

➤ AIRPORT INFORMATION: **Fredericton Airport** (✉ Lincoln Rd., ☎
506/444–6100). **Moncton Airport** (✉ Champlain Rd., ☎ 506/856–
5444). **Saint John Airport** (✉ Loch Lomond Rd., ☎ 506/638–5555).

BUS TRAVEL

SMT Eastern Ltd. runs buses within the province and connects with
most major bus lines.

➤ Bus Information: **SMT Eastern Ltd.** (☎ 506/859–5100 or 800/567–5151).

CAR RENTAL

➤ Major Agencies: **Avis** (☎ 800/331–1084; 800/879–2847 in Canada, WEB www.avis.com). **Budget** (☎ 800/527–0700, WEB www.budget.com). **Hertz** (☎ 800/654–3001; 800/263–0600 in Canada, WEB www.hertz.com). **National Car Rental** (☎ 800/227–7368, WEB www.nationalcar.com).
➤ Local Agencies: **Byways Car & Truck Rental** (☎ 800/668–4233 or 902/469–2620). **Trius Car & Truck Rental** (☎ 506/457–9000).

CAR TRAVEL

From Québec, the Trans-Canada Highway (Route 2) enters New Brunswick at St-Jacques and follows the St. John River through Fredericton and on to Moncton and the Nova Scotia border. From Maine, I–95 crosses at Houlton to Woodstock, New Brunswick, where it connects with the Trans-Canada Highway. Those traveling up the coast of Maine on Route 1, cross at Calais to St. Stephen, New Brunswick. New Brunswick's Route 1 extends to Saint John and up to Sussex, where it meets the Trans-Canada Highway.

New Brunswick has an excellent highway system with numerous facilities. The Trans-Canada Highway, marked by a maple leaf, is the same as Route 2. Route 7 joins Saint John and Fredericton. Fredericton is connected to Miramichi City by Route 8. Route 15 links Moncton to the eastern coast and to Route 11, which follows the coast to Miramichi City, around the Acadian Peninsula, and up to Campbellton. You can get a good map at a visitor information center. Tourism New Brunswick has mapped five scenic routes: the Fundy Coastal Drive, the River Valley Scenic Drive, the Acadian Coastal Drive, the Miramichi River Route, and the Appalachian Range.

EMERGENCIES

➤ Emergency Services: **Ambulance, fire, police** (☎ 911).
➤ Hospitals: **Campbellton Regional Hospital** (✉ 189 Lilly Lake Rd., Campbellton, ☎ 506/789–5000). **Chaleur Regional Hospital** (✉ 1750 Sunset Dr., Bathurst, ☎ 506/548–8961). **Dr. Everett Chalmers Hospital** (✉ Priestman St., Fredericton, ☎ 506/452–5400). **Dr. Georges Dumont Hospital** (✉ 330 Archibald St., Moncton, ☎ 506/862–4000). **Edmundston Regional Hospital** (✉ 275 Hébert Blvd., Edmundston, ☎ 506/739–2200). **Miramichi Regional Hospital** (✉ 500 Water St., Miramichi City, ☎ 506/623–3000). **Moncton City Hospital** (✉ 135 MacBeath Ave., Moncton, ☎ 506/857–5111). **Saint John Regional Hospital** (✉ Tucker Park Rd., Saint John, ☎ 506/648–6000).

OUTDOORS AND SPORTS

Whale-watching, sea kayaking, trail riding, bird-watching, garden touring, river cruising, and fishing are just a few of the province's Day Adventure programs. Packages cover a variety of skill levels and include equipment. All adventures last at least a half day; some are multiday. Information is available at New Brunswick Day Adventure centers (in some information offices, hotels, and attractions), or contact Tourism New Brunswick (☎ 800/561–0123).

BIKING

B&Bs frequently have bicycles for rent. Tourism New Brunswick (☎ 800/561–0123) has listings and free cycling maps. Baymount Outdoor Adventures operates along the Fundy shore near Hopewell Cape.
➤ Contacts: **Baymount Outdoor Adventures** (✉ 17 Elwin Jay Dr., Hillsborough, ☎ 506/734–2660).

FISHING

New Brunswick Fish and Wildlife has information on sporting licenses and can tell you where the fish are.

➤ CONTACTS: **New Brunswick Fish and Wildlife** (☎ 506/453–2440).

GOLF

The most up-to-date information about new courses and upgrades to existing courses is available at the New Brunswick Golf Association.

➤ CONTACTS: **New Brunswick Golf Association** (☎ 506/451–1324, WEB www.golfnb.nb.ca).

HIKING

The New Brunswick Trails Council has complete information on the province's burgeoning trail system.

➤ CONTACTS: **New Brunswick Trails Council** (☎ 506/459–1931 or 800/ 526–7070).

SNOWMOBILING

For information on snowmobiling, contact the New Brunswick Federation of Snowmobile Clubs, a group that maintains the province's 9,000-km trail system and issues permits.

➤ CONTACTS: **New Brunswick Federation of Snowmobile Clubs** (☎ 506/ 325–2625).

TOURS

Saint John visitor information centers have brochures for three good self-guided walking tours. Guided walking tours sponsored by the City of Saint John are also available (☎ 506/658–2855 for information).

TRAIN TRAVEL

VIA Rail offers passenger service every day but Tuesday from Campbellton, Newcastle, and Moncton to Montréal and Halifax.

➤ TRAIN INFORMATION: **VIA Rail** (☎ 800/561–8630 in Canada; 800/ 561–3949 in the U.S.).

TRANSPORTATION AROUND NEW BRUNSWICK

A car is essential outside Saint John, Moncton, and Fredericton. The inter-city bus line (SMT) has specific routes, and there are a couple of places where there are local shuttle services to small towns from the bus, but these are few and far between.

VISITOR INFORMATION

Tourism New Brunswick can provide information on day adventures, scenic driving routes, accommodations, and the seven provincial tourist bureaus. Also helpful are the city information services in Bathurst, Edmundston–St-Jacques, Fredericton, Moncton, Saint John, and St. Stephen.

➤ TOURIST INFORMATION: **Tourism New Brunswick** (✉ Box 12345, Fredericton E3B 5C3, ☎ 800/561–0123, WEB www.tourismnbcanada.com). **Bathurst** (☎ 506/548–0418). **Edmundston–St-Jacques** (☎ 506/735–2747). **Fredericton** (☎ 506/460–2041). **Moncton** (☎ 506/853–3590). **Saint John** (☎ 506/658–2990). **St. Stephen** (☎ 506/466–7390).

13 PRINCE EDWARD ISLAND

This island province, in the Gulf of St. Lawrence north of Nova Scotia and New Brunswick, seems too good to be true, with its crisply painted farmhouses, manicured green fields rolling down to sandy beaches, the warmest ocean water north of the Carolinas, and lobster boats in trim little harbors. The vest-pocket capital city, Charlottetown, is packed with architectural heritage.

W**HEN YOU EXPERIENCE** Prince Edward Island, known locally as "the Island," you'll understand instantly why Lucy Maud Montgomery's novel of youth and innocence, *Anne of Green Gables,* was framed against this land. What may have been unexpected, however, was how the story burst on the world in 1908 and is still selling untold thousands of copies every year. After potatoes and lobsters, Anne is the Island's most important product.

In 1864, Charlottetown, the Island's capital city, hosted one of the most important meetings in Canadian history, which eventually led to the creation of the Dominion of Canada in 1867. Initially, Prince Edward Island was reluctant to join, having spent years fighting for the right to an autonomous government. Originally settled by the French in 1603, the Island was handed over to the British under the Treaty of Paris in 1763. Tensions grew as absentee British governors and proprietors failed to take an active interest in the development of the land, and the resulting parliamentary government proved ineffective for similar reasons. Yet the development of fisheries and agriculture at the beginning of the 19th century strengthened the economy. Soon settlement increased, and those who were willing to take a chance on the Island prospered.

Around the middle of the 19th century, a modern cabinet government was created, and relations between tenants and proprietors worsened. At the same time, talk of creating a union with other North American colonies began. After much deliberation, and although political upheaval had begun to subside, delegates decided that it was in the Island's best economic interest to join the Canadian Confederation.

The 1997 opening of the Confederation Bridge, linking Prince Edward Island's Borden-Carleton with New Brunswick's Cape Jourimain, physically sealed the Island's connection with the mainland. The bridge was not built without controversy. Nobody doubts that it is an engineering marvel: massive concrete pillars—65 ft across and 180 ft high—-were sunk into waters more than 110 ft deep in order to cope with traffic that now brings more than 1 million visitors annually. Most locals have gotten used to the bridge, but some fear the loss of the Island's tranquillity. As you explore the crossroads villages and fishing ports, it's not hard to understand why. Outside the tourist mecca of Cavendish, otherwise known as Anne's Land, the Island seems like an oasis of peace in an increasingly busy world.

Pleasures and Pastimes

The Arts

The arts, particularly theater, are an integral part of the Island. Summer productions and theater festivals are highlights. The grandest is the Charlottetown Festival, which takes place June through mid-September at the Confederation Centre of the Arts. Theater in Summerside, Georgetown, and Victoria is also good. Traditional Celtic music, with fiddling and step dancing, can be heard almost daily.

Beaches

Prince Edward Island is ringed by beaches, most of them lightly used. Ask a dozen Islanders to recommend their favorites and you'll hear many different answers. Basin Head Beach, near Souris, is one choice—miles of singing sands, utterly deserted. West Point has lifeguards, restaurants nearby, and showers at the provincial park. At Greenwich, near St. Peter's Bay, a half-hour walk along the floating boardwalk brings you to an endless empty beach. In summer, thanks to a branch of the

Gulf Stream, the ocean beaches have the warmest water north of the Carolinas, making for fine swimming.

Dining

On Prince Edward Island, wholesome, home-cooked fare is a matter of course. Talented chefs ensure fine cuisine in each region. The service is friendly—though a little laid back at times—and the setting is generally informal. Seafood is usually good anywhere on the Island, with top honors given to lobster. Lobster suppers are offered commercially and by church and civic groups. These meals feature lobster, rolls, salad, and mountains of sweet home-baked goods. Local papers, bulletin boards at grocery stores, and visitor information centers have information about these events.

CATEGORY	COST*
$$$$	over $32
$$$	$22–$32
$$	$13–$21
$	under $13

per person, in Canadian dollars, for a main course at dinner

Lodging

Prince Edward Island has a variety of accommodations in a range of prices, from full-service resorts and luxury hotels to moderately priced motels, cottages, and lodges. Some farms take guests, too. For July and August, lodgings should be booked early, especially for long stays.

CATEGORY	COST*
$$$$	over $200
$$$	$150–$200
$$	$100–$150
$	under $100

All prices are in Canadian dollars for a standard double room, excluding 10% provincial sales tax and 7% GST.

Outdoor Activities and Sports

BIKING

The Island is popular with bike-touring companies for its moderately hilly roads and stunning scenery; trips take place throughout the province, and the Island's tourism department can recommend tour operators. There are plenty of level areas, especially east of Charlottetown to Montague and along the north shore. However, shoulderless, narrow secondary roads in some areas and summer's car traffic can be challenging. A 9-km (5½-mi) path near Cavendish Campground loops around marsh, woods, and farmland. The Confederation Trail, which extends almost the complete length of the Island, has more than 350 km (217 mi) of flat surface covered with rolled stonedust, making it an excellent family cycling path. Plum-colored entry gateways are near roadways at many points. A two-sided map–information sheet is available from Tourism PEI.

FISHING

Deep-sea fishing boats are available along the eastern end of the Island as well as in the north shore region. Although some boats can be chartered for fishing bluefin tuna, most operators offer excursions to fish for mackerel and cod. These trips stay within 6 km (4 mi) of the shore and usually last for three or four hours. The vessels have washroom facilities, approved safety equipment, and all the required gear and bait. Some operators clean and bag the catch if passengers request it.

Freshwater sport fishing for rainbow trout or salmon is also an option. A nonresident one-day fishing license may be purchased for $7 at more than 100 businesses (hardware, tackle, convenience stores) throughout PEI. A few operations rent fishing tackle and offer "no license required" fishing on private ponds.

GOLF

Prince Edward Island is a golfer's paradise with more than two dozen 9- and 18-hole courses open to the public. Several of the more beautiful ones have scenic ocean vistas, and almost all have hassle-free golfing—easily booked tee times, inexpensive rates, and uncrowded courses, particularly in fall. Brudenell River, incorporating the Brudenell Resort Golf Academy, is Atlantic Canada's only 36-hole complex.

HIKING

Hiking within the lush scenic areas of Prince Edward Island National Park and provincial parks is encouraged with marked trails, many of which are being upgraded to provide quality surfaces good for walking, hiking, or cycling. One of the trails is part of Confederation Trail, a provincial trail system created along the flat roadbed of the former railway network, which allows outdoor explorers to travel 350 km (217 mi) within the province. Contact Tourism PEI for a map.

Exploring Prince Edward Island

Prince Edward Island is irregular in shape, with deep inlets and tidal streams that nearly divide the province into three equal parts, known locally by their county names of Kings, Queens, and Prince (east to west). Roughly resembling a crescent, it is 224 km (139 mi) from one end to the other, with a width ranging from 4 km (2½ mi) to 60 km (37 mi). The Island is a rich agricultural region surrounded by sandy beaches, delicate dunes, and stunning red sandstone cliffs. The eastern and central sections consist of gentle hills. Nevertheless, the land never rises to a height of more than 500 ft above sea level, and you are never more than 15 minutes by car from a beach or waterway. To the west, from Summerside to North Cape, the terrain is flatter.

Numbers in the text correspond to numbers in the margin and on the Prince Edward Island and Charlottetown maps.

Great Itineraries

Visitors often tour only the central portion of the Island, taking Confederation Bridge from New Brunswick to Borden-Carleton and exploring Anne country and Prince Edward Island National Park. To experience the Island's character more deeply, you might visit the wooded hills of the east, including compact, bustling Montague. Another choice is to go west to superb, almost private beaches, the Acadian parish of Tignish, and the country around Summerside. Even if you're in a rush, it won't take long to get off and back on the beaten path: in most places you can cross the Island, north to south, in half an hour or so. The four areas identified in this chapter include many Island highlights: a mostly walking tour of Charlottetown, and three tours following the major scenic highways—Blue Heron Drive, Kings Byway, and Lady Slipper Drive. There are plenty of chances to get out of the car, hit the beach, or photograph wildflowers.

IF YOU HAVE 1 DAY

Leaving ⊤ **Charlottetown** ①–⑨ on Route 2 west, take Route 15 north to **Brackley Beach** ⑪. This puts you onto a 137-km-long (85-mi-long) scenic drive, marked with signs depicting a blue heron. Route 6 west takes you to **Cavendish** ⑫, an entryway to **Prince Edward Island National Park** ⑩. Cavendish is home to the fictional character Anne of Lucy Maud Montgomery's *Anne of Green Gables*. This area has enough attractions for a full day, but if you prefer to keep exploring,

Prince Edward Island

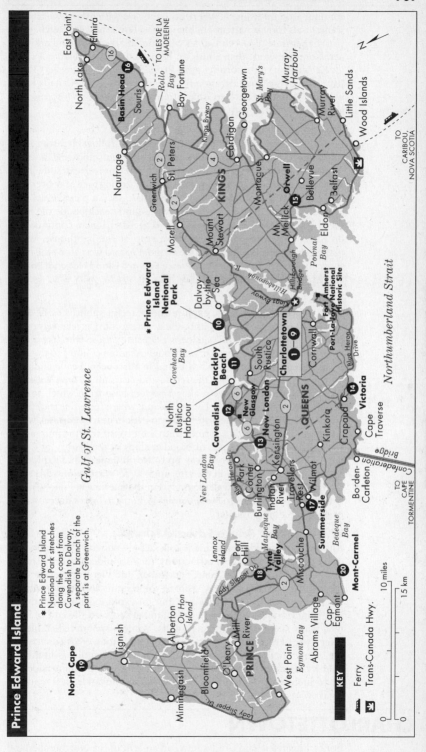

* Prince Edward Island
National Park stretches
along the coast from
Cavendish to Dalvay.
A separate branch of the
park is at Greenwich.

Gulf of St. Lawrence

Northumberland Strait

KEY

Ferry

Trans-Canada Hwy.

10 miles

15 km

TO ILES DE LA MADELEINE

TO CARIBOU, NOVA SCOTIA

TO CAPE TORMENTINE

East Point
Elmira
North Lake
Basin Head 16
Souris
Naufrage
Greenwich
St Peters
Morell
Mount Stewart
Bay Fortune
Cardigan
Georgetown
St. Mary's Bay
Murray Harbour
Murray River
Little Sands
Wood Islands
KINGS
Manague
Mt. Mellick
Orwell 15
Bellevue
Belfast
Eldon
Pownal Bay
Hillsborough Bridge
Fort Amherst National Historic Site
Port-La-Joye
Charlottetown 1–9
Cornwall
Blue Heron Drive
Victoria 14
Crapaud
Cape Traverse
QUEENS
Kinkora
Bo-den-Carleton
Confederation Bridge
Dalvay-by-the-Sea
Prince Edward Island National Park 10
Coveheaд Bay
Brackley Beach 11
South Rustico
North Rustico Harbour
Cavendish 12
New Glasgow
New London 13
Kensington
Indian River
Travellers Rest
Wilmot
Summerside
Bedeque Bay
Mont-Carmel 20
Tyne Valley 18
Port Hill
Lennox Island
Miscouche
Malpeque Bay
Park Corner
Burlington
Abrams Village
Cap-Egmont
Egmont Bay
West Point
Lady Slipper Dr.
PRINCE
Bloomfield
O'Leary
Mill River
Alberton
Tignish
Mimnegash
North Cape 19
Ou Hon Island

continue west on Route 6, where museums vie with fishing wharfs and scenic vistas for your attention. Blue Heron Drive, now Route 20, takes you to the Anne of Green Gables Museum at Silver Bush in Park Corner. Continue west, then south on Route 20 and join Route 2 south (at Kensington) until turning onto Route 1A east (at Travellers Rest). Just north of the Confederation Bridge, follow the Trans-Canada Highway east (Route 1) back to Charlottetown. **Victoria** ⑭ is a scenic fishing town along the way.

IF YOU HAVE 2 DAYS

Leaving ⌨ **Charlottetown** ①–⑨ early in the day, follow Highway 1 east to Kings Byway, a scenic drive marked by signs showing a king's crown, and on to **Orwell** ⑮, where a period farm re-creates life in the 1800s. Continue on to **Montague** for a seal-watching tour. Stay overnight in the area of ⌨ **Bay Fortune.** The next day, pack a picnic lunch and head out for a morning on the soft white-sand beach beside the Basin Head Fisheries Museum in **Basin Head** ⑯. After lunch, continue east on Kings Byway to East Point for a stop at the lighthouse, which marks the easternmost point on the Island. Proceed west along the north shore to the eastern entrance of **Prince Edward Island National Park** ⑩ and end your tour with a swim or hike.

IF YOU HAVE 3 DAYS

From **Charlottetown** ①–⑨, explore the peaceful suburbs of ⌨ **Summerside** ⑰ before heading for its bustling waterfront. The relatively undiscovered area west of Summerside is perfect for those who like a slow pace. Follow Lady Slipper Drive through Acadian country to the Acadian Museum of Prince Edward Island in **Miscouche.** Leave midafternoon and take Route 12 to the scenic and peaceful ⌨ **Tyne Valley** ⑱. This small, friendly village makes a perfect base from which to visit the Mi'Kmaq community at Lennox Island, where some fine traditional crafts are sold. Stop by the historic Green Park in nearby **Port Hill,** where you may stroll through a former shipyard or visit the fine museum to learn about the importance of wooden ships in the history of the Island. On Day 3, make your way up to **North Cape** ⑲ and explore its reef. Plan to arrive early in the afternoon at ⌨ **West Point,** where you can enjoy the beach and walking trails. Finish your time in Prince County with a south-shore tour to **Mont-Carmel** ⑳, home to one of the province's best French dinner theaters.

When to Tour Prince Edward Island

Although Prince Edward Island is considered a summer destination because of its many seasonal attractions, the "shoulder seasons" should not be overlooked. May, June, September, and October usually have spectacular weather and few visitors; some sights and restaurants are closed, however. Fall is an excellent time for exploring, hiking, and golfing. Migratory birds arrive in vast numbers toward the end of summer, many staying until the snow falls. Winters are unpredictable but offer some of the Island's most overlooked activities: cross-country skiing, snowmobiling, and ice-skating on ponds. Nightlife is limited in cold weather although many communities, including Summerside and Charlottetown, offer residents and visitors an array of festivals and cultural events.

CHARLOTTETOWN

Prince Edward Island's oldest city, on an arm of the Northumberland Strait, is named for the stylish consort of King George III. This small city, peppered with gingerbread-clad Victorian houses and tree-shaded squares, is the largest community on the Island (population 33,000).

It's often called the Cradle of Confederation, a reference to the 1864 conference that led to the union of Nova Scotia, New Brunswick, Ontario, and Québec in 1867 and, eventually, Canada itself.

Charlottetown's main activities center on government, tourism, and private commerce. While new suburbs were springing up around it, the core of Charlottetown remained unchanged, and the waterfront has been restored to recapture the flavor of earlier eras. Today the waterfront includes the Delta Prince Edward Hotel; an area known as Peake's Wharf and Confederation Landing Park, with informal restaurants and handicraft and retail shops; and a walking path painted as a blue line on the sidewalk leading visitors through some of the most interesting historical areas of the Old City. Irene Rogers's *Charlottetown: The Life in Its Buildings,* available locally, gives much detail about the architecture and history of downtown Charlottetown.

Exploring Charlottetown

Historic homes, churches, parks, and the waterfront are among the pleasures of a tour of downtown Charlottetown, and you can see many of the sights on foot. The city center is compact, so walking is the best way to explore the area.

A Good Tour

Before setting out to explore Charlottetown, brush up on local history at the **Confederation Centre of the Arts** ① on Richmond Street, in the heart of downtown. Next door, the **Province House National Historic Site** ② is the site of the first meeting to discuss federal union. If you have an interest in churches, turn left off Richmond Street onto Prince Street to see **St. Paul's Anglican Church** ③. Backtrack on Richmond two blocks and turn left onto Great George Street, home to **St. Dunstan's Basilica** ④, with its towering twin Gothic spires. Great George Street ends at the waterfront, where the boardwalks of **Confederation Landing Park** ⑤ lead past small eateries, shops, and **Founder's Hall.**

On the city's west end, the work of Robert Harris, Canada's foremost portrait artist, adorns the walls of **St. Peter's Cathedral** ⑥ in Rochford Square, bordered by Rochford and Pownal streets. It's a bit of a walk (¾ km, or ½ mi) to get there, but **Victoria Park** ⑦ provides a grassy respite edging the harborfront. Next, visit one of the finest residential buildings in the city, **Beaconsfield Historic House** ⑧, for panoramic views of its quiet garden and Charlottetown Harbour. Leave time to observe a favorite Prince Edward Island pastime—harness racing at **Charlottetown Driving Park** ⑨.

TIMING

The downtown area can be explored on foot in a couple of hours, but the wealth of historic sites and harbor views warrants a full day.

Sights to See

⑧ **Beaconsfield Historic House.** Designed by the architect W. C. Harris and built in 1877 for a wealthy shipbuilder, James Peake, Jr., this gracious Victorian home near the entrance to Victoria Park is one of the Island's finest historic homes, with 11 furnished rooms. You can tour the first and second floors and enjoy views of the garden and Charlottetown Harbour. An on-site bookstore features museum publications as well as community histories. Special events such as musical performances and history-based lectures are held regularly. A carriage house on the grounds has activities for children in summer, including a weekday morning Children's Festival during July and August (call for exact times and price). ⊠ *2 Kent St.,* ☎ *902/368–6603.* ⛫ *$3.50.* ⊙ *June–early Sept., daily 10–5; late Sept.–June, daily, call for hrs.*

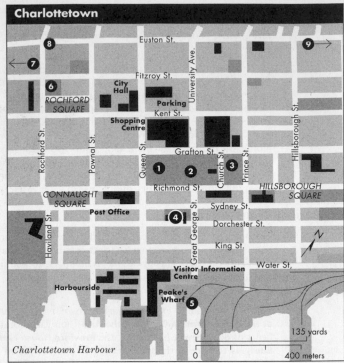

Charlottetown

Charlottetown Harbour

0   135 yards

0   400 meters

❾ Charlottetown Driving Park. Since 1890 this track at the eastern end of the city has been the home of a sport dear to Islanders—harness racing. Standardbred horses are raised around the Island, and harness racing on the ice and on country tracks has been popular for generations. In fact there are more horses per capita on the Island than in any other Canadian province. August brings **Old Home Week,** when eastern Canada's best converge for 15 races in 8 days. ⊠ *Kensington Rd.,* ☎ *902/892–6823.* ☏ *Free.* ☉ *Races June, July, and most of Aug., 3 nights per wk; Old Home Week mid-Aug., Mon.–Sat. twice daily.*

❶ Confederation Centre of the Arts. Set in Charlottetown's historic red-brick core, this modern, concrete structure houses a 1,100-seat main-stage theater and two 190-seat second-stage theaters. The center also has an outdoor amphitheater, a memorial hall, a gift shop with Canadian crafts, a seasonal theater shop, an art gallery and museum, a public library with a special Prince Edward Island collection, including first editions of Lucy Maud Montgomery's famous novel, and a restaurant. The center's art gallery is the largest east of Montréal and provides a varied year-round exhibition program that showcases both contemporary and historical Canadian art, especially as it relates to Canadian Confederation. The **Charlottetown Festival,** which runs from the end of May to mid-October, includes the professional musical adaptation *Anne of Green Gables—The Musical*™ and other world-class musical theater and comedy productions. Weather permitting, the festival also offers free summer musical entertainment at noon in the amphitheater as well as near the center's main entrance. ⊠ *145 Richmond St.,* ☎ *902/566–1267 for box office; 800/565–0278.* ☉ *Daily 9–5; hrs extended May–Oct.*

❺ Confederation Landing Park. This waterfront recreation area at the bottom of Great George Street marks the site of the historic landing of the

Fathers of Confederation in 1864. Walkways and park benches offer plenty of opportunity to survey the activity of the harbor. During summer, performers in period costume stroll about the area re-creating historical events leading up to Canadian Confederation. **Founder's Hall** heritage attraction opened in 2001. Using state-of-the-art displays, this interpretation center adds insight into Charlottetown's past. Among other activities, visitors are transported back in time to the Charlottetown Conference of 1864, eventually returning to the present day with a greater appreciation for this important event in Canadian history. The adjacent **Peake's Wharf** features casual restaurants and bars, souvenir and crafts shops, and a marina where boat tours may be arranged.

NEED A BREAK? **Cows Ice Cream** (✉ Queen St., ☎ 902/892–6969; ✉ Peake's Wharf, ☎ 902/566–4886) is the most famous ice cream on the Island. Fresh milk from PEI cows and other natural ingredients are carefully combined to create 36 flavors of premium, creamy ice cream that should be slowly savored. Cows Ice Cream can be purchased at the two Charlottetown locations, as well as at Cavendish Boardwalk, in Summerside, PEI Factory Shops in North River, Gateway Village at the approach to Confederation Bridge, and on board the PEI–Nova Scotia passenger ferry, *The Confederation.*

★ ❷ **Province House National Historic Site.** This three-story sandstone building, completed in 1847 to house the colonial government and now the seat of the Provincial Legislature, has been restored to its mid-19th-century Victorian appearance. The many restored rooms include the historic Confederation Chamber, where representatives of the 19th-century British colonies met. Special guided tours are offered for a nominal charge, historical programs may be viewed daily during the summer months, and a gift shop offers mementos. ✉ *Richmond St.,* ☎ *902/566–7626.* ▣ *Donation accepted.* ☉ *Mid-Oct.–May, weekdays 9–5; June and Sept.–mid-Oct., daily 9–5; July–Aug., daily 9–6.*

❹ **St. Dunstan's Basilica.** One of Canada's largest churches, St. Dunstan's is the seat of the Roman Catholic diocese on the Island. The church is known for its fine Italian carvings and twin Gothic spires. ✉ *Great George St.,* ☎ *902/894–3486.*

❸ **St. Paul's Anglican Church.** Erected in 1896, this is actually the third church building on this site. The first was built in 1747, making this the Island's oldest parish. You can view the paintings and artwork inside the chapel. ✉ *101 Prince St.,* ☎ *902/892–1691.*

❻ **St. Peter's Cathedral.** The murals by artist Robert Harris are found in **All Souls' Chapel,** designed in 1888 by his brother W. C. "Willy" Harris, the most celebrated of the Island's architects and the designer of many historic homes and buildings. This small chapel, which is attached to the side of the cathedral, may be open for viewing by chance; if not, you should inquire inside the cathedral. ✉ *Rochford Sq.,* ☎ *902/566–2102.*

❼ **Victoria Park.** At the southern tip of the city and overlooking Charlottetown Harbour are 40 beautiful acres that provide the perfect place to stroll, picnic, or watch a baseball game. Next to the park, on a hill between groves of white birches, is the white colonial **Government House,** built in 1835 as the official residence for the province's lieutenant governors (the house is not open to the public). The collection of antique cannons that still "guard" the city's waterfront provides a play area for children; runners enjoy the pathway that edges the harbor. ✉ *Lower Kent St.* ☉ *Park daily sunrise–sunset.*

Dining

$$–$$$$ ✕ **The Selkirk.** With its wing chairs and live piano entertainment, the Selkirk is the Island's most sophisticated dining room. The imaginative menu concentrates on regional Canadian fare—locally grown potatoes, smoked Atlantic salmon, lobster, mussels, Malpeque oysters, and Canadian beef, to name a few—served with herbs straight from the garden. A four-course extravaganza aims to satisfy even the largest appetite. ⊠ *Delta Prince Edward Hotel, 18 Queen St.,* ☎ *902/894–1208. Reservations essential. AE, DC, MC, V.*

$$–$$$ ✕ **Claddagh Room Restaurant.** Some of the best seafood in Charlotte-
      ★ town is served here. The "Galway Bay Delight," one of the Irish owner's specialties, is a savory combination of fresh scallops and shrimp sautéed with onions and mushrooms, flambéed in Irish Mist, and doused with fresh cream. Nonseafarers can choose from other dishes featuring chicken, beef, and fresh pasta. The Olde Dublin Pub upstairs has live Irish entertainment every night in summer and on weekends in winter. This friendly pub has the largest selection of beer on tap to be found anywhere on PEI. ⊠ *131 Sydney St.,* ☎ *902/892–9661. AE, DC, MC, V.*

$$–$$$ ✕ **Culinary Institute of Canada.** Students at this internationally acclaimed school cook and present lunch and dinner under the supervision of their master chef instructor as part of their training. Here's an opportunity to enjoy excellent food and top service at reasonable prices. Located at the very end of Sydney Street, next to Charlottetown Harbour, the institute has an elegant dining room with large windows that provide lovely water vistas. Many local residents come to this tastefully decorated dining room when they want a special culinary experience. Call for a schedule. ⊠ *4 Sydney St.,* ☎ *902/894–6868. Reservations essential. AE, MC, V.*

$$–$$$ ✕ **Griffon Dining Room.** Located in the Queen Anne–style Dundee Arms Inn, this cozy restaurant is filled with antiques, copper, and brass. The French Continental cuisine includes fresh Atlantic salmon, beef tenderloin, and sea scallops. The Hearth and Cricket Pub, which serves light meals and a good selection of local and imported beers, is on the same level as the dining room. ⊠ *200 Pownal St.,* ☎ *902/892–2496 or 877/638–6333. AE, DC, MC, V.*

$–$$$ ✕ **Off Broadway.** Popular with Charlottetown's young professional set, this cozy spot began modestly as a crepe-and-soup joint. You can still make a meal of the lobster or chicken crepes and the soup or Caesar salad that come with them, but now the restaurant has a fairly inventive Continental menu. Fresh local ingredients are served in strongly French-influenced preparations. The private booths won't reveal your indiscretions, including your indulgence in dessert. Upstairs, with large windows overlooking the street, is the 42nd Street Lounge, where a comfortable, casual atmosphere prevails. Light fare from the restaurant kitchen is available. ⊠ *125 Sydney St.,* ☎ *902/566–4620. AE, DC, MC, V.*

$$ ✕ **Peake's Quay Restaurant and Bar.** This great summer spot on Charlottetown's restored waterfront has daily lunch and evening specials during the summer season. The large, heated patio overlooks Confederation Landing Park and the adjoining marina. Specialties include seafood chowder, fresh scallops, and Atlantic salmon. Lobster is also featured on the menu. There's a large selection of snack food available, and live entertainment is provided Thursday through Saturday evenings from May until the end of September. ⊠ *2 Great George St.,* ☎ *902/368–1330. DC, MC, V. Closed Nov.–early May.*

$$ ✕ **Piece a Cake Restaurant.** The young chef–owner, Wesley Gallant, cooks what he likes—and it appears that the public likes what he cooks. Upstairs overlooking Grafton Street, near the Confederation Centre (and with a rear entrance to Confederation Mall), this eatery features Canadian cooking with eclectic influences. Working in an open kitchen, Gallant prepares fresh ingredients with spices and sauces inspired from around the world. The changing menu always includes a good selection of pastas. A jazz or blues group usually entertains patrons on Tuesday nights. Be sure to ask for one of the six window tables. ⊠ *119 Grafton St.,* ☎ *902/894–4585. AE, DC, MC, V. Closed Sun.*

$–$$ ✕ **Lone Star Cafe & Saloon.** This themed eatery (it bills itself as "the best little food house from Texas") serves hearty Tex-Mex fare—tacos, mesquite-grilled chicken, fajitas, and the like. Its casual country atmosphere is very popular with local residents, who come for what many consider to be the best fajitas on the Island. The café is in one of the many small strip malls that line both sides of University Avenue. ⊠ *449 University Ave.,* ☎ *902/894–7827. AE, MC, V.*

Lodging

$$$–$$$$ ⊞ **Delta Prince Edward Hotel.** A member of the Delta chain of hotels
★ and resorts, the Prince Edward has all the comforts and luxuries of its first-rate counterparts—from whirlpool baths in some suites to a grand ballroom and conference center. Guest rooms are modern, and two-thirds of the rooms in this 10-story hotel overlook the waterfront. Located next to Peake's Wharf, the Delta Prince Edward has an ideal location from which to explore both the waterfront and historic downtown areas on foot. In addition to all the conveniences you expect in a full-service hotel, there are three dining choices. The resort also has a game room and golf simulators. ⊠ *18 Queen St. (Box 2170), C1A 8B9,* ☎ *902/566–2222,* FAX *902/566–1745,* WEB *www.deltahotels.com. 211 rooms, 33 suites. 3 restaurants, bar, indoor pool, sauna, gym, health club, coin laundry. AE, DC, MC, V.*

$$$–$$$$ ⊞ **Inns on Great George.** Closely linked with the founding of Canada
★ as a nation (the so-called Fathers of Confederation stayed in these buildings during the 1864 Charlottetown Conference), this complex opened as a hotel in 1997. It includes several historic 1800s structures: the 24-room Pavilion, the five-room Wellington, and the Carriage House (a two-story house with living room and kitchen), as well as the Witter-Coombs Prime Minister's Suite and self-catering apartments. A number of the restored buildings date back to 1811. Some rooms have a four-poster bed, fireplace, claw-foot or whirlpool tub, hardwood floors, and Oriental rugs. Complimentary breakfast is served in the reception area of The Pavilion each morning. ⊠ *58 Great George St., C1A 4K3,* ☎ *902/892–0606 or 800/361–1118,* FAX *902/628–2079,* WEB *www.innsongreatgeorge.com. 29 rooms, 1 suite, 6 apartments, 1 house. AE, DC, MC, V. CP.*

$$–$$$$ ⊞ **Hillhurst Inn.** A handsome, elegant bed-and-breakfast in the heart of downtown, this grand 1897 mansion was once the home of George Longworth, a prominent Charlottetown merchant who made a fortune from building and operating ships, and has been designated a historic property. The reception area, dining room, and living room are paneled with burnished oak and beech, the work of the shipwrights Longworth employed. Each of the unique guest rooms has period furniture, and many have exquisite handmade beds. Two rooms have whirlpool baths. Deluxe breakfast is included. ⊠ *181 Fitzroy St., C1A 1S3,* ☎ *902/894–8004 or 877/994–8004,* FAX *902/892–7679,* WEB *www.hillhurst.com. 9 rooms. Air-conditioning. AE, MC, V. CP.*

$$–$$$$ ⊞ **The Shipwright Inn.** In a lovely 1860s home originally owned by the local shipbuilder James Douse are eight unique guest rooms and one

housekeeping apartment. The nautical theme is continued throughout the house in both construction and decoration. All rooms have original wood floors and Victorian memorabilia. Some units have fireplaces, whirlpool baths, and balconies. Guests enjoy innkeeper Judy Hill's memorable full breakfast and afternoon tea. ⊠ *51 Fitzroy St., C1A 1R4,* ☎ *902/368–1905 or 888/306–9966,* FAX *902/628–1905,* WEB *www.isn.net/shipwrightinn. 8 rooms, 1 apartment. Air-conditioning, fans. AE, MC, V. BP.*

$$$ 🏨 **Rodd Charlottetown—A Rodd Signature Hotel.** This five-story, red-brick hotel with white pillars and a circular driveway is just one block from the center of Charlottetown. The rooms have the latest amenities but retain the hotel's old-fashioned flavor (it was built in 1931) with reproductions of antique furnishings. The grandeur and charm of the Carvery Dining Room capture the elegance of an earlier era. ⊠ *Kent and Pownal Sts. (Box 159), C1A 7K4,* ☎ *902/894–7371 or 800/ 565–7633,* FAX *902/368–2178,* WEB *www.rodd-hotels.ca. 108 rooms, 7 suites. Restaurant, lounge, indoor pool, hot tub, sauna, gym. AE, DC, MC, V.*

$$–$$$ 🏨 **The Dundee Arms Inn.** Depending on your mood, you can choose
★ to stay in either a 1960s motel or a 1904 Queen Anne–style inn. The motel is simple, modern, and neat; the inn is homey and furnished with brass and antiques. The Dundee Arms is only minutes from downtown. ⊠ *200 Pownal St., C1A 3W8,* ☎ *902/892–2496 or 877/638–6333,* FAX *902/368–8532,* WEB *www.dundeearms.com. 15 rooms, 3 suites. Restaurant, pub, air-conditioning. AE, DC, MC, V.*

$$–$$$ 🏨 **Elmwood Heritage Inn.** One of the Atlantic Provinces' leading ar-
★ chitects, W. C. Harris, designed this handsome Victorian home in 1889. Originally part of a 20,000-acre estate, Elmwood was owned by Arthur Peters, grandson of Samuel Cunard, founder of the famous shipping line. Today it's in a quiet, residential area, set back from the road at the end of a 350-ft tree-lined driveway. The antiques-laden home has been restored, and the tastefully decorated rooms have either claw-foot tubs (in three rooms) or whirlpool baths. Some rooms have a working fireplace. A common living room has its own fireplace and second-floor balcony as well as a refrigerator, CD player, and a video-tape collection. An elegant candlelight breakfast is included in the rate. ⊠ *121 N. River Rd., C1A 3K7,* ☎ *902/368–3310 or 877/933– 3310,* FAX *902/628–8457,* WEB *www.elmwoodinn.pe.ca. 6 rooms. Air-conditioning, in-room VCRs. DC, MC, V. BP.*

Nightlife and the Arts

Ceilidhs, or live traditional entertainment combining dancing, fiddling, and comedy, can be found in and around Charlottetown. For information on locations and times, contact the Visitor Information Centre (☎ 902/368–4444). The **Benevolent Irish Society Hall** (⊠ 582 North River Rd., ☎ 902/892–2367) stages concerts on Friday, mid-May through October. There are a number of amateur and professional theater productions for adults and children, including dinner theaters. For schedules and cost, contact each one individually. **Eddie May Murder Mystery Dinner Theatre** (⊠ Piazza Joe's, 189 Kent St., ☎ 902/569–1999) combines madcap improvisation with sleuthing and dining. **Feast Dinner Theatre** (⊠ Rodd Charlottetown, corner of Kent and Pownal Sts., ☎ 902/629–2321) stages a lively show while you feast on chicken and ribs, mussels, and homemade bread. **Homefree Productions** (⊠ Beaconsfield Historic House, ☎ 902/368–6603) offers a summer-long program that may include musicals and dramas, as well as children's presentations, story-telling and concerts.

Outdoor Activities and Sports

Biking

Bicycling is a favorite sport in PEI, including its capital. There are several companies that offer bicycle repairs and rentals as well as guided city bicycle tours, among them **Cycle Smooth** (⊠ 172 Prince St., ☎ 902/566–5530).

Golf

Although there are no courses in Charlottetown, the 18-hole **Fox Meadow Golf and Country Club** (⊠ 167 Kinlock Rd., Stratford, ☎ 902/569–4653) is only a 15-minute drive from downtown. A challenging par-72 championship course, it was designed by Rob Heaslip and overlooks both the community of Stratford and Charlottetown Harbour.

Water Sports

Summertime water sports are very popular throughout the Island, and several companies operate within Charlottetown. For day sailing, contact **Saga Sailing Adventures** (⊠ Charlottetown Harbour, ☎ 902/672–1222). You can arrange pick-up service from your hotel for north shore sea kayaking. A good way to discover the area's natural beauty is to contact **Outside Expeditions** (☎ 902/963–3366 or 800/207–3899). **Peake's Wharf Boat Tours/Seal Watching** (⊠ 1 Great George St., Peake's Wharf, ☎ 902/566–4458) arranges seal-watching tours.

Shopping

The most interesting stores are at Peake's Wharf, in Confederation Court Mall (off Queen Street), and in Victoria Row on Richmond Street, between Queen and Great George streets. The zany **Cows** (⊠ Queen St., across from Confederation Centre, ☎ 902/892–6969) sells all things bovine—from T-shirts embellished with cartoon cows to delicious ice cream. **Great Northern Knitters** (⊠ 18 Queen St., ☎ 902/566–5302), in the Delta Prince Edward Hotel, has a terrific selection of handmade woolen sweaters. **Roots** (⊠ Confederation Court Mall, off Queen St., ☎ 902/566–1877) is an upscale leather-goods and clothing company with stores across Canada. There are a dozen factory outlet stores along the Trans-Canada Highway at North River Causeway near the western entrance to the city.

BLUE HERON DRIVE

From Charlottetown, Blue Heron Drive follows Route 15 north to the north shore, then winds along Route 6 through north-shore fishing villages, past the spectacular white-sand beaches of Prince Edward Island National Park, through Anne of Green Gables country, and finally along the south shore, with its red-sandstone seascapes and historic sites. The drive takes its name from the great blue heron, a stately water bird that migrates to Prince Edward Island every spring to nest in the shallow bays and marshes. The whole circuit roughly outlines Queens County and covers 190 km (118 mi). It circles some of the Island's most beautiful landscapes and best beaches, but its northern section around picturesque Cavendish and the Green Gables farmhouse is also cluttered with commercial tourist operations. For unspoiled beauty, you'll have to look beyond the fast-food outlets, tacky gift shops, and expensive carnival-type attractions and try to envision the Island's simpler days.

Prince Edward Island National Park

★ ⑩ *24 km (15 mi) north of Charlottetown.*

Prince Edward Island National Park, a narrow strip of mostly beach and dunes, stretches for more than 40 km (25 mi) along the north shore of the Island, from Cavendish to Tracadie Bay plus a separate extension, about 24 km (15 mi) further east at Greenwich. The park is blessed with nature's broadest brush strokes—sky and sea meet red-sandstone cliffs, rolling dunes, and long stretches of sand. There are six entrances to the park system off Routes 6, 13, and 15. National park information centers are at Cavendish and Brackley. The Gulfshore Highway runs through the park, giving tantalizing views of the beach and dunes. Beaches invite swimming, picnicking, and walking. Trails lead through woodlands and along streams and ponds. Among the more than 200 species of birds that pass through the area are the northern phalarope, Swainson's thrush, and the endangered piping plover. Many campgrounds span the park with varying fees and seasons. In autumn and winter, it's difficult to reach park staff—call Parks Canada (☎ 902/672–6350; 800/213–7875 for campground reservations) ahead of time for exact rates and schedules if you're planning a camping trip. 🗷 *Daily pass $3, seasonal pass $12, no charge off-season.* ☉ *Daily, full facilities open early June–mid-Sept.*

Lodging

$$$$ 🏠 **Blue Heron Hideaways Beach Houses.** Blue Heron comprises two large cottages (five- and six-bedroom) at Blooming Point (on Tracadie Bay) and two beach houses plus a studio cottage on Point Deroche, 3 mi (5 km) to the east. The private 6 mi (10 km) beach is perfect for beachcombing and has sand dunes and wildlife along with rowboats and kayaks for guest use. Units are completely equipped for cooking, and have gas barbecues and CD players. Most have whirlpool baths. From mid-June to mid-September, there are weekly rentals only. ⊠ *Meadowbank, R.R. 2, Cornwall, C0A 1H0,* ☎ *902/566–2427,* 📠 *902/368–3798. 2 cottages with 2 to 4 bedrooms; honeymoon cottage; 2 houses sleep up to 10 guests. Pool, beach, boating. No credit cards. Closed Mid-Oct.–early June.*

$$$$ 🏠 **Dalvay-by-the-Sea.** Just within the eastern border of the Prince Edward Island National Park is this Victorian house, built in 1895 as a private summer home. This historic property is the only seaside country inn on Prince Edward Island. Rooms are furnished with antiques and reproductions. You can sip cocktails or tea on the porch while viewing the inn's gardens, Dalvay Lake, or the nearby beach. Canoes and rowboats are available. Breakfast and dinner are included in the room rate. In addition to the rooms in the inn, Dalvay also has eight upscale overnight cottages. As the inn is within PEI National Park, park entrance fees apply. ⊠ *PEI National Park, Rte. 6, Grand Tracadie, near Dalvay Beach (Box 8), York C0A 1P0,* ☎ *902/672–2048,* 🌐 *www. dalvaybythesea.com. 26 rooms, 8 cottages. Restaurant, bar, driving range, 2 tennis courts, croquet, boating, shop. AE, DC, MC, V. MAP. Closed mid-Oct.–early June.*

Outdoor Activities and Sports

GOLF

The 18 holes of the links-style, par-72 course at **Stanhope Golf and Country Club** (⊠ off Rte. 6, Stanhope, ☎ 902/672–2842) are among the most challenging and scenic on the Island. It's a couple of miles west of Dalvay, along Covehead Bay.

The **Links at Crowbush Cove** (⊠ off Rte. 2 on Rte. 350, Lakeside, ☎ 902/961–7300 or 800/377–8337), an 18-hole, par-72 Scottish-style course with ocean views, is about a 20- to 30-minute drive east of the national park; *Golf Digest* has rated it Canada's only five-star public golf course.

Brackley Beach

⑪ *12 km (7 mi) west of Dalvay.*

Just outside Prince Edward Island National Park, Brackley Beach offers a variety of country-style accommodations and eating establishments. The town has a national park information service building, about a mile from the toll both at the actual park entrance. Its bays and waterways attract migratory birds and are excellent for canoeing or kayaking and windsurfing. **Northshore Rentals** (⊠ Rte. 15 at Shaw's Hotel, ☎ 902/672–2022) rents canoes, river kayaks, and rowboats.

Dining and Lodging

$$–$$$ ✕ **Dunes Café.** This stunning café shares property with a pottery stu-
★ dio, art gallery, artisans outlet, and outdoor gardens. Soaring wood ceilings produce an airy atmosphere inside, and a deck overlooks the dunes and marshlands of Covehead Bay. The chef specializes in local seafood and lamb, incorporating locally grown, fresh produce, much of which comes from the café's own gardens. Reservations are recommended. ⊠ *Rte. 15 south of the national park,* ☎ *902/672–2586. AE, MC, V. Closed early Oct.–late May.*

$$$–$$$$ ✕▦ **Shaw's Hotel and Cottages.** Each room is unique in this 1860s
★ hotel with antique furnishings, floral-print wallpapers, and hardwood floors. Shaw's is one of only two remaining hotels on PEI that have continued operating for over a century. The lovely vistas of the bay and the country elegance make this ideal for a relaxing stay or as a central base for exploring the region. Half the cottages have fireplaces. Canoes and kayaks are provided for guest use, and bicycles may be rented. If you'd like, include in your room rate a home-cooked breakfast and dinner in the Shaw's dining room, which is open to the public. The Sunday evening buffet, which features seafood, has become a popular local tradition. ⊠ *Rte. 15, Brackley Beach, C1E 1Z3,* ☎ *902/672–2022,* 𝔽𝔸𝕏 *902/672–3000,* 𝕎𝔼𝔹 *www.peisland.com/shaws/ hotel.htm. 16 rooms, 20 cottages, 3 suites. Restaurant, bar, beach, boating, playground. AE, MC, V. Closed early Oct.–May except for cottages. MAP.*

Shopping

The **Cheeselady's Gouda** (⊠ Winsloe North, Rte. 223, 8 km [5 mi] off Rte. 2, ☎ 902/368–1506) not only demonstrates how genuine Gouda is produced (for free) but also offers samples of uniquely flavored cheeses. **The Dunes Studio Gallery** (⊠ Rte. 15 south of the national park, ☎ 902/672–2586) sells the work of dozens of leading local artists, as well as craftspeople from around the world. The pottery studio is open for viewing, and a rooftop garden offers vistas of saltwater bays, dunes, and hills.

Cavendish

⑫ *21 km (13 mi) west of Brackley.*

Cavendish is the most visited Island community outside Charlottetown because of the heavy influx of visitors to Green Gables, Prince Edward Island National Park, and the amusement park–style attractions in the area. Families with children appreciate the recreational options, which range from bumper-car rides and water slides to pristine sandy beaches. In 1908, Lucy Maud Montgomery (1874–1942) entered immortality as a beloved Canadian writer of fiction. It was in that year she created a most charming and enduring character, Anne Shirley, whom Mark Twain described as "the dearest and most lovable child in fiction since the immortal Alice [in Wonderland]." Montgomery's novel *Anne of Green Gables* is still enjoyed today, and thousands of adoring fans flock to the Cavendish area to personally experience Anne by visiting some of the homes associated with Montgomery and exploring the places described in the book.

The **Site of Lucy Maud Montgomery's Cavendish Home** is where the writer lived with her maternal grandparents following the untimely death of her mother. Though the foundation and surrounding white picket fence of the home where Montgomery wrote *Anne of Green Gables* are all that remain, the homestead fields and old apple-tree gardens provide lovely walking grounds. A bookstore and museum are also on the property, which is operated by descendants of the family. ⊠ *Rte. 6,* ☎ *902/963–2231.* ▣ *$2.* ☉ *June and Sept.–mid-Oct., daily 10–5; July–Aug., daily 9–7.*

★ **Green Gables, Prince Edward Island National Park,** ½ km (¼ mi) west of Lucy Maud Montgomery's Cavendish homesite, is the green-and-white farmhouse that served as the setting for *Anne of Green Gables*. Frequently visited by Montgomery, it belonged to her grandfather's cousins. The house, farm buildings, and grounds re-create some of the settings found in the book, as do posted walking trails, the Haunted Wood, and Balsam Hollow. The site has been part of Prince Edward Island National Park since 1937. ⊠ *Rte. 6, west of Rte. 13,* ☎ *902/ 963–7874.* ▣ *$5.50; lower off-season rates.* ☉ *May–late June and Sept.– Oct., daily 9–5; late June–Aug., daily 9–8; open limited schedule Nov.– Dec. and Mar.–Apr.; by appointment only in Jan. and Feb.*

There are many amusement parks throughout the Cavendish area, but **Rainbow Valley Family Fun Park** is unique. Not only is it one of the oldest attractions in the region, but as a family-operated business it provides a full day of activities for visitors of all ages. Spread over 40 acres, this clean, friendly operation includes three boating lakes, many rides for each age group, a large play port for youngsters, six waterslides, an exciting flume ride using rubber rafts, as well as live and animatronic performances. Food service is available or visitors may bring a picnic lunch. ⊠ *Rte. 6 in Cavendish,* ☎ *902/963–2221,* WEB *www. rainbowvalley.pe.ca.* ▣ *$11.* ☉ *Early June–early Sept., Mon.–Sat. 9– 8, Sun. 11–8.*

Dining and Lodging

Due to the relatively short distances involved on PEI (to drive the total length of the Island from North Cape to East Point is only 273 km [169 mi]), visitors who stay in Charlottetown or anywhere in the north shore area are within minutes of all the major attractions in "Anne's Land." Accommodations in the Cavendish area are usually booked ahead—often a year in advance—during July and most of August. However, staying elsewhere in the central region puts visitors within minutes of Prince Edward Island National Park and other attractions, gives greater options in selecting a property, and often results in a lower cost.

$$–$$$$ ✕ **New Glasgow Lobster Supper.** Lobster suppers are held every night of the week during summer in community centers, church halls, and private restaurants. The New Glasgow Lobster Supper has been around since 1958 and is in a large, modern building edging a river. Its specialty is fresh lobster direct from a pond on the premises. Breaded scallops, hot roast beef, haddock, and ham are offered as well. All guests receive unlimited freshly baked rolls, cultivated steamed mussels,

seafood chowder, garden salad, homemade desserts, and beverages. Bar service is also available, and there's a children's menu. The dining area can seat up to 500 guests at one time, and it often fills up, but because turnover is fast there isn't usually a long wait. ⊠ *Rte. 258 at New Glasgow,* ☎ *902/964–2870,* FAX *902/964–3116. AE, DC, MC, V. Closed mid-Oct.–late May.*

$$$
★
⊞ **Sundance Cottages.** On a quiet little lane off Route 6 near the center of Cavendish is this friendly family operation, a collection of 20 one- to four-bedroom cottages in a gently sloping field. Modern, spacious, nicely decorated, and fully equipped for self-catering, each cottage has a queen-size bed, a deck with a nice country view, a picnic table, and a barbecue. Many of the cottages have whirlpool baths, a dishwasher, and a propane fireplace. Outdoors there's a vegetable garden, where you can pick fresh vegetables for meals free of charge. A national park pass is provided for each day of stay. ⊠ *R.R. 2, C0A 1N0,* ☎ *902/963–2149 or 800/565–2149,* FAX *902/963–2100,* WEB *www.peisland.com/sundance/cottages.htm. 20 cottages. In-room VCRs, pool, hot tub, gym, mountain bikes, playground, coin laundry. AE, DC, MC, V.*

$–$$$
⊞ **Kindred Spirits Country Inn and Cottages.** Green hills surround this lovely country estate, a short walk from Green Gables and a golf course. You can relax by its parlor fireplace and then retreat into a large room or suite, decorated in country Victorian style with local antiques. Breakfast is provided to inn guests. Surrounding extensive lawns and gardens are 14 large cottages in three different price ranges, from economy to luxury (the upper-end cottages have fireplaces and hot tubs); all are completely equipped for cooking and have cable TV and VCRs. ⊠ *Memory La., Rte. 6, C0A 1N0,* ☎ FAX *902/963–2434,* WEB *www.kindredspirits.ca. 25 rooms, 14 cottages. Dining room, in-room VCRs, pool, hot tub. MC, V. Closed mid-Oct.–mid-May.*

$
⚠ **Marco Polo Land Campground.** There are many campgrounds in the Cavendish region, including those in the national park and provincial parks, and those in private establishments. One of the best of the latter is Marco Polo Land, which has heated swimming pools, recreational and dining facilities, a camp store, and supervised activities—including hayrides. Its serviced lots are often reserved well in advance during July and August. Situated on Route 13 in Cavendish, it's close to all the beach and amusement areas. ⊠ *Rte. 13, Cavendish (mailing address: Box 9, Hunter River C0A 1N0),* ☎ *902/963–2352 or 800/ 665–2352; 902/964–2960 in winter. 500 sites. Dining room, 2 pools, miniature golf, tennis, shop, recreation room, coin laundry. MC, V. Closed mid-Oct.–late May.*

Outdoor Activities and Sports

GOLF

Green Gables Golf Course (⊠ Rte. 6, in Prince Edward Island National Park, ☎ 902/963–2488; 902/368–8045 in winter) is one of a half dozen golf courses in the north shore region. It was based on an original design by the golf-course architect Stanley Thompson and is a scenic 18-hole, par-72 course. Open May through October, the Green Gables also features a licensed lounge at the club house that serves refreshments and light meals. Tee times may be booked by phone.

SEA KAYAKING

Outside Expeditions (☎ 902/963–3366 or 800/207–3899), 8 km (5 mi) east of Cavendish in North Rustico Harbour, can gear a trip to suit either the new or experienced paddler. Tours include food, from light snacks to full-fledged lobster boils, depending on the expedition.

New London

🔞 *11 km (7 mi) southwest of Cavendish.*

This tiny village is best known as the birthplace of Lucy Maud Montgomery. It's also home to several seasonal gift and crafts shops and a tea shop. The wharf area is a great place to stop, rest, and watch fishing boats come and go. On the west side of New London Bay is **Cape Tryon Lighthouse,** one of a number of lighthouses around PEI. Constructed in 1905, this square, tapering, 39-ft tower stands picture-perfect at the end of a field with the Gulf of St. Lawrence beyond. Although this working lighthouse is not open to the public, the high cliff location (do not go beyond the fence) makes a great spot to take photographs or enjoy a leisurely picnic, and the site attracts many visitors each year. Inquire at the local tourist bureau for directions (it's at the end of a single-lane dirt road but worth the effort) to both this structure and nearby New London Rear Range light, a unique light station with an attached house (not open to the public).

The **Lucy Maud Montgomery Birthplace** is the modest white-and-green house overlooking New London Harbour; the author of *Anne of Green Gables* was born here in 1874. The interior of the house has been furnished with Victorian antiques to re-create the era. Among memorabilia on display are her wedding dress and personal scrapbooks filled with many of her poems and stories. ⊠ *Rtes. 6 and 20,* ☎ *902/886–2099 or 902/436–7329.* 🎟 *$2.* ⊙ *Mid-May–June and Sept.–mid-Oct., daily 9–5; July–Aug., daily 9–6.*

Northwest Corner

12 km (7 mi) west of New London.

Some of the most beautiful scenery on the Island is on Blue Heron Drive along the north shore. As the drive follows the coastline south to the other side of the Island, it passes rolling farmland and the shores of Malpeque Bay. There are a couple of lovely beaches in this area. Just north of Darnley, off Route 20, is a long sand beach with a number of sandstone caves at the end. This beach—Darnley Beach—does not have developed facilities and it is often almost entirely deserted except for the seabirds. Not far from the village of Malpeque, also on Route 20, is **Cabot Beach Provincial Park,** with camping facilities (☎ 888/734–7529), a beach, and a playground. Sets used for filming the television series *Emily of New Moon* (another of L. M. Montgomery's fictional characters) may be toured. In summer the beach area is supervised during the day, and the playground is open dawn to dusk.

Woodleigh Replicas and Gardens, in Burlington, southwest of New London, is a 45-acre park with 30 scale replicas of Great Britain's best-known architecture, including the Tower of London and Dunvegan Castle. The models, some large enough to enter, are furnished with period antiques. Children especially enjoy climbing to the top of the lookout tower that crowns a small hill surrounded by flower gardens. A medieval maze and 10 acres of English country gardens are also on the grounds, as are food service, a picnic area, a children's playground, and a unique gift shop. ⊠ *Rte. 234, Burlington,* ☎ *902/836–3401.* 🎟 *$8.50.* ⊙ *June and Sept.–Oct., daily 9–5; July–Aug., daily 9–7.*

The **Anne of Green Gables Museum at Silver Bush** was once the home of Lucy Maud Montgomery's aunt and uncle. Montgomery herself lived here for a time and was married in the parlor in 1911. Inside the house are mementos such as photographs and a quilt the writer worked on. One of the highlights of a visit to Silver Bush is a ride in Matthew's carriage (Matthew is one of the characters in *Anne of Green Gables*). Short trips around the farm property are available as well as longer excursions. **The Shining Waters Tea Room** offers a tasty array of light dishes. The property also includes a lovely crafts shop and an antiques store. ⊠ *Rte. 20, Park Corner,* ☎ *902/886–2884.* ⊠ *$2.75 (museum).* ☉ *May–June and Sept.–Oct., daily 9–5; July–Aug., daily 9–6.*

Lodging

$$–$$$ ⊡ **Malpeque Cove Cottages.** Within walking distance of Cabot Beach Provincial Park and only 21 km (13 mi) from Cavendish, these two- and three-bedroom cottages sit in an open field and have magnificent views of the rising sun over Darnley Basin. Modern and fully equipped, most have pine interiors. Each unit has a barbecue and picnic table, some have a whirlpool bath, and all have a roofed patio overlooking the harbor. From July to August, there are weekly reservations only. ⊠ *Off Rte. 20, Malpeque (Box 714, Kensington C0B 1M0),* ☎ *902/ 836–5667 or 888/283–1927,* WEB *www.malpeque.ca. 13 cottages. Coin laundry. MC, V. Closed mid-Oct.–mid-May.*

$–$$ ⊡ **Stanley Bridge Country Resort.** This collection of quality cottages, lodge units, and inn rooms overlooks picturesque New London Bay. The cottages, in a large open area, are available in several price ranges from "efficiency" to "executive," and all are fully equipped for self-catering. The lodge units have kitchenettes for light meals. Two complimentary continental breakfasts are provided per unit per day. The property's central location makes it an ideal base for exploring the whole north shore region. ⊠ *Rte. 6, Stanley Bridge (Box 8203, Kensington, C0B 1M0),* ☎ *902/886–2882 or 800/361–2882,* FAX *902/886–2940,* WEB *www.peisland.com/stanleybridge. 16 cottages, 10 lodge units, 28 inn rooms. Restaurant, lounge, pool, hot tub, gym, playground, coin laundry. MC, V. Closed late Oct.–early May. CP.*

Nightlife and the Arts

St. Mary's Church (⊠ Hwy. 104, Indian River, ☎ 902/836–4933), 5 km (3 mi) south of Park Corner, has performances by visiting artists in July and August as part of the Indian River Festival of Music. Inquire locally for schedule.

Borden-Carleton

35 km (22 mi) south of Kensington.

Once home port to the Marine-Atlantic car ferries, Borden-Carleton is now linked to the mainland via the Confederation Bridge. The 13-km (8-mi) behemoth, completed in June 1997, spans the Northumberland Strait and ends in Cape Jourimain, New Brunswick. **Gateway Village** (☎ 902/437–8539), at the foot of the bridge near the toll booths, has an interesting display related to the unique construction techniques used in completing this amazing span. Located within the village complex are a government-run visitor information center (open year-round), a liquor store, a large number of crafts and gift shops, and several food-service outlets (including a Cows Ice Cream shop). A fascinating free interactive display, **Island Home Museum,** traces the history of the Northumberland Strait crossings. The PEI section of the Trans-Canada Highway begins here and continues through Charlottetown to the Wood Islands Ferry Terminal. Many visitors to PEI enter the province across the Confederation Bridge, explore the Island, then continue on to Nova Scotia via Northumberland Ferries Ltd. (75-minute crossing).

En Route Prior to the late 1800s (when ferry service began), passengers and mail were taken across the strait in ice boats that were rowed and alternately pushed and pulled across floating ice by men. A monument on Route 10 in **Cape Traverse** commemorates their journeys.

Victoria

★ ⑭ *22 km (14 mi) east of Borden-Carleton.*

Victoria-by-the-Sea, as this charming community is known locally, is a picturesque fishing village filled with antiques, art galleries, and handicrafts shops. But the real beauty of Victoria is that it has retained its peace and integrity. The little shops and eateries are all owned by local people. Many of the artists and craftspeople who live here do so to escape the hectic life of larger centers. To truly appreciate Victoria, park on one of its several streets and walk. Stroll about the community, browse its shops, watch the fishing boats beside the wharf, admire the harbor lighthouses, and take time to chat with the locals. Be sure to take in a performance at the local live theater. The usually uncrowded **Victoria Provincial Park** is just outside the village. Here beach lovers enjoy the warm, calm waters of Northumberland Strait while walking on the sand flats at low tide. Changing rooms and washrooms, picnic tables, and a small play area are provided.

Dining and Lodging

$–$$$ ✕ **Landmark Café.** The funky little spot serves homemade soups, pasta, seafood dishes, and delicious desserts. Favorite dishes include scallops sautéed in garlic butter and dill as well as steamed salmon. ⊠ *Main St.,* ☎ *902/658–2286. MC, V. No lunch Wed. Closed mid-Sept.–late June.*

$ ✕ **Mrs. Profitt's Tea Shop.** This quaint, cozy tearoom on Victoria's Main Street serves a variety of fresh teas along with tasty treats. Homemade soup, sandwiches, and lobster rolls are featured. ⊠ *Orient Hotel, 34 Main St.,* ☎ *902/658–2503. AE, MC, V. Closed Mon. and late Sept.– late May.*

$–$$ ⌑ **Orient Hotel.** The small, historic hotel on Main Street has cozy guest rooms and suites, all with private baths. This is one of two hotels on PEI that have been in continuous operation for more than a century. Full breakfast is included and is served in the downstairs breakfast room. The Monkey's Freezer, an ice cream shop that's open from noon to dusk, June through September, is a fledgling business venture of the host's teenage son. ⊠ *34 Main St. (Box 55) C0A 2G0,* ☎ *902/658–2503 or 800/565–6743,* FAX *902/658–2078,* WEB *www3.pei.sympatico.ca/orient. 6 rooms. AE, MC, V. Closed Oct.–late May. CP.*

$ ⌑ **Victoria Village Inn.** Next door to the Victoria Playhouse, this Victorian house has four guest rooms. A tasty Continental breakfast is served up every morning. The Actor's Retreat Café is in the inn and offers dinner and theater packages for the Victoria Playhouse. ⊠ *22 Main St., Box 1, C0A 2G0,* ☎ *902/658–2483,* WEB *www.pei.sympatico.ca/victoriavillageinn. 4 rooms. MC, V. CP.*

Nightlife and the Arts

In summer, the historic **Victoria Playhouse** (⊠ Howard and Main St., ☎ 902/658–2025 or 800/925–2025, in the Maritimes) has a renowned professional theater program that celebrates Maritime comedy. From late June through September, the company mounts two plays plus a Monday night Musical Showcase Series. The Playhouse, in the historic Community Hall (built 1912–14), is widely known for its intimate interior (150 seats) and excellent acoustics. Dinner packages are available in association with the Actor's Retreat Café next door and Seawinds Restaurant.

Shopping

Island Chocolates (✉ Main St., ☎ 902/658–2320 or 800/565–2320), a chocolate factory in a 19th-century general store, sells treats made from Belgian chocolate and flavored with fruit and liqueur fillings.

Port-La-Joye–Fort Amherst National Historic Site

36 km (22 mi) east of Victoria.

In 1720 the French founded the first European settlement on the Island, Port-La-Joye; 38 years later it was usurped by the British and renamed Fort Amherst. Take time to stroll around the original earthworks of the fort; there are magnificent panoramic views. The site also includes wooded trails and a collection of antique cannons guarding the harbor, next to the picnic area. The visitor center has informative exhibits, an audiovisual presentation, a small boutique, as well as a 1720s-era café. The drive from Victoria to Rocky Point passes through the Argyle Shore to this site, which is at the mouth of Charlottetown Harbour. ✉ *Palmers La., off Rte. 19,* ☎ *902/566–7626 or 902/675–2220.* ☞ *$2.25.* ☉ *Visitor center mid-June–Labor Day, daily 9–5; grounds May–Nov. daily.*

THE KINGS BYWAY

For 375 km (233 mi), the Kings Byway follows the coastline of green and tranquil Kings County on the eastern end of the Island. The route passes wooded areas, patchwork-quilt farms, fishing villages, historic sites, and long, uncrowded beaches. In early summer, fields of blue, white, pink, and purple wild lupines slope down to red cliffs and blue sea. To get here from Charlottetown, take Route 1 east and follow the Kings Byway counterclockwise.

Orwell

★ ⑮ *27 km (17 mi) east of Charlottetown.*

For those who like the outdoors, Orwell, lined with farms that welcome guests and offer activities, is ideal. The **Orwell Corner Historic Village** is a living-history farm museum that re-creates a 19th-century rural settlement by employing methods used by Scottish and Irish settlers in the 1800s. The village contains a beautifully restored 1864 farmhouse, a school, a general store, a church, a community hall, a blacksmith shop, a refurbished shingle mill, and barns with handsome draft horses. From spring to fall the site runs many special events, including fairs and craft shows, and in summer the community hall hosts traditional music performances four evenings a week. Check locally for a schedule. ✉ *Off Trans-Canada Hwy., Rte. 1,* ☎ *902/651–8510,* ℻ *902/368–6608,* WEB *www.orwellcorner.isn.net.* ☞ *$3.50.* ☉ *Mid-June–early Sept., daily 9–5; mid-May–mid-June, weekdays 10–3; early Sept.–mid-Oct., Tues.–Sun., 9–5.*

The **Sir Andrew Macphail Homestead,** a National Historic Site, is a 140-acre farm property that contains an ecological forestry project, gardens, and three walking trails. The restored 1829 house and 19th-century outbuildings commemorate the life of Sir Andrew Macphail (1864–1938), a writer, professor, physician, and soldier. A licensed tearoom–restaurant serves traditional Scottish and contemporary fare and is open for lunch and most dinners. ✉ *Off Rte. 1,* ☎ *902/651–2789,* WEB *www.isn.net/~dhunter/macphailfoundation.html.* ☞ *Free.* ☉ *Late June–early Sept., daily 10–5; July–Aug., daily 10–9 PM.*

OFF THE
BEATEN PATH

BEN'S LAKE TROUT FARM – This pleasant attraction for the whole family is especially appreciated by aspiring young anglers. You're almost guaranteed a fish, and the staff cleans it and supplies the barbecue (for a small fee) and picnic table for a great meal. Fly fishing can also be arranged. ⊠ *Rte. 24, Bellevue,* ☎ *902/838–2706.* ⊠ *Catch $4 per pound.* ☉ *Apr.–Sept., daily 8–8; open weekends or by reservation in Oct.*

Lodging

$ 🏠 **Forest and Stream Cottages.** This collection of one- and two-bedroom cottages in a forest grove provides a secluded stay overlooking a large pond. You can use one of the rowboats to explore the winding stream or to take advantage of the property's nature trails. These traditional-style cottages have screened verandas, and each has a barbecue and picnic table. ⊠ *Murray Harbour, C0A 1V0,* ☎ FAX *902/962–3537,* WEB *www.CanadaRentals.com. 5 cottages. Boating, playground. MC, V. Closed Nov.–Apr.*

En Route   One of the Island's most historic churches, St. John's Presbyterian, is in **Belfast,** off Route 1 on Route 207. This pretty white church on a hill was built by settlers from the Isle of Skye who were brought to the Island from Scotland in 1803 by Lord Selkirk. At **Little Sands,** on Route 4, is Canada's only saltwater winery, Rossignol Estate Winery, which offers tasting for a small fee. The lighthouse at **Cape Bear** is the site of the first wireless station in Canada to receive the distress call from the *Titanic.*

Montague

20 km (12 mi) northeast of Orwell.

Montague, the business hub of eastern Prince Edward Island, is a lovely small town that straddles the Montague River and serves as a departure point for seal-watching boat tours. **Cruise Manada Seal-watching Boat Tours** (reservations recommended: ☎ 902/838–3444 or 800/986–3444, WEB www.peisland.com/cruise/manada.htm) sails past a harborseal colony and mussel farms. Boats leave from Montague Marina on Route 4 and Brudenell Resort Marina on Route 3 from mid-May through October. This is a great rainy-day activity. The restored **railway station,** overlooking the marina, is used as a tourist information center as well as for a number of small crafts shops. The Confederation Trail continues past the station and is ideal for a leisurely stroll.

Dining and Lodging

$$-$$$ ✕ **Windows on the Water Café.** Overlooking the former railway station is this old house furnished with antiques and plenty of atmosphere. You can relax inside, or out on the large deck in warm weather, with views of the Montague Marina. Winner of the Island Shellfish Chowder Competition, this lovely little eatery has tasty seafood, vegetarian fare, and chicken dishes. ⊠ *106 Sackville St.,* ☎ *902/838–2080. AE, DC, MC, V. Closed mid-Oct.–early May.*

$ 🏠 **Roseneath Bed & Breakfast.** This fine heritage home (1868) overlooks the Brudenell River. You can golf at the adjacent Brudenell course, walk or bike the Confederation Trail (which crosses the property), do a little trout fishing, or just relax and explore the 90 acres of flowers and woodlands. The fun doesn't stop in winter—there's always snowshoeing and cross-country skiing. All of the rooms have views of the river or of the property's extensive gardens, private baths (some with claw-foot tubs), and plenty of artwork and antiques. A family suite has two bedrooms with a private bath. Morning brings coffee delivered to your room and a full home-cooked breakfast downstairs. A lobster dinner may be arranged in advance during May and June. ⊠ *R.R. 6, Cardigan, C0A 1G0,*

☎ 902/838–4590 or 800/823–8933, FAX 902/838–4590, WEB *www.isn.net/~rosedew. 3 rooms, 1 family suite. Fishing, bicycles. MC, V. Closed Oct.–late May; open off-season by reservation. BP.*

Bay Fortune

38 km (24 mi) north of Georgetown.

Bay Fortune, a little-known scenic village, has been a secret refuge of American vacationers for two generations; they return year after year to relax in the peace and quiet of this charming little community.

Dining and Lodging

$$–$$$$ ✕⊞ **Inn at Bay Fortune.** This enticing, unforgettable getaway, the for-
★ mer summer home of Broadway playwright Elmer Harris and more recently of the late actress Colleen Dewhurst, is now an inn overlooking Fortune Harbour and Northumberland Strait. You'll find superb dining and genteel living. Local fresh-caught and fresh-harvested ingredients are served in an old-time ambience. The restaurant does not serve lunch, but a full breakfast is included in room rates. Two nearby summer houses are well-appointed, and provide housekeeping facilities that suit families. ✉ *Rte. 310, R.R. 4, C0A 2B0,* ☎ *902/687–3745; 860/563–6090 off-season,* WEB *www.innatbayfortune.com. 18 rooms, 2 houses. Restaurant. MC, V. Closed late Oct.–mid-May. BP.*

$$$–$$$$ ⊞ **The Inn at Spry Point.** The sister property to the Inn at Bay Fortune, this luxury retreat hugs the end of a 110-acre peninsula. In addition to 4 km (2½ mi) of shoreline walking trails, the property has a 1 km (½ mi) sandy beach. Each of the 15 guest rooms has either a private balcony or a garden terrace. Seafood and locally grown fresh produce are featured in the dining room with pan-seared scallops, halibut, and salmon taking top billing. Desserts are glorious. ✉ *Spry Point Rd.,* ☎ *902/583–2400; 860/563–6090 off-season;* FAX *902/583–2176,* WEB *www.inatsprypoint.com. 15 rooms. Restaurant. MC, V. Closed early Oct.–late May. CP.*

Souris

14 km (9 mi) north of Bay Fortune.

The Souris area is noted for its fine traditional musicians. An outdoor Scottish concert at **Rollo Bay** in July, with fiddling and step dancing, attracts thousands every year. At Souris a car ferry links Prince Edward Island with Québec's **Magdalen Islands.** Call ☎ 887/624–4437 for information about these scenic islands.

Basin Head

🔟 *13 km (8 mi) north of Rollo Bay.*

This town is noted for an exquisite silvery beach that stretches northeast for miles, backed by high grassy dunes. The lovely sand beach has been "discovered," but it's still worth spending some time here. Scuff your feet in the sand and hear it squeak, squawk, and purr at you. Known locally as "singing sand," it is a phenomenon found in only a few locations worldwide. The high silica content in the sand helps produce the sound. A boardwalk leads from the museum area at the top of the hill down to the beach area. There's a small take-out next to the museum where fish-and-chips and other fast food may be purchased and eaten at picnic tables overlooking the ocean. The nearby **Red Point Provincial Park** makes an excellent base for those who enjoy camping.

The **Basin Head Fisheries Museum** is on a headland overlooking the Northumberland Strait and has views of one of the most beautiful white-sand beaches on the island. The museum depicts the ever-changing nature of PEI's historic inshore fishing tradition through interesting displays of artifacts. The museum, part of the PEI Museum and Heritage Foundation, has an aquarium, a smokehouse, a cannery, and coastal ecology exhibits. ⊠ *Off Rte. 16,* ☎ *902/357-7233,* WEB *www.peimuseum.com.* ⊠ *$3.50.* ⊙ *Late May–Aug., daily 9–6; Sept.–Oct., daily 9–5.*

Greenwich

54 km (33 mi) southwest of East Point.

The National Park in Greenwich is known for its superior beach and massive sand dunes. These dunes are moving, gradually burying the nearby woods; here and there the bleached skeletons of trees thrust up through the sand like wooden ghosts. To get here, follow Route 16 to St. Peter's Bay and Route 313 to Greenwich. The road ends at an interpretive center, a new extension of the Prince Edward Island National Park system. Programs at the center explain to visitors the ecology of this rare land formation. Visitors are permitted to walk along designated pathways among sand hills, through beige dunes to reach the beach. Due to the rather delicate nature of the dune system, visitors must stay on the trails and refrain from touching the flora.

Outdoor Activities and Sports
Wild Winds (⊠ Savage Harbour, ☎ 902/676–2024) is one of the best of the many deep-sea fishing boats that operate from this region of PEI; half-day trips for cod and mackerel are available.

En Route   Ships from many nations have been wrecked on the reef running northeast from **East Point Lighthouse** (⊠ off Rte. 16, East Point, ☎ 902/357–2106). Guided tours are offered, and many books about life at sea are available at the gift shop in the 1908 fog-alarm building. Due to the high erosion in this area, caution should be used when approaching the high cliffs overlooking the ocean.

LADY SLIPPER DRIVE

Many visitors to the western end of PEI tend to follow the straight, flat Route 2 most of the distance, which gives a rather boring view of the Island. To truly appreciate what the western region has to offer, divert along the coastline. Follow Route 14 to West Point and continue northward along the Northumberland Strait. Try returning along the Gulf of St. Lawrence area by using Route 12, which passes the lovely beach area of Jacques Cartier Provincial Park. Both of these highways are part of the Lady Slipper Drive. This drive—named for the delicate lady's slipper orchid, the province's official flower—winds along the coast of the narrow, indented western end of the Island, known as Prince County, through very old and very small villages that still adhere to a traditional way of life. Many of these hamlets are inhabited by Acadians, descendants of the original French settlers. The area is known for its oysters and Irish moss (the dried plants of a red sea alga) but most famously for its potato farms: the province is a major exporter of seed potatoes worldwide, and half the crop is grown here.

Summerside

17   *71 km (44 mi) west of Charlottetown.*

Summerside, the second-largest city on the Island, has a beautiful waterfront area. A self-guided walking tour arranged by the Eptek Exhibition Centre is a pleasant excursion along leafy streets lined with large houses. During the third week of July, all of Summerside celebrates the eight-day **Summerside Lobster Carnival,** with livestock exhibitions, harness racing, fiddling contests, and of course, lobster suppers. Summerside has seen a renewal of the downtown area in recent years, with the addition of a number of attractions that appeal to visitors. One sign of renewal: the array of murals painted on the sides of a number of buildings in the city, most depicting historical events that helped shape the character of the community. The Confederation Trail passes through the city, and the former railway station makes an excellent starting point for walking or biking excursions. Some of the local hotels provide bicycles for their guests to explore this attractive trailway system. It takes about a half hour to drive by car from Summerside to major attractions like Cavendish in the central region of PEI.

Eptek Exhibition Centre on the waterfront has a spacious main gallery with changing Canadian-history and fine-arts exhibits, often with a strong emphasis on Prince Edward Island. In the same buildings are the 527-seat **Harbourfront Jubilee Theatre** and the **PEI Sports Hall of Fame.** ⊠ *130 Harbour Dr., Waterfront Properties,* ☎ *902/888–8373,* FAX *902/888–8375.* ⊡ *$3.50.* ☉ *Open year-round; call for hrs.*

Spinnaker's Landing, a boardwalk along the water's edge, is lined with shops and eateries. The area has a good blend of shopping, history, and entertainment. The visitors information center is a re-created lighthouse that may be climbed for panoramic views of Bedeque Bay and the city. In summer months there's often free evening entertainment (usually at 7 PM) on the outdoor stage over the water, weather permitting. Call for a schedule of events. ⊠ *130 Harbour Dr.,* ☎ *902/ 436–6692.*

Dining and Lodging

$–$$$ ✕ **Brothers Two Restaurant.** Next to the Quality Inn Garden of the Gulf, this restaurant is popular with local residents. Service is friendly, and seating is in booths, at tables, and in summer in a roofed-patio area. As with most restaurants in PEI, fish is usually featured on the menu, and dishes such as fish-and-chips can be found along with more elaborate creations. The pride of the restaurant is the homemade bread served with each meal. ⊠ *618 Water St.,* ☎ *902/436–9654. AE, DC, MC, V.*

$$–$$$$ ▦ **Quality Inn Garden of the Gulf.** Close to downtown, this clean, comfortable hotel is a convenient place to stay. The unusual layout features a high-ceiling courtyard with rooms on both sides. New Orleans–style decor creates a pleasant atmosphere. There's also a separate motor lodge–style building next to the main structure. A 9-hole, par-3 chip-and-putt golf course slopes to Bedeque Bay. ⊠ *618 Water St. E, C1N 2V5,* ☎ *902/436–2295 or 800/265–5551,* FAX *902/436–6277. 92 rooms. Coffee shop, 1 indoor and 1 outdoor pool, 9-hole golf course, shop. AE, DC, MC, V.*

$$ ▦ **Loyalist Country Inn.** Throughout this waterfront inn are detailed
★ touches that create a traditional elegance. The Loyalist combines the atmosphere of a country inn with the professionalism of a large hotel. In the heart of Summerside, the property overlooks the city waterfront, a yacht club, and a marina. The rear of the hotel faces the main downtown area, the former railway station, and the Confederation Trail— good for biking. The Prince William Dining Room has an innovative menu of seafood, steaks, and island delicacies. Thirty rooms have whirlpool baths. ⊠ *195 Harbour Dr., C1N 5R1,* ☎ *902/436–3333 or 800/361–2668,* FAX *902/436–4304. 100 rooms, 3 suites. Restaurant, lounge, indoor pool, sauna, gym. AE, DC, MC, V.*

$–$$ ▦ **Silver Fox Inn.** A fine old Victorian house and a designated historic property, this bed-and breakfast houses a tearoom, where homemade scones and Devonshire cream are served each afternoon, and a small antiques shop. Breakfasts include homemade quiche, muffins, and croissants. If you make prior arrangements, the chef will prepare dinner. Outside, a two-tier deck provides a lovely view of the garden with three koi-stocked pools. ⊠ *61 Granville St., C1N 2Z3,* ☎ *902/436–1664 or 800/565–4033,* WEB *www.silverfoxinn.net. 6 rooms. AE, DC, MC, V. CP.*

Nightlife and the Arts

The **College of Piping and Celtic Performing Arts of Canada** (⊠ 619 Water St. E, ☎ 902/436–5377 or 877/224–7473, WEB www.collegeof-piping.com) puts on a summer-long Celtic Festival incorporating bagpiping, Highland dancing, step dancing, and fiddling. The **Harbourfront Jubilee Theater** (⊠ 124 Harbour Dr., ☎ 902/888–2500 or 800/708–6505), founded in 1996, is the Island's newest professional theater. Year-round, the 527-seat main-stage theater celebrates the tradition and culture of the region with dramatic and musical productions. Call for information on current productions and schedule.

Feast Dinner Theatre (⊠ Brothers Two Restaurant, 618 Water St. E, ☎ 902/436–7674 or 888/748–1010), established in 1978, is the original dinner-theater production company in the Maritime provinces. Musical comedy is served up with heaping platefuls of Atlantic salmon, chicken, barbecue ribs, and fresh desserts.

Miscouche

10 km (6 mi) northwest of Summerside.

Many descendants of the Island's early French settlers live in this area, and a museum here commemorates their history. The **Acadian Museum/ Musée Acadien,** a National Historic Site, has a permanent exhibition on Acadian life as well as an audiovisual presentation depicting the history and culture of Island Acadians. It also has a genealogical center and an Acadian gift shop. ⊠ *Rte. 2,* ☎ *902/436–2881.* ☞ *$3.50.* ⊙ *July–Aug., daily 9:30–7; reduced hrs off-season.*

Port Hill

35 km (22 mi) north of Miscouche.

Port Hill was one of the many communities in the Tyne Valley that benefited from the shipbuilding boom of the 1800s, the era of tall-masted wooden schooners. Some beautifully restored century homes testify to the prosperity of those times.

The **Green Park Shipbuilding Museum and Yeo House** includes what was originally the home of shipbuilder James Yeo, Jr., who by the mid-1840s was the most powerful businessman on the Island. The cupola from which Yeo observed his nearby shipyard through a spyglass tops this 19th-century mansion. The modern museum building, in what has become a provincial park, details the history of the shipbuilder's craft. Those skills are brought to life at a re-created shipyard with carpentry and blacksmithing shops. The park has picnic tables and camping facilities. There's a small gift shop on site, and the museum provides an array of lectures, concerts, and activities throughout the summer. Call for schedule. ⊠ *Rte. 12,* ☎ *902/831–7947.* ☞ *$4.* ⊙ *June–Sept., daily 9–5.*

Tyne Valley

❶⑧ *8 km (5 mi) south of Port Hill.*

The charming community of Tyne Valley has some of the finest scenery on the Island. Watch for fisherfolk standing in flat boats wielding rakes to harvest the famous Malpeque oysters. A gentle river flows through the middle of the village, with lush green lawns and sweeping trees edging the water. The **Tyne Valley Oyster Festival** takes place here the first week of August. This three-day event includes fiddling, step dancing, oyster shucking, a talent contest, and a community dance. The festival is a good time to sample a fried-oyster and scallop dinner. Check locally for dates and times.

Dining and Lodging

$ ✕🖬 **Doctor's Inn Bed & Breakfast.** Beautifully landscaped, this 1860s village home is a joy in summer with its garden of herbs and flowers. In winter, cross-country skiers gather around the woodstove or living-room fireplace and share conversation over a warm drink. At the dining-room table, the local catch of the day is complemented by produce from the inn's own organic gardens. Dinner is prix fixe ($40 for guests, $50 for nonguests) and available by reservation only. There are free tours of the inn's gardens. ⊠ *Rte. 167, C0B 2C0,* ☎ *902/831–3057,* WEB *www.peisland.com/doctorsinn. 2 rooms share bath. Restaurant. MC, V. CP.*

Shopping

At **Shoreline Sweaters and Tyne Valley Studio Art Gallery** (⊠ Rte. 12, ☎ 902/831–2950), Lesley Dubey produces "Shoreline" handcrafted woolen sweaters with a unique lobster pattern and sells local crafts and honey May through October. The store is open 9 to 5:30 daily, noon to 5:30 Sunday. An art gallery displays works by accomplished Island artists.

Lennox Island, one of the largest Mi'Kmaq communities in the province, has a few shops that sell First Nations crafts. To get here, take Route 12 west to Route 163 and follow the road over the causeway leading to a large island projecting into Malpeque Bay. **Indian Art & Craft of North America** (⊠ Rte. 163, ☎ 902/831–2653) specializes in Mi'K-maq ash-split baskets as well as pottery, jewelry, carvings, and head-work. The shop, which sits on the edge of the water, has a screened-in porch where visitors may enjoy a complimentary cup of coffee along with the scenery. Earthenware figurines depicting local legends can be found at **Micmac Productions** (⊠ Rte. 163, ☎ 902/831–2277). The company is Canada's only producer of such Mi'Kmaq figurines depicting the legends and exploits of the Mi'Kmaq hero Glooscap.

O'Leary

37 km (23 mi) northeast of Tyne Valley.

The center of Prince County is composed of a loose network of small towns; many are merely a stretch of road. Many of the local residents are engaged in farming and fishing, carrying on the traditions of their forebears. Farmers driving their tractors through fields of rich, red soil, and colorful lobster boats braving the seas are common scenes in this area. This region is well known for its magnificent red cliffs, majestic lighthouses, and glistening sunsets. Woodstock, north of O'Leary, has a resort where opportunities for outdoor activities abound. The town is also a good base from which to visit one of the Island's best golf courses and a rare woolen crafts shop.

Lodging

$$ 🖬 **Rodd Mill River—A Rodd Signature Resort.** With activities ranging from night skiing to golfing, canoeing, and kayaking, this is truly an all-season resort. One of the highlights of the resort, which is inside Mill River Provincial Park, is the Mill River Golf Course. The dining room provides a perfect overview of the course. The heated pool has

a 90-ft slide. ⊠ *Rte. 136 (Box 399), Woodstock C0B 1V0,* ☎ *902/ 859–3555 or 800/565–7633,* FAX *902/859–2486,* WEB *www.rodd-ho-tels.ca. 80 rooms, 10 suites. Restaurant, bar, indoor pool, hot tub, sauna, 18-hole golf course, tennis court, gym, squash, windsurfing, boating, bicycles, ice-skating, cross-country skiing, tobogganing, pro shop. AE, DC, MC, V. Closed Nov.–Dec. and Apr.*

Outdoor Activities and Sports

The 18-hole, par-72 **Mill River Provincial Golf Course** (⊠ Rte. 136, ☎ 902/859–8873), in Woodstock's Mill River Provincial Park, is among the most scenic and challenging courses in eastern Canada. Ranked among the country's top 50 courses, it has been the site of several championship tournaments. Advance bookings are recommended.

Shopping

The **Old Mill Craft Company** (⊠ Rte. 2, Bloomfield, ☎ 902/859–3508) sells hand-quilted and woolen crafts July through August (reduced hours June and September). The adjacent **MacAusland's Woollen Mill** has been producing famous MacAusland blankets since 1932, the only producer of 100% pure virgin wool blankets in Atlantic Canada.

En Route Many things in **Tignish,** a friendly Acadian community on Route 2, 12 km (7½ mi) north of O'Leary, are cooperative, including the supermarket, insurance company, seafood plant, service station, and credit union. The imposing parish church of **St. Simon and St. Jude** (⊠ 315 School St., ☎ 902/882–2049), across from Dalton Square, has a superb 1882 Tracker pipe organ, one of the finest such instruments in eastern Canada. The church is often used for recitals by world-renowned musicians.

North Cape

★ ⑲ *14 km (9 mi) north of Tignish.*

In the northwest, the Island narrows to a north-pointing arrow of land, at the tip of which is North Cape, with its imposing lighthouse. At low tide, one of the longest reefs in the world gives way to tidal pools teeming with marine life. Seals often gather offshore here. The curious structures near the reef are wind turbines at the **Atlantic Wind Test Site,** set up on this breezy promontory to evaluate the feasibility of using wind power to generate electricity.

The **Interpretive Centre and Aquarium** has information about marine life, local history, and turbines and windmills. ⊠ *End of Rte. 12,* ☎ *902/882–2991.* ☞ *$2.* ☉ *July–Aug., daily 9–8; late May–June and Sept.– mid-Oct., daily 10–6.*

Dining and Lodging

$–$$$ ✕ **Wind & Reef Restaurant.** This restaurant serves good seafood, such as Island clams, mussels, and lobster, as well as steaks, prime rib, and chicken. There's a fine view of the Gulf of St. Lawrence and Northumberland Strait. ⊠ *End of Rte. 12,* ☎ *902/882–3535. MC, V. Closed Oct.–May.*

$–$$ ▥ **Tignish Heritage Inn.** Originally built as a convent in 1868, this large inn is close to North Cape, Mile 0 of the Confederation Trail, and the facilities offered in the town of Tignish. The pastel-colored rooms range in size from cozy to spacious and all feature wooden headboards and colorful comforters. Some of the bathrooms have cast-iron claw-foot tubs. ⊠ *Off Maple St. behind St. Simon and St. Jude Church (Box 398), C0B 2B0,* ☎ *902/882–2491 or 877/882–2491,* FAX *902/882–2500,* WEB *www.tignish.com/inn. 17 rooms, 1 suite. Dining room, coin laun-*

dry. AE, DC, MC, V. Closed Nov.–Mar., except for groups by reservation only. CP.

Miminegash

20 km (12 mi) south of North Cape.

This tiny village overlooks the ocean. The **Irish Moss Interpretive Centre** tells you everything you wanted to know about Irish moss, the fan-shape red alga found in abundance on this coast and used as a thickening agent in foods. "Seaweed pie," made with Irish moss, is served at the adjacent **Seaweed Pie Café**. ⊠ *Rte. 14,* ☎ *902/882–4313.* ⌨ *$1.* ☉ *Early June–Sept., daily 10–7.*

West Point

35 km (22 mi) south of Miminegash.

At the southern tip of the western shore, West Point has a tiny fishing harbor, campsites, and a supervised beach. **West Point Lighthouse,** built in 1875, is the tallest on the Island. When the lighthouse was automated, the community took over the building and converted it into an inn and museum, with a moderately priced restaurant. The lighthouse is open daily, late May through late September.

Lodging

$–$$ ☆ ★ 🏠 **West Point Lighthouse.** Few people can say they've actually spent the night in a lighthouse, but here's a chance to do just that. Rooms, most with ocean views, are pleasantly furnished with local antiques and handmade quilts. This inn books up in the summer months, so make your reservations early. You can enjoy clam-digging, a favorite local pastime, or perhaps try finding the buried treasure reputed to be hidden nearby. ⊠ *Rte. 14 (Box 429), O'Leary C0B 1V0,* ☎ *902/859–3605 or 800/764–6854,* ℻ *902/859–1510,* 🌐 *www.peisland.com/westpoint/light.htm. 9 rooms. Restaurant, beach, fishing. AE, DC, MC, V. Closed Oct.–May.*

En Route Lady Slipper Drive meanders from West Point back to Summerside through the **Région Évangéline,** the Island's main Acadian district. At **Cape-Egmont,** stop for a look at the Bottle Houses, two tiny houses and a chapel built by a retired carpenter entirely out of glass bottles mortared together like bricks.

Mont-Carmel

⑳ *63 km (39 mi) southeast of West Point.*

This community has a magnificent brick church overlooking Northumberland Strait. **Le Village de l'Acadie** (Acadian Pioneer Village), a reproduction of an 1820s French settlement, has a church, school, and blacksmith shop. A craft shop sells locally produced goods. There are also modern accommodations and a restaurant in which you can sample authentic Acadian dishes. ⊠ *Rte. 11,* ☎ *902/854–2227 or 800/567–3228.* ⌨ *$3.25.* ☉ *Early June–late Sept., daily 9–7.*

Nightlife and the Arts

La Cuisine à Mémé (⊠ *Rte. 11,* ☎ *902/854–2227 or 800/567–3228*), a dinner theater running June 29 to September 1, features typical Acadian step dancing and fiddle music, comedy, and song. The set dinner gives a choice of chicken, salmon, or seafood casserole, with salad, dessert and coffee. The evening, which lasts from 6:30 to about 10:15 costs $29.35 for adults, $14.54 for kids 3-12 and $27.60 for seniors.

PRINCE EDWARD ISLAND A TO Z

To research prices, get advice from other travelers, and book travel arrangements, visit www.fodors.com.

AIR TRAVEL

Air Canada (☞ Smart Travel Tips A to Z) and its regional carriers offer daily nonstop service from Charlottetown to Halifax and Toronto, both of which have connections to the rest of Canada, the United States, and beyond. Prince Edward Air is available for private charters.

➤ AIRLINES AND CONTACTS: **Prince Edward Air** (☎ 902/566–4488).

AIRPORTS

Charlottetown Airport is 5 km (3 mi) north of town.

➤ AIRPORT INFORMATION: **Charlottetown Airport** (✉ 250 Maple Hills Ave., ☎ 902/566–7997).

BOAT AND FERRY TRAVEL

Northumberland Ferries sails between Wood Islands and Caribou, Nova Scotia, from May to mid-December. The crossing takes about 75 minutes, and the round-trip costs approximately $49 per vehicle, $58 for a recreational vehicle; foot passengers pay $11 (you pay only when leaving the Island). There are 18 crossings per day in summer. Reservations are not accepted.

➤ BOAT AND FERRY INFORMATION: **Northumberland Ferries** (☎ 888/ 249–7245, WEB www.nfl-bay.com).

CAR TRAVEL

The 13-km (8-mi) Confederation Bridge connects Cape Jourimain, in New Brunswick, with Borden-Carleton, Prince Edward Island. The crossing takes about 12 minutes. The toll is $37 per car, $42.25 for a recreational vehicle; it's collected when you leave the Island.

The lack of public transportation on the Island makes having your own vehicle almost a necessity. There are more than 3,700 km (2,300 mi) of paved road in the province, including the three scenic coastal drives: Lady Slipper Drive, Blue Heron Drive, and Kings Byway. A helpful highway map of the province is available from Tourism PEI and at visitor centers on the Island.

ROAD CONDITIONS

Designated Heritage Roads are surfaced with red clay, the local soil base. The unpaved roads meander through rural and undeveloped areas, where you're likely to see lots of wildflowers and birds. A four-wheel-drive vehicle is not necessary, but in spring and inclement weather the mud can get quite deep and the narrow roads become impassable. Keep an eye open for bicycles, motorcycles, and pedestrians.

EMERGENCIES

Dial 911 for emergency police, fire, or ambulance services.

➤ HOSPITALS: **Queen Elizabeth Hospital** (✉ 60 Riverside Dr., Charlottetown, ☎ 902/894–2200 or 902/894–2095).

OUTDOORS AND SPORTS

For a publication listing golf courses in Prince Edward Island, contact **Tourism PEI** (☎ 888/734–7529). Most courses may be booked directly or by contacting **Golf Atlantic** (☎ 800/565–0001).

SHOPPING

For information on crafts outlets around Prince Edward Island, contact the **Prince Edward Island Crafts Council** (✉ 156 Richmond St., Charlottetown C1A 1H9, ☎ 902/892–5152).

TOURS

The Island has about 20 sightseeing tours, including double-decker bus tours, taxi tours, cycling tours, harbor cruises, and walking tours. Most tour companies are based in Charlottetown and offer excursions around the city and to the beaches.

DRIVING TOURS

Yellow Cab can be booked for tours by the hour or day.
➤ FEES AND SCHEDULES: **Yellow Cab** (☎ 902/892–6561).

WALKING TOURS

Island Nature Trust sells a nature-trail map of the Island. Tourism PEI has maps of the 225-km multiuse Confederation Trail.
➤ FEES AND SCHEDULES: **Island Nature Trust** (✉ Box 265, Charlottetown C1A 7K4, ☎ 902/566–9150). **Tourism PEI** (✉ Box 940, Charlottetown C1A 7M5, ☎ 902/368–7795 or 888/734–7529, FAX 902/566–4336, WEB www.peiplay.com).

VISITOR INFORMATION

Tourism PEI publishes an informative annual guide for visitors and maintains 10 Visitor Information Centres (VICs) on the Island. It also produces a map of the 350-km (217-mi) Confederation Trail. The main Visitor Information Centre is in Charlottetown and is open mid-May to October daily and November to mid-May weekdays.
➤ TOURIST INFORMATION: **Tourism PEI** (✉ Box 940, Charlottetown C1A 7M5, ☎ 902/368–7795 or 888/734–7529, FAX 902/566–4336, WEB www.peiplay.com). **Visitor Information Centre** (✉ 178 Water St., ☎ 902/368–4444).

14 NOVA SCOTIA

The rugged coastline of this Atlantic
province encloses evergreen forests and
rolling farmland. A wonderful assortment of
cultures exists here but it's no melting pot, as
each pocket of individuality works fiercely
to maintain its identity, traditions, and
language. There are Gaelic street signs
in Mabou, French masses in Chéticamp,
black gospel choirs in Halifax, Mi'Kmaq
handicrafts at Eskasoni, and German
sausage in Lunenburg. Fishing villages
abound, and in Halifax and Dartmouth,
city life coexists with small-town charm.

Updated by
Isobel Warren,
Milan
Chvostek, and
Kim Goodson

NFINITE RICHES IN A LITTLE ROOM," wrote Elizabethan playwright Christopher Marlowe. He might have been referring to Nova Scotia, Canada's second-smallest province, which packs an impossible variety of cultures and landscapes into an area half the size of Ohio.

Water, water everywhere, but that's not all. Within the convoluted coastline of Nova Scotia, you can find highlands to rival Scotland's; rugged fjords; rolling farmland; and networks of rivers, ponds, and lakes calling out to kayakers and canoers. Fifty-six kilometers (35 miles) is the farthest you can get from the sea anywhere in the province. Pounding waves in summer and the grinding ice of winter storms have sculpted the coastal rocks and reduced sandstone cliffs to stretches of sandy beach. Inland, the fertile fields of the Annapolis Valley yield peaches, corn, apples, and plums that are sold at farm stands in summer and fall. A succession of wildflowers covers the roadside with blankets of color: purple and blue lupines; yellow coltsfoot; pink fireweed. Each of the wild habitats—bogs, dry barrens, tidal wetlands, open fields, dense spruce woods, and climax hardwood forests—has its own distinctive plant life. Thousands of years ago, scouring glaciers left their scars on the land; the Halifax Citadel stands atop a drumlin, a round-topped hill left by the retreating ice. Wildlife abounds: ospreys and bald eagles; moose and deer; whales in the waters off Cape Breton and Brier Island.

The original people of Nova Scotia, the Mi'Kmaqs, have been here for 10,000 years. In the early days of European exploration, the French and English navigators found these peoples settled on the shores and harvesting the sea. In later years, waves of immigrants filled the province: Germans in Lunenburg County; Highland Scots displaced by their landlords' preference for sheep; New England Loyalists escaping the American Revolution; blacks arriving as freemen or escaped slaves; Jews in Halifax, Sydney, and industrial Cape Breton; Ukranians, Poles, West Indians, Italians, and Lebanese drawn to the Sydney steel mill. These people maintain their customs and cultures. There are Gaelic signs in Mabou and Iona, German sausage and sauerkraut in Lunenburg, Greek music festivals in Halifax. The Acadians fly their tricolored flag with pride. Scots step dance to antique fiddle airs. The fragrance of burning sweet grass mingles with the prayers of the Mi'Kmaqs' Catholic mass, blending the old ways with the new.

This is a little, buried nation, with a capital city the same size as Marlowe's London. Before Canada was formed in 1867, Nova Scotians were prosperous shipwrights and merchants, trading with the world. Who created Cunard Lines? A Haligonian, Samuel Cunard. Those days brought democracy to the British colonies, left Victorian mansions in the salty little ports, and created a uniquely Nova Scotian outlook: worldly, approachable, and sturdily independent.

Pleasures and Pastimes

Dining

Skilled chefs find their abilities enhanced by the availability of succulent blueberries, crisp apples, wild mushrooms, home-raised poultry, quality beef, fresh-from-the-sea lobster, cultivated mussels, Digby scallops, and fine Atlantic salmon. The quality of ingredients comes from the closeness of the harvest. Agriculture and fisheries (both wild harvest and aquaculture) are never far away.

Helping travelers discover for themselves the best tastes of the province, the Nova Scotian culinary industry has formed an organization called the Taste of Nova Scotia. It pulls together the producers and the pre-

parers, setting quality standards to ensure that patrons at member restaurants receive authentic Nova Scotian food. Look for their symbol: a golden oval porthole framing food and a ship.

CATEGORY	COST*
$$$$	over $32
$$$	$22–$32
$$	$13–$21
$	under $13

per person, in Canadian dollars, for a main course at dinner

Lodging

Nova Scotia's strength lies in a sprinkling of first-class resorts that have retained a traditional feel, top country inns with a dedication to fine dining and high-level accommodation, and a few superior corporate hotels. Bed-and-breakfasts, particularly those in smaller towns, are often exceptional. Most resorts and many B&Bs are seasonal, closing during the winter. Halifax and Dartmouth have some excellent hotels in addition to the reliable chains; reservations are necessary year-round. Expect to pay considerably more in the capital district than elsewhere.

CATEGORY	COST*
$$$$	over $200
$$$	$150–$200
$$	$100–$150
$	under $100

All prices are for a standard double room, excluding 15% harmonized sales tax (HST), in Canadian dollars.

Music

Scottish immigrants brought fiddles and folk airs to eastern Nova Scotia and Cape Breton, where Highland music mingled with that of the Acadians already here and the Irish soon to follow. Today the region enjoys world renown as a center of distinctive Celtic music. Watch for concerts by members of the Rankin Family or the Barra MacNeils; by outstanding fiddlers such as Natalie MacMaster, Ashley MacIsaac, Buddy MacMaster, or Wendy MacIsaac; and the Gaelic-punk sound of singer Mary Jane Lamond. Since these stars grew up here, a visitor stands a good chance of catching them at a square dance in Inverness County or at a milling frolic on Bras d'Or Lake. For 10 days in October, the Celtic Colors International Festival brings musicians from around the world to more than 20 locations throughout Cape Breton.

The Halifax pub scene is a hot spot for other musical styles. Names to watch for include the crooner Johnnie Favorite, country singer Rita MacNeil, the a cappella group Four the Moment, and the lightly punk-flavored Plumptree.

Outdoor Activities and Sports

BEACHES

The province is one big seashore, with the warmest beaches on the Northumberland Strait shore. The west coast of Cape Breton and Bras d'Or Lake also offer fine beaches and warm salt water.

BIRDING

A healthy population of bald eagles nests in Cape Breton, where they reel above Bras d'Or Lake or perch in trees along riverbanks. The Bird Islands boat tour from Big Bras d'Or circles islands where Atlantic puffins, kittiwakes, and guillemots nest in rocky cliffs. In May and August, the Bay of Fundy teems with migrating shorebirds, and the tidal marshes near the end of the Bird Islands, Merrigomish, are home to great blue-heron rookeries. The useful *Where to Find the Birds in*

Nova Scotia, published by the Nova Scotia Bird Society, is available locally in places such as the Nova Scotia Government Bookstore, opposite Province House on Granville Street in Halifax.

FISHING

Nova Scotia has more than 9,000 lakes and 100 brooks; practically all lakes and streams are open to anglers. The catch includes Atlantic salmon (June through September), brook and sea trout, bass, rainbow trout, and shad. You can get a nonresident fishing license from any Department of Natural Resources office in the province and at most sporting-goods stores. Before casting a line in national park waters, it is necessary to obtain a transferrable National Parks Fishing License, available at park offices. In May and June, many rivers and brooks have spectacular spring runs of smelt and gaspereaux (river herring or alewives). Limited quantities can be taken without a license; inquire locally for times and sites of good runs. Licenses are not required for saltwater fishing. From Barrington to Digby is the most prosperous fishing region in the province.

FOSSIL HUNTING AND ROCK HOUNDING

Coal seams and shale cliffs along Cape Breton's shores yield fossilized ferns, leaves, and petrified wood. Kempt Head on Boularderie Island, Sutherland's Corner on Sydney Mines's Shore Road, and the beach at Point Aconi are good places to search. The province's richest source of fossils is the Minas Basin, near Joggins and Parrsboro, where dinosaur fossils, agate, and amethyst are found. You can visit the Fundy Geological Museum in Parrsboro and the Joggins Fossil Center. Guided tours of the cliffs are available. Rock hounds are welcome to gather what they find along the beaches, but a permit from the Nova Scotia Museum is required to dig along the cliffs.

Wineries

Nova Scotia's wineries are becoming exceedingly popular. Local wines are featured in many restaurants, and they can be sampled for free and bought by the bottle at local vineyards. Wineries to visit include Jost Vineyards in Malagash and Sainte Famille Winery in Falmouth.

Exploring Nova Scotia

Along the coast of Nova Scotia, the wild Atlantic Ocean crashes against rocky outcrops, eddies into sheltered coves, or flows placidly over expanses of white sand. In the Bay of Fundy, which has the highest tides in the world, the receding sea reveals stretches of red-mud flats; then it rushes back in a ferocious wall that should be treated with respect. Nova Scotia also has dense forests and rolling Annapolis Valley farms. In the province's most dramatic terrain, in Cape Breton, rugged mountains plunge to meet the waves.

When arriving in Nova Scotia from New Brunswick via the Trans-Canada Highway (Highway 104), you have three ways to proceed into the province. Amherst is the first community after the border. From Amherst, Highway 104 takes you toward Halifax, a two-hour drive away. Touring alternatives lie to the north and south. Highway 6, to the north, follows the shore of the Northumberland Strait; farther east is Cape Breton. Highway 2, to the south, is a less-traveled road and a favorite because of nearby fossil-studded shores. Branch roads lead to the Annapolis Valley and other points south. Drivers should be aware that the sharply curving rural roads warrant careful attention.

Great Itineraries

The province is naturally divided into regions that can be explored in three to seven days. Some visitors do a whirlwind drive around, tak-

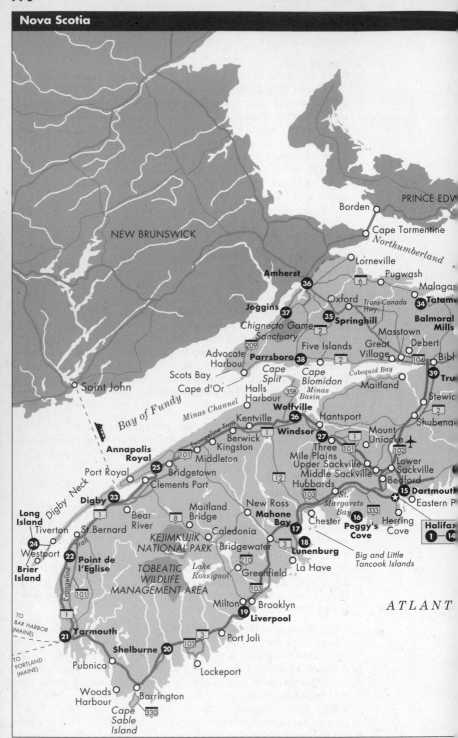

NEW BRUNSWICK

PRINCE EDW

Borden

Cape Tormentine

Northumberland

Lorneville

Pugwash

Malagas

Amherst

36

6

Oxford

34 **Tata**

Joggins

37

35

Trans-Canada Hwy.

Springhill

Balmoral Mills

Chignecto Game Sanctuary

209

2

Masstown

Debert

Bibl

Parrsboro

38

Five Islands

Great Village

104

39 **Tru**

Advocate Harbour

Cape Split

2

Cobequid Bay

Stewic

Scots Bay

Cape Blomidon

Maitland

Cape d'Or

Halls Harbour

358

Minas Basin

2

Saint John

Bay of Fundy

Minas Channel

Wolfville

Shubena

26

Hantsport

Kentville

1

Windsor

Mount Uniacke

Evangeline Trail

Berwick

27

102

Annapolis Royal

101

Kingston

Middleton

Three Mile Plains

101

1

Lower Sackville

Port Royal

25

Bridgetown

12

Upper Sackville

Middle Sackville

Bedford

Digby Neck

Clements Port

Hubbards

103

15 **Dartmouth**

Digby

23

Maitland Bridge

New Ross

St. Margarets Bay

Eastern P

Long Island

Bear River

8

Mahone Bay

Chester

16

333

Herring Cove

Halifax

Tiverton

St.Bernard

Caledonia

17

Peggy's Cove

1 — 14

24

KEJIMKUJIK NATIONAL PARK

Bridgewater

3

18

Big and Little Tancook Islands

Westport

22

Point de l'Eglise

TOBEATIC WILDLIFE MANAGEMENT AREA

Lake Rossignol

210

Lunenburg

Brier Island

101

Greenfield

La Have

103

TO BAR HARBOR (MAINE)

1

Milton

Brooklyn

ATLANT

Yarmouth

21

19

Liverpool

TO PORTLAND (MAINE)

3

Port Joli

Pubnico

Shelburne

20

103

Lockeport

Woods Harbour

Barrington

330

Cape Sable Island

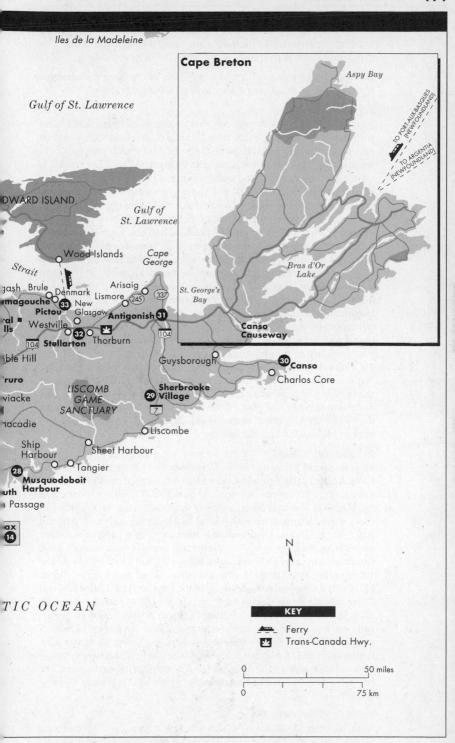

Iles de la Madeleine

Cape Breton

Aspy Bay

Gulf of St. Lawrence

TO PORT-AUX-BASQUES (NEWFOUNDLAND)

TO ARGENTIA (NEWFOUNDLAND)

DWARD ISLAND

Gulf of St. Lawrence

Wood Islands

Cape George

Bras d'Or Lake

Strait

gash   Brule   Denmark   Arisaig

Lismore

(245)   (337)

St. George's Bay

magouche   **33**   New   Glasgow   **Antigonish**   **31**

ral   Ils

Westville   **104**

ible Hill   **Stellarton**   **32**   Thorburn

Pictou

104

Canso Causeway

Truro

viacke   *LISCOMB GAME SANCTUARY*

acadie

Guysborough

30   **Canso**

Charlos Core

Sherbrooke Village   **29**   (7)

Liscombe

Ship Harbour   Sheet Harbour

28   Tangier

Musquodoboit Harbour

uth

Passage

ax   **14**

TIC OCEAN

N

KEY

Ferry

Trans-Canada Hwy.

0   50 miles

0   75 km

ing in only a few sights, but Nova Scotia's varied cultural landscape deserves careful exploration. If you have more days, try linking two or more regions. Above all, take your time: the back roads and side trips leading down to the shore are often the most rewarding.

Numbers in the text correspond to numbers in the margin and on the Nova Scotia, Halifax, and Cape Breton Island maps.

IF YOU HAVE 3 DAYS

Start in **Halifax** ①–⑭, a port city that combines old maritime charm with new architecture, lively shops, and a musical nightlife centered on a dozen friendly pubs. Explore the South Shore and Annapolis Valley, taking in the Lighthouse Route and Evangeline Trail. The two trails form a loop that begins and ends in Halifax (via Highway 3, 103, or 333, the scenic road around the shore), covering a distance of approximately 850 km (527 mi) with no side trips. Leaving Halifax, head for **Peggy's Cove** ⑯, a picturesque fishing village perched on seawashed granite and surrounded by coastal barrens. Explore the crafts shops of **Mahone Bay** ⑰ and travel on to ☒ **Lunenburg** ⑱, where the culture of Atlantic Coast fisheries is explored in the Fisheries Museum. Overnight in Lunenburg before continuing on Highway 3 or 103 to **Shelburne** ⑳ on Day 2. You can visit **Yarmouth** ㉑ and travel on to **Digby** ㉓ for a lunch of scallops. **Annapolis Royal** ㉕, with its gardens, historic sites, and harbor-front boardwalk, is a lovely spot to spend an afternoon, or you may want to drive down Digby Neck to visit **Long Island and Brier Island** ㉔ and catch a whale-watching cruise in season. Travel on to the elm-lined streets of ☒ **Wolfville** ㉖, home of Acadia University, for an overnight stay. The town is near Grand Pré National Historic Site, a tranquil park and stone church that recount the suffering of Acadians expelled from Nova Scotia in 1755. On Day 3, check tide times and plan a drive to the shore of Minas Basin, where the tides are the highest in the world. A leisurely drive will put you back in Halifax by late afternoon.

IF YOU HAVE 5 DAYS

You can spend a day or two in ☒ **Halifax** ①–⑭ before exploring the Eastern Shore, the Atlantic Coast east of the city that is perhaps the most scenic and unspoiled stretch of coastline in mainland Nova Scotia. Highway 7 winds along a deeply indented, glaciated coastline of rocky waters interspersed with pocket beaches, long and narrow fjords, and fishing villages. **Musquodoboit Harbour** ㉘ is a haven for fishing enthusiasts. Nearby is Martinique Beach, one of Nova Scotia's best. Continue northeast to **Sherbrooke Village** ㉙, full of refurbished late-19th-century structures. Highway 7 turns inland and follows the St. Mary's River toward **Antigonish** ㉛ on the Sunrise Trail. Historians will appreciate a visit to Hector Heritage Quay in ☒ **Pictou** ㉝, where the Scots landed in 1773. From Pictou, Highway 6 runs beside an apparently endless string of beaches, with many summer homes in the adjoining fields. Turn right to **Malagash,** where Jost Vineyards invites wine tasting and tours. A half-hour drive will take you to ☒ **Amherst** ㊱. Continue on to **Joggins** ㊲ and search for souvenirs in its sandstone cliffs. For more fossils, head to **Parrsboro** ㊳, which has the Fundy Geological Museum.

IF YOU HAVE 7 DAYS

With its spectacular scenery, rich musical culture, and meandering seaside highways, Cape Breton Island should not be missed. It's a perfect place for a leisurely seven-day tour. Follow the coastal route, which takes you on a west-to-east loop from the Canso Strait Causeway, taking lots of time to explore side roads. Overnight in ☒ **Mabou** ㊶, the beating heart of the island's rich musical tradition. From a base in

⚞ **Margaree Harbour** ㊷, take a day or more to explore the Cabot Trail and Cape Breton Highlands National Park and the remote fishing villages north of the park. June and July bring a profusion of wildflowers to highland meadows and bogs. You can photograph the scenery, walk the trails to hidden waterfalls, or whale-watch. There are crafts stores along St. Ann's Bay, but allow time to visit the Alexander Graham Bell National Historic Site in **Baddeck** ㊺, and spend the night in ⚞ **Iona** ㊻. A day or two in ⚞ **Sydney** ㊼ will position you for an afternoon excursion to the Glace Bay Miners' Museum in **Glace Bay** ㊽ and a daylong visit to Fortress of Louisbourg National Historic Park, the largest historic restoration in Canada, and the town of **Louisbourg** ㊾. Take Highway 4 back to Canso Causeway through **Big Pond,** home of singer Rita McNeil, and spend a day wandering the colorful Acadian villages of Isle Madame, such as **Arichat** ㊿.

When to Tour Nova Scotia

The best time of year to visit is mid-June through mid-September; in fact, many resorts, hotels, and attractions are open only during July and August. Nova Scotia, particularly the Cape Breton area, is very popular in fall because of the foliage and the 10-day Celtic Colors International Festival in October. And October—with blazing autumn colors, warm and sunny days, and cool nights—can be spectacular. Love lobster? The popular seafood is plentiful in May and June. Whale-watching and wildlife cruises as well as sea-kayaking outfitters generally operate from July to mid-September. Most golf courses stay open from June until late September, and some into October. Skiing (both downhill and cross-country) is popular at a variety of locations, including Kejimkujik and Cape Breton Highlands, from mid-December to early April.

HALIFAX AND DARTMOUTH

Halifax and Dartmouth, now combined with the surrounding County of Halifax and known as the Halifax Regional Municipality (HRM), gaze upon each other across Halifax Harbour, the second-largest natural harbor in the world. Once the point of entry to Canada for refugees and immigrants, the port remains a busy shipping center, with a flow of container ships and tugboats. Pleasure boats and yachts tie up alongside historic schooners at the Historic Properties Wharf. Pubs, shops, museums, and parks welcome visitors and locals. In summer jazz concerts and buskers, music festivals and sports events enliven the outdoor atmosphere. Art on exhibit, crafts sales, live theater, and fine food bring people here in all seasons. The film *Titanic* brought fresh attention to part of Halifax's history. Some 150 victims of the disaster are buried in three cemeteries here, and the Maritime Museum of the Atlantic has a *Titanic* display. From its harborfront life to its Victorian public gardens, Halifax is big enough to offer the pleasures of an exciting city but intimate enough to retain the ease of a small town.

Halifax

1,137 km (705 mi) northeast of Boston, 275 km (171 mi) southeast of Moncton, New Brunswick.

Salty and urbane, learned and plain-spoken, Halifax is large enough to have the trappings of a capital city, yet small enough that many of its sights can be seen on a pleasant walk downtown.

A Good Walk

Begin on Upper Water Street at **Purdy's Wharf** ① for unobstructed views of Halifax Harbour and the pier and office towers of this wharf. Continue south on Lower Water Street to the restored warehouses of **His-**

toric Properties ②, a cluster of boutiques and restaurants linked by cobblestone footpaths. Stroll south several blocks along the piers to the **Maritime Museum of the Atlantic** ③: the wharves outside frequently welcome visiting transatlantic yachts and sail-training ships. Walk to the end of the block and cross Lower Water Street to **Brewery Market** ④, a restored waterfront property. Take the elevator at the office end of Brewery Market and emerge on Hollis Street. Turn left, past several elegant Victorian town houses—notably Keith Hall—once the executive offices of the brewery.

Turn right onto Bishop Street and right again onto Barrington Street, Halifax's main downtown thoroughfare. The stone mansion on your right is **Government House** ⑤, the official residence of Nova Scotia's lieutenant governor. Take a detour from Barrington Street onto Spring Garden Road and the attractive shops in the Park Lane and Spring Garden Place shopping centers; then walk west to the **Halifax Public Gardens** ⑥, where you can rest your legs on shaded benches amid flower beds and rare trees. A block to the north, on Summer Street, is the **Nova Scotia Museum of Natural History** ⑦.

On your way back to Barrington Street on Bell Road and Sackville Street, you'll notice the **Halifax Citadel National Historic Site** ⑧, dominated by the fortress that once commanded the city. On a lot defined by Barrington, Argyle, and Prince streets lies **St. Paul's Church** ⑨; one wall within its historic confines contains a fragment of the great Halifax Explosion of 1917. A block farther north and facing City Hall is the Grand Parade, where musicians perform at noon on summer days. From here, the waterfront side of Citadel Hill, look uphill: the tall, stylish brick building is the World Trade and Convention Centre and is attached to the 10,000-seat Halifax Metro Centre—the site of hockey games, rock concerts, and political conventions. Head down the hill on Prince Street, making a left on Hollis Street to **Province House** ⑩, Canada's oldest legislative building. North of Province House, at Cheapside, is the **Art Gallery of Nova Scotia** ⑪, which showcases a large collection of folk art. Walk a block west to Granville Street and two blocks north to the **Anna Leonowens Gallery** ⑫, where you can peruse the work of local artists. Return south two blocks on Barrington to stop by the crafts displays at the **Mary E. Black Gallery** ⑬. A final stop lies to the south: **Pier 21** ⑭, a former immigration center, houses a new museum of immigration.

TIMING

The city of Halifax is fairly compact: depending on your tendency to stop and study, the above tour can take from a half to a full day. Pier 21 could take several hours in itself, so you may want to visit it separately from the walk. You can drive from sight to sight, but parking is a problem, and you will miss out on much of the flavor of the city.

Sights to See

⑫ **Anna Leonowens Gallery.** The gallery is named for the Victorian woman who served the King of Siam as governess and whose memoirs served as inspiration for Rodgers and Hammerstein's *The King and I*. Founding the Nova Scotia College of Art and Design was just another of her life's chapters. Three exhibition spaces serve as a showcase for the college faculty and students. The displays focus on contemporary studio and media art. ✉ *1891 Granville St.,* ☎ *902/494–8223.* ☞ *Free.* ☉ *Tues.–Fri. 11–5, Sat. noon–4.*

⑪ **Art Gallery of Nova Scotia.** Sheltered within this historic building is an extensive permanent collection of more than 4,000 works, including an internationally recognized collection of Maritime and folk art by artists such as wood-carver Sydney Howard and painter Joe Nor-

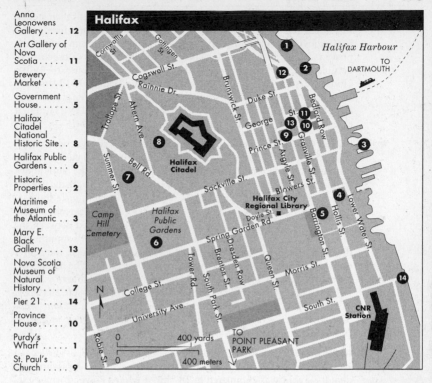

Anna Leonowens Gallery **12**
Art Gallery of Nova Scotia **11**
Brewery Market **4**
Government House **5**
Halifax Citadel National Historic Site . . **8**
Halifax Public Gardens **6**
Historic Properties . . . **2**
Maritime Museum of the Atlantic . . **3**
Mary E. Black Gallery **13**
Nova Scotia Museum of Natural History **7**
Pier 21 . . . . **14**
Province House **10**
Purdy's Wharf **1**
St. Paul's Church **9**

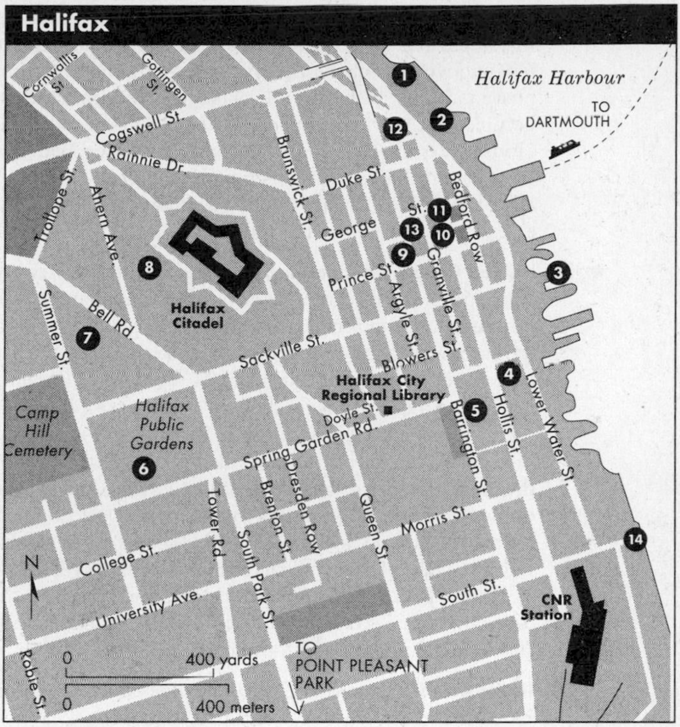

ris. Also here: the actual home of the late folk painter Maude Lewis, whose bright, cheery paintings cover the tiny structure inside and out. The collection of contemporary art has major works by Christopher Pratt, Alex Colville, John Nesbitt, and Dawn McNutt. ✉ *1741 Hollis St., at Cheapside,* ☎ *902/424–7542,* WEB *www.agns.gov.ns.ca.* 🎫 *$5.* ⏲ *June–Aug., Mon.–Wed. and Fri. 10–6, Thurs. 10–9, weekends noon–5; Sept.–May, Tues.–Fri. 10–5, weekends noon–5.*

❹ **Brewery Market.** A popular Saturday market takes place at this sprawling stone complex where Alexander Keith once brewed the beer that still bears his name. You can browse stalls laden with hand-dyed silk scarves, leatherwork, paintings, and stone carvings. Culinary temptations include Chinese and Indian snacks, farm cheese, and home-smoked sausage. Golden mountains of freshly baked bread; colorful displays of fresh local fruits and vegetables; and stalls with lamb, rabbit, and big brown eggs make this a true farmers market. Many of the city's finest chefs are regularly seen shopping here. ✉ *Between Hollis and Lower Water Sts.,* ☎ *no phone.* ⏲ *Sat. 7 AM–1 PM.*

OFF THE BEATEN PATH

FAIRVIEW CEMETERY – This cemetery is the final resting place of 121 victims of the *Titanic.* The graves can easily be located in a graceful arc of granite tombstones. One grave—marked J. Dawson—attracts particular attention from recent visitors. It's not Jack, the fictional Minnesota artist in the blockbuster film, however, but James Dawson, a coal trimmer from Ireland. Nineteen other victims are buried in Mount Olivet Catholic Cemetery, 10 in the Baron de Hirsch Jewish Cemetery. The Maritime Museum of the Atlantic has an exhibit about the disaster. ✉ *3720 Windsor St., 3 km (2 mi) north of downtown.*

❺ **Government House.** Built between 1799 and 1805 for Sir John Wentworth, the Loyalist governor of New Hampshire, and his racy wife,

Fannie (Thomas Raddall's novel *The Governor's Lady* tells their story), this house has since been the official residence of the province's lieutenant governor (currently Myra Freeman, the first woman to hold the post in almost 400 years). It is North America's oldest consecutively occupied government residence, as the older President's House (the White House) was evacuated and burned during the War of 1812. Its construction, of Nova Scotian stone, was engineered by a Virginian Loyalist, Isaac Hildrith. The house, which has been restored to its original elegance, isn't open to the public. ⊠ *1451 Barrington St.*

★ ❽ **Halifax Citadel National Historic Site.** The Citadel, erected between 1826 and 1856, was the heart of the city's fortifications and was linked to smaller forts and gun emplacements on the harbor islands and on the bluffs above the harbor entrance. Several other forts stood on the site before the present one. Kilted soldiers drill in front of the **Army Museum,** once the barracks, and a cannon is fired every day at noon. Before leaving, take in the view from the Citadel: the spiky downtown crowded between the hilltop and the harbor; the wooded islands at the harbor's mouth; and the naval dockyard under the Angus L. Macdonald Bridge, the nearer of the two bridges connecting Halifax with Dartmouth. The handsome, four-sided **Town Clock** on Citadel Hill was given to Halifax by Prince Edward, Duke of Kent, military commander from 1794 to 1800. ⊠ *Citadel Hill,* ☎ *902/426–5080,* WEB *www.parkscanada.pch.gc.ca.* ☜ *June–mid-Sept. $6; May 7–May 15 and mid-Sept.–Oct. $3.75; rest of yr free.* ☺ *July–Aug., daily 9–6; Sept.–June 14, daily 9–5.*

❻ **Halifax Public Gardens.** One of the oldest formal Victorian gardens in North America, this city oasis had its start in 1753 as a private garden. Its layout was completed in 1875 by Richard Power, former gardener to the Duke of Devonshire in Ireland. Gravel paths wind among ponds, trees, and flower beds, revealing an astonishing variety of plants from all over the world. The centerpiece is a gazebo erected in 1887 for Queen Victoria's Golden Jubilee. The gardens are closed during the winter but you can take a pleasant walk around the perimeter, along the cast-iron fence. ⊠ *Bounded by Sackville, Summer, and S. Park Sts. and Spring Garden Rd.*

❷ **Historic Properties.** These waterfront warehouses date from the early 19th century, when trade and war made Halifax prosperous. They were built by such raffish characters as Enos Collins, a privateer, smuggler, and shipper whose vessels defied Napoleon's blockade to bring American supplies to the Duke of Wellington. The buildings have since been taken over by quality shops, chic offices, and restaurants, including those in Privateer's Warehouse. ⊠ *Lower Water and Hollis Sts.*

Khyber Center for the Arts. Primarily a gallery for young and emerging artists, the Khyber hosts works in numerous genres, including performance art. Its various galleries are in a historic, turreted building. Also in the building is the Khyber Club bar, where young artists spend time discussing their work and drinking Khybeer. ⊠ *1588 Barrington St.,* ☎ *902/422–9668.* ☜ *By donation.* ☺ *Wed.–Sat. noon–5.*

❸ **Maritime Museum of the Atlantic.** The exhibits in this restored chandlery and warehouse on the waterfront include small boats once used around the coast, as well as displays describing Nova Scotia's proud sailing heritage, from the days when the province, on its own, was one of the world's foremost shipbuilding and trading nations. Other exhibits explore the Halifax Explosion of 1917, shipwrecks, and lifesaving. Permanently moored outside, after a long life of charting the coasts of Labrador and the Arctic, is the hydrographic steamer *Acadia.* At the next wharf (summer only) is Canada's naval memorial, **HMCS** *Sackville,* the sole survivor of a fleet that escorted convoys of ships from Halifax to England during World War II.

Much of the 1997 movie *Titanic* was filmed in Nova Scotia, and the museum has a permanent exhibit about the disaster. With many victims buried in Halifax, the city was, in a sense, the ship's final destination. The display includes 20 artifacts and dozens of photographs. The centerpiece is the only surviving deck chair. Also on display are a section of wall paneling; a balustrade molding and part of a newel from the dual curving staircase; a cribbage board carved from *Titanic* oak by the carpenter of one of the rescue ships; and the log kept by a wireless operator at Cape Race, Newfoundland, on the fateful night. An extensive research library is open to the public by appointment only. ⊠ *1675 Lower Water St.,* ☎ *902/424–7490 or 902/424–7491.* ☎ *$6.* ☉ *May–Oct., Mon. and Wed.–Sat. 9:30–5:30, Tues. 9:30–8, Sun. 1–5:30; Nov.–May, Wed.–Sat. 9:30–5, Tues. 9:30–8, Sun. 1–5.*

⑬ **Mary E. Black Gallery.** The exhibit space for the Nova Scotia Centre for Craft and Design presents rotating shows of quality crafts. ⊠ *1683 Barrington St.,* ☎ *902/424–4062.* ☎ *Free.* ☉ *Weekdays 9–4:30, Sat. 10–4.*

☺ ❼ **Nova Scotia Museum of Natural History.** You can learn about whales, fossils, dinosaurs, birds and mushrooms here. The Nature Centre is home to live snakes, frogs, insects, and other creatures; the Butterfly Pavilion is filled with species from around the world. Nature talks, walks, and workshops are designed to appeal to all interests and ages. The museum is most easily recognized by the huge fiberglass model of the tiny northern spring peeper (a frog) that "clings" to the side of the building May through October. ⊠ *1747 Summer St.,* ☎ *902/424–7353,* WEB *nature.museum.gov.ns.ca.* ☎ *$4.* ☉ *Mid-May–Oct., Mon.–Tues. and Thurs.–Sun. 1–5:30, Wed. 9:30–8; Nov.–mid-May, Tues. and Thurs.–Sun. 9:30–5, Wed. 9:30–8.*

⑭ **Pier 21.** From 1928 until 1971, refugees, returning troop ships, war brides, and more than a million immigrants arrived on Canadian soil through Pier 21, the front door to Canada. It's now a museum where the immigrant experience is re-created through live performances, multimedia presentations, and displays of photographs, documents, and artifacts. ⊠ *1031 Marginal Rd.,* ☎ *902/425–7770.* ☎ *$6.50.* ☉ *June–Sept., daily 9–6; Oct.–May, Tues.–Sat. 10–5, Sun. noon–5.*

Point Pleasant Park. Most of the city's secondary fortifications have been turned into public parks. This one, which encompasses 186 wooded acres with walking trails and seafront paths, is popular with joggers and dog walkers and provides the perfect vantage point from which to watch ships entering and leaving the harbor. The park was leased from the British Crown by the city for 999 years, at a shilling a year. Its major military installation is a massive round martello tower dating from the late 18th century. ⊠ *About 12 blocks down South Park Street from Spring Garden Rd.*

⑩ **Province House.** Charles Dickens proclaimed this structure, now a National Historic Site, "a gem of Georgian architecture." Erected in 1819 to house Britain's first overseas self-government, the sandstone building still serves as the meeting place for the provincial legislature. ⊠ *1726 Hollis St.,* ☎ *902/424–4661.* ☎ *Free.* ☉ *July–Aug., weekdays 9–5, weekends 10–4; Sept.–June, weekdays 8:30–4:30.*

❶ **Purdy's Wharf.** Named after a famous shipping family from the 19th century, the wharf is composed of a pier and twin office towers that stand right in the harbor. The buildings actually use ocean water to generate air-conditioning. ⊠ *Upper Water St.*

⑨ St. Paul's Church. Opened in 1750, this is Canada's oldest Protestant church and the burial site of many colonial notables. Inside, on the north end, a piece of metal is embedded in the wall. It is a fragment of the *Mont Blanc,* one of the two ships whose collision caused the Halifax Explosion of December 6, 1917, the greatest human-caused explosion prior to that at Hiroshima. ⊠ *1749 Argyle St.,* ☏ *902/429–2240.* ☉ *Sept.–May, weekdays 9–4:30; June–Aug., Mon.–Sat. 9–4:30.*

Dining and Lodging

$$$–$$$$ ✕ **Maple.** The fine and artfully presented cuisine served here is simply exquisite. Maple uses ingredients of the highest quality and mixes them up with flair in the open kitchen. The menu changes nightly according to availability. A winter combination of lobster and mango is wrapped in crisp nori and topped with sweet corn shoots. Trust the chef and order his seven-course table d'hôte. It may contain rich and tender duck breast, foie gras, or arctic char. ⊠ *1813 Granville St.,* ☏ *902/425–9100. AE, MC, V. Closed Sun.*

$$$ ✕ **da Maurizo's Dining Room.** Subdued lighting, elegant decor, and fresh flowers on the tables make dining a lovely experience at this Italian restaurant. Chef Maurizo's creativity and attention to detail create meals that are both impressive and satisfying. Seared foie gras is napped with a port sauce; pasta shells are stuffed with ricotta, radicchio, and sweet raisins, then sautéed in butter and served with Parmesan on the side. For dessert, the zabaglione is likely to leave you weak. Connoisseurs should ask to see the "specialty wine list," which tops out at $400. ⊠ *1496 Lower Water St.,* ☏ *902/423–0859. AE, MC, V. Closed Sun.*

$$–$$$ ✕ **Fid.** A fid is a graceful nautical tool used to splice rope. At this little minimalist restaurant a two-minute walk from the main gates of the Halifax Public Gardens, the chef–owner splices together unusual flavors and textures. Still, special requests and dietary requirements are accommodated here. The halibut, when available, is the most popular dish on the menu. Chocolate lovers should consider the *moelleau au chocolat,* molten chocolate-custard sauce within a shell of warm cake. ⊠ *1569 Dresden Row,* ☏ *902/422–9162. MC, V. No lunch. Closed Mon.*

$$–$$$ ✕ **The Press Gang.** Easily the hippest fine-dining establishment in Halifax, The Press Gang offers only the freshest fish available. Oysters, whether Malpeque or another delicious variety, are served with freshly grated horseradish, black pepper, and lemon, or with one of the many house salsas and dressings. You might try a fine muscadet from the well-stocked cellar to complement your seafood. Organic meats, including buffalo, venison, and rabbit, are also a specialty. The restaurant is in one of Halifax's oldest historic buildings, built in 1759; thick, cold stone walls testify to the building's era, but the atmosphere is warmed with exquisite decor and lighting. ⊠ *5218 Prince St.,* ☏ *902/423–8816. Reservations essential. AE, MC, V.*

$$–$$$ ✕ **Salty's on the Waterfront.** Overlooking Privateer's Wharf and the entire harbor, this restaurant gets the prize for the best location in the city. ★ Request a table with a window view and save room for the famous dessert, called Cadix (chocolate mousse over praline crust). The Salty Dog Bar & Grill on the ground level is less expensive and serves lunch outside on the wharf in summer (it can be very windy). ⊠ *1869 Upper Water St.,* ☏ *902/423–6818. Reservations essential. AE, DC, MC, V.*

$–$$$ ✕ **MacAskill's Restaurant.** Diners can experience Nova Scotian hospitality in this romantic dining room overlooking beautiful Halifax Harbour. The chefs create a variety of seafood dishes using the finest, freshest fish available. Specialties also include pepper steak, flambéed table-side. ⊠ *Dartmouth Ferry Terminal Bldg., 88 Alderney Dr.,* ☏ *902/466–3100. AE, DC, MC, V. No lunch weekends. Nov.–May, closed Sun.*

$–$$$ ✕ **Privateer's Warehouse.** History surrounds you in this centuries-old building, where three restaurants share early 18th-century stone walls and hewn beams. Upper Deck Waterfront Fishery & Grill, done in a nautical theme, has great views of the harbor and offers lobsters from a holding tank. Crawdads has a bistro-style atmosphere and serves innovative pastas as well as traditional cuisine; it also offers a children's menu. Lower Deck Good Time Pub is a boisterous bar with long trestle tables and a patio; fish-and-chips and other pub food are served. ⊠ *Historic Properties, Lower Water St.,* ☎ *902/422–1289, 902/426–1500, or 902/426–1501. AE, DC, MC, V.*

$–$$ ✕ **Cheelin Restaurant.** This small and informal Chinese restaurant with an open kitchen offers some of the most flavorful and freshest dishes available in the region. Each dish is prepared with individual attention and care, and the chef–owner personally checks with diners to make sure they are satisfied. Noodle and dumpling dishes are very popular, but if you're looking for something different, try the amazing fish-stuffed eggplant in black-bean sauce. ⊠ *Brewery Market, 1496 Lower Water St.,* ☎ *902/422–2252. AE, MC, V. Closed Mon.*

$–$$ ✕ **Dharma Sushi.** It's fast-paced here, but the service and food don't suffer as a result; the tidiest sushi, freshest sashimi, and feather-light tempura are artfully presented. The *chawan mushi,* a delicate egg custard with seafood, has the consistency of fine silk. ⊠ *1576 Argyle St.,* ☎ *902/ 425–7785. AE, MC, V. Closed Sun. No lunch Sat.*

$–$$ ✕ **Il Mercato Ristorante.** Enter this Italian eatery at your own risk: the gleaming display cases of antipasti and desserts—including the zucotto, a dome of chocolate and cream—are sure to tempt. On the menu, herbed lamb in wine sauce served with wild mushrooms and barley cakes is a good choice. ⊠ *5475 Spring Garden Rd.,* ☎ *902/422–2866. AE, MC, V.*

$ ✕ **Satisfaction Feast.** This small vegetarian restaurant is informal, friendly, and usually packed at lunchtime. The food is wholesome with lots of ethnic influences (think fresh whole-wheat bread and daily curries). Sweet, sharp ginger beer is brewed on the premises. Enjoy an organic coffee with one of the fine cakes or desserts. ⊠ *1581 Grafton St.,* ☎ *902/422–3540. AE, MC, V.*

$$$–$$$$ 🏨 **Westin Nova Scotian.** An enormous brick building, this grand hotel sits solidly in downtown Halifax, next door to the VIA Rail station, with the harbor behind it and Cornwallis Park in front. Comfortable, overstuffed chairs and a warm, peachy light fill the lobby, where a nautical theme prevails. Rooms are done in green or peach; some have wicker furniture. The Tradewinds Restaurant ($$–$$$) offers fresh fish and shellfish dishes as well as pastas and meatier fare. ⊠ *1181 Hollis St., B3H 2P6,* ☎ *902/421–1000 or 800/228–3000,* FAX *902/422–9465,* WEB *www.westin.com. 300 rooms, 13 suites. 3 restaurants, in-room data ports, no-smoking rooms, indoor pool, hot tub, sauna, tennis court, gym, baby-sitting, dry cleaning, laundry service. AE, DC, MC, V.*

$$–$$$$ 🏨 **Prince George Hotel.** Contemporary mahogany furnishings in this
★ luxurious and understated business-oriented hotel include writing desks. Georgio's Restaurant ($$) serves eclectic cuisine in a casual setting. The hotel is connected by underground tunnel to the World Trade and Convention Centre; walkways provide access to shops, offices, and entertainment. ⊠ *1725 Market St., B3J 3N9,* ☎ *902/425–1986; 800/ 565–1567 in Canada,* WEB *www.princegeorgehotel.com. 207 rooms, 9 suites. Restaurant, bar, pool, sauna, hot tub, gym, concierge, meeting room. AE, DC, MC, V.*

$$–$$$$ 🏨 **Sheraton Halifax.** Built low to match neighboring historic ironstone buildings, this waterfront hotel varies in appearance from others in the chain. Its convenient location in Historic Properties contributes to its elegance. Rooms are fairly spacious, all with desks and sitting areas.

A five-minute stroll through a walkway takes you to Halifax's only casino. ✉ *1919 Upper Water St., B3J 3J5,* ☎ *902/421–1700 or 800/ 325–3535,* FAX *902/422–5805,* WEB *www.sheraton.com. 335 rooms, 19 suites. Restaurant, bar, room service, indoor pool, hair salon, health club, dock, concierge, baby-sitting, dry cleaning, laundry service, meeting room, parking (fee). AE, DC, MC, V.*

$$–$$$ 🏨 **Delta Halifax.** This business-class hotel has spacious, attractive rooms, most with a panoramic harbor view. An enclosed walkway provides easy access to the Historic Properties and Scotia Square mall. The Crown Bistro ($$–$$$) includes more-refined dishes as well as lighter fare. ✉ *1990 Barrington St., B3J 1P2,* ☎ *902/425–6700 or 800/441– 1414,* FAX *902/425–6214,* WEB *www.deltahotels.com. 279 rooms, 21 suites. Restaurant, piano bar, in-room data ports (some), no-smoking rooms, indoor pool, hot tub, sauna, gym, concierge, laundry service, business services, parking (fee). AE, DC, MC, V.*

$$–$$$ 🏨 **Inn on the Lake.** A great value in a quiet location, this small country club–style hotel sits on 5 acres of parkland on the edge of Fall River Lake, 30 minutes from Halifax and 10 minutes from the airport. Rooms are spacious and have balconies. ✉ *3009 Lake Thomas Dr., Box 29, Waverly B0N 2S0,* ☎ *902/861–3480,* FAX *902/861–4883,* WEB *www.innonthelake.com. 34 rooms, 12 suites. Restaurant, lounge, beach, airport shuttle, free parking. AE, MC, V.*

$–$$$ 🏨 **Halliburton House Inn.** A historic property, this hotel is an elegant renovation of three 19th-century town houses. Period antiques, goosedown duvets, and fresh coffee await you in the comfortable rooms, lending a homey ambience. The suites have fireplaces, and there's a lovely garden. The rates here run the gamut, with some topping the $$$$ range. Local game and Atlantic seafood are served in an elegant dining room. ✉ *5184 Morris St., B3J 1B3,* ☎ *902/420–0658,* FAX *902/423–2324,* WEB *www.halliburton.ns.ca. 29 rooms, 2 suites. Restaurant, library. AE, DC, MC, V. CP.*

$–$$ 🏨 **Garden View Bed & Breakfast.** This lovely Victorian home sits on a quiet residential street near the Halifax Commons. You can relax in the living room in front of the fire or unwind with a soak in an antique bath tub. The garden is especially charming. A full breakfast is served in the dining room or in your room. ✉ *6052 Williams St., B3K 1E9,* ☎ *902/423–2943 or 888/737–0778,* FAX *902/423–4355,* WEB *www.interdesign.ca/gardenview. 3 rooms without bath. Dining room. MC, V. BP.*

$ 🏨 **Dalhousie University.** Most Halifax universities offer low prices for no-frills rooms from May through August. Dalhousie University rents single rooms for $38 and two-bedroom apartments for $55. A buffet breakfast is provided, and guests have access to the Dalplex athletic facility and parking. ✉ *6136 University Ave., B3H 4J2,* ☎ *902/494– 8840,* FAX *902/494–1219. 420 rooms without bath, 20 apartments. Indoor pool, gym, badminton. MC, V. CP.*

$ 🏨 **Queen Street Tourist Home.** Nova Scotian antiques and paintings fill this charming 19th-century Georgian house. It's just a short walk from busy Spring Garden Road, the heart of the downtown shopping district. ✉ *1266 Queen St., B3J 2H4,* ☎ *902/422–9828. 6 rooms without bath. No credit cards.*

Nightlife and the Arts

THE ARTS

Halifax has a burgeoning film industry, the product of which is presented at the **Atlantic Film Festival** (☎ *902/422–3456*), held the third week in September. The festival also showcases feature films, TV movies, and documentaries made outside of Halifax. Admission to films often includes admission to a party or gala event following the screening. During the first week of September, the **Atlantic Fringe Festival** presents 40 shows in eight venues. The **Du Maurier Atlantic Jazz Festival** (☎ 902/ 492–2225), with an eclectic selection of jazz styles, takes place in mid-July. Some concerts are free. The internationally acclaimed **Scotia Festival of Music** (☎ 902/429–9469) presents classical musicians via concert and master classes each May and June. Pierre Boulez, Philip Glass, Maureen Forrester, and Tafelmusik are just a few of the guest artists who have attended the festival to perform, teach, coach, and lecture.

The **Alderney Theatre** (✉ 2 Ochterloney St., Dartmouth, ☎ 902/461–4698) is home to the Eastern Front Theatre Company, which produces, presents, and hosts professional Canadian theater. **Grafton Street Dinner Theatre** (✉ 1741 Grafton St., ☎ 902/425–1961) holds performances Wednesday through Saturday. **Historic Feast Company** (☎ 902/420–1840) presents shows set in the 19th century at Historic Properties Thursday through Saturday evenings. The **Neptune Theatre** (✉ 1593 Argyle St., ☎ 902/429–7300; 902/429–7070 box office), Canada's oldest professional repertory playhouse, stages year-round performances ranging from classics to contemporary Canadian drama. On mild July and August evenings, **Shakespeare by the Sea** (☎ 902/422–0295) performs the Bard's works in Point Pleasant Park at the southern end of the Halifax peninsula. The natural setting—dark woods, rocky shore, and ruins of fortifications—serves as a dramatic backdrop.

NIGHTLIFE
Haligonians love their pubs and their music. At **Bearly's House of Blues and Ribs** (✉ 1269 Barrington St., ☎ 902/423–2526), a dark, low-ceilinged tavern with a couple of pool tables, you can dine on ribs, burgers, and fish-and-chips while listening to outstanding blues artists (except Monday and Wednesday). **Economy Shoe Shop Cafe and Bar, Backstage, and Dimond** (✉ 1663 Argyle St., ☎ 902/423–7463) are actually three establishments with different atmospheres combined in one space with a common menu, making for the trendiest spot in town. The eclectic decor alone is worth a visit. Live jazz can be heard every Monday; author readings are given Tuesdays. **The Marquee Club** (✉ 2037 Gottigen St., ☎ 902/429–3020), a cabaret-style venue, presents some of the hottest entertainment in town. The club buzzes until 3:30 AM with live rock, blues, and alternative bands. Downstairs there's jazz, blues, and acoustic evenings. The bar has a good selection of locally brewed beers on tap. **Merrill's Cafe and Lounge** (✉ 5171 George St., ☎ 902/425–5249) is a large, open bar with a DJ. The casual atmosphere is popular with the university crowd. **O'Carroll's Restaurant and Lounge** (✉ 1860 Upper Water St., ☎ 902/423–4405) offers a comfortable, Irish-pub setting and traditional Irish, Scottish, and local music, with the well-known duo Evans and Dougherty as Friday-night regulars. Lots of funky folk art hangs on the walls at the **Soho Kitchen** (✉ 1582 Granville St., ☎ 902/423–3049). Jazz groups perform nightly (except Monday and Wednesday) in the laid-back atmosphere. **Tom's Little Havana Café** (✉ 5428 Doyle St., ☎ 902/423–8667), a cozy pub, offers 30 types of cigars. High ceilings and a state-of-the-art air-purification system ensure that even nonsmokers can enjoy the comfort of a wing chair, bustling bar, or quiet booth.

Outdoor Activities and Sport
PARTICIPANT SPORTS
Ground Zero Climbing Gym (✉ 105 Akerley Blvd., Dartmouth, ☎ 902/ 468–8788) offers challenging indoor-climbing equipment and supervision.

Within an easy drive of downtown Halifax is **Granite Springs Golf Club** (✉ 1441 Prospect Rd., ☎ 902/852–4653), an 18-hole, par-72, semiprivate course open to greens-fee play. Lessons and golf clinics are available. The **Sackville Golf Course** (✉ Hwy. 1, ☎ 902/865–2179) is a 9-hole, par-29 public course; it also offers a driving range and a miniature golf course.

Coastal Adventures Sea Kayaking (☎ 877/404–2774) has a wide range of tours for the beginner or the experienced kayaker.

SPECTATOR SPORTS

The **Moosehead Premium Dry Speedway** (✉ 200 Prospect Rd., ☎ 902/876–8222) hosts auto races from May through October.

The **Halifax Mooseheads** (☎ 902/496–5993), a Junior A division hockey team, play at the **Halifax Metro Centre** (✉ 1800 Argyle St., ☎ 902/421–8000) September through March.

Shopping

The **Art Gallery of Nova Scotia Shop** (✉ 1741 Hollis St., ☎ 902/424–7542) carries a good selection of arts and crafts; it also has a wonderful café decorated with colorful regional art. You can find fine crafts in the **Barrington Inn Complex** (✉ 1875 Barrington St.). In addition to being a deli and bakery with great takeout, the **Italian Gourmet** (✉ 5431 Doyle St., ☎ 902/423–7880) stocks a wonderful selection of imported gift items, including ceramics, exotic foodstuffs, and cooking gadgets. **Pewter House** (✉ 1875 Granville St., ☎ 902/423–8843) sells locally made and imported pewter goods, from knickknacks and tableware to clocks and jewelry.

Ambience Home Accents (✉ 5431 Doyle St., ☎ 902/423–9200) is packed to the rafters with curios and decorative functional items from all over the province and beyond. **Attica** (✉ 1652 Granville St., ☎ 902/423–2557) presents furniture, objets d'art, and housewares by Canadian and international designers. **Drala Books** (✉ 1567 Grafton St., ☎ 902/422–2504) stocks beautiful ceramics, handmade paper, and guides to meditation and Japanese gardening. At **Nova Scotian Crystal Ltd.** (✉ Corner of George and Lower Water Sts., ☎ 902/492–5984), you can watch Waterford master craftspeople blowing glass into graceful decanters and bowls, which can be purchased in the showroom. The **Plaid Place** (✉ 1903 Barrington Pl., ☎ 902/429–6872 or 800/563–1749) has an array of tartans and Highland accessories. The **Wool Sweater Outlet** (✉ 1870 Hollis St., ☎ 902/422–9209) sells wool and cotton sweaters at reasonable prices.

Park Lane (✉ 5657 Spring Garden Rd.) is a stylish, indoor mall with everything from hand-crafted clothing to Canadian books and bath salts. **Spring Garden Road** is the liveliest street in town. Busking musicians serenade shoppers flowing in and out of **Spring Garden Place** (✉ 5640 Spring Garden Rd.), a mall. **Jennifer's of Nova Scotia** (5635 Spring Garden Rd., ☎ 902/425–3119) sells traditional crafts from around the province, soaps, hooked mats, tartan clothing, ceramics, and pewter.

Dartmouth

⑮ *Just north of Halifax via the A. Murray Mackay and Angus L. Macdonald bridges.*

Suburban in demeanor, Dartmouth was first settled by Quaker whalers from Nantucket. The 23 lakes within Dartmouth's boundaries, which have given Dartmouth the moniker "City of Lakes," provided the Mi'Kmaqs with a canoe route to the province's interior and to the Bay of Fundy. A 19th-century canal system connected the lakes for a brief time, but today there are only ruins, which have been partially restored as historic sites. You can drive or take the ferry from Halifax to Dartmouth. If you walk along the water behind the modern Law Courts in Halifax, near Historic Properties, you'll soon reach the Dartmouth ferry terminal, jammed with commuters during rush hour. The terminal is home to the oldest operational saltwater ferry service in North America, which began in 1732. If you do take the ferry, be sure to enjoy the sculptures by artist Dawn McNutt in the courtyard just outside the Dartmouth terminal. You may also want to head straight up the hill, along Pleasant Street, to explore funky little shops and cafés.

If you'd rather walk to Dartmouth, try the Angus L. Macdonald bridge, which has a walkway and a bicycle path. After you come off of the bridge you can follow the wooden boardwalk for a stroll along the water.

The **Black Cultural Centre for Nova Scotia,** in Westphal (a neighborhood of Dartmouth), is in the heart of the oldest black community in the area. The museum, library, and educational complex are dedicated to the preservation of the history and culture of blacks in Nova Scotia, who first arrived here in the 1600s. ⊠ *Hwy. 7 and Cherrybrooke Rd.,* ☎ *902/434–6223.* ⊡ *$5.* ☉ *Weekdays 9–5, Sat. 10–5.*

Dining and Lodging

$$–$$$ ✕ **La Perla.** This northern Italian restaurant with three separate dining areas, each with a distinctive ambience, overlooks the harbor and has consistently excellent food and a fine wine cellar. The food is rich and the servings are hearty. Calamari tossed with chilies and tomato has never been so tender; snails swim in a heady Gorgonzola cream sauce. ⊠ *73 Alderney Dr.,* ☎ *902/469–3241. Reservations essential. AE, MC, V.*

$$ ⊡ **Park Place Ramada Renaissance.** In Dartmouth's Burnside Industrial Park, this luxury hotel is aimed at the business traveler as well as families. There is a 108-ft indoor water slide. ⊠ *240 Brownlow Ave., B3B 1X6,* ☎ *902/468–8888; 800/561–3733 in Canada,* ℻ *902/468–8765,* Ⓦ *www.ramadans.com. 178 rooms, 30 suites. Restaurant, bar, room service, indoor pool, hot tub, sauna, gym, meeting room, free parking. AE, DC, MC, V.*

THE SOUTH SHORE AND ANNAPOLIS VALLEY

Mainland Nova Scotia is a long, narrow peninsula—no point in the province is more than 56 km (35 mi) from salt water. The South Shore is on the Atlantic side, the Annapolis Valley on the Bay of Fundy side; although they are less than an hour apart by car, the two seem like different worlds. The South Shore is rocky coast, island-dotted bays, fishing villages, and shipyards; the Annapolis Valley is lumberyards, farms, vineyards, and orchards. The South Shore is German, French, and Yankee; the valley, British. The sea is everywhere on the South Shore; in the valley the sea is blocked from view by a ridge of mountains.

Highway 103, Highway 3, and various secondary roads form the province's designated Lighthouse Route, which leads southwest from Halifax down the South Shore. It touches the heads of several big bays and small harbors, revealing a changing panorama of shoreline, inlet, and island. Small towns and fishing villages are spaced out every 50 km (31 mi) or so. The Lighthouse Route ends in Yarmouth and the Evangeline Trail begins, winding along the shore of St. Mary's Bay through a succession of Acadian villages collectively known as the French Shore. Here you notice the Acadian flag, tricolored with a gold star representing *stella maris,* the star of the sea. The star has guided the French-speaking Acadians during troubled times, which have been frequent. In 1755, after residing for a century and a half in Nova Scotia, chiefly in the Annapolis Valley, the Acadians were expelled by the British—an event that inspired Henry Wadsworth Longfellow's famous poem *Evangeline*. Some eluded capture and others slowly crept back; many settled in New Brunswick and along this shore of Nova Scotia. The villages blend into one another for about 32 km (20 mi), each one, it seems, with its own wharf, fish plant, and Catholic church. This tour mostly focuses on the towns along Highway 1, but you should follow the side roads whenever the inclination strikes; the South Shore rewards slow, relaxed exploration.

The Annapolis Valley runs northeast like a huge trench, flat on the bottom, sheltered on both sides by the North and South mountains. Occasional roads over the South Mountain lead to the South Shore; short roads over the North Mountain lead to the Fundy shore. Like the South Shore, the valley is punctuated with pleasant small towns, each with a generous supply of extravagant Victorian homes and churches. The rich soil of the valley bottom supports dairy herds, hay, grain, root vegetables, tobacco, and fruit. Apple-blossom season (late May and early June) and the fall harvest are the loveliest times to visit.

Peggy's Cove

★ ⑯ *48 km (30 mi) southwest of Halifax.*

Peggy's Cove, on Highway 333, marks the entrance to St. Margaret's Bay, which has been guarded for years by its famous octagonal lighthouse. The cove, with its houses huddled around the narrow slit in the boulders, is probably the most photographed village in Canada. A Canadian post office is in the lighthouse perched high on the rocky coast above a restless sea. Don't be tempted to venture too close—many an unwary visitor has been swept away by the mighty surf that sometimes breaks here. You can drive almost to the base of the lighthouse, but you'd do better to park in the spacious public lot below it and enjoy the village's shops and services during your three-minute walk up to the lighthouse.

A simple granite **memorial** (⊠ Hwy. 333) for 1998 Swissair Flight 111, which crashed into the waters off Peggy's Cove, commemorates "those who helped and those who died"—the 229 casualties and the courageous Nova Scotia fisherfolk for their recovery work and the unstinting comfort they offered to grieving families. Another memorial stands in the town of Blandford directly across the cove.

Dining and Lodging

$$$$ ✕ **Candleriggs Dining Room.** Authentic Scottish dishes, such as *Forfar bridie* (beef and potato in puff pastry), Scotch mushrooms in cream and whisky, Scotch onion pie, and steak-and-kidney pie, share the menu with Canadian specialties in this pleasant restaurant. ⊠ *8545 Peggy's Cove Rd., Indian Harbour (3 km, or 2 mi, from Peggy's Cove),* ☎ *902/823–2722. AE, D, DC, MC, V. Limited hrs Nov.–mid-Mar.*

$$–$$$ ✕ **Sou'wester Restaurant.** Sou'wester, at the base of the Peggy's Cove lighthouse, serves home-style fare including a wide range of Maritime specialties—try *solomon gundy* (herring and onion with sour cream)— and fish-and-chips. There's also a large souvenir shop. ⊠ *Off Hwy. 333,* ☎ *902/823–2561. AE, DC, MC, V.*

$–$$ ✕ **Gingerbread House.** Flower boxes and dark paneling decorate the outside of this restaurant 15 km (9 mi) from Peggy's Cove; home-style cooking and homemade crafts await inside. Ample portions of chowders, seafood, fettuccine, fish, steaks, and chicken are served in the dining room or out on the patio. ⊠ *10345 Peggy's Cove Rd., Glen*

Margaret, ☎ *902/823–1230. MC, V. Closed Nov.–Apr. and Mon.–Tues. in May.*

$–$$$ ⊞ **Havenside B&B.** At this luxurious home, multilevel decks overlook
★ a delightful seascape near Peggy's Cove. Saltwater swimming and ca-
noeing, a serene gathering room with fireplace and library, a games room
with a pool table, and a "breakfast that makes lunch redundant"—fresh
homemade muffins, pancakes, French toast, eggs—enhance the pack-
age. Four-night Land and Sea packages with two nights aboard a 32-
ft yacht and two nights at the B&B are an option. ✉ *225 Boutillier's
Cove Rd., Hackett's Cove B0J 3J0,* ☎ *902/823–9322 or 800/641–8272,*
FAX *902/823–9322. 3 rooms, 1 suite. Dining room, library. MC, V. BP.*

$–$$ ⊞ **Migrate In B & B and Cottage.** Perched on 56 acres overlooking St.
Margaret's Bay, this modern home is on the migration route of many
birds, including numerous shorebirds, ring-necked pheasants, red-
breasted nuthatches, hummingbirds, black-capped chickadees, and
robins. Breakfast may offer lobster quiche, homemade granola, or
waffles with Nova Scotia blueberries. A restored 1840s cottage has two
bedrooms, an eat-in kitchen, and a wood-burning stove. ✉ *9749 Hwy.
333, Hackett's Cove (7 km, or 4 mi, from Peggy's Cove) B0J 3J0,* ☎
902/823–1968 or 800/780–7471, FAX *902/823–1968,* WEB *www.mi-
gratein.com. 2 rooms, 1 suite, 1 cottage. Recreation room. MC, V. BP.*

Shopping

Beales' Bailiwick (✉ 124 Peggy's Point Rd., ☎ 902/823–2099) carries outstanding crafts—Maritime-designed clothing, pewter, jewelry,
and more. The adjoining coffee shop affords the best photo opportunity for Peggy's Cove and the lighthouse. **River'B'Quilts** (✉ 6001 St.
Margaret's Bay Rd., Head of St. Margaret's Bay, ☎ 902/826–1991),
calling itself "the biggest little quilt shop in Nova Scotia," offers quilts
and quilting supplies, including custom-made designs.

Chester

64 km (40 mi) west of Peggy's Cove.

Chester, a charming little town on Mahone Bay, is a popular summer
retreat for an established population of well-heeled Americans and
Haligonians, whose splendid homes and yachts rim the waterfront. In
fact, yachting is the town's principal summer occupation, culminating
each August in **Chester Race Week,** Atlantic Canada's largest regatta.

The **Ross Farm Living Museum of Agriculture,** a restored 19th-century
farm, illustrates the evolution of agriculture from 1600 to 1925. The
animals here are those found on a farm of the 1800s—draft horses,
oxen, and older breeds or types of animals. Blacksmithing and other
crafts are demonstrated. The Pedlar's Shop sells items made in the community. ✉ *Hwy. 12, New Ross (20-min drive inland from Chester),*
☎ *902/689–2210.* ⊠ *$3.* ☉ *June–mid-Oct., daily 9:30–5:30; Jan.–mid-
Mar., by appointment.*

A passenger-only ferry (☎ 902/275–3221) runs from the dock in
Chester to the scenic **Big and Little Tancook Islands,** 8 km (5 mi) out
in Mahone Bay. Reflecting its part-German heritage, Big Tancook
claims to make the best sauerkraut in Nova Scotia. Exploration of the
island is made easy by walking trails. The boat runs four times daily
Monday through Thursday, six times daily Friday, and twice daily on
weekends. The 45-minute ride costs $5 (round-trip ticket).

Dining and Lodging

$$–$$$ ✕ **The Galley.** Decked out in nautical bric-a-brac and providing a spec-
tacular view of the ocean, this restaurant has a pleasant, relaxed atmosphere and an outdoor dining area. The seafood chowder, lobster, and

homemade desserts are recommended. Reserve ahead for summer dining. ✉ *Hwy. 3, 115 Marina Rd., Marriot's Cove (Exit 8 off Hwy. 103, 3 km/2 mi west of Chester),* ☎ *902/275–4700. AE, D, MC, V. Closed Nov.–late Mar.*

$–$$ ✕ **Fo'c'sle Tavern.** This rustic midtown pub features nautical touches, including a deliciously ugly ship's figurehead, maps, displays of seamen's knots, and a ship's wheel. The mood is jolly, the food is abundant and affordable, and the potbellied woodstove exudes warmth and goodwill on chilly nights. The hearty pub fare includes hefty servings of fish-and-chips, seafood chowders, and steaks, as well as a Sunday breakfast buffet. ✉ *42 Queen St.,* ☎ *902/275–3912. V.*

$$$$ ✕▥ **Haddon Hall Inn.** At this luxurious resort near Chester, the large
★ guest rooms are furnished with antiques, including some canopy beds, working fireplaces, marble baths, and whirlpool tubs. Outside, tennis courts, a pool, mountain bikes, and nature await. The dining room overlooks Mahone Bay. A three-course prix fixe dinner (reservations required) may feature seafood, various meat dishes, and a vegetarian choice. The lounge is deep, dark, and rustic, with a fire in the grate on chilly evenings. ✉ *67 Haddon Hill Rd., Box 640, B0J 1J0,* ☎ *902/275–3577,* FAX *902/275–5159,* WEB *www.haddonhallinn.com. 5 rooms, 5 suites. Restaurant, lounge, pool, tennis court, mountain bikes. MC, V. Closed Nov.–Mar. MAP.*

$–$$ ✕▥ **Dauphinee Inn.** On the shore of Hubbards Cove, about 19 km (12 mi) east of Chester, this charming country inn has first-class accommodations and an excellent restaurant ($–$$). The Hot Rocks is a social dining concept where guests are invited to cook fresh vegetables, seafood, beef, or chicken on a hot slab of South Shore granite. Fresh local seafood is another specialty. Opportunities abound for bicycling, bird-watching, and deep-sea fishing and six golf courses are within a half-hour drive. ✉ *167 Shore Club Rd., Hubbards Cove (Exit 6 off Hwy. 103) B0J 1T0,* ☎ *902/857–1790 or 800/567–1790,* FAX *902/857–9555,* WEB *www.dauphineeinn.com. 4 rooms, 2 suites. Restaurant, lounge, boating, fishing. AE, D, DC, MC, V. Closed Nov.–Apr.*

Mahone Bay

★ ⑰ *24 km (15 mi) west of Chester.*

This quiet town perched on an idyllic bay of the same name comes alive each summer. Many of Nova Scotia's finest artists and artisans are represented in the studios and galleries that line the narrow streets. Three impressive churches stand shoulder to shoulder near the waterfront, their bells vying for attention each Sunday morning. You'll find sailing, kayaking, and walking opportunities. In July the annual **Wooden Boat Festival** celebrates the town's heritage as a shipbuilding center.

Dining and Lodging

$$$–$$$$ ✕ **The Innlet Café.** This pleasant restaurant commands a fine view of the town across the bay. A broad Canadian-style menu has poultry and meats, an understandable emphasis on chowders and seafoods, and a few vegetarian options. ✉ *249 Edgewater St.,* ☎ *902/624–6363. MC, V.*

$$ ▥ **Amber Rose Inn.** All the creature comforts plus expert knowledge of this historic area are available at this 125-year-old inn. The three large suites each have a private bath, whirlpool tub, refrigerator, coffeemaker, and handsome antiques. A lavish complimentary breakfast includes French toast or blueberry pancakes. ✉ *319 West Main St., Box 397, B0J 2E0,* ☎ *902/624–1060,* FAX *902/624–0997,* WEB *www.amberroseinn.com. 3 suites. Breakfast room. AE, MC, V. BP.*

$–$$ ⊡ **Manse at Mahone Bay Country Inn.** Classical music and fine art, a library of contemporary Canadian literature, and Mahone Bay's three handsome churches just down the hill distinguish this elegant mid-19th-century home, a former Presbyterian manse. Comfy chairs and binoculars near a broad bay window allow for viewing of Mahone Bay. The inn has an elegant guest parlor plus two spacious rooms in the main house; a carriage house has two huge suites. The menu is exceptional—get set for Stilton cheese–pear omelettes at a complimentary breakfast and a range of fresh seafood dishes at dinner (reservations required). ⊠ *88 Orchard St., Box 475, B0J 2E0,* ☎ *902/624–1121,* ℻ *902/624–1182,* WEB *www.bbcanada.com/manse. 2 rooms, 2 suites. Dining room. MC, V. BP.*

$ ⊡ **Countryside B&B.** Lessons in llama etiquette are part of the service at this waterfront farm with a private dock. Sheep, poultry, and llamas (the llamas protect the sheep from coyotes) share the meadows and barns. Inside, antiques and original art share space with your host's naval memorabilia. A sumptuous breakfast might include homemade treats such as wild-blueberry crepes, baked fat-free French toast, and jams. ⊠ *28 Silver Point Rd., R.R. 2, B0J 2E0,* ☎ *902/627–1308,* ℻ *902/627–1112,* WEB *www.countrysidebandb.com. 3 rooms. Dining room, dock. V. BP.*

Shopping

Amos Pewter (⊠ 589 Main St., ☎ 902/624–9547 or 800/565–3369) has been using traditional methods to make pewter for 25 years. A studio in an 1888 seaside building offers interpretive displays and demonstrations. Jewelry, sculptures, ornaments, and sand dollars are among the items available along with a new original-design Christmas ornament each year. The **Moorings Gallery & Shop** (⊠ 575 Main St., ☎ 902/624–6208) sells the work of Atlantic Canada's fine artists and artisans in many media. The **Rags to Rugs Shoppe** (⊠ 374 Clearland Woodstock Rd., ☎ 902/624–8075) specializes in the traditional hooked rugs for which Nova Scotia is famous. The owner offers her own designs and those of many other artisans.

Lunenburg

★ ⑱   *9 km (6 mi) south of Mahone Bay.*

A feast of Victorian-era architecture, wooden boats, steel draggers (a fishing boat that operates a trawl), historic inns, and good restaurants, Lunenburg delights all the senses. The center of town, known as Old Town, is a UNESCO World Heritage Site, and the fantastic old school on the hilltop is the region's finest remaining example of Second Empire architecture, an ornate style that began in 19th-century France.

Lunenburg is home port to the ***Bluenose II*** (☎ 902/634–1963 or 800/ 763–1963), a tall ship ambassador for Canada sailing out of Lunenburg, Halifax, and other ports. She's a replica of the first *Bluenose,* the great racing schooner depicted on the back of the Canadian dime— a winner of four international races and the pride of Canada. When in port, the *Bluenose II* is open for tours through the Fisheries Museum of the Atlantic. Two-hour harbor sailings in summer cost $20.

The **Fisheries Museum of the Atlantic,** on the Lunenburg waterfront, gives a comprehensive overview of Nova Scotia fisheries with demonstrations such as sail making, dory building, boat launching, and fish splitting. A touch tank with starfish, shellfish, and anemones; participatory demonstrations of rug hooking and quilting; and a day-long schedule of films at the theater make visiting here a busy yet rich experience. Add to that the *Bluenose* exhibit, celebrating the tall ship that won acclaim for Canada, plus a gift shop and seafood restaurant, and your day is full. ☒ *68 Bluenose Dr.,* ☎ *902/634–4794.* ☜ *$7.* ☉ *Mid-May–mid-Oct., daily 9:30–5:30; mid-Oct.–mid-May, by appointment.*

Dining and Lodging

$$–$$$ ✕ **Grand Banker Seafood Bar & Grill.** This bustling, big-menu establishment dispenses a wide variety of seafoods at modest prices. You can dine on scallops, shrimp, lobster in season, or all of the above in a seafood platter for those with hearty appetites. ☒ *82 Montague St.,* ☎ *902/634–3300. AE, D, MC, V.*

$$–$$$ ✕ **The Old Fish Factory Restaurant.** In the Fisheries Museum of the Atlantic, the Old Fish Factory overlooks Lunenburg Harbour. It specializes in seafood, but you can also get steaks and other dishes here. ☒ *68 Bluenose Dr.,* ☎ *902/634–3333 or 800/533–9336. AE, D, MC, V. Closed Nov.–early May.*

$–$$ ✕🏠 **Arbor View Inn.** The host is a young chef whose fresh menu ideas, based on a variety of ethnic influences, lend culinary sparkle to the gracious dining room ($$–$$$) of this grand, early-20th-century house. Though the menu changes frequently, his white-chocolate crème brûlée is a fixture. Leaded and stained-glass windows, extravagant wood trim, and handsome antiques enhance every room here. The top-floor suite has a queen-size canopy bed, a two-person whirlpool tub, and a deck. The spacious grounds invite strolls. ☒ *216 Dufferin St., B0J 2C0,* ☎ *800/890–6650,* ☎ 🖷 *902/634–3658,* 🌐 *www.arborviewinn.ns.ca. 4 rooms, 2 suites. Restaurant. MC, V. Closed Jan. BP.*

$ ✕🏠 **Lion Inn B&B.** Original works by Lunenburg artists—for show and
★   for sale—adorn the walls of this three-story 1835 town house, where the host's collection of owls stares out from all sides. Three interesting guest rooms are decorated in rich greens and burgundies and have sloping ceilings, eclectic antiques, and original artwork. The inn is noted for its outstanding dinners ($$$-$$$$); the star of the menu is rack of lamb, but you can also order good seafood and poultry and a wonderfully delicate mocha crème brûlée. ☒ *33 Cornwallis St., Box 487, B0J 2C0,* ☎ *902/634–8988 or 888/634–8988,* 🖷 *902/634–3386. 3 rooms. Restaurant. AE, MC, V. BP.*

$–$$$ 🏠 **Pelham House Bed & Breakfast.** Close to downtown, this sea captain's home, circa 1906 and decorated in the style of the era, has a large collection of books about the sea and sailing. The veranda overlooks the harbor. Full breakfast and afternoon tea are included in the room rate. ☒ *224 Pelham St., Box 358, B0J 2C0,* ☎ *902/634–7113,* 🖷 *902/ 634–7114. 3 rooms. Business services. MC, V. BP.*

$–$$ 🏠 **Boscawen Inn and MacLachlan House.** Period antiques adorn and fireplaces warm this elegant 1888 mansion and its 1905 annex in the middle of Lunenburg's historic Old Town. Guests can take afternoon tea in one of the drawing rooms or on the balcony. All rooms and suites have either water or park views. ☒ *150 Cumberland St., Box 1343, B0J 2C0,* ☎ *902/634–3325 or 800/354–5009,* 🖷 *902/634–9293,* 🌐 *www3.ns.sympatico.ca/boscawen. 20 rooms. Restaurant. AE, D, DC, MC, V. Closed Jan.–Easter.*

$–$$ 🏠 **Lunenburg Inn.** JFK's father, Joseph Kennedy, patronized this hostelry long before it became the gracious inn it is today. In those days it had 13 cell-size rooms sharing a single bathroom. Today, its two suites and seven no-smoking rooms, each with a private bath, are spacious and restful and furnished with fine antiques. An elegant main-floor parlor, awash in books, adjoins the bright blue-and-white dining room. A top-floor 775-square-ft suite includes a tiny kitchenette with a microwave and a refrigerator. ☒ *26 Dufferin St., B0J 2C0,* ☎ *902/634–3963 or 800/565–3963,* 🖷 *902/634–9419,* 🌐 *www.lunenburginn.com. 7* *rooms, 2 suites. Dining room, kitchenettes (some), no smoking rooms. AE, MC, V. BP.*

$ ⊞ **Blue Rocks Road B&B.** Vegetarians and bike enthusiasts can settle in comfortably at the Blue Rocks, which includes a bicycle shop and has bike rentals. Your host is a quilter, potter, and artist, and her unique stencil designs decorate floors, walls, and ceilings in every room. An enthusiastic dog shares hosting duties in this friendly smoke-free, meat-free home with three guest rooms. Breakfasts feature homemade granola, pancakes, French toast, or frittata with fresh herbs and vegetables from the garden. ⊠ *579 Blue Rocks Rd., RR 1, B0J 2C0,* ☎ *902/634–8033 or 800/818–3426,* FAX *902/634–7147. 3 rooms, 1 with bath. Bicycles. V. Closed mid-Oct.–mid-May. BP.*

$ ⊞ **1826 Maple Bird House B&B.** This B&B is just steps away from the Fisheries Museum and Lunenburg's fascinating waterfront. A huge garden overlooking the harbor and a golf course, an outdoor pool, and a piano in the drawing room create a relaxing ambience that characterizes this home. The hosts know a thing or two about breakfast—crepes, omelettes, cereals, and fruits appear in ample amounts as part of the complimentary meal. ⊠ *36 Pelham St., Box 278, B0J 2C0,* ☎ FAX *902/ 634–3863 or 888/395–3863,* WEB *www3.ns.sympatico.ca/barry.susie. 4 rooms. Pool. MC, V. BP.*

Outdoor Activities and Sports

June through October **Lunenburg Whale-Watching** (☎ 902/527–7175) offers three-hour trips daily from the Fisheries Museum Wharf for $35. You may spot fin, pilot, humpback, and minke whales; dolphins; seals; and myriad seabirds such as puffins, razorbills, and gannets. You can also arrange for bird-watching excursions and tours of Lunenburg Harbour.

Shopping

Black Duck Gallery and Gifts (⊠ 8 Pelham St., ☎ 902/639–3190) sells handmade kites, local art, books, and an imaginative selection of gifts. The **Houston North Gallery** (⊠ 110 Montague St., ☎ 902/634–8869) represents both trained and self-taught Nova Scotian artists as well as Inuit soapstone carvers and printmakers. It's closed in January. The **Lunenburg Forge & Metalworks Gallery** (⊠ 146 Bluenose Dr., ☎ 902/ 634–7125) is a traditional artist/blacksmith shop in a bright-blue building on the waterfront. One-of-a-kind handcrafted wrought-iron items and custom orders, including both time-honored designs and whimsical creations, are available.

Bridgewater

18 km (11 mi) west of Lunenburg.

This is the main market town of the South Shore. The **DesBrisay Museum** explores the history and people of Lunenburg County and has changing exhibits on art, science, technology, and history. The gift shop carries books by local authors and local arts and crafts. ⊠ *130 Jubilee Rd.,* ☎ *902/543–4033.* ☞ *$2 mid-May–Sept.; free rest of yr.* ☉ *Mid-May–Sept., Mon.–Sat. 9–5, Sun. 1–5; Oct.–mid-May, Tues. and Thurs.– Sun. 1–5, Wed. 1–9.*

The **Wile Carding Mill,** a water-powered mill with an overshot wheel, operated from 1860 to 1968. Interpreters tell the story of Dean Wile's woolen mill. ⊠ *242 Victoria Rd.,* ☎ *902/543–8233.* ☞ *By donation.* ☉ *June–Sept., Mon.–Sat. 9:30–5:30, Sun. 1–5:30.*

Liverpool

⑲ *46 km (29 mi) south of Bridgewater.*

Nestled on the estuary of the Mersey River, Liverpool was settled around 1760 by New Englanders and is now a fishing and paper-milling town. During the American Revolution and the War of 1812, Liverpool was a privateering center; later, it became an important shipping and trading port.

The **Hank Snow Country Music Centre Museum,** housed in a renovated CN railway station, commemorates the great country singer whose childhood home is nearby. A country-music archive and library and memorabilia of the singer's career are on view. ☒ *Off Hwy. 103,* ☎ *902/354–4675 or 888/450–5525.* ☜ *$3.* ☉ *June–mid-Oct., Mon.–Sat. 9–6, Sun. noon–6.*

The **Sherman Hines Museum of Photography** contains vintage photos and cameras and the work of the noted photographer. Changing exhibits in the galleries feature top Canadian photographers, and the research center offers a good collection of photographic books and thousands of photographs. ☒ *219 Main St.,* ☎ *902/354–2667.* ☜ *Free.* ☉ *Apr.–late Dec., Mon.–Sat. 10–5:30.*

Fort Point Lighthouse Park, on the site where explorers Samuel de Champlain and Sieur de Monts landed in 1604, overlooks Liverpool Harbour. Interpretive displays and models in the 1855 lighthouse recall the area's privateering and shipbuilding heritage. Special events include a legal marriage in 1780s style, an encampment of the King's Orange Rangers (a group that reenacts the exploits of a pro-British American Revolution brigade posted to Nova Scotia 1778–83), and opportunities to meet local artisans. ☒ *End of Main St., off Hwy. 103,* ☎ *902/354–5260.* ☜ *By donation.* ☉ *Mid-May–mid-Oct., daily 9–8.*

The **Simeon Perkins House,** built in 1766, is the historic home of privateer-turned-leading-citizen Simeon Perkins, who kept a detailed diary about colonial life in Liverpool from 1760 until his death in 1812. Built by ships' carpenters, the house gives the illusion of standing in the upside-down hull of a ship. ☒ *105 Main St.,* ☎ *902/354–4058.* ☜ *By donation.* ☉ *June–mid-Oct., Mon.–Sat. 9:30–5:30, Sun. 1–5:30.*

About 25 km (16 mi) southwest of Liverpool, **Kejimkujik Seaside Adjunct,** one of the last untouched tracts of coastline in Atlantic Canada—with isolated coves, broad white beaches, and imposing headlands—is protected by Kejimkujik National Park. A 6-km (4-mi) hiking trail leads to a pristine coastline that is home to harbor seals, eider ducks, and many other species. To protect nesting areas of the endangered piping plover, parts of the St. Catherine's River beach, the main beach, are closed to the public from late April to early August. ☒ *Off Hwy. 103, Port Joli,* ☎ *902/682–2772.* ☜ *Free.*

Dining and Lodging

$ ╳🛏 **Lane's Privateeer Inn and Bed & Breakfast.** Famed buccaneer Captain Joseph Barss once occupied this 200-year-old inn overlooking the Mersey River. Today it has 27 comfortable guest rooms as well as a restaurant serving Canadian fare ($$$–$$$$), a pub, a bookstore café, and a specialty-food shop. Next door there's a B&B, which serves a complimentary full breakfast; the inn serves a complimentary Continental breakfast. Lane's is within walking distance of Liverpool's major attractions and within 15 km (9 mi) of the Kejimkujik Seaside Adjunct. ☒ *27 Bristol Ave., B0T 1K0,* ☎ *902/354–3456 or 800/794–3332,* FAX *902/354–7220,* WEB *www3.ns.sympatico.ca/ron.lane. Inn 27 rooms, B&B 3 rooms. AE, D, MC, V. B&B closed Nov.–May. CP, BP.*

Outdoor Activities and Sports

The **Mersey River** drains Lake Rossignol, Nova Scotia's largest freshwater lake, and provides trout and salmon fishing.

Kejimkujik National Park

67 km (42 mi) northwest of Liverpool.

The gentle waterways of this 381-square-km (147-square-mi) park have been the canoe routes of the Mi'Kmaq for thousands of years. Today the routes and land trails are well marked and mapped, permitting canoeists, hikers, and campers to explore the landscape; swim in the warm lake; and glimpse white-tailed deer, beaver, owls, loons, and other wildlife. Canoes and camping equipment can be rented here. Park staffers lead interpretive hikes and canoe trips, or you can explore on your own. In late September and early October, the park's deciduous forests blaze with color. ⊠ *Hwy. 8, between Liverpool and Annapolis Royal, Maitland Bridge,* ☎ *902/682–2772.* ⊡ *$3.25 per day; camping $14–$19 a day.*

Dining and Lodging

$–$$ ✕ **Bonnie's Diner.** An unpretentious diner serves satisfying food in a homey setting. You can order a home-cooked breakfast at any time of the day, or roasted turkey, baked haddock, and other seafood. Finish off the meal with a slice of homemade cheesecake or pie. ⊠ *Hwy. 8, Caledonia,* ☎ *902/682–3481. No credit cards. Closed Mon. Sept.–mid-June.*

$ ✕ **Personal Touch Bakery.** Homemade breads, cakes, and cookies are served in a casual setting at the Personal Touch Bakery. You can also order chowders, pizza, and lasagna. ⊠ *Hwy. 8, Caledonia,* ☎ *902/682–3175. No credit cards. Closed Sun.*

$ ✕🏠 **Whitman Inn.** Just next door to Kejimkujik Park, this friendly inn offers wilderness, learning experiences, and luxurious dining. The dining room serves interesting full breakfasts and dinners ($$, reserve ahead) that feature seafood, poultry, pasta, and a vegetarian dish. The restored 1900 farmstead has a game room, library, sauna, whirlpool, and appealing rooms furnished with antiques. Nature and canoeing packages are available, and weekend workshops range from quilting, photography, and writing to stress management or wine tasting. ⊠ *12389 Hwy. 8, Kempt B0T 1B0,* ☎ *902/682–2226 or 800/830–3855,* FAX *902/682–3171,* WEB *www.whitman.ns.ca. 8 rooms, 1 2-bedroom apartment. Restaurant, indoor pool, recreation room, meeting room. MC, V.*

$$$–$$$$ 🏠 **White Point Beach Resort.** This wilderness seafront resort has something special: bunnies. They're everywhere, and bunny food is doled out at the front desk. But there's more. Just about any activity you can think of for a dynamic, luxurious holiday—golf, tennis, kayaking, surfing, fishing, nature trails, nature cruises, birding—is here. Also on the premises are a dining room, buffets, and barbeques; a spa; a games room and a playground; a gift shop; and even a summer theater. You have a choice of well-appointed rooms in one of the lodges, or housekeeping cottages, with sitting areas and fireplaces, buried among mature trees or along the beach. ⊠ *Hwy. 103, Exit 20A, White Point, Queens County B0T 1G0,* ☎ *902/354–2711 or 800/565–5068,* FAX *902/354–7278,* WEB *www.whitepoint.com. 77 rooms, 44 cottages. Dining room, indoor pool, spa, 9-hole golf course, 4 tennis courts, hiking, horseback riding, beach, surfing, fishing, mountain bikes, recreation room, theater, playground, meeting room. AE, MC, V.*

$–$$$ 🏠 **Mersey River Chalets.** Barbecues and sing-alongs around the bonfire, workshops on building kayaks or dreamcatchers, a hot tub, swimming, and outdoor sports like canoeing and kayaking fill the agenda at this 375-acre wilderness resort. A boardwalk offers nearly 2 km of
★

close-up nature, river, and waterfall scenery. Seven two-bedroom chalets are nestled in dense forest and are excellent for people with mobility problems: exterior ramps, wide doors, and roll-in showers make these accessible. And for closer encounters with nature, there are tepees built on platforms on the shore of Lake Harry. The restaurant serves Canadian fare ($–$$$); Friday night's special is planked salmon. ⊠ *Off of Hwy. 8, General Delivery, Caledonia B0T 1B0,* ☎ *902/682–2443,* FAX *902/682–2332,* WEB *www.merseyriverchalets.ns.ca. 7 chalets, 5 tepees. Restaurant, hot tub. MC, V.*

$–$$ ☷ **Apple Pie B&B.** Your host may pick up his guitar and serenade you or pick up woodworking tools and demonstrate how he crafts his handsome pine furniture. For sure, he'll welcome you to join the family in the sitting room of their century-old home for music and lively talk. The upstairs two-bedroom suite accommodates up to four visitors. For breakfast you may enjoy Morning Glory Muffins, homemade rhubarb and wild-cherry jam, or more conventional bacon and eggs. Nearby is the Kejimkujik Seaside Adjunct and three fine beaches, including Carter's Beach, which is usually deserted and strewn with shells. ⊠ *Exit 21, Hwy. 103, Box 32, Central Port Mouton B0T 1T0,* ☎ *902/683–2217 or 888/722–7753,* FAX *902/683–2180. 1 suite. Closed Nov.–Mar.*

$ ☷ **Old Homestead Bed & Breakfast.** Your host, "Auntie Pat" to numerous international visitors, offers down-home hospitality and home-cooked food in her 150-year-old farm home near Caledonia. Her sumptuous breakfasts feature homemade jams, jellies, breads, muffins, and more. The sunroom overlooks hayfields and cattle, and there's a lake for swimming and canoeing. A golf course and the wilderness of Kejimkujik Park are nearby. Pat's handmade quilts and comforters adorn the beds of the three double rooms that share a four-piece bath. ⊠ *71 Canning Rd., West Caledonia B0T 1B0,* ☎ *902/682–2654. 3 rooms without bath. V.*

Outdoor Activities and Sports

Peter Rogers of **Loon Lake Outfitters** (☎ 902/682–2220) is an 18-year veteran in canoe outfitting who offers summer canoe instruction, complete and partial canoe outfitting, and recreational guiding in and around Kejimkujik Park. At Jakes Landing, within Kejimkujik Park, **Wildcat River Outfitters** (☎ 902/682–2196 or 902/682–2822), a company owned and operated by local Mi'Kmaqs, rents bicycles, food, and camping supplies, as well as kayaks and canoes.

Shelburne

★ ⑳ *69 km (43 mi) south of Liverpool.*

The high noon of Shelburne occurred right after the American Revolution, when 16,000 Loyalists briefly made it one of the largest communities in North America—bigger than either Halifax or Montréal at the time. Today it is a fishing and shipbuilding town at the mouth of the Roseway River.

Many of Shelburne's homes date to the late 1700s, including the **Ross-Thomson House,** now a provincial museum. Inside, the only surviving 18th-century store in Nova Scotia contains all the necessities of that period. ⊠ *9 Charlotte La.,* ☎ *902/875–3141.* ⊡ *$2.* ☉ *June–mid-Oct., daily 9:30–5:30; call for winter hrs.*

Tours of some of Shelburne's historic homes are offered during periodic fund-raising endeavors. The **South Shore Tourism Association** (☎ 902/624–6466) has information.

Dining and Lodging

$–$$ ✕ **Charlotte Lane Café.** This café serves up seafood, meats, pastas, salads, and Swiss specialties. The 150-year-old historic building has a pleasant garden patio and a shop selling local crafts. ✉ *13 Charlotte La., ☎ 902/875–3314. MC, V. Closed Sun.–Mon. and Jan.–mid-Apr.*

$–$$$ ✕⌂ **Cooper's Inn and Restaurant.** One of the last cooperages in North America, on Shelburne's historic waterfront, is also a unique inn where you may purchase barrels and planters. Inside the elegant 1784 inn seven rooms are furnished with antiques and fine art. Two dining rooms ($$–$$$) offer candlelight dining with an emphasis on seafood; consider ordering scallops with pine-nut butter followed by homemade ice cream. A specialty at breakfast is Belgian waffles with maple syrup, but there are many other choices. ✉ *36 Dock St., B0T 1W0, ☎ FAX 902/875–4656 or 800/688–2011. 7 rooms. 2 restaurants. AE, DC, MC, V. Closed Nov.–Mar. BP.*

$ ⌂ **Clyde River Inn.** Queen Victoria and her pals peer down from every wall of this inn, once the main stagecoach stop between Tusket and Shelburne. The parlor, with a working organ that belonged to the host's grandmother, is as busy with artifacts and decor as its Victorian forebear might have been. Unusual bric-a-brac and fine china decorate the dining room, where a full breakfast emphasizes blueberry pancakes, homemade jams, and jellies. A golf course is a five-minute walk away, and three beaches are within a 15-minute drive, including shell-strewn Round Bay Beach, which is usually deserted. ✉ *10525 Hwy. 103, Box 2, Clyde River B0W 1R0, ☎ 902/637–3267 or 877/262–0222, FAX 902/637–1512. 4 rooms. MC, V. BP.*

Barrington

40 km (25 mi) south of Shelburne.

Tiny Barrington has a long history reflected in a clutch of interesting museums. The **Barrington Woolen Mill Museum** represents a thriving late-19th-century industry in which the mill produced durable wool for fishermen's clothing. Today it features demonstrations of hand spinning and details about sheep raising and wool processing. ✉ *2368 Hwy. 3, ☎ 902/637–2185. ⌂ By donation. ⊙ June–Sept., Mon.–Sat. 9:30–5:30, Sun. 1–5:30.*

The **Old Meeting House Museum** served as a church, town hall, and election center for New England settlers in the late 1700s. It's the oldest Nonconformist house of worship in Canada, with a historic graveyard next door. ✉ *2408 Hwy. 3, ☎ 902/637–2185. ⌂ By donation. ⊙ June–Sept., Mon.–Sat. 9:30–5:30, Sun. 1–5:30.*

The replica **Seal Island Lighthouse** is a lighthouse interpretation center that houses the original light and affords a fine view of the coastline. ✉ *Hwy. 3, ☎ 902/637–2185. ⌂ By donation. ⊙ June–Sept., Mon.–Sat. 9:30–5:30, Sun. 1–5:30.*

Cape Sable Island

8 km (5 mi) south of Barrington over the causeway.

Nova Scotia's southernmost extremity is the 21-km (13-mi) road that encircles Cape Sable Island, a Yankee community with fine beaches, connected to the mainland by a bridge. On the island the fishing village of Clark's Harbour sits on an appealing harbor sprinkled with colorful fishing boats. Hawk Point, just beyond the town, has excellent bird-watching and a fine view of the 1861 Cape Sable Island Lighthouse.

The **Archelaus Smith Museum,** named for an early New England settler, recaptures late-1700s life with household items such as quilts, toys, and cradles plus fishing gear and information about shipwrecks and sea captains. ⊠ *Hwy. 330,* ☎ *902/745–3361.* 🎟 *Free.* ☉ *Mid-June–Sept., Mon.–Sat. 9:30–5:30, Sun. 1:30–5:30.*

Pubnico

48 km (30 mi) northwest of Barrington.

Pubnico marks the beginning of the Acadian milieu; from here to Digby the communities are mostly French-speaking. Favorite local fare includes *rappie* pie, made of meat or poultry with potatoes from which much of the starch has been removed. Most restaurants along the shore between Pubnico and Digby serve some variation on rappie pie.

No fewer than seven towns bear the name Pubnico: Lower West Pubnico, Middle West Pubnico, and West Pubnico, all on the west shore of Pubnico Harbour; three East Pubnicos on the eastern shore; and just plain Pubnico, at the top of none other than Pubnico Harbour. These towns were founded by Phillipe Muis D'Entremont, and they once constituted the only barony in French Acadia. D'Entremont was a prodigious progenitor: to this day, many people in the Pubnicos are D'Entremonts, and most of the rest are D'Eons or Amiraults.

Dining and Lodging

$ ✕🏨 **Red Cap Motel and Restaurant.** This venerable establishment overlooks Pubnico Harbour and includes a six-unit motel and a café that serves an acclaimed version of a favorite Acadian dish, rappie pie. The menu also lists lobster and other seafood, chowder, and bread pudding. ⊠ *Hwy. 335, Middle West Pubnico B0W 2M0,* ☎ *902/762–2112,* 𝔽𝔸𝕏 *902/762–2887,* 🕸 *www.tusket.com/present/rest/redcap. MC, V.*

Yarmouth

㉑ *41 km (25 mi) north of Pubnico.*

Visitors have been arriving in Yarmouth for nearly three centuries, and they're still pouring in, chiefly by car ferry from Bar Harbor, Maine, and cruise ferry from Portland, Maine. In fact, the town's status as a large port city and its proximity to New England accounted for its early prosperity, and its great shipping heritage is reflected in its fine harbor, two marinas, and its museums. Handsome Victorian architecture, a pleasantly old-fashioned main street lined with friendly shops, and easy access to the Acadian villages to the north or the Lighthouse Trail to the south make Yarmouth much more than just a ferry dock.

★ The **Yarmouth County Museum** presents one of the largest collections of ship paintings in Canada; artifacts associated with the *Titanic*; exhibits of household items displayed in period rooms; musical instruments, including rare mechanical pianos and music boxes; and items that richly evoke centuries past. The museum has a preservation wing and an archival research area, where local history and genealogy are documented. Next door is the **Pelton-Fuller House,** summer home of the original Fuller Brush Man; it's maintained and furnished much as the family left it. ⊠ *22 Collins St.,* ☎ *902/742–5539,* 🕸 *www.ycn.library.ns.ca/museum/yarcomus.htm.* 🎟 *Museum $2.50, museum and Pelton-Fuller House $4, archives $5 per half day.* ☉ *Museum June–mid-Oct., Mon.–Sat. 9–5, Sun. 2–5; mid-Oct.–May, Tues.–Sun. 2–5. Pelton-Fuller House June–mid-Oct., Mon.–Sat. 9–5.*

☾ The **Firefighters Museum of Nova Scotia** recounts Nova Scotia's firefighting history through photographs and artifacts, including vintage pumpers, hose wagons, ladder trucks, and an 1863 Amoskeag Steamer. Kids love to don a fire helmet and take the wheel of a 1933 Bickle Pumper. ⊠ *451 Main St.,* ☎ *902/742–5525.* 🎟 *$2.* ☉ *June and Sept., Mon.–*

Sat. 9–5; July–Aug., Mon.–Sat. 9–9, Sun. 10–5; Oct.–May, weekdays 9–4, Sat. 1–4.

Dining and Lodging

$–$$ ✕ **Harris' Quick 'n Tasty.** This venerable establishment 4 km (2 mi) northeast of Yarmouth is a no-nonsense '50s-style diner with laminated tables, vinyl banquettes, and bright lights. It's also a penny-pincher's delight: a three-course Piggy Bank Special is only $6.95. Dishes include fresh seafood and old standbys like turkey burgers and club sandwiches. Best of all is the rappie pie, a baked and crisply refried potato and chicken casserole. The staff and management here are friendly. ⊠ *Hwy. 1, Dayton,* ☎ *902/742–3467. MC, V. Closed mid-Dec.–Feb.*

$ ✕ **Ceilidh Desserts Plus.** Homemade soups, breads, and desserts—all free of additives and preservatives—have won a loyal clientele locally and beyond for this cinnamon-scented café on Yarmouth's Main Street. The owner starts at dawn to whip up the day's baked goods and tasty lunches, which are modestly priced and served at simple wooden tables. ⊠ *276 Main St.,* ☎ *902/742–0031. AE, V. Closed Sun. mid-Oct.–mid-May.*

$ ✕⊞ **Manor Inn.** A circular rose garden is the highlight of this nine-acre waterfront property near Yarmouth. Fifty-three guest rooms are spread throughout the inn, coach house, and handsome white main lodge. Dinner specialties are fresh Nova Scotia seafood, prime rib, chicken, and pasta ($$–$$$$). The dining rooms also serve breakfast and lunch. ⊠ *Hwy. 1, Box 56, Hebron B0W 1X0,* ☎ *902/742–2487 or 888/626–6746,* FAX *902/742–8094,* WEB *www.manorinn.com. 53 rooms. 2 restaurants, 2 bars, café, pool, tennis court, boating, bicycles. AE, DC, MC, V. CP.*

$$$$ ⊞ **Trout Point Lodge.** This luxury resort consists of 200 acres situated among more than 500,000 acres of protected wilderness—the Tobeatic Wilderness Preserve to the south and Kejimkujik National Park to the north. Built of massive spruce logs with chiseled granite walls, Trout Point has eight rooms, two suites, the Great Room, a library, and a dining room. Outdoor activities include swimming, canoeing, kayaking, fishing, hiking, and wildlife-watching. Food Learning Vacations of three to five days include culinary instruction by La Ferme d'Acadie, a seaside farm at Cheboque Point. About a 40-minute drive out of Yarmouth, the lodge provides guest transportation from Yarmouth Airport or ferry terminal. You can arrange packages with or without meals. ⊠ *East Branch Rd., off Hwy. 203, East Kemptville (R.R. 2, Box 2690, Yarmouth B5A 4A6),* ☎ *902/742–0980 or 877/812–0112,* FAX *902/742–1057,* WEB *www.troutpoint.com. 8 rooms, 2 suites. Dining room, hiking, fishing, mountain bikes, meeting room. AE, MC, V. Closed Jan.–Mar.*

$$–$$$ ⊞ **Charles C. Richards House B&B.** Here is one of Nova Scotia's most
★ distinctive B&Bs. This grand old Queen Anne–style structure, directly across from the Yarmouth County Museum in the historic district, was built as a wealthy industrialist's residence in 1893, using the finest imported materials. It later served time as a Women's Army Corps barracks, the town library, and finally an apartment building. Rescued by energetic young owners who are performing every step in the restoration process themselves, it offers three spacious rooms, an orchid conservatory that opens onto a wide veranda, a patio, and a corporate suite with an in-room data port. Breakfast is an an elegant affair. ⊠ *17 Collins St., B5A 3C7,* ☎ FAX *902/742–0042.* WEB *www.charlesrichardshouse.ns.ca. 3 rooms, 1 suite. Dining room. AE, MC, V.*

$ ⊞ **Harbour's Edge B&B.** The four spacious rooms in this serene 1864 home, with its spectacular view of Yarmouth Harbour, are named for women who loved and lived here. Ornate wrought-iron fireplaces dominate the parlor and dining room, which open onto a veranda overlooking the harbor. At high tide the water laps against the lawn; at low tide myriad birds pay frequent visits. Harbour's Edge was reclaimed by new owners after a disastrous fire, and the home's phoenix-like restoration from burnt shell to elegant completion is revealed in a photo album. The restoration process at press time had moved to the exterior of the house as the owners work to restore the large garden with its century-old rhododendrons, quince, laburnum, and Japanese cherry trees. ⊠ *12 Vancouver St., B5A 2N8,* ☎ *902/742–2387,* F̲A̲X̲ *902/742–4471. 4 rooms. Dining room. MC, V.*

$ ⊞ **Murray Manor B&B.** The distinctive, pointed windows of this handsome 1825 Gothic-style house are reminiscent of a church. Century-old rhododendrons bloom in the garden and at the long dining room table, where guests share a hearty breakfast of fresh fruit, eggs with fresh garden herbs, specially ordered smoked bacon, and homemade apricot compote, and choose from a display of dozens of elegant bone china cups and saucers. ⊠ *225 Main St., B5A 1C6,* ☎ *902/742–9625 or 877/742–9629,* F̲A̲X̲ *902/742–9625. 4 rooms without bath. V. BP.*

Shopping

Professional potters Michael and Frances Morris, tired of craft shows, opened a craft shop, **At the Sign of the Whale** (⊠ 543 Hwy. 1, R.R. 1, Dayton, ☎ 902/742–8895), in their home on the outskirts of Yarmouth. Antique furniture forms a handsome backdrop for the work of 150 artisans. Wood, textiles, pewter, clothing, lovely Nova Scotian crystal, and the Morris's own excellent stoneware can be found here.

Point de l'Eglise

㉒   *70 km (43 mi) north of Yarmouth.*

Point de l'Eglise (Church Point) is the site of **Université Ste-Anne** (⊠ 1695 Hwy. 1, ☎ 888/338–8337), the only French-language institution among Nova Scotia's 17 degree-granting colleges and universities. Founded in 1891, this small university off Highway 1 is a focus of Acadian studies and culture in the province. The university offers five-week immersion French courses in summer.

St. Mary's Church, along the main road that runs through Point de l'Eglise, is the tallest and largest wooden church in North America. Completed in 1905, it is 190 ft long and 185 ft high. The steeple, which requires 40 tons of rock ballast to keep it steady in the ocean winds, can be seen for miles on the approach. Inside the church is a small museum containing an excellent collection of vestments, furnishings, and photographs. Tours are given by appointment. ⊠ *Main road,* ☎ *902/769–2832.* ⊡ *Free.* ☾ *July–mid-Oct., daily 9:30–5:30.*

Nightlife and the Arts

Evangeline, Longfellow's famous epic poem about the Acadian expulsion, comes to life in a very visual musical drama presented in Acadian French with English translation. Performances are held at 8 PM Tuesday and Saturday nights at the Université Ste-Anne (☎ 902/769–2114) June through September.

Digby

㉓   *35 km (22 mi) northeast of Point de l'Eglise.*

Digby is an underappreciated city—people tend to race to or from the ferry service connecting the town with Saint John, New Brunswick. But there's much more to Digby, including a rich history that dates to the arrival in 1783 of Loyalist refugees from New England; a famous scallop fleet that anchors in colorful profusion at the waterfront; and the plump, sweet scallops that are served everywhere. The waterfront begs leisurely strolls to view the Annapolis Basin and the boats; here you can buy ultrafresh halibut, cod, scallops, and lobster—some merchants will even cook them up for you on the spot. You can also sample Digby chicks—salty smoked herring—in pubs or buy them from fish markets. **Digby Scallop Days** is a four-day festival replete with parades, fireworks, and food in early August.

The **Admiral Digby Museum** relates the history of Digby through interesting collections of furnishings, artifacts, paintings, and maps. ⊠ *95 Montague Row,* ☎ *902/245–6322.* 🎫 *Free.* ☉ *June–Aug., daily 9–5.*

Dining and Lodging

$ ✕ **Digby's Café and Bookstore.** Bookworms with appetites will appreciate this appealing café, with a fine view of the waterfront, combined with a bookshop offering previously loved books of all persuasions. You can even browse through tomes while drinking coffee. All the food, from hearty seafood chowder to decadent pecan-butter tarts, is homemade, and the daily special, usually a soup-and-sandwich combo, pampers budgets. ⊠ *9 Water St.,* ☎ *902/245–4081. MC, V.*

$$$ ✕🏠 **Pines Resort Hotel.** Complete with fireplaces, sitting rooms, walking trails, and a view of the Annapolis Basin, this casually elegant property offers myriad comforts. It contains a Norman château–style hotel, 30 cottages, and lavish gardens. Local seafood with a French touch is served daily in the restaurant ($$–$$$$), and the lounge is perfect for quiet relaxation. ⊠ *103 Shore Rd., Box 70, B0V 1A0,* ☎ *902/245–2511 or 800/667–4637,* 🆅 *902/245–6133,* 🆆 *www.signatureresorts.com. 144 rooms. Restaurant, bar, pool, sauna, 18-hole golf course, 2 tennis courts, health club. AE, D, DC, MC. Closed mid-Oct.–May.*

$–$$ 🏠 **Thistle Down Country Inn.** A flowery haven overlooks the Annapolis Basin and Digby's fishing fleet at this historic 1904 home where wicker and antiques furnish the rooms. An annex is decorated with colonial furniture. For breakfast, consider ordering the scallop omelette. The 6:30 dinner (reservations required) celebrates fresh local seafood and ends with rich desserts. ⊠ *98 Montague Row, Box 508, B0V 1A0,* ☎ *902/245–4490 or 800/565–8081,* 🆅 *902/245–6717,* 🆆 *www.thistledown.ns.ca. 12 rooms. Restaurant. DC, MC, V. Closed Nov.–Apr. BP.*

$ 🏠 **Coastal Inn Kingfisher Motel.** Your affable host's encyclopedic knowledge and contagious enthusiasm for his adopted province open the door to little-known sights and adventures. This traditional strip motel handy to all Digby's features has wheelchair-accessible rooms (call for specifics) and a dining room. ⊠ *111 Warwick St., Box 280, B0V 1A0,* ☎ *902/245–4747 or 800/665–7829,* 🆅 *902/245–4866,* 🆆 *www.coastalinns.com. 36 rooms. AE, DC, MC, V.*

Bear River

A thriving arts-and-crafts center in summer, and almost a ghost town in winter, Bear River is called the Switzerland of Nova Scotia for the delightful vista of its deep valley, dissected by a tidal river. Some buildings have been built on stilts to stay above the tides. Craft and coffee shops line the main street, and the community center, **Oakdene Centre** (⊠ 1913 Clementsvale Rd., ☎ 902/467–3939), contains an artist-run gallery, craft workshops, and live theater and music.

The **Riverview Ethnographic Museum** houses a collection of folk costumes and artifacts from around the world. ⊠ *18 Chute Rd.,* ☎ *902/467–3762.* 🎫 *$2.* ☉ *Nov.–Sept., Tues.–Sat. 10–5.*

Long Island and Brier Island

㉔ *Two brief ferry rides between islands at East Ferry and Freeport.*

Digby Neck is extended seaward by two narrow islands, Long Island and Brier Island. Because the surrounding waters are rich in plankton, the islands attract a variety of whales, including finbacks, humpbacks, minkes, and right whales, as well as harbor porpoises. Wild orchids and other wildflowers abound here, and the islands are also an excellent spot for bird-watching.

Ferries (☎ 902/839–2302) linking the islands must scuttle sideways to fight the ferocious Fundy tidal streams coursing through the narrow gaps. They operate hourly, at a cost of $2 each way for car and passengers. One of the boats is the *Joshua Slocum,* named for Westport's most famous native; the second is the *Spray,* named for the 36-ft oyster sloop that Slocum rebuilt and in which, from 1894 to 1896, he became the first man to circumnavigate the world single-handedly. A cairn at the southern tip of Brier Island commemorates his voyage.

Dining and Lodging

$–$$ ✕⊞ **Brier Island Lodge and Restaurant.** Perched high atop a bluff at Nova Scotia's most westerly point, this rustic lodge commands a panoramic view of the Bay of Fundy. The lodge has 40 rooms, most with ocean and lighthouse views. Whale- and bird-watching are the most popular activities here, but closer to home there are hens, a flock of sheep, a pig, and some friendly dogs that children can pet. Seafood chowder, lobster-stuffed haddock, and solomon gundy (marinated herring with sour cream and onion) are dinner specialties in the attractive restaurant ($$–$$$), which also serves breakfast and can pack a box lunch for day-trippers. ⊠ *Water St., Westport, Brier Island B0V 1H0,* ☎ *902/839–2300 or 800/662–8355,* 𝖥𝖠𝖷 *902/839–2006,* 𝖶𝖤𝖡 *www.brierisland.com. 40 rooms. Restaurant, lounge. MC, V. Closed Nov.–Mar.*

$–$$ ✕⊞ **Olde Village Inn.** Halfway along Digby Neck on Highway 217, quaint Sandy Cove, population 100, snuggles the shore. The town has one of Nova Scotia's highest waterfalls and a lookout affording panoramic views of the water and sometimes whales. The Olde Village includes restored 19th-century buildings—the main inn, an annex, and various cottages—all comfortably furnished with antiques, wicker, quilts, and local art. Dinner ($$–$$$; reserve ahead) emphasizes fresh seafood and steaks. ⊠ *387 Sandy Cove Rd., Sandy Cove B0V 1E0,* ☎ *902/834–2202 or 800/834–2206,* 𝖥𝖠𝖷 *902/834–2927,* 𝖶𝖤𝖡 *www.oldevillageinn.com. 16 rooms, 1 cabin, 3 cottages. Restaurant. MC, V. Closed mid-Oct.–mid-May. BP.*

Outdoor Activities and Sports

Brier Island Whale & Seabird Cruises (☎ 902/839–2995 or 800/656–3660) offers whale-watching and seabird tours. Onboard researchers and naturalists collect data for international research organizations. The fare is $37, and a portion of the fee is used to fund the research. **Mariner Cruises** (☎ 902/839–2346 or 800/239–2189) provides whale and seabird tours with an onboard photographer and a naturalist. The 3–5-hour cruises include a light lunch; the fare is $35.

Annapolis Royal

★ ㉕ *29 km (18 mi) northeast of Digby.*

Annapolis Royal's history spans nearly four centuries, and gracious and fascinating remnants of that history abound. The town's quaint and quiet appearance belies its turbulent past. One of Canada's oldest settlements, it was founded as Port Royal by the French in 1605, destroyed by the British in 1613, rebuilt by the French as the main town of French Acadia, and fought over for a century. Finally, in 1710, New England colonists claimed the town and renamed it in honor of Queen Anne. There are approximately 150 historic sites and heritage buildings here, including the privately owned 1708 DeGannes-Cosby House, the oldest wooden house in Canada, on St. George Street, the oldest town street in Canada. A lively **market** with fresh produce, home baking, local artists, and street musicians takes place every Saturday mid-May through mid-October on St. George Street, next to Ye Olde Town Pub.

Fort Anne National Historic Site, first fortified in 1629, holds the remains of the fourth fort to be erected here and garrisoned by the British as late as 1854. Earthwork fortifications, an early 18th-century gunpowder magazine, and officers' quarters have been preserved. Four hundred years of history are depicted on the Fort Anne Heritage Tapestry. A guided candlelight tour of the historic Garrison Graveyard is a summer specialty. ⊠ *St. George St.,* ☎ *902/532–2397 or 902/532–2321.* ▨ *Grounds free, museum $3.* ☉ *Mid-May–mid-Oct., daily 9–6; mid-Oct.–mid-May, by appointment.*

The **Annapolis Royal Historic Gardens** are 10 acres of magnificent theme gardens, including a Victorian garden and a knot garden, connected to a wildlife sanctuary. ⊠ *441 Upper St. George St.,* ☎ *902/532–7018.* ▨ *$5.* ☉ *Mid-May–mid-Oct., daily 8–dusk.*

The **Annapolis Royal Tidal Power Project,** ½ km (¼ mi) from Annapolis Royal, was designed to test the feasibility of generating electricity from tidal energy. This pilot project is the only tidal generating station in North America and one of only three operational sites in the world. The interpretive center explains the process with guided tours. ⊠ *Annapolis River Causeway,* ☎ *902/532–5454.* ▨ *Free.* ☉ *Mid-May–mid-June and Sept.–mid-Oct., daily 9–5:30; mid-June–Aug., daily 9–8.*

Dining and Lodging

$$$$ ✕ **Newman's Restaurant.** Fresh flowers, fine art, and the host's handmade pottery give this quality establishment a homey air. The excellent cuisine is made with ultrafresh seafood and produce. At press time, Newman's was being put up for sale; it's likely that the restaurant will continue to maintain its good name and reputation despite a possible change of ownership. ⊠ *218 St. George St.,* ☎ *902/532–5502. MC, V. Closed Oct.–mid-Apr.*

$–$$$ ✕ **Secret Garden Restaurant.** Light lunches, snacks, and desserts are served in a sheltered open-air setting that overlooks the Annapolis Royal Historic Gardens. ⊠ *441 St. George St.,* ☎ *902/532–2200. MC, V. Closed Oct.–May.*

$–$$ ✕ **Charlie's Place.** Fresh local seafood with a Chinese flavor is served at this pleasant restaurant on the edge of town. Lobster, shrimp, scallops, meat dishes, and vegetarian fare are prepared in Cantonese or Szechuan style. ⊠ *38 Prince Albert Rd. (Hwy. 1),* ☎ *902/532–2111. AE, D, MC, V.*

$ ✕ **Ye Olde Town Pub.** This merry, low-key pub popular with locals serves down-home lunches and dinners, many prepared with regional blueberries. Diners sometimes spill out onto the patio, which is adjacent to a square where markets and music take place in summer. ⊠ *11 Church St.,* ☎ *902/532–2244. MC, V.*

$–$$ ✕▥ **Queen Anne Inn.** A lovely old Victorian mansion set within a 5-acre garden, this historic property now includes fine dining on its list of amenities. The restaurant ($$–$$$; reserve ahead) serves an eclectic dinner menu of Continental cuisine that emphasizes seafood. The 10 large guest rooms are handsomely decorated with period furniture and Victorian accessories. ✉ *494 Upper St. George St., Box 218, B0S 1A0,* ☎ *902/532–7850,* FAX *902/532–2078,* WEB *www.queenanneinn.ns.ca. 10 rooms. Restaurant. MC, V. BP.*

$ ✗🗠 **Garrison House Inn.** This structure, which faces Fort Anne and its extensive parkland, started life as an inn in 1854, when Annapolis Royal was the capital of Nova Scotia. Now carefully restored with period furniture and decor to create a Victorian ambience, it comes complete with a friendly ghost, called Emily, whose playful presence is known only to women. Three intimate dining rooms ($$$–$$$$) and a dining deck are the settings for dinners that favor fresh seafood, especially scallops and lobster. Breakfast is included in the room rate during summer months. ✉ *350 St. George St., B0S 1A0,* ☎ *902/532–5750,* FAX *902/532–5501,* WEB *www.queenanneinn.ns.ca. 7 rooms, 1 suite. 3 restaurants. AE, MC, V. Closed Jan.–Mar.*

$$ 🗠 **Bread and Roses Country Inn.** Rivalry between a doctor and a dentist gave Annapolis Royal this interesting hostelry. After the town doctor built a fine house in 1880, the dentist–pharmacist, in the spirit of competition, set out to build a better one. Today this Queen Anne–style inn is replete with exquisite architectural details and wood trim made with mahogany, black walnut, black cherry, and more. A traditional fountain is centered on the front lawn, and the garden invites sitting and strolling. The lavish breakfast may feature macadamia-nut French toast, blueberry pancakes, waffles, or quiche. ✉ *82 Victoria St., B0S 1A0,* ☎ *902/532–5727 or 888/899–0551,* WEB *www.breadandroses.ns.ca. 9 rooms. Dining room. MC, V. BP.*

$ 🗠 **Hillsdale House.** Princes, kings, and prime ministers have all visited this historic 1849 property, which is furnished with antiques and paintings and is set within 15 acres of lawns and gardens. The renovated coach house has added three bright and spacious rooms to the original 11 bedrooms. Room rates include a large breakfast with homemade breads and jams. ✉ *519 George St., Box 148, B0S 1A0,* ☎ *902/532–2345 or 877/839–2821,* FAX *905/532–2345. 14 rooms. MC, V. Closed Nov.–Apr.*

$ 🗠 **Moorings Bed & Breakfast.** Built in 1881, this tall, beautiful home overlooking Annapolis Basin has a fireplace, tin ceilings, antiques, and contemporary art. One room has a half-bath. ✉ *5287 Granville St., Box 118, Granville Ferry B0S 1K0,* ☎ FAX *902/532–2146,* WEB *www.bbcanada.com/1000.html. 3 rooms without bath. Library, bicycles. MC, V. BP.*

Port Royal

8 km (5 mi) downriver (west) from Annapolis Royal on the opposite bank.

One of the oldest settlements in Canada, Port Royal was Nova Scotia's first capital (for both French and English) until 1749, and the province's first military base. The **Port Royal National Historic Site** is a reconstruction of a French fur-trading post originally built by Sieur de Monts and Samuel de Champlain in 1605. Here, amid the hardships of the New World, North America's first social club—the Order of Good Cheer—was founded, and Canada's first theatrical presentation was written and produced by Marc Lescarbot. ✉ *Hwy. 1 to Granville Ferry, then left 12 km (7 mi) on Port Royal Rd.,* ☎ *902/532–2898 or 902/532–5589.* 🎫 *$3.* ☉ *Mid-May–mid-Oct., daily 9–6.*

Wolfville

★ ㉖ *60 km (37 mi) east of Annapolis Royal.*

Settled in the 1760s by New Englanders, Wolfville is a charming college town with stately trees and ornate Victorian homes. Chimney swifts—aerobatic birds that fly in spectacular formation at dusk—are so abundant that an interpretive display is devoted to them at the **Robie Tufts Nature Centre,** on Front Street. Dykes, built by the Acadians in the early 1700s to reclaim fertile land from the unusually high tides, can still be viewed in Wolfville at the harbor and along many of the area's back roads.

The **Atlantic Theatre Festival** (⊠ 356 Main St., ☎ 902/542–4242 or 800/337–6661) stages classical plays mid-June through September; tickets are $21–$28.

The **National Historic Site at Grand Pré,** about 5 km (3 mi) east of Wolfville on Highway 101, commemorates the expulsion of the Acadians by the British in 1755. A statue of the eponymous heroine of Longfellow's epic poem, *Evangeline,* stands outside a memorial stone church, which contains Acadian genealogical records. ⊠ *Hwy. 1, Grand Pré,* ☎ *902/542–3631.* ⊙ *Mid-May–mid-Oct., daily 9–6.*

OFF THE BEATEN PATH	**HALLS HARBOUR –** One of the best natural harbors on the upper Bay of Fundy can be reached via Highway 359. Go for a walk on a gravel beach bordered by cliffs; try sea kayaking or wilderness camping; or seek out the intaglio printmaking studio and other artists' studios, open during summer months. **CAPE BLOMIDON –** At Greenwich, take Highway 358 to Cape Blomidon via Port Williams and Canning for a spectacular view of the valley and the Bay of Fundy from the Lookoff.

Dining and Lodging

$$$–$$$$ ✗ **Acton's Grill & Café.** Refugee restaurateurs from Toronto, where their Fenton's Restaurant was *the* place to dine, have created an equally appealing dining establishment with an interesting and eclectic menu here. Consider rabbit pie, Digby scallops in fresh herbed pasta, or Fundy lobster. ⊠ *268 Main St.,* ☎ *902/542–7525. AE, MC, V. Closed Jan.*

$$$–$$$$ ✗ **Chez la Vigne.** Fresh Nova Scotia seafood, meats and poultry, and vegetarian fare are artfully presented in this pleasant century-old home. On warm summer nights, diners gather on the patio. ⊠ *17 Front St.,* ☎ *902/542–5077. AE, D, MC, V.*

$–$$$ ✗ ⌂ **Blomidon Inn.** Take time for a half-hour ramble through this inn's three-acre English country garden, with its fish-stocked ponds, roses, cacti, azaleas, and rhododendrons, plus a terraced vegetable garden that serves as a restaurant. Built by a shipbuilder in 1887, the inn still retains its teak and mahogany, marble fireplaces, and painted ceiling mural. Room rates include Continental breakfast and afternoon tea. Fresh Atlantic salmon is a specialty at the restaurant ($$$–$$$$; reserve ahead). A gift shop, in a separate house beside the inn, sells Maritime crafts, linen, garden items, and the books and prints of folk artist Maude Lewis. ⊠ *127 Main St., Box 839, B0P 1X0,* ☎ *902/542–2291 or 800/565–2291,* FAX *902/542–7461,* WEB *www.blomidon.ns.ca. 26 rooms. Restaurant, tennis court, horseshoes, shuffleboard, meeting room. MC, V. CP.*

$–$$$ ⌂ **Fundy Bay Holiday Homes B&B.** The small trek to this seaside resort 40 km (25 mi) outside of Wolfville is amply rewarded by the spectacular view of the Bay of Fundy and the north shore beyond. Set on 265 rolling wooded acres, this family-owned property has two two-bedroom houses with comfy living rooms, woodstoves, fully equipped kitchens and laundry facilities, and satellite TV. Stays at the three-room B&B include a hearty German breakfast of deli meats and sausages, European cheeses, German breads, and copious amounts of good German coffee. Groomed walking trails traverse the wooded property. ⊠ *2165 McNally Rd., Victoria Harbour, Aylesford B0P 1C0,* ☎ *902/847–*

1114, FAX *902/847–1032,* WEB *www.fundyhomes.com. 3 rooms, 2 houses. Beach. V.*

$–$$ 🏨 **Victoria's Historic Inn and Carriage House B&B.** An 8-ft-high stained-glass window imported from Britain over a century ago sets the tone for this fine Victorian home. Richly carved Nova Scotian furniture adds to the ambience. Rooms are spacious and have TVs, VCRs, and CD players; suites have double whirlpool tubs. The lavish complimentary breakfast celebrates the bounty of the Annapolis Valley. Expect plenty of blueberries to find their way to the table, along with a wide selection of breakfast staples. ✉ *416 Main St., Box 308, B0P 1X0,* ☎ *902/542–5744 or 800/556–5744,* WEB *www.valleyweb.com/victoriasinn. 9 rooms, 5 suites. AE, D, MC, V. BP.*

$ 🏨 **Farmhouse Inn B&B.** An 1860 B&B in Canning has five cozy suites, each with a whirlpool tub, a parlor, a fireplace, quilts, and whimsical dolls and critters warming the canopy beds. A full breakfast and afternoon tea are complimentary. The knowledgeable hosts may suggest day trips to nearby Blomidon Provincial Park and Cape Split, for hiking, or to the 600-ft Lookoff, which affords panoramic views of five counties. Bird-watchers are likely to enjoy the maneuvers of the chimney swifts summer evenings. ✉ *9757 Main St., Box 38, Canning B0P 1H0,* ☎ *800/928–4346,* ☎ FAX *902/582–7900,* WEB *www.farmhouseinn.ns.ca. 5 suites. Dining room. MC, V. BP.*

Shopping

The **Carriage House Gallery** (✉ 246 Main St., ☎ 902/542–3500) displays artwork from Nova Scotia in several media, including oils, acrylics, watercolors, sculpture, and quilting. **Edgemere Gallery and Crafts** (✉ 215 Main St., ☎ 902/542–1046) carries the work of Nova Scotia artists in all media, with exhibits changing monthly. Artisans from throughout the Atlantic provinces are also represented by unique quality crafts. **The Weave Shed** (✉ 232 Main St., ☎ 902/542–5504) is a cooperative craft shop selling quality work by local artisans in stained glass, pottery, wood, metal, and textiles.

Outdoor Activities and Sports

A popular hiking trail, 25 km (16 mi) north of Wolfville, leads from the end of Highway 358 to the dramatic cliffs of Cape Split, a 13-km (8-mi) round-trip.

Windsor

★ ㉗   *25 km (16 mi) southeast of Wolfville.*

Windsor claims to be the birthplace of modern hockey: the game was first played here around 1800 by students of King's-Edgehill School, the first independent school in the British Commonwealth and Canada's oldest private residential school. But the town's history dates further back—to 1703 when it was settled as an Acadian community. **Fort Edward,** an assembly point for the Acadian expulsion, is the only remaining colonial blockhouse in Nova Scotia. ✉ *Exit 6 off Hwy. 1, 1st left at King St., left up street facing fire station,* ☎ *902/542–3631.* 🎟 *Free.* ☉ *Mid-June–early Sept., daily 10–6.*

The Evangeline Express train makes a 55-km (34-mi) three-hour round-trip from Windsor to Wolfville Sundays in summer (weather permitting). The train stops at the Grand Pré National Historic Site (in Wolfville) and affords views of the Minas Basin and Annapolis Valley. ✉ *2 Water St.,* ☎ *902/798–5667.* 🎟 *$18.50.* ☉ *Late June–early Sept.; train departs at 11 AM.*

The Windsor Hockey Heritage Centre takes a fond look at Canada's favorite winter sport with photographs and antique equipment and skates. ⊠ *128 Gerrish St.,* ☎ *902/798–1800.* 🖆 *Free.* ☉ *Daily 9–5.*

☺ The **Mermaid Theatre** uses puppets and performers to retell traditional and contemporary children's classics. Props and puppets are on display. ⊠ *132 Gerrish St.,* ☎ *902/798–5841.* 🖆 *By donation.* ☉ *Jan.–Nov., weekdays 9–4:30.*

The **Haliburton House Museum,** a provincial museum on a manicured 25-acre estate, was the home of Judge Thomas Chandler Haliburton (1796–1865), a lawyer, politician, historian, and humorist. His best-known work, *The Clockmaker,* pillories Nova Scotian follies from the viewpoint of a Yankee clock peddler, Sam Slick, whose witty sayings are still commonly used. ⊠ *414 Clifton Ave.,* ☎ *902/798–2915.* 🖆 *Free.* ☉ *June–mid-Oct., Mon.–Sat. 9:30–5:30, Sun. 1–5:30.*

Tours at the family-owned **Sainte Famille Winery** in Falmouth, 5 km (3 mi) west of Windsor, combine ecological history with the intricacies of growing grapes and aging wine. Tasting is done in the gift shop, where bottles are sold at a steal. ⊠ *Dyke Rd. and Dudley Park La.,* ☎ *902/798–8311 or 800/565–0993.* 🖆 *Free.* ☉ *June–Sept., Mon.–Sat. 9–5, Sun. noon–5; call for off-season hrs and tour schedule.*

Dining and Lodging

$–$$$ ✕ **Kingsway Gardens Restaurant.** From the Bavarian decor to the homemade sauerkraut to the Black Forest cheesecake, this establishment declares its owner's German origins. Lunch and dinner specialties include German and Canadian variations on seafood, turkey, and chicken. ⊠ *Wentworth Rd., off Hwy. 101, Exit 5A,* ☎ *902/798–5075. AE, D, MC, V.*

$ ✕ **Rose Arbour Café.** True to its name, the Rose Arbour has a bright, flowery interior. Tasty food, a smiling staff, and reasonable prices make this a pleasant find. Try the fish-and-chips. ⊠ *109 Garrish St.,* ☎ *902/798–2322. V.*

$ 🏠 **Hampshire Court Motel and Cottages.** Once an elegant estate, this multi-unit property retains its splendid 1762 home, with four spacious antiques-furnished guest rooms. Four two-bedroom cottages and a strip motel are also on the property. The ample grounds include picnic tables and a tennis court. ⊠ *1081 King St., B0N 2T0,* ☎ *902/798–3133,* ℻ *902/798–2499,* 🌐 *www.hampshirecourt.ca. 4 rooms, 11 motel units, 4 cottages. Tennis court. AE, MC, V. Closed mid-Oct.–mid-May.*

THE EASTERN SHORE AND NORTHERN NOVA SCOTIA

From the rugged coastline of the Atlantic to the formidable tides of the Bay of Fundy to the gentle shores of the Northumberland Strait, the area east and north of Halifax presents remarkable contrasts within a relatively small area. The road toward Cape Breton meanders past picturesque fishing villages, forests, and remote cranberry barrens. The Northumberland Strait is bordered by sandy beaches, hiking trails and the rich heritage of its early Scottish settlers. The Bay of Fundy serves up spectacular scenery—dense forests and steep cliffs that harbor prehistoric fossils and semiprecious stones. The mighty Fundy tides—swift and dangerous—can reach 40 ft. When they recede, you can walk on the bottom of the sea.

There are two excellent driving tours you can follow here. The Sunrise Trail Heritage Tour leads to unusual and historic sights along the

Northumberland Strait, from the Tantramar Marsh in Amherst to the Heritage Museum at Antigonish and on to the still-active St. Augustine Monastery. The Fundy Shore Ecotour traces 100 million years of geology, the arrival of Samuel de Champlain, the legends of the Mi'K-maq, the Acadians, and the shipbuilders. (Tour details are available at visitor information centers or from Nova Scotia Tourism.)

This region takes in parts of three of the official Scenic Trails, including Marine Drive (315 km, or 195 mi), the Sunrise Trail (316 km, or 196 mi), and the Glooscap Trail (365 km, or 226 mi). Any one leg of the routes could be done comfortably as an overnight trip from Halifax.

Musquodoboit Harbour

28 *45 km (28 mi) east of Dartmouth.*

Musquodoboit Harbour (locals pronounce it *must*-go-*dob*-bit), with about 930 residents, is a substantial village at the mouth of the Musquodoboit River. The river offers good trout and salmon fishing, and the village touches on two slender and lovely harbors.

A 1916 train station, five rail cars, and a fine collection of railway artifacts, including a legion of lanterns dating from the late 1800s, make the volunteer-run **Musquodoboit Railway Museum** (⊠ Main Street/Hwy. 7, ☎ 902/889–2689) a must for rail buffs. A library is rich in both railway and local historical documentation and photos. The museum is open daily 9–5 late May to mid-October, by donation.

One of the Eastern Shore's best beaches, **Martinique Beach,** is about 12 km (7 mi) south of Musquodoboit Harbour, at the end of East Petpeswick Road. Clam Bay and Clam Harbour, several miles east of Martinique, are also fine beaches.

Dining and Lodging

$–$$ ✕🏠 **Salmon River House Country Inn.** Seven guest rooms and three cottages (two on the ocean and both intended for stays of a week or more; $650 to $900 a week) provide glorious water and countryside views. Guests may fish from the floating dock; hike the trails of the 30-acre property; or make use of the canoe, kayak, or rowboat. Lunch, dinner ($–$$), and a breakfast-buffet spread are served on the screened Lobster Shack dining deck. ⊠ *9931 Hwy. 7, Salmon River Bridge, Jeddore (10 km east of Musquodoboit Harbour), B0J 1P0, ☎ 902/889–3353 or 800/565–3353, ℻ 902/889–3653, WEB www.salmonriverhouse.com. 7 rooms, 3 cottages. Restaurant, boating, fishing. AE, MC, V.*

$ 🏠 **Camelot Inn.** Enthroned in her great-grandmother's rocker, surrounded by memorabilia and an enormous hoya plant, Charlie Holgate shares wit and wisdom with international guests as she has for more than 30 years. Her 5-acre wooded property borders the turbulent Musquodoboit River and is home to mink, otter, and an occasional deer. Inside, it's informal, with five unpretentious rooms, shared baths, and a robust homemade breakfast. ⊠ *8094 Hwy. 7, Box 31, B0J 2L0, ☎ 902/889–2198. 5 rooms. Lounge, library. MC, V. BP.*

Sherbrooke Village

★ **29** *166 km (103 mi) northeast of Musquodoboit Harbour.*

A living-history museum set within a contemporary village, Sherbrooke Village contains 30 restored 19th-century buildings that present life as it was lived during the town's heyday, from 1860 to 1914. Back then, this was a prime shipbuilding and lumbering center; it eventually became a gold-rush center. Artisans demonstrate weaving; wood turning; and pottery, candle, and soap making daily. A working water-powered sawmill is down the road. ✉ *Hwy. 7, Sherbrooke,* ☎ *902/ 522–2400 or 888/743–7845,* WEB *www.museum.gov.ns.ca/sv.* ✆ *$7.25.* ⊙ *June–mid-Oct., daily 9:30–5:30.*

OFF THE BEATEN PATH

PORT BICKERTON LIGHTHOUSE BEACH PARK – Two lighthouses share a lofty bluff about 20 km (12 mi) east of Sherbrooke on Highway 211. One is still a working lighthouse; the other, built in 1910, houses the Nova Scotia Lighthouse Interpretive Centre, which recounts the history, lore, and vital importance of these life-saving lights. Hiking trails and a boardwalk lead to a sandy beach. ✉ *630 Lighthouse Rd., Port Bickerton,* ☎ *902/364–2000.* ✆ *$3.* ⊙ *July–Aug., daily 9–6; Sept., daily 9–5.*

Dining and Lodging

$ ✕⬚ **Black Duck Seaside Inn.** From a third-floor picture window, equipped with binoculars and a telescope provided by the inn, you can observe birds, sea life, and maybe a star or two over Beaver Harbour. In the airy dining room ($–$$), expect lavish breakfasts of fruit and blueberry pancakes; for dinner, try the fisherman's lasagna (seafood and pasta in a cream sauce) or another seafood dish. The Black Duck is 90 km (56 mi) west of Sherbrooke Village. ✉ *25245 Hwy. 7, Port Dufferin (Box 26, Sheet Harbour B0J 3B0),* ☎ FAX *902/654–2237. 2 rooms, 2 suites. Restaurant, dock, bicycles. MC, V.*

$ ✕⬚ **Sherbrooke Village Inn & Cabins.** Woodsy chalets, a B&B suite, and a motel are all options in this comfy hostelry overlooking the St. Mary's River (open for trout fishing). The inn offers nature walks and a spectacular view. The pleasant dining room ($–$$) serves up homemade meals—full Canadian breakfasts, lunches, and dinners that lean heavily toward seafood. ✉ *7975 Hwy. 7, Box 40, Sherbrooke B0J 3C0,* ☎ *902/522–2235,* FAX *902/522–2716,* WEB *www.atyp.com/sherbrookevillageinn. 1 B&B suite, 14 motel rooms, 3 chalets. Dining room. AE, D, MC, V. Closed Dec.–mid-Apr.*

$ ⬚ **St. Mary's River Lodge.** Sherbrooke Village is steps away from this lodge with fresh and immaculate rooms. The Swiss owners, in love with their adopted countryside, are helpful in planning day trips and tours. You can also rent houses in nearby Liscombe and Port Hilford for weeklong stays. ✉ *21 Main St., B0J 3C0,* ☎ *902/522–2177,* FAX *902/522–2515,* WEB *www3.ns.sympatico.ca/lodge. 5 rooms, 2 suites, 3 houses. MC, V. BP.*

Canso

③⓪ *123 km (76 mi) east of Sherbrooke Village.*

One of Nova Scotia's oldest settlements, founded in 1605, Canso today is a busy fishing town. Each July the town hosts the **Stan Rogers Folk Festival** commemorating the much loved Canadian folk singer and composer.

The **Grassy Island National Historic Site** recounts early struggles to control the lucrative fishing industry. A free boat ride takes you to the island for an interpretive tour of what remains of a once-thriving community, a casualty in 1744 of the war between France and England. Graphics, models and audiovisuals set the scene. ✉ *Canso Waterfront, off Union St.,* ☎ *902/295–2069,* WEB *www.parkscanada.pch.gc.ca.* ✆ *$2.50.* ⊙ *June–mid-Sept., daily 10–6.*

Lodging

$–$$ ⬚ **SeaWind Landing Country Inn.** Perched on a 20-acre coastal estate just south of Canso, this restored sea captain's home—with birdwatching, interpretive nature walks, and sandy beaches—is a luxurious escape from real life. Short boat tours to offshore islands, where seals bask and bald eagles soar, include white-linen lunches served with fine wines. Home-cooked dinners favor fresh seafood. The inn is furnished with antiques, quilts, and fine art. ⊠ *1 Wharf Rd., Charlos Cove B0H 1T0,* ☏ FAX *902/525–2108,* WEB *www.seawindlanding.com. 12 rooms. Dining room, beach, boating, mountain bikes. AE, MC, V. Closed mid-Oct.–mid-May.*

Antigonish

★ ③① *85 km (53 mi) northwest of Canso.*

Antigonish, on the main route to Cape Breton Island, is home to **St. Francis Xavier University,** a center for Gaelic studies and the first coeducational Catholic institution to graduate women. The university **art gallery** (☏ 902/867–2303), open year-round, has changing exhibits. **Festival Antigonish** (☏ 902/867–3333 or 800/563–7529, WEB www.festival.antigonish.com) presents a summer-long drama program—matinées for kids, evenings for adults—in the 227-seat university theater.

The **Antigonish Heritage Museum,** in a 1908 rail station, depicts the town's early history. ⊠ *20 East Main St.,* ☏ *902/863–6160.* ⊡ *Free.* ⊙ *July–Aug., daily 10–5; Sept.–Nov. and Feb.–June, weekdays 10–noon and 1–5; Dec.–Jan., by appointment.*

The biggest and oldest **Highland Games** (☏ 902/863–4275) outside of Scotland are held here each July, complete with caber tossing, highland flinging, and pipe skirling.

Dining and Lodging

$–$$$ ✕ **Gabrieau's Bistro Restaurant.** Gabrieau's has earned a place in Antigonish hearts with its pleasant interior, highlighted by a colorful mural, and its epicurean yet affordable menu of Continental cuisine. Seafood, gourmet pizzas, luscious desserts, and several vegetarian selections are available. ⊠ *350 Main St.,* ☏ *902/863–1925. AE, MC, V. Closed Sun.*

$–$$ ✕ **Lobster Treat Restaurant.** This cozily decorated brick, pine, and stained-glass restaurant was once a two-room schoolhouse. The varied menu includes fresh seafood, chicken, pastas, and bread and pies baked on the premises. Families appreciate its relaxed atmosphere and children's menu. ⊠ *241 Post Rd. (Trans-Canada Hwy.),* ☏ *902/863–5465. AE, DC, MC, V. Closed Jan.–mid-Apr.*

$–$$ ✕⊡ **Maritime Inn.** The Main Street Café ($$–$$$) at this inn serves breakfast, lunch, and a tempting dinner menu that's heavy on seafood. Try the haddock glazed with apricot and ginger or chili pepper shrimp. One of five in a Maritime chain, this 32-room property offers standard rooms, mini-suites, and one two-bedroom family suite. ⊠ *158 Main St., B2G 2B7,* ☏ *902/863–4001 or 888/662–7484,* FAX *902/863–2672,* WEB *www.maritimeinns.com. 32 rooms. Restaurant. AE, D, DC, MC, V.*

$–$$ ⊡ **Antigonish Victorian Inn.** A mansion fit for politicians and bishops—and in fact occupied by both at various phases of its life—this luxurious establishment is a gateway to many Antigonish attractions. Rooms are commodious and handsomely appointed. The dining room serves a breakfast of cereal, fruits, French toast, and eggs. ⊠ *149 Main St., B2G 2B6,* ☏ FAX *902/863–1103 or 800/706–5558. 10 rooms. Dining room. AE, DC, MC, V.*

Outdoor Activities and Sports

A 3-km (2-mi) **walking trail** along the shoreline borders a large tidal marsh teeming with ospreys, bald eagles, and other birds.

Shopping

Lyncharm Pottery (⊠ 9 Pottery La., ☏ 902/863–6970) produces handsome functional stoneware that's sold in its own shop and exported worldwide. The **Lytesome Gallery** (⊠ 166 Main St., ☎ 902/863–5804) houses a good variety of Nova Scotian art for sale at reasonable prices.

Stellarton

③② *60 km (37 mi) west of Antigonish.*

The **Nova Scotia Museum of Industry** brings industrial heritage to life. Like factory and mine workers of old, you punch in with a time card. Hands-on exhibits show how to hook a rag mat, print a bookmark, work a steam engine, or assemble a World War II artillery shell. Interactive computer exhibits explore multimedia as a new tool of industry. Canada's oldest steam locomotives and a historic model railway layout are also displayed, and there's a restaurant. ⊠ *147 North Foord St.(Hwy. 104, Exit 24),* ☎ *902/755–5425,* WEB *www.industry.museum.gov.ns.ca.* ☞ *$7.*

Pictou

★ ③③ *20 km (12 mi) north of Stellarton.*

First occupied by the Mi'Kmaqs, this well-developed town became a Scottish settlement in 1773 when the first boat of Scottish Highlanders landed, giving the town the distinction of being "the birthplace of New Scotland." Thirty-three families and 25 unmarried men arrived aboard the *Hector,* an aging cargo ship that was reproduced in minute detail and launched in September 2000. **The Hector Heritage Quay,** where the new 110-ft fully rigged *Hector* can be toured, recounts the story of the hardy Scottish pioneers and the flood of Scots who followed them. It includes working blacksmith and carpentry shops and an interpretive center. ⊠ *33 Caladh Ave.,* ☎ *902/485–4371 or 877/574–2868.* ☞ *$4.* ☺ *Mid-May–Oct., daily 9–8.*

A lively weekend craft market at the waterfront, from June to September, showcases crafts and crafts people from the area and across the province.

Melmerby Beach, one of the warmest beaches in the province, is about 23 km (14 mi) east of Pictou. To get here, follow the shore road from Highway 104.

Dining and Lodging

$–$$$ ✕🏠 **Braeside Inn.** Collectors will covet the treasures displayed in every nook and cranny of this handsome 60-year-old inn perched on a five-acre hillside. China, crystal, silver, statuary, inlaid lacquer, and gadgets invite hours of browsing. You can stroll to the historic waterfront or watch your ship come into Pictou Harbour from the dining room ($–$$) picture window. Prime rib and seafood are specialties here, and a Sunday brunch is served. ⊠ *126 Front St., Box 1810, B0K 1H0,* ☎ *902/485–5046 or 800/613–7701,* FAX *902/485–1701,* WEB *www.nsis.com/~braeside. 18 rooms. Restaurant, meeting room. AE, MC, V.*

$–$$ ✕🏠 **Consulate Inn.** A private home in 1810 and American Consulate from 1836 to 1896, the inn is a showplace for the innkeepers' creativity— she's a skilled quilter and painter; he's an artist in the kitchen. Colorful quilted hangings and original art decorate each spacious room in the main house, the next-door annex, and a two-bedroom cottage that has a full kitchen and a deck overlooking Pictou Harbour. The dining rooms (open Tuesday to Sunday; $–$$) celebrate fresh seafood, especially salmon, plus meats and pastas. ⊠ *157 Water St., Box 1642, B0K 1H0,* ☎ *902/485–4554 or 800/424–8283,* FAX *902/485–1532,* WEB *www.consulateinn.com. 11 rooms, 1 cottage. 2 restaurants. AE, MC, V. CP.*

$$ ☎ **Customs House Inn.** In 1997 a former customs house on Pictou's waterfront metamorphosed into a nifty inn, complete with eight spacious high-ceilinged rooms overlooking the water. All have whirlpool baths. A basement pub offers Celtic entertainment and Sunday brunch. ⊠ *38 Depot St., Box 1542, B0K 1H0,* ☎ *902/485–4546,* FAX *902/485–1296,* WEB *www.pictou.nsis.com/customshouseinn. 8 rooms. Pub, in-room data ports, library, business services, meeting room. AE, DC, MC, V. CP.*

$ ☎ **Auberge Walker Inn.** A registered Heritage Property, the friendly inn is a short walk from the historic Pictou waterfront. A suite with a patio and a kitchen is on the ground floor of this compact 1865 town house. ⊠ *34 Coleraine St., B0K 1H0,* ☎ *902/485–1433 or 800/370–5553,* FAX *902/485–1222,* WEB *www.pictou.nsis.com/walkerinn. 10 rooms, 1 suite. Dining room. AE, MC, V. CP.*

Nightlife and the Arts

The **DeCoste Entertainment Centre** (⊠ Water St., ☎ 902/485–8848 or 800/353–5338) is a handsome theater presenting a summer-long program of concerts, pipe bands, highland dancing, and *ceilidhs* (Gaelic music and dance).

Shopping

The artisans' cooperative **Water Street Studio** (⊠ 110 Water St., ☎ 902/485–8398) sells clothing, weaving, silk painting, blankets, pottery, stained glass, jewelry, woodwork, handspun yarns, and other crafts.

New Glasgow

22 km (14 mi) southwest of Pictou.

The largest community along the Sunrise Trail, New Glasgow boasts a rich Scottish heritage. Since the town's prosperity has been linked to the East River, recent redevelopment of the riverfront—with restaurants, shops, and events—seems appropriate. It's the setting, in early August, of the **Riverfront Music Jubilee,** which attracts local and national performers. In mid-July, New Glasgow hosts the **Festival of the Tartans,** which includes highland dancing, piping and drumming, plus the Pictou County Pipes and Drums on Parade, a kilted golf tournament, concerts, beer gardens, and much more.

Tatamagouche

③④ *50 km (31 mi) west of Pictou.*

Despite the size of its population—all of 600 souls—Tatamagouche is a force to be reckoned with. Canada's second-largest Oktoberfest and a major quilt show are held here each fall. Summer brings strawberry and blueberry festivals, lobster and chowder suppers, and a lively farmers' market each Saturday morning. This charming town on Highway 6 on the north shore is at the juncture of two rivers: Tatamagouche is a Mi'Kmaq name meaning "meeting place of the waters." An old rail bed along the river's edge, part of the Trans-Canada Trail, is ideal for hiking, cycling, walking, and bird-watching.

The **Sunrise Trail Museum** traces the town's Mi'Kmaq, Acadian, French, and Scottish roots and its shipbuilding heritage. ⊠ *216 Main St.,* ☎ *902/657–3007.* ☞ *$1.* ⊙ *Late June–early Sept., 9–5 daily.*

The **Fraser Cultural Centre** promotes arts, crafts, and cultural activities. The 1889 Gallery displays the work of local artists; a large crafts room is used for displays and demonstrations. ⊠ *Main St.,* ☎ *902/657–3285.* 🎟 *Free.* ☾ *June–Aug., daily 10–5; Sept., 1–4.*

OFF THE
BEATEN PATH
BALMORAL GRIST MILL MUSEUM – A water-powered gristmill serves as the centerpiece of this museum near Tatamagouche. Built in 1874, it's the oldest operating mill in Nova Scotia. You can observe milling demonstrations, hike the 1-km (½-mi) walking trail, and buy freshly ground flour in the shop. ⊠ *660 Matheson Brook Rd., Balmoral Mills,* ☎ *902/657–3016,* 🖳 *museum.gov.ns.ca/bgm.* 🎟 *$2.* ☾ *June–mid-Oct., Mon.–Sat. 9:30–5:30, Sun. 1–5:30; demonstrations daily 10–noon and 2–4.*

Dining and Lodging

$–$$ ✕ **The Villager Restaurant.** This homey low-key place on Main Street serves steaks, seafood, and salads. ⊠ *Main St.,* ☎ *902/657–2029.* V.

$–$$$ 🏨 **Train Station Inn.** Railway history lives on in Tatamagouche, where
★ this unique inn offers B&B accommodation in a century-old station and in seven cabooses parked nearby. The station master's quarters include three rooms, a guest parlor, and a kitchen and laundry for guest use. Downstairs, a main-floor café, where tasty breakfasts are served, is decorated with authentic railroad memorabilia. The caboose suites include all the creature comforts (including data ports) plus touches of railroad life—signal switches and elevated conductors' cupolas with their revolving chairs. ⊠ *21 Station Rd., B0K 1V0,* ☎ *902/657–3222 or 888/724–5233,* 🖷 *902/657–9091,* 🖳 *www.trainstation.ns.ca. 3 rooms, 7 suites. Café, in-room data ports. AE, MC, V.*

$ 🏨 **The Balmoral Motel.** This small motel with 18 rooms overlooks Tatamagouche Bay. German and Canadian dishes are served in the Mill Dining Room. ⊠ *Main St., Box 178, B0K 1V0,* ☎ *902/657–2000 or 888/383–9357,* 🖷 *902/657–3343. 18 rooms. Dining room. AE, MC, V. Closed Nov.–late May.*

Shopping

At the **Sara Bonnyman Pottery Studio** (⊠ Hwy. 246, 1½ km/1 mi uphill from post office, ☎ 902/657–3215), you can watch the well-known potter at work each morning, producing her handsome stoneware pieces, bearing sunflower and blueberry motifs, and one-of-a-kind plates and bowls. She also makes 100%-wool hand-hooked rugs in colorful primitive designs. The studio is open Monday through Saturday June through mid-September, by appointment off-season.

Maritime crafts sold at the **Sunflower Crafts Shop** (⊠ 249 Main St., ☎ 902/657–3276) include the work of noted local potter Sara Bonnyman, Chéticamp hooking, pewter, wood, baskets, wrought iron, quilts, candles, and unusual framed pictures made of caribou tufting.

Malagash

17 km (11 mi) west of Tatamagouche.

Malagash is best known for a winery that flourishes in the warm climate moderated by the Northumberland Strait. **Jost Vineyards** produces a surprisingly wide range of award-winning wines, including a notable ice wine (a sweet wine made after frost has iced the grapes). There's a well-stocked wine shop, a deli-bar, a patio deck, a children's playground, and picnic area here. ⊠ *Hwy. 6, off Hwy. 104,* ☎ *902/257–2636 or 800/565–4567,* 🖳 *www.jostwine.com.* ☾ *Mid-June–mid-Sept., Mon.–Sat. 9–6, Sun. noon–6; mid-Sept.–mid-June, Mon.–Sat. 10–5, Sun. noon–5; tours mid-June–mid-Sept., daily at noon and 3.*

Springhill

㉟ *40 km (25 mi) west of Malagash.*

The coal-mining town of Springhill, on Highway 2, was the site of the famous mine disaster of the 1950s immortalized in the folk song "The Ballad of Springhill," by Peggy Seeger and Ewen McColl. You can tour a real coal mine at the **Spring Hill Miners Museum.** Retired coal miners act as guides and recount firsthand memories of mining disasters. ⊠ *Black River Rd., off Hwy. 2,* ☎ *902/597–3449.* ☜ *$5.* ☉ *May–mid-Oct., daily 10–6.*

Springhill is the hometown of internationally acclaimed singer Anne Murray, whose career is celebrated in the **Anne Murray Centre.** ⊠ *Main St.,* ☎ *902/597–8614.* ☜ *$5.* ☉ *Mid-May–mid-Oct., daily 9–5.*

OFF THE   **WILD BLUEBERRY & MAPLE CENTRE –** This center in Oxford, about 10 km
BEATEN PATH   (6 mi) outside of Springhill, details the history of two tasty industries—75% of Nova Scotia's blueberry and maple-syrup production occurs in surrounding Cumberland County. Self-guided tours, interactive displays, and a beehive tell the story. ⊠ *15 Lower Main St., Oxford,* ☎ *902/447–2908,* 𝗪𝗘𝗕 *www.town.oxford.ns.ca.* ☜ *$2.* ☉ *Mid-May–mid-Oct., daily 10–6.*

Amherst

㊱ *28 km (17 mi) northwest of Springhill.*

Amherst, near the New Brunswick border, is a quiet town today, but from the mid-1800s to early 1900s it was a bustling center of industry and influence. Four of Canada's Fathers of Confederation hailed from Amherst, including Sir Charles Tupper, who later became prime minister. The town is tame today, but the **Tantramar Marsh,** originally called Tintamarre because of the racket made by vast flocks of wildfowl, is still alive with incredible birds and wildlife. Said to be the world's largest marsh, it's a migratory route for hundreds of thousands of birds, and a breeding ground for more than 100 species.

From Amherst, the Sunrise Trail heads toward the Northumberland Strait, while the Glooscap Trail runs west through fossil country. The **Fundy Shore Ecotour** has been developed by the local tourism authority to highlight this region's six distinct eco-zones. Brochures are available at information centers (☎ 902/667–8429 or 902/667–0696 for locations).

Dining and Lodging

$$–$$$ ✕⛺ **Amherst Shore Country Inn.** This seaside country inn, with a
★   beautiful view of Northumberland Strait, has comfortable rooms, suites, and a cottage fronting 600 ft of private beach. Well-prepared four-course dinners incorporating home-grown produce are served at one daily seating (by reservation only, $29.50). ⊠ *Hwy. 366, R.R. 2, Lorneville (32 km, or 20 mi, northeast of Amherst), B4H 3X9,* ☎ 𝗙𝗔𝗫 *902/661–4800 or 800/661–2724,* 𝗪𝗘𝗕 *www.ascinn.ns.ca. 4 rooms, 4 suites, 1 cottage. Restaurant. AE, DC, MC, V. Closed weekdays Nov.–Apr.*

$$ ⛺ **Wandlyn Inn.** Just inside the Nova Scotia–New Brunswick border, this dependable inn offers a slew of amenities: an indoor pool, a hot tub, a sauna, a gym, and laundry facilities. ⊠ *Trans Canada Hwy, Victoria St. Exit. (Box 275), B4H 3Z2,* ☎ *902/667–3331 or 800/561–0000,* 𝗙𝗔𝗫 *902/667–0475,* 𝗪𝗘𝗕 *www.wandlyninns.com. 88 rooms. Restaurant, indoor pool, hot tub, sauna, gym, coin laundry. AE, MC, V.*

Joggins

37   *35 km (22 mi) southwest of Amherst.*

Joggins's main draw is the coal-age fossils embedded in its 150-ft sandstone cliffs. At the **Joggins Fossil Centre,** you can view a large collection of 300-million-year-old fossils and learn about the region's geological and archaeological history. Guided tours of the fossil cliffs are available, but departure times depend on the tides. Maps are issued for independent fossil hunters. ✉ *30 Main St.,* ☎ *902/251–2727.* ✆ *Center $3.50, tour $10.* ☉ *June–Sept., daily 9–5:30.*

Cape Chignecto and Cape d'Or

70 km (43 mi) southwest of Joggins.

Two imposing promontories—Cape Chignecto and Cape d'Or—reach into the Bay of Fundy near Chignecto Bay. Cape Chignecto, home to the newest provincial park, **Cape Chignecto Provincial Park** (✉ off Hwy. 209, West Advocate, ☎ 902/392–2085 or 902/254–3241), is an untouched wilderness of 10,000 acres of old-growth forest harboring deer, moose, and eagles. It's circumnavigated by a 50-km (31-mi) hiking trail along rugged cliffs that rise to 600 ft above the bay. Wilderness cabins and campsites are available.

Farther south is Cape d'Or (Cape of Gold), named by Samuel de Champlain for its glittering veins of copper. The region was actively mined a century ago, and at nearby Horseshoe Cove you may still find nuggets of almost pure copper on the beach as well as amethysts and other semiprecious stones. Cape d'Or's hiking trails border the cliff edge above the Dory Rips, a turbulent meeting of currents from the Minas Basin and the Bay of Fundy punctuated by a fine lighthouse.

At **Advocate Harbour,** named by Samuel de Champlain for a lawyer friend, a delightful beach walk follows the top of an Acadian dyke, built by settlers in the 1700s to reclaim farmland from the sea. Advocate Beach, noted for its tide-cast driftwood, stretches 5 km (3 mi) from Cape Chignecto to Cape d'Or.

The **Age of Sail Museum Heritage Centre** (✉ Hwy. 209, Port Greville, ☎ 902/348–2030) traces the history of the area's shipbuilding and lumbering industries. You can also see a restored 1857 Methodist church, a blacksmith shop, and a lighthouse. The center ($2) is open late May through September, daily 10–6.

Dining and Lodging

$ ✕ **Harbour Lite Restaurant.** Every bite you eat in this unpretentious roadside diner is home-cooked by the friendly owner, who is on the job 12 hours a day all summer. Clam chowder, lobster in season, and fresh seafood; sandwiches; and sweets such as feather-light cinnamon buns, muffins, pies, and cakes round out the menu. ✉ *4160 Main St., Advocate,* ☎ *902/392–2277. No credit cards. Closed Dec.–Feb.*

$$ 🏠 **Driftwood Park Retreat.** Five mist-blue cottages face the Fundy shore and its powerful tides. Four of the two-story two-bedroom units have cathedral ceilings, pine floors, gas fireplaces, well-equipped kitchens, and upstairs living rooms with fine views of the bay. The fifth cottage is a ranch unit with a sleeping loft. ✉ *47 Driftwood La., West Advocate B0M 1A0,* ☎ *902/392–2008 or 866/810–0110,* FAX *902/392–2041,* WEB *www.driftwoodparkretreat.com. 5 cottages. MC, V.*

$ 🏠 **Lightkeeper's Kitchen and Guest House.** Before automation, two lightkeepers manned the crucial light on the rocky Cape d'Or shore, and their cottages have been transformed—one to an excellent restaurant and the other to a four-room inn with a comfortable lounge and picture windows overlooking the Minas Basin. This wild and lovely place offers hiking, bird-watching, seal sightings, outdoor lobster boils and clambakes, and exceptional young hosts whose warmth, intelligence, and gourmet cooking make leaving difficult. Getting here is a bit challenging: a 5½-km (3-mi) road off Highway 209 from Advocate, then a steep gravel path down to the shore. ✉ *Cape d'Or, Advocate, B0M 1A0,* ☎ *902/670–0534,* WEB *www.capedor.ca. 4 rooms, 1 with bath. V. Closed mid–Oct.–mid–May.*

$ 🏨 **Reid's Tourist Home.** Nestled between Cape d'Or and Cape Chignecto, this cattle farm is a working operation where you can enjoy the bucolic pleasures of country life or take a short walk to the Fundy shore. Four suites, each with a sitting area, bedroom, and refrigerator, occupy a separate building near the picturesque farmhouse. Chignecto Park is just over 1 km (½ mi) away. ✉ *1391 West Advocate Rd., West Advocate (R.R. 3, Parrsboro B0M 1S0),* ☎ *902/392–2592,* FAX *902/392–2523. 4 suites. No credit cards. Closed Oct.–May.*

$ 🏨 **Spencer's Island B&B.** Once home to Captain Bigelow, who built the mysterious *Mary Celeste,* the house today is a modest and friendly B&B with three cozy rooms and an antiques-furnished parlor. Woodburning fireplaces and a vintage woodstove in the kitchen add to the ambience. Blueberry waffles or cheese soufflé are breakfast favorites. The inn is just uphill from the Spencer's Island lighthouse and the Fundy shore, and it's a 10-minute drive from the wilderness of Cape Chignecto. ✉ *Off Hwy. 209 (R.R. 3, Parrsboro B0M 1S0),* ☎ *902/392–2721. 3 rooms. No credit cards. Closed Sept.–May. BP.*

En Route   At **Spencer's Island Beach** on Highway 209, a cairn commemorates the mystery ship *Mary Celeste,* built here in 1861 and found in 1872 abandoned at sea, all sails set, undamaged, but without a trace of the crew and passengers.

Parrsboro

㊳ *55 km (34 mi) east of Cape d'Or.*

A center for rock hounds and fossil hunters, Parrsboro is the main town on this shore and hosts the **Nova Scotia Gem and Mineral Show** (third weekend of August). Among the exhibits and festivities are geological displays and concerts. The fossil-laden cliffs that rim the Minas Basin are washed by the world's highest tides twice daily. The result is a wealth of plant and animal fossils revealed in the rocks or washed down to the shore. Semiprecious stones such as amethyst, quartz, and stilbite can be found at Partridge Island, 1 km (½ mi) offshore and connected to the mainland by an isthmus.

Parrsboro is an appropriate setting for the **Fundy Geological Museum** because it's not far from the Minas Basin area, where some of the oldest dinosaur fossils in Canada were found. Two-hundred-million-year-old dinosaur fossils are showcased here alongside other mineral, plant, and animal relics. ✉ *162 Two Island Rd.,* ☎ *902/254–3814,* WEB *www.fundygeomuseum.com.* 🎟 *$4.* ☉ *June–mid-Oct., daily 9:30–5:30.*

The world's smallest dinosaur footprints, along with rare minerals, rocks, and fossils, are displayed at Eldon George's **Parrsboro Rock and Mineral Shop and Museum** (✉ 39 Whitehall Rd., ☎ 902/254–2981). Mr. George, a goldsmith, lapidarian, and wood carver, sells his work in his shop and offers tours for fossil and mineral collectors (four people minimum, $10 each). The shop closes November to April.

Although fossils have become Parrsboro's claim to fame, this harbor town was also a major shipping and shipbuilding port, and its history is described at the **Ottawa House Museum-by-the-Sea,** 3 km (2 mi) east of downtown. Ottawa House, which overlooks the Bay of Fundy, is the only surviving building from a 1700s Acadian settlement. It was later the summer home of Sir Charles Tupper (1821–1915), a former premier of Nova Scotia who was briefly prime minister of Canada. ⊠ *Whitehall Rd.,* ☎ *902/254–2376.* ⊠ *$1.* ☉ *June–mid-Sept., daily 10–8.*

Dining and Lodging

$–$$ ✕ **Harbour View Restaurant.** Expect fresh seafood at this pleasant beachfront restaurant—the owners maintain their own boats to fish for scallops and lobster, which, along with clams, flounder, and other seafood, are menu staples. The dining room, with windows overlooking the water and the lighthouse, displays paintings and photos of Parrsboro's past. It's open 7 AM–10 PM. ⊠ *476 Pier Rd.,* ☎ *902/254–3507. MC, V. Closed mid–Oct.–Apr.*

$–$$ ✕ **Stowaway Restaurant.** The menu is rich in seafood—thick chowder, fish and chips, and scallops—as well as chicken and meat dishes. Friendly and spacious, its deep window wells are stocked with interesting antiques, also for sale. In one wing, a bakery ruins diets with its fresh apple pies, donuts, and bread. There's a take-out counter, too. All three meals are served. ⊠ *69 Main St.,* ☎ *902/254–3371. AE, MC, V.*

$ ✕ **John's Café.** Here's an unexpected find—a funky café serving healthful salads, sandwiches and soups, plus decadent desserts. There's jazz, blues, and Nova Scotia music, indoors or on a pleasant patio. It's open all day. ⊠ *151 Main St.,* ☎ *902/254–3255. No credit cards. Closed mid-Dec.–early Apr.*

$–$$ 🏨 **The Maple Inn, Parrsboro.** Room 1 in this Italianate-style home built 1860–90 is popular with local residents. That's because many of them were born here when the house served time as a hospital and this was the delivery room. These days the inn offers nine dramatic rooms, including one painted black with lush, flowery touches. Parrsboro's center and the Bay of Fundy are within walking distance. ⊠ *2358 Western Ave., Box 457, B0M 1S0,* ☎ *877/627–5346,* FAX *902/254–3735,* WEB *www3.ns.sympatico.ca/mapleinn. 9 rooms. AE, MC, V. BP.*

$–$$ 🏨 **Parrsboro Mansion.** This 1880 home, set far back on a four-acre lawn, presents an imposing face; inside it's brightly modern, with contemporary European art and furnishings. The owners invite guests to join them in a morning jog and to later learn about regeneration and relaxation through magnetic-field therapy. ⊠ *15 Eastern Ave., Box 579, B0M 1S0,* ☎ FAX *902/254–2585,* WEB *www3.ns.sympatico.ca/parrsboro.m.bb. 3 rooms. Sauna, gym. AE, MC, V. Closed Nov.–June. CP.*

$ 🏨 **Gillespie House B&B.** Wild roses border the driveway leading up to this handsome home. Yoga and spa weekends can be arranged for groups; you can enjoy therapeutic massage and reflexology by reserving a few of days ahead. Four rooms with private baths, a lavish vegetarian breakfast, bikes and helmets, and tons of visitor information are all part of the service. ⊠ *358 Main St., B0M 1S0,* ☎ *902/254–3196 or 877/901–3196,* WEB *www.gillespiehouseinn.com. 4 rooms. Dining room, bikes. AE, MC, V. Closed Nov.–Apr. BP.*

Nightlife and the Arts

Ship's Company Theatre (⊠ 198 Main St., ☎ 902/254–2003 or 800/565–7469, WEB www.shipscompany.com) presents top-notch plays, comedy, and a concert series aboard the *M.V. Kipawo,* a former Minas Basin ferry, early July to early September.

Five Islands

24 km (15 mi) east of Parrsboro.

Among the most scenic areas along Highway 2 is Five Islands, which, according to Mi'Kmaq legend, was created when the god Glooscap threw handfuls of sod at Beaver, who had mocked and betrayed him. **Five Islands Provincial Park** (⊠ Hwy. 2, ☎ 902/254–2980), on the shore of Minas Basin, has a campground, a beach, and hiking trails. Interpretive displays reveal the area's interesting geology: semiprecious stones, Jurassic-age dinosaur bones, and fossils. The Five Islands Lighthouse, at Sand Point Campground, has access to good swimming and clamming; you can "walk on the ocean floor" at low tide, when the water recedes nearly a mile, but beware the awesome return of the tides, which can outrun man or beast.

Cobequid Interpretation Centre highlights the geology, history, and culture of the area, with pictures, videos and interpretive panels. A World War II observation tower offers a sweeping view of the countryside and the impressive tides. The center is home base for **Kenomee Hiking and Walking Trails** which explore the area's varied landscapes—the coast itself plus cliffs, waterfalls, and forested valleys. ⊠ 3248 Hwy. 2, Central Economy, ☎ 902/647–2600. ☞ By donation. Closed Oct.–May.

Lodging

$ ▥ **Gemstow B&B.** At this B&B 20 km (12 mi) east of Parrsboro, breakfast is served in an airy sunporch that overlooks flowery perennial beds and has a fine vista of Five Islands beyond. Photographers nab their best shots of the windswept islands from the front deck. Inside, three rooms and the lounge are tastefully furnished. Your host leads hikes to a hidden waterfall or clamming on the shore. ⊠ 463 Hwy. 2, Lower Five Islands, B0M 1N0, ☎ 902/254–2924. 3 rooms, 1 with bath. V.

Truro

❸❾ 67 km (42 mi) east of Five Islands.

Truro's central location places it on many travelers' routes, and its museums, golf course, and harness-racing track satisfy a range of interests. Throughout Truro, watch for the Truro Tree Sculptures—a creative tribute to trees killed by the dreaded Dutch Elm disease. Artists Albert Deveau, Ralph Bigney, and Bruce Wood have been transforming the dead trees into handsome sculptures of historical figures, wildlife, and cultural icons.

Truro's least known asset is also its biggest—the 1,000-acre **Victoria Park,** where, smack in the middle of town, you can find hiking trails, a winding stream flowing through a deep gorge with a 200-step climb to the top, and two picturesque waterfalls. ⊠ Park Rd., ☎ 902/893–6078. ☉ Daily dawn–dusk.

Dining and Lodging

$$$–$$$$ ✕▥ **John Stanfield Inn.** Rescued from demolition and moved to this
   ★ site by the owners of Keddy's, the John Stanfield Inn has been restored to its original Queen Anne glory, with delicate wood carvings, elaborate fireplaces, bow windows, and fine antique furniture. Three restaurants ($$–$$$) serve unusual seafood specialties including a fisherman's plate with half a dozen seafood varieties; desserts such as berries Romanoff; and a lavish Sunday brunch. ⊠ 437 Prince St., B2N 1E6, ☎ 902/895–1651 or 800/561–7666, FAX 902/893–4427, WEB www.johnstanfieldinn.com. 12 rooms. 3 restaurants, lounge, in-room data ports. AE, D, MC, V. CP.

$–$$ ▥ **Shady Maple B&B.** On this 200-acre farm 15 km (9 mi) outside of Truro, guests can hobnob with herds of Highland cattle, llamas, sheep, goats, and horses; sleep on sun-dried bed linens; and breakfast on fresh eggs and the farm's own maple syrup, jams, and jellies. The 1890 farmhouse has two rooms and a deluxe suite with a two-person jet tub. A heated pool and a hot tub are outside. ⊠ 11207 Hwy. 2, Masstown

B0M 1G0, ☎ FAX *902/662–3565 or 800/493–5844,* WEB *www.ns.sym-patico.ca/emeisses. 2 rooms without bath, 1 suite. Pool, outdoor hot tub. V.*

$ 🖭 **Keddy's Motor Inn.** Part of a five-inn Maritime chain, this comfortable establishment caters to business and family travel. The rooms, including those in a well-appointed executive wing, are modern and spacious. A large restaurant serves Canadian cuisine. ✉ *437 Prince St., B2N 1E6,* ☎ *902/895–1651 or 800/561–7666,* WEB *www.keddys.ca/truro. 115 rooms. Restaurant, pub, in-room data ports, pool, coin laundry, meeting room. AE, D, DC, MC, V.*

$ 🖭 **Suncatcher B&B.** Call this modest B&B ten minutes outside of Truro a glass act: stained glass adorns every available window, wall, and cranny. Two-day workshops in crafting stained glass are available (reservations required), too. The breakfast menu includes homemade breads, jams, and muffins; fruits in season; and eggs. The hosts, longtime B&B providers, know their province from stem to stern and cheerfully advise on itineraries and attractions. ✉ *25 Wile Crest Ave., R.R. 6, North River B2N 5B4,* ☎ FAX *902/893–7169 or 877/203–6032,* WEB *www.bbcanada.com/1853.html. 3 rooms with shared bath. V.*

Outdoor Activities and Sports

Riding the rushing tide aboard a 16-ft self-bailing Zodiac with **Shubenacadie River Runners** (✉ 8681 Hwy. 215, Maitland, ☎ 902/261–2770 or 800/856–5061, WEB www.tidalborerafting.com) is an adventure you won't soon forget. Tide conditions and time of day let you choose a mildly turbulent ride or an ultrawild one. A 3½-hour excursion costs $65, including gear and a barbecue.

The **Truro Raceway** (✉ Main St., ☎ 902/893–8075) holds year-round harness racing.

CAPE BRETON ISLAND

The highways and byways of the Island of Cape Breton, including those on the Cabot Trail, make up one of the most spectacular drives in North America. As you wind through the rugged coastal headlands of Cape Breton Highlands National Park, you can climb mountains and plunge back down to the sea in a matter of minutes. The Margaree River is a cultural dividing line: south of the river the settlements are Scottish, up the river they are largely Irish, and north of the river they are Acadian French. You can visit villages where ancient dialects can still be heard and explore a fortress where period players bring the past to life. This is a place where cultural heritage is alive, where the atmosphere is maritime, and where inventors Marconi and Bell share the spotlight with coal miners and singers like Rita MacNeil. Wherever you go in Cape Breton you are sure to experience warmth and hospitality.

Bras d'Or Lake, a vast, warm, almost-landlocked inlet of the sea, occupies the entire center of Cape Breton. The coastline of the lake is more than 967 km (600 mi) long, and people sail yachts from all over the world to cruise its serene, unspoiled coves and islands. Bald eagles have become so plentiful around the lake that they are now exported to the United States to restock natural habitats. Four of the largest communities along the shore are native Mi'Kmaq communities.

If Halifax is the heart of Nova Scotia, Cape Breton is its soul, complete with soul music—flying fiddles, boisterous rock, velvet ballads. Cape Breton musicians—weaned on Scottish jigs and reels—are among the world's finest, and in summer you can hear them at dozens of local festivals and concerts. In summer, every community in the southern end of Inverness County takes a different night of the week to offer a square dance. Propelled by driving piano and virtuoso fiddling, locals of every age whirl through "square sets," the best of them step dancing and square dancing simultaneously. Local bulletin boards and newspapers have square dance times and locations.

Allow three or four days for this meandering tour of approximately 710 km (440 mi) that begins by entering the island via the Canso Causeway on Highway 104. Turn left at the rotary and take Highway 19, the Ceilidh Trail, which winds for 129 km (80 mi) along the mountainside through glens and farms, with fine views across St. George's Bay to Cape George. This western shoreline of Cape Breton faces the Gulf of St. Lawrence and is famous for its sandy beaches and warm salt water.

Port Hood

④⓪ *45 km (28 mi) northwest of the Canso Causeway on Hwy. 19.*

At this fishing village you can buy lobster and snow crab fresh off the wharf as the boats return in mid-afternoon. With a little persuasion, one of the fisherfolk might give you a lift to **Port Hood Island,** a mile across the harbor. It's a 10-minute walk from the island's wharf to the pastel-color cliffs of wave-mottled alabaster on the seaward shore. Both the village and the island have sandy beaches ideal for swimming.

Mabou

④① *13 km (8 mi) northeast of Port Hood on Hwy. 19.*

The pretty village of Mabou is very Scottish, with its Gaelic signs and traditions of Scottish music and dancing. Most Saturday nights offer a helping of local culture in the form of a dance or kitchen party. Check bulletin boards at local businesses for information about these events. This is the hometown of national recording and performing artists such as John Allan Cameron and the Rankin Family (now defunct). Stop at a local gift shop and buy tapes to play as you drive down the long fjord of Mabou Harbour.

Dining and Lodging

$$$–$$$$ ×🏠 **Glenora Inn & Distillery Resort.** North America's only single-malt-whiskey distillery adjoins this friendly inn. Here you can sample a "wee dram" of the inn's own whiskey—billed as Canada's first legal moonshine. Even if you don't stay overnight, you can take a tour of the distillery and museum, and enjoy fine cuisine and traditional Cape Breton music. ⊠ *Hwy. 19, Box 181, Glenville B0E 1X0,* ☎ *902/258–2662 or 800/839–0491,* ℻ *902/258–3572,* ⓦⓔⓑ *www.glenoradistillery.com. 9 rooms, 6 chalets. Restaurant, pub, gift shop, convention center. AE, MC, V. Closed Nov.–mid-June.*

$–$$ ×🏠 **Duncreigan Country Inn.** These new buildings, on the shore of Mabou Harbour, suggest the early 1900s in design and furnishings. Several decks afford beautiful views and are ideal for relaxing, reading, and leaving your cares behind. The dining room, open to the public, is considered one of the top 100 in Canada. A breakfast buffet is provided in the summer, and a Continental breakfast is available in the off-season. Canoes and bicycles are available for guest use. ⊠ *Rte. 19, Box 59 B0E 1X0,* ☎ *902/945–2207; 800/840–2207 for reservations,* ℻ *902/945–2206,* ⓦⓔⓑ *www.auracom.com/˜mulldci. 7 rooms, 1 suite. Restaurant, bicycles. MC, V. CP.*

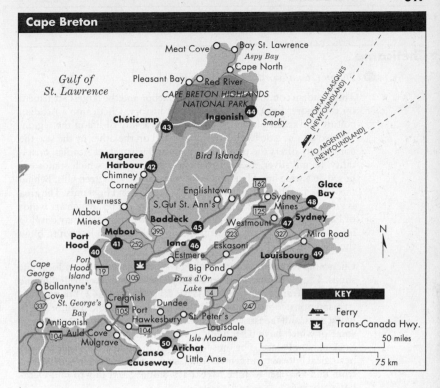

Cape Breton

Mabou Mines

10 km (6 mi) northwest of Mabou.

This quiet area, known locally as the Mines, is a place so hauntingly exquisite that you expect to meet the *sidhe*, the Scottish fairies, capering on the hillsides. Within the hills of Mabou Mines is some of the finest hiking in the province, and above the land fly bald eagles, plentiful in this region. Inquire locally or at the tourist office in Margaree Forks for information about trails.

Margaree Harbour

42 *33 km (20 mi) north of Mabou.*

The Ceilidh Trail joins the Cabot Trail at Margaree Harbour at the mouth of the Margaree River, a famous salmon-fishing stream and a favorite canoe route. Exhibits at the **Margaree Salmon Museum,** in a former schoolhouse, include fishing tackle, photographs, and other memorabilia related to salmon angling on the Margaree River. ⊠ *60 E. Big Intervale Rd.,* ☎ *902/248–2848.* ◪ *$1.* ☉ *Mid-June–mid-Oct., daily 9–5.*

Dining and Lodging

$–$$$ ✕▥ **Normaway Inn.** Nestled on 250 acres in the hills of the Margaree Valley at the beginning of the Cabot Trail, this secluded 1920s inn has distinctive rooms and cabins, most with woodstoves and screened porches, and some have hot tubs. There are films or traditional entertainment nightly as well as weekly square dances in the Barn. The restaurant is known for its country cuisine, particularly the vegetable chowders and fresh seafood ragout. ⊠ *Egypt Rd., 3 km (2 mi) off Cabot Trail (Box 101), B0E 2C0,* ☎ *902/248–2987 or 800/565–9463,* FAX *902/*

248–2600, WEB *www.normaway.com. 9 rooms, 19 cabins. Restaurant, tennis court, hiking, bicycles. MC, V. Closed mid-Oct.–mid-June.*

Chéticamp

43   *26 km (16 mi) north of Margaree Harbour.*

This Acadian community has the best harbor and the largest settlement on this shore. Even after 200 years of history, Chéticamp's Acadian culture and traditions are still very much a way of life in the region. Nestled on one side by the mountains and on the other by the sea, the community offers the pride, traditions and warmth of Acadian hospitality. Its tall silver steeple towers over the village, which stands exposed on a wide lip of flat land below a range of bald green hills. Behind these hills lies the high plateau of the Cape Breton Highlands. The area is known for its strong southeast winds, called suêtes, which are winds of 120–130 km (75–80 mi) per hour. These winds, which may develop into a force up 200 km (125 mi) per hour, have been known to blow the roofs off of buildings.

Chéticamp is famous for its hooked rugs, available at many local gift shops. The **Dr. Elizabeth LeFort Gallery and Museum: Les Trois Pignons** (✉ Cabot Trail, Box 430 B0E 1H0, ☎ 902/224–2642, WEB www.lestroispignons.com) displays artifacts and fine hooked embroidery work, rugs, and tapestries. Dr. LeFort created more than 300 tapestries, some of which have been hung in the Vatican, the White House, and Buckingham Palace. The museum is also an Acadian cultural and genealogical information center. Admission is $3.50; the museum is open from mid-October to June, weekdays 8:30–5, and July to mid-October, daily 8–6.

Dining and Lodging

$–$$ ✗ **Le Gabriel.** You can't miss Le Gabriel, with its large lighthouse entranceway. This casual tavern offers simple but good fresh fish dinners and traditional Acadian dishes. Snow crab and lobster specials are available in season. At night things heat up with live music and dancing. ✉ *Cabot Trail,* ☎ *902/224–3685,* WEB *www.legabriel.com. MC, V.*

$$ 🏠 **Cabot Trail Sea & Golf Chalets.** Right next to Le Portage Golf Course and overlooking the ocean, these chalets are ideal for families and golfers. One- and two-bedroom chalets have covered decks with gas barbecues. Some units have fireplaces and whirlpool tubs. There is a play area for children, and cribs, cots, and high chairs are available. ✉ *71 Fraser Doucet La., Box 8 B0E 1H0,* ☎ *902/224–1777 or 877/224–1777,* FAX *902/224–1999,* WEB *www.seagolfchalets.com. 13 chalets. 18-hole golf course, playground. AE, D, MC, V. Closed mid-Oct.–Apr.*

$ 🏠 **Chéticamp Outfitters' Inn B&B.** The clean and cozy rooms at this homey inn, operated by a bilingual family, overlook the ocean, mountains, and valley. The furniture includes homemade wooden pieces, paintings by the innkeeper, and quilts. Guide and outfitting services are available. ✉ *Point Cross, Box 448 B0E 1H0,* ☎ FAX *902/224–2776,* WEB *www.seatrail.com/cheticampoutfitters. 6 rooms, 3 with bath. Fishing. AE, MC, V. Closed mid-Dec.–Mar. BP.*

Outdoor Activities and Sports

Chéticamp is known for its whale-watching cruises, which depart from the government wharf twice daily in May and June, increasing in July and August to three times daily. Expect to see minke, pilot, and fin whales in their natural environment; seabird and bald-eagle sightings are also common. **Whale Cruisers Ltd.** (☎ 902/224–3376 or 800/813–3376, WEB www.whalecruises.com) is a reliable charter company, and the first of its kind in Nova Scotia.

Cape Breton Highlands National Park of Canada

★ *At the northern outskirts of Chéticamp.*

A 950-square-km (367-square-mi) wilderness of wooded valleys, plateau barrens, and steep cliffs, this park stretches across the northern peninsula of Cape Breton from the gulf shore to the Atlantic. The highway through the park (world-renowned Cabot Trail) is magnificent. It rises to the tops of the coastal mountains and descends through scenic switchbacks to the sea. In fact, the road has been compared to a 106-km (66-mi) roller coaster ride, stretching from Chéticamp to Ingonish. Good brakes and attentive driving are advised. Pull-offs provide photo opportunities. For wildlife watchers there's much to see, including moose, eagles, deer, bears, foxes, and bobcats. Your chances of seeing wildlife are better if you venture off the main road at dusk or dawn. Note that it is illegal to feed or approach any animal in the park. Always take care to observe the animals from a safe distance; in particular, you should exercise caution driving in the moose zones, marked by signs on the highway. Moose sometimes claim the road as their own and stand in the middle of it. Hitting one can be damaging to both you and the animal.

High-altitude marshlands are home to delightful wild orchids and other unique flora and fauna. If you plan to hike or camp in the park, or you want to maximize your appreciation for the nature and history of the park, stop at the Chéticamp Information Centre for advice and necessary permits. Inside the Information Centre, you can buy *Walking in the Highlands,* a guide to the park's 28 hiking trails, from the nature bookstore Les Amis du Plein Air. Trails range from easy 20-minute strolls to tough overnight treks. Five hundred fifty campsites in six spectacular locations provide a variety of facilities and services—some are even equipped with showers and cooking shelters. A park permit or pass is required for sightseeing along sections of the Cabot Trail highway when within the National Park and for use of roadside facilities such as exhibits, hiking trails, picnic areas, and washrooms. ⊠ *Entrances on Cabot Trail near Chéticamp and Ingonish,* ☎ *902/285–2535; 902/ 285–2270 in winter; 902/224–3814 bookstore,* WEB *www.parkscanada. gc.ca.* ⊠ *May–Oct. $3.50 per day, multiday and seasonal passes available; additional fees for camping.*

OFF THE BEATEN PATH

GAMPO ABBEY – The most northerly tip of the island is not part of the National Park; a spur road (take a left at Pleasant Bay) creeps along the cliffs to Red River, beyond which, on a broad flat bench of land high above the sea, is this Tibetan Buddhist Monastery. It's the only one in North America. It's possible to tour the abbey when it's not in retreat. The only way to know whether a tour is available is to drive to the abbey and check the sign at the gate. If the abbey is closed, you can continue down the road for about ½ km (¼ mi) to visit the Stupa, a large and elaborate shrine.

Outdoor Activities and Sports

On a **Pleasant Bay Whale and Seal Cruise** (☎ 902/224–1316 or 888/ 754–5112, WEB www.whaleandsealcruise.com) you may see pilot, finback, humpback, or minke whales. If you don't see them, you may at least be able to hear them with the help of an on-board hydrophone. It's also possible to catch sight of dolphins, seals, bald eagles, moose, black bears, and numerous seabirds. Cruises allow for exploration of sea caves, waterfalls, and rock and cliff formations along a remote stretch of unspoiled Cape Breton coastline. There's a money-back guarantee if you don't see a whale. **Pleasant Bay Fiddlin' Whale Tours** (☎ 902/224–2424 or 866/

688–2424) and **Wesley's Whale Watching** (☎ 902/224–1919 or 866/273–2593) are among the other outfitters in the area. For those who prefer to stay on dry land to observe sealife, stop by the **Whale Interpretive Centre** (☎ 902/224–1411, WEB www.whaleslife.com) in Pleasant Bay. Using zoom scopes on the whale-spotting deck, visitors may catch a close-up glimpse of many different species of whales that are often frolicking just off shore from the centre. Inside the modern structure, exhibits and models explain the unique world of whales. The center ($4.50) is open mid-May through October.

Bay St. Lawrence

76 km (47 mi) north of Chéticamp.

The charming fishing village of Bay St. Lawrence is nestled in a bowl-shape valley around a harbor pond. You can hike along the shore to the east and the Money Point Lighthouse, or find a quiet corner of the shoreline for a wilderness campsite. A "feed of lobster" can be purchased from the fisher who brought it up from the sea an hour before.

OFF THE
BEATEN PATH
MEAT COVE – Named for the moose and (now absent) caribou that roamed the highlands and once supplied protein for passing sailing vessels, Meat Cove feels like the end of the earth. It lies at the end of a daunting 12-km (7-mi) mostly unpaved road along a precipitous cliff marked by sudden switchbacks. It's spectacular, but for the adventurous only. To get here, leave the Cabot Trail at Cape North on the Bay St. Lawrence Road. At the foot of the hill leading into St. Margaret's, turn left and follow the sign to Capstick; that road leads to Meat Cove.

The Meat Cove Campground (☎ 902/383–2379), high on a cliff overlooking the ocean, attracts an adventurous crowd and is ideal for hiking, mountain biking, ocean swimming, and nature walks.

Lodging

$ ⊞ **Four Mile Beach Inn.** The view of Aspy Bay and the ridge of the highland mountains is spectacular from this large white historic house near Cabot's Landing. Canoeing and kayaking are possible from the small dock on the property. Rooms are clean and have a simple, country look to them. The suites have a kitchen, a private entrance, and a deck. ⊠ *R.R. 1, Box 3 B0C 1G0,* ☎ *902/383–2282 or 888/503–5551,* FAX *902/564–5877. 5 rooms, 2 suites. MC, V. Closed mid-Oct.–May. CP.*

Outdoor Activities and Sports

Capt. Cox's Whale Watch (☎ 902/383–2981 or 888/346–5556, WEB www.aco.ca/captcox) offers several tours daily—weather permitting—July through August.

Ingonish

④ *113 km (70 mi) northeast of Chéticamp.*

Ingonish, one of the leading holiday destinations on the island, is actually several villages—Ingonish Centre, Ingonish Beach, South Ingonish Harbour, and Ingonish Ferry—on two bays, divided by a long narrow peninsula called Middle Head. Each bay has a sandy beach. At Ingonish Harbour the popular local ski hill also offers ski lift rides in summer and fall. From the 1,000-ft (305-m) summit, the view of Ingonish and the surrounding highlands is breathtaking.

OFF THE
BEATEN PATH
BIRD ISLANDS – From Big Bras d'Or, 100 km (62 mi) south of Ingonish, notice the small islands on the far side of the mouth of St. Ann's Bay: these are the Bird Islands, breeding grounds for Atlantic puffins, black

guillemots, razor-billed auks, and cormorants. Boat tours are offered several times daily mid-May to mid-September from **Bird Island Boat Tour** (☎ 902/674–2384). Landing on the islands is forbidden, however.

Dining and Lodging

$$$$ ✕⊡ **Keltic Lodge.** Spread across cliffs overlooking the ocean, the provincially owned Keltic Lodge sits on the Cabot Trail in Cape Breton Highlands National Park. The setting is glorious, with stunning views of Cape Smokey and the surrounding highlands. Guests can choose among the Main Lodge, Inn at Keltic, and two- or four-bedroom cottages. A wide variety of activities is available, including live professional theater and golfing on the world-class Highlands Links. Seafood stars in the Purple Thistle Dining Room. ✉ *Middle Head Peninsula, Ingonish Beach B0C 1L0,* ☎ *902/285–2880 or 877/375–6343,* WEB *www.signatureresorts.com. 101 rooms. 2 restaurants, pool, golf, hiking, beaches, theater. AE, D, DC, MC, V. Closed Nov.–mid-May. MAP.*

$–$$ ⊡ **Castle Rock Country Inn.** Surrounded by an idyllic setting of mountains and ocean, and offering the tranquility of a library and lounge, the Castle Rock provides an excellent environment for contemplation and relaxation. This Georgian-style inn is right on the Cabot Trail in Ingonish Ferry. ✉ *39339 Cabot Trail, B0C 1L0,* ☎ *902/285–2700 or 888/884–7625,* FAX *902/285–2525,* WEB *www.ingonish.com/castlerock. 15 rooms. Dining room, library. AE, MC, V.*

$ ⊡ **Atlantic Beach Resort.** Direct beach access and a large outdoor pool are two of the attractions of this standard motel. Visit the gift shop for a selection of locally made souvenirs and handicrafts. ✉ *Cabot Trail, Box 187 B0C 1K0,* ☎ *902/285–2519 or 888/821–5551,* FAX *902/285–2538,* WEB *www.atlanticbeachresort.com. 32 rooms. Dining room, pool, beach. MC, V. Closed Nov.–Apr.*

Englishtown

65 km (40 mi) south of Ingonish on Hwy. 312.

A short (five-minute) ferry ride heads from Jersey Cove across St. Ann's Bay to Englishtown, home of the celebrated Cape Breton Giant, Angus MacAskill. Ferries run 24 hours a day; the fare is $3 per car.

The **Giant MacAskill Museum** holds artifacts of the 7'9" man who traveled with P. T. Barnum's troupe in the 1800s. His remains are buried in the local cemetery nearby. ✉ *Hwy. 312,* ☎ *902/929–2875.* 🎫 *$1.50.* ☉ *mid-June–mid-Sept., daily 9–6.*

South Gut St. Ann's

12 km (7 mi) south of Jersey Cove.

Settled by the Highland Scots, South Gut St. Ann's is home to North America's only Gaelic College. The **Great Hall of the Clans** (✉ Rte. 205, ☎ 902/295–3411, WEB www.gaeliccollege.edu) at Gaelic College depicts Scottish history and has an account of the Great Migration. The college offers courses in Gaelic language and literature, Scottish music and dancing, weaving, and other Scottish arts. There's also a Scottish gift shop. Admission to the Great Hall is $2.50, daily mid-June to early September.

From the Gaelic College, you can follow the Cabot Trail as it meanders along the hills that rim St. Ann's Bay. The 30-km (19-mi) stretch between St. Ann's and Indian Brook is home to a collection of fine crafts shops.

Baddeck

㊺ *20 km (12 mi) south of South Gut St. Ann's.*

Baddeck, the most highly developed tourist center on Cape Breton, has more than 1,000 motel beds, a golf course, fine gift shops, and many restaurants. This was also the summer home of Alexander Graham Bell until he died here at the age of 75. In summer the town celebrates the **Centre Bras d'Or Festival of the Arts,** which offers live music and drama every evening. The annual **regatta** of the Bras d'Or Yacht Club is held the first week of August. Sailing tours and charters are available, as are bus tours along the Cabot Trail. On the waterfront, the **Rose Cottage Gallery** overflows with folk art and local crafts.

In summer, a free passenger ferry shuttles between the government wharf and the sandy **Kidston Island beach** by the lighthouse.

The **Celtic Colors International Festival** (☎ 902/295–1414), 10 days spanning the second and third weekends in October, draws the world's best Celtic performers at the height of autumn splendor. International stars like the Chieftains, the Bumblebees, and Archie Fisher join homegrown performers like Rita MacNeil and Mary Jane Lamond for 30-plus performances in two dozen venues scattered around the island. The cost for each performance is $5 to $15. Workshops and seminars covering all aspects of Gaelic language, lore, history, crafts, and culture fill the festival days.

★ ☾ The **Alexander Graham Bell National Historic Site of Canada** explores Bell's inventions. Experiments, kite making, and other hands-on activities are designed for children. From films, artifacts, and photographs, you learn how ideas led Bell to create man-carrying kites, airplanes, and a marine record-setting hydrofoil boat. The site has reduced services October through May. ⊠ *Chebucto St.,* ☎ *902/295–2069,* WEB *www.parkscanada.gc.ca.* ⌸ *$4.25.* ☉ *July–Aug. daily 9–8, June and Sept. daily 9–7, Oct.–May daily 9–5.*

At the **Wagmatcook Culture & Heritage Centre,** 10 mi (16 km) west of the town of Baddeck, the ancient history and rich traditions of the native Mi'Kmaq are demonstrated. Mi'Kmaq guides provide interpretations and cultural entertainment. The on-site restaurant highlights traditional foods like moose and eel dishes, as well as more-contemporary choices. The craft shop has local native products. ⊠ *Wagmatcook First Nation, Rte. 105,* ☎ *902/295–2598.* ⌸ *$2.* ☉ *Mid-May–Oct.*

Dining and Lodging

$$–$$$$ ✕▥ **Inverary Resort.** On the shores of the magnificent Bras d'Or Lake, this resort has stunning views and lots of activities. You can choose from cozy pine-paneled cottages, modern hotel units, or the elegant 100-year-old main lodge; some rooms have fireplaces. There's boating and swimming in close proximity to the village, but the resort remains tranquil. Dining choices are the casual Lakeside Café and the elegant main dining room ($$–$$$). ⊠ *Hwy. 205 and Shore Rd., Box 190 B0E 1B0,* ☎ *902/295–3500 or 800/565–5660,* FAX *902/295–3527,* WEB *www.InveraryResort.com. 125 rooms, 14 cottages. Restaurant, café, pub, indoor pool, sauna, 3 tennis courts, boating, playground. AE, D, MC, V.*

$$–$$$ ▥ **Auberge Gisele's Inn.** An inn and motel share lovely landscaped flower gardens and overlook the Bras d'Or Lake. The atmosphere is one of tasteful hospitality. Some rooms have fireplaces. The chef prepares breakfast, lunch, and dinner by reservation in the dining room. You can also enjoy a cocktail in the smoke-free lounge and art gallery. ⊠ *387 Shore Rd., B0E 1B0,* ☎ *902/295–2849,* FAX *902/295–2033,* WEB *www.gise-*

les.com. 75 rooms, 3 suites. Dining room, in-room data ports, sauna, gym, bicycles, coin laundry. MC, V. Closed Nov.–Apr.

$$ 🏨 **Duffus House.** Facing the harbor, this quiet inn is furnished with antiques and has cozy sitting rooms and a secluded, well-tended garden. The Continental breakfast is substantial. Smoking isn't permitted. ✉ *108 Water St., Box 427 B0E 1B0,* ☎ *902/295–2172,* WEB *www.cape-bretonet.com/Baddeck/DuffusHouse. 4 rooms, 3 suites. Dock, library. V. Closed mid-Oct.–end of May. CP.*

$ 🏨 **Bain's Heritage House B&B.** In the center of Baddeck sits this tastefully appointed historic home built in the 1850s. On cooler evenings you can relax in front of the fire in the sitting room. ✉ *121 Twining St., B0E 1B0,* ☎ *902/295–1069. 3 rooms, 1 with bath. MC, V. BP.*

Outdoor Activities and Sports

The **Bell Bay Golf Club** (☎ 902/295–1333 or 800/565–3077, WEB www.bellbaygolfclub.com) has panoramic views from almost every hole on its par-72, 18-hole course. Bell Bay has the largest practice facilities in Atlantic Canada.

Iona

46 *56 km (35 mi) south of Baddeck.*

Iona, where some residents still speak Gaelic, is the site of a living-history museum. To get here from Baddeck, take Trans-Canada Highway 105 to Exit 6, which leads to Little Narrows, where you can take a ferry to the Washabuck Peninsula. The **Highland Village Museum** (✉ Hwy. 223, ☎ 902/725–2272, WEB www.highlandvillage.museum.gov.ns.ca), now part of the Nova Scotia Museum family, is set high on a mountainside, with a spectacular view of Bras d'Or Lake and the narrow Barra Strait. The village's 10 historic buildings were assembled from all over Cape Breton to depict the Highland Scots' way of life from their origins in the Hebrides to the present day. Among the staff at this museum are a smith in the blacksmith shop and a clerk in the store. The complex also houses Roots Cape Breton, a genealogy and family-history center for Cape Breton Island. The village is open from mid-May to mid-October, daily 9–6; admission is $5.

Dining and Lodging

$–$$ ✕🏨 **Highland Heights Inn.** The rural surroundings, the Scottish home-style cooking served near the restaurant's huge stone fireplace, and the view of the lake substitute nicely for the Scottish Highlands. The inn is on a hillside beside the Nova Scotia Highland Village, overlooking Iona. The salmon (or any fish in season), fresh-baked oatcakes, and homemade desserts are good choices. ✉ *4115 Hwy. 223, Iona B2C 1A3,* ☎ *902/725–2360 or 800/660–8122,* FAX *902/725–2800,* WEB *www.highlandheightsinn.com. 32 rooms. Restaurant, no-smoking rooms. D, MC, V. Closed mid-Oct.–mid-May.*

Sydney

47 *60 km (37 mi) northeast of Iona.*

The heart of Nova Scotia's second-largest urban cluster, Sydney is known as industrial Cape Breton. It encompasses villages, unorganized districts, and a half dozen towns—most of which sprang up around the coal mines, which fed the steel plant at Sydney. These are warm-hearted, interesting communities with a diverse ethnic population that includes Ukrainians, Welsh, Poles, Lebanese, West Indians, and Italians. Most residents are descendants of the miners and steelworkers who arrived a century ago when the area was booming.

Sydney has the island's only real airport, its only university, and a lively entertainment scene that specializes in Cape Breton music. It is also a departure point—fast ferries leave from North Sydney for Newfoundland, and scheduled air service to Newfoundland and the French islands of St-Pierre and Miquelon departs from Sydney Airport.

Dining and Lodging

$$ ★ **Gowrie House.** This unexpected jewel on the Shore Road between North Sydney and Sydney Mines, five minutes from the ferry to Newfoundland, is shaded by towering trees on grounds filled with gardens and flowering shrubs. Cherry trees supply the main ingredient for chilled black-cherry soup served in what some consider Nova Scotia's finest restaurant ($45 prix fixe). Antiques, fine art, and exquisite china add to the elegance. The main house has six rooms; the secluded garden house holds four more; and the caretaker's cottage provides deluxe private accommodation. Whether you stay overnight or are a guest for dinner only, dinner reservations are essential (best to book a week ahead). ✉ *139 Shore Rd., Sydney Mines B1V 1A6,* ☎ *902/544–1050 or 800/372–1115,* WEB *www.gowriehouse.com. 11 rooms. Restaurant. AE, MC, V. BP.*

$$–$$$ **Delta Sydney.** This hotel is on the harbor, beside the yacht club and close to the center of town. Guest rooms are attractive and have harbor views. The restaurant specializes in seafood and Continental cuisine. ✉ *300 Esplanade, B1P 1A7,* ☎ *902/562–7500 or 800/565–1001,* FAX *902/562–3023,* WEB *www.deltasydney.com. 152 rooms. Restaurant, lounge, indoor pool, sauna, gym. AE, DC, MC, V.*

$ **Rockinghorse Inn.** Alexander Graham Bell was a frequent guest at this historic property, which is beautifully decorated with antiques. A small dining room called the Jack Pitman Library is available for your private use by reservation only. Everything on the menu is made from scratch; the decadent desserts, prepared by the inn's owner, are the main attraction. ✉ *259 Kings Rd., B1S 1A7,* ☎ *902/539–2696 or 888/884–1010,* FAX *902/539–2696,* WEB *www.rockinghorse-inn.com. 7 rooms, 4 with bath. Dining room. MC, V.*

Nightlife and the Arts

Many fiddlers appear at the week-long **Big Pond Concert** (✉ Rte. 4, 1 km/½ mi east of Rita's Tea Room, ☎ 902/828–2373) in mid-July. At the **Casino Nova Scotia** (✉ 525 George St., ☎ 902/563–7777), you can try the slot machines, roulette, or gaming tables or enjoy live entertainment. The **University College of Cape Breton** (✉ 1250 Grand Lake Rd., ☎ 902/539–5300) has many facilities open to the public, such as the Boardmore Playhouse and the island's only public art gallery.

Glace Bay

48 *21 km (13 mi) east of Sydney.*

A coal mining town and fishing port, Glace Bay has a rich history of ★ industrial struggle. The **Glace Bay Miners' Museum** houses exhibits and artifacts illustrating the hard life of early miners in Cape Breton's undersea collieries. Former miners guide you down into the damp recesses of the mine and tell stories of working all day where the sun never shines. ✉ *42 Birkley St., Quarry Point,* ☎ *902/849–4522,* WEB *www.cbnet.ns.ca.* *$4.50 museum, $8 museum and mine tour.* ⏲ *June–Sept., Wed.–Mon. 10–6, Tues. 10–7; Sept.–June, Mon.–Fri., 9–4.*

The **Marconi National Historic Site of Canada** commemorates the site at Table Head where in 1901 Guglielmo Marconi built four tall wooden towers and beamed the first wireless messages across the Atlantic Ocean. An interpretive trail leads to the foundations of the original towers and transmitter buildings. The visitor center has large models of the towers as well as artifacts and photographs chronicling the radio pioneer's life and work. ⊠ *Timmerman St. (Hwy. 255),* ☎ *902/842–2530,* WEB *www.parkscanada.gc.ca.* ☞ *Free.* ☉ *June–mid-Sept., daily 10–6.*

Nightlife and the Arts

Glace Bay's grand Victorian-style **Savoy Theatre** (⊠ 116 Commercial St., ☎ 902/842–1577), built in 1927, is home to a variety of live drama, comedy, and music performances.

Louisbourg

⑲ *55 km (34 mi) south of Glace Bay.*

Though best known as the home of the largest historical reconstruction in North America, Louisbourg is also an important fishing community with a lovely harborfront. The **Fortress of Louisbourg National Historic Site of Canada** may be the most remarkable site in Cape Breton. After the French were forced out of mainland Nova Scotia in 1713, they established their headquarters here in a walled and fortified town on a low point of land at the mouth of Louisbourg Harbour. The fortress was twice captured, once by New Englanders and once by the British; after the second siege, in 1758, it was razed. Its capture was critical in ending the French empire in America. A quarter of the original town has been rebuilt on its foundations, just as it was in 1744, before the first siege. Costumed actors re-create the activities of the original inhabitants; you can watch a military drill, see nails and lace being made, and eat food prepared from 18th-century recipes in the town's two inns. Plan on spending at least a half day. Louisbourg tends to be chilly, so pack a warm sweater or windbreaker. ⊠ *Hwy. 22,* ☎ *902/733–2280 or 800/565–9464,* WEB *www.parkscanada.gc.ca.* ☞ *$11.* ☉ *June and Sept., daily 9:30–5; July–Aug., daily 9–6.*

At the **Sydney and Louisbourg Railway Museum,** a restored 1895 railroad station exhibits the history of the S&L Railway, railroad technology, and marine shipping. The rolling stock includes a baggage car, coach, and caboose. ⊠ *7336 Main St.,* ☎ *902/733–2157.* ☞ *Free.* ☉ *Mid-May–June and Sept.–mid-Oct., daily 9–5; July–Aug., daily 8–8.*

Both live theater performances and traditional Cape Breton music are served up at the **Louisbourg Playhouse,** a 17th-century–style theater, which was originally constructed as part of a Disney movie set. ⊠ *11 Aberdeen St.,* ☎ *902/733–2996 or 888/733–2787,* WEB *www.artscape-breton.com.* ☉ *Mid-June–Oct.*

Dining and Lodging

$–$$$ ✕ **Lobster Kettle Restaurant.** Perched on the wharf, Lobster Kettle offers a pleasant view of the Louisbourg Harbour as well as fine seafood and a variety of other dishes. A huge array of fresh salads awaits you at the all-you-can-eat salad bar. ⊠ *Bottom of Strathcona St.,* ☎ *902/733–2723. MC, V.*

$–$$ ⊡ **Cranberry Cove Inn.** This fully renovated home from the early 1900s is within walking distance of the Fortress of Louisbourg National Historic Park. Inquire about the theme guest rooms, some of which have jet tubs and gas fireplaces. Enjoy a fine meal in an antiques-filled dining room. Smoking is prohibited. ⊠ *12 Wolfe St., B1C 2J2,* ☎ *902/733–2171 or 800/929–0222,* FAX *902/733–2449,* WEB *www.louis-bourg.com/cranberrycove. 7 rooms. Dining room. AE, MC, V. CP.*

$–$$$ ⊡ **Louisbourg Harbour Inn.** In the center of the community, overlooking a fishing wharf, this renovated century-old sea captain's house affords ocean views from most rooms and balconies. All rooms have hardwood floors, high ceilings, queen-size bed, and private bath (some with whirlpool tubs). ✉ *9 Lower Warren St., B1C 1G6,* ☎ *902/733–3222 or 888/888–8466,* ᴡᴇʙ *www.louisbourg.com/louisbourgharbourinn. 8 rooms. MC, V. Closed mid-Oct.–May. CP.*

Big Pond

50 km (31 mi) west of Louisbourg.

This little town comprises just a few houses, and one of them is the home of singer-songwriter Rita MacNeil, who operates **Rita's Tea Room.** Originally a one-room schoolhouse, the building has been expanded to accommodate the multitude of visitors who come to sample Rita's Tea Room Blend Tea, which is served along with a fine selection of sandwiches and baked goods. You can visit a display room of Rita's awards and photographs and browse through her gift shop. ✉ *Hwy. 4,* ☎ *902/828–2667.* ⏲ *June–mid-Oct., daily 9–7.*

En Route   Highway 4 rolls along Bras d'Or Lake, sometimes by the shore and sometimes in the hills. At **St. Peter's** the Atlantic Ocean is connected with the Bras d'Or Lake by the century-old St. Peter's Canal, still used by pleasure craft and fishing vessels. From St. Peter's to Port Hawkesbury the population is largely Acadian French.

Arichat

⑤⓪   *62 km (38 mi) southwest of Big Pond.*

The principal town of Isle Madame, Arichat is a 27-square-km (10-square-mi) island named for Madame de Maintenon, second wife of Louis XIV. It was an important shipbuilding and trading center during the 19th century, and some fine old houses from that period still remain. Arichat was once the seat of the local Catholic diocese. **Notre Dame de l'Assumption** church, built in 1837, still retains the grandeur of its former cathedral status. Its bishop's palace is now a law office. The two cannons overlooking the harbor were installed after the town was sacked by John Paul Jones during the American Revolution.

To get here from Big Pond, take Highway 247 to Highway 320, which leads through Poulamon and D'Escousse and overlooks Lennox Passage, with its spangle of islands. Highway 206 meanders through the low hills to a maze of land and water at West Arichat. Together, the two routes encircle the island, meeting at Arichat. The island lends itself to biking, as most roads glide gently along the shore. A good half-day hike leads to Gros Nez, the "large nose" that juts into the sea.

LeNoir Forge (✉ Hwy. 320, off Hwy. 4, ☎ 902/226–9364) is a restored French 18th-century stone blacksmith shop open June through August, daily 9–5.

OFF THE
BEATEN PATH   **LITTLE ANSE –** With its red bluffs, cobble shores, tiny harbor, and brightly painted houses, Little Anse can be particularly attractive for artists and photographers. The town is at the southeastern tip of Isle Madame.

NOVA SCOTIA A TO Z

To research prices, get advice from other travelers, and book travel arrangements, visit www.fodors.com.

AIR TRAVEL
Air Atlantic, Air Canada, Air Nova, Canada 3000, and Northwest Air provide service to Halifax and Sydney from various cities. Air travel

within the area is very limited. Air Nova provides regional service to other provinces and to Sydney.

AIRPORTS

The Halifax International Airport is 40 km (25 mi) northeast of downtown Halifax. Sydney Airport is 13 km (8 mi) east of Sydney.

➤ AIRPORT INFORMATION: **Halifax International Airport** (✉ 1 Bell Blvd., Elmsdale, ☎ 902/873–1223). **Sydney Airport** (280 Airport Rd., ☎ 902/564–7720).

AIRPORT TRANSFERS

Limousine and taxi services, as well as car rentals, are available at Halifax and Sydney airports. Airport bus service to Halifax and Dartmouth hotels costs $20 round-trip, $12 one-way. Airbus has regular bus service from the airport to most major hotels in Halifax. Regular taxi fare to Halifax is $35 each way, but if you book ahead with Ace–Y, the fare is $22.70—if you share your car with another passenger. The trip takes 30–40 minutes.

➤ CONTACTS: **Ace–Y** (☎ 902/422–4437). **Airbus** (☎ 902/873–2091).

BOAT AND FERRY TRAVEL

Car ferries connect Nova Scotia with Maine and New Brunswick: Prince of Fundy Cruises sails from Portland, Maine, to Yarmouth, Nova Scotia. Bay Ferries Ltd. sails from Bar Harbor, Maine, to Yarmouth, and from Saint John, New Brunswick, to Digby, Nova Scotia. The Bar Harbor–Yarmouth service uses a high-speed catamaran, cutting the trip from 6 to 2¾ hours. The catamaran has become hugely popular recently, so reserve ahead.

From May through December, Northumberland Ferries operates between Caribou, Nova Scotia, and Wood Islands, Prince Edward Island. Marine Atlantic operates year-round between North Sydney and Port aux Basques, on the west coast of Newfoundland, and June through September between North Sydney and Argentia, on Newfoundland's east coast.

Metro Transit runs passenger ferries from the Halifax Ferry Terminal at Lower Water Street to Alderney Gate in downtown Dartmouth and to Woodside Terminal (near Dartmouth Hospital) on the hour and half hour from 6:30 AM to 11:57 PM. Ferries are more frequent during weekday rush hours; they also operate on Sunday in summer (June through September). Free transfers are available from the ferry to the bus system (and vice versa). A single crossing costs $1.50 and is worth it for the up-close view of both waterfronts.

➤ BOAT AND FERRY INFORMATION: **Bay Ferries Ltd.** (☎ 902/566–3838 or 888/249–7245). **Marine Atlantic** (☎ 902/794–5254; 709/772–7701; 800/341–7981). **Metro Transit** (☎ 902/421–6600). **Northumberland Ferries** (☎ 902/566–3838; 800/565–0201). **Prince of Fundy Cruises** (☎ 800/341–7540 in Canada; 800/482–0955 in Maine).

BUS TRAVEL

Because of conflicting schedules, getting into Nova Scotia by bus can be problematic. Greyhound Lines, from New York, and Voyageur, from Montréal, connect with Scotia Motor Tours (SMT), through New Brunswick. SMT links (inconveniently) with Acadian Lines and provides interurban service within Nova Scotia. Airbus runs between the Halifax International Airport and major hotels in Halifax and Dartmouth. Shuttle van services with convenient transportation between Halifax and Sydney include Cape Shuttle Service and Scotia Shuttle Service.

There are a number of small, regional bus services; however, connections are not always convenient. Outside of Halifax there are no innercity bus services. For information, call Nova Scotia Tourism.

Metro Transit provides bus service throughout Halifax and Dartmouth, the town of Bedford, and (to a limited extent) the county of Halifax. The base fare is $1.65, exact change only.

➤ BUS INFORMATION: **Acadian Lines** (☎ 902/454–9321). **Airbus** (☎ 902/873–2091). **Cape Shuttle Service** (☎ 800/349–1698). **Greyhound Lines** (☎ 800/231–2222). **Metro Transit** (☎ 902/421–6600). **Nova Scotia Tourism** (☎ 902/424–5000 or 800/565–0000). **Scotia Motor Tours** (☎ 506/458–6000). **Scotia Shuttle Service** (☎ 877/898–5883). **Voyageur Inc.** (☎ 613/238–5900).

CAR RENTAL

Halifax is the most convenient place from which to begin a driving tour. It is recommended that you book a car through your travel agent. Avis, Budget, Hertz, National Tilden, and Thrifty have locations in Halifax.

➤ MAJOR AGENCIES: **Avis** (✉ 5600 Sackville St., Halifax, ☎ 902/492–2847; 902/429–0963 airport). **Budget** (✉ 1558 Hollis St., Halifax, ☎ 902/492–7500 or 800/268–8900). **Hertz** (✉ Halifax Sheraton, 1919 Upper Water St., Halifax, ☎ 902/421–1763; 902/873–3700 airport). **National Tilden** (✉ 2173 Barrington St., Halifax, ☎ 902/422–4439; 902/873–3505 airport). **Thrifty** (✉ 6419 Lady Hammond, Halifax, ☎ 902/422–4455; 902/873–3527 airport).

CAR TRAVEL

Most highways in the province lead to Halifax and Dartmouth. Highways 3/103, 7, 2/102, and 1/101 terminate in the twin cities. Many of the roads in rural Nova Scotia require attentive driving, as they are not well signed, are narrow, and do not always have a paved shoulder. They are generally well surfaced and offer exquisite scenery.

Motorists can enter Nova Scotia through the narrow neck of land that connects the province to New Brunswick and the mainland. The Trans-Canada Highway (Highway 2 in New Brunswick) becomes Highway 104 on crossing the Nova Scotia border at Amherst. It is now possible to drive over the Confederation Bridge from Prince Edward Island into New Brunswick near the Nova Scotia border. Otherwise, car ferries dock at Yarmouth (from Maine), Digby (from New Brunswick), Caribou (from Prince Edward Island), and North Sydney (from Newfoundland).

ROAD MAPS

The province has 10 designated "Scenic Travelways," identified by roadside signs with icons that correspond with trail names. These lovely routes are also shown on tourist literature (maps and the provincial *Travel Guide*). Nova Scotia Tourism provides information.

RULES OF THE ROAD

Highways numbered from 100 to 199 are all-weather, limited-access roads, with 100- to 110-kph (62- to 68-mph) speed limits. The last two digits usually match the number of an older trunk highway along the same route, numbered from 1 to 99. Thus, Highway 102, between Halifax and Truro, matches the older Highway 2, between the same towns. Roads numbered from 200 to 399 are secondary roads that usually link villages. Unless otherwise posted, the speed limit on these and any roads other than the 100-series highways is 80 kph (50 mph).

EMERGENCIES

➤ CONTACTS: **Ambulance, fire, or police** (☎ 911). **Cape Breton Regional Hospital** (✉ 1482 George St., Sydney, ☎ 902/567–8000). **Queen Elizabeth II Health Sciences Centre** (✉ 5909 Jubilee Rd., Halifax, ☎ 902/473–2799 switchboard; 902/473–2043 emergencies).

LODGING

Nova Scotia has a computerized system called Check In that provides information and makes reservations with more than 700 hotels, motels, inns, campgrounds, and car-rental agencies.

➤ TOLL-FREE NUMBERS: **Check In** (☎ 902/425–5781 or 800/565–0000).

OUTDOORS AND SPORTS

BIKING

Bicycle Tours in Nova Scotia ($7) is published by Bicycle Nova Scotia. Atlantic Canada Cycling can provide information on tours and rentals.

➤ CONTACTS: **Atlantic Canada Cycling** (☎ 902/423–2453). **Bicycle Nova Scotia** (✉ 5516 Spring Garden Rd., Box 3010, Halifax B3J 3G6, ☎ 902/425–5450).

BIRD-WATCHING

Nova Scotia is on the Atlantic flyway and is an important staging point for migratory species. A fine illustrated book, *Birds of Nova Scotia,* by Robie Tufts, is a must on every ornithologist's reading list. The Nova Scotia Museum organizes walks and lectures for people interested in viewing local bird life in the Halifax area.

➤ CONTACTS: **Nova Scotia Museum** (✉ 1747 Summer St., ☎ 902/424–6475).

CANOEING

Especially good canoe routes are within Kejimkujik National Park. Canoeing information is available from Canoe NS. The publication *Canoe Routes of Nova Scotia* and route maps are available from the Nova Scotia Government Bookstore.

➤ CONTACTS: **Canoe NS** (☎ 902/425–5450 Ext. 316). **Nova Scotia Government Bookstore** (✉ 1700 Granville St., Halifax, ☎ 902/424–7580).

FISHING

You are required by law to have a valid Nova Scotia fishing license for both freshwater and saltwater fishing. For information about licenses, contact the Department of Natural Resources. Fishing charters are plentiful; contact the Nova Scotia Department of Fisheries and Aquaculture for information.

➤ CONTACTS: **Department of Natural Resources** (☎ 902/424–4467). **Nova Scotia Department of Fisheries and Aquaculture** (☎ 902/485–5056).

GOLF

➤ CONTACTS: **Golf Nova Scotia** (☎ 800/565–0001, WEB www.golfnovascotia.com).

HIKING

The province has a wide variety of trails along the rugged coastline and inland through forest glades, which enable you to experience otherwise inaccessible scenery, wildlife, and vegetation. *Hiking Trails of Nova Scotia* ($12.95) is available through Gooselane Editions.

➤ CONTACTS: **Gooselane Editions** (✉ 469 King St., Fredericton, New Brunswick, E3R 1E5, ☎ 506/450–4251).

SKIING

➤ CONTACTS: **Nova Scotia Ski Area Association** (☎ 902/798–9501).

SNOWMOBILING

Visiting snowmobilers can get information on trails, activities, clubs, and dealers through the Snowmobile Association of Nova Scotia.

➤ CONTACTS: **Snowmobile Association of Nova Scotia** (☎ 902/425–5450).

TAXIS

In Halifax, rates begin at about $2.50 and increase based on mileage and time. A crosstown trip should cost $6 to $7, depending on traffic. Hailing a taxi can be difficult, but there are taxi stands at major hotels and shopping malls. Most Haligonians simply phone for a taxi service.

➤ TAXI COMPANIES: **Casino Taxi** (☎ 902/429–6666). **Yellow Cab** (☎ 902/420–0000 or 902/422–1551).

TOURS

BOAT TOURS

Boat tours have become very popular in all regions of the province. Murphy's on the Water sails various vessels: *Harbour Queen I,* a paddle wheeler; *Haligonian III,* an enclosed motor launch; *Stormy Weather I,* a 40-ft Cape Islander (fishing boat); and *Mar II,* a 75-ft sailing ketch. All operate from mid-May to late October from berths at 1751 Lower Water Street on Cable Wharf next to the Historic Properties in Halifax. Some tours include lunch, dinner, or entertainment. A cash bar may also be available. Costs vary, but a basic tour of the Halifax Harbour ranges from $15 to $25.

Harbour Hopper Tours offers a unique amphibious tour of historic downtown Halifax and the Halifax Harbour.

➤ CONTACTS: **Harbour Hopper Tours** (☎ 902/490–8687). **Murphy's on the Water** (☎ 902/420–1015).

BUS AND RICKSHAW TOURS

Gray Line Sightseeing and Cabana Tours run coach tours through Halifax, Dartmouth, and Peggy's Cove. Halifax Double Decker Tours offers two-hour tours on double-decker buses that leave daily from Historic Properties in Halifax.

In Halifax, Yellow Cab provides clean, comfortable cars with eloquent, amicable drivers who are well versed in local history and lore. As well as local tours, day trips to locations such as Wolfville or Peggy's Cove are possible with prior arrangement. Prices vary, but you should be sure to set a fee with the tour guide before you begin.

Greater Halifax Rickshaw Service offers intimate narrated tours of downtown Halifax.

➤ CONTACTS: **Cabana Tours** (☎ 902/423–6066). **Gray Line Sightseeing** (☎ 902/454–8279). **Greater Halifax Rickshaw Service** (☎ 902/455–6677). **Halifax Double Decker Tours** (☎ 902/420–1155). **Yellow Cab** (☎ 902/420–0000 or 902/422–1551).

SPECIALIZED TOURS

Explore Halifax's rich tradition of stories of pirates, haunted houses, buried treasure, and ghosts with Halifax Ghost Walk. Tours begin at the Old Town Clock at 8:30 PM on any scheduled night.

➤ CONTACTS: **Halifax Ghost Walk** (☎ 902/469–6716).

TRAIN TOURS

VIA Rail conducts weekly first-class guided rail tours between Halifax and Sydney from May through mid-October.

➤ CONTACTS: **VIA Rail** (☎ 800/561–3949).

VISITOR INFORMATION

Nova Scotia Tourism publishes a wide range of literature, including an annual travel guide called the *Nova Scotia Doers and Dreamers Guide.* Call to have this invaluable source of information mailed to you.

Visiting pilots can obtain aviation-related information for the flying tourist from the Aviation Council of Nova Scotia.

➤ TOURIST INFORMATION: **Aviation Council of Nova Scotia** (✉ Box 100, Debert B0M 1G0, ☎ 902/895–1143). **Nova Scotia Tourism** (✉ Box 130, Halifax B3J 2M7, ☎ 902/424–5000 or 800/565–0000). **Nova Scotia Tourism Information Centre** (✉ Old Red Store at Historic Properties, Halifax, ☎ 902/424–4248). **Tourism Halifax & Nova Scotia Tourism** (✉ International Visitors Centre, 1595 Barrington St., Halifax, ☎ 902/490–5946).

15 NEWFOUNDLAND AND LABRADOR

Canada's easternmost province comprises the island of Newfoundland, at the mouth of the Gulf of St. Lawrence, and Labrador on the mainland to the northwest. Humpback whales feed near shore in the fish-rich ocean, millions of seabirds nest in almost 300 coastal colonies, and 10,000-year-old icebergs cruise by fishing villages. St. John's, the capital, is a classic harbor city offering a lively arts scene and warm hospitality.

Updated by
Ed Kirby

NEWFOUNDLAND WAS THE SITE of the first European settlement in North America. Sometime around AD 1000, a half millennium before explorers John Cabot (1497) and Gaspar Corte-Real (1500) touched down in the New World, Vikings from Iceland and Greenland built a sod hut village near Newfoundland's northern tip. They stayed only a few years and then evidence of their presence disappeared into the mists of history for centuries. Their village, part of the territory they called Vinland, was discovered only in the 1960s.

Early as they were, the Vikings were still latecomers to the area. The first people appeared in the region as the glaciers melted 9,000 years ago. The oldest known funeral monument in North America was built in southern Labrador 7,500 years ago.

When Cabot arrived, sailing under the English flag at the end of the 15th century, he reported that the fish in the ocean were so thick they could be caught with a basket. Within a decade, St. John's had become a crowded harbor. Fishing boats from France, England, Spain, and Portugal vied for a chance to catch Newfoundland's lucrative cod, which was subsequently to shape the province's history.

At one time there were 700 hardworking settlements, or "outports," dotting Newfoundland's coast, most of them devoted to catching, salting, and drying the world's most plentiful fish. Today, only about 400 of these settlements survive. Cod, Newfoundland's most famous resource, had become so scarce by 1992 that a partial fishing moratorium was declared; it's still in effect today. The cod have not yet returned, and the limited quotas may be further reduced. People have switched to catching other species, found work in other industries, or left for greener pastures. The discovery of one of the richest and largest nickel deposits in the world at Voisey's Bay in northern Labrador, near Nain, holds hope for a new industry; development is likely to begin within a few years. Several offshore oil fields are expected to go into production in the next few years, joining the Hibernia field, which began pumping oil in 1997.

For almost 400 years, before Newfoundland and Labrador joined Canada in 1949, the people had survived the vagaries of a fishing economy on their own. It was the Great Depression that forced the economy to go belly-up. After more than 50 years of confederation with Canada, the economy has improved considerably, but the people are still independent and maintain a unique language and lifestyle. E. Annie Proulx's Pulitzer prize-winning novel *The Shipping News* brought the attention of many readers to this part of the world, and a film adaptation due in 2002 promises an even wider audience. Now homegrown literary talent is finding a wider audience. Authors such as Wayne Johnston, whose novel *The Colony of Unrequited Dreams* was an artistic and commercial hit in 1999, are bringing Newfoundland and Labrador's distinctive history, ecology, and outlook to an international audience.

Visitors find themselves straddling the centuries. Old accents and customs in small towns and outports exist cheek by jowl with cable TV and the Internet. And the major cities of St. John's on Newfoundland's east coast and Corner Brook on its west coast are very much part of the 21st century.

Whether you visit an isolated outport or St. John's lively Duckworth Street, you're sure to meet some of the warmest, wittiest people in North America. Strangers have always been welcome in Newfoundland, since the days when locals brought visitors in from the cold, warmed them by the fire, and charmingly interrogated them for news of events elsewhere. Before you can shoot the breeze, though, you have to develop an ear for the strong provincial dialects. The *Dictionary of Newfoundland English* has more than 5,000 words, mostly having to do with fishery, weather, and scenery. To get started, you can practice the name of the island portion of the province—it's New-fund-*land,* with the accent on "land." However, only "livyers" ever get the pronunciation exactly right. While academics strive to preserve the old words and speech patterns, the effects of globalization combined with changes in the economy are eroding the old dialects as young people leave coastal hamlets for education and jobs in larger cities. But it is these same young people who are among the most devoted fans of Great Big Sea and other modern exponents of traditional music.

Pleasures and Pastimes

Dining

Today, despite the fishing moratorium, seafood is an excellent value in Newfoundland and Labrador. Many restaurants offer seasonal specialties with a wide variety of traditional wild and cultured species. Cod is still readily available and is traditionally prepared: panfried, baked, or poached. Aquaculture species such as steelhead trout, salmon, mussels, and sea scallops are available in better restaurants. Cold-water shrimp, snow crab, lobster, redfish, grenadier, halibut, and turbot are also good seafood choices.

Two other foods to try are partridgeberries and bakeapples. Partridgeberries, called mountain cranberries in the United States, are used for pies, jams, cakes, pancakes, and as a meat sauce. Bakeapples, also known as cloudberries, look like yellow raspberries and grow on low plants in bogs. They ripen in August, and pickers sell them by the side of the road in jars. If the ones you buy are hard, wait a few days and they'll ripen into rich-tasting fruit. The berries are popular on ice cream or spread on bread.

Only the large urban centers, especially St. John's and Corner Brook, have sophisticated restaurants. Fish is a safe dish just about everywhere, even in the lowliest takeout. Excellent meals are offered in the province's network of bed-and-breakfasts, where home cooking goes hand in hand with a warm welcome.

CATEGORY	COST*
$$$$	over $32
$$$	$22–$32
$$	$13–$21
$	under $13

per person, in Canadian dollars, for a main course at dinner

Festivals and Performing Arts Events

From the Folk Festival main stage in St. John's to the front parlor, the province is filled with music of all kinds. Newfoundlanders love a party, and from the cities to the smallest towns they celebrate their history and unique culture with festivals and events throughout the summer. "Soirees" and "times"—big parties and small parties—offer a combination of traditional music, recitation, comedy, and local food, sometimes in a dinner-theater setting.

Fishing

Newfoundland has more than 200 salmon rivers and thousands of trout streams. Fishing in these unpolluted waters is an angler's dream. The Atlantic salmon is king of the game fish. Top salmon rivers in Newfoundland include the Gander, Humber, and Exploits, while Labrador's top-producing waters are the Sandhill, Michaels, Flowers, and Eagle rivers. Lake trout, brook trout, and landlocked salmon are other favorite species. In Labrador, northern pike and arctic char can be added to that list. An upturn in returning salmon in 1998 and subsequent quota increases were followed by two years of baffling low returns to many rivers. Note: nonresidents must hire a guide or outfitter for anything other than roadside angling.

Hiking

Many provincial parks and both of the national parks in the province have hiking and nature trails, and coastal and forest trails radiate out from most small communities. The East Coast Trail on the Avalon Peninsula covers 520 km (322 mi) of coastline; the trail begins in Conception Bay South and moves north to Cape St. Francis and then south all the way down to Trepassey. It passes through two dozen communities and along clifftops that provide ideal lookouts for icebergs and seabirds. You can call individual parks or the tourist information line for specifics.

Lodging

Newfoundland and Labrador offer lodgings that range from modestly priced B&Bs, which you can find through local tourist offices, to luxury accommodations. In between, you can choose from affordable, basic, and mid-price hotels, motels, and cabins. In remote areas, be prepared to find very basic lodgings for the most part (though some of the best lodging in the province can be found in rural areas). However, the lack of amenities is usually made up for by the home-cooked meals and great hospitality.

CATEGORY	COST*
$$$$	over $200
$$$	$150–$200
$$	$100–$150
$	under $100

All prices are for a standard double room, excluding 15% harmonized sales tax (HST), in Canadian dollars.

Exploring Newfoundland and Labrador

This chapter divides the province into the island of Newfoundland, beginning with St. John's and the Avalon Peninsula and moving west, and Labrador. Labrador is considered as a whole, with suggested driving and train excursions for a number of areas.

Numbers in the text correspond to numbers in the margin and on the St. John's, Avalon Peninsula, and Newfoundland and Labrador maps.

Great Itineraries

IF YOU HAVE 3 DAYS

Pick either the west or east coast of Newfoundland. On the west coast, after arriving by ferry at **Port aux Basques** ㊻, drive through the Codroy Valley, heading north to **Gros Morne National Park** and its fjords, and overnight in 🏨 **Rocky Harbour** ㊵ or 🏨 **Woody Point** ㊳. The next day, visit **L'Anse aux Meadows National Historic Site** ㊷, where the Vikings built a village a thousand years ago; there are reconstructions of the dwellings. Spend the night in 🏨 **St. Anthony** ㊸ or nearby.

On the east coast, the ferry docks at Argentia. Explore the Avalon Peninsula, beginning in 🏨 **St. John's** ①–⑭, where you should spend your first night. The next day visit **Cape Spear,** the most easterly point in North America, and the **Witless Bay Ecological Reserve** ⑮, where you

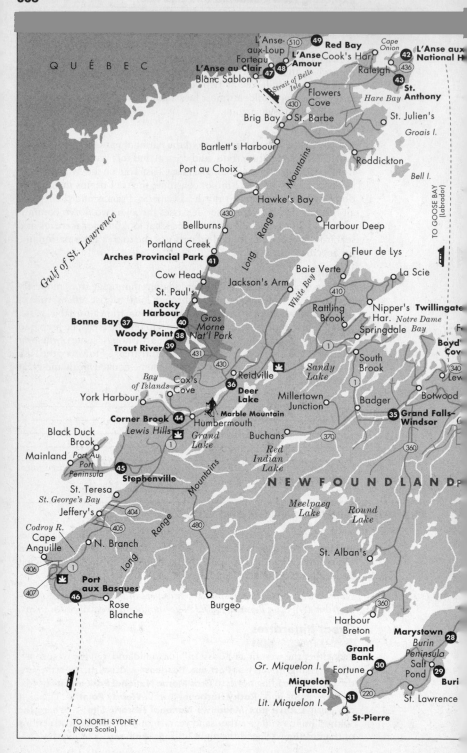

QUÉBEC

L'Anse-
aux-Loup **510** **49** **Red Bay**
Forteau **L'Anse** Cook's Har.
L'Anse au Clair **48** **Amour** Raleigh
47 **436**
Blanc Sablon Strait of Belle Isle
Flowers
Cove

Cape
Onion
L'Anse aux
National H
42

43 **St.**
Anthony

Hare Bay

St. Julien's

Groais I.

Brig Bay St. Barbe

430

Bartlett's Harbour

Roddickton

Bell I.

Port au Choix

Hawke's Bay

Mountains

Harbour Deep

TO GOOSE BAY
(Labrador)

Bellburns

430

Long

Fleur de Lys

Portland Creek

Arches Provincial Park
41

Range

Baie Verte

La Scie

Cow Head

Jackson's Arm

White Bay

St. Paul's

Rocky
Harbour

Bonne Bay **37**

40

Gros
Morne
Nat'l Park

Rattling
Brook

410

Nipper's **Twillingate**
Har. Notre Dame

Boyd'
Cov

Woody Point **38**

Springdale Bay

1

Trout River **39**

431

430

Reidville

South
Brook

1

340

Lew

Bay
of Islands Cox's
Cove

36

Deer
Lake

Sandy
Lake

Botwood

York Harbour

Millertown
Junction

Badger

Grand Falls-
Windsor
35

G

Corner Brook **44**

Lewis Hills

Marble Mountain

Humbermouth

Black Duck
Brook

Grand
Lake

Buchans

370

360

Mainland Port Au
Port
Peninsula

45

Stephenville

Red
Indian
Lake

N E W F O U N D L A N D P

St. Teresa

St. George's Bay

Jeffery's

404

Mountains

Meelpaeg
Lake

Round
Lake

Codroy R.
Cape
Anguille

N. Branch

405

Range

480

St. Alban's

406

1

Long

407

Port
aux Basques
46

Rose
Blanche

Burgeo

360

Harbour
Breton

Marystown
28

Burin
Peninsula

Grand
Bank

Salt
Pond

29

Buri

Gr. Miquelon I.

Fortune **30**

Miquelon
(France)

220

St. Lawrence

31

Lit. Miquelon I.

St-Pierre

TO NORTH SYDNEY
(Nova Scotia)

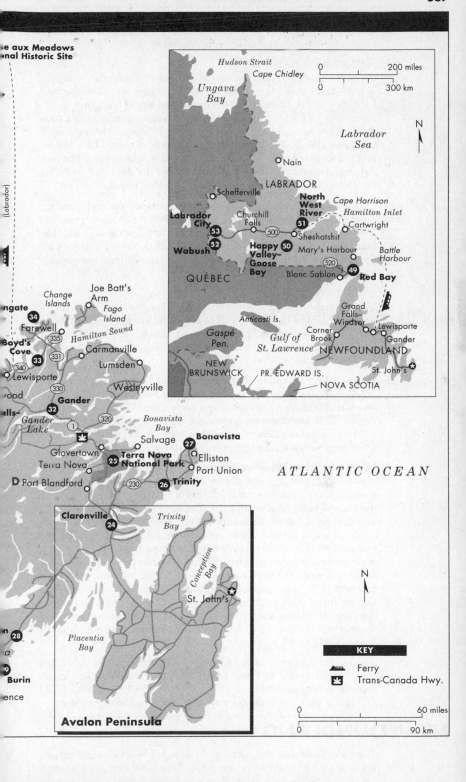

e aux Meadows
nal Historic Site

Hudson Strait
Cape Chidley

Ungava
Bay

0   200 miles
0   300 km

Labrador
Sea

N

Nain

LABRADOR

Schefferville

North
West
River

Cape Harrison
Hamilton Inlet

Labrador
City

Churchill
Falls

51

Cartwright

500

Sheshatshit

53

QUÉBEC

52

Wabush

Happy
Valley-
Goose
Bay

50

Mary's Harbour

Battle
Harbour

520

Blanc Sablon

49

Red Bay

Change
Islands

Joe Batt's
Arm

ngate

Fogo
Island

34

Farewell

335

Anticosti Is.

Grand
Falls–
Windsor

Lewisporte

Boyd's
Cove

Hamilton Sound

331

Carmanville

Gaspé
Pen.

Gulf of
St. Lawrence

Corner
Brook

Gander

33

340

Lumsden

NEWFOUNDLAND

wood

330

Wesleyville

NEW
BRUNSWICK

PR. EDWARD IS.

St. John's

Gander

32

NOVA SCOTIA

alls–

320

Gander
Lake

1

Bonavista
Bay

Salvage

Bonavista

27

Glovertown

Terra Nova
National Park

25

Elliston
Port Union

Terra Nova

Port Blandford

230

26

Trinity

D

Clarenville

24

Trinity
Bay

ATLANTIC OCEAN

N

Conception
Bay

St. John's

28

Placentia
Bay

KEY

Ferry

Burin

Trans-Canada Hwy.

ence

0   60 miles
0   90 km

Avalon Peninsula

can see whales, seabirds, and icebergs. Drive though **Placentia** ㉑ and spend your third day at ⛭ **Cape St. Mary's Ecological Reserve** ㉓, known for its gannets and dramatic coastal scenery.

IF YOU HAVE 6 DAYS

On Newfoundland's west coast, add southern Labrador to your trip. A ferry takes you from St. Barbe to Blanc Sablon on the Québec–Labrador border. Drive 96 km (60 mi) to **Red Bay** ㊾ to explore the remains of a 17th-century Basque whaling station; then head to **L'Anse Amour** ㊽ to see Canada's second-tallest lighthouse. Overnight at ⛭ **L'Anse au Clair** ㊼. Return through Gros Morne National Park and explore ⛭ **Corner Brook** ㊹, where you should stay overnight. The next day, travel west of **Stephenville** ㊺ to explore the Port au Port Peninsula, home of Newfoundland's French-speaking population.

On the east coast add ⛭ **Trinity** ㉖ to your must-see list, and spend the night there or in ⛭ **Clarenville** ㉔. The north shore of Conception Bay is home to many picturesque villages, including ⛭ **Cupids** ⑲ and **Harbour Grace** ⑳. Several half-day, full-day, and two-day excursions are possible from St. John's, and in each direction a different personality of the region unfolds.

IF YOU HAVE 9 DAYS

In addition to the places already mentioned on the west coast, take a drive into central Newfoundland and visit the lovely villages of Notre Dame Bay. Overnight in ⛭ **Twillingate** ㉞. Catch a ferry to ⛭ **Fogo** or the ⛭ **Change Islands.** Accommodations are available on both islands, but book ahead.

On the east coast add the Burin Peninsula and a trip to France—yes, France—to your itinerary. You can reach the French territory of ⛭ **St-Pierre and Miquelon** ㉛ by passenger ferry from Fortune. Explore romantic ⛭ **Grand Bank** ㉚, named for the famous fishing area just offshore, and climb Cook's Lookout in **Burin** ㉙, where Captain James Cook kept watch for smugglers from St-Pierre.

When to Tour Newfoundland and Labrador

Seasons can vary dramatically in Newfoundland and Labrador. In spring, icebergs float down from the north, and in late spring, fin, pilot, minke, and humpback whales arrive to hunt for food along the coast and stay until August. In summer, Newfoundland's bogs and meadows turn into a colorful riot of wildflowers and greenery, and the sea is dotted with boats and buoys marking traps and nets. Fall is a favored season: the weather is usually fine; hills and meadows are loaded with berries; and the woods are alive with moose, caribou, partridges, and rabbits. In winter, ski hills attract downhillers and snowboarders, and the forest trails hum with the sounds of snowmobiles and all-terrain vehicles taking anglers to lodges and lakes. Cross-country ski trails in provincial and national parks are oases of quiet populated by squirrels and birds.

The tourist season runs from June through September, when the province celebrates with festivals, fairs, concerts, plays, and crafts shows. The temperature hovers between 24°C (75°F) and 29°C (85°F) and gently cools off in the evening, providing a good night's sleep.

NEWFOUNDLAND

The rocky coasts and peninsulas of the island of Newfoundland present much dramatic beauty and many opportunities for exploring. Seaport and fishing towns such as St. John's and Grand Bank tell a fascinating story, and parks from Terra Nova National Park on the eastern side of the island to Gros Morne National Park on the west have impressive landscapes. The Avalon Peninsula includes the provincial capital of St. John's as well as the Cape Shore on the west side of the island. The Bonavista Peninsula and the Burin Peninsula as well as Notre Dame Bay have some intriguing sights, from Bonavista, associated with John Cabot's landing, to pretty towns such as Twillingate. The Great Northern Peninsula on the western side of Newfoundland holds a historic site with the remains of Viking sod houses. The west coast has Corner Brook, a good base for exploring the mountains, as well as farming and fishing communities.

St. John's

When Sir Humphrey Gilbert sailed into St. John's to establish British colonial rule for Queen Elizabeth in 1583, he found Spanish, French, and Portuguese fishermen actively working the harbor. As early as 1627, the merchants of Water Street—then known as the Lower Path—were doing a thriving business buying fish, selling goods, and supplying alcohol to soldiers and sailors. Today St. John's still encircles the snug punch-bowl harbor that helped establish its reputation.

This old seaport town (population 102,000), the province's capital, mixes English and Irish influences, Victorian architecture and modern convenience, and traditional music and rock and roll into a heady brew that finds expression in a lively arts scene and a relaxed pace—all in a setting that has the ocean on one side and unexpected greenery on the other.

Exploring St. John's

A walk downtown takes in many historic buildings, but a car is needed to explore farther-flung sights ranging from Cape Spear, south of St. John's, to parks and fishing villages.

A Good Walk

Begin at **Harbourside Park** ① on Water Street, where Gilbert planted the staff of England and claimed Newfoundland. When you leave, turn left on Water Street, right on Holloway Street, and then right onto **Duckworth Street** ②. The east end of this street is full of crafts shops and other stores. After walking east for five blocks, turn left onto Ordinance Street, just one of several streets that recall St. John's military past. Cross Military Road to **St. Thomas Anglican (Old Garrison) Church** ③, built in the 1830s as a place of worship for British soldiers.

Turn left as you leave St. Thomas and walk up King's Bridge Road. The first building on the left is **Commissariat House** ④, an officer's house restored to the style of the 1830s. North of Commissariat House, a shady lane on the left leads to the gardens of **Government House** ⑤. **Circular Road** ⑥, where the business elite moved after a fire destroyed much of the town in 1846, is across from the gardens in front of the house. Back on Military Road, cross Bannerman Road to the **Colonial Building** ⑦, the former seat of government and current home of the Provincial Archives. Walk west on Military Road until it becomes Harvey Road. The Roman Catholic **Basilica Cathedral of St. John the Baptist** ⑧ is on the right; you pass the Basilica Museum in the Bishop's Palace just before you get there.

Cross Harvey Road and turn left down Garrison Hill, so named because it once led to Fort Townshend, now home to fire and police stations. Cross Queen's Road and walk down Cathedral Street to Gower Street and the Gothic Revival **Anglican Cathedral of St. John the Baptist** ⑨. The entrance is on the west side on Church Hill. **Gower Street**

St. John's

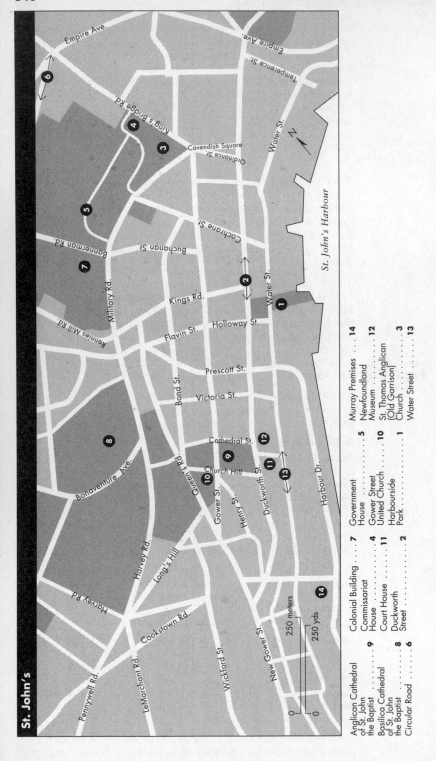

Empire Ave.

Temperance St.

Empire Ave.

King's Bridge Rd.

Cavendish Square

Ordinance St.

Water St.

St. John's Harbour

Cochrane St.

Bannerman Rd.

Buchanan St.

Water St.

Kings Rd.

Holloway St.

Military Rd.

Rennies Mill Rd.

Flavin St.

Prescott St.

Bond St.

Victoria St.

Cathedral St.

Church Hill

Duckworth St.

Queen's Rd.

Bonaventure Ave.

Gower St.

Henry St.

Harbour Dr.

Harvey Rd.

Long's Hill

Pennywell Rd.

Harvey Rd.

Cookstown Rd.

LeMarchant Rd.

Wickford St.

New Gower St.

Circular Road

250 meters

250 yds

0

0

United Church ⑩ is directly across from the cathedral on the west side of Church Hill. Continue to the bottom of Church Hill to see the Duckworth Street **Court House** ⑪, with its four turrets, each one different. Go east on Duckworth a few doors to the **Newfoundland Museum** ⑫, with exhibits on Newfoundland's natural and cultural history. Exit the museum and turn left; then go down the long set of steps to **Water Street** ⑬, one of the oldest commercial streets in North America. Turn right on Water Street to reach the last stop, the **Murray Premises** ⑭, a restored mercantile complex. It contains boutiques, a science center, offices, and—welcome after this walk—restaurants, a coffee bar, and a wine cellar.

TIMING

Downtown St. John's is compact but hilly. The walk avoids major uphill climbs. Expect to spend half a day visiting these sights, though this may vary depending on how much time you stay at each location. It's best undertaken from spring to fall.

Sights to See

❾ Anglican Cathedral of St. John the Baptist. A fine example of Gothic Revival architecture designed by Sir George Gilbert Scott, this church was first completed in the mid-1800s; it was rebuilt after the 1892 fire. Women of the parish operate a tea room in the crypt from 2:30–4:40 PM daily in summer. ⊠ *22 Church Hill,* ☎ *709/726–5677,* WEB *www.infonet.st-johns.nf.ca/cathedral.* ☞ *Free.* ☉ *Tours June–Sept., daily 10–5.*

❽ Basilica Cathedral of St. John the Baptist. This 1855 Roman Catholic cathedral in the Romanesque style has a commanding position above Military Road, overlooking the older section of the city and the harbor. A museum with vestments and religious objects is next door in the Bishop's Palace. ⊠ *200 Military Rd.,* ☎ *709/754–3660,* WEB *www.delweb.rcec.com.* ☞ *Museum $2.* ☉ *Museum June–Sept., weekdays 9–5.*

❻ Circular Road. The business elite of St. John's moved here after the devastating fire of 1846. The street contains some very fine Victorian houses and shade trees.

❼ Colonial Building. This columned building (erected 1847–50) was the seat of the Newfoundland government from the 1850s to 1960, when the legislature moved to the new Confederation Building in the north end of the city. The limestone for the building was imported from Cork, Ireland. The Colonial Building now houses the Provincial Archives, which are useful to anyone researching family or provincial history. ⊠ *Military and Bannerman Rds.,* ☎ *709/729–3065.* ☞ *Free.* ☉ *Weekdays 9–4:15, Wed. also 6:30 PM–9:45 PM.*

❹ Commissariat House. The residence and office of the British garrison's supply officer in the 1830s has been restored to reflect that era. Interpreters dress in period costume. ⊠ *King's Bridge Rd.,* ☎ *709/729–6730 or 709/729–0592.* ☞ *$2.50.* ☉ *Mid-June–early Oct., daily 10–5:30.*

⑪ Court House. The late-19th-century courthouse has an eccentric appearance: each of its four turrets is a different style. ⊠ *Duckworth St., bottom of Church Hill.*

❷ Duckworth Street. Once called the Upper Path, this has been St. John's "second street" for centuries. (Water Street has been the main street for just as long.) Stretching from the bottom of Signal Hill in the east to near City Hall in the west, Duckworth Street has restaurants, bars, antiques and crafts shops, and lawyers' offices. Lanes and stairways lead off the street down to Water Street and up to higher elevations.

⑤ Government House. This is the residence of the lieutenant governor, the Queen's representative in Newfoundland. According to popular myth, the moat around Government House was designed to keep out snakes, though there have never been snakes in Newfoundland. The house, so the story goes, was originally intended for the governor of a warmer colony, where serpents might be a problem. (In fact, the moat was actually designed to allow more light into the basement rooms.) The house, built in the 1830s, has a marvelous garden you can explore, but the building isn't open for tours. You can, however, enter the front porch and sign the guest book. Everyone who does so receives an invitation to the annual garden party held in early August. ✉ *Military Rd.,* ☎ *709/720–4494,* WEB *www.mun.ca/govhouse.* 🎟 *Garden free.* ☉ *Garden open daily.*

⑩ Gower Street United Church. This 1896 church has a redbrick facade, green turrets, 50 stained-glass windows, and a massive pipe organ. ✉ *Gower St. and Queen's Rd.,* ☎ *709/753–7286,* WEB *www.infonet. st-johns.nf.ca/providers/gowerunited.* 🎟 *Free.* ☉ *Daily; tours July–Aug., daily 2–5.*

❶ Harbourside Park. Here Sir Humphrey Gilbert claimed Newfoundland for Britain in 1583, much to the amusement of the French, Spanish, and Portuguese fishermen in port at the time. They thought him a fool, a judgment borne out a few days later when he ran his ship aground and drowned. This area, known as the Queen's Wharf, is where the harbor-pilot boat is docked. You can see boats moving around the harbor. ✉ *Water St. E.*

⑭ Murray Premises. One of the oldest buildings in St. John's, the Murray Premises dates from only 1846. The town was destroyed many times by fire, the last and worst in 1892. This restored warehouse now houses shops, offices, and restaurants. The **Newfoundland Science Centre** (☎ *709/754–0823*), open daily, with hands-on exhibits and special demonstrations, is within the Murray Premises; admission is $4.50. ✉ *Water St. and Harbour Dr., at Beck's Cove,* ☎ *709/754–0823,* WEB *www.sciencecentre.nf.ca.* ☉ *Weekdays 10–5, Sat. 10–6, Sun. noon–6.*

⑫ Newfoundland Museum. Three floors of displays focus on the province's cultural and natural history. There are also changing exhibits from the museum's collection. ✉ *285 Duckworth St.,* ☎ *709/729–0917,* WEB *www.nfmuseum.com.* 🎟 *$3.* ☉ *Mid-June–mid-Sept., daily 9:30–4:45; mid-Sept.–mid-June, Tues.–Fri. 9–4:45, Sat. 9:30–4:45, Sun. noon–4:45.*

❸ St. Thomas Anglican (Old Garrison) Church. English soldiers used to worship at this black wooden church, the oldest in the city, during the early and mid-1800s. ✉ *8 Military Rd.,* ☎ *709/576–6632.* 🎟 *Free.* ☉ *Tours June 24–Aug. 30, daily 9:30–5:30; call ahead for off-season hrs.*

⑬ Water Street. Originally called the Lower Path, Water Street has been the site of businesses since at least the 1620s. The older architecture recalls that of seaports in southwest England and Ireland.

A Good Drive

To explore attractions outside the St. John's downtown core, begin by taking Water Street west to its intersection with Route 11, which leads you to **Cape Spear National Historic Site,** 11 km (7 mi) south of St. John's. This is the easternmost point in North America—when you stand with your back to the ocean, the entire population of North America is west of you. It's also a good place to spot whales and drifting icebergs in spring and early summer.

On the drive back to St. John's, branch off to the left through **Maddox Cove** and **Petty Harbour,** two fishing villages so picture-perfect they have served as backdrops for a couple of Hollywood movies. Continue to Route 10, turn right, and head north to Waterford Bridge Road and **Bowring Park,** a traditional English-style park. Drive east through the Waterford Valley and along Water Street, Harbour Drive, and back to Water Street; turn left up Temperance Street and right again onto Duckworth Street, and then turn right to the east end of St. John's harbor and the **Battery,** a fishing village in the city. After exploring the Battery, turn right up Signal Hill Road and drive to the top, where **Cabot Tower** has a stunning view of the coastline and the city below. The **Signal Hill National Historic Site** interpretation center is also on this road, below the tower.

Heading back down the hill, turn right at the bottom onto Quidi Vidi Road and drive to its intersection with Forest Road. Turn right, drive to Cuckold's Cove Road, and continue on to **Quidi Vidi Battery,** an old French and British fort staffed by guides in period costume in summer. Return to Quidi Vidi Road, turn right, and drive through **Quidi Vidi,** another fishing village within the city. Caution: the road is very narrow here.

The final two stops on this drive are in C.A. Pippy Park in the city's north end. Take Prince Philip Drive to Allendale Road and turn north. The first turn on the left is Nagle's Place, which brings you to **The Fluvarium,** where you can view fish underwater through a large glass window. Continue north on Allendale Road to Mt. Scio Road. Turn left and head toward the native and alpine plants at **Memorial University Botanical Garden.**

TIMING

This drive goes beyond St. John's to Cape Spear, so plan to spend between a half day and a day if you want some time at each stop. Summer, when all the attractions are open, is the best time for this tour.

Sights to See

The Battery. This tiny fishing village perches precariously at the base of steep cliffs between hill and harbor. The narrow lanes snake around the houses, making this a good place to get out and walk.

Bowring Park. An expansive Victorian park west of downtown, Bowring resembles the famous city parks of London, after which it was modeled. Dotting the grounds are ponds and rustic bridges; the statue of Peter Pan just inside the east gate was cast from the same mold as the one in Kensington Park in London. The wealthy Bowring family donated the park to the city in 1911. ⊠ *Waterford Bridge Rd.,* ☏ *709/576–6134.*

Cabot Tower. This tower at the summit of Signal Hill was constructed in 1897 to commemorate the 400th anniversary of Cabot's landing in Newfoundland. The ride here along Signal Hall Road affords fine harbor and city views, as does the tower. ⊠ *Signal Hill Rd.,* ☏ *709/772–5367,* WEB *www.parkscanada.pch.gc.ca/parks/newfoundland.* ⌂ *Free.* ☉ *Early Sept.–mid-June, daily 9–5; mid-June–early Sept., daily 8:30–4:30; guides available on summer weekends.*

★ **Cape Spear National Historic Site.** At the easternmost point of land on the continent, songbirds begin their chirping in the dim light of dawn, and whales (in early summer) feed directly below the cliffs, providing an unforgettable start to the day. From April through July, you may well see icebergs floating by. **Cape Spear Lighthouse,** Newfoundland's oldest such beacon, has been lovingly restored to its original form and furnishings. ⊠ *Rte. 11,* ☎ *709/772–5367,* WEB *www.parkscanada.pch.gc.ca/ newfoundland.* ⊡ *Site free; lighthouse $2.50.* ⊙ *Site, daily 24 hrs; lighthouse mid-May–mid-Oct., daily 10–6:30.*

The Fluvarium. Underwater windows look onto a brook at the only public facility of its kind in North America. In season you can observe spawning brown and brook trout in their natural habitat. Feeding time for the fish, frogs, and eels is 4 PM daily. ⊠ *Nagles Pl., C. A. Pippy Park,* ☎ *709/754–3474,* WEB *www.fluvarium.nf.net.* ⊡ *$4.* ⊙ *Summer, daily 9–5; call ahead for other seasons.*

Maddox Cove and Petty Harbour. These picturesque fishing villages are next to each other along the coast between Cape Spear and Route 10. The wharves and sturdy seaside sheds, especially those in Petty Harbour, harken back to a time not long ago when the fishery was paramount in the economy and lives of the residents. These villages have been the setting for several Hollywood movies.

Memorial University Botanical Garden. This 110-acre garden and natural area at Oxen Pond in C. A. Pippy Park has four pleasant walking trails and many gardens, including rock gardens and scree, a Newfoundland historic-plants bed, peat and woodland beds, an alpine house, an herb wall, and native plant collections. You can see scores of varieties of rhododendron here, as well as many kinds of butterflies and the rare hummingbird moth. Guided walks are available with advance notice. ⊠ *306 Mt. Scio Rd.,* ☎ *709/737–8590,* WEB *www.mun.ca/ botgarden.* ⊡ *$2.* ⊙ *May–Nov., daily 10–5.*

Quidi Vidi. No one knows the origin of this fishing village's name. It's one of the oldest parts of St. John's. The town is best explored on foot as the roads are narrow and make driving difficult. In spring, the inlet, known as the Gut, is a good place to catch sea-run brown trout.

Quidi Vidi Battery. This small redoubt has been restored to the way it appeared in 1812. Costumed interpreters tell you about the hard, unromantic life of a soldier of the empire. ⊠ *Off Cuckold's Cove Rd.,* ☎ *709/729–2977 or 709/729–0592.* ⊡ *$2.50.* ⊙ *Mid-June–early Oct., daily 10–5:30.*

★ ⓒ **Signal Hill National Historic Site.** In spite of its height, Signal Hill was difficult to defend: throughout the 1600s and 1700s it changed hands with every attacking French, English, and Dutch force. The French and British fought the last battle of the Seven Years' War here in 1762. A wooden palisade encircles the summit of the hill, indicating the boundaries of the old fortifications. En route to the hill is the **Park Interpretation Centre,** with exhibits describing St. John's history. In July and August, cadets in 19th-century British uniform perform a tattoo of military drills and music. In 1901 Guglielmo Marconi received the first transatlantic wire transmission near **Cabot Tower,** at the top of Signal Hill. From the top of the hill it's a 500-ft drop to the narrow harbor entrance below; views are excellent. ⊠ *Signal Hill Rd.,* ☎ *709/ 772–5367,* WEB *www.parkscanada.pch.gc.ca.* ⊡ *Site free; visitor center $2.50 mid-May–mid-Oct., free rest of year.* ⊙ *Site daily 24 hrs. Center mid-June–Labor Day, daily 8:30–8; Labor Day–mid-June, daily 8:30– 4:30.*

Dining and Lodging

$$–$$$ ✕ **Bianca's.** Modern paintings lend this bright eatery the air of an art gallery. The menu changes seasonally but emphasizes fish dishes such as salmon marinated in Scotch whisky. There's a cigar room in the back. ⊠ *171 Water St.,* ☎ *709/726–9016. AE, DC, MC, V. Closed Sun.*

$$–$$$ ✕ **The Cellar.** This restaurant in a historic building on the waterfront
★ gets rave reviews for innovative Continental cuisine that uses the best
local ingredients. Menu selections include blackened fish dishes and
tiramisu for dessert. ⊠ *Baird's Cove, between Harbour and Water Sts.,*
☎ *709/579–8900. Reservations essential. AE, MC, V.*

$$–$$$ ✕ **Django's.** The menu at Django's is neither hip nor adventurous, but
the dishes are well made and satisfying. The lunch menu includes pastas, salads, and sandwiches; dinner fare consists mostly of chicken,
seafood, and steak dishes. ⊠ *184 Duckworth St.,* ☎ *709/738–4115.
AE, DC, MC, V. Closed Sun. No lunch Sat.*

$$–$$$ ✕ **Hungry Fishermen.** Salmon, scallops, halibut, mussels, cod, and
shrimp top the menu here. If you're not a fish eater, try the veal,
chicken, or five-onion soup. This restaurant in a historic 19th-century
building overlooking a courtyard has great sauces; desserts change daily
and are homemade. ⊠ *Murray Premises, 5 Beck's Cove, off Water St.,*
☎ *709/726–5790. AE, DC, MC, V.*

$$–$$$ ✕ **Margaritz Restaurant.** The fish dishes, and particularly the black-
ened salmon, are good choices at this pleasant restaurant. Other
seafood dishes include bouillabaisse; jambalaya with shrimp, mussels,
and scallops; and an appetizer of smoked-salmon pâté. You can also
order steak, chicken, lamb, and pork dishes. Margaritz has separate
levels for smokers and nonsmokers. ⊠ *188 Duckworth St.,* ☎ *709/
726–3885. AE, DC, MC, V. Closed Sun.*

$–$$$ ✕ **Chez Briann.** Pâtés, crêpes, and other French standards are served
on the second floor of a downtown Victorian townhouse. The dark
stained wood trim is well-matched by subdued decor. Heavier dishes
include scallops and garlic sautéed in olive oil and served over pasta,
medallions of lamb stuffed with spinach and feta, and several steak dishes.
⊠ *290 Duckworth St.,* ☎ *709/579–0096. AE, DC, MC, V. No lunch
weekends.*

$ ✕ **The Big R.** A fire and changes in ownership haven't dampened the
popularity of this fish-and-chips place, which draws diners from all walks
of life. Be warned: lots of schoolkids eat here at lunchtime, and it can
be noisy. ⊠ *69 Harvey Rd.,* ☎ *709/722–2256. V.*

$ ✕ **Ches's.** This fish-and-chips restaurant, which has been around since
the 1950s, caters to a steady stream of customers from noon until well
after midnight. They come from all walks of life—politicians, stu-
dents, policemen—often with a nodding acquaintance of each other,
and all devoted to the cult of "fee and chee." The owner keeps the bat-
ter recipe locked in a safe. It's strictly laminated tabletops, booths, and
plastic chairs, but the fish is hot and fresh. ⊠ *9 Freshwater Rd.,* ☎
709/722–4083. MC, V.

$ ✕ **International Flavours.** Don't be fooled by the unvarnished walls and
six small tables: the place may not look like much, but the curry with
chick peas—the one and only item on the menu—is delicious. The only
variety comes from your ordering the dish as hot or mild as you wish.
You can also buy Indian spices to use in your own curries at home. ⊠
124 Duckworth St., ☎ *709/738–4636. MC, V. Closed Sun.*

$ ✕ **Pasta Plus Café.** As the name implies, pasta is a popular item on the
menu; the local chain also serves curries, salads, and pizza. Try one of
the curry dishes, served with banana–date chutney and rice, or the pasta
stuffed with seasonally available seafood. Some of the locations have
somewhat dark lighting and decor. ⊠ *233 Duckworth St.,* ☎ *709/739–
6676;* ⊠ *Avalon Mall, Thorburn Rd.,* ☎ *709/722–6006;* ⊠ *Village
Shopping Centre, Topsail Rd.,* ☎ *709/368–3481;* ⊠ *Churchill Sq., Eliz-
abeth Ave.,* ☎ *709/739–5818. AE, DC, MC, V.*

$ ✕ **Velma's Place.** Velma's is the place to go downtown for traditional
Newfoundland fare such as fish and brewis (bread and fish soaked in
water and boiled) and Jigg's dinner (boiled beef served with potatoes,

carrots, cabbage, and turnips). The service here is friendly, and the maritime decor tastefully transcends the usual lobster-pot kitsch. ⊠ *264 Water St.,* ☎ *709/576–2264. AE, DC, MC, V.*

$$–$$$$ ✕⌷ **Delta St. John's.** Rooms in this convention hotel in downtown St. John's overlook the harbor and the city. Rooms are standard, and have temperature control, mini-bars, and coffeemakers. Deluxe and business-zone rooms have in-room fax machines and data ports.The restaurant, Portos, serves a delightful but pricey caribou dish in addition to Continental cuisine. ⊠ *120 New Gower St., A1C 6K4,* ☎ *709/739–6404 or 800/563–3838,* FAX *709/570–1622,* WEB *www.deltahotels.com. 276 rooms, 9 suites. 2 restaurants, bar, air-conditioning, business services, convention center, meeting rooms, car rental. AE, DC, MC, V.*

$$–$$$$ ✕⌷ **Fairmont Newfoundland.** St. John's residents gather at the restau-
★ rants of this comfortable modern hotel for special occasions. The hotel is noted for charming rooms that overlook the harbor, an airy atrium restaurant with live piano music, Sunday and evening buffets, and the fine cuisine of the Cabot Club. ⊠ *Cavendish Sq., Box 5637, A1C 5W8,* ☎ *709/758–8164,* FAX *709/576–0544,* WEB *www.fairmont.com. 301 rooms, 14 suites. 2 restaurants, bar, minibars, no-smoking floor, room service, indoor pool, hair salon, business services, meeting rooms, free parking. AE, DC, MC, V.*

$$–$$$ ⌷ **Holiday Inn.** The surprise at this chain hotel is the location: walking trails meander around small lakes and link into the Grand Concourse. C. A. Pippy Park is directly across the street. East Side Marios serves Italian food and burgers. ⊠ *180 Portugal Cove Rd., A1B 2N2,* ☎ *709/ 722–0506,* FAX *709/722–9756,* WEB *www.holidayinnstjohns.com. 250 rooms. Restaurant, bar, in-room data ports, no-smoking rooms, pool, gym, business services, meeting rooms, free parking. AE, DC, MC, V.*

$–$$$ ⌷ **Compton House.** A charming historic residence in the west end of
★ the city, the Victorian inn is professionally run and beautifully decorated. Twelve-foot ceilings and wide halls give the place a majestic feeling, and rooms done in pastels and chintzes add an air of coziness. Suites have fireplaces and whirlpools. ⊠ *26 Waterford Bridge Rd., A1E 1C6,* ☎ *709/739–5789,* FAX *709/738–1770,* WEB *www3.nf.sympatico.ca/comptonhouse. 5 rooms, 5 suites. In-room data ports, no-smoking room, free parking. AE, DC, MC, V.*

$–$$$ ⌷ **Waterford Manor.** The Queen Anne–style inn on the river in leafy Waterford Valley has won a heritage restoration award. Waterford Manor, or The Pink House, as it was originally known because of the color of the exterior, has deep moldings, an intricately carved wooden staircase, and the original colors of the house. The King Arthur Suite has a king-size bed, a fireplace, and a double Jacuzzi. The inn is within a few minutes' drive of Bowring Park and the downtown area. A full breakfast is included in the room rate. ⊠ *185 Waterford Bridge Rd., A1E 1C7,* ☎ *709/754–4139,* FAX *709/754–4155,* WEB *www.waterfordmanor.nf.ca. 4 rooms, 3 suites. Lounge, room service, free parking. AE, MC, V. BP.*

$–$$$ ⌷ **Winterholme Heritage Inn.** The National Historic Site in the center of old St. John's is a movie star: the gorgeous dark-wood-paneled interiors were prominently featured in the 1999 film *The Divine Ryans.* Some rooms in this Queen Anne–style inn have working fireplaces. ⊠ *79 Rennies Mill Rd., A1C 3R1,* ☎ *709/739–7979 or 800/599–7829,* FAX *709/753–9411,* WEB *www.winterholme.nf.ca. 11 suites. Room service, free parking. AE, DC, MC, V. CP.*

$$ ⌷ **Quality Hotel Harbour Front.** Like other properties in the chain, this harbor-front hotel has clean, comfortable rooms at reasonable prices. The restaurant, Rumpelstiltskins, has a splendid view and an unpretentious menu. ⊠ *Hill O'Chips, A1C 6B1,* ☎ *709/754–7788,* FAX *709/ 754–5209,* WEB *www.choicehotels.ca/cn246. 162 rooms. Restaurant, no-smoking rooms, meeting rooms. AE, DC, MC, V.*

$-$$ ⌂ **The Battery Hotel and Suites.** This hotel refers to itself as "the inn with the view" with good reason: situated halfway up Signal Hill, the Battery offers an unequaled view of the harbor and downtown St. John's. Everything else about the hotel is pretty ordinary. Not all rooms have views, so make sure you request one up front. ✉ *100 Signal Hill Rd., A1A 1B3,* ☎ *709/576–0040 or 800/563–8181,* ꜰᴀˣ *709/576–6943,* ᴡᴇʙ *www.batteryhotel.com. 86 rooms, 40 suites. Restaurant, bar, indoor pool, sauna, meeting rooms, travel services. MC, V.*

$-$$ ⌂ **Prescott Inn.** Local artwork decorates the walls of this house, one
★ of the city's most popular B&Bs. The inn has been modernized, tastefully blending the new and the old. It's central to shops and downtown attractions. Room rates include a full breakfast. ✉ *17–21 Military Rd., A1C 2C3,* ☎ *709/753–7733 or 888/263–3786,* ꜰᴀˣ *709/753–6036,* ᴡᴇʙ *www.prescottinn.nf.ca. 8 rooms, 14 suites. Kitchenettes (some), no-smoking rooms, travel services, car rental. AE, DC, MC, V. BP.*

$ ⌂ **Airport Plaza Hotel.** A half mile from the airport, this hotel offers free shuttle service to the airport and downtown. Each of the four floors has its own color scheme, and the small rooms, some of which have balconies, are decorated with textured wall coverings in soft pastels. Although refurbished in 1996, the hotel still lacks an elevator. ✉ *106 Airport Rd., A1A 5B2,* ☎ *709/753–3500 or 800/563–2489,* ꜰᴀˣ *709/ 753–3711,* ᴡᴇʙ *www.cityhotels.ca. 98 rooms, 2 suites. Restaurant, bar, room service, coin laundry, business services, meeting rooms, airport shuttle, free parking. AE, DC, MC, V.*

$ ⌂ **A Gower Street House.** Now a B&B, the gracious former home of the late photographer Elsie Holloway has been designated by the Newfoundland Historic Trust as a point of interest. It's an ideal setting for paintings by prominent local artists. The location is within walking distance of the city's main attractions. A full breakfast is included in the rate. ✉ *180 Gower St., A1C 1P9,* ☎ ꜰᴀˣ *709/754–0047,* ☎ *800/563– 3959,* ᴡᴇʙ *www.bbcanada.com/826. 4 rooms. No-smoking room, room service. AE, MC, V. BP.*

Nightlife and the Arts

Whether it's music, theater, the visual arts, literature, or film, St. John's has tremendous stylistic variety and vitality for such a small population. Theater settings include traditional spaces, courtyards, and the dramatic coastline. The best-known music is Celtic-inspired traditional and traditional rock.

The Arts

The Arts and Culture Centre (✉ Allandale Rd., ☎ 709/729–3650) houses a 1,000-seat main theater, a library, and an art gallery that displays contemporary Canadian art. The theater hosts musical and theatrical events from September through June; the library and gallery are open year-round.

The **Resource Centre for the Arts** (✉ LSPU Hall, 3 Victoria St., ☎ 709/ 753–4531) is an innovative theater with professional main-stage and experimental second-space productions year-round.

The **Ship Inn** (✉ Solomon's La., between Duckworth and Water Sts., ☎ 709/753–3870) serves as the local arts watering hole. Nighttime performances range from traditional music to flamenco dancing.

The **Newfoundland and Labrador Folk Festival** (☎ 709/576–8508, ᴡᴇʙ www.moonmusic.nfld.com/sjfac), held in St. John's in early August, is the province's best-known traditional music festival.

Nightlife

St. John's well-deserved reputation as a party town has been several hundred years in the making. **Erin's Pub** (✉ 186 Water St., ☎ 709/722–1916) is famous for Irish music. The **Fat Cat** (✉ 5 George St., ☎ 709/722–6561) is the city's blues headquarters. **George Street** downtown has dozens of pubs and restaurants; seasonal open-air concerts are held here as well.

Outdoor Activities and Sports

Golf

Neither high winds nor unforgiving temperatures can keep golfers off the links in St. John's. If you want to play, call several days in advance to book a tee time. The par-71, 18-hole Admiral's Green and the par-35, 9-hole Captain's Hill are two adjacent public courses in **C.A. Pippy Park** (✉ 290–292 Nagle's Hill, ☎ 709/753–7110) that overlook St. John's. **Clovelley** (✉ off Stavanger Dr., ☎ 709/722–7170) is a par-72, 18-hole course in the east end of St. John's. **The Woods** (✉ off Route 2 in the city's west end, ☎ 709/229–5444) has wide, forgiving fairways on its 18-hole, par-70 layout. It caters to players of moderate skill.

Scuba Diving

The ocean around Newfoundland and Labrador rivals the Caribbean in clarity, if not temperature. There are thousands of known shipwreck sites and a wealth of sea life, plus, for the truly daring, the possibility of seeing the bottom of an iceberg. **RockWater Adventures** (✉ 50 Pippy Pl., ☎ 709/738–6353 or 888/512–2227, WEB www.rockwater.nf.ca) organizes classes and excursions. One popular dive takes you to see wrecks of ships sunk by German U-boats during World War II off Bell Island in Conception Bay. Boats leave from the Foxtrap Marina in Conception Bay South.

Sea Kayaking

One of the best ways to explore the coastline is by sea kayaking, which lets you visit sea caves and otherwise inaccessible beaches. There's also a very good chance you'll see whales, icebergs, and seabirds. **Whitecap Adventures** (✉ 116 Park Ave., Mount Pearl, ☎ 709/726–9283, WEB www.whitecapadventures.com) conducts half- and full-day sea-kayaking trips.

Walking

With a well-developed marked trail system that crisscrosses the city, St. John's is a walker's dream. The **Grand Concourse** (☎ 709/737–1077) covers more than 100 km (62 mi). Some trails traverse river valleys, parks, and other open areas, while others are sidewalk routes. Well-maintained trails encircle several lakes, including Long Pond and Quidi Vidi Lake, both of which are great for bird-watching. Maps are available at tourist information centers and many hotels.

Whale-Watching

The east coast of Newfoundland, including the area around St. John's, provides spectacular whale-watching opportunities with up to 22 species of dolphins and whales visible along the coast. Huge humpback whales weighing up to 30 tons come close to shore to feed in late spring and early summer. You may be able to spot icebergs and large flocks of nesting seabirds in addition to whales on many boat tours. **Adventure Tours** (☎ 709/726–5000 or 800/779–4253, WEB www.nfld.com/scademia) operates the tour boat *Scademia* from St. John's harbor. **Dee Jay Charters** (☎ 709/753–8687, WEB www.wordplay.com/deejay) takes passengers to Cape Spear on a 42-foot Cape Islander. **J & B Schooner Tours** (☎ 709/753–7245, WEB www.schoonertours.com) operates a 62-foot schooner with bar service. **Morissey's Boat Tours** (☎ 709/748–5222, WEB www.atyp.com/morisseys) conducts whale-watching excursions.

Shopping

Antiques

Murray's Antiques (✉ 414 Blackmarsh Rd., ☎ 709/579–7344) is renowned for silver, china, and fine mahogany and walnut furniture.

Polyanna Art and Antique Gallery (⊠ 214 Duckworth St., ☎ 709/726–0936) carries antiques as well as paintings and photographs.

Art Galleries

New shows by prominent and up-and-coming artists can sell out quickly. Painters such as Barbara Pratt Wangersky typify the popularity of the new generation. The art of native peoples, especially carvings from Labrador, is also a hot item. The **Art Gallery of Newfoundland and Labrador** (⊠ Allandale Rd. and Prince Philip Dr., ☎ 709/737–8209), the province's largest public gallery, exhibits historical and contemporary Canadian arts and crafts with an emphasis on local artists and artisans. It's closed Monday. **Christina Parker Fine Art** (⊠ 7 Plank Rd., ☎ 709/753–0580) represents local and national artists in all mediums, including painting, sculpture, drawing, and prints. **David Ariss Fine Art** (⊠ 191 Water St., ☎ 709/579–4941) carries a wide variety of local painters, plus Inuit art from Labrador. **Eastern Edge Gallery** (Clift's-Baird's Cove at Harbour Dr., ☎ 709/739–1882) exhibits the works of emerging artists. **Holloway Heights Galleria** (14 Holloway St., off Duckworth St., ☎ 709/722–3777) is a small gallery that carries oils and watercolors depicting the St. John's area. **The Lane Gallery** (⊠ Hotel Newfoundland, 1st floor, Cavendish Sq., ☎ 709/753–8946) features seascapes and other works by photographer Don Lane.

Books

The **Newfoundland Bookstore** (⊠ 100 Water St., ☎ 709/722–5830) specializes in local publishers.

Handicrafts

Crafts stores display traditional patterns and techniques, modern interpretations of traditional favorites, and some bold experimentation. The **Cod Jigger** (⊠ 245 Duckworth St., ☎ 709/726–7422) carries handmade woolen sweaters and mittens as well as Newfoundland's unique Grenfell parkas. The **Craft Council Shop** (⊠ 59 Duckworth St., ☎ 709/753–2749) displays the work of local producers and showcases some innovative designs. The **Newfoundland Weavery** (⊠ 177 Water St., ☎ 709/753–0496) sells rugs, prints, lamps, books, crafts, and other gift items. **NONIA** (Newfoundland Outport Nurses Industrial Association; ⊠ 286 Water St., ☎ 709/753–8062) was founded in 1920 to give women in the outports a way to earn money to support nursing services in these remote communities. Homespun wool was used to create exquisite clothing. Today the shop continues to sell these fine homespun articles as well as lighter, more modern handmade items. The **Salt Box** (⊠ 194 Duckworth St., ☎ 709/753–0622) carries local crafts and specializes in pottery. **Wild Things** (124 Water St., ☎ 709/722–3123) sells nature-themed crafts and jewelry.

Music

Fred's Records (⊠ 198 Duckworth St., ☎ 709/753–9191) has the best selection of local recordings, as well as other music.

Avalon Peninsula

On the southern half of the peninsula, small Irish hamlets are separated by large tracts of wilderness. You can travel part of the peninsula's southern coast in one or two days, depending on how much time you have. Quaint towns line Route 10, and the natural sights are beautiful. La Manche and Chance Cove—both abandoned communities turned provincial parks—attest to the region's bounty of natural resources. At the intersection of Routes 90 and 91, in Salmonier, you can either head north toward Salmonier Nature Park and on to the towns on Conception Bay, or head west and then south to Route 100

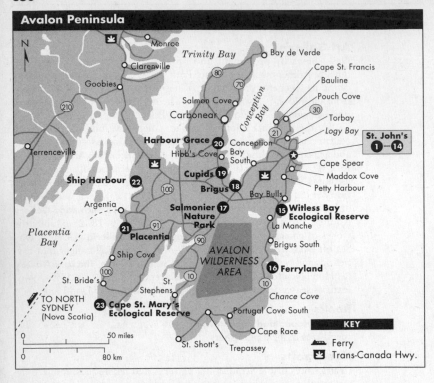

Avalon Peninsula

N

Monroe

Trinity Bay

Bay de Verde

Clarenville

Cape St. Francis

Goobies

Bauline

210

Salmon Cove

Pouch Cove

80

70

Carbonear

Conception Bay

30

Torbay

Harbour Grace 20

Conception Bay South

21

Logy Bay

St. John's 1 – 14

Hibb's Cove

Terrenceville

Cape Spear

Cupids 19

Maddox Cove

Ship Harbour 22

Brigus 18

Petty Harbour

100

Bay Bulls

Argentia

Salmonier Nature Park 17

Witless Bay Ecological Reserve 15

La Manche

Placentia

91

Brigus South

Placentia Bay

Placentia 21

90

Ship Cove

AVALON WILDERNESS AREA

100

St. Stephens

10

Ferryland 16

St. Bride's

Chance Cove

TO NORTH SYDNEY (Nova Scotia)

10

Cape St. Mary's Ecological Reserve 23

Portugal Cove South

St. Shott's

Cape Race

Trepassey

KEY

0 50 miles

0 80 km

Ferry

Trans-Canada Hwy.

to Cape St. Mary's Ecological Reserve. Each option takes about three hours. On the former route, stop in Harbour Grace; if you plan to travel on to Bay de Verde, at the northern tip of the peninsula, and down the other side of the peninsula on Route 80 along Trinity Bay, consider overnighting in the Harbour Grace–Carbonear area. Otherwise turn around and follow the same route back to Route 1.

Witless Bay Ecological Reserve

15 *29 km (18 mi) south of St. John's.*

Sometimes referred to as the Serengeti of the northwest Atlantic, the reserve is the summer home of millions of seabirds—puffins, murres, kittiwakes, razorbills, and guillemots—that nest on the reserve's four islands. The birds, and the humpback and minke whales that tarry here before continuing north to the summer grounds in the Arctic, feed on the billions of capelin that swarm inshore to spawn. The reserve is also an excellent place to see icebergs in late spring and early summer. The best views of birds and icebergs are from tour boats that operate here. ⊠ Rte. 10, ☎ 709/729–2424, WEB www.gov.nf.ca/parks&reserves. ⊠ Free. ⊘ Daily 24 hrs.

Outdoor Activities and Sports

Captain Murphy's Seabird and Whales Tours (☎ 709/334–2002 or 888/783–3467, WEB www.witlessbay.com) conducts interpretive wildlife tours. From mid-May to mid-October, **Gatherall's Puffin and Whale Watch** (☎ 709/334–2887 or 800/419–4253, WEB www.gatheralls.com) has six trips per day for viewing wildlife in the reserve. Shuttle service is available from St. John's hotels. **O'Brien's Bird Island Charters** (☎ 709/753–4850 or 877/639–4253, WEB www.netfx.ca/obriens) offers popular two-hour excursions featuring whale-, iceberg-, and seabird-watching.

En Route Although there are many pretty hamlets along the way from Witless Bay to Ferryland on Route 10, **La Manche,** accessible only on foot, and **Brigus South** have especially attractive settings and strong traditional flavors. La Manche is an abandoned fishing community between Tors Cove and Cape Broyle. The former residents moved to other towns after a storm destroyed part of the community in 1966. Brigus South, between Witless Bay and Cape Broyle, is a fishing village whose name is derived from an old French word for intrigue.

Ferryland

⑯ *43½ km (27 mi) south of Witless Bay Ecological Reserve.*

This seaside town has a long history, some of which is described in its small community museum. The major ongoing **Colony of Avalon archaeological dig** at Ferryland has uncovered the early 17th-century colony of Lord Baltimore, who abandoned the area after a decade for the warmer climes of Maryland. The site includes an archaeology laboratory and an exhibit center. Guided tours are available. ⊠ *Rte. 10, The Pool,* ☎ *709/432–3200 or 877/326–5669,* 🖳 *www.heritage.nf.ca/avalon.* 🖼 *$3.* ☉ *June–Oct., daily 9–7.*

Outdoor Activities and Sports

Diving excursions led by **Chance Cove Ventures** (☎ 709/363–2257, 🖳 www.divingtours.com) take you to explore the fascinating undersea world of shipwrecks along the southern coast of Avalon. There are more than 300 known wrecks here.

En Route In springtime, between Chance Cove and Portugal Cove South, in a stretch of land about 58 km (36 mi) long, hundreds of **caribou** and their calves gather on the barrens near Route 10. They migrate to this southern area from farther north in the Avalon Wilderness Area.

Salmonier Nature Park

⑰ *88 km (55 mi) from Ferryland, 14½ km (9 mi) north of the intersection of Rtes. 90 and 91.*

Many indigenous animal species, including moose, caribou, lynx, and otters, can be seen at this 3,000-acre wilderness reserve area. An enclosed 100-acre exhibit allows up-close viewing. ⊠ *Salmonier Line, Rte. 90,* ☎ *709/229–7189,* 🖳 *www.gov.nf.ca/snp.* 🖼 *Free.* ☉ *Early June–early Sept., daily noon–6; early Sept.–mid-Oct., daily 10–4.*

En Route From Salmonier Nature Park to Brigus, take Route 90, which passes through the scenic **Hawke Hills** before meeting up with the Trans-Canada Highway (Route 1). This reserve is the best representative of alpine barrens in Canada east of the Rockies. Turn off at Holyrood Junction (Route 62) and follow Route 70, which skirts Conception Bay.

Brigus

⑱ *19 km (12 mi) north of intersection of Rtes. 1 and 70.*

This beautiful village on Conception Bay has a wonderful public garden, winding lanes, and a teahouse. Brigus is best known as the birthplace of Captain Bob Bartlett, the famed Arctic explorer who accompanied Admiral Peary on polar expeditions during the first decade of the 20th century. **Hawthorne Cottage,** Captain Bartlett's home, is one of the few surviving examples of the picturesque cottage style, with a veranda decorated with ornamental wooden fretwork. It dates from 1830 and is a National Historic Site. ⊠ *Irishtown Rd.,* ☎ *709/ 753–9262; 709/528–4004 in summer.* 🖼 *$2.50.* ☉ *Mid-May–late June* *and early Sept.– late Oct., daily 10–6; late June–early Sept., daily 10–8; call for an appointment off-season.*

Ye Old Stone Barn Museum (the John L. Leamon Museum) displays historic town photos and artifacts, especially objects relating to its connection with the fishery. ✉ *4 Magistrate's Hill,* ☎ *709/528–3391.* 🎫 *$1.* ☉ *Mid-June–early Sept., daily 11–6.*

Lodging

$ 🏨 **Captain Bob's Berth and Breakfast.** As the name suggests, this B&B, named for the town's most famous son, is decorated with nautical touches. Rooms have brightly colored patterned quilts, brass bedsteads, and lace-trimmed curtains. Guests can browse through books on Newfoundland in the library. A full breakfast is included in the room rate. ✉ *6 Forge Rd., Box 2361, A1W 1C2,* ☎ *709/685–5438,* 📠 *709/834–6000. 3 rooms. AE, MC, V. Closed Oct.–May. BP.*

Cupids

⑲ *5 km (3 mi) north of Brigus.*

Cupids is the oldest English colony in Canada, founded in 1610 by John Guy, to whom the town erected a monument in 1910. Nearby flies a replica of the enormous Union Jack that flew during the tercentenary. When the wind snaps the flag, you can hear it half a mile away. In 1995 archaeologists began unearthing the long-lost site of the original colony here, and some of the recovered artifacts—including pots, pipes, and trade beads—are on display in the community museum, **Cupids Archaeological Site.** ✉ *Main Rd.,* ☎ *709/596–1906.* 🎫 *$2.* ☉ *July–Sept., weekdays 8:30–4:30.*

Lodging

$ 🏨 **Guy View Manor.** This nonsmoking ranch house is in an area near some good hiking and walking trails. A TV and telephone are available in the common room. ✉ *First Colony Dr., A0A 2B0,* ☎ 📠 *709/528–4248,* ☎ *800/877–4248. 4 rooms. No-smoking rooms. V. CP.*

Harbour Grace

⑳ *21 km (13 mi) north of Cupids.*

Harbour Grace, once the headquarters of 17th-century pirate Peter Easton, was a major commercial town in the 18th and 19th centuries. Beginning in 1919, the town was the departure point for many attempts to fly the Atlantic. Amelia Earhart left Harbour Grace in 1932 to become the first woman to fly solo across the Atlantic. The town has two fine churches and several registered historic houses.

Lodging

$ 🏨 **Rothesay House Inn Bed & Breakfast.** This Queen Anne–style B&B was built in the early 20th century. The front of the house has a lovely porch, and the greens, yellows, and reds of the exterior are echoed in the room colors. Rooms have brass-trimmed wooden beds, wainscotting, and antiques. The hosts recommend and arrange sightseeing, whale-watching, and boat tours. A full breakfast is included in the room rate. ✉ *34 Water St., A0A 2M0,* ☎ *709/596–2268,* 📠 *709/596–0317,* 🌐 *www.rothesay.com. 4 rooms. Dining room, no-smoking room, kennel. MC, V. BP.*

Route 100: The Cape Shore

This area is the site of an outstanding seabird colony at Cape St. Mary's. It's also culturally and historically rich. The French settlers had their capital here in Placentia. Irish influence is also strong here, in music and manner. You can reach the Cape Shore on the western side of the Avalon Peninsula from Route 1, at its intersection with Route 100. The ferry from Nova Scotia docks in Argentia, near Placentia.

Placentia

㉑ *48 km (30 mi) south of Route 1.*

Placentia was Newfoundland's French capital in the 1600s. Trust the French to select such a beautiful place for a capital! The remains of an old fort built on a hill look out over Placentia and beyond to the placid waters and wooded, steep hillsides of the inlet. **Castle Hill National Historic Site,** just north of town, is on what remains of the French fortifications. The visitor center has a "life at Plaisance" exhibit that shows the hardships endured by early English and French settlers. Performances of *Faces of Fort Royal,* a historical play about the French era, take place twice daily during July and August. ⊠ *Off Rte. 100,* ☎ *709/227–2401.* ⊠ *Historic site $2.50, play $2.* ☉ *Mid-June–early Sept., daily 8:30–8; early Sept.–mid-June, daily 8:30–4:30.*

Lodging

$ 🏠 **Fo'c's'le Bed and Breakfast.** Fo'c's'le is short for forecastle, the crew's sleeping quarters on a ship. And this pleasant B&B with nautical decor certainly has a touch of the old salt about it. But the real seaside action is out on the deck, where you can relax and watch seabirds. ⊠ *Rte. 91, A0B 2Y0,* ☎ FAX *709/227–2282,* WEB *www.bcity.com/focsle. 3 rooms. Dining room, no-smoking room. V. CP.*

$ 🏠 **Northeast Arm Motel.** The motel has a nice view of Northeast Arm and is situated on the main highway 10 minutes from the ferry to Nova Scotia in Argentia. Rooms are standard, without much in the way of frills. ⊠ *Main St., Dunville A0B 1S0,* ☎ *709/227–3560 or 877/227–3560,* FAX *709/227–5430. 13 rooms. Bar, no-smoking rooms, coin laundry. AE, DC, MC, V.*

Ship Harbour

㉒ *34 km (21 mi) north of Placentia.*

An isolated, edge-of-the-world place, Ship Harbour has historic significance. In 1941, on a ship in these waters, Franklin Roosevelt and Winston Churchill signed the Atlantic Charter and formally announced the "Four Freedoms," which still shape the politics of the world's most successful democracies: freedom of speech, freedom of worship, freedom from want, and freedom from fear. Off Route 102, amid the splendor of Placentia Bay, an unpaved road leads to a monument to the Atlantic Charter.

Cape St. Mary's Ecological Reserve

★ **㉓** *65 km (40 mi) south of Placentia.*

Cape St. Mary's Ecological Reserve is the southernmost nesting site in the world for gannets and common and thick-billed murres. A paved road takes you within a mile of the seabird colony. You can visit the interpretation center—guides are on site in summer—and then walk to within 100 ft of the colony of nesting gannets, murres, black-billed kittiwakes, and razorbills. Most birds are March through August visitors. The reserve has some of the most dramatic coastal scenery in Newfoundland. This is also a good place to spot whales. From May through September the interpretation center hosts performances of traditional music by local artists as well as an eclectic mix of musicians from else-

where in the province; call for information and times. ⊠ *Off Rte. 100,*
☎ *709/337–2473 or 709/729–2429,* WEB *www.gov.nf.ca/parks&re-*
serves. ⊠ *$3 for center; site is free.* ⊙ *Center early May–late Oct., daily*
9–7; site daily 24 hrs year-round.

Lodging

$ ⊞ **Bird Island Resort.** This pleasant lodging a half hour's drive from
Cape St. Mary's overlooks meadows and Placentia Bay. Rooms are standard and cottages have fully equipped kitchens. ⊠ *Off Rte. 100, St.*
Bride's A0B 2Z0, ☎ *709/337–2450 or 888/337–2450,* FAX *709/334–*
2903. 5 rooms, 15 cottages. Gym, coin laundry. AE, MC, V.

$ ⊞ **Capeway Motel.** The main attraction of this basic motel is its prox-
imity to the seabird sanctuary at Cape St. Mary's. The units have cable
TV and small kitchens. ⊠ *Rte. 100, General Delivery, St. Bride's A0B*
2Z0, ☎ *709/337–2163,* FAX *709/337–2028. 7 rooms. Coin laundry.*
MC, V.

Clarenville and the Bonavista Peninsula

Clarenville, about two hours northwest of St. John's via the Trans-
Canada Highway (Route 1), is the departure point for two different
excursions: the Discovery Trail, on the Bonavista Peninsula, and Terra
Nova National Park, which borders the shore of Bonavista Bay.

Clarenville

㉔   *189 km (117 mi) northwest of St. John's.*

★   If history and quaint towns appeal to you, consider following the **Dis-**
covery Trail, which begins in Clarenville on Route 230A. The trail includes two gems: the old town of Trinity, famed for its quaint architecture
and theater festival, and Bonavista, one of John Cabot's reputed landing spots.

Lodging

$–$$$ ⊞ **St. Jude Hotel.** Rooms are spacious and comfortable, if somewhat
spartan, at this modern hotel with a Mexican restaurant. Rooms
fronting the highway have a good view of the bay, but those in the back
are quieter. Even on a hot day, the air-conditioning can be a little too
cool here. ⊠ *Rte. 1, Box 2500, A0E 1J0,* ☎ *709/466–1717 or 800/*
563–7800, FAX *709/466–1714,* WEB *www.stjudehotel.nf.ca. 64 rooms.*
Restaurant, bar, no-smoking rooms. AE, MC, V.

$–$$ ⊞ **Restland Motor Inn.** The bland name doesn't do justice to the lovely
garden and excellent restaurant serving everything from burgers to curry
dishes. The rooms in this modern property are small but comfortable.
The decor is mostly bright and floral. ⊠ *Memorial Dr., A0E 1J0,* ☎
709/466–7636 or 800/205–3993, FAX *709/466–2743. 23 rooms. Restau-*
rant, no-smoking rooms. AE, DC, MC, V.

$ ⊞ **Clarenville Inn.** Formerly a Holiday Inn, the hotel in its new incar-
nation is still a no-surprises establishment. It's popular with families
because children eat free and there's a heated swimming pool. ⊠ *Rte.*
1, Box 967, A0E 1J0, ☎ *709/466–7911,* FAX *709/466–3854. 64 rooms.*
Restaurant, bar, pool. AE, DC, MC, V.

Terra Nova National Park

㉕   *24 km (15 mi) northwest of Clarenville.*

Rugged terrain, golf, sea kayaking, and fishing and camping are draws
at this park on the exposed coastline of Bonavista Bay. The Terra Nova
Park Lodge (87 rooms, 6 efficiencies) at Port Blandford has one of the
most beautiful golf courses in Canada, and the only one where two salmon

rivers cut through the 18 holes. Call ☎ 709/543–2626 for a reservation. The park also has the Marine Interpretation Center, nature walks, whale-watching and sea-kayaking tours, and a small but decent cafeteria. Eight backcountry campsites can be accessed by trails. ⊠ *Trans-Canada Hwy., Glovertown A2A 1X5,* ☎ *709/533–2801, 709/533–3186 or 800/213–7275,* WEB *www.parkscanada.pch.gc.ca/parks/newfoundland.* 🖾 *Mid-May–mid-Oct., $3.25; mid-Oct.–mid-May, free.* ☉ *Site daily 24 hrs. Center June–Aug., daily 10–9; Sept.–May, weekdays 8–4:30.*

Camping

Malady Head Campground (⊠ Rte. 310, ☎ 709/533–2801) has 99 sites and is open from July through September. The **Newman Sound Campground** (⊠ Rte. 1, ☎ 709/533–2801), with 387 campsites, is organized in clusters around playgrounds and has a store where you can rent bicycles. Winter camping is available here.

Trinity

★ **㉖** *71 km (44 mi) northeast of Clarenville.*

Trinity is one of the jewels of Newfoundland. The village's picturesque views, winding lanes, and snug houses are the main attraction. Several homes have been turned into museums and inns. In the 1700s, Trinity competed with St. John's as a center of culture and wealth. Its more contemporary claim to fame, however, is that its intricate harbor was a favorite anchorage for the British navy. Here, too, the smallpox vaccine was introduced to North America by a local rector. On West Street an information center with costumed interpreters is open daily mid-June through October. To get here, take Route 230 to Route 239.

The **Garland Mansion** is a re-creation of a fish merchant's house that was one of the most prominent 18th-century homes in Newfoundland. Next door is a 19th-century store. ⊠ *West St.,* ☎ *709/464–3706,* WEB *www3.nf.sympatico.ca/ttci.* 🖾 *$2.50.* ☉ *June 15–Sept. 15, daily 10–6.*

From July through Labor Day, the **Rising Tide Theatre** (☎ 709/738–3256 or 888/464–3377) conducts New-Founde Land Trinity Pageant walking tours (Wednesday and weekends at 2) of the town that are more theater than tour. Actors in period costume lead the way.

Dining and Lodging

$–$$ ✕ **Dock Marina.** The food at this restaurant right on the wharf is standard Canadian: pasta, salads, burgers, chicken, and local seafood. Service is prompt and friendly. ⊠ *Trinity Waterfront,* ☎ *709/464–2133. AE, DC, MC, V. Closed Nov.–Apr.*

$–$$$ 🏨 **Campbell House Bed & Breakfast.** Guest rooms in this mid-19th-century house are decorated with antiques; some have fireplaces. A full breakfast is included in the rate. ⊠ *High St., A0C 2S0,* ☎ *877/464–7700,* 🖷 FAX *709/464–3377,* WEB *www.campbellhouse.nf.ca. 6 rooms. Dining room, no-smoking room, laundry service. AE, DC, MC, V. Closed Nov.–Apr. BP.*

$–$$ 🏨 **Bishop White Manor and Eriksen Premises.** These two adjacent B&Bs with a common operator have antiques, fireplaces in some of the rooms, handcrafted furniture, and private baths. A tea room at Eriksen Premises serves inexpensive home-style cooking. Room rates include a full breakfast. ⊠ *Bishop White Manor, Gallavan's La.; Eriksen Premises, West St.; mailing address for both: Box 58, A0C 2S0,* ☎ *709/464–3698, 709/464–3299, or 877/464–3698,* FAX *709/464–2104,* WEB *www.trinityexperience.nf.ca. Bishop White 9 rooms, Eriksen 6 rooms. Dining room. MC, V. Closed Nov.–Apr. BP.*

$–$$ ⌕ **Fishers' Loft Inn.** The Fishers' Loft, just a few minutes away from the bustle of Trinity, overlooks a harbor where whales sometimes swim among small fishing boats and icebergs drift by farther out in the bay. Rooms here are bright and airy, with down duvets, handcrafted furniture, and original artwork. Four rooms have cathedral ceilings. The owners pack you a lunch and give you a map and guidance for hiking in the area. ⌂ *Mill Rd., Port Rexton A0C 2H0,* ☎ *877/464–3240,* ☎ FAX *709/464–3240,* WEB *www.fishersloft.com. 8 rooms, 4 suites. Dining room, in-room data ports, no-smoking rooms. AE, DC, MC, V. Closed Nov.–Apr.*

$ ⌕ **The Hangashore B & B.** This restored 19th-century house is the summer home of renowned Newfoundland fiddler Kelly Russell and his folklorist spouse, Tonya Kearly, who calls a mean dance at the couple's regular Wednesday traditional dance sessions. Browse the collection of rare Newfoundland books. The walls feature a changing collection of contemporary local art. Breakfast is included in the room rate. ⌂ *1 Ash's Lane (mailing address: 51 Monkstown Rd., St. John's A1C 3T4),* ☎ *709/464–3807 or 888/754–7377. 3 rooms. AE, MC, V.*

$ ⌕ **Peace Cove Inn.** This restored inn, once a schooner captain's residence, is one of the few remaining modified Second Empire houses in Newfoundland with the front and back mansard roofs and bonneted windows in Newfoundland. Rooms are large and have antiques and private baths. ⌂ *Trinity E. Rd. (Box 123, Port Rexton A0C 2H0),* ☎ *709/464–3738,* FAX *709/464–2167,* WEB *www.atlanticadventures.com. 6 rooms. Dining room, no-smoking rooms. MC, V. Closed Nov.–Apr.*

$ ⌕ **Sherwood Suites.** This accommodation has both housekeeping units and motel suites. The housekeeping units have a fully equipped kitchen, a private patio, two bedrooms, a living room, and cable TV. The motel suites have private entrances and cable TV. ⌂ *Rocky Hill Rd., Port Rexton A0C 2H0,* ☎ FAX *709/464–2130,* WEB *www.sherwoodsuites.nfld.net. 10 housekeeping units, 4 motel suites. No-smoking rooms, playground, coin laundry. V. Closed Oct.–May.*

Nightlife and the Arts

The **Rising Tide Theatre** stages the Summer in the Bight festival. Outdoor Shakespeare productions, dinner theater, and dramas and comedies fill the bill. In 2000, the troupe opened a new theatre, styled like an old mercantile warehouse, on the waterfront. Fees vary, so call for details.

Outdoor Activities and Sports

Atlantic Sailing Charters and Tours (☎ 709/464–2133 or 709/781–2255) operates a 46-ft motorized sailboat for whale-watching or just cruising Trinity Bight.

Shopping

Trinity Crafts (⌂ Church Rd., ☎ 709/464–3823) specializes in locally made quilts, woolens, and knitted goods.
Trinity Folk Art (⌂ Water St., ☎ 709/464–3760) sells a wide array of crafts from all over the province, including Innu tea dolls from Labrador.

Bonavista

㉗ *28 km (17 mi) north of Trinity.*

No one knows exactly where explorer John Cabot landed when he came to Atlantic Canada in 1497, but many believe it to have been at Bonavista. The **Ryan Premises National Historic Site** on the waterfront depicts the almost 500-year history of the commercial cod fishery in a restored fish merchant's property. ⌂ *Off Rte. 230,* ☎ *709/468–1600* or 800/213–7275, WEB *www.parkscanada.pch.gc.ca/parks/newfound-land.* ☒ *$2.50.* ⊙ *June 1–Oct. 1, daily 10–6.*

The **Cape Bonavista Lighthouse** on the point, about 1 km (½ mi) out-side town, has been restored to its condition in 1870. ☎ 709/468–7444, WEB *www.nfmuseum.com.* ☒ *$2.50 (includes Mockbeggar Plantation).* ⊙ *Mid-June–early Oct., daily 10–5:30.*

The **Mockbeggar Plantation** teaches about the life of an outport mer-chant in the years immediately before Confederation. ☒ *Off Rte. 230,* ☎ 709/729–0592 or 709/468–7300. ☒ *$2.50 (includes Cape Bonav-ista Lighthouse).* ⊙ *Mid-June–early Oct., daily 10–5:30.*

Burin Peninsula, Gander, and Notre Dame Bay

The Burin Peninsula's history is tied to the rich fishing grounds of the Grand Bank, which established this area as a center for European fish-ery as early as the 1500s. By the early 1900s, one of the world's largest fishing fleets was based on the Burin Peninsula. Today its inhabitants hope for a recovery of the fish stocks that have sustained their econ-omy for centuries. Marystown is the peninsula's commercial center.

Gander, in east-central Newfoundland, is known for its airport and its aviation history. North of it is Notre Dame Bay, an area of rugged coast-line and equally rugged islands that were once the domain of the now extinct Beothuk tribe. Only the larger islands are currently inhabited. Before English settlers moved into the area in the late 18th and early 19th centuries, it was seasonally occupied by French fisherfolk. Local dialects preserve centuries-old words that have vanished elsewhere. The bay is swept by the cool Labrador Current that carries icebergs south through Iceberg Alley; the coast is also a good whale-watching area.

The journey down to the Burin Peninsula is a three- to four-hour drive from the intersection of Routes 230 and 1 through the craggy coastal landscapes along Route 210.

Marystown

28 *283 km (175 mi) south of Bonavista.*

Marystown is built around beautiful Mortier Bay, so big it was con-sidered large enough for the entire British fleet during the early days of World War II. Shipbuilding is the main industry. Of note is the 20-ft statue of the Virgin Mary that looks out over the bay.

Lodging

$ ⛛ **Hotel Marystown.** Substantial renovations have upgraded this prop-erty, the largest hotel on the Burin Peninsula. Rooms are standard but comfortable with pastel shades, double beds, and cable TV. ☒ *Ville Marie Dr., A0E 2M0,* ☎ 709/279–1600 or 800/563–2489, FAX 709/279–4088, WEB *www.cityhotels.ca. 131 rooms. Restaurant, bar, kitchenettes (some), room service, business services, meeting rooms. AE, DC, MC, V.*

Burin

29 *17 km (11 mi) south of Marystown.*

Burin, a community built amid intricate cliffs and coves, was an ideal setting for pirates and privateers, who used to lure ships into the rocky, dead-end areas in order to plunder them. When Captain James Cook was stationed here to chart the coast in the 1760s, one of his duties was to watch for smugglers bringing in rum from the island of St-Pierre. Smuggling continues to this day. Cook's Look-out, a hill overlooking Burin, is where Cook kept watch. Trail directions for the hill are available at **Island Treasure Woodcrafts** (☎ 709/891–2516) on Main Street.

Heritage Museum, considered one of the best community museums in Newfoundland, gives you a sense of what life was like in the past in this fishing community. It has a display on the 1929 tidal wave that struck Burin and the surrounding coastal communities, and a gallery for traveling exhibits. ⊠ *Seaview Dr. off Rte. 221,* ☎ *709/891–2217,* WEB *www.schooner.nf.ca.* ☉ *Mid-May–July and early Sept.–early Oct., daily 10–6; early July–early Sept., daily 10–8.*

Lodging

$ ☷ **Sound of the Sea Bed and Breakfast.** The sound of waves crashing on the shore drifts into this B&B to create an utterly relaxing experience. Each room in this former merchant's home matches color schemes to wooden furniture: the lighter colors go with the birch furniture, the medium colors with pine, and the darker colors with the antique walnut furniture. The owners can help arrange boat tours. A full breakfast is included in the room rate. ⊠ *11A Seaview Dr., A0E 1E0,* ☎ *709/891–2115,* FAX *709/891–2377. 3 rooms. No-smoking room, coin laundry. MC, V. BP.*

Grand Bank

   ③⓪ *62 km (38 mi) from Burin.*

One of the loveliest communities in Newfoundland, Grand Bank has a fascinating history as an important fishing center. Because of trading patterns, the architecture here was influenced more by Halifax, Boston, and Bar Harbor, Maine, than by the rest of Newfoundland. A sail-shape building holds the **Southern Newfoundland Seamen's Museum,** which provides insight into the town's past. ⊠ *54 Marine Dr.,* ☎ *709/832–1484.* ☐ *$2.50.* ☉ *May–mid-June and early Sept.–Oct., daily 9–4:45; mid-June–early Sept., daily 9:30–4:45.*

Lodging

$ ☷ **Granny's Motor Inn.** The rooms here may be small, but they are comfortable, and the location is convenient, with easy access to the ferry to St-Pierre. It's also close to the town's soccer field—a five-minute walk after dinner lets you catch the most popular sport on the Burin Peninsula. ⊠ *Grandview Blvd., A0E 1W0,* ☎ *709/832–2355 or 888/275–1098,* FAX *709/832–0009. 10 rooms. Restaurant, bar, room service, coin laundry. AE, DC, MC, V.*

$ ☷ **Thorndyke Bed and Breakfast.** This 1917 Queen Anne–style mansion, a former sea captain's house, is a designated historic structure. The blown-glass objects, colored panels, and sun porch have been part of the house since it was first built. The ferry to St-Pierre is a five-minute drive away. A full breakfast is included in the price. ⊠ *33 Water St., A0E 1W0,* ☎ *709/832–0820. 4 rooms. No-smoking rooms. V. Closed Oct.–Apr. BP.*

St-Pierre and Miquelon

   ③① *70-min ferry ride from Fortune.*

The islands of St-Pierre and Miquelon, France's only territory in North America, are a ferry ride away if you crave French cuisine or a bottle of perfume. Shopping and eating are both popular pastimes here. The bakeries open early, so there's always piping hot fresh bread for breakfast. Bargain hunters can find reasonably priced wines from all over France, so a good pocket guide is most helpful. An interesting side trip via boat takes you to see seals, seabirds, and other wildlife, plus the huge sandbar (formed on the bones of shipwrecks) that now connects formerly separate Great and Little Miquelon. Visitors to the islands should carry proof of citizenship; people from outside the United States and Canada have to show valid visas and passports. Because of the ferry schedule, a trip to St-Pierre means an overnight stay in a modern hotel such as **Hotel Robert** (☎ 508/412419) or a pension, the French equivalent of a B&B. Call the **St-Pierre tourist board** (☎ 508/ 412222 or 800/565–5118) for information about accommodations.

A passenger ferry operated by **Lloyd G. Lake Ltd./St. Pierre Tours** (☎ 709/832–2006, 709/722–4103, or 800/563–2006) leaves Fortune (south of Grand Bank) daily at 2:15 PM from mid-June to late September; the crossing takes 70 minutes. The ferry leaves St-Pierre at 1 PM daily; round-trip is $55.

Gander

32 *367 km (228 mi) north of Grand Bank.*

Gander, a busy town of 12,000 people, is notable for its aviation history. It also has many lodgings and makes a good base for travel in this part of the province. During World War II, **Gander International Airport** (✉ James Blvd.) was chosen by the Canadian and U.S. air forces as a major strategic air base because of its favorable weather and secure location. After the war, the airport became an international hub for civilian travel; today it's a major air-traffic control center. The **Aviation Exhibition** in the airport's domestic passengers' lounge (☎ 709/ 256–3905) traces Newfoundland's role in the history of air travel. It's open daily 8 AM–midnight.

The **North Atlantic Aviation Museum** gives an expansive view of Gander's and Newfoundland's roles in aviation. In addition to viewing the expected models and photographs, you can climb into the cockpit of a real DC-3 parked outside next to a World War II Hudson bomber and a Canadian jet fighter. ✉ *On Rte. 1, between hospital and visitor information center,* ☎ *709/256–2923.* ➁ *$3.* ☉ *June–Sept., daily 9–9; Oct.–May, weekdays 9–5.*

Gander River Tours (☎ 709/679–2271) organizes salmon-fishing trips, canoeing excursions, and guided tours of the river and wilderness areas around Gander from April to November.

Lodging

$–$$ 🏨 **Hotel Gander.** The largest hotel in Gander has comfortable rooms and a decent dining room that serves standard Canadian fare. Children under 12 can stay and eat for free here. The staff can arrange a round of golf or a tour of the area. ✉ *100 Trans-Canada Hwy., A1V 1P5,* ☎ *709/256–3931 or 800/563–2988,* ⟨FAX⟩ *709/651–2641,* ⟨WEB⟩ *www.hotelgander.com. 154 rooms. Bar, dining room, no-smoking rooms, room service, indoor pool, coin laundry. AE, DC, MC, V.*

$–$$ 🏨 **Sinbad's Hotel and Suites.** Near nightclubs and restaurants, Sinbad's is popular with young couples. The hotel also has a lively bar of its own. Rooms are spacious and have standard amenities such as hair dryers, irons, and cable TV. ✉ *Bennett Dr., A1V 1W6,* ☎ *709/651– 2678 or 800/563–8330,* ⟨FAX⟩ *709/651–3123,* ⟨WEB⟩ *www.sinbadshotel.nf.ca. 103 rooms, 9 suites. Bar, dining room, kitchenettes (some), no-smoking rooms. AE, DC, MC, V.*

Boyd's Cove

㉝ *66 km (41 mi) north of Gander.*

Between 1650 and 1720, the Beothuks' main summer camp on the northeast coast was at the site of what is now Boyd's Cove. The coastline in and near Boyd's Cove is somewhat sheltered by Twillingate Island and New World Island. Short causeways link the shore to the islands.

The **Boyd's Cove Beothuk Interpretation Centre** offers a fresh look at the lives of the Beothuks, an extinct First Nations people who succumbed in the early 19th century to a combination of disease and battle with European settlers. The center uses traditional Beothuk building forms and adjoins an archaeological site that was inhabited from about 1650 to 1720, when pressure from settlers drove the Beothuk from this part of the coast. ⊠ *Rte. 340,* ☏ *709/656–3114 or 709/729–0592,* WEB *www.nfmuseum.com.* ⊡ *$2.50.* ☉ *Mid-June–early Oct., daily 10–5:30.*

Twillingate

㉞ *31 km (19 mi) north of Boyd's Cove.*

The inhabitants of this scenic old fishing village make their living from the sea and have been doing so for nearly two centuries. Colorful houses, rocky waterfront cliffs, a local museum, and a nearby lighthouse add to the town's appeal. Every year on the last weekend in July, the town hosts the **Fish, Fun and Folk Festival** (☏ 709/884–2678, WEB www.fishfunfolkfestival.com), where fish are cooked every possible way.

One of the best places on the island to see icebergs, Twillingate is known to the locals as Iceberg Alley. These majestic and dangerous mountains of ice are awe-inspiring to see while they're grounded in early summer. **Twillingate Island Boat Tours** (☏ 709/884–2242 or 800/611–2374) specializes in iceberg photography in the local waters. An iceberg interpretation center is right on the dock.

Lodging

$ 🏠 **Evening Sun Inn Bed and Breakfast.** You can relax on the deck and watch the sun set over the bay at this B&B. The inn has one standard room and a suite with a private entrance, a living room, and a kitchenette. Arctic terns nest nearby, and a short walk along a trail brings you to an excellent spot for watching whales and icebergs. ⊠ *319 Bayview St., A0G 4M0,* ☏ *709/884–2103,* FAX *709/884–2176. 2 rooms. No-smoking room, laundry service. V. BP.*

$ 🏠 **Toulinguest Inn Bed and Breakfast.** In this traditional home on the waterfront, rooms are old-fashioned but comfortable. You can wind down in the living room. ⊠ *56 Main St., A0G 4M0,* ☏ *709/884–2080 or 709/256–8406,* FAX *709/256–8410. 3 rooms. No-smoking rooms, coin laundry. Closed Oct.–Apr. V. BP.*

Grand Falls–Windsor

㉟ *95 km (59 mi) west of Gander.*

This central Newfoundland town is an amalgamation of the paper-making town of Grand Falls, the quintessential company town founded by British newspaper barons earlier this century, and Windsor, once an important stop on the railway. The paper mill still ships newsprint all over the world, but the railway is no more.

The **Loggers' Exhibit** (⊠ Rte. 1, ☏ 709/292–4522), a re-creation of a logging camp 2 km (1 mi) west of town, tells of the hard lives of those who supplied wood for the paper mill.

Lodging

$–$$ ☷ **Mount Peyton Hotel.** This lodging establishment has hotel and motel rooms, housekeeping units with kitchenettes, and a good steakhouse. The rooms are comfortable, if unremarkable, and have coffeemakers, hair dryers, and irons and ironing boards. ✉ *214 Lincoln Rd., A2A 1P8,* ☎ *709/489–2251 or 800/563–4894,* ⅀ *709/489–6365,* ⅏ *www. mountpeyton.com. 130 rooms, 32 housekeeping units, 4 suites. 2 restaurants, bar, kitchenettes (some), no-smoking rooms, meeting rooms. AE, DC, MC, V. Motel rooms closed Sept.–Mar.*

OFF THE   **CHANGE ISLANDS AND FOGO ISLAND –** These islands give the impression
BEATEN PATH   of a place frozen in time. Modernity came late to these outposts of the past, where old expressions and accents still survive. You can take a ferry (☎ 709/486–0733) from Farewell to either the Change Islands or Fogo Island. To get to Farewell, take Route 340 to Route 335, which takes you through scenic coastal communities.

If you choose to stay overnight, **Hart's Bed and Breakfast** (☎ 709/621–3133) is on the Change Islands and **Alma's Bed and Breakfast** (☎ 709/627–3302) is in Stag Harbour on Fogo Island.

The Great Northern Peninsula

The Great Northern Peninsula is the northernmost visible extension of the Appalachian Mountains. Its eastern side is rugged and sparsely populated. The Viking Trail—Route 430 and its side roads—snakes along its western coast through a national park, fjords, sand dunes, and communities that have relied on lobster fishing for generations. At the tip of the peninsula, the Vikings established the first European settlement in North America a thousand years ago. For thousands of years before their arrival, the area was home to native peoples who hunted, fished, and gathered berries and herbs.

Deer Lake

❸❻   *208 km (129 mi) west of Grand Falls–Windsor.*

Deer Lake was once just another small town on the Trans-Canada Highway, but the opening of Gros Morne National Park in the early '70s and the construction of a first-class paved highway passing right through to St. Anthony changed all that. Today, with an airport and car rentals available, Deer Lake is a good starting point for a fly–drive vacation.

☉   The **Newfoundland Insectarium** holds an intriguing collection of live and preserved insects, spiders, scorpions, and the like. It's in a suburb of Deer Lake, off Route 430. ✉ *Rte. 430, Reidville,* ☎ *709/635–4545,* ⅏ *www.newfoundlandinsectarium.nf.ca.* ☷ *$6.* ☉ *Mid-June–mid-Sept., daily 9–9; mid-Sept.–mid-June, Tues.–Fri. 9–5, weekends 10–5.*

Lodging

$ ☷ **Deer Lake Motel.** The guest rooms here are clean and comfortable, and the food in the café is basic, home-cooked fare. Seafood dishes are exceptionally well prepared. ✉ *Rte. 1, Box 820, A0K 2E0,* ☎ *709/635–2108 or 800/563–2144,* ⅀ *709/635–3842,* ⅏ *www.deerlakemotel.com. 54 rooms, 2 suites. Restaurant, bar, café, no-smoking rooms, meeting rooms. AE, MC, V.*

Gros Morne National Park

★ *46 km (29 mi) north of Deer Lake on Rte. 430.*

Because of its geological uniqueness and immense splendor, this park has been named a UNESCO World Heritage Site. Among the more breathtaking visions are the expanses of wild orchids in springtime. Camping and hiking are popular recreations, and boat tours are available. To see Gros Morne properly you should allow yourself at least two days. An excellent **interpretation center** (☎ 709/458–2417) in Rocky Harbour has displays and videos about the park. Scenic **Bonne Bay,** a deep, mountainous fjord, divides the park in two. You can drive around the perimeter of the fjord on Route 430 going north.

Woody Point, a charming community of old houses and imported Lombardy poplars, is in the south of the park, on Route 431. The **Tablelands,** rising behind Norris Point, are a unique rock massif that was raised from the earth's mantle through tectonic upheaval. Its rocks are toxic to most plant life, and Ice Age conditions linger in the form of persistent snow and moving rock glaciers. A **Discovery Centre** (✉ Rte. 431, on the outskirts of Woody Point heading west toward Trout River, ☎ 709/458–2417) offers educational programs on the park's geology and natural history.

The small community of **Trout River** is at the western end of Route 431 on the Gulf of St. Lawrence. You pass the scenic **Trout River Pond** along the way. The **Green Gardens Trail,** a spectacular short or long hike, is also nearby, but be prepared to do a bit of climbing on your return journey. The trail passes through the Tablelands barrens and descends sharply to a coastline of eroded cliffs and green meadows.

Head to the northern side of the park, along coastal Route 430, to visit **Rocky Harbour** with its range of restaurants, lodgings, and a luxurious indoor public pool and large hot tub—the perfect place to soothe tired limbs after a strenuous day.

The most popular attraction in the northern portion of Gros Morne is the boat tour of **Western Brook Pond.** You park at a lot on Route 430 and take a 45-minute walk to the boat dock through an interesting mix of bog and woods. Cliffs rise 2,000 ft on both sides of the gorge, and high waterfalls tumble over ancient rocks. Hikers in good shape can tackle the 16-km (10-mi) hike up **Gros Morne Mountain,** at 2,644 ft the second-highest peak in Newfoundland. Weather permitting, the reward for your effort is a unique arctic landscape and spectacular views. The park's **northern coast** has an unusual mix of sand beaches, rock pools, and trails through tangled dwarf forests known locally as tuckamore. Sunsets seen from **Lobster Cove Head Lighthouse** are spectacular. Keep an eye out for whales, and visit the lighthouse museum, devoted to the history of the area. ✉ *Gros Morne National Park, via the Viking Trail (Rte. 430),* ☎ *709/458–2417,* ℻ *709/458–2162,* ᴡᴇʙ *www.parkscanada.pch.gc.ca/grosmorne.* ✇ *Mid-May–mid-Oct., $5; free rest of yr.* ☉ *Mid-May–mid-June, daily 9 ᴀᴍ–5 ᴘᴍ; mid-June–Labor Day, daily 9–9, Labor Day–Canadian Thanksgiving Day, daily 9–5.*

Dining and Lodging

$–$$ ✕ **Fisherman's Landing.** The food here is good, but the service can be a bit slow at lunch time. Staples of Canadian fare such as hot turkey sandwiches, deep-fried chicken, and burgers are on the menu. The fish is usually a good choice, but make sure that it's fresh and not frozen. ✉ *Main St., Rocky Harbour,* ☎ *709/458–2060. AE, MC, V.*

$-$$ ✕ **Seaside Restaurant.** Fresh seafood is prepared in traditional New-foundland style at the Seaside Restaurant. You can enjoy the familiar fish-and-chips, cod, and lobster, or you can try something more adventurous in the form of batter-dipped panfried cod tongue. The tongue, denser than a fillet, has a unique combination of textures: the top has the consistency of a clam, and the underside is jellylike. Huge windows give diners a view of Bonne Bay. ⊠ *Main St., Trout River,* ☎ *709/451–3641. AE, MC, V. Closed Nov.–May.*

$-$$$ ⊡ **Gros Morne Resort.** Guest rooms in the front of this hotel overlook the ocean; those in the rear face the mountains. All of the rooms are well-appointed, spacious, and have balconies. The resort is in St. Pauls, a small community encircled by Gros Morne park. ⊠ *Rte. 430, Box 100, St. Pauls, A0K 4Y0,* ☎ *709/243–2606 or 888/243–2644,* FAX *709/243–2615. 8 rooms, 12 suites. 2 restaurants, 2 bars, minibars, hair salon. AE, MC, V.*

$-$$$ ⊡ **Sugar Hill Inn.** This small hostelry in Gros Morne National Park has quickly developed a reputation for fine wining and dining (for guests only) because of host Vince McCarthy's culinary talents and educated palate. Guided cross-country skiing and snowmobiling treks are available. ⊠ *115–129 Sexton Rd., Box 100, Norris Point A0K 3V0,* ☎ *709/ 458–2147 or 888/299–2147,* FAX *709/458–2166,* WEB *www.sugarhillinn.nf.ca. 3 rooms, 3 suites. Dining room, no-smoking rooms, hot tub, sauna, coin laundry. AE, MC, V. Closed Nov.– mid-Jan.*

$-$$ ⊡ **Gros Morne Cabins.** These modern log chalets, which overlook the Gulf of St. Lawrence, are near restaurants and stores in Rocky Harbour. Cabins can accommodate up to four people and have kitchens and TVs. ⊠ *Main St., Rocky Harbour A0K 4N0,* ☎ *709/458–2020 or 888/603–2020,* FAX *709/458–2882. 22 cabins. Grocery, playground, coin laundry. AE, DC, MC, V.*

$-$$ ⊡ **Victorian Manor Bed and Breakfast.** This modified Queen Anne house situated in Woody Point, one of the prettiest towns in the vicinity of Gros Morne, has been in the same family since it was built in the 1920s. Much of the furniture and decor of the original home, such as the valanced curtains and chandeliers, have been retained. The Victorian Manor has B&B rooms, efficiency units, and a separate guest house. The suite has a whirlpool tub. ⊠ *Water St., Woody Point A0K 1P0,* ☎ FAX *709/453–2485,* WEB *www.grosmorne.com/victorianmanor. 3 rooms, 1 suite, 3 efficiencies, 1 house. Dining room, no-smoking rooms. MC, V.*

$ ⊡ **Crocker Cabins.** These standard cabins are in Trout River in the quieter, less-developed southern part of the park. The cabins can accommodate four people. ⊠ *57 Duke St., Trout River A0K 5P0,* ☎ FAX *709/ 451–3236. 4 cabins. Fishing, playground, coin laundry. AE, MC, V.*

$ ⊡ **Frontier Cottages.** These well-appointed log cabins can hold up to six people and are ideal if you wish to do your own cooking while visiting Gros Morne. The kitchen has lots of cooking gear, and the wooden table seats six. There's a great view of the hills from the deck. It's a good idea to bring a pre-paid long-distance calling card because there are no telephones in the cabins, just a pay phone in the grocery. ⊠ *Rte. 430, Box 172, Wiltondale A0K 4N0,* ☎ *709/453–7266 or 800/668– 2520,* FAX *709/453–7272. 6 cabins. Restaurant, grocery, miniature golf, snowmobiling, playground, coin laundry. AE, DC, MC, V.*

$ ⊡ **Ocean View Motel.** The wonderful views of Rocky Harbour more than make up for the lackluster motel rooms. This is also the home base for Bontour, which conducts sightseeing boat trips. ⊠ *Main St., Rocky Harbour A0K 4N0,* ☎ *709/458–2730 or 800/563–9887,* FAX *709/ 458–2841,* WEB *www.oceanviewmotel.com. 44 rooms. Restaurant, no-smoking rooms, meeting rooms. AE, DC, MC, V.*

$ ▦ **Shallow Bay Motel and Cabins.** Shallow Bay, which has standard rooms and small cottages, is near the northern boundary of the park. Comedic dinner-theater productions from the Gros Morne Theatre Festival are held here. ⊠ *Main St., Cow Head A0K 2A0,* ☏ *709/243–2471 or 800/563–1946,* ℻ *709/243–2816,* 🕸 *www3.nf.sympatico.ca/sb.motel. 35 rooms, 17 cottages. Restaurant, pool, sauna, miniature golf, coin laundry, meeting rooms. AE, DC, MC, V.*

CAMPING

To make reservations at any of the following **campgrounds** at Gros Morne, call ☏ 709/458–2417. **Berry Hill**, in the forest on Route 430, 4 km (2 1//2 mi) north of Gros Morne, has 152 sites, kitchen shelters, playgrounds, and showers. **Lomond**, a partly exposed area on Route 431, has 29 sites, kitchen shelters, a playground, and showers. Also on Route 431 is **Trout River**, with 35 sites, kitchen shelters, showers, and a playground. **Green Point**, 10 km (6 mi) north of Rocky Harbour on Route 430, is close to the ocean and partly sheltered. It has 18 sites and kitchen shelters, but no showers. In the northern part of the park near Cow Head, **Shallow Bay** is sheltered from the ocean by sand dunes and trees. It has kitchen shelters, showers, and a huge sandy beach.

Nightlife and the Arts

The **Gros Morne Theatre Festival** (☏ 709/243–2899) provides summer entertainment in Cow Head and other venues throughout the park. Most productions are comedies, though there are some dramas based on local stories, plus an outdoor children's show.

Outdoor Activities and Sports

Gros Morne Adventures (☏ 709/458–2722 or 800/685–4624, 🕸 www.grosmorneadventures.com) has sea kayaking up the fjords and land-locked ponds of Gros Morne National Park, as well as a variety of hikes and adventures in the area.

Bon Tours (☏ 709/458–2730 or 800/563–9887, 🕸 www.oceanview-motel.com) runs sightseeing boat tours of Western Brook Pond in Gros Morne National Park and on Bonne Bay. **Tableland Boat Tours** (☏ 709/451–2101) leads tours on Trout River Pond near the southern boundary of Gros Morne National Park.

Arches Provincial Park

❹ *20 km (12 mi) north of Gros Morne National Park.*

Arches Provincial Park is a geological curiosity: the action of undersea currents millions of years ago cut a succession of caves through a bed of dolomite that was later raised above sea level by tectonic upheaval. This free park, open mid-June–mid-September, is not staffed. ⊠ *Rte. 430,* ☏ *709/729–2429,* 🕸 *www.gov.nf.ca/parks&reserves.*

En Route   Continuing north on Route 430, parallel to the Gulf of St. Lawrence, you'll find yourself refreshingly close to the ocean and the wave-tossed beaches. The **Long Range Mountains** to your right reminded Jacques Cartier, who saw them in 1534 as he was exploring the area on behalf of France, of the long, rectangular-shape farm buildings of his home village in France. Small villages are interspersed with rivers where salmon and trout grow to be "liar-size." The remains of Maritime Archaic and Dorset people have been found in abundance along this coast, and **Port au Choix National Historic Site** has an interesting interpretation center on them. An archaeological dig also has discovered an ancient village. Ask at the interpretation center for directions. ⊠ *Off Rte. 430,* ☏ *709/458–2417; 709/861–3522 in summer,* 🕸 *www.*

parkscanada.pch.gc.ca. ⌧ *$2.75.* ☉ *Mid–May–mid-June daily 9–5; mid-June–Labor Day, daily 9–9; Labor Day–Canadian Thanksgiving Day, daily 9–5.*

L'Anse aux Meadows National Historic Site

★ ㊷ *210 km (130 mi) northeast of Arches Provincial Park.*

Around the year AD 1000, Vikings from Greenland and Iceland founded the first European settlement in North America near the northern tip of Newfoundland. They arrived in the New World 500 years before Columbus, but stayed only a few years and were forgotten for centuries. It was only in 1960 that the Norwegian team of Helge and Anne Stine Ingstad discovered the remains of the Viking settlement's long sod huts. Today L'Anse aux Meadows is a UNESCO World Heritage Site. The Canadian Parks Service has a fine visitor center and has reconstructed some of the huts to give you a sense of centuries past. An interpretation program introduces you to the food, games, and way of life of that long-ago time. ⌧ *Rte. 436,* ☎ *709/623–2608; 709/458–2417 in winter;* FAX *709/623–2028 summer only.* ⌧ *$5.* ☉ *Mid–May–mid-June, daily 9–5; mid-June–Labor Day, daily 9–8; Labor Day–Canadian Thanksgiving Day, daily 9–5.*

↻ Two kilometers (1 mi) east is a second Viking attraction, **Norstead.** This reconstruction of an 11th-century Viking port, with its chieftain's hall, church, and ax-throwing arena, is a good follow-up to a stop at L'Anse aux Meadows; it's aimed more at kids, but the Viking boat-building course is designed for all ages. ⌧ *Rte 436,* ☎ *709/454–8888.* ⌧ *$7.* ☉ *Early June–late Sept., daily 10–6.*

Dining and Lodging

$ ✕ **Smith's Restaurant.** Don't let the modest facade and roadside location of Smith's Restaurant fool you—inside, huge windows frame a magnificent view of a shallow harbor, protected by an island dotted with grazing sheep, and seabirds circling overhead. The food's not bad, either. Try the Mediterranean chowder, halibut, or cod and walk it off with a stroll on the deck. The attached store sells crafts and books. ⌧ *Route 436, St. Lunaire–Griquet,* ☎ *709/623–2431. AE, DC, MC, V.*

$ ✕▥ **Tickle Inn at Cape Onion.** This refurbished, century-old fisherman's house on the beach is probably the northernmost residence on the island of Newfoundland. The Franklin stove in the parlor is good to relax by after exploring the coast or L'Anse aux Meadows (about 45 km [28 mi] away). The inn serves seafood, baked goods, and homemade jams. ⌧ *R.R. 1, Box 62, Cape Onion A0K 4J0,* ☎ *709/452–4321 June–Sept.; 709/739–5503 Oct.–May,* WEB *www3.nf.sympatico.ca/ adams.tickle. 4 rooms share bath. Dining room, no-smoking room. MC, V. CP, MAP.*

$ ▥ **Southwest Pond Cabins.** These basic cabins are a 10-minute drive from L'Anse aux Meadows. ⌧ *Rte. 430, Box 58, St. Lunaire–Griquet A0K 2X0,* ☎ *709/623–2140 or 800/515–2261,* FAX *709/623–2145. 8 cabins. Grocery, playground, coin laundry. AE, DC, MC, V. Closed Nov.–mid-May.*

$ ▥ **Valhalla Lodge Bed & Breakfast.** Comfortable and inviting, the Valhalla is 8 km (5 mi) from L'Anse aux Meadows. Some fossils are part of the rock fireplace. Hot breakfasts are included in the room rate, and other meals can be arranged. E. Annie Proulx, author of *The Shipping News,* stayed here while writing the novel. ⌧ *Gunner's Cove, St. Lunaire–Griquet A0K 2X0,* ☎ *709/623–2018 or 877/623–2018; 709/896–5476 in winter;* FAX *709/623–2144,* WEB *www.valhalla-lodge.com. 5 rooms. No-smoking room. MC, V. CP.*

$ 🖫 **Viking Nest/Viking Village Bed & Breakfast.** Each room at the Viking Nest is named after a famous person or boat from Viking legends or history. The Snorri, with a queen-size bed and private bath, is named for the first European born in the New World, at L'Anse aux Meadows. The Saga-Siglar, also with a queen-size bed, takes the name of a Viking longboat. All the guest rooms look out on the water. A full breakfast is included in the price. The Viking Village is a new five-room inn on the same property. The Viking settlement at L'Anse aux Meadows is only 1 km (½ mi) away. ⊠ *Box 127, Hay Cove A0K 2X0,* ☎ *877/858–2238,* ☎ FAX *709/623–2238,* WEB *www.bbcanada.com/2671.html. 9 rooms. No-smoking rooms. MC, V. BP.*

St. Anthony

㊸ *16 km (10 mi) south of L'Anse aux Meadows.*

The northern part of the Great Northern Peninsula served as the setting for *The Shipping News,* E. Annie Proulx's Pulitzer prize–winning novel. St. Anthony is built around a natural harbor on the eastern side of the Great Northern Peninsula, near its tip. If you take a trip out to the lighthouse, you may see an iceberg or two floating by.

The **Grenfell Mission** was founded by Sir Wilfred Grenfell, a British medical missionary who established nursing stations and cooperatives and provided medical services to the scattered villages of northern Newfoundland and the south coast of Labrador in the early 1900s. It remains the town's main employer. The main foyer of the **Charles S. Curtis Memorial Hospital** (⊠ 178–200 West St., ☎ 709/454–4010) has a decorative tile mural depicting scenes from the life of Grenfell.

The **Grenfell Historic Properties,** comprising a museum, house, and interpretation center, focus on Dr. Grenfell's life and work. ⊠ *West St.,* ☎ *709/454–4010,* WEB *www3.nf.sympatico.ca/grenfell.* ☞ *$5.* ☉ *May 1–Sept. 30, daily 9–8.*

Dining and Lodging

$ ✕ **Light Keeper's Cafe.** Good seafood and solid Canadian fare are served in this former lighthouse keeper's home overlooking the ocean. The ocean here is cold, which means the seafood—if fresh—will be succulent. Halibut, shrimp, and cod are usually good bets. If the fish isn't fresh, stick with a nonseafood dish such as pork chops. ⊠ *Fishing Point Rd.,* ☎ *709/454–4900. MC, V. Closed Oct.–Apr.*

$–$$ 🖫 **Tuckamore Country Inn.** The Scandinavian-style lodges of the Tuckamore Country Inn provide a comfortable base point from which to explore the wilderness of the area. Adventure packages, which are not covered in the basic lodging fee, include sea kayaking, wilderness viewing, and snowmobiling. This is about an hour away from St. Anthony. ⊠ *1 Southwest Pond, Box 100, Main Brook A0K 3N0,* ☎ *709/865–6361 or 888/865–6361,* FAX *709/865–2112,* WEB *www.tuckamore-lodge.nf.net. 5 rooms, 3 suites. No-smoking rooms, sauna, laundry service, airport shuttle. DC, V.*

$–$$ 🖫 **Vinland Motel.** Some rooms at this standard motel in the center of town have whirlpool baths. The restaurant isn't great, so look for other places nearby. ⊠ *West St., A0K 4S0,* ☎ *709/454–8843 or 800/563–7578,* FAX *709/454–8468. 43 rooms. Restaurant, bar, lounge, sauna, gym, coin laundry, meeting rooms. AE, DC, MC, V.*

Outdoor Activities and Sports

Northland Discovery Tours (⊠ behind the Grenfell Interpretation Centre, off West St., ☎ 709/454–3092 or 877/632–3747, WEB www3.nf.sympatico.ca/paul.alcock) offers boat tours to see whales, icebergs, and seabirds; land tours for viewing caribou, moose, and rare plants; salmon fishing; and snowmobile excursions.

Shopping

Be sure to visit the **Grenfell Handicrafts** store (✉ 227A West St., ☎ 709/454–4010) in the Grenfell Historic Properties complex. Training villagers to become self-sufficient in a harsh environment was one of Grenfell's aims. A windproof cloth that villagers turned into well-made parkas came to be known as Grenfell cloth. Mittens, caps, and coats are embroidered with motifs such as polar bears.

The West Coast

Western Newfoundland is known for the unlikely combination of world-class Atlantic salmon fishing and papermaking at two newsprint mills. This area includes Corner Brook, a major center. To the south, the Port au Port Peninsula west of Stephenville shows the French influence in Newfoundland; the farming valleys of the southwest were settled by Scots. A ferry from Nova Scotia docks at Port aux Basques in the far southwest corner.

Corner Brook

44 *50 km (31 mi) southwest of Deer Lake.*

Newfoundland's second-largest city, Corner Brook is the hub of the island's west coast. Mountains fringe three sides of the city, which has beautiful views of the harbor and the Bay of Islands. The town is also home to one of the largest paper mills in the world; you may smell it while you're here. Captain James Cook, the British explorer, charted the coast in the 1760s, and a memorial to him overlooks the bay.

Corner Brook is a convenient hub and point of departure for exploring the west coast. It's only a three-hour drive (allowing for traffic) from the Port aux Basques ferry from Nova Scotia. The town enjoys more clearly defined seasons than most of the rest of the island, and in summer it has many pretty gardens. The nearby Humber River is the best-known salmon river in the province.

The north and south shores of the Bay of Islands have fine paved roads—Route 440 on the north shore and Route 450 on the south—and both are a scenic half-day drive from Corner Brook. On both roads, farming and fishing communities exist side by side.

Dining and Lodging

$$–$$$ ✕ **13 West.** Start your meal off with oysters for an appetizer and chase them down with one of the wonderful salmon specials: strawberry salmon, mango salmon, blackened salmon, or salmon with rosemary and peppercorns. For those not interested in seafood, the rack of lamb and pork tenderloin are good choices. ✉ *13 West St.,* ☎ *709/634–1300. AE, MC, V.*

$–$$$ ✕▥ **Glynmill Inn.** This Tudor-style inn was once the staff house for the
★ visiting top brass of the paper mill. Rooms are cozy, and the dining room serves basic and well-prepared Newfoundland seafood, soups, and specialty desserts. There's also a popular steak house in the basement. ✉ *1 Cobb La., Box 550, A2H 6E6,* ☎ *709/634–5181; 800/563–4400 in Canada;* FAX *709/634–5106,* WEB *www.glynmillinn.ca. 58 rooms, 23 suites. 2 restaurants, bar, no-smoking rooms, meeting rooms. AE, DC, MC, V.*

$–$$ ✕▥ **Best Western Mamateek Inn.** The restaurant, which serves good Newfoundland home-cooked food, is known for its exquisite view of the city. Sunsets seen from here are remarkable. Rooms here are more modern than those at the Glynmill Inn. ✉ *Maple Valley Rd., Box 787, A2H 6G7,* ☎ *709/639–8901 or 800/563–8600,* FAX *709/639–7567,* WEB *www.bestwestern.com. 55 rooms. Restaurant, bar, in-room data ports, no-smoking rooms, coin laundry, business services, meeting rooms. AE, DC, MC, V.*

$-$$ 🏨 **Holiday Inn.** There's nothing special here, aside from the convenient location in town. The outdoor pool is heated, and some rooms have minibars. The restaurant is average, aside from good seasonal fish dishes. ✉ *48 West St., A2H 2Z2,* ☎ *709/634–5381,* FAX *709/634–1723,* WEB *www.holidayinncornerbrook.com. 99 rooms, 2 suites. Restaurant, lobby lounge, no-smoking rooms, room service, pool, gym. AE, D, DC, MC, V.*

$ 🏨 **Comfort Inn Corner Brook.** This is a comfortable, modern motel with pastel decor and beautiful views of the city or the Bay of Islands. ✉ *41 Maple Valley Rd., Box 1142, A2H 6T2,* ☎ *709/639–1980,* FAX *709/ 639–1549. 80 rooms. Restaurant, no-smoking rooms, meeting rooms. AE, DC, MC, V.*

Outdoor Activities and Sports

Strawberry Hill Resort (☎ 709/634–0066 or 877/434–0066, WEB www.strawberryhill.net) in Little Rapids, 12 km (7 mi) east of Corner Brook on Route 1, was once an exclusive retreat for the owner of the Corner Brook mill. Here you can enjoy Newfoundland's finest sport salmon fishing.

The growing **Marble Mountain Resort** (✉ Rte. 1, ☎ 709/637–7600 or 888/462–7253 WEB www.skimarble.com), 5 km (3 mi) east of the city in Steady Brook, has 27 downhill runs and five lifts capable of moving 6,500 skiers an hour, as well as a large day lodge, ski shop, day-care center, and restaurant. The vertical drop is 1,600 ft.

Stephenville

45   *77 km (48 mi) south of Corner Brook.*

The former Harmon Air Force Base is in Stephenville, a town best known for its summer festival. It also has a large modern paper mill. To the west of town is the Port au Port Peninsula, which was largely settled by the French, who brought their way of life and language to this small corner of Newfoundland.

The **Stephenville Festival** (☎ 709/643–4982 WEB www.stf.ca), held mid-July to mid-August, is the province's major annual summer theatrical event, with a mix of light musicals and serious drama.

En Route   As you travel down the Trans-Canada Highway toward Port aux Basques, Routes 404, 405, 406, and 407 bring you into the small Scottish communities of the **Codroy Valley.** Some of the most productive farms in the province are nestled in the valley against the backdrop of the Long Range Mountains and the Lewis Hills, from which gales strong enough to stop traffic hurl down to the coast.

Port aux Basques

46   *166 km (103 miles) south of Stephenville.*

Port aux Basques was one of seven Basque ports along Newfoundland's west coast and in southern Labrador during the 1500s and early 1600s and was given its name by the town's French successors. It's now the main ferry port connecting the island to Nova Scotia. In J. T. Cheeseman Provincial Park, 15 km (9 mi) north of town on the Trans-Canada Highway, and at Grand Bay West you may see the endangered piping plover, which nests in the sand dunes along this coast.

Lodging

$-$$ ☷ **Hotel Port aux Basques.** There's nothing special about the rooms here, but this is a good choice for families—children stay free and pets are permitted. This hotel is closer to the ferry than any other in town. ⊠ *1 Grand Bay Rd., A0M 1C0,* ☎ *709/695–2171 or 877/695–2171,* FAX *709/695–2250,* WEB *www.gatewaytonewfoundland.com. 50 rooms. Restaurant, bar, no-smoking rooms, meeting rooms. AE, DC, MC, V.*

$-$$ ☷ **St. Christopher's Hotel.** This clean, comfortable hotel has quiet, air-conditioned rooms and good food. Rooms have satellite TV. ⊠ *Caribou Rd., Box 2049, A0M 1C0,* ☎ *709/695–7034 or 800/563–4779,* FAX *709/695–9841,* WEB *www.stchrishotel.nf.net. 52 rooms, 3 suites. Restaurant, bar, no-smoking rooms, playground, meeting rooms. AE, DC, MC, V.*

$ ☷ **Caribou Bed and Breakfast.** All the rooms here are decorated in slate blue and neutral, soothing colors. The Caribou tends to be a quiet B&B because people have an early breakfast before catching the nearby ferry. A full breakfast is included in the room rate. ⊠ *42 Grand Bay Rd., A0N 1K0,* ☎ *709/695–3408,* WEB *home.thezone.net/~gibbons. 5 rooms. No-smoking rooms. MC, V. Closed Nov.–Apr. BP.*

LABRADOR

Isolated from the rest of the continent, Labrador has remained one of the world's truly wild places, although its two main centers of Labrador City–Wabush and Happy Valley–Goose Bay have all the amenities of larger urban areas. Labrador, steeped in history, is a place where the past invades the present and life evolves as it did many years ago—a composite of natural phenomena, wilderness adventure, history, and culture. This vast landscape—293,347 square km (113,261 square mi) of land and 8,000 km (5,000 mi) of coastline—is home to 30,000 people. The small but richly diverse population has a history that in some cases stretches back thousands of years; in other cases—the mining towns of Labrador West, for example—the history goes back less than four decades.

The Straits

The Straits in southeastern Labrador were a rich hunting-and-gathering ground for the area's earliest peoples, the Maritime Archaic tribes. The oldest industrial site in the New World is here—the 16th-century Basque whaling station at Red Bay.

L'Anse au Clair

❹❼ *5 km (3 mi) from Blanc Sablon, Québec (ferry from St. Barbe, Newfoundland, docks in Blanc Sablon).*

In L'Anse au Clair—French for "clear water cove" —anglers can try their luck for trout and salmon on the scenic Forteau and Pinware rivers. The French place name dates from the early 1700s when this area was settled by French speakers from Québec. Ask at the local museum for directions to The Doctor's Path where, in the 19th century, the local doctor searched out herbs and medicinal plants.

Lodging

$-$$ ☷ **Northern Light Inn.** Loads of bus-tour passengers make this a stop in summer because the Northern Light is the only accommodation of any size along Route 510. The hotel is pretty ordinary, but the food is decent and the rooms are air-conditioned. Rooms have cable TV and telephones, and there's a gift shop. ⊠ *58 Main St. (Rte. 510), A0K 3K0,*

☎ 709/931–2332 or 800/563–3188, ℻ 709/931–2708. *49 rooms, 5 suites. Restaurant, bar, coin laundry, meeting rooms. AE, DC, MC, V.*

L'Anse Amour

㊽ *19 km (12 mi) east of L'Anse au Clair.*

The elaborate **Maritime Archaic Indian burial site** (✉ Rte. 510) discovered near L'Anse Amour is 7,500 years old. A plaque marks a site that is the oldest known aboriginal funeral monument in North America. The **L'Anse Amour Lighthouse** (☎ 709/927–5825; 🎫 $2.50, ☉ mid-June–early Oct., daily 10–5:30), constructed in 1857, is 109 ft tall, the second-tallest in Canada; you can climb it.

En Route The **Labrador Straits Museum** provides a glimpse into the history and lifestyle of the area. ✉ *Rte. 510 between Forteau and L'Anse au Loup,* ☎ 709/931–2067. 🎫 *$2.* ☉ *July 15–Sept. 15, daily 9–5:30.*

Red Bay

㊾ *35 km (22 mi) from L'Anse Amour.*

The area's main attraction lies at the very end of Route 510: Red Bay, the site of a 16th-century Basque whaling station and a National Historic Site. Basque whalers began harpooning migrating whales from flimsy boats in frigid waters a few years after Cabot's discovery of the coast in 1497. Between 1550 and 1600 Red Bay was the world's whal-

★ ing capital. The **Red Bay National Historic Site** has a visitor center that interprets the Basque heritage with film and artifacts. A boat takes you on a five-minute journey over to the excavation site on Saddle Island. ✉ *Rte. 510,* ☎ 709/920–2142, 🌐 *parkscanada.pch.gc.ca.* 🎫 *Visitor center $5; boat to island $2.* ☉ *Mid-May–mid-June, daily 9–5; mid-June–Labor Day, daily 9–8; Labor Day–Canadian Thanksgiving Day, daily 9–5.*

Coastal Labrador

Along the southern coast, most villages are inhabited by descendants of Europeans, whereas farther north they are mostly Inuit and Innu. Over the years the European settlers have adopted native skills and survival strategies, and the native peoples have adopted many European technologies. In summer the ice retreats and a coastal steamer delivers goods, but in winter small airplanes and snowmobiles are the only ways in and out.

You can tour central coastal Labrador aboard a car ferry from Lewisporte, Newfoundland. A second vessel, a coastal freighter known as the *Cruising Labrador,* travels from St. Anthony, Newfoundland, to Nain, Labrador's northernmost settlement. This trip takes two weeks to complete. Both vessels carry all sorts of food and goods for people living along the coast. The coastal freighter stops at a number of summer fishing stations and coastal communities. Reservations are required.

Battle Harbour National Historic Site

12 km (7 mi) by boat from Mary's Harbour.

This island site has the only remaining intact outport fishing merchant's premises in the province. Settled in the 18th century, Battle Harbour was the main fishing port in Labrador until the first half of the 20th century. After fires destroyed some of the community, the people moved to nearby Mary's Harbour. The site also contains the oldest Anglican church in Labrador. Accommodations are available. ⊠ *Southern Labrador coast, accessible by boat from Mary's Harbour,* ☎ FAX *709/ 921–6216,* WEB *www.seascape.com/labrador/battleharbour.* ☜ *$3.50; boat from Mary's Harbour $10 one-way.* ⊙ *June–Sept., daily 10–6.*

Jones Charters and Tours (☎ 709/921–6249) offers an air and small-boat package from either St. John's or Happy Valley–Goose Bay.

Lodging
$–$$ ⊡ **Battle Harbour Inn.** This is the only game in town as far as lodging is concerned. The restored two-story house is clean and comfortable, but a bit rustic. ⊠ *Mailing address: Box 135, Mary's Harbour A0K 3P0,* ☎ FAX *709/921–6216. 5 rooms share 2 baths. Dining room. MC, V. Closed Oct.–May.*

Happy Valley–Goose Bay

❺⓿ *525 km (326 mi) from Labrador City.*

Happy Valley–Goose Bay is the chief service center for coastal Labrador. Anyone coming to Labrador to fish will probably pass through here. The town was founded in the 1940s as a top-secret air base used to ferry fleets of aircraft to Europe. It's still used as a low-level flying training base by the British, Dutch, and German air forces.

Lodging
$–$$ ⊡ **Aurora Hotel.** Rooms at this basic hotel, the best in town, are bright and decorated with pastels. The Aurora is a five-minute drive from the airport. ⊠ *382 Hamilton River Rd., A0P 1C0,* ☎ *709/896–3398 or 800/563–3066,* FAX *709/896–9608,* WEB *www.aurorahotel.com. 37 rooms, 3 suites. Bar, dining room, room service, meeting rooms. AE, MC, V.*

Outdoor Activities and Sports
Ski Mount Shana (⊠ Rte. 520, ☎ 709/896–8162), with 10 downhill runs, is between Happy Valley–Goose Bay and North West River. The vertical drop is 525 ft.

North West River

❺❶ *32 km (20 mi) northeast of Happy Valley–Goose Bay.*

North West River was founded as a Hudson's Bay trading post in the 1830s. The town was also the starting point for the Wallace–Hubbard expedition of 1903. Leonidas Hubbard and Dillon Wallace were American adventurers who attempted a journey from Lake Melville to Ungava Bay along a previously untraveled route. They took a wrong turn, got lost, and Hubbard died in the wilderness from starvation. His wife, Mina, never forgave Wallace and completed her husband's journey in 1905. Her book, *A Woman's Way Through Unknown Labrador,* is still considered a classic. These and other stories are examined at the **Labrador Heritage Museum** (☎ 709/497–8898). Call ahead for an appointment.

Labrador West

Labrador West's subarctic landscape is challenging and unforgettable. The two towns here were founded in the 1950s to exploit the huge iron-ore deposits. The best way to see this area is to ride the **Québec North Shore and Labrador Railway** (☎ 418/968–7808 or 709/944–8205), which leaves Sept-Isles, Québec, three times a week in summer and twice a week in winter. The seven- to eight-hour trip to the area takes you through nearly 600 km (372 mi) of virgin forest, past spectacular waterfalls and majestic mountains.

Wabush

52 *525 km (326 mi) west of Happy Valley–Goose Bay.*

The modern town of Wabush has all the amenities of larger centers, including accommodations, sports and recreational facilities, good shopping, and some of the warmest hospitality found anywhere.

Outdoor Activities and Sports

The **Smokey Mountain Alpine Skiing Center** (⊠ Rte. 500, ☎ 709/944–2129), west of Wabush, is open mid-November to late April and has slopes for beginners and advanced skiers. The vertical drop is 1,000 ft.

Labrador City

53 *525 km (326 mi) west of Happy Valley–Goose Bay.*

Labrador City has all the facilities of nearby Wabush. Each March, Labrador City and Wabush play host to a 192-km (120-mi) dogsled race.

Outdoor Activities and Sports

The **White Wolf Snowmobile Club** (☎ 709/944–7401 or 709/944–6833) organizes a mid-March snowmobile rally that includes tours to see the world's largest caribou herd (about 600,000 animals). White Wolf also maintains an extensive groomed trail system all winter; snowmobile rentals are available.

NEWFOUNDLAND AND LABRADOR A TO Z

To research prices, get advice from other travelers, and book travel arrangements, visit www.fodors.com.

AIR TRAVEL

Air Canada flies into Newfoundland. Regional connectors include Air Alliance (Québec to Wabush), Air Labrador, and Air Nova.

➤ AIRLINES AND CONTACTS: **Air Alliance** (☎ 888/247–6682). **Air Canada** (☎ 800/776–3000). **Air Labrador** (☎ 888/247–2262). **Air Nova** (☎ 888/247–2262). **Provincial Airlines** (☎ 709/576–1666; 800/563–2800 in Atlantic Canada).

AIRPORTS

The province's main airport is St. John's International Airport. Other airports in Newfoundland are at Stephenville, Deer Lake, St. Anthony, and Gander; airports in Labrador are in Happy Valley–Goose Bay, Wabush, and Churchill Falls.

➤ AIRPORT INFORMATION: **St. John's International Airport** (⊠ Airport Rd. off Portugal Cove Rd., St. John's, ☎ 709/772–0011).

BOAT AND FERRY TRAVEL

Marine Atlantic operates a car ferry from North Sydney, Nova Scotia, to Port aux Basques, Newfoundland (crossing time is six hours), and, from June through September, from North Sydney to Argentia, three times a week (crossing time 12–14 hours). In all cases, reservations are required.

Another car ferry, operated by the provincial government, travels from Lewisporte in Newfoundland to Cartwright, on the coast of Labrador, and then through the Hamilton inlet to Happy Valley–Goose Bay. Reservations are required. The trip takes 33 hours one-way, and two regularly scheduled return trips are made weekly.

To explore the south coast of Labrador, catch the ferry at St. Barbe on Route 430 in Newfoundland to Blanc Sablon, Québec. From here you can drive to Mary's Harbour along Route 510. Tourism Newfoundland and Labrador has information about ferry schedules.

➤ Boat and Ferry Information: **Marine Atlantic** (✉ Box 250, North Sydney, Nova Scotia B2A 3M3, ☎ 800/341–7981; 902/794–8109 TTY). **Tourism Newfoundland and Labrador** (☎ 800/563–6353).

BUS TRAVEL

DRL Coachlines runs a trans-island bus service in Newfoundland. Buses leave at 8 AM from St. John's and Port aux Basques. Small buses known as outport taxis connect the major centers with surrounding communities.

➤ Bus Information: **DRL Coachlines** (☎ 709/738–8088).

CAR TRAVEL

In winter, some highways may close during and after severe snowstorms. For winter road conditions on the west coast, call the Department of Works, Services, and Transportation. A 24-hour hot line provides winter road conditions throughout the province; calls cost 75¢. You can also log on to the Government of Newfoundland and Labrador Web site (WEB www.gov.nf.ca/roads) for information on road conditions.

Route 500 links Labrador City with Happy Valley–Goose Bay via Churchill Falls. Conditions on this 526-km (326-mi) unpaved wilderness road are best from June through October. If you plan on doing any extensive driving in any part of Labrador, you should contact the Department of Tourism, Culture, and Recreation for advice on the best routes and road conditions.

Newfoundland has an excellent highway system, and all but a handful of secondary roads are paved. The province's roads are generally uncrowded, adding to the pleasure of driving. Travel time along the Trans-Canada Highway (Route 1) from Port aux Basques to St. John's is about 13 hours, with time out for a meal. The trip from Corner Brook to St. Anthony at the northernmost tip of the island is about five hours. The drive from St. John's to Grand Bank on the Burin Peninsula takes about four hours. If you're heading for the southern coast of the Avalon Peninsula, pick up Route 10 just south of St. John's and follow it toward Trepassey.

EMERGENCY SERVICES

➤ Contacts: **Department of Tourism, Culture, and Recreation** (☎ 709/729–2830 or 800/563–6353). **Department of Works, Services, and Transportation** (☎ 709/635–4144 in Deer Lake; 709/292–4444 in Grand Falls–Windsor and Central Newfoundland; 709/466–4160 in Clarenville; 709/729–7669 in St. John's; 709/896–7888 in Happy Valley–Goose Bay depot in Labrador; 900/451–3300 for 24-hour hot line, with cost of 75¢).

EMERGENCIES

➤ Contacts: **Medical emergencies, police** (☎ 911 or 0).
➤ Hospitals: **Captain William Jackman Hospital** (✉ 410 Booth Ave., Labrador City, ☎ 709/944–2632). **Charles S. Curtis Memorial Hospital** (✉ West St., St. Anthony, ☎ 709/454–3333). **General Hospital** (✉ 300 Prince Philip Dr., St. John's, ☎ 709/737–6300). **George B. Cross Hospital** (✉ Manitoba Dr., Clarenville, ☎ 709/466–3411). **James Paton** (✉ 125 Trans-Canada Hwy., Gander, ☎ 709/651–2500). **St. Clare's Mercy Hospital** (✉ 154 Le Marchant Rd., St. John's, ☎ 709/778–3111). **Western Memorial** (✉ Brookfield Ave., Corner Brook, ☎ 709/637–5000).

OUTDOORS AND SPORTS
FISHING

Seasonal and regulatory fishing information can be obtained from the Department of Tourism, Culture, and Recreation.

➤ CONTACTS: **Department of Tourism, Culture, and Recreation** (✉ Box 8730, St. John's A1B 4K2, ☎ 709/729–2830).

TOURS
ADVENTURE

Local operators offer sea kayaking, ocean diving, canoeing, wildlife viewing, mountain biking, white-water rafting, heli-hiking, and interpretive walks in summer. In winter, snowmobiling and caribou- and seal-watching expeditions are popular. In spring and early summer, a favored activity is iceberg-watching. Before choosing an operator, contact the Department of Tourism, Culture, and Recreation to make sure you're calling an established outfit.

Eastern Edge Kayak Adventures leads east-coast sea-kayaking tours and gives white-water kayaking instruction. Maxxim Vacations in St. John's organizes packaged adventure and cultural tours. Tuckamore Wilderness Lodge, in Main Brook, uses its luxurious lodge on the Great Northern Peninsula as a base for viewing caribou, seabird colonies, whales, and icebergs, and for winter snowmobile excursions. Wildland Tours in St. John's has three weeklong guided tours that view wildlife and visit historically and culturally significant sites across Newfoundland.

➤ FEES AND SCHEDULES: **Department of Tourism, Culture, and Recreation** (✉ Box 8730, St. John's A1B 4K2, ☎ 709/729–2830). **Eastern Edge Kayak Adventures** (☎ 709/782–5925, WEB www.kayakeeo.hypersource.com). **Maxxim Vacations** (☎ 709/754–6666 or 800/567–6666, WEB www.maxximvacations.com). **Tuckamore Wilderness Lodge** (☎ 709/865–6361 or 888/865–6361, WEB www.tuckamore-lodge.nf.net). **Wildland Tours** (☎ 709/722–3123, WEB www.wildlands.com).

BY BUS

Fleetline Motorcoach Tours in Holyrood runs island-wide tours. Local tours are available for Port aux Basques, the Codroy Valley, Corner Brook, the Bay of Islands, Gros Morne National Park, the Great Northern Peninsula, and St. John's. McCarthy's Party in St. John's has guided bus tours across Newfoundland, learning vacations, and charter services.

➤ FEES AND SCHEDULES: **Fleetline Motorcoach Tours** (☎ 709/229–7600). **McCarthy's Party** (☎ 709/781–2244 or 888/660–6060, WEB www.newfoundland-tours.com).

WALKING

On the St. John's Haunted Hike, Reverend Thomas Wickam Jarvis (actor Dale Jarvis) leads popular walking tours of the supernatural on summer evenings; tours begin at the west entrance of the Anglican Cathedral on Church Hill.

➤ FEES AND SCHEDULES: **St. John's Haunted Hike** (☎ 709/576–2087).

TRAIN TRAVEL

Iron Ore Company of Canada's Québec North Shore and Labrador Railway has service between Sept-Isles, Québec, and Labrador City in Labrador.

TRAIN INFORMATION: **Iron Ore Company of Canada's Québec North Shore and Labrador Railway** (☎ 418/968–7808 OR 709/944–8205).

VISITOR INFORMATION

The Department of Tourism, Culture, and Recreation distributes brochures from its offices in the Confederation Building, West Block, St. John's. The province maintains a 24-hour, tourist-information line year-round that can help with accommodations and reservations.

From June until Labor Day, a network of Visitor Information Centres, open daily 9–9, dots the province. These centers carry information on events, accommodations, shopping, and crafts stores in their area. The airports in Gander and St. John's operate in-season visitor-information booths. The city of St. John's operates an information center in a restored railway carriage next to the harbor.

➤ TOURIST INFORMATION: **Department of Tourism, Culture, and Recreation** (✉ Box 8730, St. John's A1B 4K2, ☎ 709/729–2830; 800/563–6353 for tourist-information line).

16 WILDERNESS CANADA

THE YUKON, THE NORTHWEST TERRITORIES, AND NUNAVUT

Life above the 60th parallel in the mountainous, river-threaded Yukon, the lake-dotted Northwest Territories, and Arctic Nunavut is strange and wonderful. The landscape is austere and beautiful: the tundra plains that reach to the Arctic Ocean, the remote ice fields of Kluane National Park, white-water rivers snaking through deep canyons. This is also the last region of North America in which native peoples have managed to sustain traditional cultures relatively undisturbed.

Updated by
Tina Sebert
(the Yukon) and
Rosemary
Allerston (the
Northwest
Territories and
Nunavut)

ET IT BE STATED AS SIMPLY AS POSSIBLE: life in Canada's far north is strange—strange as in weird, strange as in wonderful, strange as in uncommon. The inherent strangeness of the world north of the 60th parallel—the latitudinal line separating Canada's provinces from the Yukon, the Northwest Territories, and Nunavut—is perceptible in empirical, practical, and mysterious ways.

Consider examples from life in the heart of strangeness:

Seasons become so overlapped in the few nonwinter months that summer wildflowers have not finished blooming by the time the foliage picks up its fall color. In winter a network of highways, built entirely of hardpacked snow over frozen rivers and lakes, opens up to automotive traffic. So cold are the snow and ice that they lose their slipperiness, making areas otherwise inaccessible relatively easy to reach. Bridges over rivers are also built of ice, and northerners must prepare for "break-up" and "freeze-up"—the few weeks in spring and fall when ice bridges are unstable but rivers are still too frozen for ferries to operate. Unprepared travelers sometimes fork over several hundred dollars or more for a helicopter to sling their cars across a river. This underscores the fact that, in a region where bush pilots are held in high regard, air transport is the way to go. To a plane with pontoons, an uncountable number of lakes means an uncountable number of watery runways.

If a single strange element of life in the far north stands out, it is the quality of light. In midsummer, sunrise and sunset merge, and north of the Arctic Circle they don't occur at all. When night does come—so belatedly in summer that it is a way of life to draw shades tightly during sunlit evenings to simulate night—there is the mystical voodoo show of the northern lights.

Most of the region is climatically classified as semiarid, much of it covered by the vast granite spread of the Canadian Shield. But because water evaporates and ice melts so slowly in Arctic climes, there is an abundance of water, mostly in the form of lakes, fjords, rivers, and ponds in the Northwest Territories and Nunavut, and as rivers in the mountainous Yukon. A good deal of it remains ice; the glaciers of the St. Elias Mountains in the Yukon's Kluane National Park, topped by 19,550-ft Mt. Logan, create the largest nonpolar ice field in the world.

This is wilderness, and the wildlife loves it. A migrating caribou herd exceeding 80,000 is not uncommon, and that's a number to keep in perspective: it represents the entire human census of the region. Indeed, people are profoundly outnumbered by nonhuman mammals: bears (black, grizzly, polar), Dall sheep, wolves, wolverines, moose, bison, and, of course, caribou. Humans are also outnumbered by fish and birds. Anglers regularly throw back trout weighing 10 pounds, because in these parts a fish that size is considered to be too small. Bald eagles are a common sight, as are the flocks of migratory waterfowl that spend their summers here.

Signs on government buildings are often inscribed in as many as eight official languages—English, French, and various First Nations languages. Native people in the far north are wielding increasing influence in governmental affairs. The main native groups are the Dene (or Athapaskan-speaking) peoples of the Yukon and the Northwest Territories; the Inland Tlingit of the Yukon; and the Métis, Inuit, Inuvialuit (western Inuit) peoples of the Mackenzie River valley, Arctic coast, and Nunavut. Many of these people go about their lives much as their ancestors did centuries before them but with the help of such 20th-century basics as electricity and motor-driven machinery—plus more sophisticated technology like computers and satellite-guided Global Positioning Systems, with which pilots and other wilderness travelers can get their bearings.

In recent years, large tracts of land have been ceded to native groups in land-claims settlements. When the Northwest Territories were divided in 1999, the new eastern territory represented the principal lands of the Inuit and was named Nunavut, meaning "our land." The Dene call the western region Denendeh, which means the same; however, since thousands of Inuvialuit, Métis, and nonnative settlers also live here, there are no plans to make this name official. The western region remains the Northwest Territories.

A visit to the far north does not happen without commitment and preparation. Lodging for less than $100 a night is rare, unless you camp or book yourself into one of the growing number of bed-and-breakfasts in the larger towns. Having to rely on planes to get from one place to another raises the cost of a visit here even more. Guides and outfitters can be expensive, too, but their fees aren't out of line with the general cost of living in the far north, and their travel packages often end up saving you money.

Visitors must be willing to abide possible discomforts and inconveniences. Outside cities and towns, mosquitoes and blackflies rule the north in summer and early fall, and anyone without insect repellent is in for big trouble. Packing gloves and insulated clothing for a visit in August might seem excessive, but such are the necessities of traveling in a world where it's not uncommon for summer temperatures to drop from above 70°F to well below freezing in a single day. And life doesn't always proceed with clockwork precision; a frontier quality still pervades in much of the far north, and a lot of business is conducted on an ad-hoc, by-the-bootstraps basis. Visiting the far north can be daunting, difficult, frightening, and even dangerous. But for those who prepare themselves for the challenge, it can be nothing short of exhilarating.

Pleasures and Pastimes

Aurora Borealis

Few spectacles on the planet rival the aurora borealis, also known as the northern lights, which fills the subarctic heavens on clear nights from September through March. Yellowknife, where there's a chance of seeing the aurora on 243 nights in a year—the best odds just about anywhere—has become a favorite destination for troops of supplicants who consider the lights to be omens of good fortune. Few would argue with them; the vast waves of shimmering green, red, and lavender seem to prance and whisper as you stand awestruck beneath the stars. The aurora is best seen away from town lights, so Yellowknife tour operators bus visitors out onto frozen Great Slave Lake, where, bundled in parkas, they can gaze to their hearts' content. If you are visiting the Yukon in summer—when 24-hour daylight makes seeing the aurora impossible—you can see a re-creation of the aurora at the Northern Lights Centre in Watson Lake.

Dining

Cuisine in the far north rarely reaches grand epicurean standards, but it can have a distinctive character. In some places and at certain times of year, a caribou steak or a moose burger may be easier to find than a fresh salad. Outside the main cities, the dining room of your hotel or lodge may well be your only choice. But if the far north is not necessarily a gastronomic paradise, it is surprising and certainly admirable given what some chefs are able to concoct with limited ingredients.

CATEGORY	COST*
$$$$	over $32
$$$	$22–$32
$$	$13–$21
$	under $13

per person, in Canadian dollars, for a main course at dinner

Lodging

Lodging prices in the far north have come down in the past decade—a reflection of the steady increase in northern tourism. Still, in some communities a single lodge or co-op hotel may be your only option, so if you don't like the price or the room, you don't have much choice. In addition, the shortness of the tourism season forces lodging proprietors to try to make ends meet in two or three months of active vacation business. Although you might think you're paying a good chunk of change for ordinary accommodations, consider the lack of quality building materials in many areas and the prohibitive costs of construction. In months other than July and August, expect better deals—room prices reduced 50% or more—but fewer choices, because many places are closed from September through June.

Wilderness lodges offer a once-in-a-lifetime experience in some of the most remote and beautiful areas of the region. A one-week stay allows you to explore the wilds during the day and then return to the comfort of a cabin and home-cooked meal in the evening. In the Yukon, Whitehorse serves as a departure point for those heading to lodges farther north. Sports lovers planning a trip to the Northwest Territories can set out from Yellowknife for backcountry lodges on the shores of Great Slave Lake or on one of the thousands of smaller lakes that, along with their barren rock underpinnings and scrub growth, are the principal geological features of the far north's interior.

Territorial, or public, campgrounds are found along all roads in the north and are open from the spring thaw until the fall freeze. Visitor information centers throughout the region can provide information on specific campground locations and facilities as well as permits. Note: It's advisable to boil or filter all water, even water that has been designated as "drinking water," at a campground.

CATEGORY	COST*
$$$$	over $200
$$$	$150–$200
$$	$100–$150
$	under $100

All prices are in Canadian dollars, for a standard double room, excluding gratuities and 7% GST.

Outdoor Activities and Sports

CROSS-COUNTRY SKIING

In a world covered by snow eight months out of the year, cross country–skiing opportunities are plentiful. The best time for skiing, however, is from February until the snow melts (the precise time varies according to latitude and elevation), when days are longer and warmer. Although short outings on skis are possible almost anywhere in the north, perhaps the most interesting extended excursions are in the Kluane area and the Arctic North. A number of backcountry lodges have begun opening in April and May for ski-touring enthusiasts.

DOGSLEDDING

Before there were planes and snowmobiles, dogsleds were the vital means of transportation in the far north. The Yukon Quest International Dogsled Race, along the Yukon River from Whitehorse to Fairbanks or Fairbanks to Whitehorse, takes place every year in mid-February. Destination/start points alternate annually. Top mushers compete for gold nuggets and cash in this 1,600-km (992-mi) trek, which is touted as the toughest dogsled race in the world. The most important race in the Northwest Territories is the Canadian Championship Dog Derby, held at Yellowknife in late March. If you want to try a little mushing yourself, there are many outfitters in the Whitehorse area. Some even take you on sections of the Yukon Quest trail. The **Yukon Visitor Reception Centre** (✉ 2nd Ave. and Hanson St., ☎ 867/667–5340, FAX 867/667–6351, WEB www.touryukon.com) has a complete list of kennels in the Yukon that offer dogsledding. Several tour operators in the Northwest Territories have dogsledding adventures near Yellowknife and Inuvik, and spring packages in Nunavut frequently include dogsled jaunts. Contact **NWT Arctic Tourism** (✉ Box 610, Yellowknife NT X1A 2N5, ☎ 867/873–7200 or 800/661–0788, FAX 867/873–4059, WEB www.nwttravel.nt.ca) or **Nunavut Tourism** (✉ Box 1450, Iqaluit NT X0A 0H0, ☎ 867/979–6551 or 800/491–7910, FAX 867/979–1261, WEB www.nunatour.nt.ca) for more information.

FISHING

Fishing in wilderness Canada is a way of life for many locals. What sustains the residents here in the north is also what attracts anglers: fish in large quantities and of considerable proportions. Lake trout between 30 and 70 pounds are not unusual. The most common catches in the far north are arctic char, grayling, pike, lake trout, and whitefish. Numerous outfitters throughout the region can guide anglers on day trips or short excursions; your best bet is to check with a regional tourist office for outfitter recommendations. Day trips from Yellowknife to Great Slave Lake are especially easy to arrange. Some lakes and streams are accessible by road in the Yukon and in the Northwest Territories. However, the more typical fishing adventure in the far north involves flying to a remote lodge for several days. Great Bear Lake, which lies astride the Arctic Circle in the Northwest Territories, is famous for its record-breaking trout. Fishing in the Arctic rivers of Nunavut is an unforgettable experience, but not one to be undertaken without a knowledgeable guide.

HIKING

Although the landscape can be spectacular, the going can be rough. Marked trails are few, and sometimes the only trails to follow are those beaten down by wild animals. The five general areas that are best for wilderness hiking are Baffin Island, Nahanni National Park, Kluane National Park, the Chilkoot Trail, and the mountains along the Dempster Highway.

MOUNTAINEERING

In the far north, the question is not what to climb but how to access the mountain. The major peaks of Kluane National Park, Mt. St. Elias, and particularly Canada's highest peak, Mt. Logan, are tops in the mountaineering world but can only be reached by helicopter or plane. For serious rock climbers, the Cirque of the Unclimbables in Nahanni National Park presents an obvious challenge. In Nunavut, the peaks of Auyuittuq National Park draw skilled climbers from around the globe.

WATER SPORTS

River travel is one of the best ways to experience the wilderness of the far north; these roads of water lead into otherwise inaccessible remote areas. Canoes of various configurations are the preferred means of travel, although for some rivers—particularly those with considerable white water—rafts or kayaks may be used. If you decide on an unguided trip, outfitters can provide both the necessary gear as well as transportation to and from the river. The South Nahanni River in Nahanni National Park is considered a classic. The Alsek and the Tatshenshini, which run primarily through British Columbia, begin in the Kluane region of the Yukon and are great for water-sports enthusiasts. With a little preparation, even beginning canoeists can follow in the footsteps of the gold-rush stampeders and float down the Yukon River from Whitehorse to Dawson City. The wild, remote rivers of the Arctic barrens and islands offer challenges to experienced paddlers. Another water adventure to consider is sailing on Great Slave Lake.

Shopping

Native arts and crafts are the most compelling buys in the far north. You may find that prices are best when buying directly from artists, craftspeople, or shops in local communities. But if you buy from galleries and stores in the cities, you'll get a wider selection of works from many regions, all of which have distinctive styles, plus information on the various artists and art forms and usually a guarantee of authenticity. Soapstone carvings, clothing, and moose- or caribou-hair tuftings (hair sewn onto velvet or hide and cut and shaped into pictures of flowers or animals) are popular purchases. Be aware before buying, however, that some products, such as those made from hides or materials from endangered species, may not be brought into the United States. In many cases—a polar-bear rug, for example—the import problem is obvious, but not in all cases; for example, jewelry made of walrus ivory may be confiscated at the border.

Exploring Wilderness Canada

The Yukon, the Northwest Territories, and Nunavut make up 3,787,800 square km (1,462,470 square mi), almost three times the size of Alaska and half the size of the rest of the United States. There are small cities—Whitehorse in the Yukon and Yellowknife in the Northwest Territories—but there are many more communities that are accessible only by plane. The landscape is reason enough to visit. Consider the tundra plains that reach to the Arctic Ocean, the remote ice fields of the St. Elias Mountains, and the glacier-sculpted cliffs of Baffin Island.

Numbers in the text correspond to numbers in the margin and on The Yukon and Northwest Territories and Nunavut maps.

Great Itineraries

The idea of exploring all of Canada's far north in a single trip is an absurdity. It would be comparable to trying to visit Florida, New England, and the Rocky Mountains on the same vacation, only with far fewer roads. Size is only one problem; expense is another. Food, gas, and lodging are typically priced higher than in other parts of Canada, but the biggest cost is transportation, especially in those vast, roadless areas where you'll need to depend on air travel. This is not to say it's difficult to get from one place to another. The large number of charter-plane operators and expert bush pilots makes getting around easier than you might think. But the cost of traveling by small planes can be dizzying.

The best strategy for exploring the far north is to focus on a specific area (e.g., Baffin Island, the Nahanni region, Dawson City) and/or an activity (e.g., fishing, wildlife viewing). Specific travel plans can save hundreds, even thousands, of dollars. The choices fall roughly into four categories: visits to main cities (Dawson City, Whitehorse, Yellowknife, Inuvik, and Iqaluit), excursions from the main cities, rambling in the backcountry wilderness, and adventures in the Arctic North. Though there are enough activities in the Yukon, the Northwest Territories, and Nunavut to keep you occupied for months, the following itineraries are geared toward the standard traveler, for whom time is an issue.

THE YUKON

If You Have 3 Days: Start your tour in ⊞ **Whitehorse** ①. The S.S. *Klondike,* the MacBride Museum, and Miles Canyon all hold a bit of character from the gold-rush era and are a good way to learn about the Yukon's colorful history. On Day 2 drive down Route 2, stopping to stretch your legs at picturesque **Carcross** ②, where you can stroll along the shores of Bennett Lake. From Carcross head to ⊞ **Skagway** ③, Alaska, along the approximate route traversed by the Klondike gold rushers in 1898. You pass through a variety of landforms, including the Carcross Desert, the alpine tundra of the White Pass, and the coastal rain forest of the Alaskan Panhandle. On the morning of your third day, ride the historic White Pass & Yukon Route railway and bus back to Whitehorse past blue glaciers and rushing waterfalls.

If You Have 5 Days: Start your trip as you would with the three-day itinerary, but on Day 3 drive eight hours from Skagway to ⊞ **Dawson City** ⑥. On your fourth day drive down Bonanza Creek Road to Dredge No. 4 and the original claim where gold was discovered in 1896. Spend Day 5 visiting Robert Service Cabin, the Palace Grand Theatre, and Diamond Tooth Gertie's Gambling Hall.

If You Have 10 Days: A 10-day itinerary allows outdoors lovers to explore the Yukon wilds. An extended stay at a fly-in wilderness lodge provides you with a base camp from which to set off for several backcountry adventures. Once you reach the lodge, your hosts help arrange hiking, boating, and fishing excursions, and they'll point you in the direction of the best wildlife-viewing areas.

A Klondike Gold Rush itinerary could include a hike over the **Chilkoot Trail** (three to four days) plus visits to ⊞ **Skagway** ③, ⊞ **Whitehorse** ①, and ⊞ **Dawson City** ⑥. If river scenery and wildlife viewing are more of an interest, a canoe trip down the Thirty-Mile section of the Yukon River, from Whitehorse to Carmacks, might fill the bill.

Some of the planet's best hiking is possible in **Kluane National Park** ④. A 10-day itinerary could take you as far back as the Donjek Glacier in the heart of Kluane's ethereal wilderness. Those wishing to stay on the Yukon's roadways could venture up the Dempster Highway, past the Arctic Circle to ⊞ **Inuvik** ⑧ in the Northwest Territories, an adventurous four-day extension of the five-day itinerary above.

THE NORTHWEST TERRITORIES AND NUNAVUT

If You Have 3 Days: You can jet north from Edmonton or Calgary across the Arctic Circle to ⊞ **Inuvik** ⑧ to see the amazing Mackenzie Delta, **Tuktoyaktuk** ⑨, and the Beaufort Sea. Two nights in Inuvik also gives you time for a flying tour over the giant estuary (where belugas romp in summer) to **Herschel Island,** a haunt of 19th-century whalers.

If You Have 5 Days: Fly to ⊞ **Yellowknife** ⑦, where you can spend your first day exploring the Old Town and the cultural attractions downtown. The focus of Day 2 could be an outdoor activity, such as a dogsled ride or a cruise on Great Slave Lake. With its good choice of dining and lodging options, Yellowknife is a fine base from which to head out and explore ⊞ **Nahanni National Park.** It's best to book a scheduled flight to Fort Simpson, where several plane and helicopter services offer flightseeing trips to the park's breathtaking Virginia Falls. Although a driving trip to Nahanni means spending Day 3 on the road, Day 4 can be worth it. If you choose to fly to Nahanni, spend two days at the park or use one day to tour historic **Fort Simpson**. ⊞ **Wood Buffalo National Park** is another possible road excursion from Yellowknife. As with the drive to Nahanni National Park, Day 3 is a travel day. On Day 4 you can explore the park's frontcountry trails; be on the look-out for bison and bald eagles. Whether you choose to drive to Nahanni National Park or to Wood Buffalo National Park, reserve Day 5 for the trip back to Yellowknife.

If You Have 7 Days: On Day 1, head for ⊞ **Iqaluit** ⑩, on Baffin Island, the capital of Nunavut. You can fly directly to Iqaluit from Ottawa, Montréal, Winnipeg, or Edmonton, via Yellowknife. Explore the town on Day 2, starting with the Unikkaarvik Visitor Centre and Nunatta Sunakkutaangit Museum. At the visitor center you can schedule an afternoon boat trip to Qaummaarviit Territorial Historic Park with a local outfitter. On Day 3, fly to the old whaling village of Pangnirtung, gateway to ⊞ **Auyuittuq National Park**; there isn't time for a full-scale back-packing expedition, but outfitters can arrange a quick introductory tour. Spend the rest of Day 3 and Days 4 and 5 hiking and camping. Depending on when you go, you can book a jaunt by dogsled or snow-mobile to see icebergs up close, try sea kayaking, or hike the tundra in search of wildflowers. On Day 6, fly back to Iqaluit and spend a relaxing afternoon in Sylvia Grinnell Territorial Park. By Day 7, you should feel well-rested for your trip back home.

When to Tour Wilderness Canada

June through August is peak season in the far north. For the remaining nine months of the year, many businesses and outfitters close, as much for lack of business as the length of winter. However, many northerners say that March and April, when daylight lengthens and the weather is perfect for such snow sports as skiing and dogsledding, are the best times to visit. September is another choice month, when the autumn colors are brilliant and ducks, geese, and caribou begin their migrations. And as harsh—and dark—as other months are, they can be prime time for visitors fascinated by the spectral displays of the northern lights.

THE YUKON

The stories and events surrounding the Klondike Gold Rush of 1896 attract many visitors to the Yukon. Although legendary, it was relatively short-lived, albeit gold continues to be mined profitably by Yukon companies. At the beginning of the 20th century, mining had already entered a new era—gold miners could no longer get rich from "just digging in the ground," as they had during the gold rush. Machinery took over, and only the large operators who could afford it remained. Most of the gold rushers packed up their money bags and abandoned the Klondike for good. To fully explore the places and events of that time, a visit of at least seven days is necessary.

If backcountry adventure is more your style, guided hiking or canoeing trips run from 6 to 14 days. The Yukon is one of the premier wilderness adventure destinations in the world. A combination of hiking, biking, canoeing, rafting, and wildlife-viewing ventures could keep you occupied for months. However, backcountry travelers should be advised that the Yukon's wilderness is truly wild. If you are an inexperienced hiker (or canoeist or snowmobiler), you should take a guided excursion into the backcountry. Even a hike over the Chilkoot Trail, which

The Yukon

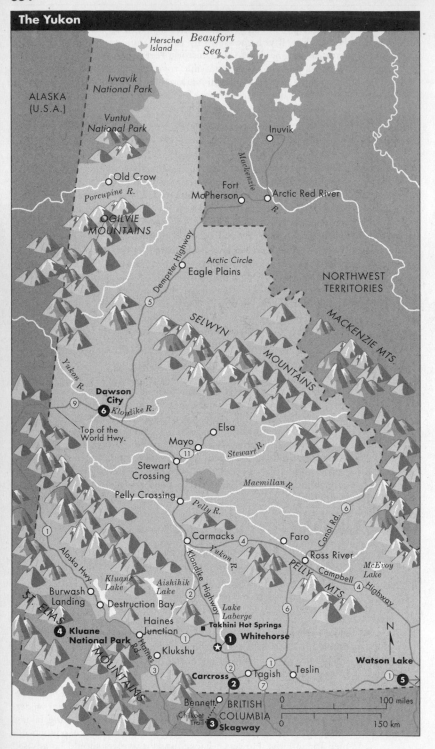

Beaufort Sea

Herschel Island

ALASKA (U.S.A.)

Ivvavik National Park

Vuntut National Park

Inuvik

Old Crow

Porcupine R.

OGILVIE MOUNTAINS

Fort McPherson

Arctic Red River

Mackenzie R.

Dempster Highway

Arctic Circle

Eagle Plains

⑤

NORTHWEST TERRITORIES

SELWYN

MOUNTAINS

MACKENZIE MTS.

Yukon R.

Dawson City

⑥ Klondike R.

⑨

Top of the World Hwy.

Elsa

Mayo

⑪

Stewart R.

Stewart Crossing

Pelly Crossing

Macmillan R.

Pelly R.

Carmacks ④

Faro

Canol Rd. ⑥

Ross River

McEvoy Lake

①

Alaska Hwy.

Kluane Lake

Aishihik Lake

Klondike Highway

Yukon R.

PELLY MTS.

Campbell Highway ④

Burwash Landing

Destruction Bay

②

Lake Laberge

⑥

N

St. ELIAS

④ **Kluane National Park**

Haines Junction

Haines Rd.

Takhini Hot Springs

① **Whitehorse**

Klukshu

MOUNTAINS

①

⑦

Watson Lake

③

Carcross ②

② Tagish

Teslin

①

① ⑤

Bennett

Chilkoot Trail

③ **Skagway**

BRITISH COLUMBIA

0 ___ 100 miles

0 ___ 150 km

is monitored by the U.S. and Canadian park services, is extremely rigorous.

Anyone expecting to see a lot of the Yukon should plan on spending a considerable amount of time in a car or a considerable amount of money on airfare. If in a car, no matter which direction you head, expect to contend with bus and RV traffic in summer; the Yukon ranks with Alaska as one of the great road-touring regions of North America. All Yukon highway signs are marked in kilometers. The Alaska Highway, however, has white mileposts that count off the 2,430 km (1,507 mi) from Dawson Creek, British Columbia, to Delta Junction, Alaska.

Whitehorse

❶ Begun as an encampment near the White Horse Rapids of the Yukon River, **Whitehorse** is 2,400 km (1,488 mi) from Vancouver. It was a logical layover for gold rushers in the late 1890s heading north from Skagway, Alaska, over the Chilkoot Trail to seek their fortune in Dawson. Today's city of 23,000 residents is the Yukon's center of commerce, communications, and transportation and is the seat of the territorial government. Though there's enough in the city to keep you occupied for a day or two, you should regard Whitehorse as a base camp from which to venture out and explore other parts of the Yukon.

The **Yukon Visitor Reception Centre** is the best place to pick up information on the Yukon and local lodgings, restaurants, shops, attractions, and special events. It's also the place to look into adventure travel; the center has information on the hundreds of tour and guide companies in the territory. A free 15-minute film provides a wonderful introduction to the Yukon's stunning scenery. ✉ *2nd Ave. and Hanson St.,* ☎ *867/667–5340,* FAX *867/667–6351,* WEB *www.touryukon.com.* ◷ *Mid-May–mid-Sept., daily 8–8; mid-Sept.–mid-May, weekdays 9– noon and 1–4:30.*

The scenic **Waterfront Walkway,** which runs along the Yukon River, is just east of the Yukon Visitor Reception Centre. Head downstream (north) to see the old White Pass & Yukon Route building on Main Street. One of Whitehorse's landmark buildings, it was erected in 1900. Today it marks the start or finish (depending on the year) of the Yukon Quest Dogsled Race.

The **MacBride Museum** encompasses more than 5,000 square ft of artifacts, natural-history specimens, historic photographs, maps, and diagrams covering prehistory to the present. Exhibits provide a historical overview of the Yukon, from the earliest exploration through the trapping era and the gold rush. The museum also houses "Rivers of Gold", an exhibit that tells the story of placer mining in the Yukon and is the largest public collection of Yukon gold in Canada. ✉ *1st Ave. and Wood St.,* ☎ *867/667–2709,* WEB *www.macbridemuseum.com.* 🎟 *$4.* ◷ *Mid-May–early Sept., daily 10–6; mid-Sept.–mid-May, Thurs.–Sat. noon–4.*

★ The **S.S. Klondike** National Historic Site, a 210-ft stern-wheeler built in 1929, was the largest boat plying the Yukon River back in the days when the river was the only transportation link between Whitehorse and Dawson. Though the boat sank in 1936, it was rebuilt a year later and, after successive restorations, is dry-docked in its 1930s glory. ✉ *Robert Service Way and 2nd Ave.,* ☎ *867/667–4511,* WEB *http:// parkscan.harbour.com/ssk.* 🎟 *$4.* ◷ *May–Sept., daily 9–6.*

The best time to visit the **Whitehorse Rapids Dam and Fish Ladder** is in August, during the longest chinook (king) salmon migration in the

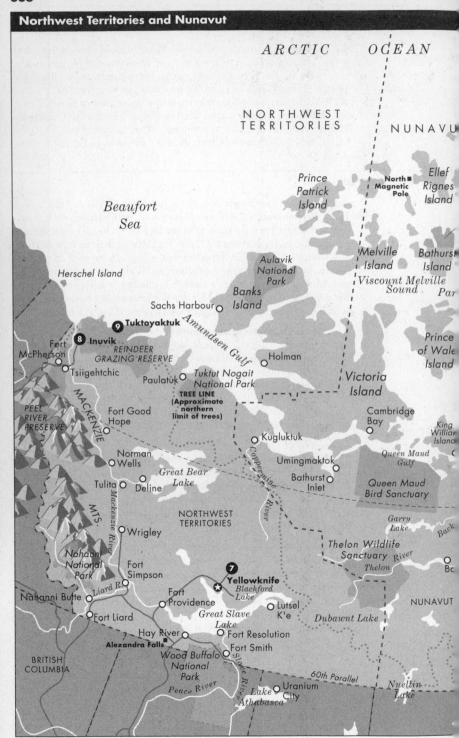

ARCTIC OCEAN

NORTHWEST TERRITORIES

NUNAVU

Prince Patrick Island

North Magnetic Pole

Ellef Rignes Island

Beaufort Sea

Melville Island

Bathurs Island

Viscount Melville Sound

Par

Herschel Island

Aulavik National Park

Banks Island

Sachs Harbour

Tuktoyaktuk

Amundsen Gulf

Holman

Victoria Island

Prince of Wale Island

Fort McPherson

Inuvik

REINDEER GRAZING RESERVE

Tsiigehtchic

Paulatuk

Tuktut Nogait National Park

TREE LINE (Approximate northern limit of trees)

Cambridge Bay

King Willia Island

MACKENZIE

PEEL RIVER PRESERVE

Fort Good Hope

Kugluktuk

Umingmaktok

Queen Maud Gulf

Norman Wells

Great Bear Lake

Coppermine River

Bathurst Inlet

Queen Maud Bird Sanctuary

Tulita

Deline

NORTHWEST TERRITORIES

Garry Lake

Back

MTS.

Mackenzie River

Wrigley

Thelon Wildlife Sanctuary

River

Thelon

Bo

Nahanni National Park

Fort Simpson

Yellowknife

Blachford Lake

NUNAVUT

Nahanni Butte

Liard R.

Fort Liard

Fort Providence

Great Slave Lake

Lutsel K'e

Dubawnt Lake

Hay River

Fort Resolution

BRITISH COLUMBIA

Alexandra Falls

Wood Buffalo National Park

Peace River

Fort Smith

Slave River

60th Parallel

Nueltin Lake

Lake Athabasca

Uranium City

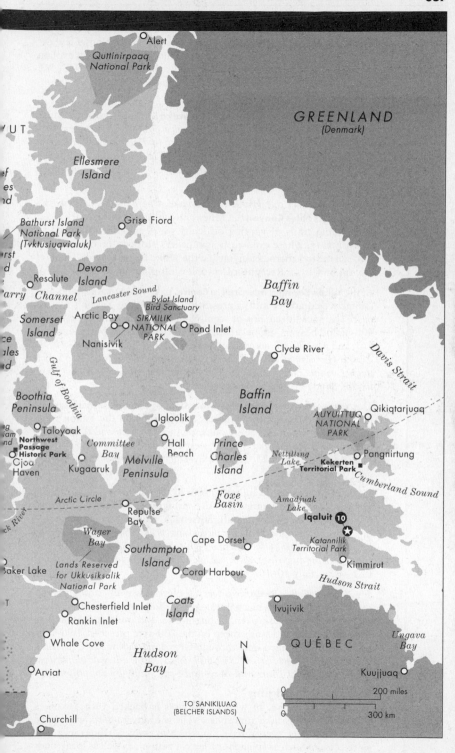

Alert

Quttinirpaaq
National Park

GREENLAND
(Denmark)

Ellesmere
Island

Grise Fiord

Bathurst Island
National Park
(Tvktusiuqvialuk)

Devon
Island

Resolute

Baffin
Bay

Parry Channel

Lancaster Sound

Bylot Island
Bird Sanctuary

Somerset
Island

Arctic Bay

SIRMILIK
NATIONAL
PARK

Pond Inlet

Nanisivik

Clyde River

Davis Strait

Gulf of Boothia

Boothia
Peninsula

Baffin
Island

AUYUITTUQ
NATIONAL
PARK

Qikiqtarjuaq

Igloolik

Taloyoak

Committee
Bay

Hall
Beach

Prince
Charles
Island

Nettilling
Lake

Kekerten
Territorial Park

Pangnirtung

Northwest
Passage
Historic Park

Gjoa
Haven

Kugaaruk

Melville
Peninsula

Cumberland Sound

Arctic Circle

Foxe
Basin

Amadjuak
Lake

Repulse
Bay

Iqaluit 10

Wager
Bay

Cape Dorset

Katannilik
Territorial Park

Baker Lake

Lands Reserved
for Ukkusiksalik
National Park

Southampton
Island

Coral Harbour

Kimmirut

Hudson Strait

Chesterfield Inlet

Coats
Island

Ivujivik

Ungava
Bay

Rankin Inlet

Whale Cove

QUÉBEC

N

Arviat

Hudson
Bay

Kuujjuaq

200 miles

TO SANIKILUAQ
(BELCHER ISLANDS)

300 km

Churchill

world. From the viewing platform overlooking the river you might spot between 150 and 2,000 salmon as they use the ladder to bypass the dam. Plan to go in the evening, when the temperature drops a few degrees and the fish swim about more freely. Interpretive displays explain the phenomenon. ⊠ *End of Nisutlin Dr.,* ☎ *867/633–5965,* WEB *www.yukonweb.com/community/yfga/fishway.html.* 🖾 *By donation.* 🕓 *June–early Sept., daily 8:30–8:30.*

A two-hour cruise aboard the **M.V. Schwatka** lets you experience Miles Canyon as Jack London did when he was a pilot on its turbulent waters. ⊠ *Schwatka Lake, 3.2 km (2 mi) south of downtown Whitehorse on Miles Canyon Rd.,* ☎ *867/668–4716.* 🖾 *$18.* 🕓 *Cruises early June–mid-June and mid-Aug.–early Sept., daily at 2* PM; *mid-June–mid-Aug., daily at 2 and 7* PM.

Two kilometers (1 mi) past Schwatka Lake, where the M.V. *Schwatka* is moored, is **Miles Canyon** (⊠ Miles Canyon Rd.), a public park laced with hiking trails of varying difficulty. A 20-minute trail leads to Canyon City, where gold-rush stampeders stopped before heading through the treacherous canyon and the White Horse Rapids. Contact the Yukon Visitor Reception Centre for information on trails.

At the **Yukon Beringia Interpretive Centre,** paleontological exhibits and interactive computer kiosks present the story of the Yukon's ice-age past. The ancient remains of woolly mammoths, giant steppe bison, 400-pound beavers, primeval horses, giant short-faced bears, scimitar cats, and American lions are among the center's holdings. ⊠ *Mi 915.4, Alaska Hwy., next to the Whitehorse Airport,* ☎ *867/667–8855,* WEB *www.beringia.com.* 🖾 *$6.* 🕓 *Mid-May–mid-Sept., daily 8* AM–9 PM; *winter, Sun. 1–5* PM *and by appointment.*

The **Yukon Transportation Museum,** north of the Yukon Beringia Interpretive Centre, displays artifacts and exhibits on the Yukon's unusual transportation legacy, from snowshoes to cars and dogsleds to airplanes. ⊠ *30 Electra Crescent, next to the Whitehorse Airport,* ☎ *867/668–4792.* 🖾 *$4.25.* 🕓 *Mid-May–late Aug., daily 10–6; early Sept., daily noon–4.*

Takhini Hot Springs, 25 minutes north of Whitehorse on Takhini Hot Springs Road, has swimming in the spring-warmed water (suits and towels are available for rental), horseback riding, cross-country skiing, a restaurant, and areas for picnicking. ⊠ *Km 9.6 on Takhini Hot Springs Rd., 10 km (6 mi) north of Whitehorse,* ☎ *867/633–2706,* WEB *http://takhinihotsprings.yk.ca.* 🖾 *$4.* 🕓 *June–Sept., daily 8* AM–10 PM; *Oct.–May, daily 10–10.*

The **Yukon Wildlife Preserve** offers a foolproof way of photographing rarely spotted animals in a natural setting. You might see elk, caribou, mountain goats, musk oxen, bison, moose, and mule deer as well as Dall, mountain, and stone sheep on the 700-acre preserve. Two-hour tours can be arranged only through Gray Line Yukon. ⊠ *Gray Line Yukon, 208G Steele St.,* ☎ *867/668–3225,* WEB *www.yukon.net/westours.* 🖾 *$15.* 🕓 *Tours mid-May–mid-Sept., daily by appointment.*

Dining and Lodging

$$–$$$ ✕ **Giorgio's Cuccina.** In winter, Giorgio's is packed with Yukoners
   ★   starved for its oasislike atmosphere. The warm terra-cotta walls lined with giant palms create a haven in which to enjoy Mediterranean-inspired cuisine such as spinach-stuffed cannelloni, as well as local foods such as halibut, salmon, king crab and arctic char. In particular, the wide variety of appetizers invites exploration—try the delectable marinated octopus when you get tired of eating moose jerky. Steaks,

seafood, pasta, and pizza round out the menu. ✉ *206 Jarvis St.,* ☎ *867/668–4050. MC, V.*

$–$$ ✕ **Sanchez Mexican Cantina.** Owner Otelina Sanchez lives many, many
★ miles away from her hometown of Veracruz, Mexico; fortunately for
the Yukon she has her family recipes with her. Everything at the
Cantina is homemade, even the tortilla chips and salsa. The always-
intriguing specials range from seafood paella to chicken mole. Off the
menu, the fresh fish seviche and chiles *rellenos* go well with the selection of perfectly chilled Mexican beers. ✉ *211 Hanson St.,* ☎ *867/
668–5858. MC, V.*

$ ✕ **Chocolate Claim.** In addition to handmade chocolates and truffles,
★ the chefs at the Claim turn out Thai soups and homespun surprises
like pumpkin cheesecake. The company is always interesting, the sandwiches are highly recommended, and the local art on the wall is for
sale. ✉ *305 Strickland St.,* ☎ *867/667–2202. V. No dinner.*

$ ✕ **Midnight Sun Coffee Roaster.** You won't find a full-course meal here,
but you can enjoy the best coffee in the Yukon—and even watch it being
fresh-roasted on the premises. The marvelous baked goods include a
zesty lemon cranberry muffin and a fragrant Morning Glory muffin
made with carrots and spices. Sandwiches and small pizzas round out
the snacking opportunities. ✉ *4th Ave. and Black St.,* ☎ *867/633–4563.
V. No dinner.*

$$ ✕⊡ **Edgewater Hotel.** On a quiet end of Main Street, this small hotel
is a good alternative if you want to avoid the tour-bus bustle. The lobby
is small and the passageway to the rooms is a bit narrow and awk-
ward, but the rooms are large, with modern furnishings. The Cellar
($–$$$$) is a somewhat elegant dining choice, with Alaska king crab
and prime rib on the menu. The more casual Gallery ($–$$), upstairs
in the hotel, serves breakfast and lunch. ✉ *101 Main St., Y1A 2A7,*
☎ *867/667–2572 or 877/484–3334,* FAX *867/668–3014,* WEB *www.edge-
waterhotel.yk.ca. 30 rooms, 2 suites. 2 restaurants, lounge. AE, DC,
MC, V.*

$$–$$$$ ⊡ **High Country Inn.** Close to the S.S. *Klondike* and the public swim-
ming pool, this comfortable inn is a great value. Rooms are clean, well
maintained, and nicely decorated in light pastel colors. The suites are
exceptional and have hot tubs, fireplaces, and canopy beds. The lobby,
restaurant, and lounge are cozy, and the Yukon Mining Company sa-
loon on the outdoor deck is a favorite Friday-night gathering spot. ✉
4051 4th Ave., Y1A 1H1, ☎ *867/667–4471 or 800/554–4471,* FAX *867/
667–6457,* WEB *www.highcountryinn.yk.ca. 70 rooms, 30 suites. Restau-
rant, bar, coin laundry. AE, DC, MC, V.*

$$–$$$ ⊡ **Westmark Whitehorse Hotel.** If it weren't for all the tour-bus bag-
gage to trip over in the hallways, this would be a fine place to stay.
Rooms are decorated with dark-wood furnishings and include TVs,
hair dryers, and coffeemakers. The hotel even has its own vaudeville
show, *Frantic Follies,* a revue playing heavily on gold-rush themes. The
restaurant can get crowded. A gift shop and a travel agency are on the
premises. ✉ *2nd Ave. and Wood St., Box 4250, Y1A 3T3,* ☎ *867/668–
4700 or 800/544–0970,* FAX *867/668–2789,* WEB *www.westmarkho-
tels.com. 181 rooms, 5 suites. Restaurant, lounge, barbershop, spa, shop.
AE, DC, MC, V.*

$$ ⊡ **Hawkins House Bed & Breakfast.** In the heart of Whitehorse, this
beautifully decorated Victorian-style home with hardwood floors is
among the best the Yukon has to offer. Gourmet breakfasts, including
homesmoked salmon pate and moose tortiere, and amenities rarely found
in this region, such as whirlpool baths, cable TV, computer hookups,
and wet bars, are more than enough reason to book a room. Breakfast is not included in the room price but at $7 per person, it's well
worth it. ✉ *303 Hawkins St., Y1A 1X5,* ☎ *867/668–7638,* FAX *867/*

668–7632, WEB *www.hawkinshouse.yk.ca. 4 rooms. Dining room, in-room data ports, minibars, laundry service. AE, MC, V.*

FLY-IN WILDERNESS LODGES

Backcountry lodges are a great way to see true Yukon wilderness. The lodges listed below provide charter service to and from Whitehorse.

$$$$ 🖪 **Inconnu Lodge.** Inconnu Lodge is a statement in relative luxury. This fly-in lodge on the shores of McEvoy Lake, about 300 km (186 mi) north-east of Whitehorse, provides accommodations in modern log cabins. The principal activities are fishing and heli-hiking, but the lodge also arranges canoe trips on nearby rivers. Wildlife is plentiful, as attested by the taxidermy displayed in the main lodge's living room. The lodge also acts as a jumping-off point for canoe and climbing trips into Nahanni National Park. Rates for five-day packages, including transportation to and from Whitehorse, are about $3,995 per person. *Mailing address:* ⊠ *Box 29008, OK, Mission, RPO, Kelowna, BC V1W 4A7,* ☎ *250/860–4187,* FAX *250/860–8894,* WEB *www.inconnulodge.com. 5 duplex cabins. Outdoor hot tub, sauna, shops, meeting rooms. MC, V.*

$$$$ 🖪 **Tincup Lake Lodge.** When this luxurious lodge was built in 1991, no expense was spared—an amazing fact considering that all materials had to be flown in to the remote site. The main lodge is surrounded by cozy log guest cabins with woodstoves, covered verandas, and private bathrooms. This was originally a fishing lodge, but recently the owners have added kayak, canoe, and wildlife-viewing excursions to the itineraries. You can even take a cooking class. A seven-day package, including the round-trip flight from Whitehorse, an hour away by plane, is about $3,250 per person. *Mailing address:* ⊠ *3641 Park Dr., R.R. 4, Victoria, BC V9C 3W3,* ☎ *250/391–0400,* FAX *250/391–0841,* WEB *www.tincup.yk.ca. 3 duplex cabins. Outdoor hot tub, sauna, laundry service.*

Outdoor Activities and Sports

A canoe trip down the Thirty-Mile section of the Yukon River lets you observe wildlife and stunning river scenery; **Kanoe People** (⊠ Box 5152, Y1A 4S3, ☎ 867/668–4899) can arrange trips.

Mountain View Golf Course (⊠ Range Rd., Box 5883, ☎ 867/633–6020), an 18-hole, par-72 course that's open May through September, has real grass and greens, and is on the scenic banks of the Yukon River.

Shopping

The revolving exhibits at the **Captain Martin House Gallery** (⊠ 305 Wood St., ☎ 867/667–4080) showcase the sculpture, paintings, photography, and crafts of both emerging and established northern artists. Native-made clothing, local artwork, and indigenous crafts ranging from moose-hair tuftings to beadwork are available at the **Indian Craft Shop** (⊠ 504 Main St., ☎ 867/667–7216). **Midnight Sun Gallery & Gifts** (⊠ 205 Main St., ☎ 867/393–8203) sells a variety of affordable Yukon and Canadian arts and crafts. **Murdoch's Gem Shop** (⊠ 207 Main St., ☎ 867/668–7867) is the Yukon's largest manufacturer of gold-nugget jewelry. The **Northend Gallery** (1st Ave. and Steele St., ☎ 867/393–3590) carries a wide range of exceptional northern art; it ships anywhere in the world. **Yukon Gallery** (⊠ 2093 2nd Ave., ☎ 867/667–2391) sells limited-edition art prints by Yukon artists. The **Whitehorse General Store** (⊠ 205 Main St., ☎ 867/668–4350) has a folksy atmosphere and sells antiques and collectibles.

Main Street in Whitehorse has some excellent outdoor stores, as well. **Coast Mountain Sports** (⊠ 208 Main St., ☎ 867/667–4074) specializes in biking and trekking. **Valhalla Pure Outfitters** (⊠ 201 B Main St., ☎ 867/668–7700) carries a wide range of paddle-sports gear.

South of Whitehorse to Skagway, Alaska

Route 2, which runs south out of the Yukon into British Columbia and on to Alaska, traverses an interesting succession of climatic zones. From Carcross, the first town of interest on this section, you'll pass by the Carcross Desert, over the alpine tundra of the White Pass, and through the coastal rain forest of the Alaskan Panhandle. By the time the road begins descending steeply into Skagway, the landscape changes dramatically to a heavily vegetated world of glacially carved fjords.

White Pass & Yukon Route

An alternative to driving from Whitehorse to Skagway is the **White Pass & Yukon Route,** a combined bus-and-rail trip. A bus travels 2½ hours from Whitehorse to Fraser, British Columbia; then the train completes the trip to Skagway in another 1¾ hours. You can do this trip in either direction. A three-hour round-trip is also available, starting and ending in Skagway. You can also take the train from Skagway to Bennett, British Columbia, Thursday–Monday. Six times a year the White Pass & Yukon Route runs a special steam-engine excursion to Bennett with historic locomotive No. 73. Call ahead for departure times. ⊠ *Box 435, Skagway, AK 99840,* ☎ *907/983–2217 or 800/343–7373,* ⓕⒶⓍ *907/983– 2734,* ⓦⒺⒷ *www.whitepassrailroad.com.* ⊠ *One-way Skagway to Whitehorse $95; round-trip Summit Excursion $82; one-way Skagway to Fraser $66.50; one-way Skagway to Bennett $65; round-trip Skagway to Bennett $128; steam excursion to Bennett $156.* ☉ *Departures mid-May–mid-Sept. daily; call for pre- and postseason schedules.*

Chilkoot Trail

You can backpack between Skagway and Bennett, British Columbia, on the 54-km (33-mi) Chilkoot Trail, a three- to five-day historic trip through spectacular scenery. Hikers begin their journey outside of Skagway in Dyea, on the Alaskan coast, and ascend through rain forest, across alpine tundra, and into boreal forest. Only those who are extremely fit should attempt to hike the trail in the reverse direction, as it is downhill and very steep. Along the way are the scattered shovels and graves of gold rushers who traveled this route a century ago.

Although the trail never reaches the Yukon, it is vitally linked with Yukon history: during the Klondike Gold Rush, prospectors trekked over the Chilkoot Pass to Bennett, where they built their own boats and sailed across Bennett and Tagish lakes to the headwaters of the Yukon River. Boats that weren't wrecked in Miles Canyon or the White Horse or Five Finger rapids eventually arrived in Dawson City.

Despite the $10 fee, reservations are recommended to hike the Chilkoot Trail; only a limited number of people are permitted to hike it at the same time, and you'll be assured of getting a site at the campground of your choice. For reservation information, contact **Canadian Heritage, Parks Canada.** ⊠ *Yukon National Historic Sites, Suite 200, 300 Main St., Whitehorse, YT Y1A 2B5,* ☎ *867/667–3910 or 800/661– 0486,* ⓦⒺⒷ *http://parkscan.harbour.com/ct.* ⊠ *$35; $10 extra to make a reservation.*

Carcross

❷ *74 km (46 mi) south of Whitehorse.*

Originally named Caribou Crossing after the herds of caribou that passed through it, Carcross is one of the Yukon's most picturesque towns. The shores of **Bennett Lake,** where thousands of gold-rush stampeders landed after a rough journey on the windy waters, are ideal for a short stroll. Near town is the **Carcross Desert,** the smallest desert (about 10 acres) in the world.

Skagway

❸ *180 km (112 mi) south of Whitehorse.*

Skagway, host to cruise ships traveling up the Alaskan coast, is an amazingly preserved artifact from one of North America's biggest, most storied gold rushes. Old false-front stores, saloons, and brothels have been restored, repainted, and refurbished by the federal government and Skagway's citizens. One of the town's most famous gold-rush characters was Jefferson Randolph "Soapy" Smith. Soapy and his gang of renegades made a fine living out of fleecing gold-rush stampeders. In his most famous con, Soapy would wrap bars of soap in banknotes—there would always be a hundred-dollar bill and a couple of twenties in the box of bars. Then he would ask people to try their luck and buy a bar of soap for $5. Two of Soapy's own men would be in the crowd and would eagerly volunteer. Once Soapy's cronies had received the bars wrapped in the big bucks, the rest of the poor dupes eagerly followed suit, but with less-profitable results. Soapy's thieves and hand artists eventually won him control over Skagway, until he was shot in July 1898 by Frank Reid, who was also killed in the exchange of gunfire. Both of their graves can be seen in the Gold Rush Cemetery. When you walk down Broadway today, the scene is not much different from what the prospectors saw in the days of 1898.

DINING AND LODGING

$$–$$$ ✕ **Portobello Ristorante.** The Portobello specializes in Italian cuisine and fresh local seafood. Alaska king crab and the halibut in the fish-and-chips taste as though they've come straight from the sea. You can even get grilled halibut on the Mediterranean pizza. If you're looking for comfort food, it's here in the form of hamburgers and pizza. Besides serving up great food, the restaurant also has a good view of the surrounding mountains and water. ⊠ *1st Ave. and Broadway,* ☎ *907/983–3459. AE, MC, V.*

$–$$ ✕▥ **Golden North Hotel.** Alaska's most historic hotel was built in
★   1898 in the heyday of the gold rush—golden dome and all—and has been lovingly restored to reflect that period. If you're looking for a bargain, the hotel has rooms with shared bath starting at $65. The garden patio area is a great place to sample one of the beers from the hotel's own microbrewery, the Skagway Brewing Company. Popular choices in the Golden North Restaurant include sourdough pancakes for breakfast; soups, salads, and sandwiches for lunch; and salmon or other fresh local seafood for dinner. ⊠ *3rd Ave. and Broadway, Box 343, Skagway, AK 99840,* ☎ *907/983–2451 or 888/222–1898,* FAX *907/983–2755,* WEB *www.alaskan.com/goldenorth. 31 rooms, 1 suite (off-premises). Restaurant. AE, DC, MC, V. Closed Nov.–Mar.*

$–$$ ✕▥ **Skagway Inn Bed & Breakfast.** Each room in this downtown inn
★   has a Victorian motif with antiques and cast-iron beds; some have mountain views. The building was constructed in 1897 and is one of Skagway's oldest. Olivia's at the Skagway Inn ($$–$$$$), the inn's summer-only restaurant, is considered by many to be Skagway's finest. Chef Wendell Fogliani trained under Lorna McDermott, a graduate of Le Cordon Bleu. The restaurant serves fresh seafood, such as halibut, crab, and salmon, with locally grown organic produce for lunch and dinner; box lunches are available for day trips and picnics. ⊠ *7th Ave. and Broadway, Box 500, Skagway, AK 99840,* ☎ *907/983–2289 or 888/752–4929,* FAX *907/983–2713,* WEB *www.skagwayinn.com. 12 rooms without bath. Restaurant. AE, DC, MC, V.*

Kluane National Park

★ ❹   Kluane National Park, the neighboring Wrangell–St. Elias National Park in Alaska, and Tatshenshini Provincial Park in British Columbia form the largest expanse of contiguous national-park land in the world. Kluane is 160 km (99 mi) west of Whitehorse. Glaciers up to 100 km (62 mi) long stretch from the huge ice fields of the interior, constituting the largest nonpolar ice mass in the world. Canada's highest mountain, Mt. Logan (19,550 ft), is another of Kluane's natural wonders. Few visitors other than experienced mountaineers (climbers must receive authorization from the Park Superintendent) get a full sense of Kluane's most extraordinary terrain, as neither roads nor trails lead into the interior. A helicopter or fixed-wing flight over the Kluane ice fields is well worth the price on a clear day. Expect to pay approximately $100 per person for helicopter rides; fixed-wing flights are slightly cheaper, but they can't offer the maneuverability of a helicopter flight. Many people are content with exploring the front ranges, which have impressive mountains with abundant wildlife—Dall sheep, black bears, and grizzly bears are the most noteworthy species.

The frontcountry trail system of Kluane National Park is the most extensive in the far north, facilitating everything from half-day hikes to multiday backpacking excursions. It's possible to make a five-day backpacking trip on marked trails, with opportunities for off-trail scrambling on mountaintops. Most marked hiking trails are relatively easy to negotiate. Keep in mind that this is bear country, and all bear precautions—especially storing food in canisters—must be taken. You might also consider buying a can of capsicum (pepper-spray) bear repellent, available in all sporting-goods stores.

The town of Haines Junction marks the junction of the Haines and Alaska highways and is the headquarters of the **Kluane National Park Reserve** (✉ Mile 1016, Alaska Hwy., ☎ 867/634–7250, WEB http://parkscan.harbour.com/kluane), a visitor center and the most logical place to begin your excursion into the park. A free 25-minute slide presentation provides an excellent introduction to the region's geology, flora, and fauna, and the amiable staff is well armed with valuable information concerning the condition of the many hiking trails—including any recent bear sightings. Day hikers should check in for a summer schedule of guided hikes. You can also pick up an overnight camping permit ($5 per person per day) and free food-storage canisters here.

More-ambitious hikers can backpack from the **Sheep Mountain Visitor Center** (✉ Mile 1019, Alaska Hwy., ☎ 867/634–2251) up the Slims River valley to the toe of the Kaskawulsh Glacier, a 27-km (17-mi) jaunt. The Sheep Mountain Center, open from May through September, is an outpost of Kluane headquarters within the park's borders.

Around Kluane National Park

Once you've explored the rugged wonders of Kluane National Park, you may want to venture south of Haines Junction on Haines Road, which hugs the park and connects a few sights worth seeing. **Rock Glacier Trail** is on the west side of Dezadeash Lake at Km 45. This 1½-km (1-mi) trail on the outskirts of Kluane National Park is well maintained and suitable for people of all ages and abilities. Kluane is home to thousands of rock glaciers, glacierlike tongues of fragmented rock that have accumulated over deep layers of ice. This trail passes over one of them. Besides offering visitors a glimpse at this curiosity, the Rock Glacier Trail provides a beautiful view of the Dezadeash Valley.

From Haines Road, the turnoff to the village of **Klukshu** is 80 km (50 mi) south of Haines Junction. On the small Klukshu River, this village is an important site of Southern Tutchone culture. For centuries, the Tutchone have been coming here from late July until September to fish for salmon. Interpretive displays along the banks of the Klukshu River explain how fish were caught over the years. Smokehouses are still used to preserve the fish. A small crafts shop sells moccasins and wood and antler carvings, and on occasion you might catch one of the elders telling stories related to the area.

The spectacular **Million Dollar Falls,** fed by the Takhanne River, are 25 km (16 mi) south of Klukshu on Haines Road. Two trails, one 1 km (½ mi) long and the other 2½ km (1½ mi) long, lead down to the falls. They're steep but well maintained, and in season you can spot salmon in the clear waters. In winter you can put on skis or snowshoes and see how the falls have been transformed into fantastic ice sculptures.

Dining and Lodging

$$ ✕🏨 **Raven Motel.** Haines Junction's finest dining and lodging estab-
★ lishment has spare, clean, and tastefully designed rooms and, unbe-
lievably, room service. The food at the Raven ($$–$$$$), which was recently named one of the top 150 restaurants in Canada, is so good that Whitehorse residents often make the two-hour drive for a special dinner. The menu at the restaurant on the second floor changes every few days, depending on what seafood or produce is freshly available. Past choices have included fresh local salmon and lake trout, home-made pasta, and juicy steaks, all topped with homegrown herbs and served at tables with views of Kluane's front ranges. ✉ *Alaska Hwy., Box 343, Haines Junction Y0B 1L0,* ☎ *867/634–2500,* 𝟠𝕏 *867/634–2517,* 𝚆𝙴𝙱 *www.yukonweb.com/tourism/raven. 12 rooms. Restaurant, room service. AE, MC, V. Closed Nov.–Apr. CP.*

$ 🏨 **Cozy Corner.** The name is anything but original, yet there is a gen-
uine coziness about this small motel. Rooms are unusually large—big enough for a bed and sofa bed—but the bathrooms are small. Some rooms have views of the front ranges of Kluane National Park. ✉ *Alaska Hwy. and Haines Rd., Box 5406, Haines Junction Y0B 1L0,* ☎ *867/634–2511,* 𝟠𝕏 *867/634–2119. 12 rooms. Restaurant. AE, MC, V.*

$ 🏨 **Gateway Hotel.** Though there's nothing remarkable about this
small hotel, it's convenient for those who want to explore Kluane Na-tional Park and the outlying area. Rooms are clean and spacious; all have cable TV. ✉ *Alaska Hwy. and Haines Rd., Box 5460, Haines Junction Y0B 1L0,* ☎ *867/634–2371,* 𝟠𝕏 *867/634–2833,* 𝚆𝙴𝙱 *www.yukonweb.com/tourism/gateway. 12 rooms. Coin laundry. AE, D, MC, V.*

Watson Lake

❺ **Watson Lake,** 450 km (279 mi) east of Whitehorse, is the gateway city
for travelers heading northwest along the Alaska Highway. The town's most remarkable feature is the **Signpost Forest.** During the construc-tion of the Alaska Highway in 1942, Carl Lindley, a homesick U.S. sol-dier, put up a proud sign displaying the name of his hometown (Danville, Illinios), as well as its distance and direction. Since then, other visitors have followed suit to the tune of more than 30,000 signs.

Watson Lake's **Northern Lights Centre** has a multimedia planetarium theater. In summer, when the midnight sun makes it impossible to see the lights, the center allows visitors to take in the spectacle of the au-rora borealis through advanced video and laser technology. The 50-minute show is presented daily at 1, 2, 3, 6:30, 7:30, and 8:30 PM. ✉ *North of Gateway Hotel on south side of Alaska Hwy.,* ☎ *867/536–7827,* 𝚆𝙴𝙱 *www.northernlightscentre.com.* 🎫 *$10.* ☉ *Mid-May–mid-Sept. daily 12:30 PM–9:30 PM.*

Lodging

$–$$ 🏨 **Big Horn Hotel.** Watson Lake's nicest hotel is in the downtown area.
Large rooms are creatively decorated with forest-theme draperies and

bedspreads and wooden headboards; all rooms have queen-size beds. The Whirlpool Suite is a great place to relax after a long day of driving the Alaska Highway. ⊠ *Mi 634, Alaska Hwy., Box 157, Y0A 1C0,* ☎ *867/ 536–2020,* FAX *867/536–2021,* WEB *www.yukonweb.com/tourism/bighorn. 29 rooms, 1 suite. Hot tub, coin laundry. AE, MC, V.*

Dawson City

★ ❻ At the turn of the 20th century, **Dawson City,** 536 km (332 mi) north of Whitehorse, was the epicenter of gold fever. Preservationists have done an admirable job not only of restoring many of the city's historic buildings but also of enforcing a zoning code that requires new structures to adopt facades conforming to a turn-of-the-20th-century look.

The **Visitor Reception Centre** covers everything from historical minutiae to lodging availability. Territory-wide information is provided by interactive computers. Walking tours and historic presentations take place daily from the end of May until mid-September. For $10 you can pick up a Parks Canada pass, which provides access to all Dawson City area National Historic Sites, including the Robert Service Cabin, the Commissioner's Residence, Dredge No. 4, and the Palace Grande Theatre; the pass also buys you a walking tour of Dawson City. If you prefer, tours are available on audio tape. ⊠ *Front and King Sts.,* ☎ *867/ 993–5566,* WEB *http://parkscan.harbour.com/khs.* ☉ *Mid-May–mid-Sept., daily 8–8.*

The **Tr'ondek Hwech'in First Nation Cultural Centre** hosts daily tours through the center that highlight Tr'ondek Hwech'in culture and history as well as weekly theatrical productions of traditional songs and dances. The center is a testament to the resilient culture of these people who endured great hardship during and after the gold rush. ⊠ *Front and King Sts.,* ☎ *867/993–5385.* ☎ *Call for fees.* ☉ *June–Aug., daily; call for hrs.*

Built in 1899, the **Palace Grand Theatre** was show-time central during gold-rush days, staging everything from opera to vaudeville. It was reconstructed in 1961 by Parks Canada, which now offers daily tours. It's home to the **Gaslight Follies,** a musical show based on gold-rush history. ⊠ *King St. between 2nd and 3rd Aves.,* ☎ *867/993–5575,* WEB *www.dawsoncity.org.* ☎ *$15–$17.* ☉ *Shows mid-May–mid-Sept., nightly at 8 PM; call Visitor Reception for tour schedule.*

The construction of the **Old Post Office** in 1900 was a symbolic affirmation of Dawson's permanence as a legitimate city rather than a boomtown of opportunism. The post office today effectively captures an aura of Dawson life in the early 20th century, and philatelists may want to purchase commemorative stamps. ⊠ *3rd Ave. and King St.* ☎ *Free.* ☉ *June–Sept., daily noon–5.*

The **Dawson City Museum** chronicles the gold rush and includes exhibits on the material culture of the local Han people, steam locomotives, and the paleontology of the region. There's a genealogical library for those trying to trace relatives who traveled to Dawson during the gold rush. ⊠ *5th Ave. between Mission and Turner Sts.,* ☎ *867/993– 5291,* WEB *www.users.yknet.yk.ca/dcpages/museum.html.* ☎ *$5.* ☉ *Mid-May–mid-Sept., daily 10–6; in winter by appointment.*

At the **Jack London Cabin and Interpretive Centre** you can visit the cabin in which the writer entertained miners with his knowledge of the classics during the winter of 1897. Works such as *The Call of the Wild* and *White Fang* were inspired by the time he spent in the Yukon wilds. The interpretive center houses an exhibit of historic photographs chronicling London's life. ⊠ *8th Ave. and 1st St.,* ☎ *867/993–5575,* WEB *www.dawsoncity.org.* ☜ *$2.* ☉ *Late May–mid-Sept., daily 10–6.*

Robert Service, primarily a poet, has been dubbed "the Bard of the Klondike." Originally from England, he came to the Yukon in the early 1900s, well after the gold rush was over. Before coming to Dawson, Service worked in Whitehorse at the Canadian Imperial Bank of Commerce. There he wrote "The Shooting of Dan McGrew," his most famous poem. The small **Robert Service Cabin** is a good representation of what many of the Dawson cabins looked like during and after the Klondike Gold Rush. The sod roof even bears raspberries in summer. ⊠ *8th Ave. and Hanson St.,* ☎ *867/993–7200.* ☜ *$6.* ☉ *Mid-May–mid-Sept., daily 9–5.*

If you want a firsthand experience of river travel, board the **Yukon Queen II,** a 100-passenger vessel docked along Front Street that makes the 173-km (107-mi) trip westward to Eagle, Alaska, in approximately five hours. Travelers who opt for a one-way ticket may return to Dawson by bus. Meals are included in the price of the trip. Tickets can be bought on the boat or purchased in advance through **Gray Line Yukon** (⊠ 208G Steele St., ☎ 867/668–3225 or 800/544–2206). ⊠ *Front St.,* ☎ *867/993–5599,* WEB *www.hollandamerica.com.* ☜ *$85 one-way, $138 round-trip.* ☉ *Departures mid-May–mid-Sept., daily; call for departure times.*

Dawson really got its start at the gold-mining sites east of town. Huge mounds of rock and slag along the roadside attest to the considerable amount of earth turned over in search of the precious metal. The most famous mining site is **Bonanza Creek,** 1 km (½ mi) south of Dawson City on Bonanza Creek Road, which produced several million-dollar claims in the days when gold went for $16 an ounce. A brass plaque on Bonanza Creek Road marks the **Discovery Claim,** staked by George Carmack in August 1896, when he and his companions Skookum Jim and Dawson Charlie discovered the gold that sparked the great Klondike Gold Rush. The creek is so rich in minerals that it's still being mined today.

If you who want to try your luck at gold panning, you can rent the necessary gear for $5 at **Claim 33** (⊠ Mi 7, Bonanza Creek Rd., ☎ 867/993–5804). You're guaranteed some gold, but don't expect to strike it rich.

Dredge No. 4, which was used to dig up the creek bed and sift gold from gravel during the height of Bonanza Creek's largesse, is approximately 15 minutes by car up Bonanza Creek Road from its intersection with the Klondike Highway. Daily tours are conducted through the dredge in summer. ⊠ *Mile 7.8, Bonanza Creek Rd.,* ☎ *867/993–7228.* ☜ *$5.* ☉ *June–mid-Sept., daily 9–5; tours given on the hr.*

Dining and Lodging

$–$$$ ✕ **Klondike Kate's.** The line at Klondike Kate's can sometimes get a
  ★   little intimidating, but the food is extremely good. Mexican and Middle Eastern dishes are often on the menu, and the smoked local king salmon is a constant standout. The latest menu addition is an extensive martini list. A large, covered outdoor deck is open in summer. The main decorative statement on the deck is a large map of the world, onto which guests are invited to stick pins marking their hometowns. ⊠ *3rd Ave. and King St.,* ☎ *867/993–6527. MC, V.*

$–$$$ ✕ **Marina's.** You'd think that being so far north you'd be inspired to order something more interesting than pizza. But Marina's thick-crust pizzas are first-rate and reasonably priced. The menu also includes pasta and salads. Because of its location across from the Westmark Inn, the dining room can fill up if there's a tour bus in town (and in summer, there usually are a few). ✉ *5th Ave. between Princess and Harper Sts.,* ☎ *867/993–6800. MC, V.*

$$ ✕🏠 **Downtown Hotel.** The Downtown is a Dawson classic, decorated with gold-rush antiques and interesting local artwork. The main building has 34 guest rooms and is open all year; the annex across the street has 25 rooms and is open only in summer. The Jack London Grill ($–$$$) evokes the atmosphere of a men's club from the early 1900s, with dark-wood siding and framed mirrors and prints. The Yukon River king salmon is exceptional. ✉ *2nd Ave. and Queen St., Box 780, Y0B 1G0,* ☎ *867/993–5346; 800/661–0514 within the Yukon and British Columbia,* FAX *867/993–5076,* WEB *www.downtown.yk.net. 59 rooms in summer, 34 rooms rest of yr. Restaurant, lounge, hot tub, meeting rooms, airport shuttle. AE, DC, MC, V.*

$$–$$$ 🏠 **Aurora Inn.** Rooms at the Aurora are spacious and have queen-size beds and contemporary wood furniture. Suites have king-size beds and hot tubs. Guests can mingle or relax and watch TV in the large sitting room. The inn doesn't serve lunch or dinner, but a Swiss-style breakfast, featuring croissants, fresh fruit, and Swiss and Dutch cheeses, is available for an additional fee. Six rooms were added in 2001. ✉ *5th Ave. and Harper St., Box 1748 Y0B 1G0,* ☎ *867/993–6860,* FAX *867/993–5689,* WEB *www.wildandwooly.yk.net. 14 rooms, 2 suites. Fans, no-smoking rooms, airport shuttle. MC, V.*

$–$$ 🏠 **Bombay Peggy's Inn & Lounge.** Opened in 2000, Bombay Peggy's is the Yukon's only restored brothel, and it revels in its past: rooms have names like "Purple Palace" and "Lipstick Room." Each of the four main rooms and two suites is decorated differently, but all have deep clawfoot tubs, velvet bed linens, and antique furnishings. Rooms are nonsmoking and have TVs, VCRs, and phones. Peggy's also has four "snugs," rooms with shared bath, starting at $79 a night. ✉ *2nd Ave. and Princess St., Box 411, Y0B 1G0,* ☎ *867/993–6969,* FAX *867/993–5403,* WEB *www.klondikeweb.com/bombay. 8 rooms, 4 with bath, 2 suites. Lounge, in-room VCRs, no-smoking rooms, airport shuttle, MC, V.*

$ 🏠 **Dawson City Bunkhouse.** Although rooms in the Bunkhouse are spare, they are comfortable and clean. Some rooms have private baths, phone, and cable TV; others do not. For budget-minded travelers, this is the best deal in town. ✉ *Front and Prince Sts. (Bag 4040), Y0B 1G0,* ☎ *867/993–6164,* FAX *867/993–6051. 32 rooms, 27 share 6 baths. Fans, no-smoking rooms, airport shuttle. MC, V. Closed early Sept.–May.*

Nightlife and the Arts

THE ARTS

The **Dawson City Music Festival** (✉ Dawson City Music Festival Association, Box 456, Y0B 1G0, ☎ 867/993–5584, WEB www.dcmf.com), which presents a variety of musicians from Alaska, Yukon, and the rest of Canada, is held each July. It's one of the most popular events in the north, so tickets can be extremely difficult to get. Write to the Festival Association in the spring to request tickets. The festival's Web site posts information on ticket availability.

NIGHTLIFE

Diamond Tooth Gertie's Gambling Hall offers a glimpse of the frolicking times of the gold rush. "Gertie" and her cancan dancers put on three shows nightly while grizzled miners sit at the poker table. Gamblers can try their luck at slot machines, blackjack, red dog, and roulette. Note: no minors are admitted. ✉ *4th Ave. and Queen St.,* ☎ *867/993–5575,* WEB *www.dawsoncity.com.* ⌧ *$6.* ☽ *Mid-May–mid-Sept., daily 7 PM–2 AM.*

Shopping

The **Gold Claim** (⊠ 3rd Ave. between Princess and Harper Sts., ☎ 867/ 993–6387) has some of the finest artwork and hand-crafted objects available in the Yukon. Most notable is the hammered-gold jewelry made by Stuart Schmidt, who co-owns the store with his wife Nancy. A wide variety of gold-nugget jewelry can be found at the **Klondike Nugget and Ivory Shop** (⊠ Front and Queen Sts., ☎ 867/993–5432).

Side Trips from Dawson City

TOP OF THE WORLD HIGHWAY

The 108-km (67-mi) trip west along the Top of the World Highway to the Yukon–Alaska border exposes you to beautiful, expansive vistas. The road partially lives up to its name, set as it is along ridge lines and high-mountain shoulders, but the dirt-and-gravel surface can hardly be called a highway. The northernmost border crossing on land between Canada and the United States is along this route; the U.S. side is in Polar Creek, Alaska—population: 2.

DEMPSTER HIGHWAY

The Dempster Highway's arctic tundra and mountain scenery are always beautiful, but are most spectacular in late August. Autumn comes early to the tundra and colors the landscape in vivid reds and yellows. The gentle rolling hills can arouse any hiker's desire to explore.

The 766-km (475-mi) journey north to Inuvik on the Dempster Highway is a much more adventurous and ambitious undertaking than driving the Top of the World Highway. The only public highway in Canada to cross the Arctic Circle, it passes through a tundra landscape that is delicate, mountainous, and ever-changing.

In its southern extreme, the highway passes first by the rugged Tombstone Mountains and then into the ranges of the Ogilvie Mountains. The route crosses Eagle Plains (approximately halfway between Dawson and Inuvik and a good stopping point for gas and supplies) before reaching the Arctic Circle, marked by a sign. From here the highway passes through the Richardson Mountains and enters the flatlands surrounding the Mackenzie River delta before reaching Inuvik. This is certainly one of *the* great wilderness drives in North America, but because there are no services for 370 km (229 mi) between the junction of the Dempster and Klondike highways and Eagle Plains, travelers should be prepared to cope with possible emergencies. You should carry a minimum of two spare tires.

THE NORTHWEST TERRITORIES

In 1999 Canada's Northwest Territories, which once encompassed four time zones from the mountainous Yukon border to Baffin Island, were divided by a boundary line that runs from Melville Island down through the Arctic islands to the Canadian mainland and south, more or less along the tree line. The land west of the boundary is still called the Northwest Territories, whereas the land to the east is now Nunavut. The Northwest Territories cover 1,171,918 square km (452,475 square mi) and its 42,000 citizens are governed by a multicultural, multilingual legislature whose elected members converge at Yellowknife's Legislative Assembly.

Aside from the regional centers used as bases for travelers (Yellowknife and Inuvik), the communities in the Northwest Territories are extremely small. Many families still support themselves by hunting, fishing, and trapping, although modern technology is becoming increasingly widespread. There are many opportunities to learn about the rich history and traditional ways of the Dene, Métis, Inuit, and Inuvialuit communities, where native languages are spoken on a par with English and French. You're especially welcome at the many local festivals and ceremonies that dot the calendar year.

Yellowknife

Back in 1934, when gold was discovered on the North Arm of Great Slave Lake, **Yellowknife,** 2,595 km (1,609 mi) from Vancouver, began as a rough-and-tumble mining camp. A center of government since the 1960s, it still thrives on hard-rock gold mining and, lately, diamonds— Lac de Gras, 350 km (217 mi) northwest of town, is the site of Ekati Mine, the Western Hemisphere's first diamond producer. A second diamond mine has been approved, with more likely to follow, and exploration for oil and gas is booming. All this activity has fueled a building surge and a buoyant outlook in the Northwest Territories' capital city, whose population has grown from 12,000 in 1991 to more than 18,000 today.

Downhill from downtown Yellowknife is **Old Town,** built around a rocky peninsula that juts into Yellowknife Bay, part of Great Slave Lake. You can reach it in 15 minutes by strolling toward the lake along Franklin Avenue; or you can drive down, perhaps taking time to turn off and explore the winding streets of historic neighborhoods first settled in the 1930s and 1940s. One of these neighborhoods is called the **Woodyard.** Once a thriving fuel depot run by a pioneer businessman, it's now known for its eccentric cabins, log dwellings, and Yellowknife's most famous street, **Ragged Ass Road,** named after hard-luck prospectors.

If you proceed north on Franklin Avenue, it becomes McDonald Drive. From McDonald Drive turn left onto Weaver Road and right onto Ingraham Drive, which travels over the **Rock,** a steep Precambrian outcropping where miners first pitched their tents more than 65 years ago. The wooden stairs at Ingraham Drive's highest point lead to the **Pilot's Monument,** a hilltop marker built in honor of the bush flyers who opened up the north. The climb is worth it: there's a 360-degree view of Great Slave Lake, neighboring islands, and Yellowknife itself.

To continue exploring the Old Town, head back down to McDonald Drive and follow it around the Rock. Watch for the **Float Plane Base,** heavy with traffic coming in and going out to mining exploration camps. You can also cross the causeway to **Latham Island,** where a handful of B&Bs and down-to-earth eateries mingle with upscale housing.

It's hard to overstress the beauty of **Great Slave Lake,** the sixth-largest freshwater lake in North America. Clean, cold, and deep, it dwarfs Yellowknife and the few other communities along its shores. The lake's East Arm, a two- to three-day sail from Yellowknife, is prime cruise country, with dramatic cliffs rising from narrow bays. For those unsure of their navigational skills, hiring a skipper is recommended, since many of the lake's small bays are still uncharted. Excursions on the lake can be arranged with any of the local operators who provide sail and motorboat charters, cruises, and sightseeing trips.

The **Prince of Wales Northern Heritage Centre,** on the shore of Frame Lake opposite City Hall, is a few minutes northwest of the city center. It houses extensive displays of such northern artifacts as caribou-hide parkas, beaded Dene clothing, and Inuit tools and stone carvings, as well as exhibits on exploration and settlement. The aviation section documents the north's history of flight. Among other displays is an exhibit devoted to the search for the Northwest Passage, which took more than 400 years as Europeans hunted for an Arctic route to the East, mapping the polar islands and the coast as they explored. ⊠ *Box 1320, X1A 2L9,* ☎ *867/873-7551,* FAX *867/873-0205,* WEB *www.pwnhc.learnnet.ca.* ☎ *Free.* ⊙ *June–Aug., daily 10:30–5:30; Sept.–May, Tues.–Fri. 10:30–5, weekends noon–5.*

A few hundred yards west of the Prince of Wales Northern Heritage Centre, the glass-domed **Legislative Assembly of the Northwest Territories** rises above the boreal forest. Free tours guide you through the splendid building in summer. You can visit the council chamber and see the translation booths that permit debates to be carried out in nine official languages. The legislature houses the ceremonial mace, a symbol of government made of Yellowknife gold, musk-ox horns, and a slender narwhal tusk. ⊠ *Turn left off Hwy. 3, northwest of town,* ☎ *867/669-2200 or 800/661-0879,* WEB *www.assembly.gov.nt.ca.* ⊙ *Tours June–July, weekdays 10:30, 1:30, and 3:30, Sun. 1:30.*

Dining and Lodging

$$–$$$ ✕ **Bullock's Bistro.** Old Town's atmospheric and popular eatery is warm, friendly, and rustic, with only a dozen or so tables, from which you can join the lively banter in the open kitchen. Bullock's specializes in a succulent variety of fish, fried to order in batter or straight in the pan. The fries are hand cut, and the catch of the day is fresh from Great Slave Lake. ⊠ *3534 Weaver Rd., X1A 2G5,* ☎ *867/873-3474. MC, V.*

$–$$ ✕ **Wildcat Cafe.** An institution as much as a restaurant, the Wildcat has been around since 1937. The low-slung log structure and split-log tables and benches inside evoke life at the frontier's edge. This is a place where strangers are expected to share tables. The food, ranging from fresh fish to vegetarian chili to caribou burgers, is excellent and moderately priced. Many people drop in at the Wildcat for coffee and desserts—mostly fresh-baked delectables. ⊠ *3904 Wiley Rd., Box 763, X1A 2NG,* ☎ *867/873-8850. MC, V. Closed Oct.–late May.*

$$–$$$ ✕📶 **Explorer Hotel.** Atop a promontory overlooking Yellowknife, the Explorer has great views of the city and the bays of Great Slave Lake. Rooms are large, bright, and clean, with natural-wood furnishings and cream-colored walls. At the Sakura Restaurant traditional Japanese dishes such as sushi with whitefish caviar are frequently made with fresh northern ingredients. You can also eat roasted eel, tuna sushi, tempura, and a variety of beef and arctic char offerings. Lord Barkley's Dining Room and its adjacent lounge serve an eclectic array of dishes, from fresh-veggie wraps to musk-ox fillet in blueberry sauce. Buffet lunches and Sunday brunch are less expensive than dinner. ⊠ *4825 49th Ave. (Postal Service 7000), X1A 2R3,* ☎ *867/873-3531; 800/661-0892 in Canada;* FAX *867/873-2789,* WEB *www.explorerhotel.nt.ca. 128 rooms, 2 suites. 2 restaurants, lounge, airport shuttle. AE, MC, V. CP.*

$–$$ ✕📶 **The Prospector.** This comfortable eatery and B&B on the waterfront, not far from the famous Wildcat Cafe, has upgraded its menu to include ambitious regional dishes such as musk-ox satay. Other unusual creations are caribou steak served with red-currant *demi-glace* (brown sauce) and arctic char baked in phyllo pastry with sun-dried tomatoes and bathed in a delicate white-wine sauce. As you dine—perhaps on the deck in warm weather—you can take in the view across Back Bay, where colorful floatplanes boom in and out all summer long. Upstairs, the Prospector offers B&B accommodations in airy, white-washed rooms with rustic, down-home furniture. Each floor has its own deck overlooking the bay. A full breakfast is included in the room rate. ⊠ *3506 Wiley Rd., Box 400, X1A 2N3,* ☎ *867/920-7620,* FAX *867/ 669-7581,* WEB *www.theprospector.net. 8 rooms, 1 suite, 1 studio. Restaurant. MC, V. BP.*

$$$ 🏨 **Yellowknife Inn.** The city's oldest hotel has a lavish marble lobby that opens into the Centre Square shopping mall. The comfortable rooms are done in muted rose, green, and beige hues. The Mackenzie Lounge, with dark-wood paneling that lends it a clubby feel, is a nice place to meet for a drink before dinner. The restaurant serves bistro-style cuisine. ⊠ *5010 49th St., Box 490, X1A 2N4,* ☎ *867/873–2601 or 800/ 661–0580,* FAX *867/873–2602,* WEB *www.yellowknifeinn.com. 125 rooms, 6 suites. Restaurant, lounge, airport shuttle. AE, DC, MC, V. CP.*

$ 🏨 **Blue Raven.** Attractively set on a bluff at the edge of Old Town and overlooking Great Slave Lake, the Blue Raven is among the best of Yellowknife's B&Bs. A Continental breakfast is served in a common room with a view of the lake. The rooms are small, modern, clean, and quiet, set apart from one another by the home's three-story configuration. ⊠ *37 Otto Dr., X1A 2T9,* ☎ *867/873–6328,* FAX *867/920–4013. 2 rooms share bath. No-smoking rooms. No credit cards. CP.*

$ 🏨 **Igloo Inn.** The Igloo is a good choice for budget-minded travelers laying over for a night before heading off to more adventurous pursuits in the territorial outback. Don't expect much more here than a small motel-style room with a TV, at a decent price. Many rooms have kitchenettes. ⊠ *4115 Franklin Ave., Box 596, X1A 2R4,* ☎ *867/873– 8511,* FAX *867/873–5547. 44 rooms. Restaurant, kitchenettes (some). AE, MC, V.*

FLY-IN WILDERNESS LODGES

If you enjoy fishing or wildlife-watching in the great outdoors, consider a backcountry trip to one of the lodges listed below. Transportation is provided to and from Yellowknife.

$$$$ 🏨 **Bathurst Inlet Lodge.** Open only about six weeks a year, this lone outpost on the tundra, 49 km (30 mi) north of the Arctic Circle, may be the most popular destination in the central Arctic, particularly for ornithologists. The lodge is actually in Nunavut, but guests are flown in from Yellowknife by bush plane. Around the lodge you can spot musk oxen, arctic foxes, wolves, falcons, hawks, and eagles. In late June or early July, as many as a half-million migrating caribou pass this way. From the lodge, you can hike (after a short airplane transfer) to Wilberforce Falls, the highest waterfall north of the Arctic Circle, where the Burnside River cuts spectacularly through a series of gorges. The lodge also arranges weeklong naturalist tours and outfits canoe or raft trips on nearby waterways. Fees start at around $4,000 per person for a seven-day stay, including flights to and from Yellowknife. ⊠ *3618 McAvoy Rd., Box 820 Yellowknife X1A 2N6,* ☎ *867/873–2595,* FAX *867/920– 4263,* WEB *www.bathurstinletlodge.com. 15 rooms in lodge, 15 cabins. Cafeteria, hiking, boating, camping, fishing, travel services. V. Closed early Aug.–late June.*

$$$$ 🏨 **Blachford Lake Lodge.** Many fishing lodges in the far north provide a minimum of services, unless patrons request otherwise. Blachford Lake Lodge is a good example of the genre. Guests are flown to and from the remote lodge (less than a half-hour flight from Yellowknife), where they stay in cabins and have the use of boats to venture out on a small lake. If you elect to bring and prepare your own food, bedding, and fishing tackle, the cost can be kept to about $300 per person per day (including the flights to and from the lodge), and less for groups of 25— modest by fly-in fishing standards. You can also choose from a variety of full-service packages, with or without guide services, at higher prices. The lodge is also open in winter for ice fishing, snowmobiling, and dogsledding. *Mailing address:* ⊠ *Box 1568, Yellowknife X1A 2P2,* ☎ *867/873–3303,* FAX *867/920–4013,* WEB *http://users.internorth.com/ ~blach/. Main lodge and 5 cabins sleep 25. Sauna, fishing, cross-country skiing, snowmobiling. V.*

$$$$ ☷ **Frontier Fishing Lodge.** On the East Arm of Great Slave Lake near the Dene community of Lutsel K'e, Frontier Lodge is typical of a full-service fishing lodge. Guests are housed in the main lodge, in outlying log cabins, and in comfortable rooms attached to the conference and recreation building. Breakfast and dinner are served daily around a big table in the main lodge. Guides take you to the best fishing waters on Great Slave as well as adjoining rivers and lakes; lake trout exceeding 25 pounds are landed regularly. Packages, including flights to and from Yellowknife, begin at around $500 per person per day. *Mailing address:* ✉ *Box 32008, Edmonton, AB T6K 4C2,* ☎ *780/465–6843,* FAX *780/466–3874,* WEB *www.frontierfishing.ab.ca. 6 rooms, 6 cabins sleep 4 to 6; shared indoor bathrooms. Sauna, fishing, meeting rooms. No credit cards. Closed mid-Sept.–mid-June. MAP.*

Nightlife and the Arts

Folk on the Rocks (✉ Box 326, X1A 2N3, ☎ 867/920–7806, WEB www.folkontherocks.com), a lakeside music festival held in mid-July, attracts musicians from throughout North America, as well as Dene and Inuit performers.

Raven Mad Daze (✉ Yellowknife Chamber of Commerce, 4807 49th St., X1A 3T5, ☎ 867/920–4944) takes place during summer solstice (the third week in June), when the sun is still out at midnight. Sidewalk sales, street vendors, concerts, and dances are part of the fun.

Outdoor Activities and Sports

The **M.S. Norweta** (✉ N.W.T. Marine Group, Box 2216, X1A 2P6, ☎ 867/873–2489 or 877/874–6001, FAX 867/873–6630) organizes short outings, dinner cruises, and multiday cruises to the legendary East Arm of Great Slave Lake and along the Mackenzie River. **Sail North** (✉ Box 2497, X1A 2P4, ☎ 867/873–8019) accommodates trips to Great Slave Lake with boat rentals (including houseboats).

Shopping

Northern Images (✉ 4910 50th Ave., X1A 3S5, ☎ 867/873–5944) sells a variety of native crafts and artwork, from sculpture to moose-hair tuftings to clothing, and has stores in several Canadian cities, including Whitehorse, Inuvik, and Yellowknife. **Polar Parkas** (✉ 5023 49th St., X1A 2P1, ☎ 867/873–3344) is the best place in Yellowknife to buy native-made parkas.

Departures from Yellowknife

Yellowknife is a transportation hub for outlying areas in the western Arctic. For driving excursions from Yellowknife, you can pass through Wood Buffalo National Park and Fort Smith to the south and through Fort Liard to the west. This is not, generally speaking, a rousing scenic drive. Long stretches of road cutting through the low-lying subarctic bush are highlighted by occasional waterfalls or the sight of wildlife on or near the highway.

Alexandra Falls

537 km (333 mi) south of Yellowknife.

Of the scenic waterfalls along the road between Yellowknife and Fort Smith, the most dramatic is Alexandra Falls, a few miles south of the town of Hay River, on Route 1 at the junction of Routes 1 and 2, where the Hay River drops 108 ft over limestone cliffs.

Wood Buffalo National Park

330 km (205 mi) southwest of Alexandra Falls, 599 km (371 mi) south of Yellowknife.

The area where you're most likely to spot wildlife is Wood Buffalo National Park, straddling the Alberta–Northwest Territories border, off Route 5. Covering 44,807 square km (17,300 square mi), this is the largest national park in Canada, home to the world's largest free-roaming bison herd (about 5,000 total). It's also a summer nesting ground for many bird species, including bald eagles, peregrine falcons, and the rare whooping crane. Much of the terrain—a flat land of bogs, swamps, salt plains, sinkholes, and meandering streams and rivers—is essentially inaccessible to visitors, but a few frontcountry trails allow exploration. Two campgrounds have 24 sites with picnic tables, firewood, running water, and playgrounds. *Mailing address:* ✉ *Superintendent, Wood Buffalo National Park, Box 750, Fort Smith, X0E 0P0,* ☎ *867/872–7900,* FAX *867/872–3910.* ⊑ *Free; camping $10 per night per person, $30 per night for groups of 8 or more.*

Nahanni National Park

★ *608 km (377 mi) west of Yellowknife.*

The principal reason to head west from Yellowknife is to visit Nahanni National Park (☒ $10). The Mackenzie and Liard rivers, which join at Fort Simpson, are the region's approximate geographical dividers, separating the low-lying bush of the east and the mountains to the west. Access to Nahanni National Park is possible only by helicopter or plane; inside the park, canoes and rafts are the principal means of travel. A well-maintained park campground near the Virginia Falls facilitates overnight excursions. For a list of air services, contact the **Nahanni National Park Reserve** (✉ Box 348, Fort Simpson, X0E 0N0, ☎ 867/695–3151, FAX 867/695–2446).

Perhaps the most impressive feature in Nahanni National Park is **Virginia Falls,** more than 410 ft high and about 656 ft wide—a thunderous wall of white water cascading around a central spire of rock. To get there contact Simpson Air (☎ 867/695–2505), one of several plane and helicopter services that offer flightseeing trips.

The spectacular **Cirque of the Unclimbables,** a breathtaking cathedral of rock towers rising as much as 3,000 vertical ft, does not entirely live up to its name, but the few who have made successful ascents here can be counted among the most proficient rock climbers in the world. Perhaps the biggest problem posed by the Cirque is that it is nearly as unreachable as it is unclimbable.

The **South Nahanni,** with its stunning scenery, is among the loveliest rivers in the far north. Two-week canoe trips start from Rabbit Kettle Lake at the park's northwestern extreme but require portage around Virginia Falls. Eight- to 12-day canoe or raft trips begin below Virginia Falls. White water along the way is minimal, so previous canoeing or rafting experience is not essential.

OUTDOOR ACTIVITIES AND SPORTS

Nahanni River Adventures (✉ Box 4869, Whitehorse, YT Y1A 4N6, ☎ 867/668–3180 or 800-297–6927, WEB www.nahanni.com) provides reliable guided river trips. **Nahanni Wilderness Adventures** (✉ Box 4, Site 6, R.R. 1, Didsbury, AB T0W 0W0, ☎ 403/637–3843 or 888/897–5223, WEB www.nahanniwild.com) specializes in canoeing and hiking adventures in Nahanni National Park.

For those interested in mountaineering, **Simpson Air** (✉ Box 260, Fort Simpson, X0E 0N0, ☎ 867/695–2505, FAX 867/695–2925, WEB www.cancom.net/~simpair) can shuttle climbers to the Cirque of the Unclimbables from Fort Simpson.

Inuvik

Overlooking the huge Mackenzie Delta, where the Mackenzie River (*Deh Cho* to the Dene people of this region) meets the Beaufort Sea, **⑧ Inuvik** is 1,086 air km (673 air mi) northwest of Yellowknife. The town's population of 3,000 mixes many major northern identities: Gwich'in Dene, Inuvialuit, Métis, and settlers from southern Canada. You can meet native peoples and experience their culture on guided tours to fishing and whaling camps with **Beaufort Delta Tours** (✉ Box 2637, X0E 0T0, ☎ 867/777–4881, 𝟙 867/777–4898).

Dining and Lodging

$$$ ✗🛏 **Finto Motor Inn.** On the outskirts of Inuvik, at the junction of the Marine Bypass and Mackenzie Road, the Finto materializes as a two-story, square structure resembling a big box that might have been flown in by a helicopter sling and dropped on the spot. The Finto may not be elegant, but the Peppermill, its restaurant, is generally considered Inuvik's best. Local foods such as arctic char and musk ox are accompanied by views of green meadows and blue water. ✉ *Box 1925, X0E 0T0,* ☎ *867/777–2647; 800/661–0843 in the Northwest Territories, Nunavut, Yukon, and Northern British Columbia;* 𝟙 *867/777– 3442. 38 rooms. Restaurant. AE, DC, MC, V.*

Nightlife and the Arts

The **Great Northern Arts Festival** (✉ Box 2921, X0E 0T0, ☎ 867/777– 3536, 🌐 www.greatart.nt.ca), in July, includes displays of carvings in wood, horn, and stone and weavings by Inuit and Inuvialuit artists, workshops focusing on various disciplines, and music and dance performances.

Departures from Inuvik

One doesn't "tour" the Northwest Territories in the usual sense of the word. Here a tour is more of an expedition. Inuvik serves as a base camp from which to make day or extended side trips in the Mackenzie Delta, along the coast, or north to the islands of the western Arctic Archipelago. Using regional airlines, you can make hops to Banks Island; to Tuktoyaktuk, overlooking the Beaufort Sea; and to Herschel Island, in the Beaufort Sea. Lodging and transportation in the Arctic North tend to be expensive even by high-end northern standards, so having a well-defined travel plan is critical to staying within a budget. Trip organizers and outfitters can be particularly helpful in tailoring a travel program to meet particular interests and budgets. Keep in mind that the prime Arctic travel season is very short: many visitor services and tour organizers operate only in July and August.

Tuktoyaktuk

⑨ *113 air km (70 air mi) north of Inuvik.*

If you're intrigued by the culture of the Arctic's original people, this small Inuvialuit community a short flight north of Inuvik is the place to experience an interesting blend of ancient culture and modern technology. As you fly in over Tuk Peninsula, you'll spot pingoes (odd conical landforms found only on the frozen borders of the Beaufort Sea) and caribou, from which the hamlet of Tuktoyaktuk derives its name, "the place where caribou cross."

From Tuktoyaktuk, it's a short hop to the coastal village of Paulatuk and the **Tuktut Nogait National Park** (mailing address: ✉ c/o Parks Canada, Box 1840, Inuvik X0E 0T0, ☎ 867/777–3248), a wilderness park without any development that was set aside to protect caribou calving grounds.

Banks Island
523 air km (324 air mi) northeast of Inuvik.

Banks Island, the most westerly of the Arctic islands, is best known for its large herd of musk oxen, now numbering in the thousands in **Aulavik National Park** (mailing address: ✉ c/o Parks Canada, Box 1840, Inuvik X0E 0T0, ☎ 867/777–3248). Arctic Tour Company conducts tours to Banks Island that include musk-oxen and caribou watching.

Herschel Island
274 air km (170 air mi) northwest of Inuvik.

Tiny Herschel Island is an excellent base for sighting beluga and bow-head whales. It's also known for its abundant bird life and its wild-flowers, which grow from the seemingly barren tundra. Historic relics include the old Anglican Rectory and the weathered grave markers of 19th-century whalers who succumbed to the island's harsh winters. Beau-fort Delta Tours offers guided day tours along the coast to Herschel, as does the Arctic Tour Company.

NUNAVUT

There are no roads to Nunavut. This fact alone makes Canada's new Arctic territory a unique travel destination. But consider its other amazements: no forests grow here—Nunavut lies entirely above the tree line. In winter, night can last around the clock. In summer, the sun never sets. It's a land of glaciers and looming peaks, where caribou out-number people. Nunavut's 27,219 residents are predominantly Inuit, and many still live by hunting and fishing in isolated settlements.

Nunavut's name means "Our Land" in Inuktitut, one of the territory's three official languages (the other two are English and French). The newest political entity in North America is also the largest, at 2,121,012 square km (818,919 square mi). The territory's northernmost bound-ary lies at latitude 83° north—only 400 km (248 mi) from the geographic North Pole. It reaches as far south as the windy Belcher Islands, deep in Hudson Bay. And it contains the geographic center of Canada—an unmarked (and little-recognized) spot on the barrens 30 km (19 mi) west of Baker Lake, in the Kivalliq (Keewatin) region.

July 9 is now celebrated as Nunavut Day in the towns and hamlets of Canada's central and eastern Arctic, from Kugluktuk in the west to Iqaluit in the east, to the High Arctic settlement of Grise Fiord, and along the coast of Hudson Bay. These small communities, 28 in all, are linked to one another by modern communications technology; all are served by regional airlines. Yet they are among the world's truly remote living places, poised on the outer edge of civilization. You won't find tidy suburban gardens or paved roads here. Instead of neatly trimmed hedges, many a front door is flanked by drying cari-bou hides and dismantled snowmobiles. The family runabout is likely to be a four-wheel motorbike or a homemade *komatik* (a long, wooden sled pulled by dogs or a snowmobile). Living here is an adventure in itself, as the Inuit cope with a harsh climate and huge distances.

Visiting is an adventure, too: experiencing the Arctic wilderness and the Inuit way of life is the lure for most travelers, even though getting around in Nunavut tends to be both time-consuming and expensive, and ameni-ties can be very basic. But if you opt for the services of the local and in-ternational outfitters who offer packages that range from outdoor adventures to cultural tours in the villages, you can often cut costs. Even in the smallest communities you'll find experienced Inuit outfitters who can help you get to know the land, the wildlife, and the local folklore.

Nunavut is vast—a fifth of Canada's landmass—and it's probably best to select a region you'd like to see most. There are three regions to consider: Baffin, Kitikmeot, and Kivalliq. To get to destinations within these regions, you must first fly to Iqaluit, the new Nunavut capital, on southwest Baffin Island, or to Yellowknife in the Northwest Territories.

Iqaluit

 On southwestern Baffin Island, overlooking Frobisher Bay, **Iqaluit,** 2,261 air km (1,402 air mi) east of Yellowknife, is the capital of Nunavut and the Arctic's transportation center. Its population—nearly 4,500 at last count—may be minuscule compared to that of other capital cities, but Iqaluit is growing fast as builders create a metropolis on the tundra. The sleek new **Government of Nunavut Building,** in the Four Corners section of town, houses the territory's elected assembly, as well as an important display of northern art. Another notable piece of architecture is **St. Jude's,** the igloo-shape Anglican cathedral in the center of town.

Nunavut's capital is notable more for the people you're likely to meet than for its architecture. Lawyers and politicos rub shoulders with village matriarchs in town to shop and hunters heading out for seals. Elderly artists carve stone on their doorsteps, while the local kids show off the latest southern gear. Nearly anyone you meet can point you in the right direction, which is a good thing, since there are no street names in Iqaluit. (At any rate, the town's small size makes it easy to navigate.)

To learn about Inuit life and culture, visit the **Nunatta Sunakkutaangit Museum,** with its excellent collection of historical artifacts, including the clothing and tools that enabled the Inuit to survive in the Arctic. The museum is in a renovated Hudson's Bay trading post down on the beach that fronts Frobisher Bay's Koojesse Inlet. ⊠ *Bldg. 212, X0A 0H0,* ☎ *867/979–5537.* ☎ *Free.* ☉ *Tues.–Sun. 1–5.*

Next door to the Nunatta Sunakkutaangit Museum is the **Unikkaarvik Visitor Centre,** where you can pick up guidebooks and brochures on the area. The center displays a collection of Inuit art and a life-size diorama of a floe edge. ⊠ *Unikkaarvik Bldg., X0A 0H0,* ☎ *867/979–4636.* ☎ *Free.* ☉ *Weekdays 10–8, weekends 1–4.*

Sylvia Grinnell Territorial Park is just 15 minutes outside of town. Trails are unmarked and of varying difficulty, so sturdy hiking boots are a must. Shallow and swift Sylvia Grinnell River is for experienced canoeists and kayakers only. Although it's mainly a day-use park, there are campsites. There's no on-site information center or staff, so contact the Unikkaarvik Visitor Centre or Nunavut Tourism for more information.

A compelling reason to visit **Qaummaarviit Territorial Historic Park,** on an island 13 km (8 mi) west of Iqaluit, is to see relics of the stone houses occupied by the Thule Inuit 1,000 years ago. A well-marked trail winds through the park, connecting the sites. Camping is not permitted on the island, so plan on a day trip only. There's no fee to enter the park, and arrangements to travel to the island can be made through the Unikkaarvik Visitor Centre.

Dining and Lodging

$$$–$$$$ ✗⌂ **Regency Frobisher Inn.** The Regency Frobisher is part of an indoor shopping and high-rise apartment complex that includes a swimming pool. Veneer-wood furnishings fill the simple, boxlike rooms, but private baths, phones, and cable TV make up for the lack of character. Rooms in the front offer good views of Frobisher Bay and Iqaluit. There's no airport shuttle, but the inn reimburses you for the taxi ride. The dining room specializes in Canadian Arctic cuisine. The hotel also provides fax services. ✉ *Box 4209, X0A 0H0,* ☎ *867/979–2222 or 877/422–9422,* FAX *867/979–0427,* WEB *www.frobisherinn.com. 95 rooms. Restaurant, lounge, indoor pool, laundry service, business services. AE, DC, MC, V.*

$$$ ✗⊞ **Discovery Lodge Hotel.** Skylights brighten the lobby and nearly every room's centerpiece is a trapezoidal bed, wider at the top than at the bottom. The Granite Room, with its granite-slab tabletops, is perhaps the best restaurant in Iqaluit, noteworthy for its use of local ingredients, including arctic char, Baffin Island shrimp, and scallops. ✉ *Box 387, X0A 0H0,* ☎ *867/979–4433,* FAX *867/979–6591,* WEB *www.arctic-travel.com/DIS/covery.html. 53 rooms, 1 suite. Restaurant, lounge, coin laundry, airport shuttle. AE, DC, MC, V.*

$$$ ✗⊞ **Navigator Inn.** Rooms here are standard, but the pervading nautical theme adds a bit of character. The inn is also a local favorite for dining, with an eclectic dinner menu that includes such Arctic specialties as caribou, char, and musk-ox chops. ✉ *1036 Ring Road, X0A 0H0,* ☎ *867/979–2222,* FAX *867/979–0422,* WEB *www.arctic-travel.com/EVAZ/navigator.html. 35 rooms. Restaurant, coffee shop, lounge, in-room data ports. AE, MC, V.*

$$ ⊞ **Accommodations-by-the-Sea.** Take in spectacular views of historic Frobisher Bay from the large windows of this B&B as you chat with visitors from all over the world. The rooms and common dining area are spacious and bright, an effect created by white walls and natural wood trim that seem in keeping with the Arctic landscape. The owner also operates Purlaavik Outfitting and Naturalist Tours and can arrange trips to Qaummaarviit Territorial Historic Park or other points of interest. ✉ *Box 341, X0A 0H0,* ☎ *867/979–6074,* FAX *867/979–1830,* WEB *www.arctictravel.com/JENS/steenburg.html. 5 rooms. Dining room, airport shuttle. No credit cards.*

The Baffin Region

Iqaluit is the gateway to magnificent Baffin Island, an awesomely rugged world where mountains meet sea and where the climates of summer and winter may be experienced on the same day. Despite the influences of modern culture, Baffin remains a stronghold of Inuit tradition, where relics of ancient peoples and 19th-century European whalers may still be seen.

From Iqaluit, visitors must choose a medium of travel: air, land, or sea. In winter, the land and sea merge under ice and snow, and April and May are ideal months for cross-country skiing, dogsledding, and snowmobiling. Those who journey into the Baffin wilderness should have an adventurous spirit. Although some tour organizers offer general sightseeing tours, Baffin is best appreciated by those inclined (and physically fit enough) to rough it.

Auyuittuq National Park
320 air km (198 air mi) northeast of Iqaluit.

The jewel of Baffin is Auyuittuq National Park, where rivers and glaciers have cut deep fjords and have carved out **Aksayook Pass** between Cumberland Sound to the south and Davis Strait to the north. The 60-km (37-mi) pass is surrounded by jagged peaks exceeding 6,600 ft that jut up from glacial ice. A marked trail leads through the pass, and in summer, backpacking groups regularly make the five- to seven-day journey. There are emergency shelters along the route, but this is still a trip only for those properly prepared and physically fit, given the length of the trip and the vagaries of weather, even in midsummer. All park visitors should sign up with a trip organizer and check in at the park headquarters in Pangnirtung for information about hiking in the park. ⊠ *Superintendent, Auyuittuq National Park, Box 353, Pangnirtung X0A 0R0,* ☎ *867/473–8828,* WEB *www.parkscanada.gc.ca.* ☉ *July–Aug., weekdays 8:30–noon, 1–5, and 6–10, weekends 1–5 and 6–10; Sept.–June, weekdays 8:30–5.* ☒ *$15 day use, $40 up to 3 nights, $100 season.*

Sirmilik National Park

1,066 air km (661 air mi) north of Iqaluit.

Its name means "place of glaciers," and Sirmilik, a park 700 km (434 mi) north of the Arctic Circle on Baffin Island, has plenty of year-round ice. But it's also rich with wildlife, from seabirds thronging the 1,000-ft cliffs to belugas and bowhead whales sporting in the frigid waters of Lancaster Sound. Sirmilik is fairly easy to get to if you first fly to one of the nearby small communities such as Pond Inlet or Arctic Bay. For more information, contact **Parks Canada** (⊠ Superintendent, Sirmilik National Park, Box 353, Pangnirtung X0A 0R0, ☎ 867/473–8828, WEB www.parkscanada.gc.ca).

Quttinirpaaq National Park

2,100 air km (1,302 air mi) northwest of Iqaluit.

Adventurous visitors can head north from Baffin Island to Ellesmere Island, home to Quttinirpaaq National Park, above 80° north latitude. Ellesmere Island, like Baffin, is intriguing as much for its climate as for its landscape. Technically a "polar desert," the island, with an annual precipitation of about 2½ inches, is one of the driest places in the Northern Hemisphere; yet, because of the water-retaining effects of ice, parts of the island can support plant and wildlife. For more information, contact **Parks Canada** (⊠ Superintendent, Quttinirpaaq National Park, Box 353, Pangnirtung X0A 0R0, ☎ 867/473–8828, WEB www.parkscanada.gc.ca).

The Kitikmeot Region

Kitikmeot is the Inuit name for the central Arctic, the Nunavut region that borders the Northwest Territories (beginning west of Kugluktuk on the Coppermine River). Some of its communities, such as Kugluktuk and Cambridge Bay on Victoria Island, are reached by scheduled flights out of Yellowknife, through Inuvik. Farther east, you must fly from Iqaluit. This is Northwest Passage country, the forbidding maze of channels and Arctic islands through which European explorers navigated for 400 years in search of a route to Asia. At Gjoa Haven, there's a historic trail commemorating the search in **Northwest Passage Territorial Park**. The **Arctic Coast Visitors Centre** (⊠ Box 91, Cambridge Bay X0C 0C0, ☎ 867/983–2224, FAX 867/983–2302, WEB www.nunavutparks.com) provides information on the area.

Major draws to Kitikmeot are its bird and wildlife sanctuaries and challenging rivers, such as the Hood, the Back, the Thelon, and the Burnside. Many outfitters offer trips by canoe or raft to these remote rivers, which wind through a vast treeless landscape that remains virtually untouched.

The Kivalliq Region

Kivalliq includes the eastern Barrenlands and the Hudson Bay coast. A rugged, thinly populated part of Nunavut, it has a fascinating Inuit history, still visible in the form of old stone caches, tent rings, and kayak stands. In summer, you might spot polar bears, whales, walrus colonies, wildfowl nurseries, or caribou herds. Local outfitters take you to

Southampton and Coats islands, to fishing rivers, and on paddling adventures. You can reach the Kivalliq region by flying from Iqaluit or Yellowknife to Rankin Inlet, which serves as a way station to smaller villages like Arviat, Whale Cove, and Chesterfield Inlet.

Rankin Inlet

1,200 air km (744 air mi) from Iqaluit.

Founded as a nickel mining center in the 1950s, Rankin Inlet is now a bustling hamlet and regional transportation hub. Inuit constitute 77% of its tiny population of 2,058. The nickel mine has been closed for nearly 40 years, but mineral explorers are once again searching the nearby tundra for gold and base metals, and future mining appears likely. In summer, **Ijiraliq (Meliadine) River Historic Park,** 8 km (5 mi) from town, offers hiking, fishing, bird-watching, and berry-picking opportunities. The park also contains the remains of stone houses built centuries ago. **Kivalliq Regional Visitors' Centre** (✉ Rankin Inlet X0C 0G0, ☎ 867/645-3838, FAX 867/645-3904) provides information on the area.

Dining and Lodging

$$$$ ✕🏨 **Siniktarvik Hotel.** In the center of town, the Siniktarvik offers basic but comfortable rooms, and dining in the Captain's Galley restaurant. The food, ranging from lasagne to a grilled steak and shrimp platter, is satisfying without being exceptional. ✉ *Box 190, Rankin Inlet X0C 0G0,* ☎ *867/645-2807,* FAX *867/645-2999,* WEB *www.arctic-travel.com/EVAZ/siniktarvik.html. 48 rooms. Restaurant, lounge. AE, DC, MC, V.*

Fly-in Wilderness Lodge

$$$$ 🏨 **Sila Lodge.** A rather spartan facility, Sila Lodge is noteworthy for its exceptional location on Wager Bay, 80 km (50 mi) south of the Arctic Circle and teeming with wildlife, especially polar bears and peregrine falcons. In addition to wildlife viewing, the lodge offers programs on Inuit culture, excellent hiking opportunities, and tours across the tundra to Baker Lake and Churchill, Manitoba. *Mailing address:* ✉ *173 Ragsdill Rd., Winnipeg, MB R2G 4C6,* ☎ *204/949-2050 or 800/663-9832,* FAX *204/663-6375,* WEB *www.frontiersnorth.com. 5 cabins, each sleeps 6. V. Closed Sept.–June.*

WILDERNESS CANADA A TO Z

To research prices, get advice from other travelers, and book travel arrangements, visit www.fodors.com.

AIR TRAVEL

Air Canada can arrange connecting service from the United States through scheduling agreements with Delta Air Lines. Air Canada serves destinations throughout the Northwest Territories and Nunavut in partnership with First Air, which flies to 28 destinations across the North, from main gateways in Ottawa, Montréal, Winnipeg, Edmonton, Whitehorse, and Yellowknife.

Canadian North offers scheduled passenger service from Yellowknife, Ottawa, and Edmonton to key regional destinations throughout the far north. In summer, Canada 3000 offers service to Whitehorse and Yellowknife from Vancouver.

➤ AIRLINES AND CONTACTS: **Air Canada** (☎ 888/247-2262, WEB www.air-canada.com). **Canadian North** (☎ 867/669-4000 or 800/661-1505, FAX 867/669-4040, WEB www.canadiannorth.com). **Canada 3000** (☎ 888/226-3000, WEB www.canada3000.ca). **Delta Air Lines** (☎ 800/221-1212, WEB www.deltaair.com). **First Air** (☎ 613/839-3340 or 800/267-1247, FAX 613/839-5690, WEB www.firstair.ca).

AIRPORTS AND TRANSFERS

Whitehorse International Airport, 5 km (3 mi) from downtown White-horse, is the Yukon's major airport. Yellowknife Airport, the main fa-cility for the Northwest Territories, is 5 km (3 mi) northwest of the city center. Iqaluit Airport is Nunavut's main hub, with connections to regional centers.

➤ AIRPORT INFORMATION: **Iqaluit Airport** (☎ 867/979–5224). **White-horse International Airport** (☎ 867/667–8440). **Yellowknife Airport** (☎ 867/873–4049).

BUS TRAVEL

Greyhound Lines of Canada has service from Edmonton to Hay River and Yellowknife, Northwest Territories. Greyhound also has service from Edmonton or Vancouver to Whitehorse in the Yukon.

In the Yukon, Alaska Direct Transport and Bus Line offers scheduled service from Whitehorse to many Alaskan communities, as well as Haines Junction, Dawson City, Burwash Landing, and Beaver Creek. Alaskon Express has service between Whitehorse and cities in Alaska from mid-May to mid-September. Frontier Coachlines offers service connecting Fort Smith, Fort Providence, Hay River, and Yellowknife. Summer bus service between Dawson and Inuvik is offered by Gold City Tours. Nor-line Coaches has service between Dawson City and Whitehorse.

➤ BUS INFORMATION: **Alaska Direct Transport and Bus Line** (⊠ 4051 4th Ave., Whitehorse, YT Y1A 1H1, ☎ 867/668–4833, FAX 867/667–7411). **Alaskon Express** (⊠ 208-G Steele St., Whitehorse, YT Y1A 2C4, ☎ 867/668–3225 or 800/544–2206, FAX 867/667–4494). **Frontier Coachlines** (⊠ 16-102 St., Hay River, NT X0E 0R9, ☎ 867/874–2566, FAX 867/874–2388; ⊠ 328 Old Airport Rd., Yellowknife, NT X1A 3T3, ☎ 867/873–4892). **Gold City Tours** (⊠ Box 960, Dawson City, YT Y0B 1G0, ☎ 867/993–5175, FAX 867/993–5261). **Greyhound Lines of Canada** (☎ 800/661–8747, WEB www.greyhound.com). **Norline Coaches** (⊠ 34 MacDonald Rd., Whitehorse, YT Y1A 4L2, ☎ 867/633–3864, FAX 867/633–3849).

CAR RENTAL

Rental agencies in Whitehorse and Yellowknife typically rent trucks and four-wheel-drive vehicles in addition to cars. Avis is in Fort Smith; Budget has outlets at the Whitehorse and Yellowknife airports, as does National Tilden.

Whitehorse and Yellowknife also have several recreational-vehicle rental agencies.

➤ MAJOR AGENCIES: **Avis** (☎ 800/272–5871, WEB www.avis.com). **Bud-get** (☎ 800/268–8900, WEB www.budget.com). **National Tilden** (☎ 800/387–4747, WEB www.nationalcar.com).

➤ RECREATIONAL-VEHICLE AGENCIES: **Ambassador Motor Home & Recreational Services Ltd.** (⊠ Box 4147, 37 Boswell Crescent, White-horse, YT Y1A 3S9, ☎ 867/667–4130, FAX 867/633–2195). **CanaDream Inc.** (⊠ 110 Copper Rd., Whitehorse, YT Y1A 2Z6, ☎ 867/668–3610, FAX 867/668–3795). **Frontier Rentals** (⊠ Box 1088-EG, Yellowknife, NT X1A 2N7, ☎ 867/873–5413, FAX 867/873–5417). **Klondike Recre-ational Rentals** (⊠ Box 5156, Whitehorse, YT Y1A 4S3, ☎ 867/668–2200 or 800/665–4755, FAX 867/668–6567).

CAR TRAVEL

It hardly needs to be said that getting to the Yukon or the Northwest Territories by car calls for a good deal of driving. The best route into the region is the Alaska Highway (Route 97 in British Columbia), ac-cessible from Edmonton via Routes 43, 34, and 2 and from Vancou-ver via Route 1. After Fort Nelson, British Columbia, Routes 7, 1, and

3 lead to Yellowknife; the Alaska Highway (also known as Route 1 in the Yukon) continues on to Whitehorse. The good news is that with so few roads in the region it's difficult to make a wrong turn. With relatively little lodging along the way, you might want to embark on the trip in a camper or recreational vehicle. There are no roads to Nunavut.

In general, exploring by car is a more sensible idea in the Yukon than in the Northwest Territories. The only part of the Northwest Territories with any kind of highway network is the southwest, where the roads are paved from the Alberta border to Fort Providence, and again near Yellowknife. Farther north and west, they are hard-packed gravel. And there are no roads connecting the hamlets of Nunavut. Many highways in the Yukon are paved, the scenery along the way considerable, and roadside services more extensive.

Anyone traveling by car in the far north should take precautions. At least one good spare tire is essential, and many residents of the region carry more, especially when traveling long distances. It is also advisable to carry extra parts (air filter, fan belt) and fluids. Another common practice is to cover headlights, grills, and even windshields with plastic shields or wire mesh to protect against flying gravel. Be sure your vehicle has good suspension, even if you plan to stick to the major highways; shifting permafrost regularly damages paved roads, and ruts and washboard occasionally appear on unpaved roads, especially after periods of bad weather.

Winter driving requires extra precautionary measures. Many a far-north resident can tell you a tale about overnighting on the road and waiting out fierce weather. Take along emergency survival gear, including an ax, shovel, flashlight, plenty of matches, kindling (paper or wood) to start a fire, sleeping bag, rugged outerwear, and food. Also, you should have a properly winterized car, with light engine oil and transmission fluid, a block heater, tire chains, and good antifreeze.

GASOLINE

As you drive farther north, gas stations are few and gas is very expensive. Distances from one service area to the next typically exceed 160 km (100 mi), so make sure to monitor your fuel gauge.

ROAD CONDITIONS

Several river crossings in the Northwest Territories don't have real bridges. In summer you ride a free car ferry; in winter you cross on ice bridges. However, there are the seasons known as "freeze-up" and "break-up," in fall and spring, respectively, when ice bridges aren't solid but rivers are too frozen for ferries to run. Call for daily ferry reports, available late May to late October for the south Mackenzie region, and June to late October for areas farther north.

Information about winter road conditions and the Yukon Highway also are available.
➤ CONTACTS: **Ferry crossings** (☎ 800/661–0751 for Routes 1 and 3; 800/661–0752 for the Dempster Highway). **Road conditions** (☎ 800/661–0750 for Routes 1 through 7; 800/661–0752 for the Dempster Highway, WEB www.nwttravel.nt.ca/html/highway.htm). **Yukon Highway information** (☎ 867/667–8215).

EMERGENCIES

It's a good idea when traveling in the far north—especially in remote wilderness areas and if unescorted by a guide or outfitter—to give a detailed itinerary to someone at home or to the police, to facilitate emergency rescue.

For emergency services in the Yukon, the Northwest Territories, and Nunavut, dial 0 for the operator and explain the nature of the emergency. You will then be connected with the police, fire department, or medical service, as needed. In Whitehorse dial 911 for emergencies.

Medical services, with staff on call 24 hours a day, are available at Watson Lake Hospital, Stanton Yellowknife Hospital, Fort Smith Health Services, H. H. Williams Memorial Hospital in Hay River, Inuvik Regional Hospital, and Baffin Regional Hospital in Iqaluit. You may also call a Royal Canadian Mounted Police toll-free number for medical assistance from anywhere in the Yukon.

Pharmacies can be found in major settlements of the Yukon, the Northwest Territories, and Nunavut, but late-night service is rare; after hours contact the nearest hospital or nursing station. If you have a preexisting medical condition that requires special medication, be sure you are well supplied before your trip, as getting unusual prescriptions filled can be difficult or impossible.

➤ DOCTORS: **Fort Smith Health Services** (✉ Byrant St., ☎ 867/872–6200).

➤ EMERGENCY SERVICES: **Royal Canadian Mounted Police** (☎ 867/669–1111 in Yellowknife; 867/667–5555 toll-free emergency number; 867/667–3333 for medical assistance).

➤ HOSPITALS: **Baffin Regional Hospital** (✉ northern section of town, Iqaluit, ☎ 867/979–7300). **H. H. Williams Memorial Hospital** (✉ 3 Gates Dr., Hay River, ☎ 867/874–6512). **Inuvik Regional Hospital** (✉ 185 Mackenzie Rd., ☎ 867/777–2955). **Stanton Yellowknife Hospital** (✉ 550 Byrne Rd., ☎ 867/669–4111). **Watson Lake Hospital** (✉ Liard Dr. and 9th St. N, ☎ 867/536–4444).

LODGING

B&BS

The Northern Network of Bed and Breakfasts publishes a brochure with more than 80 listings in wilderness Canada as well as in Alaska, Alberta, and British Columbia.

➤ RESERVATION SERVICES: **Northern Network of Bed and Breakfasts** (✉ Box 954, Dawson City, YT Y0B 1G0, ☎ 867/993–5644, FAX 867/993–5648).

HOTELS

Inns North is an organization of locally operated hotels throughout the far north.

➤ RESERVING A ROOM: **Inns North** (✉ Arctic Cooperatives Ltd., Hotel Division, 1645 Inkster Blvd., Winnipeg, MB R2X 2W1, ☎ 204/697–1625 or 888/866–6784, WEB www.arctictravel.com/INNSN/innsnorth.html).

TOURS

THE NORTHWEST TERRITORIES

Aurora-viewing and river tours are available through Arctic Nature Tours. Arctic Tour Company arranges various day and multiday trips in the Mackenzie River delta, including visits to Tuktoyaktuk. One of the largest adventure-travel companies in Canada, Black Feather Wilderness Adventures leads canoeing and hiking trips in Nahanni National Park, the Mackenzie Mountains, and the central Arctic. The N.W.T. Marine Group offers a 1,600-km (992-mi) 10-day cruise along the Mackenzie River from Yellowknife to Inuvik aboard the M.S. *Norweta*. Raven Tours conducts tours of Yellowknife and the Great Slave Lake area, including aurora-viewing tours in winter. The specialty of Subarctic Wildlife Adventures is primarily wildlife-viewing tours in Wood Buffalo National Park and the nearby Slave River Rapids corridor, but it also arranges canoeing, hiking, and dogsledding trips.

➤ CONTACTS: **Arctic Nature Tours** (✉ Box 1530 [EX], Inuvik NT X0E 0T0, ☎ 867/777–3300, WEB www.arcticnaturetours.com). **Arctic Tour Company** (✉ Box 325, Tuktoyaktuk NT X0E 1C0, ☎ 867/977–2230, FAX 867/977–2276, WEB www.auroranet.nt.ca/atc). **Black Feather Wilderness Adventures** (✉ 1960 Scott St., Ottawa ON K1Z 8L8, ☎ 613/722–9717 or 800/574–8375, WEB www.blackfeather.com). **N.W.T. Marine Group** (✉ Box 2216, Yellowknife NT X1A 2P6, ☎ 867/873–2489 or 877/874–6001, FAX 867/873–6630, WEB www.denendeh.com/norweta). **Raven Tours** (✉ Box 2435, Yellowknife NT X1A 2P8, ☎ 867/873–4776, FAX 867/873–4856, WEB www.raventours.yk.com). **Subarctic Wildlife Adventures** (✉ Box 685, Fort Smith NT X0E 0P0, ☎ 867/872–2467, FAX 867/872–2126, WEB www.subarcticwildlife.nt.ca).

NUNAVUT

Adventure Canada sets up trips to the Arctic North, including excursions to the North Pole. Backpacking, dogsledding, canoeing, and wildlife viewing are among the activities arranged. Central Arctic Tours and Outfitters operates bus and dogsled tours along the south coast of Victoria Island. Ecosummer Expeditions leads guided sea-kayaking trips on Ellesmere Island. Naturalist tours and expeditions to the high Arctic are the specialty of Northwinds Arctic Adventures. Nuna Tours offers tours of Kekerten Territorial Park, Auyuittuq National Park, and Cumberland Sound, with opportunities to watch whales, birds, and sea-mammals. Qimuk Adventure Tours arranges aurora-viewing trips and cultural adventures from Iqaluit by snowmobile, boat, and dog team. Whitewolf Adventure Expeditions offers guided trips on the Coppermine and Burnside rivers. Fully escorted canoeing, kayaking, and hiking trips in Nunavut are available through the Wilderness Adventure Company.

➤ CONTACTS: **Adventure Canada** (✉ 14 Front St. S, Mississauga ON L5H 2C4, ☎ 800/363–7566, WEB www.adventurecanada.com). **Central Arctic Tours and Outfitters** (✉ Box 1199, Cambridge Bay NT X0E 0C0, ☎ 867/983–2024, FAX 867/983–2821). **Ecosummer Expeditions** (✉ Box 1765, Clearwater BC V6H 3S4, ☎ 800/465–8884, WEB www.ecosummer.com). **Northwinds Arctic Adventures** (✉ Box 888, Iqaluit NT X0A 0H0, ☎ 867/979–0551 or 800/549–0551, FAX 867/979–0573, WEB www.northwinds-arctic.com). **Nuna Tours** (✉ Box 365, Pangnirtung NT X0A 0R0, ☎ 867/473–8692). **Qimuk Adventure Tours** (✉ Box 797, Iqaluit NT X0A 0H0, ☎ 867/979–2777, FAX 867/979–1554, WEB http://pooka.nunanet.com/~qimuk). **Whitewolf Adventure Expeditions** (✉ Box 4869, Whitehorse YT Y1A 4N6, ☎ 604/944–5500 or 800/661–6659, WEB www.nahanni.com). **The Wilderness Adventure Company** (✉ R.R. 3, Parry Sound ON P2A 2W9, ☎ 705/746–1372 or 888/849–7668, FAX 705/746–7048, WEB www.wildernessadventure.com).

THE YUKON

Access Yukon arranges river trips, canoe rentals, heli-hiking, camper and four-wheel-drive rentals, and trail riding and has information on sightseeing opportunities, wilderness lodges, and transportation throughout the Yukon. Canadian River Expeditions coordinates six- to 12-day wilderness and natural-history expeditions on the Tatshenshini, Alsek, and Firth rivers. Gray Line Yukon conducts package tours to Dawson City and Alaska as well as Yukon River cruises and sightseeing tours of the Yukon Wildlife Preserve.

Holland America Westours organizes bus tours through the Yukon and Alaska as well as combined cruise-ship–bus tours that link in Skagway, Alaska. Kanoe People arranges guided and unguided canoe trips, from a half day to two weeks, on several rivers. Nahanni River Adventures conducts guided river trips on the Tatshenshini, Yukon, Nahanni, and other northern rivers. Rainbow Tours runs tours by van throughout the Yukon.

➤ CONTACTS: **Access Yukon** (✉ 212 Lambert St., Whitehorse Y1A 1Z4, ☎ 867/668–1233 or 800/661–0468, FAX 867/668–5595). **Canadian River Expeditions** (✉ Box 1023, Whistler, BC V0N 1B0, ☎ 604/938–6651 or 800/898–7238). **Gray Line Yukon** (✉ Box 4157, 208-G Steele St., Whitehorse Y1A 2C4, ☎ 867/668–3225, FAX 867/667–4494). **Holland America Westours** (✉ 300 Elliott Ave. W, Seattle, WA, 98119, ☎ 206/281–3535 or 888/252–7524). **Kanoe People** (✉ Box 5152, Whitehorse Y1A 4S3, ☎ 867/668–4899, FAX 867/668–4891). **Nahanni River Adventures** (✉ Box 4869, Whitehorse Y1A 4N6, ☎ 867/668–3180 or 800/297–6927, FAX 867/668–3056). **Rainbow Tours** (✉ 212 Lambert St., Whitehorse Y1A 1Z4, ☎ 867/668–5598 or 800/661–0468, FAX 867/668–5595).

TRANSPORTATION AROUND WILDERNESS CANADA

Once you are outside the Yukon and the southwest section of the Northwest Territories, flying is pretty much the only way to get around in wilderness Canada. Air Nunavut, Canadian North, and First Air have regularly scheduled service within the Northwest Territories and Nunavut. Air North, Alkan Air, Buffalo Airways, Calm Air, North-Wright Airways, and Ptarmigan Airways all also offer charter air service, an option worth considering for groups of four or more and usually the only option for getting to and from remote wilderness areas. Check with regional tourist offices for other charter services operating locally and regionally.

Pilots visiting the Northwest Territories can order a copy of the *Air Tourist's Information brochure* by contacting NWT Arctic Tourism.

YUKON
➤ CONTACTS: **Air North** (☎ 867/668–2228). **Alkan Air** (☎ 867/668–2107 or 800/661–0432).

THE NORTHWEST TERRITORIES
➤ CONTACTS: **Buffalo Airways** (☎ 867/873–6112). **Calm Air** (☎ 800/839–2256, WEB www.calmair.com). **North-Wright Airways** (☎ 867/587–2288 or 800/661–0702, WEB www.north-wrightairways.com). **NWT Arctic Tourism** (✉ 4916 47th St., 3rd floor, Yellowknife, NT X1A 1L7; mailing address: ✉ Box 610, Yellowknife NT X1A 2N5, ☎ 867/873–7200 or 800/661–0788, FAX 867/873–4059, WEB www.nwttravel.nt.ca). **Ptarmigan Airways** (☎ 867/873–5209 or 800/661–0808).

NUNAVUT
➤ CONTACTS: **Air Nunavut** (☎ 867/979–4018, WEB www.inuit.pail.ca/air-nunavut.htm).

VISITOR INFORMATION
YUKON
Tourism Yukon publishes the Yukon "Vacation Guide" and is the central source of information for the entire area. It also operates six regional information centers, open mid-May to mid-September, in Beaver Creek, Carcross, Dawson City, Haines Junction, Watson Lake, and Whitehorse.

➤ CONTACTS: **Tourism Yukon** (✉ Box 2703, Whitehorse, YT Y1A 2C6, ☎ 867/667–5340, FAX 867/667–3546). **Beaver Creek** (✉ Km 1,934, or Mi 1,202, on Alaska Hwy., ☎ 867/862–7321). **Carcross** (✉ Old Train Depot, ☎ 867/821–4431). **Dawson City** (✉ Front and King Sts., ☎ 867/993–5566). **Haines Junction** (✉ Kluane National Park Visitor

Centre, ☎ 867/634–2345). **Watson Lake** (✉ Rtes. 1 and 4, ☎ 867/536–7469). **Whitehorse** (✉ 100 Hanson St., at 2nd Ave., ☎ 867/667–2915). **Yukon Visitor Reception Centre** (2nd Ave. and Hanson St., ☎ 867/667–5340, FAX 867/667–6351, WEB www.touryukon.com).

NORTHWEST TERRITORIES
For general information and a copy of the Northwest Territories "Explorers' Guide," contact NWT Arctic Tourism.

The Northern Frontier Visitors Association has information about Yellowknife and its environs. For the far northwest, contact the Western Arctic Regional Visitors Center.
➤ CONTACTS: **NWT Arctic Tourism** (✉ 4916 47th St., 3rd floor, Yellowknife, NT X1A 1L7; mailing address: ✉ Box 610, Yellowknife NT X1A 2N5, ☎ 867/873–7200 or 800/661–0788, FAX 867/873–4059, WEB www.nwttravel.nt.ca). **Northern Frontier Visitors Association** (✉ 4807 49th St., Box 1107, Yellowknife NT X1A 3T5, ☎ 867/873–4262 or 877/881–4262, FAX 867/873–3654, WEB www.northernfrontier.com). **Western Arctic Regional Visitors Center** (✉ Bag Service No. 1, Inuvik NT X0E 0T0, ☎ 867/777–4727 or 867/777–7237).

NUNAVUT
For a complete guide to traveling in Nunavut, contact Nunavut Tourism. For information on the Arctic coastal region, contact the Arctic Coast Visitors Centre. For Baffin and Ellesmere islands, contact the Unikkaarvik Visitor Centre. For the Kivalliq (Keewatin) region, which includes the western coast of Hudson Bay, contact Kivalliq Regional Visitors Centre.
➤ CONTACTS: **Arctic Coast Visitors Centre** (✉ Box 91, Cambridge Bay NT X0C 0C0, ☎ 867/983–2224, FAX 867/983–2302). **Kivalliq Regional Visitors Centre** (✉ Rankin Inlet Airport, Rankin Inlet, NT X0C 0G0, ☎ 867/645–3838, FAX 867/645–3904). **Nunavut Tourism** (✉ Box 1450, Iqaluit NT X0A 0H0, ☎ 867/979–6551 or 800/491–7910, FAX 867/979–1261, WEB www.nunatour.nt.ca). **Unikkaarvik Visitor Centre** (✉ Box 1450, Iqaluit NT X0A 0H0, ☎ 867/979–4636, FAX 867/979–1261).

FRENCH VOCABULARY

One of the trickiest French sounds to pronounce is the nasal final *n* sound (whether or not the *n* is actually the last letter of the word). You should try to pronounce it as a sort of nasal grunt—as in "huh." The vowel that precedes the *n* will govern the vowel sound of the word, and in this list we precede the final *n* with an *h* to remind you to be nasal.

Another problem sound is the ubiquitous but untransliterable *eu*, as in *bleu* (blue) or *deux* (two), and the very similar sound in *je* (I), *ce* (this), and *de* (of). The closest equivalent might be the vowel sound of "stood."

English	French	Pronunciation
Basics		
Yes/no	Oui/non	wee/nohn
Please	S'il vous plaît	seel voo play
Thank you	Merci	mair-**see**
You're welcome	De rien	deh ree-**ehn**
That's all right	Il n'y a pas de quoi	eel nee ah pah de kwah
Excuse me, sorry	Pardon	pahr-**dohn**
Sorry!	Désolé(e)	day-zoh-**lay**
Good morning/ afternoon	Bonjour	bohn-**zhoor**
Good evening	Bonsoir	bohn-**swahr**
Goodbye	Au revoir	o ruh-**vwahr**
Mr. (Sir)	Monsieur	muh-**syuh**
Mrs. (Ma'am)	Madame	ma-**dam**
Miss	Mademoiselle	mad-mwa-**zel**
Pleased to meet you	Enchanté(e)	ohn-shahn-**tay**
How are you?	Comment allez-vous?	kuh-mahn-tahl-ay-**voo**
Very well, thanks	Très bien, merci	tray bee-ehn, mair-**see**
And you?	Et vous?	ay voo?
Numbers		
one	un	uhn
two	deux	deuh
three	trois	twah
four	quatre	**kaht**-ruh
five	cinq	sank
six	six	seess
seven	sept	set
eight	huit	wheat
nine	neuf	nuf
ten	dix	deess
eleven	onze	ohnz
twelve	douze	dooz

thirteen	treize	trehz
fourteen	quatorze	kah-torz
fifteen	quinze	kanz
sixteen	seize	sez
seventeen	dix-sept	deez-**set**
eighteen	dix-huit	deez-**wheat**
nineteen	dix-neuf	deez-**nuf**
twenty	vingt	vehn
twenty-one	vingt-et-un	vehnt-ay-**uhn**
thirty	trente	trahnt
forty	quarante	ka-**rahnt**
fifty	cinquante	sang-**kahnt**
sixty	soixante	swa-**sahnt**
seventy	soixante-dix	swa-sahnt-**deess**
eighty	quatre-vingts	kaht-ruh-**vehn**
ninety	quatre-vingt-dix	kaht-ruh-vehn-**deess**
one-hundred	cent	sahn
one-thousand	mille	meel

Colors

black	noir	nwahr
blue	bleu	bleuh
brown	brun/marron	bruhn/mar-**rohn**
green	vert	vair
orange	orange	o-**rahnj**
pink	rose	rose
red	rouge	rouge
violet	violette	vee-o-**let**
white	blanc	blahnk
yellow	jaune	zhone

Days of the Week

Sunday	dimanche	dee-**mahnsh**
Monday	lundi	luhn-**dee**
Tuesday	mardi	mahr-**dee**
Wednesday	mercredi	mair-kruh-**dee**
Thursday	jeudi	zhuh-**dee**
Friday	vendredi	vawn-druh-**dee**
Saturday	samedi	sahm-**dee**

Months

January	janvier	zhahn-vee-**ay**
February	février	feh-vree-**ay**
March	mars	marce
April	avril	a-**vreel**
May	mai	meh
June	juin	zhwehn
July	juillet	zhwee-**ay**
August	août	ah-**oo**
September	septembre	sep-**tahm**-bruh
October	octobre	awk-**to**-bruh
November	novembre	no-**vahm**-bruh
December	décembre	day-**sahm**-bruh

Useful Phrases

Do you speak English?	Parlez-vous anglais?	par-lay **voo** ahn-**glay**
I don't speak French	Je ne parle pas français	zhuh nuh parl pah frahn-**say**
I don't understand	Je ne comprends pas	zhuh nuh kohm-**prahn** pah
I understand	Je comprends	zhuh kohm-**prahn**
I don't know	Je ne sais pas	zhuh nuh say **pah**
I'm American/ British	Je suis américain/ anglais	zhuh sweez a-may-ree-**kehn**/ahn-**glay**
What's your name?	Comment vous appelez-vous?	ko-mahn voo za-pell-ay-**voo**
My name is . . .	Je m'appelle . . .	zhuh ma-**pell** . . .
What time is it?	Quelle heure est-il?	kel air eh-**teel**
How?	Comment?	ko-**mahn**
When?	Quand?	kahn
Yesterday	Hier	yair
Today	Aujourd'hui	o-zhoor-**dwee**
Tomorrow	Demain	duh-**mehn**
This morning/ afternoon	Ce matin/cet après-midi	suh ma-**tehn**/set ah-pray-mee-**dee**
Tonight	Ce soir	suh **swahr**
What?	Quoi?	kwah
What is it?	Qu'est-ce que c'est?	kess-kuh-**say**
Why?	Pourquoi?	poor-**kwa**
Who?	Qui?	kee
Where is . . .	Où est . . .	oo ay
the train station?	la gare?	la gar
the subway station?	la station de métro?	la sta-**syon** duh may-**tro**
the bus stop?	l'arrêt de bus?	la-**ray** duh **booss**
the terminal (airport)?	l'aérogare?	lay-ro-**gar**
the post office?	la poste?	la post
the bank?	la banque?	la bahnk
the . . . hotel?	l'hôtel . . .?	lo-**tel**
the store?	le magasin?	luh ma-ga-**zehn**
the cashier?	la caisse?	la **kess**
the . . . museum?	le musée . . .?	luh mew-**zay**
the hospital?	l'hôpital?	lo-pee-**tahl**
the elevator?	l'ascenseur?	la-sahn-**seuhr**
the telephone?	le téléphone?	luh tay-lay-**phone**
Where are the restrooms?	Où sont les toilettes?	oo sohn lay twah-**let**
Here/there	Ici/là	ee-**see**/la
Left/right	A gauche/à droite	a goash/a drwaht

Straight ahead	Tout droit	too drwah
Is it near/far?	C'est près/loin?	say pray/lwehn
I'd like . . .	Je voudrais . . .	zhuh voo-**dray**
a room	une chambre	ewn **shahm**-bruh
the key	la clé	la clay
a newspaper	un journal	uhn zhoor-**nahl**
a stamp	un timbre	uhn **tam**-bruh
I'd like to buy . . .	Je voudrais acheter . . .	zhuh voo-**dray** ahsh-**tay**
a cigar	un cigare	uhn see-**gar**
cigarettes	des cigarettes	day see-ga-**ret**
matches	des allumettes	days a-loo-**met**
dictionary	un dictionnaire	uhn deek-see-oh-**nare**
soap	du savon	dew sah-**vohn**
city plan	un plan de ville	uhn plahn de **veel**
road map	une carte routière	ewn cart roo-tee-**air**
magazine	une revue	ewn reh-**vu**
envelopes	des enveloppes	dayz ahn-veh-**lope**
writing paper	du papier à lettres	dew pa-pee-**ay** a **let**-ruh
airmail writing paper	du papier avion	dew pa-pee-**ay** a-vee-**ohn**
postcard	une carte postale	ewn cart pos-**tal**
How much is it?	C'est combien?	say comb-bee-**ehn**
It's expensive/cheap	C'est cher/pas cher	say share/pa share
A little/a lot	Un peu/beaucoup	uhn peuh/bo-**koo**
More/less	Plus/moins	plu/mwehn
Enough/too (much)	Assez/trop	a-say/tro
I am ill/sick	Je suis malade	zhuh swee ma-**lahd**
Call a doctor	Appelez un docteur	a-play uhn dohk-**tehr**
Help!	Au secours!	o suh-**koor**
Stop!	Arrêtez!	a-reh-**tay**
Fire!	Au feu!	o fuh
Caution!/Look out!	Attention!	a-tahn-see-**ohn**

Dining Out

A bottle of . . .	une bouteille de . . .	ewn boo-**tay** duh
A cup of . . .	une tasse de . . .	ewn tass duh
A glass of . . .	un verre de . . .	uhn vair duh
Ashtray	un cendrier	uhn sahn-dree-**ay**
Bill/check	l'addition	la-dee-see-**ohn**
Bread	du pain	dew pan
Breakfast	le petit-déjeuner	luh puh-**tee** day-zhuh-**nay**
Butter	du beurre	dew burr

Cheers!	A votre santé!	ah vo-truh sahn-**tay**
Cocktail/aperitif	un apéritif	uhn ah-pay-ree-**teef**
Dinner	le dîner	luh dee-**nay**
Dish of the day	le plat du jour	luh plah dew **zhoor**
Enjoy!	Bon appétit!	bohn a-pay-**tee**
Fixed-price menu	le menu	luh may-**new**
Fork	une fourchette	ewn four-**shet**
I am diabetic	Je suis diabétique	zhuh swee dee-ah-bay-**teek**
I am on a diet	Je suis au régime	zhuh sweez o ray-**jeem**
I am vegetarian	Je suis végétarien(ne)	zhuh swee vay-zhay-ta-ree-**en**
I cannot eat . . .	Je ne peux pas manger de . . .	zhuh nuh **puh** pah mahn-**jay** deh
I'd like to order	Je voudrais commander	zhuh voo-**dray** ko-mahn-**day**
I'm hungry/thirsty	J'ai faim/soif	zhay fahm/swahf
Is service/the tip included?	Est-ce que le service est compris?	ess kuh luh sair-**veess** ay comb-**pree**
It's good/bad	C'est bon/mauvais	say bohn/mo-**vay**
It's hot/cold	C'est chaud/froid	say sho/frwah
Knife	un couteau	uhn koo-**toe**
Lunch	le déjeuner	luh day-zhuh-**nay**
Menu	la carte	la cart
Napkin	une serviette	ewn sair-vee-**et**
Pepper	du poivre	dew **pwah**-vruh
Plate	une assiette	ewn a-see-**et**
Please give me . . .	Donnez-moi . . .	doe-nay-**mwah**
Salt	du sel	dew sell
Spoon	une cuillère	ewn kwee-**air**
Sugar	du sucre	dew **sook**-ruh
Waiter!/Waitress!	Monsieur!/ Mademoiselle!	muh-**syuh**/ mad-mwa-**zel**
Wine list	la carte des vins	la cart day **van**

INDEX

NOTES

NOTES

NOTES

NOTES

NOTES

NOTES

NOTES

NOTES